PEARSON

ALWAYS LEARNING

Series Editor Mary Anne Poatsy
Series Created by Dr. Robert T. Grauer

Exploring Microsoft® Excel and Access 2013

Custom Edition for University of Notre Dame MGT 20600

Taken from:
Exploring Microsoft® Excel 2013: Comprehensive
by Series editor Mary Anne Poatsy;
Series created by Dr. Robert T. Grauer

Exploring Microsoft® Access 2013: Comprehensive
by Series editor Mary Anne Poatsy;
Series created by Dr. Robert T. Grauer

Cover Art: Courtesy of Pearson Learning Solutions.

Taken from:

Exploring Microsoft® Excel 2013: Comprehensive
by Series editor Mary Anne Poatsy; Series created by Dr. Robert T. Grauer
Copyright © 2014 by Pearson Education, Inc.
New York, New York 10013

Exploring Microsoft® Access 2013: Comprehensive
by Series editor Mary Anne Poatsy; Series created by Dr. Robert T. Grauer
Copyright © 2014 by Pearson Education, Inc.
New York, New York 10013

This special edition published in cooperation with Pearson Learning Solutions.

Pearson Learning Solutions, 330 Hudson Street, New York, New York 10013
A Pearson Education Company
www.pearsoned.com

Printed in the United States of America

1 2 3 4 5 6 7 8 9 10 V092 19 18 17 16

000200010272023583

NC

ISBN 10: 1-323-32528-x
ISBN 13: 978-1-323-32528-5

Brief Contents

Contents

Microsoft Office Excel 2013

■ CHAPTER ONE **Introduction to Excel:** What Is a Spreadsheet? 1

■ CHAPTER TWO **Formulas and Functions:** Performing Quantitative Analysis 75

■ CHAPTER SEVEN **Subtotals, PivotTables, and PivotCharts:** Summarizing and Analyzing Data 337

■ CHAPTER EIGHT **What-If Analysis:** Using Decision-Making Tools 387

■ CHAPTER NINE **Templates, Styles, and Macros:** Standardizing Workbooks 431

Microsoft Office Access 2013

■ CHAPTER TEN Introduction to Access: Finding Your Way Through an Access Database   481

■ CHAPTER ELEVEN Tables and Queries in Relational Databases: Designing Databases and Extracting Data   539

■ CHAPTER SIXTEEN **Get Connected:** Exchanging Data Between Access and Other Applications   **797**

■ CHAPTER SEVENTEEN **Fine-Tuning the Database:** Analyzing and Improving Database Performance   **869**

Excel

Introduction to Excel

CHAPTER 1

What Is a Spreadsheet?

Yuri Arcurs/Shutterstock

OBJECTIVES | AFTER YOU READ THIS CHAPTER, YOU WILL BE ABLE TO:

1. Explore the Excel window p. 2
2. Enter and edit cell data p. 5
3. Create formulas p. 12
4. Use Auto Fill p. 14
5. Display cell formulas p. 15
6. Manage worksheets p. 22
7. Manage columns and rows p. 25
8. Select, move, copy, and paste data p. 34
9. Apply alignment and font options p. 42
10. Apply number formats p. 44
11. Select page setup options p. 51
12. Preview and print a worksheet p. 55

CASE STUDY | OK Office Systems

You are an assistant manager at OK Office Systems (OKOS) in Oklahoma City. OKOS sells a wide range of computer systems, peripherals, and furniture for small- and medium-sized organizations in the metropolitan area. To compete against large, global, big-box office supply stores, OKOS provides competitive pricing by ordering directly from local manufacturers rather than dealing with distributors.

Alesha Bennett, the general manager, asked you to calculate the retail price, sale price, and profit analysis for selected items on sale this month. Using markup rates provided by Alesha, you need to calculate the retail price, the amount OKOS charges its customers for the products. For the sale, Alesha wants to give customers between a 10% and 30% discount on select items. You need to use those discount rates to calculate the sale prices. Finally, you will calculate the profit margin to determine the percentage of the final sale price over the cost.

After you create the initial pricing spreadsheet, you will be able to change values and see that the formulas update the results automatically. In addition, you will be able to insert data for additional sale items or delete an item based on the manager's decision.

Although your experience with Microsoft Office Excel 2013 may be limited, you are excited to apply your knowledge and skills to your newly assigned responsibility. In the Hands-On Exercises for this chapter, you will create and format the analytical spreadsheet to practice the skills you learn.

Introduction to Spreadsheets

Organizing, calculating, and evaluating quantitative data are important skills needed today for personal and managerial decision making. You track expenses for your household budget, maintain a savings plan, and determine what amount you can afford for a house or car payment. Retail managers create and analyze their organizations' annual budgets, sales projections, and inventory records. Charitable organizations track the donations they receive, the distribution of those donations, and overhead expenditures.

You can use a spreadsheet to maintain data and perform calculations. A *spreadsheet* is an electronic file that contains a grid of columns and rows used to organize related data and to display results of calculations, enabling interpretation of quantitative data for decision making.

Performing calculations using a calculator and entering the results into a ledger can lead to inaccurate values. If an input value is incorrect or needs to be updated, you have to recalculate the results manually, which is time-consuming and can lead to inaccuracies. A spreadsheet makes data entry changes easy. If the formulas are correctly constructed, the results recalculate automatically and accurately, saving time and reducing room for error.

In this section, you will learn how to design spreadsheets. In addition, you will explore the Excel window and learn the name of each window element. Then, you will enter text, values, and dates in a spreadsheet.

Exploring the Excel Window

In Excel, a *worksheet* is a single spreadsheet that typically contains descriptive labels, numeric values, formulas, functions, and graphical representations of data. A *workbook* is a collection of one or more related worksheets contained within a single file. By default, new workbooks contain one worksheet. Storing multiple worksheets within one workbook helps organize related data together in one file and enables you to perform calculations among the worksheets within the workbook. For example, you can create a budget workbook of 13 worksheets, one for each month to store your personal income and expenses and a final worksheet to calculate totals across the entire year.

Excel contains the standard interface of Microsoft Office applications:

- **Quick Access Toolbar:** Save, Undo, and Redo/Repeat commands
- **Title bar:** File name (such as Book1) and software name (such as Excel)
- **Control buttons:** Microsoft Excel Help, Full Screen Mode, Minimize, Restore Down, and Close
- **Ribbon:** Commands (such as Align Left) organized within groups (such as Alignment) on various tabs (such as Home)
- **Scroll bars:** Tools to scroll vertically and horizontally through a worksheet

Identify Excel Window Elements

Figure 1.1 identifies elements specific to the Excel window, and Table 1.1 lists and describes the Excel window elements.

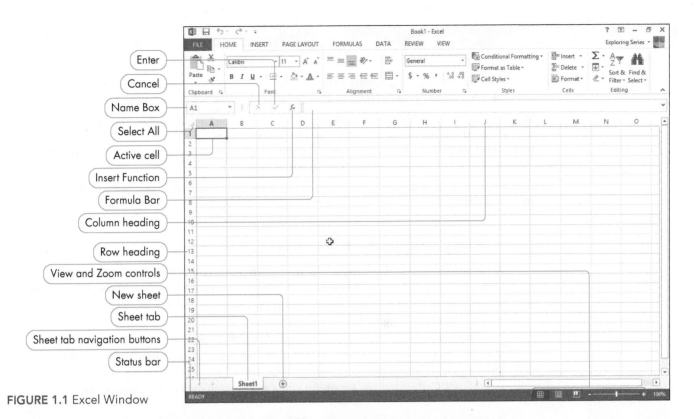

FIGURE 1.1 Excel Window

TABLE 1.1	Excel Elements
Element	**Description**
Name Box	The **Name Box** is an identifier that displays the address of the current cell in the worksheet. Use the Name Box to go to a cell, assign a name to one or more cells, or select a function.
Cancel ☒	When you enter or edit data, click Cancel to cancel the data entry or edit and revert back to the previous data in the cell, if any. The Cancel icon changes from gray to red when you position the mouse pointer over it.
Enter ☑	When you enter or edit data, click Enter to accept data typed in the active cell and keep the current cell active. The Enter icon changes from gray to blue when you position the mouse pointer over it.
Insert Function ƒx	Click to display the Insert Function dialog box to search for and select a function to insert into the active cell. The Insert Function icon changes from gray to green when you position the mouse pointer over it.
Formula Bar	The **Formula Bar** shows the contents of the active cell. You can enter or edit cell contents here or directly in the active cell. Drag the bottom border of the Formula Bar down to increase the height of the Formula Bar to display large amounts of data or a long formula contained in the active cell.
Select All ◣	The triangle at the intersection of the row and column headings in the top-left corner of the worksheet. Click it to select everything contained in the active worksheet.
Column headings	The letters above the columns, such as A, B, C, and so on.
Row headings	The numbers to the left of the rows, such as 1, 2, 3, and so on.
Active cell	The active cell is the current cell, which is indicated by a dark green border.
Sheet tab	A **sheet tab** shows the name of a worksheet contained in the workbook. When you create a new Excel workbook, the default worksheet is named Sheet1.
New sheet ⊕	Inserts a new worksheet to the right of the current worksheet.
Sheet tab navigation buttons	If your workbook contains several worksheets, Excel may not show all the sheet tabs at the same time. Use the buttons to display the first, previous, next, or last worksheet.

TABLE 1.1   Excel Elements *(continued)*

Element	Description
Status bar	Displays information about a selected command or operation in progress. For example, it displays *Select destination and press ENTER or choose Paste* after you use the Copy command.
View controls	Click a view control to display the worksheet in Normal, Page Layout, or Page Break Preview. Normal view displays the worksheet without showing margins, headers, footers, and page breaks. Page Layout view shows the margins, header and footer area, and a ruler. Page Break Preview indicates where the worksheet will be divided into pages.
Zoom control	Drag the zoom control to increase the size of the worksheet onscreen to see more or less of the worksheet data.

Identify Columns, Rows, and Cells

A worksheet contains columns and rows, with each column and row assigned a heading. Columns are assigned alphabetical headings from columns A to Z, continuing from AA to AZ, and then from BA to BZ until XFD, which is the last of the possible 16,384 columns. Rows have numeric headings ranging from 1 to 1,048,576.

The intersection of a column and row is a *cell*; a total of more than 17 billion cells are available in a worksheet. Each cell has a unique *cell address*, identified by first its column letter and then its row number. For example, the cell at the intersection of column A and row 9 is cell A9. Cell references are useful when referencing data in formulas, or in navigation.

Navigate In and Among Worksheets

The *active cell* is the current cell. Excel displays a dark green border around the active cell in the worksheet, and the cell address of the active cell appears in the Name Box. The contents of the active cell, or the formula used to calculate the results of the active cell, appear in the Formula Bar. You can change the active cell by using the mouse to click in a different cell. If you work in a large worksheet, use the vertical and horizontal scroll bars to display another area of the worksheet and click in the desired cell to make it the active cell.

To navigate to a new cell, click it or use the arrow keys on the keyboard. When you press Enter, the next cell down in the same column becomes the active cell. Table 1.2 lists the keyboard navigation methods. The Go To command is helpful for navigating to a cell that is not visible onscreen.

TABLE 1.2   Keystrokes and Actions

Keystroke	Used to
↑	Move up one cell in the same column.
↓	Move down one cell in the same column.
←	Move left one cell in the same row.
→	Move right one cell in the same row.
Tab	Move right one cell in the same row.
Page Up	Move the active cell up one screen.
Page Down	Move the active cell down one screen.
Home	Move the active cell to column A of the current row.
Ctrl+Home	Make cell A1 the active cell.
Ctrl+End	Make the rightmost, lowermost active corner of the worksheet—the intersection of the last column and row that contains data—the active cell. Does not move to cell XFD1048576 unless that cell contains data.
F5 or Ctrl+G	Display the Go To dialog box to enter any cell address.

To display the contents of another worksheet within the workbook, click the sheet tab at the bottom-left corner of the workbook window. The active sheet tab has a white background color. After you click a sheet tab, you can then navigate within that worksheet.

Entering and Editing Cell Data

You should plan the structure before you start entering data into a worksheet. Using the OKOS case presented at the beginning of the chapter as an example, use the following steps to plan the worksheet design, enter and format data, and complete the workbook:

Plan the Worksheet Design

1. **State the purpose of the worksheet.** The purpose of the OKOS worksheet is to store data about products on sale and to calculate important details, such as the retail price based on markup, the sales price based on a discount rate, and the profit margin.

2. **Decide what input values are needed.** Input values are the initial values, such as variables and assumptions. You may change these values to see what type of effects different values have on the end results. For the OKOS worksheet, the input values include the costs OKOS pays the manufacturers, the markup rates, and the proposed discount rates for the sale. In some worksheets, you can create an *input area*, a specific region in the worksheet to store and change the variables used in calculations. For example, if you applied the same Markup Rate and same Percent Off for all products, it would be easier to create an input area at the top of the worksheet to change the values in one location rather than in several locations.

3. **Decide what outputs are needed to achieve the purpose of the worksheet.** Outputs are the results you need to calculate. For the OKOS worksheet, the outputs include columns to calculate the retail price (i.e., the selling price to your customers), the sale price, and the profit margin. In some worksheets, you can create an *output area*, the region in the worksheet to contain formulas dependent on the values in the input area.

Enter and Format the Data

4. **Enter the labels, values, and formulas in Excel.** Use the design plan (steps 2–3) as you enter labels, input values, and formulas to calculate the output. In the OKOS worksheet, descriptive labels (the product names) appear in the first column to indicate that the values on a specific row pertain to a specific product. Descriptive labels appear at the top of each column, such as Cost and Retail Price, to describe the values in the respective column. Change the input values to test that your formulas produce correct results. If necessary, correct any errors in the formulas to produce correct results. For the OKOS worksheet, change some of the original costs and markup rates to ensure the calculated retail price, selling price, and profit margin percentage results update correctly.

5. **Format the numerical values in the worksheet.** Align decimal points in columns of numbers and add number formats and styles. In the OKOS worksheet, use Accounting Number Format and the Percent Style to format the numerical data. Adjust the number of decimal places as needed.

6. **Format the descriptive titles and labels so that they stand out.** Add bold and color to headings so that they stand out and are attractive. Apply other formatting to headings and descriptive labels. In the OKOS worksheet, you will center the main title over all the columns, bold and center column labels over the columns, and apply other formatting to the headings. Figure 1.2 shows the completed OKOS worksheet.

Complete the Workbook

7. **Document the workbook as thoroughly as possible.** Include the current date, your name as the workbook author, assumptions, and purpose of the workbook. You can provide this documentation in a separate worksheet within the workbook. You can also add some documentation in the *Properties* section when you click the File tab.

8. **Save and share the completed workbook.** Preview and prepare printouts for distribution in meetings, send an electronic copy of the workbook to those who need it, or upload the workbook on a shared network drive or in the cloud.

	A	B	C	D	E	F	G	H
1	OK Office Systems Pricing Information							
2	9/1/2016							
3								
4	Product	Cost	Markup Rate	Retail Price	Percent Off	Sale Price	Profit Amount	Profit Margin
5	**Electronics**							
6	Computer System	$ 475.50	50.0%	$ 713.25	15.0%	$ 606.26	$ 130.76	21.6%
7	Color Laser Printer	$ 457.70	75.5%	$ 803.26	20.0%	$ 642.61	$ 184.91	28.8%
8	28" Monitor	$ 195.00	83.5%	$ 357.83	10.0%	$ 322.04	$ 127.04	39.4%
9	**Furniture**							
10	Desk Chair	$ 75.00	100.0%	$ 150.00	25.0%	$ 112.50	$ 37.50	33.3%
11	Solid Oak Computer Desk	$ 700.00	185.7%	$1,999.90	30.0%	$1,399.93	$ 699.93	50.0%
12	Executive Desk Chair	$ 200.00	100.0%	$ 400.00	25.0%	$ 300.00	$ 100.00	33.3%
13								

Callouts: Centered title • Formatted output range (calculated results) • Formatted column labels • Formatted input range (Cost, Markup Rate, and Percent Off) • Product data organized into rows

FIGURE 1.2 Completed OKOS Worksheet

Enter Text

Text is any combination of letters, numbers, symbols, and spaces not used in calculations. Excel treats phone numbers, such as 555-1234, and Social Security numbers, such as 123-45-6789, as text entries. You enter text for a worksheet title to describe the contents of the worksheet, as row and column labels to describe data, and as cell data. In Figure 1.2, the cells in column A, row 1, and row 4 contain text, such as *Product*. Text aligns at the left cell margin by default. To enter text in a cell, do the following:

STEP 1 »

1. Make sure the cell is active where you want to enter text.
2. Type the text.
3. Do one of the following to make another cell the active cell after entering data:

   • Press Enter on the keyboard.
   • Press an arrow key on the keyboard.
   • Press Tab on the keyboard.

   Do one of the following to keep the current cell the active cell after entering data:

   • Press Ctrl+Enter.
   • Click Enter (the check mark between the Name Box and the Formula Bar).

As soon as you begin typing a label into a cell, the *AutoComplete* feature searches for and automatically displays any other label in that column that matches the letters you typed. For example, *Computer System* is typed in cell A6 in Figure 1.2. When you start to type *Co* in cell A7, AutoComplete displays *Computer System* because a text entry previously typed starts with *Co*. Press Enter to accept the repeated label, or continue typing to enter a different label, such as *Color Laser Printer*.

Enter Values

STEP 2 >>

Values are numbers that represent a quantity or a measurable amount. Excel usually distinguishes between text and value data based on what you enter. The primary difference between text and value entries is that value entries can be the basis of calculations, whereas text cannot. In Figure 1.2, the data below the *Cost*, *Markup Rates*, and *Percent Off* labels are values. Values align at the right cell margin by default. After entering values, you can align decimal places and apply formatting by adding characters, such as $ or %.

Enter Dates

STEP 3 >>

You can enter dates and times in a variety of formats in cells, such as 9/1/2016; 9/1/16; September 1, 2016; or 1-Sep-16. You can also enter times, such as 1:30 PM or 13:30. You should enter a static date to document when you create or modify a workbook or to document the specific point in time when the data were accurate, such as on a balance sheet or income statement. Later, you will learn how to use formulas to enter dates that update to the current date. In Figure 1.2, cell A2 contains a date. Dates are values, so they align at the right cell margin. However, the date in Figure 1.2 has been centered by the user.

Excel displays dates differently from the way it stores dates. For example, the displayed date 9/1/2016 represents the first day in September in the year 2016. Excel stores dates as serial numbers starting at 1 with January 1, 1900, so 9/1/2016 is stored as 42614 so that you can create formulas, such as to calculate how many days exist between two dates.

Enter Formulas

Formulas combine cell references, arithmetic operations, values, and/or functions used in a calculation. You must start the formula with an equal sign (=). In Figure 1.3, the data below the *Retail Price*, *Sale Price*, *Profit Amount*, and *Profit Margin* labels contain formulas. When a cell containing a formula is the active cell, the formula displays in the Formula Bar, and the result of the formula displays in the cell.

Edit and Clear Cell Contents

You can edit a cell's contents by doing one of the following:

- Click the cell, click in the Formula Bar, make the changes, and then click Enter (the check mark between the Name Box and the Formula Bar) to keep the cell the active cell.
- Double-click the cell, make changes in the cell, and then press Enter.
- Click the cell, press F2, make changes in the cell, and then press Enter.

You can clear a cell's contents by doing one of the following:

- Click the cell and press Delete.
- Click the cell, click Clear in the Editing group on the HOME tab, and then select Clear Contents.

1. What are two major advantages of using an electronic spreadsheet instead of a paper-based ledger? *p. 2*

2. What visual indicators let you know which cell is the active cell? *p. 3*

3. What steps should you perform before entering data into a worksheet? *p. 5*

4. What are four major things you can enter into a cell? Give an example (different from those in the book) for each type. *pp. 6–7*

Hands-On Exercises

1 Introduction to Spreadsheets

As the assistant manager of OKOS, you need to create a worksheet that shows the cost (the amount OKOS pays its suppliers), the markup percentage (the amount by which the cost is increased), and the retail selling price. You also need to list the discount percentage (such as 25% off) for each product, the sale price, and the profit margin percentage.

Skills covered: Enter Text • Enter Values • Enter a Date and Clear Cell Contents

STEP 1 >> ENTER TEXT

Now that you have planned the OKOS worksheet, you are ready to enter labels for the title, column labels, and row labels. You will type a title in cell A1, product labels in the first column, and row labels in the fourth row. Refer to Figure 1.3 as you complete Step 1.

Step b: Title

Step f: Labels for other columns

Step e: Label for second column

Step c: Label for first column

Step d: Name of products

	A	B	C	D	E	F	G	H
1	OK Office Systems Pricing Information							
2								
3								
4	Product	Cost	Markup R:	Retail Pric	Percent O	Sale Price	Profit Margin	
5	Computer System							
6	Color Laser Printer							
7	Filing Cabinet							
8	Desk Chair							
9	Solid Oak Computer Desk							
10	28" Monitor							
11								
12								

FIGURE 1.3 Text Entered in Cells

a. Start Excel and open a new blank workbook. Save the new workbook as **e01h1Markup_LastFirst**.

   When you save files, use your last and first names. For example, as the Excel author, I would save my workbook as *e01h1Markup_MulberyKeith*.

b. Type **OK Office Systems Pricing Information** in **cell A1** and press **Enter**.

   When you press Enter, the next cell down—cell A2 in this case—becomes the active cell. The text does not completely fit in cell A1, and some of the text appears in cells B1, C1, D1, and possibly E1. If you make cell B1, C1, D1, or E1 the active cell, the Formula Bar is empty, indicating that nothing is stored in those cells.

c. Click **cell A4**, type **Product**, and then press **Enter**.

d. Continue typing the rest of the text in **cells A5** through **A10** as shown in Figure 1.4. Text in column A appears to flow into column B.

   When you start typing *Co* in cell A6, AutoComplete displays a ScreenTip suggesting a previous text entry starting with *Co—Computer System*—but keep typing to enter *Color Laser Printer* instead. You just entered the product labels to describe the data in each row.

e. Click **cell B4** to make it the active cell. Type **Cost** and press **Tab**.

   Instead of pressing Enter to move down column B, you pressed Tab to make the cell to the right the active cell.

f. Type the following text in the respective cells, pressing **Tab** after typing each of the first four column labels and pressing **Enter** after the last column label:

- **Markup Rate** in **cell C4**
- **Retail Price** in **cell D4**
- **Percent Off** in **cell E4**
- **Sale Price** in **cell F4**
- **Profit Margin** in **cell G4**

The text looks cut off when you enter data in the cell to the right. Do not worry about this now. You will adjust column widths and formatting later in this chapter.

> **TROUBLESHOOTING:** If you notice a typographical error, click in the cell containing the error and retype the label. Or press F2 to edit the cell contents, move the insertion point using the arrow keys, press Backspace or Delete to delete the incorrect characters, type the correct characters, and then press Enter. If you type a label in an incorrect cell, click the cell and press Delete.

g. Save the changes you made to the workbook.

You should develop a habit of saving periodically. That way if your system unexpectedly shuts down, you will not lose everything you worked on.

STEP 2 ≫ ENTER VALUES

Now that you have entered the descriptive labels, you need to enter the cost, markup rate, and percent off for each product. Refer to Figure 1.4 as you complete Step 2.

Steps e–f: Percent Off values

Steps c–d: Markup Rate values

Steps a–b: Cost values

	A	B	C	D	E	F	G	H
1	OK Office Systems Pricing Information							
2								
3								
4	Product	Cost	Markup Ra	Retail Pric	Percent O	Sale Price	Profit Margin	
5	Computer	400	0.5		0.15			
6	Color Lase	457.7	0.75		0.2			
7	Filing Cab	68.75	0.905		0.1			
8	Desk Chai	75	1		0.25			
9	Solid Oak	700	1.857		0.3			
10	28" Monit	195	0.835		0.1			
11								
12								

FIGURE 1.4 Values Entered in Cells

a. Click **cell B5**, type **400**, and then press **Enter**.

b. Type the remaining costs in **cells B6** through **B10** shown in Figure 1.4.

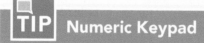 **TIP** Numeric Keypad

To improve your productivity, use the number keypad (if available) on the right side of your keyboard. It is much faster to type values and press Enter on the number keypad rather than using the numbers on the keyboard. Make sure Num Lock is active before using the number keypad to enter values.

c. Click **cell C5**, type **0.5**, and then press **Enter**.

You entered the markup rate as a decimal instead of a percentage. You will apply Percent Style later, but now you can concentrate on data entry. When you enter decimal values less than zero, you can type the period and value without typing the zero first, such as .5. Excel will automatically add the zero. You can also enter percentages as 50%, but the approach this textbook takes is to enter raw data without typing formatting such as % and to use number formatting options through Excel to display formatting symbols.

d. Type the remaining markup rates in **cells C6** through **C10** as shown in Figure 1.4.

e. Click **cell E5**, type **0.15**, and then press **Enter**.

You entered the Percent Off or markdown sale value as a decimal.

f. Type the remaining Percent Off values in **cells E6** through **E10** as shown in Figure 1.4 and save the workbook.

STEP 3 ≫ ENTER A DATE AND CLEAR CELL CONTENTS

As you review the worksheet, you realize you need to provide a date to indicate when the sale starts. Refer to Figure 1.5 as you complete Step 3.

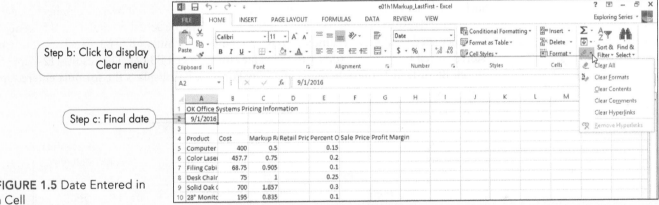

FIGURE 1.5 Date Entered in a Cell

a. Click **cell A2**, type **9/1**, and then press **Enter**.

The date aligns on the right cell margin by default. Excel displays *1-Sep* instead of *9/1*.

b. Click **cell A2**, click **Clear** in the Editing group on the HOME tab, and then select **Clear All**.

The Clear All command clears both cell contents and formatting in the selected cell(s).

c. Type **9/1/2016** in **cell A2** and press **Enter**.

> **TROUBLESHOOTING:** If you did not use Clear All and typed 9/1/2016 in cell A2, Excel would have retained the previous date format and displayed 1-Sep again.

d. Save the workbook. Keep the workbook open if you plan to continue with the next Hands-On Exercise. If not, close the workbook and exit Excel.

Mathematics and Formulas

Formulas transform static numbers into meaningful results that can update as values change. For example, a payroll manager can build formulas to calculate the gross pay, deductions, and net pay for an organization's employees, or a doctoral student can create formulas to perform various statistical calculations to interpret his or her research data.

You can use formulas to help you analyze how results will change as the input data change. You can change the value of your assumptions or inputs and explore the results quickly and accurately. For example, if the interest rate changes from 4% to 5%, how would that affect your monthly payment? Analyzing different input values in Excel is easy after you build formulas. Simply change an input value and observe the change in the formula results.

In this section, you will learn how to use mathematical operations in Excel formulas. You will refresh your memory of mathematical order of precedence and how to construct formulas using cell addresses so that when the value of an input cell changes, the result of the formula changes without you having to modify the formula.

Creating Formulas

Start a formula by typing the equal sign (=), followed by the arithmetic expression. Do not include a space before or after the arithmetic operator. Figure 1.6 shows a worksheet containing data and results of formulas. The figure also displays the actual formulas used to generate the calculated results. For example, cell B6 contains the formula =B2+B3. Excel uses the value stored in cell B2 (10) and adds it to the value stored in cell B3 (2). The result—12—appears in cell B6 instead of the actual formula. The Formula Bar displays the formula entered into the active cell.

	A	B	C	D	E	F
1	Description	Values		Description	Results	Formulas in Column E
2	First input value	10		Sum of 10 and 2	12	=B2+B3
3	Second input value	2		Difference between 10 and 2	8	=B2-B3
4				Product of 10 and 2	20	=B2*B3
5				Results of dividing 10 by 2	5	=B2/B3
6				Results of 10 to the 2nd power	100	=B2^B3

FIGURE 1.6 Formula Results

> **TROUBLESHOOTING:** If you type B2+B3 without the equal sign, Excel does not recognize that you entered a formula and stores the data as text.

Use Cell References in Formulas

STEP 1 »
STEP 2 »
STEP 3 »

You should use cell references instead of values in formulas where possible. You may include values in an input area—such as dates, salary, or costs—that you will need to reference in formulas. Referencing these cells in your formulas, instead of typing the value of the cell to which you are referring, keeps your formulas accurate if the values change.

When you create a formula, you can type the cell references in uppercase, such as =B2+B3, or lowercase, such as =b2+b3. Excel changes cell references to uppercase.

In Figure 1.6, cell B2 contains 10, and cell B3 contains 2. Cell E2 contains =B2+B3 but shows the result, 12. If you change the value of cell B3 to 5, cell E2 displays the new result, which is 15. However, if you had typed actual values in the formula, =10+2, you would have to edit the formula each time an input value changes. This would be problematic, as you might forget to edit the formula or you might have a typographical error if you edit the formula. Always design worksheets in such a way as to be able to change input values without having to modify your formulas if an input value changes later.

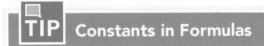
Apply the Order of Precedence

The **_order of precedence_** (also called order of operations) is a rule that controls the sequence in which arithmetic operations are performed, which affects the results of the calculation. Excel performs mathematical calculations left to right in this order: **P**ercent, **E**xponentiation, **M**ultiplication or **D**ivision, and finally **A**ddition or **S**ubtraction. Some people remember the order of precedence with the phrase *Please Excuse My Dear Aunt Sally*.

Table 1.3 lists the complete order of precedence. This chapter focuses on orders 4, 5, and 6.

TABLE 1.3 Order of Precedence

Order	Description	Symbols
1	Reference Operators	colon (:), space, and comma (,)
2	Negation	-
3	Percent	%
4	Exponentiation	^
5	Multiplication and Division	* and / (respectively)
6	Addition and Subtraction	+ and – (respectively)
7	Concatenation	ampersand symbol (&) to connect two text strings
8	Comparison	Equal sign (=), greater than (>), and less than (<)

Figure 1.7 shows formulas, the sequence in which calculations occur, calculations, the description, and the results of each order of precedence. The highlighted results are the final formula results. This figure illustrates the importance of symbols and use of parentheses.

	A	B	C	D	E	F
1	Input		Formula	Sequence	Description	Result
2	2		=A2+A3*A4+A5	1	3 (cell A3) * 4 (cell A4)	12
3	3			2	2 (cell A2) + 12 (order 1)	14
4	4			3	14 (order 2) + 5 (cell A5)	19
5	5					
6			=(A2+A3)*(A4+A5)	1	2 (cell A2) + 3 (cell A3)	5
7				2	4 (cell A4) + 5 (cell A5)	9
8				3	5 (order 1) * 9 (order 2)	45
9						
10			=A2/A3+A4*A5	1	2 (cell A2) / 3 (cell A3)	0.666667
11				2	4 (cell A4) * 5 (cell A5)	20
12				3	0.666667 (order 1) + 20 (order 2)	20.66667
13						
14			=A2/(A3+A4)*A5	1	3 (cell A3) + 4 (cell A4)	7
15				2	2 (cell A2) / 7 (order 1)	0.285714
16				3	0.285714 (order 2) * 5 (cell A5)	1.428571
17						
18			=A2^2+A3*A4%	1	4 (cell A4) is converted to percentage	0.04
19				2	2 (cell A2) to the power of 2	4
20				3	3 (cell A3) * 0.04 (order 1)	0.12
21				4	4 (order 2) + 0.12 (order 3)	4.12

FIGURE 1.7 Formula Results Based on Order of Precedence

Use Semi-Selection to Create a Formula

To decrease typing time and ensure accuracy, you can use *semi-selection*, a process of selecting a cell or range of cells for entering cell references as you create formulas. Semi-selection is often called *pointing* because you use the mouse pointer to select cells as you build the formula. To use the semi-selection technique to create a formula, do the following:

1. Click the cell where you want to create the formula.
2. Type an equal sign (=) to start a formula.
3. Click the cell or drag to select the cell range that contains the value(s) to use in the formula. A moving marquee appears around the cell or range you select, and Excel displays the cell or range reference in the formula.
4. Type a mathematical operator.
5. Continue clicking cells, selecting ranges, and typing operators to finish the formula. Use the scroll bars if the cell is in a remote location in the worksheet, or click a worksheet tab to see a cell in another worksheet.
6. Press Enter to complete the formula.

Using Auto Fill

Auto Fill enables you to copy the contents of a cell or a range of cells by dragging the *fill handle* (a small green square appearing in the bottom-right corner of the active cell) over an adjacent cell or range of cells. To use Auto Fill, do the following:

1. Click the cell with the content you want to copy to make it the active cell.
2. Point to the fill handle in the bottom-right corner of the cell until the mouse pointer changes to the fill pointer (a thin black plus sign).
3. Drag the fill handle to repeat the content in other cells.

Copy Formulas with Auto Fill

STEP 4 ›› After you enter a formula in a cell, you can duplicate the formula without retyping it by using the fill handle to copy the formula in the active cell down a column or across a row, depending on how the data are organized. Excel adapts each copied formula based on the type of cell references in the original formula.

Complete Sequences with Auto Fill

You can also use Auto Fill to complete a sequence. For example, if you enter January in a cell, you can use Auto Fill to enter the rest of the months in adjacent cells. Other sequences you can complete are quarters (Qtr 1, etc.), weekdays, and weekday abbreviations, by typing the first item and using Auto Fill to complete the other entries. For numeric sequences, however, you must specify the first two values in sequence. For example, if you want to fill in 5, 10, 15, and so on, you must enter 5 and 10 in two adjacent cells, select the two cells, and then use Auto Fill so that Excel knows to increment by 5. Figure 1.8 shows the results of filling in months, abbreviated months, quarters, weekdays, abbreviated weekdays, and increments of 5.

	A	B	C	D	E	F	G	H	I
1	January	Jan	Qtr 1	Monday	Mon	5			
2	February	Feb	Qtr 2	Tuesday	Tue	10			
3	March	Mar	Qtr 3	Wednesday	Wed	15			
4	April	Apr	Qtr 4	Thursday	Thu	20			
5	May	May		Friday	Fri	25			
6	June	Jun		Saturday	Sat	30			
7	July	Jul		Sunday	Sun	35			
8	August	Aug							
9	September	Sep					○ Copy Cells		
10	October	Oct					◉ Fill Series		
11	November	Nov					○ Fill Formatting Only		
12	December	Dec					○ Fill Without Formatting		
13							○ Flash Fill		
14									
15									

Incremented values filled in

Click to see Auto Fill Options

FIGURE 1.8 Auto Fill Examples

Immediately after you use Auto Fill, Excel displays the Auto Fill Options button in the bottom-right corner of the filled data (see Figure 1.8). Click Auto Fill Options to display five fill options: Copy Cells, Fill Series, Fill Formatting Only, Fill Without Formatting, or Flash Fill.

TIP **Double-Clicking the Fill Handle**

You can double-click the fill handle to quickly copy a formula down a column. Excel will copy the formula in the active cell for each row of data to calculate in your worksheet.

Displaying Cell Formulas

Excel shows the result of the formula in the cell (see the top half of Figure 1.9); however, you might want to display the formulas instead of the calculated results in the cells (see the bottom half of Figure 1.9). To display cell formulas, do one of the following:

STEP 5 ❯❯

- Press Ctrl and the grave accent (`) key, sometimes referred to as the tilde key, in the top-left corner of the keyboard, below the Esc key.
- Click Show Formulas in the Formula Auditing group on the FORMULAS tab.

To hide the formulas and display the formula results again, repeat the preceding process.

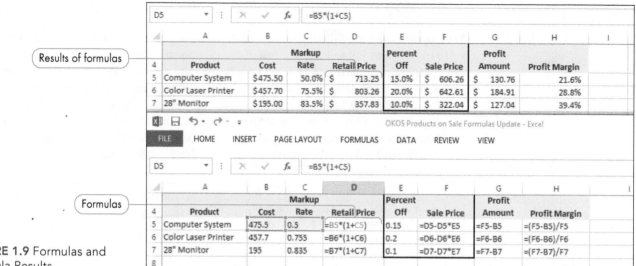

Results of formulas

| D5 | fx | =B5*(1+C5) |

▲	A	B	C	D	E	F	G	H	I
			Markup			Percent		Profit		
4	Product	Cost	Rate	Retail Price	Off	Sale Price	Amount	Profit Margin	
5	Computer System	$475.50	50.0%	$ 713.25	15.0%	$ 606.26	$ 130.76	21.6%	
6	Color Laser Printer	$457.70	75.5%	$ 803.26	20.0%	$ 642.61	$ 184.91	28.8%	
7	28" Monitor	$195.00	83.5%	$ 357.83	10.0%	$ 322.04	$ 127.04	39.4%	

OKOS Products on Sale Formulas Update - Excel

FILE HOME INSERT PAGE LAYOUT FORMULAS DATA REVIEW VIEW

| D5 | fx | =B5*(1+C5) |

Formulas

▲	A	B	C	D	E	F	G	H	I
			Markup			Percent		Profit		
4	Product	Cost	Rate	Retail Price	Off	Sale Price	Amount	Profit Margin	
5	Computer System	475.5	0.5	=B5*(1+C5)	0.15	=D5-D5*E5	=F5-B5	=(F5-B5)/F5	
6	Color Laser Printer	457.7	0.755	=B6*(1+C6)	0.2	=D6-D6*E6	=F6-B6	=(F6-B6)/F6	
7	28" Monitor	195	0.835	=B7*(1+C7)	0.1	=D7-D7*E7	=F7-B7	=(F7-B7)/F7	
8									

FIGURE 1.9 Formulas and Formula Results

Quick Concepts ✓

1. What is the order of precedence? Provide and explain two examples that use four different operators, one with parentheses and one without. *p. 13*

2. What is the purpose of Auto Fill? Provide an example of data you can complete using Auto Fill. *p. 14*

3. Why would it be useful to display formulas instead of formula results in a worksheet? *p. 15*

Hands-On Exercises

2 Mathematics and Formulas

In Hands-On Exercise 1, you created the basic worksheet for OKOS by entering text, values, and a date for items on sale. Now you need to insert formulas to calculate the missing results—specifically, the retail (before sale) value, sale price, and profit margin. You will use cell addresses in your formulas, so when you change a referenced value, the formula results will update automatically.

Skills covered: Use Cell References in a Formula and Apply the Order of Precedence • Use the Semi-Selection Method to Enter a Formula • Use Cell References in a Formula and Apply the Order of Precedence • Copy Formulas with Auto Fill • Change Values and Display Cell Formulas

STEP 1 ≫ USE CELL REFERENCES IN A FORMULA AND APPLY THE ORDER OF PRECEDENCE

The first formula you need to create will calculate the retail price. The retail price is the price you originally charge. It is based on a percentage of the original cost so that you earn a profit. Refer to Figure 1.10 as you complete Step 1.

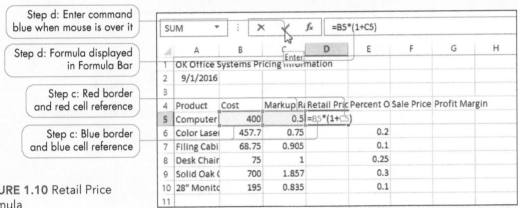

FIGURE 1.10 Retail Price Formula

a. Open *e01h1Markup_LastFirst* if you closed it at the end of Hands-On Exercise 1 and save it as **e01h2Markup_LastFirst**, changing *h1* to *h2*.

> **TROUBLESHOOTING:** If you make any major mistakes in this exercise, you can close the file, open *e01h1Markup_LastFirst* again, and then start this exercise over.

b. Click **cell D5**, the cell where you will enter the formula to calculate the retail selling price of the first item.

c. Type **=B5*(1+C5)** and view the formula and the colored cells and borders on the screen.

   As you type or edit a formula, each cell address in the formula displays in a specific color, and while you type or edit the formula, the cells referenced in the formula have a temporarily colored border. For example, in the formula =B5*(1+C5), B5 appears in blue, and C5 appears in red. Cell B5 has a temporarily blue border and cell C5 has a temporarily red border to help you identify cells as you construct your formulas (see Figure 1.10).

An alternative formula also calculates the correct retail price: =B5*C5+B5 or =B5+B5*C5. In this formula, 400 (cell B5) is multiplied by 0.5 (cell C5); that result (200) represents the dollar value of the markup. Excel adds the value 200 to the original cost of 400 to obtain 600, the retail price. You were instructed to enter =B5*(1+C5) to demonstrate the order of precedence.

d. Click **Enter** (the check mark ✓ between the Name Box and the Formula Bar) and view the formula in the Formula Bar to check it for accuracy.

The result of the formula, 600, appears in cell D5, and the formula displays in the Formula Bar. This formula first adds 1 (the decimal equivalent of 100%) to 0.5 (the value stored in cell C5). Excel multiplies that sum of 1.5 by 400 (the value stored in cell B5). The theory behind this formula is that the retail price is 150% of the original cost.

> **TROUBLESHOOTING:** If the result is not correct, click the cell and look at the formula in the Formula Bar. Click in the Formula Bar, edit the formula to match the formula shown in Step c, and then click Enter (the check mark between the Name Box and the Formula Bar). Make sure you start the formula with an equal sign.

e. Save the workbook with the new formula.

STEP 2 ≫ USE THE SEMI-SELECTION METHOD TO ENTER A FORMULA

Now that you have calculated the retail price, you need to calculate a sale price. This week, the computer is on sale for 15% off the retail price. Refer to Figure 1.11 as you complete Step 2.

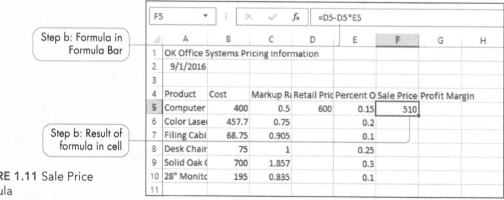

Step b: Formula in Formula Bar

Step b: Result of formula in cell

FIGURE 1.11 Sale Price Formula

a. Click **cell F5**, the cell where you will enter the formula to calculate the sale price.

b. Type =, click **cell D5**, type -, click **cell D5**, type *, and then click **cell E5**. Notice the color-coding in the cell addresses. Press **Ctrl+Enter** to keep the current cell the active cell.

You used the semi-selection method to enter a formula. The result is 510. Looking at the formula, you might think D5–D5 equals zero; remember that because of the order of precedence rules, multiplication is calculated before subtraction. The product of 600 (cell D5) and 0.15 (cell E5) equals 90, which is then subtracted from 600 (cell D5), so the sale price is 510. If it helps to understand the formula better, add parentheses: =D5-(D5*E5).

c. Save the workbook with the new formula.

You should check the result for logic. Use a calculator to spot-check the accuracy of formulas. If you mark down merchandise by 15% of its regular price, you are charging 85% of the regular price. You can spot-check your formula to ensure that 85% of 600 is 510 by multiplying 600 by 0.85.

STEP 3 ≫ USE CELL REFERENCES IN A FORMULA AND APPLY THE ORDER OF PRECEDENCE

After calculating the sale price, you want to know the profit margin OKOS will earn. OKOS paid $400 for the computer and will sell it for $510. The profit of $110 is then divided by the $400 cost, which gives OKOS a profit margin of 21.57%. Refer to Figure 1.12 as you complete Step 3.

Step b: Formula in Formula Bar

| G5 | ▾ | : | ✕ | ✓ | *fx* | =(F5-B5)/F5 |

◢	A	B	C	D	E	F	G	H
1	OK Office Systems Pricing Information							
2	9/1/2016							
3								
4	Product	Cost	Markup Ra	Retail Pric	Percent O	Sale Price	Profit Margin	
5	Computer	400	0.5	600	0.15	510	0.215686	
6	Color Laser	457.7	0.75		0.2			
7	Filing Cabi	68.75	0.905		0.1			
8	Desk Chair	75	1		0.25			
9	Solid Oak C	700	1.857		0.3			
10	28" Monito	195	0.835		0.1			
11								

Step b: Result of formula in cell

FIGURE 1.12 Profit Margin Formula

a. Click **cell G5**, the cell where you will enter the formula to calculate the profit margin.

   The profit margin is the profit (difference in sales price and cost) percentage of the sale price.

b. Type **=(F5-B5)/F5** and notice the color-coding in the cell addresses. Press **Ctrl+Enter**.

   The formula must first calculate the profit, which is the difference between the sale price (510) and the original cost (400). The difference (110) is then divided by the sale price (510) to determine the profit margin of 0.215686, or 21.6%.

┌──┐
│ **TROUBLESHOOTING:** If you type a backslash (\) instead of a forward slash (/), Excel will │
│ display an error message box. Make sure you type / as the division operator. │
└──┘

c. Look at the Formula Bar and save the workbook with the new formula.

STEP 4 ≫ COPY FORMULAS WITH AUTO FILL

After double-checking the accuracy of your calculations for the first product, you are ready to copy the formulas down the columns to calculate the retail price, sale price, and profit margin for the other products. Refer to Figure 1.13 as you complete Step 4.

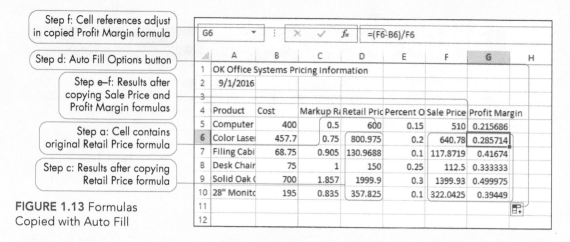

Step f: Cell references adjust in copied Profit Margin formula

Step d: Auto Fill Options button

Step e–f: Results after copying Sale Price and Profit Margin formulas

Step a: Cell contains original Retail Price formula

Step c: Results after copying Retail Price formula

FIGURE 1.13 Formulas Copied with Auto Fill

a. Click **cell D5**, the cell containing the formula to calculate the retail price for the first item.

b. Position the mouse pointer on the **cell D5 fill handle**. When the pointer changes from a white plus sign to a thin black plus sign, double-click the **fill handle**.

Excel's Auto Fill feature copies the retail price formula for the remaining products in your worksheet. Excel detects when to stop copying the formula when it encounters a blank row, such as in row 11.

c. Click **cell D6**, the cell containing the first copied retail price formula, and look at the Formula Bar.

The formula in cell D5 is =B5*(1+C5). The copied formula in cell D6 is =B6*(1+C6). Excel adjusts the cell addresses in the formula as it copies the formula down a column so that the results are based on each row's data rather than using the original formula's cell addresses for other products.

> **TROUBLESHOOTING:** The result in cell D7 may show more decimal places than shown in Figure 1.13. This may be due to different screen resolutions. Do not worry about this slight difference.

d. Select the **range F5:G5**. Double-click the **fill handle** in the bottom-right corner of **cell G5**.

Auto Fill copies the selected formulas down their respective columns. Auto Fill Options are available down and to the right of the cell G10 fill handle, indicating you could select different fill options if you want.

> **TROUBLESHOOTING:** If Excel displays pound symbols, such as ####, instead of results, that means the column is not wide enough to show results. You will learn how to adjust column widths in the third section.

e. Click **cell F6**, the cell containing the first copied sale price formula, and view the Formula Bar.

The original formula was =D5-D5*E5. The copied formula in cell F6 is adjusted to =D6-D6*E6 so that it calculates the sales price based on the data in row 6.

f. Click **cell G6**, the cell containing the first copied profit margin formula, and look at the Formula Bar. Save the workbook.

The original formula was =(F5-B5)/F5, and the copied formula in cell G6 is =(F6-B6)/F6.

STEP 5 ›› CHANGE VALUES AND DISPLAY CELL FORMULAS

You want to see how the prices and profit margins are affected when you change some of the original cost values. For example, the supplier might notify you that the cost to you will increase. In addition, you want to see the formulas displayed in the cells temporarily. Refer to Figures 1.14 and 1.15 as you complete Step 5.

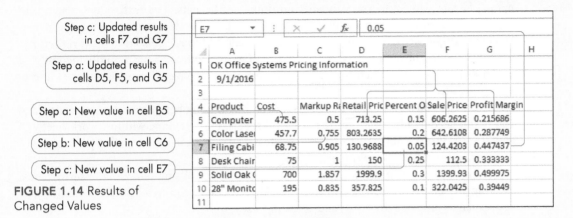

Step c: Updated results in cells F7 and G7

Step a: Updated results in cells D5, F5, and G5

Step a: New value in cell B5

Step b: New value in cell C6

Step c: New value in cell E7

FIGURE 1.14 Results of Changed Values

a. Click **cell B5**, type **475.5**, and then press **Enter**.

   The results of the retail price, sale price, and profit margin formulas change based on the new cost.

b. Click **cell C6**, type **0.755**, and then press **Enter**.

   The results of the retail price, sale price, and profit margin formulas change based on the new markup rate.

c. Click **cell E7**, type **0.05**, and then press **Ctrl+Enter**.

   The results of the sale price and profit margin formulas change based on the new markdown rate. Note that the retail price did not change, since that formula is not based on the markdown rate.

d. Press **Ctrl+`** (the grave accent mark).

   The workbook now displays the formulas rather than the formula results (see Figure 1.15). This is helpful when you want to review several formulas at one time.

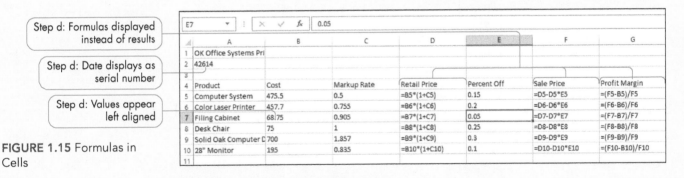

Step d: Formulas displayed instead of results

Step d: Date displays as serial number

Step d: Values appear left aligned

FIGURE 1.15 Formulas in Cells

e. Press **Ctrl+`** (the grave accent mark).

   The workbook now displays the formula results in the cells again.

f. Save the workbook. Keep the workbook open if you plan to continue with the next Hands-On Exercise. If not, close the workbook and exit Excel.

Workbook and Worksheet Management

When you start a new blank workbook in Excel, the workbook contains one worksheet named Sheet1. However, you can add additional worksheets. The text, values, dates, and formulas you enter into the individual sheets are saved under one workbook file name. Having multiple worksheets in one workbook is helpful to keep related items together. For example, you might want one worksheet for each month to track your monthly income and expenses for one year. When tax time comes around, you have all your data stored in one workbook file.

Although you should plan the worksheet and workbook before you start entering data, you might need to add, delete, or rename worksheets. Furthermore, within a worksheet you may want to insert a new row to accommodate new data, delete a column that you no longer need, or adjust the size of columns and rows.

In this section, you will learn how to manage workbooks by renaming, inserting, and deleting worksheets. You will also learn how to make changes to worksheet columns and rows, such as inserting, deleting, and adjusting sizes.

Managing Worksheets

Creating a multiple-worksheet workbook takes some planning and maintenance. Worksheet tab names should reflect the contents of the respective worksheets. In addition, you can insert, copy, move, and delete worksheets within the workbook. You can even apply background color to the worksheet tabs so that they stand out onscreen. Figure 1.16 shows a workbook in which the sheet tabs have been renamed, colors have been applied to worksheet tabs, and a worksheet tab has been right-clicked so that the shortcut menu appears.

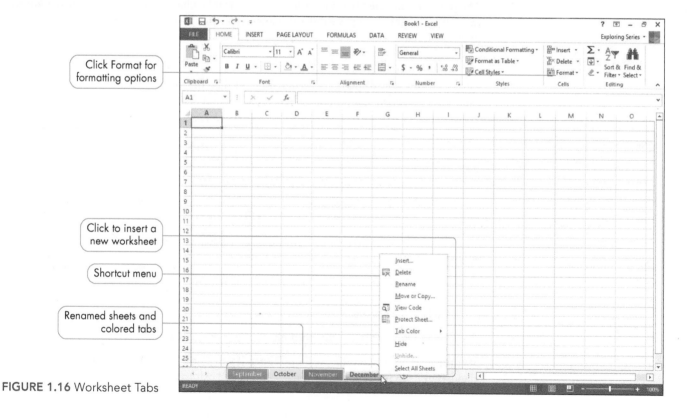

FIGURE 1.16 Worksheet Tabs

Rename a Worksheet

STEP 1 » The default worksheet name Sheet1 does not describe the contents of the worksheet. You should rename worksheet tabs to reflect the sheet contents. For example, if your budget workbook contains monthly worksheets, name the worksheets September, October, etc. Although you can have spaces in worksheet names, keep worksheet names relatively short. The longer the worksheet names, the fewer sheet tabs you will see at the bottom of the workbook window without scrolling.

To rename a worksheet, do one of the following:

- Double-click a sheet tab, type the new name, and then press Enter.
- Click the sheet tab for the sheet you want to rename, click Format in the Cells group on the HOME tab (refer to Figure 1.16), select Rename Sheet (see Figure 1.17), type the new sheet name, and then press Enter.
- Right-click the sheet tab, select Rename from the shortcut menu (see Figure 1.16), type the new sheet name, and then press Enter.

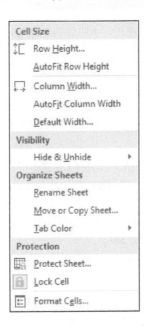

FIGURE 1.17 Format Menu

Change Worksheet Tab Color

STEP 1 » The active worksheet tab is white with a green bottom border. When you use multiple worksheets, you might want to apply a different color to each worksheet tab to make the tab stand out or to emphasize the difference between sheets. For example, you might apply red to the September tab, green to the October tab, dark blue to the November tab, and purple to the December tab.

To change the color of a worksheet tab, do one of the following:

- Click the sheet tab for the sheet you want to rename, click Format in the Cells group on the HOME tab (refer to Figure 1.16), point to Tab Color (refer to Figure 1.17), and then click a color on the Tab Color palette.
- Right-click the sheet tab, point to Tab Color on the shortcut menu (refer to Figure 1.16), and then click a color on the Tab Color palette.

Insert and Delete a Worksheet

STEP 2 >> Sometimes you need more than one worksheet in the workbook. For example, you might create a workbook that contains 12 worksheets—a worksheet for each month of the year. To insert a new worksheet, do one of the following:

- Click *New sheet* to the right of the last worksheet tab.
- Click the Insert arrow—either to the right or below Insert—in the Cells group on the HOME tab and select Insert Sheet.
- Right-click any sheet tab, select Insert from the shortcut menu (refer to Figure 1.16), click Worksheet in the Insert dialog box, and then click OK.
- Press Shift+F11.

TIP Ribbon Commands with Arrows

Some commands, such as Insert in the Cells group, contain two parts: the main command and an arrow. The arrow may be below or to the right of the command, depending on the command, window size, or screen resolution. Instructions in the Exploring Series use the command name to instruct you to click the main command to perform the default action, such as *Click Insert in the Cells group* or *Click Delete in the Cells group*. Instructions include the word arrow when you need to select an additional option, such as *Click the Insert arrow in the Cells group* or *Click the Delete arrow in the Cells group*.

If you no longer need the data in a worksheet, delete the worksheet. Doing so will eliminate extra data in a file and reduce file size. To delete a worksheet in a workbook, do one of the following:

- Click the Delete arrow—either to the right or below Delete—in the Cells group on the HOME tab and select Delete Sheet.
- Right-click any sheet tab and select Delete from the shortcut menu (refer to Figure 1.16).

If the sheet you are trying to delete contains data, Excel will display a warning: *You can't undo deleting sheets, and you might be removing some data. If you don't need it, click Delete.* If you try to delete a blank worksheet, Excel will not display a warning; it will immediately delete the sheet.

Move or Copy a Worksheet

After inserting and deleting worksheets, you can arrange the worksheet tabs in a different sequence, especially if the newly inserted worksheets do not fall within a logical sequence. To move a worksheet, do one of the following:

- Drag a worksheet tab to the desired location. As you drag a sheet tab, the pointer resembles a piece of paper. A down-pointing triangle appears between sheet tabs to indicate where the sheet will be placed when you release the mouse button.
- Click Format in the Cells group on the HOME tab (refer to Figure 1.16) and select *Move or Copy Sheet*, or right-click the sheet tab you want to move and select *Move or Copy* to display the *Move or Copy* dialog box (see Figure 1.18). You can move the worksheet within the current workbook, or you can move the worksheet to a different workbook. In the *Before sheet* list, select the worksheet you want to come after the moved worksheet and click OK. For example, you have just created a new worksheet named August and you want it to come before the September worksheet. You would select September in the *Before sheet* list.

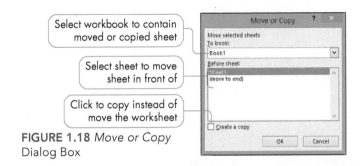

Select workbook to contain
moved or copied sheet

Select sheet to move
sheet in front of

Click to copy instead of
move the worksheet

FIGURE 1.18 *Move or Copy*
Dialog Box

After creating a worksheet, you may want to copy it to use as a template or starting point for similar data. For example, if you create a worksheet for your September budget, you can copy the worksheet and then easily edit the data on the copied worksheet to enter data for your October budget. Copying the entire worksheet would save you a lot of valuable time in entering and formatting the new worksheet. The process for copying a worksheet is similar to moving a sheet. To copy a worksheet, press and hold Ctrl as you drag the worksheet tab. Alternatively, display the *Move or Copy* dialog box, select the *To book* and *Before sheet* options (refer to Figure 1.18), click the *Create a copy* check box, and then click OK.

Managing Columns and Rows

As you enter and edit worksheet data, you can adjust the row and column structure. You can add rows and columns to add new data, or you can delete data you no longer need. Adjusting the height and width of rows and columns, respectively, can present the data better.

Insert Cells, Columns, and Rows

STEP 3》

After you construct a worksheet, you might need to insert cells, columns, or rows to accommodate new data. For example, you might need to insert a new column to perform calculations or a new row to list a new product. When you insert cells, rows, and columns, cell addresses in formulas adjust automatically.

To insert a new column or row, do one of the following:

- Click in the column or row for which you want to insert a new column to the left or a new row above, respectively. Click the Insert arrow in the Cells group on the HOME tab and select Insert Sheet Columns or Insert Sheet Rows.

- Right-click the column (letter) or row (number) heading for which you want to insert a new column to the left or a new row above, respectively, and select Insert from the shortcut menu.

Excel inserts new columns to the left of the current column and new rows above the active row. If the current column is column C and you insert a new column, the new column becomes column C, and the original column C data are now in column D. Likewise, if the current row is 5 and you insert a new row, the new row is row 5, and the original row 5 data are now in row 6.

Inserting a cell is helpful when you realize that you left out an entry in one column after you have entered columns of data. Instead of inserting a new row for all columns, you just want to move the existing content down in one column to enter the missing value. You can insert a single cell in a particular row or column. To insert a cell, click in the cell where you want the new cell, click the Insert arrow in the Cells group on the Home tab, and then select Insert Cells. Select an option from the Insert dialog box (see Figure 1.19) to position the new cell and click OK. Alternatively, click Insert in the Cells group. The default action of clicking Insert is to insert a cell at the current location, which moves existing data down in that column only.

FIGURE 1.19 Insert Dialog
Box

Delete Cells, Columns, and Rows

STEP 4 ≫ If you no longer need a cell, column, or row, you can delete it. In these situations, you are deleting the entire cell, column, or row, not just the contents of the cell to leave empty cells. As with inserting new cells, any affected formulas adjust the cell references automatically. To delete a column or row, do one of the following:

- Click the column or row heading for the column or row you want to delete. Click Delete in the Cells group on the HOME tab.

- Click in any cell within the column or row you want to delete. Click the Delete arrow in the Cells group on the HOME tab and select Delete Sheet Columns or Delete Sheet Rows, respectively.

- Right-click the column letter or row number for the column or row you want to delete and select Delete from the shortcut menu.

To delete a cell or cells, select the cell(s), click the Delete arrow in the Cells group, and then select Delete Cells to display the Delete dialog box (see Figure 1.20). Click the appropriate option to shift cells left or up and click OK. Alternatively, click Delete in the Cells group. The default action of clicking Delete is to delete the active cell, which moves existing data up in that column only.

FIGURE 1.20 Delete Dialog
Box

Adjust Column Width

STEP 5 ≫ After you enter data in a column, you often need to adjust the *column width*—the number of characters that can fit horizontally using the default font or the number of horizontal pixels—to show the contents of cells. For example, in the worksheet you created in Hands-On Exercises 1 and 2, the labels in column A displayed into column B when those adjacent cells were empty. However, after you typed values in column B, the labels in column A appeared cut off. You will need to widen column A to show the full name of all of your products.

TIP | Pound Signs Displayed

Numbers appear as a series of pound signs (######) when the cell is too narrow to display the complete value, and text appears to be truncated.

To widen a column to accommodate the longest label or value in a column, do one of the following:

- Position the pointer on the vertical border between the current column heading and the next column heading. When the pointer displays as a two-headed arrow, double-click the border. For example, if column B is too narrow to display the content in that column, double-click the border between the column B and C headings.
- Click Format in the Cells group on the HOME tab (refer to Figure 1.16) and select AutoFit Column Width (refer to Figure 1.17).

To widen a column to an exact width, do one of the following:

- Drag the vertical border to the left to decrease the column width or to the right to increase the column width. As you drag the vertical border, Excel displays a ScreenTip specifying the width (see Figure 1.21) from 0 to 255 characters and in pixels.
- Click Format in the Cells group on the HOME tab (refer to Figure 1.16), select Column Width (refer to Figure 1.17), type a value in the Column width box in the Column Width dialog box, and then click OK.

ScreenTip displaying column width

Mouse pointer as you drag the border between column headings

Current column width

Column width when you release the mouse button

	A	B	C	D	E	F	G	H
1	OK Office Systems Pricing Information							
2	9/1/2016							
3								
4	Product	Cost	Markup R	Retail Pric	Percent O	Sale Price	Profit Margin	
5	Computer	475.5	0.5	713.25	0.15	606.263	0.275	
6	Color Lase	457.7	0.755	803.264	0.2	642.611	0.404	
7	Filing Cabi	68.75	0.905	130.969	0.05	124.42	0.80975	
8	Desk Chai	75	1	150	0.25	112.5	0.5	
9	Solid Oak	700	1.857	1999.9	0.3	1399.93	0.9999	
10	28" Monit	195	0.835	357.825	0.1	322.043	0.6515	

D14 | Width: 10.57 (79 pixels)

FIGURE 1.21 Changing Column Width

Adjust Row Height

When you increase the font size of cell contents, Excel automatically increases the *row height*—the vertical measurement of the row. However, if you insert a line break or wrap text to create multiple lines of text in a cell, Excel might not increase the row height. You can adjust the row height in a way similar to how you change column width by double-clicking the border between row numbers or by selecting Row Height or AutoFit Row Height from the Format menu (refer to Figure 1.17). In Excel, row height is a value between 0 and 409 based on point size (abbreviated as pt) and pixels. Whether you are measuring font sizes or row heights, one point size is equal to 1/72 of an inch. Your row height should be taller than your font size. For example, with an 11-pt font size, the default row height is 15.

TIP | Multiple Column Widths and Row Heights

You can set the size for more than one column or row at a time to make the selected columns or rows the same size. Drag across the column or row headings for the area you want to format, and then set the size using any method.

Hide and Unhide Columns and Rows

STEP 6 >> If your worksheet contains confidential information, you might need to hide some columns and/or rows before you print a copy for public distribution. However, the column or row is not deleted. If you hide column B, you will see columns A and C side by side. If you hide row 3, you will see rows 2 and 4 together. Figure 1.22 shows that column B and row 3 are hidden. Excel displays a double line between **column headings** (such as between A and C), indicating one or more columns are hidden, and a double line between row headings (such as between 2 and 4), indicating one or more rows are hidden.

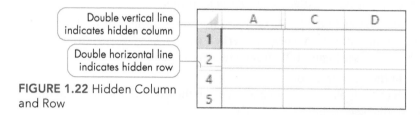

Double vertical line indicates hidden column

Double horizontal line indicates hidden row

FIGURE 1.22 Hidden Column and Row

To hide a column or row, do one of the following:

- Click in the column or row you want to hide, click Format in the Cells group on the HOME tab (refer to Figure 1.16), point to Hide & Unhide (refer to Figure 1.17), and then select Hide Columns or Hide Rows, depending on what you want to hide.
- Right-click the column or row heading(s) you want to hide and select Hide.

You can hide multiple columns and rows at the same time. To select adjacent columns (such as columns B through E) or adjacent rows (such as rows 2 through 4), drag across the adjacent column or row headings. To hide nonadjacent columns or rows, press and hold Ctrl while you click the desired column or row headings. After selecting multiple columns or rows, use any acceptable method to hide the selected columns or rows.

To unhide a column or row, select the columns or rows on both sides of the hidden column or row. For example, if column B is hidden, drag across column letters A and C. Then do one of the following:

- Click Format in the Cells group on the HOME tab (refer to Figure 1.16), point to Hide & Unhide (refer to Figure 1.17), and then select Unhide Columns or Unhide Rows, depending on what you want to display again.
- Right-click the column(s) or row(s) you want to hide and select Unhide.

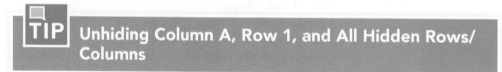

TIP   Unhiding Column A, Row 1, and All Hidden Rows/ Columns

Unhiding column A or row 1 is different because you cannot select the row or column on either side. To unhide column A or row 1, type A1 in the Name Box and press Enter. Click Format in the Cells group on the Home tab, point to Hide & Unhide, and then select Unhide Columns or Unhide Rows to display column A or row 1, respectively. If you want to unhide all columns and rows, click Select All and use the Hide & Unhide submenu.

Quick Concepts ✓

1. What is the benefit of renaming a worksheet? ***p. 23***
2. What are two ways to insert a new row in a worksheet? ***p. 25***
3. How can you delete cell B5 without deleting the entire row or column? ***p. 26***
4. When should you adjust column widths instead of using the default width? ***p. 26***

Hands-On Exercises

Watch the Video for this Hands-On Exercise!

MyITLab®
HOE3 Training

3 Workbook and Worksheet Management

After reviewing the OKOS worksheet, you decide to rename the worksheet, change the worksheet tab color, insert a worksheet, and delete an empty worksheet. In addition, you need to insert a column to calculate the amount of markup and delete a row containing data you no longer need. You also need to adjust column widths to display the labels in the columns.

Skills covered: Rename a Worksheet and Select a Tab Color • Insert, Move, and Delete a Worksheet • Insert a Column and Rows • Delete a Row • Adjust Column Width and Row Height • Hide and Unhide Columns

STEP 1 ≫ RENAME A WORKSHEET AND SELECT A TAB COLOR

You want to rename Sheet1 to describe the worksheet contents and add a color to the sheet tab. Refer to Figure 1.23 as you complete Step 1.

FIGURE 1.23 Renamed Worksheet with Tab Color

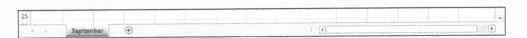

a. Open *e01h2Markup_LastFirst* if you closed it at the end of Hands-On Exercise 2 and save it as **e01h3Markup_LastFirst**, changing *h2* to *h3*.

b. Double-click the **Sheet1 sheet tab**, type **September**, and then press **Enter**.

   You renamed Sheet1 September.

c. Right-click the **September sheet tab**, point to *Tab Color*, and then click **Red** in the *Standard Colors* section.

   The worksheet tab color is red.

d. Save the workbook.

STEP 2 ≫ INSERT, MOVE, AND DELETE A WORKSHEET

Your supervisor asks you to add another worksheet to the workbook. She wants you to place it before the September worksheet so that she can add August data. After you do this, she calls you on the phone and tells you that she won't be adding the August data after all. Therefore, you will delete that worksheet. Refer to Figure 1.24 as you complete Step 2.

Step a: Click to insert new sheet
Step b: New sheet moved to the left

FIGURE 1.24 New Sheet Inserted

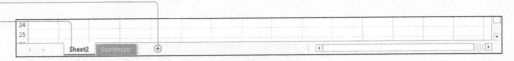

a. Click **New sheet**, the plus icon to the right of the September sheet tab.

   Excel adds a new worksheet named either Sheet1 or Sheet2 to the right of the previously active sheet.

b. Drag the **Sheet tab** to the left of the September sheet tab.

c. Click the **Sheet tab**, click the **Delete arrow** in the Cells group on the HOME tab, and then select **Delete Sheet**.

   You deleted the blank worksheet from the workbook.

> **TROUBLESHOOTING:** Delete in the Cells group, like some other commands in Excel, contains two parts: the main command icon and an arrow. Click the main command icon when instructed to click Delete to perform the default action. Click the arrow when instructed to click the Delete arrow for additional command options.

> **TROUBLESHOOTING:** Notice that Undo is unavailable on the Quick Access Toolbar. You cannot undo deleting a worksheet. It is deleted!

d. Save the workbook.

STEP 3 ≫ INSERT A COLUMN AND ROWS

You decide that you need a column to display the amount of profit. Because profit is a dollar amount, you want to keep the profit column close to another column of dollar amounts. Therefore, you will insert the profit column before the profit margin (percentage) column. You also want to insert new rows for product information and category names. Refer to Figure 1.25 as you complete Step 3.

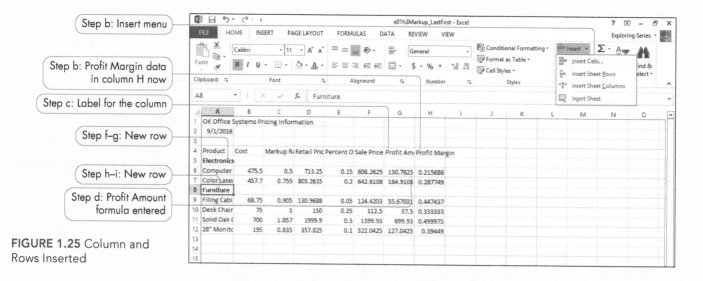

Step b: Insert menu
Step b: Profit Margin data in column H now
Step c: Label for the column
Step f–g: New row
Step h–i: New row
Step d: Profit Amount formula entered

FIGURE 1.25 Column and Rows Inserted

a. Click **cell G5** (or any cell in column G), the column containing the Profit Margin.

You want to insert a column between the Sale Price and Profit Margin columns so that you can calculate the profit amount in dollars.

b. Click the **Insert arrow** in the Cells group and select **Insert Sheet Columns**.

You inserted a new, blank column G. The data in the original column G are now in column H.

c. Click **cell G4**, type **Profit Amount**, and then press **Enter**.

d. Make sure the active cell is **cell G5**. Type **=F5-B5** and click **Enter** (the check mark between the Name Box and the Formula Bar). Double-click the **cell G5 fill handle** to copy the formula down the column.

You calculated the profit amount by subtracting the original cost from the sale price. Although steps e and f below illustrate one way to insert a row, you can use other methods presented in this chapter.

e. Right-click the **row 5 heading**, the row containing the Computer System data.

Excel displays a shortcut menu consisting of commands you can perform.

f. Select **Insert** from the shortcut menu.

You inserted a new blank row 5, which is selected. The original rows of data move down a row each.

g. Click **cell A5**. Type **Electronics** and press **Ctrl+Enter**. Click **Bold** in the Font group on the HOME tab.

You typed and bolded the category name *Electronics* above the list of electronic products.

h. Right-click the **row 8 heading**, the row containing the Filing Cabinet data, and select **Insert** from the shortcut menu.

i. Click **cell A8**. Type **Furniture** and press **Ctrl+Enter**. Click **Bold** in the Font group on the HOME tab.

You typed and bolded the category name *Furniture* above the list of furniture products.

j. Save the workbook.

STEP 4 ≫ DELETE A ROW

You just realized that you do not have enough filing cabinets in stock to offer on sale, so you need to delete the Filing Cabinet row. Refer to Figure 1.26 as you complete Step 4.

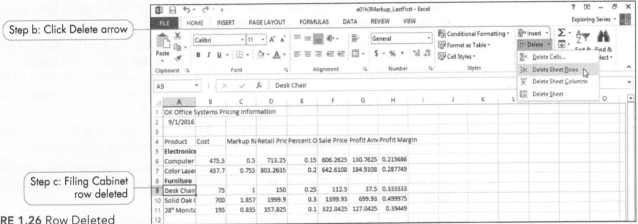

Step b: Click Delete arrow

Step c: Filing Cabinet row deleted

FIGURE 1.26 Row Deleted

a. Click **cell A9** (or any cell on row 9), the row that contains the Filing Cabinet data.

b. Click the **Delete arrow** in the Cells group.

c. Select **Delete Sheet Rows** and save the workbook.

The Filing Cabinet row is deleted and the remaining rows move up one row.

> **TROUBLESHOOTING:** If you accidentally delete the wrong row or accidentally select Delete Sheet Columns instead of Delete Sheet Rows, click Undo on the Quick Access Toolbar to restore the deleted row or column.

STEP 5 ≫ ADJUST COLUMN WIDTH AND ROW HEIGHT

As you review your worksheet, you notice that the labels in column A appear cut off. You need to increase the width of that column to display the entire product names. In addition, you want to make row 1 taller. Refer to Figure 1.27 as you complete Step 5.

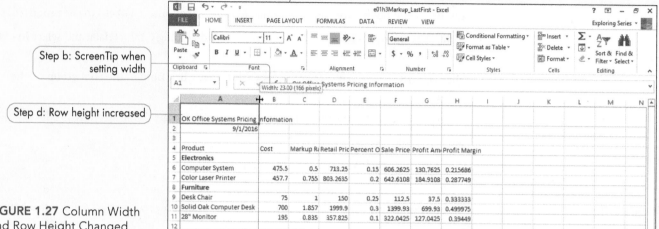

Step b: ScreenTip when setting width

Step d: Row height increased

FIGURE 1.27 Column Width and Row Height Changed

a. Position the pointer between the column A and B headings. When the pointer looks like a double-headed arrow, double-click the border.

When you double-click the border between two columns, Excel adjusts the width of the column on the left side of the border to fit the contents of that column. Excel increased the width of column A based on the cell containing the longest content (the title in cell A1, which will eventually span over all columns). Therefore, you want to decrease the column to avoid so much empty space in column A.

b. Position the pointer between the column A and B headings again. Drag the border to the left until the ScreenTip displays **Width: 23.00 (166 pixels)**. Release the mouse button.

You decreased the column width to 23 for column A. The longest product name is visible. You will not adjust the other column widths until after you apply formats to the column headings in Hands-On Exercise 5.

c. Click **cell A1**. Click **Format** in the Cells group and select **Row Height** to display the Row Height dialog box.

d. Type **30** in the **Row height box** and click **OK**. Save the workbook.

You increased the height of the row that contains the worksheet title so that it is more prominent.

STEP 6 >> HIDE AND UNHIDE COLUMNS

To focus on the dollar amounts, you decide to hide the markup rate, discount rate, and profit margin columns. Refer to Figure 1.28 as you complete Step 6.

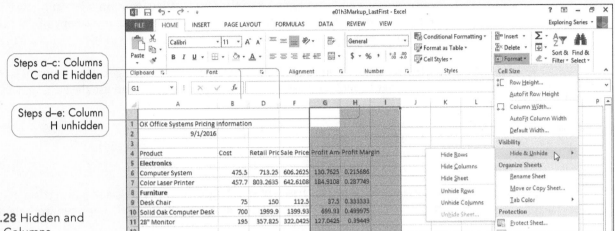

FIGURE 1.28 Hidden and Unhidden Columns

a. Click the **column C heading**, the column containing the Markup Rate values.

b. Press and hold **Ctrl** as you click the **column E heading** and the **column H heading**. Release Ctrl after selecting the headings.

   Holding down Ctrl enables you to select nonadjacent ranges. You want to hide the rate columns temporarily.

c. Click **Format** in the Cells group, point to *Hide & Unhide*, and then select **Hide Columns**.

   Excel hides the selected columns. You see a gap in column heading letters, indicating columns are hidden (refer to Figure 1.28).

d. Drag to select the **column G and I headings**.

   You want to unhide column H, so you must select the columns on both sides of the hidden column.

e. Click **Format** in the Cells group, point to *Hide & Unhide*, and then select **Unhide Columns**.

   Column H, which contains the Profit Margin values, is no longer hidden. You will keep the other columns hidden and save the workbook as evidence that you know how to hide columns. You will unhide the remaining columns in the next Hands-On Exercise.

f. Save the workbook. Keep the workbook open if you plan to continue with the next Hands-On Exercise. If not, close the workbook and exit Excel.

Clipboard Tasks

Although you plan worksheets before entering data, you might decide to move data to a different location in the same worksheet or even in a different worksheet. Instead of deleting the original data and then typing it in the new location, you can select and move data from one cell to another. In some instances, you might want to create a copy of data entered so that you can explore different values and compare the results of the original data set and the copied and edited data set.

In this section, you will learn how to select different ranges. Then you will learn how to move a range to another location, make a copy of a range, and use the Paste Special feature.

Selecting, Moving, Copying, and Pasting Data

You may already know the basics of selecting, cutting, copying, and pasting data in other programs, such as Microsoft Word. These tasks are somewhat different when working in Excel.

Select a Range

STEP 1 ≫ A *range* refers to a group of adjacent or contiguous cells. A range may be as small as a single cell or as large as the entire worksheet. It may consist of a row or part of a row, a column or part of a column, or multiple rows or columns, but will always be a rectangular shape, as you must select the same number of cells in each row or column for the entire range. A range is specified by indicating the top-left and bottom-right cells in the selection. For example, in Figure 1.29, the date is a single-cell range in cell A2, the Color Laser Printer data are stored in the range A6:G6, the cost values are stored in the range B5:B10, and the sales prices and profit margins are stored in range F5:G10. A *nonadjacent range* contains multiple ranges, such as C5:C10 and E5:E10. At times, you need to select nonadjacent ranges so that you can apply the same formatting at the same time, such as formatting the nonadjacent range C5:C10 and E5:E10 with Percent Style.

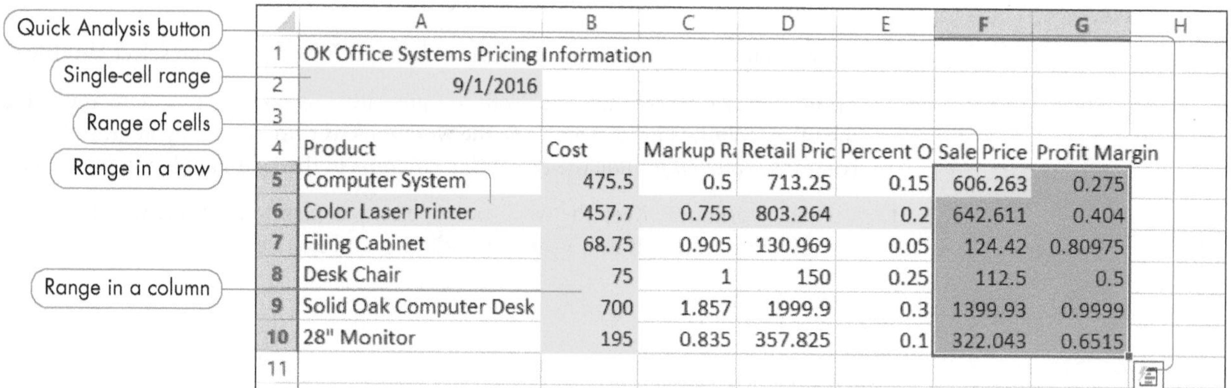

	A	B	C	D	E	F	G	H
1	OK Office Systems Pricing Information							
2	9/1/2016							
3								
4	Product	Cost	Markup R:	Retail Pric	Percent O	Sale Price	Profit Margin	
5	Computer System	475.5	0.5	713.25	0.15	606.263	0.275	
6	Color Laser Printer	457.7	0.755	803.264	0.2	642.611	0.404	
7	Filing Cabinet	68.75	0.905	130.969	0.05	124.42	0.80975	
8	Desk Chair	75	1	150	0.25	112.5	0.5	
9	Solid Oak Computer Desk	700	1.857	1999.9	0.3	1399.93	0.9999	
10	28" Monitor	195	0.835	357.825	0.1	322.043	0.6515	
11								
12								

Quick Analysis button
Single-cell range
Range of cells
Range in a row
Range in a column

FIGURE 1.29 Sample Ranges

Table 1.4 lists methods you can use to select ranges, including nonadjacent ranges.

TABLE 1.4 Selecting Ranges

To Select:	Do This:
A range	Drag until you select the entire range. Alternatively, click the first cell in the range, press and hold Shift, and then click the last cell in the range.
An entire column	Click the column heading.
An entire row	Click the row heading.
Current range containing data	Click in the range of data and press Ctrl+A.
All cells in a worksheet	Click Select All or press Ctrl+A twice.
Nonadjacent range	Select the first range, press and hold Ctrl, and then select additional range(s).

A green border appears around a selected range, and the Quick Analysis button displays in the bottom-right corner of the selected range. Any command you execute will affect the entire range. The range remains selected until you select another range or click in any cell in the worksheet.

TIP Name Box

You can use the Name Box to select a range by clicking in the Name Box, typing a range address such as B15:D25, and then pressing Enter.

Move a Range to Another Location

STEP 1 ⟫ You can move cell contents from one range to another. For example, you might need to move an input area from the right side of the worksheet to above the output range. When you move a range containing text and values, the text and values do not change. However, any formulas that refer to cells in that range will update to reflect the new cell addresses. To move a range, do the following:

1. Select the range.
2. Use the Cut command to copy the range to the Clipboard. Unlike cutting data in other Microsoft Office applications, the data you cut in Excel remain in their locations until you paste them elsewhere. After you click Cut, a moving dashed green border surrounds the selected range and the status bar displays *Select destination and press ENTER or choose Paste*.
3. Make sure the destination range—the range where you want to move the data—is the same size or greater than the size of the cut range. If any cells within the destination range contain data, Excel overwrites that data when you use the Paste command.
4. Click in the top-left corner of the destination range, and then use the Paste command to insert the data contained in the selected range and remove that data from the original range.

Copy and Paste a Range

STEP 2 ⟫ You may need to copy cell contents from one range to another. For example, you might copy your January budget to another worksheet to use as a model for creating your February budget. When you copy a range, the original data remain in their original locations. Cell references in copied formulas adjust based on their relative locations to the original data. To copy a range, do the following:

1. Select the range.
2. Use the Copy command to copy the contents of the selected range to the Clipboard. After you click Copy, a moving dashed green border surrounds the selected range and the status bar displays *Select destination and press ENTER or choose Paste*.
3. Make sure the destination range—the range where you want to copy the data—is the same size or greater than the size of the copied range. If any cells within the destination range contain data, Excel overwrites that data when you use the Paste command.
4. Click in the top-left corner of the destination range where you want the duplicate data, and then use the Paste command. The original range still has the moving dashed green border, and the pasted copied range is selected with a solid green border. Figure 1.30 shows a selected range and a copy of the range.
5. Press Esc to turn off the moving dashed border around the originally selected range.

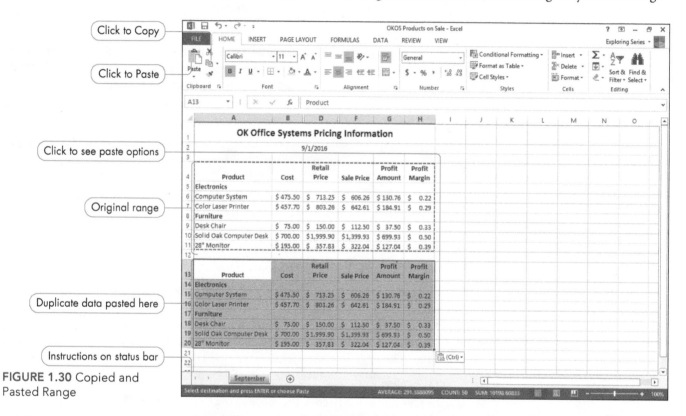

FIGURE 1.30 Copied and Pasted Range

TIP Copy as Picture

Instead of clicking Copy, if you click the Copy arrow in the Clipboard group, you can select Copy (the default option) or Copy as Picture. When you select Copy as Picture, you copy an image of the selected data. You can then paste the image elsewhere in the workbook or in a Word document or PowerPoint presentation. However, when you copy the data as an image, you cannot edit individual cell data after you paste the image.

Use Paste Options and Paste Special

STEP 3 Sometimes you might want to paste data in a different format than they are in the Clipboard. For example, you might want to copy a range containing formulas and cell references, and paste the range as values in another workbook that does not have the referenced cells. If you want to copy data from Excel and paste them into a Word document, you can paste the Excel data as a worksheet object, as unformatted text, or in another format. To paste data from the Clipboard into a different format, click the Paste arrow in the Clipboard group, and hover over a command to see a ScreenTip and a preview of how the pasted data will look. In Figure 1.31, the preview shows that a particular paste option will maintain formulas and number formatting; however, it will not maintain the text formatting, such as font color and centered text. After previewing different paste options, click the one you want in order to apply it.

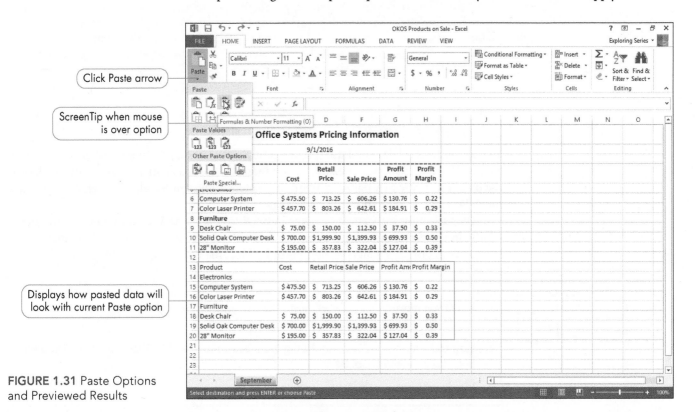

Click Paste arrow

ScreenTip when mouse is over option

Displays how pasted data will look with current Paste option

FIGURE 1.31 Paste Options and Previewed Results

For more specific paste options, click the Paste arrow, and then select Paste Special to display the Paste Special dialog box (see Figure 1.32). This dialog box contains more options than the Paste menu. Click the desired option and click OK.

FIGURE 1.32 Paste Special Dialog Box

Paste Options Button

When you copy or paste data, Excel displays the *Paste Options button* in the bottom-right corner of the pasted data (refer to Figure 1.30). Click Paste Options to see different results for the pasted data.

After entering data into a worksheet, you might want to transpose the columns and rows so that the data in the first column appear as column labels across the first row, or the column labels in the first row appear in the first column. To transpose worksheet data, select and copy the original range, click the top-left corner of the destination range, click the Paste arrow, and then click Transpose.

Copy Excel Data to Other Programs

You can copy Excel data and use it in other applications, such as in a Word document or in a PowerPoint slide show. For example, you might perform statistical analyses in Excel, copy the data into a research paper in Word or create a budget in Excel, and then copy the data into a PowerPoint slide show for a meeting.

After selecting and copying a range in Excel, you must decide how you want the data to appear in the destination application. Click the Paste arrow in the destination application, such as Word, to see a gallery of options or to select the Paste Special option.

Quick Concepts

1. When you move or copy a worksheet, what are some of the decisions you must make? *pp. 34–38*

2. How can you select nonadjacent ranges, such as B5:B10 and F5:F10? Why would you select nonadjacent ranges? *pp. 34–35*

3. Why would you use the Paste Special options in Excel? *p. 36*

Hands-On Exercises

4 Clipboard Tasks

You realize the 28" Monitor data is in the Furniture category instead of the Electronics category. You need to move the product to its appropriate location. In addition, your supervisor will ask you to enter data for a new product. Because it is almost identical to an existing product, you can copy the original data and edit the copied data to save time. You also want to experiment with the Paste Special option to see the results of using it in the OKOS workbook.

Skills covered: Select a Range and Move a Row to a New Location • Copy and Paste a Range • Use Paste Special

STEP 1 ≫ SELECT A RANGE AND MOVE A ROW TO A NEW LOCATION

You want to move the 28" Monitor product to be immediately after the Color Laser Printer product. Before moving the 28" Monitor row, you need to insert a blank row between the Color Laser Printer and Furniture rows. Refer to Figure 1.33 as you complete Step 1.

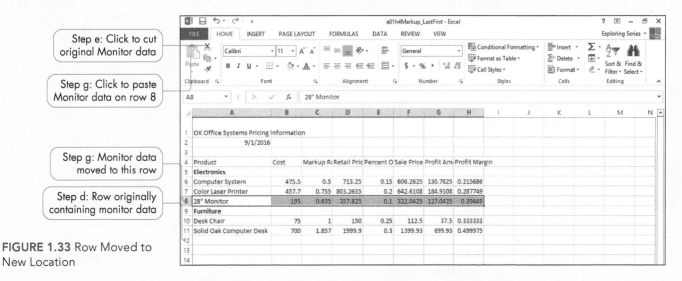

Step e: Click to cut original Monitor data

Step g: Click to paste Monitor data on row 8

Step g: Monitor data moved to this row

Step d: Row originally containing monitor data

FIGURE 1.33 Row Moved to New Location

a. Open *e01h3Markup_LastFirst* if you closed it at the end of Hands-On Exercise 3 and save it as **e01h4Markup_LastFirst**, changing *h3* to *h4*.

b. Select the **column B, D, and F headings**. Unhide columns C and E as you learned in Hands-On Exercise 3.

   You kept those columns hidden when you saved the *e01h3Markup_LastFirst* workbook to preserve evidence that you know how to hide columns. Now you need the columns visible to continue.

c. Right-click the **row 8 heading** and select **Insert** from the menu.

   You need to insert a blank row so that you can move the *28" Computer Monitor* data to be between the *Color Laser Printer* and *Furniture* rows.

d. Select the **range A12:H12**.

   You selected the range of cells containing the 28" Monitor data.

e. Click **Cut** in the Clipboard group.

   A moving dashed green border outlines the selected range. The status bar displays the message *Select destination and press ENTER or choose Paste*.

f. Click **cell A8**, the new blank row you inserted in step c.

This is the first cell in the destination range.

g. Click **Paste** in the Clipboard group and save the workbook.

The 28" Monitor data are now located on row 8.

> **TROUBLESHOOTING:** If you cut and paste a row without inserting a new row first, Excel will overwrite the original row of data, which is why you inserted a new row in step c. If you forgot to do step c, click Undo until the 28" Monitor data is back in its original location and start with step c again.

STEP 2 ≫ COPY AND PASTE A RANGE

Alesha told you that a new chair is on its way. She asked you to enter the data for the Executive Desk Chair. Because most of the data is the same as the Desk Chair data, you will copy the original Desk Chair data, edit the product name, and then change the cost to reflect the cost of the second chair. Refer to Figure 1.34 as you complete Step 2.

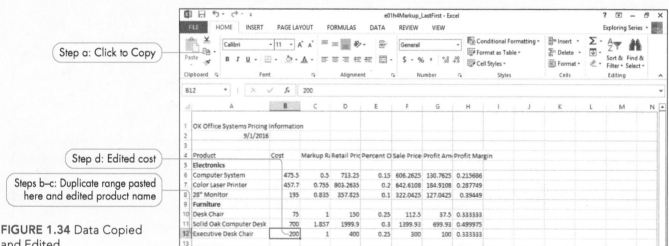

FIGURE 1.34 Data Copied and Edited

a. Select the **range A10:H10**, the row containing the Desk Chair product data, and click **Copy** in the Clipboard group.

b. Click **cell A12**, the location for the duplicate data, and click **Paste** in the Clipboard group. Press **Esc**.

The pasted range is selected in row 12.

c. Click **cell A12**, press **F2** to activate Edit Mode, press **Home**, type **Executive**, press **Spacebar**, and then press **Enter**.

You edited the product name.

d. Change the value in **cell B12** to **200**. Save the workbook.

The formulas calculate the results based on the new cost of 200 for the Executive Desk Chair.

STEP 3 ≫ USE PASTE SPECIAL

During your lunch break, you want to experiment with some of the Paste Special options. Particularly, you are interested in pasting Formulas and Value & Source Formatting. First, you will bold the title and apply a font color to help you test these Paste Special options. Refer to Figure 1.35 as you complete Step 3.

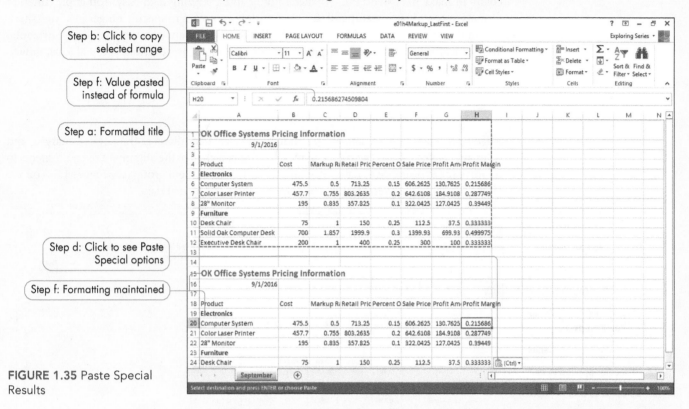

FIGURE 1.35 Paste Special Results

a. Click **cell A1**. Apply these font formats to the title: **14 pt**, **Bold**, and **Gold, Accent 4, Darker 50% font color** in the Font group on the HOME tab.

   You need to format text to see the effects of using different Paste Special options.

b. Select the **range A1:H12** and click **Copy** in the Clipboard group.

c. Click **cell A15**, the top-left corner of the destination range.

d. Click the **Paste arrow** in the Clipboard group and position the mouse pointer over *Formulas*.

   Without clicking the command, Excel shows you a preview of what that option would do. The pasted copy would not contain the font formatting you applied to the title or the bold on the two category names. In addition, the pasted date would appear as a serial number. The formulas would be maintained.

e. Position the mouse pointer over *Values & Source Formatting*.

   This option would preserve the formatting, but it would convert the formulas into the current value results.

f. Click **Values & Source Formatting**, click **cell H6** to see a formula, and then click **cell H20**. Press **Esc** to turn off the border.

   Cell H6 contains a formula, but in the pasted version, the equivalent cell H20 has converted the formula result into an actual value. If you were to change the original cost on row 20, the contents of cell H20 would not change. In a working environment, this is useful only if you want to capture the exact value in a point in time before making changes to the original data.

g. Save the workbook. Keep the workbook open if you plan to continue with the next Hands-On Exercise. If not, close the workbook and exit Excel.

Formatting

After entering data and formulas, you should format the worksheet. A professionally formatted worksheet—through adding appropriate symbols, aligning decimals, and using fonts and colors to make data stand out—makes finding and analyzing data easy. You apply different formats to accentuate meaningful details or to draw attention to specific ranges in a worksheet.

In this section, you will learn to apply different alignment options, including horizontal and vertical alignment, text wrapping, and indent options. In addition, you will learn how to format different types of values.

Applying Alignment and Font Options

Alignment refers to how data are positioned in cells. Text aligns at the left cell margin, and dates and values align at the right cell margin. You can change the alignment of cell contents to improve the appearance of data within the cells. The Alignment group (see Figure 1.36) on the Home tab contains several features to help you align and format data.

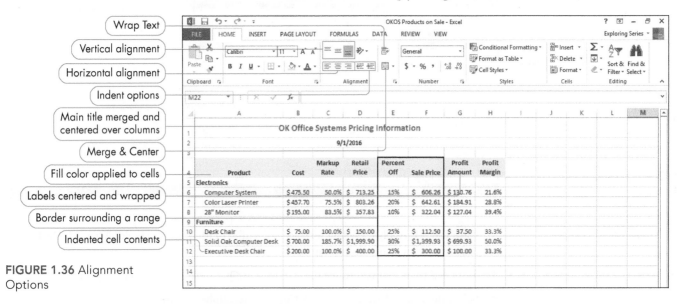

FIGURE 1.36 Alignment Options

 TIP   Alignment Options

The Format Cells dialog box contains additional alignment options. To open the Format Cells dialog box, click the Dialog Box Launcher in the Alignment group on the Home tab. The Alignment tab in the dialog box contains the options for aligning data.

Merge and Center Labels

STEP 1 ≫ You may want to place a title at the top of a worksheet and center it over the columns of data in the worksheet. You can center main titles over all columns in the worksheet, and you can center category titles over groups of related columns. To create a title, enter the text in the far left cell of the range. Select the range of cells across which you want to center the title and click Merge & Center in the Alignment group on the Home tab. Only data in the far left cell (or top right cell) are merged. Any other data in the merged cells are deleted. Excel merges the selected cells together into one cell, and the merged cell address is that of the original cell on the left. The data are centered between the left and right sides of the merged cell.

If you merge too many cells and want to split the merged cell back into its original multiple cells, click the merged cell and click Merge & Center. Unmerging places the data in the top-left cell.

For additional options, click the Merge & Center arrow. Table 1.5 lists the four merge options.

TABLE 1.5 Merge Options	
Option	**Results**
Merge & Center	Merges selected cells and centers data into one cell.
Merge Across	Merges the selected cells but keeps text left aligned or values right aligned.
Merge Cells	Enables you to merge a range of cells on multiple rows as well as in multiple columns.
Unmerge Cells	Separates a merged cell into multiple cells again.

Change Horizontal and Vertical Cell Alignment

STEP 2 ❯❯ *Horizontal alignment* specifies the position of data between the left and right cell margins, and *vertical alignment* specifies the position of data between the top and bottom cell margins. Bottom Align is the default vertical alignment (as indicated by the light green background), and Align Left is the default horizontal alignment for text. In Figure 1.36, the labels on row 4 have Center horizontal alignment and the title in row 1 has Middle Align vertical alignment.

If you increase row height, you might need to change the vertical alignment to position data better in conjunction with data in adjacent cells. To change alignments, click the desired alignment setting(s) in the Alignment group on the Home tab.

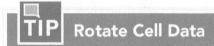

TIP Rotate Cell Data

People sometimes rotate headings in cells. You can rotate data in a cell by clicking Orientation in the Alignment group and selecting an option, such as Angle Clockwise.

Wrap Text

STEP 2 ❯❯ Sometimes you have to maintain specific column widths, but the data do not fit entirely. You can use *wrap text* to make data appear on multiple lines by adjusting the row height to fit the cell contents within the column width. When you click Wrap Text in the Alignment group, Excel wraps the text on two or more lines within the cell. This alignment option is helpful when the column headings are wider than the values contained in the column. In Figure 1.36, the *Markup Rate* and *Percent Off* labels on row 4 are examples of wrapped text.

Increase and Decrease Indent

STEP 3 ❯❯ To offset labels, you can indent text within a cell. *Indenting* helps others see the hierarchical structure of data. Accountants often indent the word *Totals* in financial statements so that it stands out from a list of items above the total row. To indent the contents of a cell, click Increase Indent in the Alignment group on the Home tab. The more you click Increase Indent, the more text is indented in the cell. To decrease the indent, click Decrease Indent in the Alignment group. In Figure 1.36, *Computer System* and *Desk Chair* are indented.

TIP | **Indenting Values**

Values right align by default. You should align the decimal places in a column of values. If the column label is wide, the values below it appear too far on the right. To preserve the values aligning at the decimal places, use the Align Right horizontal alignment and click Increase Indent to shift the values over to the left a little for better placement.

Apply Borders and Fill Color

STEP 4 You can apply a border or fill color to accentuate data in a worksheet. A *border* is a line that surrounds a cell or a range of cells. You can use borders to offset some data from the rest of the worksheet data. To apply a border, select the cell or range that you want to have a border, click the Borders arrow in the Font group, and then select the desired border type. In Figure 1.36, a border surrounds the range E4:F12. To remove a border, select No Border from the Borders menu.

To add some color to your worksheet to add emphasis to data or headers, you can apply a fill color. *Fill color* is a background color that displays behind the data. You should choose a fill color that contrasts with the font color. For example, if the font color is Black, you might want to choose Yellow fill color. If the font color is White, you might want to apply Blue or Dark Blue fill color. To apply a fill color, select the cell or range that you want to have a fill color, click the Fill Color arrow on the Home tab, and then select the color choice from the Fill Color palette. In Figure 1.36, the column labels in row 4 contain the Gold, Accent 4, Lighter 80% fill color. If you want to remove a fill color, select No Fill from the bottom of the palette.

For additional border and fill color options, click the Dialog Box Launcher in the Font group to display the Format Cells dialog box. Click the Border tab to select border options, including the border line style and color. Click the Fill tab to set the background color, fill effects, and patterns.

Applying Number Formats

Values have no special formatting when you enter data. You should apply *number formats* based on the type of values in a cell, such as applying either the Accounting or Currency number format to monetary values. Changing the number format changes the way the number displays in a cell, but the format does not change the number's value. If, for example, you enter 123.456 into a cell and format the cell with the Currency number type, the value shows as $123.46 onscreen, but the actual value 123.456 is used for calculations. When you apply a number format, you can specify the number of decimal places to display onscreen.

Apply a Number Format

STEP 5 The default number format is General, which displays values as you originally enter them. General does not align decimal points in a column or include symbols, such as dollar signs, percent signs, or commas. Table 1.6 lists and describes the primary number formats in Excel.

TABLE 1.6 Number Formats

Format Style	Display
General	A number as it was originally entered. Numbers are shown as integers (e.g., 12345), decimal fractions (e.g., 1234.5), or in scientific notation (e.g., 1.23E+10) if the number exceeds 11 digits.
Number	A number with or without the 1,000 separator (e.g., a comma) and with any number of decimal places. Negative numbers can be displayed with parentheses and/or red.
Currency	A number with the 1,000 separator and an optional dollar sign (which is placed immediately to the left of the number). Negative values are preceded by a minus sign or are displayed with parentheses or in red. Two decimal places display by default.
Accounting Number Format	A number with the 1,000 separator, an optional dollar sign (at the left border of the cell, vertically aligned within a column), negative values in parentheses, and zero values as hyphens. Two decimal places display by default. Changes alignment slightly within the cell.
Comma	A number with the 1,000 separator. Used in conjunction with Accounting Number Style to align commas and decimal places.
Date	The date in different ways, such as Long Date (March 14, 2016) or Short Date (3/14/16 or 14-Mar-16).
Time	The time in different formats, such as 10:50 PM or 22:50.
Percent Style	The value as it would be multiplied by 100 (for display purpose), with the percent sign. The default number of decimal places is zero if you click Percent Style in the Number group or two decimal places if you use the Format Cells dialog box. However, you should typically increase the number of decimal points to show greater accuracy.
Fraction	A number as a fraction; use when no exact decimal equivalent exists. A fraction is entered into a cell as a formula such as =1/3. If the cell is not formatted as a fraction, the formula results display.
Scientific	A number as a decimal fraction followed by a whole number exponent of 10; for example, the number 12345 would appear as 1.23E+04. The exponent, +04 in the example, is the number of places the decimal point is moved to the left (or right if the exponent is negative). Very small numbers have negative exponents.
Text	The data left aligned; is useful for numerical values that have leading zeros and should be treated as text, such as postal codes or phone numbers. Apply Text format before typing a leading zero so that the zero displays in the cell.
Special	A number with editing characters, such as hyphens in a Social Security number.
Custom	Predefined customized number formats or special symbols to create your own customized number format.

The Number group on the Home tab contains commands for applying *Accounting Number Format*, *Percent Style*, and *Comma Style* numbering formats. You can click the Accounting Number Format arrow and select other denominations, such as English pounds or euros. For other number formats, click the Number Format arrow and select the numbering format you want to use. For more specific numbering formats than those provided, select More Number Formats from the Number Format menu or click the Number Dialog Box Launcher to open the Format Cells dialog box with the Number tab options readily available. Figure 1.37 shows different number formats applied to values.

	A	B
1	General	1234.567
2	Number	1234.57
3	Currency	$1,234.57
4	Accounting	$ 1,234.57
5	Comma	1,234.57
6	Percent	12%
7	Short Date	3/1/2016
8	Long Date	Tuesday, March 1, 2016

FIGURE 1.37 Number Formats

Increase and Decrease Decimal Places

STEP 5 ⟫ After applying a number format, you may need to adjust the number of decimal places that display. For example, if you have an entire column of monetary values formatted in Accounting Number Format, Excel displays two decimal places by default. If the entire column of values contains whole dollar values and no cents, displaying *.00* down the column looks cluttered. You can decrease the number of decimal places to show whole numbers only.

To change the number of decimal places displayed, click Increase Decimal in the Number group on the Home tab to display more decimal places for greater precision or Decrease Decimal to display fewer or no decimal places.

Quick Concepts ✓

1. What is the importance of formatting a worksheet? *p. 42*

2. Describe five alignment and font formatting techniques used to format labels that are discussed in this section. *pp. 42–44*

3. What are the main differences between Accounting Number Format and Currency format? Which format has its own command on the Ribbon? *p. 45*

5 Formatting

In the first four Hands-On Exercises, you entered data about products on sale, created formulas to calculate markup and profit, and inserted new rows and columns to accommodate the labels *Electronics* and *Furniture* to identify the specific products. You are ready to format the worksheet. Specifically, you need to center the title, align text, format values, and then apply other formatting to enhance the readability of the worksheet.

Skills covered: Merge and Center the Title • Align Text Horizontally and Vertically and Wrap Text • Increase Indent • Apply Borders and Fill Color • Apply Number Formats and Increase and Decrease Decimal Places

STEP 1 ≫ MERGE AND CENTER THE TITLE

To make the title stand out, you want to center it over all the data columns. You will use the Merge & Center command to merge cells and center the title at the same time. Refer to Figure 1.38 as you complete Step 1.

Step e: Date merged, centered, and bold A2:H2

	A	B	C	D	E	F	G	H	I
1	OK Office Systems Pricing Information								
2	9/1/2016								
3									
4	Product	Cost	Markup Ra	Retail Pric	Percent O	Sale Price	Profit Am	Profit Margin	
5	Electronics								
6	Computer System	475.5	0.5	713.25	0.15	606.2625	130.7625	0.215686	
7	Color Laser Printer	457.7	0.755	803.2635	0.2	642.6108	184.9108	0.287749	
8	28" Monitor	195	0.835	357.825	0.1	322.0425	127.0425	0.39449	
9	Furniture								
10	Desk Chair	75	1	150	0.25	112.5	37.5	0.333333	
11	Solid Oak Computer Desk	700	1.857	1999.9	0.3	1399.93	699.93	0.499975	
12	Executive Desk Chair	200	1	400	0.25	300	100	0.333333	
13									

FIGURE 1.38 Title and Date Merged and Centered

a. Open *e01h4Markup_LastFirst* if you closed it at the end of Hands-On Exercise 4 and save it as **e01h5Markup_LastFirst**, changing *h4* to *h5*.

b. Select the **range A15:H26** and press **Delete**.

You maintained a copy of your Paste Special results in the *e01h4Markup_LastFirst* workbook, but you do not need it to continue.

c. Select the **range A1:H1**.

You want to center the title over all columns of data.

d. Click **Merge & Center** in the Alignment group.

Excel merges cells in the range A1:H1 into one cell and centers the title horizontally within the merged cell, which is cell A1.

> **TROUBLESHOOTING:** If you merge too many or not enough cells, you can unmerge the cells and start again. To unmerge cells, click in the merged cell. The Merge & Center command is shaded in green when the active cell is merged. Click Merge & Center to unmerge the cell. Then select the correct range to merge and use Merge & Center again.

e. Select the **range A2:H2**. Merge and center the date and bold it.

> **TROUBLESHOOTING:** If you try to merge and center data in the range A1:H2, Excel will keep the top-left data only and delete the date. To merge separate data on separate rows, you must merge and center data separately.

f. Save the workbook.

STEP 2 >> ALIGN TEXT HORIZONTALLY AND VERTICALLY AND WRAP TEXT

You will wrap the text in the column headings to avoid columns that are too wide for the data, but which will display the entire text of the column labels. In addition, you will horizontally center column labels between the left and right cell margins. Refer to Figure 1.39 as you complete Step 2.

Step d: Title with Middle (vertical) Align

Steps b–c: Column labels wrapped, centered, and bold

	A	B	C	D	E	F	G	H	I
1	OK Office Systems Pricing Information								
2	9/1/2016								
3									
4	Product	Cost	Markup Rate	Retail Price	Percent Off	Sale Price	Profit Amount	Profit Margin	
5	Electronics								
6	Computer System	475.5	0.5	713.25	0.15	606.2625	130.7625	0.215686	
7	Color Laser Printer	457.7	0.755	803.2635	0.2	642.6108	184.9108	0.287749	
8	28" Monitor	195	0.835	357.825	0.1	322.0425	127.0425	0.39449	
9	Furniture								
10	Desk Chair	75	1	150	0.25	112.5	37.5	0.333333	
11	Solid Oak Computer Desk	700	1.857	1999.9	0.3	1399.93	699.93	0.499975	
12	Executive Desk Chair	200	1	400	0.25	300	100	0.333333	
13									

FIGURE 1.39 Formatted Column Labels

a. Select the **range A4:H4** to select the column labels.

b. Click **Wrap Text** in the Alignment group.

The multiple-word column headings are now visible on two lines within each cell.

c. Click **Center** in the Alignment group. Bold the selected column headings.

The column headings are centered horizontally between the left and right edges of each cell.

d. Click **cell A1**, which contains the title, click **Middle Align** in the Alignment group, and then save the workbook.

Middle Align vertically centers data between the top and bottom edges of the cell.

STEP 3 >> INCREASE INDENT

As you review the first column, you notice that the category names, Electronics and Furniture, do not stand out. You decide to indent the labels within each category to better display which products are in each category. Refer to Figure 1.40 as you complete Step 3.

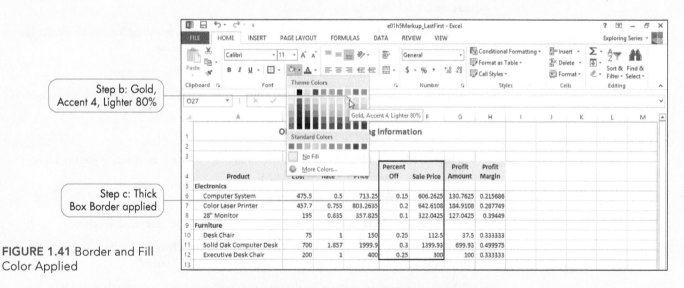

Step d: Column A width increased to 26.00

Step b: Electronics product labels indented twice

Step c: Furniture product labels indented twice

	A	B	C	D	E	F	G	H	I
1	OK Office Systems Pricing Information								
2	9/1/2016								
3									
4	Product	Cost	Markup Rate	Retail Price	Percent Off	Sale Price	Profit Amount	Profit Margin	
5	Electronics								
6	Computer System	475.5	0.5	713.25	0.15	606.2625	130.7625	0.215686	
7	Color Laser Printer	457.7	0.755	803.2635	0.2	642.6108	184.9108	0.287749	
8	28" Monitor	195	0.835	357.825	0.1	322.0425	127.0425	0.39449	
9	Furniture								
10	Desk Chair	75	1	150	0.25	112.5	37.5	0.333333	
11	Solid Oak Computer Desk	700	1.857	1999.9	0.3	1399.93	699.93	0.499975	
12	Executive Desk Chair	200	1	400	0.25	300	100	0.333333	
13									

FIGURE 1.40 Indented Cell Contents

a. Select the **range A6:A8**, the cells containing electronic products labels.

b. Click **Increase Indent** in the Alignment group twice.

The three selected product names are indented below the *Electronics* heading.

c. Select the **range A10:A12**, the cells containing furniture products, and click **Increase Indent** twice.

The three selected product names are indented below the *Furniture* heading. Notice that the one product name appears cut off.

d. Increase the column A width to **26.00**. Save the workbook.

STEP 4 ⟩⟩ APPLY BORDERS AND FILL COLOR

You want to apply a light gold fill color to highlight the column headings. In addition, you want to emphasize the percent off and sale prices. You will do this by applying a border around that range. Refer to Figure 1.41 as you complete Step 4.

Step b: Gold, Accent 4, Lighter 80%

Step c: Thick Box Border applied

FIGURE 1.41 Border and Fill Color Applied

a. Select the **range A4:H4** and click the **Fill Color arrow** in the Font group.

b. Click **Gold, Accent 4, Lighter 80%** in the *Theme Colors* section. It is the second color down in the third column from the right.

You applied a fill color to the selected cells to draw attention to these cells.

    c. Select the **range E4:F12**, click the **Border arrow** in the Font group, and then select **Thick Box Border**.

    You applied a border around the selected cells.

    d. Click in an empty cell below the columns of data to deselect the cells. Save the workbook.

STEP 5 » APPLY NUMBER FORMATS AND INCREASE AND DECREASE DECIMAL PLACES

You need to format the values to increase readability and look more professional. You will apply number formats and adjust the number of decimal points displayed. Refer to Figure 1.42 as you complete Step 5.

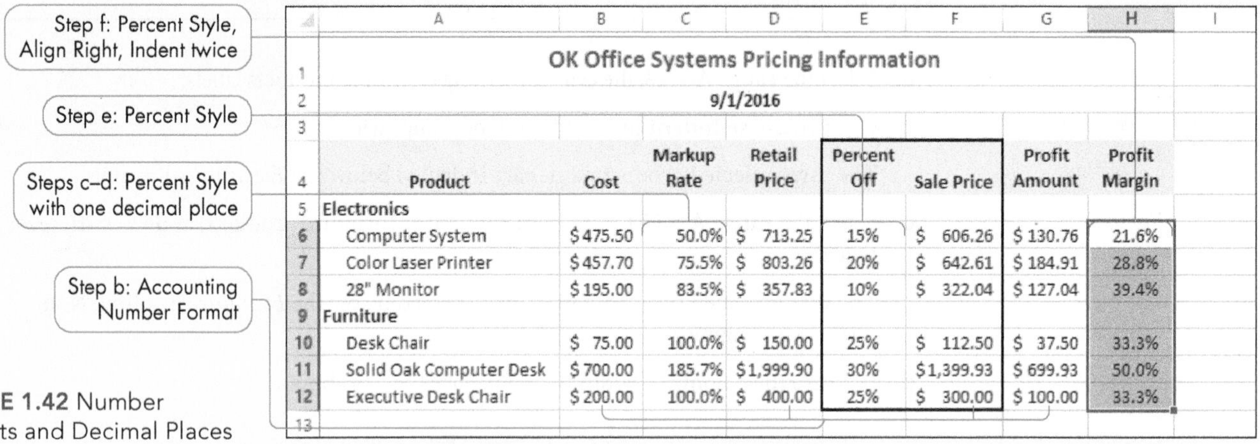

	A	B	C	D	E	F	G	H	I
1	OK Office Systems Pricing Information								
2	9/1/2016								
3									
4	Product	Cost	Markup Rate	Retail Price	Percent Off	Sale Price	Profit Amount	Profit Margin	
5	Electronics								
6	Computer System	$475.50	50.0%	$ 713.25	15%	$ 606.26	$ 130.76	21.6%	
7	Color Laser Printer	$457.70	75.5%	$ 803.26	20%	$ 642.61	$ 184.91	28.8%	
8	28" Monitor	$195.00	83.5%	$ 357.83	10%	$ 322.04	$ 127.04	39.4%	
9	Furniture								
10	Desk Chair	$ 75.00	100.0%	$ 150.00	25%	$ 112.50	$ 37.50	33.3%	
11	Solid Oak Computer Desk	$700.00	185.7%	$1,999.90	30%	$1,399.93	$ 699.93	50.0%	
12	Executive Desk Chair	$200.00	100.0%	$ 400.00	25%	$ 300.00	$ 100.00	33.3%	
13									

Callouts:
- Step f: Percent Style, Align Right, Indent twice
- Step e: Percent Style
- Steps c–d: Percent Style with one decimal place
- Step b: Accounting Number Format

FIGURE 1.42 Number Formats and Decimal Places

    a. Select the **range B6:B12**. Press and hold **Ctrl** as you select the **ranges D6:D12 and F6:G12**.

    Because you want to format nonadjacent ranges with the same formats, you hold down Ctrl.

    b. Click **Accounting Number Format** in the Number group. If some cells contain pound signs, increase the column widths as needed.

    You formatted the selected nonadjacent ranges with the Accounting Number Format. The dollar signs align on the left cell margins and the decimals align.

    c. Select the **range C6:C12** and click **Percent Style** in the Number group.

    You formatted the values in the selected ranges with Percent Style, showing whole numbers only.

    d. Click **Increase Decimal** in the Number group.

    You increased the decimal to show one decimal place to avoid misleading your readers by displaying the values as whole percentages.

    e. Apply **Percent Style** to the **range E6:E12**.

    f. Select the **range H6:H12**, apply **Percent Style**, and then click **Increase Decimal**.

    g. Select the **range E6:E12**, click **Align Right**, and then click **Increase Indent** twice. Select the **range H6:H12**, click **Align Right**, and then click **Increase Indent**.

    With values, you want to keep the decimal points aligned, but you can then use Increase Indent to adjust the indent so that the values appear more centered below the column labels.

    h. Save the workbook. Keep the workbook open if you plan to continue with the next Hands-On Exercise. If not, close the workbook and exit Excel.

Page Setup and Printing

Although you might distribute workbooks electronically as e-mail attachments or you might upload workbooks to a corporate server, you should prepare the worksheets in the workbook for printing. You should prepare worksheets in case you need to print them or in case others who receive an electronic copy of your workbook need to print the worksheets. The Page Layout tab provides options for controlling the printed worksheet (see Figure 1.43).

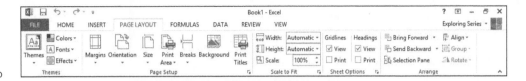

FIGURE 1.43 Page Layout Tab

In this section, you will select options on the Page Layout tab. Specifically, you will use the Page Setup, Scale to Fit, and Sheet Options groups. After selecting page setup options, you are ready to print your worksheet.

Selecting Page Setup Options

The Page Setup group on the Page Layout tab contains options to set the margins, select orientation, specify page size, select the print area, and apply other options. The *Scale to Fit* group contains options for adjusting the scaling of the spreadsheet on the printed page. When possible, use the commands in these groups to apply page settings. Table 1.7 lists and describes the commands in the Page Setup group.

TABLE 1.7 Page Setup Commands

Command	Description
Margins	Displays a menu to select predefined margin settings. The default margins are 0.75" top and bottom and 0.7" left and right. You will often change these margin settings to balance the worksheet data better on the printed page. If you need different margins, select Custom Margins.
Orientation	Displays orientation options. The default page orientation is portrait, which is appropriate for worksheets that contain more rows than columns. Select landscape orientation when worksheets contain more columns than can fit in portrait orientation. For example, the OKOS worksheet might appear better balanced in landscape orientation because it has eight columns.
Size	Displays a list of standard paper sizes. The default size is 8 1/2" by 11". If you have a different paper size, such as legal paper, select it from the list.
Print Area	Displays a list to set or clear the print area. When you have very large worksheets, you might want to print only a portion of that worksheet. To do so, select the range you want to print, click Print Area in the Page Setup group, and then select Set Print Area. When you use the Print commands, only the range you specified will be printed. To clear the print area, click Print Area and select Clear Print Area.
Breaks	Displays a list to insert or remove page breaks.
Background	Enables you to select an image to appear as the background behind the worksheet data when viewed onscreen (backgrounds do not appear when the worksheet is printed).
Print Titles	Enables you to select column headings and row labels to repeat on multiple-page printouts.

Specify Page Options

STEP 1 ❯❯ To apply several page setup options at once or to access options not found on the Ribbon, click the Page Setup Dialog Box Launcher. The Page Setup dialog box organizes options into four tabs: Page, Margins, Header/Footer, and Sheet. All tabs contain Print and Print Preview buttons. Figure 1.44 shows the Page tab.

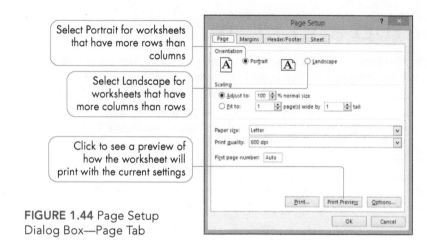

Select Portrait for worksheets that have more rows than columns

Select Landscape for worksheets that have more columns than rows

Click to see a preview of how the worksheet will print with the current settings

FIGURE 1.44 Page Setup Dialog Box—Page Tab

The Page tab contains options to select the orientation and paper size. In addition, it contains scaling options that are similar to the options in the *Scale to Fit* group on the Page Layout tab. You use scaling options to increase or decrease the size of characters on a printed page, similar to using a zoom setting on a photocopy machine. You can also use the *Fit to* option to force the data to print on a specified number of pages.

Set Margins Options

STEP 2 >> The Margins tab (see Figure 1.45) contains options for setting the specific margins. In addition, it contains options to center the worksheet data horizontally or vertically on the page. To balance worksheet data equally between the left and right margins, Excel users often center the page horizontally.

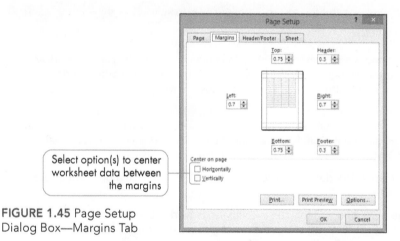

Select option(s) to center worksheet data between the margins

FIGURE 1.45 Page Setup Dialog Box—Margins Tab

Create Headers and Footers

STEP 3 >> The Header/Footer tab (see Figure 1.46) lets you create a header and/or footer that appears at the top and/or bottom of every printed page. Click the arrows to choose from several preformatted entries, or alternatively, you can click Custom Header or Custom Footer, insert text and other objects, and then click the appropriate formatting button to customize your headers and footers. You can use headers and footers to provide additional information about the worksheet. You can include your name, the date the worksheet was prepared, and page numbers, for example.

You can create different headers or footers on different pages, such as one header with the file name on odd-numbered pages and a header containing the date on even-numbered pages. Click the *Different odd and even pages* check box in the Page Setup dialog box (see Figure 1.46).

You might want the first page to have a different header or footer from the rest of the printed pages, or you might not want a header or footer to show up on the first page but want the header or footer to display on the remaining pages. Click the *Different first page* check box in the Page Setup dialog box to specify a different first page header or footer (see Figure 1.46).

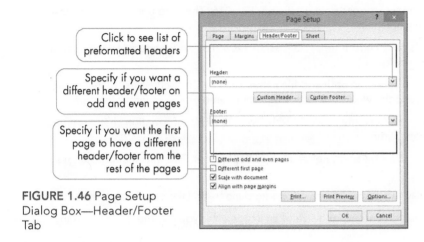

Click to see list of preformatted headers

Specify if you want a different header/footer on odd and even pages

Specify if you want the first page to have a different header/footer from the rest of the pages

FIGURE 1.46 Page Setup Dialog Box—Header/Footer Tab

Instead of creating headers and footers using the Page Setup dialog box, you can click the Insert tab and click Header & Footer in the Text group. Excel displays the worksheet in *Page Layout view* with the insertion point in the center area of the header. You can click inside the left, center, or right section of a header or footer. When you do, Excel displays the Header & Footer Tools Design contextual tab (see Figure 1.47). You can enter text or insert data from the Header & Footer Elements group on the tab. Table 1.8 lists and describes the options in the Header & Footer Elements group. To get back to *Normal view*, click any cell in the worksheet and click Normal in the Workbook Views group on the View tab.

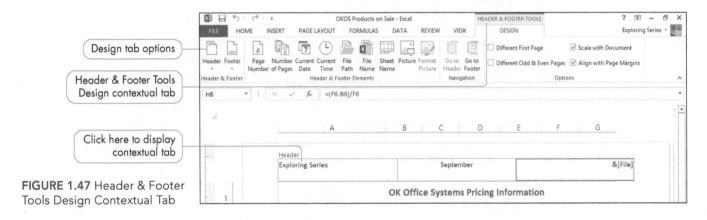

Design tab options

Header & Footer Tools Design contextual tab

Click here to display contextual tab

FIGURE 1.47 Header & Footer Tools Design Contextual Tab

TABLE 1.8 Header & Footer Elements Options

Option Name	Result
Page Number	Inserts the code &[Page] to display the current page number.
Number of Pages	Inserts the code &[Pages] to display the total number of pages that will print.
Current Date	Inserts the code &[Date] to display the current date, such as 5/19/2016. The date updates to the current date when you open or print the worksheet.
Current Time	Inserts the code &[Time] to display the current time, such as 5:15 PM. The time updates to the current time when you open or print the worksheet.
File Path	Inserts the code &[Path]&[File] to display the path and file name, such as C:\Documents\e01h4Markup. This information changes if you save the workbook with a different name or in a different location.
File Name	Inserts the code &[File] to display the file name, such as e01h4Markup. This information changes if you save the workbook with a different name.
Sheet Name	Inserts the code &[Tab] to display the worksheet name, such as September. This information changes if you rename the worksheet.
Picture	Inserts the code &[Picture] to display and print an image as a background behind the data, not just the worksheet.
Format Picture	Enables you to adjust the brightness, contrast, and size of an image after you use the Picture option.

TIP View Tab

If you click the View tab and click Page Layout, Excel displays an area *Click to add header* at the top of the worksheet.

Select Sheet Options

STEP 5 » The Sheet tab (see Figure 1.48) contains options for setting the print area, print titles, print options, and page order. Some of these options are also located in the Sheet Options group on the Page Layout tab on the Ribbon. By default, Excel displays gridlines onscreen to show you each cell's margins, but the gridlines do not print unless you specifically select the Gridlines check box in the Page Setup dialog box or the Print Gridlines check box in the Sheet Options group on the Page Layout tab. In addition, Excel displays row (1, 2, 3, etc.) and column (A, B, C, etc.) headings onscreen. However, these headings do not print unless you click the *Row and column headings* check box in the Page Setup dialog box or click the Print Headings check box in the Sheet Options group on the Page Layout tab.

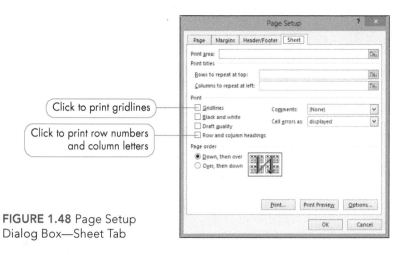

FIGURE 1.48 Page Setup Dialog Box—Sheet Tab

TIP Printing Gridlines and Headings

For most worksheets, you do not need to print gridlines and row/column headings. However, when you want to display and print cell formulas instead of formula results, you might want to print the gridlines and row/column headings. Doing so will help you analyze your formulas. The gridlines help you see the cell boundaries, and the headings help you identify what data are in each cell. At times, you might want to display gridlines to separate data on a regular printout to increase readability.

Previewing and Printing a Worksheet

STEP 4 >> Before printing a worksheet, you should click the File tab and select Print. The Microsoft Office Backstage view displays print options and displays the worksheet in print preview mode. This mode helps you see in advance if the data are balanced on the page or if data will print on multiple pages.

You can specify the number of copies to print and which printer to use to print the worksheet. The first option in the Settings area enables you to specify what to print. The default option is Print Active Sheets. You can choose other options, such as Print Entire Workbook or Print Selection. You can also specify which pages to print. If you are connected to a printer capable of duplex printing, you can print on only one side or print on both sides. You can also collate, change the orientation, specify the paper size, adjust the margins, and adjust the scaling.

The bottom of the Print window indicates how many pages will print. If you do not like how the worksheet will print, click the Page Layout tab so that you can adjust margins, scaling, column widths, and so on until the worksheet data appear the way you want them to print.

 TIP Printing Multiple Worksheets

To print more than one worksheet at a time, select the sheets you want to print. To select adjacent sheets, click the first sheet tab, press and hold Shift, and then click the last sheet tab. To select nonadjacent sheets, press and hold Ctrl as you click each sheet tab. When you display the Print options in the Microsoft Office Backstage view, Print Active Sheets is one of the default settings. If you want to print all of the worksheets within the workbook, change the setting to Print Entire Workbook.

Quick
Concepts

1. What helps determine whether you use portrait or landscape orientation for a worksheet? *p. 51*

2. Why would you select a *Center on page* option if you have already set the margins? *p. 52*

3. List at least five elements you can insert in a header or footer. *p. 54*

4. Why would you want to print gridlines and row and column headings? *p. 54*

Hands-On Exercises

Watch the Video for this Hands-On Exercise!

MyITLab®
HOE6 Training

6 Page Setup and Printing

You are ready to complete the OKOS worksheet. Before printing the worksheet for your supervisor, you want to make sure the data will appear professional when printed. You will adjust some page setup options to put the finishing touches on the worksheet.

Skills covered: Set Page Orientation • Set Margin Options • Create a Header • View in Print Preview and Print • Adjust Scaling and Set Sheet Options

STEP 1 ≫ SET PAGE ORIENTATION

Because the worksheet has several columns, you decide to print it in landscape orientation.

a. Open *e01h5Markup_LastFirst* if you closed it at the end of Hands-On Exercise 5 and save it as **e01h6Markup_LastFirst**, changing *h5* to *h6*.

b. Click the **PAGE LAYOUT tab**.

c. Click **Orientation** in the Page Setup group.

d. Select **Landscape** from the list. Save the workbook.

If you print the worksheet, the data will print in landscape orientation.

STEP 2 ≫ SET MARGIN OPTIONS

You want to set a 1" top margin and center the data between the left and right margins.

a. Click **Margins** in the Page Setup group on the PAGE LAYOUT tab.

As you review the list of options, you notice the list does not contain an option to center the worksheet data horizontally.

b. Select **Custom Margins**.

The Page Setup dialog box opens with the Margins tab options displayed.

c. Click the **Top spin arrow** to display **1**.

You set a 1" top margin. For the OKOS worksheet, you do not need to change the left and right margins because you will center the worksheet data horizontally between the original margins.

d. Click the **Horizontally check box** in the *Center on page* section and click **OK**. Save the workbook.

The worksheet data are centered between the left and right margins.

TIP **Page Setup Dialog Box**

You can click the Page Setup Dialog Box Launcher in the Page Setup group to quickly display the Page Setup dialog box. From there, you can click the Margins tab and set the desired margins.

STEP 3 » CREATE A HEADER

To document the worksheet, you want to include your name, the current date, and the worksheet tab name in a header. Refer to Figure 1.49 as you complete Step 3.

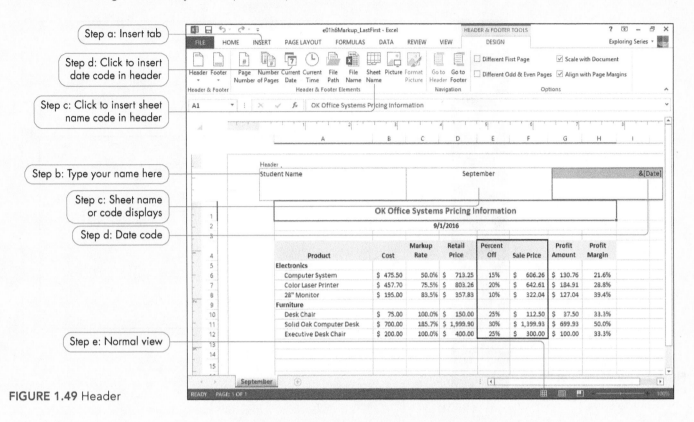

FIGURE 1.49 Header

a. Click the **INSERT tab** and click **Header & Footer** in the Text group.

Excel displays the DESIGN tab and the worksheet displays in Page Layout view, which displays the header area, margin space, and ruler. The insertion point blinks inside the center section of the header.

b. Click in the left section of the header and type your name.

c. Click in the center section of the header and click **Sheet Name** in the Header & Footer Elements group on the DESIGN tab.

Excel inserts the code &[Tab]. This code displays the name of the worksheet. If you change the worksheet tab name, the header will reflect the new sheet name.

d. Click in the right section of the header and click **Current Date** in the Header & Footer Elements group on the DESIGN tab.

Excel inserts the code &[Date]. This code displays the current date based on the computer clock when you print the worksheet. If you want a specific date to appear regardless of the date you open or print the worksheet, you would have to type that date manually. When you click in a different header section, the codes, such as &[Tab], display the actual tab name instead of the code.

e. Click in any cell in the worksheet, click **Normal** on the status bar, and then save the workbook.

Normal view displays the worksheet, but does not display the header or margins.

Before printing the worksheet, you should preview it. Doing so helps you detect margin problems and other issues, such as a single row or column of data flowing onto a new page. Refer to Figure 1.50 as you complete Step 4.

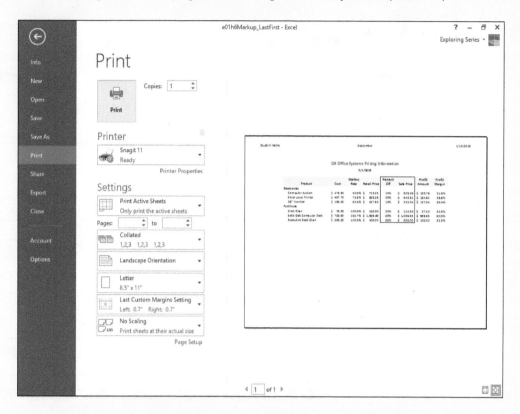

FIGURE 1.50 Worksheet in Print Preview

a. Click the **FILE tab** and click **Print**.

The Microsoft Office Backstage view displays print options and a preview of the worksheet.

b. Verify the Printer box displays the printer that you want to use to print your worksheet.

c. Click **Print** to print the worksheet and save the workbook.

Check your printed worksheet to make sure the data are formatted correctly. After you click Print, the HOME tab displays. If you decide not to print at this time, click the **Back arrow** to display the Ribbon again.

STEP 5 ≫ ADJUST SCALING AND SET SHEET OPTIONS

You want to print a copy of the worksheet formulas to check the logic of the formulas. You need to display the formulas, select options to print gridlines and headings, and then decrease the scaling so that the data print on one page. Refer to Figure 1.51 as you complete Step 5.

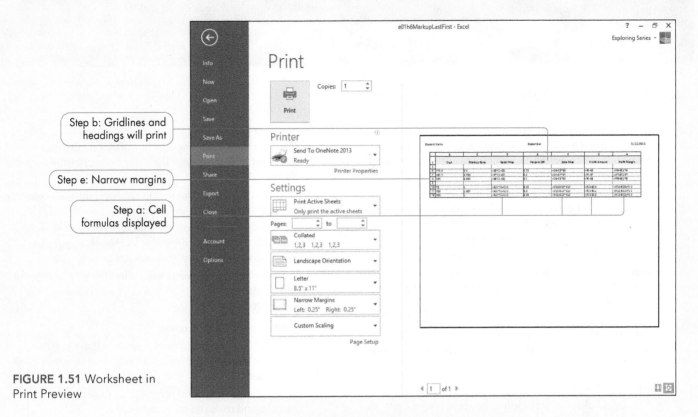

FIGURE 1.51 Worksheet in Print Preview

Step b: Gridlines and headings will print

Step e: Narrow margins

Step a: Cell formulas displayed

a. Press **Ctrl+`** to display cell formulas.

b. Click the **PAGE LAYOUT tab**. Click the **Print Gridlines check box** in the Sheet Options group and click the **Print Headings check box** in the Sheet Options group.

   Because you want to print cell formulas, it is helpful to display the gridlines and row and column headings on that printout.

c. Click the **FILE tab** and click **Print**.

   The bottom of the Print Preview displays 1 of 2, indicating the worksheet no longer prints on one page.

d. Click **Next Page** (the right triangle at the bottom of the Microsoft Office Backstage view) to view the contents of the second page and click the **Back arrow** to display the Ribbon again.

e. Click **Margins** in the Page Setup group and select **Narrow**.

f. Select the **range B4:H12**, click **Print Area** in the Page Setup group, and then select **Set Print Area**.

g. Click the **Scale spin arrow** in the *Scale to Fit* group on the PAGE LAYOUT tab until it displays **90%**.

   If you want to verify that the worksheet will print on one page, display it in print preview.

h. Save and close the workbook, and submit based on your instructor's directions.

   Check your printed worksheet to make sure the data are formatted correctly.

Chapter Objectives Review

After reading this chapter, you have accomplished the following objectives:

1. Explore the Excel window.

- A worksheet is a single spreadsheet containing data. A workbook is a collection of one or more related worksheets contained in a single file.
- Identify Excel window elements: The Name Box displays the name of the current cell. The Formula Bar displays the contents of the current cell. The active cell is the current cell. A sheet tab shows the name of the worksheet.
- Identify columns, rows, and cells: Columns have alphabetical headings, such as A, B, C. Rows have numbers, such as 1, 2, 3. A cell is the intersection of a column and row and is indicated like A5.
- Navigate in and among worksheets: Use the arrow keys to navigate within a sheet, or use the Go To command to go to a specific cell. Click a sheet tab to display the contents on another worksheet.

2. Enter and edit cell data.

- You should plan the worksheet design by stating the purpose, deciding what input values are needed, and then deciding what outputs are needed. Next, you enter and format data in a worksheet. Finally, you document, save, and then share a workbook.
- Enter text: Text may contain letters, numbers, symbols, and spaces. Text aligns at the left side of a cell.
- Enter values: Values are numbers that represent a quantity. Values align at the right side of a cell by default.
- Enter dates: Excel stores dates as serial numbers so that you can calculate the number of days between dates.
- Enter formulas: A formula is used to perform calculations. The formula results display in the cells.
- Edit and clear contents: You can clear the cell contents and/or formats.

3. Create formulas.

- Use cell references in formulas: Use references, such as =B5+B6, instead of values within formulas.
- Apply the order of precedence: The most commonly used operators are performed in this sequence: Exponentiation, Multiplication, Division, Addition, and Subtraction. Use parentheses to perform a lower operation first.
- Use semi-selection to create a formula: When building a formula, you can click a cell containing a value to enter that cell reference in the formula.

4. Use Auto Fill.

- Copy formulas with Auto Fill: To copy a formula down a column or across a row, double-click or drag the fill handle.
- Complete sequences with Auto Fill: Use Auto Fill to copy formulas, number patterns, month names, etc.

5. Display cell formulas.

- By default, the results of formulas appear in cells.
- You can display formulas by pressing Ctrl+`.

6. Manage worksheets.

- Rename a worksheet: The default worksheet tab name is Sheet1, but you can change the name to describe the contents of a worksheet.
- Change worksheet tab color: You can apply different colors to the sheet tabs so they stand out.
- Insert and delete a worksheet: You can insert new worksheets to include related data within one workbook, or you can delete extra worksheets you do not need.
- Move or copy a worksheet: Drag a sheet tab to rearrange the worksheets. You can copy a worksheet within a workbook or to another workbook.

7. Manage columns and rows.

- Insert cells, columns, and rows: Insert a cell to move the remaining cells down or to the right. Insert a new column or row for data.
- Delete cells, columns, and rows: You can delete cells, columns, and rows you no longer need.
- Adjust column width: Double-click between the column headings to widen a column based on the longest item in that column, or drag the border between column headings to increase or decrease a column width.
- Adjust row height: Drag the border between row headings to increase or decrease the height of a row.
- Hide and unhide columns and rows: Hiding rows and columns protects confidential data from being displayed.

8. Select, move, copy, and paste data.

- Select a range: A range may be a single cell or a rectangular block of cells.
- Move a range to another location: After selecting a range, cut it from its location. Then make the top-left corner of the destination range the active cell and paste the range there.
- Copy and paste a range: After selecting a range, click Copy, click the top-left corner of the destination range, and then click Paste to make a copy of the original range.
- Use Paste Options and Paste Special: The Paste Special option enables you to specify how the data are pasted into the worksheet.
- Copy Excel data to other programs: You can copy Excel data and paste it in other programs, such as in Word or PowerPoint.

9. Apply alignment and font options.

- Merge and center labels: Type a label in the left cell, select a range including the data you typed, and then click Merge & Center to merge cells and center the label within the newly merged cell.
- Change horizontal and vertical cell alignment: The default horizontal alignment depends on the data entered, and the default vertical alignment is Bottom Align.

- Wrap text: Use the Wrap Text option to present text on multiple lines in order to avoid having extra-wide columns.
- Increase and decrease indent: To indicate hierarchy of data or to offset a label you can increase or decrease how much the data are indented in a cell.
- Apply borders and fill colors: Borders and fill colors help improve readability of worksheets.

10. Apply number formats.

- The default number format is General, which does not apply any particular format to values. Apply appropriate formats to values to present the data with the correct symbols and decimal alignment. For example, Accounting Number Format is a common number format for monetary values.
- Increase and decrease decimal places: After applying a number format, you can increase or decrease the number of decimal places displayed.

11. Select page setup options.

- The Page Layout tab on the Ribbon contains options for setting margins, selecting orientation, specifying page size, selecting the print area, and applying other settings.
- Specify page options: Page options include orientation, paper size, and scaling.
- Set margin options: You can set the left, right, top, and bottom margins. In addition, you can center worksheet data horizontally and vertically on a page.
- Create headers and footers: You can insert a header or footer to display documentation, such as your name, date, time, and worksheet tab name.
- Select sheet options: Sheet options control the print area, print titles, print options, and page order.

12. Preview and print a worksheet.

- Before printing a worksheet, you should display a preview to ensure the data will print correctly. The Print Preview helps you see if margins are correct or if isolated rows or columns will print on separate pages.
- After making appropriate adjustments, you can print the worksheet.

Key Terms Matching

Match the key terms with their definitions. Write the key term letter by the appropriate numbered definition.

a. Alignment
b. Auto Fill
c. Cell
d. Column width
e. Fill color
f. Fill handle
g. Formula
h. Formula Bar
i. Input area
j. Name Box

k. Order of precedence
l. Output area
m. Range
n. Row height
o. Sheet tab
p. Text
q. Value
r. Workbook
s. Worksheet
t. Wrap text

1. _____ A spreadsheet that contains formulas, functions, values, text, and visual aids. **p. 2**

2. _____ A file containing related worksheets. **p. 2**

3. _____ A range of cells containing values for variables used in formulas. **p. 5**

4. _____ A range of cells containing results based on manipulating the variables. **p. 5**

5. _____ Identifies the address of the current cell. **p. 3**

6. _____ Displays the content (text, value, date, or formula) in the active cell. **p. 3**

7. _____ Displays the name of a worksheet within a workbook. **p. 3**

8. _____ The intersection of a column and row. **p. 4**

9. _____ Includes letters, numbers, symbols, and spaces. **p. 6**

10. _____ A number that represents a quantity or an amount. **p. 7**

11. _____ Rules that control the sequence in which Excel performs arithmetic operations. **p. 13**

12. _____ Enables you to copy the contents of a cell or cell range or to continue a sequence by dragging the fill handle over an adjacent cell or range of cells. **p. 14**

13. _____ A small green square at the bottom-right corner of a cell. **p. 14**

14. _____ The horizontal measurement of a column. **p. 26**

15. _____ The vertical measurement of a row. **p. 27**

16. _____ A rectangular group of cells. **p. 34**

17. _____ The position of data between the cell margins. **p. 42**

18. _____ Formatting that enables a label to appear on multiple lines within the current cell. **p. 43**

19. _____ The background color appearing behind data in a cell. **p. 44**

20. _____ A combination of cell references, operators, values, and/or functions used to perform a calculation. **p. 7**

Multiple Choice

1. What is the first step in planning an effective worksheet?

   (a) Enter labels, values, and formulas.

   (b) State the purpose of the worksheet.

   (c) Identify the input and output areas.

   (d) Decide how to format the worksheet data.

2. What Excel interface item displays the address of the current cell?

   (a) Quick Access Toolbar

   (b) Formula Bar

   (c) Status bar

   (d) Name Box

3. Given the formula =B1*B2+B3/B4^2 where B1 contains 3, B2 contains 4, B3 contains 32, and B4 contains 4, what is the result?

   (a) 14

   (b) 121

   (c) 76

   (d) 9216

4. Why would you press Ctrl+` in Excel?

   (a) To display the print options

   (b) To undo a mistake you made

   (c) To display cell formulas

   (d) To enable the AutoComplete feature

5. Which of the following is a nonadjacent range?

   (a) C15:D30

   (b) L15:L65

   (c) A1:Z99

   (d) A1:A10, D1:D10

6. If you want to balance a title over several columns, what do you do?

   (a) Enter the data in the cell that is about midway across the spreadsheet.

   (b) Merge and center the data over all columns.

   (c) Use the Increase Indent command until the title looks balanced.

   (d) Click Center to center the title horizontally over several columns.

7. Which of the following characteristics is not applicable to the Accounting Number Format?

   (a) Dollar sign immediately on the left side of the value

   (b) Commas to separate thousands

   (c) Two decimal places

   (d) Zero values displayed as hyphens

8. You selected and copied worksheet data containing formulas. However, you want the pasted copy to contain the current formula results rather than formulas. What do you do?

   (a) Click Paste in the Clipboard group on the Home tab.

   (b) Click the Paste arrow in the Clipboard group and select Formulas.

   (c) Click the Paste arrow in the Clipboard group and select Values & Source Formatting.

   (d) Display the Paste Special dialog box and select *Formulas and number formats.*

9. Assume that the data on a worksheet consume a whole printed page and a couple of columns on a second page. You can do all of the following except what to force the data to print all on one page?

   (a) Decrease the Scale value.

   (b) Increase the left and right margins.

   (c) Decrease column widths if possible.

   (d) Select a smaller range as the print area.

10. What should you do if you see a column of pound signs (###) instead of values or results of formulas?

    (a) Increase the zoom percentage.

    (b) Delete the column.

    (c) Adjust the row height.

    (d) Increase the column width.

Practice Exercises

1 Mathematics Review

You want to brush up on your math skills to test your logic by creating formulas in Excel. You realize that you should avoid values in formulas most of the time. Therefore, you created an input area that contains values you will use in your formulas. To test your knowledge of formulas, you will create an output area that will contain a variety of formulas using cell references from the input area. You also need to include a formatted title, the date prepared, and your name. After creating and verifying formula results, you will change input values and observe changes in the formula results. You want to display cell formulas, so you will create a picture copy of the formulas view. This exercise follows the same set of skills as used in Hands-On Exercises 1–4 and 6 in the chapter. Refer to Figure 1.52 as you complete this exercise.

▲	A	B	C	D	E
1				**Excel Formulas and Order of Precedence**	
2	Date Created:	42614		Student Name	
3					
4	**Input Area:**			**Output Area:**	
5	First Value	2		Sum of 1st and 2nd values	=B5+B6
6	Second Value	4		Difference between 4th and 1st values	=B8-B5
7	Third Value	6		Product of 2nd and 3rd values	=B6*B7
8	Fourth Value	8		Quotient of 3rd and 1st values	=B7/B5
9				2nd value to the power of 3rd value	=B6^B7
10				1st value added to product of 2nd and 4th values and difference between sum and 3rd value	=B5+B6*B8-B7
11				Product of sum of 1st and 2nd and difference between 4th and 3rd values	=(B5+B6)*(B8-B7)
12				Product of 1st and 2nd added to product of 3rd and 4th values	=(B5*B6)+(B7*B8)

FIGURE 1.52 Formula Practice

a. Open *e01p1Math* and save it as **e01p1Math_LastFirst**.

b. Type the current date in **cell B2** in this format: 9/1/2016. Type your first and last names in **cell D2**.

c. Adjust the column widths by doing the following:
   - Click in any cell in column A and click **Format** in the Cells group.
   - Select **Column Width**, type **12.57** in the **Column width box**, and then click **OK**.
   - Click in any cell in column B and set the width to **11**.
   - Click in any cell in column D and set the width to **35.57**.

d. Select the **range A1:E1**, click **Merge & Center** in the Alignment group, click **Bold**, and then apply **14 pt font size**.

e. Select the **range B5:B8** and click **Center** in the Alignment group.

f. Select the **range D10:D12** and click **Wrap Text** in the Alignment group.

g. Enter the following formulas in column E:
   - Click **cell E5**. Type =B5+B6 and press **Enter**. Excel adds the value stored in cell B5 (1) to the value stored in cell B6 (2). The result (3) appears in cell E5, as described in cell D5.
   - Enter appropriate formulas in **cells E6:E8**, pressing **Enter** after entering each formula. Subtract to calculate a difference, multiply to calculate a product, and divide to calculate a quotient.
   - Type =B6^B7 in **cell E9** and press **Enter**. Calculate the answer: 2*2*2 = 8.
   - Enter =B5+B6*B8-B7 in **cell E10** and press **Enter**. Calculate the answer: 2*4 = 8; 1+8 = 9; 9−3 = 6. Multiplication occurs first, followed by addition, and finally subtraction.
   - Enter =(B5+B6)*(B8-B7) in **cell E11** and press **Enter**. Calculate the answer: 1+2 = 3; 4−3 = 1; 3*1 = 3. This formula is almost identical to the previous formula; however, calculations in parentheses occur before the multiplication.
   - Enter =B5*B6+B7*B8 in **cell E12** and press **Enter**. Calculate the answer: 1*2 = 2; 3*4 = 12; 2+12 = 14.

h. Edit a formula and the input values:
- Click **cell E12** and click in the Formula Bar to edit the formula. Add parentheses as shown: **=(B5*B6)+(B7*B8)** and click **Enter** to the left side of the Formula Bar. The answer is still 14. The parentheses do not affect order of precedence because multiplication occurred before the addition. The parentheses help improve the readability of the formula.
- Type **2** in **cell B5**, **4** in **cell B6**, **6** in **cell B7**, and **8** in **cell B8**.
- Double-check the results of the formulas using a calculator or your head. The new results in cells E5:E12 should be 6, 6, 24, 3, 4096, 28, 12, and 56, respectively.

i. Double-click the **Sheet1 tab**, type **Results**, and then press **Enter**. Right-click the **Results tab**, select **Move or Copy**, click **(move to end)** in the *Before sheet* section, click the **Create a copy check box**, and then click **OK**. Double-click the **Results (2) tab**, type **Formulas**, and then press **Enter**.

j. Click the **FORMULAS tab** and click **Show Formulas** in the Formula Auditing group. Double-click between the column A and column B headings to adjust the column A width. Double-click between the column B and column C headings to adjust the column B width. Set **24.0 width** for column D.

k. Select the **range A1:E12**, click the **HOME tab**, click the **Copy arrow** in the Clipboard group, and then select **Copy as Picture**. In the Copy Picture dialog box, click **As shown on screen** and click **OK**.

l. Press **Delete** to delete the selected worksheet data and click **Paste**.

> **TROUBLESHOOTING:** If you do not delete the worksheet data, the pasted picture image will display over the data, creating a double effect.

m. Make sure the Formulas worksheet is active, click the **PAGE LAYOUT tab**, and then do the following:
- Click **Orientation** in the Page Setup group and select **Landscape**.
- Click the **View Gridlines check box** in the Sheet Options group to deselect it. The worksheet gridlines are hidden, but the gridlines in the picture still display.

n. Click the **FILE tab** and click **Print**. Verify that the worksheet will print on one page. Press **Esc** to close the Print Preview.

o. Save and close the file, and submit based on your instructor's directions.

2 Calendar Formatting

FROM SCRATCH

You want to create a calendar for May 2016. The calendar will enable you to practice alignment settings, including center, merge and center, and indents. In addition, you will need to adjust column widths and increase row height to create cells large enough to enter important information, such as birthdays, in your calendar. You will create a formula and use Auto Fill to complete the days of the week and the days within each week. To improve the appearance of the calendar, you will add fill colors, font colors, borders, and clip art. This exercise follows the same set of skills as used in Hands-On Exercises 1–6 in the chapter. Refer to Figure 1.53 as you complete this exercise.

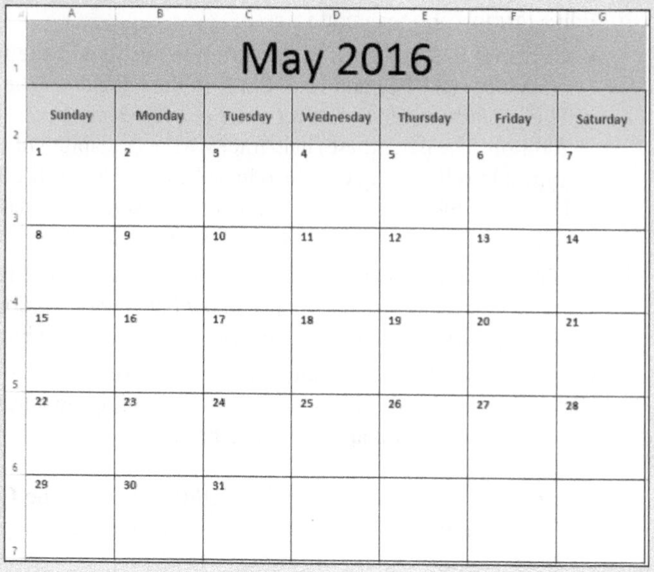

FIGURE 1.53 May 2016 Calendar

a. Click the **FILE tab**, select **New**, and then click **Blank workbook**. Save the workbook as **e01p2May2016_LastFirst**.

b. Type **'May 2016** in **cell A1** and click **Enter** on the left side of the Formula Bar.

> **TROUBLESHOOTING:** If you do not type the apostrophe before *May 2016*, the cell will display *May-16* instead of *May 2016*.

c. Format the title:
   - Select the **range A1:G1** and click **Merge & Center** in the Alignment group.
   - Apply **48 pt font size**.
   - Click the **Fill Color arrow** and click **Green, Accent 6, Lighter 40%** in the *Theme Colors* section of the color palette.

d. Complete the days of the week:
   - Type **Sunday** in **cell A2** and click **Enter** on the left side of the Formula Bar.
   - Drag the **cell A2 fill handle** across the row through **cell G2** to use Auto Fill to complete the rest of the weekdays.
   - Click the **Fill Color arrow** and select **Green, Accent 6, Lighter 60%**. Click the **Font Color arrow** and click **Green, Accent 6, Darker 50%**. Apply bold and **14 pt font size**. Click **Middle Align** and click **Center** in the Alignment group.

e. Complete the days of the month:
   - Type **1** in **cell A3** and press **Ctrl+Enter**. Drag the **cell A3 fill handle** across the row through **cell G3**. Click **Auto Fill Options** in the bottom-right corner of the filled data and select **Fill Series**.
   - Type **=A3+7** in **cell A4** and press **Ctrl+Enter**. Usually you avoid numbers in formulas, but the number of days in a week is always 7. Drag the **cell A4 fill handle** down through **cell A7** to get the date for each Sunday in May.
   - Keep the **range A4:A7** selected and drag the fill handle across through **cell G7**. Select the **range D7:G7** and press **Delete** to delete the extra days.

f. Format the columns and rows:
   - Select **columns A:G**. Click **Format** in the Cells group, select **Column Width**, type **16** in the **Column width box**, and then click **OK**.
   - Select **row 2**. Click **Format** in the Cells group, select **Row Height**, type **54**, and then click **OK**.

- Select **rows 3:7**. Set an **80 row height**.
- Select the **range A2:G7**. Click the **Borders arrow** in the Font group and select **All Borders**.
- Select the **range A3:G7**. Click **Top Align** and **Align Left** in the Alignment group. Click **Increase Indent**. Bold the numbers and apply **12 pt font size**.

g. Double-click the **Sheet1 tab**, type **May**, and then press **Enter**.

h. Deselect the range and click the **PAGE LAYOUT tab**. Click **Orientation** in the Page Setup group and select **Landscape**.

i. Click the **INSERT tab** and click **Header & Footer** in the Text group. Click in the left side of the header and type your name. Click in the center of the header and click **Sheet Name** in the Header & Footer Elements group on the DESIGN tab. Click in the right side of the header and click **File Name** in the Header & Footer Elements group on the DESIGN tab. Click in any cell in the workbook and click **Normal** on the status bar.

j. Save and close the file, and submit based on your instructor's directions.

3 Downtown Theatre

You are the assistant manager at Downtown Theatre, where touring Broadway plays and musicals are performed. You need to complete a spreadsheet to help you analyze ticket sales by seating chart for each performance. The spreadsheet will identify the seating sections, total seats in each section, and the number of seats sold for a performance. You will then calculate the percentage of seats sold and unsold. This exercise follows the same set of skills as used in Hands-On Exercises 1–6 in the chapter. Refer to Figure 1.54 as you complete this exercise.

	A	B	C	D	E
1	**Downtown Theatre**				
2	Ticket Sales by Seating Section				
3	3/31/2016				
4					
5	**Section**	**Available Seats**	**Seats Sold**	**Percentage Sold**	**Percentage Unsold**
6	Box Seats	25	12	48.0%	52.0%
7	Front Floor	120	114	95.0%	5.0%
8	Back Floor	132	108	81.8%	18.2%
9	Tier 1	40	40	100.0%	0.0%
10	Mezzanine	144	138	95.8%	4.2%
11	Balcony	106	84	79.2%	20.8%

FIGURE 1.54 Theatre Seating Data

a. Open *e01p3TicketSales* and save it as **e01p3TicketSales_LastFirst**.

b. Double-click the **Sheet1 tab**, type **Seating**, and then press **Enter**.

c. Type **3/31/2016** in **cell A3** and press **Enter**.

d. Adjust alignments and font attributes by doing the following from the Alignment and Font groups on the HOME tab:
- Select the **range A1:E1**, click **Merge & Center**, click **Bold**, click the **Font Size arrow**, and then select **16**.
- Use the Merge & Center command to merge the **range A2:E2** and center the subtitle.
- Use the Merge & Center command to merge the **range A3:E3** and center the date.
- Select the **range A5:E5**, click **Wrap Text**, click **Center**, and then click **Bold** to format the column labels.

e. Right-click the **row 9 heading** and select **Insert** from the shortcut menu to insert a new row. Type the following data in the new row: **Back Floor, 132, 108**.

f. Move the Balcony row to be the last row by doing the following:
- Click the **row 6 heading** and click **Cut** in the Clipboard group on the HOME tab.
- Right-click the **row 12 heading** and select **Insert Cut Cells** from the menu.

g. Adjust column widths by doing the following:
- Double-click between the column A and column B headings.
- Select **columns B** and **C headings** to select the columns, click **Format** in the Cells group, select **Column Width**, type **9** in the **Column width box**, and then click **OK**. Because columns B and C contain similar data, you set the same width for these columns.
- Set the width of columns D and E to **12**.

h. Select the **range B6:C11**, click **Align Right** in the Alignment group on the HOME tab, and then click **Increase Indent** twice in the Alignment group.

i. Calculate and format the percentage of sold and unsold seats by doing the following:
- Click **cell D6**. Type **=C6/B6** and press **Tab** to enter the formula and make cell E6 the active cell. This formula divides the number of seats sold by the total number of Box Seats.
- Type **=(B6-C6)/B6** and click **Enter** on the left side of the Formula Bar to enter the formula and keep cell E6 the active cell. This formula must first subtract the number of sold seats from the available seats to calculate the number of unsold seats. The difference is divided by the total number of available seats to determine the percentage of unsold seats.
- Select the **range D6:E6**, click **Percent Style** in the Number group on the HOME tab, and then click **Increase Decimal** in the Number group. Keep the range selected.
- Double-click the **cell E6 fill handle** to copy the selected formulas down their respective columns. Keep the range selected.
- Click **Align Right** in the Alignment group and click **Increase Indent** twice in the Alignment group. These actions will help center the data below the column labels. Do not click Center; doing so will center each value and cause the decimal points not to align. Deselect the range.

j. Display and preserve a screenshot of the formulas by doing the following:
- Click **New sheet**, double-click the **Sheet1 tab**, type **Formulas**, and then press **Enter**.
- Click **Select All** in the top-left corner above the row headings and to the left of the column headings, click the **Fill Color arrow** in the Font group, and then click **White, Background 1**. Applying this fill color will prevent the cell gridlines from bleeding through the screenshot you are about to embed.
- Click the **Seating sheet tab**, click the **FORMULAS tab**, and then click **Show Formulas** in the Formula Auditing group to display cell formulas.
- Click **cell A1** and drag down to **cell E11** to select the range of data. Click the **HOME tab**, click **Copy arrow** in the Clipboard group, select **Copy as Picture**, and then click **OK**.
- Click the **Formulas sheet tab**, click **cell A1**, and then click **Paste**.
- Click the **PAGE LAYOUT tab**, click **Orientation** in the Page Setup group, and then select **Landscape**.
- Click the **Seating sheet tab**, click the **FORMULAS tab**, and then click **Show Formulas** in the Formula Auditing group to hide the cell formulas.

k. Click **cell A1**. Click the **PAGE LAYOUT tab**, click **Margins** in the Page Setup group, and then select **Custom Margins**. Click the **Horizontally check box** and click **Print Preview**. Excel centers the data horizontally based on the widest item. Press **Esc** to leave the Print Preview mode.

l. Click the **Page Setup Dialog Box Launcher**, click the **Header/Footer tab** in the Page Setup dialog box, click **Custom Footer**, type your name in the **Left section box**, click in the **Center section box**, click **Insert File Name**, click in the **Right section box**, click **Insert Sheet Name**, and then click **OK**. Click **OK**.

m. Save and close the file, and submit based on your instructor's directions.

1 Restaurant Receipt

Matt, the owner of Matt's Sports Grill in Toledo, Ohio, asked you to help him create a receipt spreadsheet that he can use until his new system arrives. He wants an input area for the total food and beverage purchases, the sales tax rate, and the tip rate. The formatted receipt should include the subtotal, tax, tip, and total amount for a customer. Refer to Figure 1.55 as you complete this exercise.

	A	B	C	D	E
1	**Input Area**			**Matt's Sports Grill**	
2	Food & Beverages	$ 9.39		Toledo, Ohio	
3	Sales Tax Rate	6.5%			
4	Tip Rate	18.0%		Food & Beverages	$ 9.39
5				Sales Tax Amount	0.61
6				Subtotal	$ 10.00
7				Tip Amount	1.69
8				**Total Bill**	**$ 11.69**
9					
10				*Thank you for dining with us.*	

FIGURE 1.55 Matt's Sports Grill Receipt

a. Open a new Excel workbook, save it as **e01m1Receipt_LastFirst**, and then rename *Sheet1* as **Receipt**.

b. Enter the four labels in the **range A1:A4** in the Input Area as shown in Figure 1.56. Type **9.39**, **0.065**, and **.18** in the **range B2:B4**. Apply these formats to the Input Area:
   - Merge and center the *Input Area* title over both columns. Apply bold and **Blue, Accent 1, Lighter 40% fill color** to the title. Adjust the width of the first column.
   - Apply the **Accounting Number Format** and **Percent Style** format with the respective decimal places as shown in the **range B2:B4**.

c. Enter the labels in the receipt area in column D. Use Format Painter to copy the formats of the title in **cells A1** and **D1**. Merge and center the city and state in the **range D2:E2**. Change the width of column D to **17**. Indent the *Subtotal* and *Tip Amount* labels twice each. Apply bold to *Total Bill* and apply italic to *Thank you for dining with us*.

d. Enter the following formulas for the receipt:
   - **Food & Beverages:** Enter a formula that reads the value in the Input Area; do not retype the value in cell E4.
   - **Sales Tax Amount:** Calculate the product of the food & beverages and the sales tax rate.
   - **Subtotal:** Determine the formula needed.
   - **Tip Amount:** Calculate the tip based on the pretax amount and the tip rate.
   - **Total Bill:** Determine the formula needed.

e. Apply **Accounting Number Format** to the *Food & Beverages*, *Subtotal*, and *Total Bill* values, if necessary. Apply **Comma Style** and underline to the *Sales Tax Amount* and *Tip Amount* values. Apply the **Double Underline style** to the *Total Bill* value.

f. Set **1.5"** top margin and center the data horizontally on the page.

g. Insert a footer with your name on the left side, the sheet name code in the center, and the file name code on the right side.

h. Create a copy of the Receipt worksheet, move the new sheet to the end, and then rename the copied sheet **Formulas**. Display cell formulas on the Formulas worksheet, select **Landscape orientation**, and then select the options to print gridlines and headings. Adjust column widths so that the data will fit on one page.

DISCOVER

i. Open the Excel Options dialog box while displaying the Formulas worksheet. In the Advanced category, under *Display options for this worksheet:*, select the **Show formulas in cells instead of their calculated results check box**. This option will make sure the active worksheet will display the formulas when you open the workbook again. The Receipt worksheet will continue showing the results.

j. Save and close the file, and submit based on your instructor's directions.

2 Guest House Rental Rates

ANALYSIS CASE

You manage a beach guest house in Ft. Lauderdale containing three types of rental units. Prices are based on peak and off-peak times of the year. You need to calculate the maximum daily revenue for each rental type, assuming all units are rented. In addition, you need to calculate the discount rate for off-peak rental times. Finally, you will improve the appearance of the worksheet by applying font, alignment, and number formats.

a. Open *e01m2Rentals* and save it as **e01m2Rentals_LastFirst**.

b. Merge and center *Peak Rentals* in the **range C4:D4**, over the two columns of peak rental data. Apply **Dark Red fill color** and **White, Background 1 font color**.

c. Merge and center *Off-Peak Rentals* in the **range E4:G4** over the three columns of off-peak rental data. Apply **Blue fill color** and **White, Background 1 font color**.

d. Center and wrap the headings on row 5. Adjust the width of columns D and F, if needed. Center the data in the **range B6:B8**.

e. Create and copy the following formulas:
   • Calculate the Peak Rentals Maximum Revenue by multiplying the number of units by the peak rental price per day.
   • Calculate the Off-Peak Rentals Maximum Revenue by multiplying the number of units by the off-peak rental price per day.
   • Calculate the Discount rate for the Off-Peak rental price per day. For example, using the peak and off-peak per day values, the studio apartment rents for 75% of its peak rental rate. However, you need to calculate and display the off-peak discount rate, which is .24975.

f. Format the monetary values with **Accounting Number Format**. Format the Discount Rate formula results in **Percent Style** with one decimal place.

DISCOVER

g. Apply **Blue, Accent 1, Lighter 80% fill color** to the **range E5:G8**.

h. Select the **range C5:D8** and apply a custom color with **Red 242**, **Green 220**, and **Blue 219**.

i. Answer the four questions below the worksheet data. If you change any values to answer the questions, change the values back to the original values.

j. Set **1"** top, bottom, left, and right margins. Center the data horizontally on the page.

k. Insert a footer with your name on the left side, the sheet name code in the center, and the file name code on the right side.

l. Create a copy of the Rental Rates worksheet, place the new sheet to the right side of the original worksheet, and rename the new sheet **Formulas**. On the Formulas worksheet, select **Landscape orientation** and the options to print gridlines and headings. Delete the question and answer section on the Formulas sheet.

DISCOVER

m. Open the Excel Options dialog box while displaying the Formulas worksheet. In the Advanced category, under *Display options for this worksheet:*, select the **Show formulas in cells instead of their calculated results check box**. This option will make sure the active worksheet will display the formulas when you open the workbook again. The Rental Rates worksheet will continue showing the results. Adjust column widths so that the data will fit on one page.

n. Save and close the file, and submit based on your instructor's directions.

---

3 Real Estate Sales Report

You own a small real estate company in Indianapolis. You want to analyze sales for selected properties. Your assistant has prepared a spreadsheet with sales data. You need to calculate the number of days that the houses were on the market and their sales percentage of the list price. In one situation, the house was involved in a bidding war between two families that really wanted the house. Therefore, the sale price exceeded the list price.

a. Open *e01m3Sales* and save it as **e01m3Sales_LastFirst**.

b. Delete the row that has incomplete sales data. The owners took their house off the market.

c. Calculate the number of days each house was on the market. Copy the formula down that column.

d. Format prices with **Accounting Number Format** with zero decimal places.

e. Calculate the sales price percentage of the list price. The second house was listed for $500,250, but it sold for only $400,125. Therefore, the sale percentage of the list price is 79.99%. Format the percentages with two decimal places.

f. Wrap the headings on row 4.

g. Insert a new column between the *Date Sold* and *List Price* columns. Move the *Days on Market* column to the new location. Apply **Align Right** and increase the indent on the days on market formula results. Then delete the empty column B.

h. Edit the list date of the 41 Chestnut Circle house to be **4/22/2016**. Edit the list price of the house on Amsterdam Drive to be **$355,000**.

i. Select the property rows and set a **20 row height**. Adjust column widths as necessary.

j. Select **Landscape orientation** and set the scaling to **130%**. Center the data horizontally and vertically on the page.

k. Insert a header with your name, the current date code, and the current time code.

l. Save and close the file, and submit based on your instructor's directions.

4 | Problem-Solving with Classmates

COLLABORATION CASE

Your instructor wants all students in the class to practice their problem-solving skills. Pair up with a classmate so that you can create errors in a workbook and then see how many errors your classmate can find in your worksheet and how many errors you can find in your classmate's worksheet.

a. Create a folder named **Exploring** on your OneDrive and give access to that drive to a classmate and your instructor.

b. Open *e01h6Markup_LastFirst*, which you created in the Hands-On Exercises, and save it as **e01m4Markup_LastFirst**.

c. Edit each main formula to have a deliberate error (such as a value or incorrect cell reference) in it and then copy the formulas down the columns.

d. Save the workbook to your shared folder on your OneDrive.

e. Open the workbook your classmate saved on his or her OneDrive and save the workbook with your name after theirs, such as *e01m4Markup_MulberyKeith_KrebsCynthia*.

f. Find the errors in your classmate's workbook, insert comments to describe the errors, and then correct the errors.

g. Save the workbook back to your classmate's OneDrive and submit based on your instructor's directions.

Beyond the Classroom

Credit Card Rebate

RESEARCH CASE

FROM SCRATCH

You recently found out the Costco TrueEarnings® American Express credit card earns annual rebates on all purchases. You want to see how much rebate you would have received had you used this credit card for purchases in the past year. Use the Internet to research the percentage rebates for different categories. Plan the design of the spreadsheet. Enter the categories, rebate percentages, amount of money you spent in each category, and a formula to calculate the amount of rebate. Use the Excel Help feature to learn how to add several cells using a function instead of adding cells individually and how to apply a Double Accounting underline. Insert the appropriate function to total your categorical purchases and rebate amounts. Apply appropriate formatting and page setup options for readability. Underline the last monetary values for the last data row and apply the **Double Accounting underline style** to the totals. Insert a header. Save the workbook as **e01b2Rebate_LastFirst**. Close the workbook and submit based on your instructor's directions.

Net Proceeds from House Sale

DISASTER RECOVERY

Garrett Frazier is a real estate agent. He wants his clients to have a realistic expectation of how much money they will receive when they sell their houses. Sellers know they have to pay a commission to the agent and pay off their existing mortgages; however, many sellers forget to consider they might have to pay some of the buyer's closing costs, title insurance, and prorated property taxes. The realtor commission and estimated closing costs are based on the selling price and the respective rates. The estimated property taxes are prorated based on the annual property taxes and percentage of the year. For example, if a house sells three months into the year, the seller pays 25% of the property taxes. Garrett created a worksheet to enter values in an input area to calculate the estimated deductions at closing and calculate the estimated net proceeds the seller will receive. However, the worksheet contains errors. Open *e01b3Proceeds* and save it as **e01b3Proceeds_LastFirst**.

Use Help to learn how to insert comments into cells. As you identify the errors, insert comments in the respective cells to explain the errors. Correct the errors, including formatting errors. Apply **Landscape orientation**, **115% scaling**, **1.5" top margin**, and center horizontally. Insert your name on the left side of the header, sheet name code in the center, and the file name code on the right side. Save and close the workbook, and submit based on your instructor's directions.

Goal Setting

SOFT SKILLS CASE

FROM SCRATCH

After watching the Goal Setting video, start a new Excel workbook and save it as **e01b4Goals_LastFirst**. List three descriptive goals in column A relating to your schoolwork and degree completion. For example, maybe you usually study three hours a week for your algebra class, and you want to increase your study time by 20%. Enter *Algebra homework & study time (hours)* in column A, *3* in column B, the percentage change in column C, and create a formula that calculates the total goal in column D. Adjust column widths as needed.

Insert column labels above each column. Format the labels and values using information you learned earlier in the chapter. Merge and center a title at the top of the worksheet. Use the Page Setup dialog box to center the worksheet horizontally. Rename Sheet1 using the term, such as *Fall 2016*. Create a footer with your name on the left side, sheet name code in the center, and file name code on the right side. Save and close the workbook, and submit based on your instructor's directions.

Capstone Exercise

You manage a publishing company that publishes and sells books to bookstores in Austin. Your assistant prepared a standard six-month royalty statement for one author. You need to insert formulas, format the worksheets, and then prepare royalty statements for other authors.

Enter Data into the Worksheet

You need to format a title, enter the date indicating the end of the statement period, and delete a blank column. You also need to insert a row for the standard discount rate, a percentage that you discount the books from the retail price to sell to the bookstores.

a. Open *e01c1Royalty* and save it as **e01c1Royalty_LastFirst**.

b. Merge and center the title over the **range A1:D1**.

c. Type **6/30/2016** in **cell B3** and left align the date.

d. Delete the blank column between the Hardback and Paperback columns.

e. Insert a new row between Retail Price and Price to Bookstore. Enter **Standard Discount Rate**, **0.55**, and **0.5**. Format the two values as **Percent Style**.

Calculate Values

You need to insert formulas to perform necessary calculations.

a. Enter the Percent Returned formula in **cell B10**. The percent returned indicates the percentage of books sold but returned to the publisher.

b. Enter the Price to Bookstore formula in **cell B15**. This is the price at which you sell the books to the bookstore. It is based on the retail price and the standard discount. For example, if a book has a $10 retail price and a 55% discount, you sell the book for $4.50.

c. Enter the Net Retail Sales formula in **cell B16**. The net retail sales is the revenue from the net units sold at the retail price. Gross units sold minus the returned units equals net units sold.

d. Enter the Royalty to Author formula in **cell B20**. Royalties are based on net retail sales and the applicable royalty rate.

e. Enter the Royalty per Book formula in **cell B21**. This amount is the author's earnings on every book sold but not returned.

f. Copy the formulas to the Paperback column.

Format the Values

You are ready to format the values to improve readability.

a. Apply **Comma Style** with zero decimal places to the **range B8:C9**.

b. Apply **Percent Style** with one decimal place to the **range B10:C10** and **Percent Style** with two decimal places to the **range B19:C19**.

c. Apply **Accounting Number Format** to all monetary values.

Format the Worksheet

You want to improve the appearance of the rest of the worksheet.

a. Select the **range B6:C6**. Apply bold, right alignment, and **Purple font color**.

b. Click **cell A7**, apply **Purple font color**, and then apply **Gray-25%, Background 2, Darker 10% fill color**. Select the **range A7:C7** and select **Merge Across**.

c. Use Format Painter to apply the formats from **cell A7** to **cells A12** and **A18**.

d. Select the **ranges A8:A10, A13:A16, and A19:A21**. Indent the labels twice. Widen column A as needed.

e. Select the **range A7:C10** (the *Units Sold* section) and apply the **Outside Borders** border style. Apply the same border style to the *Pricing* and *Royalty Information* sections.

Manage the Workbook

You will apply page setup options insert a footer, and, then duplicate the royalty statement worksheet to use as a model to prepare a royalty statement for another author.

a. Select the margin setting to center the data horizontally on the page. Insert a footer with your name on the left side, the sheet name code in the center, and the file name code on the right side.

b. Copy the Jacobs worksheet, move the new worksheet to the end, and then rename it **Lopez**.

c. Change the Jacobs sheet tab to **Red**. Change the Lopez sheet tab to **Dark Blue**.

d. Make these changes on the Lopez worksheet: **Lopez** (author), **5000** (hardback gross units), **14000** (paperback gross units), **400** (hardback returns), **1925** (paperback returns), **19.95** (hardback retail price), and **6.95** (paperback retail price).

Display Formulas and Print the Workbook

You want to print the formatted Jacobs worksheet to display the calculated results. To provide evidence of the formulas, you want to display and print cell formulas in the Lopez worksheet.

a. Display the cell formulas for the Lopez worksheet.

b. Select options to print the gridlines and headings.

c. Change the Options setting to make sure the formulas display instead of cell results on this worksheet when you open it again.

d. Adjust the column widths so that the formula printout will print on one page.

e. Save and close the workbook, and submit based on your instructor's directions.

Formulas and Functions

CHAPTER 2

Performing Quantitative Analysis

Yuri Arcurs/Shutterstock

OBJECTIVES | AFTER YOU READ THIS CHAPTER, YOU WILL BE ABLE TO:

1. Use relative, absolute, and mixed cell references in formulas p. 76
2. Correct circular references p. 78
3. Insert a function p. 84
4. Insert basic math and statistics functions p. 86
5. Use date functions p. 91
6. Determine results with the IF function p. 99
7. Use lookup functions p. 102
8. Calculate payments with the PMT function p. 105
9. Create and maintain range names p. 110
10. Use range names in formulas p. 112

CASE STUDY | Townsend Mortgage Company

You are an assistant to Erica Matheson, a mortgage broker at the Townsend Mortgage Company. Erica spends her days reviewing mortgage rates and trends, meeting with clients, and preparing paperwork. She relies on your expertise in using Excel to help analyze mortgage data.

Today, Erica provided you with sample mortgage data: loan number, house cost, down payment, mortgage rate, and the length of the loan in years. She asked you to perform some basic calculations so that she can check the output provided by her system to verify if it is calculating results correctly. She needs you to calculate the amount financed, the periodic interest rate, the total number of payment periods, the percent of the house cost that is financed, and the payoff year for each loan. In addition, you will calculate totals, averages, and other basic statistics.

Furthermore, you need to complete another worksheet that uses functions to look up interest rates from another table, calculate the monthly payments, and determine how much (if any) the borrower will have to pay for private mortgage insurance (PMI).

Formula Basics

When you increase your understanding of formulas, you can build robust workbooks that perform a variety of calculations for quantitative analysis. Your ability to build sophisticated workbooks and to interpret the results increases your value to any organization. By now, you should be able to build simple formulas using cell references and mathematical operators and using the order of precedence to control the sequence of calculations in formulas.

In this section, you will create formulas in which cell addresses change or remain fixed when you copy them. Finally, you will learn how to identify and prevent circular references in formulas.

Using Relative, Absolute, and Mixed Cell References in Formulas

When you copy a formula, Excel either adjusts or preserves the cell references in the copied formulas based on how the cell references appear in the original formula. Excel uses three different ways to reference a cell in a formula: relative, absolute, and mixed. When you create a formula that you will copy to other cells, ask yourself the following question:

> Do the cell references need to adjust for the copied formulas, or should the cell references always refer to the same cell location, regardless of where the copied formula is located?

Use a Relative Cell Reference

STEP 1 » A *relative cell reference* indicates a cell's relative location, such as five rows up and one column to the left, from the cell containing the formula. When you copy a formula containing a relative cell reference, the cell references in the copied formula change relative to the position of the copied formula. Regardless of where you copy the formula, the cell references in the copied formula maintain the same relative distance from the cell containing the copied formula, as the cell references the relative location to the original formula cell.

In Figure 2.1, the formulas in column F contain relative cell references. When you copy the original formula =D2-E2 from cell F2 down to cell F3, the copied formula changes to =D3-E3. Because you copy the formula *down* the column to cell F3, the column letters in the formula stay the same, but the row numbers change to reflect the row to which you copied the formula. Using relative cell addresses to calculate the amount financed ensures that each borrower's down payment is subtracted from his or her respective house cost.

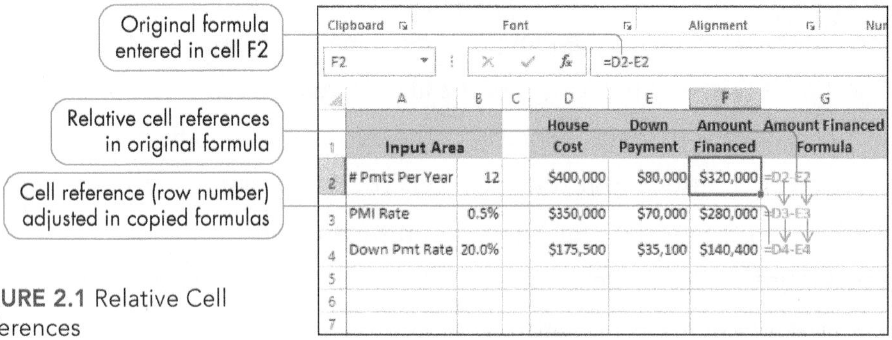

FIGURE 2.1 Relative Cell References

Use an Absolute Cell Reference

STEP 2 » An *absolute cell reference* provides a permanent reference to a specific cell. When you copy a formula containing an absolute cell reference, the cell reference in the copied formula does not change, regardless of where you copy the formula. An absolute cell reference appears with a dollar sign before both the column letter and row number, such as $B$4.

In Figure 2.2, each down payment is calculated by multiplying the respective house cost by the down payment rate (20%). Cell E2 contains =D2*$B$4 ($400,000*20.0%) to calculate the first borrower's down payment ($80,000). When you copy the formula down to the next row, the copied formula in cell E3 is =D3*$B$4. The relative cell reference D2 changes to D3 (for the next house cost) and the absolute cell reference $B$4 remains the same to refer to the 20.0% down payment rate. This formula ensures that the cell reference to the house cost changes for each row but that the house cost is always multiplied by the rate in cell B4.

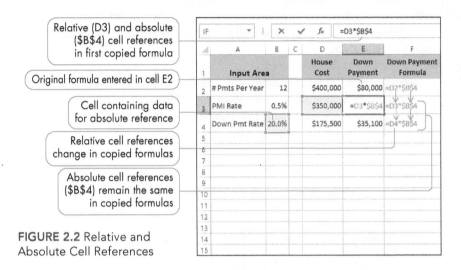

Relative (D3) and absolute ($B$4) cell references in first copied formula

Original formula entered in cell E2

Cell containing data for absolute reference

Relative cell references change in copied formulas

Absolute cell references ($B$4) remain the same in copied formulas

FIGURE 2.2 Relative and Absolute Cell References

TIP Input Area and Absolute Cell References

Figure 2.2 illustrates an input area, a range in a worksheet that contains values that you can change. You build formulas using absolute references to the cells in the input area. By using cell references from an input area, you can change the value in the input area and the formulas that refer to those cells will update automatically. If an input value changes (e.g., the down payment rate changes from 20% to 25%), enter the new input value in only one cell (e.g., B4), and Excel recalculates the amount of down payment for all the formulas.

Figure 2.3 shows what happens if the down payment formula used a relative reference to cell B4. If the original formula in cell E2 is =D2*B4, the copied formula becomes =D3*B5 in cell E3. The relative cell reference to B4 changes to B5 when you copy the formula down. Because cell B5 is empty, the $350,000 house cost in cell D3 is multiplied by 0, giving a $0 down payment, which is not a valid down payment amount.

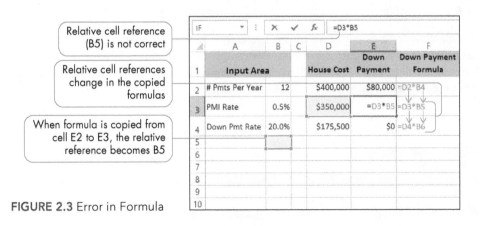

Relative cell reference (B5) is not correct

Relative cell references change in the copied formulas

When formula is copied from cell E2 to E3, the relative reference becomes B5

FIGURE 2.3 Error in Formula

Use a Mixed Cell Reference

STEP 3 » A *mixed cell reference* combines an absolute cell reference with a relative cell reference. When you copy a formula containing a mixed cell reference, either the column letter or the row number that has the absolute reference remains fixed while the other part of the cell reference that is relative changes in the copied formula. $B4 and B$4 are examples of mixed cell references. In the reference $B4, the column B is absolute, and the row number is relative; when you copy the formula, the column letter, B, does not change, but the row number will change. In the reference B$4, the column letter, B, changes, but the row number, 4, does not change. To create a mixed reference, type the dollar sign to the left of the part of the cell reference you want to be absolute.

In the down payment formula, you can change the formula in cell E2 to be =D2*B$4. Because you are copying down the same column, only the row reference 4 must be absolute; the column letter stays the same. Figure 2.4 shows the copied formula =D3*B$4 in cell E3. In situations where you can use either absolute or mixed references, consider using mixed references to shorten the length of the formula.

Mixed cell references in original formula

Row numbers stay the same for copied mixed cell references

Copied formulas still point to cell B4 with mixed cell reference

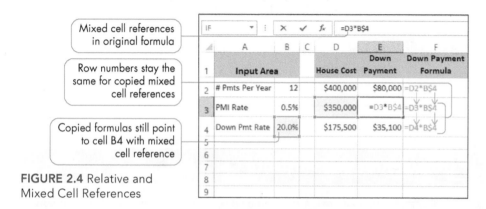

FIGURE 2.4 Relative and Mixed Cell References

> **TIP** **The F4 Key**
>
> The F4 key toggles through relative, absolute, and mixed references. Click a cell reference within a formula on the Formula Bar and press F4 to change it. For example, click in B4 in the formula =D2*B4. Press F4 and the relative cell reference (B4) changes to an absolute cell reference ($B$4). Press F4 again and $B$4 becomes a mixed reference (B$4); press F4 again and it becomes another mixed reference ($B4). Press F4 a fourth time and the cell reference returns to the original relative reference (B4).

Correcting Circular References

If a formula contains a direct or an indirect reference to the cell containing the formula, a *circular reference* exists. Figure 2.5 shows an example of a circular reference in a formula. The formula in cell E2 is =E2*$B$4. Because the formula is in cell E2, using the cell address E2 within the formula creates a circular reference.

Active cell

Formula contains reference to active cell

Error message

FIGURE 2.5 Circular Reference

STEP 4 Circular references usually cause inaccurate results. Excel displays a warning message when you enter a formula containing a circular reference or when you open an Excel workbook that contains an existing circular reference. Click Help to display the *Find and fix a circular reference* Help topic or click OK to accept the circular reference. Until you resolve a circular reference, the status bar indicates the location of a circular reference, such as CIRCULAR REFERENCES: E2.

 TIP | **Green Triangles**

Excel displays a green triangle in the top-left corner of a cell if it detects a potential error in a formula. Click the cell to see the Trace Error button (yellow diamond with exclamation mark). When you click Trace Error, Excel displays information about the potential error and how to correct it. In some cases, Excel may anticipate an inconsistent formula or the omission of adjacent cells in a formula. For example, if a column contains values for the year 2016, the error message indicates that you did not include the year itself. However, the year 2016 is merely a label and should not be included; therefore, you would ignore that error message.

Quick Concepts ✓

1. What happens when you copy a formula containing a relative cell reference one column to the right? *p. 76*

2. Why would you use an absolute reference in a formula? *p. 76*

3. What is a circular reference? Provide an example. *p. 78*

Watch the Video for this Hands-On Exercise!

MyITLab®
HOE1 Training

1 Formula Basics

Erica prepared a workbook containing data for five mortgages financed with the Townsend Mortgage Company. The data include house cost, down payment, mortgage rate, number of years to pay off the mortgage, and the financing date for each mortgage.

Skills covered: Use a Relative Cell Reference in a Formula • Use an Absolute Cell Reference in a Formula • Use a Mixed Cell Reference in a Formula • Correct a Circular Reference

---

STEP 1 ›› USE A RELATIVE CELL REFERENCE IN A FORMULA

You need to calculate the amount financed by each borrower by creating a formula with relative cell references that calculates the difference between the house cost and the down payment. After verifying the results of the amount financed by the first borrower, you will copy the formula down the Amount Financed column to calculate the other borrowers' amounts financed. Refer to Figure 2.6 as you complete Step 1.

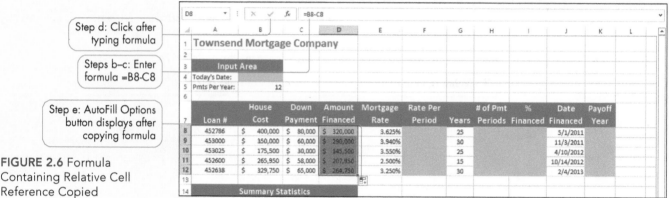

Step d: Click after typing formula

Steps b–c: Enter formula =B8-C8

Step e: AutoFill Options button displays after copying formula

FIGURE 2.6 Formula Containing Relative Cell Reference Copied

a. Open *e02h1Loans* and save it as **e02h1Loans_LastFirst**.

> **TROUBLESHOOTING:** If you make any major mistakes in this exercise, you can close the file, open *e02h1Loans* again, and then start this exercise over.

The workbook contains two worksheets: Details (for Hands-On Exercises 1 and 2) and Payment Info (for Hands-On Exercises 3 and 4). You will enter formulas in the shaded cells.

b. Click **cell D8** in the Details sheet. Type = and click **cell B8**, the cell containing the first borrower's house cost.

c. Type - and click **cell C8**, the cell containing the down payment by the first borrower.

d. Click **Enter** (the check mark between the Name Box and Formula Bar) to complete the formula.

The first borrower financed (i.e., borrowed) $320,000, the difference between the cost ($400,000) and the down payment ($80,000).

e. Double-click the **cell D8 fill handle**.

You copied the formula down the Amount Financed column for each mortgage row.

TIP Auto Fill Options

The Auto Fill Options button appears in the bottom-right corner of the copied formulas. If you click it, you can see that the default is Copy Cells. If you want to copy only formatting, click Fill Formatting Only. If you want to copy data only, click Fill Without Formatting.

f. Click **cell D9** and view the formula in the Formula Bar.

The formula in cell D8 is =B8-C8. The formula pasted in cell D9 is =B9-C9. Because the original formula contained relative cell references, when you copy the formula down to the next row, the row numbers for the cell references change. Each result represents the amount financed for that particular borrower.

g. Press ⬇ and look at the cell references in the Formula Bar to see how the references change for each formula you copied. Save the workbook with the new formula you created.

STEP 2 ≫ USE AN ABSOLUTE CELL REFERENCE IN A FORMULA

Column E contains the annual percentage rate (APR) for each mortgage. Because the borrowers will make monthly payments, you need to calculate the monthly interest rate by dividing the APR by 12 (the number of payments in one year) for each borrower. Refer to Figure 2.7 as you complete Step 2.

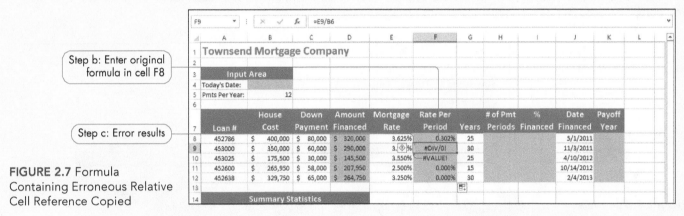

FIGURE 2.7 Formula Containing Erroneous Relative Cell Reference Copied

a. Click **cell F8**.

You need to create a formula to calculate the monthly interest rate for the first borrower.

b. Type **=E8/B5** and click **Enter** (the checkmark between the Name Box and the Formula Bar).

Typically, you should avoid typing values directly in formulas. Although the number of months in one year is always 12, use a reference to cell B5, where the number of payments per year is placed in the input area, so that the company can change the payment period to bimonthly (24 payments per year) or quarterly (four payments per year) without adjusting the formula.

c. Double-click the **cell F8 fill handle**, click **cell F9**, and then view the results (see Figure 2.7).

An error icon displays to the left of cell F9, cell F9 displays #DIV/0!, and cell F10 displays #VALUE!. The original formula was =E8/B5. Because you copied the formula =E8/B5 down the column, the first copied formula is =E9/B6, and the second copied formula is =E10/B7. Although you want the mortgage rate cell reference (E8) to change (E9, E10, etc.) from row to row, you do not want the divisor (cell B5) to change. You need all formulas to divide by the value stored in cell B5, so you will edit the formula to make B5 an absolute reference.

d. Click **Undo** in the Quick Access Toolbar to undo the Auto Fill process. Click within or to the right of **B5** in the Formula Bar.

e. Press **F4** and click **Enter** (the checkmark between the Name Box and the Formula Bar).

Excel changes the cell reference from B5 to $B$5, making it an absolute cell reference.

f. Copy the formula down the Rate Per Period column. Click **cell F9** and view the formula in the Formula Bar. Save the workbook.

The formula in cell F9 is =E9/$B$5. The reference to E9 is relative and the reference to B5 is absolute.

STEP 3 ≫ USE A MIXED CELL REFERENCE IN A FORMULA

The next formula you create will calculate the total number of payment periods for each loan. Refer to Figure 2.8 as you complete Step 3.

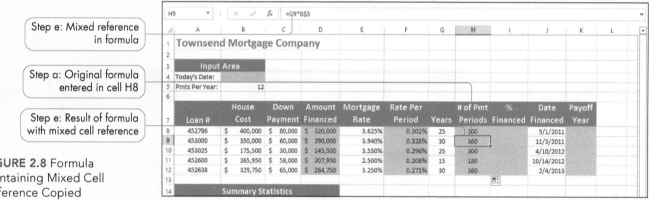

FIGURE 2.8 Formula Containing Mixed Cell Reference Copied

a. Click **cell H8** and type **=G8*B5**.

You need to multiply the number of years (25) by the number of payment periods in one year (12) using cell references.

b. Press **F4** to make the B5 cell reference absolute and click **Enter** (the checkmark between the Name Box and Formula Bar).

You want B5 to be absolute so that the cell reference remains B5 when you copy the formula. The product of 25 years and 12 months is 300 months or payment periods.

c. Copy the formula down the # of Pmt Periods column.

The first copied formula is =G9*$B$5, and the result is 360. You want to see what happens if you change the absolute reference to a mixed reference and copy the formula again. Because you are copying down a column, the column letter B can be relative because it will not change either way, but the row number 5 must be absolute.

d. Click **Undo** on the Quick Access Toolbar to undo the copied formulas.

Cell H8 is the active cell.

e. Click within the **$B$5 cell reference** in the Formula Bar. Press **F4** to change the cell reference to a mixed cell reference: B$5. Press **Ctrl+Enter** and copy the formula down the # of Pmt Periods column. Click **cell H9**. Save the workbook.

The first copied formula is =G9*B$5 and the result is still 360. In this situation, using either an absolute reference or a mixed reference provides the same results.

STEP 4 >> CORRECT A CIRCULAR REFERENCE

Erica wants to know what percentage of the house cost each borrower will finance. As you create the formula, you enter a circular reference. After studying the results, you correct the circular error and plan future formulas that avoid this problem. Refer to Figure 2.9 as you complete Step 4.

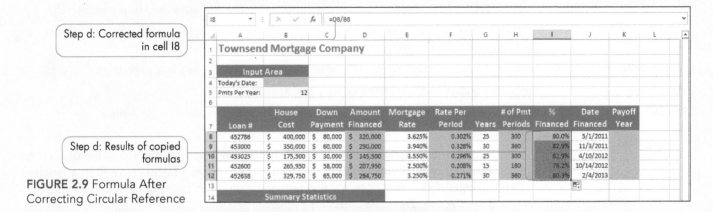

Step d: Corrected formula in cell I8

Step d: Results of copied formulas

FIGURE 2.9 Formula After Correcting Circular Reference

a. Click **cell I8**, type **=I8/B8**, and then press **Enter**.

The Circular Reference Warning message box displays.

> **TROUBLESHOOTING:** If the message box does not display, close the workbook and exit Excel. Start Excel, open the workbook again, and then repeat Step 4a. Sometimes the message box appears only once while Excel is running. If you had previously experimented with a circular reference during a work session, the message box might not display. However, exiting Excel and opening it again will enable the message box to display.

b. Read the description of the error and click **Help**.

The Excel Help window opens, displaying information about circular references.

c. Read the circular reference information, close the Excel Help window, and then click **OK** in the message box.

The left side of the status bar displays *CIRCULAR REFERENCES: I8*.

Because the formula is stored in cell I8, the formula cannot refer to the cell itself. You need to divide the value in the Amount Financed column by the value in the House Cost column.

d. Click **cell I8** and edit the formula to be **=D8/B8**. Copy the formula down the % Financed column.

The first borrower financed 80% of the cost of the house: $320,000 financed divided by $400,000 cost.

e. Save the workbook. Keep the workbook open if you plan to continue with the next Hands-On Exercise. If not, close the workbook and exit Excel.

Function Basics

An Excel *function* is a predefined computation that simplifies creating a formula that performs a complex calculation. Excel contains more than 400 functions, which are organized into 14 categories. Table 2.1 lists and describes the primary function categories used in this chapter.

TABLE 2.1	Function Categories and Descriptions
Category	**Description**
Date & Time	Provides methods for manipulating date and time values.
Financial	Performs financial calculations, such as payments, rates, present value, and future value.
Logical	Performs logical tests and returns the value of the tests. Includes logical operators for combined tests, such as AND, OR, and NOT.
Lookup & Reference	Looks up values, creates links to cells, or provides references to cells in a worksheet.
Math & Trig	Performs standard math and trigonometry calculations.
Statistical	Performs common statistical calculations, such as averages and standard deviations.

When using functions, you must adhere to correct *syntax*, the rules that dictate the structure and components required to perform the necessary calculations. Start a function with an equal sign, followed by the function name, and then its arguments in parentheses.

- The function name describes the purpose of the function. For example, the function name SUM indicates that the function sums, or adds, values.

- A function's *arguments* specify the inputs—such as cells, values, or arithmetic expressions—that are required to complete the operation. In some cases, a function requires multiple arguments separated by commas.

In this section, you will learn how to insert common functions using the keyboard and the Insert Function and Function Arguments dialog boxes.

Inserting a Function

To insert a function by typing, first type an equal sign, and then begin typing the function name. *Formula AutoComplete* displays a list of functions and defined names that match letters as you type a formula. For example, if you type =SU, Formula AutoComplete displays a list of functions and names that start with *SU* (see Figure 2.10). You can double-click the function name from the list or continue typing the function name. You can even scroll through the list to see the ScreenTip describing the function.

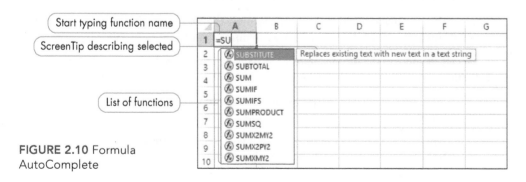

FIGURE 2.10 Formula AutoComplete

After you type the function name and opening parenthesis, Excel displays the **function ScreenTip**, a small pop-up description that displays the function's arguments. The argument you are currently entering is bold in the function ScreenTip (see Figure 2.11). Square brackets indicate optional arguments. For example, the SUM function requires the number1 argument, but the number2 argument is optional. Click the argument name in the function ScreenTip to select the actual argument in the formula you are creating if you want to make changes to the argument.

	A	B	C	D	E	F	G
1	=SUM(						
2	SUM(**number1**, [number2], ...)						
3							

FIGURE 2.11 Function ScreenTip

You can also use the Insert Function dialog box to search for a function, select a function category, and select a function from the list (see Figure 2.12). The dialog box is helpful if you want to browse a list of functions, especially if you are not sure of the function you need and want to see descriptions.

To display the Insert Function dialog box, click Insert Function *fx* (located between the Name Box and the Formula Bar) or click Insert Function in the Function Library group on the Formulas tab. From within the dialog box, select a function category, such as Most Recently Used, and select a function to display the syntax and a brief description of that function. Click *Help on this function* to display details about the selected function.

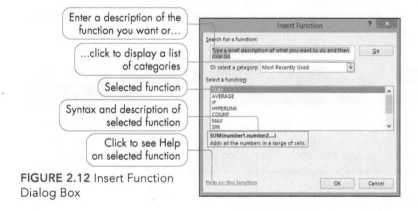

Enter a description of the function you want or...

...click to display a list of categories

Selected function

Syntax and description of selected function

Click to see Help on selected function

FIGURE 2.12 Insert Function Dialog Box

When you find the function you want, click OK. The Function Arguments dialog box opens so that you can enter the arguments for that specific function (see Figure 2.13). The following list explains the arguments in the Function Arguments dialog box:

- Argument names in **bold** (such as Number1 in the SUM function) are required.
- Argument names that are not bold (such as Number2 in the SUM function) are optional. The function can operate without the optional argument, which is used when you need additional specifications to calculate a result.

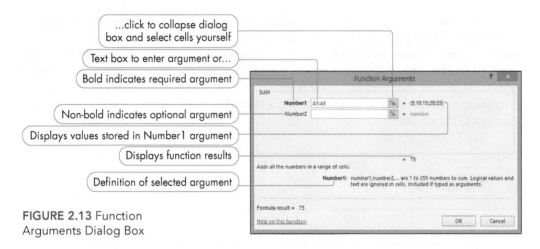

...click to collapse dialog box and select cells yourself

Text box to enter argument or...

Bold indicates required argument

Non-bold indicates optional argument

Displays values stored in Number1 argument

Displays function results

Definition of selected argument

FIGURE 2.13 Function Arguments Dialog Box

Type the cell references in the argument boxes or click a collapse button to the right side of an argument box to collapse the dialog box and select the cell or range of cells in the worksheet to designate as that argument. If you click the collapse button to select a range, you need to click the expand button to expand the dialog box again. The value, or results, of a formula contained in the argument cell displays on the right side of the argument box (such as 5; 10; 15; 20; 25—the values stored in the range A1:A5 used for the Number1 argument). If the argument is not valid, Excel displays an error description on the right side of the argument box.

The bottom of the Function Arguments dialog box displays a description of the function and a description of the argument containing the insertion point. As you enter arguments, the bottom of the dialog box also displays the results of the function, such as 75.

> **TIP** **#Name?**
>
> If you enter a function and #NAME? displays in the cell, you might have mistyped the function name. To avoid this problem, select the function name from the Formula AutoComplete list as you type the function name, or use the Insert Function dialog box. You can type a function name in lowercase letters. If you type the name correctly, Excel converts the name to all capital letters when you press Enter, indicating that you spelled the function name correctly.

Inserting Basic Math and Statistics Functions

Excel includes commonly used math and statistical functions that you can use for a variety of calculations. For example, you can insert functions to calculate the total amount you spend on dining out in a month, the average amount you spend per month downloading music from iTunes®, your highest electric bill, and your lowest time to run a mile this week.

Calculate a Total with the SUM Function

STEP 1 ≫ The **SUM function** totals values in two or more cells and displays the result in the cell containing the function. This function is more efficient to create when you need to add the values contained in three or more cells. For example, to add the contents of cells A2 through A14, you could enter =A2+A3+A4+A5+A6+A7+A8+A9+A10+A11+A12+A13+A14, which is time-consuming and increases the probability of entering an inaccurate cell reference, such as entering a cell reference twice or accidentally leaving out a cell reference. Instead, you should use the SUM function, =SUM(A2:A14).

=SUM(number 1, [number 2],...)

The SUM function contains one required argument (Number1) that represents a range of cells to add. The range, such as A2:A14, specifies the first and last cells containing values to SUM. Excel will sum all cells within that range. The Number2 optional argument is used when you want to sum values stored in nonadjacent cells or ranges, such as =SUM(A2:A14,F2:F14). The ellipsis in the function syntax indicates you can add as many additional ranges as desired, separated by commas.

To insert the SUM function (for example, to sum the values in the range A2:A14), do one of the following:

- Type =SUM(A2:A14) and press Enter.
- Type =SUM(and drag to select the range A2:A14 with the mouse. Type the ending #) and press Enter.
- Click in cell A15, click Sum in the Editing group on the HOME tab, press Enter to select the suggested range or type (or drag to select) A2:A14, and then press Enter.
- Click in cell A15, click Sum in the Function Library group on the FORMULAS tab, press Enter to select the suggested range or type A2:A14, and then press Enter.

Figure 2.14 shows the result of using the SUM function in cell D2 to total scores (898).

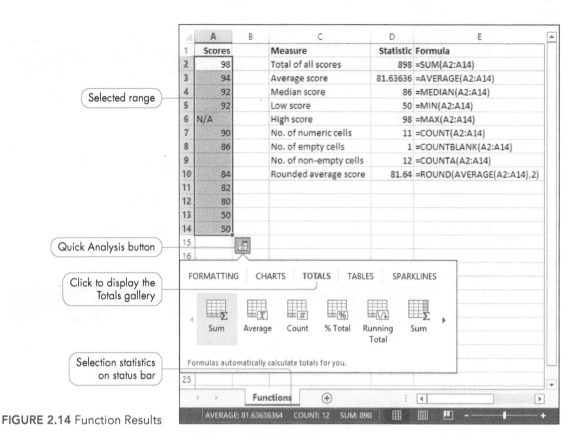

Selected range

Quick Analysis button

Click to display the Totals gallery

Selection statistics on status bar

FORMATTING   CHARTS   **TOTALS**   TABLES   SPARKLINES

Sum   Average   Count   % Total   Running Total   Sum

Formulas automatically calculate totals for you.

AVERAGE: 81.63636364   COUNT: 12   SUM: 898

FIGURE 2.14 Function Results

TIP Sum Arrow

If you click Sum, Excel inserts the SUM function. However, if you click the Sum arrow in the Editing group on the Home tab or in the Function Library group on the Formulas tab, Excel displays a list of basic functions to select: Sum, Average, Count Numbers, Max, and Min. If you want to insert another function, select More Functions from the list.

Find Central Tendency with AVERAGE and MEDIAN

STEP 2 ≫   People often describe data based on central tendency, which means that values tend to cluster around a central value. Excel provides two functions to calculate central tendency: AVERAGE and MEDIAN. The **AVERAGE function** calculates the arithmetic mean, or average, for the values in a range of cells. You can use this function to calculate the class average on a biology test or the average number of points scored per game by a basketball player. In Figure 2.14, =AVERAGE(A2:A14) in cell D3 returns 81.63636 as the average test score. The AVERAGE function ignores empty cells and cells containing N/A or text.

=AVERAGE(number 1,[number2],...)

STEP 3 ≫   The **MEDIAN function** finds the midpoint value, which is the value that one half of the data set is above or below. The median is particularly useful because extreme values often influence arithmetic mean calculated by the AVERAGE function. In Figure 2.14, the two extreme test scores of 50 distort the average. The rest of the test scores range from 80 to 98. Cell D4 contains =MEDIAN(A2:A14). The median for test scores is 86, which indicates that half the test scores are above 86 and half the test scores are below 86. This statistic is more reflective of the data set than the average is. The MEDIAN function ignores empty cells and cells containing N/A or text.

=MEDIAN(number 1,[number 2],...)

Identify Low and High Values with MIN and MAX

STEP 4 » The **MIN function** analyzes an argument list to determine the lowest value, such as the lowest score on a test. Manually inspecting a range of values to identify the lowest value is inefficient, especially in large spreadsheets. If you change values in the range, the MIN function will identify the new lowest value and display it in the cell containing the MIN function. In Figure 2.14, =MIN(A2:A14) in cell D5 identifies that 50 is the lowest test score.

=MIN(number 1,[number 2],...)

The **MAX function** analyzes an argument list to determine the highest value, such as the highest score on a test. Like the MIN function, when the values in the range change, the MAX function will display the new highest value within the range of cells. In Figure 2.14, =MAX(A2:A14) in cell D6 identifies 98 as the highest test score.

=MAX(number 1,[number 2],...)

 TIP Nonadjacent Ranges

You can use multiple ranges as arguments, such as finding the largest number within two nonadjacent (nonconsecutive) ranges. For example, you can find the highest test score where some scores are stored in cells A2:A14 and others are stored in cells K2:K14. Separate each range with a comma in the argument list, so that the formula is =MAX(A2:A14,K2:K14).

Identify the Total Number with COUNT Functions

Excel provides three basic count functions—COUNT, COUNTBLANK and COUNTA—to count the cells in a range that meet a particular criterion. The **COUNT function** tallies the number of cells in a range that contain values you can use in calculations, such as numerical and date data, but excludes blank cells or text entries from the tally. In Figure 2.14, the selected range spans 13 cells; however, =COUNT(A2:A14) in cell D7 returns 11, the number of cells that contain numerical data. It does not count the cell containing the text *N/A* or the blank cell.

The **COUNTBLANK function** tallies the number of cells in a range that are blank. In Figure 2.14, =COUNTBLANK(A2:A14) in cell D8 identifies that one cell in the range A2:A14 is blank. The **COUNTA function** tallies the number of cells in a range that are not blank, that is, cells that contain data, whether a value, text, or a formula. In Figure 2.14, =COUNTA(A2:A14) in cell D9 returns 12, indicating the range A2:A14 contains 12 cells that contain some form of data. It does not count the blank cell.

=COUNT(number 1,[number 2],...)
=COUNTBLANK(number 1,[number 2],...)
=COUNTA(number 1,[number 2],...)

 TIP Status Bar Statistics: Average, Count, and Sum

When you select a range of cells containing values, by default Excel displays the average, count, and sum of those values on the status bar (see Figure 2.14). You can customize the status bar to show other selection statistics, such as the minimum and maximum values for a selected range. To display or hide particular selection statistics, right-click the status bar and select the statistic.

Perform Calculations with Quick Analysis Tools

Excel 2013 contains a new feature called *Quick Analysis*, which is a set of analytical tools you can use to apply formatting, create charts or tables, and insert basic functions. When you select a range of data, the Quick Analysis button displays in the bottom-right corner of the selected range. Click the Quick Analysis button to display the Quick Analysis gallery and select the analytical tool to meet your needs.

Figure 2.14 shows the TOTALS options so that you can sum, average, or count the values in the selected range. Select % Total to display the percentage of the grand total of two or more columns. Select Running Total to provide a cumulative total at the bottom of multiple columns.

Use Other Math and Statistical Functions

In addition to the functions you have learned in this chapter, Excel provides more than 100 other math and statistical functions. Table 2.2 lists and describes some of these functions that you might find helpful in your business, education, and general statistics courses.

TABLE 2.2 Math and Statistical Functions	
Function Syntax	**Description**
=ABS(number)	Displays the absolute (i.e., positive) value of a number.
=FREQUENCY(data_array,bins_array)	Counts how often values appear in a given range.
=INT(number)	Rounds a value number down to the nearest whole number.
=MODE.SNGL(number1,[number2],…)	Displays the most frequently occurring value in a list.
=RANK.AVG(number,ref,[order])	Identifies a value's rank within a list of values; returns an average rank for identical values.
=RANK.EQ(number,ref,[order])	Identifies a value's rank within a list of values; the top rank is identified for all identical values.
=ROUND(number,num_digits)	Rounds a value to a specific number of digits. Rounds numbers of 5 and greater up and those less than 5 down.

TIP Round Versus Decrease Decimal Points

When you click Decrease Decimal in the Number group to display fewer or no digits after a decimal point, Excel still stores the original value's decimal places so that those digits can be used in calculations. The ROUND function changes the stored value to its rounded state.

Nest Functions as Arguments

A *nested function* occurs when one function is embedded as an argument within another function. Each function has its own set of arguments that must be included. For example, cell D10 in Figure 2.14 contains =ROUND(AVERAGE(A2:A14),2). The ROUND function requires two arguments: number and num_digits.

The AVERAGE function is nested in the *number* argument of the ROUND function. AVERAGE(A2:A14) returns 81.63636. That value is then rounded to two decimal places, indicated by 2 in the *num_digits* argument. The result is 81.64. If you change the second argument from 2 to 0, such as =ROUND(AVERAGE(A2:A14),0), the result would be 82.

Using Date Functions

Because Excel treats dates as serial numbers, you can perform calculations using dates. For example, assume today is January 1, 2016, and you graduate on May 6, 2016. To determine how many days until graduation, subtract today's date from the graduation date. Excel uses the serial numbers for these dates (42370 and 42494) to calculate the difference of 126 days.

Insert the TODAY Function

 The **TODAY function** displays the current date, such as 6/14/2016, in a cell. Excel updates the function results when you open or print the workbook. The TODAY() function does not require arguments, but you must include the parentheses. If you omit the parentheses, Excel displays #NAME? in the cell with a green triangle in the top-left corner of the cell. When you click the cell, an error icon appears that you can click for more information.

=TODAY()

Insert the NOW Function

The **NOW function** uses the computer's clock to display the date and military time, such as 6/14/2016 15:30, that you last opened the workbook. (Military time expresses time on a 24-hour period where 1:00 is 1 a.m. and 13:00 is 1 p.m.) The date and time will change every time the workbook is opened. Like the TODAY function, the NOW function does not require arguments, but you must include the parentheses. Omitting the parentheses creates a #NAME? error.

=NOW()

> ### TIP Update the Date and Time
>
> Both the TODAY and NOW functions display the date/time the workbook was last opened or last calculated. These functions do not continuously update the date and time while the workbook is open. To update the date and time, press F9 or click the Formulas tab and click *Calculate now* in the Calculation group.

Use Other Date & Time Functions

Excel contains a variety of other date functions. You can use these functions to calculate when employees are eligible for certain benefits, what the date is six months from now, or what day of the week a particular date falls on. Table 2.3 describes and Figure 2.15 shows examples of some date functions.

TABLE 2.3 Date Functions

Function Syntax	Description
=DATE(year,month,day)	Returns the serial number for a date.
=DAY(serial_number)	Displays the day (1–31) within a given month for a date or its serial number.
=EDATE(start_date,months)	Displays the serial number using the General format of a date a specified number of months in the future (using a positive value) or past (using a negative value). Displays the actual future or past date in Short Date format.
=EOMONTH(start_date,months)	Identifies the serial number of the last day of a month using General format or the exact last day of a month using Short Date format for a specified number of months from a date's serial number.
=MONTH(serial_number)	Returns the month (1–12) for a serial number, where 1 is January and 12 is December.
=WEEKDAY(serial_number, [return_type])	Identifies the weekday (1–7) for a serial number, where 1 is Sunday and 7 is Saturday (the default with no second argument); can specify a second argument for different numbers assigned to weekdays (see Help).
=YEAR(serial_number)	Identifies the year for a serial number.
=YEARFRAC(start_date,end_date,[basis])	Calculates the fraction of a year between two dates based on the number of whole days.

	A	B	C	D	E	F
1	Inputs:	7	11	2016	10/17/2016	
2						
3	Description			Format	Result	Formula
4	Today's Date			Short Date	10/17/2016	=TODAY()
5	Today's Date			Other Date	October 17, 2016	=TODAY()
6	Today's Date and Military Time			Date/Time	10/17/2016 17:15	=NOW()
7	Serial # of Date			General	42562	=DATE(D1,B1,C1)
8	Serial # of Date			Short Date	7/11/2016	=DATE(D1,B1,C1)
9	Day within the Month			General	17	=DAY(E4) or =DAY(TODAY())
10	Serial # of Date 3 Months in Future			General	42752	=EDATE(E4,3)
11	Date 3 Months in Future			Short Date	1/17/2017	=EDATE(E4,3)
12	Date 3 Years in Future			Short Date	10/17/2019	=EDATE(E4,3*12)
13	Date 2 Months Ago			Short Date	8/17/2016	=EDATE(E4,-2)
14	Serial # of Date 6 Months in Future			General	42746	=EDATE(DATE(D1,B1,C1),6)
15	Serial # of Last Day in 6 Months			General	42855	=EOMONTH(E4,6) or =EOMONTH(TODAY())
16	Last Day of 6 Months in Future			Short Date	4/30/2017	=EOMONTH(E4,6) or =EOMONTH(TODAY())
17	Month Number (where 6=June)			General	10	=MONTH(E5) or =MONTH(TODAY())
18	Week day (1=Sunday; 7=Saturday)			General	2	=WEEKDAY(E4)
19	Week day (1=Monday; 7=Sunday)			General	1	=WEEKDAY(E4,2)
20	Year for a Serial Date			General	2016	=YEAR(E4) or =YEAR(TODAY())
21	Fraction of Year 7/11/2016-10/17/2016			General	0.266666667	=YEARFRAC(DATE(D1,B1,C1),E1)

FIGURE 2.15 Date Function Examples

You can nest a date function inside another date function, such as =DAY(TODAY()). This nested function TODAY() first identifies today's date, and from that date, the DAY function identifies the day of the month. In Figure 2.15, cell E21 contains =YEARFRAC(DATE(D1,B1,C1),E1). The DATE function is nested to combine values in three cells (D1, B1, and C1) to build a date (7/11/2016). Excel finds the number of days between that date and 10/17/2016, the date stored in cell E1. From there, the YEARFRAC function calculates the fraction of a year (26.667%) between those two dates. Had 7/11/2016 been stored as a date in a single cell, the formula would simplify to something like =YEARFRAC(D1,E1).

TIP **Date Functions and Arithmetic Operations**

You can combine date functions with arithmetic operations. For example, you sign a lease on June 14, 2016, for three years. The starting date is stored in cell E4. What date does your lease expire? Enter =EDATE(E4,3*12)-1 to calculate the expiration date. The first argument, E4, is the cell containing the start date, and the second argument, 3*12, equals three years containing 12 months each, or 36 months. (In an actual worksheet, you should store the value 36 in a cell instead of typing numbers in the argument.) That result is June 14, 2019, but the lease actually expires the day before. So you must then subtract 1 from the function result to calculate the June 13, 2019, date.

Quick
Concepts

1. What visual features help guide you through typing a function directly in a cell? ***pp. 84–85***

2. What type of data do you enter in a Function Arguments dialog box, and what are four things the dialog box tells you? ***pp. 85–86***

3. What is the difference between the AVERAGE and MEDIAN functions? ***p. 88***

4. What is a nested function, and why would you create one? ***p. 90***

5. Provide three examples of using date functions to determine something specific. ***p. 91***

Hands-On Exercises

Watch the Video for this Hands-On Exercise!

MyITLab®
HOE2 Training

2 Function Basics

The Townsend Mortgage Company's worksheet contains an area in which you must enter summary statistics. In addition, you need to include today's date and identify the year in which each mortgage will be paid off.

Skills covered: Use the SUM Function • Use the AVERAGE Function • Use the MEDIAN Function • Use the MIN, MAX, and COUNT Functions • Use the TODAY and YEAR Functions

STEP 1 >> USE THE SUM FUNCTION

The first summary statistic you need to calculate is the total value of the houses bought by the borrowers. You will use the SUM function. Refer to Figure 2.16 as you complete Step 1.

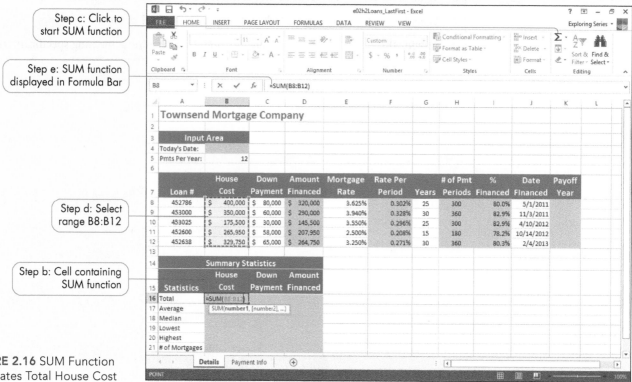

FIGURE 2.16 SUM Function Calculates Total House Cost

a. Open *e02h1Loans_LastFirst* if you closed it at the end of Hands-On Exercise 1 and save it as **e02h2Loans_LastFirst**, changing *h1* to *h2*.

b. Make sure the Details worksheet is active and click **cell B16**, the cell where you will enter a formula for the total house cost.

c. Click **Sum** in the Editing group on the HOME tab.

> **TROUBLESHOOTING:** Click the main part of the Sum command. If you click the Sum arrow, select Sum.

Excel anticipates the range of cells containing values you want to sum based on where you enter the formula—in this case, A8:D15. This is not the correct range, so you must enter the correct range.

d. Select the **range B8:B12**, the cells containing house costs.

As you use the semi-selection process, Excel enters the range in the SUM function.

> **TROUBLESHOOTING:** If you entered the function without changing the arguments, repeat steps b–d or edit the arguments in the Formula Bar by deleting the default range, typing B8:B12 between the parentheses and pressing Enter.

e. Click **Enter** (the checkmark between the Name Box and Formula Bar) and save the workbook.

Cell B16 contains the function = SUM(B8:B12), and the result is $1,521,200.

STEP 2 ➤➤ USE THE AVERAGE FUNCTION

Before copying the functions to calculate the total down payments and amounts financed, you want to calculate the average house cost bought by the borrowers in your list. Refer to Figure 2.17 as you complete Step 2.

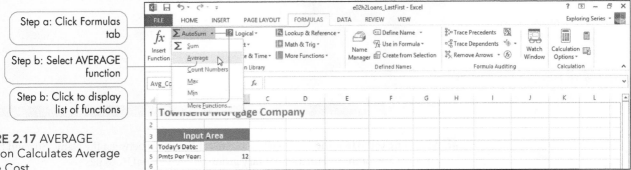

Step a: Click Formulas tab

Step b: Select AVERAGE function

Step b: Click to display list of functions

FIGURE 2.17 AVERAGE Function Calculates Average House Cost

a. Click the **FORMULAS tab** and click **cell B17**, the cell where you will display the average cost of the houses.

b. Click the **Sum arrow** in the Function Library group and select **Average**.

Excel selects cell B15, which is the total cost of the houses. You need to change the range.

> **TROUBLESHOOTING:** Sum, like some other commands in Excel, contains two parts: the main command icon and an arrow. Click the main command icon when instructed to click Sum to perform the default action. Click the arrow when instructed to click the Sum arrow for additional options. If you accidentally clicked Sum instead of the arrow, press Esc to cancel the SUM function from being completed and try step b again.

c. Select the **range B8:B12**, the cells containing the house costs.

The function is =AVERAGE(B8:B12).

d. Press **Enter**, make **cell B18** the active cell, and save the workbook.

The average house cost is $304,240.

STEP 3 >> USE THE MEDIAN FUNCTION

You realize that extreme house costs may distort the average. Therefore, you decide to identify the median house cost to compare it to the average house cost. Refer to Figure 2.18 as you complete Step 3.

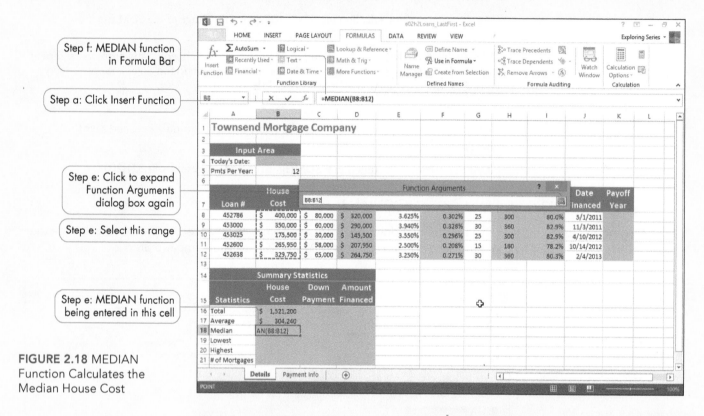

FIGURE 2.18 MEDIAN Function Calculates the Median House Cost

a. Make sure **cell B18** is the active cell. Click **Insert Function** between the Name Box and the Formula Bar, or in the Function Library group on the FORMULAS tab.

The Insert Function dialog box opens. Use this dialog box to select the MEDIAN function since it is not available on the Ribbon.

b. Type **median** in the **Search for a function box** and click **Go**.

Excel displays a list of functions in the *Select a function* list. The MEDIAN function is selected at the top of the list; the bottom of the dialog box displays the syntax and the description.

c. Read the MEDIAN function's description and click **OK**.

The Function Arguments dialog box opens. It contains one required argument, Number1, representing a range of cells containing values. It has an optional argument, Number2, which you can use if you have nonadjacent ranges that contain values.

d. Click the **collapse button** to the right of the Number1 box.

You collapsed the Function Arguments dialog box so that you can select the range.

e. Select the **range B8:B12** and click the **expand button** in the Function Arguments dialog box.

The Function Arguments dialog box expands, displaying B8:B12 in the Number1 box.

f. Click **OK** to accept the function arguments and close the dialog box. Save the workbook.

Half of the houses purchased cost more than the median, $329,750, and half of the houses cost less than this value. Notice the difference between the median and the average: The average is lower because it is affected by the lowest-priced house, $175,500.

STEP 4 ≫ USE THE MIN, MAX, AND COUNT FUNCTIONS

Erica wants to know the least and most expensive houses so that she can analyze typical customers of the Townsend Mortgage Company. You will use the MIN and MAX functions to obtain these statistics. In addition, you will use the COUNT function to tally the number of mortgages in the sample. Refer to Figure 2.19 as you complete Step 4.

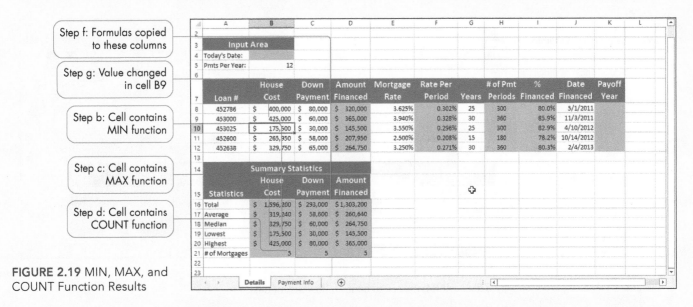

Step f: Formulas copied to these columns

Step g: Value changed in cell B9

Step b: Cell contains MIN function

Step c: Cell contains MAX function

Step d: Cell contains COUNT function

FIGURE 2.19 MIN, MAX, and COUNT Function Results

a. Click **cell B19**, the cell to display the cost of the lowest-costing house.

b. Click the **Sum arrow** in the Function Library group, select **Min**, select the **range B8:B12**, and then press **Enter**.

   The MIN function identifies that the lowest-costing house is $175,500.

c. Click **cell B20**, if necessary. Click the **Sum arrow** in the Function Library group, select **Max**, select the **range B8:B12**, and then press **Enter**.

   The MAX function identifies that the highest-costing house is $425,000.

d. Click **cell B21**, if necessary. Type **=COUNT(B8:B12)** and press **Enter**.

   As you type the letter *C*, Formula AutoComplete suggests functions starting with *C*. As you continue typing, the list of functions narrows. After you type the beginning parenthesis, Excel displays the function ScreenTip, indicating the arguments for the function. The range B8:B12 contains five cells.

e. Select the **range B16:B21**.

   You want to select the range of original statistics to copy the cells all at one time to the next two columns.

f. Drag the fill handle to the right by two columns to copy the functions. Click **cell D21**.

   Because you used relative cell references in the functions, the range changes from =COUNT(B8:B12) to =COUNT(D8:D12).

g. Change the value in **cell B9** to **425000**. Save the workbook.

   The results of several formulas and functions change, including the total, average, and max house costs.

STEP 5 ≫ USE THE TODAY AND YEAR FUNCTIONS

You have two date functions (TODAY and YEAR) to enter to complete the first worksheet. The TODAY function will display today's date, and you will use the YEAR function in a formula to calculate the payoff year for each mortgage. Refer to Figure 2.20 as you complete Step 5.

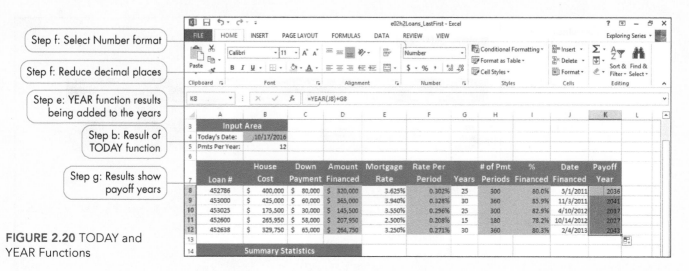

Step f: Select Number format

Step f: Reduce decimal places

Step e: YEAR function results being added to the years

Step b: Result of TODAY function

Step g: Results show payoff years

FIGURE 2.20 TODAY and YEAR Functions

a. Click **cell B4**, the cell to contain the current date.

b. Click **Date & Time** in the Function Library group, select **TODAY** to display the Function Arguments dialog box, and then click **OK** to close the dialog box.

  The Function Arguments dialog box opens, although no arguments are necessary for this function. Excel inserts the current date in Short Date format, such as 1/2/2016, based on the computer system's date.

c. Click **cell K8**, click **Date & Time** in the Function Library group, scroll through the list, and then select **YEAR**.

  The Function Arguments dialog box opens so that you can enter the argument, a serial number for a date.

d. Click **cell J8** to enter it in the **Serial_number box**. Click **OK**.

  The function returns 2011, the year the first mortgage was taken out. However, you want the year the mortgage will be paid off. The YEAR function returns the year from a date. You need to add the years to the result of the function to calculate the year that the borrower will pay off the mortgage.

e. Press **F2** to edit the formula stored in **cell K8**. With the insertion point on the right side of the closing parenthesis, type **+G8** and press **Ctrl+Enter**.

  Pressing Ctrl+Enter is the alternative to clicking Enter by the Formula Bar. It keeps the current cell as the active cell. The results show a date: 7/28/1905. You need to apply the Number format to display the year.

f. Click the **HOME tab**, click the **Number Format arrow** in the Number group, and then select **Number**. Decrease the number of decimal places to show the value as a whole number.

  You applied the Number format instead of the Comma format because although the Comma format is correct for quantities, such as 2,036 units, it is not appropriate for the year 2036.

g. Copy the formula down the Payoff Year column.

h. Save the workbook. Keep the workbook open if you plan to continue with the next Hands-On Exercise. If not, close the workbook and exit Excel.

Logical, Lookup, and Financial Functions

As you prepare complex spreadsheets using functions, you will frequently use three function categories: logical, lookup and reference, and finance. Logical functions test the logic of a situation and return a particular result. Lookup and reference functions are useful when you need to look up a value in a list to identify the applicable value. Financial functions are useful to anyone who plans to take out a loan or invest money.

In this section, you will learn how to use the logical, lookup, and financial functions.

Determining Results with the IF Function

STEP 3 >> The most common logical function is the *IF function*, which returns one value when a condition is met or is true and returns another value when the condition is not met or is false. For example, a company gives a $500 bonus to employees who sold *over* $10,000 in merchandise this week, but no bonus to employees who did not sell over $10,000 in merchandise. Figure 2.21 shows a worksheet containing the sales data for three representatives and their bonuses, if any.

Result if condition is false
Condition to be tested
Result if condition is true

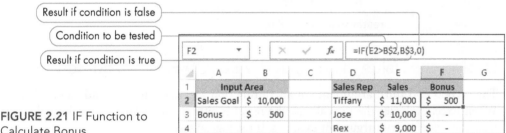

FIGURE 2.21 IF Function to Calculate Bonus

The IF function has three arguments: (1) a condition that is tested to determine if it is either true or false, (2) the resulting value if the condition is true, and (3) the resulting value if the condition is false.

=IF(logical_test,value_if_true,value_if_false)

You might find it helpful to create two flowcharts to illustrate an IF function. First, construct a flowchart that uses words and numbers to illustrate the condition and results. For example, the left flowchart in Figure 2.22 illustrates the condition to see if sales are greater than $10,000, and the $500 bonus if the condition is true or $0 if the condition is false. Then, create a second flowchart similar to the one on the right side of Figure 2.22 that replaces the words and values with actual cell references. Creating these flowcharts can help you construct the IF function that is used in cell F2 in Figure 2.21.

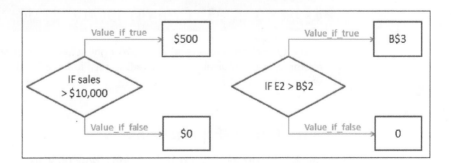

FIGURE 2.22 Flowcharts Illustrating IF Function

Design the Logical Test

The first argument for the IF function is the logical test. The **logical test** is a formula that contains either a value or an expression that evaluates to true or false. The logical expression is typically a binary expression, meaning that it requires a comparison between at least two variables, such as the values stored in cells E2 and B2. Table 2.4 lists and describes the logical operators to make the comparison in the logical test.

In Figure 2.21, cell F2 contains an IF function where the logical test is E2>B$2 to determine if Tiffany's sales in cell E2 are greater than the sales goal in cell B2. The reference to cell B2 can be mixed B$2 or absolute $B$2. Either way, copying the function down the column will compare each sales representative's sales with the $10,000 value in cell B2.

TABLE 2.4 Logical Operators	
Operator	**Description**
=	Equal to
<>	Not equal to
<	Less than
>	Greater than
<=	Less than or equal to
>=	Greater than or equal to

Design the Value_If_True and Value_If_False Arguments

The second and third arguments of an IF function are value_if_true and value_if_false. When Excel evaluates the logical test, the result is either true or false. If the logical test is true, the value_if_true argument executes. If the logical test is false, the value_if_false argument executes. Only one of the last two arguments is executed; both arguments cannot be executed, because the logical test is either true or false but not both.

The value_if_true and value_if_false arguments can contain text, cell references, formulas, or constants (not recommended unless –1, 1, or 0). In Figure 2.21, cell F2 contains an IF function in which the value_if_true argument is B$3 and the value_if_false argument is 0. Because the logical test (E2>B$2) is true—that is, Tiffany's sales of $11,000 are greater than the $10,000 goal—the value_if_true argument is executed, and the result displays $500, the value that is stored in cell B3.

Jose's sales of $10,000 are not *greater than* $10,000, and Rex's sales of $9,000 are not *greater than* $10,000. Therefore, the value_if_false argument is executed and returns no bonus in cells F3 and F4.

 TIP | At Least Two Possible Right Answers

Every IF function can have at least two right solutions to produce the same results. For example, if the logical test is E2<=B$2 for Figure 2.21, the value_if_true is 0, and the value_if_false is B$3.

Create Other IF Functions

Figure 2.23 illustrates several IF functions, how they are evaluated, and their results. The input area contains values that are used in the logical tests and results. You can create this worksheet with the input area and IF functions to develop your understanding of how IF functions work.

⊿	A	B	C
1	**Input Values**		
2	$1,000		
3	$2,000		
4	10%		
5	5%		
6	$250		
7			
8	**IF Function**	**Evaluation**	**Result**
9	=IF(A2=A3,A4,A5)	$1,000 is equal to $2,000: FALSE	5%
10	=IF(A2<A3,A4,A5)	$1,000 is less than $2,000: TRUE	10%
11	=IF(A2<>A3,"Not Equal","Equal")	$1,000 and $2,000 are not equal: TRUE	Not Equal
12	=IF(A2>A3,(A2*A4),(A2*A5))	$1,000 is greater than $2,000: FALSE	$50
13	=IF(A2>A3,A2*A4,MAX(A2*A5,A6))	$1,000 is greater than $2,000: FALSE	$250
14	=IF(A2*A4=A3*A5,A6,0)	$100 (A2*A4) is equal to $100 (A3*A5): TRUE	$250

FIGURE 2.23 Sample IF Functions

- **Cell A9.** The logical test A2=A3 compares the values in cells A2 and A3 to see if they are equal. Because $1,000 is not equal to $2,000, the logical test is false. The value_if_false argument is executed, which displays 5%, the value stored in cell A5.

- **Cell A10.** The logical test A2<A3 determines if the value in cell A2 is less than the value in A3. Because $1,000 is less than $2,000, the logical test is true. The value_if_true argument is executed, which displays the value stored in cell A4, which is 10%.

- **Cell A11.** The logical test A2<>A3 determines if the values in cells A2 and A3 are not equal. Because $1,000 and $2,000 are not equal, the logical test is true. The value_if_true argument is executed, which displays the text *Not Equal*.

- **Cell A12.** The logical test A2>A3 is false. The value_if_false argument is executed, which multiplies the value in cell A2 ($1,000) by the value in cell A5 (5%) and displays $50. The parentheses in the value_if_true (A2*A4) and value_if_false (A2*A5) arguments are optional. They are not required but may help you read the function arguments better.

- **Cell A13.** The logical test A2>A3 is false. The value_if_false argument, which contains a nested MAX function, is executed. The MAX function, MAX(A2*A5,A6), multiplies the values in cells A2 ($1,000) and A5 (5%) and returns the higher of the product ($50) and the value stored in cell A6 ($250).

- **Cell A14.** The logical test A2*A4=A3*A5 is true. The contents of cell A2 ($1,000) are multiplied by the contents of cell A4 (10%) for a result of $100. That result is then compared to the result of A3*A5, which is also $100. Because the logical test is true, the function returns the value of cell A6 ($250).

 TIP Using Text in Formulas

You can use text within a formula. For example, you can build a logical test comparing the contents of cell A1 to specific text, such as A1="Input Values". The IF function in cell A11 in Figure 2.23 uses "Not Equal" and "Equal" in the value_if_true and value_if_false arguments. When you use text in a formula or function, you must enclose the text in quotation marks. However, do not use quotation marks around formulas, cell references, or values.

 TIP Nest Functions in IF Functions

You can nest functions in the logical test, value_if_true, and value_if_false arguments of the IF function. When you nest functions as arguments, make sure the nested function contains the required arguments for it to work and that you nest the function in the correct argument to calculate accurate results. For example, cell C13 in Figure 2.23 contains a nested MAX function in the value_if_false argument.

Using Lookup Functions

You can use lookup and reference functions to look up values to perform calculations or display results. For example, when you order merchandise on a Web site, the Web server looks up the shipping costs based on weight and distance, or at the end of a semester, your professor uses your average, such as 88%, to look up the letter grade to assign, such as B+.

Create the Lookup Table

A *lookup table* is a range containing a table of values or text that can be retrieved. The table should contain at least two rows and two columns, not including headings. Figure 2.24 illustrates a college directory with three "columns." The first column contains professors' names. You look up a professor's name in the first column to see his or her office (second "column") and phone extension (third "column").

Brazil, Estivan	GT 218b	7243
Fiedler, Zazilia	CS 417	7860
Lam, Kaitlyn	SC 124a	7031
Rodriquez, Lisa	GT 304	7592
Yeung, Bradon	CS 414	7314

FIGURE 2.24 College Directory Lookup Table Analogy

It is important to plan the table so that it conforms to the way in which Excel can utilize the data in it. Excel cannot interpret the structure of Table 2.5. To look up a value in a range (such as the range 80–89), you must arrange data from the lowest to the highest value and include only the lowest value in the range (such as 80) instead of the complete range. If the values you look up are *exact* values, you can arrange the first column in any logical order. The lowest value for a category or in a series is the *breakpoint*. The first column contains the breakpoints—such as 60, 70, 80, and 90—or the lowest values to achieve a particular grade. The lookup table contains one or more additional columns of related data to retrieve. Table 2.6 shows how to construct the lookup table in Excel.

TABLE 2.5	Grading Scale
Range	**Grade**
90–100	A
80–89	B
70–79	C
60–69	D
Below 60	F

TABLE 2.6	Grades Lookup Table
Range	**Grade**
0	F
60	D
70	C
80	B
90	A

Understand the VLOOKUP Function Syntax

STEP 1 » The *VLOOKUP function* accepts a value, looks the value up in a vertical lookup table, and returns a result. Use VLOOKUP to search for exact matches or for the nearest value that is less than or equal to the search value, such as assigning a B grade for an 87% class average. The VLOOKUP function has the following three required arguments and one optional argument: (1) lookup_value, (2) table_array, (3) col_index_number, and (4) range_lookup.

=VLOOKUP(lookup_value,table_array,col_index_number,[range_lookup])

Figure 2.25 shows a partial grade book that contains a vertical lookup table, as well as the final scores and letter grades. The function in cell F3 is =VLOOKUP(E3,$A$3:$B$7,2).

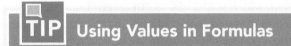

Callout	
Value (final score) to look up	
Table array range	
Use second column within the table to return letter grade	

| F3 | ▾ | : | × | ✓ | fx | =VLOOKUP(E3,$A$3:$B$7,2) |

⊿	A	B	C	D	E	F	G
1	Grading Scale			Partial Gradebook			
2	Breakpoint	Grade		Names	Final Score	Letter Grade	
3	0	F		Abbott	85	B	
4	60	D		Carter	69	D	
5	70	C		Hon	90	A	
6	80	B		Jackson	74	C	
7	90	A		Miller	80	B	
8				Nelsen	78	C	

FIGURE 2.25 VLOOKUP Function for Grade Book

The *lookup value* is the cell reference of the cell that contains the value to look up. The lookup value for the first student is cell E3, which contains 85. The *table array* is the range that contains the lookup table: $A$3:$B$7. The table array range must be absolute and cannot include column labels for the lookup table. The *column index number* is the column number in the lookup table that contains the return values. In this example, the column index number is 2.

> ## TIP | Using Values in Formulas
>
> You know to avoid using values in formulas because the input values in a worksheet cell might change. However, the value 2 is used in the col_index_number argument of the VLOOKUP function. The 2 refers to a particular column within the lookup table and is an acceptable use of a number within a formula.

Understand How Excel Processes the Lookup

Here is how the VLOOK function works:

1. The function identifies the value-stored cell used as the lookup value argument.
2. Excel searches the first column of the lookup table until it (a) finds an exact match (if possible) or (b) identifies the correct range if the lookup table contains breakpoints for range.
3. If Excel finds an exact match, it returns the value stored in the column designated by the column index number on that same row. If breakpoints are used and the lookup value is larger than the breakpoint, it looks to the next breakpoint to see if the lookup value is larger than that breakpoint also. When Excel detects that the lookup value is not greater than the next breakpoint, it stays on that row. It then uses the column index number to identify the column containing the value to return for the lookup value. Because Excel goes sequentially through the breakpoints, it is mandatory that the breakpoints are arranged from the lowest value to the highest value for ranges.

In Figure 2.25, the VLOOKUP function assigns letter grades based on final scores. Excel identifies the lookup value (85 in cell E3) and compares it to the values in the first column of the lookup table (range A3:B7). It tries to find an exact match of 85; however, the table contains breakpoints rather than every conceivable score. Because the lookup table is arranged from the lowest to the highest breakpoints, Excel detects that 85 is greater than the 80 breakpoint but is not greater than the 90 breakpoint. Therefore, it stays on the 80 row. Excel looks at the second column (column index number of 2) and returns the letter grade of B. The B grade is then stored in cell F3.

Use the Range_Lookup Argument

Instead of looking up values in a range, you can look up a value for an exact match using the optional range_lookup argument in the VLOOKUP function. By default, the range_lookup is set implicitly to TRUE, which is appropriate to look up values in a range. Omitting the optional argument or typing TRUE in it enables the VLOOKUP function to find the closest match in the table to the lookup value.

To look up an exact match, enter FALSE in the range_lookup argument. For example, if you are looking up product numbers, you must find an exact match to display the price. The function would look like this: =VLOOKUP(D15,$A$1:$B$50,2,FALSE). The function returns a value for the first lookup value that matches the first column of the lookup table. If no exact match is found, the function returns #N/A.

Nest Functions Inside the VLOOKUP Function

You can nest functions as arguments inside the VLOOKUP function. For example, Figure 2.26 illustrates shipping amounts that are based on weight and location (Boston or Chicago). In the VLOOKUP function in cell C3, the lookup_value argument looks up the weight of a package in cell A3. That weight (14 pounds) is looked up in the table_array argument, which is $E$3:$G$5. To determine which column of the lookup table to use, an IF function is nested as the column_index_number argument. The nested IF function compares the city stored in cell B3 to the text *Boston*. If cell B3 contains *Boston*, it returns 2 to use as the column_index_number to identify the shipping value for a package that is going to Boston. If cell B3 does not contain *Boston* (i.e., the only other city in this example is *Chicago*), the column_index_number is 3.

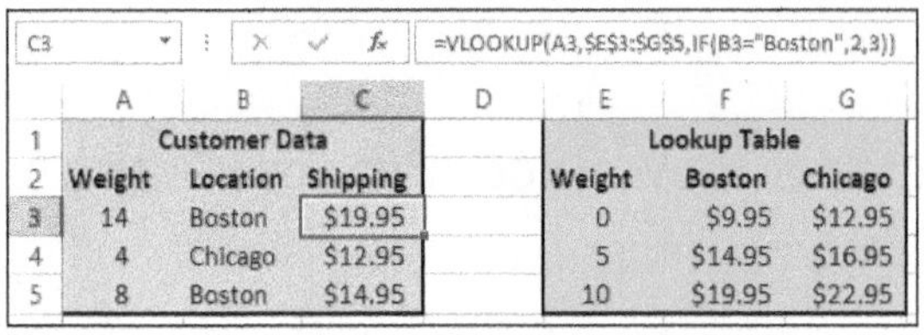

FIGURE 2.26 IF Function Nested in VLOOKUP Function

Use the HLOOKUP Function

You can design a lookup table horizontally where the first row contains the values for the basis of the lookup or the breakpoints, and additional rows contain data to be retrieved. With a horizontal lookup table, use the ***HLOOKUP function***. Table 2.7 shows how the grading scale would look as a horizontal lookup table.

TABLE 2.7 Horizontal Lookup Table

0	60	70	80	90
F	D	C	B	A

The syntax is almost the same as the syntax for the VLOOKUP function, except the third argument is row_index_number instead of col_index_number.

=HLOOKUP(lookup_value,table_array,row_index_number,[range_lookup])

Calculating Payments with the PMT Function

STEP 2 >>

Excel contains several financial functions to help you perform calculations with monetary values. If you take out a loan to purchase a car, you need to know the monthly payment, which depends on the price of the car, the down payment, and the terms of the loan, in order to determine if you can afford the car. The decision is made easier by developing the worksheet in Figure 2.27 and by changing the various input values as indicated.

B9	▼	:	×	✓	f_x	=PMT(B6,B8,-B3)

◢	A	B	C	D
1	Purchase Price	$25,999.00		
2	Down Payment	$ 5,000.00		
3	Amount to Finance	$20,999.00		
4	Payments per Year	12		
5	Interest Rate (APR)	3.500%		
6	Periodic Rate (Monthly)	0.292%		
7	Term (Years)	5		
8	No. of Payment Periods	60		
9	Monthly Payment	$ 382.01		
10				

FIGURE 2.27 Car Loan Worksheet

Creating a loan model helps you evaluate options. You realize that the purchase of a $25,999 car is prohibitive because the monthly payment is $382.01. Purchasing a less expensive car, coming up with a substantial down payment, taking out a longer-term loan, or finding a better interest rate can decrease your monthly payments.

The *PMT function* calculates payments for a loan with a fixed amount at a fixed periodic rate for a fixed time period. The PMT function uses three required arguments and up to two optional arguments: (1) rate, (2) nper, (3) pv, (4) fv, and (5) type.

=PMT(rate,nper,pv,[fv],[type])

The *rate* is the periodic interest rate, the interest rate per payment period. If the annual percentage rate (APR) is 12% and you make monthly payments, the periodic rate is 1% (12%/12 months). With the same APR and quarterly payments, the periodic rate is 3% (12%/4 quarters). Divide the APR by the number of payment periods in one year. However, instead of dividing the APR by 12 within the PMT function, calculate the periodic interest rate in cell B6 in Figure 2.27 and use that calculated rate in the PMT function.

The *nper* is the total number of payment periods. The term of a loan is usually stated in years; however, you make several payments per year. For monthly payments, you make 12 payments per year. To calculate the nper, multiply the number of years by the number of payments in one year. Instead of calculating the number of payment periods in the PMT function, calculate the number of payment periods in cell B8 and use that calculated value in the PMT function.

The *pv* is the present value of the loan. The result of the PMT function is a negative value because it represents your debt. However, you can display the result as a positive value by typing a minus sign in front of the present value cell reference in the PMT function.

Quick Concepts ✓

1. Describe the three arguments for an IF function. *pp. 99–100*

2. How should you structure a vertical lookup table if you need to look up values in a range? *p. 104*

3. What are the first three arguments of a PMT function? Why would you have to divide by or multiply an argument by 12? *p. 105*

Hands-On Exercises

Watch the Video
for this Hands-
On Exercise!

MyITLab®
HOE3 Training

3 Logical, Lookup, and Financial Functions

Erica wants you to complete another model that she might use for future mortgage data analysis. As you study the model, you realize you need to incorporate logical, lookup, and financial functions.

Skills covered: Use the VLOOKUP Function • Use the PMT Function • Use the IF Function

STEP 1 » USE THE VLOOKUP FUNCTION

Rates vary based on the number of years to pay off the loan. Erica created a lookup table for three common mortgage years, and she entered the current APR. The lookup table will provide efficiency later when the rates change. You will use the VLOOKUP function to display the correct rate for each customer based on the number of years of the respective loans. Refer to Figure 2.28 as you complete Step 1.

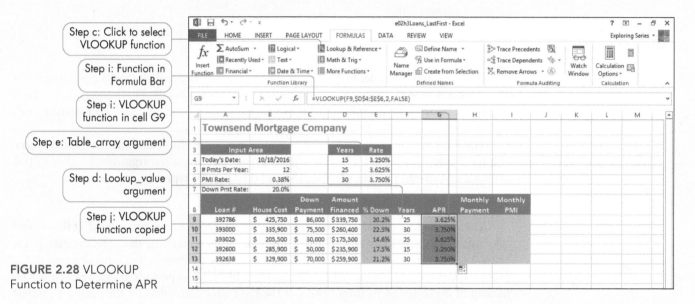

Step c: Click to select VLOOKUP function

Step i: Function in Formula Bar

Step i: VLOOKUP function in cell G9

Step e: Table_array argument

Step d: Lookup_value argument

Step j: VLOOKUP function copied

FIGURE 2.28 VLOOKUP Function to Determine APR

a. Open *e02h2Loans_LastFirst* if you closed it at the end of Hands-On Exercise 2 and save it as **e02h3Loans_LastFirst**, changing *h2* to *h3*.

b. Click the **Payment Info worksheet tab** to display the worksheet containing the data to complete. Click **cell G9**, the cell that will store the APR for the first customer.

c. Click the **FORMULAS tab**, click **Lookup & Reference** in the Function Library group, and then select **VLOOKUP**.

   The Function Arguments dialog box opens.

d. Click **F9** to enter F9 in the **Lookup_value box**.

   Cell F9 contains the value you need to look up from the table: 25 years.

> **TROUBLESHOOTING:** If you cannot see the cell you need to use in an argument, click the Function Arguments dialog box title bar and drag the dialog box on the screen until you can see and click the cell you need for the argument. Alternatively, you can click the collapse button to the right of the argument box to collapse the dialog box so that you can select the range. After selecting the range, click the expand button to expand the dialog box.

e. Press **Tab** and select the **range D4:E6** in the **Table_array box**.

This is the range that contains that data for the lookup table. The Years values in the table are arranged from lowest to highest. Do **not** select the column labels for the range.

Anticipate what will happen if you copy the formula down the column. What do you need to do to ensure that the cell references always point to the exact location of the table? If your answer is to make the table array cell references absolute, then you answered correctly.

f. Press **F4** to make the range references absolute.

The Table_array box now contains $D$4:$E$6.

g. Press **Tab** and type **2** in the **Col_index_num box**.

The second column of the lookup table contains the APRs that you want to return and display in the cells containing the formulas.

h. Press **Tab** and type **False** in the **Range_lookup box**.

You want the formula to display an error if an incorrect number of years has been entered. To ensure an exact match to look up in the table, you enter *False* in the optional argument.

i. Click **OK**.

The VLOOKUP function looks up the first person's years (25), finds an exact match in the first column of the lookup table, and then returns the corresponding APR, which is 3.625%.

j. Copy the formula down the column and save the workbook.

Spot check the results to make sure the function returned the correct APR based on the number of years.

STEP 2 ≫ USE THE PMT FUNCTION

The worksheet now has all the necessary data for you to calculate the monthly payment for each loan: the APR, the number of years for the loan, the number of payment periods in one year, and the initial loan amount. You will use the PMT function to calculate the monthly payment, which includes paying back the principal amount with interest. This calculation does not include escrow amounts, such as property taxes or insurance. Refer to Figure 2.29 as you complete Step 2.

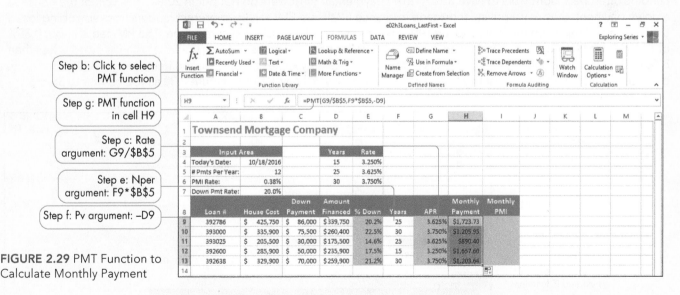

FIGURE 2.29 PMT Function to Calculate Monthly Payment

a. Click **cell H9**, the cell that will store the payment for the first customer.

b. Click **Financial** in the Function Library group, scroll through the list, and then select **PMT**.

> **TROUBLESHOOTING:** Make sure you select PMT, not PPMT. The PPMT function calculates the principal portion of a particular monthly payment, not the total monthly payment itself.

The Function Arguments dialog box opens.

c. Type **G9/B5** in the **Rate box**.

Think about what will happen if you copy the formula. The argument will be G10/B6 for the next customer. Are those cell references correct? G10 does contain the APR for the next customer, but B6 does not contain the correct number of payments in one year. Therefore, you need to make B5 an absolute cell reference because the number of payments per year does not vary.

d. Press **F4** to make the reference to cell B5 absolute.

e. Press **Tab** and type **F9*$B$5** in the **Nper box**.

You calculate the nper by multiplying the number of years by the number of payments in one year. You must make B5 an absolute cell reference so that it does not change when you copy the formula down the column.

f. Press **Tab** and type **-D9** in the **Pv box**.

The bottom of the dialog box indicates that the monthly payment is 1723.73008 or $1,723.73.

> **TROUBLESHOOTING:** If the payment displays as a negative value, you probably forgot to type the minus sign in front of the D9 reference in the Pv box. Edit the function and type the minus sign in the correct place.

g. Click **OK**. Copy the formula down the column and save the workbook.

STEP 3 ▶▶ USE THE IF FUNCTION

Lenders often want borrowers to have a 20% down payment. If borrowers do not put in 20% of the cost of the house as a down payment, they pay a private mortgage insurance (PMI) fee. PMI serves to protect lenders from absorbing loss if the borrower defaults on the loan, and it enables borrowers with less cash to secure a loan. The PMI fee is about 0.38% of the amount financed. Some borrowers have to pay PMI for a few months or years until the balance owed is less than 80% of the appraised value. The worksheet contains the necessary values input area. You need to use the IF function to determine which borrowers must pay PMI and how much they will pay. Refer to Figure 2.30 as you complete Step 3.

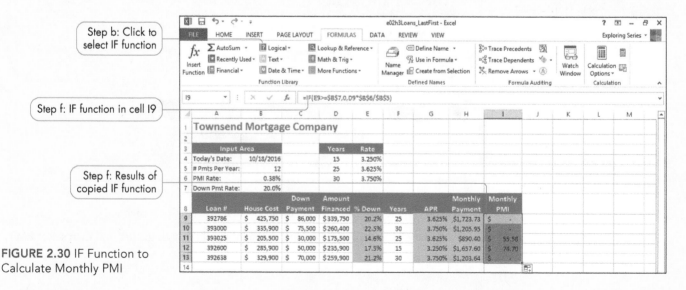

FIGURE 2.30 IF Function to Calculate Monthly PMI

a. Click **cell I9**, the cell that will store the PMI, if any, for the first customer.

b. Click **Logical** in the Function Library group and select **IF**.

The Function Arguments dialog box opens. You need to enter the three arguments.

c. Type **E9>=$B$7** in the **Logical_test box**.

The logical test compares the down payment percentage to see if the customer's down payment is at least 20%, the threshold stored in B7, of the amount financed. The customer's percentage cell reference needs to be relative so that it will change when you copy it down the column; however, cell B7 must be absolute because it contains the threshold value.

d. Press **Tab** and type **0** in the **Value_if_true box**.

If the customer makes a down payment that is at least 20% of the purchase price, the customer does not pay PMI. The first customer paid 20% of the purchase price, so he or she does not have to pay PMI.

e. Press **Tab** and type **D9*$B$6/$B$5** in the **Value_if_false box**.

If the logical test is false, the customer must pay PMI, which is calculated by dividing the yearly PMI (0.38%) by 12 and multiplying the result by the amount financed.

f. Click **OK** and copy the formula down the column.

The third and fourth customers must pay PMI because their respective down payments were less than 20% of the purchase price.

TROUBLESHOOTING: If the results are not as you expected, check the logical operators. People often mistype < and > or forget to type = for >= situations. Correct any errors in the original formula and copy the formula again.

---

g. Save the workbook. Keep the workbook open if you plan to continue with the next Hands-On Exercise. If not, close the workbook and exit Excel.

Range Names

To simplify entering ranges in formulas, you can use range names. A ***range name*** is a word or string of characters assigned to one or more cells. Think of range names in this way: Your college identifies you by your student ID; however, your professors call you by an easy-to-remember name, such as Micah or Vanessa. Similarly, instead of using cell addresses, you can use descriptive range names in formulas. Going back to the VLOOKUP example shown in Figure 2.25, you can assign the range name *Grades* to cells A3:B7 and modify the VLOOKUP function to be =VLOOKUP(E3,Grades,2), using the range name *Grades* in the formula. Another benefit of using range names is that they are absolute references, which helps ensure accuracy in your calculations.

In this section, you will work with range names. First, you will learn how to create and maintain range names. Then you will learn how to use a range name in a formula.

Creating and Maintaining Range Names

Each range name within a workbook must be unique. For example, you cannot assign the name *COST* to ranges on several worksheets or on the same sheet. After you create a range name, you might need to change its name or range. If you no longer need a range name, you can delete it. You can also insert in the workbook a list of range names and their respective cell ranges for reference.

Create a Range Name

STEP 1 » A range name can contain up to 255 characters, but it must begin with a letter or an underscore. You can use a combination of upper- or lowercase letters, numbers, periods, and underscores throughout the range name. A range name cannot include spaces or special characters. You should create range names that describe the range of cells being named, but names cannot be identical to the cell contents. Keep the range names short to make them easier to use in formulas. Table 2.8 lists acceptable and unacceptable range names.

TABLE 2.8	Range Names
Name	**Description**
Grades	Acceptable range name
COL	Acceptable abbreviation for cost-of-living
Tax_Rate	Acceptable name with underscore
Commission Rate	Unacceptable name; cannot use spaces in names
Discount Rate %	Unacceptable name; cannot use special symbols and spaces
2016_Rate	Unacceptable name; cannot start with a number
Rate_2016	Acceptable name with underscore and numbers

To create a range name, select the range you want to name and do one of the following:

- Click in the Name Box, type the range name, and then press Enter.
- Click the FORMULAS tab, click Define Name in the Defined Names group to open the New Name dialog box (see Figure 2.31), type the range name in the Name Box, and then click OK.
- Click the FORMULAS tab, click Name Manager in the Defined Names group to open the Name Manager dialog box, click New, type the range name in the Name Box, click OK, and then click Close.

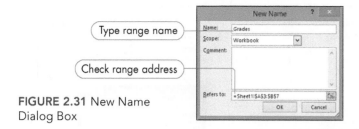

FIGURE 2.31 New Name Dialog Box

Type range name

Check range address

You can create several range names at the same time if your worksheet includes ranges with values and descriptive labels. To do this, select the range of cells containing the labels that you want to become names and the cells that contain the values to name, click *Create from Selection* in the Defined Named group on the Formulas tab, and then select an option in the *Create Names from Selection* dialog box (see Figure 2.32).

FIGURE 2.32 Create Names from Selection Dialog Box

Edit or Delete a Range Name

STEP 2 Use the Name Manager dialog box to edit, delete, and create range names. To open the Name Manager dialog box shown in Figure 2.33, click Name Manager in the Defined Names group on the Formulas tab. To edit a range or range name, click the range name in the list and click Edit. In the Edit Name dialog box, make your edits and click OK.

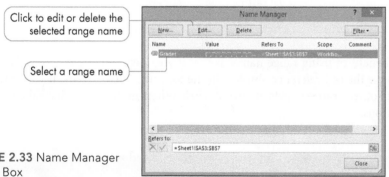

Click to edit or delete the selected range name

Select a range name

FIGURE 2.33 Name Manager Dialog Box

To delete a range name, open the Name Manager dialog box, select the name you want to delete, click Delete, and then click OK in the confirmation message box.

If you change a range name, any formulas that use the range name reflect the new name. For example, if a formula contains =cost*rate and you change the name rate to tax_rate, Excel updates the formula to be =cost*tax_rate. If you delete a range name and a formula depends on that range name, Excel displays #NAME?—indicating an Invalid Name Error.

Insert a Table of Range Names

STEP 4 You can document a workbook by inserting a list of range names in a worksheet. To insert a list of range names, click *Use in Formula* in the Defined Names group on the Formulas tab and select Paste Names. The Paste Name dialog box opens (see Figure 2.34), listing all range names in the current workbook. Click Paste List to insert a list of range names in alphabetical order. The first column contains a list of range names, and the second column contains the worksheet names and range locations.

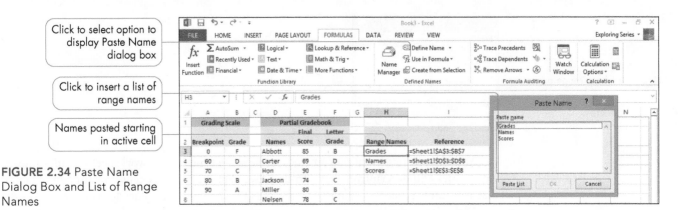

Click to select option to display Paste Name dialog box

Click to insert a list of range names

Names pasted starting in active cell

FIGURE 2.34 Paste Name Dialog Box and List of Range Names

Using Range Names in Formulas

STEP 3 You can use range names in formulas instead of cell references. For example, if cell C15 contains a purchase amount, and cell C5 contains the sales tax rate, instead of typing =C15*C5, you can type the range names in the formula, such as =purchase*tax_rate. When you type a formula, Formula AutoComplete displays a list of range names, as well as functions, that start with the letters as you type (see Figure 2.35). Double-click the range name to insert it in the formula.

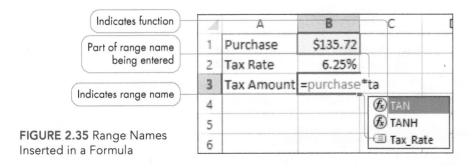

Indicates function

Part of range name being entered

Indicates range name

FIGURE 2.35 Range Names Inserted in a Formula

Another benefit of using range names is that if you have to copy the formula, you do not have to make the cell reference absolute in the formula. Furthermore, if you share your workbook with others, range names in formulas help others understand what values are used in the calculations.

TIP Go to a Range Name

Use the Go To dialog box to go to the top-left cell in a range specified by a range name.

Quick Concepts

1. What is a range name? *p. 110*

2. List at least five guidelines and rules for naming a range. *p. 110*

3. What is the purpose of inserting a list of range names in a worksheet? What is contained in the list, and how is it arranged? *p. 112*

Hands-On Exercises

4 Range Names

You decide to simplify the VLOOKUP function by using a range name for the APR rates lookup table instead of the actual cell references. After creating a range name, you will modify some range names Erica created and create a list of range names.

Skills covered: Create a Range Name • Edit and Delete Range Names • Use a Range Name in a Formula • Insert a List of Range Names

STEP 1 ≫ CREATE A RANGE NAME

You want to assign a range name to the lookup table of years and APRs. Refer to Figure 2.36 as you complete Step 1.

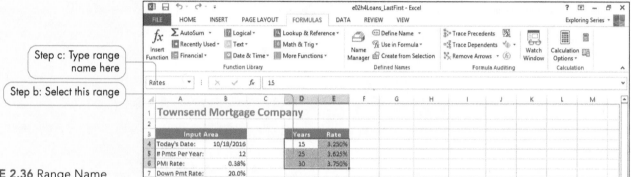

FIGURE 2.36 Range Name

a. Open *e02h3Loans_LastFirst* if you closed it at the end of Hands-On Exercise 3 and save it as **e02h4Loans_LastFirst**, changing *h3* to *h4*.

b. Make sure the **Payment Info worksheet tab** is active. Select **range D4:E6** (the lookup table).

c. Click in the **Name Box**, type **Rates**, and then press **Enter**. Save the workbook.

STEP 2 ≫ EDIT AND DELETE RANGE NAMES

You noticed that Erica added some range names. You will use the Name Manager dialog box to view and make changes to the range names, such as reducing the length of two range names and deleting another range name. Refer to Figure 2.37 as you complete Step 2.

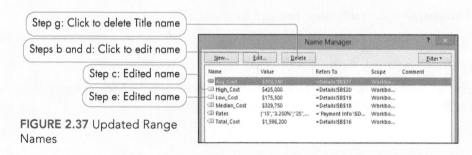

FIGURE 2.37 Updated Range Names

a. Click **Name Manager** in the Defined Names group on the FORMULAS tab.

   The Name Manager dialog box opens.

b. Select **Highest_House...** and click **Edit** to open the Edit Name dialog box.

c. Type **High_Cost** in the **Name Box** and click **OK**.

d. Select **Lowest_House...** and click **Edit**.

e. Type **Low_Cost** in the **Name Box** and click **OK**.

f. Select **Title** in the Name Manager dialog box.

This range name applies to a cell containing text, which does not need a name as it cannot be used in calculations. You decide to delete the range name.

g. Click **Delete**, read the warning message box, and then click **OK** to confirm the deletion of the Title range name.

h. Click **Close** and save the workbook.

STEP 3 ≫ USE A RANGE NAME IN A FORMULA

You will modify the VLOOKUP function by replacing the existing Table_array argument with the range name. This will help Erica interpret the VLOOKUP function. Refer to Figure 2.38 as you complete Step 3.

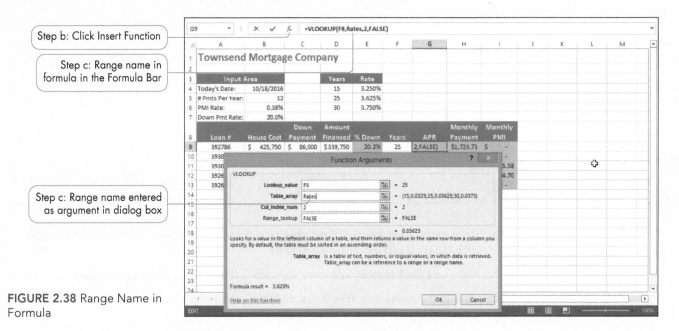

FIGURE 2.38 Range Name in Formula

a. Click **cell G9**, the cell containing the VLOOKUP function.

b. Click **Insert Function** between the Name Box and the Formula Bar to open the Function Arguments dialog box.

The Table_array argument contains $D$4:$E$6, the absolute reference to the lookup table.

c. Select **$D$4:$E$6** in the **Table_array box**, type **Rates**, and then click **OK**.

The new function is =VLOOKUP(F9,Rates,2,FALSE).

d. Copy the updated formula down the column and save the workbook.

The results are the same as they were when you used the absolute cell references. However, the formulas are shorter and easier to read with the range names.

STEP 4 >> INSERT A LIST OF RANGE NAMES

Before submitting the completed workbook to Erica, you want to create a documentation worksheet that lists all of the range names in the workbook. Refer to Figure 2.39 as you complete Step 4.

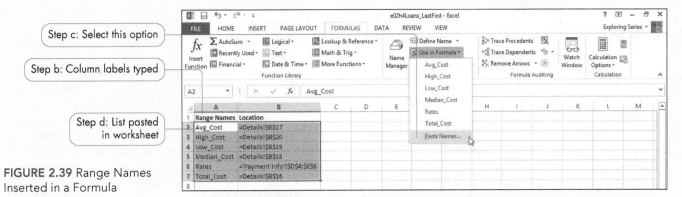

FIGURE 2.39 Range Names Inserted in a Formula

a. Click **New sheet** to the right of the worksheet tabs and double-click the default sheet name, **Sheet1**. Type **Range Names** and press **Enter**.

You inserted and renamed the new worksheet to reflect the data you will add to it.

b. Type **Range Names** in cell **A1** and type **Location** in **cell B1**. Bold these headings.

These column headings will display above the list of range names.

c. Click **cell A2**, click **Use in Formula** in the Defined Names group on the FORMULAS tab, and then select **Paste Names**.

The Paste Name dialog box opens, displaying all of the range names in the workbook.

d. Click **Paste List**.

Excel pastes an alphabetical list of range names starting in cell A2. The second column displays the locations of the range names.

e. Increase the widths of columns A and B to fit the data.

f. Save and close the workbook, and submit based on your instructor's directions.

TIP List of Range Names

When you paste range names, the list will overwrite any existing data in a worksheet, so consider pasting the list in a separate worksheet. If you add, edit, or delete range names, the list does not update automatically. To keep the list current, you would need to paste the list again.

Chapter Objectives Review

After reading this chapter, you have accomplished the following objectives:

1. Use relative, absolute, and mixed cell references in formulas.

- Use a relative cell address: A relative reference indicates a cell's location relative to the formula cell. When you copy the formula, the relative cell reference changes.
- Use an absolute cell reference: An absolute reference is a permanent pointer to a particular cell, indicated with $ before the column letter and row number, such as $B$5. When you copy the formula, the absolute cell reference does not change.
- Use a mixed cell reference: A mixed reference contains part absolute and part relative reference, such as $B5 or B$5. Either the column or row reference changes, while the other remains constant when you copy the formula.

2. Correct circular references.

- A circular reference occurs when a formula refers to the cell containing the formula. The status bar indicates the location of a circular reference.

3. Insert a function.

- A function is a predefined formula that performs a calculation. It contains the function name and arguments. Formula AutoComplete, function ScreenTips, and the Insert Function dialog box help you select and create functions. The Function Arguments dialog box guides you through entering requirements for each argument.

4. Insert basic math and statistics functions.

- Calculate the total with the SUM function: The SUM function calculates the total of a range of values. The syntax is =SUM(number1,[number2],…).
- Find central tendency with AVERAGE and MEDIAN: The AVERAGE function calculates the arithmetic mean of values in a range. The MEDIAN function identifies the midpoint value in a set of values.
- Identify low and high values with MIN and MAX: The MIN function identifies the lowest value in a range, whereas the MAX function identifies the highest value in a range.
- Identify the total number with COUNT functions: The COUNT function tallies the number of cells in a range, whereas the COUNTBLANK function tallies the number of blank cells in a range.
- Use other math and statistical functions: Excel contains other math and statistical functions, such as MODE.
- Nest functions as arguments: You can nest one function inside another function's argument, such as nesting the AVERAGE function inside the ROUND function: =ROUND(AVERAGE(A2:A14),2).

5. Use date functions.

- Insert the TODAY function: The TODAY function displays the current date.
- Insert the NOW function: The NOW function displays the current date and time.
- Use other date functions: Excel contains a variety of date and time functions.

6. Determine results with the IF function.

- Design the logical test: The IF function is a logical function that evaluates a logical test using logical operators, such as <, >, and =, and returns one value if the condition is true and another value if the condition is false.
- Design the value_if_true and value_if_false arguments: The arguments can contain cell references, text, or calculations. If a logical test is true, Excel executes the value_if_true argument. If a logical test is false, Excel executes the value_if_false argument.
- Create other IF functions: You can nest or embed other functions inside one or more of the arguments of an IF function to create more complex formulas.

7. Use lookup functions.

- Create the lookup table: Design the lookup table using exact values or the breakpoints for ranges. If using breakpoints, the breakpoints must be in ascending order.
- Understand the VLOOKUP syntax: The VLOOKUP function contains the required aruguments lookup_value, table_array, and col_index_num and one optional argument, range_lookup.
- Understand how Excel processes the lookup: The VLOOKUP function looks up a value for a particular record, compares it to a lookup table, and returns a result in another column of the lookup table.
- Use the range_lookup argument: If an exact match is required, the optional fourth argument should be FALSE; otherwise, the fourth argument can remain empty.
- Nest functions inside the VLOOKUP function: You can nest functions inside one or more arguments.
- Use the HLOOKUP function: The HLOOKUP function looks up values by row (horizontally) rather than by column (vertically).

8. Calculate payments with the PMT function.

- The PMT function calculates periodic payments for a loan with a fixed interest rate and a fixed term. The PMT function requires the periodic interest rate, the total number of payment periods, and the original value of the loan.

9. Create and maintain range names.

- Create a range name: A range name may contain letters, numbers, and underscores, but must start with either a letter or an underscore.
- Edit or delete a range name: Use the Name Manager dialog box to edit, create, or delete range names.
- Insert a table of range names: The first column contains an alphabetical list of range names, and the second column contains a list of their ranges.

10. Use range names in formulas.

- You can use range names in formulas to make the formulas easier to interpret by using a descriptive name for the value(s) contained in a cell or range.

Key Terms Matching

Match the key terms with their definitions. Write the key term letter by the appropriate numbered definition.

a. Absolute cell reference
b. Argument
c. AVERAGE function
d. Circular reference
e. COUNT function
f. IF function
g. Logical test
h. Lookup table
i. MAX function
j. MEDIAN function
k. MIN function

l. Mixed cell reference
m. NOW function
n. PMT function
o. Range name
p. Relative cell reference
q. SUM function
r. Syntax
s. TODAY function
t. VLOOKUP function

1. _____ A set of rules that governs the structure and components for properly entering a function. **p. 84**

2. _____ Displays the current date. **p. 84**

3. _____ Indicates a cell's specific location; the cell reference does not change when you copy the formula. **p. 76**

4. _____ Occurs when a formula directly or indirectly refers to itself. **p. 78**

5. _____ An input, such as a cell reference or value, needed to complete a function. **p. 84**

6. _____ Identifies the highest value in a range. **p. 89**

7. _____ Tallies the number of cells in a range that contain values. **p. 89**

8. _____ Looks up a value in a vertical lookup table and returns a related result from the lookup table. **p. 103**

9. _____ A range that contains data for the basis of the lookup and data to be retrieved. **p. 102**

10. _____ Calculates the arithmetic mean, or average, of values in a range. **p. 88**

11. _____ Identifies the midpoint value in a set of values. **p. 88**

12. _____ Displays the current date and time. **p. 91**

13. _____ Evaluates a condition and returns one value if the condition is true and a different value if the condition is false. **p. 99**

14. _____ Calculates the total of values contained in two or more cells. **p. 86**

15. _____ Calculates the periodic payment for a loan with a fixed interest rate and fixed term. **p. 105**

16. _____ Indicates a cell's location from the cell containing the formula; the cell reference changes when the formula is copied. **p. 76**

17. _____ Contains both an absolute and a relative cell reference in a formula; the absolute part does not change but the relative part does when you copy the formula. **p. 78**

18. _____ A word or string of characters that represents one or more cells. **p. 110**

19. _____ An expression that evaluates to true or false. **p. 100**

20. _____ Displays the lowest value in a range. **p. 89**

Multiple Choice

1. If cell D15 contains the formula =$C$5*D$15, what is the D15 in the formula?

   (a) Relative reference

   (b) Absolute reference

   (c) Circular reference

   (d) Range name

2. What function would most appropriately accomplish the same thing as =(B5+C5+D5+E5+F5)/5?

   (a) =SUM(B5:F5)/5

   (b) =AVERAGE(B5:F5)

   (c) =MEDIAN(B5:F5)

   (d) =COUNT(B5:F5)

3. When you start =AV, what displays a list of functions and defined names?

   (a) Function ScreenTip

   (b) Formula AutoComplete

   (c) Insert Function dialog box

   (d) Function Arguments dialog box

4. A formula containing the entry =$B3 is copied to a cell one column to the right and two rows down. How will the entry appear in its new location?

   (a) =$B3

   (b) =B3

   (c) =$C5

   (d) =$B5

5. Cell B10 contains a date, such as 1/1/2016. Which formula will determine how many days are between that date and the current date, given that the cell containing the formula is formatted with Number Format?

   (a) =TODAY()

   (b) =CURRENT()-B10

   (c) =TODAY()-B10

   (d) =TODAY()+NOW()

6. Given that cells A1, A2, and A3 contain values 2, 3, and 10, respectively, and B6, C6, and D6 contain values 10, 20, and 30, respectively, what value will be returned by the function =IF(B6>A3,C6*A1,D6*A2)?

   (a) 10

   (b) 40

   (c) 60

   (d) 90

7. Given the function =VLOOKUP(C6,$D$12:$F$18,3), the entries in:

   (a) Range D12:D18 are in ascending order.

   (b) Range D12:D18 are in descending order.

   (c) The third column of the lookup table must be text only.

   (d) Range D12:D18 contain multiple values in each cell.

8. The function =PMT(C5,C7,-C3) is stored in cell C15. What must be stored in cell C5?

   (a) APR

   (b) Periodic interest rate

   (c) Loan amount

   (d) Number of payment periods

9. Which of the following is *not* an appropriate use of the SUM function?

   (a) =SUM(B3:B45)

   (b) =SUM(F1:G10)

   (c) =SUM(A8:A15,D8:D15)

   (d) =SUM(D15-C15)

10. Which of the following is *not* an acceptable range name?

    (a) FICA

    (b) Test_Weight

    (c) Goal for 2016

    (d) Target_2015

1 Blue Canadian Skies Airlines

You are an analyst for Blue Canadian Skies Airlines, a regional airline headquartered in Victoria. Your assistant developed a template for you to store daily flight data about the number of passengers per flight. Each regional aircraft can hold up to 70 passengers. You need to calculate the occupancy rate (the percent of each flight that is occupied), daily statistics (such as total number of passengers, averages, least full flights, etc.), and weekly statistics per flight number. This exercise follows the same set of skills as used in Hands-On Exercises 1 and 2 in the chapter. Refer to Figure 2.40 as you complete this exercise.

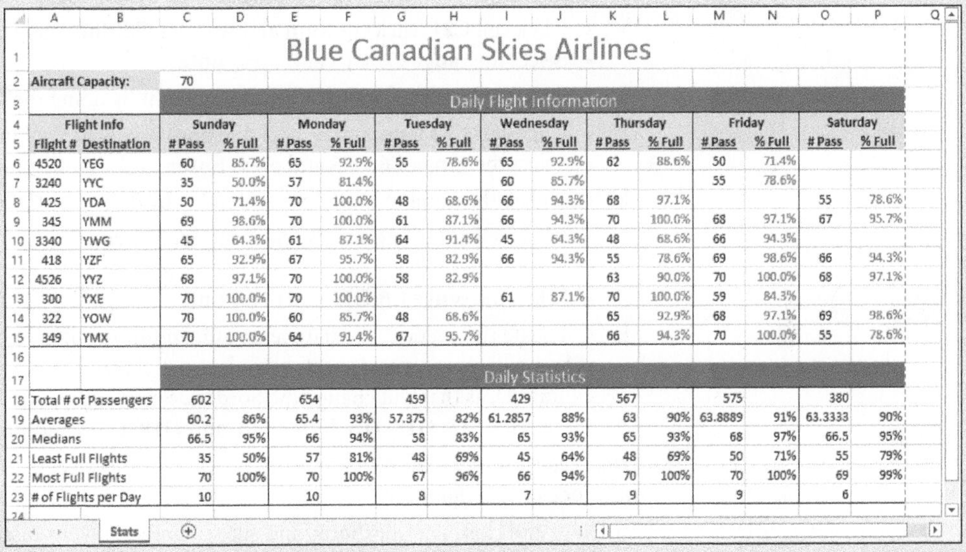

FIGURE 2.40 Blue Canadian Skies Airlines

a. Open *e02p1Flights* and save it as **e02p1Flights_LastFirst**.

b. Click **cell D6**, the cell to display the occupancy percent for Flight 4520 on Sunday, and do the following:
   - Type **=C6/$C$2** and click **Enter** (the checkmark between the Name Box and the Formula Bar). The occupancy rate of Flight 4520 is 85.7%.
   - Double-click the **cell D6 fill handle** to copy the formula down the column.

c. Click **cell D7**. When you copy a formula, Excel also copies the original cell's format. The cell containing the original formula did not have a bottom border, so when you copied the formula down the column, Excel formatted it to match the original cell with no border. To reapply the border, click **cell D15**, click the **Border arrow** in the Font group on the HOME tab, and then select **Bottom Border**.

d. Select the **range D6:D15**, click **Copy**, click **cell F6**, and then click **Paste**. The formula in cell F6 is =E6/$C$2. The first cell reference changes from C6 to E6, maintaining its relative location from the pasted formula. $C$2 remains absolute so that the number of passengers per flight is always divided by the value stored in cell C2. The copied range is still in the Clipboard. Paste the formula into the remaining % Full columns (columns H, J, L, N, and P). Press **Esc**.

e. Clean up the data by deleting *0.0%* in cells, such as H7. The 0.0% is misleading, as it implies the flight was empty; however, some flights do not operate on all days. Check your worksheet against the *Daily Flight Information* section in Figure 2.40.

f. Calculate the total number of passengers per day by doing the following:
   - Click **cell C18** and click **Sum** in the Editing group.
   - Select the **range C6:C15** and press **Enter**.

g. Calculate the average number of passengers per day by doing the following:
- Click **cell C19**, click the **Sum arrow** in the Editing group, and then select **Average**.
- Select the **range C6:C15** and click **Enter** (the checkmark between the Name Box and the Formula Bar).

h. Calculate the median number of passengers per day by doing the following:
- Click **cell C20**.
- Click **Insert Function**, type **median** in the **Search for a function box**, and then click **Go**.
- Click **MEDIAN** in the **Select a function box** and click **OK**.
- Select the **range C6:C15** to enter it in the **Number1 box** and click **OK**.

i. Calculate the least number of passengers on a daily flight by doing the following:
- Click **cell C21**, click the **Sum arrow** in the Editing group, and then select **Min**.
- Select the **range C6:C15** and press **Enter**.

j. Calculate the most passengers on a daily flight by doing the following:
- Click **cell C22** if necessary, click the **Sum arrow** in the Editing group, and then select **Max**.
- Select the **range C6:C15** and press **Enter**.

k. Calculate the number of flights for Sunday by doing the following:
- Click **cell C23** if necessary, click the **Sum arrow** in the Editing group, and then select **Count Numbers**.
- Select the **range C6:C15** and press **Enter**.

l. Calculate the average, median, least full, and most full percentages in **cells D19:D22**. Format the values with Percent Style with zero decimal places. Do not copy the formulas from column C to column D, as that will change the borders. Select **cells C18:D23**, copy the range, and then paste in these cells: **E18, G18, I18, K18, M18,** and **O18**. Press **Esc** after pasting.

m. Create a footer with your name on the left side, the sheet name code in the center, and the file name code on the right side.

n. Save and close the workbook, and submit based on your instructor's directions.

2 Steggel Consulting Firm Salaries

You work in the Human Resources Department at Steggell Consulting Firm. You are preparing a model to calculate bonuses based on performance ratings, where ratings between 1 and 1.9 do not receive bonuses, ratings between 2 and 2.9 earn $100 bonuses, ratings between 3 and 3.9 earn $250 bonuses, ratings between 4 and 4.9 earn $500 bonuses, and ratings of 5 or higher earn $1,000 bonuses. In addition, you need to calculate annual raises based on years employed. Employees who have worked five or more years earn a 3.25% raise; employees who have not worked at least five years earn a 2% raise. This exercise follows the same set of skills as used in Hands-On Exercises 1–4 in the chapter. Refer to Figure 2.41 as you complete this exercise.

a. Open *e02p2Salary* and save it as **e02p2Salary_LastFirst**.

b. Click **cell B4**, click the **FORMULAS tab**, click **Date & Time** in the Function Library group, select **TODAY**, and then click **OK** to enter today's date in the cell.

c. Enter a formula to calculate the number of years employed by doing the following:
- Click **cell C11**, click **Date & Time** in the Function Library group, scroll through the list, and then select **YEARFRAC**.
- Click **cell A11** to enter the cell reference in the **Start_date box**.
- Press **Tab** and click **cell B4** to enter the cell reference in the **End_date box**.
- Press **F4** to make **cell B4** absolute and click **OK**. (Although you could have used the formula =($B$4-A11)/365 to calculate the number of years, the YEARFRAC function provides better accuracy because it accounts for leap years and the divisor 365 does not. The completed function is =YEARFRAC(A11,$B$4).
- Double-click the **cell C11 fill handle** to copy the YEARFRAC function down the Years Employed column. Your results will differ based on the date contained in cell B4.

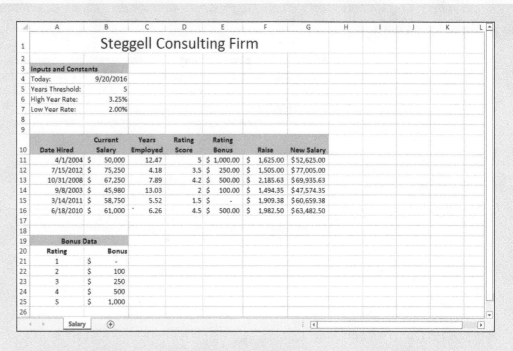

	A	B	C	D	E	F	G
1			Steggell Consulting Firm				
2							
3	**Inputs and Constants**						
4	Today:	9/20/2016					
5	Years Threshold:	5					
6	High Year Rate:	3.25%					
7	Low Year Rate:	2.00%					
8							
9							
10	Date Hired	Current Salary	Years Employed	Rating Score	Rating Bonus	Raise	New Salary
11	4/1/2004	$ 50,000	12.47	5	$ 1,000.00	$ 1,625.00	$52,625.00
12	7/15/2012	$ 75,250	4.18	3.5	$ 250.00	$ 1,505.00	$77,005.00
13	10/31/2008	$ 67,250	7.89	4.2	$ 500.00	$ 2,185.63	$69,935.63
14	9/8/2003	$ 45,980	13.03	2	$ 100.00	$ 1,494.35	$47,574.35
15	3/14/2011	$ 58,750	5.52	1.5	$ -	$ 1,909.38	$60,659.38
16	6/18/2010	$ 61,000	6.26	4.5	$ 500.00	$ 1,982.50	$63,482.50
17							
18							
19	**Bonus Data**						
20	**Rating**		**Bonus**				
21	1	$ -					
22	2	$ 100					
23	3	$ 250					
24	4	$ 500					
25	5	$ 1,000					
26							

Salary

FIGURE 2.41 Steggell Consulting Firm

d. Enter the breakpoint and bonus data for the lookup table by doing the following:
- Click **cell A21**, type **1**, and then press **Ctrl+Enter**.
- Click the **HOME tab**, click **Fill** in the Editing group, and then select **Series**. Click **Columns** in the *Series in* section, leave the **Step value** at **1**, type **5** in the **Stop value box**, and then click **OK**.
- Click **cell B21**. Enter **0, 100, 250, 500**, and **1000** down the column. The cells have been formatted with Accounting Number Format with zero decimal places.
- Select **range A21:B25**, click in the **Name Box**, type **Bonus**, and then press **Enter**.

e. Enter the bonus based on rating by doing the following:
- Click **cell E11** and click the **FORMULAS tab**.
- Click **Lookup & Reference** in the Function Library group and select **VLOOKUP**.
- Type **D11** in the **Lookup_value box**, type **Bonus** in the **Table_array box**, type **2**, and then click **OK**. The completed function is =VLOOKUP(D11,Bonus,2).
- Double-click the **cell E11 fill handle** to copy the formula down the Rating Bonus column.

f. Enter the raise based on years employed by doing the following:
- Click **cell F11**, click **Logical** in the Function Library group, and then select **IF**.
- Type **C11>=$B$5** to compare the years employed to the absolute reference of the five-year threshold in the **Logical_test box**.
- Press **Tab** and type **B11*$B$6** to calculate a 3.25% raise for employees who worked five years or more in the **Value_if_true box**.
- Press **Tab** and type **cell B11*$B$7** to calculate a 2% raise for employees who worked less than five years in the Value_if_false box. Click **OK**. The completed function is =IF(C11>=$B$5,B11*$B$6,B11*$B$7).
- Double-click the **cell F11 fill handle** to copy the formula down the Raise column.

g. Click **cell G11**. Type =B11+E11+F11 to add the current salary, the bonus, and the raise to calculate the new salary. Double-click the **cell G11 fill handle** to copy the formula down the column.

h. Create a footer with your name on the left side, the sheet name code in the center, and the file name code on the right side.

i. Save and close the workbook, and submit based on your instructor's directions.

After obtaining a promotion at work, you want to buy a luxury car, such as a Lexus or Infinity. Before purchasing a car, you want to create a worksheet to estimate the monthly payment based on the purchase price (including accessories, taxes, and license plate), APR, down payment, and years. You will assign range names and use range names in the formulas to make them easier to analyze. This exercise follows the same set of skills as used in Hands-On Exercises 1–4 in the chapter. Refer to Figure 2.42 as you complete this exercise.

	A	B	C
1	Car Loan		
2			
3	**Inputs**		
4	Cost of Car*	45000	
5	Down Payment	10000	
6	APR	0.0399	
7	Years	5	
8	Payments Per Year	12	
9	*Includes taxes, etc.		
10			
11	**Outputs**		
12	Loan	=Cost-Down	
13	Monthly Payment	=PMT(APR/Months,Years*Months,-Loan)	
14	Total to Repay Loan	=Years*Months*Payment	
15	Total Interest Paid	=Repaid-Loan	
16			

FIGURE 2.42 Car Loan

a. Open *e02p3CarLoan* and save it as **e02p3CarLoan_LastFirst**.

b. Name the input values by doing the following:
- Select the **range A4:B8**.
- Click the **FORMULAS tab** and click **Create from Selection** in the Defined Names group.
- Make sure *Left column* is selected and click **OK**.
- Click each input value cell in the **range B4:B8** and look at the newly created names in the Name Box.

DISCOVER

c. Edit the range names by doing the following:
- Click **Name Manager** in the Defined Names group.
- Click **Cost_of_Car**, click **Edit**, type **Cost**, and then click **OK**.
- Change *Down_Payment* to **Down**.
- Change *Payments_Per_Year* to **Months**.
- Click **Close** to close the Name Manager.

d. Name the output values in the **range A12:B15** using the *Create from Selection* method you used in step b to assign names to the empty cells in the range B12:B15. However, you will use the range names as you build formulas in the next few steps. Edit the range names using the same approach you used in step c.
- Change *Monthly_Payment* to **Payment.**
- Change *Total_Interest_Paid* to **Interest**.
- Change *Total_to_Repay_Loan* to **Repaid**.
- Click **Close** to close the Name Manager.

e. Enter the formula to calculate the amount of the loan by doing the following:
- Click **cell B12**. Type **=Cos** and double-click **Cost** from the Function AutoComplete list. If the list does not appear, type the entire name **Cost**.
- Press - and type **do**, and then double-click **Down** from the Function AutoComplete list.
- Press **Enter** to enter the formula =Cost-Down.

f. Calculate the monthly payment of principal and interest by doing the following:
- Click the **FORMULAS tab**. Click **cell B13**. Click **Financial** in the Function Library group, scroll down, and then select **PMT**.
- Type **APR/Months** in the **Rate box**.
- Press **Tab** and type **Years*Months** in the **Nper box**.
- Press **Tab**, type **-Loan** in the **Pv box**, and then click **OK**. The completed function is =PMT(APR/Months,Years*Months,-Loan).

DISCOVER

g. Enter the total amount to repay loan formula by doing the following:
- Click **cell B14**. Type = to start the formula.
- Click **Use in Formula** in the Defined Names group and select **Years**.
- Type *, click **Use in Formula** in the Defined Names group, and then select **Months**.
- Type *, click **Use in Formula** in the Defined Names group, and then select **Payment**.
- Press **Enter**. The completed formula is =Years*Months*Payment.

h. Use the skills from step g to enter the formula **=Repaid-Loan** in **cell B15**.

i. Select the **range B12:B15**, click the **HOME tab**, and then click **Accounting Number Format** in the Number group.

j. Select the option to center the worksheet data between the left and right margins in the Page Setup dialog box.

k. Create a footer with your name on the left side, the sheet name code in the center, and the file name code on the right side.

l. Right-click the **Car sheet tab**, select **Move or Copy** from the menu, click **(move to end)** in the *Before sheet* section, click the **Create a copy check box**, and then click **OK**. Rename the Car (2) sheet **Formulas**.

m. Make sure the Formulas sheet is active. Click the **FORMULAS tab** and click **Show Formulas** in the Formula Auditing group. Widen column B to display entire formulas.

n. Click the **PAGE LAYOUT tab** and click the **Gridlines Print check box** and the **Headings Print check box** in the Sheet Options group to select these two options.

o. Insert a new sheet, name it **Names**, type **Range Name** in **cell A1**, and then type **Location** in **cell B1**. Apply bold to these column labels. Click **cell A2**, click the **FORMULAS tab**, click **Use in Formula**, select **Paste Names**, and then click **Paste List** to paste an alphabetical list of range names in the worksheet. Adjust the column widths. Apply the same Page Setup settings and footer to the Formulas and Cars worksheets.

p. Save and close the workbook, and submit based on your instructor's directions.

Mid-Level Exercises

1 Metropolitan Zoo Gift Shop Weekly Payroll

ANALYSIS CASE

As manager of the gift shop at the Metropolitan Zoo, you are responsible for managing the weekly payroll. Your assistant developed a partial worksheet, but you need to enter the formulas to calculate the regular pay, overtime pay, gross pay, taxable pay, withholding tax, FICA, and net pay. In addition, you want to total pay columns and calculate some basic statistics. As you construct formulas, make sure you use absolute and relative cell references correctly in formulas and avoid circular references.

a. Open the *e02m1Payroll* workbook and save it as **e02m1Payroll_LastFirst**.

b. Study the worksheet structure and read the business rules in the Notes section.

c. Use IF functions to calculate the regular pay and overtime pay based on a regular 40-hour work-week in **cells E5** and **F5**. Pay overtime only for overtime hours. Calculate the gross pay based on the regular and overtime pay. Abram's regular pay is $398. With 8 overtime hours, Abram's over-time pay is $119.40.

d. Create a formula in **cell H5** to calculate the taxable pay. Multiply the number of dependents by the deduction per dependent and subtract that from the gross pay. With two dependents, Abram's tax-able pay is $417.40.

e. Use a VLOOKUP function in **cell I5** to identify and calculate the federal withholding tax. With a taxable pay of $417.40, Abram's tax rate is 25% and the withholding tax is $104.35. The VLOOKUP function returns the applicable tax rate, which you must then multiply by the taxable pay.

f. Calculate FICA in **cell J5** based on gross pay and the FICA rate and calculate the net pay in **Cell K5**.

g. Calculate the total regular pay, overtime pay, gross pay, taxable pay, withholding tax, FICA, and net pay on row 17.

h. Copy all formulas down their respective columns.

i. Apply **Accounting Number Format** to the **range C5:C16**. Apply **Accounting Number Format** to the first row of monetary data and to the total row. Apply **Comma Style** to the monetary values for the other employees. Underline the last employee's monetary values and use the Format Cells dialog box to apply **Double Accounting Underline** for the totals.

j. Insert appropriate functions to calculate the average, highest, and lowest values in the Summary Statistics area (the **range I21:K23**) of the worksheet.

DISCOVER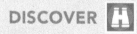

k. At your instructor's discretion, use Help to learn about the FREQUENCY function. The Help feature contains sample data for you to copy and practice in a new worksheet to learn about this function. You can close the practice worksheet containing the Help data without saving it. You want to determine the number (frequency) of employees who worked less than 20 hours, between 20 and 29 hours, between 30 and 40 hours, and over 40 hours. **Cells J28:J31** list the ranges. You need to translate this range into correct values for the Bin column in **cells I28:I31** and enter the FREQUENCY function in **cells K28:K31**. The function should identify one employee who worked between 0 and 19 hours and six employees who worked more than 40 hours.

l. Apply other page setup formats as needed.

 m. Insert a new sheet named **Overtime**. List the number of overtime hours for the week. Calculate the yearly gross amount spent on overtime assuming the same number of overtime hours per week. Add another row with only half the overtime hours (using a formula). What is your conclusion and recommendation on overtime? Format this worksheet.

n. Insert a footer with your name on the left side, the sheet name code in the center, and the file name code on the right side of both worksheets.

o. Save and close the workbook, and submit based on your instructor's directions.

2 Mortgage Calculator

FROM SCRATCH

As a financial consultant, you work with people who are planning to buy a new house. You want to create a worksheet containing variable data (the price of the house, down payment, date of the first payment, and borrower's credit rating) and constants (property tax rate, years, and number of payments in one year). Borrowers pay 0.5% private mortgage insurance (PMI) on the loan amount if they do not make at least a 20% down payment. A borrower's credit rating determines the required down payment percentage and APR. For example, a person with an excellent credit rating may make only a 5% down payment with a 3.25% APR loan. A person with a fair credit rating will make a 15% down payment and have a higher APR at 5.25%. Your worksheet needs to perform various calculations. The filled cells in column F indicate cells containing formulas, not values. Refer to Figure 2.43 as you complete this exercise.

	A	B	C	D	E	F
1			Mortgage Calculator			
2						
3	Inputs				Intermediate Calculations	
4	Negotiated Cost of House		$ 375,000.00		APR Based on Credit Rating	3.25%
5	Additional Down Payment		$ 5,000.00		Min Down Payment Required	$ 18,750.00
6	Date of First Payment		5/1/2016		Annual Property Tax	$ 2,812.50
7	Credit Rating		Excellent		Annual PMI	$ 1,756.25
8						
9	Constants				Outputs	
10	Property Tax Rate		0.75%		Total Down Payment	$ 23,750.00
11	Down Payment to Avoid PMI		20.00%		Amount of the Loan	$351,250.00
12	PMI Rate		0.50%		Monthly Payment (P&I)	$1,528.66
13	Term of Loan in Years		30		Monthly Property Tax	234.38
14	# of Payments Per Year		12		Monthly PMI	146.35
15					Total Monthly Payment	$ 1,909.39
16	Credit	Down Payment	APR		Date of Last Payment	4/1/2046
17	Excellent	5%	3.25%			
18	Good	10%	3.50%			
19	Fair	15%	4.25%			
20	Poor	20%	5.25%			
21						

FIGURE 2.43 Mortgage Data

a. Start a new Excel workbook, save it as **e02m2Loan_LastFirst**, rename Sheet1 **Payment**, add a new sheet, and then rename it **Range Names**.

b. Select the **Payment sheet**, type **Mortgage Calculator** in **cell A1**, and then merge and center the title on the first row in the **range A1:F1**. Apply bold, **18 pt size**, and **Gold, Accent 4, Darker 25% font color**.

c. Create and format the Inputs and Constants areas by doing the following:
   - Type the labels in the **range A3:A20**. For each label, such as *Negotiated Cost of House*, merge the cells, such as the **range A4:B4**, and apply **Align Text Left**. You will have to merge cells for nine labels.
   - Enter and format the *Inputs* and *Constants* values in column C.

d. Create the lookup table in the **range A16:C20** to use the credit ratings to identify the appropriate required percentage down payment and the respective APR by doing the following:
   - Type **Credit, Down Payment**, and **APR** in the **range A16:C16**.
   - Type the four credit ratings in the first column, the required down payment percentages in the second column, and the respective APRs in the third column.
   - Format the percentages, apply **Align Text Right**, and then indent the percentages in the cells as needed.

e. Assign range names to cells containing individual values in the *Inputs* and *Constants* sections. Do *not* use the *Create from Selection* feature because the labels are stored in merged cells. Assign a range name to the lookup table.

f. Type labels in the *Intermediate Calculations* and *Outputs* sections in column E and assign a range name to each cell in the **ranges F4:F7** and **F10:F12**. Widen column E as needed.

g. Enter formulas in the *Intermediate Calculations* and *Outputs* sections using range names to calculate the following:

- **APR** based on the borrower's credit rating by using a lookup function. Include the range_lookup argument to ensure an *exact match*. For example, a borrower who has an Excellent rating gets a 3.25% APR.
- **Minimum down payment required** amount by using a lookup function and calculation. Include the range_lookup argument to ensure an *exact match*. For example, a borrower who has an Excellent rating is required to pay a minimum of 5% down payment of the negotiated purchase price. Multiply the function results by the negotiated cost of the house. Hint: The calculation comes after the closing parenthesis.
- **Annual property tax** based on the negotiated cost of the house and the annual property tax rate.
- **Annual PMI**. If the borrower's total down payment (required and additional) is 20% or higher of the negotiated purchase price (multiply the cost by the PMI avoidance percentage), PMI is zero. If the total down payment is less than 20%, the borrower has to pay PMI based on multiplying the amount of the loan by the PMI rate.
- **Total down payment**, which is sum of the required minimum down payment (calculated previously) and any additional down payment entered in the Inputs section.
- **Amount of the loan**, which is the difference between the negotiated cost of the house and the total down payment.
- **Monthly payment** of principal and interest using the PMT function.
- **Monthly property tax**, the **monthly PMI**, and the **total monthly payment**.
- **Last payment date** using the EDATE function. The function's second argument must calculate the correct number of months based on the total length of the loan. For example, if the first payment date is 5/1/2016, the final payment date is 4/1/2046 for a 30-year loan. The last argument of the function must subtract 1 to ensure the last payment date is correct. If the last payment date calculated to 5/1/2046, you would be making an extra payment.

h. Format each section with fill color, bold, underline, number formats, borders, and column widths as shown in the figure.

i. Paste a list of range names in the Range Names worksheet. Insert a row above the list and type and format column labels above the two columns in the list of range names.

j. Center the worksheet data horizontally between the left and right margins.

k. Insert a footer with your name on the left side, the sheet name code in the center, and the file name code on the right side of both sheets.

l. Save and close the workbook, and submit based on your instructor's directions.

3 Professor's Grade Book

You are a teaching assistant for Dr. Denise Gerber, who teaches an introductory C# programming class at your college. One of your routine tasks is to enter assignment and test grades into the grade book. Now that the semester is almost over, you need to create formulas to calculate category averages, the overall weighted average, and the letter grade for each student. In addition, Dr. Gerber wants to see general statistics, such as average, median, low, and high for each graded assignment and test, as well as category averages and total averages. Furthermore, you need to create the grading scale on the documentation worksheet and use it to display the appropriate letter grade for each student.

a. Open *e02m3Grades* and save it as **e02m3Grades_LastFirst**.

b. Use breakpoints to enter the grading scale in the correct structure on the Documentation worksheet and name the grading scale range **Grades**. The grading scale is as follows:

95+	A
90–94.9	A–
87–89.9	B+
83–86.9	B
80–82.9	B–
77–79.9	C+
73–76.9	C
70–72.9	C–
67–69.9	D+
63–66.9	D
60–62.9	D–
0–59.9	F

c. Calculate the total lab points earned for the first student in **cell T8** in the Grades worksheet. The first student earned 93 lab points.

d. Calculate the average of the two midterm tests for the first student in **cell W8**. The student's midterm test average is 87.

e. Calculate the assignment average for the first student in **cell I8**. The formula should drop the lowest score before calculating the average. Hint: You need to use a combination of three functions: SUM, MIN, and COUNT. The argument for each function for the first student is B8:H8. Find the total points and subtract the lowest score. Then divide the remaining points by the number of assignments minus 1. The first student's assignment average is 94.2 after dropping the lowest assignment score.

f. Calculate the weighted total points based on the four category points (assignment average, lab points, midterm average, and final exam) and their respective weights (stored in the **range B40:B43**) in **cell Y8**. Use relative and absolute cell references as needed in the formula. The first student's total weighted score is 90.

g. Use a VLOOKUP function to calculate the letter grade equivalent in **cell Z8**. Use the range name in the function. The first student's letter grade is A–.

h. Copy the formulas down their respective columns for the other students.

i. Name the passing score threshold in **cell B5** with the range name **Passing**. Use an IF function to display a message in the last grade book column based on the student's semester performance. If a student earned a final score of 70 or higher, display *Enroll in CS 202*. Otherwise, display *RETAKE CS 101*. Remember to use quotation marks around the text arguments.

j. Calculate the average, median, low, and high scores for each assignment, lab, test, category average, and total score. Display individual averages with no decimal places; display category and final score averages with one decimal place. Display other statistics with no decimal places.

k. Insert a list of range names in the designated area in the Documentation worksheet. Complete the documentation by inserting your name, today's date, and a purpose statement in the designated areas.

DISCOVER

l. At your instructor's discretion, add a column to display each student's rank in the class. Use Help to learn how to insert the RANK function.

m. Select page setup options as needed to print the Grades worksheet on one page.

n. Insert a footer with your name on the left side, the sheet name code in the center, and the file name code on the right side of each worksheet.

o. Save and close the workbook, and submit based on your instructor's directions.

4 Facebook and YouTube

COLLABORATION CASE

FROM SCRATCH

Social media extends past friendships to organizational and product "fan" pages. Organizations such as Lexus, Pepsi, and universities create pages to provide information about their organizations. Some organizations even provide product details, such as the Lexus ES350. Facebook includes a wealth of information about Microsoft Office products. People share information, pose questions, and reply with their experiences.

a. Log in to your Facebook account. If you do not have a Facebook account, sign up for one and add at least two classmates as friends. Search for Microsoft Excel and click **Like**.

b. Review postings on the Microsoft Excel wall. Notice that some people post what they like most about Excel or how much it has improved their productivity. Post a note about one of your favorite features about Excel that you have learned so far or how you have used Excel in other classes or on the job. Start Word and, using the Snipping Tool, insert a screenshot of your posting. Save the document as **e02t1_LastFirst**.

c. Click the **Discussions link** on the Microsoft Excel Facebook page and find topics that relate to IF or VLOOKUP functions. Post a response to one of the discussions. Take a screenshot of your posting and insert it into your Word document.

d. Create a team of three students. Create one discussion that asks people to describe their favorite use of any of the nested functions used in this chapter. Each team member should respond to the posting. Monitor the discussion and, when you have a few responses, capture a screenshot of the dialogue and insert it into your Word document.

e. Save and close the document. Submit it based on your instructor's directions.

f. Go to www.youtube.com and search for one of these Excel topics: absolute references, mixed references, semi-selection, IF function, VLOOKUP function, circular references, statistical functions shown in Table 2.2, date functions shown in Table 2.3, or range names.

g. Watch several video clips and find one of particular interest to you.

h. Post the URL on your Facebook wall. Specify the topic and describe why you like this particular video.

i. Watch videos from the links posted by other students on their Facebook walls. Comment on at least two submissions. Point out what you like about the video or any suggestions you have for improvement.

j. If required by your instructor, insert screenshots of your postings in a Word document. Save and submit based on your instructor's directions.

Beyond the Classroom

College Sports Scores

You want to create a spreadsheet to display data for your favorite college sports team. Conduct an Internet search to identify the game dates, your team's scores, the opponent, and the opponent's score for each game for the last complete season. Enter the data into a new workbook and save the workbook as **e02b2Sports_LastFirst**. Games are usually scheduled seven days apart. Enter this value on a second sheet, assign a range name, and then use the range name in a formula to calculate the game dates based on the original game date. In some instances, you may have to enter a date if more or fewer days exist between two game dates. In the fifth column, use an IF function to determine if your team won or lost each game; display either *Win* or *Lose*. In the sixth column, use an IF function to calculate by how many points your team won each game or display an empty string by entering "" in the value_if_false argument if your team lost.

Create a statistics area to calculate the average, median, low, and high scores for your team. Below the won-by points column, use two different count functions to count the number of games won and lost. Use Help to learn about the COUNTIF function and use this function to count the number of games won based on the number of *Win* entries. Use mixed references in the function's first argument, copy the function, and then edit the second argument of the copied COUNTIF function to calculate the number of games lost. The summary area should have four count functions. Add titles and column labels, format data within the columns, and then include the URL of where you got the data. Include a footer with your name on the left side, the date code in the center, and the file name code on the right side. Save and close the workbook, and submit based on your instructor's directions.

Park City Condo Rental

You and some friends are planning a Labor Day vacation to Park City, Utah. You have secured a four-day condominium that costs $1,200. Some people will stay all four days; others will stay part of the weekend. One of your friends constructed a worksheet to help calculate each person's cost of the rental. The people who stay Thursday night will split the nightly cost evenly. To keep the costs down, everyone agreed to pay $30 per night per person for Friday, Saturday, and/or Sunday nights. Depending on the number of people who stay each night, the group may owe more money. Kyle, Ian, Isaac, and Daryl agreed to split the difference in the total rental cost and the amount the group members paid. Open *e02b3ParkCity*, address the circular reference error message that displays, and save the workbook as **e02b3ParkCity_LastFirst**.

Review the worksheet structure, including the assumptions and calculation notes at the bottom of the worksheet. Check the formulas and functions, making necessary corrections. With the existing data, the number of people staying each night is 5, 7, 10, and 10, respectively. The total paid given the above assumptions is $1,110, giving a difference of $90 to be divided evenly among the first four people. Kyle's share should be $172.50. In the cells containing errors, insert comments to describe the error and fix the formulas. Verify the accuracy of formulas by entering an IF function in **cell I1** to ensure the totals match. Nick, James, and Body inform you they can't stay Sunday night, and Rob wants to stay Friday night. Change the input accordingly. The updated total paid is now $1,200, and the difference is $150. Include a footer with your name on the left side, the date code in the center, and the file name code on the right side. Save and close the workbook, and submit based on your instructor's directions.

Interview Walkthough

SOFT SKILLS CASE

FROM SCRATCH

After watching the video, create a workbook named **e02b4Interview_LastFirst** that lists five to seven common interview questions in the first column. In the second column, enter a percentage weight for each question. For example, the first question might count 5% of the total. The total weights should be 100%. Include columns to rate five interviewees on the questions using a scale of 1–5 where 1 is low and 5 is high. Incude a column label with a first name for each interviewee. At the bottom of the first interviewee's column, use the AVERAGE function with the argument to multiply that person's individual scores by their respective weights using relative and absolute references correctly. Copy the formula to the other candidates.

Add an input area for a minimum weighted score of 4.5. Assign a range name to the score. On the row below the weighted scores, add a row labeled *Second Interview?* Enter an IF function for the first candidate: If the weighted score is greater than or equal to 4.5, then display *Yes*; otherwise, display *No*. Copy the function for the other candidates. Include a footer with your name on the left side, the date code in the center, and the file name code on the right side. Save and close the workbook, and submit based on your instructor's directions.

You are a sales representative at the local fitness center, Health & Fitness Gym. Your manager expects each representative to track weekly new membership data, so you created a spreadsheet to store data. Membership costs are based on membership type. Clients can rent a locker for an additional annual fee. You are required to collect a down payment based on membership type, determine the balance, and then calculate the monthly payment based on a standard interest rate. In addition, you need to calculate general statistics to summarize for your manager. Spot-check results to make sure you created formulas and functions correctly.

Perform Preliminary Work

You need to open the starting workbook you created, acknowledge the existing circular reference error, and assign a range name to the membership lookup table. You will correct the circular reference error later.

a. Open the *e02c1Gym* workbook, click **Help**, read about circular references, close the Help window that displays, and then save the workbook as **e02c1Gym_LastFirst**.

b. Assign the name **Membership** to the **range A18:C20**.

c. Insert a function to display the current date in **cell B2**.

Calculate Cost, Annual Total, and Total Due

You are ready to calculate the basic annual membership cost and the total annual cost. The basic annual membership is determined based on each client's membership type, using the lookup table.

a. Insert a lookup function in **cell C5** to display the basic annual membership cost for the first client.

b. Use an IF function in **cell E5** to calculate the annual total amount, which is the sum of the basic cost and locker fees for those who rent a locker. For people who do not rent a locker, the annual cost is only the cost shown in column C. The Locker column displays *Yes* for clients who rent a locker and *No* for those who don't.

c. Calculate the total amount due in **cell G5** for the first client based on the annual total and the number of years in the contract.

d. Copy the three formulas down their respective columns.

Determine the Down Payment and Balance

You need to collect a down payment based on the type of membership for each new client. Then you must determine how much each client owes.

a. Insert a lookup function in **cell H5** to display the amount of down payment for the first client based on the membership type.

b. Find and correct the circular reference for the balance. The balance is the difference between the total due and the down payment.

c. Copy the two formulas for the rest of the clients.

Calculate the Monthly Payment

Clients pay the remainder by making monthly payments. Monthly payments are based on the number of years specified in the client's contract and a standard interest rate.

a. Insert the function in **cell J5** to calculate the first client's monthly payment, using appropriate relative and absolute cell references.

b. Copy the formula down the column.

c. Edit the formula by changing the appropriate cell reference to a mixed cell reference. Copy the formula down.

Finalize the Workbook

You need to perform some basic statistical calculations and finalize the workbook with formatting and page setup options.

a. Calculate totals on row 14.

b. Insert the appropriate functions in the *Summary Statistics* section of the worksheet: **cells H18:H22**. Format the payments with **Accounting Number Format** and format the number of new members appropriately.

c. Format the other column headings on rows 4 and 17 to match the fill color in the **range E17:H17**. Wrap text for the column headings.

d. Format the monetary values for Andrews and the total row with **Accounting Number Format**. Use zero decimal places for whole amounts and display two decimal places for the monthly payment. Apply **Comma Style** to the internal monetary values. Underline the values before the totals and apply **Double Accounting Underline** (found in the Format Cells dialog box) for the totals.

e. Set **0.3"** left and right margins and ensure the page prints on only one page.

f. Insert a footer with your name on the left side, the date code in the center, and the file name code on the right side.

g. Save and close the workbook, and submit based on your instructor's directions.

Charts

CHAPTER **3**

Depicting Data Visually

Yuri Arcurs/Shutterstock

CASE STUDY | Computer Job Outlook

You are an academic advisor for the School of Computing at a private university in Seattle, Washington. You will be visiting high schools in the state over the next few weeks to discuss the computing programs at the university and to inform students about the job outlook in the computing industry.

Your assistant, Doug Demers, researched growing computer-related jobs in the *Occupational Outlook Handbook* published by the Bureau of Labor Statistics on the U.S. Department of Labor's Web site. In particular, Doug listed seven jobs, the number of those jobs in 2010, the projected number of jobs by 2020, the growth in percentage increase and number of jobs, and the 2010 median pay. This data set shows an 18%–31% increase in computer-related jobs in that 10-year time period.

To prepare for your presentation to encourage students to enroll in your School of Computing, you want to create several charts that depict the job growth in the computer industry. You know that different charts provide different perspectives on the data. After you complete the charts, you will be able to use them in a variety of formats, such as presentations, fliers, brochures, and press releases.

Chart Creation Basics

The expression "a picture is worth a thousand words" means that a visual can be a more effective way to communicate or interpret data than words or numbers. Storing, organizing, and performing calculations on quantitative data are important, but you must also be able to analyze the data. A *chart* is a visual representation of numerical data that compares data and helps reveal trends or patterns to help people make informed decisions. An effective chart depicts data in a clear, easy-to-interpret manner and contains enough data to be useful without overwhelming your audience.

A chart may include several chart elements. The *chart area* contains the entire chart and all of its elements, including the plot area, titles, legend, and labels. The *plot area* is the region containing the graphical representation of the values in the data series. Two axes form a border around the plot area.

The *X-axis* is a horizontal border that provides a frame of reference for measuring data horizontally. The *Y-axis* is a vertical border that provides a frame of reference for measuring data vertically. Excel refers to the axes as the category axis and value axis. The *category axis* displays descriptive group names or labels (such as college names, cities, or equal amounts of time) to identify data. Categories are usually defined by column or row labels (such as job titles or years) in the worksheet. The *value axis* displays incremental numbers to identify the worksheet values (such as number of jobs or revenue) used to create the chart. A *legend* is a key that identifies the color, gradient, picture, texture, or pattern assigned to each data series in a chart. For example, blue might represent values for 2010, and orange might represent values for 2020.

In this section, you will select the data source, choose the best chart type to represent numerical data, and designate the chart's location.

Selecting the Data Source

Before creating a chart, organize the worksheet data so that the values in columns and rows are on the same value system (such as dollars or units), make sure labels are descriptive, and delete any blank rows or columns that exist in the primary data set. Look at the structure of the worksheet—the column labels, the row labels, the quantitative data, and the calculated values. Decide what you want to convey to your audience by answering these questions:

- Does the worksheet hold a single set of data, such as average snowfall at one ski resort, or multiple sets of data, such as average snowfall at several ski resorts?

- Do you want to depict data for one specific time period or over several time periods, such as several years or decades?

Identify the data range by selecting values and labels that you want to include in the chart. If the values and labels are not stored in adjacent cells, hold Ctrl while selecting the nonadjacent ranges. Do not select worksheet titles or subtitles; doing so would add unnecessary data to the chart.

Figure 3.1 shows a worksheet containing computer-related job titles, the number of jobs in 2010, the projected number of jobs by 2020, and other details. Row 3 contains labels merged and centered over individual column labels in row 5. Row 4 is blank and hidden. It is a good practice to insert a blank row between merged labels and individual column labels. Without the blank row, you would not be able to correctly sort data; the column headings would be sorted with the data.

Each cell containing a value is a *data point*. For example, the value 110,800 is a data point for the number of Database Administrators in 2010. A group of related data points that display in row(s) or column(s) in the worksheet create a *data series*. For example, the values 110,800 and 144,800 comprise the Database Administrators data series. Row and column labels (such as job titles, years, growth, etc.) are used to create *category labels* in charts.

	A	B	C	D	E	F
1	Computer-Related Jobs					
2						
3		# of Jobs		Job Growth		Median Pay
5		2010	2020 Est.	% Growth	# of New Jobs	2010
6	Database Administrators	110,800	144,800	31%	34,000	$ 73,490
7	Info Security Analysts	302,300	367,900	22%	65,600	$ 75,600
8	CIS Managers	307,900	363,700	18%	55,800	$ 115,780
9	Network/System Admins	347,200	443,800	28%	96,600	$ 69,160
10	Programmers	363,100	406,800	12%	43,700	$ 71,380
11	Software App Developers	520,800	664,500	28%	143,700	$ 90,530
12	Systems Analysts	544,400	664,800	22%	120,400	$ 77,740
14	Source: Bureau of Labor Statistics, U.S. Department of Labor, *Occupational Outlook Handbook, 2012-13 Edition*, on the Internet at http://www.bls.gov/					

FIGURE 3.1 Sample Data Set

 TIP **Avoid Using Data Aggregates and Individual Values**

Make sure that each data series uses the same scale. For example, do not include data aggregates (such as totals or averages) with individual values. The data source used to create the chart in Figure 3.2 mixes individual number of jobs by title with the total number of jobs, which distorts the scale from the comparison of the number of jobs for each job title.

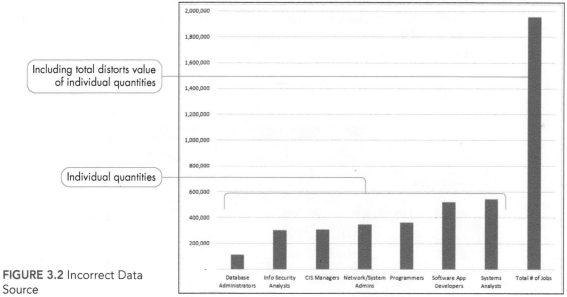

Including total distorts value of individual quantities

Individual quantities

FIGURE 3.2 Incorrect Data Source

TIP **Charts Update When Data Change**

After you create a chart, you may need to change the worksheet data. When you change the worksheet data, Excel updates any charts that you created based on the data.

Choosing a Chart Type

When you select a range of cells and position the mouse pointer over that selected range, Excel displays the Quick Analysis button in the bottom-right corner of the selected area. The Excel 2013 Quick Analysis tool enables you to use analytical tools, such as charts, to quickly examine data. You should select a chart type that appropriately represents the data and tells a story. You can create different charts from the same data set, but each chart tells a different story. For example, one chart might compare the number of computer-related jobs between 2010 and 2020, and another chart might indicate the percentage of new jobs by job title. The most commonly used chart types are column, bar, line, and pie (see Table 3.1). Each chart type is designed to provide a unique perspective to the selected data.

TABLE 3.1 Common Chart Types

Chart	Chart Type	Description
	Column	Displays values in vertical columns where the height represents the value; the taller the column, the larger the value. Categories display along the horizontal (category) axis.
	Bar	Displays values in horizontal bars where the width represents the value; the wider the bar, the larger the value. Categories display along the vertical (category) axis.
	Line	Displays category data on the horizontal axis and value data on the vertical axis. Appropriate to show continuous data to depict trends over time, such as months, years, or decades.
	Pie	Shows proportion of individual data points to the sum of all those data points.

To create a chart, do the following:

1. Select the data and click the Quick Analysis button.
2. Click CHARTS in the Quick Analysis gallery (see Figure 3.3).
3. Position the mouse over each recommended chart thumbnail to see the type of chart that would be created from the selected data.
4. Click the thumbnail of the chart you want to create.

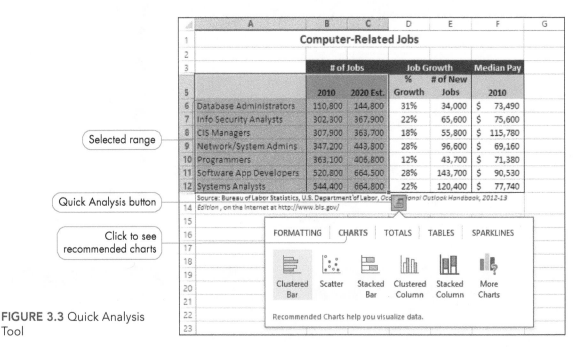

FIGURE 3.3 Quick Analysis Tool

Another way to create a chart is to click the Insert tab and do one of the following:

- Click the chart type (such as Column) in the Charts group and click a chart subtype (such as Clustered Column) from the chart gallery (see Figure 3.4).
- Click Recommended Charts in the Charts group to open the Insert Chart dialog box (see Figure 3.5), click a thumbnail of the chart you want, and then click OK.

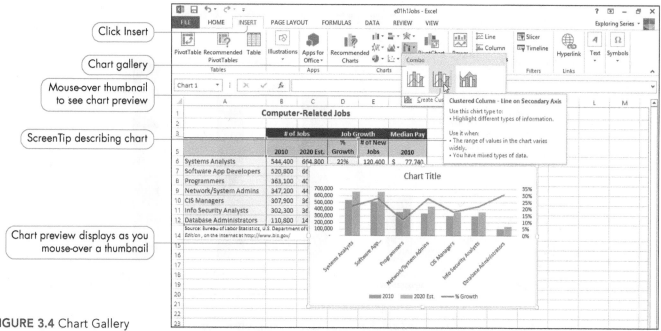

Click Insert

Chart gallery

Mouse-over thumbnail to see chart preview

ScreenTip describing chart

Chart preview displays as you mouse-over a thumbnail

FIGURE 3.4 Chart Gallery

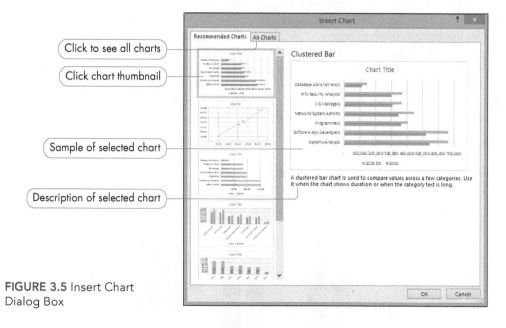

Click to see all charts

Click chart thumbnail

Sample of selected chart

Description of selected chart

FIGURE 3.5 Insert Chart Dialog Box

Create a Column Chart

STEP 1 ❯❯

A *column chart* displays data vertically in columns. Create a column chart to compare values across different categories, such as population among cities in a state or number of computer-related jobs between two years. Column charts are most effective when they are limited to seven or fewer categories. If more categories exist, the columns appear too close together, making it difficult to read the labels.

The column chart in Figure 3.6 compares the number of projected jobs by job title for 2020 using the data in Figure 3.1. The first four job titles stored in the first column (range A6:A9) form the category axis, and the increments of the number of jobs in 2020 (range C6:C9) form the value axis. The height of each column represents the value of individual data points: The larger the value, the taller the column. For example, the Info Security Analysts column is taller than the Database Administrators column, indicating that more jobs are projected for Info Security Analysts than Database Administrators.

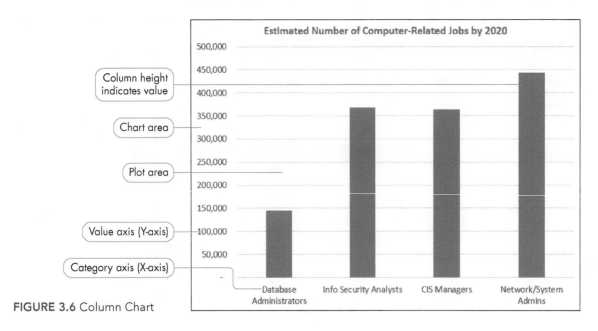

FIGURE 3.6 Column Chart

A *clustered column chart* compares groups—or clusters—of columns set side by side for easy comparison. The clustered column chart facilitates quick comparisons across data series, and it is effective for comparing several data points among categories. Figure 3.7 shows a clustered column chart created from the data in Figure 3.1. By default, the row labels appear on the category axis, and the yearly data series appear as columns with the value axis showing incremental numbers. Excel assigns a different color to each yearly data series and includes a legend so that you will know what color represents which data series. The 2010 data series is light blue, and the 2020 data series is dark blue. This chart makes it easy to compare the predicted job growth from 2010 to 2020 for each job title and then to compare the trends among job titles.

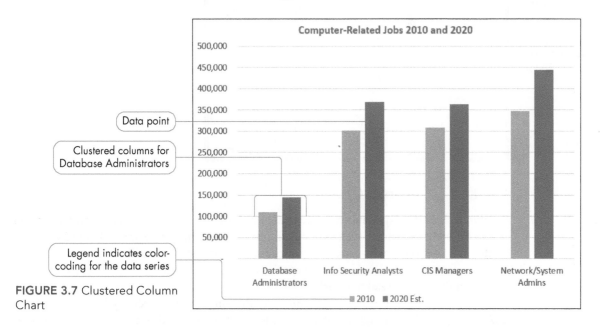

FIGURE 3.7 Clustered Column Chart

Figure 3.8 shows a clustered column chart in which the categories and data series are reversed. The years appear on the category axis, and the job titles appear as color-coded data series and in the legend. This chart gives a different perspective from that in Figure 3.7 in that it compares the number of jobs within a given year, such as 2010.

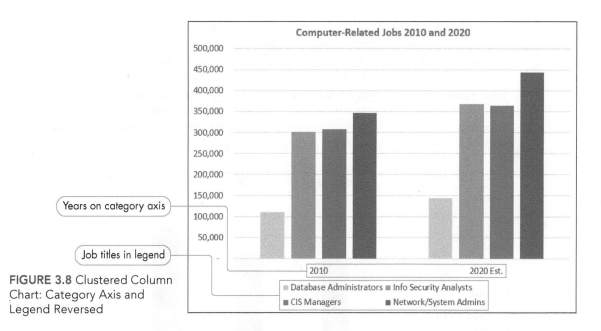

FIGURE 3.8 Clustered Column Chart: Category Axis and Legend Reversed

A *stacked column chart* shows the relationship of individual data points to the whole category. A stacked column chart displays only one column for each category. Each category within the stacked column is color-coded for one data series. Use the stacked column chart when you want to compare total values across categories, as well as to display the individual category values. Figure 3.9 shows a stacked column chart in which a single column represents each categorical year, and each column stacks color-coded data-point segments representing the different jobs. The stacked column chart enables you to compare the total number of computer-related jobs for each year. The height of each color-coded data point enables you to identify the relative contribution of each job to the total number of jobs for a particular year. A disadvantage of the stacked column chart is that the segments within each column do not start at the same point, making it more difficult to compare individual segment values across categories.

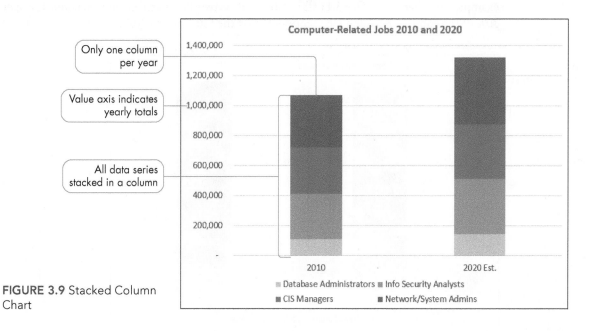

FIGURE 3.9 Stacked Column Chart

When you create a stacked column chart, make sure data are *additive*: each column represents a sum of the data for each segment. Figure 3.9 correctly uses years as the category axis and the jobs as data series. Within each year, Excel adds the number of jobs, and the columns display the total number of jobs. For example, the estimated total number of computer-related jobs in 2020 is about 1,300,000. Figure 3.10 shows an incorrectly constructed stacked column chart because the yearly number of jobs by job title is *not* additive. It is incorrect to state that about 800,000 Network/System Admin jobs exist. Be careful when constructing stacked column charts to ensure that they lead to logical interpretation of data.

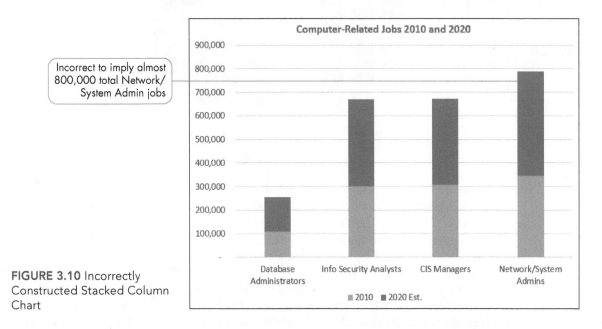

FIGURE 3.10 Incorrectly Constructed Stacked Column Chart

A **100% stacked column chart** converts individual data points into percentages of the total value. Each data series is a different color of the stack, representing a percentage. The total of each column is 100%. This type of chart depicts contributions to the whole. For example, the chart in Figure 3.11 illustrates that Network/System Admins account for over 30% of the computer-related jobs represented by the four job categories.

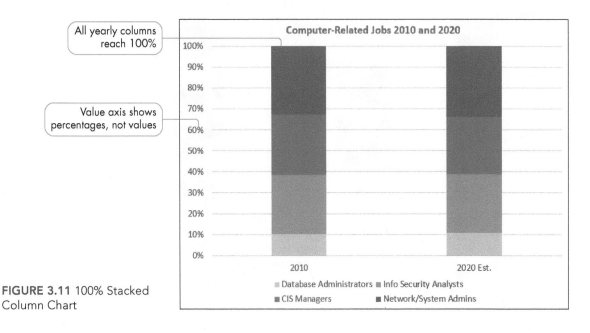

FIGURE 3.11 100% Stacked Column Chart

TIP | Avoid 3-D Charts

Avoid creating 3-D charts, because the third dimension is a superficial enhancement that usually distorts the charted data. For example, some columns appear taller or shorter than they actually are because of the angle of the 3-D effect, or some columns might be hidden by taller columns in front of them.

Create a Bar Chart

STEP 3》 A *bar chart* compares values across categories using horizontal bars. The horizontal axis displays values, and the vertical axis displays categories (see Figure 3.12). Bar charts and column charts tell a similar story: they both compare categories of data. A bar chart is preferable when category names are long, such as *Database Administrators*. A bar chart enables category names to appear in an easy-to-read format, whereas a column chart might display category names at an awkward angle or in a smaller font size. The overall decision between a column and a bar chart may come down to the fact that different data may look better with one chart type than the other.

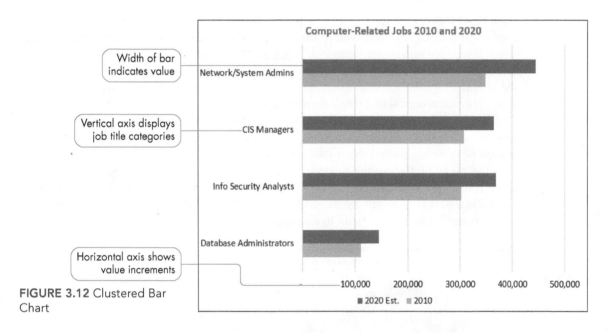

FIGURE 3.12 Clustered Bar Chart

Create a Line Chart

A *line chart* displays lines connecting data points to show trends over equal time periods. Excel displays each data series with a different line color. The category axis (X-axis) represents time, such as 10-year increments, whereas the value axis (Y-axis) represents the value, such as money or quantity. A line chart enables you to detect trends because the line continues to the next data point. To show each data point, choose the Line with Markers chart type. Figure 3.13 shows a line chart indicating the number of majors from 2005 to 2020 at five-year increments. The number of Arts majors remains relatively constant, but the number of Tech & Computing majors increases significantly over time, especially between the years 2010 and 2020.

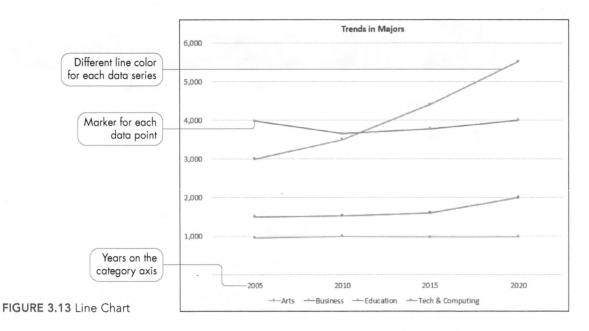

Different line color for each data series

Marker for each data point

Years on the category axis

FIGURE 3.13 Line Chart

Create a Pie Chart

STEP 4 >> A *pie chart* shows each data point as a proportion to the whole data series. The pie chart displays as a circle, or "pie," where the entire pie represents the total value of the data series. Each slice represents a single data point. The larger the slice, the larger percentage that data point contributes to the whole. Use a pie chart when you want to convey percentage or market share. Unlike column, bar, and line charts that typically chart multiple data series, pie charts represent a single data series only.

The pie chart in Figure 3.14 divides the pie representing the estimated number of new jobs into seven slices, one for each job title. The size of each slice is proportional to the percentage of total computer-related jobs for that year. The chart depicts a single data series from the range E6:E12 on the worksheet in Figure 3.1. Excel creates a legend to indicate which color represents which pie slice. When you create a pie chart, limit it to about seven slices. Pie charts with too many slices appear too busy to interpret, or shades of the same color scheme become too difficult to distinguish.

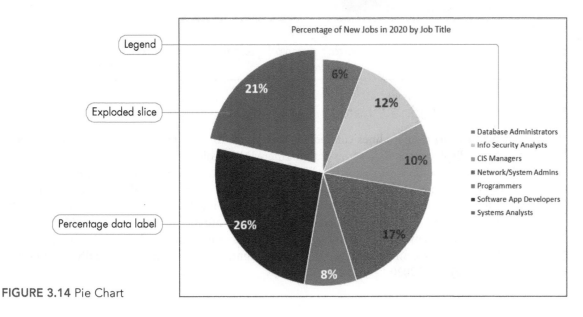

Legend

Exploded slice

Percentage data label

FIGURE 3.14 Pie Chart

The projected number of new Systems Analyst jobs is 33,900, which accounts for 21% of the new jobs. You can focus a person's attention on a particular slice by separating one or more slices from the rest of the chart in an *exploded pie chart*, as shown in Figure 3.14.

Change the Chart Type

After you create a chart, you may decide that the data would be better represented by a different type of chart. For example, you might decide a bar chart would display the labels better than a column chart. When you select a chart, Chart Tools displays on the Ribbon with the Design and Format tabs. To change the type of an existing chart, do the following:

1. Select the chart and click the DESIGN tab.
2. Click Change Chart Type in the Type group to open the Change Chart Type dialog box, which is similar to the Insert Chart dialog box.
3. Click the ALL CHARTS tab within the dialog box.
4. Click a chart type on the left side of the dialog box.
5. Click a chart subtype on the right side of the dialog box and click OK.

Create Other Chart Types

Two other chart types that are used for specialized analysis are X Y (scatter) charts and stock charts.

An *X Y (scatter) chart* shows a relationship between two numerical variables using their X and Y coordinates. Excel plots one variable on the horizontal X-axis and the other variable on the vertical Y-axis. Scatter charts are often used to represent data in educational, scientific, and medical experiments. Figure 3.15 shows the relationship between the number of minutes students view a training video and their test scores.

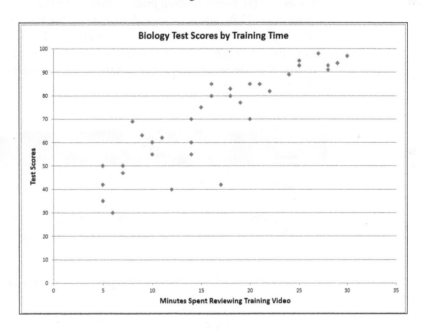

FIGURE 3.15 X Y (Scatter) Chart

A *stock chart* shows fluctuations in stock changes. You can select one of four stock subtypes: High-Low-Close, Open-High-Low-Close, Volume-High-Low-Close, and Volume-Open-High-Low-Close. The High-Low-Close stock chart marks a stock's trading range on a given day with a vertical line from the lowest to the highest stock prices. Rectangles mark the opening and closing prices. Figure 3.16 shows three days of stock prices for a particular company.

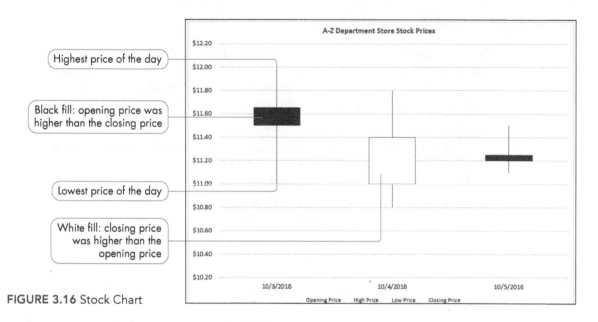

FIGURE 3.16 Stock Chart

The rectangle represents the difference in the opening and closing prices. If the rectangle has a white fill, the closing price is higher than the opening price. If the rectangle has a black fill, the opening price is higher than the closing price. In Figure 3.16, on October 3, the opening price was $11.65, and the closing price was $11.50. A line below the rectangle indicates that the lowest trading price is lower than the opening and closing prices. The lowest price was $11.00 on October 3. A line above the rectangle indicates the highest trading price is higher than the opening and closing prices. The highest price was $12.00 on October 3. If no line exists below the rectangle, the lowest price equals either the opening or closing price, and if no line exists above the rectangle, the highest price equals either the opening or closing price.

TIP | Arrange Data for a Stock Chart

To create an Open-High-Low-Close stock chart, you must arrange data with Opening Price, High Price, Low Price, and Closing Price as column labels in that sequence. If you want to create other variations of stock charts, you must arrange data in a structured sequence required by Excel.

Table 3.2 lists and describes other types of charts you can create in Excel.

TABLE 3.2 Other Chart Types

Chart	Chart Type	Description
	Area	Similar to a line chart in that it shows trends over time; however, the area chart displays colors between the lines to help illustrate the magnitude of changes.
	Surface	Represents numeric data and numeric categories. Takes on some of the same characteristics as a topographic map of hills and valleys.
	Doughnut	A derivative of a pie chart showing relationship of parts to a whole, but the doughnut chart can display more than one data series.
	Bubble	A derivative of a scatter chart in which both the horizontal and vertical axes are value axes. The third value determines the size of the bubble, where the larger the value, the larger the bubble. Do not select the column labels, as they might distort the data.
	Radar	Uses each category as a spoke radiating from the center point to the outer edges of the chart. Each spoke represents each data series, and lines connect the data points between spokes, similar to a spider web. You can create a radar chart to compare aggregate values for several data series.
	Combo	Combines two chart types (such as column and line) to plot different data types (such as values and percentages).

Moving, Sizing, and Printing a Chart

Excel inserts the chart as an embedded object in the current worksheet, often to the right side of, but sometimes on top of and covering up, the data area. After you insert a chart, you usually need to move it to a different location, adjust its size, and prepare to print it.

Move a Chart

To move the chart on the active worksheet, position the mouse pointer over the chart area. When you see the Chart Area ScreenTip and the mouse pointer includes the white arrow-head and a four-headed arrow, drag the chart to the desired location.

You can place the chart in a separate worksheet, called a *chart sheet*. A chart sheet contains a single chart only; you cannot enter data and formulas on a chart sheet. If you leave the chart in the same worksheet, you can print the data and chart on the same page. If you want to print or view a full-sized chart, move the chart to its own chart sheet. To move a chart to another sheet or a chart sheet, do the following:

1. Select the chart.
2. Click the DESIGN tab and click Move Chart in the Location group to open the Move Chart dialog box (see Figure 3.17).
3. Select one of these options to indicate where you want to move the chart:

   - Click *New sheet* to move the chart to its own sheet.
   - Click *Object in*, click the *Object in* arrow, and select the worksheet to which you want to move the chart. The default chart sheet is Chart1, but you can rename it in the Move Chart dialog box or similarly to the way you rename other sheet tabs. Click OK.

Design tab

Click to move selected chart

Select location to place chart

FIGURE 3.17 Design Tab and Move Chart Dialog Box

Size a Chart

If you keep a chart in a worksheet, you can size it to fit in a particular range or to ensure the chart elements are proportional. To change the chart size, do the following:

1. Select the chart.
2. Position the mouse pointer on the outer edge of the chart where you see eight small white-filled squares, called *sizing handles*.
3. When the mouse pointer changes to a two-headed arrow, drag the border to adjust the chart's height or width. Drag a corner sizing handle to increase or decrease the height and width of the chart at the same time. Press and hold down Shift as you drag a corner sizing handle to change the height and width proportionately.

You can also change the chart size by clicking the Format tab and changing the height and width values in the Size group (see Figure 3.18).

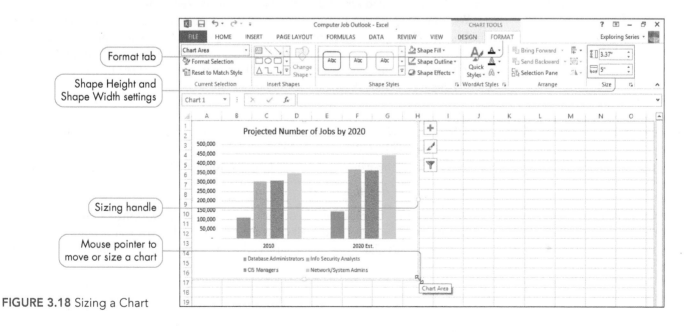

Format tab

Shape Height and Shape Width settings

Sizing handle

Mouse pointer to move or size a chart

FIGURE 3.18 Sizing a Chart

Print a Chart

If you embedded a chart on the same sheet as the data source, you need to decide if you want to print the data only, the data *and* the chart, or the chart only. To print the data only, select the data, click the File tab, click Print, click the first arrow in the Settings section and select Print Selection, and then click Print. To print only the chart, select the chart, click the File tab, click Print, make sure the default setting is Print Selected Chart, and then click Print to print the chart as a full-page chart. If the data and chart are on the same worksheet, print the worksheet contents to print both, but do not select either the chart or the data before displaying the Print options. The preview shows you what will print. Make sure it displays what you want to print before clicking Print.

If you moved the chart to a chart sheet, the chart is the only item on that worksheet. When you display the print options, the default is Print Active Sheets, and the chart will print as a full-page chart.

Quick
Concepts

1. Why should you not include aggregates, such as totals or averages, along with individual data series in a chart? **p. 135**

2. What is the purpose of each of these chart types: (a) column, (b) bar, (c) line, and (d) pie? **p. 136**

3. How can you use the Quick Analysis button to create a chart? **p. 136**

4. After you create a chart, where is it located by default? What do you usually do to the chart immediately after creating it? **p. 145**

Watch the Video for this Hands-On Exercise!

MyITLab®
HOE1 Training

1 Chart Creation Basics

Doug Demers, your assistant, gathered data about seven computer-related jobs from the *Occupational Outlook Handbook* online. He organized the data into a structured worksheet that contains the job titles, the number of jobs in 2010, the projected number of jobs by 2020, and other data. Now you are ready to transform the data into visually appealing charts.

Skills covered: Create a Clustered Column Chart • Create a Bar Chart • Change the Chart Position, Size, and Type • Create a Pie Chart

STEP 1 >> CREATE A CLUSTERED COLUMN CHART

You want to compare the number of jobs in 2010 to the projected number of jobs in 2020 for all seven computer-related professions that Doug entered into the worksheet. You decide to create a clustered column chart to depict this data. After you create this chart, you will move it to its own chart sheet. Refer to Figure 3.19 as you complete Step 1.

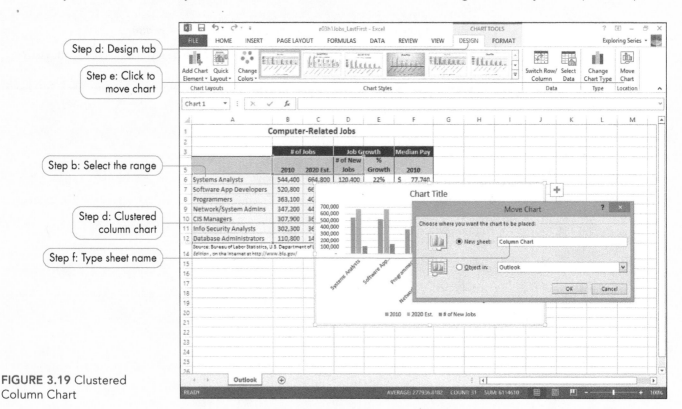

FIGURE 3.19 Clustered Column Chart

a. Open *e03h1Jobs* and save it as **e03h1Jobs_LastFirst**.

> **TROUBLESHOOTING:** If you make any major mistakes in this exercise, you can close the file, open *e03h1Jobs* again, and then start this exercise over.

b. Select the **range A5:D12**.

> You selected the job titles, the number of jobs in 2010, the projected number of jobs in 2020, and the number of new jobs.

c. Click the **Quick Analysis button** at the bottom-right corner of the selected range and click **CHARTS**.

The Quick Analysis gallery displays recommended charts based on the selected range.

d. Position the mouse pointer over *Clustered Column* to see a live preview of what the chart would look like and click **Clustered Column**.

Excel inserts a clustered column chart based on the selected data.

The DESIGN tab displays on the Ribbon.

e. Click **Move Chart** in the Location group to open the Move Chart dialog box.

f. Click **New sheet**, type **Column Chart**, and click **OK**. Save the workbook.

Excel moves the clustered column chart to a new sheet called Column Chart. Later, you will modify the chart.

STEP 2 ≫ CREATE A BAR CHART

You want to create a bar chart to depict the number of jobs in 2010 and the number of new jobs that will be created by 2020. Refer to Figure 3.20 as you complete Step 2.

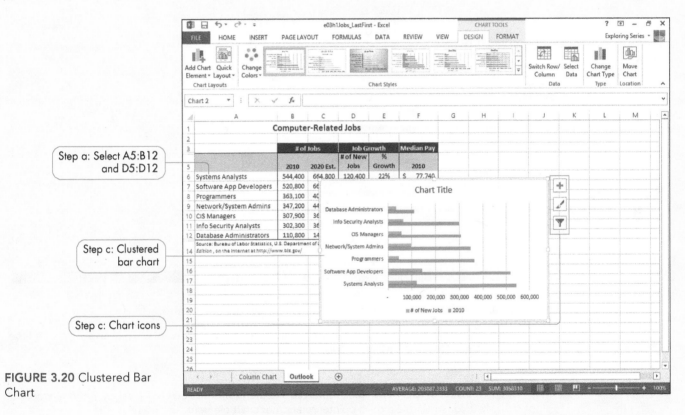

FIGURE 3.20 Clustered Bar Chart

a. Click the **Outlook sheet tab**, select the **range A5:B12**, press and hold **Ctrl**, and then select the range **D5:D12**.

You selected the job title labels, the number of jobs in 2010, and the number of new jobs.

 **Parallel Ranges**

Nonadjacent ranges should be parallel so that the legend will correctly reflect the data series. This means that each range should contain the same number of related cells. For example, A5:A12, B5:B12, and D5:D12 are parallel ranges.

b. Click the **INSERT tab** and click **Insert Bar Chart** in the Charts group.

A gallery containing thumbnails of different bar charts displays.

c. Click **Clustered Bar** in the 2-D Bar group. Save the workbook.

Excel inserts the clustered bar chart in the worksheet. Three icons display to the right side of the selected chart: Chart Elements, Chart Styles, and Chart Filters.

STEP 3 ≫ CHANGE THE CHART POSITION, SIZE, AND TYPE

Because the bar chart overlaps the data, you need to move it. You decide to position it below the job outlook data and adjust its size. Finally, you want to change the chart to a stacked bar chart to show the total jobs in 2020 based on the number of jobs in 2010 and the number of new jobs. Refer to Figure 3.21 as you complete Step 3.

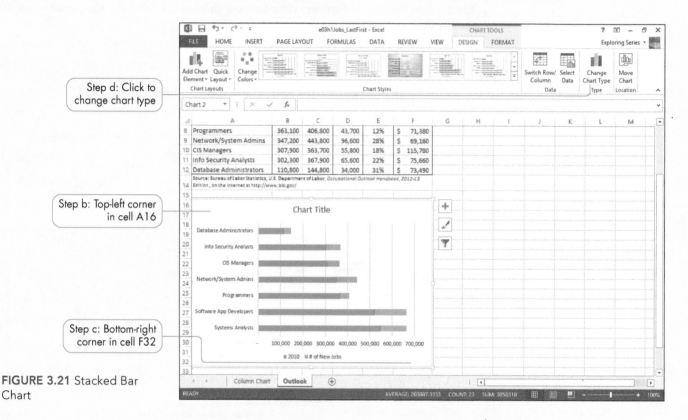

FIGURE 3.21 Stacked Bar Chart

a. Position the mouse pointer over the empty area of the chart area.

The mouse pointer includes a four-headed arrow with the regular white arrowhead, and the Chart Area ScreenTip displays.

> **TROUBLESHOOTING:** Make sure you see the Chart Area ScreenTip as you perform step b. If you move the mouse pointer to another chart element—such as the legend—you will move or size that element instead of moving the entire chart.

b. Drag the chart so that the top-left corner of the chart appears in **cell A16**.

You positioned the chart below the worksheet data.

c. Drag the bottom-right sizing handle through **cell F32**.

You changed both the height and the width at the same time.

d. Click **Change Chart Type** in the Type group, click **Stacked Bar** in the top center of the dialog box, and then click **OK**. Save the workbook.

Excel stacks the 2010 number of new jobs data series into one column per job title. This chart tells the story of where the projected number of jobs in 2020 come from: the number of existing jobs in 2010 (blue) and the number of new jobs (orange).

STEP 4 ≫ CREATE A PIE CHART

You decide to create a pie chart that depicts the percentage of new jobs by job title created out of the total number of new jobs created, which is 559,800. After creating the pie chart, you will move it to its own sheet. Finally, you want to draw attention to the job that has the largest slice by exploding it. Refer to Figure 3.22 as you complete Step 4.

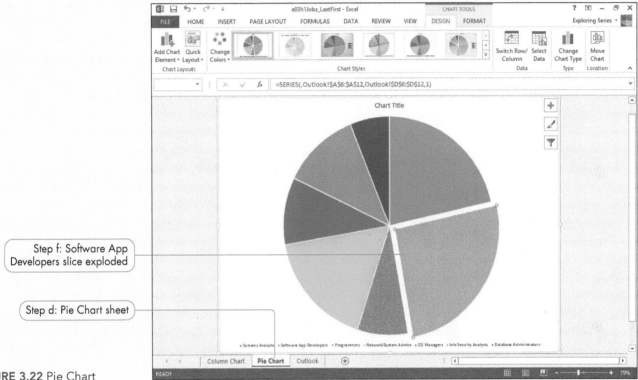

FIGURE 3.22 Pie Chart

a. Select the **range A6:A12** and press and hold **Ctrl** as you select the **range D6:D12**.

> **TROUBLESHOOTING:** Do not select cells A5 and D5 this time because you are creating a pie chart. Doing so would add unnecessary data to the chart.

b. Click the **INSERT tab**, click **Insert Pie or Doughnut** in the Charts group, and then select **Pie** in the 2-D Pie group on the gallery.

The pie chart may overlap part of the worksheet data and the stacked bar chart.

c. Click **Move Chart** in the Location group on the DESIGN tab.

The Move Chart dialog box opens.

d. Click **New sheet**, type **Pie Chart**, and then click **OK**.

Excel creates a new sheet called Pie Chart. The pie chart is the only object on that sheet.

e. Click the **Software App Developers orange slice**, pause, and then click it again.

The first click selects all slices of the pie. The second click selects only the Software App Developers slice.

> **TROUBLESHOOTING:** If you double-click the pie chart, the Format Data Series task pane opens on the right side of the chart. Click its Close button and click the orange slice one time.

    f. Drag the **Software App Developers orange slice** away from the pie a little bit.

    g. Save the workbook. Keep the workbook open if you plan to continue with the next Hands-On Exercise. If not, close the workbook and exit Excel.

Chart Elements

After you create a chart, you usually need to add components to describe the chart. Adding descriptive text for labels provides information for the reader to comprehend the chart. When you create a chart, one or more components may display by default. For example, when you created the charts in Hands-On Exercise 1, Excel displayed a placeholder for the chart title and displayed a legend so that you know which color represents which data series.

When you select a chart, Excel displays three icons to the right side the chart, the first of which is Chart Elements. In addition, the Design tab contains the Chart Layouts group so that you can add and customize chart elements.

In this section, you will learn how to add and format chart elements.

Adding Chart Elements

A *chart element* is a component that completes or helps clarify the chart. Some chart elements, such as chart titles, should be included in every chart. Other elements are optional. Table 3.3 describes the chart elements, and Figure 3.23 illustrates several chart elements.

TABLE 3.3 Chart Elements

Element	Description
Axes	Category axis labels, such as job titles, and the value axis quantities in increments in column, bar, and line charts. Axes display by default.
Axis titles	Labels that describe the category and value axes. You can display axis titles, such as *In Millions of Dollars* or *Top 7 Computer Job Titles*, to clarify the axes. Axis titles are not displayed by default.
Chart title	Label that describes the entire chart. It should reflect the purpose of the chart. For example, *Houses Sold* is too generic, but *Houses Sold in Seattle in 2016* indicates the what (Houses), the where (Seattle), and the when (2016). The default is *Chart Title*.
Data labels	Descriptive labels that show exact value or name of a data point. Data labels are not displayed by default.
Data table	A grid that contains the data source values and labels. If you embed a chart on the same worksheet as the data source, you might not need to include a data table. Only add a data table with a chart that is on a chart sheet.
Error bars	Visuals that indicate the standard error amount, a percentage, or a standard deviation for a data point or marker. Error bars are not displayed by default.
Gridlines	Horizontal or vertical lines that span across the chart to help people identify the values plotted by the visual elements, such as a column. Excel displays horizontal gridlines for column, line, scatter, stock, surface, and bubble charts and vertical gridlines for bar charts. Gridlines may display by default, depending on the chart type.
Legend	A key that identifies the color, gradient, picture, texture, or pattern assigned to each data series. The legend is displayed by default for particular charts.
Trendline	A line that depicts trends or helps forecast future data, such as estimating future sales or number of births in a region. You can add a trendline to column, bar, line, stock, scatter, and bubble charts. Excel will analyze the current trends to display a line indicating future values based on the current trend.

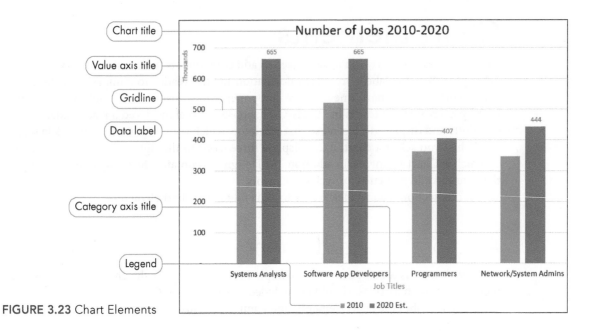

FIGURE 3.23 Chart Elements

To add a chart element, do the following:

1. Click the Chart Elements button to the right side of the chart (see Figure 3.24).
2. Click an empty check box to display an element, or position the mouse pointer on an element and click the triangle to select more specific chart elements. For example, if you click the triangle to the right of Axis Titles, you select on which axis to include a title.
3. If you selected a title, type the text for the title, and then press Enter.
4. Click the Chart Elements button again to close the menu.

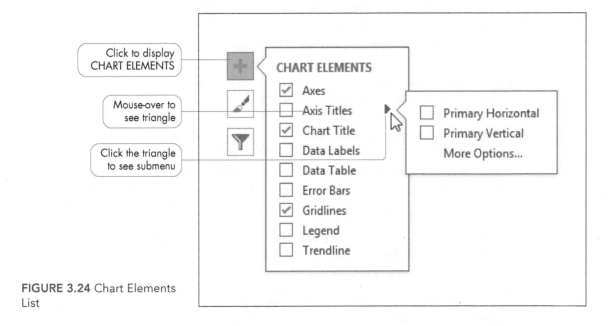

FIGURE 3.24 Chart Elements List

TIP **Remove an Element**

To remove an element, click Chart Elements and deselect a check box. Alternatively, click Add Chart Element in the Chart Layouts group on the Chart Tools Design tab, position the mouse pointer over the element name, and then select None.

To use the Design tab to add or remove a chart element, do the following:

1. Click the DESIGN tab.
2. Click Add Chart Element in the Chart Layouts group.
3. Point to an element and select from that element's submenu (see Figure 3.25).
4. If you selected a title, type the text for the title and press Enter.

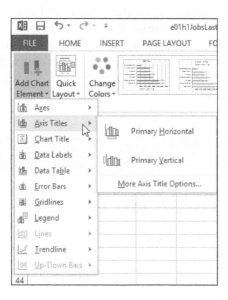

FIGURE 3.25 Chart Elements Menu and Submenu

Position the Chart Title

Excel includes the placeholder text *Chart Title* above the chart when you create a chart. You should replace that text with a descriptive title. To change the chart title text, click the Chart Title placeholder, type the text, and then press Enter. You can select the position of the title by doing the following:

1. Click the Chart Elements button to the right side of the chart.
2. Position the mouse pointer over Chart Title and click the triangle on the right side.
3. Select one of the options:
   - Above Chart: Centers the title above the plot area, decreasing the plot area size to make room for the chart title.
   - Centered Overlay: Centers the chart title horizontally without resizing the plot area; the title displays over the top of the plot area.
   - More Options: Opens the Format Chart Title task pane so that you can apply fill, border, and alignment settings.
4. Click the Chart Elements button to close the menu.

Include and Position Axis Titles

STEP 2 ≫ Excel does not include axis titles by default; however, you can display titles. When you click Chart Elements and click the triangle on the right side of Axis Titles, you can select Primary Horizontal and Primary Vertical. The horizontal axis title displays below the category labels, and the rotated vertical axis title displays on the left side of the value axis. After including these titles, you can click the respective title, type the text for the title, and then press Enter.

Include and Position Data Labels

STEP 3 ≫ Excel does not include data labels by default; however, you can display the exact values of the data points in the chart. When you click Chart Elements and click the triangle on the right side of Data Labels, you can select where the labels display.

By default, Excel adds data labels to all data series. If you want to display data labels for only one series, select the data labels for the other data series and press Delete. In Figure 3.23, data labels are included for the 2020 data series but not the 2010 data series.

Position the Legend

When you create a multiple series chart, the legend displays, providing a key to the color-coded data series. You can position the legend to the right, top, bottom, or left of the plot area. Choose the position based on how the legend's placement affects the chart. Make sure that the columns, bars, or lines appear proportionate and well balanced after you position the legend. You may need to adjust the height and/or width of the entire chart to achieve a balanced appearance.

TIP Quick Layout

Use Quick Layout to apply predefined layouts to a chart. Specifically, you can apply a layout to add several chart elements at one time. Click Quick Layout in the Chart Layouts group on the Design tab (see Figure 3.26) and select a layout. Each layout contains predefined chart elements and their positions.

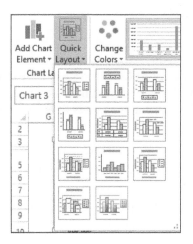

FIGURE 3.26 Quick Layout Gallery

Formatting Chart Elements

When you position the mouse pointer over the chart, Excel displays a ScreenTip with the name of that chart element. To select a chart element, click it when you see the ScreenTip, or click the Format tab, click the Chart Elements arrow in the Current Selection group, and then select the element from the list.

STEP 1 ≫ After you select a chart element, you can format it. For example, you might want to apply 18-pt font size to the chart title. In addition, you might want to change the fill color of a data series to red. You can apply these formats from the Home tab:

- Font for titles, axes, and labels
- Font Size for titles, axes, and labels
- Font Color for titles, axes, and labels
- Fill Color for column, bar, and line data series or background fill color behind titles and labels

Format the Chart Area, Plot Area, and Data Series

STEP 4>> You can apply multiple settings, such as fill colors and borders, at once using a Format task pane. To display a chart element's task pane, double-click the chart element. Figure 3.27 displays the Format Chart Area, Format Plot Area, and Format Data Series task panes. All three task panes include the same fill and border elements. After you select a fill option, such as *Gradient fill*, the remaining options change in the task pane.

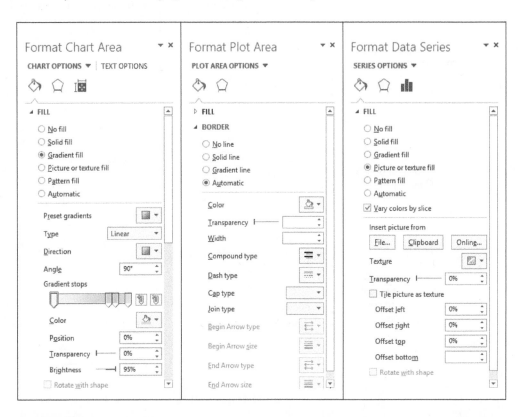

FIGURE 3.27 Format Task Panes

TIP Use Images or Textures

For less formal presentations, you might want to use images or a texture to fill the data series, chart area, or plot area instead of a solid fill color. To use an image or a texture, click the Fill & Line icon at the top of the task pane, click Fill, and then click *Picture or texture fill* in the Format Data Series task pane. Click File or Online in the *Insert picture from* section and insert an image file or search online to insert an image. The image is stretched by default, but you can select the Stack option to avoid distorting the image. To add a texture, click *Picture or texture fill*, click Texture, and then select a textured background from the gallery of textures. Generally, do not mix images and textures.

Format Axes

Based on the data source values and structure, Excel determines the starting, incremental, and stopping values that display on the value axis when you create the chart. You might want to adjust the value axis. For example, when working with large values such as 4,567,890, the value axis displays increments, such as 4,000,000 and 5,000,000. You can simplify the value axis by displaying values in millions, so that the values on the axis are 4 and 5 with the word *Millions* placed by the value axis to indicate the units. Figure 3.28 shows the Format Axis task pane. Diagonal black triangles, such as Axis Options, indicate all of a category's options are displayed (see the left task pane in Figure 3.28). Triangles with a white fill, such as Number, indicate the category options are not displayed (see the left task pane in Figure 3.28). You might need to scroll down and click a category name, such as Number, to see additional options. The task pane on the right side of Figure 3.28 shows the Number options after clicking the triangle.

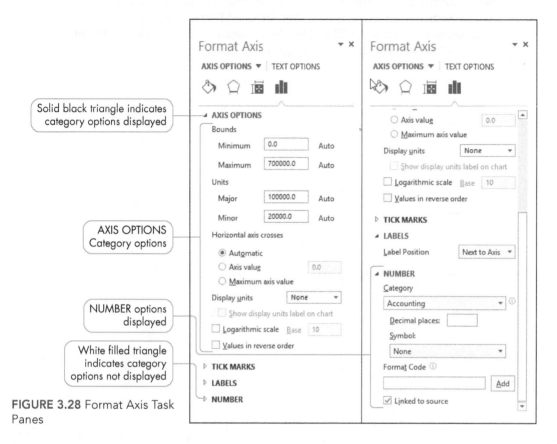

FIGURE 3.28 Format Axis Task Panes

Insert and Format Data Labels

When you select a data label, Excel selects all data labels in that data series. To format the labels, double-click a data label to open the Format Data Labels task pane (see Figure 3.29). The Format Data Labels task pane enables you to specify what to display as the label. The default setting for Label Contains options is Value, but you can display additional label contents, such as the Category Name. However, displaying too much label content can clutter the chart. You can also specify the Label Position, such as Center or Outside End. If the numeric data labels are not formatted, click Number and apply number formats.

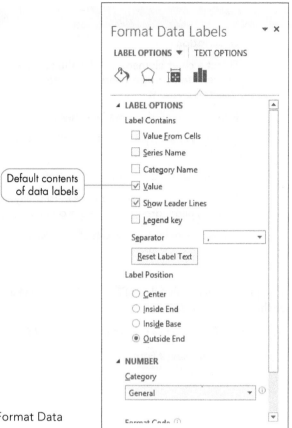

Default contents of data labels

FIGURE 3.29 Format Data Labels Task Pane

> ### TIP Pie Chart Data Labels
>
> When you first create a pie chart, Excel generates a legend to identify the category labels for the different slice colors, but it does not display data labels. You can display Values, Percentages, and even Category Labels on or next to each slice. Pie charts often include percentage data labels. If you also include category labels, remove the legend to avoid duplicating elements.

Use the Chart Tools Format Tab

The Format tab contains options to select a chart element, insert shapes, apply shape styles, apply WordArt styles, arrange objects, and specify the size of an object. Table 3.4 lists and describes the groups on the Format tab.

TABLE 3.4 Chart Tools Format Tab

Group	Description
Current Selection	Select a chart element, display the task pane to format the selected element, and clear custom formatting of the selected element.
Insert Shapes	Insert a variety of shapes in a chart.
Shape Styles	Specify a chart style, fill color, outline color, and shape effect.
WordArt Styles	Add artistic style, text fill, and text effects to an object.
Arrange	Bring an object forward or backward to layer multiple objects; align, group, and rotate objects.
Size	Adjust the height and width of the selected object.

Quick
Concepts

1. List at least four types of appropriate labels that describe chart elements. What types of things can you do to customize these labels? ***pp. 153–155***

2. How can you change the fill color of a data series in a column chart? ***p. 157***

3. What types of formats can you apply by using a Format task pane for a chart element? ***p. 157***

Hands-On Exercises

 Watch the Video for this Hands-On Exercise!

 MyITLab® HOE2 Training

2 Chart Elements

You want to enhance the computer job column, bar, and pie charts by adding some chart elements. In particular, you need to enter a descriptive chart title for each chart, add and format axis titles for the bar chart, add and format data labels for the pie chart, and change fill colors in the pie chart.

Skills covered: Add and Format Chart Titles • Add and Format Axis Titles • Add and Format Data Labels • Apply Fill Colors

---

STEP 1 ≫ ADD AND FORMAT CHART TITLES

When you created the column, bar, and pie charts in Hands-On Exercise 1, Excel displayed *Chart Title* at the top of each chart. You need to type chart titles that appropriately describe each chart. In addition, you want to format the chart titles by applying bold to them and enlarging their font sizes. Refer to Figure 3.30 as you complete Step 1.

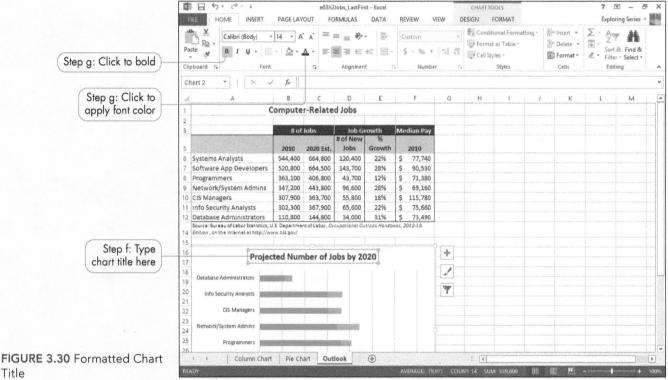

FIGURE 3.30 Formatted Chart Title

a. Open *e03h1Jobs_LastFirst* if you closed it at the end of Hands-On Exercise 1 and save it as **e03h2Jobs_LastFirst**, changing *h1* to *h2*.

b. Make sure the Pie Chart sheet is the active sheet, select the **Chart Title placeholder**, type **New Computer-Related Jobs by 2020** in the Formula Bar, and then press **Enter**.

Excel displays the text you typed in the chart title.

> **TROUBLESHOOTING:** If you double-click a title and type directly into the title placeholder, do *not* press Enter after typing the new title. Doing so will add a blank line. If you select the title placeholder only and type text, the text will appear in the Formula Bar.

c. Click the **HOME tab**, click **Bold**, click the **Font Size arrow**, and then select **18**.

You formatted the pie chart's title so that it stands out better.

d. Click the **Column Chart sheet tab**, select the **Chart Title placeholder**, type **Number of Computer-Related Jobs 2010 and 2020** in the Formula Bar, and then press **Enter**.

e. Click **Bold**, click the **Font Size arrow**, and then select **18**.

f. Click the **Outlook sheet tab**, select the **Chart Title placeholder**, type **Projected Number of Jobs by 2020**, and then press **Enter**.

g. Click **Bold**, click the **Font Size arrow**, and then select **14**. Click the **Font Color arrow** and click **Dark Blue** in the *Standard Colors* section. Save the workbook.

You formatted the bar chart title to be consistently formatted with the worksheet title.

STEP 2 ❯❯ ADD AND FORMAT AXIS TITLES

For the bar chart, you want to add and format a title to describe the job titles on the vertical axis. In addition, you want to simplify the horizontal axis values to avoid ,000 for each increment and add the title *Thousands*. Refer to Figure 3.31 as you complete Step 2.

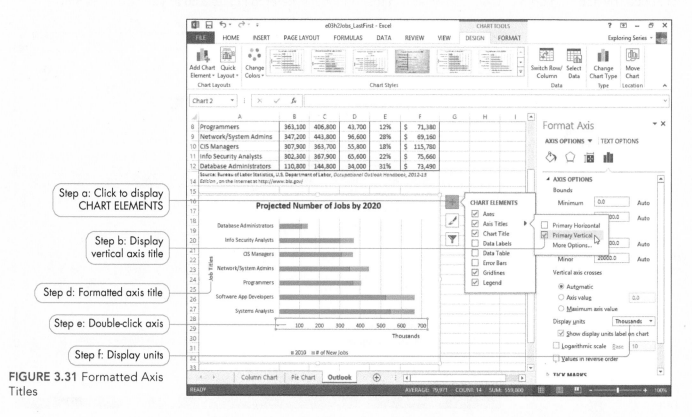

FIGURE 3.31 Formatted Axis Titles

a. Make sure the bar chart is selected in the Outlook worksheet and click the **Chart Elements button** to the right of the chart.

Excel displays the CHART ELEMENTS menu.

b. Position the mouse pointer over *Axis Titles*, click the **Axis Titles arrow**, and then click the **Primary Vertical check box**.

Excel displays *Axis Title* on the left side of the vertical axis.

c. Make sure the *Axis Title* placeholder is selected, type **Job Titles** in the Formula Bar, and then press **Enter**.

d. Click **Font Color** to apply the default Dark Blue font color to the selected axis title.

e. Double-click the values on the horizontal axis.

Excel displays the Format Axis task pane so that you can format the value axis.

f. Click **AXIS OPTIONS**, if necessary, click the **Display units arrow,** and then select **Thousands**.

The axis now displays values such as 700 instead of 700,000. The title *Thousands* displays in the bottom-right corner of the horizontal axis.

g. Click the **HOME tab**, make sure the title *Thousands* is selected, and then apply **Dark Blue font color** in the Font group. Close the task pane. Save the workbook.

STEP 3 » ADD AND FORMAT DATA LABELS

The pie chart includes a legend to identify which color represents which computer-related job; however, it does not include numerical labels to help you interpret what percentage of all computer-related jobs will be hired for each position. You want to insert and format percentage value labels. Refer to Figure 3.32 as you complete Step 3.

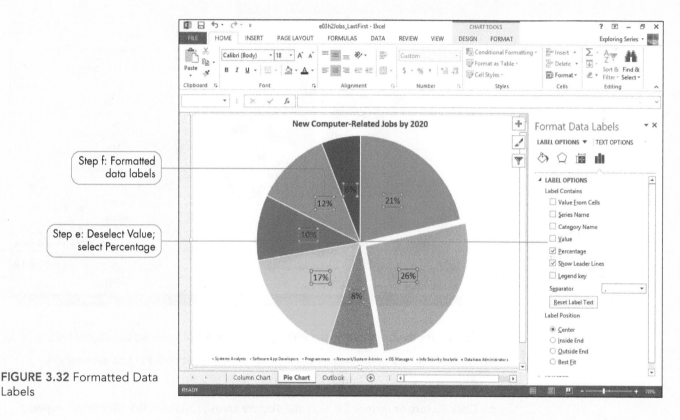

FIGURE 3.32 Formatted Data Labels

a. Click the **Pie Chart Sheet tab** and click the **Chart Elements button**.

b. Click the **Data Labels arrow** and select **Center**.

You added data labels to the pie slices.

> **TROUBLESHOOTING:** If the Chart Elements menu remains open, click the Chart Elements button to close the menu.

c. Double-click one of the data labels to display the Format Data Labels task pane.

d. Click the **Label Options icon** in the Format Data Labels task pane, if necessary.

e. Click the **LABEL OPTIONS triangle**, if necessary, click the **Percentage check box** to select it, and then click the **Value check box** to deselect it.

Typically, pie chart data labels show percentages instead of values.

f. Change the font size to **18** to make the data labels larger. Save the workbook.

STEP 4 ≫ APPLY FILL COLORS

You want to apply a texture fill to the chart area and change the fill colors for the Software Apps Developers' and the Database Administrators' slices. Refer to Figure 3.33 as you complete Step 4.

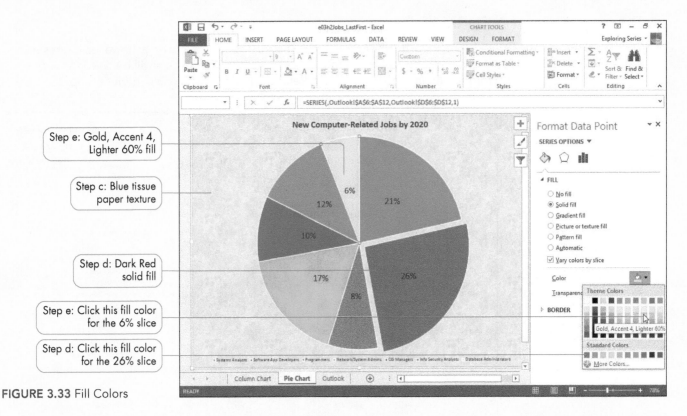

Step e: Gold, Accent 4, Lighter 60% fill

Step c: Blue tissue paper texture

Step d: Dark Red solid fill

Step e: Click this fill color for the 6% slice

Step d: Click this fill color for the 26% slice

FIGURE 3.33 Fill Colors

a. Position the mouse pointer in the white space and click when you see the Chart Area ScreenTip.

b. Click **Fill & Line** in the Format Chart Area task pane and click **FILL**, if necessary.

The task pane displays different fill options.

c. Click **Picture or texture fill**, click the **Texture arrow**, and then click **Blue tissue paper**.

The chart area now has the blue tissue paper texture fill.

d. Click the pie chart, pause, and then click the **26% orange slice**. Click **Solid fill**, click the **Color arrow**, and then click **Dark Red** in the *Standard Colors* section.

The Software Apps Developers slice is now dark red.

e. Click the **6% slice**, click **Solid fill**, click the **Color arrow**, and then click **Gold, Accent 4, Lighter 60%**.

The new color for the Database Administrators slice makes it easier to read the percentage data label.

f. Save the workbook. Keep the workbook open if you plan to continue with the next Hands-On Exercise. If not, close the workbook and exit Excel.

Chart Design and Sparklines

After you add and format chart elements, you might want to experiment with other features to enhance a chart. The Chart Tools Design tab contains two other groups: Chart Styles and Data. These groups enable you to apply a different style or color scheme to a chart or manipulate the data that are used to build a chart. You can also click the Chart Styles and Chart Filters buttons to the right of a chart to change the design of a chart.

At times, you might want to insert small visual chart-like images within worksheet cells to illustrate smaller data series rather than a large chart to illustrate several data points. Excel enables you to create small chart-like images in close proximity to individual data points to help you visualize the data.

In this section, you will learn how to apply chart styles and colors, filter chart data, and insert and customize miniature charts (sparklines) within individual cells.

Applying a Chart Style and Colors

 You can apply a different *chart style*, a collection of formatting that controls the color of the chart area, plot area, and data series. Styles also affect the look of the data series, such as flat, 3-D, or beveled. Figure 3.34 shows the options when you click the Chart Styles button to the right side of the chart, and Figure 3.35 shows the Chart Styles gallery when you click Chart Styles on the Design tab.

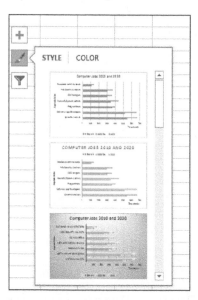

FIGURE 3.34 Chart Styles

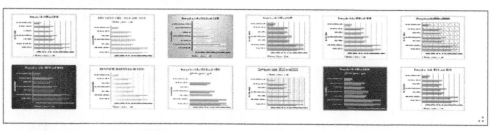

FIGURE 3.35 Chart Styles Gallery

TIP | Choosing Appropriate Chart Styles

When choosing a chart style, make sure the style complements the chart data and is easy to read. Also, consider whether you will display the chart onscreen in a presentation or print the chart. If you will display the chart in a presentation, consider selecting a style with a black background.

You can change the color scheme by clicking the Chart Styles button on the right side of the chart and clicking Color or click Change Colors in the Chart Styles group on the Design tab. You can select from the Colorful and Monochromatic sections.

Modifying the Data Source

The data source is the range of worksheet cells that are used to construct a chart. Although you should select the data source carefully before creating a chart, you may decide to alter that data source after you create and format the chart. The Data group on the Design tab is useful for adjusting the data source.

Create Chart Filters

STEP 2 ≫   A *chart filter* controls which data series and categories are visible in a chart. By default, all the data you selected to create the chart are used to construct the data series and categories. However, you can apply a chart filter to hide extraneous data. Click the Chart Filter button to the right side of the chart to display the options (see Figure 3.36). A check mark indicates the data series or category currently displayed in the chart. Click a check box to deselect or hide a data series or category.

FIGURE 3.36 Chart Filter Options

You can click Select Data in the Data group on the Design tab to open the Select Data Source dialog box (see Figure 3.37). This dialog box is another way to filter which categories and data series are visible in your chart.

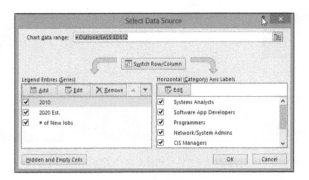

FIGURE 3.37 Select Data Source Dialog Box

Switch Row and Column Data

You can switch data used to create the horizontal axis and the legend. In Figure 3.38, the chart on the left uses the job titles to build the data series and legend, and the years display on the horizontal axis. The chart on the right shows the results after switching the data: the job titles build the horizontal axis, and the years build the data series and legend. To switch the data, click Switch Row/Column in the Data group on the Design tab.

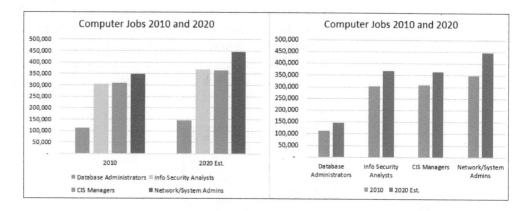

FIGURE 3.38 Original Chart and Chart with Reversed Rows/Columns

Creating and Customizing Sparklines

A *sparkline* is a small line, column, or win/loss chart contained in a single cell. The purpose of a sparkline is to present a condensed, simple, succinct visual illustration of data. Unlike a regular chart, a sparkline does not include a chart title or axis labels. Inserting sparklines next to data helps your audience understand data quickly without having to look at a full-scale chart.

Figure 3.39 shows three sample sparklines: line, column, and win/loss. The line sparkline shows trends over time, such as each student's trends in test scores. The column sparkline compares test averages. The win/loss sparkline depicts how many points a team won or lost each game.

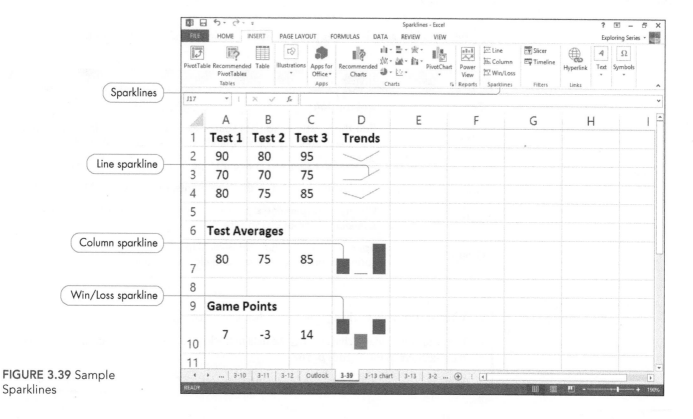

FIGURE 3.39 Sample Sparklines

Create a Sparkline

STEP 3 » Before creating a sparkline, identify which data you want to depict and where you want to place them. To create a sparkline, do the following:

1. Click the INSERT tab.
2. Click Line, Column, or Win/Loss in the Sparklines group. The Create Sparklines dialog box opens (see Figure 3.40).
3. Type the cell references containing the values in the Data Range box, or click the Collapse Dialog button (if necessary), select the range, and then click the Collapse Dialog button to display the dialog box again.
4. Enter or select the range where you want the sparkline to display in the Location Range box and click OK. The default cell location is the active cell unless you change it.

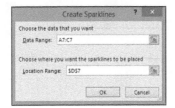

FIGURE 3.40 Create Sparklines Dialog Box

Customize a Sparkline

After you insert a sparkline, the Sparkline Tools Design tab displays (see Figure 3.41), with options to customize the sparkline.

FIGURE 3.41 Sparkline Tools Design Tab

Table 3.5 lists and describes the groups on the Sparkline Tools Design tab.

TABLE 3.5	Sparkline Tools Design Tab
Group	**Description**
Sparkline	Edit the location and data source for a group or individual data point that generates a group of sparklines or an individual sparkline
Type	Change the selected sparkline type (line, column, win/loss)
Show	Display points, such as the high points, or markers within a sparkline
Style	Change the sparkline style, similar to a chart style, change the sparkline color, or change the marker color
Group	Specify the horizontal and vertical axis settings, group objects together, ungroup objects, and clear sparklines

Quick
Concepts

1. What are two ways to change the color scheme of a chart? *p. 165*
2. How can you change a chart so that the data in the legend are on the X-axis and the data on the X-axis are in the legend? *p. 167*
3. What is a sparkline, and why would you insert one? *p. 167*

3 Chart Design and Sparklines

Now that you have completed the pie chart, you want to focus again on the bar chart. You are not satisfied with the overall design and want to try a different chart style. In addition, you would like to include sparklines to show trends for all jobs between 2010 and 2020.

Skills covered: Apply a Chart Style • Apply Chart Filters • Insert and Customize Sparklines

STEP 1 ≫ APPLY A CHART STYLE

You want to give more contrast to the bar chart. Therefore, you will apply the Style 2 chart style. That style formats the chart area with a dark fill color and helps highlight the data series. Refer to Figure 3.42 as you complete Step 1.

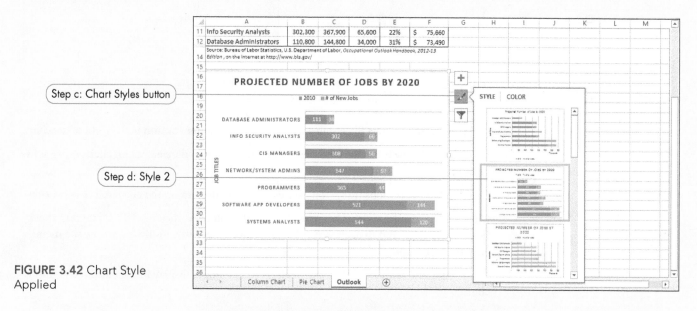

FIGURE 3.42 Chart Style Applied

a. Open *e03h2Jobs_LastFirst* if you closed it at the end of Hands-On Exercise 2 and save it as **e03h3Jobs_LastFirst**, changing *h2* to *h3*.

b. Click the **Outlook Sheet tab** and click the bar chart to select it.

c. Click the **Chart Styles button** to the right of the chart.

The gallery of chart styles opens.

d. Click **Style 2**. Click the **Chart Styles button** to close the gallery. Save the workbook.

Excel applies the Style 2 chart style to the chart, which displays value data labels in white font color within each stack of the bar chart. The chart title and the category labels display in all capital letters. The legend displays above the plot area.

STEP 2 ≫ APPLY CHART FILTERS

When you first created the clustered column chart, you included the number of new jobs as well as the number of 2010 jobs and the projected number of 2020 jobs. However, you decide that the number of new jobs is implied by comparing the 2010 to the 2020 jobs. Therefore, you want to set a chart filter to exclude the number of new jobs. Refer to Figure 3.43 as you complete Step 2.

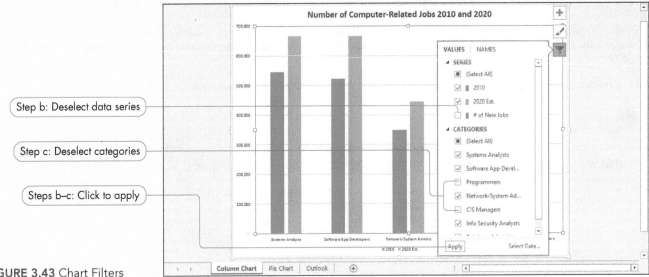

Step b: Deselect data series

Step c: Deselect categories

Steps b–c: Click to apply

FIGURE 3.43 Chart Filters

a. Click the **Column Chart Sheet tab** and click the **Chart Filters button** to the right of the chart.

b. Click the **# of New Jobs check box** in the SERIES group to deselect it and click **Apply** at the bottom of the filter window.

The number of new jobs (gray) data series no longer displays in the clustered column chart.

c. Click the **Programmers check box** to deselect the category, click the **CIS Managers check box** to deselect it, and then click **Apply**. Click the **Chart Filters button** to close the menu. Save the workbook.

The Programmers and CIS Managers categories no longer display in the clustered column chart.

STEP 3 ≫ INSERT AND CUSTOMIZE SPARKLINES

You want to insert sparklines to show the trends between 2010 and 2020. After inserting the sparklines, you want to display the high points to show that all jobs will have major increases by 2020. Refer to Figure 3.44 as you complete Step 3.

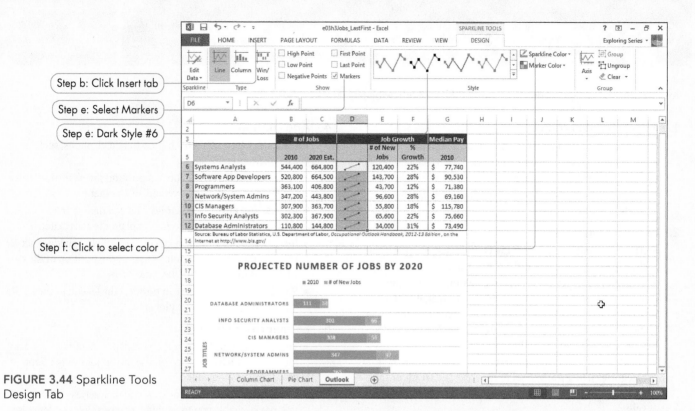

Step b: Click Insert tab

Step e: Select Markers

Step e: Dark Style #6

Step f: Click to select color

FIGURE 3.44 Sparkline Tools Design Tab

a. Click the **Outlook sheet tab**, select **cell D6**, click the **HOME tab**, click the **Insert arrow** in the Cells group, and then select **Insert Sheet Columns**.

You inserted a new column to place the sparklines close to the data you want to visualize.

b. Click the **INSERT tab** and click **Line** in the Sparklines group.

c. Select the **range B6:C12** to enter that range in the Data Range box.

You can select multiple rows at one time to create a group of sparklines.

d. Press **Tab** and select the **range D6:D12** to enter that range in the Location Range box. Click **OK**.

Excel inserts sparklines in the range D6:D12 with each sparkline representing data on its respective row. The Sparkline Tools Design tab displays.

e. Click the **Markers check box** in the Show group to select it and click **Sparkline Style Dark #6** in the Style group.

f. Click **Sparkline Color** in the Style group and click **Red**.

g. Save and close the workbook, and submit based on your instructor's directions.

Chapter Objectives Review

After reading this chapter, you have accomplished the following objectives:

1. Select the data source.

- Decide which data you want to include in a chart.
- Each value is a data point, and several related data points create a data series in a chart.
- Select the range of data, including appropriate labels. The labels become the legend and the category axis.

2. Choose a chart type.

- After selecting a range, click the Quick Analysis button and click Charts to display a gallery of recommended chart types.
- Create a column chart: A clustered column chart compares groups of side-by-side columns where the height of the column indicates its value. The taller the column, the larger the value. A stacked column chart shows relationships of individual data points to the whole.
- Create a bar chart: A bar chart compares values across categories using horizontal bars where the width of the bar indicates its value. The wider the bar, the larger the value.
- Create a line chart: A line chart compares trends over time. Values are displayed on the value axis, and time periods are displayed on the category axis.
- Create a pie chart: A pie chart indicates proportions to the whole for one data series. The size of the slice indicates the size of the value. The larger the pie slice, the larger the value.
- Select other chart types based on the intended purpose.
- Change the chart type: After creating a chart, you can change it to a different type using the Change Chart Type command.
- Create other chart types: An X Y (scatter) chart shows a relationship between two numerical variables. A stock chart shows fluctuations in prices of stock, such as between the opening and closing prices on a particular day.

3. Move, size, and print a chart.

- Move a chart: The Move Chart dialog box enables you to select a new sheet and name the new chart sheet.
- Size a chart: Adjust the chart size by dragging a sizing handle or specifying exact measurements in the Size group on the Format tab.
- Print a chart: To print a chart with its data series, the chart needs to be on the same worksheet as the data source. To ensure both the data and the chart print, make sure the chart is not selected. If the chart is on its own sheet or if you select the chart on a worksheet containing other data, the chart will print as a full-sized chart.

4. Add chart elements.

- Click the Chart Elements button to add elements, such as axis titles and data labels.
- Position the chart title: You can position the chart title above the chart, centered and overlaid, or in other locations.
- Include and position axis titles: You can display titles for the value and category axes to help explain the axes better.
- Include and position data labels: Data labels provide exact values for a data series. You can select the position of the data labels and the content of the data labels.
- Position the legend: You can position the legend to the right, top, bottom, or left of the plot area.

5. Format chart elements.

- You can select and format each element separately. For basic formatting, such as font color, use the options in the Font group on the Home tab.
- Format the chart area, plot area, and data series: The Format task panes enable you to apply fill colors, select border colors, and apply other settings.
- Format axes: You can specify number formats for the value axis. You can specify measurement units, such as Millions, to simplify the value axis increments.
- Insert and format data labels: You can specify what is displayed in data labels and how to format the labels.
- Use the Chart Tools Format tab: This tab enables you to select a chart element and insert and format shapes.

6. Apply a chart style and colors.

- You can apply a chart style, which determines formatting, such as the background color and the data series color.

7. Modify the data source.

- You can add or remove data from the data source to change the data in the chart.
- Create chart filters: The Select Data Source dialog box enables you to modify the ranges used for the data series.
- Switch row and column data: Excel usually places the first column of data as the category axis and the first row of data as the legend, but you can switch these.

8. Create and customize sparklines.

- Create a sparkline: A sparkline is a miniature chart in a cell representing a single data series.
- Customize a sparkline: You can customize sparklines by changing the data source, location, and style. You can display markers and change line or marker colors.

Match the key terms with their definitions. Write the key term letter by the appropriate numbered definition.

a. Axis title
b. Bar chart
c. Category axis
d. Chart area
e. Chart title
f. Clustered column chart
g. Data label
h. Data point
i. Data series
j. Gridline

k. Legend
l. Line chart
m. Pie chart
n. Plot area
o. Sizing handle
p. Sparkline
q. Stock chart
r. Task pane
s. Value axis
t. X Y (scatter) chart

1. _____ Chart type to compare multiple categories of data vertically. **p. 138**

2. _____ Miniature chart contained in a single cell. **p. 167**

3. _____ Chart type that shows trends over time in which the value axis indicates quantities and the horizontal axis indicates time. **p. 141**

4. _____ Label that describes the chart. **p. 153**

5. _____ Label that describes either the category axis or the value axis. **p. 153**

6. _____ Key that identifies the color, gradient, picture, texture, or pattern fill assigned to each data series in a chart. **p. 134**

7. _____ Chart type that compares categories of data horizontally. **p. 141**

8. _____ Chart that shows each data point in proportion to the whole data series. **p. 142**

9. _____ Numeric value that decribes a single value on a chart. **p. 134**

10. _____ Chart that shows the high, low, and close prices for individual stocks over time. **p. 143**

11. _____ Indicators that enable you to adjust the height and width of a selected chart. **p. 146**

12. _____ Horizontal or vertical line that extends from the horizontal or vertical axis through the plot area. **p. 153**

13. _____ Chart type that shows the relationship between two variables. **p. 143**

14. _____ Group of related data points that display in row(s) or column(s) in a worksheet. **p. 134**

15. _____ Window of options to format and customize chart elements. **p. 157**

16. _____ Provides descriptive group names for subdividing a data series. **p. 134**

17. _____ Section of a chart that contains graphical representation of the values in a data series. **p. 134**

18. _____ Boundary that contains the entire chart and all of its elements, including the plot area, titles, legends, and labels. **p. 134**

19. _____ Descriptive label that shows the exact value of the data points on the value axis. **p. 153**

20. _____ Displays incremental numbers to identify approximate values, such as dollars or units, of data points in a chart. **p. 134**

Multiple Choice

1. Which type of chart is the *least* appropriate for depicting yearly rainfall totals for five cities for four years?

   (a) Pie chart

   (b) Line chart

   (c) Column chart

   (d) Bar chart

2. What is the typical sequence for creating a chart?

   (a) Select the chart type, select the data source, and then size and position the chart.

   (b) Select the data source, size the chart, select the chart type, and then position the chart.

   (c) Select the data source, select the chart type, and then size and position the chart.

   (d) Click the cell to contain the chart, select the chart type, and then select the data source.

3. Which of the following applies to a sparkline?

   (a) Chart title

   (b) Single-cell chart

   (c) Legend

   (d) Multiple data series

4. If you want to show exact values for a data series in a bar chart, which chart element should you display?

   (a) Chart title

   (b) Legend

   (c) Value axis title

   (d) Data labels

5. The value axis currently shows increments such as 50,000 and 100,000. What do you select to display increments of 50 and 100?

   (a) More Primary Vertical Axis Title Options

   (b) Show Axis in Thousands

   (c) Show Axis in Millions

   (d) Show Right to Left Axis

6. You want to create a single chart that shows each of five divisions' proportion of yearly sales for each year for five years. Which type of chart can accommodate your needs?

   (a) Pie chart

   (b) Surface chart

   (c) Clustered bar chart

   (d) 100% stacked column chart

7. Currently, a column chart shows values on the value axis, years on the category axis, and state names in the legend. What should you do if you want to organize data with the states on the category axis and the years shown in the legend?

   (a) Change the chart type to a clustered column chart.

   (b) Click Switch Row/Column in the Data group on the Design tab.

   (c) Click Layout 2 in the Chart Layouts group on the Design tab and apply a different chart style.

   (d) Click Legend in the Labels group on the Layout tab and select Show Legend at Bottom.

8. Which tab contains commands to apply a predefined chart layout that controls which elements are included, where, and their color scheme?

   (a) Design

   (b) Layout

   (c) Format

   (d) Page Layout

9. Which icon does *not* display to the right of a selected chart?

   (a) Chart Elements

   (b) Chart Styles

   (c) Chart Filters

   (d) Chart Quick Analysis

10. What indicates that the closing price was higher than the opening price in a stock chart?

    (a) A double vertical line between the price markers

    (b) A positive data label above the data series for a particular day

    (c) A rectangle with a white fill color

    (d) A rectangle with a black fill color

1 | Hulett Family Utility Expenses

Your cousin, Alex Hulett, wants to analyze his family's utility expenses for 2016. He gave you his files for the electric, gas, and water bills for the year. You created a worksheet that lists the individual expenses per month, along with yearly totals per utility type and monthly totals. You will create some charts to depict the data. This exercise follows the same set of skills as used in Hands-On Exercises 1–3 in the chapter. Refer to Figure 3.45 as you complete this exercise.

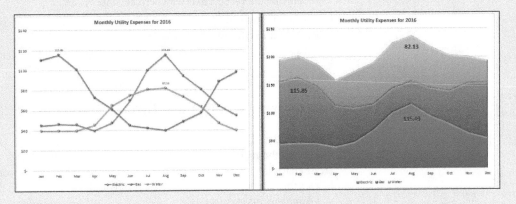

FIGURE 3.45 Hulett Family Utility Expenses

a. Open *e03p1Utilities* and save it as **e03p1Utilities_LastFirst**.

b. Select the **range A4:E17**, click the **Quick Analysis button**, and then click **CHARTS**.

c. Click **Clustered Column**, click the **Chart Filters button** to the right of the chart, and then do the following:
  • Deselect the **Monthly Totals check box** in the SERIES group.
  • Scroll through the CATEGORIES group and deselect the **Yearly Totals check box**.
  • Click **Apply** to remove totals from the chart. Click **Chart Filters** to close the menu.

d. Position the mouse pointer over the chart area. When you see the Chart Area ScreenTip, drag the chart so that the top-left edge of the chart is in **cell A19**.

e. Click the **FORMAT tab** and change the size by doing the following:
  • Click in the **Shape Width box** in the Size group, type **6"**, and then press **Enter**.
  • Click in the **Shape Height box** in the Size group, type **3.5"**, and then press **Enter**.

f. Click the **DESIGN tab**, click **Quick Layout** in the Chart Layouts group, and then click **Layout 3**.

g. Select the **Chart Title placeholder** and type **Monthly Utility Expenses for 2016**.

h. Click the **More button** in the Chart Styles group and click **Style 8**.

i. Select the chart, if necessary, click **Copy** on the HOME tab, click **cell A37**, and then click **Paste**. With the second chart selected, do the following:
  • Click the **DESIGN tab**, click **Change Chart Type** in the Type group, click **Line** on the left side of the dialog box, select **Line with Markers** in the top-center section, and then click **OK**.
  • Click the **Electric data series line** to select it and click the highest marker to select only that marker. Click the **Chart Elements button** and click **Data Labels**.
  • Repeat and adapt the previous bulleted step to add a data label to the highest Gas and Water markers. Click the **Chart Elements button** to close the menu.
  • Select the chart, copy it, and then paste it in **cell A55**.

j. Make sure the third chart is selected and do the following:
  • Click the **DESIGN tab**, click **Change Chart Type** in the Type group, select **Area** on the left side, click **Stacked Area**, and then click **OK**.
  • Click **Move Chart** in the Location group, click **New sheet**, type **Area Chart**, and then click **OK**.
  • Select each data label, click **Bold**, and select **18-pt font size**. Move the data label up closer to the top of the respective shaded area.
  • Select the value axis, select **12-pt font size**, and then select **Black, Text 1 font color**.

- Right-click the value axis and select **Format Axis**. Scroll down in the Format Axis task pane, click **NUMBER**, and then type **0** in the **Decimal places box**. Close the task pane.
- Apply **12-pt font size** and **Black, Text 1 font color** to the category axis and to the legend.

k. Click the **Expenses sheet tab**, select the line chart, and then do the following:
- Click the **DESIGN tab**, click **Move Chart** in the Location group, click **New sheet**, type **Line Chart**, and then click **OK**.
- Apply **12-pt font size** to the value axis, category axis, and legend.
- Format the vertical axis with zero decimal places.

l. Create a footer with your name on the left side, the sheet name code in the center, and the file name code on the right side of each sheet.

m. Save and close the workbook, and submit based on your instructor's directions.

2 Trends in Market Value of Houses on Pine Circle

You are considering buying a house on Pine Circle, a quiet cul-de-sac in a suburban area. Recently, you researched the market value and square footage of the five houses on Pine Circle. Now, you want to create charts to visually depict the data to determine which house you might want to buy. This exercise follows the same set of skills as used in Hands-On Exercises 1–3 in the chapter. Refer to Figure 3.46 as you complete this exercise.

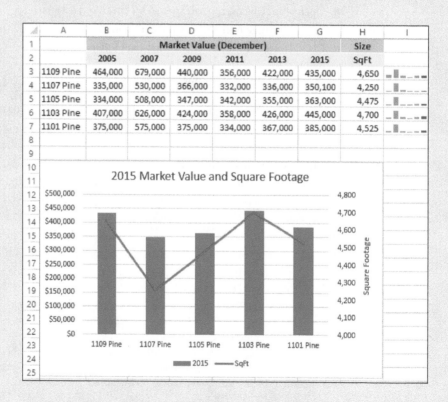

FIGURE 3.46 Market Values

a. Open *e03p2Pine* and save it as **e03p2Pine_LastFirst**.

b. Select the **range A2:G7**, click the **Quick Analysis button**, click **CHARTS**, and then click **Line**.

c. Click **Move Chart** in the Location group, click **New sheet**, type **Line**, and then click **OK**.

d. Select the **Chart Title placeholder** and do the following:
- Type **Market Value of Pine Circle Houses** and press **Enter**.
- Bold the title, apply **20-pt size**, and select **Olive Green, Accent 3, Darker 50% font color**.

e. Click the value axis on the left side of the chart and do the following:

- Apply **12-pt font size** and **Olive Green, Accent 3, Darker 50% font color**.
- Double-click the value axis to display the Format Axis task pane. If necessary, click the **Axis Options icon** and click **AXIS OPTIONS** to display options.
- Type **300000** in the **Minimum Bounds box** and press **Enter**. The Maximum Bounds box should change to 700000 automatically.
- Scroll down in the Format Axis task pane and click **NUMBER** to display those options.
- Click the **Category arrow** and select **Currency**.
- Close the Format Axis task pane.

f. Click the **Chart Elements button**, click the **Axis Titles triangle**, and then click the **Primary Vertical check box**. Type **December Market Values** in the **Axis Title placeholder** and press **Enter**.

g. Make sure the Chart Elements menu is showing, click the **Gridlines triangle**, and then click the **Primary Minor Horizontal check box**. Click **Chart Elements** to close the menu.

h. Select the category axis, apply **12-pt font size**, and apply **Olive Green, Accent 3, Darker 50% font color**.

i. Right-click the legend and select **Format Legend**. Click **Top** in the *Legend Position* section of the Format Legend task pane and close the task pane.

j. Click the **Pine Circle Sheet tab** and select the **ranges A2:A7, G2:G7, and H2:H7**.

k. Click the **INSERT tab**, click **Insert Combo Chart** in the Charts group, and then click the **Clustered Column – Line on Secondary Axis thumbnail**.

l. Do the following to the chart:

- Drag the chart to fill the **range A10:H25**.
- Select the **Chart Title Placeholder** and type **2015 Market Value and Square Footage**.
- Double-click the value axis on the left side, scroll down in the Format Axis task pane, click **NUMBER**, click the **Category arrow**, and then select **Currency**.
- Click the **Chart Elements button**, click the **Axis Titles triangle**, click the **Secondary Vertical check box**, type **Square Footage**, and then press **Enter**. Close the Format Axis Title task pane.

m. Select the **range B3:G7**, click the **INSERT tab**, click **Column** in the Sparklines group, make sure B3:G7 displays in the Data Range box, type **I3:I7** in the **Location Range box**, and then click **OK**.

n. Customize the sparklines by doing the following:

- Click **More** in the Style group and select **Sparkline Style Accent 6, Darker 25%**.
- Click **Last Point** in the Show group.

o. Create a footer with your name on the left side, the sheet name code in the center, and the file name code on the right side of both sheets.

p. Save and close the workbook, and submit based on your instructor's directions.

Mid-Level Exercises

1 Airport Passenger Counts

ANALYSIS CASE As an analyst for the airline industry, you track the number of passengers at major U.S. airports. One worksheet you created lists the number of total yearly passengers at the top five airports for four years. To prepare for an upcoming meeting, you need to create a chart to compare the number of passengers for each airport. In addition, you want to insert sparklines to visually represent trends in passengers at each airport.

a. Open *e03m1Airports* and save it as **e03m1Airports_LastFirst**.

b. Create a clustered column chart for the **range A4:E9**. Position the chart to fit in the **range A15:F34**.

c. Customize the chart style by doing the following:
  - Apply **Style 8 chart style**.
  - Select **Color 6** in the *Monochromatic* section of the Change Colors gallery.
  - Change the fill color of the 2011 data series to **White, Background 1**.

d. Enter **Passengers by Top U.S. Airports** as the chart title.

 e. Adjust the value axis by doing the following:
  - Change the display units to **Millions** for the value axis.
  - Edit the axis title to display **MILLIONS OF PASSENGERS**.

f. Display data labels above the columns for the 2011 data series only.

g. Insert Line sparklines in the **range F5:F9** to illustrate the data in the **range B5:E9**. This should insert a sparkline to represent yearly data for each airport.

h. Customize the sparklines by doing the following:
  - Show the high and low points in each sparkline.
  - Apply **Black, Text 1 color** to the high point marker in each sparkline.
  - Apply **Dark Red color** to the low point marker in each sparkline.

i. Merge cells in the **range A36:F41**, wrap text, and then apply **Top Align** and **Align Left** alignments.

 j. Compose a paragraph that analyzes the trends depicted by the airport sparklines. Notice the overall trends in decreased and increased number of passengers and any unusual activity for an airport. Spell check the worksheet and correct any errors.

k. Insert a footer with your name on the left side, the sheet name code in the center, and the file name code on the right side on all worksheets.

l. Save and close the workbook, and submit based on your instructor's directions.

2 Grade Analysis

You are a teaching assistant for Dr. Monica Unice's introductory psychology class. You have maintained her grade book all semester, entering three test scores for each student and calculating the final average. Dr. Unice wants to see a chart that shows the percentage of students who earn each letter grade. You decide to create a pie chart. She wants to see if a correlation exists between attendance and students' final grades, so you will create a scatter chart.

a. Open *e03m2Psych* and save it as **e03m2Psych_LastFirst**.

b. Create a pie chart from the Final Grade Distribution data located below the student data and move the pie chart to its own sheet named **Grades Pie**.

c. Customize the pie chart with these specifications:
  - Style 7 chart style
  - Chart title: **PSY 2030 Final Grade Distribution - Fall 2016**
  - B grade slice exploded
  - Legend: none

d. Add centered data labels and customize the labels with these specifications:
   - Label captions: **Percentage** and **Category Name**; no values
   - 28-pt size; Black, Text 1 font color, and bold

DISCOVER

e. Create a Scatter with only Markers chart using the attendance record and final averages from the Grades worksheet. Move the scatter chart to its own sheet named **Scatter Chart**.

f. Apply these label settings to the scatter chart:
   - Legend: none
   - Chart title: **Attendance-Final Average Relationship**
   - Primary horizontal axis title: **Percentage of Attendance**
   - Primary vertical axis title: **Student Final Averages**

g. Use Help to learn how to apply the following axis settings:
   - Vertical axis: 40 minimum bounds, 100 maximum bounds, 10 major units, and a number format with zero decimal places
   - Horizontal axis: 40 minimum bounds, automatic maximum bounds, automatic units

h. Apply **12 pt font size** to the vertical axis title, vertical axis, horizontal axis title, and horizontal axis.

i. Add the **Parchment texture fill** to the plot area and insert a linear trendline.

j. Insert a footer with your name on the left side, the sheet name code in the center, and the file name code on the right side for the two chart sheets.

k. Save and close the workbook, and submit based on your instructor's directions.

3 Box Office Movies

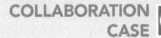

You and two of your friends like to follow the popularity of new movies at the theater. You will research current movies that have been showing for four weeks and decide which movies to report on. Work in teams of three for this activity. After obtaining the data, your team will create applicable charts to illustrate the revenue data. Team members will critique each other's charts.

a. Have all three team members log in to a chat client and engage in a dialogue about which movies are currently playing. Each member should research a different theater to see what is playing at that theater. Decide on six movies that have been in theaters for at least four weeks to research. Save a copy of your instant message dialogue and submit based on your instructor's directions.

b. Divide the six movies among the three team members. Each member should research the revenue reported for two movies for the past four weeks. Make sure your team members use the same source to find the data.

Student 1:

c. Create a new Excel workbook and enter appropriate column labels and the four-week data for all six movies. Name Sheet1 **Data**.

d. Format the data appropriately. Save the workbook as **e03t1CurrentMovies_GroupName**. Upload the workbook to a shared location, such as OneDrive, and contact the next student.

Student 2:

e. Create a line chart to show the trends in revenue for the movies for the four-week period.

f. Add a chart title, format the axes appropriately, select a chart style, and then apply other formatting.

g. Move the chart to its own sheet named **Trends**. Save the workbook, upload it to the shared location, and then contact the next student.

Student 3:

h. Add a column to the right of the four-week data and total each movie's four-week revenue.

i. Create a pie chart depicting each movie's percentage of the total revenue for your selected movies.

j. Add a chart title, explode one pie slice, add data labels showing percentages and movie names, and then apply other formatting.

k. Move the chart to its own sheet named **Revenue Chart**. Save the workbook, upload it to the shared location, and then contact the first student.

Student 1:

l. Critique the charts. Insert a new worksheet named **Chart Critique** that provides an organized critique of each chart. Type notes that list each team member's name and specify what each student's role was in completing this exercise.

m. Save the workbook, upload it to the shared location, and then contact the second student.

Student 2:

n. Read the critique of the line chart and make any appropriate changes for the line chart. On the critique worksheet, provide a response to each critique and why you made or did not make the suggested change.

o. Save the workbook, upload it to the shared location, and then contact the third student.

Student 3:

p. Read the critique of the pie chart and make any appropriate changes for the pie chart. On the critique worksheet, provide a response to each critique and why you made or did not make the suggested change.

q. Save and close the workbook. Submit based on your instructor's directions.

Beyond the Classroom

Historical Stock Prices

RESEARCH CASE

FROM SCRATCH

You are interested in investing in the stock market. First, you need to research the historical prices for a particular stock. Launch a Web browser, go to money.msn.com/investing/, type a company name, such as Apple, and then select the company name from a list of suggested companies. Click the **Historical Prices link**. Copy the stock data (date, high, low, open, close, volume) for a six-month period and paste it in a new workbook, adjusting the column widths to fit the data. Save the workbook as **e03b2StockData_LastFirst**. Rename Sheet1 **Data**. Display data for only the first date listed for each month; delete rows containing data for other dates. Sort the list from the oldest date to the newest date. Use Help if needed to learn how to sort data and how to create a Volume-Open-High-Low-Close chart. Then rearrange the data columns in the correct sequence. Format the data and column labels. Insert a row to enter the company name and insert another row to list the company's stock symbol, such as AAPL. Copy the URL from the Web browser and paste it as a source below the list of data and the date you obtained the data. Merge the cells containing the company name and stock symbol through the last column of data and word-wrap the URL.

Create a Volume-Open-High-Low-Close chart on a new chart sheet named **Chart**. Type an appropriate chart title. Set the primary vertical axis (left side) unit measurement to millions and include an axis title **Volume in Millions**. Include a secondary vertical axis (right side) title **Stock Prices**. Apply **Currency number style** with 0 decimal places for the secondary axis values. Apply **11-pt size** to the vertical axes and category axis. Use Help to research how to insert text boxes. Insert a text box that describes the stock chart: white fill rectangles indicate the closing price was higher than the opening price; black fill rectangles indicate the closing price was lower than the opening price; etc. Create a footer with your name, the sheet name code, and the file name code on both worksheets. Save and close the workbook, and submit based on your instructor's directions.

Harper County Houses Sold

DISASTER RECOVERY

You want to analyze the number of houses sold by type (e.g., rambler, two story, etc.) in each quarter during 2012. Your intern created an initial chart, but it contains a lot of problems. Open *e03b3Houses* and save it as **e03b3Houses_LastFirst**. Identify the errors and poor design for the chart. Below the chart, list the errors and your corrections in a two-column format. Then correct problems in the chart. Create a footer with your name, the sheet name code, and the file name code. Adjust the margins and scaling to print the worksheet data, including the error list, and the chart on one page. Save and close the workbook, and submit based on your instructor's directions.

Time Management

SOFT SKILLS

FROM SCRATCH

After reviewing the video on time-management skills, start a new workbook and save it as **e03b4Time_LastFirst**. List the major activities you do each week (e.g., sleeping, attending classes, eating, etc.) in the first column. In the second column, enter the number of hours per week you spend on each task. For example, if you sleep 8 hours each night, enter 56 (8 hours × 7 nights). Insert the SUM function to total the hours. The total hours per week is 168, so the total time of all activities should be 168. Adjust any values until the total is correct. Create a pie chart based on this data, include and format percentage data labels, and include an appropriate chart title. Below the data and chart, type a recommendation for yourself to improve your time-management skills. Create a footer with your name, the sheet name code, and the file name code. Save and close the workbook, and submit based on your instructor's directions.

Capstone Exercise

You are an assistant manager at Premiere Movie Source, an online company that enables customers to download movies for a fee. You need to track movie download sales by genre. You gathered the data for November 2016 and organized it in an Excel workbook. You are ready to create charts to help represent the data so that you can make a presentation to your manager later this week.

Set Chart Filters, Position, and Size

You created a clustered column chart, but you selected too many cells for the data source. You need to open the workbook and set chart filters to exclude extraneous data sources. In addition, you want to position and size the chart below the data.

a. Open the *e03c1Movies* workbook and save it as **e03c1Movies_LastFirst**.

b. Set chart filters to remove the Category Totals and the Weekly Totals.

c. Position and size the chart to fill the **range A18:K37**.

d. Change the row and column orientation so that the weeks appear in the category axis and the genres appear in the legend.

Add Chart Labels

You need to enter text for the chart title and add a value axis title. In addition, you want to position the legend on the right side because it is easier to read a vertical, alphabetical list rather than a horizontal list of genres.

a. Enter the text **November 2016 Downloads by Genre** as the chart title, bold the title, and then apply **Black, Text 1 font color**.

b. Add a value axis title: **Number of Downloads**. Apply **Black, Text 1 font color**.

c. Move the legend to the right side of the chart.

Format Chart Elements

You are ready to apply the finishing touches to the clustered column chart. You will format the category axis by adjusting the font size and applying a darker font color. You will add and adjust data labels to the Drama data series to emphasize this series.

a. Format the category axis with **11-pt size** and **Black, Text 1 font color**.

b. Select the **Drama data series** and add data labels in the Outside End position.

c. Add a **Gradient fill** to the data labels.

Insert and Format Sparklines

You want to show weekly trends for each genre by inserting sparklines in the column to the right of Category Totals.

a. Click **cell G5** and insert Line Sparklines for the weekly data for each category and the weekly totals, but do not include the category totals for the data range. The location range should be **G5:G15**.

b. Apply the **Sparkline Style Accent 3 (no dark or light) sparkline style**.

c. Show the high point and markers.

d. Change the high point marker color to **Red**.

Create a Stacked Bar Chart

You want to create a bar chart to show how the weekly totals contribute to the month totals by genre.

a. Select the **range A4:E14**. Create a clustered bar chart.

b. Move the chart to its own sheet named **Bar Chart**.

c. Change the chart type to a stacked bar chart.

d. Add a chart title above the chart and enter **November 2016 Weekly Downloads**.

Format the Bar Chart

You want to enhance the appearance of the chart by applying a chart style and adjusting the axis values.

a. Apply bold and **Blue, Accent 5 font color** to the chart title.

b. Apply **11-pt font size** to the category axis, value axis, and the legend.

c. Use the AXIS OPTIONS to display the value axis in units of **Thousands**, set the Major Units to **500**, and apply the **Number format** with 1 decimal place.

d. Use the AXIS OPTIONS to format the category axis so that the category labels are in reverse order.

Finalizing the Charts

You want to prepare the workbook in case someone wants to print the data and charts. To ensure the worksheet data and chart print on the same page, you need to adjust the page setup options.

a. Create a footer on each worksheet with your name, the sheet name code, and the file name code.

b. Apply **landscape orientation** for the Data worksheet.

c. Set **0.2"** left, right, top, and bottom margins for the original worksheet.

d. Change the scaling so that the worksheet fits on only one page.

e. Save and close the workbook, and submit based on your instructor's directions.

Multiple-Sheet Workbook Management

CHAPTER 4

Ensuring Quality Control

OBJECTIVES AFTER YOU READ THIS CHAPTER, YOU WILL BE ABLE TO:

1. Work with grouped worksheets p. 184
2. Manage windows and workspaces p. 187
3. Insert hyperlinks p. 189
4. Insert a 3-D formula p. 197

5. Link workbooks p. 199
6. Audit formulas p. 207
7. Set up a Watch Window p. 209
8. Validate data p. 210

CASE STUDY | Circle City Sporting Goods

You are the regional manager of Circle City Sporting Goods (CSG), which has locations in Indianapolis, Bloomington, and South Bend. CSG is a comprehensive retailer that sells athletic apparel, exercise equipment, footwear, camping gear, sports gear, and sports nutrition items. Each store manager gathers data for every department monthly and prepares a quarterly worksheet. Because each store contains the same departments, the worksheets are identical. Having an identical structure helps you consolidate sales data for all three locations.

You want to review sales data for the past fiscal year. Before consolidating data, you need to format the worksheets, copy data to the summary sheet, and then insert hyperlinks from the summary sheet back to the individual quarterly sheets in the Indianapolis workbook. Later, you will consolidate data from the Indianapolis, Bloomington, and South Bend workbooks into a regional workbook. Finally, you will use auditing tools to identify errors in the Bloomington workbook and add validation to ensure users enter correct data.

Multiple Worksheets

A workbook can contain one or more worksheets of related data. Deciding how to structure data into multiple worksheets and how to manage these worksheets is important. You should determine how much data to enter on each worksheet, when to divide data among several worksheets, and how to format worksheets efficiently. You might also want to create links among the worksheets to enable efficient navigation. For example, you can create a documentation worksheet and then insert links to each worksheet.

After you design multiple worksheets in a workbook, you might want to display worksheets side by side or in a particular arrangement. You can also save the worksheet view layout so that it retains a specific view when you open the workbook again.

In this section, you will work with multiple worksheets and insert hyperlinks from one worksheet to other worksheets. In addition, you will group worksheets together to enter data and apply formatting. Finally, you will manage windows by controlling worksheet visibility, opening and arranging windows, splitting a window, and saving a workspace.

Working with Grouped Worksheets

You often work with workbooks that contain several worksheets. For example, a workbook might contain sales data on one worksheet, a column chart on another sheet, and a PivotTable on a third sheet. In addition, you might create scenarios with Scenario Manager, generate a scenario summary report on a new worksheet or create a Solver model, and then generate a Solver answer report on a new worksheet. In these situations, in order to organize data, the original data are separated into separate worksheets from the consolidated analysis.

Worksheets within a workbook often contain similar content and formatting. For example, a budget workbook might contain detailed monthly data on separate worksheets. By placing monthly data on separate worksheets, you can focus on one month's data at a time instead of presenting the entire year's worth of data on only one worksheet. When worksheets contain similar data but for different time periods—such as months—or different company locations—such as department store locations in various states—you should structure and format the data the same on all worksheets. For example, each monthly worksheet in the yearly budget workbook should contain an identical structure and format for the list of income and expenses. The only differences among the worksheets are the actual values and the column labels that identify the respective months.

Creating worksheets with identical structure and formatting provides consistency and continuity when working with the same type of data on multiple worksheets. In addition, it helps you locate particular items quickly on all worksheets because you know the structure is identical.

Group and Ungroup Worksheets

STEP 1 ≫ Although you can design and format worksheets individually, you can improve your productivity by designing and formatting the worksheets as a group. *Grouping* is the process of selecting two or more worksheets so that you can perform the same action at the same time on all selected worksheets. Table 4.1 describes how to group worksheets. Excel displays grouped worksheet tabs with a white background color and green line spanning the length of all grouped worksheets, and [Group] appears in the title bar.

TABLE 4.1   Grouping Worksheets

To Group:	Do This:
All worksheets	Right-click a worksheet tab and select Select All Sheets.
Adjacent worksheets	Click the first worksheet tab, press and hold Shift, and then click the last worksheet tab.
Nonadjacent worksheet tabs	Click the first worksheet tab, press and hold Ctrl, and then click each additional worksheet tab.

Ungrouping is the process of deselecting grouped worksheets so that actions performed on one sheet do not affect other worksheets. To ungroup worksheets, click a worksheet tab for a sheet that is not grouped. If you grouped all worksheets, right-click a worksheet tab and select Ungroup Sheets.

TIP Caution with Grouping!

Make sure that you ungroup worksheets when you want to perform a task on only one worksheet. If you forget to ungroup sheets, you could potentially ruin several worksheets by overwriting data on all worksheets instead of just the active worksheet.

Enter Data and Format Grouped Worksheets

STEP 2 » Grouping worksheets enables you to improve your productivity by performing the same tasks on the grouped worksheets at the same time instead of performing the tasks individually on each worksheet. Grouping worksheets helps you enter data, change the worksheet structure, apply page layouts, and print worksheets. Whatever you do to the active worksheet also affects the other grouped worksheets.

Data Entry

You can enter labels, values, dates, and formulas efficiently on grouped worksheets, saving you from entering the same data on each worksheet individually. For example, if you enter row labels in the range A5:A10 to describe the different types of monthly income and expenses, Excel enters the same data in the same location (the range A5:A10) on the other grouped worksheets. When you enter a formula on grouped worksheets, Excel enters the formula in the same cell address on all grouped worksheets. For example, if you enter =A4-B4 in cell C4 on the active worksheet, Excel enters =A4-B4 in cell C4 on all grouped worksheets. The formulas use the values on the respective worksheets.

Structural Changes

If you insert a row between rows 4 and 5 and widen column B on the active worksheet, Excel inserts a row between rows 4 and 5 and widens column B on all grouped worksheets. You can cut, copy, and paste data to the same locations and delete cell contents, rows, and columns on grouped worksheets. You can also copy, delete, or hide a group of worksheets.

Formatting

You can apply font formats (e.g., font, font size, bold, font color), alignment settings (e.g., top-left vertical alignment, center horizontal alignment, wrap text), and number formats (e.g., Accounting Number Format, Percent Style, and decimal points) in the same cells on grouped worksheets. Figure 4.1 shows worksheets that were grouped to enter and format data.

Page Layouts and Printing

You can group worksheets, and then apply identical headers, set the page orientation, set the print areas, and adjust the scaling all at one time instead of applying these page layouts individually to each worksheet. After grouping worksheets, you can display them in Print Preview, select print settings, and then finally print the grouped worksheets.

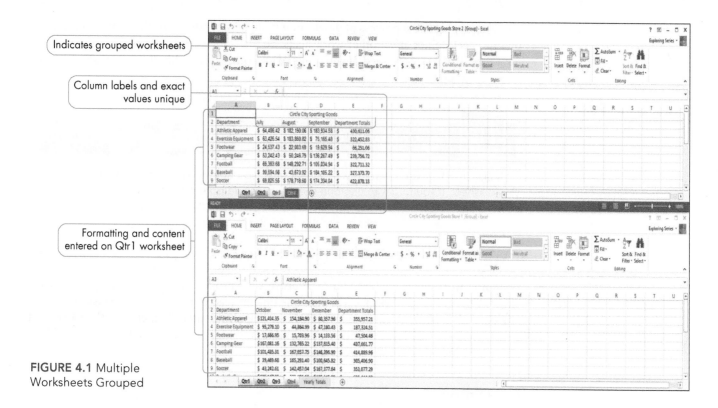

Indicates grouped worksheets

Column labels and exact values unique

Formatting and content entered on Qtr1 worksheet

FIGURE 4.1 Multiple Worksheets Grouped

 **Unavailable Tasks**

Some tasks are not available on grouped worksheets. These tasks appear grayed out on the Ribbon or in menus. For example, you cannot apply conditional formatting or format data as a table on grouped worksheets. Most commands such as PivotTable on the Insert tab are unavailable for grouped worksheets.

Fill Across Worksheets

The previous discussion assumes you are entering new data or formatting existing data across several worksheets at the same time. However, you might have created and formatted only one worksheet, and now you want to copy the data and formats to other worksheets. Instead of using the Copy and Paste commands or copying the entire worksheet, you can fill the data to other worksheets to save time and reduce potential errors, such as formatting the wrong area or forgetting to format a worksheet. To fill data and/or formats from one sheet to other sheets, do the following:

1. Click the worksheet tab that contains the data and/or formats you want to copy. Select the range that you want to fill across the worksheets.
2. Press Ctrl while you click the destination worksheet tabs—the worksheets that you want the data and/or formats applied to.
3. Click the HOME tab, click Fill in the Editing group, and then select Across Worksheets to open the Fill Across Worksheets dialog box (see Figure 4.2).
4. Click All to copy data and formats, click Contents to copy the data only without the formatting, or click Formats to copy only the formatting to the other grouped worksheets. Click OK.

FIGURE 4.2 Fill Across Worksheet Dialog Box

Excel copies the data and/or formatting to the same cells in the other worksheets. For example, if cell A1 in the original worksheet contains the text *Heartland Department Store* bold, centered, and in 14-pt font, Excel copies this text and formatting to cell A1 in the grouped worksheets.

TIP **Conditional Formatting**

Excel disables the Conditional Formatting feature when you group worksheets. You cannot group worksheets and then create and manage conditional formats. However, you can create a conditional formatting rule on one worksheet, group the worksheets, and then use the Fill Across Worksheets command to replicate the conditional formatting rule to a range on other worksheets.

Managing Windows and Workspaces

Because a workbook may contain several worksheets, you need to be able to manage the worksheets onscreen to help you focus on particular worksheets and reduce information overload. To help you manage worksheet windows, you can control worksheet visibility, open and arrange windows for ease of use, split a window to see different parts of a worksheet, and save the layout of the worksheet windows.

Control Visibility of Worksheets

STEP 4 » If a workbook contains so many worksheets that each corresponding tab is not visible, use the worksheet scroll buttons on the left side of the worksheet tabs to find the worksheet you need. If you do not need to view a worksheet, you can hide it. Hiding worksheets is helpful to keep visible only those worksheet tabs that you are currently working on to minimize scrolling through worksheet tabs or when you want to display worksheets on a projector in a meeting but you do not want to accidently click a worksheet containing confidential data. To hide a worksheet, right-click a worksheet tab and select Hide, or do the following:

1. Select the worksheet or worksheets you want to hide. If you want to hide a single worksheet, click the respective worksheet tab. If you want to hide two or more worksheets, select their tabs in a similar way to that with which you group worksheets.
2. Click the HOME tab and click Format in the Cells group.
3. Point to Hide & Unhide and select Hide Sheet.

When you need to display a hidden worksheet again, click Format in the Cells group, point to Hide & Unhide, and then select Unhide Sheet. Excel then opens the Unhide dialog box (see Figure 4.3). Select the worksheet that you want to display and click OK.

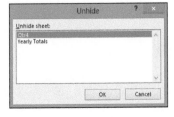

FIGURE 4.3 Unhide Dialog Box

Open and Arrange Windows

You might want to see the contents of two worksheets in the same workbook at the same time. For example, you might want to compare the Qtr1 and Qtr2 worksheets simultaneously. Instead of clicking back and forth between worksheet tabs, you can open another window of the same workbook, and then display different worksheets within each window.

Open Another Window. To open another window of the current workbook, click the View tab, and then click New Window in the Window group. Excel opens another window of the workbook. The title bar adds *:1* to the original workbook view and *:2* to the second window. Although only one window appears maximized, both windows are open. There is no limit to the number of windows that can be opened.

Arrange the Windows. To see all windows of the same workbook, click Arrange All in the Window group. Select one of the options from the Arrange Windows dialog box (see Figure 4.4). You can display windows in a tiled arrangement, horizontally, vertically, or in a cascaded view. If you have other workbooks open when you click Arrange All, Excel includes those workbook windows. To display windows for the current workbook only, click the *Windows of active workbook* check box.

FIGURE 4.4 Arrange Windows Dialog Box

Split a Window

When you work with very large, complex worksheets, you may need to view different sections at the same time. For example, you may need to look at input data on rows 5 and 6 and see how changing the data affects overall results on row 150. To see these different worksheet sections at the same time, split the worksheet window. *Splitting* is the process of dividing a worksheet window into two or four resizable panes so you can view separate parts of a worksheet at the same time (see Figure 4.5). All panes are part of the one worksheet. Any changes you make to one pane affect the entire worksheet.

To divide a worksheet into panes, click Split in the Window group on the View tab. Depending on which cell is the active cell, Excel splits the worksheet into two or four panes with *split bars*—vertical and horizontal lines that frame the panes—above and to the left of the active cell. If the active cell is in row 1, the worksheet appears in two *vertical* panes. If the active cell is in column A, the worksheet appears in two *horizontal* panes. If the active cell is cell A1 or any cell besides in the first row or first column, the worksheet appears in four panes.

Once the window is split, you can further customize the display by dragging the horizontal or vertical line that appears. Drag the vertical split bar to divide the worksheet into left and right (vertical) panes. Drag the horizontal split bar to divide the worksheet into upper and lower (horizontal) panes. While the active cell will be mirrored across all split panes, you can scroll each pane to the desired range you wish to see.

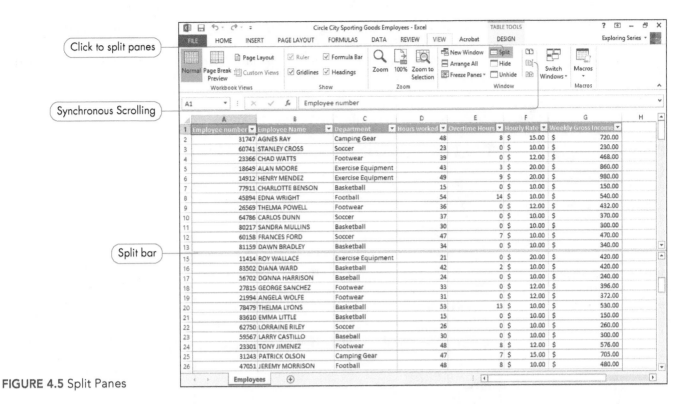

FIGURE 4.5 Split Panes

To remove panes, click Split in the Window group, or double-click the split bar, or drag a vertical split bar to the left or right edge of the worksheet window or a horizontal split bar to the top or bottom of the worksheet window.

> ### TIP | Other Window Settings
>
> The Window group on the View tab contains options to enable you to view two worksheet windows side by side and synchronize the scrolling for both windows or enable separate scrolling. If you have adjusted the window sizes, you can reset the open worksheet windows to share the screen equally. In addition, you can hide a worksheet if you do not want to display it, or you can display a previously hidden worksheet window. However, you cannot use the Freeze Panes settings and split bars at the same time.

Inserting Hyperlinks

STEP 3 When you create a workbook that has multiple worksheets, you might want to include a documentation worksheet that is similar to a table of contents. On the documentation worksheet, enter labels to describe each worksheet, and then create hyperlinks to the respective worksheets. A *hyperlink*, or link, is an electronic marker that, when clicked, connects to another location in the same or a different worksheet, another file, a Web page, or an e-mail. To create a hyperlink, click the cell that will contain the hyperlink or select an object, such as an image, that you want to use as the hyperlink, and then do one of the following:

1. Click the INSERT tab and click Hyperlink in the Links group.
2. Right-click the cell or object and select Hyperlink.
3. Click a cell or object and press Ctrl+K.

The Insert Hyperlink dialog box opens so that you can specify the conditions of the hyperlink. In addition, you can click ScreenTip and enter the text to appear as a ScreenTip when the mouse pointer hovers over a hyperlink. Based on the type of link you select on the left side of the dialog box, the options change to complete the hyperlink specifications (see Figures 4.6 and 4.7).

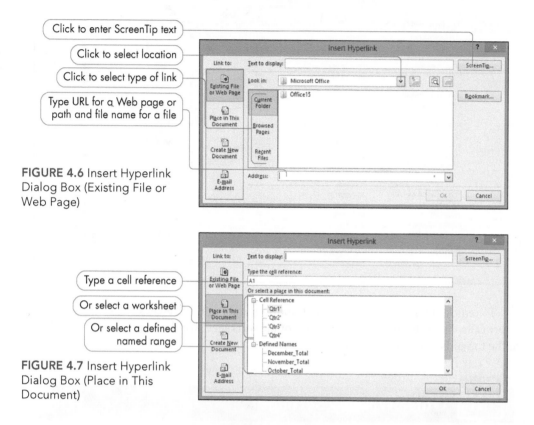

FIGURE 4.6 Insert Hyperlink Dialog Box (Existing File or Web Page)

FIGURE 4.7 Insert Hyperlink Dialog Box (Place in This Document)

TIP Hyperlink Objects

You have the ability to add hyperlinks to more than just text. You have the ability to add links to inserted images and objects as well.

Workbook hyperlinks are similar to Web page hyperlinks. Textual hyperlinks appear blue with a blue underline. When you position the mouse pointer over a hyperlink, the pointer looks like a hand, and Excel displays a default ScreenTip indicating where the link will take you or the custom ScreenTip if you created one in the Set Hyperlink ScreenTip dialog box (see Figure 4.8). Click the link to jump to the link's destination. After you click a hyperlink, the color changes to purple so that you can distinguish between links you have clicked and links you have not clicked. The hyperlink color changes back to blue after a period of time.

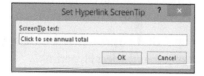

FIGURE 4.8 Set Hyperlink ScreenTip Dialog Box

TIP Edit or Remove a Hyperlink

To modify a hyperlink, right-click it, and then select Edit Hyperlink to open the Edit Hyperlink dialog box, which is similar to the Insert Hyperlink dialog box. Make the desired changes and click OK. To remove a hyperlink, right-click it and select Remove Hyperlink. This action removes the hyperlink but does not delete the cell contents or object.

Quick Concepts

1. What are the benefits of grouping worksheets? *p. 184*

2. What are the benefits of using Split window? *p. 188*

3. Besides linking inside a worksheet, where else can hyperlinks lead the user? *p. 189*

1 Multiple Worksheets

After reviewing last year's fiscal data, you need to improve the appearance of the worksheets for Circle City Sporting Goods. You need to enter a missing heading on the summary worksheet and enter formulas across the quarterly worksheets. To save time, you will group the worksheets to perform tasks to all grouped worksheets at the same time. After you complete the quarterly worksheets, you will insert hyperlinks from the yearly worksheet to the quarterly worksheets.

Skills covered: Group and Fill Across Worksheets • Enter and Format Data Across Worksheets • Insert Hyperlinks • Open and Arrange Worksheets

STEP 1 ≫ GROUP AND FILL ACROSS WORKSHEETS

You noticed that the main title and the row headings are displayed only in the Qtr1 worksheet in the Indianapolis workbook. You need to fill in the title and row headings for the other three quarterly and the yearly worksheets. Refer to Figure 4.9 as you complete Step 1.

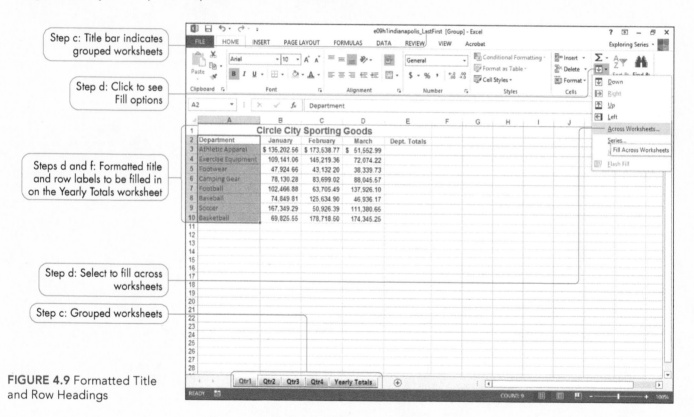

FIGURE 4.9 Formatted Title and Row Headings

a. Open *e09h1Indianapolis* and save it as **e09h1Indianapolis_LastFirst**.

> **TROUBLESHOOTING:** If you make any major mistakes in this exercise, you can close the file, open *e09h1Indianapolis* again, and then start this exercise over.

b. Click the **Qtr1 worksheet tab** and click each worksheet tab to see the differences.

The Qtr1 worksheet contains a title and row labels, whereas the Qtr2, Qtr3, and Qtr4 worksheets are missing the title, row labels, and number formatting. The Yearly Totals worksheet is empty.

c. Click the **Qtr1 worksheet tab**, press and hold **Shift**, and then click the **Yearly Totals worksheet tab**.

You grouped all worksheets together. Anything you do now affects all grouped worksheets. The title bar displays *[Group]* after the file name.

d. Click cell **A1** in the Qtr1 worksheet to select it, click **Fill** in the Editing group on the HOME tab, and then select **Across Worksheets**.

The Fill Across Worksheets dialog box opens so that you can select what to fill from the active worksheet to the other grouped worksheets. The default option is All, which will fill in both the content and the formatting.

e. Click **OK**.

Excel fills in the formatted title from the Qtr1 worksheet to the other worksheets.

f. Select the **range A2:A10** on the Qtr1 worksheet, click **Fill** in the Editing group on the HOME tab, select **Across Worksheets**, and then click **OK**.

> **TROUBLESHOOTING:** Do not select the range A1:D9 to fill across worksheets. If you do, you will overwrite the other worksheet data with the January, February, and March labels and data. If this happens, click Undo to restore data in the other worksheets.

g. Right-click the **Yearly Totals worksheet tab** and select **Ungroup Sheets**. Click each worksheet to review the results. Save the workbook once review is complete.

You ungrouped the worksheets. Now all grouped worksheets contain the formatted title and row labels that were copied across worksheets.

STEP 2 » ENTER AND FORMAT DATA ACROSS WORKSHEETS

You need to regroup the worksheets so that you can increase the width of column A. In addition, you want to insert monthly and department totals for the quarterly worksheets. Refer to Figure 4.10 as you complete Step 2.

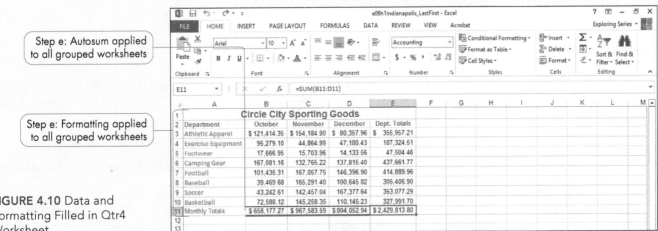

Step e: Autosum applied to all grouped worksheets

Step e: Formatting applied to all grouped worksheets

FIGURE 4.10 Data and Formatting Filled in Qtr4 Worksheet

a. Right-click the **Yearly Totals worksheet tab** and select **Select All Sheets**.

b. Click cell **A2**, click **Format** in the Cells group, select **Column Width**, type **18** in the **Column width box**, and then click **OK**.

You set the column width to 18 for the first column in the grouped worksheets, ensuring that column A's width is identical among the worksheets.

c. Right-click the **Qtr1 worksheet tab** and select **Ungroup Sheets**.

d. Press and hold **Shift** and click the **Qtr4 worksheet tab**.

You have to ungroup sheets and group only the four quarterly worksheets to perform the next few steps.

e. Do the following to the grouped quarterly worksheets:

- Select the **range B3:E11** and click **AutoSum** in the Editing group to insert department totals in column E and monthly totals in row 11.
- Apply **Accounting Number Format** to the **ranges B3:E3** and **B11:E11** to display $ and commas for the first and total rows.
- Type **Monthly Totals** in **cell A11**. Apply bold, increase indent, and **Purple font color**.
- Type **Dept. Totals** in **cell E2**. Use Format Painter to copy the formats from **cell D2** to **cell E2**.
- Select the **range B11:E11**, click the **Border arrow** in the Font group, and then select **Top and Double Bottom Border**.

You applied the Top and Double Bottom Border style to the monthly totals to conform to standard accounting formatting practices.

f. Right-click the **Qtr4 worksheet tab**, select **Ungroup Sheets**, click each quarterly worksheet tab to ensure the formats were applied to each worksheet, and then save the workbook.

STEP 3 ≫ INSERT HYPERLINKS

You want to insert hyperlinks on the Yearly Totals worksheet so that you can click a hyperlink to jump back to the respective quarterly worksheet quickly. Refer to Figure 4.11 as you complete Step 3.

FIGURE 4.11 Hyperlinks

a. Click the **Yearly Totals worksheet tab**, type **Qtr1** in **cell B2**, and then use the fill handle to fill in the remaining quarter labels in the **range C2:E2**. Type **Dept. Totals** in **cell F2**. Center the labels. Increase the width of column F to **12**.

b. Click **cell B2**, click the **INSERT tab**, and then click **Hyperlink** in the Links group.

The Insert Hyperlink dialog box opens so that you can specify the destination when the user clicks the hyperlink.

c. Click **Place in This Document** in the *Link to* section on the left side of the dialog box.

d. Type **E2:E11** in the **Type the cell reference box**, click **'Qtr1'** in the **Or select a place in this document list**, and then click **OK**.

You created a hyperlink to the range E2:E11 in the Qtr1 worksheet. Note that if you do not specify a reference cell for the link it will default to cell A1.

e. Create the following hyperlinks by adapting steps b through d:

- **Cell C2**: Create a hyperlink to the **range E2:E11** in the Qtr2 worksheet.
- **Cell D2**: Create a hyperlink to the **range E2:E11** in the Qtr3 worksheet.
- **Cell E2**: Create a hyperlink to the **range E2:E11** in the Qtr4 worksheet.

f. Position the mouse pointer over cell E2.

The ScreenTip informs you where the hyperlink's destination is (see Figure 4.11). The path and file name shown on your screen will differ from those shown in the figure. If you had created a ScreenTip in the Insert Hyperlink dialog box, that text would appear instead of the destination.

g. Click the hyperlink in **cell E2**.

The hyperlink jumps to the destination: the range E2:E11 in the Qtr4 worksheet.

h. Click the **Yearly Totals worksheet tab** and click the other hyperlinks to ensure they work. When you are done, click the **Yearly Totals worksheet tab** and save the workbook.

> **TROUBLESHOOTING:** If a hyperlink does not jump to the correct range and worksheet, right-click the cell containing the wrong hyperlink, click Edit Hyperlink, and then edit the hyperlink in the Edit Hyperlink dialog box.

STEP 4 ≫ OPEN AND ARRANGE WORKSHEETS

You want to see the four quarterly sales data worksheets at the same time. To do this, you need to open additional windows of the workbook, and then arrange them. Refer to Figure 4.12 as you complete Step 4.

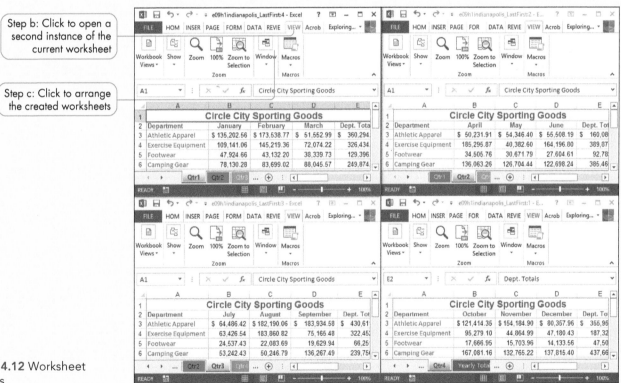

Step b: Click to open a second instance of the current worksheet

Step c: Click to arrange the created worksheets

FIGURE 4.12 Worksheet Windows

a. Click the **VIEW tab** and click **New Window** in the Window group.

You opened another window of the same workbook. The title bar displays the same file name with *:2* at the end of the name.

b. Click **New Window** on the **VIEW tab** in the Window group twice.

Two new windows open with :3 and :4 at the end of each file name. You now have four windows open.

c. Click **Arrange All** in the Window group on the VIEW tab.

The Arrange Windows dialog box opens so you can specify how you want to arrange the open worksheet windows.

d. Click **Tiled**, if necessary, click the **Windows of active workbook check box**, and then click **OK**.

Clicking the *Windows of active workbook* check box ensures that the windows display for the active workbook. If you have other workbooks open, those windows do not display.

Excel arranges the four windows of the same workbook. Currently, all the windows display the Yearly Totals worksheet, but you will display a different worksheet in each window.

e. Click the **Qtr1 worksheet tab** twice in the top-left window, click the **Qtr2 worksheet tab** twice in the top-right window, click the **Qtr3 worksheet tab** twice in the bottom-left window, and click the **Qtr4 worksheet tab** twice in the bottom-right window.

f. Save the workbook. Keep the workbook open if you plan to continue with Hands-On Exercise 2. If not, close the workbook and exit Excel.

3-D Formulas and Linked Workbooks

Excel workbooks often contain data from different time periods, geographic regions, or products. For example, a workbook might contain a worksheet to store data for each week in a month, data for each location of a chain of department stores, or data for sales of each type of automobile produced by one manufacturer. While you have experience creating formulas and functions to perform calculations within one worksheet, you need to be able to consolidate, or combine, data from multiple worksheets into one. For example, you might want to consolidate sales data from all of your department store locations into one worksheet for the year.

Additional data analysis occurs over time. To avoid overloading a workbook with detailed sales data for several years, you might have detailed sales data in individual worksheets in one workbook for a specific year. You then might want to determine the average yearly sales for the past 10 years.

In this section, you will create a 3-D formula to consolidate data from several worksheets. In addition, you will learn how to link data from several workbooks to one workbook.

Inserting a 3-D Formula

 You have referenced other cells in the same worksheet. For example, when you created a one-variable data table, you entered a reference, such as =B12, to display the contents of a formula in cell B12 instead of performing the calculation again in the one-variable data table. At times, you need to consolidate data from multiple worksheets into one worksheet. For example, you might want to create a yearly budget by consolidating values from monthly worksheets, or you might want to calculate average daily occupancy rates for a hospital from detailed weekly occupancy worksheets. When you create formulas that involve reference cells on different worksheets, you include worksheet references. A *3-D reference,* is a pointer to a cell in another worksheet, such as October!E3, which references cell E3 in the October worksheet. An exclamation point separates the worksheet name and the cell reference. If the value in cell E3 in the October worksheet changes, you do not have to edit the value in another worksheet; the reference does that for you automatically.

'Worksheet Name'!RangeOfCells

You can use worksheet references in formulas. For example, a formula that adds the values of cell E3 in the October, November, and December worksheets looks like this: =October!E3+November!E3+December!E3. If a worksheet name contains words separated by a space such as *October Sales*, single quotation marks surround the worksheet name, such as ='October Sales'!E3+'November Sales'!E3+'December Sales'!E3.

> ## TIP CamelCase Notation
>
> CamelCase notation is a file naming convention that eliminates spaces and capitalizes compound words—for example, OctoberSales.xlsx versus October sales.xlsx. By using a naming convention such as CamelCase, you can reduce some of the complexity of a 3-D formula by eliminating the need for single quotation marks.

STEP 2 >>   Entering this type of formula manually or by using the semi-selection process is time-consuming to ensure you click every worksheet and every cell within the respective worksheets. When individual worksheets have an identical structure (i.e., totals for the Jewelry Department are in cell E7 in each quarterly worksheet), you can improve your efficiency in creating formulas by using a *3-D formula*, which is a formula or function that refers to the same cell or range in multiple worksheets. The term *3-D formula* comes from having a reference with three dimensions: worksheet name, column letter, and row number. It is a convenient way to reference several identically structured worksheets in which the cells in each worksheet contain the same type of data, such as when you consolidate sales information from different branches into the Summary worksheet. For example, =SUM('Qtr1:Qtr4'!E3) is a 3-D formula that adds the values in cell E3 in each worksheet, starting in the Qtr1 worksheet and ending in the Qtr4 worksheet, including worksheets between those two. You can type a 3-D reference directly into a cell formula or function, but using the semi-selection method is more efficient. To create a 3-D formula, do the following:

1. Click the cell in which you will enter the 3-D formula.
2. Type =, type the name of the function, such as SUM, and then type an opening parenthesis.
3. Click the first worksheet tab, such as Qtr1.
4. Press and hold Shift as you click the last worksheet tab for adjacent worksheets, or press and hold Ctrl as you click nonadjacent worksheet tabs.
5. Click the cell or select the range that contains the value(s) you want to use in the function argument and press Enter. Figure 4.13 shows the process of creating a 3-D formula before you press Enter.

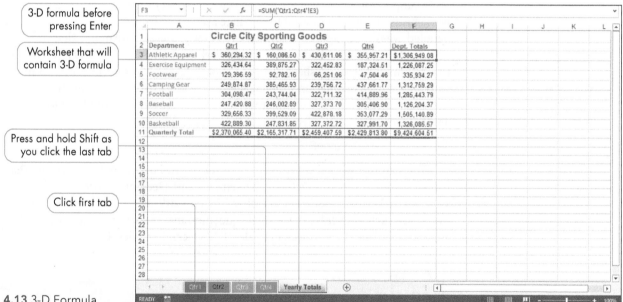

FIGURE 4.13 3-D Formula

=SUM('First Worksheet:Last Worksheet'!RangeOfCells)

You can use a variety of functions for 3-D formulas. Some of these functions include SUM, AVERAGE, COUNT, MIN, and MAX. You can create 3-D formulas using some standard deviation and variance functions. Other functions, such as PMT, VLOOKUP, and COUNTIF, do not work with 3-D formulas.

Linking Workbooks

Workbook linking is another way of consolidating data. When you link workbooks, you consolidate the data from several workbooks into another workbook. *Linking* is the process of creating external cell references from worksheets in one workbook to cells on a worksheet in another workbook. For example, you might have three workbooks—Indianapolis, Bloomington, and South Bend—one for each store location. Each store manager maintains a workbook to record sales by department—such as exercise equipment, footwear, and camping gear—for a particular time period. As district manager, you want to consolidate the data from each workbook into one workbook. Instead of reentering the data, you can create links from specific cells of data in the individual workbooks to your active workbook.

Before creating links, identify the source and destination files. A *source file* is one that contains original data that you need elsewhere. For example, the individual department store workbooks—Indianapolis, Bloomington, and South Bend—are source files. The *destination file* is a file containing a pointer to receive data from the source files—that is, the target file that needs the data. When you link workbooks, you create a connection between the source and destination files. If data change in the source file, the destination file's data update also. Linking ensures that the destination file always contains the most up-to-date data.

Create an External Reference

STEP 3»

When you create a link between source and destination files, you establish an external reference or pointer to one or more cells in another workbook. The external reference is similar to the worksheet reference that you created for 3-D formulas. However, an external reference must include the workbook name to identify which workbook contains the linked worksheet and cell reference. For example, to create a link to cell E3 in the Qtr3 worksheet in the Indianapolis file, type =[Indianapolis.xlsx]Qtr3!E3. You must type the workbook name, including the file name extension, between brackets, such as [Indianapolis.xlsx]. After the closing bracket, type the worksheet name, such as Qtr3, followed by an exclamation mark and the cell reference, such as E3. Table 4.2 lists additional rules to follow when entering external references.

[WorkbookName]WorksheetName!RangeOfCells

TABLE 4.2 External References

Situation	Rule	Example
Workbook and worksheet names do not contain spaces; source and destination files are in the same folder.	Type brackets around the workbook name and an exclamation mark between the worksheet name and range.	[Indianapolis.xlsx]Qtr3!A1
Workbook or worksheet name contains spaces; source and destination files are in the same folder.	Type single quotation marks on the left side of the opening bracket and the right side of the worksheet name.	'[South Bend.xlsx]Qtr3'!A1
Worksheet name contains spaces; source and destination files are in the same folder.	Type single quotation marks on the left side of the opening bracket and the right side of the worksheet name.	'[Bloomington.xlsx]Qtr 3 Sales'!A1
Source workbook is in a different folder than the destination workbook.	Type a single quotation mark, and then the full path—drive letter and folder name—before the opening bracket and a single quotation mark after the worksheet name.	'C:\Data[Indianapolis.xlsx] Sheet1'!A1

Excel displays formulas with external references in two ways, depending on whether the source workbook is open or closed. When the source is open, the external reference shows the file name, worksheet, and cell reference. When the source workbook is closed, the external reference shows the full path name in the Formula Bar. By default, Excel creates absolute cell references in the external reference. However, you can edit the external reference to create a relative or mixed cell reference. To create an external reference between cells in different workbooks:

1. Open the destination workbook and all source workbooks.
2. Select the cell or cells to hold the external reference.
3. Type =. If you want to perform calculations or functions on the external references, type the operator or function.
4. Switch to the source workbook and click the worksheet that contains the cells to which you want to link.
5. Select the cells you want to link to and press Enter.

TIP Drive and Folder Reference

Excel updates an external reference regardless of whether the source workbook is open. The source workbooks must be in the same folder location as when you created the link to update the destination workbook. If the location of the workbooks changes, as may happen if you copy the workbooks to a different folder, click Edit Links in the Connections group on the Data tab.

Manage and Update Linked Workbooks

If you create an external reference when both the source and destination files are open, changes you make to the source file occur in the destination file as well. However, if the destination file is closed when you change data in the source file, the destination file does not automatically update to match the source file. Excel does not update linked data in a destination workbook automatically to protect the workbook against malicious activity, such as viruses.

When you open the destination file the first time, Excel displays the Security Warning Message Bar between the Ribbon and Formula Bar with the message *Automatic updates of links has been disabled*. If you are confident that the source files contain safe data, enable the links in the destination file. Click Enable Content to update the links and save the workbook. The next time you open the destination file, Excel displays a message box that prompts the user to update, do not update, or select help. Click Update to update the links. Figure 4.14 has been contrived to show you both ways of updating links.

Reference link to another workbook

Click to update links if the toolbar displays

Security Warning Message Bar

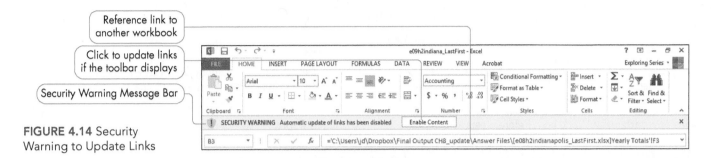

FIGURE 4.14 Security Warning to Update Links

External references identify the workbook names and locations. If you rename or move the source workbook, you must ensure that the external reference in the destination file matches the name of the new source workbook. Otherwise, when you open a destination file that contains external links that cannot be updated, Excel displays an error message, *This workbook contains one or more links that cannot be updated.* Click Edit Links to display the Edit Links dialog box and modify the source links (see Figure 4.15).

Click to change source file

Click to open source file

Click to disable the current link

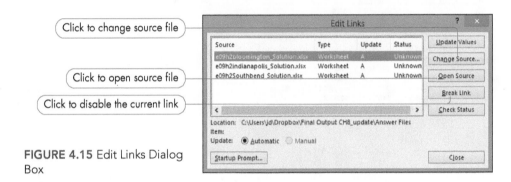

FIGURE 4.15 Edit Links Dialog Box

The Status column displays OK if the external reference link to the source file still works. If a problem exists, the Status column indicates the type of error, such as *Error: Source not found.* Click the source that contains an error and click Change Source to find and select the renamed or moved source file.

Quick Concepts

1. What is a 3-D formula? *p. 198*

2. What are the benefits of 3-D formulas? *p. 198*

3. How do you create an external reference? *pp. 199–200*

Hands-On Exercises

Watch the Video
for this Hands-
On Exercise!

MyITLab®
HOE2 Training

2 3-D Formulas and Linked Workbooks

Previously, you set up the four quarterly worksheets and the yearly total worksheet for Circle City Sporting Goods. Next, you want to calculate total yearly sales for each department as well as the overall total sales. In addition, you want to link sales data from all three locations into one workbook.

Skills covered: Insert Worksheet References • Insert 3-D Formulas • Link Workbooks • Complete the Linked Workbook

STEP 1 ≫ INSERT WORKSHEET REFERENCES

Each quarterly worksheet calculates the quarterly sales totals for a three-month period for each department. You want to insert references from each quarterly worksheet to consolidate the quarterly sales on the Yearly Totals worksheet. Refer to Figure 4.16 as you complete Step 1.

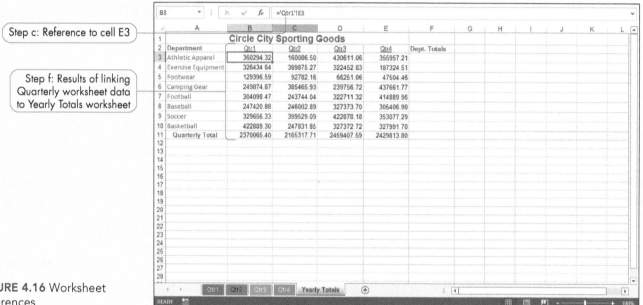

FIGURE 4.16 Worksheet References

a. Open *e09h1Indianapolis_LastFirst* and save it as **e09h2Indianapolis_LastFirst**, changing *h1* to *h2*.

b. Click the **Yearly Totals worksheet tab**. Type **Quarterly Total** in **cell A11**. Bold, indent, and apply **Purple font color** to the label.

c. Click **cell B3**, type =, click the **Qtr1 worksheet tab**, click **cell E3** in that worksheet, and then press **Ctrl+Enter**.

   Look at the Formula Bar. The formula is ='Qtr1'!E3, where Qtr1 refers to the worksheet, and E3 refers to the cell within that worksheet.

d. Double-click the **cell B3 fill handle** to copy the formula down the column.

   The formula's cell reference is relative, so it changes as you copy the formula down the column. The formula in cell B4 is ='Qtr1'!E4.

e. Click **cell C3** in the Yearly Totals worksheet, type **=**, click the **Qtr2 worksheet tab**, click **cell E3** in that worksheet, and then press **Ctrl+Enter**. Double-click the **cell C3 fill handle** to copy the formula down the column.

Look at the Formula Bar. The formula is ='Qtr2'!E3, where Qtr2 refers to the worksheet and E3 refers to the cell within that worksheet.

f. Adapt step e to enter references to the appropriate totals in the Qtr3 and Qtr4 worksheets.

g. Increase the four quarterly column widths to **13**. Save the workbook.

STEP 2 ≫ INSERT 3-D FORMULAS

You want to calculate the total annual sales by department. Although you could simply sum the values in the Yearly Totals worksheet, you want to use a 3-D formula to provide a cross-check that the totals are correct. Refer to Figure 4.17 as you complete Step 2.

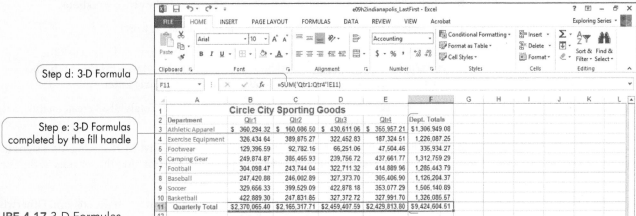

FIGURE 4.17 3-D Formulas

a. Click **cell F3** in the Yearly Totals worksheet.

This cell needs to calculate the total yearly sales for the Men's Clothing Department.

b. Type **=SUM(**

You start the 3-D formula with =, the function name, and the opening parenthesis.

c. Click the **Qtr1 worksheet tab**, press and hold **Shift**, and then click the **Qtr4 worksheet tab**.

You grouped the worksheets together so that you can use a common cell reference for the range of cells to sum.

d. Click **cell E3**, the cell containing the quarterly sales, and press **Ctrl+Enter**.

Look at the Formula Bar. The formula is =SUM('Qtr1:Qtr4'!E3). If you select the range B3:E3, the status bar shows that the sum is $1,306,949.08, the same value that appears when you inserted the 3-D formula.

e. Double-click the **cell F3 fill handle** to copy the formula down the column.

The cell reference is relative, so it changes as you copy the 3-D formula.

f. Apply **Accounting Number Format** to the **ranges B3:F3** and **B11:F11**. Apply **Comma Style** to the **range B4:F10**. Increase the width of column F to **13**. Apply the **Top and Double Bottom Border** to the **range B11:F11**. Bold **cell F2** and change the color to **purple**. Save the workbook.

STEP 3 ≫ LINK WORKBOOKS

You need to link the Indianapolis, Bloomington, and South Bend workbooks to display their totals in the Indiana workbook. The South Bend and Bloomington workbooks have the same structure as the Indianapolis workbook on which you have been working. Refer to Figure 4.18 as you complete Step 3.

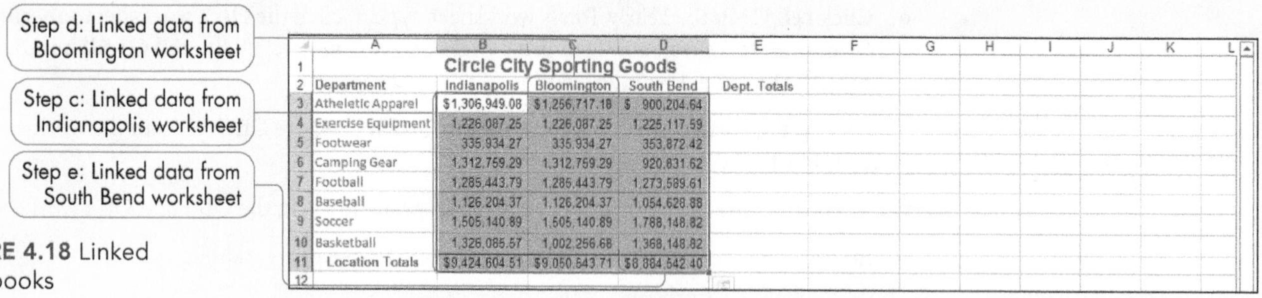

Step d: Linked data from
Bloomington worksheet

Step c: Linked data from
Indianapolis worksheet

Step e: Linked data from
South Bend worksheet

FIGURE 4.18 Linked Workbooks

a. Open *e09h2Bloomington* and save it as **e09h2Bloomington_LastFirst**; open *e09h2SouthBend* and save it as **e09h2SouthBend_LastFirst**; and then open *e09h2Indiana* and save it as **e09h2Indiana_LastFirst**, making sure you save the workbooks in the same folder as your *e09h2Indianapolis_LastFirst* workbook.

b. Click *e09h2Indiana_LastFirst* on the taskbar to make it the active workbook.

   This workbook will contain the links to the three location workbooks.

c. Click **cell B3**, type =, point to the Excel icon on the Windows taskbar, select the *e09h2Indianapolis_LastFirst* workbook, click the **Yearly Totals worksheet tab**, click **cell F3** containing the yearly department totals, and then press **Ctrl+Enter**.

   The formula =‘[e09h2Indianapolis_LastFirst.xlsx]Yearly Totals’!$F$3 creates a link to the Indianapolis workbook.

d. Edit the cell reference in the formula to make cell F3 relative by removing the $ signs in the Formula Bar and pressing **Ctrl+Enter** or placing the cursor after the formula in the Formula Bar and pressing **F4** three times.

   You must make this cell reference relative before copying it down the column. Otherwise, the results will show the value for cell F3 for the other Indianapolis departments.

e. Click **cell C3**, type =, point to the Excel icon on the Windows taskbar, select the *e09h2Bloomington_LastFirst* workbook, click the **Yearly Totals worksheet tab**, click **cell F3**, and then press **Ctrl+Enter**.

   You created a link to the Bloomington workbook. The formula appears as =‘[e09h2Bloomington_LastFirst.xlsx]Yearly Totals’!$F$3.

f. Edit the cell reference in the formula to make cell F3 relative.

g. Adapt steps e and f to create a link to the South Bend workbook's yearly totals.

h. Copy the formulas down the columns in the *e09h2Indiana_LastFirst* workbook. Save the workbook.

STEP 4 ≫ COMPLETE THE LINKED WORKBOOK

You need to insert department totals for all three locations and format the linked workbook. Refer to Figure 4.19 as you complete Step 4.

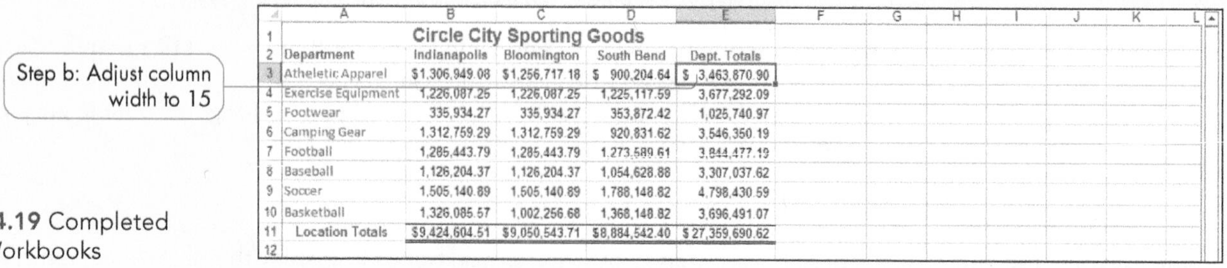

Step b: Adjust column
width to 15

FIGURE 4.19 Completed Linked Workbooks

a. Click **cell E3** in the *e09h2Indiana_LastFirst* workbook.

b. Insert the SUM function to enter **=SUM(B3:D3)**. Copy the formula down column E. Adjust the width of column E to **15**.

You calculated the total yearly sales across all three locations by department.

c. Format the **range B4:E10** with **Comma Style**.

d. Apply **Top and Double Bottom Border** to the **range B11:E11**.

e. Save and close all open workbooks, and submit based on your instructor's directions.

Formula Audits and Data Validation

Errors can occur in a worksheet in several ways. Sometimes, an error may occur with a function name, such as =AVG(B1:E1) when the formula should be =AVERAGE(B1:E1). A *syntax error* is an error that occurs because a formula or function violates correct construction, such as a misspelled function name or illegal use of an operator. Syntax errors also include illegal mathematical construction, such as attempting to divide a value by zero. You must correct syntax errors to obtain a viable result. Excel helps you detect and correct syntax errors. For example, Excel displays #DIV/0! if the formula divides a value by zero to inform you that a result cannot be calculated. Table 4.3 lists some common syntax errors and the reasons for those errors.

TABLE 4.3	Syntax Errors Explained
Error	**Reasons**
#DIV/0!	Formula attempts to divide a value by zero or an empty cell
#NAME?	Misspelled or invalid range name or function name, such as VLOKUP instead of VLOOKUP
	Parentheses missing for function, such as =TODAY instead of =TODAY( )
	Omitted quotation marks around text, such as using *text* instead of *"text"* in the function =IF(A4="text",A5,A6)
	Missing colon in a range reference, such as =SUM(A1A8)
#N/A	Function is missing one or more required arguments, or VLOOKUP, HLOOKUP, or MATCH functions do not return a match
#NULL!	Incorrect range separator
	Formula requires cell ranges to intersect and they do not
#NUM!	Invalid arguments used in a function
#REF!	Reference to cell that contains no data or deleted data
#VALUE!	Incorrect type of data used in an argument, such as referring to a cell that contains text instead of a value

More difficult to detect are errors that appear to be correct but are not because an incorrect range was entered, such as =AVERAGE(B1:D1) when the range should be =AVERAGE(B1:E1). *Logic errors* are the result of a syntactically correct formula but logically incorrect construction, which produces inaccurate results. Logic errors occur when a formula contains the wrong operator or cell reference.

You can design worksheets to help facilitate correct data entry, such as ensuring that a user enters a value, not text. Doing so helps prevent formula errors because the user must enter valid data. Although you can design workbooks to require valid data, you might work with workbooks that other people created that contain errors in the formulas.

In this section, you will learn how to use formula auditing tools to detect errors. In addition, you will apply data validation rules to make sure users enter correct data into input cells.

Auditing Formulas

Recall that you can press Ctrl+` (grave accent key) to display cell formulas instead of cell results. Displaying the formulas may help you identify some errors, but you might not be able to detect all errors immediately. Especially challenging to detect are errors in 3-D formulas or formulas that link workbooks. To help you detect and correct formula errors, you can use *formula auditing*, a set of tools that enable you to display or trace relationships for formula cells, show formulas, check for errors, and evaluate formulas. The Formula Auditing group on the Formulas tab contains commands to help you audit a workbook (see Figure 4.20).

FIGURE 4.20 Formula Auditing Group

 Green Triangle

Excel detects potential logic errors even if the formula does not contain a syntax error. For example, Excel might detect that =SUM(B2:B5) contains a potential error if cell B1 contains a value, assuming the possibility that the function might need to include B1 in the range of values to add. When this occurs, Excel displays a green triangle in the top-left corner of the cell. Click the cell containing the green triangle and click the error icon, the yellow diamond with the exclamation mark, to see a list of options to correct the error.

Trace Precedents and Dependents

STEP 1 » Although Excel displays error messages, you might not know what cell is causing the error to appear in the formula cell. Even if your worksheet does not contain errors, you might want to use formula auditing tools to identify which cells are used in formulas. Formulas involve both precedent and dependent cells. *Precedent cells* are cells that are referenced in a formula. For example, assume an hourly pay rate ($10.25) is stored in cell A1, hours worked (40) is stored in cell A2, and the formula =A1*A2 is stored in cell A3 to calculate the gross pay. Cells A1 and A2 are precedent cells to the formula in cell A3. *Dependent cells* contain formulas that refer to other cells. These cells *depend* on other cells to generate their values. For example, if cell A3 contains the formula =A1*A2, cell A3 is a dependent of cells A1 and A2.

You use Trace Precedents and Trace Dependents to display *tracer arrows* that show the relationship between cells and formulas (see Figure 4.21). The tracer starts in a precedent cell with the arrowhead ending in the dependent cell. To trace precedents, select the cell that contains the formula for which you will find precedent cells and click Trace Precedents in the Formula Auditing group. To trace dependent cells, click the cell for which you will find dependents and click Trace Dependents in the Formula Auditing group. The tracer arrows help you identify cells that cause errors. Blue arrows show cells with no errors. Red arrows show cells that cause errors.

Red indicates error

FIGURE 4.21 Trace
Precedents

TIP **Remove Tracer Arrows**

Click Remove Arrows in the Formula Auditing group on the Formulas tab to remove all tracer arrows, or click the Remove Arrows arrow and select Remove Arrows, Remove Precedent Arrows, or Remove Dependent Arrows.

Check For and Repair Errors

STEP 2 >> When the tracing of precedents or dependents shows errors in formulas, or if you want to check for errors that have occurred in formulas anywhere in a worksheet, you can use Error Checking in the Formula Auditing group. When Excel identifies an error, the Error Checking dialog box opens (see Figure 4.22) and identifies the cell containing an error and describes the error.

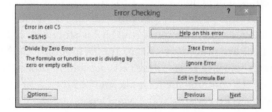

FIGURE 4.22 Error Checking
Dialog Box

Click *Help on this error* to see a description of the error. Click Show Calculation Steps to open the Evaluate Formula dialog box (see Figure 4.23), which provides an evaluation of the formula and shows which part of the evaluation will result in an error. Clicking Ignore Error either moves to the next error or indicates that Error Checking is complete. When you click *Edit in Formula Bar*, you can correct the formula in the Formula Bar.

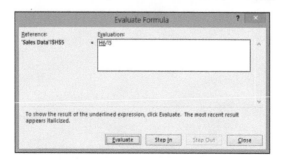

FIGURE 4.23 Evaluate
Formula Dialog Box

Evaluate a Formula

Using nested formulas can make it difficult to understand the formula evaluation. Understanding how a nested formula calculates is hard because intermediate calculations and logical tests exist. You can use the Evaluate Formula dialog box to view different parts of a nested formula and evaluate each part. To use the Evaluate Formula dialog box, do the following:

1. Select the cell you want to evaluate.
2. Click Evaluate Formula in the Formula Auditing group to see the Evaluate Formula dialog box (see Figure 4.23).
3. Click Evaluate to examine the value of the reference that is underlined.
4. If the underlined part of the formula is a reference to another formula, click Step In to display the other formula in the Evaluation box.
5. Click Step Out to return to the previous cell and formula.
6. Continue until you have evaluated the entire formula and click Close.

Use the IFERROR Function to Detect Errors

If you create a workbook for others to use, you should anticipate errors the users will introduce so that you can provide a way to identify and correct those errors. The **IFERROR function** is a logical function that checks a cell to determine if that cell contains an error or if a formula will result in an error. If no error exists, the IFERROR function returns the value of the formula. The *value* argument contains the value being checked for an error, and the *value_if_error* argument is the value to return if the formula evaluates to an error. IFERROR detects the following types of errors: #N/A, #VALUE!, #REF!, #DIV/0!, #NUM!, #NAME?, and #NULL, although the output does not indicate the type of error.

Typically, you use a text string enclosed in quotation marks to return an error message. For example, if you divide the contents of cells in row 2 by cell B1 and anticipate that a #DIV/0! error might occur when copying the formula, you can use =IFERROR(A2/B1,"You cannot divide by zero. Change the value of cell B1 to a value higher than 0.").

=IFERROR(value,value_if_error)

TIP **Information Functions**

The Information functions contain additional functions you can use for error checking. Of particular interest are the ERROR.TYPE and ISERROR functions. Use Help to learn how to incorporate these functions in error-checking tasks.

Setting Up a Watch Window

STEP 3 ▶▶ When you are working with a worksheet containing a large dataset, formulas in cells that are not visible can be "watched" using the Watch Window. You do not need to keep scrolling to different parts of the worksheet if you are using a Watch Window. The **Watch Window** enables you to create a small window so you can conveniently inspect, audit, or confirm formula calculations involving cells not immediately visible on the screen. You can double-click a cell in the Watch Window to jump to that cell quickly. To add cells to the Watch Window, do the following:

1. Click Watch Window in the Formula Auditing group.
2. Click Add Watch in the Watch Window toolbar.
3. Select the cells to watch in the Add Watch dialog box and click Add. The Watch Window shows the cells and formulas you selected to watch (see Figure 4.24).

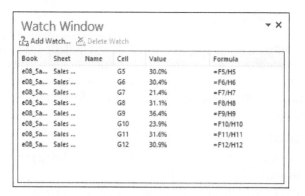

FIGURE 4.24 Watch Window

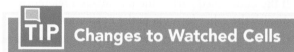

TIP Changes to Watched Cells

Any time you make a change to the watched cell(s), the Watch Window shows you the current value of the watched cell(s).

Validating Data

STEP 4 ⟫ **Data validation** enables you to control the data that can be entered into a cell. It warns and prevents people from entering "wrong" data in a cell, or it can provide a list of valid data from which to choose. Data validation enables you to specify and correct the kind of data that can be entered, specify an input message alerting users when they click a cell that only specific types of data can be entered in that cell, and specify error messages that appear when others persist and attempt to enter incorrect data. To set up a data validation rule, click the cell for which the rule will be applied, and then click Data Validation in the Data Tools group on the Data tab.

Specify Data Validation Criteria

In the Data Validation dialog box, use the Settings tab to specify the **validation criteria**—the rules that dictate the type of data that can be entered in a cell. Click the Allow arrow to specify what type of data you will allow the user to enter, such as a whole number, a value that is part of a specific list, or a date that is within a particular date range. For example, if you specify whole number and the user attempts to enter a decimal, Excel displays an error message. You can also specify that the data must be between two values and specify the minimum and maximum values permitted. Figure 4.25 shows a validation rule in which the cell contents must be (a) a whole number and (b) between a minimum and maximum value, which are stored respectively in cells G5 and G6.

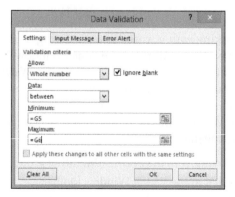

FIGURE 4.25 Data Validation Settings Tab: Criteria

To make data entry easier or to limit items to certain defined items and thereby be more accurate, you can create a list of valid entries from data contained in cells. When you create a list, Excel displays an arrow in the cell. The user clicks the arrow, and then selects the desired entry. The user cannot enter invalid data. To create a list, do the following:

1. Create a list of valid entries in a single column or row without blank cells.
2. Click the cell for which you want to create a validation rule.
3. Click the DATA tab and select Validation in the Data Tools group to show the Data Validation dialog box.
4. Click the Settings tab, click the Allow arrow, and then select List.
5. Enter a reference to the list in the Source box (see Figure 4.26).
6. Make sure that the *In-cell dropdown* check box is selected and that the *Ignore blank* check box is clear and click OK.

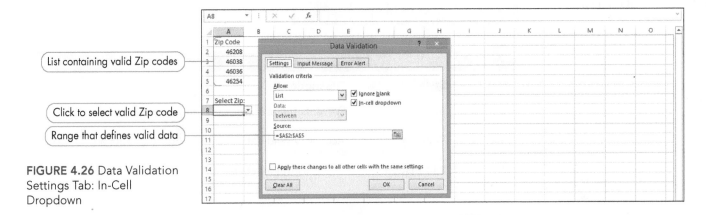

FIGURE 4.26 Data Validation Settings Tab: In-Cell Dropdown

Create an Input Message

STEP 5 ≫   *Input messages* are descriptive text or instructions for data entry that can be entered in the Data Validation dialog box. You add input messages to cells, and Excel displays these messages when a user moves to a cell that has a data-entry restriction. Input messages consist of two parts: a title and an input message (see Figure 4.27). These messages should describe the data validation and explain or show how to enter data correctly. For example, an input message might be *Enter hire date in the form: mm/dd/yyyy* or *Enter Employee name: last name, first name.*

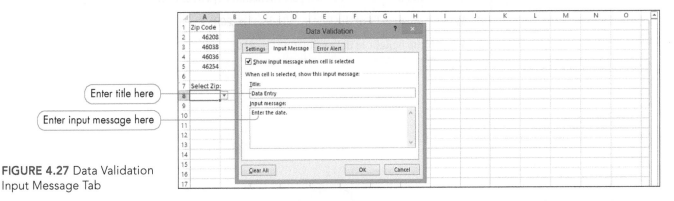

FIGURE 4.27 Data Validation Input Message Tab

Create an Error Alert

Sometimes, no matter how descriptive you are with an input message, users will attempt to enter invalid data in a cell. Instead of using Excel's default error message, you can create an *error alert*, a message that displays when a user enters invalid data in a cell that has a validation rule applied to it. To create an error alert, specify the style, title, and error message on the Error Alert tab (see Figure 4.28). The error alert message should be polite and clearly state what the error is. Cryptic, nondescriptive alert messages do not help users understand the data-entry problem. Table 4.4 shows the error styles that control the icon that appears with the error message.

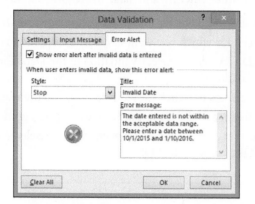

FIGURE 4.28 Data Validation Error Tab

Icon	Style	Description
		**TABLE 4.4 Error Style**		
⊗	Stop	Prevents the user from entering invalid data
⚠	Warning	Accepts invalid data but warns user that data are invalid
ⓘ	Information	Accepts invalid data but provides information to user

TIP   Circle Text

After defining data validation rules, you can display circles around invalid text. To display circles for invalid data, click the Data Validation arrow in the Data Tools group and select Circle Invalid Data. When the user corrects the invalid data, the circles disappear.

Quick
Concepts

1. What is the difference between precedent and dependent cells? *p. 207*

2. What is the benefit of the Watch Window? *p. 209*

3. What is the benefit of data validation? *p. 210*

Hands-On Exercises

Watch the Video for this Hands-On Exercise!

MyITLab®
HOE3 Training

3 Formula Audits and Data Validation

A colleague prepared a worksheet based on projected data if the company opened a store in Fort Wayne. Unfortunately, your colleague introduced several errors. You will use auditing tools to identify and correct the errors. In addition, you will insert validation rules to ensure only valid data are entered in the future.

Skills covered: Trace Precedents and Dependents • Check for Errors • Set Up a Watch Window • Create a Validation Rule • Specify Inputs and Alerts

STEP 1 >> TRACE PRECEDENTS AND DEPENDENTS

You want to display precedent and dependent arrows to identify sources and destinations for cells being used in formulas in the Fort Wayne workbook. Refer to Figure 4.29 as you complete Step 1.

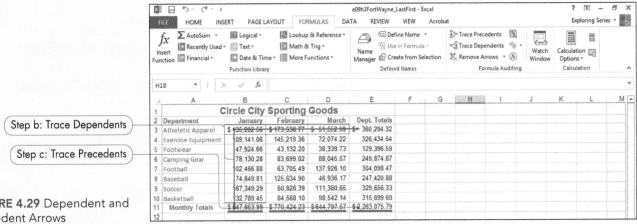

FIGURE 4.29 Dependent and Precedent Arrows

a. Open *e09h3FortWayne*, click **OK** when prompted to fix a circular error, and then save it as **e09h3FortWayne_LastFirst**.

b. Click **cell B3**, click the **FORMULAS tab**, and then click **Trace Dependents** in the Formula Auditing group.

Excel displays a tracer arrow from cell B3 to cells E3 and B11, indicating that cell B3's value is used in formulas in cells E3 and B11.

c. Click **cell E11** and click **Trace Precedents** in the Formula Auditing group.

Excel displays a tracer error showing that the values in the range B11:D11 are used within the current cell's formula.

d. Click **Remove Arrows** in the Formula Auditing group. Save the workbook.

STEP 2 >> CHECK FOR ERRORS

The Qtr2 worksheet contains errors. You will use the Error Checking dialog box and trace precedents to identify the errors. Refer to Figure 4.30 as you complete Step 2.

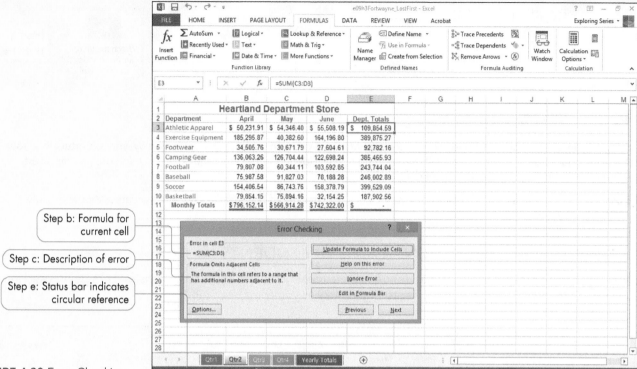

Step b: Formula for current cell

Step c: Description of error

Step e: Status bar indicates circular reference

FIGURE 4.30 Error Checking

a. Click the **Qtr2 worksheet tab**, look for the green error checking error in cell E3, and then click **cell A1**.

b. Click the **Error Checking arrow** in the Formula Auditing group and select **Error Checking**.

The Error Checking dialog box opens, indicating an error in cell E3. Excel detects that the formula omits an adjacent cell.

c. Click **Update Formula to Include Cells**.

Excel modifies the formula from =SUM(C3:D3) to =SUM(B3:D3) to include the April sales.

d. Click **OK** in the message box that informs you that error checking is complete.

When you opened the workbook, an error message stated that the workbook contains a circular reference. However, the Error Checking dialog box did not locate that circular reference. The status bar still indicates that a circular reference exists.

e. Click the **Error Checking arrow** in the Formula Auditing group, point to *Circular References*, and then select **$E$11**.

A circular reference occurs when a formula refers to itself. In this case, cell E11's formula includes itself in the function argument.

f. Edit the formula to be =**SUM(B11:D11)**. Save the workbook.

The circular reference notation on the status bar disappears.

STEP 3 ≫ SET UP A WATCH WINDOW

You want to set up a Watch Window to watch the results of formulas in the Yearly Totals worksheet when you change values in another worksheet. Refer to Figure 4.31 as you complete Step 3.

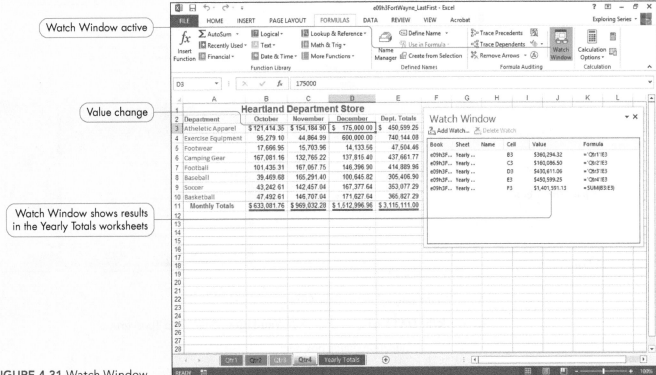

FIGURE 4.31 Watch Window

a. Click the **Yearly Totals worksheet tab**.

b. Select the **range B3:F3**.

   You selected the range you want to watch to ensure formulas work correctly.

c. Click **Watch Window** in the Formula Auditing group and click **Add Watch** in the Watch Window.

   The Add Watch dialog box opens, indicating the worksheet and cells you selected.

d. Click **Add**.

   The Watch Window adds a watch for every cell in the selected range. It shows the workbook name, worksheet name, cell address, current value, and formula.

e. Click the **Qtr4 worksheet tab**.

   The Watch Window remains onscreen. The current Athletic apparel total is $355,957.21, shown in cell E3 and in the Watch Window. The Watch Window also shows the total Athletic Apparel sales to be $1,306,949.08.

f. Click **cell D3**, enter **175000**, and then press **Ctrl+Enter**.

   The Qtr4 Athletic Apparel total changed to $450,599.25 in cell E3 and in the Watch Window. The Watch Window also shows that the total Athletic Apparel sales are now $1,401,591.13.

g. Click **Watch Window** in the Formula Auditing group to hide the Watch Window. Save the workbook.

STEP 4 ≫ CREATE A VALIDATION RULE

You want to insert a validation rule for the Exercise Equipment, Footwear, and Camping Gear values on the Qtr4 worksheet. Based on projections, you believe the maximum revenue would be no more than $500,000. Refer to Figure 4.32 as you complete Step 4.

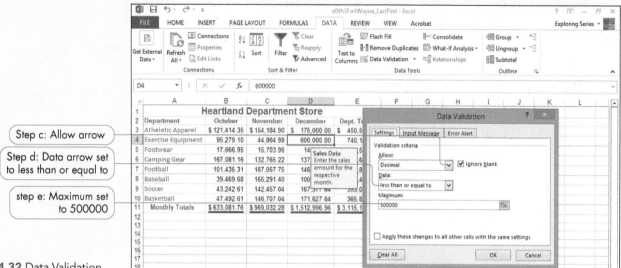

FIGURE 4.32 Data Validation

a. Select the **range B4:D4** on the Qtr4 worksheet.

b. Click the **DATA tab** and click **Data Validation** in the Data Tools group.

The Data Validation dialog box opens.

c. Click the **Allow arrow** and select **Decimal** to allow for dollar-and-cent entries.

The dialog box displays Data, Minimum, and Maximum options.

d. Click the **Data arrow** and select **less than or equal to**.

e. Type **500000** in the **Maximum box**. Keep the Data Validation dialog box open for the next step.

STEP 5 ≫ SPECIFY INPUTS AND ALERTS

You will specify the input message and an alert if a user enters more than 500,000 however, you will let the incorrect value be entered. Refer to Figure 4.33 as you complete Step 5.

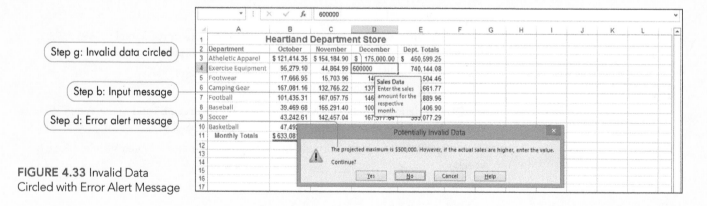

FIGURE 4.33 Invalid Data Circled with Error Alert Message

a. Click the **Input Message tab** in the Data Validation dialog box.

TROUBLESHOOTING: If you wish to edit the validation message that was set up after completing the prior step, you can edit the validation rule by reentering the data validation menu.

---

b. Type **Sales Data** in the **Title box** and type **Enter the sales amount for the respective month.** in the **Input message box**.

c. Click the **Error Alert tab** in the Data Validation dialog box, click the **Style arrow**, and then select **Warning**.

The stop style would prevent values outside the acceptable maximum from being entered. However, your sales projections might be wrong, so you want to allow values over the maximum.

d. Type **Potentially Invalid Data** in the **Title box** and type **The projected maximum is $500,000. However, if actual sales are higher, enter the actual value.** in the **Error message box**. Click **OK**.

e. Click **cell D4**, notice the input message you created from step b, type **600000**, and then press **Enter**.

The error message you created appears (see Figure 4.33).

f. Click **Yes**. Note that even though 600000 is beyond the validation limit, the user is still able to enter the number by clicking **Yes**.

g. Click the **Data Validation arrow** in the Data Tools group and select **Circle Invalid Data**.

Excel circles the value in cell D4, indicating that the value violates the validation rule.

h. Save and close the workbook, and submit it based on your instructor's directions.

Chapter Objectives Review

After reading this chapter, you have accomplished the following objectives:

1. **Work with grouped worksheets.**
   - Group and ungroup worksheets: Allows you to perform the same action simultaneously to grouped worksheets.
   - Enter data and format grouped worksheets: Data entry, structural changes, formatting, and page layout can be edited on grouped worksheets.
   - Fill across worksheets: Selecting Fill Across Worksheets from the Fill button on the Ribbon will copy formatting across all grouped worksheets.

2. **Manage windows and workspaces.**
   - Control visibility of worksheets: You have the ability to hide or unhide worksheets from the Format drop down in the cells group located in the Home tab.
   - Open and arrange windows: The Arrange Window dialog box allows you to display multiple windows as tiled, horizontal, vertical, or cascade.
   - Split a window: Divides the current worksheet window into resizable panes.

3. **Insert hyperlinks.**
   - Insert hyperlink: Hyperlinks are markers that connect one cell to another cell in the same worksheet, different worksheet, or different worksheet in another workbook. You can also create hyperlinks to link to Web pages or e-mail.

4. **Insert a 3-D formula.**
   - Insert a 3-D formula: A 3-D formula is used to consolidate data among two or more worksheets.

5. **Link workbooks.**
   - Create an external reference: An established external reference or pointer to one or more cells in an external worksheet.
   - Manage and update linked workbooks: When a destination file is first opened, you will be prompted to enable automatic link updates.

6. **Audit formulas.**
   - Trace precedent and dependents: Shows arrows that depict the relationships between precedent and dependent cells.
   - Precedent cells are cells referenced in a formula, dependent cells contain formulas that refer to other cells.
   - Check for and repair errors: Check and repair errors by selecting *Error checking* from the Formula Auditing group on the Formulas tab.
   - Evaluate a formula: Provides an evaluation of a formula that shows the portion that returns an error.
   - Use IFERROR function to detect errors: Checks a value and returns the results if possible or an error message.

7. **Set up a Watch Window.**
   - Set up a Watch Window: When you work with large datasets, you can watch formulas in cells that are not visible by using the Watch Window feature. Click Watch Window in the Formula Auditing group and then select Add Watch.

8. **Validate data.**
   - Specify data validation criteria: To specify criteria, use the Settings tab in the Data Validation dialog box.

Key Terms Matching

Match the key terms with their definitions. Write the key term letter by the appropriate numbered definition.

a.	3-D formula	**k.**	Linking
b.	Data validation	**l.**	Logic error
c.	Dependent cell	**m.**	Precedent cell
d.	Destination file	**n.**	Source file
e.	Error alert	**o.**	Split bar
f.	Formula auditing	**p.**	Splitting
g.	Grouping	**q.**	Syntax error
h.	Hyperlink	**r.**	Tracer arrow
i.	IFERROR function	**s.**	Ungrouping
j.	Input message	**t.**	Validation criteria

1. _____ Occurs when formula construction rules are violated. **p. 206**

2. _____ An electronic marker to another location in a worksheet, workbook, file, Web page, or e-mail. **p. 189**

3. _____ Rules that dictate the data to enter a cell. **p. 210**

4. _____ Checks a value and returns the result if possible or an error message. **p. 209**

5. _____ A file that contains a pointer to the source file. **p. 199**

6. _____ Requires that rules be followed in order to allow data to be entered in a cell. **p. 210**

7. _____ Tools to enable you to detect and correct errors in formulas by identifying relationships among cells. **p. 207**

8. _____ A colored line that indicates relationships between precedent and dependent cells. **p. 207**

9. _____ The process of connecting cells between worksheets. **p. 199**

10. _____ The process of selecting worksheets to perform the same action at the same time. **p. 184**

11. _____ The process of dividing a worksheet window. **p. 188**

12. _____ The process of deselecting worksheets that were grouped. **p. 185**

13. _____ A vertical or horizontal line that frames panes in a worksheet and enables the user to resize the panes. **p. 188**

14. _____ A cell containing a formula that is dependent on other cells to obtain its value. **p. 207**

15. _____ Occurs when a formula adheres to syntax rules but produces inaccurate results. **p. 206**

16. _____ A formula or function that refers to the same range in multiple worksheets. **p. 198**

17. _____ A file that contains original data. **p. 199**

18. _____ A cell that is referenced by a formula in another cell. **p. 207**

19. _____ A message that appears when the user enters invalid data in a cell containing a validation rule. **p. 211**

20. _____ A description or instructions for data entry. **p. 211**

Multiple Choice

1. You have a workbook that contains sales data for different regional sales reps of a company. Which task is the least likely to be done while the worksheets are grouped?

   (a) Fill the sales categories across the worksheets.
   (b) Format the column and row labels at the same time.
   (c) Enter specific values for the first sales rep.
   (d) Format the values with an appropriate number style.

2. Your manager sent you a workbook that contains data validation rules. One rule specifies a maximum value of 15% with a warning alert. You try to enter 22% in that cell. What happens?

   (a) Excel enters the 22% with no message boxes.
   (b) Excel enters the 22% and provides a message box to inform you that your entry violates the validation rule.
   (c) Excel displays a message box and prevents you from entering 22%.
   (d) Excel displays a message box informing you the value is above the maximum value and lets you choose to go ahead and enter that value or a different value.

3. The function =FV(D10,D8,-D5) is entered in cell D12. Which cell is a dependent of cell D8?

   (a) D10
   (b) D12
   (c) D5
   (d) D1

4. If you want to display a portion of all three worksheets in a workbook, what should you do?

   (a) Open two new workbook windows, arrange windows, and then click a different worksheet tab in each window.
   (b) Use the Freeze Panes option and cascade the title bars of all open workbooks.
   (c) Double-click the split boxes to display four window panes, click within each pane, and then click the worksheet tab to display its content.
   (d) Use the Split, Freeze Panes, and Arrange All commands at the same time.

5. Which function cannot be used in a 3-D formula?

   (a) SUM
   (b) AVERAGE
   (c) MIN
   (d) PMT

6. A personal trainer stores how much weight each person can lift in several categories. Each week's data are stored in a separate worksheet within the same workbook, and each worksheet has an identical structure. Assume cell F5 contains the weight the first person can bench press. What function can identify that person's highest amount bench-pressed in all worksheets?

   (a) =COUNT(Week 1,Week4:F5)
   (b) =SUM(Week 1:Week4:F5)
   (c) =MAX('Week 1:Week 4'!F5)
   (d) =MAX(Week1:Week4:'F5')

7. You want to create a hyperlink within your document to the SEC Web site. Which type of link do you create?

   (a) Existing File or Web Page
   (b) Place in This Document
   (c) Create New Document
   (d) E-Mail Address

8. To study the results of a formula on the Summary worksheet when you change an input value on the Input worksheet, what can you do?

   (a) Create a watch for the formula and display the Watch Window while changing the input value on the Input worksheet.
   (b) Create a watch for the input cell and display the Watch Window on the Summary worksheet.
   (c) Display the trace precedents and dependents arrows on both worksheets as you change the input value.
   (d) Create a hyperlink from the results to the input cell and from the input cell to the formula.

9. You are preparing an accreditation report for your university. You have several workbooks of data for each college, such as Arts, Sciences, and Business. Assuming the individual workbooks are stored in the same folder as the University workbook, how would a link to cell B15 in the Digital Media worksheet in the School of Computing workbook appear in the University workbook?

   (a) =Computing.xlsx:Digital Media:B15
   (b) ="School of Computing"!'Digital Media'!B15
   (c) ='[School of Computing.xlsx]Digital Media'!$B$15
   (d) ='School of Computing'![Digital Media]:$B$15

10. Which dialog box specifies a cell containing an error and the type of error, such as *Divide by Zero Error*?

    (a) Watch Window
    (b) Circular Reference
    (c) Evaluate Formula
    (d) Error Checking

Practice Exercises

1 Range Free Foods Corporation

The Range Free Foods Corporation began operation last year in Phoenix by opening three stores in different areas of the city. The manager of each store prepared a workbook that summarizes the first-quarter results. As the assistant to the general manager, you need to complete the Downtown workbook, and then link data from the three workbooks to a consolidated workbook. This exercise follows the same set of skills as used in Hands-On Exercises 1 and 2 in the chapter. Refer to Figure 4.34 as you complete this exercise.

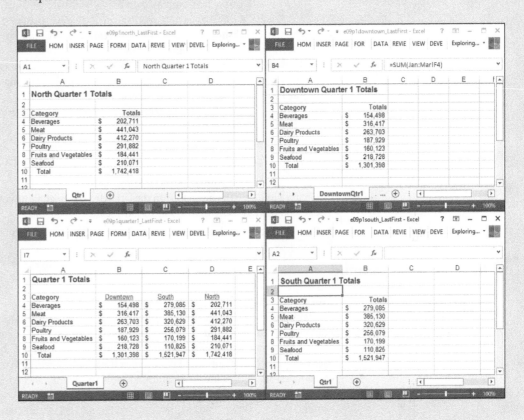

FIGURE 4.34 Range Free Foods Corporation

a. Open *e09p1Downtown* and save it as **e09p1Downtown_LastFirst**. Click each worksheet tab to see what work has been done and what work you will do.

b. Click the **Jan worksheet tab**, press and hold **Shift**, click the **Mar worksheet tab**, and then do the following:

 - Click **cell A1**, click the **HOME tab**, click **Fill** in the Editing group, and then select **Across Worksheets**. Click **Formats** in the Fill Across Worksheets dialog box and click **OK**.
 - Select the **range B4:F10** and click **Sum** in the Editing group.

c. Click the **DowntownQtr1 worksheet**, click **cell B4**, and then insert a 3-D formula by doing the following:

 - Type **=SUM(**
 - Click the **Jan worksheet tab**, press and hold **Shift**, and then click the **Mar worksheet tab**.
 - Click **cell F4** and press **Ctrl+Enter**.
 - Double-click the **cell B4 fill handle** to copy the formula down the column.

d. Open *e09p1South* and save it as **e09p1South_LastFirst**, open *e09p1North* and save it as **e09p1North_LastFirst**, and then open *e09p1Quarter1* and save it as **e09p1Quarter1_LastFirst**.

e. Click the **VIEW tab**, click **Switch Windows** in the Window group, and then select *e09p1North_ LastFirst*.

f. Click the **Jan worksheet**, hold **Shift**, click the **Mar tab** to group the worksheets, and then select **Hide**.

g. Adapt steps e and f to hide the Jan, Feb, and Mar worksheets in *e09p1South_LastFirst.*

h. Click **Switch Windows** in the Window group and select *e09p1Quarter1_LastFirst.*

i. Click **Arrange All** in the Window group, click the **Windows of active workbook check box** to deselect it if necessary, and then click **OK** in the dialog box.

j. Add links by doing the following:

- Click **cell B4** in the Quarter1 worksheet. Type =, display *e09p1Downtown_LastFirst*, click **cell B4** in the DowntownQtr1 worksheet, and then press **Ctrl+Enter**. Edit the formula to change *$B$4* to **B4**. Copy the formula down the Downtown column.
- Click **cell C4** in the Quarter1 worksheet. Type =, display *e09p1South_LastFirst*, click **cell B4** in the Qtr1 worksheet, and then press **Ctrl+Enter**. Edit the formula to change *$B$4* to **B4**. Copy the formula down the South column.
- Click **cell D4** in the Quarter1 worksheet. Type =, display *e09p1North_LastFirst*, click **cell B4** in the Qtr1 worksheet, and then press **Ctrl+Enter**. Edit the formula to change *$B$4* to **B4**. Copy the formula down the North column.
- Format the monetary values with **Accounting Number Format** with zero decimal places in the Quarter1 worksheet.

k. Click **cell B3** in the Quarter1 worksheet, click the **INSERT tab**, click **Hyperlink** in the Links group, scroll through the list of files, select *e09p1Downtown_LastFirst.xlsx*, and then click **OK**.

l. Adapt step k to create hyperlinks in **cells C3** and **C4** to their respective files.

m. Create a footer with your name on the left side, the sheet name code in the center, and the file name code on the right side of the Quarter1 worksheet.

n. Save and close the workbooks, and submit based on your instructor's directions.

2 Retirement Planning

An associate created a worksheet to help people plan retirement based on a set of annual contributions to a retirement account. A user indicates the age to start contributions, projected retirement age, the number of years in retirement, and the rate of return expected to earn on the money when the user retires. The worksheet determines the total amount the user will have contributed, the amount the user will have accumulated, and the value of the monthly retirement amount. However, the worksheet contains errors. You will use the auditing tools to identify and correct errors. Then you will specify validation rules to ensure users enter valid data. This exercise follows the same set of skills as used in Hands-On Exercise 3 in the chapter. Refer to Figure 4.34 as you complete this exercise.

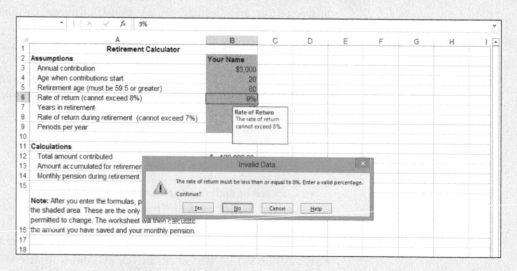

FIGURE 4.34 Retirement Planning

a. Open *e09p2Retire* and save it as **e09p2Retire_LastFirst**.

b. Click **cell B14**, click the **FORMULAS tab**, and then click **Trace Precedents** in the Formula Auditing group.

c. Click the **Error Checking arrow** in the Formula Auditing group and select **Error Checking**.

d. Click **Show Calculation Steps** in the Error Checking dialog box. The Evaluate Formula dialog box opens, showing the formula and stating that the next evaluation will result in an error. Click **Evaluate** to see the error replace the argument in the function: #DIV/0!. Click **Step In** to see the value and click **Step Out** to return to the evaluation. Repeat the Step In and Step Out process and click **Close**. Click **Next** in the Error Checking dialog box and click **OK** in the message box. Find the *0* in **cell B9** and change it to **12**.

e. Click **Remove Arrows** in the Formula Auditing group to remove the precedents arrow.

f. Click **Watch Window** in the Formula Auditing group and click **Add Watch**. Move the dialog boxes so that you can see the data, select the **range B12:B14**, and then click **Add**.

g. Create a data validation rule to ensure the retirement age is greater than 59.5 by doing the following:
   - Click **cell B5**, click the **DATA tab**, and then click **Data Validation** in the Data Tools group.
   - Click the **Settings tab**, click the **Allow arrow**, and then select **Decimal**.
   - Click the **Data arrow** and select **greater than or equal to**.
   - Type **59.5** in the **Minimum box**.
   - Click the **Input Message tab** and type **Retirement Age** in the **Title box**.
   - Type **Federal law does not permit payout prior to 59.5.** in the **Input message box**.
   - Click the **Error Alert tab**, click the **Style arrow**, and then select **Warning**.
   - Type **Invalid Data** in the **Title box**, type **Age must be greater than 59.5.** in the **Error message box**, and then click **OK**.

h. Adapt step g to create a validation rule for **cell B6** to ensure the rate of return will not exceed 8%. Include appropriate titles and messages.

i. Adapt step g to create a validation rule for **cell B8** to ensure the rate of return during retirement will not exceed 7%. Include appropriate titles and messages.

j. Type **50** in **cell B5**. Click **No** when the error message displays, change the value to **60**, and then press **Enter**.

k. Type **8.5%** in **cell B6**. Click **No** when the error message displays, change the value to **8%**, and then press **Enter**.

l. Type **7.5%** in **cell B8**. Click **No** when the error message displays, change the value to **7%**, and then press **Enter**. Close the Watch Window.

m. Create a footer with your name on the left side, the sheet name code in the center, and the file name code on the right side.

n. Save and close the workbook, and submit it based on your instructor's directions.

Mid-Level Exercises

1 Sales Data

ANALYSIS CASE

You are an accountant for a pharmaceutical sales company. As part of your tasks, you compile an annual report that documents regional sales information into one standardized worksheet. As part of this process, you group the worksheets and insert descriptive rows and columns, apply formatting, and insert functions. Your last step is to create a sales summary worksheet and provide basic information for management to evaluate.

a. Open *e09m1Sales* and save it as **e09m1Sales_LastFirst**.

b. Group the five regional worksheets and do the following:

- Insert a new row above row 1 of the existing data. Type **Agent** in **cell A1**. Apply the **Heading 2 style** from the styles group.
- Type **Qtr1** in **cell B1**. Use the fill handle to add Qtr2-Qtr4 in **cells C1:E1**. Apply **Heading 3 format** to **cells B1:E1**.
- Type **Total** in **cell F1**. In **cell F2**, enter the following function: =**SUM(B2:E2)**. Use the fill handle to complete the summary information for the rest of column F.

c. Keep the five worksheets grouped (not including the Summary sheet) and do the following:

- Type **Total** in **cell A20**. In **cell B20**, insert a function to total Qtr1 sales. Copy the function to the **range C20:F20**.
- Format **cells B2:F20** with the **Accounting Number Format**. Set the column width for the **range B1:F20** to **20**.
- Apply **Heading 2 style** to **cell F1**. Add Top and Double Bottom Borders to **cells B20:F20**.

d. Ungroup the worksheets, click the **Summary worksheet tab**, and then apply **Accounting Number Format** to **cells B2:E6.** Select **cells F2:F6** and press **ALT** = to add totals to column F. Set the column width to **18**.

e. Highlight **cells F2:F6** and apply flag indicator conditional formatting.

f. Using the data in the Summary sheet answer the summary questions in the worksheet labeled **Q&A**.

g. Save and close the workbook, and submit it based on your instructor's directions.

2 Temperature Comparisons

As a weather analyst, you have been tracking daily high and low temperatures for Oklahoma City, Tulsa, and Lawton during June, July, and August. Each month's data are stored in their own workbooks, with each city's data stored in its own worksheet. You need to apply consistent formatting and enter formulas for all worksheets. On each workbook, you need to create the summary worksheet to identify the record high and low temperatures by day and identify the respective cities. Finally, you will link the data to a master workbook.

a. Open *e09m2June* and save it as **e09m2June_LastFirst**.

b. Group the city worksheets and do the following:

- Fill the formatting of **cells A1, A2,** and **A5:C5** from the OKC worksheet to the other city worksheets.
- Enter dates 6/1 to 6/30 in this date format (no year) in the Date column. Apply **Orange, Accent 6, Lighter 60% fill** to the dates.
- Split the window after 6/10. Scroll down in the second window to see the Monthly Records section. Note that only the active window in the grouped worksheets is split.
- Enter a function in **cell B39** to calculate the highest temperature of the month. Enter a function in **cell C39** to calculate the lowest temperature of the month.
- Use a nested MATCH function within the INDEX function in **cell B40** to identify the date for the highest temperature. The dataset may contain several identical highest temperatures, but the nested function will identify the first date containing the match.
- Use a nested MATCH function within the INDEX function in **cell C40** to identify the date for the lowest temperature.
- Right-click the **OKC worksheet** and select **ungroup**.

DISCOVER

c. Use a Web browser to go to **www.wunderground.com**, a weather Web site. Locate and click the **History Data link** below the Local Weather menu and do a search for **OKC**. Copy the URL and create a hyperlink to this Web page for **cell A3** in the OKC worksheet. Add a ScreenTip stating **Click to see weather history for Oklahoma City.**

d. Adapt step c to create hyperlinks for the Tulsa and Lawton worksheets as well. Continue to use **www.wunderground.com** for the weather link. Check each hyperlink to ensure it works correctly.

e. Enter the following 3-D formulas in the appropriate cell in the Summary worksheet:

- Calculate the highest temperature from the three cities for 6/1. Copy the formula down the High column.
- Calculate the lowest temperature from the three cities for 6/1. Copy the formula down the Low column.

DISCOVER

- Enter a nested IF function in **cell C6** to determine which city had the highest temperature. Remember to enclose city names in double quotation marks. Use Help if needed to help you understand a nested IF statement. Copy the formula down the High-City column.
- Enter a nested IF function in **cell E6** to determine which city had the lowest temperature. Copy the formula down the Low-City column.

f. Enter formulas in the shaded *Monthly Records* section (below the daily data) on the summary worksheet to identify the highest and lowest temperatures. Enter nested INDEX and MATCH functions to identify the dates and cities for the respective highest and lowest temperatures.

g. Create a footer with your name on the left side, the sheet name code in the center, and the file name code on the right side of each worksheet. Select the option to center the worksheet data horizontally on each sheet. Save the workbook.

h. Open *e09m2July* and save it as **e09m2July_LastFirst**. Open *e09m2August* and save it as **e09m2August_LastFirst**. Study the workbooks and adapt steps b and e above as necessary to enter formulas on grouped city worksheets and to enter 3-D formulas on the Summary worksheets for these two workbooks. The formatting and hyperlinks are done for you. Add your name on the left side of the footer for each worksheet.

i. Open *e09m2Summer* and save it as **e09m2Summer_LastFirst**. Insert external reference links to the respective cells on the monthly Summary worksheets. Format dates and labels appropriately. Enter your name on the left side of the footer. Save the workbook.

j. Save and close the workbooks, and submit them based on your instructor's directions.

---

3 **Book Club**

COLLABORATION CASE

FROM SCRATCH

You have decided to join a book club. As part of the book club, each member has the ability to choose a book from any popular genre. To help make the decision process easier, you have decided to create an Excel spreadsheet that has links to popular media Web sites to allow members of the club to browse the options. You will save this file on OneDrive to allow each member to access the links as needed.

Student 1

a. Log in to your OneDrive account using your Windows ID. Do the following to create a shared folder for the rest of the participants.

- Click **Create**, click **Folder**, and then type **Book Club shared folder**.
- Click the newly created folder and click **Excel workbook** from the Create menu.
- Save the newly created file as **e09m3BookClub_LastFirst**.

b. Type **Popular media websites** in cell A1.

c. Expand the width of column A to allow the full text to be seen.

d. Name the worksheet **Movie Links**.

e. Close the worksheet to return to the OneDrive home screen. From the home screen, complete the following steps:

- Right-click the *e09m3BookClub_LastFirst* file and click **Sharing**.
- Type the e-mail address of a student you will be collaborating with in the pop-up window and click **Share**.

Student 2

a. Open the e-mail that contains the shared Excel workbook.

b. Click **Edit in Excel Online** from the Edit Workbook menu.

c. Click **cell A2**. Click the **INSERT tab** on the Ribbon and create a hyperlink to **www.amazon.com**.

d. Click **cell A3** and create a hyperlink to **www.barnesandnoble.com**.

e. Click **cell A4** and create a hyperlink to **www.ebookstore.sony.com**.

f. Click **cell A5** and create a hyperlink to **www.apple.com/apps/ibooks**.

g. Save the file as **e09p3BookClub_LastFirst** and close.

h. Save and close the workbooks, and submit them based on your instructor's directions

Beyond the Classroom

Europe Trip

RESEARCH CASE

Your grandparents are giving you a trip to Europe as a graduation present. You need to plan your trip and get cost estimates for their approval. Open *e09b2Trip* and save it as **e09b2Trip_LastFirst**. This workbook will summarize your trip expenditures. You will visit two countries, with two major excursions in each country. Open *e09b2Country* and save it as **e09b2Country1_LastFirst** for the first country you plan to visit. Open *e09b2Country* again and save it as **e09b2Country2_LastFirst**. Each workbook should contain a worksheet for each excursion and a country cost summary worksheet where the cost fields are linked in case your projections change. Convert all costs to U.S. dollars.

Include hyperlinks to Web sites from which you obtained your information in case your grandparents have questions. For ease of visibility, display the Summary worksheet for each country workbook and the trip summary from the trip workbook. Link the country workbook's key financial fields to the overall trip workbook summary area. Set a Watch Window on the total expenditure cell to oversee that a formula error does not occur. Close the Watch Window. Create a footer with your name on the left side, the sheet name code in the center, and the file name code on the right side of each worksheet. Save and close the workbooks, and submit them based on your instructor's directions.

Gradebook Errors

DISASTER RECOVERY

You are taking a teaching methods course at your college to prepare you to be a secondary education teacher. One course module teaches students about gradebook preparation, in which you learn how to create formulas to assign grades based on course assessment instruments. Your methods professor assigned a flawed gradebook to see how well you and the other future teachers will do in identifying and correcting the errors. Open *e09b3Grades*, and then save it as **e09b3Grades_LastFirst**. Set validation rules for the range of quiz and final exam scores to accept scores between 0 and 100 only. Create appropriate input and error messages. Use the feature to circle invalid data. Start Microsoft Word, click the Insert tab, and then click Screenshot in the Illustrations group to capture a screenshot for the Excel window. Copy the screenshot in Word, and then paste it on the right side of the worksheet data. Adjust the screenshot sizes as needed so that the entire worksheet will print on only two pages. Insert a comment in each cell containing invalid data describing what is wrong with the data and how to fix it. Then fix the data-entry errors.

Use the auditing tools to find errors, and then display precedents and dependents to identify errors. From Microsoft Word, insert a screenshot of the Excel window, and then copy the screenshot in Word and paste it below the first screenshot in the workbook. Correct the errors in the formulas. Insert comments indicating the errors found and how you corrected the formulas. Create a footer with your name on the left side, the sheet name code in the center, and the file name code on the right side of the worksheet. Save and close the workbook, and submit it based on your instructor's directions.

Managing Your Personal Space

SOFT SKILLS CASE [S]

You work for E&L Financial, a large financial management company that specializes in department store management. You have been assigned as the account manager of Dickson's department store. As part of your task, you will review the past year's earnings. Moving forward you will continue to manage their earnings, therefore you have decided to create a custom workspace to help manage the data.

Open the file *e09b3Workspace*. Save the file as **e09b4Workspace_LastFirst**. Click New Window in the View tab three times to open three additional copies of the document. Arrange the four workbooks in tiled view. Make the Qtr2 worksheet active in the worksheet located in the top-right corner. Make the Qtr3 worksheet active in the bottom-left corner and the Qtr4 worksheet active in the bottom-right corner. Save the layout as a workspace with the name **e09b4Workspace_LastFirst**. Close the workbook and submit it based on your instructor's directions.

Capstone Exercise

You are an accounting assistant for Downtown Theater in San Diego. The theater hosts touring Broadway plays and musicals five days a week, including matinee and evening performances on Saturday. You want to analyze weekly and monthly ticket sales by seating type.

Data Validation

You notice a few occurrences in which it appears more tickets were sold than seats were available. Therefore, you decide to set a validation rule for Week 1.

a. Open *e09c1Theater10* and save it as **e09c1Theater10_LastFirst**.

b. Select the number of daily Orchestra Front tickets sold for Week 1 in the **range C3:G3**.

c. Create a validation rule to accept only numbers that are less than or equal to the available value in cell B3 (i.e., whole numbers between 0 and 86). The input message should display the ticket type in the title bar and should instruct the user to **Enter the number of tickets sold per day.** Use a Stop icon for invalid data, with a title and specific instructions on what to do to correct invalid data entry.

d. Create respective validation rules for the number of tickets sold for the remaining ticket types.

e. Circle invalid data entry. Change each invalid entry to the maximum number of available seats. Save the workbook.

Group Worksheets and Enter Formulas

You need to calculate the daily revenue by seating type (such as Orchestra Front), the weekly seating totals, and the total daily revenue in the weekly worksheets.

a. Group the four weekly worksheets.

b. Enter a formula to calculate Sunday's Orchestra Front revenue, which is based on the number of seats sold and the price per seat found in cells B15:B22. Use relative and mixed cell references correctly.

c. Copy the formula for the Sunday column to the other weekdays. If you constructed the formula correctly, you should not have to edit the copied formulas.

d. Insert formulas to calculate the weekly seating totals in column H and the total daily revenue in row 23. Include the revenue grand total for the week. Save the workbook.

Format Grouped Worksheets

You want to indent the word *Totals*, format the monetary values in the revenue area, and then insert underlines for readability. You also realize the October worksheet needs similar formatting for the descriptions for each section.

a. Indent and bold the word *Totals* in **cells A11** and **A23** on the grouped worksheets.

b. Apply **Accounting Number Format** with zero decimal places to the Orchestra Front revenue and the Total revenue row.

c. Apply **Comma Style** with zero decimal places to the remaining seating revenue rows.

d. Apply a regular underline to the Balcony Level 2 revenue and apply a **Double Underline** for the total revenue values on Total row.

e. Use Format Painter to copy the formats from **cells A2:H2** to **cells A14:H14**.

f. Ungroup the worksheets. Look at the October worksheet to see that the titles above the column headings lack formatting. Fill the formats of **cells C1** and **C13** from the Week 4 worksheet to the October worksheet *without* copying the content. Save the workbook.

Create Hyperlinks

Because several accountants will review the workbook, you want to add hyperlinks from the documentation worksheet to the other worksheets.

a. Select the **Documentation worksheet**, enter your name and the current date in the respective cells, and then create a hyperlink from the Week 1 label to the Week 1 worksheet.

b. Create the hyperlinks from the Documentation worksheet to the other worksheets.

c. Select the **Week 1 worksheet**. Create a hyperlink in **cell A1** back to the Documentation worksheet. Group the weekly and October worksheets and use the Fill Across Worksheets command to copy the link and formatting for the other weekly and summary worksheets.

d. Test all hyperlinks and make any necessary corrections. Save the workbook.

Create 3-D Formulas

You need to consolidate data from the weekly worksheets to the October worksheet to see the percentage of total daily sales and the total revenue by day/seat type.

a. Insert a 3-D formula that calculates the total Sunday Orchestra Front revenue for all four weeks in **cell C15** in the October worksheet. Copy the formula for the remaining seating types, weekdays, total row, and total column.

b. Use the Week 4 worksheet to fill the revenue number formatting to the October revenue.

c. Enter a 3-D formula in **cell C3** on the October worksheet that calculates the overall percentage of total Sunday Orchestra Front tickets sold based on the total available Orchestra Front seating. The result is 97.7%, based on the sum of 336 Sunday Orchestra Front tickets sold (86+84+80+86) out of 344 (86 available for each performance) available tickets. The 3-D formula must perform several internal calculations, avoid raw numbers, and use an appropriate mix of relative and mixed references to derive the correct percentage. Format the result with **Percent Style** with one decimal place.

d. Copy the formula down the Sunday column through the Avg. Daily Capacity row and then across to the Saturday Evening column.

e. Calculate the average daily revenue for each seating type. Format the results with **Percent Style** with one decimal place and copy the formula down the column. Save the workbook.

Audit a Workbook

You need to identify and correct some errors in the November workbook using the Auditing Tools.

a. Open *e09c1Theater11*, click **OK** to acknowledge the error, and then save the workbook as **e09c1Theater11_LastFirst**.

b. Show precedents for **cell H15** and fix the error in the formula.

c. Activate the Error Checking dialog box to find the first potential error. Display the precedent arrows for that formula. If the formula is correct, click **Ignore Error**. If the formula contains an error, fix it. Continue ignoring correct formulas and fix the error in **cell H23** when detected.

d. Use Error Checking to identify a circular reference. Display the precedents arrow and fix the error. Save the workbook.

Link Workbooks

You need to consolidate monthly revenue into the fourth quarter workbook using links. To make it easier to create the links, you will tile windows.

a. Open *e09c1Theater12* and save it as **e09c1Theater12_LastFirst**.

b. Open *e09c1TheaterQ4* and save it as **e09c1TheaterQ4_LastFirst**.

c. Tile the four windows, making sure the monthly totals worksheets are active.

d. Create links in the *e09c1TheaterQ4_LastFirst* workbook to the individual monthly seat revenue and monthly totals. Save the workbooks.

e. Set up a Watch Window to watch the formulas in the quarterly workbook. Close the Watch Window.

Finalize the Workbooks

You are ready to finalize the workbooks.

a. Create a footer on all worksheets with your name on the left side, the sheet name code in the center, and the file name code on the right side.

b. Apply **landscape orientation** and center the worksheet horizontally on the printouts. Save the workbooks.

c. Save and close the workbooks, and submit them based on your instructor's directions.

Specialized Functions

Logical, Lookup, Databases, and Finances

OBJECTIVES AFTER YOU READ THIS CHAPTER, YOU WILL BE ABLE TO:

1. Create a nested logical function p. 232
2. Use MATCH and INDEX lookup functions p. 236
3. Use advanced filtering p. 243

4. Manipulate data with database functions p. 245
5. Create a loan amortization table p. 252
6. Perform other financial calculations p. 254

CASE STUDY | Transpayne Filtration

You are an assistant accountant in the Human Resources (HR) Department for Transpayne Filtration, a company that sells water filtration systems to residential customers. Transpayne has locations in Atlanta, Boston, and Chicago, with a manager at each location who oversees several account representatives. You have an Excel workbook that contains names, locations, titles, hire dates, and salaries for the 20 managers and account representatives. To prepare for your upcoming salary analyses, you downloaded salary data from the corporate database into the workbook.

The HR manager wants you to perform several tasks based on locations and job titles. You will use logical functions to calculate annual bonus amounts and database functions to help analyze the data. Finally, you will review financial aspects of automobiles purchased for each manager.

Logical and Lookup Functions

Logical functions enable you to test conditions to determine if the condition is true or false. You have used the IF function, which is the most popular logical function, to perform different actions based on whether the logical test is true or false. Lookup and reference functions are valuable when you need to look up a value contained elsewhere in a workbook. For example, the VLOOKUP and HLOOKUP functions enable you to take an identified value, such as the number of months for a certificate of deposit (CD) to mature, look up that value in a vertical or horizontal lookup table, and then obtain a related value, such as the annual percentage rate (APR). Excel contains additional logical and lookup functions to perform more complex calculations and analyses.

In this section, you will learn how to create a nested logical function using the IF function. In addition, you will learn how to use the MATCH and INDEX lookup functions.

Creating a Nested Logical Function

The IF function contains three arguments: logical_test, Value_if_true, and Value_if_false. You can enter formulas within both the Value_if_true and Value_if_false arguments to perform calculations. For situations with multiple outcomes based on conditions, you can nest IF functions within the Value_if_true and Value_if_false arguments. A nested function is a function that is embedded within an argument of another function. Excel permits up to 64 IF statements in one formula.

Nested IF Within an IF Function

STEP 1 » Figure 5.1 illustrates three bonus rates based on employee hire date. If a representative was hired before 1/1/2005, the rep receives 9% of her or his total salary as a bonus. If a representative was hired between 1/1/2005 and 1/1/2010, the rep earns a 5% bonus. Lastly, anyone hired after 1/1/2010 receives a 3% bonus.

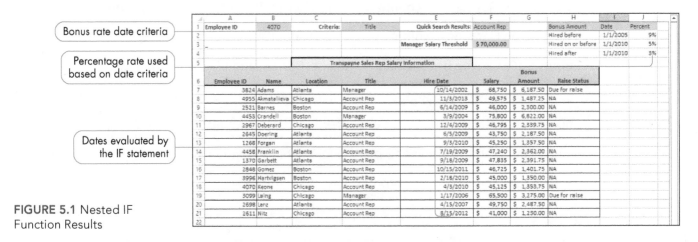

FIGURE 5.1 Nested IF Function Results

Figure 5.2 illustrates the process as a flowchart. Diamonds are logical_test arguments and rectangles are Value_if_true and Value_if_false arguments. The second IF function is stored in the outer Value_if_false argument. Figure 5.3 illustrates the process with cell references.

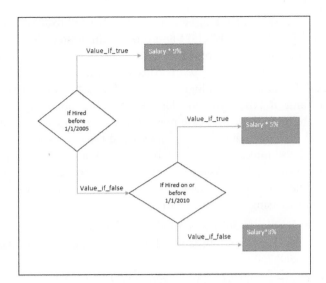

FIGURE 5.2 Nested IF Function Flowchart

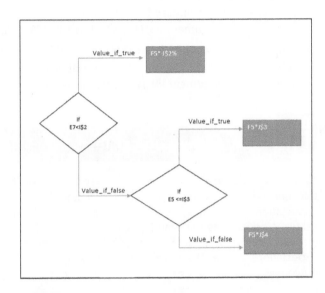

FIGURE 5.3 Nested IF Function Flowchart with Cell References

Figure 5.4 shows the nested IF function as the argument in the Value_if_false box in the Function Arguments dialog box. The function uses relative cell references for the hire date (cell E7) so that the cell reference will change to the next sales rep's hire date when you copy the formula down the column. The formula uses mixed references for the date thresholds (I$2 and I$3) and for the bonus percentages (J$2, J$3, and J$4) so that the references will point to the same rows when you copy the formulas down the column. You could use absolute instead of mixed references, such as $J$4, but doing so creates a longer formula and makes it a little more difficult to read. In the Formula Bar, the nested IF statement looks like this:

=IF(E5<J$7, F5*K$7,IF(E5<=J$8,F5*K$8,F5*K$9))

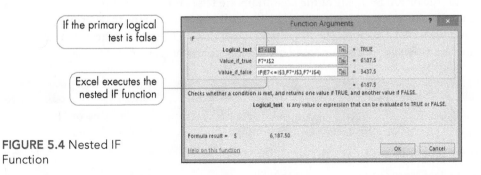

FIGURE 5.4 Nested IF Function

Because you have three outcomes, you need to have two logical tests: one for the primary IF statement (E7<I$2) and one for the nested IF statement (E7<=I$3). The primary logical test evaluates a rep's hire date in cell E7 against the first hire date cutoff stored in cell I2. If the primary logical test is true, Excel multiplies the salary in cell F7 by the rate stored in cell J2. If the primary logical test (E7<I$2) is false, Excel executes the nested IF function in the Value_if_false argument. The nested IF function then evaluates its logical test (E7<=I$3) to determine if the hire date meets the second bonus cutoff level. If that logical test is true, Excel multiplies the salary by the second bonus rate stored in cell J3. If that logical test is false, Excel multiples the salary by the third bonus rate stored in cell J4. You do not need a third logical test to execute the remaining outcome.

The following statements explain how the bonus is calculated for the individual representatives using the nested IF function:

- Employee 3824 was hired on 10/14/2002. In this situation, the logical test (E7<I$2) is true. This causes Excel to execute the Value_if_true argument J2*F$7, which is $68,750 * 9%.

- Employee 4955 was hired on 11/3/2013. In this situation, the logical test (E8<I$2) is false, as is the secondary logical test (E8<=I$3). This causes Excel to execute the Value_if_false argument F8*J$4, which is $49,575 * 3%.

- Employee 2521 was hired on 6/14/2009. In this situation, the logical test (E9<I$2) is false; however, the secondary logical test is true. This causes Excel to execute the Value_if_true argument F9*J$2, which is $46,000 * 5%.

TIP | How Many Logical Tests?

To determine how many logical tests you need, count the number of outcomes and subtract one. For example, if you have three outcomes (such as Exceeds Expectations, Meets Expectations, and Below Expectations), you need only two logical tests. The first logical test produces one outcome (Exceeds Expectations). The nested logical test produces a second outcome (Meets Expectations) if true or produces the third outcome (Below Expectations) if false. Therefore, you do not need a third logical test to produce the third outcome.

Nest AND, OR, and NOT Functions

STEP 2 >> At times, you might need to evaluate *multiple* conditions *at the same time* to determine the result. For example, you might want to evaluate all employees that make less than $50,000 and who are managers for an equity-based salary increase. Excel contains three additional functions to determine whether certain conditions are true or false. These functions are AND, OR, and NOT. You can use these functions individually (which has limited usefulness) or nest them inside another function, such as inside an IF statement (which can increase the capabilities of the function).

The **AND function** accepts two or more logical tests and displays TRUE if *all* conditions are true or FALSE if *any* of the conditions are false. You can test up to 255 conditions. Programmers often create truth tables to help analyze the conditions to determine the overall result. Table 5.1 illustrates the AND truth table that a professor might use to determine whether a student earns a bonus based on attendance and homework submissions.

TABLE 5.1 AND Truth Table

	All Homework Submitted	Missing One or More Homework Scores
Perfect Attendance	TRUE	FALSE
Absent 1 or More Days	FALSE	FALSE

The bonus is awarded (TRUE) only when a student has perfect attendance *and* has completed all homework assignments, as shown in column D in Figure 5.5. Only Zach had perfect attendance and completed all assignments. All other combinations of attendance and homework submissions result in FALSE. Although Bill had perfect attendance, he missed one assignment, so he does not get the bonus.

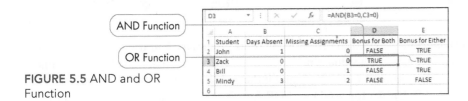

FIGURE 5.5 AND and OR Function

=AND(logical1,logical2)

You can nest the AND function inside the logical_test argument of an IF function to test to see if multiple conditions are met. For example, =IF(AND(B2=0,C2=0),10,0) where B2 contains the number of days absent, C2 contains the number of homework assignments missed, 10 represents the number of bonus points if both conditions are met, and 0 represents that no bonus points are awarded if either condition is false.

> ## TIP AND Results
>
> If the logical argument contains text or empty cells, those values are ignored. If no values exist in the logical argument, the AND function returns the #VALUE! error.

The **OR function** also accepts two or more conditions and returns TRUE if any of the conditions are true. It returns FALSE only if all conditions are false. You can test up to 255 conditions. Table 5.2 illustrates the OR truth table that a professor might use to determine whether a student earns a bonus based on attendance and homework submissions.

TABLE 5.2   OR Truth Table

	All Homework Submitted	Missing One or More Homework Scores
Perfect Attendance	TRUE	TRUE
Absent 1 or More Days	TRUE	FALSE

In column E in Figure 5.5, the bonus is awarded (TRUE) when the student had either perfect attendance *or* if the student completed all assignments. The only time the student does not earn a bonus is if the student is absent one or more days and is also missing one or more homework scores. Mindy was the only student who did not earn the bonus using the OR condition. See Table 5.3 for more detail on the differences between AND and OR functions.

=OR(logical1,logical2)

Table 5.3 displays the differences between AND and OR functions.

TABLE 5.3 AND vs. OR

	All conditions are true	At least one condition is true	At least one condition is false	All conditions are false
AND	TRUE	FALSE	FALSE	FALSE
OR	TRUE	TRUE	TRUE	FALSE

The ***NOT function*** reverses the truth value of its argument. You use the NOT function when you want to make sure a value is not equal to a particular value. If the logical argument is false, the NOT function returns TRUE, and if the logical argument is true, the NOT function returns FALSE. Unlike the AND and OR functions that require two or more logical arguments, the NOT function contains only one logical argument.

=NOT(logical)

Using MATCH and INDEX Lookup Functions

You have used the VLOOKUP and HLOOKUP functions to look up a value, compare it to a lookup table, and then return a result from the lookup table. Two other lookup functions that are helpful when the order of data is not conducive to VLOOKUP or HLOOKUP are MATCH and INDEX. Figure 5.6 demonstrates the MATCH, INDEX, and nested functions.

	A	B	C
1	Agent	Sales	
2	Judy	$10,251.00	
3	Randy	$14,147.00	
4	Bill	$ 8,454.00	
5	Jack	$ 9,254.00	
6			
7	Condition	Results	Formula
8	High Sales amount	$14,147.00	=MAX(B2:B5)
9	Position of High Sales	2	=MATCH(B8,B2:B5,0)
10	Rep w/ Highest Sales	Randy	=INDEX(A2:B5,B8,1)
11	Rep w/ Highest Sales	Randy	=INDEX(A2:B5,MATCH(MAX(B2:B5),B2:B5,0),1)

FIGURE 5.6 MATCH, INDEX, and Nested Functions

Use the MATCH Function

The ***MATCH function*** returns the position of a value in a list. Think of it like a reverse phone number lookup. Instead of using directory assistance to look up a person's phone number, it would be like using the phone number to look up the person. You should use the MATCH function, not the VLOOKUP function, when you have the value, such as $14,147, but want to identify its row position within a list, such as third row. Whereas the MATCH function is often nested inside other functions, you should understand how it works on its own. The MATCH function contains three arguments: lookup_value, lookup_array, and match_type. In Figure 5.6, the MATCH function in cell B9 returns 2, the position of $14,147 within the sales range. The following list explains the arguments of the MATCH function.

=MATCH(lookup_value,lookup_array,[match_type])

- **Lookup_value.** The lookup_value argument is the value that you want to find in the array or list. It can be a value, label, logical value, or cell reference that contains one of these items. In Figure 5.6, the lookup_value argument for the MATCH function in cell B9 refers to the cell containing the MAX function: B8.
- **Lookup_array.** This argument is a range of contiguous cells that contain potential lookup values. In Figure 5.6, the lookup_array argument for the MATCH function in cell B9 is the range of cells containing the sales values: B2:B5.

- **Match_type.** This argument is 1, 0, or -1 to indicate which value to return. Use 1 to find the largest value that is less than or equal to the lookup_value when the values in the lookup_array are arranged in ascending order. Use -1 to find the smallest value that is greater than or equal to the lookup_value when the values in the lookup_array are in descending order. Use 0 to find the first value that is identical to the lookup_value when the values in the lookup_array have no particular order. In Figure 5.6, the match_type is 0 to find an exact match of the highest sales amount.

Use the Index Function

The *INDEX function* returns a value or the reference to a value within a range based on X and Y coordinates. So, for example, it will return the value in the intersection of a specific row and column such as the 3rd value in the 2nd column of a worksheet. When you select this function, the Select Arguments dialog box opens so that you can select an array form or a reference form. The array form is the more commonly used option. It displays the value of an element in a table based on either a row or column number.

`=INDEX(array,row_num,[column_num])`

- **Array.** This argument is one or more ranges. In Figure 5.6, the array argument in the INDEX function in cell B10 is the range containing the agents and their respective sales: A2:B5.

- **Row_num.** This argument identifies the row number within the array range. In the INDEX function in cell B10 in Figure 5.6, the row_num argument is B9, the cell containing the MATCH function results. Recall that the MATCH function in cell B8 determined the position of the highest sales amount from the list of Sales values in cells B2:B5. Therefore, the INDEX function refers to cell B10, which then uses the second row of the array in the range A2:B5.

- **Column_num.** This argument identifies the column within the reference that contains the value you want. In Figure 5.6, the column_num is 1 to identify the first column within the range A2:B5. The first column contains the agent names. So, after the MATCH function identifies the row (2) containing the highest sales value ($14,147.00), the column_num argument (1) identifies the name (Randy) in the first column that corresponds to the highest sales value.

The array in the range A2:B5 contains more than one row and column; therefore, row_num and column_num arguments were required. If an array contains only one row, the column_num is required, and if the array contains only one column, the row_num is required.

 INDEX Function in Reference Form

The reference form displays the cell reference of a row and column intersection. The syntax for the reference form is =INDEX(reference,row_num,[column_num],[area_num]). Use Help to learn about the arguments and to see an example of its usage.

You can reduce the number of cells containing functions by nesting the MATCH function inside the INDEX function. For example, cell B11 in Figure 5.6 contains a nested MAX function inside the MATCH function, which is then nested inside the INDEX function to identify which sales rep had the highest amount of sales.

Nest Functions in Other Functions

STEP 3 You can use the Insert Function and Function Arguments dialog boxes to insert functions as arguments for another function instead of typing the entire nested function directly in the Formula Bar. For example, to create =INDEX(A2:B5,MATCH(MAX(B2:B5),B2:B5,0),1) in dialog boxes, do the following:

1. Click Insert Function, select the outer function, such as INDEX, and then click OK to display the Function Arguments dialog box.

2. Click in the argument box where the nested function is needed, click the Name Box arrow on the Formula Bar, and then select the desired function from the list of recently used functions, or select More Functions from the Name Box drop-down list, select the function, such as MATCH, in the Insert Function dialog box, and then click OK to open the Function Arguments dialog box for the nested function.

3. Enter the arguments for the nested function. Click in the outer function's name—INDEX—in the Formula Bar to display the Function Arguments dialog box for the outer function again.

4. Continue entering or nesting other arguments. When the entire function is complete, click OK in the outer function's Function Arguments dialog box.

Quick
Concepts ✓

1. What is the difference between a single IF statement and a nested IF statement? *p. 232*

2. In what situation would you use an AND function over a nested IF statement? *p. 234*

3. What is the benefit of nesting the MATCH function inside the INDEX function? *p. 237*

1 Logical and Lookup Functions

As the Transpayne accounting assistant, you have been asked to identify underpaid account representatives to bring their salaries up to a new minimum standard within the corporation. In addition, you want to calculate annual bonus amounts based on hire date as well as create a quick search lookup field to allow for instant access to individual information.

Skills covered: Create a Nested IF Function • Nest an AND Function Inside an IF Function • Create a Lookup Field Using INDEX and MATCH Functions

STEP 1 » CREATE A NESTED IF FUNCTION

Your first task is to calculate the annual bonus amount for each employee. The company uses a tiered bonus system that awards a specific percentage of salary based on hire date. Employees hired before 1/1/2005 receive 9%. Employees hired on or before 1/1/2010 receive 5%, and employees that were hired after 1/1/2010 receive 3%. You plan to use a nested IF function to calculate each employee's bonus. You will then use the fill handle to replace the function in the rest of the column. Refer to Figure 5.7 as you complete Step 1.

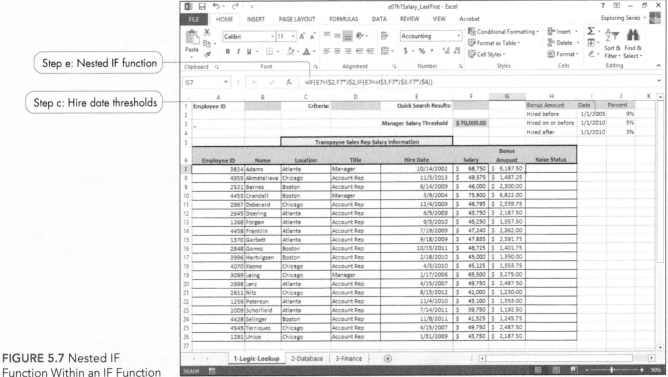

FIGURE 5.7 Nested IF Function Within an IF Function

a. Open *e07h1Salary* and save it as **e07h1Salary_LastFirst**. Click the **1-Logic-Lookup worksheet tab**.

> **TROUBLESHOOTING:** If you make any major mistakes in this exercise, you can close the file, open *e07h1Salary* again, and then start this exercise over.

b. Click **cell G7**, click the **FORMULAS tab** if necessary, click **Logical** in the Function Library group, and then select **IF**.

c. Type E7<I$2 in the **Logical_test box**.

The logical test compares the hire date to the first bonus threshold, 1/1/2005. Because you will copy the formula down the column and want to make sure the reference to the employee's hire date changes, use a relative cell reference to cell E7. To ensure that the reference to the date threshold remains constant, use a mixed cell reference to cell I$2. You could use an absolute reference, but because you are copying the formula down, the column letter I will remain the same. Using a mixed reference keeps the formula shorter and easier to read.

d. Type F7*J$2 in the **Value_if_true box**.

This will multiply the salary by the bonus percentage if the logical test provided is true. If the logical test is not true, it will move on to the next argument created in step e.

e. Type IF(E7<=I$3,F7*J$3,F7*J$4) in the **Value_if_false box**.

By entering an IF statement in the Value_if_false box, you have created a nested function that evaluates the second threshold, 1/1/2010 (cell I3). If the hire date does not fall within the first or second thresholds defined by the primary and secondary logical tests, it will then by default trigger the Value_if_false, (F7*J$4). This will calculate the bonus based on the lowest bonus amount, 3% (cell J4). Use relative cell references for the employee's hire date (cell E7), because it should change when you copy the formula down the column. Use a mixed (or an absolute) reference for the threshold date (cell I$3) to ensure it does not change as you copy the formula down the column. Again, using mixed references keeps the formula shorter and easier to read than absolute references, but both produce the same results.

f. Click **OK** in the Function Arguments dialog box.

The function returns the value 6,188. This is calculated by multiplying the current salary, $68,750 (cell F7), by the bonus percentage rate of 9% (cell J2).

g. Double-click the **cell G7 fill handle** to copy the function down the column.

h. Select the **range G7:G26** and apply **Accounting Number Format**.

i. Save the workbook.

STEP 2 ≫ NEST AN AND FUNCTION INSIDE AN IF FUNCTION

The Human Resources Director recommends that the company pay managers at least $70,000. You would like to nest an AND function inside an IF function to determine which managers should receive pay raises based on their current salary level. The salary threshold is located in cell F3 in the 1-Logic-Lookup worksheet. Refer to Figure 5.8 as you complete Step 2.

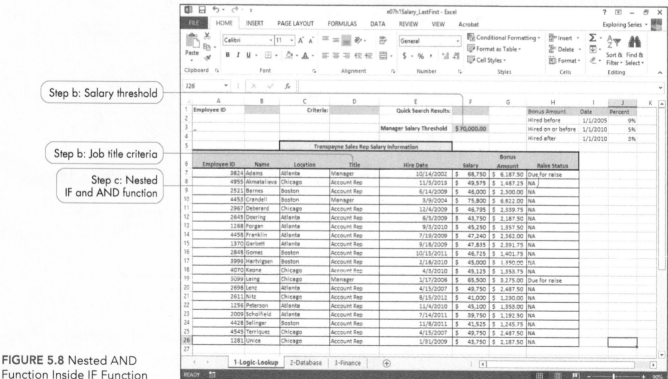

FIGURE 5.8 Nested AND Function Inside IF Function

a. Click **cell H7**, click the **FORMULAS tab**, click **Logical** in the Function Library group, and then select **IF**.

b. Type **AND(D7="manager",F7<F$3)** in the **Logical_test box**.

Using the AND function nested in the logical test of the IF statement gives you the ability to add multiple arguments. In this scenario, you have the criteria if the employee is a manager (D7="manager" and makes less than $70,000 (F7<F$3).

c. Type **"Due for raise"** in the **Value_if_true box**.

If both conditions specified in the AND function are true, the employee is eligible for a raise. You use a mixed reference in cell F3 to ensure that row number 3 does not change when you copy the formula down the column.

d. Type **"NA"** in the **Value_if_false box**.

> **TROUBLESHOOTING:** Do not make cells D7 or F7 absolute or mixed. If you do, the function will use the incorrect values and return the first person's salary of $68,750, in the range H7:H26.

e. Click **OK**, double-click the **cell H7 fill handle** to copy the formula down the column, and then save the workbook.

The function now evaluates the employee's title and salary. If both arguments in the AND function are true, then *Due for raise* is displayed; if not, *NA* is displayed.

STEP 3 ≫ CREATE A LOOKUP FIELD USING INDEX AND MATCH FUNCTIONS

You want to provide a simple search feature so that users can enter an employee number in cell B1 and then display employee title information in cell F1. For example, if Employee ID 4070 is entered in cell B1, cell F1 displays "Account Rep." Refer to Figure 5.9 as you complete Step 3.

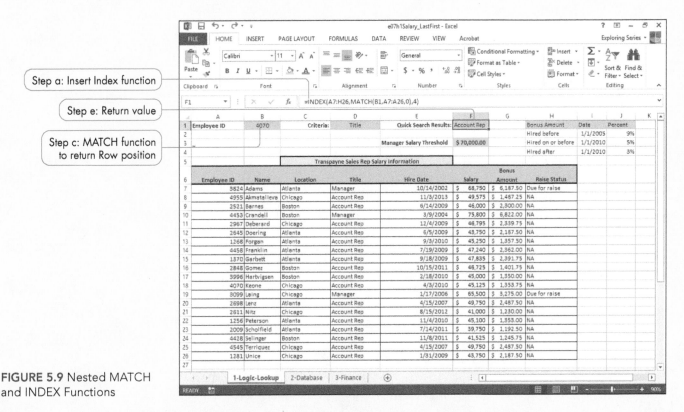

FIGURE 5.9 Nested MATCH and INDEX Functions

a. Click **cell F1**, click **Lookup & Reference** in the Function Library group, and then select **INDEX**. Choose **array, row_num, column_num** from the Select Arguments dialog box and click **OK**.

b. Select **range A7:H26** in the Array box.

This defines the data pool from which Excel will pull information.

c. Type **MATCH(B1,A7:A26,0)** in the **Row_num box**.

If you nest the MATCH function in the Row_num box of the index function, Excel will look up the position of the employee number in cell B1 within the range A7:A26 and return the relative position, which for employee 4070 is 12. Currently, the function returns #N/A because cell B1 is blank.

d. Type **4** in the **Column_num box**. Click **OK**.

If you enter the number 4 in the Column_num box, the function returns information from the fourth column in the data set.

e. Type **4070** in **cell B1**.

Cell F1 now displays the current position of employee 4070. It does this by matching the Employee ID in column A to the Title in column D.

f. Save and leave the workbook open if you plan to continue with Hands-On Exercise 2. If not, save and close the workbook, and exit Excel.

Database Filtering and Functions

Databases are prevalent in most organizations today to store and manipulate data, such as inventory details about automobiles at a particular dealership or financial transaction details for your credit card. Whereas Microsoft Access is more appropriate for relational database modeling, people often use Excel for basic database storage and manipulation. You have some experience in using Excel tables to perform basic database tasks, such as sorting and filtering data. However, you may need to perform more advanced filtering or calculations.

In this section, you will learn how to use advanced filtering techniques and insert database functions. Specifically, you will define a criteria range and extract data that meet certain criteria. Then you will insert the DSUM and DAVERAGE functions to calculate results based on filtered data.

Using Advanced Filtering

Data become more useful in decision making when you reduce the records to a subset of data that meets specific conditions. For example, a manager might want to identify account reps who earn more than $30,000 in Chicago. The manager can use the filter arrows to filter the table data by job title, salary, and location, and Excel will filter the original dataset by hiding records that do not meet the conditions. Sometimes, however, it may be important to keep the original dataset visible and create a copy of only those records that meet these conditions in another location of the worksheet. To do so, the manager can use advanced filtering techniques.

Define a Criteria Range

STEP 1 ▷▷ Before you apply advanced filtering techniques, you must define a criteria range. A *criteria range* is a separate range of cells—often several rows above or below the table—that specifies the conditions used to filter the table. A criteria range must contain at least two rows and one column. The first row contains the column labels as they appear in the table, and the second row contains the conditions (e.g., values) for filtering the table. Figure 5.10 shows the original table, criteria range, and copy of records that meet the conditions.

	Employee ID	Name	Location	Title	Salary	Bonus Amount	Raise Status
6							
7	3824	Adams	Atlanta	Manager	$ 68,750	$ 6,187.50	Due for raise
8	4955	Akmatalieva	Chicago	Account Rep	$ 49,575	$ 1,487.25	NA
9	2521	Barnes	Boston	Account Rep	$ 46,000	$ 2,300.00	NA
10	4453	Crandell	Boston	Manager	$ 75,800	$ 6,822.00	NA
11	2967	Deberard	Chicago	Account Rep	$ 46,795	$ 2,339.75	NA
12	2645	Doering	Atlanta	Account Rep	$ 43,750	$ 2,187.50	NA
13	1268	Forgan	Atlanta	Account Rep	$ 45,250	$ 1,357.50	NA
14	4458	Franklin	Atlanta	Account Rep	$ 47,240	$ 2,362.00	NA
15	1370	Garbett	Atlanta	Account Rep	$ 47,835	$ 2,391.75	NA
16	2848	Gomez	Boston	Account Rep	$ 46,725	$ 1,401.75	NA
17	3996	Hartvigsen	Boston	Account Rep	$ 45,000	$ 1,350.00	NA
18	4070	Keone	Chicago	Account Rep	$ 45,125	$ 1,353.75	NA
19	3099	Laing	Chicago	Manager	$ 65,500	$ 3,275.00	Due for raise
20							
21							
22	Employee ID	Name	Location	Title	Salary		
23			Chicago	Account Rep	>30000		
24							
25	Employee ID	Name	Location	Title	Salary		
26	4955	Akmatalieva	Chicago	Account Rep	$ 49,575		
27	2967	Deberard	Chicago	Account Rep	$ 46,795		
28	4070	Keone	Chicago	Account Rep	$ 45,125		
29	2611	Nitz	Chicago	Account Rep	$ 41,000		
30	4545	Terriquez	Chicago	Account Rep	$ 49,750		

- Criteria set on the second row of the criteria range
- Original data
- Labels on the first row of the criteria range
- Copy of records meeting criteria

FIGURE 5.10 Data, Criteria Range, and Output

Because you want to display records that meet all three conditions, you enter the conditions on the second row of the criteria range, immediately below their respective labels: Chicago below Location, Account Rep below Title, and >30000 below Salary. By default, Excel looks for an exact match. If you want to avoid an exact match for values, enter relational operators. For example, entering >30000 sets the condition for salaries that are greater than $30,000. You can use <, >, <=, >=, and <> relational operators, similar to using relational operators in the logical_test argument of an IF function. Excel copies only the records that meet all three conditions. Therefore, Adams earning $68,750 from Atlanta is excluded because Adams is a manager, not an account rep, and is not from Chicago. You can set an OR condition in the criteria range. For example, you want to display (a) Chicago account reps who earn more than $30,000 *or* (b) Atlanta account reps regardless of salary. Figure 5.11 shows the conditions in the criteria range. Notice that the criteria range contains three rows: column labels on the first row, the first set of conditions on the second row, and the second set of conditions on the third row. Each column of conditions sets an AND condition; that is, each criterion must be met. Each additional row sets an OR condition.

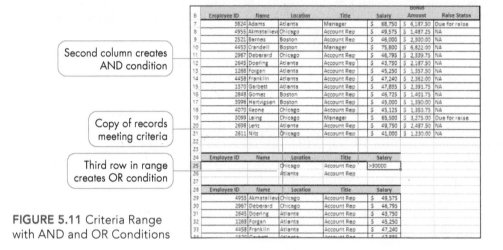

Second column creates AND condition

Copy of records meeting criteria

Third row in range creates OR condition

FIGURE 5.11 Criteria Range with AND and OR Conditions

TIP Using = and <>

Using equal (=) and unequal (<>) symbols with the criteria values selects records with empty and nonempty fields, respectively. An equal with nothing after it will return all records with no entry in the designated column. An unequal (<>) with nothing after it will select all records with an entry in the column. An empty cell in the criteria range returns every record in the list.

Apply the Advanced Filter

STEP 2 ›› After you create the criteria range, you are ready to apply the advanced filter using the Advanced Filter dialog box. This dialog box enables you to filter the table in place or copy the selected records to another area in the worksheet, specify the list range, specify the criteria range, or display unique records only. To apply the advanced filter, do the following:

1. Click a cell in the data table.
2. Click Advanced in the Sort & Filter group on the DATA tab.
3. Click the desired action: *Filter the list, in-place* to filter the range by hiding rows that do not match your criteria or *Copy to another location* if you want to copy the rows that match your criteria instead of filtering the original dataset.
4. Make sure the *List range* displays the range containing the original dataset, including the column headings.
5. Enter the criteria range, including the criteria labels, in the *Criteria range* box. To perform the advanced filter for the OR condition in Figure 5.11, you must select all three rows of the criteria range: the column labels, the row containing the criteria for Chicago account reps earning more than $30,000, and the row containing criteria for Atlanta account reps.

6. Specify the *Copy to* range if you selected *Copy to another location* in Step 3. Notice that you enter only the starting row. Excel will copy the column labels and fill in the rows below the heading with the records that meet the conditions you set. Make sure the *Copy to* range contains sufficient empty rows to accommodate the copied records. If you do not include enough rows, Excel will replace existing data with the copied records. Click OK.

Figure 5.12 shows the Advanced Filter dialog box with settings to produce the advanced filter shown in Figure 5.11.

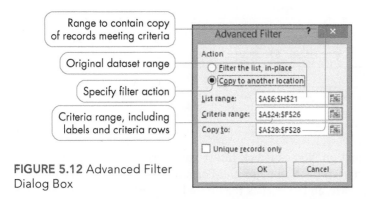

Range to contain copy of records meeting criteria

Original dataset range

Specify filter action

Criteria range, including labels and criteria rows

FIGURE 5.12 Advanced Filter Dialog Box

> **TIP** **Auto Range Names**
>
> When you use the Advanced Filter dialog box, Excel assigns the range name *Criteria* to the criteria range and *Extract* to the output range.

Manipulating Data with Database Functions

Database functions analyze data for selected records only in a database table. These functions are similar to statistical functions (SUM, AVERAGE, MAX, MIN, COUNT) except that database functions are exclusively used for database tables; these functions affect only records that satisfy the specified criteria. Data not meeting the specified criteria are filtered out. All database functions use a criteria range that defines the filter parameters. Using range names can simplify the construction of database functions.

Database functions have three arguments: database, field, and criteria.

- **Database.** The database argument is the entire table, including column labels and all data, on which the function operates. The database reference may be represented by a range name. In Figure 5.13, the Database argument is A6:H21.

- **Field.** The field argument is the database column that contains the values operated on by the function. You can enter the name of the column label in quotation marks, such as "Salary," or you can enter the number that represents the location of that column within the table. For example, if the Salary column is the fifth column in the table, you can enter a 5 for the field argument. You can also enter a cell reference, for example, F6, as shown in Figure 5.13.

- **Criteria.** The criteria argument defines the conditions to be met by the function. This range must contain at least one column label and a cell below the label that specifies the condition. The criteria argument may include more than one column with conditions for each column label, indicated by a range such as A24:F25 or a range name.

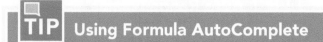

DSUM function

	A	B	C	D	E	F	G	H
4								Hired after
5			Transpayne Sales Rep Salary Information					
6	Employee ID	Name	Location	Title		Salary	Bonus Amount	Raise Status
7	3824	Adams	Atlanta	Manager		$ 68,750	$ 6,187.50	Due for raise
8	4955	Akmatalieva	Chicago	Account Rep		$ 49,575	$ 1,487.25	NA
9	2521	Barnes	Boston	Account Rep		$ 46,000	$ 2,300.00	NA
10	4453	Crandell	Boston	Manager		$ 75,800	$ 6,822.00	NA
11	2967	Deberard	Chicago	Account Rep		$ 46,795	$ 2,339.75	NA
12	2645	Doering	Atlanta	Account Rep		$ 43,750	$ 2,187.50	NA
13	1268	Forgan	Atlanta	Account Rep		$ 45,250	$ 1,357.50	NA
14	4458	Franklin	Atlanta	Account Rep		$ 47,240	$ 2,362.00	NA
15	1370	Garbett	Atlanta	Account Rep		$ 47,835	$ 2,391.75	NA
16	2848	Gomez	Boston	Account Rep		$ 46,725	$ 1,401.75	NA
17	3996	Hartvigsen	Boston	Account Rep		$ 45,000	$ 1,350.00	NA
18	4070	Keone	Chicago	Account Rep		$ 45,125	$ 1,353.75	NA
19	3099	Laing	Chicago	Manager		$ 65,500	$ 3,275.00	Due for raise
20	2698	Lenz	Atlanta	Account Rep		$ 49,750	$ 2,487.50	NA
21	2611	Nitz	Chicago	Account Rep		$ 41,000	$ 1,230.00	NA
22								
23								
24	Employee ID	Name	Location	Title		Salary		Total Salaries Paid
25			Atlanta	Account Rep				$ 233,825.00
26								
27								

Function results

DSUM criteria

FIGURE 5.13 DSUM Function

To insert a database function, you can click Insert Function in the Function Library group or Insert Function between the Name Box and Formula Bar. Then click the *Or select a category* arrow, select Database, and then click the desired database function in the *Select a function* list.

> ## TIP Using Formula AutoComplete
>
> Alternatively, to begin using a database function, you can type =D in a cell. Excel displays the Formula AutoComplete list, showing a list of functions that start with the letter D. Select the appropriate database function from the list.

Use DSUM and DAVERAGE Functions

STEP 3 >>

The **DSUM function** adds the values in a numeric database column based on conditions you specify in a criteria range. In Figure 5.13, the criteria range sets conditions for Boston and account rep. You then use the criteria range to calculate the total salaries for records meeting those two conditions.

=DSUM(database,field,criteria)

The DSUM function is shorter and easier to read than other conditional summary functions, but you must create a criteria range to complete the conditions first. Note that the criteria argument does not need to include the entire database range A6:H21; it only needs to include the column labels and conditions such as A24:F25.

The **DAVERAGE function** determines the arithmetic mean, or average, of numeric entries in a database column that match conditions you specify. For example, you might want to determine the average salary of account reps in Boston using =DAVERAGE(A6:H21, "Salary",A24:F25).

=DAVERAGE(database,field,criteria)

TIP | Division by Zero—#DIV/0—and How to Avoid It

The DAVERAGE function displays a division-by-zero error message if no records meet the specified criteria. You can hide the error message by nesting the DAVERAGE function inside the IFERROR function, which detects the error: =IFERROR(DAVERAGE(A6:H21, "Salary",A24:F25),"No Records Match the Criteria").

Identify Values with DMAX and DMIN

STEP 4 » The **DMAX function** identifies the highest value in a database column that matches conditions you specify. For example, you can use the DMAX function to determine the highest salary ($49,750) of account reps in Boston. The **DMIN function** identifies the lowest value ($43,750) in a database column that matches conditions you specify. For example, you can use the DMIN function to determine the lowest salary for account reps in Boston.

=DMAX(database,field,criteria)

=DMIN(database,field,criteria)

Identify the Total Number with DCOUNT

STEP 5 » The **DCOUNT function** counts the cells that contain numbers in a database column that match conditions you specify. For example, you can use the DCOUNT function to count the number of account reps in Boston, which is four. However, if one of the records is missing a value, DCOUNT excludes that record from being counted. If after completing the DCOUNT, you decide you would like to change the match conditions, you can do so by altering the information entered in the criteria area. To count records containing an empty cell, use DCOUNTA instead.

=DCOUNT(database,field,criteria)

=DCOUNTA(database,field,criteria)

TIP | Additional Database Functions

Excel contains additional database functions, such as DSTDEV to calculate the sample population standard deviation for values in a database column and DVAR to estimate the sample population variance for values in a database column when specified conditions are met.

Quick Concepts

1. Why would you use advanced filtering over basic filtering? **p. 243**

2. What are the benefits of database functions? **p. 245**

3. Why would you use a database function over advanced filtering? **p. 245**

Hands-On Exercises

2 Database Filtering and Functions

Other assistant accountants want to be able to enter criteria to see a list of records that meet the conditions they specify. In addition, these assistants then want to calculate summary statistics based on the filtered results.

Skills covered: Create Criteria and Output Ranges • Perform an Advanced Filter • Insert a DAVERAGE Function • Use DMIN, DMAX, and DCOUNT Functions • Change the Filter Criteria

---

STEP 1 ›› CREATE CRITERIA AND OUTPUT RANGES

You want to set up the workbook with a criteria range and an output range. This will enable other assistant accountants to enter criteria of their choosing to filter the list of salary data. Refer to Figure 5.14 as you complete Step 1.

Step c: Pasted label range

Step d: Second copy of label range for output range use

FIGURE 5.14 Criteria and Output Ranges

a. Open *e07h1Salary_LastFirst* and save it as **e07h2Salary_LastFirst**, replacing *h1* with *h2*. Click the **2-Database worksheet tab**.

b. Select the **range A2:F2** and copy the range.

c. Paste the data in **cell A25**.

d. Click **cell A30**, paste another copy of the data, and then press **Esc**. Save the workbook.

> You copied the original column labels and pasted them in the range A25:F25, the area for the Criteria Range, and another copy of the headings for the Output Range in cells A30:F30.

STEP 2 ›› PERFORM AN ADVANCED FILTER

You are ready to enter conditions to restrict the output list to Account Reps in Boston. Refer to Figure 5.15 as you complete Step 2.

Step a: Advanced filter criteria

Step g: Advanced filter results

FIGURE 5.15 Conditions and Output

a. Type **Boston** in **cell C26** and type **Account Rep** in **cell D26**.

You entered the conditions on the first row below the labels in the criteria range. Because you entered both conditions on the same row, you created an AND condition. Both conditions must be met in order to display employee data in the output range.

b. Click in **cell D19** (or any cell within the dataset).

c. Click the **DATA tab** and click **Advanced** in the Sort & Filter group.

The Advanced Filter dialog box opens so that you can specify the desired filter action, the list, the criteria range, and other details.

d. Click **Copy to another location**.

e. Click in the **List range box** and select the **range A2:F22**.

f. Click in the **Criteria range box** and select the **range A25:F26**.

You selected the labels and the row containing the conditions for the criteria range.

g. Click in the **Copy to box**, select the **range A30:F30**, and then click **OK**.

Make sure you select only the labels for the output range.

h. Scroll down to see the output records. Save the workbook.

Four employees are account reps in Boston.

STEP 3 ≫ INSERT A DAVERAGE FUNCTION

Regardless of the criteria entered in the criteria range A25:F26, you want to calculate the average salary for the records that meet those conditions. You will insert a DAVERAGE function to perform the calculation. Refer to Figure 5.16 as you complete Step 3.

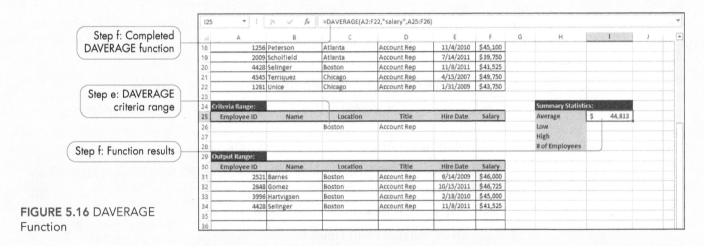

FIGURE 5.16 DAVERAGE Function

a. Click **cell I25** and click **Insert Function** in the Function Library group on the FORMULAS tab.

b. Click the **Or select a category arrow**, select **Database**, select **DAVERAGE** in the *Select a function* list if necessary, and then click **OK**.

c. Select the **range A2:F22** to enter that range in the Database box.

The database argument must include the column labels and original dataset.

d. Click in the **Field box** and type **Salary**.

Excel enters the quotation marks for you within the dialog box. If you want, you can enter the field name in quotation marks yourself, or you can enter the column number (6) of the column that contains the data you wish to average.

> **TROUBLESHOOTING:** If you type the function instead of using the dialog box, make sure you type the double quotation marks (") around text. Otherwise, Excel will display an error message.

e. Click in the **Criteria box** and select the **range A25:F26**.

Excel might display *Criteria* instead of the range in the Criteria box.

f. Click **OK**. Save the workbook.

The average salary of account reps in Boston is $44,813.

STEP 4 ➤➤ USE DMIN, DMAX, AND DCOUNT FUNCTIONS

The other accounting assistants would like to see the lowest and highest salaries based on the database conditions. In addition, you want to insert the DCOUNT function to count the number of records that meet the specified conditions. Refer to Figure 5.17 as you complete Step 4.

Steps b–c: DMIN function

Steps d–e: DMAX function

Step f: DCOUNT function

FIGURE 5.17 DMIN, DMAX, DCOUNT Functions

a. Click **cell I26** and click **Insert Function** in the Function Library group.

The Database functions should be listed because that was the last function category you selected.

b. Select **DMIN** in the *Select a function* list and click **OK**.

c. Select the **range A2:F22** in the Database box, select the **cell F2** in Field box, select the **range A25:F26** in the Criteria box, and then click **OK**.

The lowest salary for account reps in Boston is $41,525.

d. Click **cell I27** and click **Insert Function** in the Function Library group. Select **DMAX** in the *Select a function* list and click **OK**.

e. Select the **range A2:F22** in the Database box, select the **cell F2** in Field box, select the **range A25:F26** in the Criteria box, and then click **OK**.

The highest salary for account reps in Boston is $46,725.

f. Type **=DCOUNT(A2:F22,"Salary",A25:F26)** in **cell I28**. Save the workbook.

The company has four account reps in the Boston location.

You want to change the criteria to see the managers' salary data. Refer to Figure 5.18 as you complete Step 5.

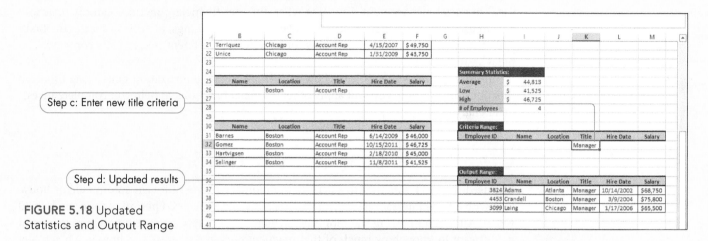

Step c: Enter new title criteria

Step d: Updated results

FIGURE 5.18 Updated Statistics and Output Range

a. Copy the data in the **range A24:F26** and paste the copied data in **cell H30**.

b. Delete the contents in **cells J32** and **K32**.

c. Type **Manager** in **cell K32** and press **Enter**.

d. Copy **cell A29** and paste it in **cell H35**.

e. Click anywhere in the original dataset. Repeat Steps 2c through f using the **data range A2:F22**.

Excel updates the filtered list in the output range.

f. Save the workbook. Keep the workbook onscreen if you plan to continue with Hands-On Exercise 3. If not, close the workbook and exit Excel.

Financial Functions

Excel's financial functions are helpful for business financial analysts and for you in your personal financial management. Knowing what different financial functions can calculate and how to use them will benefit you as you plan retirement savings, identify best rates to obtain your financial goals, and evaluate how future values of different investments compare with today's values.

In this section, you will learn how to prepare a loan amortization table using financial functions. In addition, you will apply other financial functions to help you complete investment analyses.

Creating a Loan Amortization Table

STEP 2 » You used the PMT function to calculate the monthly payment for an automobile or house loan with a fixed interest rate (such as 5.75% APR) for a specified period of time (such as 30 years). Although knowing the monthly payment is helpful to analyze a potential loan, you might want to know how much of that payment contains interest and how much actually goes toward paying off the loan balance. Interest is not identical for every month of the loan. Interest is calculated on the balance of the loan. As you continue making monthly payments, the loan balance continually decreases; therefore, the amount of interest decreases and the principal increases each month. Because your monthly payments are constant throughout the life of the loan, with each payment, more of the payment goes toward paying off the loan. To see the interest and principal portions of each monthly payment and the reduction in the loan amount, you can create a *loan amortization table*, which is a schedule that calculates the interest, principal repayment, and remaining balance.

Figure 5.19 shows the top and bottom portions of an amortization schedule (rows 22:51 are hidden) for an automobile loan of $30,000 with an APR of 5.25% for a four-year loan with a monthly payment of $694.28, rounded to the nearest penny. The borrower pays a total of $33,325.51 (48 payments of $694.28). These payments equal the principal of $30,000 plus $3,325.51 in interest over the life of the loan.

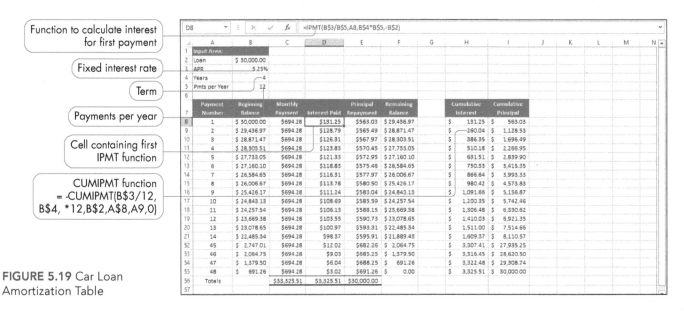

FIGURE 5.19 Car Loan Amortization Table

Perform Internal Calculations

The body of the worksheet shows how principal and interest comprise each payment. The balance of the loan at the beginning of the first period is $30,000. The monthly payment includes interest and principal repayment. The interest for the first month ($131.25) is calculated on the beginning balance for the period, which is the original loan amount ($30,000) for the first payment at a monthly interest rate (5.25%/12).

The principal repayment is the amount of the monthly payment that is left over after deducting the monthly interest. For the first payment, the principal repayment is $563.03 ($694.28 – $131.25).

The remaining balance is the difference between the previous remaining balance and the principal repayment. For the first month, subtract the principal repayment from the original loan amount ($30,000 – $563.03).

The interest for the second month ($128.79) is less than interest for the previous period because the remaining balance to start that period is less ($29,436.97 * 5.25%/12). As each month's beginning balance decreases, so does the monthly interest. The principal repayment is higher for the second month because the interest is less than for the first month.

 TIP Extra Principal Payment

Many homebuyers choose a 30-year mortgage to keep the monthly payment low but opt to pay extra toward the principal each month to reduce the length of the mortgage and the total interest paid. This reduction in interest can be substantial. For example, paying an extra $100 a month on a 30-year, $350,000 mortgage with an interest rate of 3.24% APR can save more than $40,000 in interest over the life of the mortgage and pay off the mortgage before its original payoff date.

Calculate Interest and Principal Payments with IPMT and PPMT Functions

The financial category contains additional functions to calculate results for loan payments: IPMT and PPMT. You can use these functions in isolation or within the body of a loan amortization table if the table does not allow additional principal payments. If your loan amortization enables users to pay additional principal, these functions will not provide accurate results.

The *IPMT function* calculates the periodic interest for a specified payment period on a loan or an investment given a fixed interest rate, term, and periodic payments. In Figure 5.19, you use the IPMT function to calculate the interest payment for each period (for example, the calculation for interest for the first period is: =IPMT(B$3/B$5,A8,B$4*B$5,-B$2)). A benefit of the IPMT function is that you can use it to identify the interest for any given payment without having to create a loan amortization table. The IPMT function has four required arguments and two optional arguments:

=IPMT(rate,per,nper,pv,[fv],[type])

- **Rate.** The rate argument is the periodic interest rate. If the APR is 5.25% (cell B3) and monthly payments are made, the rate is 5.25%/12 (B3/12), or 0.438%.

- **Per.** The per argument is the specific payment or investment period to use to calculate the interest where the first payment period is 1. It is best to include a payment number column as in Figure 5.19. You can use a relative cell reference to avoid having raw numbers in the argument.

- **Nper.** The nper argument represents the total number of payment or investment periods. With a four-year loan consisting of monthly payments, the nper is 48. You should perform the calculation using the input cells, such as $B$4*$B$5, in the nper argument instead of typing the value 48 in case the number of years or number of payments per year changes.

- **Pv.** The pv argument represents the present value of the loan or investment. Enter a minus sign in front of the cell reference to avoid having a negative interest payment returned. In this example, pv would be –B$2.

- **Fv.** The optional fv argument represents the future value of the loan or investment. If you omit this argument, Excel defaults to 0. For loan payments, the balance should be zero after you pay off your loan.

- **Type.** The optional type argument represents the timing of the payments. Enter 0 if the payments are made at the end of the period, or enter 1 if the payments are made at the beginning of the period. If you omit this argument, Excel assumes a default of 0.

The *PPMT function* calculates the principal payment for a specified payment period on a loan or an investment given a fixed interest rate, term, and periodic payments. In Figure 5.19, you can use the PPMT function to calculate the principal repayment in column E. For example, cell E8 contains =PPMT(B$3/B$5,A8,B$4*B$5,-B$2). The first month's total payment of $694.28 includes $563.03 principal repayment. The PPMT function has the same four required arguments and two optional arguments as the IPMT function:

=PPMT(rate,per,nper,pv,[fv],[type])

Calculate Cumulative Interest and Principal Payments with CUMIPMT and CUMPRINC Functions

STEP 3》 Although the IPMT function calculates the amount of interest paid in one particular loan payment, it does not determine the amount of interest paid over a specific number of payments. You can use the *CUMIPMT function* to calculate the cumulative interest throughout a loan amortization table. This function accumulates the interest paid between selected payments or throughout the entire loan. For the first payment, the cumulative interest is the same as the periodic interest. From that point on, you can calculate the cumulative interest, such as the sum of the interest paid for the first two periods, as shown in cell H9 in Figure 5.19. If you do not want to calculate a running total for the entire loan, you can specify the interest between two periods, such as between payment periods 5 and 10, to calculate the total interest paid for the second year of the loan. The CUMIPMT contains six arguments:

=CUMIPMT(rate,nper,pv,start_period,end_period,type)

The rate, nper, pv, and type arguments are the same arguments that you use in the IPMT and PPMT functions. The start_period argument specifies the first period you want to start accumulating the interest, and the end_period argument specifies the last payment period you want to include. In Figure 5.19, the first cumulative interest payment formula in cell G8 uses 1 for both the start_period and end_period arguments. From that point on, the start_period is still 1, but the end_period changes to reflect each payment period, using the payment numbers in column A.

STEP 4》 You can use the *CUMPRINC function* to calculate the cumulative principal throughout a loan amortization table. This function accumulates the principal repayment between selected payments or throughout the entire loan. For the first payment, the cumulative principal paid is the same as the first principal repayment. From that point on, you can calculate the cumulative principal payment, such as the sum of the principal repayment paid for the first two periods, as shown in cell H9 in Figure 5.19. If you do not want to calculate a running total for the entire loan, you can specify the principal repayment between two periods, such as between payment periods 5 and 10, to calculate the total principal repaid for the second year of the loan. The CUMPRINC contains six arguments:

=CUMPRINC(rate,nper,pv,start_period,end_period,type)

Performing Other Financial Calculations

In addition to using financial functions to calculate monthly payments on a loan and to build a loan amortization table, you might want to make other investment-related calculations. For example, you can calculate present or future values, rates, and number of payment periods. Figure 5.20 illustrates the results of several financial functions.

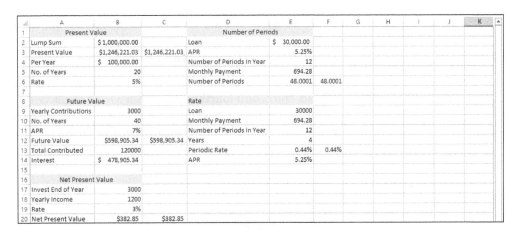

	A	B	C	D	E	F	G	H	I	J	K
1	Present Value			Number of Periods							
2	Lump Sum	$1,000,000.00		Loan	$ 30,000.00						
3	Present Value	$1,246,221.03	$1,246,221.03	APR	5.25%						
4	Per Year	$ 100,000.00		Number of Periods in Year	12						
5	No. of Years	20		Monthly Payment	694.28						
6	Rate	5%		Number of Periods	48.0001	48.0001					
7											
8	Future Value			Rate							
9	Yearly Contributions	3000		Loan	30000						
10	No. of Years	40		Monthly Payment	694.28						
11	APR	7%		Number of Periods in Year	12						
12	Future Value	$598,905.34	$598,905.34	Years	4						
13	Total Contributed	120000		Periodic Rate	0.44%	0.44%					
14	Interest	$ 478,905.34		APR	5.25%						
15											
16	Net Present Value										
17	Invest End of Year	3000									
18	Yearly Income	1200									
19	Rate	3%									
20	Net Present Value	$382.85	$382.85								

FIGURE 5.20 Financial Functions

Calculate Present and Future Values

STEP 1 » The **PV function** calculates the total present (i.e., current) value of a series of payments that will be made in the future. This function illustrates the time value of money in which the value of $1 today is worth more than the value of $1 received at some time in the future, given that you can invest today's $1 to earn interest in the future. For example, you might want to use the PV function to compare a lump-sum payment versus annual payments if you win the lottery to see which is better: receiving $100,000 per year for the next 20 years or $1 million now. The PV function has three required arguments (rate, nper, and pmt) and two optional arguments (fv and type). The rate, nper, and type arguments have the same definitions as in other financial functions. The pmt argument is the fixed periodic payment. The fv argument represents the future value of the investment. If you do not know the payment, you must enter a value for the fv argument. In Figure 5.20, cell B3 contains the PV function. The yearly payments of $100,000 invested at 5% yield a higher present value ($1,246,221.03) than the $1 million lump-sum payment.

=PV(rate,nper,pmt,[fv],[type])

The **FV function** calculates the future value of an investment, given a fixed interest rate, term, and periodic payment. You can use the FV function to determine how much an individual retirement account (IRA) would be worth at a future date. The FV function has three required arguments (rate, nper, and pmt) and two optional arguments (pv and type). If you omit the pmt argument, you must enter a value for the pv argument.

=FV(rate,nper,pmt,[pv],[type])

Assume that you plan to contribute $3,000 a year to an IRA for 40 years and that you expect the IRA to earn 7% interest annually. The future value of that investment—the amount you will have at age 65— would be $598,905.34! In Figure 5.20, cell B12 contains the FV function. You would have contributed $120,000 ($3,000 a year for 40 years). The extra $478,905.34 results from compound interest you will earn over the life of your $120,000 investment!

The **NPV function** calculates the net present value of an investment, given a fixed discount rate (rate of return) and a set of given cash inflows. Specifically, it considers periodic future income and payments. The NPV and PV functions are very similar in concept. The difference is that the PV function requires equal payments at the end of a payment period, whereas the NPV function can have unequal but constant payments. The NPV function contains two required arguments (rate and value1) and additional optional arguments (such as value2). If an investment returns a positive net present value, the investment is profitable. If an investment returns a negative net present value, the investment will lose money.

=NPV(rate,value1,value2,)

- **Rate.** The rate argument is the discount rate for one period. It is also called the rate of return or the percentage return on your investment. If an investment pays 12% per year and each period is one month, the rate is 1%.

- **Value1.** The value arguments represent a sequence of payments and income during the investment period. To provide an accurate net present value, the cash flows must occur at equally spaced-out time periods and must occur at the end of each period.

Assume you invest $3,000 at the end of the first year and receive $1,200 during the second, third, and fourth years with a 3% discount rate. In Figure 5.20, cell B20 contains the NPV function. The net present value would be $382.85. However, if you pay the $3,000 at the beginning of the first year instead of the end of the first year, you cannot discount the $3,000 since it is already in today's value. You would then subtract it after the function: =NPV(B19,B18,B18,B18)–B17. By investing $3,000 immediately, the net present value is higher at $394.33.

Use NPER and RATE Functions

The **NPER function** calculates the number of payment periods for an investment or loan given a fixed interest rate, periodic payment, and present value. You can use NPER to calculate the number of monthly payments given a car loan of $30,000, an APR of 5.25%, and a monthly payment of $694.28. In Figure 5.20, cell E6 contains the NPER function. The NPER would be 48.0001, or about 48 payments. The NPER function contains three required arguments (rate, pmt, and pv) and two optional arguments (fv and type).

=NPER(rate,pmt,pv,[fv],[type])

The **RATE function** calculates the periodic rate for an investment or loan given the number of payment periods, a fixed periodic payment, and present value. You can use RATE to calculate the periodic rate of a four-year car loan of $30,000 and a monthly payment of $694.28. In Figure 5.20, cell E13 contains the RATE function. The periodic rate would be 0.44%. Keep in mind that this is the periodic or monthly rate. The APR is then found by multiplying the periodic rate by 12: 5.25%. The RATE function contains three required arguments (nper, pmt, and pv) and two optional arguments (fv and type).

=RATE(nper,pmt,pv,[fv],[type])

Quick
Concepts

1. In what situation would you use IPMT and PPMT? ***p. 253***
2. What is the difference between IPMT and CUMIPMT? ***p. 254***
3. What is the difference between PV and NPV calculations? ***p. 255***

3 Financial Functions

The location managers want new company cars. Angela Khazen, the chief financial officer, has determined that the company can afford $450 monthly payments based on a 5.25% APR for four-year loans. She wants you to prepare a loan amortization table and running totals for interest and principal repayment.

Skills covered: Calculate the Present Value of the Loan • Enter Formulas in the Amortization Table • Calculate Cumulative Interest • Calculate Cumulative Principal Paid

STEP 1 ≫ CALCULATE THE PRESENT VALUE OF THE LOAN

Because Angela determined the monthly payment for an automobile, you must use the PV function to calculate the loan amount. Other variables, such as trade-in value of the current vehicle, need to be considered, but you will exclude those variables at the moment. Refer to Figure 5.21 as you complete Step 1.

Steps d–e: Enter PV function

	A	B	C	D	E
E2			fx	=PV(E3,E4,-B2)	
1	Input Area:			Basic Output Area:	
2	Payment	$ 450.00		Loan	$ 19,444.57
3	APR	5.25%		Periodic Rate	0.438%
4	Years	4		# of Payments	48
5	Pmts per Year	12			
6					

FIGURE 5.21 PV Function

a. Open *e07h2Salary_LastFirst* and save it as **e07h3Salary_LastFirst**, replacing *h2* with *h3*. Click the **3-Finance worksheet tab**.

You will calculate the periodic interest rate and number of payment periods before you can calculate the present value of the loan.

b. Click **cell E3**, type **=B3/B5**, and then press **Enter**.

The periodic rate, 0.438%, is the result of dividing the APR by the number of payments per year.

c. Type **=B4*B5** in **cell E4** and press **Enter**.

The total number of monthly payments, 48, is the product of the number of years the loan is outstanding and the number of payments per year.

d. Click **cell E2**, click **Financial** in the Function Library group on the FORMULAS tab, scroll through the list, and then select **PV**.

e. Click **cell E3** to enter that cell reference in the Rate box, click in the **Nper box**, and then click **cell E4**. Click in the **Pmt box**, type **-B2**, and then click **OK**. Save the workbook.

The result is $19,444.57 based on four years of $450 monthly payments with an APR of 5.25%. You entered a negative sign to the left of the B2 reference. If you do not enter a negative sign, Excel will display the loan as a negative value.

STEP 2 ≫ ENTER FORMULAS IN THE AMORTIZATION TABLE

Angela wants you to create an amortization table. The column labels and payment numbers have already been entered into the worksheet. Now you will enter formulas to show the beginning loan balance for each payment, the monthly payment, interest paid, and principal repayment. Refer to Figure 5.22 as you complete Step 2.

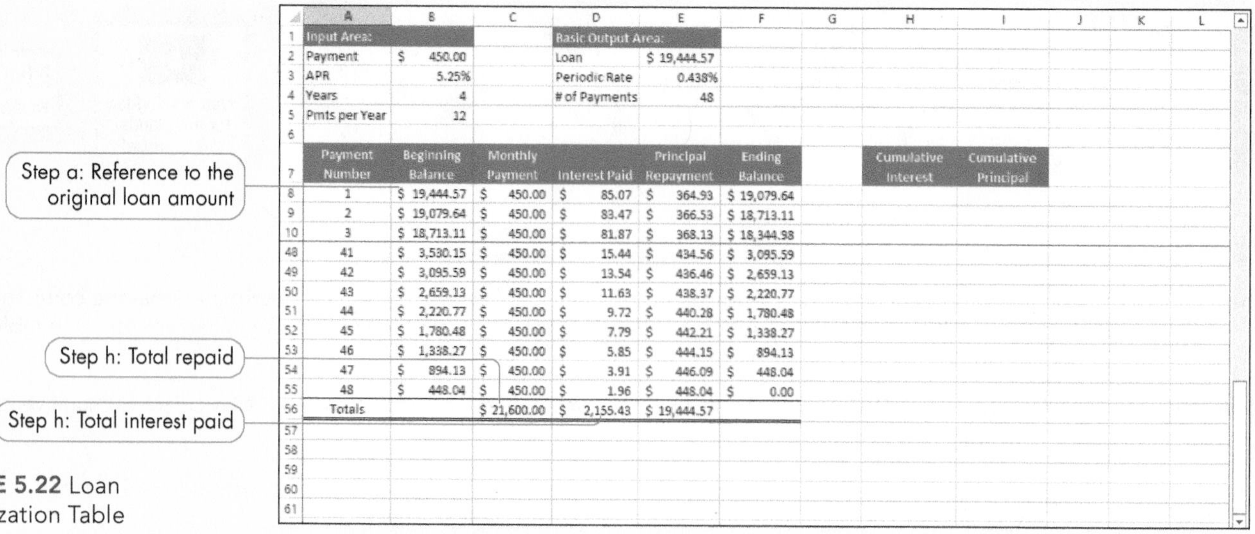

FIGURE 5.22 Loan Amortization Table

Step a: Reference to the original loan amount

Step h: Total repaid

Step h: Total interest paid

a. Click **cell B8**, type **=E2**, and then press **Tab**.

You entered a reference to the original loan amount because that is the beginning balance to start the first payment period. Referencing the original cell is recommended instead of typing the value directly in the cell due to internal rounding. Furthermore, if you change the original input values, the calculated loan amount will change in both cells B8 and E2.

b. Type **=B$2** in **cell C8** and press **Ctrl+Enter**. Use the fill handle to copy the payment down the column ending in **cell C55**.

The monthly payment is $450.00. You entered a reference to the original monthly payment so that if you change it in cell B2, Excel will update the values in the Monthly Payment column automatically. The cell reference must be a mixed (B$2) or absolute ($B$2) reference to prevent the row number from changing when you copy the formula down the column later.

c. Type **=IPMT** in **cell D8**, press **Tab**, and click the **Insert Function button**. Type E$3 for the rate, A8 for per, E$4 for the NPER, and -E$2 for the PV and click **OK**. Use the fill handle to copy the function down the rest of the column.

The IPMT function calculates the interest of a specific payment based on the starting balance of $19,444.57 with a periodic interest of .438% over 48 payments. By not making cell A8 absolute, the function is able to adjust the period to match the specific period of evaluation.

d. Type **=PPMT** in **cell E8** and press **Tab**. Click the **Insert Function button**. Type E$3 for the rate, A8 for per, E$4 for the NPER, and -E$2 for the PV and click **OK**. Use the fill handle to copy the function down the rest of the column.

To manually calculate interest, the interest of the first payment $85.07 is subtracted from the monthly payment of $450. The remaining portion of the payment $364.93 goes toward paying down the principal owed. Using the PPMT function automatically completed these calculations.

e. Click in **cell F8** and type **=B8-E8**.

This calculates the ending balance after the first payment is made. The ending balance is calculated by subtracting the amount of principal in the payment $364.93 from the balance currently owed $19,444.57.

f. Click in **cell B9**, type **=F8**, and then press **Ctrl+Enter**.

The beginning balance of the second payment is also the ending balance of the first payment. The easiest method to populate the column is by referencing the ending balance from the prior month (cell F8). However, this can also be calculated by subtracting the previous principal repayment value (such as $364.93) from the previous month's beginning balance (such as $19,444.57).

g. Use the fill handle to copy the cell reference in **cell B9** down the rest of the column, ending in **cell B55**.

h. Click **cell F8** and use the fill handle to copy the formula down, ending in **cell F55**.

i. Type SUM functions in **cells C56, D56,** and **E56**. Select the **range A56:F56** and apply the **top and double bottom border**. Save the workbook.

You calculated totals for the appropriate columns, noting that column B is a running balance and cannot be logically totaled. Figure 5.22 shows the top and bottom portions of the amortization table using Freeze Panes.

STEP 3 ≫ CALCULATE CUMULATIVE INTEREST

The loan amortization table shows how much of each payment is interest and how much pays down the principal. However, Angela wants you to include a column to show the cumulative interest after each payment. Refer to Figure 5.23 as you complete Step 3.

Steps a–b: Enter CUMIPMT function

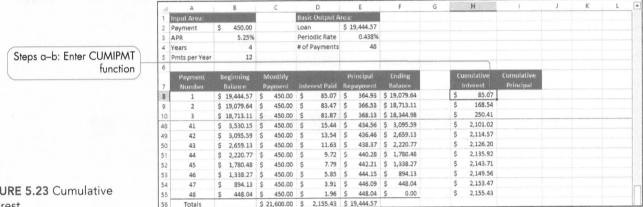

FIGURE 5.23 Cumulative Interest

	A	B	C	D	E	F	H	I
1	Input Area:			Basic Output Area:				
2	Payment	$ 450.00		Loan	$ 19,444.57			
3	APR	5.25%		Periodic Rate	0.438%			
4	Years	4		# of Payments	48			
5	Pmts per Year	12						
6								
7	Payment Number	Beginning Balance	Monthly Payment	Interest Paid	Principal Repayment	Ending Balance	Cumulative Interest	Cumulative Principal
8	1	$ 19,444.57	$ 450.00	$ 85.07	$ 364.93	$ 19,079.64	$ 85.07	
9	2	$ 19,079.64	$ 450.00	$ 83.47	$ 366.53	$ 18,713.11	168.54	
10	3	$ 18,713.11	$ 450.00	$ 81.87	$ 368.13	$ 18,344.98	250.41	
48	41	$ 3,530.15	$ 450.00	$ 15.44	$ 434.56	$ 3,095.59	2,101.02	
49	42	$ 3,095.59	$ 450.00	$ 13.54	$ 436.46	$ 2,659.13	2,114.57	
50	43	$ 2,659.13	$ 450.00	$ 11.63	$ 438.37	$ 2,220.77	2,126.20	
51	44	$ 2,220.77	$ 450.00	$ 9.72	$ 440.28	$ 1,780.48	2,135.92	
52	45	$ 1,780.48	$ 450.00	$ 7.79	$ 442.21	$ 1,338.27	2,143.71	
53	46	$ 1,338.27	$ 450.00	$ 5.85	$ 444.15	$ 894.13	2,149.56	
54	47	$ 894.13	$ 450.00	$ 3.91	$ 446.09	$ 448.04	2,153.47	
55	48	$ 448.04	$ 450.00	$ 1.96	$ 448.04	$ 0.00	2,155.43	
56	Totals		$ 21,600.00	$ 2,155.43	$ 19,444.57			

a. Click **cell H8**, click **Financial** in the Function Library group on the FORMULAS tab, and then select **CUMIPMT**.

The Function Arguments dialog box displays so that you can enter the arguments for the CUMIPMT function.

b. Type the following arguments: **E$3** in the **Rate box**, **E$4** in the **Nper box**, **E$2** in the **Pv box**, and **A$8** in the **Start_period box**.

Make sure the cell references you enter in Rate, Nper, Pv, and Start_period boxes are mixed as shown to prevent the row number from changing as you copy the formula down the column.

 TIP Mixed or Absolute References

You can also use absolute references; however, the entire formula is easier to read (and is shorter) in the Formula Bar when you use mixed instead of absolute references.

c. Type **A8** in the **End_period box**.

This reference should be relative so that it reflects the current month's payment number as you copy the formula down the column.

d. Press **Tab**, type **0** in the **Type box**, and then click **OK**.

The cumulative interest for the first payment is the same as the first payment's interest. However, the formula displays a negative result, as indicated by the parentheses.

e. Edit the function by typing - between = and *CUMIPMT* to convert the results to a positive value.

Unlike other functions, placing a - before the PV variable of the function will not return the intended result. To circumvent the issue, you place the - before the start of the CUMIPMT function after the = sign.

f. Copy the formula through **cell H55**. Save the workbook.

The cumulative interest in cell H55 should match the total interest paid calculated in cell D56: $2,155.43.

STEP 4 ≫ CALCULATE CUMULATIVE PRINCIPAL PAID

Angela wants to see the cumulative principal paid after making each loan payment. You will use the CUMPRINC function to calculate the cumulative principal paid. Refer to Figure 5.24 as you complete Step 4.

Steps a–b: Enter CUMPRINC function

	A	B	C	D	E	F	G	H	I	J	K	L
1	Input Area:			Basic Output Area:								
2	Payment	$ 450.00		Loan	$ 19,444.57							
3	APR	5.25%		Periodic Rate	0.438%							
4	Years	4		# of Payments	48							
5	Pmts per Year	12										
6												
7	Payment Number	Beginning Balance	Monthly Payment	Interest Paid	Principal Repayment	Ending Balance		Cumulative Interest	Cumulative Principal			
8	1	$ 19,444.57	$ 450.00	$ 85.07	$ 364.93	$ 19,079.64		$ 85.07	$ 364.93			
9	2	$ 19,079.64	$ 450.00	$ 83.47	$ 366.53	$ 18,713.11		$ 168.54	$ 731.46			
10	3	$ 18,713.11	$ 450.00	$ 81.87	$ 368.13	$ 18,344.98		$ 250.41	$ 1,099.59			
48	41	$ 3,530.15	$ 450.00	$ 15.44	$ 434.56	$ 3,095.59		$ 2,101.02	$ 16,348.98			
49	42	$ 3,095.59	$ 450.00	$ 13.54	$ 436.46	$ 2,659.13		$ 2,114.57	$ 16,785.43			
50	43	$ 2,659.13	$ 450.00	$ 11.63	$ 438.37	$ 2,220.77		$ 2,126.20	$ 17,223.80			
51	44	$ 2,220.77	$ 450.00	$ 9.72	$ 440.28	$ 1,780.48		$ 2,135.92	$ 17,664.08			
52	45	$ 1,780.48	$ 450.00	$ 7.79	$ 442.21	$ 1,338.27		$ 2,143.71	$ 18,106.29			
53	46	$ 1,338.27	$ 450.00	$ 5.85	$ 444.15	$ 894.13		$ 2,149.56	$ 18,550.44			
54	47	$ 894.13	$ 450.00	$ 3.91	$ 446.09	$ 448.04		$ 2,153.47	$ 18,996.53			
55	48	$ 448.04	$ 450.00	$ 1.96	$ 448.04	$ 0.00		$ 2,155.43	$ 19,444.57			
56	Totals		$ 21,600.00	$ 2,155.43	$ 19,444.57							

FIGURE 5.24 Cumulative Principal Paid

a. Click **cell I8**, click **Financial** in the Function Library group, and then select **CUMPRINC**.

The Function Arguments dialog box displays so that you can enter the arguments for the CUMPRINC function.

b. Type the following arguments: **E$3** in the **Rate box**, **E$4** in the **Nper box**, **E$2** in the **Pv box**, **A$8** in the **Start_period box**, **A8** in the **End_period box**, and **0** in the **Type box**.

c. Click **OK** and edit the function by typing - between = and *CUMPRINC*.

d. Copy the formula through **cell I55**.

The cumulative principal in cell I55 should match the total principal repayment calculated in cell E56: $19,444.57.

e. Save and close the workbook, and submit based on your instructor's directions.

Chapter Objectives Review

After reading this chapter, you have accomplished the following objectives:

1. **Create a nested logical function.**
   - A nested IF function is one that contains one or more additional IF functions nested inside one or more arguments. This type of nested function helps derive calculations for complex situations with multiple outcomes.
   - Nested IF within an IF function: When more than two outcomes are possible, you can nest additional IF statements within an IF statement.
   - Nest AND, OR, and NOT functions: Nested AND, OR, and NOT statements give you the ability to evaluate multiple conditions at the same time.

2. **Use MATCH and INDEX lookup functions.**
   - Use the MATCH function: The MATCH function returns the position of a value in a list.
   - Use the INDEX function: The INDEX function returns a value or the reference to a value within a range.
   - Nest functions in other functions: Nest the MATCH function inside the INDEX function to identify a location and then return related data.

3. **Use advanced filtering.**
   - Create a criteria range that is separate from the table or list, contains column labels, and lists the conditions.
   - If multiple conditions must be met, enter those criteria on the same row.
   - If the advanced filter should be an either/or case, enter the second set of criteria on the row below the first row of criteria.
   - Define a criteria range: Before you apply advanced filtering, you must define the criteria range.
   - Apply the Advanced Filter: Once applied, the Advanced Filter only displays information that meets predefined criteria.

4. **Manipulate data with database functions.**
   - Database functions help calculate aggregates for databases in which you have created an advanced filter.
   - Use DSUM and DAVERAGE functions: The DSUM functions adds the values in a numeric database column based on predefined conditions. The DAVERAGE function averages the values in a numeric database based on predefined conditions.

   - Identify values with DMAX and DMIN: The DMAX function returns the highest value in a database column that matches predefined criteria. In contrast, the DMIN function returns the lowest value in a database column that matches predefined criteria.
   - Identify the total number with DCOUNT: The DCOUNT function counts the cells that contain numbers in a database column that match predefined criteria.

5. **Create a loan amortization table.**
   - A loan amortization table is a schedule of monthly payments, interest per period, principal repayment per period, and balances.
   - Perform internal calculations: Use basic arithmetic operations to manually calculate interest and principal payments.
   - Calculate interest and principal payments with IPMT and PPMT functions: The IPMT function calculates the periodic interest for a specified payment period on a loan or investment. The PPMT function calculates the principal payment for a specified payment period on a loan or investment.
   - Calculate cumulative interest and principal payments with CUMIPMT and CUMPRINC functions: The CUMIPMT function calculates the cumulative interest throughout a loan. The CUMPRINC function calculates the cumulative principal throughout a loan.

6. **Perform other financial calculations.**
   - Several financial functions are available to calculate payment or investment values.
   - Calculate present and future values: The FV function calculates the future value of an investment. The PV function calculates the present value of an investment.
   - Use NPER and RATE functions: Use the NPER function to calculate the number of payment periods for a loan or an investment if the other variables are given. Use the RATE function to calculate the periodic interest rate if other variables are given.

Key Terms Matching

Match the key terms with their definitions. Write the key term letter by the appropriate numbered definition.

a. AND function
b. CUMIPMT function
c. CUMPRINC function
d. Database function
e. DAVERAGE function
f. DCOUNT function
g. DMAX function
h. DMIN function
i. DSUM function
j. FV function

k. INDEX function
l. IPMT function
m. Loan amortization table
n. MATCH function
o. NOT function
p. NPER function
q. NPV function
r. OR function
s. PPMT function
t. PV function

1. _____ Calculates the number of periods for an investment of loan. **p. 256**

2. _____ Calculates the future value of an investment. **p. 255**

3. _____ Calculates the net present value of an investment with periodic payments and a discount rate. **p. 255**

4. _____ Calculates cumulative principal for specified payment periods. **p. 254**

5. _____ Calculates the present value of an investment. **p. 255**

6. _____ Calculates cumulative interest for specified payment period. **p. 254**

7. _____ A schedule showing monthly payments, interest per payment, amount toward paying off the loan, and the remaining balance for each payment. **p. 252**

8. _____ Calculates the principal payment for a specified payment period given a fixed interest rate, term, and periodic payments. **p. 254**

9. _____ Calculates periodic interest for a fixed-term, fixed-rate loan or investment. **p. 253**

10. _____ Counts the cells that contain a number in a database column based on specified conditions. **p. 247**

11. _____ Identifies the highest value in a database column based on specified conditions. **p. 247**

12. _____ Identifies the lowest value in a database column based on specified conditions. **p. 247**

13. _____ Averages values in a database column based on specified conditions. **p. 246**

14. _____ Adds values in a database column based on specified conditions. **p. 246**

15. _____ Analyzes data for selected records in a table. **p. 245**

16. _____ Returns a value or reference to a value within a range. **p. 237**

17. _____ Identifies a searched item's position in a list. **p. 236**

18. _____ Returns TRUE if the argument is false and FALSE if the argument is true. **p. 236**

19. _____ Returns TRUE if any argument is true and returns FALSE if all arguments are false. **p. 235**

20. _____ Returns TRUE when all arguments are true and FALSE when at least one argument is false. **p. 234**

Multiple Choice

1. A workbook contains a list of university students. You want to identify the total number of students who are seniors and who are majoring in biology. Without modifying the original student dataset, what function can you use to find the answer to your question?

   (a) Nested IF
   (b) COUNTA
   (c) DCOUNT
   (d) COUNT

2. The original mortgage loan was for $300,000 with a 5% APR for 30 years. You want to calculate the interest on the last monthly payment at the end of the 15th year. What value should be referenced for the *per* argument in the IPMT function?

   (a) 15
   (b) 180
   (c) 30
   (d) 0.05/12

3. A local police office wants to create a rule that if an officer pulls over a person for exceeding the speed limit by at least five miles per hour or if that person has two or more speeding violations on record, the officer will fine the speeder the higher of $200 or $50 for each mile over the speed limit. Otherwise, the fine is $45. The speed limit is entered in cell B5, the person's speed is entered in cell B10, and the person's number of previous tickets is entered in cell B11. What function derives the correct answer?

   (a) =IF(AND(B10>B5,B11>=2),200,45)
   (b) =IF(AND(B10-B5>=5,B11<2),MAX(200, (B10-B5)*50),45)
   (c) =IF(OR(B10-B5>=5,B11>=2),MAX(200, (B10-B5)*50),45)
   (d) =IF(OR(B10>B5,B11>=2),MAX(200,50),45)

4. How much interest is paid on the first payment of a $15,000 auto loan financed at 3.25% interest paid monthly over 6 years?

   (a) $50.25
   (b) $40.63
   (c) $47.55
   (d) None of the above

5. A worksheet contains the times in which runners completed a race, with the times organized from fastest to slowest. You will use the MATCH function to identify what place a runner came in given a time of 4:05 (four minutes and five seconds). Which argument should contain the specific runner's time?

   (a) Lookup_value
   (b) Lookup_array
   (c) Match_type
   (d) Row_num

6. What function would you use to calculate the total principal paid on a loan over a specific start and end date?

   (a) CUMIPMT
   (b) IPMT
   (c) PPMT
   (d) CUMPRINC

7. Which database function would you use to count a range of cells that have some cells that are blank without excluding the blank cells?

   (a) DCOUNT
   (b) DCOUNTA
   (c) COUNT
   (d) DSUM

8. Which function should you use to calculate the total interest paid for all monthly payments for the second year of a four-year automobile loan?

   (a) CUMPRINC
   (b) PPMT
   (c) IPMT
   (d) CUMIPMT

9. In the Advanced Filter dialog box, where do you enter the location for placing the output?

   (a) Copy to
   (b) List range
   (c) Criteria range
   (d) Unique records only

10. What function would you use to calculate the total number of periods in a loan or investment?

    (a) NPER
    (b) RATE
    (c) PV
    (d) FV

1 Financial Investments

Some of your friends are in a business finance class. They are studying for their first test and will have to use financial calculators. As they practice for the test, they want to make sure they are calculating investment variables correctly. You volunteered to set up an investment model in which they enter the input variables to check their answers against formula calculations you will enter. This exercise follows the same set of skills as used in Hands-On Exercise 3 in the chapter. Refer to Figure 5.25 to complete this exercise.

	A	B	C	D	E
1	Instructions:	Enter input values in cells with light blue.			
2					
3	Investment Variable	PMT/FV	PV	NPER/FV	RATE/FV
4	Payments Per Year	12	12	12	12
5	Present Value	$ 100,000.00	$ 100,000.00	$ 100,000.00	$ 100,000.00
6	APR	10.00%	10.00%	10.00%	10.00%
7	Rate	0.83%	0.83%	0.83%	0.83%
8	Term	20	20	20	20
9	No. of Payments	240	240	240	240
10	Periodic Payment	$ 965.02	$ 965.02	$ 965.02	$ 965.02
11	Future Value	$1,465,614.73	$ 1,465,614.73	$1,465,614.73	$1,465,614.73
12					
13					

FIGURE 5.25 Financial Functions

a. Open *e07p1Finance* and save it as **e07p1Finance_LastFirst**.

b. Calculate the periodic rate, number of periods, periodic payment, and future value in column B by completing the following:
   - Click **cell B7** and type =**B6/B4** to calculate the periodic rate.
   - Click **cell B9** and type =**B8*B4** to calculate the number of payment periods.
   - Click **cell B10**, click the **FORMULAS tab**, click **Financial** in the Function Library group, scroll down, and then select **PMT**. Type **B7** in the **Rate box**, type **B9** in the **Nper box**, and then type **-B5** in the **PV box**. Click **OK** to calculate the monthly payment.
   - Click **cell B11**, click **Financial** in the Function Library group, and then select **FV**. Type **B7** in the **Rate box**, type **B9** in the **Nper box**, type **B10** in the **Pmt box**, and then type **B5** in the **Pv box**. Click **OK** and edit the formula by typing - on the right side of =.

c. Calculate the number of payments, periodic rate, and present value in column C by completing the following:
   - Click **cell C9** and type =**C8*C4** to calculate the number of payment periods.
   - Click **cell C7** and type =**C6/C4** to calculate the periodic rate.
   - Click **cell C5**, click **Financial** in the Function Library group, and then select **PV**. Type **C7** in the **Rate box**, type **C9** in the **Nper box**, and then type **C10** in the **Pmt box**. Click **OK** and edit the formula by typing - on the right side of =.

d. Calculate the rate, number of payment periods, term, and future value in column D by completing the following:
   - Click **cell D7** and type =**D6/D4** to calculate the periodic rate.
   - Click **cell D9**, click **Financial** in the Function Library group, and then select **NPER**. Type **D7** in the **Rate box**, type **D10** in the **Pmt box**, type **-D5** in the **Pv box**, and then click **OK**.
   - Click **cell D8** and type =**D9/D4** to calculate the term (i.e., number of years).
   - Click **cell D11** and type =-**FV(D7,D9,D10,D5)** to calculate the future value.

e. Calculate the number of payment periods, rate, APR, and future value in column E by completing the following:
   - Click **cell E9** and type =**E8*E4** to calculate the number of payment periods.
   - Click **cell E7**, click **Financial** in the Function Library group, and then select **RATE**. Type **E9** in the **Nper box**, type **-E10** in the **Pmt box**, type **E5** in the **Pv box**, and then click **OK**.
   - Click **cell E6** and type =**E7*E4** to calculate the APR.
   - Click **cell E11** and type =-**FV(E7,E9,E10,E5)** to calculate the future value.

f. Create a footer with your name on the left side, the sheet name code in the center, and the file name code on the right side.

g. Save and close the workbook, and submit based on your instructor's directions.

2 Detailed Loan Amortization

You are planning to buy a house soon, so you want to set up a detailed loan amortization table. So far, you have designed a worksheet with a loan parameters area (i.e., input area), a summary area, and amortization table column labels. You want to build in mechanisms to prevent formula errors if input data are missing and to hide zeros from displaying if you take out a shorter-term loan or pay it off early. However, you must keep formulas in place for a traditional 30-year loan. In addition, you will notice overpayments on the last payment if you pay extra toward the principal each month. To make the amortization table as flexible as possible and to avoid errors, you will create several nested IF functions. This exercise follows the same set of skills as used in Hands-On Exercise 3 in the chapter. Refer to Figure 5.26 as you complete this exercise.

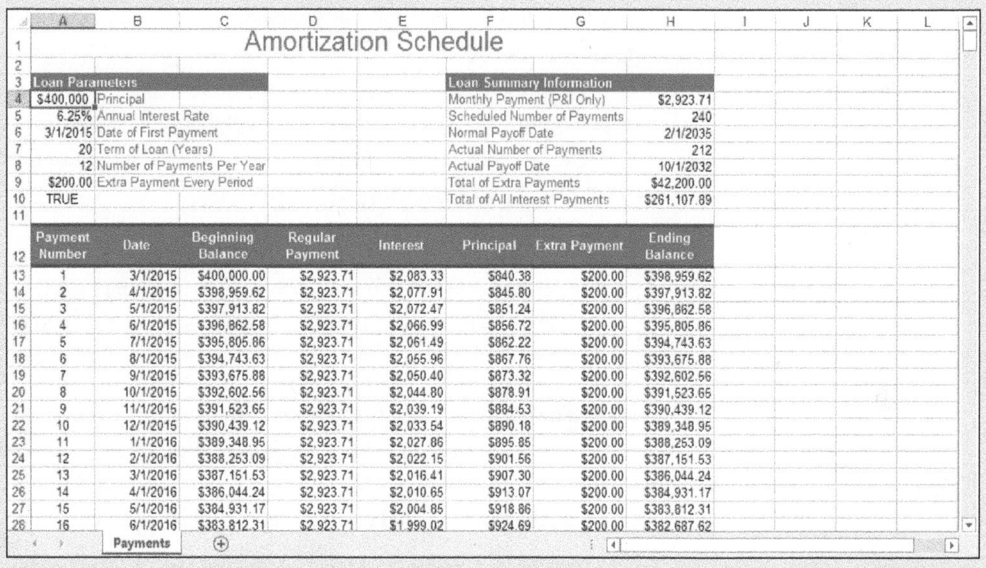

Amortization Schedule

Loan Parameters		Loan Summary Information	
$400,000	Principal	Monthly Payment (P&I Only)	$2,923.71
6.25%	Annual Interest Rate	Scheduled Number of Payments	240
3/1/2015	Date of First Payment	Normal Payoff Date	2/1/2035
20	Term of Loan (Years)	Actual Number of Payments	212
12	Number of Payments Per Year	Actual Payoff Date	10/1/2032
$200.00	Extra Payment Every Period	Total of Extra Payments	$42,200.00
TRUE		Total of All Interest Payments	$261,107.89

Payment Number	Date	Beginning Balance	Regular Payment	Interest	Principal	Extra Payment	Ending Balance
1	3/1/2015	$400,000.00	$2,923.71	$2,083.33	$840.38	$200.00	$398,959.62
2	4/1/2015	$398,959.62	$2,923.71	$2,077.91	$845.80	$200.00	$397,913.82
3	5/1/2015	$397,913.82	$2,923.71	$2,072.47	$851.24	$200.00	$396,862.58
4	6/1/2015	$396,862.58	$2,923.71	$2,066.99	$856.72	$200.00	$395,805.86
5	7/1/2015	$395,805.86	$2,923.71	$2,061.49	$862.22	$200.00	$394,743.63
6	8/1/2015	$394,743.63	$2,923.71	$2,055.96	$867.76	$200.00	$393,675.88
7	9/1/2015	$393,675.88	$2,923.71	$2,050.40	$873.32	$200.00	$392,602.56
8	10/1/2015	$392,602.56	$2,923.71	$2,044.80	$878.91	$200.00	$391,523.65
9	11/1/2015	$391,523.65	$2,923.71	$2,039.19	$884.53	$200.00	$390,439.12
10	12/1/2015	$390,439.12	$2,923.71	$2,033.54	$890.18	$200.00	$389,348.95
11	1/1/2016	$389,348.95	$2,923.71	$2,027.86	$895.85	$200.00	$388,253.09
12	2/1/2016	$388,253.09	$2,923.71	$2,022.15	$901.56	$200.00	$387,151.53
13	3/1/2016	$387,151.53	$2,923.71	$2,016.41	$907.30	$200.00	$386,044.24
14	4/1/2016	$386,044.24	$2,923.71	$2,010.65	$913.07	$200.00	$384,931.17
15	5/1/2016	$384,931.17	$2,923.71	$2,004.85	$918.86	$200.00	$383,812.31
16	6/1/2016	$383,812.31	$2,923.71	$1,999.02	$924.69	$200.00	$382,687.62

Payments

FIGURE 5.26 Detailed Amortization Table

a. Open *e07p2House* and save it as **e07p2House_LastFirst.**

b. Click in each cell in the **range B13:H13** to look at the formulas in the Formula Bar. Delete the contents of **cell A7** and look at the #NUM! errors.

c. Click **cell A10**, click the **FORMULAS tab**, click **Logical**, and then select **AND.** Do the following in the Function Arguments dialog box:

- Type **A4>0** in the **Logical1 box.**
- Type **A5>0** in the **Logical2 box.**
- Type **A6>0** in the **Logical3 box.**
- Type **A7>0** in the **Logical4 box.**
- Type **A8>0** in the **Logical5 box** and click **OK.**

The arguments ensure that if any required input value is missing, the AND function returns FALSE. You will use cell A10's results to avoid error messages in calculated cells. Currently, the result is FALSE because you deleted the contents of cell A7.

d. Assign the range name **DataEntered** to **cell A10** so that you can use a range name in formulas that refer to this cell.

e. Enter the following replacement functions on row 13 to test if data have been entered or if cell A13 contains a value greater than zero. If data have been entered, calculations occur. If not, the functions return zeros:

- **Cell A13: =IF(DataEntered,1,0)**
  If DataEntered (cell A10) is TRUE, display **1** for first payment number. If DataEntered is FALSE, display **0** for first payment number.
- **Cell B13: =IF(A13>0,A6,"")**
  If DataEntered (cell A13) is TRUE, display date of first payment as entered in cell A6. If DataEntered is FALSE, an empty cell displays.
- **Cell C13: =IF(A13>0,A4,0)**
- **Cell D13: =IF(A13>0,H$4,0)**
- **Cell E13: =IF(A13>0,C13*A$5/A$8,0)**
- **Cell F13: =IF(A13>0,D13-E13,0)**
- **Cell G13: =IF(A13>0,A$9,0)**
- **Cell H13: =IF(A13>0,C13-F13-G13,0)**

f. Edit the formula in **cell H4** to be **=IF(DataEntered,PMT(A5/A8,H5,-A4),0)**. Edit the formula in **cell H5** to be **=IF(DataEntered,A7*A8,0)**.

All error messages should be gone now.

g. Type **30** in **cell A7** to see calculated results appear.

Because all required input values are entered, the AND function in cell A10 indicates TRUE, which is then used in several IF functions that display calculated results if all required inputs are entered.

h. Type the following formulas on row 14 to calculate values for the second payment:

- **Cell A14: =IF(H13>0,A13+1,0)**
  This function calculates the next payment number only if the previous ending balance is greater than zero.
- **Cell B14: =IF(A14>0,DATE(YEAR(B13),MONTH(B13)+1,DAY(B13)),0)**
  The date functions identify the specific year, month, and day and add 1 to increase each due date to the next month. The result is 42095 because it is a serial date so far. You will format it soon.
- **Cell C14: =IF(A14>0,H13,0)**
  The beginning balance is equal to the ending balance from the previous period.

i. Format **cell B14** as **Short Date** and format **range C13:H14** as **Currency** (not Accounting Number Format).

j. Select the **range D13:H13** and drag the fill handle down to copy the formulas to row 14. Select the **range A14:H14** and drag the fill handle down to copy the formulas to row 372—the end of the 360th payment in which the 30-year loan is paid off.

k. Click **cell A7** and change the value to **20** years. Scroll down the amortization table to row 252—the end of the 240th payment in which the 20-year loan is paid off. Notice that row 253 contains a negative balance (due to rounding) and rows 254 through 372 contain zeros because the loan is paid off.

l. Click the **FILE tab**, click **Options**, and then click **Advanced** to see *Advanced Options for working with Excel*.

m. Scroll through the options to see *Display options for this worksheet: Payments*, click the **Show a zero in cells that have zero value check box** to deselect it, and then click **OK**. Deselecting this option hides the zeros in rows 254 through 372, but Excel keeps the formulas intact in case the results change, and the negative values on row 253 still display. If you change the term to 30 years again, the results will display in the otherwise empty cells. Also note that if you used Accounting Number Format, you would see $ - instead of empty cells.

n. Type **200** in **cell A9** and format it as **Currency**. Scroll down and notice that you have a negative balance, indicating that you overpaid. You need to modify the regular payment and extra payments to prevent overpayment on the last payment.

o. Click **cell D13** and type **=IF(A13>0,IF(C13>$H$4,$H$4,C13*A$5/A$8+C13),0)**. If cell A13 is 0, then the result shows zero. If the logical_test is true, the nested IF statement checks the current balance against the regular monthly payment. If the balance is greater, you pay the monthly payment.

If the monthly payment is higher, you pay the balance plus the interest on the balance only to avoid overpayment. Double-click the **cell D13 fill handle** to copy the formula down the column through **cell D372**.

p. Click **cell G13** and type: **=IF(AND(A13>0,C13-F13>=A$9),A$9,0)**. The nested AND in the logical_test makes sure that the payment number is greater than 0 *and* the difference between the beginning balance and principal is greater than or equal to the extra payment. If so, you pay the extra payment. If not, the extra payment is zero. This prevents paying an extra principal payment during the last payment and overpaying the final balance. Double-click the **cell G13 fill handle** to copy the formula down the column through **cell G372**.

q. Click **cell H6**, type **=IF(DataEntered,DATE(YEAR(A6),MONTH(A6)+(A7-1)*A8+11,DAY (A6)),0)**, and then format it as **Short Date** to determine the normal payoff date if you do not make any extra payments.

r. Click **cell H7** and type **=IF(DataEntered,MATCH(0,EndingBalance,-1),0)**. The MATCH function searches the existing range name EndingBalance for the smallest value that is greater than or equal to zero. The balance never goes exactly to zero because of a rounding error. Thus, the row above the match corresponds to the number of actual payments.

s. Click **cell H8** and type **=IF(DataEntered,INDEX(AmortizationTable,H7,2),0)**. Apply the **Short Date format** to **cell H8**. The INDEX function returns the date from column 2 of the row within the table that was returned by the MATCH function in the above step.

t. Click **cell H9**, type **=SUM(ExtraPayment)**, and then format it as **Currency**.

This calculates the total of all extra payments made. Note the ExtraPayment range name used in this step and Interest range name used in the next step were predefined in the student data file.

u. Click **cell H10**, type **=SUM(Interest)**, and then format it as **Currency**. Note that you cannot use the CUMIPMT to calculate total interest because that function does not incorporate extra payments.

v. Create a footer with your name on the left side, the sheet name code in the center, and the file name code on the right side.

w. Save and close the workbook, and submit based on your instructor's directions.

3 Retirement Planning

FROM SCRATCH

You have recently taken a position as a financial planner, and your first client would like assistance planning for retirement. Your client is currently 30 years old and would like to retire at the age of 60. Your client would like to contribute $300.00 a month until retirement. You plan on investing the $300 in an interest-earning savings account that earns 2.75% APR. Your client would like you to create a worksheet that details the investment and calculates the future value of the investment.

a. Open Excel and create a new document. Save the document as **e07p3Retirement_LastFirst**.

b. Click **cell A1** and type **Retirement Goal**. Press **Enter** and type the following headings in column A:
- **Cell A2: Current Age**
- **Cell A3: Retirement Goal**
- **Cell A4: Monthly Investment**
- **Cell A5: APR**
- **Cell A6: Periodic Rate**
- **Cell A7: NPER**
- **Cell A8: Number of payments per year**
- **Cell A9: Future value at retirement**

c. Click **cell B2** and type **30**. Press **Enter** and type the following data:
- **Cell B3: 60**
- **Cell B4: 300**
- **Cell B5: 2.75%**
- **Cell B6: =B5/12**, if necessary format to display two decimal positions.
- **Cell B7: =(B3-B2)*12**
- **Cell B8: 12**

d. Type the following function in **cell B9**: **=FV(B6,B7,-B4)**.

e. Increase the width of column A and apply **Accounting Number Format** to **cell B9**.

f. Create a footer with your name on the left side, the sheet name code in the center, and the file name code on the right side.

g. Save and close the workbook, and submit based on your instructor's directions.

Mid-Level Exercises

1 West Coast University Admissions Office

You work in the Admissions Office for West Coast University, a mid-sized regional university in California. Your assistant entered a list of college applicants for the Fall 2015 semester. You determine if a student qualifies for early admission or early rejection based on SAT and GPA. After determining the immediate admissions and rejections, you calculate a total score based on SAT and GPA to determine regular admissions and rejections.

a. Open *e07m1Admissions* and save it as **e07m1Admissions_LastFirst**.

b. Enter a nested logical function in the Admit Early column to display either Yes or No. The university admits a student early if that student meets *both* the early admission criteria for the SAT and GPA. That is, the student's SAT score must be 2000 or higher, and the GPA must be 3.80 or higher. Use appropriate references to the cells in the Admission Criteria range. Based on the requirements, the first student, Julie Alevy will be admitted early.

c. Enter a nested logical function in the Reject Early column to display either Yes or No. The university rejects a student early if that student has *either* an SAT score less than 1000 *or* a GPA below 1.80. Use appropriate references to the cells in the Admission Criteria range.

d. Enter a formula in the Score column to calculate an applicant's admission score. Apply the multiplier (found in the Miscellaneous Standards & Filter range) to the student's GPA and add that score to the SAT. Julie Alevy's score is 4700.

e. Enter a nested IF function inside a main IF function in the Final Decision column. The decision text should be one of the following: Early Admission, Early Rejection, Admit, or Reject. *Hint:* Two logical tests are based on the Yes/No displayed in the Admit Early and Reject Early columns. For regular admission, a student must have a combined admission score that is 2900 or higher. A student is rejected if his or her score is lower than the threshold. Use appropriate references to the cell in the Miscellaneous Standards & Filter range.

f. Copy the formulas down the Admit Early, Reject Early, Score, and Final Decision columns.

g. Enter a database function to count the total number of admissions with >= threshold scores.

h. Enter a database function to count the total number of in-state early admissions.

i. Enter database functions to calculate the average SAT and GPA for all early admits with admissions scores at or above the threshold. Note that you cannot merely average the existing averages because the counts are different for Early Admits and Regular Admits. You can use the database function without performing an advanced filter with an output range.

j. Calculate the average GPA for all in-state early admits.

k. Create a footer with your name on the left side, Page 1 of 28 codes in the middle, and the file name code on the right side.

l. Save and close the workbook, and submit based on your instructor's directions.

2 Artwork Database

You are an analyst for an art gallery that is an authorized Greenwich Workshop fine art dealer (www.greenwichworkshop.com). Customers in your area are especially fond of James C. Christensen's art. You prepared a list of artwork: art, type, edition size, release date, issue price, and estimated market value. You want to identify highly sought-after pieces based on age, percentage of value increase, and sold-out status. In addition, you want to perform an advanced filter and identify specific details from the filtered data.

DISCOVER

a. Open *e07m2Art* and save it as **e07m2Art_LastFirst**.

b. Make sure the Valuable worksheet is active and enter a nested logical function in the Comments column to display *Highly Valuable* if either condition is met:

- The release date is on or before December 31, 1989, *or*
- The sold-out status is Yes, the percentage increase in value is at least 500%, or the Edition Size was less than 400.

Enter an empty text string if the conditions are not met. Hint: You will need to nest two logical functions within the logical test argument. Use cell references to the two conditions.

c. Enter conditional math and statistical functions in the **range N8:N10** to calculate the number of pieces, average estimate value, and total estimate value of the highly valuable pieces of artwork indicated in column K.

d. Display the Database worksheet. Assign a range name called **database** to the **range A14:J178**. Assign a range name called **Criteria** to the **range A7:J9**.

e. Create column labels for the Criteria range and replace the Edition Size with a second Release Date column label. Set the following conditions in the Criteria range:

- Sold-out limited-edition canvases released after 1/1/2000 and before 12/31/2003
- Sold-out limited-edition prints released after 1/1/2000 and before 12/31/2003

f. Create an advanced filter using the database list and Criteria range. Filter the records in place.

g. Enter the appropriate database function in **cell C2** in the Summary Statistics area to calculate the highest estimated value of the filtered records. Apply **Currency format** and left-align the value.

DISCOVER

h. Enter a nested function using INDEX and MATCH to display the title (in cell C3) and the release date (in cell C4) for highest estimated valued filtered artwork. Left-align and format the date.

i. Create a footer with your name on the left side, the sheet name code in the center, and the file name code on the right side on each worksheet.

j. Save and close the workbook, and submit based on your instructor's directions.

---

3 Personal Financial Management

An out-of-state family member asked for your assistance with financial planning. First, he is considering purchasing a house and would like you to create a detailed amortization table and calculate cumulative principal paid, as well as cumulative interest throughout the loan, total amount of interest, and interest for selected years. In addition, he is considering a five-year investment in which you invest $75 per month. He would like you to calculate the interest earned per month and the ending values. Once you have completed the work, you will upload your file to OneDrive to allow for review.

Student 1:

a. Open *e07m3Personal* and save it as **e07m3Personal_LastFirst**.

b. Enter formulas on the Loan worksheet to complete the Calculations area.

c. Enter values 1 through 360 in the Payment Number column.

d. Calculate values for the first payment using appropriate relative, mixed, and absolute references:

- Beginning Balance: Create a reference to the appropriate value above the amortization table.
- Monthly Payment: Enter a reference to the calculated monthly payment.
- Interest Paid: Use the appropriate financial function to calculate the interest payment for the given period.
- Principal Repayment: Use the appropriate financial function to calculate the principal repayment for the given period.
- Ending Balance: Enter the formula to calculate the ending balance after you make the first payment.

e. Type a reference to display the beginning balance for the second period. Copy formulas down their respective columns. Apply **Accounting Number Format** to the monetary values.

f. Calculate the following cumulative values:

- Total Interest: Enter the appropriate function to calculate the total interest for the entire loan in **cell I6**.
- Cumulative Interest: Use the appropriate financial function to calculate the cumulative interest for each period, starting in **cell H10**. The final value in cell H369 should be identical to the value calculated in cell I6.
- Cumulative Principal: Use the appropriate financial function to calculate the cumulative principal for each period, starting in **cell I10**. The final value in cell I369 should match the loan amount in cell E3.
- Interest Paid Summary: Enter individual financial functions to calculate total interest paid during specific years in the **range I2:I5**. The first function calculates total interest for the fifth year only, which is $13,441.15.

g. Format monetary values with **Accounting Number Format**.

h. Set appropriate margins and page scaling to fit one page so that if you decide to print the Loan worksheet, all columns fit across each page. Repeat the headings on row 9 on all pages. Create a footer with your name and the worksheet tab code on the right side of the Loan worksheet.

i. Display the Investment worksheet and in **cell A12**, enter a reference to the original start of the first investment period date. In **cell A13**, enter the DATE function with nested YEAR, MONTH, and DAY functions with appropriate arguments. Ensure that the month number represents the next month. Copy the formula down the column and apply different but complementary shading, such as progressive shading of blue, to each 12-month period of dates. Apply right horizontal alignment and increase the indent three times for the dates in column A.

j. Enter formulas for the first period:

- Beginning Value: Type **0**.
- Interest Earned: Enter a formula to calculate the interest for the first period. Use relative and mixed references only.
- End-of-Period Invest: Enter a reference to the Deposit per Period found in the Input Area.
- Ending Value: Calculate the Ending Value, which includes the beginning Value, Interest Earned, and End-of-Period Investment.

k. Calculate the second period's Beginning Value by referencing the previous period's Ending Value. Copy formulas down the columns.

l. Enter the appropriate financial function in **cell E75** to calculate the final value of the investment. This value should be identical to the value shown in cell E71.

m. Format monetary values with **Accounting Number Format**.

n. Adjust margins and insert a page break so that the first three years of investment display on page 1. Center the worksheet data between the left and right margins, and repeat the column headings at the top of page 2. Create a footer with your name on the left side, the sheet name code in the center, and the file name code on the right side of the Investment worksheet.

o. Save the file to OneDrive to share with student 2.

Student 2:

p. Open *e07m3Personal_LastFirst*.

q. Click the Loan worksheet and change the value in **cell B2** to **$350,000**.

r. Click the Investment worksheet and change **cell B5** to **$125.00**.

s. Answer the questions on the Q&A worksheet.

t. Save and close the workbook, and submit based on your instructor's directions.

Beyond the Classroom

Home Renovation

RESEARCH CASE

You are considering a home renovation project. You plan on investing in a mixed-market savings account (MMA) to reach your monetary goal faster. You will invest $100.00 a month for three years to save for the project. You will research the interest rates of MMA accounts and use the data to calculate the future value of your investment. Open *e07b2Renovation* and save it as **e07b2Renovation_LastFirst**. Research current MMA interest rates online and populate the **range F4:F8** with the names of the top five institutions offering MMA savings accounts. Enter the interest rates for each of the institutions in the **range G4:G8**. In **cell I4**, enter a future value function to calculate the value of your investment at the end of the three-year period. Use the fill handle to copy the function down to fill the **range I5:I8**. Fill the top cells containing the two highest values with green. Create a footer with your name, the sheet name, and the file name on each worksheet. Save and close the workbook, and submit based on your instructor's directions.

Cruises

DISASTER RECOVERY

You just started working for a travel agency that specializes in working with cruise companies departing from Miami and travelling to the Caribbean and Mexico/Central America. Carter, your predecessor, created a database in Excel that lists details about each cruise, such as number of days of the cruise, departure date, destination, cruise line, ship name, and posted rates by cabin type. In addition, Carter calculated 10% discounts on Outside and Balcony cabins and discounts for Interior and Deluxe cabins based on these rules:

- 15% discount on Deluxe/Suite cabins for either 4- OR 5-day cruises
- 20% discount on Interior cabins with both (a) 7 or more day cruise AND (b) 4 rating
- 25% discount on Interior cabins with both (a) 7 or more day cruise AND (b) 3.5 rating

Open *e07b3Cruises* and save it as **e07b3Cruises_LastFirst**. Correct the errors with the discount formula in the Adj-Suite column and in the Adj-Interior column. Insert comments in **cells K10** and **N10** describing the errors and what you did to correct the errors. Carter also created a Criteria Range to be able to filter records for seven-day cruises to the Caribbean that depart before May 1, 2012, with a rating of either four or five. Correct and document errors in this range and perform the advanced filter again, copying the results in the Output Range. Carter created an Adjusted Rate Statistics area using database functions to identify the lowest, highest, and average adjusted rates for the four cabin types. In addition, he calculated the number of cabins meeting the criteria. Correct and document errors in this section. Create a footer with your name, the sheet name, and the file name. Save and close the workbook, and submit based on your instructor's directions.

Course Evaluation

SOFT SKILLS CASE S

You are helping create a course-assessment survey for your university. Open *e07b4Evaluation* and save it as **e07b4Evaluation_LastFirst**. Enter a function in **cell C18** to total the cells C7, C9, C11, C13, C15. In **cell D18**, enter a nested IF function that returns *Eligible for teaching award* if the total score is 50 and *Forward to Dean* if the value is less than or equal to 20; all other scores should return the text *Forward to instructor*. Create a footer with your name, the sheet name, and the file name on each worksheet. Save and close the workbook, and submit based on your instructor's directions.

Capstone Exercise

You work for a company that owns five apartment complexes in Nevada. The owners want some specific information about rentals by apartment size (e.g., number of bedrooms per apartment). The owners are also considering purchasing a sixth apartment complex and asked you to perform some financial calculations and analyses.

Apartment Unit Statistics

The owners decided that unoccupied units should be remodeled if the last remodel took place before 2005. Furthermore, they have decided to calculate the pet deposit based on the number of bedrooms and remodel date.

a. Open *e07c1Apartment*, click the **Summary worksheet**, and then save it as **e07c1Apartment_LastFirst**.

b. Insert functions in the Pet Deposit column to calculate the required pet deposit for each unit. If the unit has two or more bedrooms and was remodeled after 2008, the deposit is $125; if not, it is $75.

c. Enter a nested function in the Recommendation column to indicate *Need to remodel* if the apartment is unoccupied and was last remodeled before 2005. For all other apartments, display *No change*.

Create a Search

The owners would like to be able to perform a simple search by ranking to identify which apartment complex is at that ranking.

a. Type **101** in **cell B2**; this is the cell the owners will use to research apartment unit prices.

b. Insert a nested lookup function in **cell E2** that will look up the rental price in column D using the apartment number referenced in cell B2.

Manage a Database List

The Database worksheet contains an identical list of apartments. One of the owners wants to know how many two- and three-bedroom apartments should be remodeled, the value of lost rent,

and the year of the oldest remodel on those units. You need to perform an advanced filter and enter some database functions to address the owner's concerns.

a. Click the **Database worksheet tab**.

b. Enter conditions in the Criteria Range for unoccupied two- and three-bedroom apartments that need to be remodeled.

c. Perform an advanced filter based on the criteria range. Filter the existing database in place.

d. Enter database functions to calculate the database statistics in the **range C8:C10**.

Loan Amortization

The owners are considering purchasing a sixth apartment complex for $850,000 with a down payment of $375,000 for 30 years at 5.75%, with the first payment due on March 20, 2015. You will perform internal calculations and build a loan amortization table.

a. Click the **Loan worksheet tab**.

b. Enter the loan parameters in the Input Area and insert formulas to perform calculations in the Summary Calculations.

c. Complete the loan amortization table. Use a date function for the Payment Date column and financial functions for the Interest Paid and Principal Payment columns.

d. Create a footer with your name on the left side, the sheet name code in the center, and the file name code on the right side of each worksheet. Adjust page setup options as needed.

e. Save and close the workbook, and submit based on your instructor's directions.

Datasets and Tables

Managing Large Volumes of Data

OBJECTIVES | AFTER YOU READ THIS CHAPTER, YOU WILL BE ABLE TO:

1. Freeze rows and columns p. 277
2. Print large datasets p. 277
3. Design and create tables p. 285
4. Apply a table style p. 289
5. Sort data p. 296

6. Filter data p. 298
7. Use structured references and a total row p. 307
8. Apply conditional formatting p. 314
9. Create a new rule p. 318

CASE STUDY | Reid Furniture Store

Vicki Reid owns Reid Furniture Store in Portland, Oregon. She divided her store into four departments: Living Room, Bedroom, Dining Room, and Appliances. All merchandise is categorized into one of these four departments for inventory records and sales. Vicki has four sales representatives: Chantalle Desmarais, Jade Gallagher, Sebastian Gruenewald, and Ambrose Sardelis. The sales system tracks which sales representative processed each transaction.

The business has grown rapidly, and Vicki hired you to analyze the sales data in order to increase future profits. For example, which department generates the most sales? Who is the leading salesperson? Do most customers purchase or finance? Are sales promotions necessary to promote business, or will customers pay the full price?

You downloaded March 2016 data from the sales system into an Excel workbook. To avoid extraneous data that is not needed in the analysis, you did not include customer names, accounts, or specific product numbers. The downloaded file contains transaction numbers, dates, sales representative names, departments, general merchandise description, total price, payment type, transaction type, and the total price.

Large Datasets

So far you have worked with worksheets that contain small datasets, a collection of structured, related data in a limited number of columns and rows. In reality, you will probably work with large datasets consisting of hundreds or thousands of rows and columns of data. When you work with small datasets, you can usually view most or all of the data without scrolling. When you work with large datasets, you probably will not be able to see the entire dataset onscreen even on a large, widescreen monitor set at high resolution. You might want to keep the column and row labels always in view, even as you scroll throughout the dataset. Figure 6.1 shows the Reid Furniture Store's March 2016 sales transactions. Because it contains a lot of transactions, the entire dataset is not visible. You could decrease the zoom level to display more transactions; however, doing so decreases the text size onscreen, making it hard to read the data.

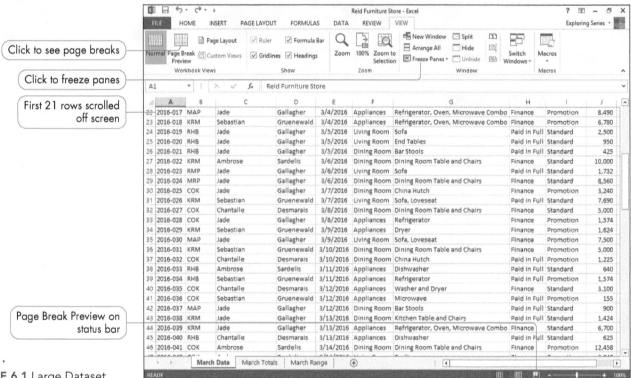

FIGURE 6.1 Large Dataset

As you work with larger datasets, realize that the data will not always fit on one page. You will need to preview the automatic page breaks and probably insert some manual page breaks in more desirable locations, or you might want to print only a selected range within the large dataset to distribute to others.

In this section, you will learn how to keep labels onscreen as you scroll through a large dataset. In addition, you will learn how to manage page breaks, print only a range instead of an entire worksheet, and print column labels at the top of each page of a large dataset.

TIP Go to a Specific Cell

You can navigate through a large worksheet by using the Go To command. Click Find & Select in the Editing group on the Home tab and select Go To (or press F5 or Ctrl+G) to display the Go To dialog box, enter the cell address in the Reference box, and then press Enter to go to the cell.

You can also click in the Name Box, type the cell reference, and then press Enter to go to a specific cell.

Freezing Rows and Columns

When you scroll to parts of a dataset not initially visible, some rows and columns disappear from view. When the row and column labels scroll off the screen, you may not remember what each column represents. You can keep labels onscreen by freezing them. *Freezing* is the process of keeping rows and/or columns visible onscreen at all times even when you scroll through a large dataset. Table 6.1 describes the three freeze options.

TABLE 6.1 Freeze Options

Option	Description
Freeze Panes	Keeps both rows and columns above and to the left of the active cell visible as you scroll through a worksheet.
Freeze Top Row	Keeps only the top row visible as you scroll through a worksheet.
Freeze First Column	Keeps only the first column visible as you scroll through a worksheet.

STEP 1 To freeze labels, click the View tab, click Freeze Panes in the Window group, and then select a freeze option. To freeze one or more rows and columns, use the Freeze Panes option. Before selecting this option, make the active cell one row below and one column to the right of the rows and columns you want to freeze. For example, to freeze the first five rows and the first column, make cell B6 the active cell before clicking the Freeze Panes option. As Figure 6.2 shows, Excel displays a horizontal line below the last frozen row (row 5) and a vertical line to the right of the last frozen column (column A). Unfrozen rows (such as rows 6–14) and unfrozen columns (such as columns B and C) are no longer visible as you scroll down and to the right, respectively.

Rows 1–5 and column A frozen

Vertical line to the right of last frozen column

Horizontal line below last frozen row

FIGURE 6.2 Freeze Panes Set

To unlock the rows and columns from remaining onscreen as you scroll, click Freeze Panes in the Window group and select Unfreeze Panes, which only appears on the menu when you have frozen rows and/or columns. After you unfreeze the panes, the Freeze Panes option appears instead of Unfreeze Panes on the menu again.

When you freeze panes and press Ctrl+Home, the first unfrozen cell is the active cell instead of cell A1. For example, with column A and rows 1 through 5 frozen in Figure 6.2, pressing Ctrl+Home makes cell B6 the active cell. If you need to edit a cell in the frozen area, click the particular cell to make it active and edit the data.

Printing Large Datasets

For a large dataset, some columns and rows may print on several pages. Analyzing the data on individual printed pages is difficult when each page does not contain column and row labels. To prevent wasting paper, always use Print Preview. Doing so enables you to adjust page settings until you are satisfied with how the data will print.

The Page Layout tab (see Figure 6.3) contains options to help you prepare large datasets to print. Previously, you changed the page orientation, set different margins, and adjusted the scaling. In addition, you can manage page breaks, set the print area, and print titles.

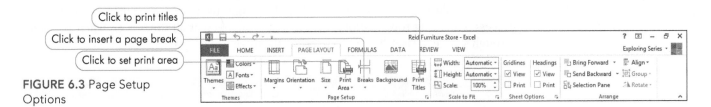

FIGURE 6.3 Page Setup Options

Display and Change Page Breaks

Based on the paper size, orientation, margins, and other settings, Excel identifies how much data can print on a page. Then it displays a *page break*, indicating where data will start on another printed page. To identify where these automatic page breaks will occur, click Page Break Preview on the status bar or in the Workbook Views group on the View tab. In Page Break Preview, Excel displays watermarks, such as *Page 1*, indicating the area that will print on a specific page. Blue dashed lines indicate where the automatic page breaks occur, and solid blue lines indicate manual page breaks.

If the automatic page breaks occur in undesirable locations, you can adjust the page breaks. For example, if you have a worksheet listing sales data by date, the automatic page break might occur within a group of rows for one date, such as between two rows of data for 3/14/2016. To make all rows for that date appear together, you can either insert a page break above the first data row for that date or decrease the margins so that all 3/14/2015 transactions fit at the bottom of the page. To do this, drag a page break line to the desired location.

Manual Page Break: Do the following to set a manual break at a specific location:

STEP 2 >>

1. Click the cell that you want to be the first row and column on a new printed page. For example, click cell A50 if you want cell A50 to start a new page. If you click cell D50, you create a page for columns A through C, and then column D starts a new page.
2. Click the PAGE LAYOUT tab.
3. Click Breaks in the Page Setup group and select Insert Page Break. Excel displays a solid blue line in Page Break Preview or a dashed line in Normal view to indicate the manual page breaks you set. Figure 6.4 shows a worksheet with both automatic and manual page breaks.

Remove a Manual Page Break: To remove a manual page break, do the following:

1. Click a cell below a horizontal page break or a cell to the right of a vertical page break.
2. Click Breaks in the Page Setup group and select Remove Page Break.

Reset Page Breaks: To reset all page breaks back to the automatic page breaks, do the following:

1. Click Breaks in the Page Setup group.
2. Select Reset All Page Breaks.

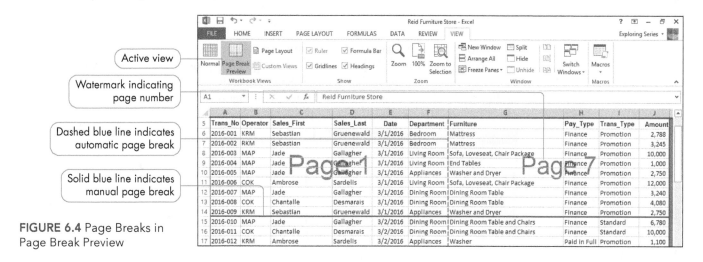

Active view

Watermark indicating page number

Dashed blue line indicates automatic page break

Solid blue line indicates manual page break

FIGURE 6.4 Page Breaks in Page Break Preview

Set and Clear a Print Area

The default Print settings send an entire dataset on the active worksheet to the printer. However, you might want to print only part of the worksheet data. If you display the worksheet in Page Break view, you can identify which page(s) you want to print. Then click the File tab and select Print. Type the number(s) of the page(s) you want to print. For example, to print page 2 only, type 2 in the Pages text box and in the *to* text box.

You can further restrict what is printed by setting the ***print area***, which is the range of cells that will print. For example, you might want to print only an input area or just the transactions that occurred on a particular date. To set a print area, do the following:

STEP 3》

1. Select the range you want to print.
2. Click the PAGE LAYOUT tab and click Print Area in the Page Setup group.
3. Select Set Print Area.

In Page Break Preview, the print area has a white background and solid blue border; the rest of the worksheet has a gray background (see Figure 6.5). In Normal view or Page Layout view, the print area is surrounded by thin gray lines.

Dark blue lines indicate boundaries in Page Break Preview

Click to set print area

Gray background indicates nonprinting area in Page Break Preview

FIGURE 6.5 Print Area in Page Break Preview

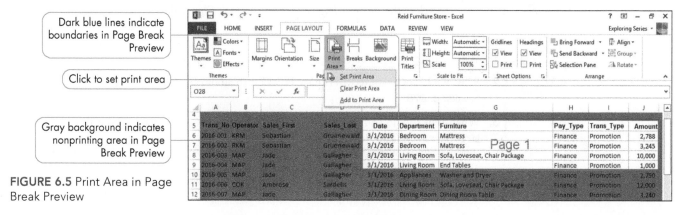

To add print areas where each print area will print on a separate page, select the range you want to print, click Print Area, and then select *Add to Print Area*. To clear the print area, click Print Area in the Page Setup group and select Clear Print Area.

TIP **Print a Selection**

Another way to print part of a worksheet is to select the range you want to print. Click the File tab and click Print. Click the first arrow in the *Settings* section and select Print Selection.

Print Titles

STEP 4 » When you print large datasets, it is helpful that every page contains descriptive column and row labels. When you click Print Titles in the Page Setup group on the Page Layout tab, Excel opens the Page Setup dialog box with the Sheet tab active so that you can select which row(s) and/or column(s) to repeat on each printout (see Figure 6.6).

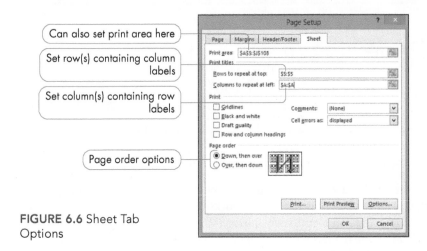

Can also set print area here

Set row(s) containing column labels

Set column(s) containing row labels

Page order options

FIGURE 6.6 Sheet Tab Options

To print the column labels at the top of each page, select the row(s) that contain the labels or titles (such as row 5) in the *Rows to repeat at top* box to display $5:$5. To print the row labels at the left side of each page, select the column(s) that contain the labels or titles (such as column A) in the *Columns to repeat at left* box to display AA.

Control Print Page Order

Print order is the sequence in which the pages are printed. By default, the pages print in this order: top-left section, bottom-left section, top-right section, and bottom-right section. However, you might want to print the entire top portion of the worksheet before printing the bottom portion. To change the print order, open the Page Setup dialog box, click the Sheet tab, and then select the desired *Page order* option (see Figure 6.6).

Quick Concepts

1. What is the purpose of freezing panes in a worksheet? *p. 277*

2. Why would you want to insert page breaks instead of using the automatic page breaks? *p. 278*

3. What steps should you take to ensure that column labels display on each printed page of a large dataset? *p. 280*

Hands-On Exercises

Watch the Video for this Hands-On Exercise!

MyITLab®
HOE1 Training

1 Large Datasets

You want to review the large dataset that shows the March 2016 transactions for Reid Furniture Store. You will need to view the data and adjust some page setup options so that you can print necessary labels on each page.

Skills covered: Freeze Rows and Columns • Manage Page Breaks • Set and Clear a Print Area • Print Titles

STEP 1 » FREEZE ROWS AND COLUMNS

Before printing the March 2016 transaction dataset, you want to view the data. The dataset contains more rows than will display onscreen at the same time. You decide to freeze the column and row labels to stay onscreen as you scroll through the transactions. Refer to Figure 6.7 as you complete Step 1.

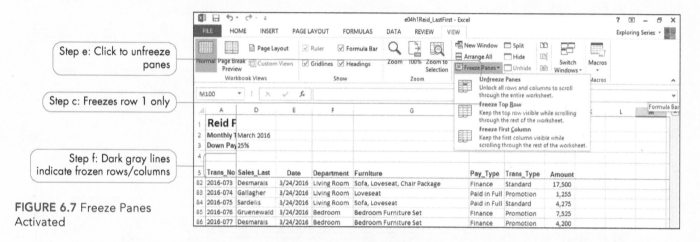

FIGURE 6.7 Freeze Panes Activated

a. Open *e04h1Reid* and save it as **e04h1Reid_LastFirst**.

> **TROUBLESHOOTING:** If you make any major mistakes in this exercise, you can close the file, open *e04h1Reid* again, and then start this exercise over.

The workbook contains three worksheets: March Data (for Hands-On Exercises 1–3), March Totals (for Hands-On Exercise 4), and March Range (for Hands-On Exercise 5).

b. Press **Page Down** four times to scroll through the dataset. Then press **Ctrl+Home** to go back to the top of the worksheet.

After you press Page Down, the column labels in row 5 scroll off the screen, making it challenging to remember what type of data are in some columns.

c. Click the **VIEW tab**, click **Freeze Panes** in the Window group, and then select **Freeze Top Row**.

A dark gray horizontal line displays between rows 1 and 2.

d. Press **Page Down** to scroll down through the worksheet.

As rows scroll off the top of the Excel window, the first row remains frozen onscreen. The title by itself is not helpful; you need to freeze the column labels as well.

e. Click **Freeze Panes** in the Window group and select **Unfreeze Panes**.

f. Click **cell B6**, the cell below the row and one column to the right of what you want to freeze. Click **Freeze Panes** in the Window group and select **Freeze Panes**.

Excel displays a vertical line between columns A and B, indicating that column A is frozen, and a horizontal line between rows 5 and 6, indicating the first five rows are frozen.

g. Press **Ctrl+G**, type **M100** in the **Reference box** of the Go To dialog box, and then click **OK** to make cell M100 the active cell. Save the workbook.

Rows 6 through 81 and columns B and C are not visible because they scrolled off the screen.

> **TROUBLESHOOTING:** Your screen may differ from Figure 6.7 due to different Windows resolution settings. If necessary, continue scrolling right and down until you see columns and rows scrolling offscreen.

STEP 2 ≫ MANAGE PAGE BREAKS

You plan to print the dataset so that you and Vicki Reid can discuss the transactions in your weekly meeting. Because the large dataset will not fit on one page, you want to see where the automatic page breaks are and then insert a manual page break. Refer to Figure 6.8 as you complete Step 2.

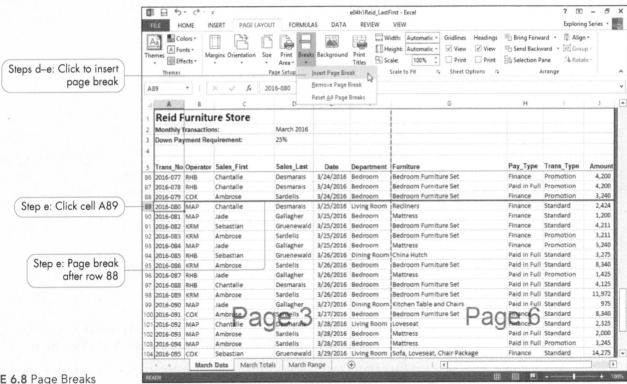

FIGURE 6.8 Page Breaks

a. Press **Ctrl+Home** to move to **cell B6**, the first cell in the unfrozen area. Click the **VIEW tab**, if necessary, and click **Page Break Preview** in the Workbook Views group or on the status bar.

Excel displays blue dashed lines to indicate the automatic page breaks.

b. Scroll down until you see row 44 below the frozen column labels.

The automatic horizontal page break is between rows 46 and 47 (or between rows 45 and 46). You do not want transactions for a particular day to span between printed pages, so you need to move the page break up to keep all 3/13/2016 transactions together.

c. Click **cell A45**, the first cell containing 3/13/2016 data and the cell to start the top of the second page.

d. Click the **PAGE LAYOUT tab**, click **Breaks** in the Page Setup group, and then select **Insert Page Break**.

You inserted a page break between rows 44 and 45 so that the 3/13/2016 transactions will be on one page.

e. Click **cell A89**, click **Breaks** in the Page Setup group, and then select **Insert Page Break**. Save the workbook.

You inserted a page break between rows 88 and 89 to keep the 3/25/2016 transactions on the same page.

TIP Using the Mouse Pointer to Move Page Breaks

To use the mouse pointer to adjust a page break, position the mouse pointer on the page break line to see the two-headed arrow and drag the line to where you want the page break to occur.

STEP 3 ≫ SET AND CLEAR A PRINT AREA

You want to focus on the transactions for only March 1, 2016. To avoid printing more data than you need, you will set the print area to print transactions for only that day. Refer to Figure 6.9 as you complete Step 3.

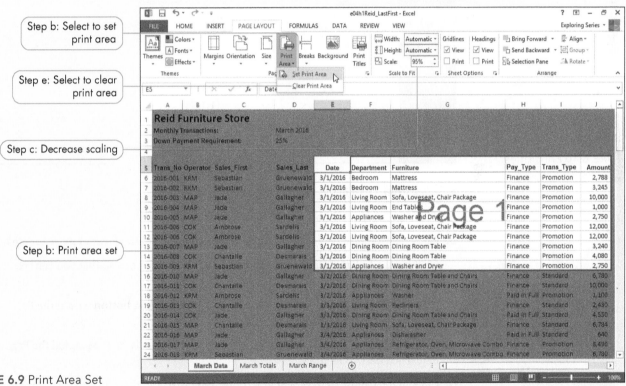

FIGURE 6.9 Print Area Set

a. Scroll up to see the first row of March data. Select the **range E5:J15**, the range of data for March 1, 2016.

b. Click the **PAGE LAYOUT tab**, if necessary, click **Print Area** in the Page Setup group, and then select **Set Print Area**.

Excel displays the print area with a solid blue border. A dotted blue line displays between columns I and J, indicating an automatic page break. The rest of the worksheet displays with a gray background.

c. Click **cell E5** and click the **Scale arrow** down one time in the *Scale to Fit* group.

The selected print area will print on one page.

d. Press **Ctrl+P** to see that only the print area will print. Press **Esc**.

e. Click **Print Area** in the Page Setup group and select **Clear Print Area**. Save the workbook.

STEP 4 ≫ PRINT TITLES

Only the first page will print both row and column labels. Pages 2 and 3 will print the remaining row labels, Page 4 will print the remaining column labels, and Pages 5 and 6 will not print either label. You want to make sure the column and row labels print on all pages. To do this, you will print titles. Refer to Figure 6.10 as you complete Step 4.

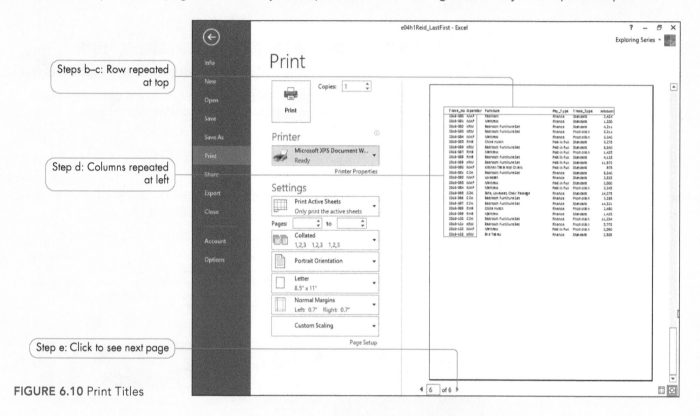

FIGURE 6.10 Print Titles

a. Click **Print Titles** in the Page Setup group.

The Page Setup dialog box opens, displaying the Sheet tab.

b. Click the **Collapse Dialog box button** on the right side of the *Rows to repeat at top* box.

Clicking the *Collapse Dialog box* button reduces the dialog box so that you can select a range in the worksheet easily.

c. Click the **row 5 heading** and click the **Collapse Dialog box button** within the Page Setup: Rows to repeat at top dialog box.

You selected the fifth row, which contains the column labels, and expanded the Page Setup dialog box back to its full size.

d. Click in the **Columns to repeat at left box**, type **A:B**, and then click **Print Preview**.

e. Click **Next Page** at the bottom of the Microsoft Office Backstage view. Click **Next Page** until the sixth page displays.

Figure 6.10 shows a preview of the sixth page. The column labels and the first two columns appear on all pages.

f. Click the **Back arrow** in the top-left corner of the Microsoft Office Backstage view.

g. Save the workbook. Keep the workbook onscreen if you plan to continue with the next Hands-On Exercise. If not, close the workbook and exit Excel.

Excel Tables

All organizations maintain lists of data. Businesses maintain inventory lists, educational institutions maintain lists of students and faculty, and governmental entities maintain lists of contracts. Although more complicated related data should be stored in a database-management program, such as Access, you can maintain structured lists in Excel tables. A *table* is a structured range that contains related data organized in such a way as to facilitate data management and analysis. Although you can manage and analyze a range of data, a table provides many advantages over a range of data:

- Column headings remain onscreen without having to use Freeze Panes.
- Filter arrows are available for efficient sorting and filtering.
- Table styles easily format table rows and columns with complementary fill colors.
- Calculated columns where the formulas copy down the columns automatically are available to create and edit.
- Calculated total row enables the user to implement a variety of summary functions.
- Structured references can be used instead of cell references in formulas.
- Table data can export to a SharePoint list.

In this section, you will learn table terminology and rules for structuring data. You will create a table from existing data, manage records and fields, and remove duplicates. Then you will apply a table style to format the table.

Designing and Creating Tables

A table is a group of related data organized in a series of rows and columns that is managed independently from any other data on the worksheet. Each column represents a *field*, which is an individual piece of data, such as last names or quantities sold. Each field should represent the smallest possible unit of data. For example, instead of a Name field, separate name data into First Name and Last Name fields. Instead of one large address field, separate address data into Street Address, City, State, and ZIP Code fields. Separating data into the smallest units possible enables you to manipulate the data in a variety of ways for output. Each row in a table represents a *record*, which is a collection of related data about one entity. For example, all data related to one particular transaction form a record in the Reid Department Store worksheet.

You should plan the structure before creating a table. The more thoroughly you plan, the fewer changes you will have to make to the table after you create it. To help plan your table, follow these guidelines:

- Enter field (column) names on the top row.
- Keep field names short, descriptive, and unique. No two field names should be identical.
- Format the field names so that they stand out from the data.
- Enter data for each record on a row below the field names.
- Do not leave blank rows between records or between the field names and the first record.
- Delete any blank columns between fields in the dataset.
- Make sure each record has something unique, such as a transaction number or ID.
- Insert at least one blank row and one blank column between the table and other data, such as the main titles. When you need multiple tables in one workbook, a best practice is to place each table on a separate worksheet.

Create a Table

When your worksheet data are structured correctly, you can easily create a table. To create a table from existing data, do the following:

1. Click within the existing range of data.
2. Click the INSERT tab and click Table in the Tables group. The Create Table dialog box opens (see Figure 6.11), prompting you to enter the range of data.

    *   If Excel does not correctly predict the range, select the range for the *Where is the data for your table?* box.
    *   If the existing range contains column labels, select the *My table has headers* check box.

3. Click OK to create the table.

FIGURE 6.11 Create Table Dialog Box

Quick Analysis Table Creation

You can also create a table by selecting a range, clicking the Quick Analysis button, clicking TABLES (see Figure 6.12) in the Quick Analysis gallery, and then clicking Table. While Quick Analysis is efficient for tasks such as creating a chart, it may take more time to create a table because you have to select the entire range first. Some people find that it is faster to create a table from the Insert tab.

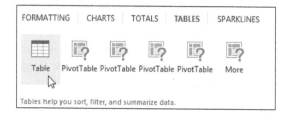

FIGURE 6.12 Quick Analysis Gallery

After you create a table, the Table Tools Design tab displays. Excel applies the default Table Style Medium 2 style to the table, and each cell in the header row has arrows, also called *filtering arrows* or *filtering buttons* in Excel Help (see Figure 6.13). This book uses the term *filter arrows* for consistency. Excel assigns a name to each table, such as Table 1. You can change the table name by clicking in the Table Name box in the Properties group, typing a new name using the same rules you applied when assigning range names, and then pressing Enter.

FIGURE 6.13 Excel Table in Default Format

Labels pointing to the figure:
- Table Tools contextual tab
- Table name
- Click to show or hide filtering arrows in the header row
- Filtering arrow
- Alternating fill colors applied

Instead of converting a range to a table, you can create a table structure first and add data to it later. Select an empty range and follow the previously listed steps to create the range for the table. The default column headings are Column1, Column2, and so on. Click each default column heading and type a descriptive label. Then enter the data into each row of the newly created table.

TIP Converting a Table to a Range

To convert a table back to a range, click within the table range, click the Table Tools Design tab, click *Convert to Range* in the Tools group, and then click Yes in the message box asking, *Do you want to convert the table to a normal range?*

Add and Delete Fields

STEP 2 » After creating a table, you might want to add a new field. For example, you might want to add a field for product numbers to the Reid Furniture Store transaction table. To insert a field:

1. Click in any data cell (but not the cell containing the field name) in a field that will be to the right of the new field. For example, to insert a new field between the fields in columns A and B, click any cell in column B.
2. Click the HOME tab and click the Insert arrow in the Cells group.
3. Select *Insert Table Columns to the Left*.

TIP Adding a New Field on the Right Side of a Table

If you want to add a field at the end of the right side of a table, click in the cell to the right of the last field name and type a label. Excel will extend the table to include that field and will format the cell as a field name.

You can also delete a field if you no longer need any data for that particular field. Although deleting records and fields is easy, you must make sure not to delete data erroneously. If you accidentally delete data, click Undo immediately. To delete a field, do the following:

1. Click a cell in the field that you want to delete.
2. Click the Delete arrow in the Cells group on the HOME tab.
3. Select Delete Table Columns.

Add, Edit, and Delete Records

After you create a table, you might want to add new records, such as adding a new client or a new item to an inventory table. To add a record to a table, do the following:

1. Click a cell in the record below which you want the new record inserted. If you want to add a new record below the last record, click the row containing the last record.
2. Click the HOME tab and click the Insert arrow in the Cells group.
3. Select Insert Table Rows Above to insert a row above the current row, or select Insert Table Row Below if the current row is the last one and you want a row below it.

> **TIP** **Adding a New Record at the End of a Table**
>
> You can also add a record to the end of a table by clicking in the row immediately below the table and typing. Excel will extend the table to include that row as a record in the table and will apply consistent formatting.

You might need to change data for a record. For example, when a client moves, you need to change the client's address and phone number. You edit data in a table the same way you edit data in a regular worksheet cell.

Finally, you can delete records. For example, if you maintain an inventory of artwork in your house and sell a piece of art, delete that record from the table. To delete a record from the table:

1. Click a cell in the record that you want to delete.
2. Click the HOME tab and click the Delete arrow in the Cells group.
3. Select Delete Table Rows.

Remove Duplicate Rows

A table might contain duplicate records, which can give false results when totaling or performing other calculations on the dataset. For a small table, you might be able to detect duplicate records by scanning the data. For large tables, it is more difficult to identify duplicate records by simply scanning the table with the eye. To remove duplicate records, do the following:

1. Click within the table and click the DESIGN tab.
2. Click Remove Duplicates in the Tools group to display the Remove Duplicates dialog box (see Figure 6.14).
3. Click Select All to set the criteria to find a duplicate for every field in the record and click OK. If you select individual column(s), Excel looks for duplicates in the specific column(s) only and deletes all but one record of the duplicated data. Excel will display a message box informing you of how many duplicate rows it removed.

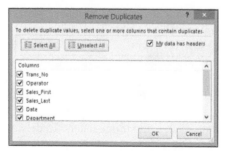

FIGURE 6.14 Remove Duplicates Dialog Box

TIP **Data Tab to Delete Duplicates**

You can also click the Data tab and click Remove Duplicates in the Data Tools group to open the Remove Duplicates dialog box.

Applying a Table Style

STEP 5 » Excel applies a table style when you create a table. *Table styles* control the fill color of the header row (the row containing field names) and rows of records. In addition, table styles specify bold and border lines. You can change the table style to a color scheme that complements your organization's color scheme or to emphasize data the header rows or columns. Click Quick Styles in the Table Styles group to display the Table Styles gallery (see Figure 6.15). To see how a table style will format your table using Live Preview, position the pointer over a style in the Table Styles gallery. After you identify a style you want, click it to apply it to the table.

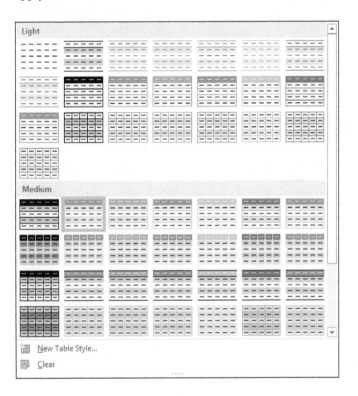

FIGURE 6.15 Table Styles Gallery

After you select a table style, you can control what the style formats. The Table Style Options group contains check boxes to select specific format actions in a table. Table 6.2 lists the options and the effect of each check box. Avoid overformatting the table. It is not good to apply so many formatting effects that the message you want to present with the data is obscured or lost.

TABLE 6.2	Table Style Options
Check Box	**Action**
Header Row	Displays the header row (field names) when checked; removes field names when not checked. Header Row formatting takes priority over column formats.
Total Row	Displays a total row when selected. Total Row formatting takes priority over column formats.
First Column	Applies a different format to the first column so that the row headings stand out. First Column formatting takes priority over Banded Rows formatting.
Last Column	Applies a different format to the last column so that the last column of data stands out; effective for aggregated data, such as grand totals per row. Last Column formatting takes priority over Banded Rows formatting.
Banded Rows	Displays alternate fill colors for even and odd rows to help distinguish records.
Banded Columns	Displays alternate fill colors for even and odd columns to help distinguish fields.
Filter Button	Displays a filter button on the right side of each heading in the header row.

Quick
Concepts

1. List at least four guidelines for planning a table in Excel. ***p. 285***

2. Why would you convert a range of data into an Excel table? ***p. 285***

3. What are six options you can control after selecting a table style? ***p. 289***

2 Excel Tables

You want to convert the March data to a table. As you review the table, you will delete the unnecessary Operator field, add two new fields, insert a missing furniture sale transaction, and remove duplicate transactions. Finally, you will enhance the table appearance by applying a table style.

Skills covered: Create a Table • Add and Delete Fields • Add Records • Remove Duplicate Rows • Apply a Table Style

STEP 1 >> CREATE A TABLE

Although the Reid Furniture Store's March transaction data are organized in an Excel worksheet, you know that you will have additional functionality if you convert the range to a table. Refer to Figure 6.16 as you complete Step 1.

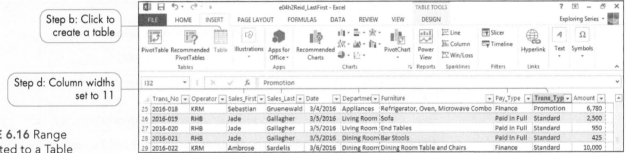

Step b: Click to create a table

Step d: Column widths set to 11

FIGURE 6.16 Range Converted to a Table

a. Open *e04h1Reid_LastFirst* if you closed it at the end of Hands-On Exercise 1 and save it as **e04h2Reid_LastFirst**, changing *h1* to *h2*. Click **Normal** on the status bar.

b. Click in any cell within the transactional data, click the **INSERT tab**, and then click **Table** in the Tables group.

The Create Table dialog box opens. The *Where is the data for your table?* box displays =$A$5:$I$112. Keep the *My table has headers* check box selected so that the headings on the fifth row become the field names for the table.

c. Click **OK** and click **cell A5**.

Excel creates a table from the data range and displays the DESIGN tab, filter arrows, and alternating fill colors for the records. The columns widen to fit the field names, although the wrap text option is still applied to those cells.

d. Set column width to **11** for the Sales_First, Sales_Last, Department, Pay_Type, and Trans_Type fields.

e. Unfreeze the panes and scroll through the table. Save the workbook.

With a regular range of data, column labels scroll off the top of the screen if you do not freeze panes. When you scroll within a table, the table's header row remains onscreen by moving up to where the Excel column (letter) headings usually display (see Figure 6.16).

STEP 2 >> ADD AND DELETE FIELDS

The original range included a column for the data entry operators' initials. You will delete this column because you do not need it for your analysis. In addition, you want to add a field to display down payment amounts in the future. Refer to Figure 6.17 as you complete Step 2.

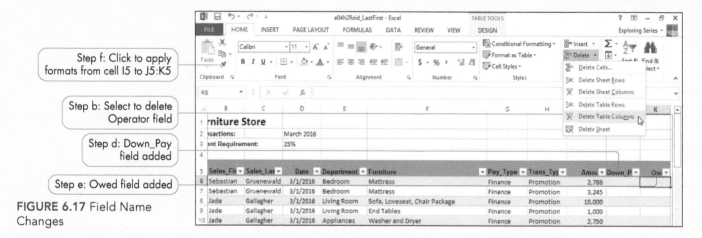

Step f: Click to apply formats from cell I5 to J5:K5

Step b: Select to delete Operator field

Step d: Down_Pay field added

Step e: Owed field added

FIGURE 6.17 Field Name Changes

a. Click **cell B25** or any cell containing a value in the Operator column.

   You need to make a cell active in the field you want to remove.

b. Click the **HOME tab**, click the **Delete arrow** in the Cells group, and then select **Delete Table Columns**.

   Excel deletes the Operator column and may adjust the width of other columns.

c. Adjust the widths of columns E, F, and G as necessary. Click **cell J5**, the first blank cell on the right side of the field names.

d. Type **Down_Pay** and press **Ctrl+Enter**.

   Excel extends the table formatting to column J automatically. A filter arrow appears for the newly created field name, and alternating fill colors appear in the rows below the field name. The fill color is the same as the fill color for other field names; however, the font color is White, Background 1, instead of Black Text 1.

e. Click **cell K5**, type **Owed**, and then press **Ctrl+Enter**.

f. Click **cell I5**, click **Format Painter** in the Clipboard group, and then select the **range J5:K5** to copy the format. Save the workbook.

STEP 3 ≫ ADD RECORDS

As you review the March 2016 transaction table, you notice that two transactions are missing: 2016-68 and 2016-104. After finding the paper invoices, you are ready to add records with the missing transaction data. Refer to Figure 6.18 as you complete Step 3.

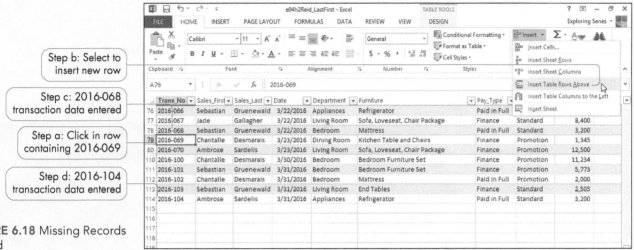

Step b: Select to insert new row

Step c: 2016-068 transaction data entered

Step a: Click in row containing 2016-069

Step d: 2016-104 transaction data entered

FIGURE 6.18 Missing Records Added

a. Click **cell A78** or any cell within the table range on row 78.

The missing record 2016-68 needs to be inserted between 2016-67 on row 77 and 2016-69 on row 78.

b. Click the **HOME tab**, click the **Insert arrow** in the Cells group, and then select **Insert Table Row Above**.

Excel inserts a new table row on row 78, between the 2016-67 and 2016-69 transactions.

c. Enter the following data in the respective fields on the newly created row.

2016-68, Sebastian, Gruenewald, 3/22/2016, Bedroom, Mattress, Paid in Full, Standard, 3200

d. Click **cell A114** and enter the following data in the respective fields. Save the workbook.

2016-104, Ambrose, Sardelis, 3/31/2016, Appliances, Refrigerator, Paid in Full, Standard, 1500

When you start typing 2016-104 in the row immediately below the last record, Excel immediately includes and formats row 114 as part of the table. Review Figure 6.18 to ensure you inserted the records in the correct locations. Rows 81–109 are hidden to display both new records in one screenshot.

STEP 4 ≫ REMOVE DUPLICATE ROWS

You noticed that the 2016-006 transaction is duplicated on rows 11 and 12 and that the 2016-118 transaction is duplicated on rows 24 and 25. You think the table may contain other duplicate rows. To avoid having to look at the entire table row by row, you want to have Excel find and remove the duplicate rows for you. Refer to Figure 6.19 as you complete Step 4.

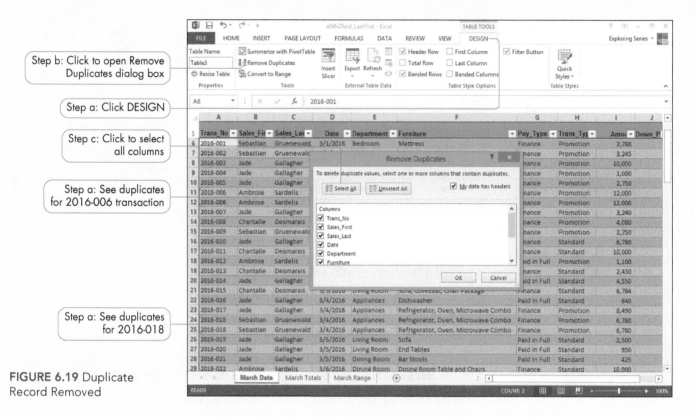

FIGURE 6.19 Duplicate Record Removed

a. Scroll to see rows 11 and 12. Click the **DESIGN tab**.

The records on rows 11 and 12 are identical. Rows 24 and 25 are also duplicates. You need to remove the extra rows.

b. Click **Remove Duplicates** in the Tools group.

The Remove Duplicates dialog box opens.

c. Click **Select All**, make sure the **My data has headers check box** is selected, and then click **OK**.

Excel displays a message box indicating *5 duplicate records found and removed; 104 unique values remain.*

d. Click **OK** in the message box. Press **Page Down** until you see the last record. Save the workbook.

Transaction 2016-104 is located on row 109 after the duplicate records are removed.

STEP 5 >> APPLY A TABLE STYLE

Now that you have finalized the fields and added missing records to the March 2016 transaction table, you want to apply a table style to format the table. Refer to Figure 6.20 as you complete Step 5.

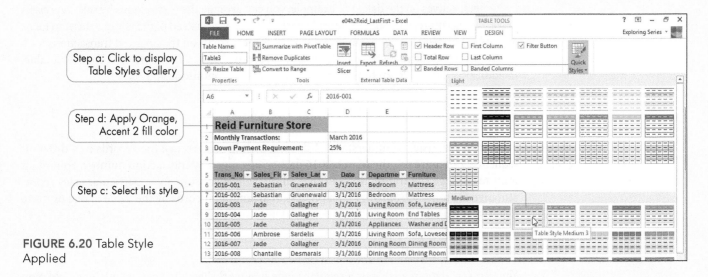

FIGURE 6.20 Table Style Applied

a. Click the **DESIGN tab** and click **Quick Styles** in the Table Styles group to open the Table Styles gallery.

b. Position the mouse pointer over the fourth style on the second row in the *Light* section.

   Live Preview shows the table with the Table Style Light 10 style but does not apply it.

c. Click **Table Style Medium 3**, the third style on the first row in the *Medium* section.

   Excel formats the table with the Table Style Medium 3, which applies Orange, Accent 2 fill color to the header row and Orange, Accent 2, Lighter 80% fill color to every other record.

d. Press **Ctrl_Home** to go to cell A1. Select the **range A1:C1**, click the **Fill Color arrow** in the Font group on the HOME tab, and then click **Orange, Accent 2**.

   You applied a fill color for the title to match the fill color of the field names on the header row in the table.

e. Save the workbook. Keep the workbook onscreen if you plan to continue with the next Hands-On Exercise. If not, close the workbook and exit Excel.

Table Manipulation

You have a variety of options to manipulate table data, in addition to managing fields, adding records, and applying table styles. You can arrange the records in different sequences to get different perspectives on the data. For example, you can arrange the transactions by sales representative. Furthermore, you can display only particular records instead of the entire dataset to focus on a subset of the data. For example, you might want to focus on the financed transactions.

In this section, you will learn how to sort records by text, numbers, and dates in a table. In addition, you will learn how to filter data based on conditions you set.

Sorting Data

Table data are easier to understand and work with if you arrange the records in a different sequence. In Figure 6.1, the March 2016 data are arranged by transaction number. You might want to arrange the transactions so that all of the transactions for a particular sales representative are together. *Sorting* is the process of arranging records by the value of one or more fields within a table.

Sort One Field

STEP 1 » You can sort data in a table or a regular range in a worksheet. To sort by only one field, you can use any of the following methods for either a range of data or a table:

- Click in a cell within the field you want to sort and click Sort & Filter in the Editing group on the HOME tab.
- Click in a cell within the field you want to sort and click *Sort A to Z*, *Sort Z to A*, or Sort in the Sort & Filter group on the DATA tab.
- Right-click the field to sort, point to Sort on the shortcut menu, and then select the type of sort you want.
- Click the filter arrow in the header row and select the desired sort option.

Table 6.3 lists sort options by data type.

TABLE 6.3	Sort Options	
Data Type	**Options**	**Explanation**
Text	Sort A to Z	Arranges data in alphabetical order.
	Sort Z to A	Arranges data in reverse alphabetical order.
Dates	Sort Oldest to Newest	Displays data in chronological order, from oldest to newest.
	Sort Newest to Oldest	Displays data in reverse chronological order, from newest to oldest.
Values	Sort Smallest to Largest	Arranges values from the smallest value to the largest.
	Sort Largest to Smallest	Arranges values from the largest value to the smallest.
Color	Sort by Cell Color	Arranges data together for cells containing a particular fill color.
	Sort by Font Color	Arranges data together for cells containing a particular font color.

Sort Multiple Fields

STEP 2 » At times, sorting by only one field yields several records that have the same information. For example, the same last name or the same department could display several times. In those instances, you may want to add a sort on a second field. A second sort will help to uniquely identify a record. You might need both last name and first name to identify an individual. Using multiple level sorts enables like records in the primary sort to be further organized by additional sort levels. For example, you might want to sort by department, then by sales representative, and finally by sales amount. Excel enables you to sort data on 64 different levels. To perform a multiple level sort:

1. Click in any cell in the table.
2. Click Sort in the Sort & Filter group on the Data tab to display the Sort dialog box.
3. Select the primary sort level by clicking the *Sort by* arrow, selecting the field to sort by, and then clicking the Order arrow and selecting the sort order from the list.
4. Click Add Level, select the second sort level by clicking the *Then by* arrow, select the column to sort by, click the Order arrow, and then select the sort order from the list.
5. Continue to click Add Level and add sort levels until you have entered all sort levels. See Figure 6.21. Click OK.

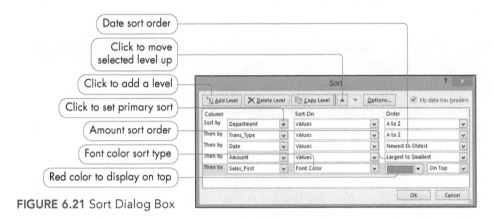

FIGURE 6.21 Sort Dialog Box

Create a Custom Sort

Excel arranges data in defined sequences, such as alphabetical order. For example, days of the week are sorted alphabetically: Friday, Monday, Saturday, Sunday, Thursday, Tuesday, and Wednesday. However, you might want to create a custom sort sequence. For example, you can create a custom sort to arrange days of the week in order from Sunday to Saturday.

To create a custom sort sequence:

1. Click Sort in the Sort & Filter group on the DATA tab.
2. Click the Order arrow and select Custom List to display the Custom Lists dialog box (see Figure 6.22).
3. Select an existing sort sequence in the *Custom lists* box, or select NEW LIST.
4. Click Add and type the entries in the desired sort sequence in the *List entries* box, pressing Enter between entries.
5. Click Add and click OK.

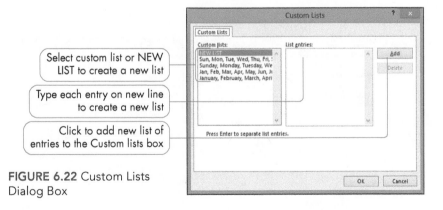

FIGURE 6.22 Custom Lists Dialog Box

Filtering Data

Filtering is the process of specifying conditions to display only those records that meet certain conditions. For example, you might want to filter the data to show transactions for only a particular sales representative. To filter records by a particular field, click the filter arrow for that field. The list displays each unique label, value, or date contained in the column. Deselect the (Select All) check box and click the check box for each value you want to include in the filtered results.

Often you will need to apply more than one filter to display the needed records. You can filter more than one field. Each additional filter is based on the current filtered data and further reduces a data subset. To apply multiple filters, click each field's filter arrow and select the values to include in the filtered data results.

> ## TIP Copying Before Filtering Data
>
> Often, you need to show different filters applied to the same dataset. You can copy the worksheet and filter the data on the copied worksheet to preserve the original dataset.

Apply Text Filters

STEP 3 » When you apply a filter to a text field, the filter menu displays each unique text item. You can select one or more text items from the list. For example, select Gallagher to show only her records. To display records for both Gallagher and Sardelis, deselect the (Select All) check mark and click the Gallagher and Sardelis check boxes. You can also select Text Filters to see a submenu of additional options, such as *Begins With*, to select all records for which the name begins with the letter G, for example.

Figure 6.23 shows the Sales_Last filter menu with two names selected. Excel displays records for these two reps only. The records for the other sales reps are hidden but not deleted. The filter arrow displays a filter icon, indicating which field is filtered. Excel displays the row numbers in blue, indicating that you applied a filter. The missing row numbers indicate hidden rows of data. When you remove the filter, all the records display again.

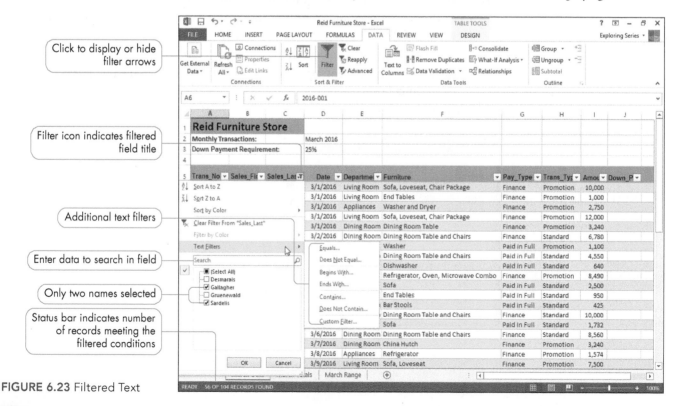

FIGURE 6.23 Filtered Text

TIP | Filter Arrows

Click the Filter Button check box in the Table Style Options group on the Design tab to display or hide the filter arrows. For a range of data instead of a table, click Filter in the Sort & Filter group on the Data tab to display or hide the filter arrows.

Apply Number Filters

STEP 4 ▶▶

When you filter a field of numbers, you can select specific numbers. You might want to filter numbers by a range, such as numbers greater than $5,000 or numbers between $4,000 and $5,000. The submenu enables you to set a variety of number filters. In Figure 6.24, the amounts are filtered to show only those that are above the average amount. In this situation, Excel calculates the average amount as $4,512. Only records above that amount display.

If the field contains a large number of unique entries, you can click in the Search box and then type a value, text label, or date. Doing so narrows the visible list so that you do not have to scroll through the entire list. For example, if you enter $7, the list will display only values that start with $7.

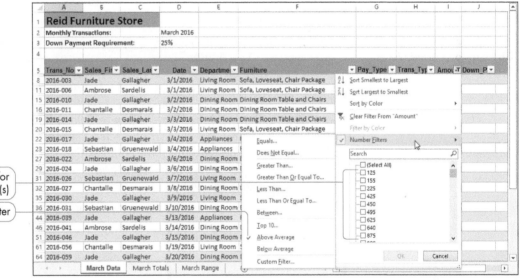

FIGURE 6.24 Filtered Numbers

The Top 10 option enables you to specify the top records. Although the option name is Top 10, you can specify the number or percentage of records to display. For example, you can filter the list to display only the top five or the bottom 7%. Figure 6.25 shows the Top 10 AutoFilter dialog box. Click the first arrow to select either Top or Bottom, click the spin arrows to indicate a value, and then click the last arrow to select either Items or Percent.

FIGURE 6.25 Top 10 AutoFilter Dialog Box

Apply Date Filters

STEP 5 >>

When you filter a field of dates, you can select specific dates or a date range, such as dates after 3/15/2016 or dates between 3/1/2016 and 3/7/2016. The submenu enables you to set a variety of date filters. For more specific date options, point to Date Filters, point to *All Dates in the Period*, and then select a period, such as Quarter 2 or October. Figure 6.26 shows the Date Filter menu.

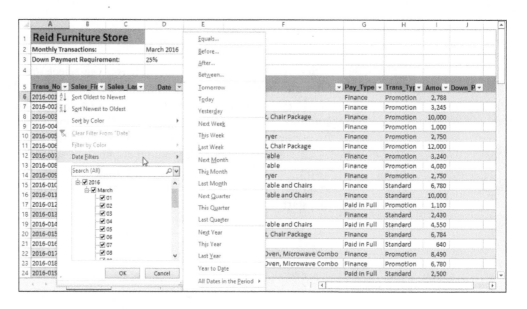

FIGURE 6.26 Filtered Dates

Apply a Custom Filter

If you select options such as *Greater Than* or *Before*, Excel displays the Custom AutoFilter dialog box (see Figure 6.27). You can also select Custom Filter from the menu to display this dialog box, which is designed for more complex filtering requirements.

FIGURE 6.27 Custom AutoFilter Dialog Box

The dialog box indicates the column being filtered. To set the filters, click the arrows to select the comparison type, such as equals or contains. Click the arrow on the right to select a specific text, value, or date entry, or type the data yourself. For ranges of dates or values, click And, and then specify the comparison operator and value or date for the next condition row. For text, click Or. For example, if you want both Gallagher and Desmarais, you must select Or because each data entry contains either Gallagher or Desmarais but not both at the same time.

You can use wildcards to represent characters. For example, to select all states starting with New, type *New ** in the second box to obtain results such as New York or New Mexico. The asterisk (*) represents any number of characters. If you want a wildcard for only a single character, type the question mark (?).

Clear Filters

You can remove the filters from one or more fields to expand the dataset again. To remove only one filter and keep the other filters, click the filter arrow for the field from which you wish to clear the filter and select Clear Filter From.

To remove all filters and display all records in a dataset, do one of the following:

- Click Filter in the Sort & Filter group on the DATA tab.
- Click Sort & Filter in the Editing group on the HOME tab and select Filter.

Quick
Concepts

1. What is the purpose of sorting data in a table? *p. 296*

2. What are two ways to arrange (sort) dates? *p. 296*

3. List at least five ways you can filter numbers. *p. 299*

4. Assume you are filtering a list and want to display records for people who live in Boston or New York. What settings do you enter in the Custom AutoFilter dialog box for that field? *p. 300*

Watch the Video for this Hands-On Exercise!

MyITLab®
HOE3 Training

3 Table Manipulation

You want to start analyzing the March 2016 transactions for Reid Furniture Store by sorting and filtering data in a variety of ways to help you understand the transactions better.

Skills covered: Sort One Field • Sort Multiple Fields • Apply Text Filters • Apply a Number Filter • Apply a Date Filter

STEP 1 ≫ SORT ONE FIELD

First, you want to compare the number of transactions by sales rep, so you will sort the data by the Rep_Last field. After reviewing the transactions by sales reps, you want to arrange the transactions from the one with the largest purchase first to the smallest purchase last. Refer to Figure 6.28 as you complete Step 1.

Step b: Click to sort alphabetically by last name

Step c: Click to sort amount from largest to smallest

FIGURE 6.28 Sorted Data

a. Open *e04h2Reid_LastFirst* if you closed it at the end of Hands-On Exercise 2. Save it as **e04h3Reid_LastFirst**, changing *h2* to *h3*.

b. Click the **Sales_Last filter arrow** and select **Sort A to Z**.

Excel arranges the transactions in alphabetical order by last name, starting with Desmarais. Within each sales rep, records display in their original sequence by transaction number. If you scan the records, you can see that Gallagher completed the most sales transactions in March. The up arrow icon on the Sales_Last filter arrow indicates records are sorted in alphabetical order by that field.

TIP | Name Sorts

Always check the data to determine how many levels of sorting you need to apply. If your table contains several people with the same last name but different first names, you would first sort by the Last Name field, then sort by First Name field. All the people with the last name Desmarais would be grouped together and further sorted by first name, such as Amanda and then Bradley.

c. Click the **Amount filter arrow** and select **Sort Largest to Smallest**. Save the workbook.

The records are no longer sorted by Sales_Last. When you sort by another field, Excel arranges the data for that field. In this case, Excel arranges the transactions from the one with the largest amount to the smallest amount, indicated by the down arrow icon in the Amount filter arrow.

STEP 2 ≫ SORT MULTIPLE FIELDS

You want to review the transactions by payment type (financed or paid in full). Within each payment type, you want to further compare the transaction type (promotion or standard). Finally, you want to compare costs within the sorted records by displaying the highest costs first. You will use the Sort dialog box to perform a three-level sort. Refer to Figure 6.29 as you complete Step 2.

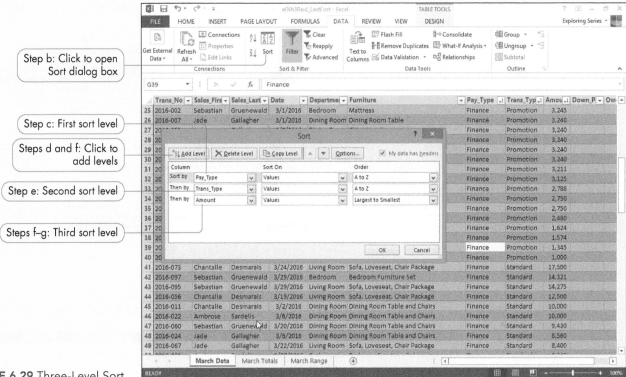

FIGURE 6.29 Three-Level Sort

a. Click inside the table and click the **DATA tab**.

Both the DATA and HOME tabs contain commands to open the Sort dialog box.

b. Click **Sort** in the Sort & Filter group to open the Sort dialog box.

c. Click the **Sort by arrow** and select **Pay_Type**. Click the **Order arrow** and select **A to Z**.

You start by specifying the column for the primary sort. In this case, you want to sort the records first by the Payment Type column.

d. Click **Add Level**.

The Sort dialog box adds the *Then by* row, which adds a secondary sort.

e. Click the **Then by arrow** and select **Trans_Type**.

The default order is A to Z, which will sort in alphabetical order by Trans_Type. Excel will first sort the records by the Pay_Type (Finance or Paid in Full). Within each Pay_Type, Excel will further sort records by Trans_Type (Promotion or Standard).

f. Click **Add Level** to add another *Then by* row. Click the second **Then by arrow** and select **Amount**.

g. Click the **Order arrow** for the Amount sort and select **Largest to Smallest**.

Within the Pay_Type and Trans_Type sorts, this will arrange the records with the largest amount first in descending order to the smallest amount.

h. Click **OK** and scroll through the records. Save the workbook.

Most customers finance their purchases instead of paying in full. For the financed transactions, more than half were promotional sales. For merchandise paid in full, a majority of the transactions were standard sales, indicating that people with money don't necessarily wait for a promotional sale to purchase merchandise.

STEP 3 ≫ APPLY TEXT FILTERS

Now that you know Jade Gallagher had the most transactions for March, you will filter the table to focus on her sales. You notice that she sells more merchandise from the Dining Room department, so you will filter out the other departments. Refer to Figure 6.30 as you complete Step 3.

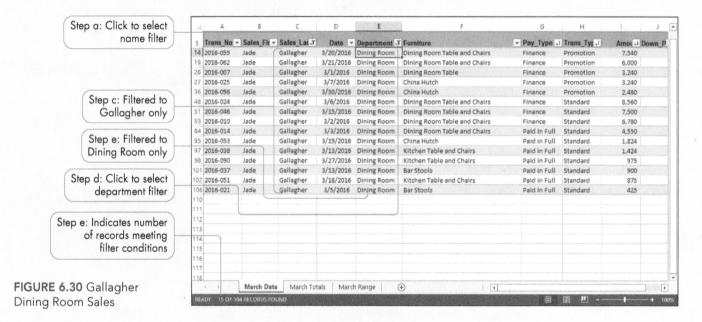

FIGURE 6.30 Gallagher Dining Room Sales

a. Click the **Sales_Last filter arrow**.

The (Select All) check box is selected.

b. Click the **(Select All) check box** to deselect all last names.

c. Click the **Gallagher check box** and click **OK**.

The status bar indicates that 33 out of 104 records meet the filtering condition. The Sales_Last filter arrow includes a funnel icon, indicating that this column is filtered.

d. Click the **Department filter arrow**.

e. Click the **(Select All) check box** to deselect all departments, click the **Dining Room check box** to focus on that department, and then click **OK**. Save the workbook.

The remaining 15 records show Gallagher's dining room sales for the month. The Department filter arrow includes a funnel icon, indicating that this column is also filtered.

STEP 4 » APPLY A NUMBER FILTER

Vicki is considering giving a bonus to employees who sold the high-end dining room furniture during a specific time period (3/16/2016 to 3/31/2016). You want to determine if Jade Gallagher qualifies for this bonus. In particular, you are interested in how much gross revenue she generated for dining room furniture that cost at least $5,000 or more. Refer to Figure 6.31 as you complete Step 4.

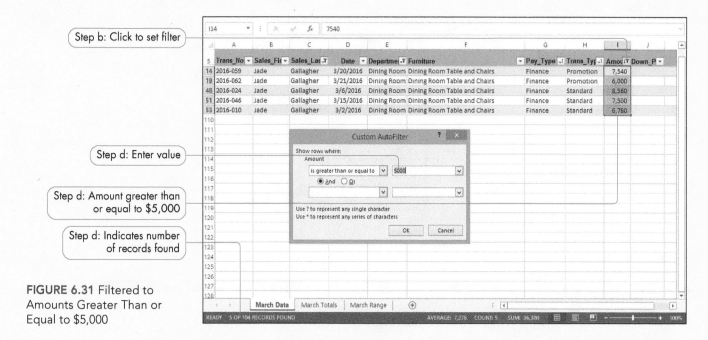

FIGURE 6.31 Filtered to Amounts Greater Than or Equal to $5,000

a. Select the **range I14:I108** of the filtered list and then view the status bar.

The average transaction amount is $3,754 with 15 transactions (i.e., 15 filtered records).

b. Click the **Amount filter arrow**.

c. Point to **Number Filters** and select **Greater Than Or Equal To**.

The Custom AutoFilter dialog box opens. The default comparison *is greater than or equal to* is displayed.

d. Type **5000** in the box to the right of *is greater than or equal to* and click **OK**. Save the workbook.

When typing numbers, you can type raw numbers such as 5000 or formatted numbers such as $5,000. Out of Gallagher's original 15 dining room transactions, only 5 transactions (one-third of her sales) were valued at $5,000 or more.

> **TROUBLESHOOTING:** If no records display or if too many records display, you might have entered 500000 or 500. Repeat steps b through d.

STEP 5 ≫ APPLY A DATE FILTER

Finally, you want to study Jade Gallagher's sales records for the last half of the month. You will add a date filter to identify those sales records. Refer to Figure 6.32 as you complete Step 5.

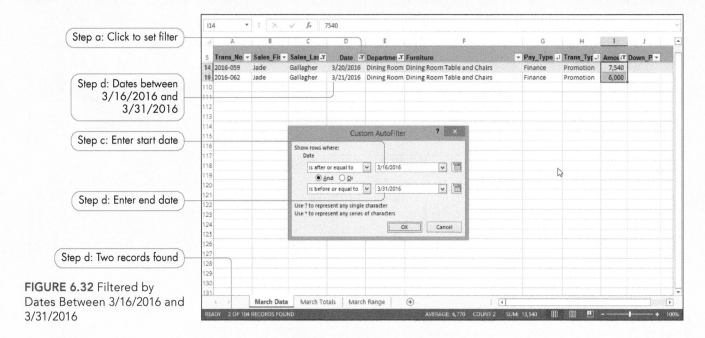

FIGURE 6.32 Filtered by Dates Between 3/16/2016 and 3/31/2016

a. Click the **Date filter arrow**.

b. Point to **Date Filters** and select **Between**.

The Custom AutoFilter dialog box opens. The default comparisons are *is after or equal to* and *is before or equal to*, ready for you to enter the date specifications.

c. Type **3/16/2016** in the box on the right side of *is after or equal to*.

You specified the starting date of the range of dates to include. You will keep the *And* option selected.

d. Type **3/31/2016** in the box on the right side of *is before or equal to*. Click **OK**.

Gallagher had only two dining room sales greater than $5,000 during the last half of March.

e. Save the workbook. Keep the workbook onscreen if you plan to continue with the next Hands-On Exercise. If not, close the workbook and exit Excel.

Table Aggregation

In addition to sorting and filtering tables to analyze the data, you might want to add fields that perform calculations using existing fields. For example, you might want to calculate a required down payment on the amount purchased. Furthermore, you might want to perform aggregate calculations, such as AVERAGE, for a field of numeric data.

In this section, you will learn how to insert structured references to build formulas within a table. In addition, you will learn how to add a row at the end of the table to display basic statistical calculations.

Using Structured References and a Total Row

Excel aids you in quantitative analysis. Your value to an organization increases with your ability to create sophisticated formulas, aggregate data in a meaningful way, and interpret those results. Although you can create complex formulas that you understand, you should strive to create formulas that other people can understand. Creating easy-to-read formulas helps you present self-documenting formulas that require less explanation on your part. When you create formulas for tables, you can use built-in functionality (such as structured references and a total row) that assists you in building understandable formulas.

Create Structured References in Formulas

Your experience in building formulas involves using cell references, such as =SUM(B1:B15) or =H6*$B$3, or range names, such as grades in =VLOOKUP(E5,grades,2). You can use cell references and range names in formulas to perform calculations in a table, as well as another type of reference for formulas in tables: structured references. A *structured reference* is a tag or use of a table element, such as a field heading, as a reference in a formula. Structured references in formulas clearly indicate which type of data is used in the calculations.

STEP 1 ❯❯

A structured reference requires brackets around column headings or field names, such as =[Amount]–[Down_Pay]. The use of field headings without row references in a structured formula is called an *unqualified reference*. Formula AutoComplete displays a list of field headings after you type the equal sign and the opening bracket (see Figure 6.33). Type or double-click the column name from the list and type the closing bracket. Excel displays a colored border around the referenced column. When you enter a formula using structured references, Excel copies the formula down the rest of the table column automatically, compared to typing references in formulas and manually copying the formula down a column.

Type =[to start structured reference

Formula AutoComplete displays field names

FIGURE 6.33 Structured Reference Creation

You can also use the semiselection process to create a formula. As you point to cells to enter a formula in a table, Excel builds a formula like this: =[@Amount]–[@Down_Pay], where the @ indicates the current row. If you use the semiselection process to create a formula outside the table, the formula includes the table and field names, such as =Table1 [@Amount]–Table1[@Down_Pay]. Table1 is the name of the table; Amount and Down_Pay are field names. This structured formula that includes references, such as table numbers, is called a *fully qualified structured reference*. When you build formulas *within* a table, you can use either unqualified or fully qualified structured references. If you need to use table data in a formula *outside* the table boundaries, you must use fully qualified structured references.

Add a Total Row

At times, aggregating data provides more meaningful quantitative interpretation than individual values. For regular ranges of data, you use basic statistical functions, such as SUM, AVERAGE, MIN, and MAX, to provide meaning for a dataset. An Excel table provides the advantage of being able to display a total row automatically without creating the aggregate function yourself. A *total row* displays below the last row of records in an Excel table and enables you to display summary statistics, such as a sum of values displayed in a column.

To display and use the total row:

STEP 2》

1. Click the DESIGN tab.
2. Click Total Row in the Table Style Options group. Excel displays the total row below the last record in the table. Excel displays *Total* in the first column of the total row. Excel either sums or counts data for the last field, depending on the type of data stored in that field. If the last field consists of values, Excel sums the values. If the last field is text, Excel counts the number of records.
3. Click a cell in the total row, click that cell's total row arrow, and then select the function results that you desire. To add a summary statistic to another column, click in the empty cell for that field in the total row and click the arrow to select the desired function. Select None to remove the function.

Figure 6.34 shows the active total row with totals applied to the Amount, Down_Pay, and Owed fields. A list of functions displays to change the function for the last field.

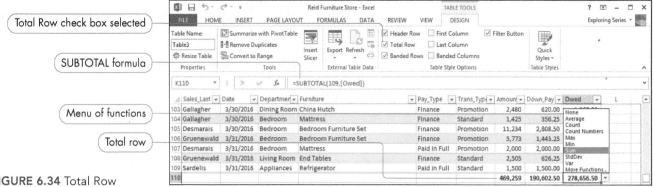

Total Row check box selected

SUBTOTAL formula

Menu of functions

Total row

FIGURE 6.34 Total Row

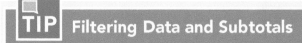

TIP Filtering Data and Subtotals

If you filter the data and display the total row, the SUBTOTAL function's 109 argument ensures that only the displayed data are summed; data for hidden rows are not calculated in the aggregate function.

The calculations on the total row use the SUBTOTAL function. The **SUBTOTAL function** calculates an aggregate value, such as totals or averages, for values in a range or database. If you click in a calculated total row cell, the SUBTOTAL function displays in the Formula Bar. The function for the total row looks like this: =SUBTOTAL(function_num,ref1). The function_num argument is a number that represents a function (see Table 6.4). The ref1 argument indicates the range of values to calculate. The SUBTOTAL function to total the values in the Owed field would be =SUBTOTAL(109,[Owed]), where the number 109 represents the SUM function, and [Owed] represents the Owed field. A benefit of the SUBTOTAL function is that it subtotals data for filtered records, so you have an accurate total for the visible records.

=SUBTOTAL(function_num,ref1,...)

TABLE 6.4	SUBTOTAL Function Numbers	
Function	Database Number	Table Number
AVERAGE	1	101
COUNT	2	102
COUNTA	3	103
MAX	4	104
MIN	5	105
PRODUCT	6	106
STDEV	7	107
STDEVP	8	108
SUM	9	109
VAR	10	110
VARP	11	111

Quick
Concepts

1. What is a structured reference? What is the general format for including a field name in a formula? Give an example. *p. 307*

2. What are the benefits of displaying a total row and selecting functions instead of adding functions yourself below a table? *p. 308*

Hands-On Exercises

Watch the Video
for this Hands-
On Exercise!

MyITLab®
HOE4 Training

4 Table Aggregation

You further analyze the March 2016 transactions for Reid Furniture Store: You want to calculate the required down payment amount and how much customers owe for their purchases. Finally, you will convert the table back to a range.

Skills covered: Create Structured References in Formulas • Add a Total Row • Convert a Table to a Range

STEP 1 ≫ CREATE STRUCTURED REFERENCES IN FORMULAS

To continue reviewing the March transactions, you need to calculate the required down payment for customers who financed their purchases. The required down payment is located above the table data so that you can change that value if needed. In addition, you want to calculate how much customers owe on their purchases if they did not pay in full. You will use structured formulas to perform these calculations. Refer to Figure 6.35 as you complete Step 1.

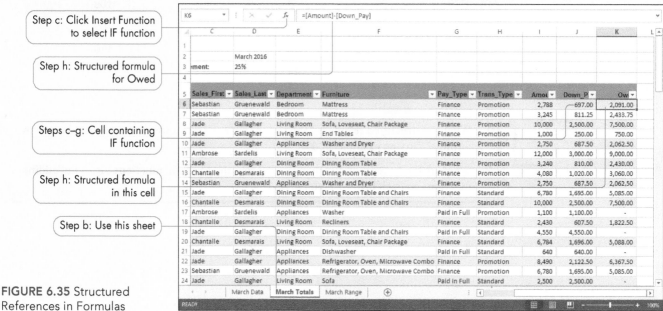

FIGURE 6.35 Structured
References in Formulas

a. Open *e04h3Reid_LastFirst* if you closed it at the end of Hands-On Exercise 3. Save it as **e04h4Reid_LastFirst**, changing *h3* to *h4*.

b. Click the **March Totals worksheet tab** and make **cell J6** the active cell.

    To preserve the integrity of the sorting and filtering in case your instructor wants to verify your work, you will continue with an identical dataset on another worksheet.

c. Click **Insert Function** to open the Insert Function dialog box, select **IF** in the **Select a function list**, and then click **OK**.

d. Type **[Pay_Type]="Paid in Full"** in the **Logical_test box**.

    The logical test evaluates whether a customer paid in full, indicated in the Pay_Type field. Remember to type the brackets around the column label.

e. Type **[Amount]** in the **Value_if_true box**.

    If a customer pays in full, the down payment is the full amount.

f. Type **[Amount]*$D$3** in the **Value_if_false box**.

If a customer does not pay in full, he or she must pay a required down payment. You use [Amount] to refer to the Amount field in the table. Enclose the field labels in brackets. The amount is multiplied by the absolute reference to D3, the cell containing the required down payment percentage. Make this cell reference absolute so that it does not change when Excel copies the formula down the Down_Pay column.

g. Click **OK** to enter the formula.

The formula looks like this in the Formula Bar: =IF([Pay_Type]= "Paid in Full",[Amount],[Amount]*$D$3). Because you are entering formulas in a table, Excel copies the formula down the column automatically. The first customer must pay a $697 down payment (25% of $2,788). The columns in the current worksheet have been formatted as Comma Style for you.

> **TROUBLESHOOTING:** If the results seem incorrect, check your function. Errors will result if you do not enclose the field names in brackets, if you have misspelled a field name, if you omit the quotation marks around *Paid in Full*, and so on. Correct any errors.

h. Click **cell K6**. Type the formula =**[Amount]**–**[Down_Pay]** and press **Enter**. Save the workbook.

The formula calculates how much customers owe if they finance their purchases. Excel copies the formula down the column.

STEP 2 ⟩⟩ ADD A TOTAL ROW

You want to see the monthly totals for the Amount, Down_Pay, and Owed columns. Instead of entering SUM functions yourself, you will add a total row. Refer to Figure 6.36 as you complete Step 2.

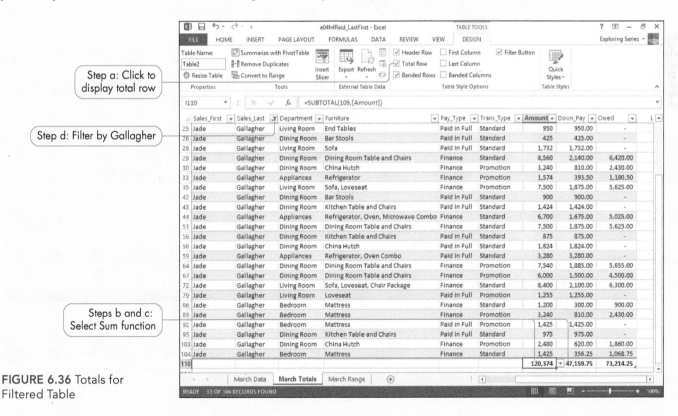

FIGURE 6.36 Totals for Filtered Table

a. Click the **DESIGN tab** and click **Total Row** in the Table Style Options group.

Excel displays the total row after the last record. It sums the last field of values automatically. The total amount customers owe is $278,656.50.

b. Click the **Down_Pay cell** in row 110, click the **total arrow**, and then select **Sum**.

You added a total to the Down_Pay field. The total amount of down payment collected is $190,602.50. The formula displays as =SUBTOTAL(109,[Down_Pay]) in the Formula Bar.

c. Click the **Amount cell** in row 110, click the **total arrow**, and then select **Sum**.

You added a total to the Amount column. The total amount of merchandise sales is $469,259. The formula displays as =SUBTOTAL(109,[Amount]) in the Formula Bar.

d. Filter by Gallagher again. Save the workbook.

The total row values change to display the totals for only Gallagher: $120,374 (Amount), 47,159.75 (Down_Pay), and 73,214.25 (Owed). This is an advantage of using the Total Row, which uses the SUBTOTAL function, as opposed to if you had inserted the SUM function manually. The SUM function would provide a total for all data in the column, not just the filtered data.

STEP 3 ≫ CONVERT A TABLE TO A RANGE

Your last task for now is to convert a copy of the table to a range again so that you can apply other formats. Refer to Figure 6.37 as you complete Step 3.

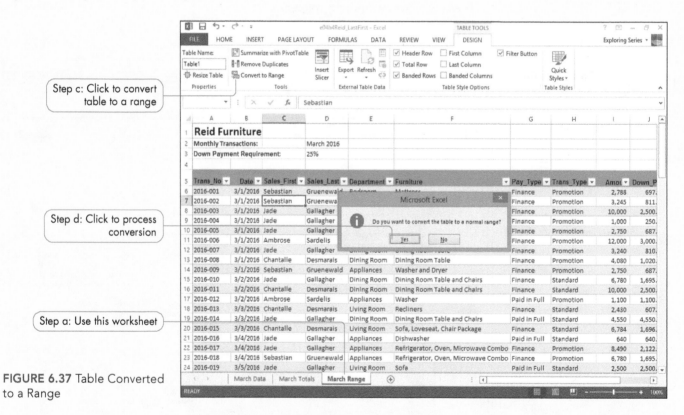

FIGURE 6.37 Table Converted to a Range

a. Click the **March Range worksheet tab**.

To preserve the integrity of the sorting and filtering in case your instructor wants to verify your work, you will continue with an identical dataset on another worksheet.

b. Click within the table and click the **DESIGN tab**, if necessary.

c. Click **Convert to Range** in the Tools group.

Excel displays a message box asking if you want to convert the table to a range.

d. Click **Yes**.

Excel converts the table to a range. The filter arrows disappear, and the Design tab no longer displays. The range is still formatted using a table style. The structured formula =[Amount]-[Down_Pay] in cell K6 changes to ='March Range'!$I$6:$I$109-'March Range'!$J$6:$J$109.

e. Save the workbook. Keep the workbook onscreen if you plan to continue with the next Hands-On Exercise. If not, close the workbook and exit Excel.

Conditional Formatting

You use table styles, or a variety of font, alignment, and number formats on the Home tab, to format a worksheet. You can also apply special formatting to cells that contain particular values or text using conditional formatting. ***Conditional formatting*** applies special formatting to highlight or emphasize cells that meet specific conditions. For example, a sales manager might want to highlight cells containing the top 10 sales amounts, or a professor might want to highlight test scores that fall below the average. You can also apply conditional formatting to point out data for a specific date or duplicate values in a range.

In this section, you will learn about the five conditional formatting categories and how to apply conditional formatting to a range of values based on a condition you set.

Applying Conditional Formatting

Conditional formatting helps you and your audience understand a dataset better because it adds a visual element to the cells. The term is called *conditional* because the formatting occurs when a condition is met. This is similar logic to the IF function you have used. Remember with an IF function, you create a logical test that is evaluated. If the logical or conditional test is true, the function produces one result. If the logical or conditional test is false, the function produces another result. With conditional formatting, if the condition is true, Excel formats the cell automatically based on that condition. If the condition is false, Excel does not format the cell. If you change a value in a conditionally formatted cell, Excel examines the new value to see if it should apply the conditional format.

Apply Conditional Formatting with the Quick Analysis Tool

When you select a range and click the Quick Analysis button, the FORMATTING options display in the Quick Analysis gallery. Position the mouse over a thumbnail to see how it will affect the selected range (see Figure 6.38). You can also apply conditional formatting by clicking Conditional Formatting in the Styles group on the Home tab.

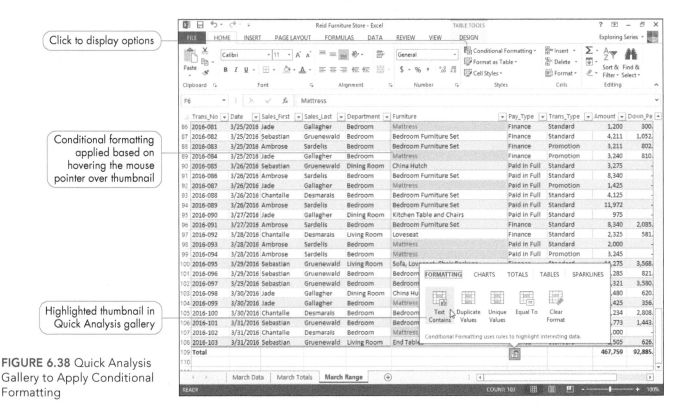

FIGURE 6.38 Quick Analysis Gallery to Apply Conditional Formatting

Table 6.5 describes the conditional formatting options in the Quick Analysis gallery.

TABLE 6.5 Conditional Formatting Options in Quick Analysis Gallery	
Options	**Description**
Text Contains	Formats cells that contain the text in the first selected cell. In Figure 6.38, the first selected cell contains Mattress. If a cell contains Mattress and Springs, Excel would format that cell also because it *contains* Mattress.
Duplicate Values	Formats cells that are duplicated in the selected range.
Unique Values	Formats cells that are unique; that is, no other cell in the selected range contains the same data.
Equal To	Formats cells that are exactly like the data contained in the first selected cell.
Clear Format	Removes the conditional formatting from the selected range.

Table 6.6 lists and describes a number of different conditional formats that you can apply if you want more specific rules.

TABLE 6.6 Conditional Formatting Options	
Options	**Description**
Highlight Cells Rules	Highlights cells with a fill color, font color, or border (such as Light Red Fill with Dark Red Text) if values are greater than, less than, between two values, equal to a value, or duplicate values; text that contains particular characters; or dates when a date meets a particular condition, such as *In the last 7 days*.
Top/Bottom Rules	Formats cells with values in the top 10 items, top 10%, bottom 10 items, bottom 10%, above average, or below average. You can change the exact values to format the top or bottom items or percentages, such as top 5 or bottom 15%.
Data Bars	Applies a gradient or solid fill bar in which the width of the bar represents the current cell's value compared to other cells' values.
Color Scales	Formats different cells with different colors, assigning one color to the lowest group of values and another color to the highest group of values, with gradient colors to other values.
Icon Sets	Inserts an icon from an icon palette in each cell to indicate values compared to each other.

To apply a conditional format, select the cells for which you want to apply a conditional format, click the Home tab, click Conditional Formatting in the Styles group, and then select the conditional formatting category you want to apply.

Apply the Highlight Cells Rules

STEP 1 ≫ The Highlight Cells Rules category enables you to apply a highlight to cells that meet a condition, such as a value greater than a particular value. This option contains predefined combinations of fill colors, font colors, and/or borders. This category is useful because it helps you identify and format automatically values of interest. For example, a weather tracker who developed a worksheet containing the temperatures for each day of a month might want to apply a conditional format to cells that contain temperatures between 70 and 75 degrees. To apply this conditional formatting, she would select Highlight Cells Rules and then select

Between. In the Between dialog box (see Figure 6.39), the weather tracker would type 70 in the *Format cells that are BETWEEN* box and 75 in the *and* box, select the type of conditional formatting, such as *Light Red Fill with Dark Red Text*, and then click OK to apply the formats.

FIGURE 6.39 Between Dialog Box

Figure 6.40 shows two columns of data that contain conditional formats. The Department column is conditionally formatted to highlight text with a Light Red Fill with Dark Red Text for cells that contain *Living Room*, and the Amount column is conditionally formatted to highlight with Red Border values between $5,000 and $10,000.

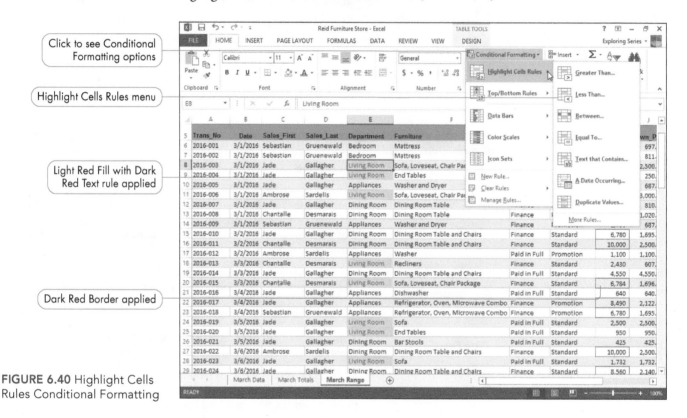

FIGURE 6.40 Highlight Cells Rules Conditional Formatting

Specify Top/Bottom Rules

STEP 2 ❯ You might be interested in identifying the top five sales to reward the sales associates, or want to identify the bottom 15% of automobile dealers so that you can close underperforming locations. The Top/Bottom Rules category enables you to specify the top or bottom number, top or bottom percentage, or values that are above or below the average value in that range. In Figure 6.41, the Amount column is conditionally formatted to highlight the top five amounts. (Some rows are hidden so that all top five values display in the figure.) Although the menu option is Top 10 Items, you can specify the exact number of items to format.

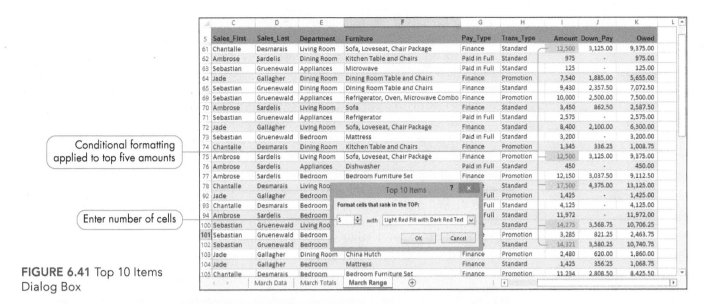

Conditional formatting applied to top five amounts

Enter number of cells

FIGURE 6.41 Top 10 Items Dialog Box

Display Data Bars, Color Scales, and Icon Sets

STEP 3 ▶▶ *Data bars* indicate the value of a cell relative to other cells (see Figure 6.42). The width of the data bar represents the value in a cell, with a wider bar representing a higher value and a narrower bar a lower value. Use data bar conditional formatting to identify high and low values. Excel locates the largest value and displays the widest data bar in that cell. Excel then finds the smallest value and displays the smallest data bar in that cell. Excel sizes the data bars for the remaining cells based on their values relative to the high and low values in the column. If you change the values, Excel updates the data bar widths. Excel uses the same color for each data bar, but each bar differs in size based on the value in the respective cells.

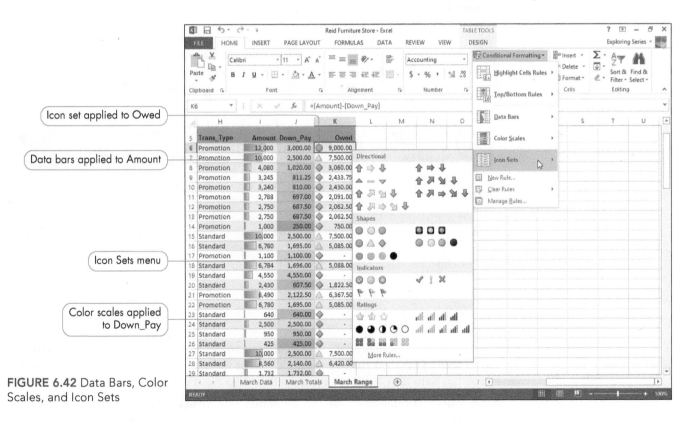

Icon set applied to Owed

Data bars applied to Amount

Icon Sets menu

Color scales applied to Down_Pay

FIGURE 6.42 Data Bars, Color Scales, and Icon Sets

Color scales format cells with different colors based on the relative value of a cell compared to other selected cells. You can apply a two- or three-color scale. This scale assists in comparing a range of cells using gradations of those colors. The shade of the color represents higher or lower values. In Figure 6.42, for example, the red color scales display for the lowest values, the green color displays for the highest values, and gradients of yellow and orange represent the middle range of values in the Down_Pay column. Use color scales to understand variation in the data to identify trends, for example, to view good stock returns and weak stock returns.

Icon sets are symbols or signs that classify data into three, four, or five categories, based on the values in a range. Excel determines categories of value ranges and assigns an icon to each range. In Figure 6.42, a three-icon set was applied to the Owed column. Excel divided the range of values between the lowest value $0 and the highest value of $13,125 into thirds. The red diamond icon displays for the cells containing values in the lowest third ($0 to $4,375), the yellow triangle icon displays for cells containing the values in the middle third ($4,376 to $8,750), and the green circle icon displays for cells containing values in the top third ($8,751 to $13,125). Most purchases fall into the lowest third.

 Don't Overdo It!

Although conditional formatting helps identify trends, you should use this feature wisely. Apply conditional formatting when you want to emphasize important data. When you decide to apply conditional formatting, think about which category is best to highlight the data. Sometimes simple highlighting will suffice when you want to point out data meeting a particular condition; other times, you might want to apply data bars to point out relative differences among values. Finally, do not apply conditional formatting to too many columns.

Clear Rules

To clear conditional formatting from the entire worksheet, click Conditional Formatting in the Styles group on the Home tab, point to Clear Rules, and then select *Clear Rules from Entire Sheet*. To remove conditional formatting from a range of cells, select cells. Then click Conditional Formatting, point to Clear Rules, and then select *Clear Rules from Selected Cells*.

 Sort and Filter Using Conditional Formatting

You can sort and filter by conditional formatting. For example, if you applied the Highlight Cells Rules conditional formatting, you can sort the column by color so that all cells containing the highlight appear first or last. To do this, display the filter arrows, click the arrow for the conditionally formatted column you wish to sort, point to Sort by Color, and then click the fill color or No Fill in the *Sort by Cell Color* area. If you applied the Icon Sets conditional formatting, you can filter by icon.

Creating a New Rule

The default conditional formatting categories provide a variety of options. Excel also enables you to create your own rules to specify different fill colors, borders, or other formatting if you do not want the default settings. Excel provides three ways to create a new rule:

- Click Conditional Formatting in the Styles group and select New Rule.
- Click Conditional Formatting in the Styles group, select Manage Rules to open the Conditional Formatting Rules Manager dialog box, and then click New Rule.
- Click Conditional Formatting in the Styles group, select a rule category such as Highlight Cells Rules, and then select More Rules.

The New Formatting Rule dialog box opens (see Figure 6.43) so that you can define your new conditional formatting rule. First, select a rule type, such as *Format all cells based on their values*. The *Edit the Rule Description* section changes, based on the rule type you select. With the default rule type selected, you can specify the format style (2-Color Scale, 3-Color Scale, Data Bar, or Icon Sets). You can then specify the minimum and maximum values, the fill colors for color sets or data bars, or the icons for icon sets. After you edit the rule description, click OK to save your new conditional format.

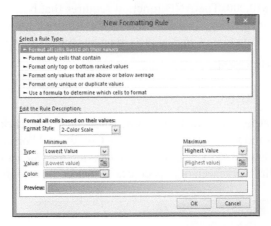

FIGURE 6.43 New Formatting Rule Dialog Box

If you select any rule type except the *Format all cells based on their values* rule, the dialog box contains a Format button. When you click Format, the Format Cells dialog box opens so that you can specify number, font, border, and fill formats to apply to your rule.

TIP | Format Only Cells That Contain

This option provides a wide array of things you can format: values, text, dates, blanks, no blanks, errors, or no errors. Formatting blanks is helpful to see where you are missing data, and formatting cells containing errors helps you find those errors quickly.

Use Formulas in Conditional Formatting

STEP 4 >> If you need to create a complex conditional formatting rule, you can select a rule that uses a formula to format cells. For example, you might want to format merchandise amounts of financed items *and* amounts that are $10,000 or more. Figure 6.44 shows the Edit Formatting Rule dialog box and the corresponding conditional formatting applied to cells.

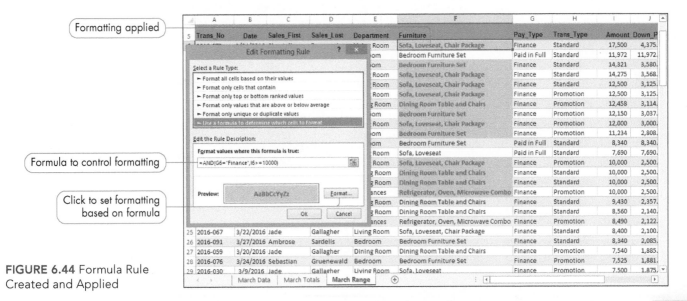

FIGURE 6.44 Formula Rule Created and Applied

To create a formula-based conditional formatting rule, select the data and create a new rule. In the New Formatting Rule dialog box, select *Use a formula to determine which cells to format* and type the formula, using cell references in the first row, in the *Format values where this formula is true* box. Excel applies the general formula to the selected range, substituting the appropriate cell reference as it makes the comparisons. In the Figure 6.44 example, =AND(G6="Finance",I6>=10000) requires that the text in the Pay_Type column (column F) contain *Finance* and the Amount column (column I) contain a value that is greater than or equal to $10,000. The AND function requires that both logical tests be met to apply the conditional formatting. Two logical tests are required; however, you can include additional logical tests. Note that *all* logical tests must be true to apply the conditional formatting.

= AND(logical1,logical2,...)

Manage Rules

To edit or delete conditional formatting rules you create, click Conditional Formatting in the Styles group and select Manage Rules. The Conditional Formatting Rules Manager dialog box opens (see Figure 6.45). Click the *Show formatting rules for* arrow and select from current selection, the entire worksheet, or a specific table. Select the rule and click Edit Rule or Delete Rule.

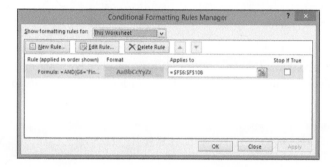

FIGURE 6.45 Conditional Formatting Rules Manager Dialog Box

Quick Concepts

1. How is conditional formatting similar to an IF function? *p. 314*

2. What conditional formatting would be helpful to identify the three movies with the highest revenue playing at theaters? *p. 315*

3. How is data bar conditional formatting helpful when reviewing a column of data? *p. 317*

Hands-On Exercises

Watch the Video for this Hands-On Exercise!

MyITLab®
HOE5 Training

5 Conditional Formatting

Vicki Reid wants to review the transactions with you. She is interested in Sebastian Grunewald's sales record and the three highest transaction amounts. In addition, she wants to compare the down payment amounts visually. Finally, she wants you to analyze the amounts owed for sales completed by Sebastian.

Skills covered: Highlight Cells Rules • Specify Top/Bottom Rules • Display Data Bars • Use a Formula in Conditional Formatting

STEP 1 ≫ HIGHLIGHT CELLS RULES

You want to identify Sebastian's sales for March 2016 without filtering the data. You will apply a conditional format to apply a fill and font color so that cells containing his first name stand out. Refer to Figure 6.46 as you complete Step 1.

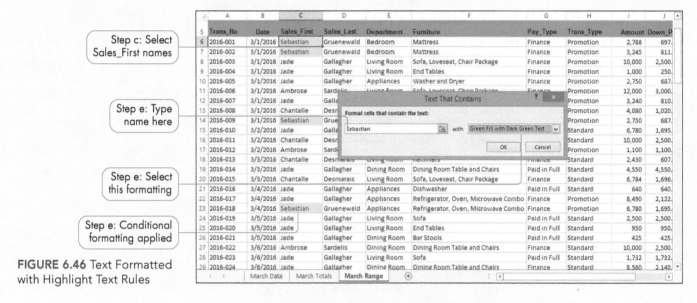

Step c: Select Sales_First names

Step e: Type name here

Step e: Select this formatting

Step e: Conditional formatting applied

FIGURE 6.46 Text Formatted with Highlight Text Rules

a. Open *e04h4Reid_LastFirst* if you closed it at the end of Hands-On Exercise 4. Save the workbook as **e04h5Reid_LastFirst**, changing *h4* to *h5*.

b. Select **row headings 6 through 109** in the March Range worksheet. Click the **HOME tab**, if necessary, click the **Fill Color arrow**, and then select **No Fill**.

You removed the previous table style with banded rows. This will avoid having too many fill colors when you apply conditional formatting rules.

c. Select the **range C6:C109**, which is the column containing the sales representatives' first names.

d. Click **Conditional Formatting** in the Styles group, point to *Highlight Cells Rules*, and then select **Text that Contains**.

The Text That Contains dialog box opens.

e. Type **Sebastian** in the box, click the **with arrow**, and then select **Green Fill with Dark Green Text**. Click **OK**. Deselect the range and save the workbook.

Excel formats only cells that contain Sebastian with the fill and font color.

Hands-On Exercise 5   321

STEP 2 » SPECIFY TOP/BOTTOM RULES

Vicki is now interested in identifying the highest three sales transactions in March. Instead of sorting the records, you will use the Top/Bottom Rules conditional formatting. Refer to Figure 6.47 as you complete Step 2.

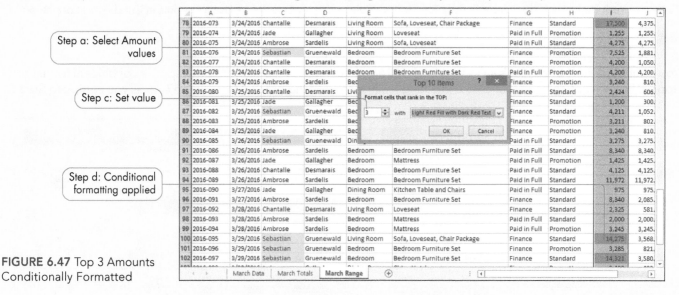

FIGURE 6.47 Top 3 Amounts Conditionally Formatted

a. Select the **range I6:I109**, the range containing the amounts.

b. Click **Conditional Formatting** in the Styles group, point to *Top/Bottom Rules*, and then select **Top 10 Items**.

The Top 10 Items dialog box opens.

c. Click the spin arrow to display *3* and click **OK**.

d. Scroll through the worksheet to see the top three amounts. Save the workbook.

STEP 3 » DISPLAY DATA BARS

Vicki wants to compare all of the down payments. Data bars would add a nice visual element as she compares down payment amounts. Refer to Figure 6.48 as you complete Step 3.

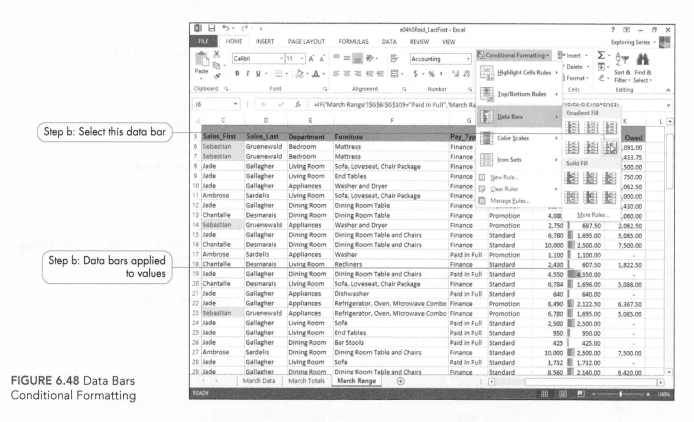

Step b: Select this data bar

Step b: Data bars applied to values

FIGURE 6.48 Data Bars Conditional Formatting

a. Select the **range J6:J109**, which contains the down payment amounts.

b. Click **Conditional Formatting** in the Styles group, point to *Data Bars*, and then select **Purple Data Bar** in the *Gradient Fill* section. Scroll through the list and save the workbook.

Excel displays data bars in each cell. The larger bar widths help Vicki quickly identify the largest down payments. However, the largest down payments are identical to the original amounts when the customers pay in full. This result illustrates that you should not accept the results at face value. Doing so would provide you with an inaccurate analysis.

STEP 4 ≫ USE A FORMULA IN CONDITIONAL FORMATTING

Vicki's next request is to analyze the amounts owed by Sebastian's customers. In particular, she wants to highlight the merchandise for which more than $5,000 is owed. To do this, you realize you need to create a custom rule that evaluates both the Sales_First column and the Owed column. Refer to Figure 6.49 as you complete Step 4.

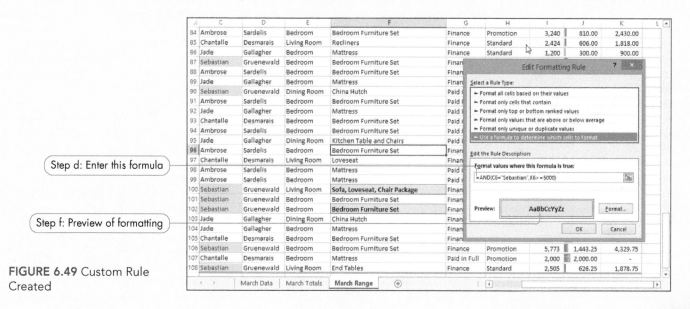

Step d: Enter this formula

Step f: Preview of formatting

FIGURE 6.49 Custom Rule Created

a. Select the **range F6:F109**, which contains the merchandise.

b. Click **Conditional Formatting** in the Styles group and select **New Rule**.

The New Formatting Rule dialog box opens.

c. Select **Use a formula to determine which cells to format**.

d. Type **=AND(C6="Sebastian",K6>5000)** in the **Format values where this formula is true box**.

Because you are comparing the contents of cell C6 to text, you must enclose the text within quotation marks.

e. Click **Format** to open the Format Cells dialog box.

f. Click the **Font tab**, if necessary, and then click **Bold** in the **Font style list**. Click the **Border tab**, click the **Color arrow**, select **Blue, Accent 5**, and then click **Outline**. Click the **Fill tab**, click **Blue, Accent 5, Lighter 80% background color** (the second color from the right on the first row below the first horizontal line), and then click **OK**.

Figure 6.49 shows the Edit Formatting Rule dialog box, but the options are similar to the New Formatting Rule dialog box.

g. Click **OK** in the New Formatting Rule dialog box and scroll through the list to see which amounts owed are greater than $5,000 for Sebastian only.

> **TROUBLESHOOTING:** If the results seem incorrect, click Conditional Formatting and select Manage Rules. Edit the rule you just created and make any corrections to the formula.

h. Save and close the workbook, and submit based on your instructor's directions.

Chapter Objectives Review

After reading this chapter, you have accomplished the following objectives:

1. Freeze rows and columns.
- The Freeze Panes setting freezes the row(s) above and the column(s) to the left of the active cell. When you scroll, those rows and columns remain onscreen.
- Use Unfreeze Panes to clear the frozen rows and columns.

2. Print large datasets.
- Display and change page breaks: Display the data in Page Break Preview to see the automatic page breaks. Dashed blue lines indicate automatic page breaks. You can insert manual page breaks, indicated by solid blue lines.
- Set and clear a print area: If you do not want to print an entire worksheet, select a range and set a print area.
- Print titles: Select rows to repeat at top and/or columns to repeat at left to print the column and row labels on every page of a printout of a large dataset.
- Control print page order: You can control the sequence in which the pages will print.

3. Design and create tables.
- A table is a structured range that contains related data. Tables have several benefits over regular ranges. The column labels, called *field names*, display on the first row of a table. Each row is a complete set of data for one record.
- You should plan a table before you create it. Create unique field names on the first row of the table and enter data below the field names, avoiding blank rows.
- Create a table: You can create a table from existing data. Excel applies the Table Style Medium 2 format and assigns a name, such as Table1, to the table. When the active cell is within a table, the Table Tools Design tab displays.
- Add and delete fields: You can insert and delete table rows and columns to adjust the structure of a table.
- Add, edit, and delete records: You can add table rows, edit records, and delete table rows.
- Remove duplicate rows: Use the Remove Duplicates dialog box to remove duplicate records in a table. Excel will display a dialog box telling you how many records are deleted.

4. Apply a table style.
- Table styles control the fill color of the header row and records within the table.

5. Sort data.
- Sort one field: You can sort text in alphabetical or reverse alphabetical order, values from smallest to largest or largest to smallest, and dates from oldest to newest or newest to oldest. Click the filter arrow and select the sort method from the list.
- Sort multiple fields: Open the Sort dialog box and add column levels and sort orders.

- Create a custom sort: You can create a custom sort for unique data, such as ensuring the months sort in sequential order rather than alphabetical order.

6. Filter data.
- Filtering is the process of specifying conditions for displaying records in a table. Only records that meet those conditions display; the other records are hidden.
- Apply text filters: A text filter can find exact text, text that does not equal a condition, text that begins with a particular letter, and so forth.
- Apply number filters: A number filter can find exact values, values that do not equal a particular value, values greater than or equal to a value, and so on.
- Apply date filters: You can set filters to find dates before or after a certain date, between two dates, yesterday, next month, and so forth.
- Clear filters: If you do not need filters, you can clear the filters.

7. Use structured references and a total row.
- Create structured references in formulas: A structured reference uses field names instead of cell references, such as =[Amount]−[Down Payment]. Field names must display in brackets within the formula.
- Add a total row: You can display a total row after the last record. You can add totals or select a different function, such as Average.

8. Apply conditional formatting.
- Apply conditional formatting with the Quick Analysis Tool: After selecting text, click FORMATTING on the Quick Analysis gallery to apply a conditional format.
- Apply the highlight cells rules: This rule highlights cell contents with a fill color, font color, and/or border color where the contents match a particular condition.
- Specify top/bottom rules: This rule enables you to highlight the top *x* number of items or percentage of items.
- Display data bars, color scales, and icon sets: Data bars compare values within the selected range. Color scales indicate values that occur within particular ranges. Icon sets display icons representing a number's relative value compared to other numbers in the range.
- Clear rules: If you no longer want conditional formatting applied, you can clear a rule.

9. Create a new rule.
- You can create conditional format rules. The New Formatting Rule dialog box enables you to select a rule type.
- Use formulas in conditional formatting: You can create rules based on content in multiple columns.
- Manage rules: Use the Conditional Formatting Rules Manager dialog box to edit and delete rules.

Key Terms Matching

Match the key terms with their definitions. Write the key term letter by the appropriate numbered definition.

a. Color scale
b. Conditional formatting
c. Data bar
d. Field
e. Filtering
f. Freezing
g. Icon set
h. Page break
i. Print area
j. Print order
k. Record
l. Sorting
m. Structured reference
n. SUBTOTAL function
o. Table
p. Table style
q. Total row

1. _____ A conditional format that displays horizontal gradient or solid fill indicating the cell's relative value compared to other selected cells. **p. 317**

2. _____ The process of listing records or text in a specific sequence, such as alphabetically by last name. **p. 296**

3. _____ The process of specifying conditions to display only those records that meet those conditions. **p. 298**

4. _____ A set of rules that applies specific formatting to highlight or emphasize cells that meet specifications. **p. 314**

5. _____ A group of related fields representing one entity, such as data for one person, place, event, or concept. **p. 285**

6. _____ The rules that control the fill color of the header row, columns, and records in a table. **p. 289**

7. _____ An indication of where data will start on another printed page. **p. 278**

8. _____ A table row that appears below the last row of records in an Excel table and displays summary or aggregate statistics, such as a sum or an average. **p. 308**

9. _____ A conditional format that displays a particular color based on the relative value of the cell contents to the other selected cells. **p. 318**

10. _____ The sequence in which the pages are printed. **p. 280**

11. _____ A tag or use of a table element, such as a field label, as a reference in a formula. Field labels are enclosed in square brackets, such as [Amount] within the formula. **p. 307**

12. _____ A conditional format that displays an icon representing a value in the top third, quarter, or fifth based on values in the selected range. **p. 318**

13. _____ The range of cells within a worksheet that will print. **p. 279**

14. _____ A predefined formula that calculates an aggregate value, such as totals, for values in a range, a table, or a database. **p. 308**

15. _____ The smallest data element contained in a table, such as first name, last name, address, and phone number. **p. 285**

16. _____ A structure that organizes data in a series of records (rows), with each record made up of a number of fields (columns). **p. 285**

17. _____ The process of keeping rows and/or columns visible onscreen at all times even when you scroll through a large dataset. **p. 277**

Multiple Choice

1. You have a large dataset that will print on several pages. You want to ensure that related records print on the same page with column and row labels visible and that confidential information is not printed. You should apply all of the following page setup options *except* which one to accomplish this?

   (a) Set a print area.
   (b) Print titles.
   (c) Adjust page breaks.
   (d) Change the print page order.

2. You are working with a large worksheet. Your row headings are in column A. Which command(s) should be used to see the row headings and the distant information in columns X, Y, and Z?

   (a) Freeze Panes command
   (b) Hide Rows command
   (c) New Window command and cascade the windows
   (d) Split Rows command

3. Which statement is *not* a recommended guideline for designing and creating an Excel table?

   (a) Avoid naming two fields with the same name.
   (b) Ensure no blank columns separate data columns within the table.
   (c) Leave one blank row between records in the table.
   (d) Include field names on the first row of the table.

4. You have a list of all the employees in your organization. The list contains employee name, office, title, and salary. You want to list all employees in each office branch. The branches should be listed alphabetically, with the employee earning the highest salary listed first in each office. Which is true of your sort order?

   (a) Branch office is the primary sort and should be in A to Z order.
   (b) Salary is the primary sort and should be from highest to lowest.
   (c) Salary is the primary sort and should be from lowest to highest.
   (d) Branch office is the primary sort and should be in Z to A order.

5. You suspect a table has several identical records. What should you do?

   (a) Do nothing; a logical reason probably exists to keep identical records.
   (b) Use the Remove Duplicates command.

   (c) Look at each row yourself and manually delete duplicate records.
   (d) Find the duplicate records and change some of the data to be different.

6. Which check box in the Table Style Options group enables you to apply different formatting to the records in a table?

   (a) Header Row
   (b) Banded Rows
   (c) Banded Columns
   (d) Total Row

7. Which date filter option enables you to specify criteria for selecting a range of dates, such as between 3/15/2016 and 7/15/2016?

   (a) Equals
   (b) Before
   (c) All Dates in the Period
   (d) Between

8. You want to display a total row that identifies the oldest date in a field in your table. What function do you select from the list?

   (a) Max
   (b) Sum
   (c) Min
   (d) Count

9. What type of conditional formatting displays horizontal colors in which the width of the bar indicates relative size compared to other values in the selected range?

   (a) Color Scales
   (b) Icon Sets
   (c) Data Bars
   (d) Sparklines

10. When you select the _____ rule type, the New Formatting Rule dialog box does not show the Format button.

    (a) Format all cells based on their values
    (b) Format only cells that contain
    (c) Use a formula to determine which cells to format
    (d) Format only unique or duplicate values

Practice Exercises

1 Fiesta® Items and Replacement Values

Marie Maier has collected Fiesta dinnerware, manufactured by the Homer Laughlin China Company, since 1986. Between 1986 and 2012, the company produced 30 colors, each with a unique name. Marie created a table in Word that lists the name, number, year introduced, and year retired (if applicable) for each color. She created another table in Word that lists the item number, item, replacement value, and source of information for each item in her collection. Her main sources for replacement values are Homer Laughlin (www.fiestafactorydirect.com), Replacements, Ltd. (www.replacements.com), eBay (www.ebay.com), and two local antique stores. She needs your help to convert the data to Excel tables, apply table formatting, delete duplicate records, insert functions, and sort and filter the data. This exercise follows the same set of skills as used in Hands-On Exercises 1–3 in the chapter. Refer to Figure 6.50 as you complete this exercise.

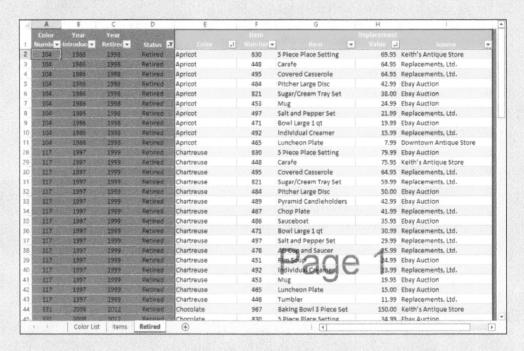

FIGURE 6.50 Fiesta® Collection

a. Open *e04p1Colors* in Word. Do the following to copy the Word table data into Excel and prepare the data to be used as a lookup table:
   - Click the **table icon** in the top-left corner of the table and click **Copy** in the Clipboard group.
   - Start a new Excel workbook, click the **Paste arrow** in the Clipboard group in Excel, and then select **Match Destination Formatting (M)**.
   - Bold and horizontally center the labels on the first row. Center the data in the first, third, and fourth columns. Widen the second and third columns to fit the data.
   - Select the **range A2:D31**, click in the **Name Box**, type **colors**, and then press **Enter** to assign a name to the selected range.
   - Click **cell A2**, click **Sort & Filter** in the Editing group, and then select **Sort Smallest to Largest**. Remember that you must sort the first column in ascending order to use the table for an exact match for a VLOOKUP function.
   - Save the Excel workbook as **e04p1Collection_LastFirst**. Close the Word document.

b. Open *e04p1Items* in Word. Select and copy the table, display the Excel workbook, add a new sheet, make sure **cell A1** is the active cell in the new sheet, and then paste the table in the same way you did in step a. Widen column E. Rename *Sheet2* **Items**. Close the Word document.

c. Click **cell A2** in the Items sheet, click the **VIEW tab**, click **Freeze Panes** in the Window group, and then select **Freeze Top Row**.

d. Press **Ctrl+End** to go to the last data cell. The first row is frozen so that the column labels remain onscreen. Press **Ctrl+Home** to go back to **cell A2**.

e. Click the **INSERT tab**, click **Table** in the Tables group, and then click **OK** in the Create Table dialog box.

f. Click **Quick Styles** in the Table Styles group and click **Table Style Medium 5**.

g. Click the **DATA tab**, click **Remove Duplicates** in the Data Tools group, and then click **OK** in the Remove Duplicates dialog box. Click **OK** in the message box that informs you that *12 duplicate values were found and removed; 356 unique values remain.*

h. Click **cell B2**, click the **HOME tab**, click the **Insert arrow** in the Cells group, and then select **Insert Table Columns to the Left**. Then insert two more columns to the left. Do the following to insert functions and customize the results in the three new table columns:

- Type **Year Introduced** in **cell B1**, **Year Retired** in **cell C1**, and **Color** in **cell D1**.
- Click **cell B2**, type **=VLOOKUP([Color Number],colors,3,False)**, and then press **Enter**. Excel copies the function down the Year Introduced column. This function looks up each item's color number using the structured reference [Color Number], looks up that value in the colors table, and then returns the year that color was introduced, which is in the third column of that table.
- Click **cell B2**, click **Copy**, click **cell C2**, and then click **Paste**. Change the *3* to **4** in the col_index_num argument of the pasted function. Excel copies the function down the Year Retired column. This function looks up each item's color number using the structured reference [Color Number], looks up that value in the colors table, and then returns the year that color was retired, if applicable, which is in the fourth column of that table. The function returns 0 if the retired cell in the lookup table is blank.

DISCOVER

- Click the **FILE tab**, click **Options**, click **Advanced**, scroll down to the *Display options for this worksheet* section, click the **Show a zero in cells that have zero value check box** to deselect it, and then click **OK**. The zeros disappear. (This option hides zeros in the active worksheet. While this is not desirable if you need to show legitimate zeros, this worksheet is designed to avoid that issue.)
- Click **cell C2**, click **Copy**, click **cell D2**, and then click **Paste**. Change the *4* to **2** in the col_index_num argument of the pasted function. Excel copies the function down the Color column. This function looks up each item's color number using the structured reference [Color Number] to look up that value in the colors table and returns the color name, which is in the second column of that table.

i. Apply wrap text, horizontal centering, and **30.75 row height** to the column labels row. Adjust column widths. Center data horizontally in the Color Number, Year Introduced, Year Retired, and Item Number columns. Apply **Comma Style** to the Replacement Values. Deselect the data.

j. Click **Sort & Filter** in the Editing group and select **Custom Sort** to display the Sort dialog box. Do the following in the Sort dialog box:

- Click the **Sort by arrow** and select **Color**.
- Click **Add Level**, click the **Then by arrow**, and then select **Replacement Value**.
- Click the **Order arrow** and select **Largest to Smallest**. Click **OK**.

k. Right-click the **Items sheet tab**, select **Move or Copy**, click **(move to end)**, click the **Create a copy check box**, and then click **OK**. Rename the copied sheet **Retired**.

l. Make sure the active sheet is Retired. Insert a table column between the Year Retired and Color columns.

- Type **Status** in **cell D1** as the column label.
- Click **cell D2**, type **=IF([Year Retired]=0, "Current","Retired")**, and then press **Enter**. This function determines that if the cell contains a 0 (which is hidden), it will display the word *Current*. Otherwise, it will display *Retired*.

m. Click the **Status filter arrow**, deselect the **Current check box**, and then click **OK** to filter out the current colors and display only retired colors.

n. Click the **DESIGN tab** and click **Total Row** in the Table Style Options group. Press **Ctrl+End** to go to the total row, click the **Source total cell** (which contains a count of visible items), click the

Source total arrow**, and then select **None**. Click **cell H358**, the *Replacement Value total* cell, click the **Replacement Value total arrow**, and then select **Sum**.

o. Prepare the Retired worksheet for printing by doing the following:
- Set **0.2"** left and right page margins.
- Select the **range E1:I358**, click the **PAGE LAYOUT tab**, click **Print Area** in the Page Setup group, and then select **Set Print Area**.
- Click **Print Titles** in the Page Setup group, click the **Rows to repeat at top Collapse Dialog box button**, click the **row 1 header**, and then click the **Collapse Dialog box button**. Click **OK**.
- Click the **VIEW tab** and click **Page Break Preview** in the Workbook Views group. Decrease the top margin to avoid having only one or two records print on the last page.

p. Create a footer with your name on the left side, the sheet name code in the center, and the file name code on the right side of each worksheet.

q. Save and close the workbook, and submit based on your instructor's directions.

2 Dentist Association Donation List

The Midwest Regional Dentist Association is planning its annual meeting in Lincoln, Nebraska, this spring. Several members donated items for door prizes at the closing general session. You will organize the list of donations and format it to highlight particular data for your supervisor, who is on the conference board of directors. This exercise follows the same set of skills as used in Hands-On Exercises 2–5 in the chapter. Refer to Figure 6.51 as you complete this exercise.

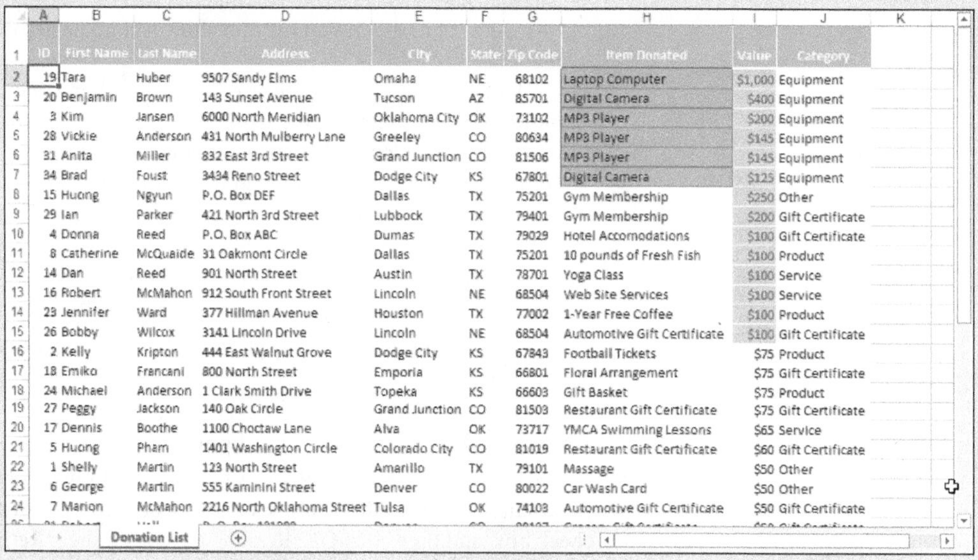

ID	First Name	Last Name	Address	City	State	Zip Code	Item Donated	Value	Category
19	Tara	Huber	9507 Sandy Elms	Omaha	NE	68102	Laptop Computer	$1,000	Equipment
20	Benjamin	Brown	143 Sunset Avenue	Tucson	AZ	85701	Digital Camera	$400	Equipment
3	Kim	Jansen	6000 North Meridian	Oklahoma City	OK	73102	MP3 Player	$200	Equipment
28	Vickie	Anderson	431 North Mulberry Lane	Greeley	CO	80634	MP3 Player	$145	Equipment
31	Anita	Miller	832 East 3rd Street	Grand Junction	CO	81506	MP3 Player	$145	Equipment
34	Brad	Foust	3434 Reno Street	Dodge City	KS	67801	Digital Camera	$125	Equipment
15	Huong	Ngyun	P.O. Box DEF	Dallas	TX	75201	Gym Membership	$250	Other
29	Ian	Parker	421 North 3rd Street	Lubbock	TX	79401	Gym Membership	$200	Gift Certificate
4	Donna	Reed	P.O. Box ABC	Dumas	TX	79029	Hotel Accomodations	$100	Gift Certificate
8	Catherine	McQuaide	31 Oakmont Circle	Dallas	TX	75201	10 pounds of Fresh Fish	$100	Product
14	Dan	Reed	901 North Street	Austin	TX	78701	Yoga Class	$100	Service
16	Robert	McMahon	912 South Front Street	Lincoln	NE	68504	Web Site Services	$100	Service
23	Jennifer	Ward	377 Hillman Avenue	Houston	TX	77002	1-Year Free Coffee	$100	Product
26	Bobby	Wilcox	3141 Lincoln Drive	Lincoln	NE	68504	Automotive Gift Certificate	$100	Gift Certificate
2	Kelly	Kripton	444 East Walnut Grove	Dodge City	KS	67843	Football Tickets	$75	Product
18	Emiko	Francani	800 North Street	Emporia	KS	66801	Floral Arrangement	$75	Gift Certificate
24	Michael	Anderson	1 Clark Smith Drive	Topeka	KS	66603	Gift Basket	$75	Product
27	Peggy	Jackson	140 Oak Circle	Grand Junction	CO	81503	Restaurant Gift Certificate	$75	Gift Certificate
17	Dennis	Boothe	1100 Choctaw Lane	Alva	OK	73717	YMCA Swimming Lessons	$65	Service
5	Huong	Pham	1401 Washington Circle	Colorado City	CO	81019	Restaurant Gift Certificate	$60	Gift Certificate
1	Shelly	Martin	123 North Street	Amarillo	TX	79101	Massage	$50	Other
6	George	Martin	555 Kaminini Street	Denver	CO	80022	Car Wash Card	$50	Other
7	Marion	McMahon	2216 North Oklahoma Street	Tulsa	OK	74103	Automotive Gift Certificate	$50	Gift Certificate

FIGURE 6.51 Donation List

a. Open *e04p2Donate* and save it as **e04p2Donate_LastFirst**.

b. Click the **DESIGN tab**, click **Remove Duplicates** in the Tools group, and then click **OK**. Click **OK** in the message box that tells you that Excel removed three duplicate records.

c. Click **Convert to Range** in the Tools group and click **Yes** in the message box.

d. Select the **range A2:J35**, click the **HOME tab**, click the **Fill Color arrow** in the Font group, and then select **No Fill** to remove the table fill colors.

e. Select the **range I2:I35**. Click **Conditional Formatting** in the Styles group, point to *Highlight Cells Rules*, and then select **Greater Than**. Type **99** in the **Format cells that are GREATER THAN box** and click **OK**.

f. Select **cells H2:H35**. Create a custom conditional format by doing the following:

- Click **Conditional Formatting** in the Styles group and select **New Rule**.
- Click **Use a formula to determine which cells to format**.
- Type =(J2="Equipment") in the **Format values where this formula is true box**. The basic condition is testing to see if the contents of cell J2 equal the word *Equipment*. You type *Equipment* in quotation marks because you are comparing text instead of a value.
- Click **Format**, click the **Fill tab** if necessary, and then click **Red, Accent 2, Lighter 60%** (sixth background color on the second row below the first horizontal line).
- Click the **Border tab**, click the **Color arrow**, click **Dark Red**, and then click **Outline**.
- Click **OK** in each dialog box.

DISCOVER

g. Click in the table to deselect the range. Click **Sort & Filter** in the Editing group and select **Custom Sort**. The dialog box may contain existing sort conditions for the State and City fields, which you will replace. Set the following sort conditions:

- Click the **Sort by arrow** and select **Item Donated**. Click the **Sort On arrow** and select **Cell Color**. Click the **Order arrow** and select the **RGB(146, 205, 220) fill color**. The fill color displays for the Order.
- Click the **Then by arrow** and select **Value**. Click the **Order arrow** and select **Largest to Smallest**.
- Click **OK**.

h. Select **Landscape orientation**, set appropriate margins, and then adjust column widths so that all the data will print on one page. Do not decrease the scaling.

i. Create a footer with your name on the left side, the sheet name code in the center, and the file name code on the right side.

j. Save and close the workbook, and submit based on your instructor's directions.

Mid-Level Exercises

1 Biology Department Teaching Schedule

As the department head of the biology department at a university, you prepare and finalize the faculty teaching schedule. Scheduling preparation takes time because you must ensure that you do not book faculty for different courses at the same time or double-book a classroom with two different classes. You downloaded the Spring 2015 schedule as a starting point and edited it to prepare the Spring 2016 schedule, and now you need to sort and filter the schedule to review it from several perspectives.

DISCOVER

a. Open *e04m1Classes* and save it as **e04m1Classes_LastFirst**.

b. Freeze the panes so that the column labels do not scroll offscreen.

c. Convert the data to a table and name the table **Spring2016**.

d. Apply **Table Style Light 14** to the table.

e. Sort the table by Instructor, then Days, and then Start Time. Create a custom sort order for Days so that it appears in this sequence: MTWR, MWF, MW, M, W, F, TR, T, R. (The day abbreviations are as follows: M = Monday, T = Tuesday, W = Wednesday, R = Thursday, F = Friday.)

f. Remove duplicate records from the table. Excel should find and remove three duplicate records.

g. Copy the Faculty sheet, place the copied worksheet to the right of the Faculty sheet, and then rename the duplicate worksheet **Rooms**. Sort the data in the Rooms sheet by Room in ascending order, then by Days using the custom sort order you created in step e, and finally by Start Time from earliest to latest time.

h. Copy the Rooms sheet, place the copied worksheet to the right of the Rooms sheet, and then rename the duplicate worksheet **Prime Time**.

i. Filter the table in the Prime Time sheet to show only classes scheduled on any combination of Monday, Wednesday, and Friday. Include classes that meet four days a week (MTWR). Do not include any other combination of Tuesday or Thursday classes, though. Also filter the table by classes that start between 9:00 AM and 12:00 PM. The status bar indicates 20 of 75 records found.

j. Insert a field on the right side of the Credits field in the Faculty sheet. Type the label **Capacity**. Insert a lookup function that looks up the room number, compares it to the lookup table in the Room Capacity worksheet, and returns the room capacity. Make sure the function copies down the entire column.

k. Select the first three sheet tabs and set **0.2"** left and right margins, **Landscape orientation**, and **95% scaling**. Repeat the column labels on all pages. On the Faculty sheet, decrease some column widths so that the Capacity column will print on the same page as the other columns.

l. Display the Faculty sheet in Page Break Preview. Adjust any page breaks so that classes for a particular instructor do not split between pages.

m. Display the Rooms sheet in Page Break Preview. Adjust any page breaks so that classes for a particular room do not split between pages, if necessary. Set the worksheet to print 1 page wide and 3 pages tall.

n. Insert a footer with your name on the left side, the sheet name code in the center, and the file name code on the right side of all four sheets.

o. Save and close the workbook, and submit based on your instructor's directions.

2 Artwork

ANALYSIS CASE

You work for a gallery that is an authorized Greenwich Workshop fine art dealer (www .greenwichworkshop.com). Customers in your area are especially fond of James C. Christensen's art. Although customers can visit the Web site to see images and details about his work, they have requested a list of all his artwork. Your assistant prepared a list of artwork: art, type, edition size, release date, and issue price. In addition, you included a column to identify which pieces are sold out at the publisher, indicating the rare, hard-to-obtain artwork that is available on the secondary market. You now want to convert the data to a table so that you can provide information to your customers.

a. Open *e04m2FineArt* and save it as **e04m2FineArt_LastFirst**.

b. Convert the data to a table and apply **Table Style Medium 5**.

c. Add a row (below the *The Yellow Rose* record) for this missing piece of art: **The Yellow Rose**, **Masterwork Canvas Edition**, **50** edition size, **May 2009** release date, **$895** issue price. Enter **Yes** to indicate the piece is sold out.

d. Sort the table by Type in alphabetical order and then by release date from newest to oldest.

e. Add a total row that shows the largest edition size and the most expensive issue price. Delete the Total label in **cell A205**. Add a descriptive label in **cell C205** to reflect the content on the total row.

f. Create a custom conditional format for the Issue Price column with these specifications:
   - 4 Traffic Lights icon set (Black, Red, Yellow, Green)
   - Red icon when the number is greater than 1000
   - Yellow icon when the number is less than or equal to 1000 and greater than 500
   - Green icon when the number is less than or equal to 500 and greater than 250
   - Black icon when the number is less than or equal to 250.

g. Filter the table by the Red Traffic Light conditional formatting icon.

h. Answer the questions in the range D211:D215 based on the filtered data.

i. Set the print area to print the **range C1:H205**, select the **first row to repeat at the top of each printout**, set **1"** top and bottom margins, set **0.3"** left and right margins, and then select **Landscape orientation**. Set the option to fit the data to 1 page.

j. Wrap text and horizontally center column labels and adjust column widths and row heights as needed.

k. Create a footer with your name on the left side, the sheet name code in the center, and the file name code on the right side.

l. Save and close the workbook, and submit based on your instructor's directions.

3 Party Music

COLLABORATION CASE

FROM SCRATCH

You are planning a weekend party and want to create a mix of music so that most people will appreciate some of the music you will play at the party. To help you decide what music to play, you have asked five classmates to help you create a song list. The entire class should decide on the general format, capitalization style, and sequence: song, musician, genre, year released, and approximate song length.

a. Conduct online research to collect data for your favorite 25 songs.

b. Enter the data into a new workbook in the format, capitalization style, and sequence that was decided by the class.

c. Save the workbook as **e04m3PlayList_LastFirst**.

d. Upload the file to a shared folder on OneDrive or Dropbox that everyone in the class can access.

e. Download four workbooks from friends and copy and paste data from their workbooks into yours.

f. Convert the data to a table and apply a table style of your choice.

g. Detect and delete duplicate records. Make a note of the number of duplicate records found and deleted.

h. Sort the data by genre in alphabetical order, then by artist in alphabetical order, and then by release date with the newest year first.

i. Set a filter to hide songs that were released before 2000.

j. Display the total row and select the function to count the number of songs displayed.

k. Insert comments in the workbook to indicate which student's workbooks you used, the number of duplicate records deleted, and number of filtered records.

l. Save and close the workbook. Submit the workbook based on your instructor's directions.

Beyond the Classroom

Flight Arrival Status

As an analyst for an airport, you want to study the flight arrivals for a particular day. Select an airport and find its list of flight arrival data. Some airport websites do not list complete details, so search for an airport that does, such as Will Rogers World Airport or San Diego International Airport. Copy the column labels and arrival data (airline, flight number, city, gate, scheduled time, status, etc.) for one day and paste them in a new workbook. The columns may be in a different sequence from what is listed here. However, you should format the data as needed. Leave two blank rows below the last row of data and enter the URL of the Web page from which you got the data, the date, and the time. Save the workbook as **e04b2Flights_LastFirst**. Convert the list to a table and apply a table style.

Sort the table by scheduled time and then by gate number. Apply conditional formatting to the Status column to highlight cells that contain the text *Delayed* (or similar text). Add a total row to calculate the MODE for the gate number and arrival time. You must select **More Functions** from the list of functions in the total row and search for and select **MODE**. Change the label in the first column from *Total* to **Most Frequent**. Use Help to refresh your memory on how to nest an IF function inside another IF function. Add a calculated column on the right side of the table using a nested IF function and structured references to display *Late* if the actual time was later than the scheduled time, *On Time or Early* if the actual time was earlier or equal to the scheduled time, or *Incomplete* if the flight has not landed yet.

Name the worksheet **Arrival Time**. Copy the worksheet and name the copied worksheet **Delayed**. Filter the list by delayed flights. Include a footer with your name on the left side, the sheet name code in the center, and the file name code on the right side of both worksheets. Adjust the margins on both worksheets as necessary. Save and close the workbook, and submit based on your instructor's directions.

U.S. Population

A colleague at an advertising firm downloaded U.S. population information from the government Web site. In the process of creating tables, he made some errors and needs your help. Open *e04b3Populate* and save it as **e04b3Populate_LastFirst**. As you find the errors, document them on the Errors worksheet and make the corrections. Your documentation should include these columns: Error Number, Location, Problem, and Solution. Both tables in the U.S. Population worksheet should show grand total populations per year. The state table should be sorted by region and then by state. Your colleague wants to emphasize the top 15% state populations for the most recent year in the state table. The last column should show percentage changes from year to year, such as 0.6%. Your colleague wants to print only the state data. Select the sorted data population for one region at a time to compare to the regional totals in the first table to crosscheck the totals. For example, when you select the July 1, 2008, Midwest values in the second table, the status bar should display the same value as shown for the Midwest July 1, 2008, values in the first table. Create a footer with your name, the sheet name code, and the file name code. Save and close the workbook, and submit based on your instructor's directions.

Performance Evaluation

FROM SCRATCH

After watching the Performance Evaluation video, create a workbook that lists at least 10 performance traits mentioned in the video or other common performance traits, such as "arriving to work on time." Use the second column for a self-evaluation and the third column for manager evaluation. Below the list, create a description to describe ratings 1 through 5. For example, Exemplary—exceeds expectations is a 5, and Unacceptable—grounds for probation is a 1. Enter your own scores for each performance trait and enter scores based on your manager's review. Save the workbook as **e04b4Performance_LastFirst**.

Convert the list to a table and sort the table alphabetically by performance trait descriptions. Add a total row and select the AVERAGE function for the two ratings columns. Create a conditional formatting rule to highlight cells in the ratings columns for values less than 3. Insert three rows at the top for a title, your name, and the current date. Create a footer with your name on the left side, the date code in the center, and the filename code on the right side. Save and close the workbook, and submit based on your instructor's directions.

You work at Mountain View Realty. A coworker developed a spreadsheet listing houses listed and sold during the past several months. She included addresses, location, list price, selling price, listing date, and date sold. You need to convert the data to a table. You will manage the large worksheet, prepare the worksheet for printing, sort and filter the table, include calculations, and then format the table.

Prepare the Large Worksheet as a Table

You will freeze the panes so that labels remain onscreen. You also want to convert the data to a table so that you can apply table options.

a. Open the *e04c1Houses* workbook and save it as **e04c1Houses_LastFirst**.

b. Freeze the first row on the Sales Data worksheet.

c. Convert the data to a table and apply the **Table Style Medium 17**.

d. Remove duplicate records.

Add Calculated Fields and a Total Row

The office manager asked you to insert a column to display the percentage of list price. The formula finds the sale price percentage of the list price. For example, if a house was listed at $100,000 and sells for $75,000, the percentage of list price is 75%. In some cases, the percentage is more than 100%. This happens when a bidding war occurs and buyers increase their offers, which results in the seller getting more than the list price.

a. Insert a new field to the right of the Selling Price field. Name the new field **Percent of List Price**.

b. Create a formula with structured references to calculate the percentage of the list price.

c. Format the field with **Percent Style** with one decimal place.

d. Insert a new field to the right of the Sale Date field. Name the new field **Days on Market**.

e. Create a formula with structured references to calculate the number of days on the market. Apply the **General number format** to the values.

f. Add a total row to display the average percentage of list price and average number of days on market. Format the average number of days on market as a whole number. Use an appropriate label for the total row.

Sort and Print the Table

To help the office manager compare house sales by city, you will sort the data. Then you will prepare the large table to print.

a. Sort the table by city in alphabetical order and add a second level to sort by days on market with the houses on the market the longest at the top within each city.

b. Adjust column widths so that the data are one page across (three pages total). Wrap the column labels.

c. Repeat the field names on all pages.

d. Change page breaks so that city data do not span between pages and change back to Normal view.

e. Add a footer with your name on the left side, the sheet name code in the center, and the file name code on the right side.

Copy and Filter the Data

The office manager needs to focus on houses that took longer than 30 days to sell within three cities. To keep the original data intact for the agents, you will copy the table data to a new sheet and use that sheet to display the filtered data.

a. Copy the Sales Data sheet and place the duplicate sheet to the right of the original sheet tab. Convert the table to a range of data and delete the average row.

b. Rename the duplicate worksheet **Filtered Data**.

c. Display the filter arrows for the data.

d. Filter the data to display the cities of Alpine, Cedar Hills, and Eagle Mountain.

e. Filter the data to display records for houses that were on the market 30 days or more.

Apply Conditional Formatting

To highlight housing sales to illustrate trends, you will apply conditional formatting. Because data are sorted by city, you will use an icon set to color-code the number of days on market. You will also apply data bar conditional formatting to the sale prices to help the office manager visualize the differences among the sales.

a. Apply the **3 Arrows (Colored) icon set** to the *Days on Market* values.

b. Apply the **Light Blue Data Bar conditional formatting** in the *Gradient Fill* section to the selling prices.

c. Create a new conditional format that applies yellow fill and bold font to values that contain 95% or higher for the *Percent of List Price* column.

d. Edit the conditional format you created so that it formats values 98% or higher.

Finalize the Workbook

You are ready to finalize the workbook by adding a footer to the new worksheet and saving the final workbook.

a. Add a footer with your name on the left side, the sheet name code in the center, and the file name code on the right side.

b. Remove all page breaks in the Filtered Data worksheet.

c. Select **Landscape orientation** and set appropriate margins so that the data will print on one page.

d. Save and close the workbook, and submit based on your instructor's directions.

Subtotals, PivotTables, and PivotCharts

CHAPTER 7

Summarizing and Analyzing Data

Yuri Arcurs/Shutterstock

OBJECTIVES | AFTER YOU READ THIS CHAPTER, YOU WILL BE ABLE TO:

1. Subtotal data p. 338

2. Group and ungroup data p. 341

3. Create a PivotTable p. 346

4. Modify a PivotTable p. 349

5. Filter and slice a PivotTable p. 359

6. Create a calculated field p. 362

7. Format a PivotTable p. 369

8. Use PowerPivot Functionality p. 370

9. Create a PivotChart p. 372

CASE STUDY | Ivory Halls Publishing Company

You are the new Vice President of the Sociology Division at Ivory Halls Publishing Company. The sociology domain has many disciplines, such as introductory sociology, family, research, gender issues, and more. Ivory Halls publishes several textbooks in each discipline to appeal to a vast array of university professors and students.

Your assistant prepared a list of books, their disciplines, and other pertinent data. The current list is not easy to analyze. You need to organize the data so that you can study the sales trends by discipline and area. The list contains current editions of all sociology textbooks. Some books are brand new—in their first edition—while other books are in their 10th edition. All of the books on the list have publication dates between 2014 and 2017.

One of your first tasks in your new position is to analyze sales for all books published in the Sociology Division. To do this, you need to organize data so that you can group data by discipline and then insert subtotal rows. You will also use Excel's PivotTable tool to gain a variety of perspectives of aggregated data. Finally, you will create a PivotChart to depict the aggregated data visually.

Subtotals and Outlines

When you use large datasets, you develop an appreciation for functionality that enables you to manage the data and quickly provide answers to imperative questions. Data alone are meaningless; data translated into meaningful information increase your knowledge so that you can make well-informed decisions. Previously, you used analytical tools such as sorting, filtering, conditional formatting, tables, and charts. These tools help translate raw data into information so that you can identify trends, patterns, and anomalies in a dataset. Now you are ready to explore other functionalities that help you consolidate and analyze large amounts of data.

In this section, you will learn how to insert subtotals for categories. Then you will learn how to group data to create an outline, collapse and expand groups within the outline, and ungroup data to return them to their original state.

Subtotaling Data

Decision makers often want to calculate subtotals by groups within large dataset. You can use the Subtotal feature to insert subtotal rows by categories for a regular data range.

For example, the Ivory Halls Publishing Company's dataset contains a list of sociology textbooks organized by discipline, such as Family. Textbooks are further classified by a specific area within the discipline. For example, the Family discipline contains specific areas such as *Family Interaction* and *Marriage and Family*. You can calculate the number of books sold and the total sales per area. Adding subtotals can help you identify which disciplines and which areas contribute the highest revenue for the company and which disciplines and areas produce the lowest revenue. You can then analyze the data to determine to continue publishing books in high-revenue–generating areas or discontinue the publication of books in low-selling areas. To add subtotals to a dataset, do the following:

STEP 1»

1. Sort the data on a primary category (such as Discipline in the sociology textbook example) that has the same values, such as the same city, state, or department name for several records in one column. **NOTE: If the data are not sorted by a major category, the subtotaled results will not be correct.**
2. Convert the table to range (if the dataset is a table).
3. Click in the dataset and click the DATA tab.
4. Click Subtotal in the Outline group to open the Subtotal dialog box.
5. Click the *At each change in* arrow and select the column by which the data are sorted (see Figure 7.1). **NOTE: You must select the column by which you sorted data in Step 1.**
6. Click the *Use function* arrow and select the function you want to apply.
7. Select the appropriate column heading check boxes in the *Add subtotal to* list for each field you want to subtotal. You can use all functions for columns that contain numeric data. For text columns, you can only count the number of rows within the group.
8. Select any other check boxes you want to use and click OK.

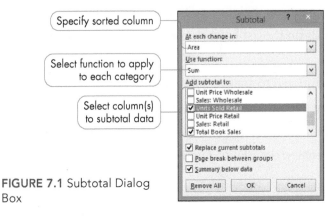

FIGURE 7.1 Subtotal Dialog Box

The dataset must be sorted by categorical labels. For example, the Sociology Textbooks dataset is sorted first by discipline. When you use the Subtotal feature, Excel inserts a *subtotal*, a row within the dataset containing at least one aggregated value when the category you specified in the *At a change in* option changes. For example, when Excel detects a change from Family to Introductory, a subtotal row is inserted on row 35 (see Figure 7.2). (NOTE: Subtotal rows for discipline are highlighted in yellow in the figure; however, the Subtotal feature does not add highlighting.) The subtotal of the number of Family discipline books sold at wholesale was 76,710, and the subtotal of the number of Introductory discipline books sold at wholesale was 179,415, indicating that the number of Introductory books sold is more than double the number of Family books sold. A grand total row is inserted at the end of the dataset to indicate the grand total values (not shown in the figure).

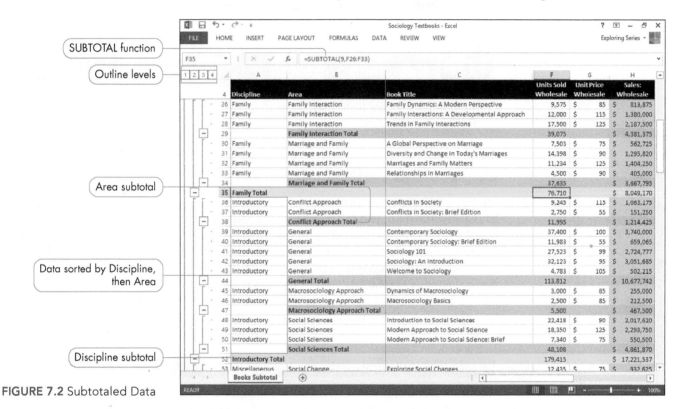

FIGURE 7.2 Subtotaled Data

Excel uses the SUBTOTAL function to calculate the subtotals. Cell F35 contains =SUBTOTAL(9,F26:F33) to sum the values in the range F26:F33. The first argument indicates which summary function is used to calculate the subtotal. Use 1-11 to summarize data including hidden values; use 101-111 to summarize visible data only. Table 7.1 lists some of the summary functions and their respective argument values. For example, 9 sums all values in the range specified in the second argument. If you create a subtotal to average the gross sales, the first argument in the function would be 1 instead of 9.

TABLE 7.1 SUBTOTAL Function_Num Argument		
Summary Function	Argument to Include Hidden Values	Argument to Ignore Hidden Values
AVERAGE	1	101
COUNT	2	102
COUNTA	3	103
MAX	4	104
MIN	5	105
SUM	9	109

Add a Second Level of Subtotals

You can add a second level of subtotals to a dataset. Adding a second level preserves the primary subtotals and adds another level of subtotals for subcategories. In the Sociology Textbook example, Figure 7.2 shows the discipline subtotals as well as the areas subcategory subtotals. To add a second level of subtotals while maintaining the existing subtotals, do the following:

STEP 2 ≫

1. Perform a two-level sort based on primary and secondary categorical data.
2. Click the DATA tab and click Subtotal in the Outline group.
3. Click the *At a change in* arrow and specify the column that was used for the secondary sort.
4. Select the function and columns to be subtotaled.
5. Deselect the *Replace current subtotals* check box and click OK.

TIP Removing Subtotals

The subtotal rows are temporary. To remove them, display the Subtotals dialog box and click Remove All.

Collapse and Expand the Subtotals

STEP 3 ≫

The Subtotal feature creates an *outline*, a hierarchical structure of data. When a dataset contains a structured list, you can collapse or expand the categories after using the Subtotal feature. Table 7.2 explains the outline buttons that appear on the left side of the subtotaled data. Figure 7.3 shows a dataset that is collapsed to display the discipline subtotals and the grand total after the user clicked the outline button 2. The number of outline buttons depends on the total number of subtotals created. Because the data in Figure 7.2 contained discipline and area subtotals, four outline buttons appear in Figure 7.3. If the dataset contained only one level of subtotals, only three outline buttons would appear.

TABLE 7.2 Outline Buttons

Button	Description
1	Collapse outline to display the grand total only.
2	Display subtotals by the main subtotal category and the grand total.
3	Displays subtotals by the main subtotal category, the secondary subtotal category, and the grant total.
4	Display the entire list.
+	Expand an outline group to see its details.
–	Collapse an outline group to see its category name only.

Click to show category subtotals and grand total

Click to expand a particular area to show its details

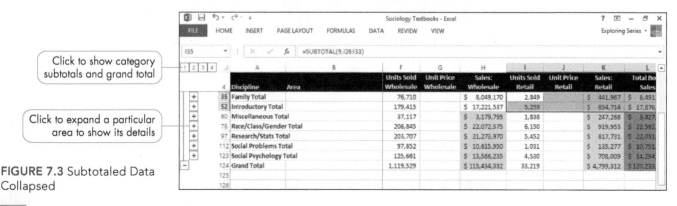

FIGURE 7.3 Subtotaled Data Collapsed

Grouping and Ungrouping Data

STEP 4 » The Subtotals feature outlines data into categories by rows. You can create outlines by columns of related data as well. For Excel to outline by columns, the dataset must contain formulas or aggregate functions. If Excel cannot create the outline, it displays the message box *Cannot create an outline*. To create an outline by columns, do the following:

1. Click the DATA tab.
2. Click the Group arrow in the Outline group.
3. Select Auto Outline.

For more control in creating an outline, you can create groups. **Grouping** is the process of joining rows or columns of related data together into a single entity. After you create groups in the dataset, you can click a collapse button (–) to collapse a group to show the outsider column or click the expand button (+) to expand groups of related columns to view the internal columns of data. Grouping enables you to hide raw data while you focus on key calculated results. To group data, do the following:

1. Select the rows or columns you want to group. For column groups, you often select columns containing details but not aggregate columns, such as totals or averages. (Rows are automatically grouped if you use the Subtotals feature.)
2. Click the DATA tab.
3. Click Group in the Outline group. If the Group dialog box opens, choose the option to group by columns or rows and click OK.

In Figure 7.4, Excel grouped the data by columns. Because the Units Sold Retail and Unit Price Retail columns are grouped, you can click the collapse button above Sales Retail to collapse the columns and focus on the Sales Retail column. Currently, some of the wholesale columns are hidden, showing only the Sales: Wholesale column. You can click the expand button above the Sales: Wholesale column to display the related wholesale columns.

Group related columns

Ungroups the dataset

Click to collapse column groups

Click to expand a group of columns

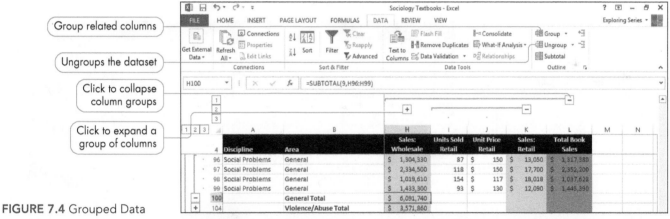

FIGURE 7.4 Grouped Data

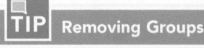 **Removing Groups**

To remove groups, select all grouped columns or rows and click Ungroup in the Outline group.

Quick Concepts

1. Why must a dataset be sorted by a category before using the Subtotal feature? Within the Subtotal dialog box, which option do you set to match the column you used to sort the data? *p. 338*

2. Explain the SUBTOTAL function as it is used by the Subtotal feature. *p. 339*

3. How can you expand or collapse outlined groups of columns? *p. 341*

Hands-On Exercises

Watch the Video
for this Hands-
On Exercise!

MyITLab®
HOE1 Training

1 Subtotals and Outlines

As VP of the Sociology Division at Ivory Halls Publishing Company, you want to conduct a preliminary analysis of your current textbook offerings. Each textbook falls within a general discipline, and each discipline is divided into several areas. Details for each textbook include the title, current edition, and copyright year. The company tracks units sold, unit prices, and gross sales by two major types of sales: (1) wholesale sales to bookstores and (2) retail sales to individual consumers. You will organize the data and include area subtotals. Your assistant applied Freeze Panes to keep the column headings in row 4 and the disciplines and areas in columns A and B visible regardless of where you scroll.

Skills covered: Subtotal the Data • Add a Second Subtotal • Collapse and Expand the Subtotals • Group and Ungroup Data

STEP 1 >> SUBTOTAL THE DATA

Before you use the Subtotal feature, you must sort the data by discipline and then by area. After sorting the data, you will insert subtotals for each discipline. You want to see the totals for the wholesale sales, retail sales, and combined book sales. Refer to Figure 7.5 as you complete Step 1.

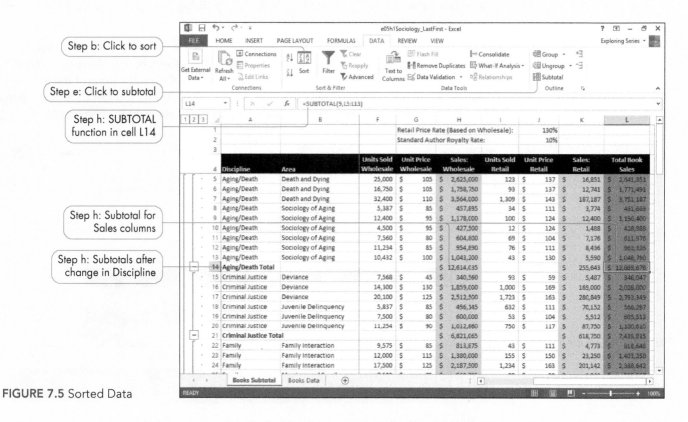

FIGURE 7.5 Sorted Data

a. Open *e05h1Sociology* and save it as **e05h1Sociology_LastFirst**.

> **TROUBLESHOOTING**: If you make any major mistakes in this exercise, you can close the file, open *e05h1Sociology* again, and then start this exercise over.

The workbook contains two worksheets: Books Subtotal for Hands-On Exercise 1 and Books Data for Hands-On Exercises 2–4.

b. Click the **DATA tab** and click **Sort** in the Sort & Filter group.

c. Click the **Sort by arrow** and select **Discipline** in the Sort dialog box.

d. Click **Add Level**, click the **Then by arrow**, and then select **Area**. Click **OK**.

Excel sorts the data by discipline in alphabetical order. Within each discipline, Excel sorts the data further by area. The data are sorted first by disciplines so that you can apply subtotals to each discipline.

e. Click **Subtotal** in the Outline group.

The Subtotal dialog box opens. The default *At each change in* is the Discipline column, and the default *Use function* is Sum. These settings are correct.

f. Click the **Sales: Wholesale check box** in the *Add subtotal to* section.

g. Click the **Sales: Retail check box** in the *Add subtotal to* section.

Excel selected the last column—Total Book Sales—automatically. You selected the other two sales columns to total. You will leave the *Replace current subtotals* and *Summary below data* check boxes selected.

h. Click **OK**. Scroll to the right to see the subtotals and click **cell L14** to see the SUBTOTAL function for the total book sales for the Aging/Death discipline. Save the workbook.

Excel inserts subtotal rows after each discipline category. The subtotal rows include labels and subtotals for the wholesale sales, retail sales, and book sales columns.

TROUBLESHOOTING: If your subtotals do not match the totals in Figure 7.5, open the Subtotal dialog box, click Remove All, click OK, and repeat steps b through h again.

STEP 2 ≫ ADD A SECOND SUBTOTAL

Displaying subtotals by discipline helps you compare sales data better; however, you want to add another level to see subtotals for each area within each discipline. To insert two levels of subtotals, you must subtotal the primary category first (Discipline) and then add a subtotal to the second category (Area). As you use the Subtotal dialog box, you want to keep the original subtotals intact. Refer to Figure 7.6 as you complete Step 2.

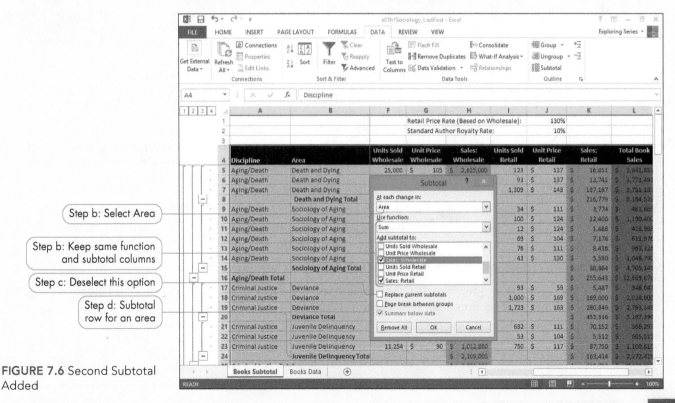

FIGURE 7.6 Second Subtotal Added

a. Click **Subtotal** in the Outline group to open the Subtotal dialog box again.

b. Click the **At each change in arrow** and select **Area**.

The *Use function* is still Sum, and Excel remembers the last columns you selected in the *Add subtotal to* section—Sales: Wholesale, Sales: Retail, and Total Book Sales.

c. Click the **Replace current subtotals check box** to deselect it.

Deselecting this check box will keep the discipline subtotals.

d. Click **OK** and click **cell L15**. Save the workbook.

Excel inserts subtotal rows after each area. The Formula Bar displays =SUBTOTAL(9,L9:L14). Your data have discipline subtotals and area subtotals within each discipline.

> **TROUBLESHOOTING:** If you subtotal the area first and then discipline, Excel adds several discipline subtotals, which repeat the area subtotals. That is why you must subtotal by the primary category first and then subtotal by the secondary category.

STEP 3 ≫ COLLAPSE AND EXPAND THE SUBTOTALS

You want to compare wholesale, retail, and book sales among the disciplines and then among areas within a discipline. Refer to Figure 7.7 as you complete Step 3.

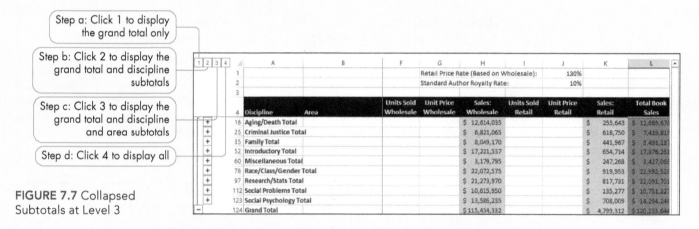

Step a: Click 1 to display the grand total only

Step b: Click 2 to display the grand total and discipline subtotals

Step c: Click 3 to display the grand total and discipline and area subtotals

Step d: Click 4 to display all

FIGURE 7.7 Collapsed Subtotals at Level 3

a. Click the **1** in the top-left outline area (to the left of the column headings).

You collapsed the outline to show the grand totals only.

b. Click the **2** in the top-left outline area.

You expanded the outline to show the grand and discipline subtotals. Which two disciplines had the highest wholesale and retail sales? Which discipline had the lowest total sales?

c. Click the **3** in the top-left outline area.

You expanded the outline to show the grand, discipline, and area subtotals (see Figure 7.7). Within the Introductory discipline, which area had the lowest sales? How do wholesale and retail sales compare? Are they proportionally the same within each area?

d. Click the **4** in the top-left outline area. Save the workbook.

You expanded the outline to show all details again. If you had not added the second subtotal, the outline would have had three levels instead of four.

STEP 4 ≫ GROUP AND UNGROUP DATA

You want to apply an outline to the columns so that you can collapse or expand the units sold and unit prices columns. Refer to Figure 7.8 as you complete Step 4.

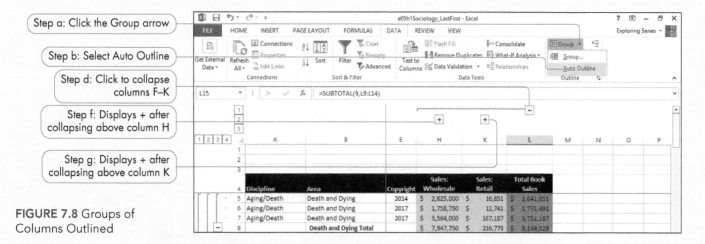

FIGURE 7.8 Groups of Columns Outlined

a. Click the **Group arrow** in the Outline group on the DATA tab.

You want to see if Excel can create a column outline for you so that you do not have to select columns and group them individually.

b. Select **Auto Outline**.

Excel displays the message box *Modify existing outline?* because it recognizes that an existing outline exists—the row subtotals outline.

c. Click **OK**.

Excel maintains the outlined subtotals and adds column subtotals. Horizontal lines and collapse buttons appear above the columns. The formula in column H is =F5*G5, so Excel creates an outline for these columns. The formula in column K is =I5*J5, so Excel creates an outline for these columns. It also creates a hierarchical outline of columns F through K, since the formula in column L sums the values in columns H and K.

d. Click the **collapse (–) button** above column L.

You collapsed columns F through K to display disciplines, areas, and total sales by title.

e. Click the **expand (+) button** above column L.

You expanded the outline to show columns F through K again.

f. Click the **collapse (–) button** above column H.

You collapsed the outline to hide columns F and G so you can focus on the wholesale sales without the distraction of the Units Sold or Unit Price columns.

g. Click the **collapse (–) button** above column K.

You collapsed the outline to hide columns I and J so you can focus on the retail sales without the distraction of the Units Sold or Unit Price columns.

h. Save the workbook. Keep the workbook open if you plan to continue with Hands-On Exercise 2. If not, close the workbook and exit Excel.

PivotTable Basics

Analyzing large amounts of data is important for making solid decisions. Entering data is the easy part; retrieving data in a structured, meaningful way is more challenging. ***Data mining*** is the process of analyzing large volumes of data, using advanced statistical techniques, and identifying trends and patterns in the data. Managers use data-mining techniques to address a variety of questions, such as the following:

- What snack foods do customers purchase most when purchasing Pepsi® products?
- What age group from what geographic region downloads the most top 10 songs from iTunes?
- What hotel chain and rental car combinations are most popular among Delta Air Lines passengers flying into Salt Lake City?

Questions similar to those above help organizations prepare their marketing plans to capitalize on consumer spending patterns. The more you know about your customer demographics, the better you can focus your strategic plans to increase market share.

A ***PivotTable*** is a powerful, interactive data-mining feature that enables you to summarize and analyze data, especially helpful when working with large datasets. An advantage of using a PivotTable is that you can group data into one or more categories and perform a variety of calculations without altering the original dataset. The most important benefit of a PivotTable is that it is dynamic. You can easily and quickly *pivot*, or rearrange, data to analyze them from different viewpoints, such as expanding or collapsing details, organizing and grouping data differently, and switching row and column categories. Viewing the PivotTable from different perspectives helps you more easily identify trends and patterns among the variables in the data that might not be obvious from looking at the data from only one viewpoint.

In this section, you will learn how to create a PivotTable by organizing data into columns and rows to aggregate data.

Creating a PivotTable

Before you create a PivotTable, ensure the data source is well structured. Applying the rules for good table design is a start: Use meaningful column labels, ensure data accuracy, and avoid blank rows and columns in the dataset. To consolidate and aggregate data, at least one column must have duplicate values, such as the same city, state, or department name for several records. You then use these columns of duplicate values to create categories for organizing and summarizing data. Another column must have numeric values that can be aggregated to produce quantitative summaries, such as averages or sums.

Create a PivotTable from the Quick Analysis Gallery

You can create a PivotTable from the Quick Analysis gallery. A benefit of this method is that Excel displays recommended PivotTables based on the data. To create a PivotTable using Quick Analysis, do the following:

STEP 1 »
1. Select the entire dataset, including the field names (column labels).
2. Click the Quick Analysis button in the bottom-right corner of the selected range.
3. Click TABLES in the Quick Analysis gallery.
4. Position the mouse pointer over the PivotTable thumbnails to see a preview of the different recommended PivotTables (see Figure 7.9).
5. Click the PivotTable thumbnail to create the desired PivotTable.

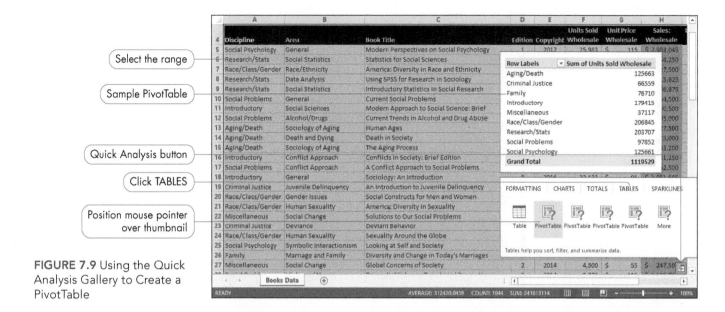

Select the range

Sample PivotTable

Quick Analysis button

Click TABLES

Position mouse pointer over thumbnail

FIGURE 7.9 Using the Quick Analysis Gallery to Create a PivotTable

---

TIP **PivotTable or Subtotals?**

At first glance, PivotTables are similar to subtotals because they both produce subtotals, but PivotTables are more robust. PivotTables provide more flexibility than subtotals provide. If you need complex subtotals cross-referenced by two or more categories with filtering and other specifications, create a PivotTable.

Create a PivotTable from the Ribbon

You can also create a PivotTable by using commands on the Ribbon. The Insert tab contains PivotTable and Recommended PivotTables commands. If you click PivotTable, Excel displays the Create PivotTable dialog box so that you can create a blank PivotTable from scratch. However, if you click Recommended PivotTables, Excel displays a dialog box so that you can select from a gallery of PivotTables. This option is similar to using the Quick Analysis gallery. To create a recommended PivotTable using the Ribbon, do the following:

1. Click inside the dataset (the range of cells or table).
2. Click the INSERT tab and click Recommended PivotTables in the Tables group to open the Recommended PivotTables dialog box (see Figure 7.10).
3. Click a thumbnail in the gallery on the left side of the dialog box to see a preview of the PivotTable on the right side.
4. Click OK to create the desired PivotTable.

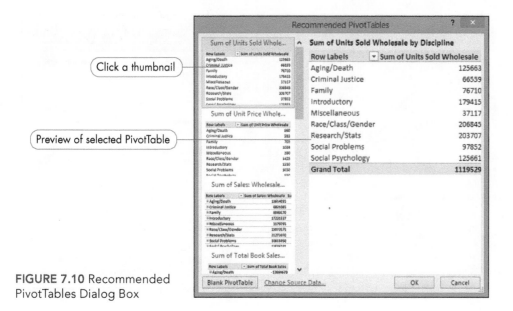

Click a thumbnail

Preview of selected PivotTable

FIGURE 7.10 Recommended PivotTables Dialog Box

After you use the Recommended PivotTables dialog box or the Quick Analysis gallery, Excel creates a PivotTable on a new worksheet (see Figure 7.11). The ROWS area contains the category names of the summarized data. For example, each discipline, such as Family, is listed in only one row, regardless of how many times each category name appears in the original dataset.

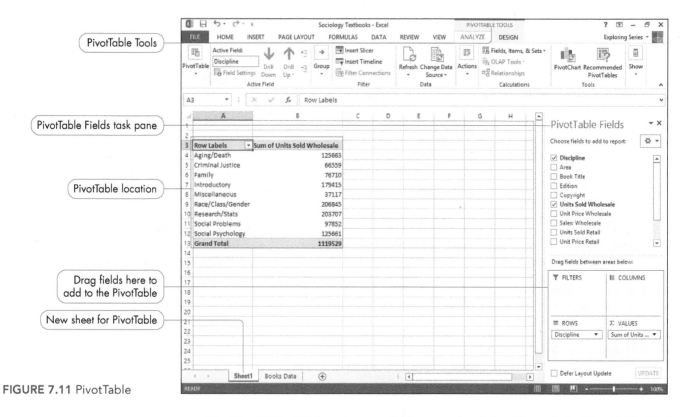

PivotTable Tools

PivotTable Fields task pane

PivotTable location

Drag fields here to add to the PivotTable

New sheet for PivotTable

FIGURE 7.11 PivotTable

The PivotTable Fields task pane displays on the right side, and the PivotTable Tools Analyze and Design contextual tabs appear on the Ribbon. If you click outside the PivotTable, the contextual tabs and the task pane disappear. Click within the PivotTable to display these elements again.

The **PivotTable Fields task pane** contains two sections. The *Choose fields to add to report* section lists all the fields or column labels from the original data source. You can click either drag a field to an area in the bottom of the task pane or click the check box to add the field to the PivotTable. Use the *Drag fields between areas below* section to arrange fields in one of the four PivotTable areas. Table 7.3 describes the areas of a PivotTable.

TABLE 7.3   Areas of a PivotTable

Area	Description
Filters Area	Filters the data to display results based on particular conditions you set.
Columns Area	Subdivides data into one or more additional categories.
Rows Area	Organizes and groups data into categories on the left side. Each group name occupies a single row.
Values Area	Displays summary statistics, such as totals or averages.

Modifying a PivotTable

After you create a PivotTable, you might want to modify it to see the data from a different perspective. For example, you might want to add fields to the rows, values, and columns areas of the PivotTable. In addition, you might want to collapse the PivotTable to show fewer details or expand it to show more details.

Add Rows

You can add fields to provide a more detailed analysis. For example, you might want to organize data by discipline by adding the Discipline field to the ROWS area in the PivotTable Fields task pane. To add a field as a row, do one of the following:

STEP 2»

- Click the field's check box in the *Choose fields to add to report* section. Excel adds the field to a PivotTable area based on the type of data stored in the field. If the field contains text, Excel usually places that field in the ROWS area.

- Drag the field from the *Choose fields to add to report* section and drop it in the ROWS area.

- Right-click the field name in the *Choose fields to add to report* section and select *Add to Row Labels*.

Add Values

A PivotTable has meaning when you include quantitative fields, such as quantities and monetary values, to aggregate the data. For example, you might want to display the total wholesale sales for each discipline and area. To add values, do one of the following:

- Click the field's check box in the *Choose fields to add to report* section. Excel makes it the value aggregate, such as *Sum of Sales*.

- Drag the field from the *Choose fields to add to report* section and drop it in the VALUES area.
- Right-click the field name in the *Choose fields to add to report* section and select *Add to Values*.

Excel sums the values for each group listed in the ROWS area. For example, the total number of units sold wholesale for the Family discipline is 76,710. If you drag a text field, such as Book Title, to the VALUES area, Excel counts the number of records for each group listed in the ROWS area. In this case, Excel counts seven books in the Family discipline.

Add Columns

Although you can create subdivisions of data by adding more fields to the ROWS area, you might want to arrange the subdivision categories in columns. Doing so minimizes the redundancy of duplicating subdivision row labels and helps consolidate data. To subdivide data into columns, drag a field from the *Choose fields to add to report* section and drop it in the COLUMNS area. Excel updates the aggregated values by the combination of row and column categories.

Figure 7.12 shows a PivotTable that uses the Discipline field as rows, the *Sum of Units Sold Wholesale* field as values, and Copyright field as columns. Each discipline label and each copyright year label appears only once in the PivotTable. This added level of detail enables you to see the total sales for each discipline based on its copyright year. The PivotTable includes grand totals for each discipline and grand totals for each year.

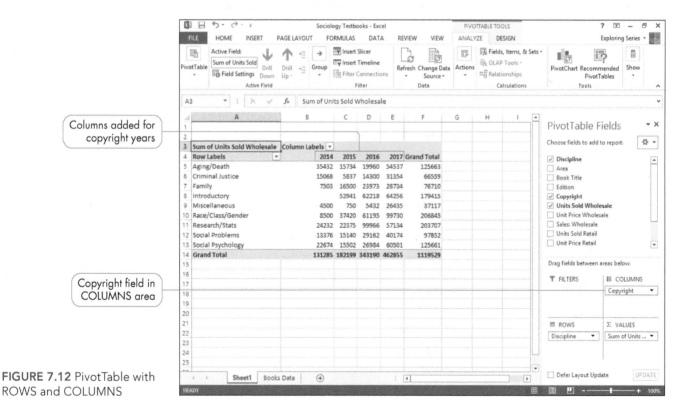

Columns added for copyright years

Copyright field in COLUMNS area

FIGURE 7.12 PivotTable with ROWS and COLUMNS

Collapse and Expand Items

If you include two fields as ROWS, the PivotTable displays more depth but may be overwhelming. You can hide or collapse the secondary field rows. For example, if the PivotTable contains both Discipline and Copyright row labels, you might want to collapse copyright years for some disciplines. The collapse and expand buttons display to the left of the row labels. If they do not, click Show and click the +/– buttons on the Analyze tab. Figure 7.13 shows the collapse and expand buttons.

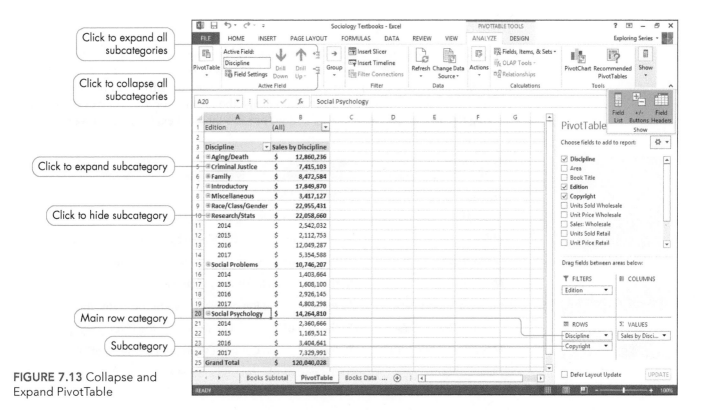

Click to expand all subcategories

Click to collapse all subcategories

Click to expand subcategory

Click to hide subcategory

Main row category

Subcategory

FIGURE 7.13 Collapse and Expand PivotTable

To hide the subcategories for a particular category, click the collapse button (–) on the left side of the specific category you wish to collapse. Excel hides the subcategories for that particular category and shows only the aggregated totals for the category. Continue collapsing other categories as needed to focus on a particular category's details.

To expand the subcategories again, click the expand button (+) on the left side of the category labels.

TIP **Collapse and Expand All**

You can collapse all categories at one time by clicking Collapse Field in the Active Field group on the Analyze tab. To expand all categories at one time, click Expand Field. This approach is faster than collapsing or expanding each category individually.

Remove Fields

You can remove fields to reduce the amount of data to analyze. To remove a field from the PivotTable, do one of the following:

- Click the field name in the *Drag fields between areas below* section and select Remove Field.
- Deselect the check box next to the field name in the *Choose fields to add to report* section.
- Drag a field name in the *Drag fields between areas below* section outside the PivotTable Fields task pane.

Rearrange Fields

You can rearrange fields in a PivotTable to improve readability. For example, you might want more columns than rows, so you can switch the fields in the ROWS and COLUMNS areas in the task pane. To move a field from one area to another, drag the field in the *Drag fields between areas below* section. You can also change the location or hierarchy of the fields by clicking the field arrow and selecting a Move option. Table 7.4 explains the Move options.

TABLE 7.4 Move Options	
Option	**Moves the Field...**
Move Up	Up one position in the hierarchy within the same area
Move Down	Down one position in the hierarchy within the same area
Move to Beginning	To the beginning of all fields in the same area
Move to End	To the end of all fields in the same area
Move to Report Filter	To the end of the Report Filter area of the PivotTable
Move to Row Labels	To the end of the Row Labels area of the PivotTable
Move to Column Labels	To the end of the Column Labels area of the PivotTable
Move to Values	To the end of the VALUES area of the PivotTable

Change the Values Field Settings

Although Excel uses the SUM function as the default summary statistic for numerical fields, you can select a different function. For example, you might want to calculate the average, lowest, or highest value within each group, or identify the lowest sales for each discipline/copyright year combination to see if the older books have decreased sales. In addition to changing the summary statistic, you might want to change the column label that appears above the summary statistics. By default, words indicate the summary statistic function applied, such as *Sum of Total Sales by Book* or *Average of Total Sales by Book*, depending on the summary statistic applied to the values. Finally, you might need to format the aggregated values. To modify any of these value settings, do the following:

STEP 4 ⟫

1. Click a value in the appropriate field in the PivotTable and click Field Settings in the Active Field group on the ANALYZE tab. Alternatively, click the field's arrow in the VALUES area of the task pane and select Value Field Settings. The Value Field Settings dialog box opens (see Figure 7.14).
2. Type the name you want to appear as the column label in the Custom Name box. For example, you might want the heading to appear as *Total Sales* instead of *Sum of Total Book Sales*.
3. Select the summary statistical function you want to use to summarize the values in the *Summarize value field by* list.
4. Click Number Format to open an abbreviated version of the Format Cells dialog box. Select a number type, such as Accounting, in the Category list; select other settings, such as number of decimal places in the *Decimal places* spin arrow; and then click OK.
5. Click OK in the Value Field Settings dialog box.

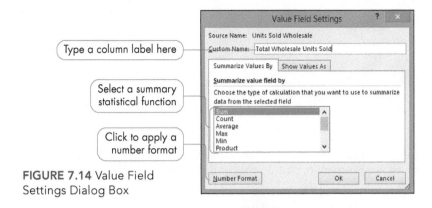

Type a column label here

Select a summary
statistical function

Click to apply a
number format

FIGURE 7.14 Value Field
Settings Dialog Box

 Multiple Summary Statistics

You can display more than one function for a field. For example, you might want to show *both* the total book sales and the average book sales. To display multiple summary statistics, drag another copy of the same field to the VALUES area and set each value setting separately.

Refresh a PivotTable

Although PivotTables are powerful, they do not update automatically if you make any changes to the underlying data in the data source. For example, if you change a sales value or delete a row in the data source, the PivotTable does not reflect the changed data. Unfortunately, this causes PivotTable summary statistics to be outdated with inaccurate results. If you change the data source, you must update the PivotTable by doing the following:

STEP 5»
1. Click in the PivotTable.
2. Click the ANALYZE tab.
3. Click Refresh in the Data group to refresh the current PivotTable only, or click the Refresh arrow and select Refresh All to refresh all PivotTables in the workbook.

If you want to ensure your PivotTable is up to date when you open the workbook, click the Analyze tab, click the PivotTable arrow on the left side of the Ribbon, select Options to open the PivotTable Options dialog box, click the Data tab, select *Refresh data when opening the file*, and then click OK.

Quick
Concepts

1. What are the advantages of using a PivotTable instead of a subtotal? *p. 346*
2. What is the main benefit of creating a PivotTable using the Quick Analysis gallery or from the Recommended PivotTables dialog box over creating a blank PivotTable? *pp. 346–347*
3. List the four areas of a PivotTable. *p. 349*

MyITLab®
HOE2 Training

2 PivotTable Basics

After exhausting the possibilities of outlines and subtotals, you want to create a PivotTable to analyze the sociology book sales. You realize you can see the data from different perspectives, enabling you to have a stronger understanding of the sales by various categories.

Skills covered: Create a PivotTable • Add Rows, Values, and Columns • Remove and Rearrange Fields • Change the Values Field Settings • Refresh a PivotTable

---

STEP 1 ≫ CREATE A PIVOTTABLE

Because you want to keep the subtotals you created in the Books Subtotal worksheet, you will create a PivotTable from the Books Data worksheet. Refer to Figures 7.10 and 7.15 as you complete Step 1.

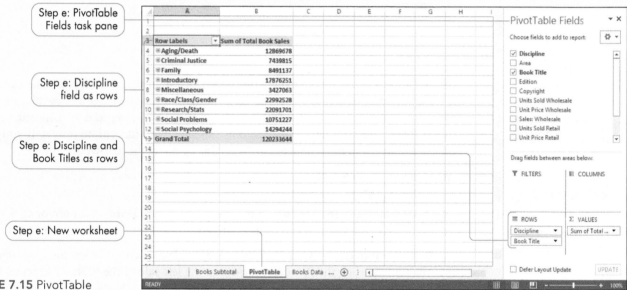

FIGURE 7.15 PivotTable

a. Open *e05h1Sociology_LastFirst* if you closed it at the end of Hands-On Exercise 1 and save it as **e05h2Sociology_LastFirst**, changing *h1* to *h2*.

b. Click the **Books Data worksheet tab**.

   Excel does not let you create a PivotTable using subtotaled data. To preserve the subtotals you created in Hands-On Exercise 1, you will use the dataset in the Books Data worksheet.

c. Click in **cell A5**, click the **INSERT tab**, and then click **Recommended PivotTables** in the Tables group.

   The Recommended PivotTables dialog box opens (see Figure 7.10).

d. Scroll the thumbnails of recommended PivotTables and click the **Sum of Total Book Sales by Discipline thumbnail**. (NOTE: Hover the mouse pointer over the thumbnails to see the full names.)

   You selected this PivotTable to show the overall total book sales for each discipline. The dialog box shows a preview of the selected PivotTable.

e. Click **OK** and click within the PivotTable, if necessary. Rename Sheet1 as **PivotTable**. Save the workbook.

Excel inserts a new Sheet1 worksheet, which you renamed as PivotTable, with the PivotTable on the left side and the PivotTable Fields task pane on the right side (see Figure 7.15).

STEP 2 ≫ ADD ROWS, VALUES, AND COLUMNS

You want to compare sales combinations by discipline, copyright year, and edition. The discipline field is already in the PivotTable, but you need to add the copyright year and edition fields. Refer to Figure 7.16 as you complete Step 2.

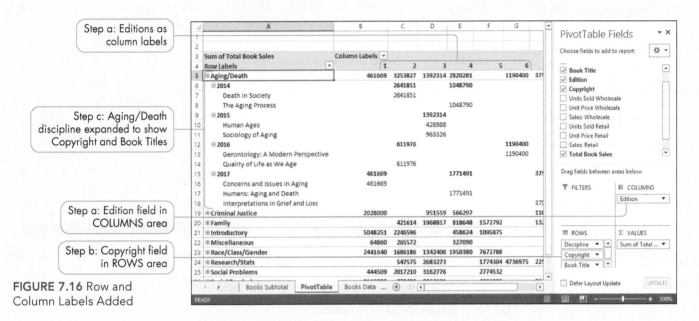

Step a: Editions as column labels

Step c: Aging/Death discipline expanded to show Copyright and Book Titles

Step a: Edition field in COLUMNS area

Step b: Copyright field in ROWS area

FIGURE 7.16 Row and Column Labels Added

a. Drag the **Edition field** to the COLUMNS area in the PivotTable Fields task pane.

Excel displays the total book sales by a combination of discipline and edition. This enables you to compare sales of current editions within each discipline. Blanks appear in the PivotTable when a discipline does not have a specific edition. For example, the Family discipline does not have any first-edition books currently being published.

b. Drag the **Copyright field** to be between the Discipline and Book Title fields in the ROWS area.

The Copyright and Book Titles are not showing because they are collapsed within the Discipline rows.

c. Click the **Aging/Death expand (+) button**. Save the workbook.

You expanded the Aging/Death discipline to show the copyright years and titles.

 **Field ScreenTip**

It may be confusing to see *Sum of Total...* in the VALUES box. Position the pointer over a field name in the area to see a ScreenTip with the full name, such as *Sum of Total Book Sales*.

Although it is informative to compare sales by edition, you think that the PivotTable contains too much detail, so you will remove the Edition field. In addition, the ROWS area contains the Book Titles field, but those data are collapsed; therefore, you will remove it as well. After you remove the fields, you will rearrange other fields to simplify the PivotTable. Refer to Figure 7.17 as you complete Step 3.

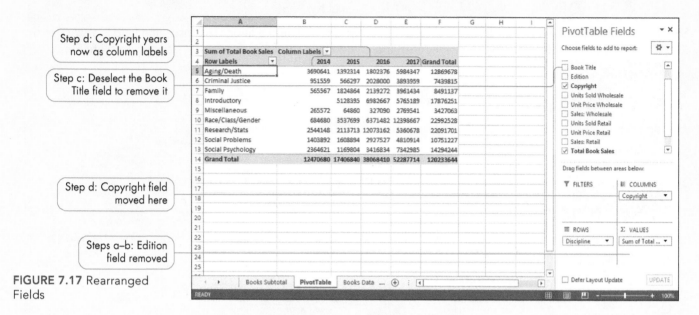

Step d: Copyright years now as column labels

Step c: Deselect the Book Title field to remove it

Step d: Copyright field moved here

Steps a–b: Edition field removed

FIGURE 7.17 Rearranged Fields

a. Click the **Edition arrow** in the Column Labels area.

   Excel displays a menu of options to apply to this field.

b. Select **Remove Field** on the menu.

   You removed the Edition field from the PivotTable. Instead of several sales columns, Excel consolidates the sales into one sales column. Although you find it helpful to have sales breakdowns by copyright year, you think the PivotTable will be easier to read if you move the Copyright field to the COLUMNS area.

c. Deselect the **Book Title check box** in the *Choose fields to add to report* section of the task pane.

   You removed the Book Title field from the PivotTable.

d. Drag the **Copyright field** from the ROWS area to the COLUMNS area. Save the workbook.

   This arrangement consolidates the data better. Instead of repeating the copyright years for each discipline, the copyright years are listed only once each at the top of the sales columns.

STEP 4 >> CHANGE THE VALUES FIELD SETTINGS

After selecting the PivotTable fields, you want to improve the appearance of the sociology textbook PivotTable. You will format the values for Accounting Number Format and replace the generic Row Labels description with a label that indicates the sociology disciplines. Refer to Figure 7.18 as you complete Step 4.

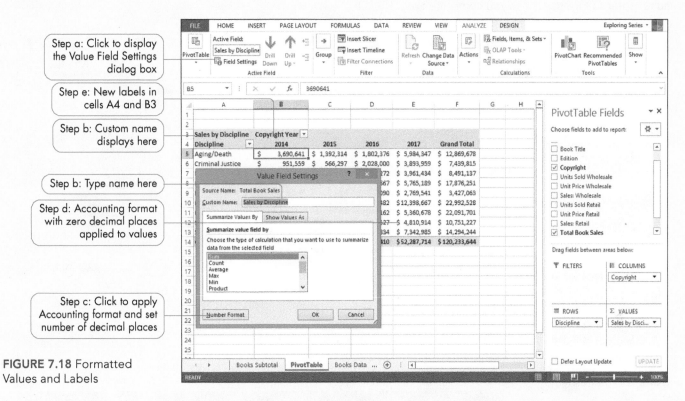

Step a: Click to display the Value Field Settings dialog box

Step e: New labels in cells A4 and B3

Step b: Custom name displays here

Step b: Type name here

Step d: Accounting format with zero decimal places applied to values

Step c: Click to apply Accounting format and set number of decimal places

FIGURE 7.18 Formatted Values and Labels

a. Click **cell B5** and click **Field Settings** in the Active Field group on the ANALYZE tab.

The Value Field Settings dialog box opens so that you can format the field.

b. Type **Sales by Discipline** in the **Custom Name box**.

Leave Sum as the selected calculation type in the *Summarize value field by* section.

c. Click **Number Format**.

Excel opens a Format Cells dialog box with only one tab: the Number tab.

d. Click **Accounting** in the Category list, change the **Decimal places value** to **0**, click **OK** in the Format Cells dialog box, and then click **OK** in the Value Field Settings dialog box.

You formatted the values with Accounting Number Format with no decimal places, and the heading *Sales by Discipline* appears in cell A3.

e. Type **Discipline** in **cell A4** and type **Copyright Year** in **cell B3**.

You replaced the generic *Row Labels* heading with *Discipline* to describe the contents of the first column, and you replaced the *Column Labels* heading with *Copyright Year*. Although you can create custom names for values, you cannot create custom names for row and column labels. However, you can edit the labels directly in the cells.

f. Select the **range B4:F4** and center the labels horizontally. Save the workbook.

STEP 5 ›› REFRESH A PIVOTTABLE

After consulting with the Accounting Department, you realize that the retail prices are incorrect. The unit retail prices are based on a percentage of the wholesale price. The retail unit price is 30% more than the wholesale unit price, but it should be 25%. You will edit the input cell in the original worksheet and refresh the PivotTable to see the corrected results. Refer to Figure 7.19 as you complete Step 5.

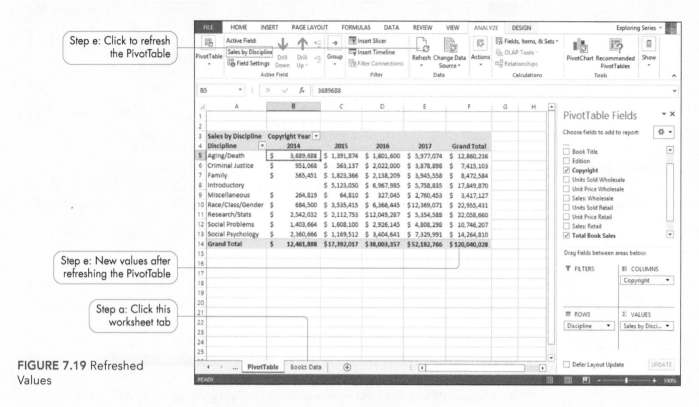

FIGURE 7.19 Refreshed Values

a. Click the **Books Data worksheet tab**.

You need to locate and change the retail price percentage.

b. Click **cell J1**, the cell that contains the current retail price percentage.

c. Type **125%** and press **Enter**. Save the workbook to update the formula results on the Books Data worksheet.

> **TROUBLESHOOTING**: If the formula results in the Unit Price Retail, Sales: Retail, and Total Book Sales columns do not change after you edit the data in step c, the workbook may be set for manual calculation. To ensure that formulas update automatically, click the File tab, click Options, click Formulas, click Automatic as the Workbook Calculation setting, and then click OK.

d. Click the **PivotTable worksheet tab**.

Notice that the PivotTable aggregate values did not change. The grand total is $120,233,644. You must refresh the PivotTable.

e. Click the **ANALYZE tab** and click **Refresh** in the Data group.

Excel updates the PivotTable values based on the change you made in the Books Data worksheet.

f. Save the workbook. Keep the workbook open if you plan to continue with Hands-On Exercise 3. If not, close the workbook and exit Excel.

PivotTable Options

As you have experienced, PivotTables consolidate and aggregate large amounts of data to facilitate data analysis. You can customize the PivotTable for more in-depth analysis. In the previous section, you used the Analyze tab to display the Value Field Settings dialog box and refresh the PivotTable. However, the Analyze tab contains more ways for you to customize your PivotTable. For example, you can filter groups, display or hide particular groups temporarily, and add subtotals.

In this section, you will learn how to filter data in a PivotTable. In addition, you will create a calculated field and display subtotals.

Filtering and Slicing a PivotTable

By default, PivotTables display aggregated data for each category. However, you may want to set a filter to exclude particular categories or values. You can specify a particular field to use to filter the PivotTable. In addition, you can include slicers to easily set filters to designate which specific data to include in the PivotTable.

Add Filters

Although PivotTables consolidate data from the original data source into groups, the PivotTable might contain more details than you want. You can apply filters to show only a subset of the PivotTable. Drag a field to the FILTERS area in the task pane when you want to engage a filter based on a particular field. For example, you might want to filter the PivotTable to show only aggregates for first- and second-edition books. When you drag a field to the FILTERS area, Excel displays the field name in cell A1 with a filter arrow in cell B1. To set the filter, click the filter arrow and do one of the following and then click OK:

STEP 1 »

- Select the value in the list to filter the data by that value only.
- Click the *Select Multiple Items* check box if you want to select more than one value to filter the PivotTable. Then click the check boxes by each value you want to set (see Figure 7.20).
- Type a value in the Search box if the list is too long and you want to find a value quickly.

Only a subset of the data that meet those conditions appears in the PivotTable; Excel hides the unselected items.

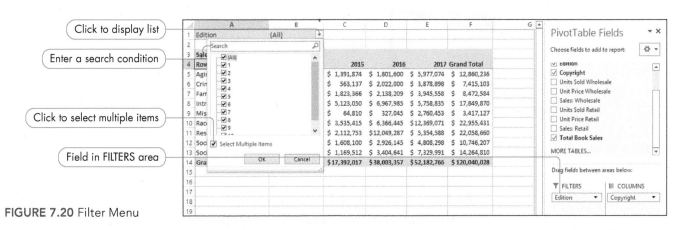

FIGURE 7.20 Filter Menu

Cell B1 displays (All) when no filter is enabled, the value if one filter is enabled, or (Multiple Items) if more than one item is selected. To remove the filter entirely, remove it from the FILTER area. To remove the filter temporarily, click the filter arrow in cell B1, select (All), and then click OK.

You can apply additional filters based on the row and column label groupings. For example, you can apply date filters to display summary statistics for data occurring within a particular time frame or apply filters for values within a designated range. To apply group filters, click the Row Labels or Column Labels arrow in the PivotTable and specify the settings (see Figure 7.21). Excel calculates the summary statistics based on the filtered data rather than the complete dataset.

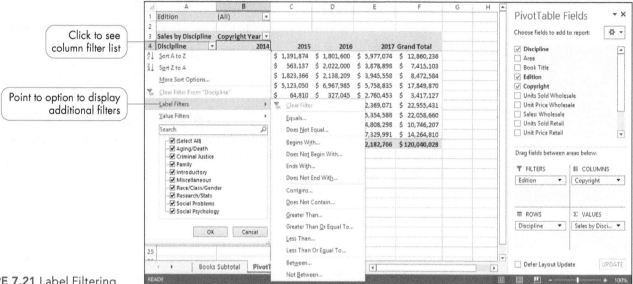

Click to see column filter list

Point to option to display additional filters

FIGURE 7.21 Label Filtering

Insert Slicers

You can insert a *slicer*, a small window containing one button for each unique item in a field so that you can filter the PivotTable quickly. Slicers are especially helpful to filter data when a PivotTable is based on multiple tables. The visual representation is easier to manipulate than adding more fields to the FILTERS area and then setting each field's filter through drop-down lists. To insert a slicer, do the following:

STEP 2»

1. Click the ANALYZE tab.
2. Click Insert Slicer in the Filter group to display the Insert Slicers dialog box (see Figure 7.22).
3. Click one or more field check boxes to display one or more slicers and click OK.

FIGURE 7.22 Insert Slicers Dialog Box

Excel inserts slicers into the worksheet. You can manipulate a slicer by doing the following:

- **Move the Slicer.** Drag a slicer to move it onscreen.
- **Filter Data.** Click the slicer button to filter by the value represented by the button. Press Ctrl to select several slicers to apply additional filters. Excel highlights the item to make it clear how you filtered the PivotTable. For example, in Figure 7.23, the Discipline field is filtered by Family, Introductory, and Social Problems. Although

no filter has been enabled for the Edition field, the 6th and 9th edition buttons are unavailable because the three disciplines selected do not have books that are in their 6th or 9th editions.

- **Remove a Filter.** Click Remove Filter in the top-right corner of the slicer window.

FIGURE 7.23 Slicers

Customize Slicers

When you select a slicer, the Slicer Tools Options tab displays so that you can customize a slicer. The default slicer caption displays the field name only. The *slicer caption* is text that displays in the header at the top of the slicer window. However, you can customize the slicer by changing its caption. In Figure 7.23, the left slicer's caption displays an instruction to the user, whereas the right slicer's caption displays the default field name. Table 7.5 lists and describes the commands on the Slicer Tools Options tab.

TABLE 7.5 Slicer Tools Commands	
Group	Commands
Slicer	Enables you to change the slicer caption, display the Slicer Settings dialog box for further customization, and manage the PivotTable connected to the slicer. In Figure 7.23, the Edition slicer has been sorted in ascending order. The light blue items 6 and 9 do not apply to the selected disciplines.
Slicer Styles	Applies a style to the slicer by specifying the color of the filtered item in the slicer. For example, given the workbook theme, the default active filters appear in blue and unavailable items appear in light blue. In Figure 7.23, Slicer Style Dark 2 has been applied to the Discipline style.
Arrange	Specifies the slicer's placement in relation to other groups, such as placing a slicer on top of other slicers.
Buttons	Defines how many columns are displayed in the selected slicer and the height and width of each button inside the slicer. For example, the Edition slicer contains two columns, and the Discipline slicer contains one column in Figure 7.23.
Size	Sets the height and width of the slicer window. For example, the Discipline slicer's height is 3.07" in Figure 7.23.

Creating a Calculated Field

You can create a *calculated field*, which is a user-defined field that does not exist in the original dataset. It derives its values based on performing calculations on other original dataset values. For example, you can create a calculated field that converts totals to percentages for easier relative comparison among categories, or you might want to create a calculated field that determines what the number of units a 10% increase in units sold for the upcoming year would be. To create a calculated field, do the following:

STEP 3 »

1. Select a cell within the PivotTable.
2. Click the PIVOTTABLE TOOLS ANALYZE tab.
3. Click Fields, Items, & Sets in the Calculations group and select Calculated Field to display the Insert Calculated Field dialog box (see Figure 7.24).

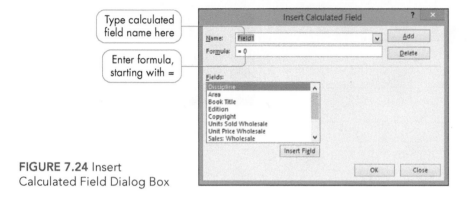

FIGURE 7.24 Insert Calculated Field Dialog Box

Type a descriptive label for the calculated field in the Name box. Build a formula starting with the equal sign (=). Instead of using cell references, insert the field names and other operands. For example ='Total Book Sales'*.1 calculates a 10% royalty amount on the total book sales. Click OK to insert the calculated field in the PivotTable. Format the numerical values in the calculated field column as needed.

Show Values as a Specific Calculation Result

In addition to creating calculated fields, you can apply built-in custom calculations that display relationships between values in rows and columns in the PivotTable. For example, you can show each value as a percentage of the grand total or each value's percentage of the row total. To display values in relation to others, do the following:

STEP 4 »

1. Click the field in the VALUES area of the task pane and select Value Field Settings (or click within the field in the PivotTable and click Field Settings in the Active Field group on the ANALYZE tab).
2. Click the Show Values As tab within the Value Field Settings dialog box.
3. Click the *Show values as* arrow and select the desired calculation type. Table 7.6 lists and describes some of the calculation options.
4. Click Number Format to set number formats, click OK to close the Format Cells dialog box, and then click OK to close the Value Field Settings dialog box.

TABLE 7.6 Calculation Options	
Option	**Description**
% of Grand Total	Displays each value as a percentage of the grand total.
% of Column Total	Displays each value as a percentage of the respective column total. The values in each column total 100%.
% of Row Total	Displays each value as a percentage of the respective row total. The values in each row total 100%.
% of Parent Row Total	Displays values as: (value for the item) / (value for the parent item on rows).
Running Total	Displays values as running totals.
Rank Smallest to Largest	Displays the rank of values in a specific field where 1 represents the smallest value.
Rank Largest to Smallest	Displays the rank of values in a specific field where 1 represents the largest value.

Quick
Concepts

1. What is the purpose of applying a filter to a PivotTable? How do you apply a main filter and additional filters? *p. 359*

2. What is a slicer? What do the three different colors indicate in a slicer? *p. 360*

3. When would you create a calculated field in a PivotTable? *p. 362*

Hands-On Exercises

Watch the Video
for this Hands-
On Exercise!

MyITLab®
HOE3 Training

3 PivotTable Options

The PivotTable you created has been beneficial for you to review sales data by discipline for each copyright year. In addition, you have used the PivotTable to compare grand total sales among disciplines and grand totals by copyright year. Now you want to extend your analysis. You will calculate author royalties from the sales and impose filters to focus your attention on each analysis.

Skills covered: Set Filters • Insert and Customize a Slicer • Create a Calculated Field • Show Values as Calculations

STEP 1 ≫ SET FILTERS

The level of success of the first two editions especially determines the likelihood of approving subsequent revisions and editions. To display aggregated sales for these editions, you need to set a filter to remove the other editions from being included in the calculated sales data. After you review the first- and second-edition data, you will enable additional filters to review books published in the past two years. Refer to Figure 7.25 as you complete Step 1.

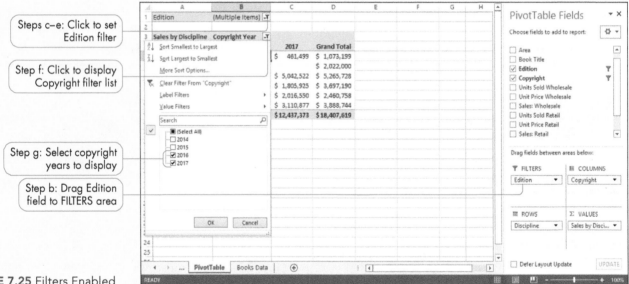

Steps c–e: Click to set Edition filter

Step f: Click to display Copyright filter list

Step g: Select copyright years to display

Step b: Drag Edition field to FILTERS area

FIGURE 7.25 Filters Enabled

a. Open *e05h2Sociology_LastFirst* if you closed it at the end of Hands-On Exercise 2 and save it as **e05h3Sociology_LastFirst**, changing *h2* to *h3*.

> **TROUBLESHOOTING:** Click in the PivotTable to display the PivotTable Field task pane if necessary.

b. Make sure the PivotTable worksheet tab is active and drag the **Edition field** from the *Choose fields to add to report* section to the FILTERS area.

You can now filter the PivotTable based on the Edition field. Cell A1 displays the field name, and cell B1 displays (All) and the filter arrow.

c. Click the **Edition filter arrow** in **cell B1** and click the **Select Multiple Items check box**.

The list displays a check box for each item.

d. Click the **(All) check box** to deselect it.

e. Click the **1** and **2 check boxes** and click **OK**.

The summary statistics reflect sales data for only first- and second-edition publications. The filter arrow changes to a funnel icon in cell B1.

f. Click the **Copyright Year filter arrow** in **cell B3** and click the **(Select All) check box** to deselect it.

g. Click the **2016** and **2017 check boxes** and click **OK**.

Excel filters out data for years that do not meet the condition you set. The filter arrow changes to a funnel icon in cell B3.

h. Save the workbook.

STEP 2 >> INSERT AND CUSTOMIZE A SLICER

You might distribute the workbook to colleagues who are not as skilled in Excel as you are. To help them set their own filters, you insert slicers. Refer to Figure 7.26 as you complete Step 2.

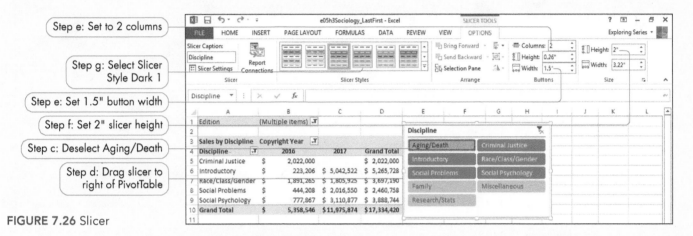

FIGURE 7.26 Slicer

a. Click **Insert Slicer** in the Filter group on the ANALYZE tab.

The Insert Slicers dialog box opens, listing each field name.

b. Click **Discipline** and click **OK**.

Excel inserts the Discipline slicer in the worksheet. Six slicer buttons are blue, indicating that those disciplines are selected. The grayed-out buttons at the bottom of the slicer indicate those disciplines are not applicable based on other engaged filters you set (first and second editions and 2016 and 2017 copyright years).

c. Press and hold **Ctrl** as you click **Aging/Death** in the Discipline slicer.

This deselects the Aging/Death discipline.

> **TROUBLESHOOTING**: Because several disciplines are selected, if you click Aging/Death instead of pressing Ctrl as you click it, you set Aging/Death as the only discipline. The others are filtered out. If this happens, immediately click Undo and repeat step c.

d. Drag the slicer to the right side of the PivotTable.

You moved the slicer so that it does not cover up data in the PivotTable.

e. Change the **Columns value** to **2** in the Buttons group on the SLICER TOOLS OPTIONS tab. Change the button **Width** to **1.5"** in the Buttons group.

The slicer now displays buttons in two columns. You changed the width of the buttons to 1.5" to display the full discipline names within the buttons.

f. Change the slicer **Height** to **2** in the Size group.

The slicer window is now only 2" tall.

g. Click the **More button** in the Slicer Styles group and click **Slicer Style Dark 1**. Save the workbook.

Based on the selected workbook theme, Slicer Style Dark 1 applies a dark blue fill color for selected disciplines, dark gray and black font for available but not currently selected disciplines, and light gray fill with medium gray font for nonapplicable disciplines.

STEP 3 ≫ CREATE A CALCULATED FIELD

You want to calculate the amount of the sales returned to the authors as royalties. Although the 10% royalty rate is stored in cell J2 in the Books Data worksheet, the value must be used in the calculated field because range names and cell references outside the PivotTable cannot be used. Refer to Figure 7.27 as you complete Step 3.

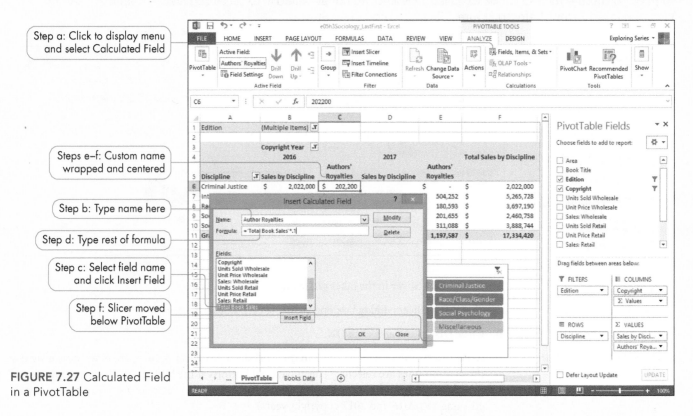

FIGURE 7.27 Calculated Field in a PivotTable

a. Click within the PivotTable, click the **ANALYZE tab**, click **Fields, Items, & Sets** in the Calculations group, and then select **Calculated Field**.

The Insert Calculated Field dialog box opens.

b. Type **Author Royalties** in the **Name box**.

c. Scroll down the Fields list, click **Total Book Sales**, and then click **Insert Field**.

Excel starts to build the formula, which is currently ='Total Book Sales'.

d. Type *.1 at the end of the **Formula box** and click **OK**.

Excel adds Sum of Author Royalties calculated field columns, one for each copyright year category. It calculates the authors' royalties as 10% of the total sales for each copyright year.

e. Right-click the **Sum of Author Royalties heading** in cell C5, select **Value Field Settings**, type **Authors' Royalties** in the **Custom Name box**, and then click **OK**.

f. Move the slicer below the PivotTable. Select **cells C5 and E5**, wrap text for field names, set **30** row height, **12** column widths, and center column labels.

g. Save the workbook.

STEP 4 ➤➤ SHOW VALUES AS CALCULATIONS

You want to see what copyright year generated the largest sales for each discipline, which discipline contributes the largest percentage of the total sociology sales, and which introductory book has the largest sales contribution within that discipline. Refer to Figure 7.28 as you complete Step 4.

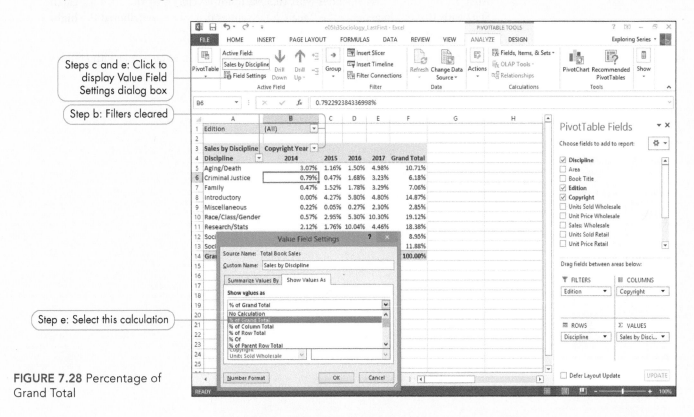

FIGURE 7.28 Percentage of Grin Total

a. Right-click the **PivotTable worksheet tab**, select **Move or Copy**, click **Books Data** in the *Before sheet* list, click the **Create a copy check box**, and then click **OK**.

   You copied the PivotTable worksheet to maintain the previous tasks you completed as evidence. You will work with the PivotTable (2) worksheet, which is the active worksheet.

b. Do the following to remove filters, slicer, and Authors' Royalties field:
   • Click the **Edition filter** in **cell B1**, click the **(All) check box**, and then click **OK** to clear the Edition filter.
   • Click the **Discipline filter** in **cell A5** and select **Clear Filter From "Discipline"**.
   • Click the **Copyright Year filter** in **cell B3** and select **Clear Filter From "Copyright"**.
   • Select the slicer and press **Delete**.
   • Click the **Authors' Royalties** in the VALUES area of the task pane and select **Remove Field**.

c. Click within any value in the PivotTable, click the **ANALYZE tab**, and then click **Field Settings** in the Active Field group.

   The Value Field Settings dialog box opens.

d. Click the **Show Values As tab**, click the **Show values as arrow**, select **% of Row Total**, and then click **OK**.

   Excel displays each copyright year's values as percentages for that discipline. All disciplines except Introductory and Research/Stats had the highest percentage of sales for the books with a 2017 copyright. These two disciplines had their highest percentage of sales for books with a 2016 copyright.

e. Click the **Field Settings** in the Active Field group, click the **Show Values As tab** within the dialog box, select **% of Grand Total**, and then click **OK**.

See Figure 7.28. Each discipline's yearly value displays as a percentage of the total sales. Which discipline and for what copyright year produces the highest percentage of total sales? Answer: 2017 Race/Class/Gender with 10.30%, followed closely by the 2016 Research/Stats with 10.04%. In general, the Race/Class/Gender discipline contributed the highest percentage of the total sales with 19.12%.

f. Save the workbook and keep the workbook open if you plan to continue with Hands-On Exercise 4. If not, close the workbook and exit Excel.

PivotTable Design and PivotCharts

After you create and modify the structure of a PivotTable, you can focus on the overall appearance and format of the PivotTable. The PivotTable Tools Design tab enables you to control the position of grouped calculations and the PivotTable style. In addition to finalizing the PivotTable's appearance, you might want to create a PivotChart to depict the consolidated data in a visual form.

In this section, you will apply a different style to and change the layout of a PivotTable. In addition, you will create and format a PivotChart.

Formatting a PivotTable

Excel applies basic formatting to PivotTables. For example, it formats primary row labels in bold to distinguish those categories from the subcategories. In addition, the subtotals are bold to offset these values from the subcategory values. The PivotTable Tools Design tab contains commands for enhancing the format of a PivotTable (see Figure 7.29).

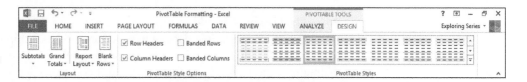

FIGURE 7.29 PivotTable Tools Design Tab

STEP 1 »

A PivotTable style controls bold formatting, font colors, shading colors, and border lines. To change the style, click the PivotTable Tools Design tab and click the More button in the PivotTable Styles group to display the PivotTable Styles gallery (see Figure 7.30). Select the most appropriate style that accentuates the data in your PivotTable. As you move the pointer over the gallery, Excel shows how that style will affect the PivotTable. Click a style to apply it to the PivotTable.

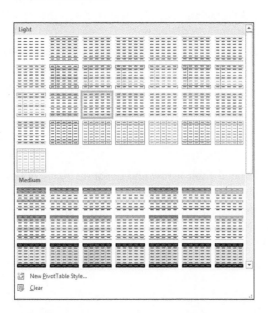

FIGURE 7.30 PivotTable Styles

After you apply a style, you can select which areas of the PivotTable are affected by the style. Select check boxes in the PivotTable Style Options group to apply formats to row headers, column headers, banded rows, and banded columns.

By default, the VALUES area consolidates data by showing subtotals for each category. You can customize the location of subtotals by clicking Subtotals in the Layout group on the

Design tab. For example, when the PivotTable is large, displaying the subtotals at the top of the group draws attention to the totals and enables you to scroll to view all of the supporting data if necessary. Table 7.7 describes the Subtotals options.

TABLE 7.7   PivotTable Subtotals Options

Option	Description
Do Not Show Subtotals	Removes subtotals for each category but retains the category names and displays aggregated values for the subcategories.
Show All Subtotals at Bottom of Group	Displays category subtotals below the last subcategory value within each category. Subtotal labels and values appear in bold.
Show All Subtotals at Top of Group	Displays category subtotals at the top of the list on the same row as the category labels. This approach takes up fewer rows than Show All Subtotals at Bottom of Group.
Include Filtered Items in Totals	Includes values for filtered items in the total rows and columns. (Active only when a filter has been applied.)

Using PowerPivot Functionality

PowerPivot is a built-in add-in program in Excel 2013 that enables you to import millions of rows of data from multiple data sources, create a relationship between two or more related tables within one workbook (similar to creating relationships among tables in Access), and maintain connections. For example, one table contains sales representatives' names and IDs. A related table contains the sales dates and sales amounts but only the sales reps' IDs to avoid mistyping a person's name. You must create a relationship based on a common field (such as ID) between the tables. A *relationship* is an association between two related tables where both tables contain a related field of data, such as IDs.

After you create a relationship between tables, you can use PowerPivot to create a PivotTable from both tables. After you create the relationship, you can use the common field to display the sales reps' names instead of their IDs. To create a relationship, do the following:

1. Click the DATA tab and click Relationships in the Data Tools group to open the Manage Relationships dialog box.
2. Click New in the dialog box to open the Create Relationship dialog box (see Figure 7.31).
3. Click the Table arrow and select the name of the primary table. The primary table in this example is SALES.
4. Click the Column (Foreign) arrow and select the name of the column that contains a relationship to the related or lookup table. For example, the column that relates to the other table is REPS.
5. Click the Related Table arrow and select the name of the related or lookup table. For example, the related table is REPS.
6. Click the Related Column (Primary) arrow and select the name of the column that is related to the primary table. For example, the ID column relates to the Rep column in the SALES table. Click OK.

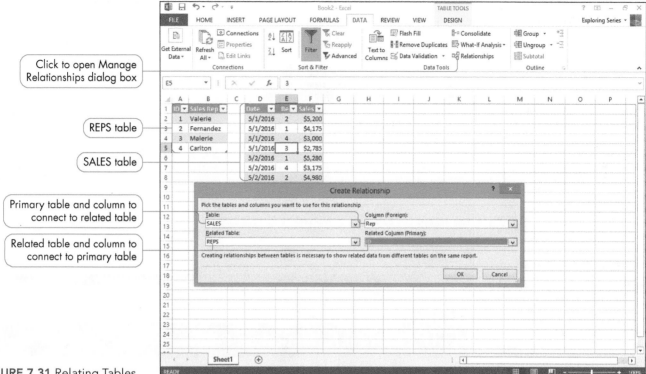

Click to open Manage Relationships dialog box

REPS table

SALES table

Primary table and column to connect to related table

Related table and column to connect to primary table

FIGURE 7.31 Relating Tables

After you create a relationship between the tables, you can use PowerPivot to create a PivotTable based on the relationship. Do the following to create a PivotTable using two related tables:

1. Click within the primary table.
2. Click the INSERT tab and click PivotTable in the Tables group to open the Create PivotTable dialog box (see Figure 7.32).
3. Make sure the primary table name displays in the Table/Range box.
4. Click the *Add this data to the Data Model* check box and click OK.

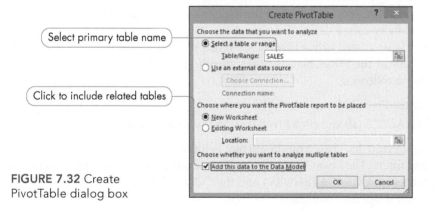

Select primary table name

Click to include related tables

FIGURE 7.32 Create PivotTable dialog box

In the PivotTable Fields task pane, click ALL to display the names of all related tables. Then click the table names to display their field names. From there, you can arrange the fields in the different area boxes at the bottom of the task pane (see Figure 7.33).

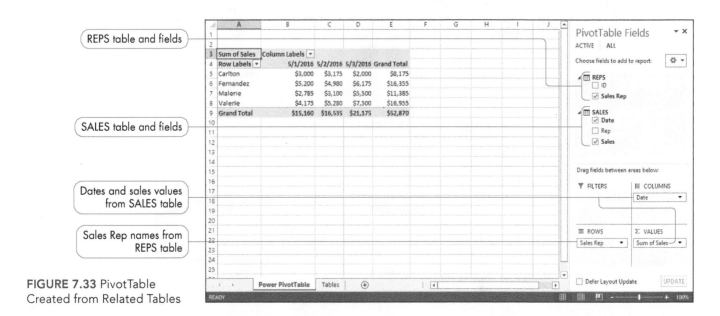

REPS table and fields

SALES table and fields

Dates and sales values from SALES table

Sales Rep names from REPS table

FIGURE 7.33 PivotTable Created from Related Tables

TIP | **More Information on Power PivotTables**

Look up the topic *What's new in PowerPivot in Excel 2013* to learn more about the PowerPivot functionality and how to create PivotTables from related tables. The Help menu also informs you which versions of Microsoft Office 2013 contain this feature and how you can enable it.

Creating a PivotChart

Charts display data visually. This visual representation may help you and your audience understand the data better than merely presenting the data in a spreadsheet. Although PivotTables help reduce the amount of data to analyze, PivotTables can be overwhelming. Another way to display a PivotTable's aggregated data is through a PivotChart. A *PivotChart* is an interactive graphical representation of the data in a PivotTable. A PivotChart presents the consolidated data visually.

A PivotChart is associated with a PivotTable. When you change the position of a field in either the PivotTable or the PivotChart, the corresponding object changes as well. To create a PivotChart, do the following:

1. Click inside the PivotTable.
2. Click the ANALYZE tab and click PivotChart in the Tools group.

Excel creates a PivotChart based on the current PivotTable settings—row labels, column labels, values, and filters. The PivotChart contains elements that enable you to set filters. The ROWS area changes to AXIS (CATEGORY) and the COLUMNS area changes to LEGEND (SERIES) when you select the PivotChart (see Figure 7.34).

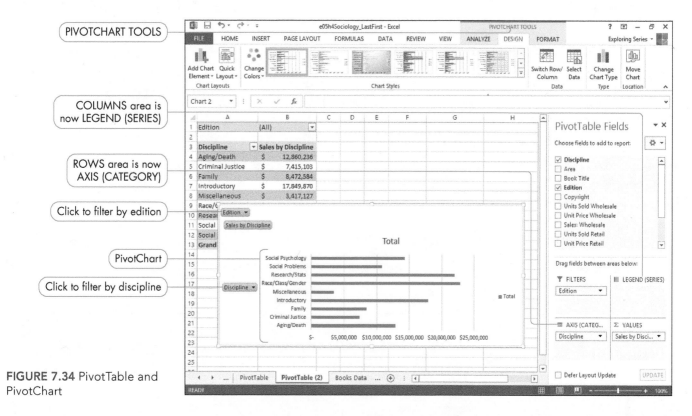

PIVOTCHART TOOLS

COLUMNS area is now LEGEND (SERIES)

ROWS area is now AXIS (CATEGORY)

Click to filter by edition

PivotChart

Click to filter by discipline

FIGURE 7.34 PivotTable and PivotChart

Although Excel creates the PivotChart based on the current PivotTable settings, you can change the settings using the PivotTable Field List. Click the FILTERS arrow and select values to filter the chart. Click the AXIS (CATEGORY) arrows to sort or filter the categories and subcategories in rows. Click the LEGEND (SERIES) to filter the chart representation based on the values. Changes you make to the PivotChart also affect the corresponding PivotTable. For example, if you apply a filter to the PivotChart, Excel also filters the PivotTable.

The Chart Tools Analyze tab contains the same options that you used to customize a PivotTable. In addition, the Actions group contains the Move Chart option so that you can move a PivotChart to a different worksheet.

The Chart Tools Design tab contains options to add a chart element, apply a layout, change colors, and apply a chart style. In addition, you can switch the data between the category axis and the legend, select the data used to create the chart, change the chart type, and move the chart to a different worksheet.

You can further customize PivotChart elements the same way you can customize regular charts—display data labels, change the fill color for a data series, display axis titles, and so forth. Use Help to learn more about customizing PivotCharts.

Quick Concepts

1. What types of specific elements can you select to be controlled by PivotTable styles? **p. 369**

2. What must be done to create a PivotTable from more than one table? **p. 370**

3. What replaces the ROWS and COLUMNS in the task pane when you create a PivotChart? **p. 372**

Hands-On Exercises

Watch the Video for this Hands-On Exercise!

MyITLab®
HOE4 Training

4 PivotTable Design and PivotCharts

You want to format the PivotTable to make it easier for you to analyze the sales data. In addition, you want to create a PivotChart to depict sales data.

Skills covered: Apply a PivotTable Style • Create a PivotChart

STEP 1 ⟫ APPLY A PIVOTTABLE STYLE

To enhance the readability of the sociology textbook PivotTable, you will apply a style. Refer to Figure 7.35 as you complete Step 1.

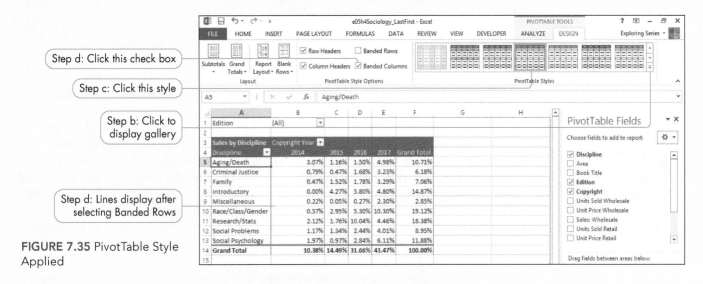

FIGURE 7.35 PivotTable Style Applied

a. Open *e05h3Sociology_LastFirst* if you closed it at the end of Hands-On Exercise 3 and save it as **e05h4Sociology_LastFirst**, changing *h3* to *h4*.

b. Make sure the PivotTable (2) sheet is active. Click a cell within the PivotTable, click the **DESIGN tab**, and then click the **More button** in the PivotTable Styles group.

   The PivotTable Style gallery displays styles that you can apply.

c. Click **Pivot Style Medium 3** to apply a dark red style to the PivotTable.

d. Click the **Banded Columns check box** in the PivotTable Style Options group to add dark red vertical lines between the columns. Save the workbook.

You want to create a PivotChart to depict the sales data by discipline. Refer to Figure 7.36 as you complete Step 2.

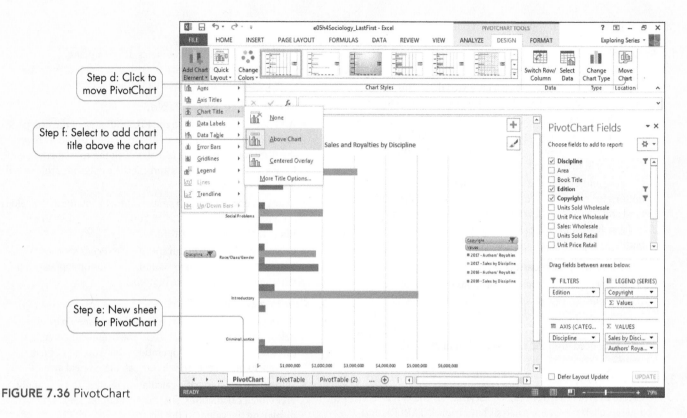

Step d: Click to move PivotChart

Step f: Select to add chart title above the chart

Step e: New sheet for PivotChart

FIGURE 7.36 PivotChart

a. Click the **PivotTable sheet tab** and click inside the PivotTable.

b. Click the **ANALYZE tab** and click **PivotChart** in the Tools group.

   The Insert Chart dialog box opens.

c. Click **Bar** and click **OK**.

   Excel creates a clustered bar PivotChart based on the PivotTable. Any changes you make to the PivotChart will also affect the PivotTable.

d. Click the **PIVOTCHART TOOLS DESIGN tab** and click **Move Chart** in the Location group.

   The Move Sheet dialog box opens.

e. Click **New sheet**, type **PivotChart**, and then click **OK**.

   The PivotChart is now on its own sheet.

f. Click the **DESIGN tab**, click **Add Chart Element**, point to *Chart Title*, and then select **Above Chart**.

   A Chart Title placeholder displays above the plot area in the PivotChart.

g. Type **Sales and Royalties by Discipline** and press **Enter**.

h. Save and close the workbook, and submit based on your instructor's directions.

Chapter Objectives Review

After reading this chapter, you have accomplished the following objectives:

1. **Subtotal data.**
   - The Subtotal dialog box enables you to insert subtotals, such as sums or averages, based on sorted data. This feature detects changes between categories arranged in rows to insert the subtotal rows.
   - Add a second level of subtotals: To keep the first level and add a second level, deselect the *Replace current* subtotals check box in the Subtotals dialog box.
   - Collapse and expand the subtotals: Click the outline level buttons to collapse the subtotals to the grand total, grand total and subtotals, or entire dataset. Click a particular collapse button to collapse a category, or click an expand button to expand a particular category.

2. **Group and ungroup data.**
   - If the data contain columns of formulas based on other columns and/or row subtotals, use the auto outline process to create an outline based on the data structure. You can then collapse and expand the outline as you review the data. If you no longer need grouped data, select and ungroup the data again.

3. **Create a PivotTable.**
   - Create a PivotTable from the Quick Analysis Gallery: Select a range, click the Quick Analysis button, click TABLES, and click the desired PivotTable thumbnail.
   - Create a PivotTable from the Ribbon: Use the Ribbon to create a blank PivotTable or to display the Recommended PivotTables dialog box to create a PivotTable.

4. **Modify a PivotTable.**
   - Add rows and values: Drag fields to the ROWS and VALUES areas of the PivotTable Fields task pane to add row categories and columns of aggregated values.
   - Add columns: Drag fields to the COLUMNS area to add additional columns of details.
   - Collapse and expand items: Click the collapse button to collapse subcategory rows and click the expand button to expand a subcategory of details.
   - Remove fields: Click a field name in the respective area of the task pane and select Remove Field.
   - Rearrange fields: Drag fields from one area to another in the task pane to rearrange fields in the PivotTable.
   - Change the value field settings: You can select a different function to calculate the statistics in the PivotTable. You can also apply number formatting and specify a custom column heading for value columns.

   - Refresh a PivotTable: PivotTables do not update automatically if you change the original dataset. You must click Refresh to update the PivotTable.

5. **Filter and slice a PivotTable.**
   - Add filters: Drag a field to the FILTERS area of the task pane and click the Filter arrow at the top of the PivotTable to set the filter conditions. You can also click the row labels arrow in cell A4 to set row filters and click the column arrow in cell B3 to set column filters.
   - Insert slicers: A slicer is a small window containing the values for a particular field. You click buttons in the slicer to set filters for that particular field.
   - Customize slicers: You can specify the slicer's style and size. You can specify how many columns of buttons appear in the slicer and the size of those buttons.

6. **Create a calculated field.**
   - A calculated field is a user-defined field based on other fields. This field does not exist in the original dataset. You can use basic arithmetic operations, but you cannot use cell references or range names in the calculated field syntax.
   - Show values as a specific calculation results: You can apply predefined calculations, such as *% of Grand Total*, for displaying the values in the PivotTable.

7. **Format a PivotTable.**
   - The PivotTable Tools Design tab enables you to improve the appearance of a PivotTable by applying a PivotTable style. The style controls the fill color, bold formatting, and other formatting aspects of data in the PivotTable.

8. **Use PowerPivot Functionality.**
   - You can create relationships between two or more related tables within one workbook. After creating the relationships, you can use PowerPivot to create a PivotTable that uses fields from the related tables.

9. **Create a PivotChart.**
   - The PivotChart is similar to creating a regular chart, except it is based on the categories and structure of the PivotTable, not the original dataset. You can customize a PivotChart with the same methods you use to customize a regular chart. If you change fields or sort in either the PivotTable or the PivotChart, Excel automatically adjusts the corresponding pivot object.

Key Terms Matching

Match the key terms with their definitions. Write the key term letter by the appropriate numbered definition.

a. Calculated field
b. Columns area
c. Data mining
d. Filters area
e. Grouping
f. Outline
g. PivotChart
h. PivotTable

i. PivotTable Fields task pane
j. PowerPivot
k. Relationship
l. Rows area
m. Slicer
n. Slicer caption
o. Subtotal
p. Values area

1. _____ An association created between two tables where both tables contain a matching field. **p. 370**

2. _____ A hierarchical structure of data. **p. 340**

3. _____ A row within a dataset that displays the total or another statistic for a particular category. **p. 339**

4. _____ A process of joining related rows or columns of related data. **p. 341**

5. _____ The process of analyzing large volumes of data to identify patterns and trends. **p. 346**

6. _____ An organized structure that summarizes large amounts of data without altering the original dataset. **p. 346**

7. _____ A user-defined field that performs a calculation based on other fields in a PivotTable. **p. 362**

8. _____ A window listing all items in a field and enabling efficient filtering. **p. 360**

9. _____ Drag fields here to display categories horizontally in a PivotTable. **p. 349**

10. _____ Drag fields here to display data as aggregates, such as sums or averages. **p. 349**

11. _____ Drag fields here to be able to specify which values or content to include or exclude in the PivotTable. **p. 349**

12. _____ Drag fields here to add more vertical data to a PivotTable. **p. 349**

13. _____ A graphical representation of aggregated data derived from a PivotTable. **p. 372**

14. _____ A window that enables you to drag fields to particular areas to build and arrange data in a PivotTable. **p. 349**

15. _____ The label that appears at the top of a slicer window. By default, it displays the name of the field used. **p. 361**

16. _____ A built-in add-in program that enables users to create a PivotTable from multiple related tables. **p. 370**

Multiple Choice

1. A worksheet contains data for businesses that are sponsoring this year's Arts Festival. The worksheet contains these columns in this sequence: Business Name, Address, City, State, and Donation Amount. Data are sorted by State and then by City. What is the default *At a change in* setting within the Subtotal dialog box, and what would be a more appropriate setting?

   (a) Business Name (default field), Donation Amount (correct field)
   (b) Business Name (default field), State (correct field)
   (c) Donation Amount (default field), Address (correct field)
   (d) Address (default field), Donation Amount (correct field)

2. You created an outline for a dataset. What does the + button indicate to the left of a row heading?

   (a) You can add a new row at that location only.
   (b) One or more columns are hidden.
   (c) You can click it to collapse the details of that category.
   (d) You can click it to expand the details of that category.

3. A worksheet contains a PivotTable placeholder and the PivotTable Fields task pane. Where do you drag the State field if you want a list of each state in the first column of the PivotTable?

   (a) FILTERS area
   (b) COLUMNS area
   (c) ROWS area
   (d) VALUES area

4. You just created a slicer for the State field in a PivotTable. Which of the following does *not* characterize the initial slicer?

   (a) The slicer buttons are set to filter out all records.
   (b) The slicer caption is State.
   (c) The slicer contains one column of state names or abbreviations.
   (d) The slicer may display on top of the PivotTable data.

5. You created a PivotTable and made some changes to values in the original dataset from which the PivotTable was created. How does this affect the PivotTable?

   (a) The PivotTable updates automatically when you make changes to the dataset.
   (b) You must create a new PivotTable if you want updated results in a PivotTable.
   (c) Click the DATA tab and click Update to update the PivotTable to reflect changes you made in the dataset.
   (d) Click Refresh in the Data group on the ANALYZE tab to update the PivotTable.

6. You created a PivotTable to summarize salaries by department. What is the default summary statistic for the salaries in the PivotTable?

   (a) Average
   (b) Sum
   (c) Count
   (d) Max

7. What settings should you select for a PivotTable if you want to apply a different color scheme and display different fill colors for main category rows and horizontal lines within the PivotTable?

   (a) Banded Rows and Banded Columns check boxes
   (b) Banded Columns check box and a different PivotTable style
   (c) Banded Rows check box and a different PivotTable style
   (d) A different PivotTable style only

8. Which PivotTable calculated field is correctly constructed to calculate a 20% tip on a meal at a restaurant?

   (a) =Meal Cost * 20%
   (b) ='Meal Cost'*.2
   (c) ="Meal Cost"*.2
   (d) =B5*1.2

9. You have created a PivotChart showing sales by quarter by sales rep. Before presenting it to management, you notice the name of a rep who has since been fired. How do you remove this rep from the chart without deleting the data?

   (a) Filter the Sales Rep field in the PivotChart and deselect the employee's check box.
   (b) Make the employee's data points and axis titles invisible.
   (c) You cannot delete the rep from the chart without first deleting the data.
   (d) Hide that rep's row(s) in the underlying list, which automatically removes that rep from the chart.

10. Currently, the House Types field is in the Row Labels area, the Real Estate Agent field is in the Column Labels area, and Sum of List Prices is in the VALUES area. How can you modify the PivotTable to display the agent names as subcategories within the house types in the first column?

    (a) Drag the Real Estate Agent field from the Column Labels area and drop it above the House Types field in the Row Labels area.
    (b) Drag the House Types field from the ROWS area and drop it below the Real Estate Agent field in the COLUMNS area.
    (c) Drag the House Types field from the ROWS area to the FILTERS area and drag the Real Estate Agent field from the COLUMNS area to the ROWS area.
    (d) Drag the Real Estate Agent field from the COLUMNS area and drop it below the House Types field in the ROWS area.

1 The Men's Store

You work at the Men's Store, a men's department store in Cheyenne, Wyoming. You need to analyze a year's worth of transactions to determine which salesperson had the highest overall sales and which salesperson had the best sales in the Dress Shirts and Ties category. You will use the Subtotal feature and outline the list of transactions for the year. This exercise follows the same set of skills as used in Hands-On Exercise 1 in the chapter. Refer to Figure 7.37 as you complete this exercise.

	Order Date	Salesperson	Category	Sale Item	Total Amount
22			Accessories Total		$ 8,673.23
70			Casual wear Total		$ 32,870.22
101			Dress Shirts and Ties Total		$ 19,280.39
126			Sport Jackets and Slacks Total		$ 28,679.05
175			Suits Total		$ 71,981.32
188			Underwear Total		$ 1,024.91
189		Adams Total			$ 162,509.12
220			Accessories Total		$ 8,893.02
296			Casual Wear Total		$ 41,884.53
322			Dress Shirts and Ties Total		$ 12,167.17
360			Sport Jackets and Slacks Total		$ 41,201.04
408			Suits Total		$ 80,843.55
421			Underwear Total		$ 1,248.57
422		Baker Total			$ 186,237.88
443			Accessories Total		$ 6,527.99
489			Casual wear Total		$ 22,565.30
511			Dress Shirts and Ties Total		$ 9,878.98
535			Sport Jackets and Slacks Total		$ 24,945.13
576			Suits Total		$ 59,443.75
591			Underwear Total		$ 1,680.33
592		Davis Total			$ 124,841.48
613			Accessories Total		$ 8,595.89
654			Casual Wear Total		$ 19,318.44
687			Dress Shirts and Ties Total		$ 18,170.45
716			Sport Jackets and Slacks Total		$ 29,509.26
763			Suits Total		$ 68,538.25
772			Underwear Total		$ 785.42
773		Goodman Total			$ 144,917.71
774		Grand Total			$ 618,506.18
775					

FIGURE 7.37 Subtotals

a. Open *e05p1MensStore* and save it as **e05p1MensStore_LastFirst**.

b. Sort the list by salesperson and then by category within salesperson.

c. Click the **DATA tab** and click **Subtotal** in the Outline group. Do the following in the Subtotal dialog box:
  • Click the **At each change in arrow** and select **Salesperson**.
  • Click the **Order Amount check box** and the **Sales Tax check box** in the *Add subtotal to* list.
  • Keep the *Total Amount* check box selected. Click **OK**.

d. Add a second-level subtotal by category by doing the following:
  • Click **Subtotal** in the Outline group.
  • Click the **At each change in arrow** and select **Category**.
  • Keep the *Order Total*, *Sales Tax*, and *Total Amount* check boxes selected.
  • Click the **Replace current subtotals check box** to deselect it. Click **OK**.

e. Click **2** to collapse the list to see the salesperson subtotals. Who had the highest order totals for the year? Who had the lowest order totals for the year?

f. Click **3** to expand the list to see category subtotals for each salesperson. Who had the highest dress shirts and tie sales for the year? Is this the same person who had the overall highest order totals for the year?

g. Click the **Group arrow** in the Outline group on the DATA tab and select **Auto Outline**. Click **OK** when prompted to modify the existing outline. Click the **collapse button** above column G to collapse the columns.

h. Create a footer with your name on the left side, the sheet name code in the center, and the file name code on the right side.

i. Save and close the workbook, and submit based on your instructor's directions.

Your college friend Cirio owns a successful Greek restaurant in Denver, Colorado. He tracks daily dinner revenue but needs your assistance to consolidate data for the entire year. Specifically, he wants to compare quarterly totals by weekday, and he wants to take a closer look at the fourth-quarter revenue. You will insert two functions to complete the main worksheet and then create a relationship between that table and a related table of weekday names. You will build a PivotTable and a PivotChart to help Cirio analyze the weekday revenue by quarters. This exercise follows the same set of skills as used in Hands-On Exercises 2–4 in the chapter. Refer to Figure 7.38 as you complete this exercise.

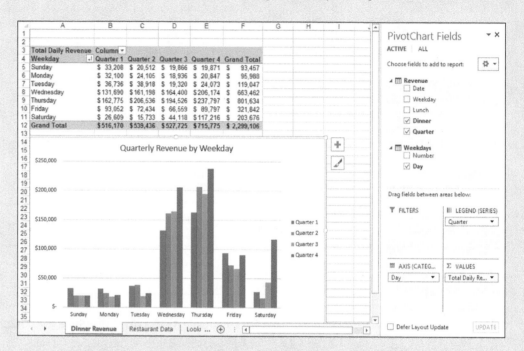

FIGURE 7.38 PivotTable and PivotChart

a. Open *e05p2Dinner* and save it as **e05p2Dinner_LastFirst**. Click the **Lookup Tables worksheet tab** to see the two datasets. The first dataset is a table named Weekdays that will be used to relate the day numbers (such as 2) with the names of the weekdays (such as Monday). The second dataset is a lookup table range-named Quarters so that you can create a VLOOKUP function to look up a value within a breakpoint, identified by month numbers, and return which quarter the month is in. For example, the fifth month (5) returns Quarter 2.

b. Create two formulas to calculate missing values by doing the following:

- Click the **Restaurant Data worksheet tab**, click in **cell B2**, type **=WEEKDAY(A2)**, and then press **Enter**. For 1/1/2016, the WEEKDAY function returns 6, which represents Friday.
- Click **cell E2**, type **=VLOOKUP(MONTH(A2),Quarters,2)**, and then press **Enter**. MONTH(A2) returns the month from the data in cell A2, which is 1. The VLOOKUP function looks up the month number in the lookup table that is range-named Quarters and returns the quarter of the year for that date. For example, months 1 through 3 return Quarter 1.

DISCOVER

c. Create a relationship between the Revenues table in the Restaurant Data worksheet and the Weekdays table in the Lookup Tables worksheet by doing the following:

- Click the **DATA tab** and click **Relationships** in the Data Tools group to open the Manage Relationships dialog box.
- Click **New** to open the Create Relationships dialog box.
- Click the **Table arrow** and select **Revenue** (the main table). Click the **Column (Foreign) arrow** and select **Weekday**.
- Click the **Related Table arrow** and select **Weekdays**. Click the **Related Column (Primary) arrow** and select **Number**.
- Click **OK** to close the Create Relationships dialog box. Click **Close** to close the Manage Relationships dialog box.

d. Use PowerPivot to create a PivotTable using the related tables by doing the following:
- Click the **INSERT tab** and click **PivotTable** in the Tables group to open the Create PivotTable dialog box.
- Click the **Add this data to the Data Model check box** in the *Choose whether you want to analyze multiple tables* section. Click **OK**.
- Click **ALL** at the top of the PivotTable Fields task pane to display all table names.
- Click **Revenue** at the top of the task pane to display the fields for the Revenue table.
- Click the **Dinner** and **Quarter check boxes** in the task pane and drag **Quarter** from the ROWS area to the COLUMNS area.
- Scroll down, if necessary, and click **Weekdays** in the task pane to display the fields for the Weekdays table.
- Click the **Day check box** in the task pane to add this field to the ROWS area.

e. Modify the PivotTable by doing the following:
- Click the **Row Labels arrow** in **cell A4** and select **Sort A to Z**. (Note that this action sorts in sequential order by weekday, not alphabetical order by weekday name.)
- Click **cell A4**, type **Weekday**, and then press **Enter**.
- Click the **DESIGN tab**, click the **More button** in the PivotTable Styles group, and then click **Pivot Style Light 15**.

f. Format the values by doing the following:
- Click **cell B5**, click the **ANALYZE tab**, and then click **Field Settings** in the Active Field group.
- Type **Total Daily Revenue** in the **Custom Name box**.
- Click **Number Format**, click **Accounting**, click the **Decimal places spin arrow** to display *0*, click **OK** in the Format Cells dialog box, and then click **OK** in the Value Field Settings dialog box.
- Set a column width of **9** for column B.

g. Create a PivotChart from the PivotTable by doing the following.
- Click **PivotChart** in the Tools group on the ANALYZE tab and click **OK** in the Insert Chart dialog box to create a default column chart.
- Click the **DESIGN tab**, click **Quick Layout** in the Chart Layouts group, and then click **Layout 1**.
- Click the **Chart Title placeholder**, type **Quarterly Revenue by Weekday**, and then press **Enter**.
- Move the chart so that the top-left corner starts in **cell A14**. Resize the chart to extend through **cell H35**.
- Click the **ANALYZE tab**, click **Field Buttons** in the Show/Hide group, and then select **Hide All** to hide the buttons within the chart area.

h. Rename the Sheet1 worksheet **Dinner Revenue**. Create a footer with your name on the left side, the sheet name code in the center, and the file name code on the right side on each worksheet.

i. Save and close the workbook, and submit based on your instructor's directions.

Greek Restaurant Combined Revenue

Cirio needs to conduct additional revenue analysis. Now he wants you to create a PivotTable that displays the daily percentage of revenue that contributes to the total lunch and dinner revenues, respectively. Because he has a list of several ways to view the data, you decide to insert slicers so that Cirio can filter the PivotTable data himself. This exercise follows the same set of skills as used in Hands-On Exercises 2–4 in the chapter. Refer to Figure 7.39 as you complete this exercise.

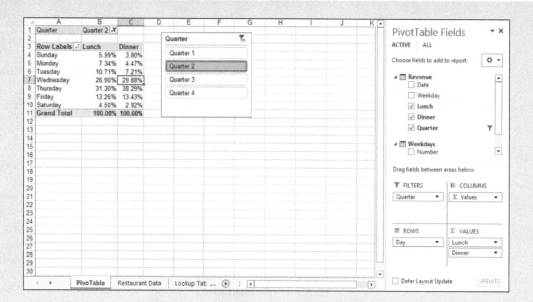

FIGURE 7.39 PivotTable and Slicers

a. Open *e05p3Revenue* and save it as **e05p3Revenue_LastFirst**.

b. Use PowerPivot to create a PivotTable using the related tables by doing the following:
  - Click the **INSERT tab** and click **PivotTable** in the Tables group to open the Create PivotTable dialog box.
  - Click the **Add this data to the Data Model check box** in the *Choose whether you want to analyze multiple tables* section. Click **OK**.
  - Click **ALL** at the top of the PivotTable Fields task pane to display all table names.
  - Click **Weekdays** at the top of the task pane to display the fields for the Weekday table.
  - Drag **Day** to the ROWS area.
  - Click **Revenue** in the task pane to display the fields for the Revenue table.
  - Drag the **Quarter field** to the FILTERS area.
  - Click the **Lunch** and **Dinner check boxes** to add them to the VALUES area.
  - Click the **Row Labels arrow** in **cell A3** and select **Sort A to Z**.

c. Display the daily revenue as a percentage of total weekly sales for lunch by doing the following:
  - Click **cell B4** and click **Field Settings** in the Active Field group to open the Value Field Settings dialog box.
  - Type **Lunch** in the **Custom Name box**.
  - Click the **Show Values As tab** in the dialog box, click the **Show Value As arrow**, and then select **% of Column Total**. Click **OK** in the Value Field Settings dialog box.
  - Apply the custom name **Dinner** to **cell C4** and show the values as *% of Column Total*. Click **OK** to close the dialog box.

d. Click **Insert Slicer** in the Filter group, click the **Quarter check box** in the Insert Slicer dialog box, and then click **OK**.

e. Move the slicer to the right of the PivotTable, click the **SLICER TOOLS OPTIONS tab**, enter **1.8** in the **Width box** in the Size group, and then enter **1.77** in the **Height box** in the Size group.

f. Click the **Quarter 2 slicer slice** to filter the PivotTable by the second quarter of the year.

g. Create a footer with your name on the left side, the sheet name code in the center, and the file name code on the right side on each worksheet.

h. Save and close the workbook, and submit based on your instructor's directions.

1 Mountain View Realty

ANALYSIS CASE

You are a real estate analyst who works for Mountain View Realty in the North Utah County area. You have consolidated a list of houses sold during the past few months and need to start analyzing the data. For a simple analysis, you will outline the data and use the Subtotal feature. Then you will create a PivotTable to give you a way to perform more in-depth analysis.

a. Open *e05m1RealEstate* and save it as **e05m1RealEstate_LastFirst**.

b. Make sure the Sales Subtotals worksheet is the active sheet. Insert a column between the Selling Price and Listing Date columns. Enter the heading **% of Asking Price** and double-click between the column G and H headings to increase the column width. Insert a formula in **cell G2** to calculate the selling price percentage of the asking price, format it with **Percent Style** with one decimal place, and then copy the formula down the column.

c. Enter the heading **Days on Market** on the right side of the last column and double-click between the column J and K headings to increase the column width. Calculate the number of days between the listing date and sale date. Copy the formula down the column.

d. Sort the list by city in alphabetical order, then by selling agent in alphabetical order, and finally by listing date in chronological order.

e. Use the Subtotal feature to calculate the average selling price, percentage of asking price, and days on market by city.

f. Apply an automatic outline to the columns. Collapse the outline to hide the listing and sale dates. Click the appropriate button to display the grand average and city average rows only. Format the average days on market to zero decimal places. Apply wrap text, **10.00** column width, and increased row height to **cells G1 and J1**. Set a print area for the **range C1:J88**.

⭐ g. Go to **cell C95** in the Sales Subtotals worksheet. Read the questions and provide the appropriate answers in the respective highlighted cells in the **range G96:G100**.

h. Click the **Sales Data worksheet** and create a PivotTable on a new worksheet. Name the new worksheet **PivotTable**.

i. Display the cities in the first row of the PivotTable, selling agents in the first column, and asking and selling prices in additional columns.

j. Modify the PivotTable. Display averages rather than sums with **Accounting Number Format** with zero decimal places. Pivot the data by placing the cities in columns and the selling agents in rows.

k. Add a group filter to display only Alpine and Cedar Hills.

l. Adjust column widths, wrap text as needed, insert a bottom border line below the city names, and then add a more descriptive label for the first column and any other columns that need more descriptive labels. Adjust row heights so that column labels fully display.

m. Go back to the Sales Data worksheet. You realize that a selling price is incorrect. Change the selling price for Number 40 from *$140,000* to **$1,400,000**. Refresh the PivotTable.

n. Create a footer with your name on the left side, the sheet name code in the center, and the file name code on the right side for the Sales Subtotals and the PivotTable worksheets. Adjust the margins and scaling to fit on one page.

o. Save and close the workbook, and submit based on your instructor's directions.

2 Fiesta® Collection

Your Aunt Laura has been collecting Fiesta dinnerware, a popular brand from the Homer Laughlin China Company, since 1986. You help her maintain an inventory. So far, you and Aunt Laura have created a table of color numbers, color names, year introduced, and year retired, if applicable. In a second table, you entered color numbers, item numbers, items, current value, and source. Previously, you helped her research current replacement costs from Homer Laughlin's Web site (www.hlchina.com), Replacements, Ltd. (www.replacements.com), and eBay (www.ebay.com); however, you believe the retired colors may be worth more now. Laura is especially interested in the values of retired colors so that she can provide this information for her insurance agent. You will build a PivotTable and add slicers to help her with the analysis.

a. Open *e05m2Fiesta* and save it as **e05m2Fiesta_LastFirst**.

b. Create a relationship between the Items table using the Color Number field and the Colors table using the Number field.

c. Create a blank PivotTable from within the Items table to analyze multiple tables. Place the PivotTable on a new worksheet and name the worksheet **Retired Colors**.

d. Display the names of both tables in the PivotTable Fields task pane.

e. Display the Color names as ROWS and the sum of the Replacement Value field as VALUES.

f. Add a FILTER to display aggregates for retired colors only. Note that current colors do not have a retirement date, so you must filter out the blanks.

g. Apply the **Pivot Style Medium 7**.

h. Format the values with **Accounting Number Format** with two decimal places. Create a custom heading named **Replacement Value**. Change *Row Labels* in **cell A3** to **Retired Colors**.

i. Add a calculated field by doing the following:

- Display the Excel Options dialog box, click **Customize Ribbon** on the left side of the dialog box, click the **POWERPIVOT check box** in the *Customize the Ribbon* section on the right side, and then click **OK**.
- Use the Calculated Fields command to create a new calculated field.
- Enter the formula to multiply [Sum of Replacement Value] by 1.15.
- Type the custom name **Updated Replacement Values**. Word-wrap and center the label.
- Apply the same number format that you did for the Replacement Values column.

j. Add slicers for the Color field. Select these colors to display: **Apricot**, **Chartreuse**, **Lilac**, **Marigold**, **Pearl Gray**, and **Sapphire**.

k. Apply the **Slicer Style Light 6 style**.

l. Create a footer with your name on the left side, the sheet name code in the center, and the file name code on the right side of the Retired Colors worksheet.

m. Save and close the workbook, and submit based on your instructor's directions.

3 Facebook® Social Phenomenon

COLLABORATION CASE

FROM SCRATCH

Facebook has experienced phenomenal growth since its creation in 2004. What is it that has made Facebook a huge success story, starting a decade after many of the other Web company startups? To understand how people use Facebook, look at its applications. Work with another student to conduct this research, obtain data, and create PivotTables.

a. Open www.checkfacebook.com in a Web browser to read about Facebook's history.

b. Start a new Excel workbook and save it as **e05m3Facebook_LastFirst**.

c. Go to **http://statistics.allfacebook.com** and use this site to build a worksheet that lists at least 200 application leaders for 10 categories, two of which must be Business and Just For Fun. Each student should find 100 different application leaders. Use collaboration tools to make sure you and your team member use the same format and do not duplicate data.

d. Include data for these columns: Category, Name, Daily Average Use (DAU), Monthly Average Use (MAU), and Daily Growth.

e. Copy your team member's worksheet as a new worksheet in your workbook. Then create a third worksheet to combine the data. Name the sheets appropriately.

f. Format the data and headings appropriately in the combined worksheet.

g. Create a PivotTable based on the data to reflect one perspective of analysis. Format the values and apply desired filters.

h. Have your teammate copy the combined sheet and create his or her own PivotTable with a different perspective, formatting, and desired filters.

i. Discuss your analysis with your team member.

j. Create a footer with your name and your team member's name on the left side, sheet name code in the center, and the file name code on the right side of each worksheet.

k. Save and close the workbook, and submit based on your instructor's directions.

Beyond the Classroom

Departing Flights

RESEARCH CASE →

You want to research morning flight departures at Oklahoma City Will Rogers Airport. Find the airport's departing flight schedule and copy the morning departing flight information to a new worksheet. Name the workbook as **e05b2OKC_LastFirst**. Clean up the data after copying it. Name the worksheet as **Morning Departures**. Create a PivotTable using the *Count of Departing To by Airline* recommendation. Display the Status field as a column so that you can see canceled, on-time, and delayed flights. Add the Gate information as a secondary row label. Apply **PivotStyle Medium 13 style**. Type **Airlines and Gates** in **cell A4**. Type **Status** in **cell B3**. Adjust column widths as needed. Name the worksheet **PivotTable**.

Create a PivotChart from the original dataset. Use the Airline field as the Axis and the Flight # as the Value. Change the chart type to a pie chart. Add a chart title and percentage data labels. Adjust the chart size and location as needed. Name the sheet as **PivotChart**. Create a footer with your name, the sheet name code, and the file name code on each worksheet. Save and close the workbook, and submit based on your instructor's directions.

Innovative Game Studio

DISASTER RECOVERY

You work as an assistant to Terry Park, the producer for a video game studio in Phoenix, Arizona. The company produces games for the PlayStation®, Xbox®, and Wii™ consoles. The producer tracks salaries and performance for everyone on a particular team, which consists of artists, animators, programmers, and so forth. Terry tried to create a PivotTable to organize the data by department and then by title within department. He also wants to display total salaries by these categories and filter the data to show aggregates for team members who earned only Excellent and Good performance ratings. In addition, he wants to see what the percentages of total salaries for each job title are of each department's budget. For example, the total salary for Senior Artists is $263,300. That represents 50.27% of the Art Department's salary budget for Excellent- and Good-rated employees. However, the percentages are not displayed correctly. Terry called you in to correct his PivotTable.

Open *e05b3Games* and save it as **e05b3Games_LastFirst**. Identify the errors and make a list of these errors starting on row 41 in the PivotTable worksheet. Correct the errors and improve the format, including a medium Pivot Style, throughout the PivotTable. Create a footer with your name, the sheet name code, and the file name code. Save and close the workbook, and submit based on your instructor's directions.

Job Fair

SOFT SKILLS CASE Ⓢ

FROM SCRATCH

You are ready to help your college create a worksheet to organize the companies that will participate. Create a list of companies, the cities in which they are located, and the number of active openings they are advertising. Include any other details that help classify the companies. Sort the list by a major classification and then display subtotals to indicate the total number of jobs by classification. Save the workbook as **e05b4JobFair_LastFirst**. Create a footer with your name, the sheet name code, and the file name code. Save and close the workbook, and submit based on your instructor's directions.

Capstone Exercise

You are an analyst for an authorized Greenwich Workshop® fine art dealer (www.greenwichworkshop.com). Customers are especially fond of James C. Christensen's art. You prepared a list of artwork: art, type, edition size, release date, issue price, and estimated current market value. Studying the data will help you discuss value trends with art collectors.

Sort, Subtotal, and Outline Data

You need to organize data to facilitate using the Subtotal feature. Then you will further outline the list so that you can collapse and expand groups.

a. Open *e05c1FineArt* and save it as **e05c1FineArt_LastFirst**.

b. Click the **Subtotals worksheet**. Sort the data by type and further sort it by the name of the art, both in alphabetical order.

c. Use the Subtotal feature to identify the highest Issue Price and Est. Value.

d. Select and group the first and last name columns.

e. Collapse the names created by the grouping.

f. Study the list to see the Est. Value in each type.

Create a PivotTable

Although creating an outline and subtotaling data are helpful for an initial analysis of the artwork values, you will create a PivotTable for further analysis.

a. Click the **Christensen worksheet** and create a blank PivotTable from the data.

b. Use the Type, Release Date, and Issue Price fields, enabling Excel to determine where the fields go.

c. Remove the Release Date field. Add the Est. Value field.

Format the PivotTable

You will calculate averages within each art type. You will format the values and provide clear headings in the PivotTable.

a. Modify the value fields to determine the average issue price and average estimated market value by type.

b. Insert a calculated field to determine percent change in values by type.

c. Format the three columns of values appropriately, using whole numbers for dollar values and two decimal places for percentages.

d. Edit the custom names for the values columns. Apply these formats to the three values column headings: wrap text, center horizontally, **30** row height, and **9.7** column widths.

e. Enter appropriate labels for the first column and the grand total label.

Filter the PivotTable and Apply a Style

You want to focus on average values for sold-out art because these pieces typically increase in value on the secondary market. In addition, you want to narrow the list to particular types. After filtering the data, you will apply a style.

a. Set a filter to display only sold-out art (indicated by *Yes*).

b. Set a Type filter to *omit* Hand Colored Print, Limited Edition Hand Colored Print, Open Edition Print, and Poster types.

c. Apply **Pivot Style Medium 5**.

d. Display banded columns and banded rows.

Create a PivotChart

To help interpret the consolidated values of the art, you want to create a PivotChart. You realize that displaying both monetary values and percentages on the same chart is like mixing apples and oranges. If you modify the PivotChart, you will change the PivotTable; therefore, you will create a PivotChart from the original data source.

a. Use the Christensen worksheet to create a PivotChart.

b. Use the Type, Issue Price, and Est. Value fields. Find the average issue price and average estimated value.

c. Set filters as you did for the first PivotTable.

d. Apply formatting as you did for the first PivotTable.

e. Change the chart type to **Bar**.

f. Move the PivotChart below the PivotTable, resize the PivotChart, and hide the field buttons in the PivotChart.

g. Insert an appropriate chart title reflecting the contents and the filter. Set a **12-pt font size** for the chart title.

h. Set the upper limit of the value axis to **2000** if needed.

i. Sort the PivotTable in such a way that its effect on the PivotChart is to display the category labels alphabetically.

j. Type **Art Type** in cell A3 and type **Overall Averages** in cell A13.

Finalizing Your Workbook

You need to finalize your workbook.

a. Rename the first PivotTable worksheet **PivotTable**.

b. Rename the second PivotTable/PivotChart worksheet **PivotChart**.

c. Select landscape orientation and adjust the top and bottom margins for the Subtotals worksheet.

d. Create a footer on all four worksheets with your name, the sheet name code, and the file name code.

e. Save and close the workbook, and submit based on your instructor's directions.

What-If Analysis

CHAPTER **8**

Using Decision-Making Tools

OBJECTIVES | AFTER YOU READ THIS CHAPTER, YOU WILL BE ABLE TO:

1. Create a one-variable data table p. 388

2. Create a two-variable data table p. 392

3. Identify an input value with Goal Seek p. 399

4. Use Scenario Manager p. 400

5. Generate scenario summary reports p. 402

6. Load the Solver add-in p. 408

7. Optimize results with Solver p. 409

CASE STUDY | Personal Finance: Buying Your First Home

After several years of living with friends after college, you have decided to purchase your first home. After doing some preliminary research on prices, you developed a spreadsheet to help you calculate your monthly mortgage payment, total amount to repay the loan, and the total amount of interest you will pay. Your total budget for the home is $150,000 including taxes, closing costs, and other miscellaneous fees. You plan to take $10,000 out of your savings account for a down payment. You are currently investigating loan interest rates at various banks and credit unions. You realize that you may need to find a less expensive home or increase your down payment. Although you can change input values to see how different values affect the monthly payment, you want to be able to see the comparisons at the same time. In addition, you want to look at your budget to review the impact of purchasing a new home on your income and expenses.

You will use Excel to help you analyze the variables that affect the mortgage payment, total amount to repay the loan, and the total interest paid. To help you make a decision, you will use several tools, each with specific purposes, benefits, and restrictions. With these tools, you will have a better understanding of how a mortgage payment will affect your overall budget.

One- and Two-Variable Data Tables

You are now ready to explore Excel's powerful what-if analysis tools. **What-if analysis** enables you to experiment with different variables or assumptions so that you can observe and compare how these changes affect a related outcome. A **variable** is an input value that can change to other values to affect the results of a situation. People in almost every industry perform some type of what-if analysis to make educated decisions. For example, business people perform what-if analysis to see the impact that producing different quantities of a product will have on revenue. Remember that these what-if analysis tools are just that—tools. While these tools do not provide the definitive, perfect solution to a problem, they will help you analyze data and interpret data, but you or another human must make ultimate decisions based on the data.

In this section, you will learn how to create one- and two-variable data tables to perform what-if analysis. You will design the data tables, insert formulas, and complete the data tables to compare the results for different values of the variables.

Creating a One-Variable Data Table

A **one-variable data table** is a structured range that contains different values for *one variable* to compare how these values affect one or more calculated results. For example, you can use a one-variable data table to compare monthly payments on a mortgage. As you recall, monthly payments are based on the interest rate, the number of payment periods, and the amount of the loan. Holding the number of payment periods and loan amount constant, you can compare how different values of the interest rate (the one variable) affect the calculated results: monthly payment, total amount to repay the loan, and total interest paid.

When setting up a one-variable data table, you must decide which one variable you want to use. After you decide on an input variable, then you select one or more formulas that depend on that input variable for calculations.

Set Up the Substitution Values

STEP 1 Your first step is to decide which one variable, such as the interest rate, to manipulate. Then you need to specify the substitution values. A **substitution value** is a value that replaces the original input value of the variable in a data table. For example, the original interest rate is 4.5%, but you might want to substitute 5%, 5.5%, 6%, 6.5%, and 7% to see how changing the interest rate affects the results.

Locate a range to the right of or below the regular worksheet data to create the one-variable data table. Leave at least one blank row and one blank column between the dataset and the data table. Enter the substitution values down one column or across one row. With one variable and several results, a vertical orientation for the substitution values is recommended because people often look up a value in the first column of a table and then read across to see corresponding values.

You can enter the substitution values yourself or use the Series dialog box to help complete a series of values. To use the Series dialog box, do the following:

1. Type the first substitution value (such as 5%) in cell D4 and keep that cell as the active cell (see Figure 8.1, cell D4).
2. Click the HOME tab, click Fill in the Editing group, and then select Series to open the Series dialog box (see Figure 8.1).
3. Click Rows to place the series of substitution values in a row or click Columns to place the series of substitution values down a column.

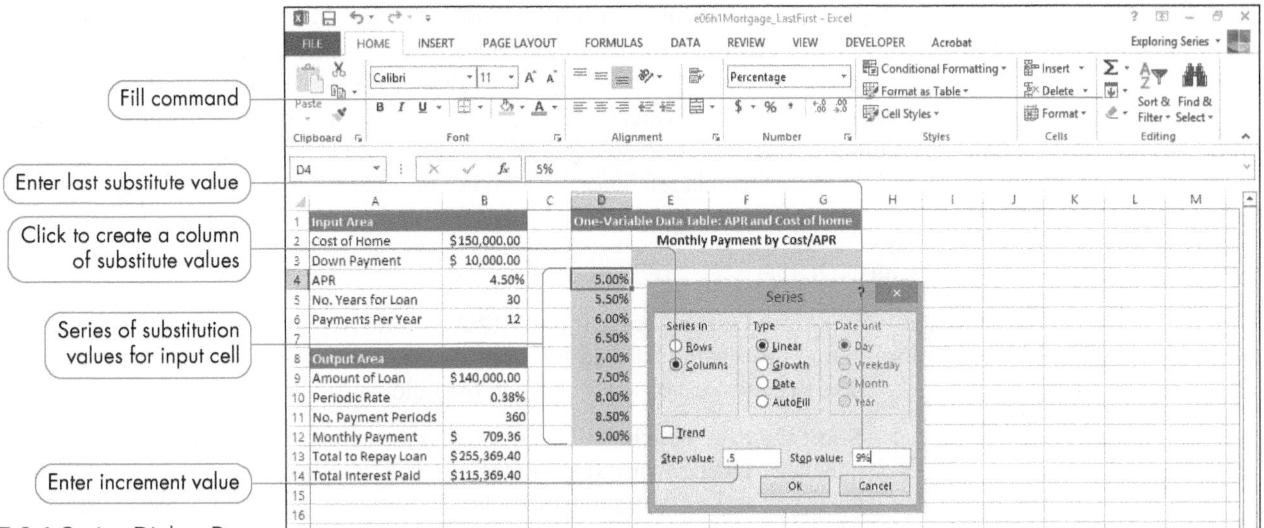
Fill command
Enter last substitute value
Click to create a column of substitute values
Series of substitution values for input cell
Enter increment value
Series
Series in
Rows
Columns
Type
Linear
Growth
Date
AutoFill
Date unit
Day
Weekday
Month
Year
Trend
Step value: .5
Stop value: 9%
OK
Cancel
One-Variable Data Table: APR and Cost of home
Monthly Payment by Cost/APR

FIGURE 8.1 Series Dialog Box

4. Enter the value increment in the *Step value* box and enter the ending value for the series in the *Stop value* box. For example, if you want to create a list of incremental interest rates, such as 5%, 5.5%, and 6% up to 9%, then enter 0.5% in the *Step value* box and 9% in the *Stop value* box.
5. Click OK. Excel fills in a series of values, as shown in Figure 8.1. You may need to format the percentages to show one or more decimal places. If decimal places are not displayed, the interest rate values will appear rounded to the nearest integer.

TIP Auto Fill a Series of Substitution Values

Instead of using the Series dialog box, you can use Auto Fill to complete a series of substitution values. To do this, enter the first two substitution values (such as 5% and 5.5%). Select the cells containing these two values and drag the fill handle down until the ScreenTip displays the last substitution value you want. Excel sets the increment pattern based on the difference between the first two values.

Add Formulas to the Data Table

STEP 2›› After you enter the substitution values in either a column or row, you must add one or more formulas that relate mathematically to the variable for which you are using substitution values. Although you can create formulas directly in the data table, referencing cells containing existing formulas outside the data table is preferable because the formulas are often already created. You can save time and reduce errors by referencing the original formula. Within the data table range, the formula references must be entered in a specific location based on the location of your substitution values (see Table 8.1).

TABLE 8.1 Locations for Formula References

Location of Substitution Values	Enter the First Formula Reference	Enter Additional Formula References
Vertically in a column	On the row above and one column to the right of the first substitution value	To the right of the first formula reference
Horizontally in a row	On the row below and one column to the left of the first substitution value	Below the first formula reference

For example, assume you want to compare the effect of different interest rates on the monthly payment, the total amount repaid, and the total interest paid. As shown in Figure 8.2, you need to set up three columns to show the calculated results. The first formula reference for monthly payment (=B12) goes in cell E3. To compare the effects of substitution values on other results, the second formula reference for total repaid (=B13) goes in cell F3, and the third formula reference for total interest paid (=B14) goes in cell G3.

Complete the Results

STEP 3≫ It is important that you enter the substitution values and formula references in the correct locations. This sets the left and top boundaries of the soon-to-be-completed data table. To complete the one-variable data table, do the following:

1. Select the data table boundaries, starting in the blank cell in the top-left corner of the data table. Drag down and to the right, if there is more than one column, to select the last blank cell at the intersection of the last substitution value and the last formula reference.
2. Click the DATA tab, click What-If Analysis in the Data Tools group, and then select Data Table to open the Data Table dialog box (see Figure 8.2).
3. Enter the cell reference of the cell containing the original variable for which you are substituting values. If you listed the substitution values in a row, enter the original variable cell reference in the *Row input cell* box. If you listed the substitution values in a column, enter the original variable cell reference in the *Column input cell* box. In Figure 8.2, for example, click cell B4—the original interest rate variable—in the *Column input cell* box because you entered the substitution interest rates in a column. Note that the cell reference is automatically made absolute so that Excel always refers to the original input cell as it performs calculations in the data table.
4. Click OK.

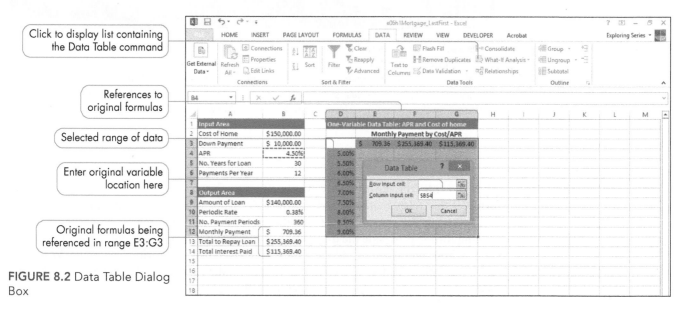

FIGURE 8.2 Data Table Dialog Box

When you create the one-variable data table, Excel uses the substitution values individually to replace the original variable's value, which is then used in the formulas to produce the results in the body of the data table. In Figure 8.3, the data table shows the substitution values of different interest rates, whereas the formulas produce the monthly payments (column E), total payments (column F), and total interest paid (column G) for the respective interest rates.

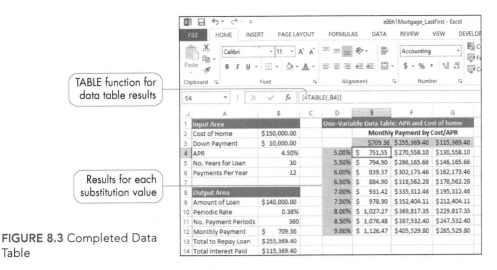

TABLE function for data table results

Results for each substitution value

FIGURE 8.3 Completed Data Table

Format the Data Table

After creating the data table, you should format the values with Accounting Number Format. To reduce confusion, you should also create custom formats to disguise the formula references as column labels. To create custom formats, do the following:

1. Click in the cell containing a formula reference in the data table.
2. Click the Number Dialog Box Launcher in the Number group on the HOME tab to open the Format Cells dialog box with the Number tab active.
3. Click Custom in the Category list, scroll up in the Type list, and then select General in the list.
4. Select General in the Type box above the Type list and type what you want to appear as a column heading. Enter the text within quotation marks, such as "Payment," and click OK. Note that you must include the word to be displayed within quotation marks or the custom format will not display properly (see Figure 8.4).
5. Click OK.

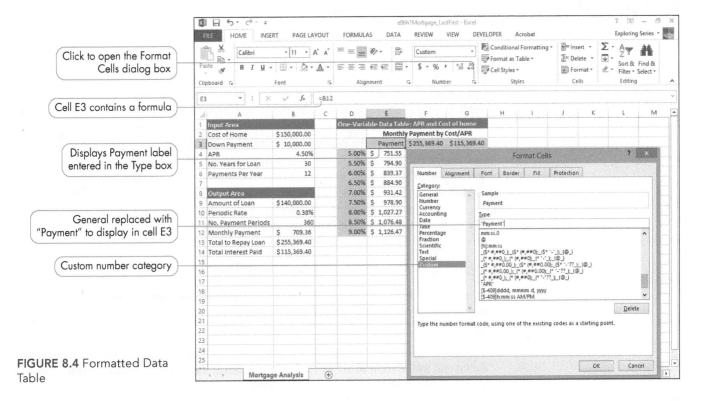

Click to open the Format Cells dialog box

Cell E3 contains a formula

Displays Payment label entered in the Type box

General replaced with "Payment" to display in cell E3

Custom number category

FIGURE 8.4 Formatted Data Table

You can then apply bold and centering to the column headings. If you see pound signs, the column is too narrow to display the text, indicating you need to wrap the text or expand the column width. Although you are using a custom number format that displays text, Excel remembers that the actual contents are values derived from formulas.

Creating a Two-Variable Data Table

Although a one-variable data table is effective for comparing results for different values for one variable, you might want to compare results for two variables. For example, you might want to compare the combined effects of various interest rates (such as 5%, 5.5%, and 6%) and different down payments (such as $10,000, $15,000, and $20,000) on the monthly payment. A *two-variable data table* is a structured range that contains different values for *two variables* to compare how these differing values affect the results for one calculated value.

Set Up the Substitution Values for Two Variables

STEP 4 ▶▶ Create the two-variable data table separate from regular worksheet data, similar to the method used for a one-variable data table. For a two-variable data table, you use the top row for one variable's substitution values and the first column for the other variable's substitution values. Figure 8.5 shows substitution interest rates in the first column (range D4:D12) and substitution down payments in the first row (range E3:G3).

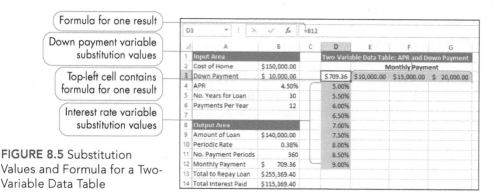

FIGURE 8.5 Substitution Values and Formula for a Two-Variable Data Table

Add a Formula to the Data Table

The two-variable data table enables you to use two variables, but you are restricted to only one result instead of multiple results. With the one-variable data table, you use the interest rate variable to compare multiple results: monthly payment, total to repay the loan, and total interest paid. However, for the two-variable data table, decide which result you want to focus on based on the two variables. In the case of a home loan, you might want to focus on comparing the effects that changes in interest rates and down payments (the two variables) have on different monthly payments (the result). Enter the formula or reference to the original formula in the blank cell in the top-left corner. For example, enter the cell reference for the monthly payment (=B12) in cell D3 as shown in Figure 8.5.

Complete the Two-Variable Data Table

STEP 5 ▶▶ After entering the substitution values and the reference to one formula result, you are ready to complete the table to see the results. To complete the two-variable data table, do the following:

1. Select the data table boundaries, starting in the top-left corner of the data table. Drag down and to the right to select the last blank cell at the intersection of the last substitution value for both the column and the row.

2. Click the DATA tab, click What-If Analysis in the Data Tools group, and then select Data Table. The Data Table dialog box opens.

3. Enter the cell that contains the original value for the substitution values in the first row in the *Row input cell* box. Enter the cell that contains the original value for the substitution values in the first column in the *Column input cell* box. For example, the original row (down payment) variable value is stored in cell B3, and the original column (APR) variable value is stored in cell B4.

4. Click OK.

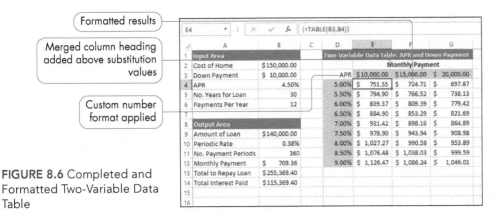

FIGURE 8.6 Completed and Formatted Two-Variable Data Table

After you complete the data table, to reduce confusion, you should format the results by applying a custom number format to the formula cell to appear as a heading and add a merged heading above the row substitution values (see Figure 8.6).

Quick Concepts ✓

1. What is the first step to creating a one-variable data table? **p. 388**

2. Why is it preferable to reference formula cells outside of a one-variable data table versus entering the formula manually? **p. 389**

3. What is the difference between a one- and two-variable data table? **p. 392**

Hands-On Exercises

Watch the Video
for this Hands-
On Exercise!

MyITLab®
HOE1 Training

1 One- and Two-Variable Data Tables

As you consider different options for a home purchase, you want to use data tables to compare how different interest rates and price will affect your monthly payment. You decide to create both one- and two-variable data tables to analyze the results.

Skills covered: Enter Substitution Values for a One-Variable Data Table • Enter Formulas and Complete the Data Table • Format the One-Variable Data Table • Set Up the Structure for a Two-Variable Data Table • Complete the Two-Variable Data Table

STEP 1 ≫ ENTER SUBSTITUTION VALUES FOR A ONE-VARIABLE DATA TABLE

You want to compare monthly mortgage payments, total amounts to repay a loan, and total interest you will pay based on several interest rates—the variable. The interest rates range from 4% to 6% in 0.25% increments. Your first step is to enter a series of substitution values for the interest rate. Refer to Figure 8.7 as you complete Step 1.

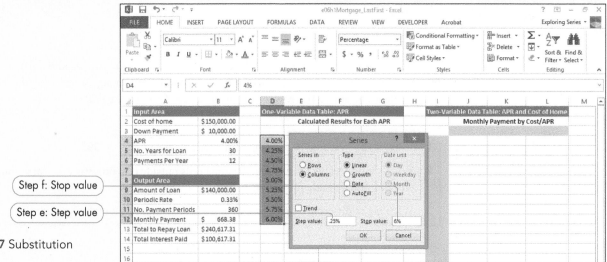

FIGURE 8.7 Substitution Values

a. Open the *e06h1Mortgage* workbook and save it as **e06h1Mortgage_LastFirst**.

> **TROUBLESHOOTING:** If you make any major mistakes in this exercise, you can close the file, open *e06h1Mortgage* again, and then start this exercise over.

b. Click **cell D4**, type **4%**, and then press **Ctrl+Enter**.

   Cell D4 is the first cell containing a substitution value. Make sure cell D4 is still the active cell.

c. Click **Fill** in the Editing group on the HOME tab and select **Series**.

   The Series dialog box opens.

d. Click **Columns**.

   You changed the *Series in* option to Columns because you want the series of substitution values listed vertically in column D.

e. Delete the existing value in the **Step value box** and type **0.25%**.

f. Type **6%** in the **Stop value box** and click **OK**.

Excel fills in the series of values; however, you need to increase the number of decimal points to see the full percentages.

> **TROUBLESHOOTING:** If you forget to type the decimal point in step e and/or the percent sign in steps e or f, the series will be incorrect. If this happens, click Undo and repeat steps c through f.

STEP 2 ›› ENTER FORMULAS AND COMPLETE THE DATA TABLE

In the next steps, you will enter references to the monthly payment, total amount to repay the loan, and total interest formulas. Then, you will complete the table to compare the results for different interest rates ranging from 4% to 6%. Refer to Figure 8.8 as you complete Step 2.

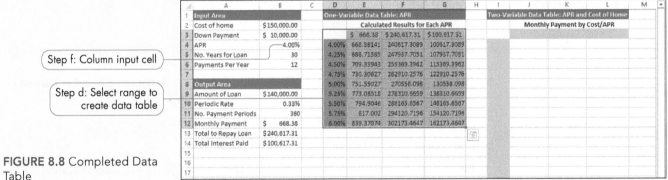

Step f: Column input cell

Step d: Select range to create data table

FIGURE 8.8 Completed Data Table

a. Click **cell E3**, type **=B12**, and then press **Tab**.

You entered a reference to the original monthly payment formula. When the results of cell B12 change, they are reflected in cell E3.

b. Type **=B13** in **cell F3** and press **Tab**.

You entered a reference to the original total amount to repay the loan.

c. Type **=B14** in **cell G3** and press **Enter**.

You entered a reference to the original total interest paid.

d. Select the **range D3:G12**.

You select the entire range of the data table, starting in the blank cell in the top-left corner. Note that you did not select the titles or headings in cells D1:G2.

e. Click the **DATA tab**, click **What-If Analysis** in the Data Tools group, and then select **Data Table**.

f. Click in the **Column input cell box**, click **cell B4**, and then click **OK**. Save the workbook.

Because the substitution values are in a column, you reference cell B4 in the *Column input* box. Excel inserts the TABLE array function in the empty result cells and substitutes the values in range D4:D12 individually for the original APR to calculate the respective monthly payments, total amounts, and total interest payments. The higher the APR, the higher the monthly payment, total amount to repay the loan, and total interest.

STEP 3 ≫ FORMAT THE ONE-VARIABLE DATA TABLE

You want to format the results to show dollar signs and to display rounded values to the nearest penny. In addition, you want to add column headings to provide more detail to the data table and add custom formats to the cells to appear as column headings. Refer to Figure 8.9 as you complete Step 3.

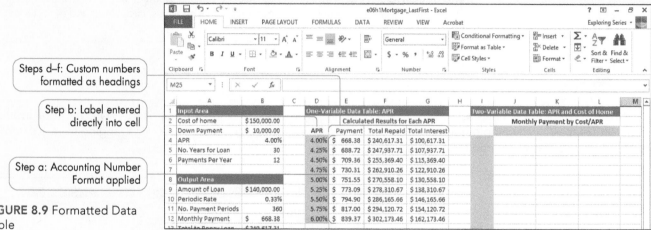

FIGURE 8.9 Formatted Data Table

a. Select the **range E4:G12**, click the **HOME tab**, and then click **Accounting Number Format** in the Number group.

The values look more professional now that you have formatted them.

b. Click **cell D3**, type **APR**, and then press **Tab**.

Because cell D3 was empty, you can type the label directly in the cell without adding a custom format. Cell E3 should now be the active cell.

c. Click the **Number Dialog Box Launcher** in the Number group on the HOME tab of the Ribbon.

d. Select **Custom** in the **Category list**, scroll up through the Type list, and then select **General** in the list.

e. Select **General** in the **Type box**, type **"Payment"**, and then click **OK**.

The formula result $668.38 now appears as Payment in cell E3.

f. Repeat and adapt steps c through e to enter the following custom number formats: **"Total Repaid"** for **cell F3** and **"Total Interest"** for **cell G3**.

> **TROUBLESHOOTING:** If you forget the quotation marks, the cell contents will contain a mix of numbers and characters. If this happens, open the Format Cells dialog box again and edit the contents of the Type box to display the text surrounded by quotation marks.

g. Center and bold the **range E3:G3**. Save the workbook.

Now you want to focus on how a combination of interest rates and different costs will affect just the monthly payment. The interest rates range from 4% to 8% at .25% increments with costs of $200,000, $225,000, and $250,000. Refer to Figure 8.10 as you complete Step 4.

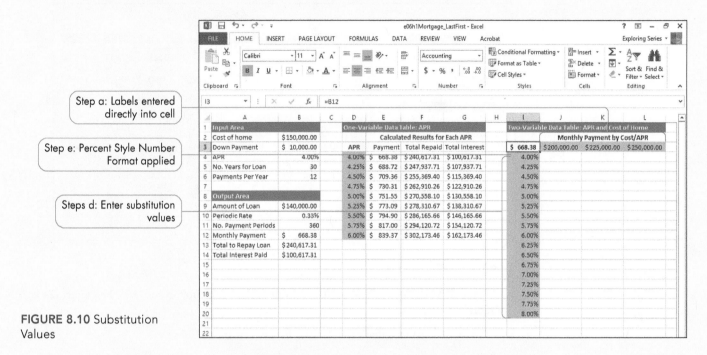

FIGURE 8.10 Substitution Values

a. Enter **200000, 225000,** and **250000** in the **range J3:L3**. Format these values with **Accounting Number Format**.

> **TROUBLESHOOTING:** After formatting the numbers, you may see ### displayed in the cells. The pound signs indicate the number is larger than the width of the column. To automatically expand the column to the proper width, click the HOME tab, click Format from the Cells group, and then select Auto Fit Column Width.

b. Click **cell I4**, type **4%**, and then press **Ctrl+Enter**.

c. Click **Fill** in the Editing group, select **Series**, and then click **Columns**.

d. Replace the existing value in the **Step value box** with **0.25%**, type **8%** in the **Stop value box**, and then click **OK**.

e. Format the **range I4:I20** with **Percent Style** with two decimal places.

f. Click **cell I3**, type **=B12**, and then press **Ctrl+Enter**. Save the workbook.

You inserted the reference to the formula in the top-left cell of the two-variable data table. The cell displays pound signs, indicating the column is too narrow to display the value; you will apply a custom number format in Step 5.

You complete the data table, format the monthly payment results, and apply a custom number format to the cell containing the formula reference so that it displays the text APR. Refer to Figure 8.11 as you complete Step 5.

Step e: Custom number format

Step c: Row input value

Step d: Column input value

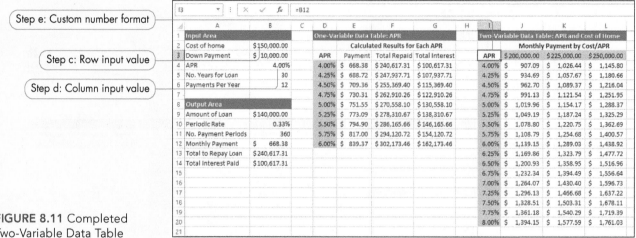

FIGURE 8.11 Completed Two-Variable Data Table

a. Select the **range I3:L20**.

b. Click the **DATA tab**, click **What-If Analysis** in the Data Tools group, and then select **Data Table**.

c. Click **cell B2** to enter that cell reference in the **Row input cell box**.

   Because you entered the purchase price substitution values in the top row of the data table, you entered the reference to the cell containing the original cost in the Row input cell box.

d. Click in the **Column input cell box**, click **cell B4**, and then click **OK**.

   Because you entered the interest rate substitution values in the left column of the data table, you entered the reference to the cell containing the original APR variable in the Column input cell box.

e. Click **cell I3** and apply a custom number format to display *APR*. Center and bold the contents in **cell I3**.

f. Save the workbook. Keep the workbook open if you plan to continue with Hands-On Exercise 2. If not, close the workbook and exit Excel.

Goal Seek and Scenario Manager

Although data tables are useful for particular situations to compare effects of different values for one or two variables, other what-if analysis tools such as Goal Seek and Scenario Manager are better suited for other situations. For example, you might want to use Goal Seek to determine exactly the down payment required to acquire a desired payment. In this situation, you would not need all of the data provided by a data table. You may also want to weigh the options between various options of down payments, purchase costs, and interest rates. If more than two variables are required, data tables would not be a viable option.

In this section, you will learn when and how to use both Goal Seek and Scenario Manager to assist you in making decisions. These tools enable you to perform what-if analysis to make forecasts or predictions involving quantifiable data.

Identifying an Input Value with Goal Seek

STEP 1 » Suppose the most you can afford for a monthly payment on a mortgage is $800. How can you determine the down payment amount needed to meet that monthly payment? *Goal Seek* is a tool that enables you to specify a desired result from a formula ($800 monthly payment) without knowing what input value achieves that goal. Goal Seek works backward to identify the exact value for a variable to reach your goal. In this case, you can use Goal Seek to determine the required down payment. Unlike variable data tables, Goal Seek uses the original worksheet data to change an input instead of displaying various combinations of results in a separate table. Goal Seek manipulates only one variable and one result; it does not produce a list of values to compare. To use Goal Seek, do the following:

1. Click What-If Analysis in the Data Tools group on the DATA tab.
2. Select Goal Seek to open the Goal Seek dialog box.
3. Enter the cell reference for the cell to be optimized in the *Set cell* box. This cell must contain a formula, such as the monthly payment.
4. Enter the result you want to achieve (such as the $800 goal) in the *To value* box.
5. Enter the cell reference that contains the variable to adjust (such as the down payment) in the *By changing cell* box as shown in Figure 8.12. This cell must be a value, not a formula, which has a mathematical relationship with the cell containing the formula or goal.
6. Click OK.

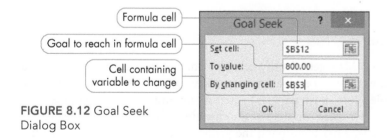

FIGURE 8.12 Goal Seek Dialog Box

Excel varies the input value until the desired result is achieved, if possible, and displays the Goal Seek Status dialog box. Click OK to accept the target value and change the value of the input cell you entered in Step 5 to achieve the goal you specified in Steps 3 and 4. Click Cancel to keep the original input cell value instead of changing it. If Excel cannot determine a solution given the input cell and the desired results, it displays a message box.

Using Scenario Manager

You may want to compare several variables and their combined effects on multiple calculated results. This type of analysis involves identifying and setting up *scenarios*, which are detailed sets of values that represent different possible situations. Business managers often create a best-case scenario, worst-case scenario, and most likely scenario to compare outcomes. For example, a best-case scenario could reflect an increase in units sold and lower production costs. A worst-case scenario could reflect fewer units sold and higher production costs.

Scenario Manager is a what-if analysis tool that enables you to define and manage up to 32 scenarios to compare their effects on calculated results. You can perform more sophisticated what-if analyses with Scenario Manager than with data tables with the increased number of variables and results. The Scenario Manager dialog box (see Figure 8.13) enables you to create, edit, and delete scenario names. Each scenario represents different sets of what-if conditions to assess the outcome of spreadsheet models. Each scenario is stored under its own name and defines cells whose values change from scenario to scenario.

Scenario names —
Click to manage scenarios —
Cell containing variables —

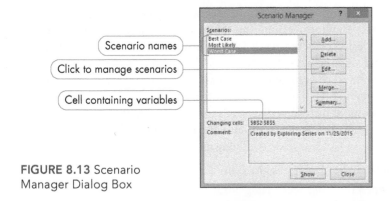

FIGURE 8.13 Scenario Manager Dialog Box

TIP Scenarios on Different Worksheets

When you create scenarios, Excel maintains those scenarios on the worksheet that was active when you created them. You can create scenarios for each worksheet in a workbook. The Scenario Manager dialog box displays only those scenarios you have created on the active worksheet.

Create and Edit Scenarios

STEP 2 » Before you start the Scenario Manager, identify cells that contain the variables you want to change or manipulate. For example, in evaluating home loans, you might want to manipulate the values for these variables: cost, down payment, interest rate, and the duration of the loan. You enter the cell references for these variables as the changing cells because you change the values to compare the results. After identifying the variables you want to change, identify one or more cells containing formulas that generate results you want to compare. Note these formulas must directly impact the change cell. To create a scenario, do the following:

1. Click What-If Analysis in the Data Tools group on the DATA tab.
2. Select Scenario Manager to open the Scenario Manager dialog box.
3. Click Add to open the Add Scenario dialog box (see Figure 8.14).
4. Enter a meaningful name in the *Scenario name* box.
5. Enter the input cells for the scenario in the *Changing cells* box. These are the cells containing variable values that Scenario Manager will adjust or change. The changing cells must be identical cell references across all scenarios.

6. Click in the Comment box. Excel enters the name of the person who created the scenarios in the Comment box; however, you can change the name and enter additional descriptions and rationales for the scenarios.

7. Click OK to open the Scenario Values dialog box (see Figure 8.15), which lists the changing cell references that you specified in the previous dialog box. In each respective box, type the value you want to use for that particular scenario.

STEP 3 ≫

8. Click Add to add another scenario and specify its values. After you enter values for the last scenario, click OK to return to the Scenario Manager dialog box.

FIGURE 8.14 Add Scenario Dialog Box

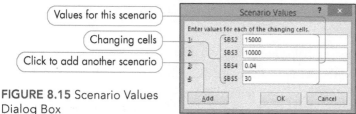

FIGURE 8.15 Scenario Values Dialog Box

TIP Range Names

To help you know what data to enter for the changing cells, you might want to assign a range name to the variable cells before using Scenario Manager. If you do this, the range names, rather than the cell references, appear in the Scenario Values dialog box.

If you need to modify the parameters of a scenario, such as the name or input values, open the Scenario Manager dialog box, select the scenario you want to modify in the Scenarios list, and then click Edit. The Edit Scenario dialog box opens so that you can change the values. Click OK after making the necessary changes.

If you have scenarios in several worksheets or workbooks, you can combine them. Click Merge in the Scenario Manager dialog box to open the Merge Scenarios dialog box. Select the workbook and worksheet and click OK. Use Help to learn more about merging scenarios.

View Scenarios

After you create the scenarios, you can view each of them. To view your scenarios, click What-If Analysis in the Data Tools group on the Data tab, select Scenario Manager, select the name of the scenario you want to view in the Scenarios list, and then click Show. Excel places the defined values in the respective changing cells and displays the results.

Generating Scenario Summary Reports

STEP 4 »

 TIP **Updated Scenario Reports**

Unlike one- and two-variable data tables that update results if you change other values in the input area, scenario reports do not update. If you change other values or assumptions, or if you add, edit, or delete scenarios, you will have to generate a new scenario report. To avoid this problem, do your best to double-check the scenarios to ensure they are perfect before you generate a scenario summary report.

Although you can view the defined values and their results individually, you will probably want to compare all scenarios in a table. A ***scenario summary report*** is an organized structured table of the scenarios, their input values, and their respective results. The summary report appears in the form of a worksheet outline and enables you to compare the results based on different values specified by the respective scenarios. Excel can produce two types of reports: scenario summary and scenario PivotTable report. PivotTable reports summarize the data in a pivot table. This provides the same functionality as any other pivot table. Scenario summary reports display the results of each scenario in a new worksheet. The data reported in the summary are formatted without gridlines, and the report is easily printable. To create a scenario summary report, do the following:

1. Open the Scenario Manager dialog box.
2. Click Summary to open the Scenario Summary dialog box (see Figure 8.16).
3. Click *Scenario summary* or click *Scenario PivotTable report*. Enter the reference for the cell(s) whose values change in the scenarios in the *Result cells* box. Drag to select a range of adjacent results cells, or press Ctrl as you click cells in nonadjacent ranges. For example, in Figure 8.16, the result cells are monthly payment (B12) and total interest (B14).
4. Click OK. Excel creates the Scenario Summary on a new worksheet (see Figure 8.17).

FIGURE 8.16 Scenario Summary Dialog Box

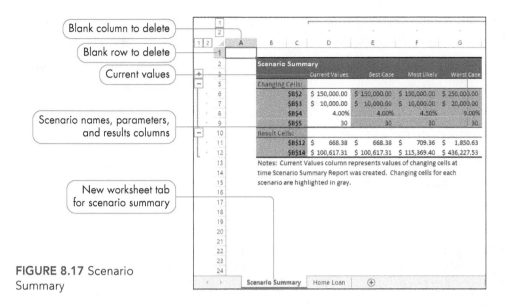

Blank column to delete

Blank row to delete

Current values

Scenario names, parameters, and results columns

New worksheet tab for scenario summary

FIGURE 8.17 Scenario Summary

The scenario summary contains a column listing the changing and result cell references, current values and result values, and a column of values and results for each defined scenario. This organized structure helps you compare the results as you analyze the scenarios. You should modify the structure and format the data for a more professional look. Typically, you should do the following:

- Delete the blank row 1 and the blank column A.
- Delete the Current Values column if it duplicates a defined scenario or if you do not want that data.
- Replace cell reference labels with descriptive labels in the first column.
- Delete the explanatory paragraph below the table and replace it with a narrative analysis relevant to the data.

Quick Concepts

1. What is the difference between Goal Seek and Scenario Manager? *p. 400*

2. What is the difference between a scenario summary report and a PivotTable report? *p. 402*

3. Will scenario summary reports automatically update when variables are changed? *p. 402*

2 Goal Seek and Scenario Manager

You want to use Goal Seek and Scenario Manager to perform additional what-if analyses with your mortgage data.

Skills covered: Use Goal Seek • Create a Scenario • Create Additional Scenarios • Generate and Format a Summary Report

STEP 1 ≫ USE GOAL SEEK

Given the current interest rate with a 30-year mortgage and your planned down payment, you want to identify the most that you can afford and maintain a $600.00 monthly payment. You will use Goal Seek to work backward from your goal to identify the ideal home purchase price. Refer to Figure 8.18 as you complete Step 1.

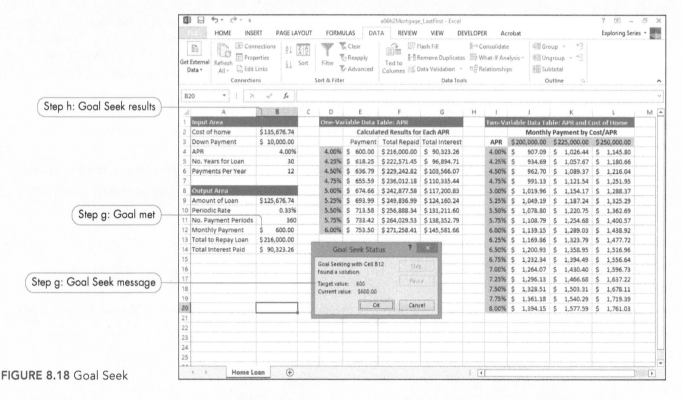

FIGURE 8.18 Goal Seek

a. Open the *e06h1Mortgage_LastFirst* workbook and save it as **e06h2Mortgage_LastFirst**, replacing *h1* with *h2*.

b. Click the **DATA tab**.

c. Click **What-If Analysis** in the Data Tools group and select **Goal Seek**.

   The Goal Seek dialog box opens.

d. Click **cell B12** to enter the cell reference in the **Set cell box**.

   You indicated which cell contains the formula that produces the goal.

e. Click in the **To value box** and type **600**.

   You want the monthly payment to be $600.

f. Click in the **By changing cell box** and click **cell B2**, the cell containing the cost of the home.

   Cell B2 is the cell whose value will be determined using the Goal Seek analysis tool.

g. Click **OK**.

The Goal Seek Status dialog box opens, indicating that it reached the target monthly payment goal of $600.

h. Click **OK** to accept the solution and to close the Goal Seek Status dialog box. Save the workbook.

To achieve a $600 monthly mortgage payment, you need to purchase a home that costs up to $135,676.74, instead of the original $150,000, assuming the other variables (down payment, interest rate, and term of loan) stay the same.

STEP 2 >> CREATE A SCENARIO

You want to use Scenario Manager to explore different scenarios. Your first scenario is a best-case scenario with these parameters: $250,000 home, $10,000 down payment, special no-interest financing for 30 years. Refer to Figure 8.19 as you complete Step 2.

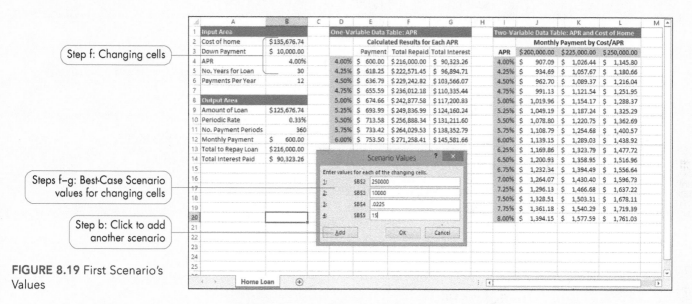

FIGURE 8.19 First Scenario's Values

a. Click the **DATA tab**, if necessary, click **What-If Analysis** in the Data Tools group, and then select **Scenario Manager**.

The Scenario Manager dialog box opens.

b. Click **Add**.

The Add Scenario dialog box opens so that you can assign a scenario name and select the changing cells.

c. Click in the **Scenario name box** and type **Best-Case Scenario**.

d. Delete existing contents in the *Changing cells* box and select the **range B2:B5**.

Excel enters this range in the *Changing cells* box.

e. Edit the Comment box, if needed, to display your name and the date the scenario is created, such as *Created by Jason Davidson on 8/01/2015*, and click **OK**.

The Scenario Values dialog box opens so that you can enter the parameters for the scenario.

f. Type **250000** in the **$B$2 box** and press **Tab** twice to accept the current $10,000 down payment.

You entered 250000 as the cost of the home.

g. Type **.0225** in the **$B$4 box**, press **Tab**, and then type **15** in the **$B$5 box**.

h. Click **OK** and click **Close**. Save the workbook.

While you could have kept the Scenario Values dialog box open to continue to the next step, you closed it so that you could save the workbook.

You will add two more scenarios: a worst-case scenario and a most likely scenario. In the worst-case scenario, you assume you will have to settle for a higher down payment, higher interest rate, and a longer loan period. In the most likely scenario, you will enter values that are between those in the other two scenarios.

a. Click **What-If Analysis** in the Data Tools group and select **Scenario Manager**.

b. Click **Add**, type **Worst-Case Scenario**, and then click **OK**.

The *Changing cells* box displays *B2:B5*, the range you selected for the first scenario.

c. Type the following values in the respective changing cells boxes:

Changing Cell Box	Value
$B$2	250000
$B$3	15000
$B$4	6%
$B$5	45

For the cell $B$4 box, you can enter the value as a percentage (6%) or as a decimal equivalent (0.06).

d. Click **Add**.

e. Type **Most Likely Scenario** and click **OK** in the Add Scenario dialog box.

f. Type the following values in the respective changing cells boxes:

Changing Cell Box	Value
$B$2	250000
$B$3	8500
$B$4	4.25%
$B$5	30

g. Click **OK**.

The Scenario Manager dialog box lists the three scenarios you created.

> **TROUBLESHOOTING:** If you believe you made any data entry errors, or if you want to double-check your values, select a scenario and click Edit. You can then change values in the Edit Scenario dialog box and click OK.

h. Click **Close** to close the Scenario Manager dialog box. Save the workbook.

STEP 4 ≫ GENERATE AND FORMAT A SUMMARY REPORT

You want to generate a scenario summary report to compare the three home loan scenarios you created. Refer to Figures 8.17 and 8.20 as you complete Step 4.

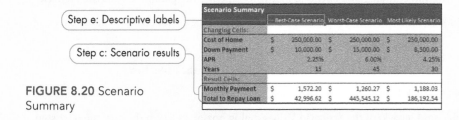

FIGURE 8.20 Scenario Summary

Step e: Descriptive labels

Step c: Scenario results

Scenario Summary

	Best-Case Scenario	Worst-Case Scenario	Most Likely Scenario
Changing Cells:			
Cost of Home	$ 250,000.00	$ 250,000.00	$ 250,000.00
Down Payment	$ 10,000.00	$ 15,000.00	$ 8,500.00
APR	2.25%	6.00%	4.25%
Years	15	45	30
Result Cells:			
Monthly Payment	$ 1,572.20	$ 1,260.27	$ 1,188.03
Total to Repay Loan	$ 42,996.62	$ 445,545.12	$ 186,192.54

a. Click **What-If Analysis** in the Data Tools group and select **Scenario Manager**.

b. Click **Summary**.

Excel may select a range within a data table.

c. Select the **range B12:B14** to enter it in the *Result cells* box and click **OK**.

Excel generates the summary on a new worksheet named Scenario Summary. The results are similar to Figure 8.17 except your summary also includes $B$13 results. You need to make a few deletions and add descriptive labels.

d. Delete the following:

- Column A
- Row 1
- Current Values column
- Notes in the **range A12:A15**

e. Enter descriptive labels in the following cells:

- **Cost of home** in **cell A5**
- **Down Payment** in **cell A6**
- **APR** in **cell A7**
- **Years** in **cell A8**
- **Monthly Payment** in **cell A10**
- **Total to Repay Loan** in **cell A11**
- **Total Interest Paid** in **cell A12**

The labels describe data contained in each row. Now you can delete column B, which displays the cell references.

f. Delete column B and increase the width of column A.

The Best-Case Scenario provides the lowest monthly payment.

g. Save the workbook. Keep the workbook open if you plan to continue with Hands-On Exercise 3. If not, close the workbook and exit Excel.

 TIP Scenario Worksheets

Each time you generate a summary, Excel inserts another Scenario Summary worksheet. You can delete a summary worksheet if you no longer need the data.

Solver

Add-ins are programs that can be added to Excel to provide enhanced functionality. *Solver* is an add-in application that searches for the best or optimum solution to a problem by manipulating the values for several variables within restrictions that you impose. You can use Solver to create optimization models. *Optimization models* find the highest, lowest, or exact value for one particular result by adjusting values for selected variables. Solver is one of the most sophisticated what-if analysis tools, and people use Solver in a variety of situations and industries. For example, a cellular phone manufacturing facility can use Solver to maximize the number of phones made or minimize the number of labor hours required while conforming to other production specifications. A financial planner might use Solver to help a family adjust its expenses to stay within its monthly income.

In this section, you will learn how to load the Solver add-in. Then, you will use Solver to set a target, select changing cells, and create constraints.

Loading the Solver Add-In

STEP 1 » Because other companies create the add-ins, they are not active by default. You must load the Solver add-in before you can use it. To load Solver, do the following:

1. Click the FILE tab and select Options.
2. Click Add-Ins to see a list of active and inactive add-in applications. The Active Application Add-ins list displays currently enabled add-ins, and the Inactive Application Add-ins list displays add-ins that are not currently enabled.
3. Click the Manage arrow, select Excel Add-ins, and then click Go to open the Add-Ins dialog box (see Figure 8.21).
4. Click the Solver Add-in check box in the *Add-Ins available* list and click OK.

FIGURE 8.21 Add-Ins Dialog Box

When you load Solver, Excel displays Solver in the Analysis group on the Data tab (see Figure 8.22), where it remains until you remove the Solver add-in. However, if you are in a campus computer lab that resets software settings when you log off, you will have to load Solver again each time you log into the lab's network.

Solver command

FIGURE 8.22 Solver on Data Tab

TIP Solver

Optimizing Results with Solver

Solver may be the best what-if analysis tool to solve complex linear and nonlinear problems. You can use it for complex equation solving and for constrained optimization where a set of constraints is specified and you want the outcome to be minimized or maximized. With Solver, you are able to change the values of several variables at once to achieve the desired result. For example, a business analyst might want to use Solver to maximize profits by changing selected variables while adhering to required limitations. Or a fulfillment company might want to determine the lowest shipping costs to transfer merchandise from a distribution center to retail stores.

Identify the Objective Cell and Changing Cells

STEP 2 »

Before using Solver, review your spreadsheet as you specify the goal, identify one or more variables that can change to reach the desired goal, and determine the limitations of the model. You will use these data to specify three parameters in Solver: objective cell, changing cells, and constraints.

The **objective cell** specifies the cell that contains a formula that produces a value that you want to optimize (that is, maximize, minimize, or set to a value) by manipulating values of one or more variables. The formula in the objective cell relates directly or indirectly to the changing cells and constraints. Using the mortgage case study as an example, the objective cell is B14 (the cell containing the total interest paid formula), and your goal is to minimize the total interest.

The **changing variable cells** are the cells containing variables whose values change within the constraints until the objective cell reaches its optimum value. The changing variable cells typically contain values, not formulas, but these cells have a mathematical relationship to the formula in the objective. In the home loan example, the changing variable cells are B3 (down payment) and B5 (number of years). You can select up to 200 changing variable cells. To specify the objective and changing cells, do the following:

1. Click Solver in the Analysis group on the Data tab to open the Solver Parameters dialog box (see Figure 8.23).

2. Enter the cell containing the formula for which you want to optimize its value in the Set Objective box.

3. Click an option in the *To* section to specify what type of value you need to find for the target cell. Click Max to maximize the value, Min to find the lowest value, or Value Of, and then specify the value in the Value Of box.

4. Enter the cell references that contain variables in the By Changing Variable Cells box. These are the variables that you want to change to reach the objective.

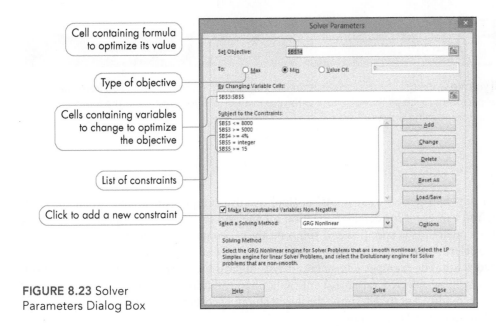

Cell containing formula to optimize its value

Type of objective

Cells containing variables to change to optimize the objective

List of constraints

Click to add a new constraint

FIGURE 8.23 Solver Parameters Dialog Box

Define the Constraints

STEP 3» The *constraints* specify the restrictions or limitations imposed on a spreadsheet model as Solver determines the optimum value for the objective cell. Rules govern every business model, based on historical requirements, physical limitations, and other decisions. Probably the most challenging process in using Solver is identifying all legitimate limitations. You may identify limitations through conversations with your supervisor, by reading policy statements, gathering information in meetings, and so on. Even after you enter data into Solver and run a report, you may gain knowledge of other limitations that you must build into the model. Using the home loan example, a constraint might be that the down payment must be between $5,000 and $8,000.

To add constraints to the Solver, do the following inside the Solver Parameters dialog box:

1. Click Add to the right of the *Subject to the Constraints* list to open the Add Constraint dialog box.
2. Enter the cell reference, the operator to test the cell references, and the constraint the cell needs to match (see Figure 8.24). The cell reference contains a variable whose value you want to constrain or restrict to a particular value or range. The operator defines the relationship between the variable and the constraint. For example, cell B3 (the down payment) is restricted to being less than or equal to $8,000. Solver will not allow the cost to be higher than this value.
3. Click OK to add the constraint and return to the Solver Parameters dialog box, or click Add to add the constraint and create another constraint.

TIP | Integer Constraint

One of the constraint operators is integer. This constraint requires the changing variable cell to be an integer, or whole number. For example, a manufacturing plant does not produce partial units such as 135.62 units, and a department store does not sell 18.32 shirts. To ensure that Solver produces realistic results, you should create integer constraints for these types of quantities. In Figure 8.23, the constraint $B$5 = integer limits the number of years for the loan to be a whole number.

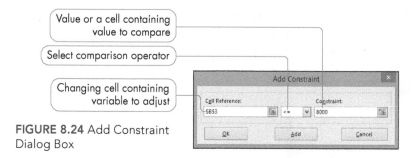

Value or a cell containing value to compare

Select comparison operator

Changing cell containing variable to adjust

FIGURE 8.24 Add Constraint Dialog Box

To modify a constraint's definition, select the constraint in the *Subject to the Constraints* list and click Change. Make changes in the Change Constraint dialog box and click OK to update the definition. If you no longer need a constraint, select it in the *Subject to the Constraints* list and click Delete. Be careful when using Delete; Solver does not prompt you to confirm the deletion. Solver deletes the selected constraint immediately, and you cannot restore the deleted constraint.

> **TIP** **Greater-Than-Zero Constraint**
>
> Another often-overlooked constraint is the requirement that the value of a variable cell be greater than or equal to zero. Physically, it makes no sense to produce a negative number of products in any category. Mathematically, however, a negative value in a changing variable cell may produce a higher value for the objective cell. By default, the Make Unconstrained Variables Non-Negative check box is selected to ensure variable values are greater than or equal to zero. If you want to allow the lower end of a variable's value to be a negative value, you can create a constraint such as B2>=-100. That constraint takes priority over the Make Unconstrained Variables Non-Negative check box.

Create a Solver Report

STEP 4 ≫ After defining the objective, changing variable cells, and constraints, select a solving method. Solver uses the selected solving method to determine which type of algorithms it executes to reach the objective. The Solver add-in for Excel 2013 contains these solving methods: GRG Nonlinear, Simplex LP, and Evolutionary. Look up *Solver* in Help to link to a specific set of descriptions of these methods. You can also review additional information and download additional add-ins on www.solver.com. For the purposes of this chapter, accept the default option, GRG Nonlinear.

You are now ready to use Solver to find a solution to the problem. Solver uses an iterative process of using different combinations of values in the changing variable cells to identify the optimum value for the objective cell. It starts with the current values and adjusts those values in accordance with the constraints. Once it finds the best solution, given the parameters you set, it identifies the values for the changing variable cells and shows you the optimum value in the objective value. If Solver cannot determine an optimum value, it does not enable you to generate summary reports. To create a Solver report, do the following:

1. Click Solve in the Solver Parameters dialog box. When Solver completes the iterative process, the Solver Results dialog box appears (see Figure 8.25). If it finds a solution, the Reports list displays available report types. If Solver cannot reach an optimal solution, no reports are available. Solutions are unattainable if a logic error exists or if the constraints do not allow sufficient elasticity to achieve a result. For example, a constraint between 10 and 11 may not allow sufficient flexibility, or a constraint greater than 20 but also less than 10 is illogical. If this happens, check each constraint for range constraints or errors in logic.

2. Click Keep Solver Solution to keep the changed objective and variable values, or click Restore Original Values to return to the original values in the worksheet. If you keep the changed values, Excel makes those changes to the actual worksheet. Do this if you are comfortable with those changes. If you want to maintain the original values, you should restore the original values.

3. Select a report from the Reports list. Generating a report is appropriate to see what changes Solver made while preserving the original values in the worksheet from Step 2.

4. Click OK to generate the summary on a separate worksheet.

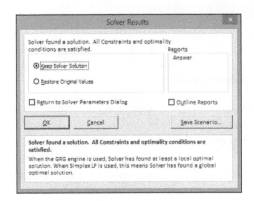

FIGURE 8.25 Solver Results Dialog Box

Solver creates a new worksheet for the Solver summary report containing four major sections (see Figure 8.26). The first section displays information about the Solver report. Specifically, it displays the report type, file name and worksheet containing the dataset, date and time the report was generated, Solver Engine details, and Solver Options that were set at the time the report was generated.

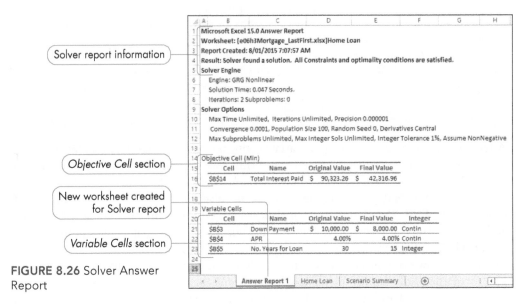

FIGURE 8.26 Solver Answer Report

The remaining sections of the report help you analyze the results. The section displays the objective cell information. Specifically, this section shows the original and final objective cell values. For example, using the original worksheet values, the original total interest paid in cell B14 was $100,617.31. The final minimized total interest paid is $47,064.23.

The third section displays the variable cells. Specifically, it displays the cell references, the variable cell names, original values, and final values. For example, the original down payment was $10,000, and the final value is $8,000.

The final section lists the constraints. Specifically, it displays the cell reference, description, new cell value, formula, status, and slack for each defined constraint. In this case, the down payment slack ($3,000) is the difference between the lower constraint ($5,000) and the final value ($8,000). The Status column indicates Binding or Not Binding. A ***binding constraint*** is a rule that Solver has to enforce to reach the objective value. That is, the value hits the maximum allowable value for a less-than-or-equal-to, minimum allowable value for a greater-than-or-equal-to, equal to, or integer constraint. For example, $B$3<=8000 is a binding constraint. That is, the down payment was raised to its maximum limit of $8,000 to identify the optimal least amount of total interest paid. If this constraint had not been set, Solver could have identified a higher down payment to obtain a lower value for the objective cell. A *nonbinding constraint* is one that does not restrict the target value that Solver finds. For example, $B$3>=5000 is nonbinding. Solver did not have to stop at a lowest down payment of $3,000 to reach the optimal total interest paid value.

If you change any of the Solver parameters—objective cell, changing variable cells, or constraints—you need to generate another report. Solver does not update the report automatically. Each time you generate a report, Solver creates another new worksheet with names like Answer Report 1, Answer Report 2, and so on. Delete any reports you no longer need to minimize the file size of your workbook.

TIP Save Scenario

If you want to save the solution parameters to use in Scenario Manager, click Save Scenario in the Solver Results dialog box and type a name for the scenario in the *Scenario name* box.

Configure Solver

You can closely monitor the trial solutions prior to reaching the final solution. Solver is a mathematical modeling operation, and you can determine solutions using the associated mathematics. However, stepping through Solver enables you to view the steps Solver performs. To step through trial solutions, do the following:

1. Click Options in the Solver Parameters dialog box to open the Options dialog box.
2. Select the Show Iteration Results check box to see the values of each trial solution and click OK.
3. Click Solve in the Solver Parameters dialog box.
4. When the Show Trial Solution dialog box appears, either:

   - Click Stop to stop the process and open the Solver Results dialog box, or
   - Click Continue to continue the process and display the next trial solution.

You can also use the Options dialog box to customize Solver further. Because Solver uses an iterative approach, you can specify the number of iterations to try, how much time to take to solve the problem, and how precise the answer should be (i.e., accuracy to what number of decimal places), among other settings.

Save and Restore a Solver Model

When you use Solver, Excel keeps track of your settings and saves only the most recent Solver settings. In some cases, you may want to save the parameters of a model so that you can apply them again in the future. Saving a Solver model is helpful if the original data source might change and you want to compare results by generating multiple Solver answer reports. When you save a Solver model, you save the objective value, the changing variable cells, and the constraints.

Saving a Solver model places the information in a small block of cells on a worksheet. The number of cells required to save the Solver model is dependent on the number of constraints in the model. To save Solver settings, do the following:

1. Click Load/Save in the Solver Parameters dialog box.
2. Click in the worksheet where the first cell is to be placed. Make sure the worksheet has sufficient empty cells so the Solver information does not overwrite Excel data.
3. Click Save to return to the Solver Parameters dialog box.

If you want to use an existing Solver model with new or updated data, you must return to a previous Solver model. When you want to use a Solver model that you saved, do the following:

1. Click Load/Save in the Solver Parameters dialog box.
2. Select the worksheet cells that contain the Solver data. You must select all cells with the Solver data.
3. Click Load to load the model's values and return to the Solver Parameter dialog box.

Quick
Concepts

1. Is Solver preloaded in Excel? *p. 408*
2. What three optimization goals can Solver calculate? *p. 408*
3. What is the advantage of Solver over Goal Seek? *p. 409*

Hands-On Exercises

 Watch the Video for this Hands-On Exercise!

3 Solver

Although Goal Seek and Scenario Manager were helpful in further analyzing your home purchase, you want to ensure the spreadsheet model imposes constraints on the situation. Therefore, you will continue your analysis by using Solver.

Skills covered: Load the Solver Add-In • Set the Objective and Variable Cells • Define the Constraints • Generate a Report

STEP 1 » LOAD THE SOLVER ADD-IN

Before you can use Solver to analyze your home loan model, you need to load Solver. If Solver is already loaded, skip Step 1 and start with Step 2. Refer to Figure 8.27 as you complete Step 1.

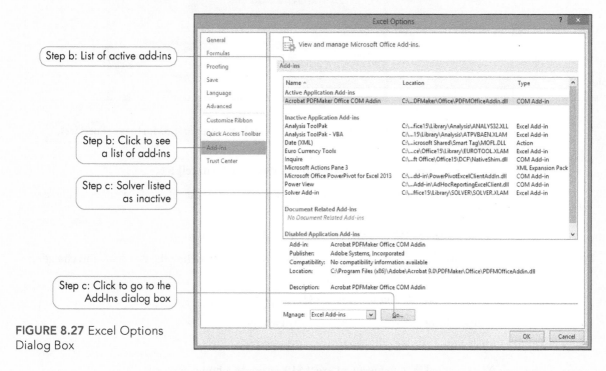

FIGURE 8.27 Excel Options Dialog Box

a. Click the **FILE tab** and click **Options**.

The Excel Options dialog box opens so that you can customize Excel settings.

b. Click **Add-Ins** on the left side of the Excel Options dialog box.

The Excel Options dialog box displays a list of active and inactive application add-ins.

c. Check to see where Solver is listed. If Solver is listed in the Active Application Add-ins list, click **OK**, and then skip step d. If Solver is listed in the Inactive Application Add-ins list, click the **Manage arrow**, select **Excel Add-ins** if necessary, and then click **Go**.

The Add-Ins dialog box opens, containing a list of available add-in applications.

d. Click the **Solver Add-in check box** in the **Add-Ins available list** and click **OK**.

STEP 2 ≫ SET THE OBJECTIVE AND VARIABLE CELLS

Before using Solver, you want to reset the variables to their original values. After entering the original variable values again, you will specify the monthly payment cell as the objective cell and the home cost, down payment, APR, and number of years for the loan as the changing variable cells. Refer to Figure 8.28 as you complete Step 2.

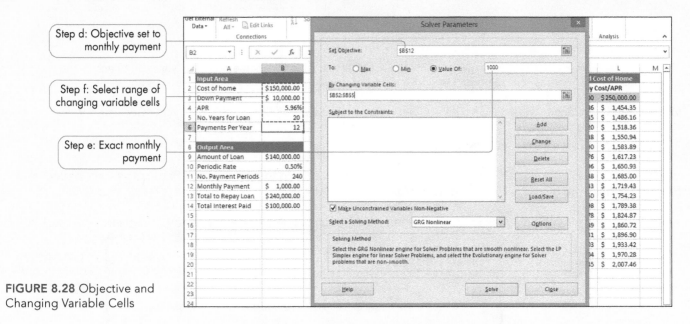

Step d: Objective set to monthly payment

Step f: Select range of changing variable cells

Step e: Exact monthly payment

FIGURE 8.28 Objective and Changing Variable Cells

a. Open the *e06h2Mortgage_LastFirst* workbook and save it as **e06h3Mortgage_LastFirst**, replacing *h2* with *h3*.

b. Click the **Home Loan worksheet tab** and type **150000** in **cell B2**.

Now that you have reset the values to your original spreadsheet model, you are ready to use Solver.

c. Click the **DATA tab** and click **Solver** in the Analysis group.

The Solver Parameters dialog box opens so that you can define the objective and changing variable cells.

d. Click **cell B12** to enter it in the **Set Objective box**.

You set the objective cell as the monthly payment.

e. Click **Value Of** and type **1000** in the **Value Of box**.

You specified that you want an exact $1000 monthly home payment.

f. Click in the **By Changing Variable Cells box** and select the **range B2:B5**. Click **Close** and save the workbook.

> **TROUBLESHOOTING:** Be careful to select the correct range. If you accidentally select cell B6, Solver might produce inaccurate results.

STEP 3 >> DEFINE THE CONSTRAINTS

You define the constraints: $100,000 to $300,000 cost, $5,000 to $10,000 down payment, 4% to 6% APR, and 15- to 30-year loan. In addition, you set an integer constraint for the years so that Solver does not produce a fractional year, such as 5.71. Refer to Figure 8.29 as you complete Step 3.

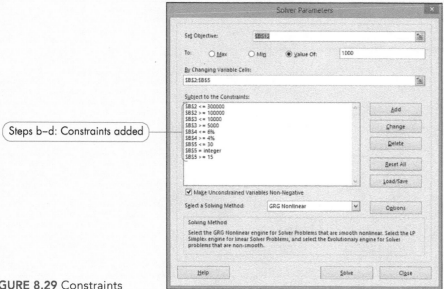

Steps b–d: Constraints added

FIGURE 8.29 Constraints

a. Click **Solver** in the Analysis group and click **Add**.

The Add Constraint dialog box opens so that you can define the first constraint.

b. Click **cell B2**, make sure <= is selected, click in the **Constraint box**, and then type **300000**.

You defined a constraint that the total home cost cannot exceed $300,000.

c. Click **Add** to define another constraint. Click **cell B2**, click the **operator arrow**, select >=, click in the **Constraint box**, and then type **100000**.

The second constraint specifies that the cost of the home must be at least $100,000.

d. Add the following constraints in a similar manner. After you enter the last constraint, click **OK** in the Add Constraint dialog box.

- B3<=10000
- B3>=5000
- B4<=6%
- B4>=4%
- B5<=30
- B5>=15
- B5 int

> **TROUBLESHOOTING:** Click Add to complete the current constraint and open an Add Constraint dialog box to enter another constraint. Click OK in the Add Constraint dialog box only when you have completed the last constraint and want to return to the Solver Parameters dialog box to solve the problem.

e. Check the constraints carefully against those shown in Figure 8.29 and step d. Click **Close** and save the workbook.

STEP 4 >> GENERATE A REPORT

Now that you have completed the parameters for restricting the result based on the cost of the home, the down payment, the APR, and the number of years for the loan, you are ready to generate a Solver report. Refer to Figure 8.30 as you complete Step 4.

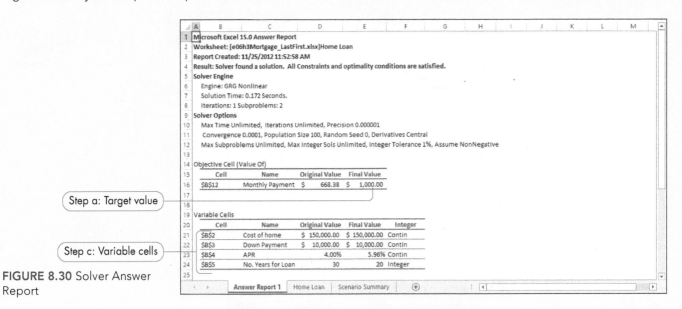

Step a: Target value

Step c: Variable cells

FIGURE 8.30 Solver Answer Report

a. Click **Solver** in the Analysis group and click **Solve**.

The Solver Results dialog box opens. If you look at the worksheet data, the new values appear in the changing cells, and the $1000 target monthly payment appears in cell B12.

b. Select **Answer** in the **Reports list** and click **OK**.

Solver generates a report and displays it in a new worksheet named Answer Report 1.

> **TROUBLESHOOTING:** If you see the error message, *Solver: An unexpected internal error occurred, or available memory was exhausted*, close Solver, click Undo, remove Solver as an add-in, save and close the workbook, open the workbook again, and then enable the Solver add-in again. Then click Solver in the Analysis group, click Solve, select Answer Report, and then click OK.

c. Click the **Answer Report 1 worksheet tab**.

Solver adjusts the values in the changing cells B2:B5 to obtain the exact value of $1000 for the objective cell B12. The report shows the previous and final values of the objective and variable cells. *Your final values may vary slightly from those shown in the figure.*

d. Scroll down through the worksheet to see the constraints.

In addition, the report displays the constraints—cell references, descriptive labels, current cell values, formulas, status (binding/not binding), and slack. Although not specified, integer constraints are always binding. Had you not constrained the years to a whole number, Solver might have found different values for the variable cells. However, you need to enforce that constraint because the term of the mortgage is a whole year. The 4% APR constraint is binding, meaning that Solver found the lowest possible APR to produce its answer. Finally, the 30-year limit is binding, meaning that Solver could not use a larger number of years for the loan to derive its answer.

e. Save and close the workbook, and submit based on your instructor's directions.

Chapter Objectives Review

After reading this chapter, you have accomplished the following objectives:

1. **Create a one-variable data table.**
   - A one-variable data table enables you to compare different values for one variable to compare their effects on one or more results.
   - Set up the substitution values: Substitution values replace the original value of a variable in a data table.
   - Add formulas to the data table: After entering a substitution value, a formula must be added to relate mathematically to the substation values.
   - Complete the results: Excel uses the substitution values individually to replace the original variable's to populate the data table.
   - Format the data table: After completing the data table, all values should be appropriately formatted.

2. **Create a two-variable data table.**
   - A two-variable data table enables you to compare results for two variables at the same time but for only one result.
   - Set up the substitution values for two variables: Use the top row for one variable's substitution values and the first column for the second variable's substitution values.
   - Add a formula to the data table: Enter the required formula in the top-left corner of the data table.
   - Complete the two-variable data table: Select the data table boundaries, then choose Data Table from the What-If Analysis menu on the Ribbon.

3. **Identify an input value with Goal Seek.**
   - Use Goal Seek to work backward with a problem when you know what you want for the result but you do not know the value of a variable to achieve that goal. If you accept the results, Excel enters the identified input value directly in the variable cell.

4. **Use Scenario Manager.**
   - Use Scenario Manager to create a set of scenarios, each with multiple variables.
   - The Scenario Manager dialog box enables you to add, delete, and change scenarios.
   - For each scenario, you specify a name, the changing cells, and the values for those changing cells.
   - Create and edit scenarios: Click What-If Analysis in the Data Tools group of the Data tab. Select Scenario Manager. Click Add to open the scenario dialog box.
   - View scenarios: To view a created scenario, click What-If Analysis in the Data Tools group of the Data tab. Select Scenario Manager, click the name of the scenario you would like to review, and then click show.

5. **Generate scenario summary reports.**
   - After you create the scenarios with specific values, you can generate a summary report.
   - Excel creates the summary report in a structured format on a new worksheet and displays the values for the changing cells and their effects on the results cells so that you can compare the results easily.

6. **Load the Solver add-in.**
   - Solver is an add-in program for Excel. When you enable Solver, Excel places Solver in the Analysis group on the Data tab.

7. **Optimize results with Solver.**
   - Solver is an optimization technique that enables you to maximize or minimize the value of an objective function, such as profit or cost. Solver uses an iterative process to use different values for variable cells until it finds the optimum objective value within the constraints you set.
   - Identify the objective cell and changing cells: The objective cell contains the information that is to be set to value of, minimum, or maximum by Solver.
   - Define the constraints: Set in the Solver dialog box, constraints are limitations that are imposed on Solver.
   - Create a Solver report: In the Solver Results dialog box, choose an option under Reports to have Excel create a report on a new worksheet.
   - Configure Solver: Solver's calculation settings can be configured by clicking the Options button in the Solver Parameters dialog box.
   - Save and restore a Solver model: A Solver model can be imported or exported by clicking Load/Save in the Solver Parameters dialog box.

Key Terms Matching

Match the key terms with their definitions. Write the key term letter by the appropriate numbered definition.

a. Add-in
b. Binding constraint
c. Changing variable cell
d. Constraint
e. Goal Seek
f. Nonbinding constraint
g. Objective cell
h. One-variable data table
i. Optimization model

j. Scenario
k. Scenario Manager
l. Scenario summary report
m. Solver
n. Substitution value
o. Two-variable data table
p. Variable
q. What-if analysis

1. _____ A constraint that Solver enforces to reach the target value. **p. 412**

2. _____ A cell containing a variable whose value changes until Solver optimizes the value in the objective cell. **p. 409**

3. _____ An add-in application that manipulates variables based on constraints to find the optimal solution to a problem. **p. 408**

4. _____ A data analysis tool that provides various results based on changing one variable. **p. 388**

5. _____ A set of values that represent a possible situation. **p. 400**

6. _____ The cell that contains the formula-based value that you want to maximize, minimize, or set to a value in Solver. **p. 409**

7. _____ Finds the highest, lowest, or exact value for one particular result by adjusting values for selected variables. **p. 408**

8. _____ A constraint that does not restrict the target value that Solver finds. **p. 413**

9. _____ The process of changing variables to observe how changes affect calculated results. **p. 388**

10. _____ A value that you can change to see how that change affects other values. **p. 388**

11. _____ Replaces the original value of a variable in a data table. **p. 388**

12. _____ A limitation that imposes restrictions on Solver. **p. 410**

13. _____ A program that can be added to Excel to provide enhanced functionality. **p. 408**

14. _____ A worksheet that contains scenario results. **p. 402**

15. _____ A data analysis tool that provides results based on changing two variables. **p. 392**

16. _____ A tool that identifies the necessary input value to obtain a desired goal. **p. 399**

17. _____ Enables you to define and manage scenarios to compare how they affect results. **p. 400**

1. Which what-if analysis tool is the best option for complex calculations requiring constrained optimization?

   (a) Goal Seek

   (b) Scenario Manager

   (c) Data Tables

   (d) Solver

2. Which tools are best suited to calculate the impact of multiple interest rates on an auto loan? (Check all that apply.)

   (a) Goal Seek

   (b) Scenario Manager

   (c) One-variable data table

   (d) Solver

3. Which tool is most effective when comparing the impacts of various combinations of interest rates and down payments on a mortgage?

   (a) Goal Seek

   (b) Solver

   (c) Two-variable data table

   (d) Scenario Manager

4. This tool calculates the value required in a single cell to produce a desired result with in a related cell.

   (a) Goal Seek

   (b) Solver

   (c) One- or Two-variable data table

   (d) Scenario Manager

5. This analysis tool has the ability to handle multiple adjustable cells while minimizing, maximizing, or meeting goals.

   (a) Goal Seek

   (b) Solver

   (c) One- or Two-variable data table

   (d) Scenario Manager

6. Which of the following is an Excel add-in?

   (a) Goal Seek

   (b) Solver

   (c) One- or Two-variable data table

   (d) Scenario Manager

7. Doug would like to purchase a new automobile. He has budgeted for $600 per month. If the interest and number of payments are constant variables that cannot change, which analysis tool should Doug use to calculate the amount to spend on a car?

   (a) Goal Seek

   (b) Solver

   (c) One- or Two-variable data table

   (d) Scenario Manager

8. Which dialog box enables you to specify the result cells for a scenario summary report?

   (a) Scenario Summary

   (b) Scenario Values

   (c) Add Scenario

   (d) Solver Options

9. Which of the following tools can incorporate constraints?

   (a) Goal Seek

   (b) Solver

   (c) Data Tables

   (d) Scenario Manager

10. How can you determine if the Solver add-in is active? (Check all that apply.)

    (a) Solver is an option in the Home tab of the Ribbon.

    (b) Solver is available via right-click.

    (c) Solver appears in the Data tab of the Ribbon.

    (d) Solver appears in the Goal Seek dialog box to make it appear as a label.

Practice Exercises

1 Annual Bonuses

You manage a software development company in Portland. Employees earn an annual bonus that ranges from 0.5% to 5% of their gross salary. You are required by law to withhold applicable income taxes. To minimize employee disappointment from knowing what their qualified bonus is versus seeing the bonus on their paychecks, you developed a model that you can distribute to employees to help them predict their net bonus amount. You create a one-variable data table to list various bonus rates and their effects on the gross bonus, taxes withheld, and net bonus. Then you create a two-variable data table that compares combinations of various bonus rates and sample gross salaries to show net bonuses. This exercise follows the same set of skills as used in Hands-On Exercise 1 in the chapter. Refer to Figure 8.31 as you complete this exercise.

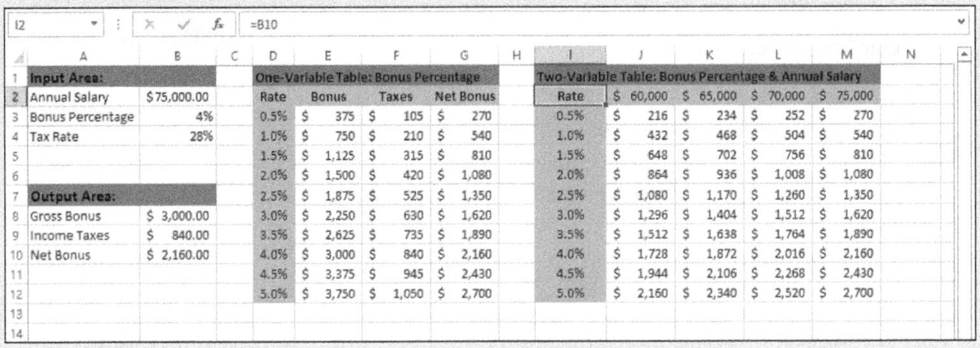
I2 =B10

	A	B	C	D	E	F	G	H	I	J	K	L	M
1	Input Area:			One-Variable Table: Bonus Percentage					Two-Variable Table: Bonus Percentage & Annual Salary				
2	Annual Salary	$75,000.00		Rate	Bonus	Taxes	Net Bonus		Rate	$ 60,000	$ 65,000	$ 70,000	$ 75,000
3	Bonus Percentage	4%		0.5%	$ 375	$ 105	$ 270		0.5%	$ 216	$ 234	$ 252	$ 270
4	Tax Rate	28%		1.0%	$ 750	$ 210	$ 540		1.0%	$ 432	$ 468	$ 504	$ 540
5				1.5%	$ 1,125	$ 315	$ 810		1.5%	$ 648	$ 702	$ 756	$ 810
6				2.0%	$ 1,500	$ 420	$ 1,080		2.0%	$ 864	$ 936	$ 1,008	$ 1,080
7	Output Area:			2.5%	$ 1,875	$ 525	$ 1,350		2.5%	$ 1,080	$ 1,170	$ 1,260	$ 1,350
8	Gross Bonus	$ 3,000.00		3.0%	$ 2,250	$ 630	$ 1,620		3.0%	$ 1,296	$ 1,404	$ 1,512	$ 1,620
9	Income Taxes	$ 840.00		3.5%	$ 2,625	$ 735	$ 1,890		3.5%	$ 1,512	$ 1,638	$ 1,764	$ 1,890
10	Net Bonus	$ 2,160.00		4.0%	$ 3,000	$ 840	$ 2,160		4.0%	$ 1,728	$ 1,872	$ 2,016	$ 2,160
11				4.5%	$ 3,375	$ 945	$ 2,430		4.5%	$ 1,944	$ 2,106	$ 2,268	$ 2,430
12				5.0%	$ 3,750	$ 1,050	$ 2,700		5.0%	$ 2,160	$ 2,340	$ 2,520	$ 2,700
13													
14													

FIGURE 8.31 Bonus Variable Data Tables

a. Open *e06p1Bonus* and save it as **e06p1Bonus_LastFirst.**

b. Click **cell D3** and do the following to enter a series of substitution values for the bonus percentage:
- Type **0.5%** and press **Ctrl+Enter** to keep **cell D3** active.
- Click **Fill** in the Editing group on the HOME tab and select **Series.**
- Click **Columns** in the *Series in* section, type **0.5%** in the **Step value box**, type **5%** in the **Stop value box**, and then click **OK.**

c. Enter the references to formulas in the following cells:
- **Cell E2: =B8**
- **Cell F2: =B9**
- **Cell G2: =B10**

d. Complete the one-variable data table by doing the following:
- Select the **range D2:G12.**
- Click the **DATA tab**, click **What-If Analysis** in the Data Tools group, and then select **Data Table.**
- Click in the **Column input cell box**, click **cell B3**, and then click **OK.**
- Select the **range E3:G12**, click the **HOME tab**, and then apply **Accounting Number Format** with zero decimal places.

e. Create column headings for the data table by doing the following:
- Type **Rate** in **cell D2.**
- Click **cell E2** and click the **Number Dialog Box Launcher** in the Number group.
- Click **Custom** in the **Category list**, scroll up in the **Type list**, and then select **General.**
- Select **General** in the Type box, type **Bonus**, and then click **OK.**
- Adapt the above steps to create a custom number format to display *Taxes* in **cell F2** and **Net Bonus** in **cell G2.**
- Center and bold the **range D2:G2.**

f. Set up the variables for the two-variable data table by copying the **range D3:D12** and pasting it in the **range I3:I12.** Enter **60000** in **cell J2** and use the Series dialog box to fill the row data to **75000** in steps of **5000.**

g. Enter **=B10** in **cell I2.**

h. Complete the two-variable data table by doing the following:

- Select the **range I2:M12**.
- Click the **DATA tab**, click **What-If Analysis** in the Data Tools group, and then select **Data Table**.
- Click **cell B2** to enter that reference in the **Row input cell box**.
- Click in the **Column input cell box**, click **cell B3**, and then click **OK**.
- Select the **range J3:M12** and apply **Accounting Number Format** with zero decimal places.
- Create a custom number format to display *Rate* in **cell I2**. Bold and center data in this cell.

i. Select **landscape orientation** and set **0.4"** left and right margins.

j. Create a footer with your name on the left side, the date code in the center, and the file name code on the right side.

k. Save and close the workbook, and submit it based on your instructor's directions.

2 Sue's Bakery

Sue has opened a bakery specializing in cupcakes. Her budget must account for fixed expenses, such as her facility lease, utilities, and credit card equipment fees. In addition, she accounts for variable costs including cost of goods sold and credit card processing fees. You will use Goal Seek to determine how many cupcakes she must sell to earn a net profit of $3,500. Then you will use Scenario Manager to evaluate several possible situations. This exercise follows the same set of skills as used in Hands-On Exercise 2 in the chapter. Refer to Figure 8.32 as you complete this exercise.

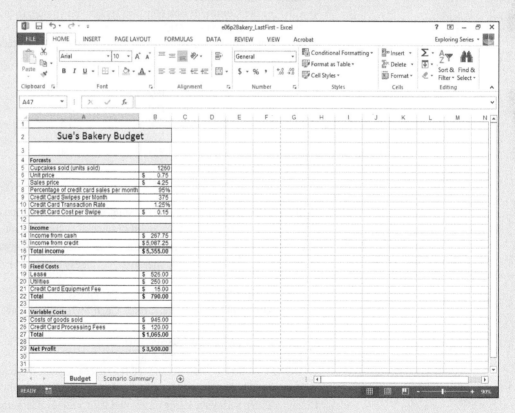

FIGURE 8.32 Sue's Bakery Budget

a. Open *e06p2Bakery* and save it as **e06p2Bakery_LastFirst**.

b. Enter the following formulas:
- **Cell B14: =B16-B16*B8** to calculate the projected cash sales amount of the total sales.
- **Cell B15: =B16-B14** to calculate the amount of income from credit card transactions.
- **Cell B25: =B5*B6** to calculate the cost of goods sold, which is the product of the units sold and unit cost.
- **Cell B26: =(B10*B15)+(B9*B11)** to calculate credit card processing fees, which are currently 1.25% of credit card amounts and $0.15 cents per transaction.
- **Cell B29: =B16-B22-B27** to calculate the net profit.

c. Click the **DATA tab**, click **What-If Analysis** in the Data Tools group, and then select **Goal Seek**.

d. Complete the Goal Seek by doing the following:
- Click **cell B29** to add the cell reference to the *Set cell* box.
- Click in the **To value box** and type **3500**.
- Click in the **By changing cell box** and click **cell B5**.
- Click **OK** in the Goal Seek dialog box and click **OK** in the Goal Seek Status dialog box. How many cupcakes must Sue sell to reach her net profit goal of $3,500? Answer: 1,260.

e. Click **What-If Analysis** in the Data Tools group and select **Scenario Manager**.

f. Create the first scenario by doing the following:
- Click **Add** and type **Current Conditions** in the **Scenario name box**.
- Click in the **Changing cells box**, select the **range B5:B7**, and then press and hold **Ctrl** while you select the **range B9:B10**.
- Click in the **Comment box** edit it to reflect your name, such as *Created by Jason Davidson on 9/4/2015*, and then click **OK**.
- Type **700** in the **$B$5 box**, leave the other current values intact, and then click **OK**.

g. Create the following three scenarios, clicking either **Add** or **OK** as indicated:

Scenario Name	Ideal Case	Increased Costs	Low Sales
$B$4	1,260	700	500
$B$5	.75	.75	.75
$B$6	4.25	4.50	4.00
$B$8	375	275	150
$B$9	1.25%	2.49%	1.25%
Button	Add	Add	OK

h. Click **Summary**, select and delete the suggested range in the **Result cells box**, press and hold **Ctrl** as you click **cells B16, B22, B27, and B29** to enter these cells, and then click **OK**.

i. Make these changes to the summary on the Scenario Summary worksheet:
- Delete the blank column A, the Current Values column, the blank row 1, and the notes in the **range A16:A18**.
- Click in **cell A5**, type **Units Sold**, and then press **Enter**.
- Enter **Unit Cost, Sale Price, Credit Card Swipes**, and **Card Transaction Rate** in the **range A6:A9**.
- Enter **Gross Sales, Fixed Costs, Variable Costs**, and **Profit** in the **range A11:A14**.
- Increase the width of column A to display the labels.
- Delete column B containing the cell references because these references would have no meaning if you distribute only the scenario summary worksheet to others.

j. Create a footer with your name on the left side, and the file name code on the right side for both worksheets.

k. Save and close the workbook, and submit it based on your instructor's directions.

1 Housing Construction Cost Variables

Your friends, Elijah and Valerie Foglesong, want to build their dream house. They identified tentative costs, but they cannot afford the $414,717 estimated cost. You will use Goal Seek to determine an estimate of the total finished square footage they can afford. To help provide more flexibility in their decision making, you will create a data table listing various finished square footages and their effects on the base house cost and total cost. Finally, you will create another data table showing combinations of square footages and lot prices to identify total costs. Although a builder's overall house design specifies the square footage, the Foglesongs can use your data tables to help guide them in their decision.

a. Open *e06m1House* and save it as **e06m1House_LastFirst**.

b. Use Goal Seek to determine the total finished square footage to meet the total cost goal of $350,000.

c. Enter a series of total square footages ranging from 1,800 to 3,600 in increments of 200 in the **range D6:D15**. Apply **Blue font** and **Comma Style** with zero decimal places to the series. Enter references to the base cost and total cost in the appropriate cells on row 5.

d. Complete the data table using the appropriate input cell. Apply custom number formats to give appropriate descriptions to the second and third columns. Apply these formats to the headings: bold, center, and **Blue font**.

e. Identify the square footage, base price, and total cost that come closest to their goal. Apply **Blue, Accent 1, Lighter 40% fill color** to those cells in the data table.

f. Copy the square footage substitution values to the **range H6:H15** and remove the fill color. Enter these lot price substitution values in the **range I5:K5: 90000, 96000**, and **102675**. Format these values with **Accounting Number Format** with zero decimal places and **Blue font**.

g. Enter the reference to the total cost formula in the appropriate location for the second data table. Complete the data table using the appropriate input cells. Apply a custom number format to the reference to the formula cell. Apply bold and **Blue font color** to that cell. Apply **Blue, Accent 1, Lighter 40% fill color** to the total price in each column that comes closest to their goal.

h. Format results in both tables with **Accounting Number Format** with zero decimal places.

i. Create a footer with your name on the left side, the sheet name code in the center, and the file name code on the right side. Adjust the orientation, margins, and scaling to fit on one page.

j. Save and close the workbook, and submit it based on your instructor's directions.

2 Ray's Heating and Air

ANALYSIS CASE

You are the Chief Financial Officer for Ray's Heating and Air. You have been given the task of increasing gross income from $91,000 to $120,000 per year. Ray's income is earned through service calls. Customers are charged trip and hourly charges as pictured in the table below. Your goal is to create a spreadsheet to allow you to evaluate the most economically feasible option for increasing gross income while adhering to the following constraints. The maximum amount of hours billed without hiring additional technicians is 2,500. The trip charge may not exceed $50.00, and the service hourly rate/trip charge must all be whole numbers. The calls/hourly rate/trip charge must all be whole numbers.

Current Service Calls	Hourly rate	Trip Charge	Hours Billed
640	$30.00	$25.00	2500

a. Open *e06m2RaysAC* and save it as **e06m2RaysAC_LastFirst**.

b. Use the formula service calls * trip charge + hours billed * hourly rate to determine gross income.

c. If not loaded, load the Solver add-in.

d. Set the objective cell to $120,000.

e. Set constraints to ensure service calls, hourly rate, and trip charge are integers.

f. Set a constraint to ensure hours billed cannot exceed 2,500.

g. Set a constraint to ensure the trip charge does not exceed $50.00.

h. Set a constraint to ensure hourly rate does not drop below $30.00

i. Create an Answer Report to outline your findings.

j. After solving, answer the questions in the Q&A section.

3 College Budget

COLLABORATION CASE

FROM SCRATCH

You are beginning your freshman year of college. Prior to leaving for school, you worked a summer job and were able to save $1,500 for expenses such as books, supplies, and a university parking pass. After arriving on campus, you discovered your computer was out of date, and you need to purchase a newer model. Your books cost $700, a mini fridge for your room costs $250.00, and you are estimating your parking pass will cost $350.00. After researching pricing for newer computers, you determine a new computer will cost $750.00. Your parents have agreed to give you the additional money required to purchase the computer; however, they will only do so if you send them an Excel workbook outlining your expenses and the amount of money that they must contribute to the purchase. You have decided to create this document and then share the file with your parents through your family's OneDrive account.

Student 1:

a. Open Excel and create a blank document. Save this document as **e06m3CollegeBudget_LastFirst**.

b. Click in **cell A1** and type item **Description**. Press **Tab** and type **Expense** in **cell B1**.

c. Click in **cell A2**, type the name of your first expense—for example, **Parking Pass**—and then enter the corresponding cost in **cell B2**.

d. Continue entering your expenses in **cells A3:B3** for books and in **cell A4:B4** for the mini fridge. Type **Total expenses** in **cell A5** and enter a SUM function in **cell B5** to total your expenses.

e. Highlight **cells A5:B5** and apply the **Bad style** from the styles group located in the HOME tab of the Ribbon.

f. Click **cell D1**, type **Summer Savings**, and then type **1500** in **cell D2**. Then complete the following tasks:
   - Type **Savings after expenses** in **cell A6**.
   - Type **Computer cost** in **cell A7**.
   - Type **Parental contribution** in **cell A8**.
   - Type **Deficit** in **cell A9**.
   - Type **750** in **cell B7**.
   - Type **0** in **cell B8**.

g. Click in **cell B9** and enter the following formula: **=B7-B6-B8**. This calculates the financial deficit after the computer has been purchased. The goal is for this cell to have a value of zero after your parents' contribution.

h. Use Goal Seek to set the deficit to **0** by changing your parents' contribution amount.

i. Format the worksheet with the font and color of your choice. Apply **Currency format** to all numbers.

j. Save the workbook to OneDrive.

Student 2:

k. Open the worksheet and review the proposed budget.

l. Based on the budget, navigate to www.amazon.com and research the going rates on a college size mini fridge. If you are able to locate a better price, update the dollar amount and upload back to sky drive.

Beyond the Classroom

Too Cold to Snow

RESEARCH CASE

Have you ever wondered whether it could be too cold to snow? Actually, it is much more likely to snow if the temperature is close to freezing than if it is much below. The reason is because the air gets too dry to snow. As the air gets colder, it holds less water vapor for making snow. This explains why Nashville, Tennessee, typically gets more snowfall each year than frigid Barrow, Alaska! Because snow in northern Alaska does not melt as quickly as snow in Nashville, the area appears to get more snow.

You are a high school science teacher preparing a lesson on the effect of temperature and water vapor on snowfall. The dew point is the temperature at which water vapor condenses and forms into liquid or frozen precipitation, and the wet bulb temperature is the lowest temperature that can be reached by the evaporation of water only. Typically, the greater the difference between wet bulb and air temperatures, the drier the air. Because drier air is less likely to produce snow, you will use the wet bulb temperature to approximate the dryness of the air and the potential for snow. Use the Internet to find the temperature and dew point of Nashville on January 6 of the current year and develop an estimate of the wet bulb temperature.

Open *e06b2Snow* and save it as **e06b2Snow_LastFirst**. Use Scenario Manager to create a Most Likely and Least Likely projection of wet bulb temperature for Nashville. The Most Likely statistics are those that you identified for January 6. The Least Likely statistics are a temperature of 18° and a dew point of 5°. Wet bulb temperature is calculated by subtracting dew point from temperature and dividing the result by 3. Edit the summary as specified in the *Generating Scenario Summary Reports* section in the chapter. Insert a text box and write an analysis about your results. Create a footer with your name, the sheet name code, and the file name code. Save and close the workbook, and submit it based on your instructor's directions.

Mining Company

DISASTER RECOVERY

You work for an investment corporation that is considering purchasing a coal mine. One of your colleagues developed a spreadsheet model and started a what-if analysis using Solver. Unfortunately, Solver is unable to solve the problem given the parameters entered. You need to identify and correct the errors and then generate an answer report. Open *e06b3Mining* and save it as **e06b3Mining_LastFirst**. Make sure that Solver is loaded. If not, load the Solver add-in. The objective is to maximize the rate of return by the end of the fifth year. The investment firm is considering paying between $20 and $25 million for the mine with an anticipated 1 to 1.5 million tons sold in the first year. Research indicates the price per ton to be between $12.35 and $14.50 initially. The price-per-ton increase should range from 0.5% to 1.25%. Before you run the Solver report, change the number of iterations to 1,500 in the Solver Options dialog box. Insert notes to describe the parameter errors, correct the errors, and run a Solver answer report. Create a footer with your name, the sheet name code, and the file name code on the report. Adjust the left and right margins on the Answer Report 1 worksheet so that the data can print on one page. Deselect the options that print gridlines and headings on the Forecast worksheet. Save and close the workbook, and submit it based on your instructor's directions.

Payment Options

You have been hired by a debt management company and given the task of working with recent graduates to help manage student loan debt. While the goal of your company is to make money, they value the importance of transparency in payment options. As part of your daily tasks, you will use Excel to build scenarios based on payment options to determine the best repayment choice for each graduate.

Open the file *e06b4Repayment*. Save the file as **e06b4Repayment_LastFirst**. Use Scenario Manager to create three scenarios to share with your client. Name the first scenario **Early payment**. Select **cell C5** as the change cell and use the value **8**. Create a second scenario named **Normal payment**. Select **cell C5** as the change cell and use the value **10**. Create a third scenario named **Extended payment**. Select **cell C5** as the change cell and use the value **20**. Create a scenario summary report using **cells C7** and **F3**. Be sure to format the scenario report accordingly, removing the extra row and column created by Excel. The client has expressed that he is most comfortable with a repayment plan that is no more than 7% of his monthly income. Based on the scenarios you created, enter the repayment plan you recommend in **cell E12.** Once completed, save and close the workbook, and submit it based on your instructor's directions.

You are on the budget committee for the formal Valentine's Day Ball at your university. The ball includes dinner and dancing. Your committee prepared a tentative budget outlining income and expenses. The primary sources of income are contributions from student organizations and ticket prices. Expenses include the actual cost of the dinner, facilities, parking, and other costs at a luxurious hotel in the city. Your goal is to balance the income and expenses, decide on the most appropriate ticket price per student, and ensure your budget falls within the limitations you must work with.

Goal Seek

Currently, the estimated budget has a deficit. The fastest way to try to reconcile the income and expenses is to use Goal Seek. The goal is to break even, that is, to have a zero balance. Your instinct is to adjust the ticket price per person to reach the goal.

a. Open *e06c1Dance* and save it as **e06c1Dance_LastFirst**.

b. Use Goal Seek to achieve a $0 balance by changing the ticket price per person.

c. Enter the value of the ticket price per person variable in the Q&A worksheet.

One-Variable Data Table

You believe that between 200 and 500 students will attend. Because the ticket revenue, chair setup, catering cost, and valet parking expenses are dependent on the number of students, you decide to create a one-variable data table to compare the budget effects based on different numbers of students attending.

a. Start in **cell E3**. Complete the series of substitution values ranging from 200 to 500 at increments of 20 students vertically down column E.

b. Enter references to the total revenue, total expenses, and balance formulas in the correct location for a one-variable data table.

c. Complete the one-variable data table, and then format the results with **Accounting Number Format** with two decimal places.

d. Apply custom number formats to make the formula references appear as descriptive column headings. Bold and center the headings and substitution values.

e. Answer questions 2 through 4 on the Q&A worksheet. Save the workbook.

Two-Variable Data Table

The break-even point for the one-variable data table is identical to the current model because all other variables are held constant. You want to compare the balances of different combinations of attendees and ticket prices per person using a two-variable data table.

a. Copy the number of attendees substitution values from the one-variable data table, and then paste the values starting in **cell E22**.

b. Type **$50** in **cell F21**. Complete the series of substitution values from $50 to $100 at $10 increments.

c. Enter the reference to the total income formula in the correct location for a two-variable data table.

d. Complete the two-variable data table and format the results with **Accounting Number Format** with two decimal places.

e. Apply a fill color to the cells closest to break-even without creating a deficit.

f. Apply a custom number format to make the formula reference appear as a descriptive column heading. Bold and center the headings and substitution values.

g. Answer questions 5 and 6 on the Q&A worksheet. Question 6 requires three combinations to list. Save the workbook.

Scenario Manager

You negotiated different cost per meal and ballroom rental rates based on 500, 400, 300, or 200 attendees. You estimated tentative ticket prices per attendee. To help you decide the target number of attendees, you need to use Scenario Manager.

a. Create a scenario named **500 Attend**, using the number of attendees, meal cost per person, ticket price per person, and ballroom rental variables as the changing cells. Enter these values for the scenario: **500, 15.95, 75,** and **12500**.

b. Create a second scenario named **400 Attend**, using the same changing cells. Enter these values for the scenario: **400, 17.95, 85,** and **12500**.

c. Create a third scenario named **300 Attend**, using the same changing cells. Enter these values for the scenario: **300, 19.95, 90,** and **11995**.

d. Create a fourth scenario named **200 Attend**, using the same changing cells. Enter these values for the scenario: **200, 22.95, 95,** and **11995**.

e. Generate a scenario summary report using the total revenue, total expenses, and balance as the results.

f. Clean up the summary as discussed in the chapter.

g. Answer questions 7 through 9 on the Q&A worksheet. Save the workbook.

Use Solver

You realize a perfect break-even point may be unrealistic, but you will donate any positive balance to charity. For this analysis, you will use Solver to keep the expenses constant while changing the number of attendees and ticket price per person.

a. Load the Solver add-in if it is not already loaded.

b. Set the objective to calculate the highest balance possible.

c. Use the number of attendees and the ticket price per person as changing variable cells.

d. Look at the *Limitations* section of the spreadsheet model.

e. Set a constraint for the number of attendees.

f. Set constraints for the ticket price per person.

g. Set an appropriate integer constraint.

h. Set a constraint that ensures the valet parking expense is less than or equal to the product of the number of parking stalls and the valet price per vehicle.

i. Solve the problem, but keep the original values in the Budget worksheet. Generate the Answer Report. If you get an internal memory error message, remove Solver as an add-in, close the workbook, open the workbook, add Solver in again, and finish using Solver.

j. Answer questions 10 through 13 on the Q&A worksheet. Apply **landscape orientation** to the Q&A worksheet. Save the workbook.

k. Create a footer on all four worksheets with your name on the left side, the sheet name code in the center, and the file name code on the right side.

l. Save and close the workbook, and submit it based on your instructor's directions.

Templates, Styles, and Macros

CHAPTER **9**

Standardizing Workbooks

Yuri Arcurs/Shutterstock

OBJECTIVES AFTER YOU READ THIS CHAPTER, YOU WILL BE ABLE TO:

1. Select a template p. 432
2. Apply themes and backgrounds p. 433
3. Apply cell styles p. 435
4. Create and use a template p. 441
5. Protect a cell, a worksheet, and a workbook p. 442

6. Create a macro p. 451
7. Create macro buttons p. 454
8. Set macro security p. 455
9. Create a sub procedure p. 461
10. Create a custom function p. 463

CASE STUDY | Staff Accounting Services

Recently, you took a position as the manager of staff accounting at EBL, Ltd., a regional information technology (IT) company based in Denver, Colorado, with additional offices in Salt Lake City, Utah, and Reno, Nevada. The company provides computer and data network consultation services to individuals, small businesses, and nonprofits. The previous manager used a paper-based system to prepare expense reports, invoices, and payroll statements. However, this was a time-consuming process and required manual recalculation when any values changed.

Because of your extensive experience using Excel, you want to start automating these tasks. You decide to start with the monthly travel expense report form. Because each office utilizes the same procedures, you want to adapt an Excel template to use as a model for travel expense documentation. The template needs to be generic enough to accommodate a range of options, but it also needs to maintain a standard design to facilitate easy data entry.

You will customize the template by applying cell styles to give the form a more polished look and then create macros to perform a series of tasks, such as clearing the values to reset the form if needed and printing the expense report worksheet for management approval.

Templates, Themes, and Styles

Designing the perfect workbook can be time consuming. By now, you know you have to plan the layout before you enter data to minimize data-entry changes later. You decide what column and row labels are needed to describe the data, where to place the labels, and how to format the labels. In addition, you enter and format quantitative data, such as applying Accounting Number Format and decreasing the number of decimal places. The longer you work for the same department or organization, the more you will notice that you create the same types of workbooks. Excel has the right tools to improve your productivity in developing consistently formatted workbooks. Some of these tools include templates, themes, backgrounds, and styles.

In this section, you will select an Excel template. After opening the template, you will apply a theme, display a background, and apply cell styles.

Selecting a Template

STEP 1 » A ***template*** is a partially completed document that you use as a model to create other documents that have the same structure and purpose. A template typically contains standard labels, formulas, and formatting but may contain little or no quantitative data. Templates help ensure consistency and standardization for similar workbooks, such as detailed sales reports for all 12 months of a year. When you start Excel, you are presented with a gallery of templates. If you are already working within a workbook, click the File tab and click New. The Backstage view displays a gallery of featured templates (see Figure 9.1). You can select from templates you have recently used, sample templates that were installed with the software, or templates you created, or download new templates. To create a workbook based on a template, do the following:

1. Click a sample template, such as *Travel expense report*.
2. A pop-up window will display a sample of the selected template (see Figure 9.2).
3. Click Create to load the template data as a new workbook.

FIGURE 9.1 Template Thumbnails

The *Search for online templates* box allows you to search Office.com for a particular template by entering your search conditions and pressing Enter. Start searching, or you can select a template from a category, such as Budgets. These templates are created by Microsoft, a Microsoft partner, or a member of the Microsoft community. To download an Office.com template, do the following:

1. Click a template category, such as Expense. The Backstage view then displays thumbnails representing the various templates in that category.
2. Click the template thumbnail representing the template you want to download. A pop-up window displays information about the selected template, such as the template name and creator and the download size (see Figure 9.2).
3. Click Create. The Download Template message box displays briefly, after which the template is opened as a workbook in Excel.

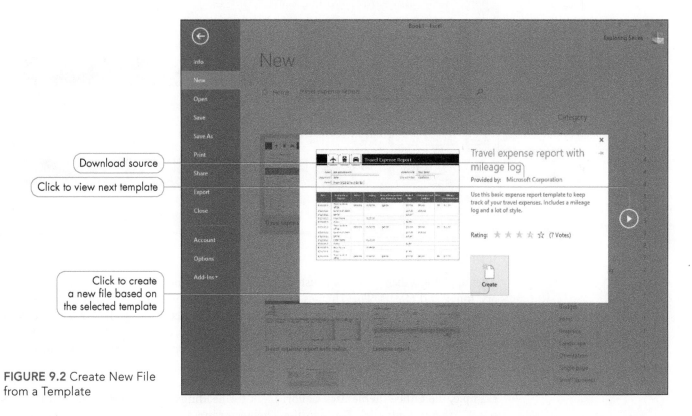

FIGURE 9.2 Create New File from a Template

Downloading the template does not save it to a storage location. You must save the workbook on a storage device. When you save a workbook from a downloaded template for the first time, the Save As dialog box defaults to OneDrive in Windows 8.1.1; however, you can select another location in which to save the workbook.

Applying Themes and Backgrounds

STEP 2 ≫ In addition to selecting a template, you might want to apply a theme or insert a background to create a consistent look with the workbooks you create. A ***theme*** is a collection of formats that include coordinating colors, fonts, and special effects to provide a stylish appearance. You can apply a theme to a workbook to give it a consistent look with other workbooks used in your department or organization. Most organizations have a style that encompasses particular fonts, colors, and a logo or trademark on corporate stationery, advertisements, and Web pages. You can use themes in Excel workbooks to match the corporate "look and feel." Some of the Excel theme names match theme names in other Office applications so that you can provide continuity and consistency in all of your documents. To apply a theme to all worksheets in a workbook, do the following:

1. Click the PAGE LAYOUT tab.
2. Click Themes in the Themes group. The Office theme is presented first; the other built-in themes are listed alphabetically in the Themes gallery (see Figure 9.3).
3. Position the pointer over each theme to display a Live Preview of how the theme would format existing data on the current worksheet.
4. Click a theme to make it active.

FIGURE 9.3 Themes Gallery

Customize a Theme

After applying a theme, you can customize the three elements that comprise the theme: colors, fonts, and effects. The Themes group on the Page Layout tab contains commands to customize your theme. When you click Colors, you can select from a gallery of colors, or you can select Customize Colors to define the text, background, accent, hyperlink, and followed hyperlink colors. If you create and name your own color theme, that theme name will appear in the *Custom* section of the Colors menu.

Theme fonts contain a coordinating heading and body text font for each theme. For example, the Office theme uses Calibri Light for headings and Calibri for cell entries. To select a theme font, click Fonts in the Themes group and select a theme font, or select Customize Fonts to define your own theme fonts.

Theme effects are special effects that control the design differences in objects, such as shapes, SmartArt, and object borders. To select a theme effect, click Effects in the Themes group, position the mouse pointer over an effect to see a Live Preview of how that effect will affect objects, and click the desired effect to apply it to your workbook.

Apply a Background

STEP 3 ▶▶

Excel enables you to use graphics as the background of a worksheet. The effect is similar to placing a background on a Web page. A *background* is an image placed behind the worksheet data. For example, you might want to use the corporate logo as your background, or you might want a "Confidential" graphic image to remind onscreen viewers that the worksheet contains corporate trade secrets. (If you want an image to appear behind data on a printed worksheet, insert the image as a watermark in a header.) Be careful in selecting and using backgrounds, because the images can distract users from comprehending the quantitative data. A subtle, pale image is less likely to distract a workbook user than a bright, vividly colored image. To add a background to a worksheet, do the following:

1. Click Background in the Page Setup group on the PAGE LAYOUT tab to open the Insert Pictures dialog box.

2. Select the picture file, such as a jpeg or bitmap file, that you want to use as a background.

3. Click Insert.

The image, like background images in Web pages, is tiled across your worksheet (see Figure 9.4). The background image displays only in the worksheet onscreen; it does not print. Notice that Delete Background replaces Background in the Page Setup group after you insert a background for a specific worksheet.

Delete background replaces Background command

Background image appears behind text

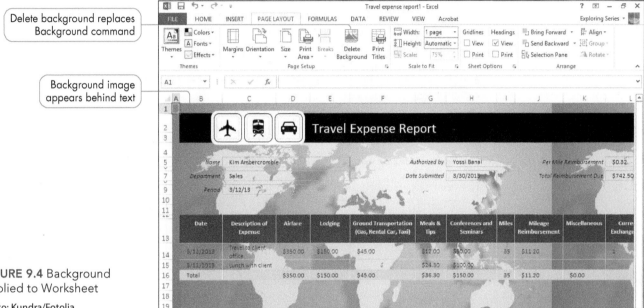

FIGURE 9.4 Background Applied to Worksheet

Photo: Kundra/Fotolia

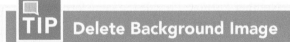 **Background Visibility**

You can turn off the gridlines to increase the visibility of the background image and the worksheet data. Click the Page Layout tab and deselect the Gridlines View check box in the Sheet Options group.

TIP **Delete Background Image**

To delete a background picture, click Delete Background in the Page Setup group on the Page Layout tab.

Applying Cell Styles

STEP 4 ▶▶

Different areas of a worksheet have different formatting. For example, titles may be centered in 16-pt size; column labels may be bold, centered, and dark blue font; and input cells may be formatted differently from output cells. A *cell style* is a collection of format settings based on the currently selected theme to provide a consistent appearance within a worksheet and among similar workbooks. Cell styles control the following formats:

- Font attributes, such as font and font size
- Borders and fill styles and colors
- Vertical and horizontal cell alignment

- Number formatting, such as Currency and number of decimal places
- Cell-protection settings

The currently selected theme controls cell styles. If you change the theme, Excel updates cells formatted by cell styles to reflect the new theme. For example, if you change from Facet theme to Integral, particular fill colors change from shades of green to blue. To apply a style to a cell or range of cells, do the following:

1. Click the HOME tab and click Cell Styles in the Styles group to display the Cell Styles gallery (see Figure 9.5).
2. Position the mouse pointer over a style name to see a Live Preview of how that style will affect the active cell.
3. Click a style to apply it to the active cell or range.

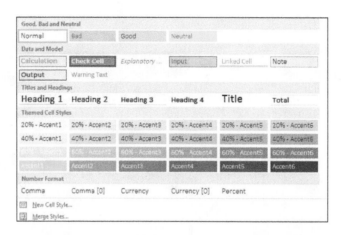

FIGURE 9.5 Cell Styles

The gallery contains the following five predefined cell categories:

- **Good, Bad, and Neutral:** Use to emphasize bad, good, or neutral results, or click Normal to reset a cell to its original default setting.
- **Data and Model:** Use to indicate special cell contents, such as a calculated result, input cell, output cell, or warning.
- **Titles and Headings:** Use to format titles and headings, such as column and row labels, for emphasis.
- **Themed Cell Styles:** Use Accent styles for visual emphasis. These cell styles are dependent on the currently selected theme.
- **Number Format:** Provide the same formatting as commands in the Number group on the Home tab.

Create Custom Cell Styles

You can create your own custom cell styles if the predefined cell styles do not meet your needs. For example, you might want to create custom cell styles that match the color, font, and design of your corporate logo or stationery to help brand your workbooks with the company image. After you create custom cell styles, you can apply them in multiple workbooks instead of formatting each workbook individually. To create a custom cell style do the following:

1. Click the cell that contains the desired formatting.
2. Click the HOME tab and click Cell Styles in the Styles group.
3. Select New Cell Style at the bottom of the gallery to open the Style dialog box (see Figure 9.6).
4. Type the name for your new style in the *Style name* box.

5. Click the check boxes to select the style options you want in the *Style Includes (By Example)* section. (If you are not creating a style using the active cell as an example, click Format to open the Format Cells dialog box and select the formats just as you would format an individual cell.)

6. Click OK to close the Style dialog box.

After you create a custom style, Excel displays another section, *Custom*, at the top of the Cell Styles gallery. This section lists the custom styles you create.

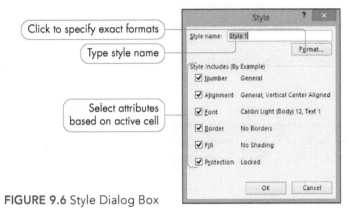

FIGURE 9.6 Style Dialog Box

Modify and Remove Custom Cell Styles

After you create and apply custom styles to worksheet cells, you might decide to change the format. For example, you might want to change the font size or fill color. The primary advantage to creating and applying styles is that you can modify the style, and Excel updates all cells for which you applied the style automatically. To modify a style, do the following:

1. Right-click the style in the *Custom* section of the Cell Styles palette.
2. Select Modify to open the Style dialog box.
3. Make the desired format changes and click OK.

If you no longer need a cell style, you can delete it. However, if you delete a cell style that has been applied to worksheet cells, Excel will remove all formatting from those cells. To delete a cell style, right-click the style name in the *Custom* section of the Cell Styles palette and select Delete. Excel does not ask for confirmation before deleting the style.

TIP | Use Styles in Other Workbooks

When you create your own cell styles, the styles are saved with the workbook in which you created the styles. However, you may want to apply those styles in other workbooks as well. To do this, open the workbook that contains the custom cell styles (the source) and open the workbook in which you want to apply those custom styles (the destination). In the destination workbook, click Cell Styles in the Styles group on the Home tab. Select Merge Styles at the bottom of the Cell Styles gallery to open the Merge Styles dialog box. In the *Merge styles from* list, select the name of the workbook that contains the styles you want and click OK. When you click Cell Styles again, the custom styles appear in the gallery.

Quick Concepts

1. What are the benefits of using templates? *p. 432*

2. How do you print worksheets with background images? *p. 434*

3. Why would you create a custom cell style? *p. 436*

Hands-On Exercises

Watch the Video
for this Hands-
On Exercise!

MyITLab®
HOE1 Training

1 Templates, Themes, and Styles

You need to get up and running quickly since you took over at EBL, Ltd. You decide to use the Travel Expense Report template that is part of the Office 2013 template downloads. After opening the template, you will modify it by applying a theme, theme color, background, and cell styles.

Skills covered: Select a Template • Apply a Theme • Apply a Background • Apply Cell Styles

STEP 1 ≫ SELECT A TEMPLATE

To save time, you would like to create a new report using a template. After reviewing the templates available in the template gallery, you decided the Travel Expense Report template shown in Figure 9.7 was sufficient to build your company's report. Your first step is to download the Travel Expense Report template. Refer to Figure 9.7 as you complete Step 1.

FIGURE 9.7 Travel Expense Report Template Saves as a Workbook

a. Open Excel, type **Travel expense report** in the **Search for online templates box**, and then press **Enter**.

b. Click **Travel expense report with mileage log** to select it; a pop-up window will appear with a brief description of the template.

Since there are several templates with the same name, choose the template that is the same format as the template shown in Figure 9.7.

> **TROUBLESHOOTING**: Any Microsoft Office user has the ability to submit personally created templates to Office.com. If when searching you discover several templates with the name *Travel Expense Report*, be sure to select the option that resembles the image in Figure 9.7.
> If you are unable to locate the required template, a copy of the file *e12h1ExpenseReport* is included with the start files for this chapter.

c. Click **Create** below the preview on the right side of the Backstage view.

Excel opens a copy of the Travel Expense Report as a new workbook. The template contains labels, fill colors, sample data, and formulas.

d. Save the workbook as **e12h1ExpenseReport_LastFirst**.

STEP 2 ›› APPLY A THEME

The Travel Expense Report template provides the basic design you need, but you want to apply a different theme to the workbook. Refer to Figure 9.8 as you complete Step 2.

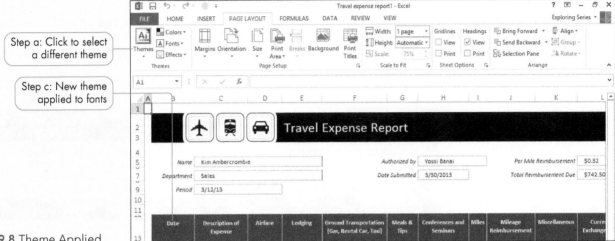

FIGURE 9.8 Theme Applied

a. Click the **PAGE LAYOUT tab** and click **Themes** in the Themes group.

b. Move the pointer over the Banded and Office themes to see the Live Preview of how those themes will affect the workbook.

c. Click **Basis** to apply that theme to the workbook. Save the workbook.

STEP 3 ›› APPLY A BACKGROUND

To enhance the professional look and feel of the Travel Expense Report, you will add a clip art background image. Refer to Figure 9.9 as you complete Step 3.

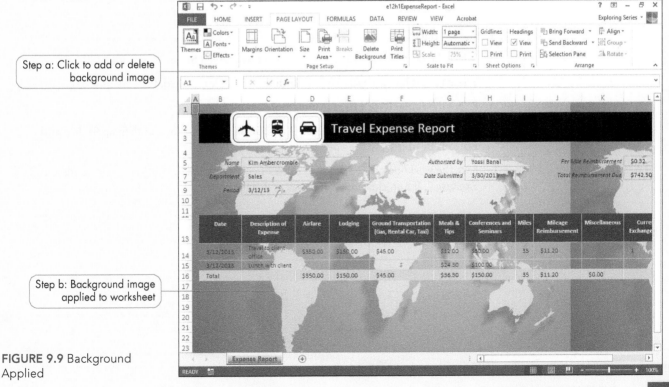

FIGURE 9.9 Background Applied

a. Click the **PAGE LAYOUT tab**, if necessary, and click **Background** in the Page Setup group.

b. Select *e12h1Map.jpg* from the student data file folder and click **Insert**.

   The image is tiled across and down the worksheet and appears behind the worksheet data. Because the original template did not include fill colors, the background image can be seen underneath the cells in the worksheet.

c. Save the workbook.

STEP 4 ≫ APPLY CELL STYLES

You want to further customize the Travel Expense Report workbook by applying different cell styles. For example, you want fill colors in the cells that contain data labels for rows 4:9. You also would like an accent color for rows 14:15 to make the data easier to view. Refer to Figure 9.10 as you complete Step 4.

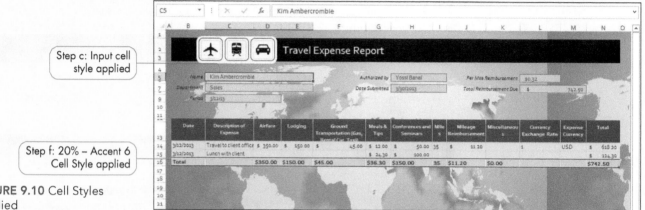

FIGURE 9.10 Cell Styles Applied

a. Select **cell C5**, press and hold **Ctrl**, and then select **cell C7**.

b. Click the **HOME tab** and click **Cell Styles** in the Styles group.

   The Cell Styles gallery opens so that you can apply a cell style to the selected cells.

c. Click **Input** in the *Data and Model* section.

d. Adapt steps b and c to apply **Input cell style** to **cell C9**, the **range H5:I5**, **cell H7**, **cell L5**, and **cell L7**.

e. Apply **Short Date number format** to **cell C9**.

f. Select the **range B14:N15**. Apply **20% – Accent 6 Cell Style**.

   These ranges had no background. With the cell styles applied, they are now easier to read.

g. Select the **range B16:N16** and apply **Bold** font format.

h. Select the **range B16:N16**, if necessary, click the **HOME tab**, and then apply **Top and Bottom Border** from the Font group.

i. Save the workbook. Keep the workbook open if you plan to continue with Hands-On Exercise 2. If not, close the workbook and exit Excel.

Custom Templates and Workbook Protection

Using Excel templates helps save time when designing workbooks, but these templates will not always meet your needs. When this is the case, you can create a workbook with the specifications you need and save it as a template so that you can use it as a model to create identically structured workbooks for unique data. For example, after downloading the Travel Expense Report template, you applied a theme, a background, and several cell styles. You want the company's employees to be able to use this modified workbook to create individual reports. However, creating a new workbook from scratch for each employee is time consuming. When you find yourself needing the same workbook design for several unique workbooks, you should develop and use a template that can be accessed by each employee and modified as needed.

You can protect cells or worksheets from unauthorized or accidental changes. Doing so ensures that people do not change areas of a worksheet, such as formulas, when you distribute the worksheet on an organization's server.

In this section, you will learn how to save a workbook as a template. In the process, you will learn how to protect cells and worksheets from being changed.

Creating and Using a Template

The Travel Expense Report template you used contains labels, sample values, and formulas. The formulas calculate category totals, such as the total airfare and total of the lodging category expenses. You can remove the sample expenses from the workbook and save it as a template so that you have an empty report for each employee to fill out.

When you create a template from scratch instead of starting with an existing template, adhere to the following guidelines:

- Keep in mind that a template should contain formatted, descriptive labels, empty cells, and formulas.
- Avoid values when possible in formulas; use cell references instead.
- Use an appropriate function to trap errors.
- Include data-validation settings (valid data rules, warning messages, input messages).
- Include instructions for the template.
- Turn off worksheet gridlines, if desired, for clarity.
- Apply appropriate formatting to the template.
- Give worksheets meaningful names and delete worksheets that are not used.

 TIP | **Trap Errors with the IFERROR Function and Set Data Validation**

Formulas used in workbooks display zeros or error messages when you remove values to create a template. You can use the IFERROR function to check a cell to see if it contains errors or if a formula will result in an error. If no error exists, the IFERROR function returns the value of the formula. You can enter an argument in the function to display a customized error message instead of a default error, such as #DIV/0! In addition, you can set validation rules so template users will enter correct data.

After you finalize your workbook, you need to save it. To save a workbook as a template, do the following:

1. Click the FILE tab and click Export.
2. Click Change File Type.
3. Click Template in the Change File Type scrollable list and click Save As at the bottom of the Backstage view to open the Save As dialog box. Notice that the *Save as type* is set to Excel Template.
4. Select the desired location, type a name in the *File name* box, and then click Save. **Note: This method does not default to the "correct" Template folder to provide easy access.**

To save the template so that it automatically is included in the Templates gallery, do the following:

1. From the Backstage view, click Save As and click Computer to open the Save As dialog box.
2. Click the *Save as type* arrow and select Excel Template. Excel then selects the C:\Users\username\Documents\CustomOfficeTemplates folder automatically.
3. Type a name in the *File name* box and click Save.

TIP | Templates Folder

Templates use a different file extension (.xltx) than Excel workbooks (.xlsx). In order for your template to appear in the Template gallery in the Backstage view, be sure to save it in the correct folder, C:\Users\username\Documents\CustomOfficeTemplates in Windows 8.1.1 and Windows 7. If you use File Explorer to find the Templates folder, you will need to display hidden folders to do so. If you save your custom templates in the correct location, you can use them to create new workbooks by clicking the File tab, clicking New, and then clicking Personal in the Templates gallery of the Backstage view. The New dialog box displays thumbnails and names for the templates you created.

Protecting a Cell, a Worksheet, and a Workbook

Most templates protect worksheets by enabling users to change only particular cells in a worksheet. For example, users are permitted to enter data in input cells, but they cannot change formulas or alter formatting or worksheet structure. In Hands-On Exercise 2, you will protect the formula cells in the Travel Expense Report template. This will prevent users from changing the formulas. Protecting worksheets prevents modification of formulas and text but enables you to change values in unprotected cells.

Lock and Unlock Cells

STEP 1 ›› A *locked cell* is one that prevents users from editing the contents or formatting of that cell in a protected worksheet. By default, all cells are locked as indicated by the blue border around the padlock icon for the Lock Cell option on the Format menu in the Cells group on the Home tab. Locked cells are not enforced until you protect the worksheet. Locking or unlocking cells has no effect if the worksheet has not been protected. Before protecting the worksheet, you should unlock the cells that you want users to be able to edit. For example, you will unlock the Per Mile Reimbursement and Date Submitted cells in the Travel Expense Report template so that users can enter unique values. However, you will keep the cells containing formulas locked. To unlock input cells, do the following:

1. Select the cells in which you want users to be able to enter or edit data.
2. Click the HOME tab and click Format in the Cells group (see Figure 9.11). Note that Lock Cell is active by default.
3. Select Lock Cell in the *Protection* section to unlock the active cell or selected range of cells.

   To relock cells, repeat the above process.

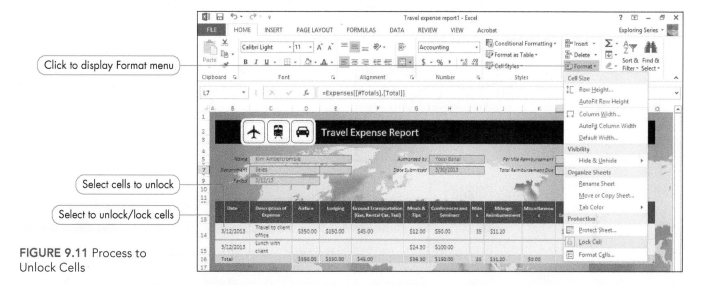

FIGURE 9.11 Process to Unlock Cells

 TIP Using the Format Cells Dialog Box

Alternatively, after selecting a cell or range of cells to unlock, you can open the Format Cells dialog box, click the Protection tab, deselect the Locked check box, and then click OK.

Protect a Worksheet

STEP 2 After unlocking cells that you want the users to be able to modify, you are ready to protect the worksheet. When you protect a worksheet, you prevent users from altering the locked cells. During the process of protecting a worksheet, you can enter a password to ensure that only those who know the password can unprotect the worksheet. Protecting the template is typically the final step in the creation of a custom template because you need to enter standard labels, create formulas, and unprotect input cells first. If you protect the worksheet before finalizing the content, you will have to unprotect the worksheet, make content changes, and then protect the worksheet again. To protect a worksheet, do the following:

STEP 3 1. Click the HOME tab and click Format in the Cells group.
2. Select Protect Sheet in the *Protection* section (or click Protect Sheet in the Changes group on the REVIEW tab) to open the Protect Sheet dialog box (see Figure 9.12).
3. Select the check boxes for actions you want users to be able to do in the *Allow all users of this worksheet to* list.
4. Type a password in the *Password to unprotect sheet* box and click OK. The Confirm Password dialog box opens (see Figure 9.13). Type the same password in the *Reenter password to proceed* box.
5. Read the caution statement and click OK.

FIGURE 9.12 Protect Sheet Dialog Box

FIGURE 9.13 Confirm Password Dialog Box

> ### TIP | Passwords
>
> Passwords can be up to 255 characters, including letters, numbers, and symbols. Passwords are case sensitive, so *passWORD* is not the same as *Password*. Make sure you record your password in a secure location or select a password that you will always remember. If you forget the password, you will not be able to unprotect the worksheet.

After you protect a worksheet, most commands on the Ribbon are dimmed, indicating that they are not available. If someone tries to enter or change data in a locked cell on a protected workbook, Excel displays the warning message and instructs the user how to remove the protection (see Figure 9.14). To unprotect a worksheet, do the following:

1. Click Unprotect Sheet in the Changes group on the REVIEW tab, or click Format in the Cells group on the HOME tab and select Unprotect Sheet. The Unprotect Sheet dialog box opens.
2. Type the password in the Password box and click OK. The worksheet is then unprotected so that you can make changes.

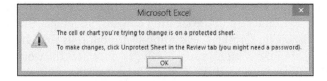

FIGURE 9.14 Warning Message

Protect a Workbook

Although locking cells and protecting a worksheet prevents unauthorized modifications, users might make unwanted changes to other parts of the workbook. You can prevent users from inserting, deleting, renaming, moving, copying, and hiding worksheets within the workbook by protecting the workbook with a password. Protecting an entire workbook does not disable the unlocked cells within a workbook; it merely prevents worksheet manipulation from occurring. That is, individual cells must still be unlocked even if a workbook is unprotected. To protect a workbook, do the following:

1. Click the REVIEW tab and click Protect Workbook in the Changes group. The Protect Structure and Windows dialog box opens (see Figure 9.15).
2. Click the check boxes for the desired action in the *Protect workbook for* section.
3. Type a password in the *Password (optional)* box and click OK. The Confirm Password dialog box opens.
4. Type the same password in the *Reenter password to proceed* box and click OK.

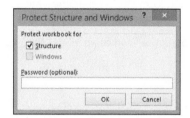

FIGURE 9.15 Protect Structure and Windows Dialog Box

TIP Unprotect a Workbook

To unprotect a workbook, click the Review tab, click Protect Workbook, type the password in the Password box in the Unprotect Workbook dialog box, and then click OK.

STEP 4 »

Once a workbook is completed and the appropriate cells are locked, the last step is to save the file as a template. Saving the file as a template not only stores the files as a template in the Custom Office Templates folder on your computer, it also displays the file as a personal template in the Backstage gallery. To save a workbook as a template, do the following:

STEP 5 »
1. Click the FILE tab.
2. Click Save As, click Computer, and then click Browse.
3. Select Excel Template from the *Save as type* menu.
4. Click Save.

Quick
Concepts

1. What is the default file extension for a template? *p. 442*
2. Where are templates saved in Windows 8.1.1? *p. 442*
3. Why would you protect a workbook? *p. 445*

Hands-On Exercises

Watch the Video
for this Hands-
On Exercise!

MyITLab®
HOE2 Training

2 Custom Templates and Workbook Protection

After customizing the Travel Expense Report, you want to ensure consistency of use within the company by saving the workbook as a template. As the manager, you do not want your staff deleting formulas or other imperative sections of the expense form you have created. Your next set of steps will include protecting the workbook and then saving it as a template.

Skills covered: Unlock Input Cells • Delete Sample Values • Protect the Worksheet • Save the Workbook as a Template • Use the Template to Create a Sample Expense Report

STEP 1 ≫ UNLOCK INPUT CELLS

Before protecting the worksheet, you will unlock input cells. You need to ensure the input cells are unlocked so that each employee can enter specific lodging, mileage, and miscellaneous costs. Refer to Figure 9.16 as you complete Step 1.

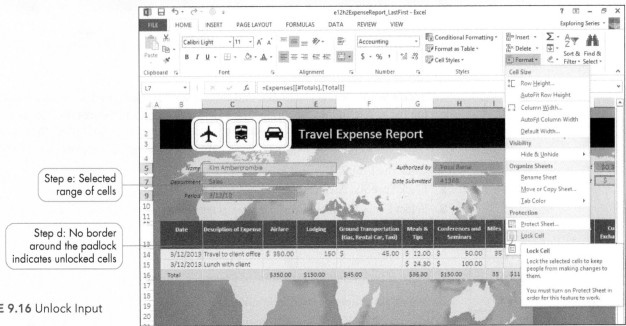

Step e: Selected range of cells

Step d: No border around the padlock indicates unlocked cells

FIGURE 9.16 Unlock Input Cells

a. Open the *e12h1ExpenseReport_LastFirst* workbook and save it as **e12h2ExpenseReport_LastFirst**, changing *h1* to *h2*.

b. Select **cell C5**.

    This cell will be the input area for the name of the creator of the report.

c. Click the **HOME tab**, if necessary, and click **Format** in the Cells group.

    The Format menu opens.

d. Select **Lock Cell** in the *Protection* section.

The Lock Cell option does not change to Unlock Cell. However, when you unlock a cell, the Lock Cell command does not have a blue border around the padlock icon on the menu. The selected range of cells is unlocked and will remain unlocked when you protect the worksheet later.

e. Press **Ctrl** while selecting the following cells and range and repeat steps c and d to unlock the cells and range:

- **Cell C7**
- **Cell C9**
- **Cell H5**
- **Cell H7**
- **Cell L5**
- **Range B14:M15**

> **TROUBLESHOOTING:** If you unlock too many cells, select the cells that should be locked, click Format, and then select Lock Cell to lock them again.

f. Save the workbook.

STEP 2 ›› DELETE SAMPLE VALUES

Although you unlocked the input cells for Name, Department, Period, Authorized by, Date Submitted, Per Mile Reimbursement, and Total Reimbursement, you need to delete the sample values to create a ready-to-use empty form before you protect the worksheet and save it as a template. Refer to Figure 9.17 as you complete Step 2.

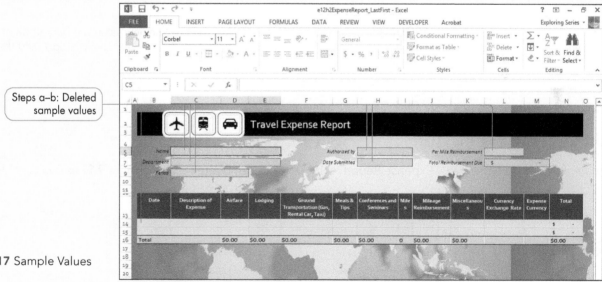

FIGURE 9.17 Sample Values Removed

a. Select **cell C5** and press **Delete**.

b. Delete the sample values in the following cells and range:

- **Cell C7**
- **Cell C9**
- **Cell H5**
- **Cell H7**
- **Cell L5**
- **Range B14:M15**

c. Save the workbook.

STEP 3 ≫ PROTECT THE WORKSHEET

Now that you have unlocked input cells and deleted sample expense values, you are ready to protect the Expense Report worksheet. The other cells in the worksheet still have the Lock Cell property enabled. So, after you protect the worksheet, those cells will not be able to be modified.

a. Press **Ctrl+Home**.

b. Click **Format** in the Cells group and select **Protect Sheet**. If not already checked, check *Select locked cells* and *Select unlocked cells*.

The Protect Sheet dialog box opens. The *Protect worksheet and contents of locked cells* check box is selected by default. In addition, the users are allowed to *Select locked cells* and *Select unlocked cells*. Although they can select locked cells, they will not be able to change those cells. Notice that users are not allowed to format data, insert columns or rows, or delete columns or rows.

c. Type **eXploring** in the **Password to unprotect sheet box**.

Remember that passwords are case sensitive and that you must remember the password. If you forget it, you will not be able to unprotect the sheet.

d. Click **OK**.

The Confirm Password dialog box opens with a caution.

e. Read the caution, type **eXploring** in the **Reenter password to proceed box**, and then click **OK**.

f. Click **cell N14** and try to type **1000**.

Excel displays the warning box that the cell is protected with instructions on how to unprotect the worksheet.

> **TROUBLESHOOTING**: If you are allowed to enter the new value without the warning box, the cell is not locked. Click Undo to restore the formula, review Step 1, and then lock this cell.

g. Click **OK** to close the warning box and save the workbook.

STEP 4 ≫ SAVE THE WORKBOOK AS A TEMPLATE

You are ready to save the Travel Expense Report workbook as a template. Refer to Figure 9.18 as you complete Step 4.

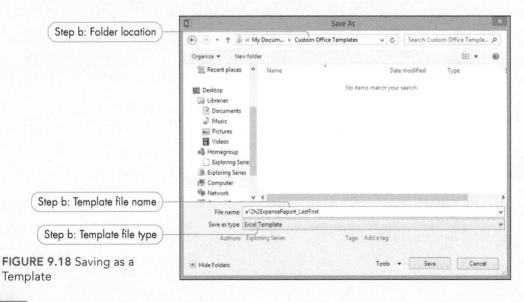

FIGURE 9.18 Saving as a Template

a. Click the **FILE tab**, click **Save As**, click **Browse**, and then click the **Save as type arrow**.

b. Select **Excel Template** and save the file to the default folder, Custom Office Templates, as **e12h2ExpenseReportTemplate_LastFirst**.

The Save As dialog box opens, displaying the current workbook name and Excel Workbook as the default file type.

> **TROUBLESHOOTING**: When saving a template, Excel changes the file location to C:\Users\ Username\My Documents\CustomOfficeTemplates. You may not have the ability to save a template to the hard drive of your school's computer lab, or your instructor may request you submit the file. To ensure you do not lose the template, be sure to change the save location to your student data folder. Note that if you do change the default location, the template will not display in the Personal template gallery and you will need to manually open the file from your student data folder to continue.

c. Click **Save**.

This will save the workbook as a template and exit the backstage area.

d. Click the **FILE tab** and click **Close**.

STEP 5 » USE THE TEMPLATE TO CREATE A SAMPLE EXPENSE REPORT

Now that you have created a Travel Expense Report template, you are ready to enter data for one of your coworkers. Refer to Figure 9.19 as you complete Step 5.

FIGURE 9.19 Create a New Workbook from a Personal Template

a. Click the **FILE tab** and click **New**.

The Backstage view displays a gallery of available templates.

b. Click **PERSONAL** in the *gallery* section.

This displays personal templates saved on your computer.

> **TROUBLESHOOTING**: If you were not able to save the template to the Custom Office Templates folder in Step 4, you will not see the template in the Personal template gallery. If this is the case, the file can be located by searching Recent Workbooks from the Open menu in the Backstage view.

c. Click *e12h2ExpenseReportTemplate_LastFirst* and click **OK**.

The template creates a new workbook based on the same file name but with a number appended to the end, such as *e12h2ExpenseReportTemplate_LastFirst1*.

d. Type **Your Name** in **cell C5**.

e. Type the following values in the appropriate cells:

Cell	Value
C7	Finance
H7	1/28/2015
L5	.35
B14	1/3/2015
C14	Sales Conference
D14	250.00
E14	125.00
F14	35.00

f. Press **Ctrl+Home** and save the workbook as **e12h2Sample_LastFirst** in the Excel Workbook file format. Close the workbook and submit based on your instructor's directions.

Macros

By now, you have used most of the tabs on the Ribbon to perform a variety of tasks. Often, you repeat the execution of the same commands as you develop and modify workbooks. Although the sequence to execute commands is easy, you lose productivity when you repeat the same procedures frequently. Previously, you learned how to apply styles and themes and how to create and use templates as models to develop similar workbooks. However, you can automate other routine tasks to increase your productivity. For example, think about how often you set a print range, adjust scaling, set margins, insert a standard header or footer, and specify other page setup options.

You can automate a series of routine or complex tasks by creating a macro. A *macro* is a set of instructions that execute a sequence of commands to automate repetitive or routine tasks. While the term *macro* often intimidates people, you should view macros as your personal assistants that do routine tasks for you! After you create a macro, you can execute the macro to perform all the tasks with minimal work on your part. When you run a macro, the macro executes all of the tasks the same way each time, and faster than you could execute the commands yourself, thus reducing errors while increasing efficiency.

The default Excel Workbook file format (.xlsx) cannot store macros. When you save a workbook containing macros, click the *Save as type* arrow in the Save As dialog box, and select one of the following file formats that support macros:

- Excel Macro-Enabled Workbook (.xlsm)
- Excel Binary Workbook (.xlsb)
- Excel Macro-Enabled Template (.xltm)

In this section, you will learn how to use the Macro Recorder to record a macro. You will also learn how to run a macro, edit a macro, create macro buttons, and review macro security issues.

Creating a Macro

Excel provides two methods for creating macros. You can use the Macro Recorder or type instructions using *Visual Basic for Applications (VBA)*. VBA is a robust programming language that is the underlying code of all macros. While programmers use VBA to create macros, you do not have to be a programmer to write macros. It is relatively easy to use the *Macro Recorder* within Excel to record your commands, keystrokes, and mouse clicks to store Excel commands as VBA code within a workbook. Before you record a macro, keep the following points in mind:

- Remember that once you begin recording a macro, most actions you take are recorded in the macro. If you click something in error, you have to edit the code or undo the action to correct it.

- Practice the steps before you start recording the macro so that you will know the sequence in which to perform the steps when you record the macro.

- Ensure your macros are broad enough to apply to a variety of situations or an action you perform often for the workbook.

- Determine whether cell references should be relative, absolute, or mixed if you include cell references in the macro.

Use the Macro Recorder

You can access the Macro Recorder in a variety of ways: from the View tab, from the Developer tab, or from the status bar. The following list briefly describes what each method includes:

- The View tab contains the Macros group with the Macros command. You can click the Macros arrow to view macros, record a macro, or use relative references.

STEP 1 ⟫

- The Developer tab, when displayed, provides more in-depth tools that workbook developers use. The Code group contains the same commands as the Macros arrow on the View tab, but it also includes commands to open the Visual Basic editor and set macro security.
- The status bar displays the Macro Recording button so that you can quickly click it to start and stop recording macros.

To display the Developer tab on the Ribbon, do the following:

1. Click the FILE tab and click Options to open the Excel Options dialog box.
2. Click Customize Ribbon on the left side to display the *Customize the Ribbon* options.
3. Click the Developer check box in the Main Tabs list to select it and click OK. Figure 9.20 shows the DEVELOPER tab.

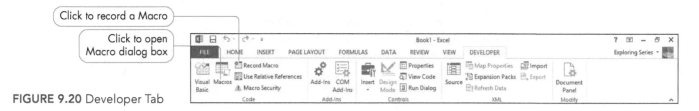

FIGURE 9.20 Developer Tab

Record a Macro

STEP 2 ⟫

Recording a macro is relatively straightforward: You initiate the macro recording, perform a series of commands as you normally do, then stop the macro recording. Be careful and thorough when recording a macro to ensure that it performs the task it is designed to do and to avoid the need to edit the macro in the VBA Editor. Before recording a macro, you should practice it first and make sure you know the sequence of tasks you want to perform. After planning a macro, you are ready to record it. To record a macro, do the following:

1. Click the VIEW tab, click the Macros arrow in the Macros group, and then select Record Macro; or click the DEVELOPER tab and click Record Macro in the Code group; or click Macro Recording on the status bar. The Record Macro dialog box opens (see Figure 9.21 and Figure 9.22).
2. Type a name for the macro in the *Macro name* box. Macro names cannot include spaces or special characters and must start with a letter. Use CamelCasing (capitalize the first letter of each word but without a space), a programming naming convention, to increase readability of the macro name.
3. Assign a keyboard shortcut, if desired, for your macro in the *Shortcut key* box. Use caution, because many Ctrl+ shortcuts are already assigned in Excel. To be safe, it is best to use Ctrl+Shift+, such as Ctrl+Shift+C instead of Ctrl+C, because Ctrl+C is the existing keyboard shortcut for the Copy command.
4. Click the *Store macro in* arrow and select a storage location, such as This Workbook.
5. Type a description of the macro and its purpose in the Description box and click OK to start recording the macro.
6. Perform the commands that you want to record.
7. Click the VIEW tab, click Macros in the Macros group, and then select Stop Recording; or click the DEVELOPER tab and click Stop Recording in the Code group; or click Stop Recording on the status bar.

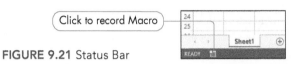

Click to record Macro

FIGURE 9.21 Status Bar

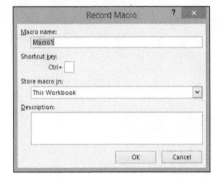

FIGURE 9.22 Record Macro
Dialog Box

Use Relative References

It is important to determine if your macro should use relative, absolute, or mixed references as you record the macro. By default, when you select cells when recording a macro, the macro records the cells as absolute references. When you run the macro, the macro executes commands on the absolute cells, regardless of which cell is the active cell when you run the macro. If you want flexibility in that commands are performed relative to the active cell when you run the macro, click the Macros arrow in the Macros group on the View tab and select Use Relative References *before* you perform the commands. Relative references look like this in the VBA Editor:

```
ActiveCell.Offset(3,-2).Range("A1").Select
```

This code moves the active cell down three rows and back to the left by two cells. If the active cell is D1 when you run the macro, the active cell becomes B4 (down three rows; to the left by two cells).

Run a Macro

STEP 3 » After you record a macro, you should run a test to see if it performs the commands as you had anticipated. When you run a macro, Excel performs the tasks in the sequence in which you recorded the steps. To run a macro, do the following:

1. Select the location where you will test the macro. It is recommended to test a macro in a new, blank workbook if you recorded it so that it is available for multiple workbooks. If you saved it to the current workbook only, insert a new worksheet to test the macro.

2. Click the VIEW tab, click the Macros arrow in the Macros group, and then select View Macros; or click the DEVELOPER tab and click Macros in the Code group. The Macro dialog box opens (see Figure 9.23).

3. Select the macro from the *Macro name* list and click Run.

TIP | Delete a Macro

If you no longer need a macro, use the Macro dialog box to select the macro and click Delete. Excel will prompt you with a message box asking if you want to delete the selected Macro. Click Yes to confirm the deletion.

FIGURE 9.23 Macro Dialog Box

Creating Macro Buttons

STEP 4 » For the most part, it will be a rare macro that is so all-encompassing that it would rate a place on the Quick Access Toolbar. On the other hand, you may create a macro that is frequently used in a particular workbook. The easiest way to access frequently used macros within a workbook is to assign a macro to a button on a worksheet. That way, when you or other people use the workbook, it is easy to click the button to run the macro. To add a macro button to a worksheet, do the following:

1. Click the DEVELOPER tab, click Insert in the Controls group, and then click Button (Form Control) in the *Form Controls* section of the Insert gallery. See Figure 9.24.

2. Drag the crosshair pointer to draw the button on the worksheet. When you release the mouse button, the Assign Macro dialog box opens (see Figure 9.25).

3. Select the macro to assign to the button and click OK.

4. Right-click the button, select Edit Text, delete the default text, and then type a more descriptive name for the button.

5. Click the worksheet to complete the button.

6. Click a cell, if necessary, that should be the active cell when the macro runs and click the button to execute the macro assigned to the button.

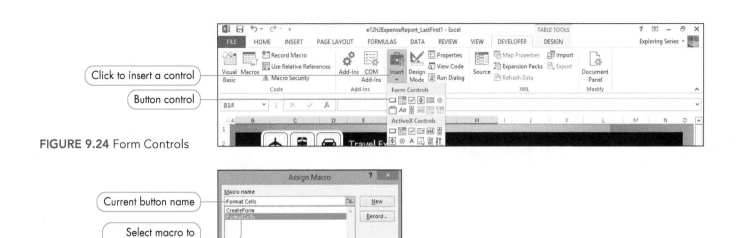

Click to insert a control

Button control

FIGURE 9.24 Form Controls

Current button name

Select macro to
assign to the button

FIGURE 9.25 Assign Macro
Dialog Box

TIP **Other Controls**

You can insert other controls in a worksheet such as images and artwork and then assign macros to them. For example, you can insert combo boxes, check boxes, and option buttons by clicking Insert in the Controls group on the Developer tab and selecting the desired control. Drag an area on the worksheet to draw the control, right-click the object, and then select Assign Macro to assign a macro action for that particular control.

Setting Macro Security

Macro security is a concern for anyone who uses files containing macros. A macro virus is nothing more than actions written in VBA set to perform malicious actions when run. The proliferation of macro viruses has made people more cautious about opening workbooks that contain macros. By default, Excel automatically disables the macros and displays a security warning that macros have been disabled (see Figure 9.26). Click Enable Content to use the workbook and run macros.

Excel Security Warning

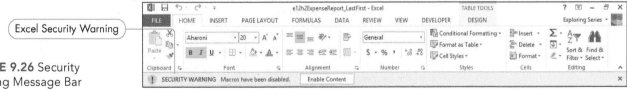

FIGURE 9.26 Security
Warning Message Bar

You can use the Trust Center dialog box to change settings to make it easier to work with macros. The Trust Center can direct Excel to trust files in particular folders, trust workbooks created by a trusted publisher, and lower the security settings to allow macros. To open the Trust Center, do the following:

1. Click the FILE tab and click Options.
2. Click Trust Center on the left side of the Excel Options dialog box.
3. Click Trust Center Settings. The Trust Center dialog box displays the sections described in Table 9.1 on the left side of the dialog box (see Figure 9.27).

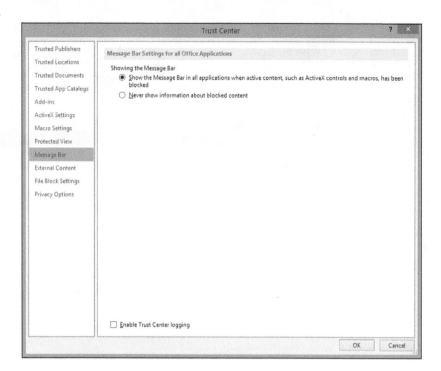

FIGURE 9.27 Trust Center Dialog Box

TABLE 9.1	Trust Center Options
Item	**Description**
Trusted Publishers	Directs Excel to trust digitally signed workbooks by certain creators.
Trusted Locations	Enables you to select places on your computer to store workbooks securely.
Trusted Documents	Enables you to trust network documents to open without Excel displaying any security warnings.
Trusted App Catalogs	Enables you to trust third-party Office Apps that run inside Excel.
Add-Ins	Enables you to specify which add-ins will be allowed to run given the desired level of security.
ActiveX Settings	Enables you to adjust how Excel deals with ActiveX controls.
Macro Settings	Enables you to specify how Excel deals with macros.
Protected View	Opens potentially dangerous files in a restricted mode but without any security warnings.
Message Bar	Enables you to specify when Excel shows the message bar when it blocks macros.
External Content	Enables you to specify how Excel deals with links to other workbooks and data from other sources.
File Block Settings	Enables you to select which types of files, such as macros, to open in Protected View or which file type to prevent saving a file in.
Privacy Options	Enables you to deal with nonmacro privacy issues.

Quick
Concepts

1. What is the purpose of a macro? *p. 451*

2. How are macros accessed after they have been recorded? *p. 454*

3. What potential risks are associated with macros? *p. 455*

Hands-On Exercises

3 Macros

Because you want all employees to use the Travel Expense Report template to report expenditures each month, you want to create a macro to clear the form. In addition, you want to create a button to run the macro so that other users can easily clear the form if they do not know what a macro is or how to run it.

Skills covered: Display Developer Tab • Record a Macro • Run a Macro • Add a Macro Button

STEP 1 ≫ DISPLAY DEVELOPER TAB

The average employee at your company does not use developer tools; therefore, they are not enabled on your workstation. You would like to display the Developer tab so that you can record the macro.

a. Open *e12h2ExpenseReportTemplate_LastFirst* and save it with the file name **e12h3ExpenseReportTemplate_LastFirst**, changing *h2* to *h3*.

When you use Open or Recent to open a template, you open it as a template to edit. When you use New, you make a copy of the template as a workbook.

> **TROUBLESHOOTING**: If you do not see Templates in Recent Places, click Open and navigate to the local directory that contains your student files.

b. Click the **FILE tab** and click **Options** to open the Excel Options dialog box.

c. Click **Customize Ribbon**, click the **Developer check box** in the Main Tabs list, and then click **OK**.

The Developer tab is added to the Ribbon.

STEP 2 ≫ RECORD A MACRO

You do not want to assume the level of Excel expertise throughout your company; therefore, you want to craft a macro that will automate as much as possible. The macro you would like to create needs to automatically clear existing values and then display an instruction for users to enter specific data. Although the template is empty to start, users might open the template, save a workbook, and then want to use that workbook to prepare future months' reports. Therefore, you need the macro to clear cells even though the original template has no values. Refer to Figure 9.28 as you complete Step 2.

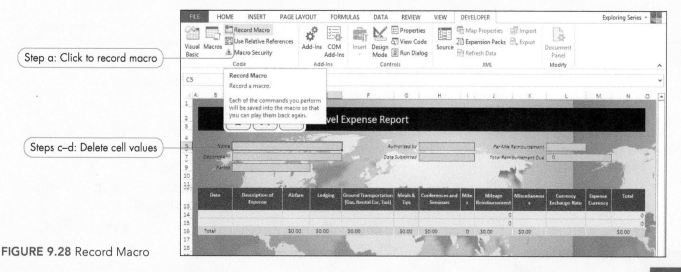

FIGURE 9.28 Record Macro

a. Click the **DEVELOPER tab** and click **Record Macro** in the Code group.

The Record Macro dialog box opens so that you can name and describe the macro.

b. Type **ClearForm** in the **Macro name box**, click in the **Description box**, type **This macro clears existing values in the current Travel Expense Report**, and then click **OK**.

TROUBLESHOOTING: Read through steps c–g in advance before you proceed. Remember most actions taken in Excel are recorded by the macro recorder. Practice the steps below before activating the recorder. If you make a major mistake, delete the macro and repeat steps b through j.

---

c. Select **cell C5** and press **Delete**.

Even though the cells are empty now, they may contain values at some point. You want the macro to delete any values that might exist in this range.

d. Adapt step c for the following cells and ranges:

- **Cell C7**
- **Cell C9**
- **Cell H5**
- **Cell H7**
- **Cell L5**
- **Range B14:I15**
- **Range K14:M15**

You deleted ranges that might contain values after the user enters data into any workbooks created from the template. It is always good to plan for various possibilities in which data might be entered even if those ranges do not contain values now.

e. Press **Ctrl+G**, type **C5** in the **Reference box** of the Go To dialog box, and then click **OK**.

f. Type **Enter Name Here** in **cell C5** and press **Ctrl+Enter**.

Pressing Ctrl+Enter keeps cell C5 the active cell so that users can immediately enter the label when they open a workbook from the template.

g. Click **cell C7**, type **Enter Department Name**, and then press **Ctrl+Enter**.

h. Click **Stop Recording** in the Code group on the DEVELOPER tab.

i. Save the *e12h3ExpenseReportTemplate_LastFirst* template; click **No** when prompted that the workbook cannot be saved with the macro in it.

Excel opens the Save As dialog box so that you can select the file type.

j. Click the **Save as type arrow**, select **Excel Macro-Enabled Template**, and then click **Save**.

TROUBLESHOOTING: Make sure you select Excel Macro-Enabled Template, not Excel Macro-Enabled Workbook, because you want the file saved as a template, not a workbook. Because the template contains macros, you must save it as an Excel Macro-Enabled Template, not just a template.

STEP 3 ≫ RUN A MACRO

You want to make sure the ClearForm macro does what you want it to do. First, you will add some sample data and run the macro.

a. Type your name in **cell C5**, type **Finance** in **cell C7**, type **1/25/2015** in **cell H7**, type **1/5/2015** in **cell B14**, type **Sales Meeting** in **cell C14**, and then type **$75.00** in **cell G14**.

You entered some sample values in various cells to test the ClearForm macro to verify if it will delete those values.

b. Click the **DEVELOPER tab**, if necessary, and click **Macros** in the Code group.

The Macro dialog box opens and displays the ClearForm macro, which should be selected in the Macro name box.

c. Select **ClearForm**, if necessary, and click **Run**.

The ClearForm macro quickly goes through the worksheet, erasing the values in the specified ranges, goes to cells C5 and C7, enters descriptive labels, and then stops.

> **TROUBLESHOOTING**: If the macro does not delete sample values, delete the macro and rerecord it.

STEP 4 ≫ ADD A MACRO BUTTON

Your colleagues are probably not Excel experts and do not know how to run a macro. To make it easier to clear values from the form, you want to assign the ClearForm macro to a button. The users can then click the button to clear the form to use it for another month. Refer to Figure 9.29 as you complete Step 4.

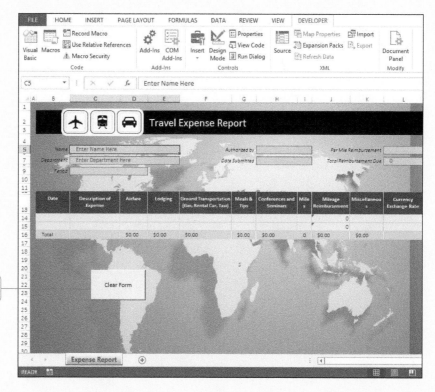

Steps b–d: Create macro button

FIGURE 9.29 Macro Button

a. Click the **HOME tab**, click **Format** in the Cells group, select **Unprotect Sheet**, type **eXploring** in the **Password box** in the Unprotect Sheet dialog box, and then click **OK**.

You have to unprotect the worksheet before you can insert a macro button.

b. Click the **DEVELOPER tab**, click **Insert** in the Controls group, and then click **Button (Form Control)** in the *Form Controls* section of the gallery.

c. Click the top of **cell C20** and drag down and to the right to the bottom of **cell D23** to create the area where the button will be placed.

The Assign Macro dialog box opens.

d. Select **ClearForm** in the Macro name list and click **OK**.

This action assigns the ClearForm macro to the button. The button appears in cells C20:D23, is selected, and displays *Button 1*. You will provide descriptive text to appear on the button.

e. Right-click **Button 1** and select **Edit Text**. Select the **Button 1 text**, type **Clear Form**, and then click any cell on the worksheet outside the button.

The button now shows *Clear Form*, which is more descriptive of the button's purpose than *Button 1*.

f. Right-click the **Expense Report worksheet tab**, select **Protect Sheet**, type **eXploring** in the **Password to protect sheet box**, click **OK**, type **eXploring** in the **Reenter password to proceed box**, and then click **OK**.

You need to protect the worksheet after creating the macro button.

g. Type **6/1/2015** in cell **B14** and type **6/29/2015** in **cell B15** to enter sample data.

h. Click **Clear Form** in the worksheet.

When you click Clear Form, Excel runs the ClearForm macro.

i. Save the Macro-Enabled Template. Keep the workbook open if you plan to continue with Hands-On Exercise 4. If not, close the workbook and exit Excel.

Visual Basic for Applications

As you perform commands while recording a macro, those commands are translated into programming code called Visual Basic for Applications (VBA). VBA is a robust programming language that can be used within various software packages to enhance and automate functionality. While many casual users will be able to complete required tasks using just the macro recorder, more advanced VBA macros can be created by authoring code directly into modules within the Visual Basic Editor. A *module* is a file in which macros are stored. The ***Visual Basic Editor*** is an application used to create, edit, execute, and debug Office application macros using programming code. These macros can then be used within a Macro-Enabled Workbook or Template. The two types of VBA macros are sub procedures and custom functions. ***Sub procedures***, which are also created when using the macro recorder, perform actions on a workbook, such as the ClearForm example earlier in the chapter. For example, you can create a sub procedure to insert the current date in a worksheet. Similar to the hundreds of built-in functions in Excel, custom functions have the ability to manipulate input variables and return a value.

Creating a Sub Procedure

STEP 1 ▶ The first step to creating a sub procedure is inserting a new module or editing data in an existing module within the VBA editor. To access the VBA Editor, press Alt+F11 on your keyboard. The left side of the VBA window contains the Project Explorer, which is similar in concept and appearance to the File Explorer except that it displays only open workbooks and/or other Visual Basic projects (see Figure 9.30).

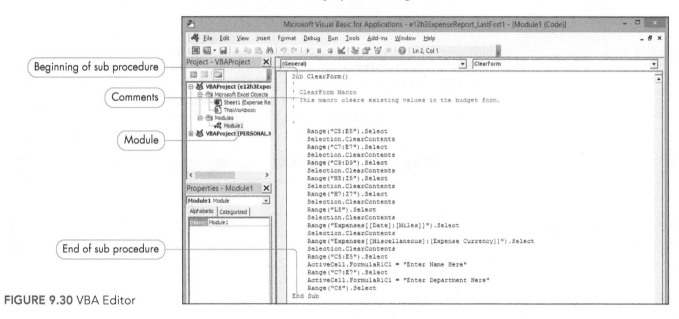

FIGURE 9.30 VBA Editor

The Visual Basic statements appear in the Code window on the right side. A Visual Basic module consists of at least one *procedure*, which is a named sequence of statements stored in a macro. In this example, Module1 contains the ClearForm procedure, which is also the name of the macro created in Excel. Module1 is stored in the Travel Expense Report workbook.

A procedure or macro always begins and ends with the Sub and End Sub statements. The Sub statement contains the name of the macro, such as Sub ClearForm() in Figure 9.30. The End Sub statement is the last statement and indicates the end of the macro. Sub and End Sub are Visual Basic keywords and appear in blue. *Keywords* are special programming syntax that have special meaning with the programming language and must be used for their intended purposes.

Comments, which are indicated by an apostrophe and appear in green, provide information about the macro but do not affect its execution and are considered documentation. Comments can be entered manually or are inserted automatically by the macro recorder to document the macro name, its author, and shortcut key (if any). You can add, delete, or modify comments. To create a basic sub procedure that would enter a date into a cell, complete the following steps:

1. From the VBA Editor, select Module from the Insert menu.
2. Type *sub currentdate()* and press Enter.
3. Type '*This macro will insert the current date in cell H7.*
4. Type *range("H7") = date* and press Enter.
5. Type *range("H7").font.bold = true.*
6. Save and exit the Visual Basic Editor.

Table 9.2 explains some of the lines of code used to create the previous sub procedure. The first word, *range*, refers to an object. An **object** is a variable that contains both data and code and represents an element of Excel such as Range or Selection. A period follows the object name, and the next word is often a behavior or attribute, such as Select or ClearContents, that describes a behavior or action performed on the object.

TABLE 9.2 VBA Editor Code

Code	Explanation
range("H7")	Identifies the range H7
= date	Applies the current date to the cell
font.bold = true	Applies object property, setting the font to bold. To disable, change *true* to *false*.

Use VBA with Protected Worksheets

Run time errors can sometimes occur when running VBA scripts on protected worksheets. A **run time error** is a software or hardware problem that prevents a program from working correctly. This is most commonly due to a procedure such as *range("H7").font.bold = true*, attempting to alter a locked cell. There are several methods to correct this issue. The simplest, as shown in Figure 9.31, is to encase your current VBA script with a statement that will unprotect the worksheet, run the current script, and reprotect the worksheet before ending the procedure.

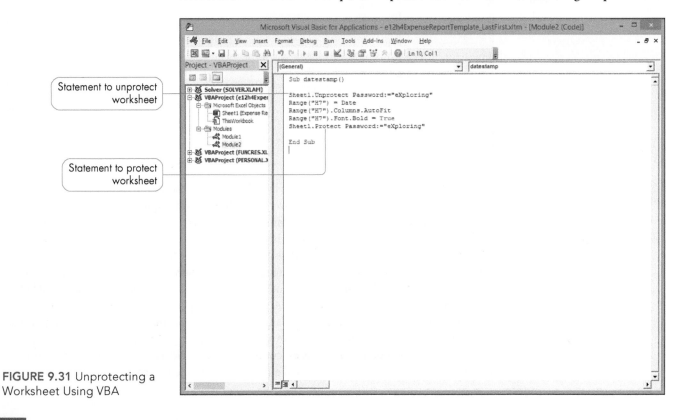

Statement to unprotect worksheet

Statement to protect worksheet

FIGURE 9.31 Unprotecting a Worksheet Using VBA

In the example given, cell H7 is formatted and the column size is altered. However, this will create a run time error because the worksheet is protected. The statement *Sheet1. Unprotect Password:= "eXploring"* unprotects the worksheet to allow the format changes to occur. The statement *Sheet1.Protect Password:= "eXploring"* then reprotects the worksheet.

Edit a Macro in the Visual Basic Editor

STEP 2>> If you work with a workbook that has macros that were created by a coworker or you used the macro recorder, you can edit the existing macro using the Visual Basic Editor. For example, if you record a macro to apply bold, Arial font, 12-pt size, and Red font color, each command appears in a separate statement (see Figure 9.32). The two statements to apply bold and italic start with Selection.Font, indicating that a font attribute will be applied to the current selection. The statement continues with a period and behavior, such as *Bold = True,* indicating that bold is activated. If the sub procedure is turning off bold, the statement looks like this:

```
Selection.Font.Bold = False
```

The With statement enables you to perform multiple actions on the same object. All commands between the With and the corresponding End With statement are executed collectively. Although the font and font size were changed in the macro, the macro also indicates that other attributes, such as superscript and subscript, are turned off. You can delete those lines of code if you want.

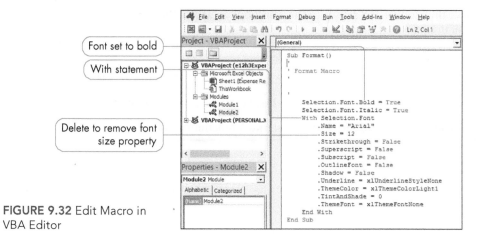

FIGURE 9.32 Edit Macro in VBA Editor

Creating a Custom Function

STEP 4>> There are several hundred built-in functions in Excel that can perform tasks as simple as capitalizing the first letter of a word, such as the Proper function, or as complex as a multiconditional sum, as created with SumIFs. In the event that one of the numerous built-in functions does not meet your needs, you have the ability to create your own custom function using VBA. Custom functions are virtually limitless. However, like sub procedures, they are still saved in modules. This means that if they are not saved to a Personal Macro Workbook, they will only be available within the Macro-Enabled Workbook in which they were created.

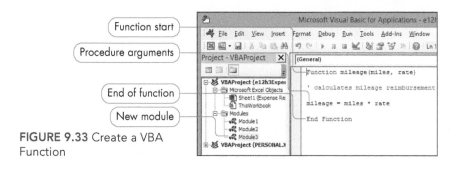

FIGURE 9.33 Create a VBA Function

When creating a custom function in VBA, you must start by creating a new module and typing *function* followed by the name of the function you are creating and the arguments that the function will use inside parentheses (see Figure 9.32).

After entering arguments on the next line, you have the ability to add comments in the same manner they were added to sub procedures. Your next step is to enter the statement that defines your function such as:

Mileage = miles * rate

After completing the statement, you end the function by typing End Function. However, this step should automatically be completed by the VBA editor.

Once a custom function is completed, it can be viewed within Excel under User Defined functions within the Insert Function command in the Function Library. Furthermore, you can access the function by simply typing = in the cell of your choice and the name of the function. This will allow you to use the custom function in the same manner as any of the built-in Excel functions. To create the VBA function described above, complete the following steps:

1. Press Alt+F11 to open the VBA Editor.
2. From the INSERT tab, select Module.
3. Type *Function mileage (rate, miles)* and press Enter.
4. Type *mileage = rate * miles*.
5. Type End Function.
6. Save the module and return to the workbook to access the newly created custom function.

Quick
Concepts

1. When using Excel, why would you want to access the VBA editor? *p. 461*

2. What are the two types of VBA macros that can be created in the VBA editor? *p. 461*

3. Why would it be necessary to create a custom function? *p. 463*

Hands-On Exercises

Watch the Video
for this Hands-
On Exercise!

MyITLab®
HOE4 Training

4 Visual Basic for Applications

You would like to automate as much of the Travel Expense Report as possible. Therefore, you will create a sub procedure assigned to a macro button to automatically insert the current date into the worksheet. You would also like to add an additional function that will allow the user to estimate mileage reimbursement prior to submission.

Skills covered: Create a Sub Procedure • Edit a Macro • Assign a Macro to an Image • Create a Custom Function

STEP 1 ≫ CREATE A SUB PROCEDURE

Before you create the sub procedure, you will open the template you created in Hands-On Exercise 3 and save it as a template with another name to preserve the original template in case you make any mistakes.

a. Open the Macro-Enabled Template *e12h3ExpenseReportTemplate_LastFirst*, click **Enable Content** to activate the prior macro, and save it as **e12h4ExpenseReportTemplate_LastFirst**, changing *h3* to *h4*.

When you use Open or Recent to open a template, you open it as a template to edit. When you use New, you make a copy of the template as a workbook.

b. Press **Alt+F11** on your keyboard to open the Visual Basic Editor.

c. Click the **Insert menu** and select **Module**.

d. Type *sub datestamp ()* on the first line of the newly created module and press **Enter**.

e. Type **Sheet1.Unprotect Password:= "eXploring"** and press **Enter**.

This unprotects the workbook to allow the remaining changes to take place..

f. Type **range("H7") = date** and press **Enter**.

This enters the current date.

g. Type **range("H7").columns.autofit** and press **Enter**.

This sets the selected column to autofit, which will ensure proper display of the date.

h. Type **range("H7").Font.Bold = True**.

This sets the newly entered date to bold.

i. Type **Sheet1.Protect Password:= "eXploring"** and press **Enter**.

j. Save the macro and press **F5** to test the newly created macro.

When run, the newly created sub procedure unprotects the worksheet, adds and formats the current date, sets the column width to auto, and reprotects the document.

STEP 2 ≫ EDIT A MACRO

After running the created sub procedure, you have decided that the newly inserted date should be italicized instead of bold. You will make this change in the VBA Editor by editing the bold property.

a. Press **Alt+F11** on your keyboard if the VBA Editor is not open.

Excel opens the VBA Editor so that you can edit the macro programming language.

b. Click **module 2**, if it is not already selected, to display the sub procedure created in Step 1. Select the line **Range("H7").Font.Bold = True** and replace the word *Bold* with **Italic**.

This edits the command to set the inserted date to italics instead of bold.

c. Save and exit the VBA Editor.

STEP 3 ≫ ASSIGN A MACRO TO AN IMAGE

After creating the sub procedure to insert the current date in the worksheet, you would like to enhance the usability of the document by creating a calendar icon to activate the macro. Refer to Figure 9.34 as you complete Step 3.

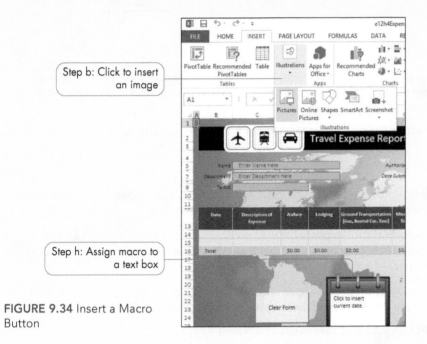

FIGURE 9.34 Insert a Macro Button

a. Right-click the **Expense Report worksheet tab**, select **Unprotect Sheet**, type **eXploring** in the **Password to unprotect sheet box**, and then click **OK**.

b. Click the **INSERT tab** and select **Pictures** from the Illustrations group.

c. Insert the image **e12h4Calendar.png** and position the image to the right of Clear Form.

d. Right-click the inserted image and click **Assign Macro**. Click the **datestamp macro**.

e. Click the **INSERT tab**, if necessary, and click **Text Box** in the Text group.

f. Draw a text box inside the image inserted in step b.

g. Type **Click to insert current date** in the text box.

h. Right-click the text box and click **Assign Macro**. Click the **datestamp macro box**.

   You decided to assign the macro to both the inserted image and the text box to make sure that the macro activates no matter where the end user clicks on the image.

i. Click the newly created button to verify the current date. Once the date is verified, click **Clear Form** and save the template.

STEP 4 ≫ CREATE A CUSTOM FUNCTION

Even though the Travel Expense Report has the ability to automatically calculate travel mileage reimbursement, you have decided to create a custom function to allow users to manually calculate their mileage reimbursement if they choose.

a. Press **Alt +F11** on your keyboard to open the Visual Basic Editor.

b. Click the **Insert menu** and select **Module**.

c. Type **function mileage(miles,rate)** on the first line of the newly created module and press **Enter**.

d. Type **This function will calculate mileage reimbursement**. Press **Enter**.

   This will appear as a comment in the module. However, it will not impact the calculation of the function.

e. Type the statement **mileage = miles * rate** and press **Enter**.

f. Save and exit the VBA Editor.

This creates a custom function that can be used in a similar fashion to any built-in function within Excel.

g. Click **cell H21** and type **=mileage(32,0.75)**. This returns the value 24.

You entered 32 miles at the rate of $.75 per mile to test the newly created function.

h. Delete the contents of **cell H21**.

i. Right-click the **Expense Report worksheet tab**, select **Protect Sheet**, type **eXploring** in the **Password to protect sheet box**, click **OK**, type **eXploring** in the **Reenter password to proceed box**, and then click **OK**.

j. Save the workbook and submit based on your instructor's directions.

Chapter Objectives Review

After reading this chapter, you have accomplished the following objectives:

1. **Select a template.**
   - A template is a partially created workbook that you can use as a model to create a workbook. You can create a workbook based on sample templates stored on your computer, or you can download a template from Office.com to create a new workbook.

2. **Apply themes and backgrounds.**
   - A theme is a collection of colors, fonts, and special effects. You can apply themes to various workbooks to develop a consistent look for your organization's workbooks.
     - Customize a theme: After applying a theme, you can customize the colors, fonts, and effects.
     - Apply a background: Excel has the ability to use graphics as a background of a worksheet.

3. **Apply cell styles.**
   - A cell style is a collection of format settings to provide a consistent look for fonts, borders, fill colors, alignment, and number formatting.
   - The Cell Styles gallery provides a variety of existing cell styles. If you change the cell style formatting, all cells affected by that style assume the new formatting, thus saving you valuable time so that you do not have to reformat cells individually.
     - Create custom cell styles: You can create a new custom style from the Styles group in the Home tab.
     - Modify and remove custom cell styles: Create custom styles that can be modified or removed by right-clicking the style and selecting the desired change in the Styles group.

4. **Create and use a template.**
   - You can save a workbook as a template when existing templates do not provide the structure you need.
   - When you save a template, Excel saves it in the C:\Users\ username\Documents\CustomOfficeTemplates folder so that the templates are available when you click the File tab and click New.
   - Templates have an .xltx file name extension.

5. **Protect a cell, a worksheet, and a workbook.**
   - By default, the Locked property is selected for all cells in all new workbooks you create; however, this property has no effect until you protect the worksheet.
   - Before protecting the worksheet, you should unlock cells that you want a user to be able to change, such as input cells.

   - For greater security, you can assign a password that is required to unprotect the worksheet.
   - For additional protection, you can protect an entire workbook to prevent users from inserting, deleting, renaming, or moving worksheets.

6. **Create a macro.**
   - A macro is a stored procedure that performs multiple, routine, or complex tasks.
   - The Developer tab contains commands to record, run, and edit macros.
     - Use the Macro Recorder: The Macro Recorder translates user actions into VBA. It can be accessed by pressing Alt+F11.
     - Record a macro: When recording a macro, all user actions will be recorded by the Macro Recorder and stored in VBA.
     - Record a Personal Macro workbook: Personal Macro workbooks allow user-created macros to be available at all times. They are stored in the XL Start folder in Windows 8.1.1.
     - Run a macro: After macros are created, they can be run from the assigned keyboard shortcut, a macro button, or from the View Macro dialog box.

7. **Create macro buttons.**
   - To facilitate the running of a macro, you can assign a macro to a button. The Developer tab contains controls, such as buttons, you can insert in a worksheet.

8. **Set macro security.**
   - The proliferation of Excel macro viruses has made it dangerous to open workbooks that contain macros. To counter this threat, Excel automatically disables the macros and displays a security warning message that macros have been disabled.

9. **Creating a sub procedure.**
   - Sub procedures can be created using the Macro Recorder or entered manually in the VBA Editor. Sub procedures only perform actions and cannot return values.
     - Edit a macro in the VBA Editor: After a sub procedure has been created, it can be edited in the VBA Editor.

10. **Creating a custom function.**
    - If the built-in Excel functions do not meet your needs, you can create a custom function using VBA. All custom functions are noted in VBA with the Open function and the Close End function.

Key Terms Matching

Match the key terms with their definitions. Write the key term letter by the appropriate numbered definition.

a. Background
b. Cell Style
c. Comment
d. Keyword
e. Locked Cell
f. Macro
g. Macro Recorder
h. Module
i. Object

j. Personal Macro Workbook
k. Procedure
l. Run Time Error
m. Sub Procedure
n. Template
o. Theme
p. Visual Basic for Applications (VBA)
q. Visual Basic Editor

1. _____ A special workbook file used as a model to create similarly structured workbooks. **p. 432**

2. _____ A collection of colors, fonts, and special effects. **p. 433**

3. _____ An image that appears behind the worksheet data onscreen; it does not print. **p. 434**

4. _____ A set of formatting options applied to worksheet cells. **p. 435**

5. _____ Prevents users from making changes to a specific cell in a protected worksheet. **p. 442**

6. _____ A set of instructions that tells Excel which commands to execute. **p. 451**

7. _____ A tool that records a series of commands in the sequence performed by a user and converts the commands into programming syntax. **p. 451**

8. _____ A hidden workbook stored in the XL Start folder that contains macros and opens automatically when you start Excel. **p. 453**

9. _____ The Office application used to create, edit, execute, and debug macros using programming language. **p. 461**

10. _____ A named sequence of statements that can be executed by the user or a macro. **p. 461**

11. _____ A special programming syntax used for a specific purpose that appears in blue in the Visual Basic Editor. **p. 461**

12. _____ Documents programming code, starts with an apostrophe, and appears in green in the VBA Editor. **p. 461**

13. _____ Command lines written in the VBA Editor that have the ability to perform actions in Excel. **p. 461**

14. _____ A file that stores sub procedures and functions. **p. 461**

15. _____ A variable that contains both data and code and represents an element of Excel. **p. 462**

16. _____ A software or hardware problem that prevents a program from working correctly. **p. 462**

17. _____ A robust programming language that can be used within various software packages to enhance and automate functionality. **p. 451**

Multiple Choice

1. Which would you do to start using a calendar template from Office.com Templates?

   (a) Open the Backstage view, click Open, and then choose a template from the Office.com gallery.

   (b) Open the Backstage view, click New, and then click Calendars in the Suggested Searches options.

   (c) Click the Office.com option in the Template Manager on the Developer tab.

   (d) Open the Backstage view, click Options, and then choose the Office.com templates in the Template Manager.

2. You created an invoice template to prepare invoices for your consulting business. In Windows 8.1.1, where would you save the template so it is available in the available templates list in the Backstage view?

   (a) C:\Users\user_name\Libraries\Documents

   (b) Submit it to Office.com.

   (c) C:\Users\username\Documents\CustomOfficeTemplates

   (d) None of the above

3. Your company just had a new corporate logo designed. What do you do in Excel to present professional-looking reusable workbooks to share with clients?

   (a) Replace the old logo with the new logo in all templates used by the company.

   (b) Create a theme that complements the colors, fonts, and effects of the new logo and apply the theme to all templates.

   (c) Create a cell style that complements the new logo and update cell styles in all of the templates used by the company.

   (d) All of the above

4. How do you print a background image?

   (a) In Print Options, select Print Background.

   (b) A background image is printable only from the Print Preview options.

   (c) Backgrounds print automatically when the worksheet prints.

   (d) Backgrounds are not printable.

5. What is the keyboard shortcut to access the VBA Editor?

   (a) Alt+F8

   (b) Command-T

   (c) F4

   (d) Alt+F11

6. If you forget the password you used to protect an Excel worksheet, how do you reset it?

   (a) You cannot reset it.

   (b) You can reset it in Excel Options in Backstage view.

   (c) You can e-mail it to Office.com for reset.

   (d) There is a password reset in the Properties pane for each Excel workbook.

7. In which programming language are Excel macros written?

   (a) Java

   (b) C++

   (c) VBA

   (d) SQL

8. When you get ready to write a macro:

   (a) Be careful and thorough as you plan which actions to record so you do not inadvertently record unnecessary steps.

   (b) You can record steps and easily delete extraneous steps while using the Macro Recorder.

   (c) Neither A nor B

   (d) Both A and B

9. Which of the following statements is true about macro security?

   (a) When you add a Macro-Enabled Workbook to the Trust Center, you must enable the content of that file each time you open it.

   (b) Setting your Trust Center options to include files in a specific folder and then saving macro-enabled files in that folder allows you to open those files with the content enabled.

   (c) Set macro security options on the Developer tab to Secured.

   (d) Macro-enabled files cannot contain viruses.

10. Which of the following Workbook file extensions support macros?

   (a) .xlsm

   (b) .xlsb

   (c) .xltm

   (d) All of the above

1 Blood Pressure Tracker

FROM SCRATCH Inner City Health Clinic is located in downtown San Francisco. As a physician's assistant, you help monitor each patient's blood pressure. It is important for some patients to track their blood pressure throughout the week between office visits, so you want to create a template that you can e-mail to them. You will create a template from scratch, select a theme, add a background image, and apply styles. After you are satisfied with the appearance, you will then save the workbook as a new template that you can e-mail to your computer-savvy patients so that they can track their blood pressure at home. This exercise follows the same set of skills as used in Hands-On Exercises 1 and 2 in the chapter. Refer to Figure 9.35 as you complete this exercise.

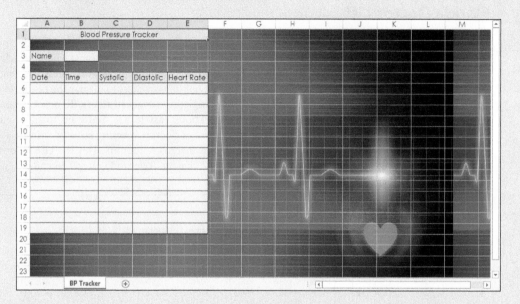

FIGURE 9.35 Blood Pressure Tracker Template

Photo: psdesign1/Fotolia

a. Start Excel and click **Blank workbook** from the Backstage view.

b. Save the workbook as a template with the file name **e12p1BpTracker_LastFirst**.

c. Name the worksheet **BP Tracker**.

d. Click the **PAGE LAYOUT tab**, click **Themes** in the Themes group, and then select **Slice**.

e. Click **Background** in the Page Setup group, click **Browse**, and then navigate to your student data files. Select *e12p1Bpressure.jpg* in the Sheet Background dialog box and click **Insert**.

f. Merge and center the **range A1:E1** and complete the following tasks:
   - Type **Blood Pressure Tracker** in **cell A1** and apply **20% – Accent 5 cell style**.
   - Type **Name** in **cell A3** and apply **20% – Accent 5 cell style**.
   - Apply the **Output cell style** to **cell B3**.

g. Select the **range A5:E5**, click **Borders** in the Font group on the HOME tab, apply **All Borders,** and then apply **20% – Accent 5 cell style**.

h. Enter the following text as column headings in row 5:
   - **Cell A5: Date**
   - **Cell B5: Time**
   - **Cell C5: Systolic**
   - **Cell D5: Diastolic**
   - **Cell E5: Heart Rate**

i. Click **cell E5**, click the **HOME tab**, and then select **Format** from the Cells group. Select **AutoFit Column Width**.

j. Select **range A6:E19** and apply the **Output cell style**.

k. Select **cell B3**, press and hold **Ctrl**, and then select the **range A6:E19**. Click **Format** in the Cells group of the HOME tab and select **Lock Cell**.

l. Protect the worksheet by doing the following:
- Right-click the **BP Tracker sheet tab**, select **Protect Sheet**, type **eXploring** in the **Password (optional) box**, and then click **OK**.
- Type **eXploring** in the **Reenter password to proceed box** and click **OK**.

m. Click the **FILE tab**, click **Save As**, and then navigate to your student data files. Click the **Save as type arrow**, select **Excel Template**, keep the default name, and then click **Save**.

n. Save and close the workbook. Submit based on your instructor's directions.

2 Florida Doctor List

The Florida Medical Referral Agency maintains a list of select doctors, cities, specialties, genders, and board certification data. In addition, the list indicates whether each doctor is accepting new patients (Yes) or not (No). The workbook contains three worksheets: the Doctor List, Criteria Settings to enter advanced criteria, and the Output worksheet to display the results of an advanced filter. You will create range names to use for completing advanced filters. To assist the employees who run the call center, you want to make the workbook easy to use. You want to create three macros: two macros to filter the database to display a list of doctors meeting selected criteria and one macro to clear the output results. You will then assign macros to buttons. This exercise follows the same set of skills as used in Hands-On Exercise 3 in the chapter. Refer to Figures 9.36 and 9.37 as you complete this exercise.

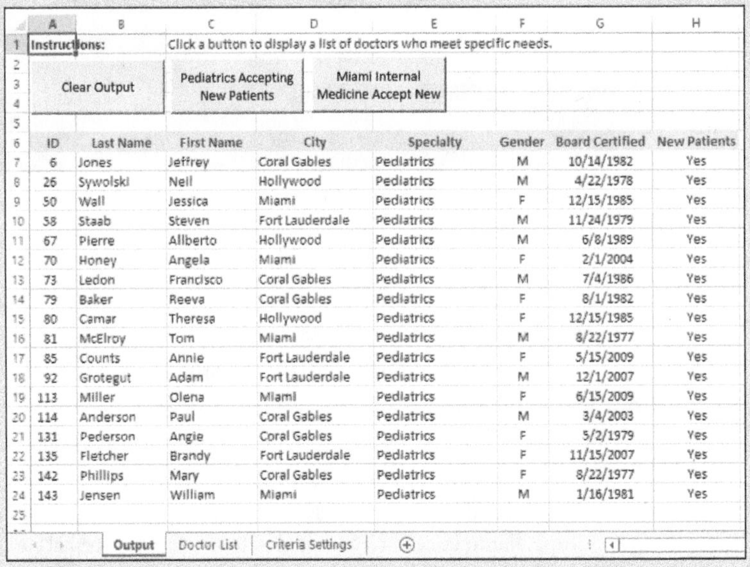

	A	B	C	D	E	F	G	H
1	Instructions:		Click a button to display a list of doctors who meet specific needs.					
2								
3		Clear Output	Pediatrics Accepting New Patients	Miami Internal Medicine Accept New				
4								
5								
6	ID	Last Name	First Name	City	Specialty	Gender	Board Certified	New Patients
7	6	Jones	Jeffrey	Coral Gables	Pediatrics	M	10/14/1982	Yes
8	26	Sywolski	Neil	Hollywood	Pediatrics	M	4/22/1978	Yes
9	50	Wall	Jessica	Miami	Pediatrics	F	12/15/1985	Yes
10	58	Staab	Steven	Fort Lauderdale	Pediatrics	M	11/24/1979	Yes
11	67	Pierre	Alberto	Hollywood	Pediatrics	M	6/8/1989	Yes
12	70	Honey	Angela	Miami	Pediatrics	F	2/1/2004	Yes
13	73	Ledon	Francisco	Coral Gables	Pediatrics	M	7/4/1986	Yes
14	79	Baker	Reeva	Coral Gables	Pediatrics	F	8/1/1982	Yes
15	80	Camar	Theresa	Hollywood	Pediatrics	F	12/15/1985	Yes
16	81	McElroy	Tom	Miami	Pediatrics	M	8/22/1977	Yes
17	85	Counts	Annie	Fort Lauderdale	Pediatrics	F	5/15/2009	Yes
18	92	Grotegut	Adam	Fort Lauderdale	Pediatrics	M	12/1/2007	Yes
19	113	Miller	Olena	Miami	Pediatrics	F	6/15/2009	Yes
20	114	Anderson	Paul	Coral Gables	Pediatrics	M	3/4/2003	Yes
21	131	Pederson	Angie	Coral Gables	Pediatrics	F	5/2/1979	Yes
22	135	Fletcher	Brandy	Fort Lauderdale	Pediatrics	F	11/15/2007	Yes
23	142	Phillips	Mary	Coral Gables	Pediatrics	F	8/22/1977	Yes
24	143	Jensen	William	Miami	Pediatrics	M	1/16/1981	Yes
25								

Output | Doctor List | Criteria Settings

FIGURE 9.36 Results of Running Pediatrics New Macro

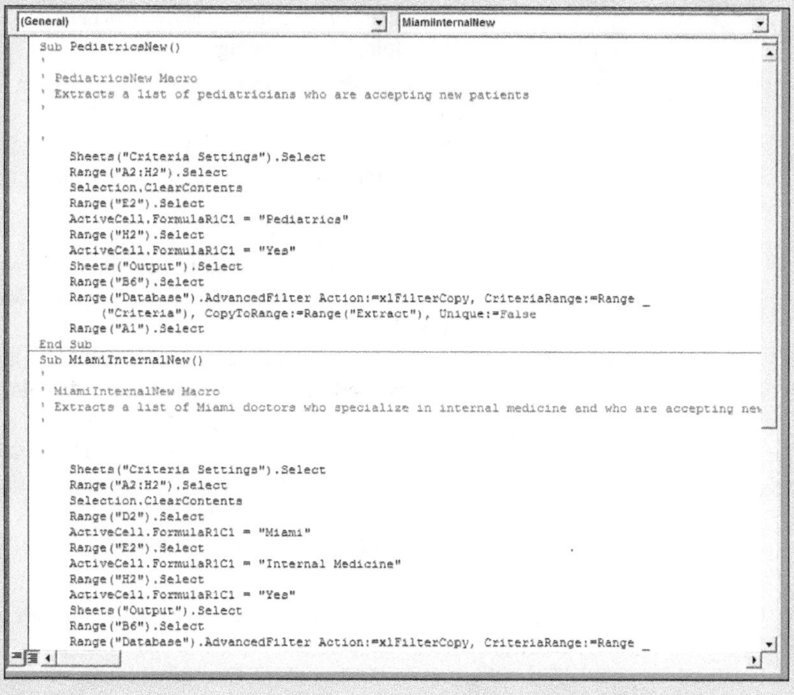

FIGURE 9.37 Macro Code in VBA Window

a. Open *e12p2Doctors* and save it as **e12p2Doctors_LastFirst** in the Excel Macro-Enabled Workbook file format.

b. Create range names by doing the following:
- Click the **Output sheet tab**, select the **range A6:H6**, type **Extract** in the **Name Box**, and then press **Enter**.
- Click the **Doctor List sheet tab**, select the **range A1:H151**, type **Database** in the **Name Box**, and then press **Enter**.
- Click the **Criteria Settings sheet tab**, select the **range A1:H2**, type **Criteria** in the **Name Box**, and then press **Enter**.

c. Check the Ribbon to see if it contains the DEVELOPER tab. If not, click the **FILE tab**, click **Options**, click **Customize Ribbon** in the Excel Options dialog box, click the **Developer check box** in the Main Tabs list, and then click **OK**.

d. Click the **Output sheet tab** and create a macro that filters the database to show pediatric doctors who are accepting new patients by doing the following:
- Click the **DEVELOPER tab** and click **Record Macro** in the Code group to open the Record Macro dialog box.
- Type **PediatricsNew** in the **Macro name box**, type **Extracts a list of pediatricians who are accepting new patients** in the **Description box**, and then click **OK**.
- Click the **Criteria Settings sheet tab**, select the **range A2:H2**, and then press **Delete** to delete any existing conditions that might exist later.
- Click **cell E2**, type **Pediatrics**, click **cell H2**, type **Yes**, and then press **Ctrl+Enter**.
- Click the **Output sheet tab** and click **cell B6** to place the active cell in the Extract range.
- Click the **DATA tab** and click **Advanced** in the Sort & Filter group to open the Advanced Filter dialog box.
- Click the **Copy to another location option**, type **Database** in the **List range box**, type **Criteria** in the **Criteria range box**, type **Extract** in the **Copy to box**, and then click **OK**.
- Press **Ctrl+Home** to position the active cell in **cell A1**.
- Click the **DEVELOPER tab** and click **Stop Recording** in the Code group.

e. Create a macro that filters the database to show internal medicine doctors in Miami who are accepting new patients by doing the following:

- Click the **DEVELOPER tab** if necessary and click **Record Macro** in the Code group to open the Record Macro dialog box.
- Type **MiamiInternalNew** in the **Macro name box**, type **Extracts a list of Miami doctors who specialize in internal medicine and who are accepting new patients** in the **Description box**, and then click **OK**.
- Click the **Criteria Settings sheet tab**, select the **range A2:H2**, and then press **Delete** to delete any conditions that a user might enter to perform their own filter.
- Click **cell D2**, type **Miami**, click **cell E2**, type **Internal Medicine**, click **cell H2**, type **Yes**, and then press **Ctrl+Enter**.
- Click the **Output sheet tab** and click **cell B6** to place the active cell in the Extract range.
- Click the **DATA tab** and click **Advanced** in the Sort & Filter group to open the Advanced Filter dialog box.
- Click the **Copy to another location option**, type **Database** in the **List range box**, type **Criteria** in the **Criteria range box**, type **Extract** in the **Copy to box**, and then click **OK**.
- Press **Ctrl+Home** to position the active cell in **cell A1**.
- Click the **DEVELOPER tab** and click **Stop Recording** in the Code group. Save the workbook.

f. Create a macro that clears the criteria range and the output by doing the following:

- Click the **DEVELOPER tab** if necessary and click **Record Macro** in the Code group to open the Record Macro dialog box.
- Type **Clear** in the **Macro name box**, type **Clears the criteria range and the output** in the **Description box**, and then click **OK**.
- Click the **Criteria Settings sheet tab**, select the **range A2:H2**, and then press **Delete** to delete any existing conditions that might exist later.
- Click **cell A2**, type **-100** as a dummy value, and then press **Ctrl+Enter**.
- Click the **Output sheet tab** and click **cell B6** to place the active cell in the Extract range.
- Click the **DATA tab** and click **Advanced** in the Sort & Filter group to open the Advanced Filter dialog box.
- Click the **Copy to another location option**, type **Database** in the **List range box**, type **Criteria** in the **Criteria range box**, type **Extract** in the **Copy to box**, and then click **OK**.
- Press **Ctrl+Home** to position the active cell in **cell A1**.
- Click the **DEVELOPER tab** and click **Stop Recording** in the Code group.

g. Create a macro button and assign the Clear macro to it by doing the following:

- Click the **DEVELOPER tab** if necessary, click **Insert** in the Controls group, and then click **Button (Form Control)** in the *Form Controls* section.
- Click in **cell A2** and create a button that fills the range A2:B4. When you release the mouse button, the Assign Macro dialog box opens.
- Select **Clear** in the *Macro name* list and click **OK**. The button displays *Button 1*.
- Right-click the button, select **Edit Text**, select **Button 1**, type **Clear Output**, and then click in **cell A1**. Save the workbook.

h. Create a macro button and assign the PediatricsNew macro to it by doing the following:

- Click **Insert** in the Controls group and click **Button (Form Control)** in the *Form Controls* section.
- Drag to create a button on the right side of the Clear Output button. Make sure the second button is approximately the same height and width as the Clear Output button.
- Select **PediatricsNew** in the *Macro name* list and click **OK**. The button displays *Button 2*.
- Right-click the button, select **Edit Text**, select **Button 2**, type **Pediatrics Accepting New Patients**, and then click in **cell A1**. If you need to resize the button to display the button text, press **Ctrl** as you click the button to select it. Then resize the button as necessary. Save the workbook.

i. Adapt step h to create a macro button on the right side of the Pediatrics button and assign the MiamiInternalNew macro to it. Display the text **Miami Internal Medicine Accept New** and click in **cell A1**. Save the workbook.

j. Run the macros by doing the following:

- Click **Pediatrics Accepting New Patients**. The Output sheet should display 18 records (see Figure 9.35).
- Click **Miami Internal Medicine Accept New**. The Output sheet should display 4 records.
- Click **Clear Output**.

k. Edit any macro that does not run correctly: Click the **DEVELOPER tab**, click **Macros** in the Code group, select the macro that contains errors, and then click **Edit**. Edit the code as necessary in the VBA Editor (see Figure 9.36), click **Save**, close the VBA Editor, and then run the macro again.

l. Create a footer with your name on the left side, the sheet name code in the center, and the file name code on the right side of all three worksheets.

m. Save and close the workbook, and submit based on your instructor's directions.

Mid-Level Exercises

1 Little League Statistics

You volunteered to coach for your community Little League program. You are working with the Pirates, a team of 10- to 12-year-olds who respond well to seeing their batting statistics. You created a workbook to record the Pirates' batting data and calculate their statistics. The recreation department manager is a friend of yours from high school and is impressed with your workbook. He wondered if you could make something similar for the other coaches when he saw how you were recording statistics.

a. Open *e12m1Pirates* and save it as **e12m1Pirates_LastFirst**.

b. Apply the **Title cell style** to cell A1, the **Heading 2 cell style** to the **range A2:R2**, the **Heading 4 cell style** to the **range A4:A20**, and **Output style** to the **range B3:R20**.

c. Apply the **Wood Type theme** and apply the **Red theme colors**.

d. Add *e12m1Pirate.jpg* as a background image for the worksheet.

e. Save the Excel workbook and save it as a template named **e12m1Baseball_LastFirst**.

f. Delete the background from the Statistics worksheet and insert *e12m1Baseball.jpg* as the background image for the template before distributing the template to the other teams.

g. Select the **Game 1 worksheet**, delete all players' names and batting information from the **range A3:M16**. Right-align the labels in the **range C2:M2**.

h. Unlock cells in **cell A1**, the **range A3:M16** of the Game 1 worksheet, and **cell A1** in the Statistics worksheet. Right-align the labels in the **range B2:R2** in the Statistics worksheet.

i. Set **0.2"** left and right margins on both worksheets. Set a width of **6.00** for columns B:H and J:O on the Statistics worksheet.

j. Create a footer with your name on the left side, the sheet name code in the center, and the file name code on the right side of both worksheets.

k. Protect all worksheets with a password of **eXploring**. Allow all users to format cells, columns, and rows.

l. Save and close the template.

m. Create a new workbook from the *e12m1Baseball_LastFirst* template and save the workbook as **e12m1Broncos_LastFirst**.

n. Edit the league name from *Pirates* to **Broncos** in **cell A1** of each worksheet and enter player names and data for 14 players in the Games 1 worksheet.

o. Save the workbook and submit based on your instructor's directions.

2 Jackson Municipal Airport

ANALYSIS CASE

Hulett Enterprises is located in Jackson, Mississippi. In the past, you have created Web queries to find departure and arrival information for your supervisors, Denise Petrillo and Omar Vincent, who travel frequently for business meetings. Because of your Excel experience, other managers are interested in having you develop a workbook with this information they can use. You decide to create macros to update the Web queries, adjust formatting of the imported data, and then print the worksheets. Finally, you will assign the macros to macro buttons.

a. Open *e12m2Airport* and save it as **e12m2Airport_LastFirst** as an Excel Macro-Enabled Workbook file format.

b. Create a Web query in **cell A8** to **http://www.jmaa.com/JAN/FlightInfo_arr.asp** to the arrival schedule table on the Arrivals worksheet.

c. Create a Web query in **cell A8** to **http://www.jmaa.com/JAN/FlightInfo_arr.asp** to the departure schedule table on the Departures worksheet.

d. Apply **conditional formatting** to the Status column (the **range F9:F50**) to highlight DELAYED flights with **Light Red Fill with Dark Red Text formatting** on both worksheets.

DISCOVER

e. Display the Arrivals worksheet and record a macro named **Update** to do the following:
   - Refresh all Web queries.
   - Bold the column labels on row **8**.
   - Set **cell A1** as the active cell.

f. Create a button on each worksheet in the **range A4:C6** that is assigned to the Update macro and displays *Refresh the List* on the button.

g. Click **Refresh the List** on each worksheet to ensure it works.

h. Create a footer with your name on the left side, the sheet name code in the center, and the file name code on the right side on each worksheet.

 i. Answer the questions on the Q&A worksheet.

j. Save and close the workbook, and submit based on your instructor's directions.

---

3 Fundraiser

COLLABORATION CASE

You work for a regional philanthropic organization that helps raise money for underprivileged youth. To help meet an end-of-the-year fundraising goal, you have decided to deploy regional donation agents to help collect contributions. You would like to make a worksheet to help track donations. Once the worksheet is completed, you will share the file via e-mail with a collaborator in the region who will update the numbers.

Student 1:

a. Open *e12m3FundRaiser* and save it as **e12m3FundRaiser_LastFirst**.

b. Select **cell B2** and apply the **Heading 2 cell style**.

c. Select the **range B3:E10**, click the **HOME tab**, click **Format** and then unlock the cells.

d. Click **Format** and protect the worksheet using the password **eXploring**.

e. Click the **FILE tab** and select **Share** in the Backstage view.

f. Select **EMAIL** and choose **Send as Attachment**.

g. E-mail the worksheet to your collaborator.

Student 2:

h. Open the e-mail and the attachment and enter the following data:

Date	Name	Donation	Collector
12/20/2015	Smith	$350.00	
12/22/2015	Williams	$125.00	
12/23/2015	Wilky	$110.00	
12/23/2015	Barns	$500.00	

i. Type your name as the **collector** in column E.

j. Create a footer with your name on the left side, the sheet name code in the center, and the file name code on the right side on each worksheet.

k. Save and close the workbook, and submit based on your instructor's directions.

Trust Center

So far, you have worked with the default Trust Center settings. You want to learn more about the Trust Center. Open the Trust Center dialog box in Excel and display the Macro Settings options. Start Word and insert a screenshot of the default Macro Settings. Set a **3"** shape height for the screenshot. Save the Word document as **e12b2Trust_LastFirst**. Compose a short explanation of the default Macro Settings option. Display the File Block Settings options and select the Excel 2007 and later Macro-Enabled Workbooks and Templates Open and Save check boxes. Insert a screenshot in your Word document and set a **3"** shape height. Click **OK** in each open dialog box.

In Excel, open *e12h3ExpenseReportTemplate_LastFirst.xltm*, the Macro-Enabled Template. In Word, explain what happens when you open this template and what happens when you try to run the macro by clicking **Clear Form**. Close the Macro-Enabled Template and deselect the check boxes you just selected in the File Block Settings. In the Word document, insert a footer with your name on the left side and a file name field on the right side. Save the document and submit based on your instructor's directions.

Real Estate Listings

You are a real estate analyst who works for Mountain View Realty in the North Utah County area. Your assistant, Joey, compiled a list of houses sold during the past few months in a Macro-Enabled Workbook. Joey created three macros: (1) a Clear macro to clear the existing Criteria Range and run the filter to empty the Output Range, (2) a CedarHills macro to set a criterion in the Criteria Range to filter the list for Cedar Hills only, and (3) a CityAgentCombo interactive macro with input boxes to prompt the user for the city and agent, enter those in respective cells, and run the advanced filter. In addition, Joey created three macro buttons, one to run each macro. However, the macros and buttons have errors. Open *e12b3RealEstate.xlsm* and save it as a Macro-Enabled Workbook named **e12b3RealEstate_LastFirst**. Find the errors in the macros, document the problems in the macro code using programming comments, and then fix the errors. Find and correct the macro button errors. Create a footer with your name on the left side, the sheet name code in the center, and the file name code on the right side of the Input-Output worksheet. Save and close the workbook, and submit based on your instructor's directions.

Interview Techniques

 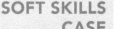

Soon you will graduate from college and, in preparation for graduation, you will be participating in several job interviews. As part of your preparation, you would like to do research on interview techniques. Your next goal is to create an Excel worksheet to help rate your overall feelings toward your performance during each interview.

After completing your research, create a workbook named **e12b4Evaluation_LastFirst**. Name the worksheet **Interview Notes**. Type the heading **Company** in **cell A1**, **Position** in **cell B1**, **Date** in **cell C1**, and **Notes** in **cell D1**. Format the cells with the **Heading 2 cell style**. Highlight the **range A1:D1** and ensure the cells are locked. Your last step is to protect the worksheet, using the password **eXploring**. Create a footer with your name on the left side, the sheet name code in the center, and the file name code on the right side of the Input-Output worksheet. Save and close the workbook, and submit based on your instructor's directions.

Capstone Exercise

As the department head of the Information Systems Department at a university, you are responsible for developing the class teaching schedules for your faculty. You have a tentative Fall 2015 schedule developed in sequence, but you want to ensure that you are not double-booking classrooms or faculty. To help you review room and faculty schedules, you will need to sort the original list in various ways. In addition, you want to create a model to use as a template for future semesters and to share with other department heads.

Create a Template

You want to convert the existing Fall 2015 schedule into a template so that you can use it to develop future semester schedules. In addition, you want to apply cell styles to format the template.

a. Open *e12c1Schedule* and save it as **e12c1Schedule_LastFirst** in Macro-Enabled Template file format.

b. Apply the **Retrospect theme**.

c. Apply the **Heading 3 cell style** to the column labels in the **range A4:K4** in the Sequential worksheet.

d. Apply the **Aspect theme color**.

e. Save the template.

Create the RoomSort Macro

You will sort the table by room number to ensure you do not have any room conflicts, such as double-booking a room. To avoid having to create a custom sort each time you want to perform this sort, you will record the steps as a macro.

a. Record a macro named **RoomSort**.

b. Display the Room worksheet data, use the Name Box to select the **range A4:M100**, and then delete the selected range. (This process will delete any existing data to ensure empty cells before copying new data to this worksheet.)

c. Display the Sequential worksheet, use the Go To command to go to **cell A4**, and then press **Ctrl+Shift+End** to select the scheduling data. Copy the selected range and paste it starting in **cell A4** of the Room worksheet. Use the Go To command to go to **cell A4**.

d. Create a custom sort with these settings:

- Sort by Room in alphabetical order.
- Sort then by Days with a custom order by adding entries in this order: MWF, MW, M, W, TR, T, R, S.
- Sort then by Start Time from earliest to latest.
- Perform the sort.

e. Display the Sequential worksheet, use the Go To command to go to **cell A1**, and then stop recording the macro.

f. Save the file as a Macro-Enabled Template.

Create the FacultySort Macro

You want to sort the table by faculty, days, and times to ensure you do not have any scheduling conflicts, such as double-booking a faculty member with two classes at the same time. To avoid having to create a custom sort each time you want to perform this sort, you will record the steps as a macro.

a. Record a macro named **FacultySort**.

b. Display the Faculty worksheet data, use the Name Box to select the **range A4:M100**, and then delete the selected range. (This process will delete any existing data to ensure empty cells before copying new data to this worksheet.)

c. Display the Sequential worksheet, use the Go To command to go to **cell A4**, and then press **Ctrl+Shift+End** to select the scheduling data. Copy the selected range and paste it starting in **cell A4** of the Faculty worksheet. Use the Go To command to go to **cell A4**.

d. Create a custom sort with these settings:

- Sort by Instructor in alphabetical order.
- Sort then by Days with a custom order you created previously.
- Sort then by Start Time from earliest to latest.
- Perform the sort.

e. Display the Sequential worksheet, use the Go To command to go to **cell A1**, and then stop recording the macro. Save the Macro-Enabled Template.

Create Macro Buttons

To create a user-friendly interface for yourself and others who might use your Macro-Enabled Template, you will insert two macro buttons, one for each macro, on the Sequential worksheet.

a. Insert a button at the top of the worksheet and assign it to the RoomSort macro.

b. Edit the text that appears on the button to display appropriate text.

c. Create, place, and edit a button for the second macro.

d. Right-click each macro button and set **0.5"** height and **1.5"** width. Ensure all buttons are the same distance from the top of the worksheet and the same distance apart.

e. Save the Macro-Enabled Template.

Finalize the Template

You will save the current data as a Macro-Enabled Workbook to preserve the data. Then you will prepare the file to be a template without the data.

a. Save the workbook as **e12c1InfoSys_LastFirst** in the Excel Macro-Enabled Workbook file type.

b. Delete the specific scheduling data on all three worksheets, but do not delete the macro buttons or column labels in the Sequential worksheet.

c. Save the file as **e12c1InfoSys_LastFirst** in the Excel Macro-Enabled Template file format. Close the template.

Use the Template

Another department head gave you a copy of her partial schedule. You want to select the template you created, import her data, and run the macros you created.

a. Use the New dialog box to select the *e12c1InfoSys* Macro-Enabled Template you created.

b. Open *e12c1Office*, copy the data, and then paste the data below the column headings in the Sequential worksheet. Center data horizontally in the ID, Prefix, Number, and Section columns.

c. Click the macro buttons to sort the data on the respective worksheets.

d. Save the file as **e12c1Office_LastFirst** in the Excel Macro-Enabled Workbook file format.

e. Close the files and submit based on your instructor's directions.

Introduction to Access

Finding Your Way Through an Access Database

OBJECTIVES AFTER YOU READ THIS CHAPTER, YOU WILL BE ABLE TO:

1. Understand database fundamentals p. 482

2. Use an existing database p. 489

3. Sort table data on one or multiple fields p. 500

4. Create, modify, and remove filters p. 501

5. Know when to use Access or Excel to manage data p. 509

6. Understand relational power p. 510

7. Create a database p. 517

CASE STUDY | Managing a Business in the Global Economy

Northwind Traders* is an international gourmet food distributor that imports and exports specialty foods from around the world. Northwind's products include meats, seafood, dairy products, beverages, and produce. Keeping track of customers, vendors, orders, and inventory is a critical task. The owners of Northwind have just purchased an order-processing database created with Microsoft Office Access 2013 to help manage their customers, suppliers, products, and orders.

You have been hired to learn, use, and manage the database. Northwind's owners are willing to provide training about their business and Access. They expect the learning process to take about three months. After three months, your job will be to support the order-processing team as well as to provide detail and summary reports to the sales force as needed. Your new job at Northwind Traders will be a challenge, but it is also a good opportunity to make a great contribution to a global company. Are you up to the task?

*Northwind Traders was created by the Microsoft Access Team as a sample database for Access 2003. Access 2013 does not include a sample database, so you will use a modified version of Northwind Traders. The names of companies, products, people, characters, and/or data are fictitious.

Databases Are Everywhere!

A **database** is a collection of data organized as meaningful information that can be accessed, managed, stored, queried, sorted, and reported. You probably participate in data collection and are exposed to databases on a regular basis. For example, your community college or university uses a database to store registration data. When you enrolled at your institution, you created a profile that was saved in a database. When you registered for this course, your data was entered into a database. If you have a bank account, have a Social Security card, have a medical history, or have booked a flight with an airline, your information is stored in a record in a database.

If you use the Internet, you probably use databases often because the Internet can provide you with easy access to databases. For example, when you shop online or check your bank statement online, you connect to a database. Even when you type a search phrase into Google and click Search, you are using Google's massive database with all of its stored Web page references and keywords. Look for something on Amazon, and you are searching Amazon's database to find a product that you might want to buy. Need a new driver for golfing? Log on to Amazon, search for "golf clubs driver" (see Figure 10.1), and find the right driver with your preferred loft, hand orientation, flex, shaft material, and price range. All of this information is stored in Amazon's products database.

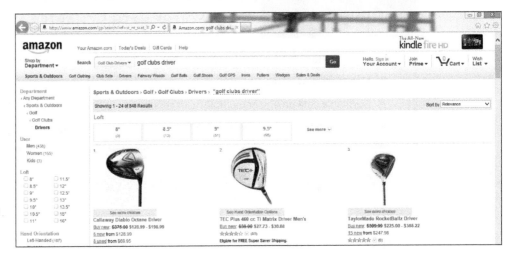

FIGURE 10.1 Amazon Web Site

Photo: Copyright © 2013 Amazon.com, Inc.

Organizations rely on data to conduct daily operations, regardless of whether the organization exists as a profit or not-for-profit environment. Organizations maintain data about their customers, employees, orders, volunteers, activities, and facilities. Organizations maintain data about their customers, employees, orders, volunteers, activities, and facilities, and this data needs to be stored, organized, and made available for analysis. *Data* and *information* are two terms that are often used interchangeably. However, when it comes to databases, the two terms mean different things. *Data* is what is entered into a database. *Information* is the finished product that is produced by the database. Data is converted to information by selecting, calculating, sorting, or summarizing records. Decisions in an organization are usually based on information produced by a database, rather than raw data.

In this section, you will learn the fundamentals of organizing data in a database, explore what Access database objects are and what their purpose is, and examine the Access interface.

Understanding Database Fundamentals

People use databases to store collections of data. A **database management system (DBMS)** is a software system that provides the tools needed to create, maintain, and use a database. Database management systems make it possible to access and control data and display the information in a variety of formats such as lists, forms, and reports. **Access** is the database management system included in the Office 2013 Professional suite and the Office 2013 Professional Academic suite. Access is a valuable decision-making tool that many organizations are using. Advanced Access users and software developers can even use Microsoft Access to develop software applications for specific solutions to the needs of organizations. For example, a health organization uses Access to track and understand disease reports.

Organize Information in a Database and Recognize Access Objects

STEP 2 ❯❯ An Access database is a structured collection of *objects*, the main components that are created and used to make the database function. The main object types in an Access database are listed below and discussed in the following paragraphs.

- Tables
- Forms
- Queries
- Reports
- Macros
- Modules

The objects that make up an Access database are available from the *Navigation Pane*. The Navigation Pane is an Access interface element that organizes and lists the database objects in an Access database. You will learn about the object types and their benefits in the remainder of this section. Later you will learn to create and use these objects.

The foundation of every database is a *table*, the object in which data, such as a person's name or a product number, is stored. The other objects in a database are based on one or more underlying tables. To understand how an Access database works and how to use Access effectively, you should learn the structure of a table. Tables organize data into columns and rows. Columns display a *field*, the smallest data element of a table. For example, in the Northwind database, a table containing information about customers would include a Customer ID field. Another field would contain the Company Name. Fields may be required or optional—a contact name may be required, for example, but a contact title may be optional.

Each row in a table contains a *record*, a complete set of all the fields (data elements) about one person, place, event, or concept. A customer record, for example, would contain all of the fields about a single customer, including the Customer ID, the Company Name, Contact Name, Contact Title, Address, City, etc. Figure 10.2 shows the Northwind database with the Customers table selected in the Navigation Pane. The Customers table is open and shows the records of Northwind customers in the table rows. Each record contains multiple fields, with the field name displaying at the top of each column.

FIGURE 10.2 Customers Table

A *form* is an object that gives a user a way of entering and modifying data in databases. Forms enable you to enter, modify, or delete table data. They enable you to manipulate data in the same manner that you would in a table. The difference is that you can create a form that will limit the user to viewing only one record at a time. This helps the user to focus on the data being entered or modified and also provides for more reliable data entry. As an Access user, you will add, delete, and edit records in Form view. As the Access designer, you will create and edit the form structure.

A *query* is a question that you ask about the data in your database. For example, how many of our customers live in Boston? The answer is shown in the query results. A query can be used to display only records that meet certain conditions and only the fields that you require. In addition to helping you find and retrieve data that meets the conditions that you specify, you can use a query to update or delete records and to perform predefined or custom calculations with your data.

A *report* contains professional-looking formatted information from underlying tables or queries. Reports enable you to print the information in your database and are an effective way to present database information. You have control over the size and appearance of everything in a report. Access provides different views for designing, modifying, and running reports.

Two other object types, macros and modules, are used less frequently unless you are a power Access user. A *macro* object is a stored series of commands that carry out an action. You can create a macro to automate simple tasks by selecting an action from a list of macro actions. A *module* is similar to a macro, as it is an object that adds functionality to a database, but modules are written using the VBA (Visual Basic for Applications) programming language.

Figure 10.3 displays the different object types in Access with the foundation object—the table—in the center of the illustration. The purpose each object serves is explained underneath the object name. The flow of information between objects is indicated by single arrowhead arrows if the flow is one direction only. Two arrowhead arrows indicate that the flow goes both directions. For example, you can use forms to view, add, delete, or modify data from tables.

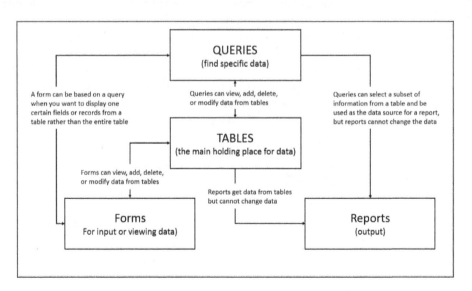

FIGURE 10.3 Object Types and Flow of Information

Examine the Access Interface

While Access includes the standard elements of the Microsoft Office applications interface such as the title bar, the Ribbon, the Home tab, the Backstage view, and scroll bars, it also includes elements unique to Access.

The Access Ribbon has five tabs that will always display, as well as contextual tabs that appear only when particular objects are open. The File tab leads to the Backstage view, which gives you access to a variety of database tools such as Save, Save As, Compact and Repair, Backup Database, and Print. The Home tab, the default Access tab, contains basic editing functions, such as cut and paste, filtering, find and replace, and most formatting actions. This tab also contains the features that enable you to work with record creation and deletion, totals, and spelling.

The Create tab contains all the tools used to create new objects in a database whereas the External Data tab contains all of the operations used to facilitate data import and export. Finally, the Database Tools tab contains the feature that enables users to create relationships between tables and enables use of the more advanced features of Access, such as setting relationships between tables, analyzing a table or query, and migrating data to SharePoint.

On the left side of the screen, you will see the Navigation Pane. The Navigation Pane organizes and lists all of the objects that are needed to make the current database function. You can open any object by double-clicking the object's name in the list. You can also open an object by right-clicking the object name and selecting Open from the shortcut menu. Right-clicking provides other options, such as renaming the object, cutting the object, and copying the object.

Most databases contain multiple tables, queries, forms, and reports. By default, the objects display in groups by object type in the Navigation Pane. If you wish, you can collapse the contents of an object group by clicking the group heading or the double arrows to the right of the group heading. To expand the contents of an object group that has been hidden, click the heading again or click the double arrows to the right of the group heading again. If you wish to change the way objects are grouped in the Navigation Pane, click the list arrow on the Navigation Pane title bar and select your preferred configuration of the available options.

By default, Access uses a Tabbed Documents interface. That means that each object that is open has its own tab beneath the Ribbon and to the right of the Navigation Pane. You can switch between open objects by clicking a tab to make that object active. Figure 10.4 shows the Access interface for the Northwind Traders database, which was introduced in the Case Study at the beginning of the chapter. The Navigation Pane is grouped by object type. The Tables and Reports groups in the Navigation Pane are expanded. The Table Tools contextual tab displays because the Employees table is open. The Employees table shows the records for nine employees. The employee records contain multiple fields about each employee, including the employee's Last Name, First Name, Hire Date, Region, and so on. Occasionally a field does not contain a value for a particular record. For example, one of the employees, Nancy Davolio, has not been assigned a title yet. The value of that field is missing. Access shows a blank cell when data is missing.

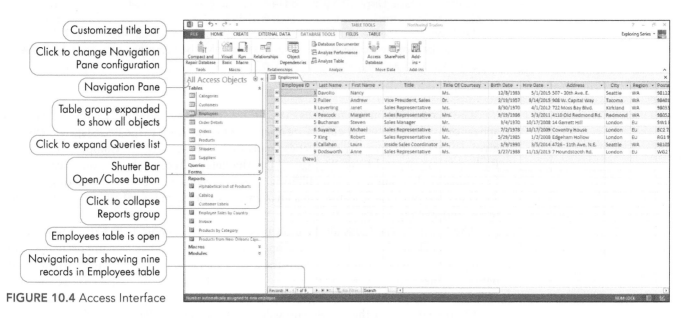

FIGURE 10.4 Access Interface

Explore Access Views

Access provides two different ways to view a table: the Datasheet view and the Design view. To switch between views:

- Click the HOME tab and click View in the Views group to toggle between the current view and the previous view.
- Click the HOME tab, click the View arrow in the Views group, and then select the view you want to use.
- Right-click the object tab and select the view you want to use.
- Right-click the object in the Navigation Pane and select the view you want to use.
- Click one of the view shortcuts in the lower-right corner of the Access window.

The **Datasheet view** is a grid containing fields (columns) and records (rows), similar to an Excel spreadsheet. You can view, add, edit, and delete records in the Datasheet view. Figure 10.5 shows the Datasheet view for the Northwind Customers table. Each row contains a record for a specific customer. Click the **record selector** at the beginning of a row to select the record. Each column represents a field or one attribute about a customer. Click the **field selector**, or column heading, to select a column.

Customers table is open

Pencil in record selector indicates the record is being edited

Navigation bar indicates record 9 of 91 customers in the table is selected

Datasheet view

FIGURE 10.5 Customers Table in Datasheet View

The navigation bar at the bottom of Figure 10.5 shows that the Customers table has 91 records and that record number 9 is the current record. The vertical scroll bar on the right side of the window displays only when the table contains more records than can appear in the window at one time. Similarly, the horizontal scroll bar at the bottom of the window displays only when the table contains more fields than can appear in the window at one time.

The pencil symbol to the left of Record 9 indicates that the data in that record is being edited and that changes have not yet been saved. The pencil symbol disappears when you move to another record. It is important to understand that Access saves data automatically as soon as you move from one record to another. This may seem counterintuitive at first because other Office applications, such as Word and Excel, do not save changes and additions automatically.

Figure 10.6 shows the navigation buttons on the *navigation bar* that you use to move through the records in a table, query, or form. The buttons enable you to go to the first record, the previous record, the next record, or the last record. The button with the yellow asterisk is used to add a new (blank) record. You can also type a number directly into the current record field, and Access will take you to that record. Finally, the navigation bar enables you to find a record based on a single word. Type the word in the search box, and Access will locate the first record that contains the word.

Type in a single search word

Create a new (blank) record

Go to the last record

Go to the next record

Type in the record you want to go to

Go to the previous record

Go to the first record

FIGURE 10.6 Navigation Buttons

You can also use the Find command in the Find group on the Home tab to locate specific records within a table, form, or query. You can search for a single field or the entire record, match all or part of the selected field(s), move forward or back in a table, or specify a case-sensitive search. The Replace command can be used to substitute one value for another. Select Replace All if you want Access to automatically search for and replace every instance of a value without first checking with you. Be careful when using the Replace All option for global replacement, however, because unintended replacements are possible.

The *Design view* gives you a detailed view of the table's structure and is used to create and modify a table's design by specifying the fields it will contain, the fields' data types, and their associated properties. Data types define the type of data that will be stored in a field, such as short text, long text, numeric, currency, etc. For example, if you need to store the hire date of an employee, you would enter the field name Hire Date and select the Date/Time data type. The *field properties* define the characteristics of the fields in more detail. For example, for the field Hire Date, you could set a field property that requires a Short Date format.

Figure 10.7 shows the Design view for the Customers table. In the top portion, each row contains the field names, the data type, and an optional description for each field in the table. In the bottom portion, the Field Properties pane contains the properties (details) for each field. Click on a field, and the properties for that field will be displayed in the bottom portion of the Design view window.

Figure 10.7 also shows the primary key. The *primary key* is the field (or combination of fields) that uniquely identifies each record in a table. The CustomerID field is the primary key in the Customers table; it ensures that each record in the table can be distinguished from every other record. It also helps prevent the occurrence of duplicate records. Primary key fields may be numbers, letters, or a combination of both. In Figure 10.7, the primary key has an *AutoNumber* data type (a number that is generated by Access and is automatically incremented each time a record is added). Another example of a primary key is an automatically generated Employee ID.

FIGURE 10.7 Customers Table in Design View

Open an Access File and Work with Content Security

STEP 1 ≫ When Access is first launched, the Backstage view displays. The left side of the view provides a list of databases you have recently used. Beneath the list of recently used databases is the Open Other Files option. Click Open Other Files to access the Open options. You will see a list of the places your account allows you to open a file from: a recent location, your OneDrive account, your computer, or from any additional places you have added to your Places list. You can also add a new place by clicking the *Add a Place* option. If you select your OneDrive or another place and the desired database is not in the recent list, you will need to click Browse to open the Open dialog box. Then you can locate and select the database and click Open.

If you are currently using Access and wish to open another database, do the following:

1. Click the FILE tab.
2. Click Open in Backstage view to access Open options.
3. Select the place where the database is stored.

4. Click Browse to open the Open dialog box.

5. Locate and select the database and click Open.

If you open a database from a location you have not designated as a trusted location or open a database that does not have a digital signature from a publisher you can trust, Access will display a message bar immediately below the Ribbon. The message bar displays a security warning designed to prevent you from opening a database that may contain harmful code that can be hidden in macros or VBA modules. Click the Enable Content button if you trust the database's source—it becomes a trusted location. After you click Enable Content, Access closes the database and reopens the file to enable the content. Access also adds the database to its list of trusted documents so you will not see the security message again. All content from this publisher and associated with this book can be trusted.

Using an Existing Database

Databases must be carefully managed to keep information accurate. Records need to be edited when changes occur and when new records are added, and records may need to be deleted on occasion. All of these processes are easily accomplished using Access. Managing a database also requires that you understand when data is saved and when you need to use the Save commands.

Understand the Difference Between Working in Storage and Memory

STEP 3>> The way Access performs its save function is different from the other Microsoft Office applications. Word, Excel, and PowerPoint all work primarily from memory. In those applications, your work is not automatically saved to your storage location. You must save your work. This could be catastrophic if you are working with a PowerPoint presentation and you forget to save it. If the power is lost, you may lose your presentation. Access, on the other hand, works primarily from storage. As you enter and update the data in an Access database, the changes are automatically saved to the storage location you specified when you saved the database. If a power failure occurs, you will lose only the changes to the record that you are currently editing.

When you make a change to a record's content in an Access table (for example, changing a customer's cell phone number), Access saves your changes as soon as you move the insertion point to a different record. However, you are required to save after you modify the design of a table, a query, a form, or a report. When you modify an object's design, such as widening a field display on the Customers form, and then close it, Access will prompt you with the message "Do you want to save changes to the design of form 'Customers'?" Click Yes to save your changes.

Also in Access, you can click Undo to reverse the most recent change (the phone number you just modified) to a single record immediately after making changes to that record. However, unlike other Office programs that enable multiple Undo steps, you cannot use Undo to reverse multiple edits in Access.

With an Access database file, several users can work in the same file at the same time. Databases are often located on company servers, making it easy to have multiple users working in the same database at the same time. As long as multiple users do not attempt to change the same record at the same time, Access will let these users access the database simultaneously. So one person can be adding records to the Customers table while another can be creating a query based on the Products table. Two users can even work on the same table as long as they are not working on the same record.

Add, Edit, and Delete Records

STEP 4 » To add a new record, click New in the Records group on the Home tab or click *New (blank) record* on the navigation bar. In a table, you can also click the first column of the blank row beneath the last record. As soon as you begin typing, the asterisk record indicator changes to a pencil icon to show that you are in editing mode. Press Tab to move to the next column so that you can enter the data for the next field. Pressing Tab in the last column in the record saves the record and moves the insertion point to the next record. You can also press Shift+Enter at any time in the record to save the record. The easiest way to save the record is to press the up or down arrow on your keyboard, which moves you to another record. As soon as you move to another record Access automatically saves the changes to the record you created or changed.

To edit a record, tab to the field you want to modify and type the new data. When you start typing, you erase all existing data in the field because the entire field is selected. You can switch to Edit mode by pressing F2. In Edit mode, you will not automatically delete all the data in the field. Instead, you can position your insertion point and make the changes you want.

REFERENCE Keyboard Shortcuts for Entering Data

Keystroke	Result
Up arrow (↑)	Moves insertion point up one row.
Down arrow (↓)	Moves insertion point down one row.
Left arrow (←)	Moves insertion point left one field in the same row.
Right arrow (→)	Moves insertion point right one field in the same row.
Tab or Enter	Moves insertion point right one field in the same row.
Shift+Tab	Moves insertion point left one field in the same row.
Home	Moves insertion point to the first field in the current row.
End	Moves insertion point to the last field in the current row.
Page Up	Moves insertion point up one screen.
Page Down	Moves insertion point down one screen.
Ctrl+Home	Moves insertion point to the first field in the first row.
Ctrl+End	Moves insertion point to the last field in the last row.
Esc	Cancels any changes made in the current field while in Edit mode.
Ctrl+Z	Reverses the last edit.
Ctrl+semicolon (;)	Enters the current date.
Ctrl+Alt+Spacebar	Enters the default value of a field.
Ctrl+single quote	Enters the value from the same field in the previous record.
Ctrl+plus sign (+)	Moves to a new record row.
Ctrl+minus sign (−)	Deletes the current record.

STEP 5 » To delete a record, click the row selector for the record you want to delete and click Delete in the Records group on the Home tab. You can also delete a selected record by pressing Delete on the keyboard, or by right-clicking the row selector and selecting Delete Record from the shortcut menu.

Save As, Compact and Repair, and Back Up Access Files

STEP 6 >> The Backstage view gives you access to the Save As command. When you click the Save As command, you can choose the file type you want to save: the database or the current object. Having the option of saving the entire database or just a component of it distinguishes Access from Word, Excel, and PowerPoint. Those applications have only one thing being saved—the primary document, workbook, or presentation. Save Database As enables you to select whether you want to save the database in the default database format (Access 2007–2013 file format), in one of the earlier Access formats, or as a template. Save Object As enables you to make a copy of the current Access object or publish a copy of the object as a PDF or XPS file. A PDF or XPS file looks the same on most computers because these file types preserve the object's formatting. PDF and XPS files also have a small file size. You can also click Save on the Quick Access Toolbar to save an active object—clicking Save on the Quick Access Toolbar does not save the database.

To help you manage your database so that it operates efficiently and securely, Access provides two utilities to help protect the data within a database: *Compact and Repair*, which reduces the size of the database, and *Back Up Database*, which creates a duplicate copy of the database.

Databases have a tendency to expand with everyday use and may become corrupt, so Access provides the *Compact and Repair Database* utility. Entering data, creating queries, running reports, and adding and deleting objects will all cause a database file to expand. This growth may increase storage requirements and may also impact database performance. When you run the Compact and Repair utility, it creates a new database file behind the scenes and copies all the objects from the original database into the new one. As it copies the objects into the new file, Access removes temporary objects and unclaimed space due to deleted objects, which results in a smaller database file. *Compact and Repair* will also defragment a fragmented database file if needed. When the utility is finished copying the data, it deletes the original file and renames the new one with the same name as the original. This utility can also be used to repair a corrupt database. In most cases, only a small amount of data—the last record modified—will be lost during the repair process. You should compact your database every day. To compact and repair an open database, do the following:

1. Close all open objects in the database.
2. Click the FILE tab.
3. Click *Compact and Repair Database* in the Info options.

As an alternative, you can click the Database Tools tab and click *Compact and Repair Database* in the Tools group.

The Back Up Database utility makes a copy of the entire database to protect your database from loss or damage. Imagine what would happen to a firm that loses the orders placed but not shipped, a charity that loses the list of donor contributions, or a hospital that loses the digital records of its patients. Making backups is especially important when you have multiple users working with the database. When you use the Back Up Database utility, Access provides a file name for the backup that uses the same file name as the database you are backing up, an underscore, and the current date. This makes it easy for you to keep track of databases by the date they were created. To back up a database, do the following:

1. Click the FILE tab and click Save As.
2. Click Save Database As under File Types, if necessary.
3. Click Back Up Database under the Advanced group.
4. Click Save As. Revise the location and file name if you want to change either and click Save.

In Hands-On Exercise 1, you will work with the Northwind Traders database discussed in the Case Study at the beginning of the chapter. You open the database and examine the interface and Access views, organize information, work with records, and save, compact, repair, and back up the database.

Quick
Concepts

1. Name the six objects in an Access database and briefly describe the purpose of each. **p. 483**
2. What is the difference between Datasheet view and Design view in a table? **p. 486**
3. What is meant by the statement "Access works from storage"? **p. 489**
4. What is the purpose of the *Compact and Repair* utility? **p. 491**

Hands-On Exercises

1 Databases Are Everywhere!

Northwind purchases food items from suppliers around the world and sells them to restaurants and specialty food shops. Northwind depends on the data stored in its Access database to process orders and make daily decisions. In your new position with Northwind Traders, you need to spend time getting familiar with the Access database. You will open Northwind's database, examine the Access interface, review the existing objects in the database, and explore Access views. You will add, edit, and delete records using both tables and forms. Finally, you will compact and repair, and back up the database.

Skills covered: Open an Access File and Work with Content Security • Examine the Access Interface, Explore Access Views, Organize Information in a Database, and Recognize Access Objects and Edit a Record and Understand the Difference Between Working in Storage and Memory • Add a Record • Delete a Record • Save As, Compact and Repair, and Back Up the Database

---

STEP 1 ≫ OPEN AN ACCESS FILE AND WORK WITH CONTENT SECURITY

This exercise introduces you to the Northwind Traders database. You will use this database to learn the fundamentals of working with database files. Refer to Figure 10.8 as you complete Step 1.

Click to enable content

Security Warning message

Message Bar

FIGURE 10.8 Message Bar Displaying Security Warning

a. Open Access, click **Open Other Files**, click **Computer**, and then click **Browse**. Navigate to the folder location designated by your instructor. Click *a01h1Traders* and click **Open**.

b. Click the **FILE tab**, click **Save As**, click **Save Database As**, and then verify *Access Database* is selected under *Database File Types*. Click **Save As** and save the file as **a01h1Traders_LastFirst**.

   When you save files, use your last and first names. For example, as the Access author, I would save my database as *a01h1traders_KrebsCynthia*. The Security Warning message bar appears below the Ribbon, indicating that some database content is disabled.

c. Click **Enable Content** on the Security Warning message bar.

   When you open an Access file from the student files associated with this book, you will need to enable the content. You may be confident of the trustworthiness of the files for this book. Keep the database open for the rest of the exercise.

STEP 2 ≫ EXAMINE THE ACCESS INTERFACE, EXPLORE ACCESS VIEWS, ORGANIZE INFORMATION IN A DATABASE, AND RECOGNIZE ACCESS OBJECTS

Now that you have opened Northwind Traders, you examine the Navigation Pane, objects, and views to become familiar with these fundamental Access features. Refer to Figure 10.9 as you complete Step 2.

Step e: Tabs showing open table objects

Step a: Expanded Tables group

Step f: Shutter Bar Open/Close button

Step h: Collapsed Forms group

Step g: Expanded Reports group

FIGURE 10.9 Access Navigation Pane and Open Objects

a. Scroll through the Navigation Pane and note the Access objects listed under each expanded group.

The Tables group and the Forms group are expanded, displaying all of the tables and forms objects. The Queries, Reports, Macros, and Modules groups are collapsed so that the objects in those groups are not displayed.

b. Right-click the **Customers table** in the Navigation Pane and select **Open**.

The Customers table opens. The Customers tab displays below the Ribbon indicating the table object is open. The data contained in the table displays. Each customer's record displays on a table row. The columns of the table display the fields that comprise the records. You are viewing the table in Datasheet view.

c. Click **View** in the Views group on the HOME tab.

The view of the Customers table switches to Design view. The top portion of the view displays each field that comprises a customer record, the field's data type, and an optional description of what the field should contain. The bottom portion of the view displays the field properties (attributes) for the selected field.

d. Click **View** in the Views group on the HOME tab again.

Because View is a toggle button, your view returns to the Datasheet view, which resembles an Excel worksheet.

e. Double-click **Employees** in the Navigation Pane Tables group and double-click **Products** in the same location.

The tabs for three table objects display below the Ribbon: Customers, Employees, and Products.

f. Click the **Shutter Bar Open/Close button** on the title bar of the Navigation Pane to contract the Navigation Pane. Click the button again to expand the Navigation Pane.

The Shutter Bar Open/Close button toggles to allow you to view more in the open object window, or to enable you to view your database objects.

g. Scroll down in the Navigation Pane and click **Reports**.

The Reports group expands, and all report objects display.

h. Click the arrows to the right of Forms in the Navigation Pane.

The Forms group collapses and individual form objects no longer display.

STEP 3 >> EDIT A RECORD AND UNDERSTAND THE DIFFERENCE BETWEEN WORKING IN STORAGE AND MEMORY

You need to learn to edit the data in the Northwind database, because data can change. For example, employees will change their address and phone numbers when they move, and customers will change their order data from time to time. Refer to Figure 10.10 as you complete Step 3.

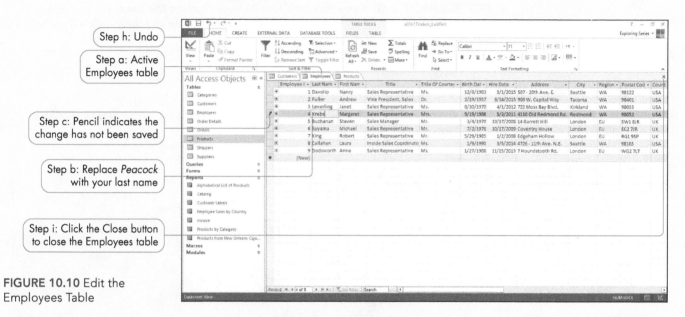

FIGURE 10.10 Edit the Employees Table

a. Click the **Employees tab** to activate the Employees table.

b. Click the **Last Name field** in the fourth row. Double-click **Peacock**; the entire name highlights. Type your last name to replace *Peacock*.

Your last name replaces Peacock. For example, as the Access author, my last name, Krebs, replaces Peacock.

c. Press **Tab** to move to the next field in the fourth row. Replace *Margaret* with your first name and press **Tab**.

Your first name replaces Margaret. For example, as the Access author, my first name, Cynthia, replaces Margaret. You have made changes to two fields in the same record. The pencil symbol in the row selector box indicates that the record has not yet been saved.

d. Click **Undo** on the Quick Access Toolbar.

Your first and last names revert back to *Margaret Peacock* because you have not yet left the record.

e. Type your first and last names again to replace *Margaret Peacock*. Press **Tab**.

You should now be in the title field and your title, *Sales Representative*, is selected. The record has not been saved, as indicated by the pencil symbol in the row selector box.

f. Click anywhere in the third row where Janet Leverling's data is stored.

The pencil symbol disappears, indicating your changes have been saved.

g. Click the **Address field** in the first record, Nancy Davolio's record. Select the entire address and then type **4004 East Morningside Dr**. Click anywhere on the second record, Andrew Fuller's record.

h. Click **Undo**.

Nancy Davolio's address reverts back to 507- 20th Ave. E. However, the Undo command is now faded. You can no longer undo the change that you made replacing Margaret Peacock's name with your own.

i. Click the **Close (X) button** at the top of the table to close the Employees table.

The Employees table closes. You are not prompted to save your changes; they have already been saved for you because Access works in storage, not memory. If you reopen the Employees table, you will see your name in place of Margaret Peacock's name.

> **TROUBLESHOOTING:** If you click the Close (X) button on the title bar at the top right of the window and accidentally close the database, locate the file and double-click it to reopen the file.

STEP 4 ≫ ADD A RECORD

You need to add new products to the Northwind database because the company is adding a new line of products. Refer to Figure 10.11 as you complete Step 4.

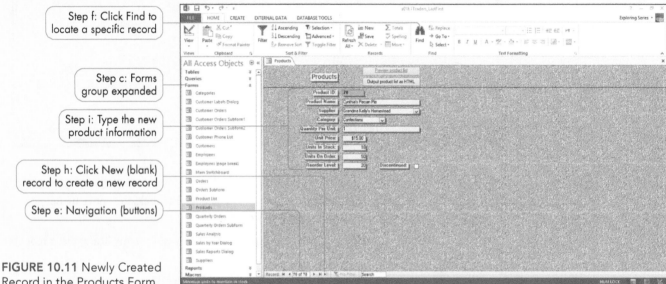

FIGURE 10.11 Newly Created Record in the Products Form

a. Right-click the **Customers tab** and click **Close All**.

b. Click the **Tables group** in the Navigation Pane to collapse it and collapse the **Reports group**.

c. Click the **Forms group** in the Navigation Pane to expand the list of available forms.

d. Double-click the **Products form** to open it.

e. Locate the navigation buttons at the bottom of the Access window. Practice moving from one record to the next. Click **Next record** and click **Last record**; click **Previous record** and click **First record**.

f. Click **Find** in the Find group on the HOME tab, type **Grandma** in the **Find What box**, click the **Match arrow**, and then select **Any Part of Field**. Click **Find Next**.

You should see the data for Grandma's Boysenberry Spread. Selecting the Any Part of the Field option will return a match even if it is contained in the middle of a word.

g. Close the Find dialog box.

h. Click **New (blank) record** on the navigation bar.

i. Enter the following information for a new product.

Field Name	Value to Type
Product Name	*Your name*'s Pecan Pie
Supplier	Grandma Kelly's Homestead (click the arrow to select from the list of Suppliers)
Category	Confections (click the arrow to select from the list of Categories)
Quantity Per Unit	1
Unit Price	15.00
Units in Stock	18
Units on Order	50
Reorder Level	20
Discontinued	No (leave the check box unchecked)

As soon as you begin typing in the product name box, Access assigns a Product ID, in this case 78, to the record. The Product ID is used as the primary key in the Products table.

j. Click anywhere on the Pecan Pie record you just entered. Click the **FILE tab**, click **Print**, and then click **Print Preview**.

The first four records display in the Print Preview.

k. Click **Last Page** in the navigation bar and click **Previous Page** to show the new record you entered.

The beginning of the Pecan Pie record is now visible. The record continues on the next page.

l. Click **Close Print Preview** in the Close Preview group.

m. Close the Products form.

STEP 5 ≫ DELETE A RECORD

To help you understand how Access stores data, you verify that the new product is in the Products table. You also attempt to delete a record. Refer to Figure 10.12 as you complete Step 5.

FIGURE 10.12 Deleting a Record with Related Records

a. Click the **Forms group** in the Navigation Pane to collapse it and expand the **Tables group**.

b. Double-click the **Products table** to open it.

c. Click **Last record** in the navigation bar.

The Pecan Pie record you entered in the Products form is listed as the last record in the Products table. The Products form was created from the Products table. Your newly created record, Pecan Pie, is stored in the Products table even though you added it using the form.

d. Navigate to the fifth record in the table, *Chef Anton's Gumbo Mix.*

e. Use the horizontal scroll bar to scroll right until you see the Discontinued field.

The check mark in the Discontinued check box tells you that this product has been discontinued.

f. Click the **row selector** to the left of the fifth record.

The row highlights with a red-colored border to show that it is selected.

g. Click **Delete** in the Records group and read the error message.

The error message that displays tells you that you cannot delete this record because the table 'Order Details' has related records. (Customers ordered this product in the past.) Even though the product is now discontinued and no stock remains, it cannot be deleted from the Products table because related records exist in the Order Detail table.

h. Click **OK**.

i. Navigate to the last record and click the **row selector** to highlight the entire row.

j. Click **Delete** in the Records group. Read the warning.

The warning box that appears tells you that this action cannot be undone. Although this product can be deleted because it was just entered and no orders were created for it, you do not want to delete the record.

k. Click **No**. You do not want to delete this record. Close the Products table.

> **TROUBLESHOOTING:** If you clicked Yes and deleted the record, return to Step i. Reenter the information for this record. You will need it later in the lesson.

STEP 6 ❯❯ SAVE AS, COMPACT AND REPAIR, AND BACK UP THE DATABASE

You will protect the Northwind Traders database by using the two built-in Access utilities—Compact and Repair and Back Up Database. Refer to Figure 10.13 as you complete Step 6.

Step c: Save As contains the Back Up Database option

Step d: Back Up Database option

FIGURE 10.13 Back Up Database Utility

a. Click the **FILE tab** to open the Backstage view.

b. Click Compact & Repair Database.

Using the *Compact and Repair* utility helps improve the performance of your database.

c. Click the **FILE tab**, click **Save As**, and then click **Save Database As** under *File Types*, if necessary.

d. Double-click **Back Up Database** under the Advanced group to open the **Save As** dialog box.

The backup utility assigns the default name by adding a date to your file name.

e. Verify the *Save in* folder displays the location where you want your file saved and click **Save**.

You just created a backup of the database after completing Hands-On Exercise 1. The original database *a01h1traders_LastFirst* remains onscreen.

f. Keep the database open if you plan to continue with Hands-On Exercise 2. If not, close the database and exit Access.

Sorts and Filters

Access provides you with many tools that you can use to change the order of information and to identify and extract only the data needed at the moment. For example, you might need to display information by customer name in alphabetical order. Or you might need to know which suppliers are located in New Orleans or which customers have outstanding orders that were placed in the last seven days. You might use that information to identify possible disruptions to product deliveries or customers who may need a telephone call to let them know the status of their orders.

In this section, you will learn how to sort information and to isolate records in a table based on certain criteria.

Sorting Table Data on One or Multiple Fields

You can change the order of information by sorting one or more fields. A *sort* lists records in a specific sequence, such as alphabetically by last name or by ascending EmployeeID. To sort a table on one criteria, do the following:

STEP 4 >>

1. Click in the field that you want to use to sort the records.
2. Click Ascending or Descending in the Sort & Filter group on the HOME tab.

Ascending sorts a list of text data in alphabetical order or a numeric list in lowest to highest order. *Descending* sorts a list of text data in reverse alphabetical order or a numeric list in highest to lowest order. Figure 10.14 shows the Customers table for a bank sorted in ascending order by state.

FIGURE 10.14 Customers Table Sorted by State

Access can sort records by more than one field. Access sorts multiple criteria by first sorting the column on the left. The column immediately to the right of that column is sorted next. Because of this, you must arrange your columns in this order. To move a column, select the column and hold down the left mouse button. A heavy black bar appears to the left of the column. Drag the column to the position where you want it for the multiple sort.

Creating, Modifying, and Removing Filters

In Hands-On Exercise 1, you added Pecan Pie to the Products table with a category of Confections, but you also saw many other products. Suppose you wanted to see a list of just the products in the Confections category. To obtain this list, you would open the Products table in Datasheet view and create a filter. A *filter* displays a subset of records based on specified criteria. A *criterion* (or criteria, plural) is a number, a text phrase, or an expression used to select records from a table. Therefore, to view a list of all Confections, you would need to filter the Category field of the Products table using Confections as the criterion.

You can use filters to analyze data quickly. Applying a filter does not delete any records; filters only *hide* records that do not match the criteria. Two types of filters are discussed in this section: *Filter by Selection* and *Filter by Form*.

Use, Modify, and Remove a Filter

Filter by Selection displays only the records that match a criterion you select. To use *Filter by Selection*, do the following:

STEP 1 ≫

1. Click in any field that contains the criterion on which you want to filter.
2. Click Selection in the Sort & Filter group on the HOME tab.
3. Select *Equals "criterion"* from the list of options.

Figure 10.15 displays a Customers table with 10 records. The records in the table are displayed in sequence according to the CustomerID, which is also the primary key (the field or combination of fields that uniquely identifies a record). The navigation bar at the bottom indicates that the active record is the first row in the table. *Owner* in the Job Title field is selected.

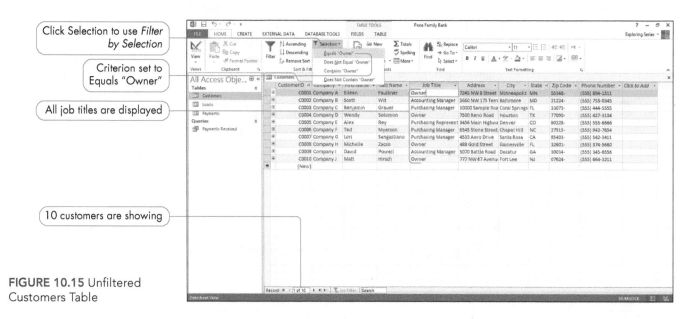

FIGURE 10.15 Unfiltered Customers Table

Figure 10.16 displays a filtered view of the Customers table, showing records with the job title *Owner*. The navigation bar shows that this is a filtered list containing 4 records matching the criteria. (The Customers table still contains the original 10 records, but only 4 records are visible with the filter applied.)

Click Toggle Filter to remove filter

Only records with the job title *Owner* are displayed

Filter icons

Only four customers are showing

FIGURE 10.16 Filtered Customers Table Shows Owners

Filter by Form is a more versatile method of selecting data because it enables you to display table records based on multiple criteria. When you use *Filter by Form*, all of the records are hidden and Access creates a blank form in a design grid. You see only field names with an arrow in the first field. Click on other fields and an arrow displays. Click an arrow and a list opens for you to use to specify your criterion. You can specify as many criteria as you need. When you apply the filter, Access displays the records that meet your criteria.

STEP 3 »

An advantage of using this filter method is that you can specify AND and OR logical operators. If you use the AND operator, a record is included in the results if all the criteria are true. If you use the OR operator, a record is included if at least one criterion is true. Another advantage of *Filter by Form* is that you can use a comparison operator. A *comparison operator* is used to evaluate the relationship between two quantities. For example, a comparison operator can determine if quantities are equal or not equal. If they are not equal, a comparison operator determines which one is greater than the other. Comparison operator symbols include: equal (=), not equal (<>), greater than (>), less than (<), greater than or equal to (>=), and less than or equal to (<=). To use *Filter by Form*, do the following:

1. Click Advanced in the Sort & Filter group on the HOME tab.
2. Click *Filter by Form*.
3. Click in the field you want to use as a criterion. Click the arrow to select the criterion from existing data.
4. Add additional criterion and comparison operators as needed.
5. Click Toggle Filter in the Sort & Filter group on the HOME tab to apply the filter.

In Figure 10.17, the Northwind Traders Products table is open. *Filter by Form* is set to select products with an inventory (Units in Stock) level greater than 30 (>30).

Click Advanced to access *Filter by Form*

Filter By Form

Filter set to display products with more than 30 units in stock

Add criteria by clicking the Or tab

FIGURE 10.17 Filter by Form Design Grid

The sort and filter operations can be done in any order; that is, you can sort a table first and apply a filter. Conversely, you can filter a table first to show only selected records and sort the filtered table to display the records in a certain order. It does not matter which operation is performed first.

STEP 2 ▶▶ You can also filter the table further by applying a second, third, or more criteria. For example, in the Products table shown in Figure 10.17, you can apply *Filter by Form* by clicking in the Supplier cell, selecting Exotic Liquids from the list, and then applying the filter. Then you could click Beverages and apply *Filter by Selection* to display all the beverages supplied by Exotic Liquids. You can also click Toggle Filter at any time to remove all filters and display all the records in the table. Filters are a temporary method for examining table data. If you close the filtered table and reopen it, the filter will be removed and all of the records will be restored.

> **TIP** **Use Undo After Applying a Filter by Selection**
>
> You can apply one *Filter by Selection* to a table, and then a second, and then a third to display certain records based on three criteria. If you click Toggle Filter, all three filters will be removed. What if you only want the last filter removed? Click Undo to remove only the last filter. Click Undo again and remove the second-to-last filter. This feature will help you apply and remove multiple filters, one at a time.

Quick Concepts

1. What are the benefits of sorting the records in a table? *p. 500*

2. What is the purpose of creating a filter? *p. 501*

3. What is the difference between *Filter by Selection* and *Filter by Form*? *pp. 501–502*

4. What is a comparison operator and how is it used in a filter? *p. 502*

Hands-On Exercises

Watch the Video
for this Hands-
On Exercise!

MyITLab®
HOE2 Training

2 Sorts and Filters

The sales manager at Northwind Traders needs quick answers to her questions about customer orders. You use the Access database to filter tables to answer these questions, then sort the records based on the manager's needs.

Skills covered: Use Filter by Selection with an Equal Condition • Use Filter by Selection with a Contains Condition • Use Filter by Form with a Comparison Operator • Sort a Table

---

STEP 1 ≫ USE FILTER BY SELECTION WITH AN EQUAL CONDITION

The sales manager asks for a list of customers who live in London. You use *Filter by Selection* with an equal condition to locate these customers. Refer to Figure 10.18 as you complete Step 1.

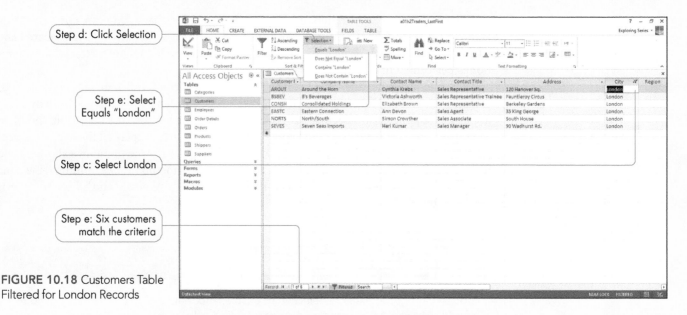

FIGURE 10.18 Customers Table Filtered for London Records

a. Open the *a01h1traders_LastFirst* database if you closed it after the last Hands-On Exercise and save it as **a01h2Traders_LastFirst**, changing *h1* to *h2*.

> **TROUBLESHOOTING:** If you make any major mistakes in this exercise, you can close the file, open *a01h1Traders_LastFirst* again, and then start this exercise over.

b. Double-click the **Customers table** in the Navigation Pane under *Tables*, navigate to record 4, and then replace *Thomas Hardy* with your name in the Contact Name field.

c. Scroll right until the City field is visible. The fourth record has a value of *London* in the City field. Click the field to select it.

d. Click **Selection** in the Sort & Filter group on the HOME tab.

e. Select **Equals "London"** from the menu. Note that six customers were located.

The navigation bar display shows that six records that meet the *London* criterion are available. The other records in the Customers table are hidden. The Filtered icon also displays on the navigation bar, indicating that the Customers table has been filtered.

f. Click **Toggle Filter** in the Sort & Filter group to remove the filter.

g. Click **Toggle Filter** again to reset the filter. Leave the Customers table open for the next step.

STEP 2 ≫ USE FILTER BY SELECTION WITH A CONTAINS CONDITION

The sales manager asks you to narrow the list of London customers so that it displays only Sales Representatives. To accomplish this task, you add a second layer of filtering using the *Filter by Selection* feature. Refer to Figure 10.19 as you complete Step 2.

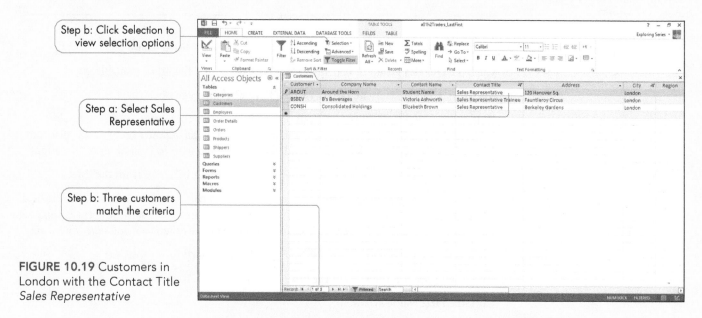

FIGURE 10.19 Customers in London with the Contact Title *Sales Representative*

a. Click in any field in the Contact Title column that contains the value *Sales Representative*.

b. Click **Selection** in the Sort & Filter group and click **Contains "Sales Representative"**. Locate your name in the filtered table. Compare your results to those shown in Figure 10.19.

Three records match the criteria you set. You have applied a second layer of filtering to the customers in London. The second layer further restricts the display to only those customers who have the words *Sales Representative* contained in their titles.

> **TROUBLESHOOTING:** If you do not see the record for Victoria Ashworth, you selected *Equals "Sales Representative"* instead of *Contains "Sales Representative"*. Repeat steps a and b, making sure you select *Contains "Sales Representative"*.

c. Close the Customers table. Click **Yes** if a dialog box asks if you want to save the design changes to the Customers table.

STEP 3 ≫ USE FILTER BY FORM WITH A COMPARISON OPERATOR

You are asked to provide a list of records that do not match just one set of criteria. You are asked to provide a list of all extended prices less than $50 for a specific sales representative. Use *Filter by Form* to provide the information when two or more criteria are needed. You also preview the results in Print Preview to see how the list would print. Refer to Figure 10.20 as you complete Step 3.

Step i: Enter <50 for the
ExtendedPrice criteria

Step d: Click Advanced to
select Filter by Form

Steps f–h: Select your
first and last names

FIGURE 10.20 Filter by Form
Selection Criteria

a. Click the **Tables group** in the Navigation Pane to collapse the listed tables.

b. Click the **Queries group** in the Navigation Pane to expand the list of available queries.

c. Locate and double-click the **Order Details Extended query** to open it.

This query contains information about orders. It has fields containing information about the sales person, the Order ID, the product name, the unit price, quantity ordered, the discount given, and an extended price. The extended price is a field used to total order information.

d. Click **Advanced** in the Sort & Filter group and select **Filter by Form** from the list.

All of the records are now hidden, and you see only field names and an arrow in the first field. Although you are applying *Filter by Form* to a query, you can use the same process as applying *Filter by Form* to a table. You are able to enter more than one criterion using *Filter by Form*.

e. Click in the first row under the First Name field, if necessary.

An arrow appears at the right of the box.

f. Click the **First Name arrow**.

A list of all available first names appears. Your name should be on the list. Figure 10.20 shows *Cynthia Krebs*, which replaced Margaret Peacock in Hands-On Exercise 1.

> **TROUBLESHOOTING:** If you do not see your name and you do see Margaret on the list, you probably skipped steps in Hands-On Exercise 1. Close the query without saving changes, return to the first Hands-On Exercise, and then rework it, making sure not to omit any steps. Then you can return to this location and work the remainder of this Hands-On Exercise.

g. Select your first name from the list.

h. Click in the first row under the Last Name field to reveal the arrow. Locate and select your last name by clicking it.

i. Scroll right until you see the Extended Price field. Click in the first row under the Extended Price field and type **<50**.

This will select all of the items that you ordered where the total was under $50. You ignore the arrow and type the expression needed.

j. Click **Toggle Filter** in the Sort & Filter group.

You have specified which records to include and have executed the filtering by clicking Toggle Filter. You should have 31 records that match the criteria you specified.

k. Click the **FILE tab**, click **Print**, and then click **Print Preview**.

You instructed Access to preview the filtered query results. The preview displays the query title as a heading. The current filter is applied, as well as page numbers.

l. Click **Close Print Preview** in the Close Preview group.

m. Close the Order Details Extended query. Click **Yes** if a dialog box asks if you want to save your changes.

TIP Deleting Filter by Form Criterion

While working with *Filter by Selection* or *Filter by Form*, you may inadvertently save a filter. To view a saved filter, open the table or query that you suspect may have a saved filter. Click Advanced in the Sort & Filter group and click *Filter by Form*. If criteria appear in the form, then a filter has been saved. To delete a saved filter, toggle the filter, click Advanced, and then click Close All Filters. Close and save the table or query.

STEP 4 » SORT A TABLE

The Sales Manager is pleased with your work; however, she would like some of the information to appear in a different order. You will now sort the records in the Customers table using the manager's new criteria. Refer to Figure 10.21 as you complete Step 4.

FIGURE 10.21 Customers Table Sorted by Country, Then City

a. Click the **Queries group** in the Navigation Pane to collapse the listed queries.

b. Click the **Tables group** in the Navigation Pane to expand the list of available tables and double-click the **Customers table** to open it.

   This table contains information about customers. The table is sorted in alphabetical order by Company Name.

c. Click the **Shutter Bar Open/Close button** in the Navigation Pane to close the Navigation Pane.

   It will be easier to locate fields in the Customer table if the Navigation Pane is closed.

d. Click any field in the Customer ID column, the first field in the table. Click **Descending** in the Sort & Filter group on the HOME tab.

   Sorting in descending order on a character field produces a reverse alphabetical order.

e. Scroll right until you can see both the Country and City fields.

f. Click the **Country column heading**.

   The entire column is selected.

g. Click the **Country column heading** again and hold down the **left mouse button**.

   A thick dark blue line displays on the left edge of the Country field.

h. Check to make sure that you see the thick blue line. Drag the **Country field** to the left until the thick black line moves between the City and Region fields. Release the mouse and the Country field position moves to the right of the City field.

You moved the Country field next to the City field so that you can easily sort the table based on both fields. In order to sort by two or more fields, they need to be placed adjacent to each other.

i. Click any city name in the City field and click **Ascending** in the Sort & Filter group.

The City field displays the cities in alphabetical order.

j. Click any country name in the Country field and click **Ascending**.

The countries are sorted in alphabetical order. The cities within each country also are sorted alphabetically. For example, the customer in Graz, Austria, is listed before the customer in Salzburg, Austria.

k. Close the Customers table. Click **Yes** to save the changes to the design of the table.

l. Click the **Shutter Bar Open/Close button** in the Navigation Pane to open the Navigation Pane.

m. Click the **FILE tab** to open the Backstage view and click **Compact & Repair Database**.

n. Click the **FILE tab**, click **Save As**, and then click **Save Database As** in File Types, if necessary.

o. Double-click **Back Up Database** under the Advanced group to open the Save As dialog box.

p. Verify the *Save in* folder displays the location where you want your file saved and click **Save**.

q. Close the database and submit based on your instructor's directions. Leave Access open if you plan to continue with Hands-On Exercise 3. If not, exit Access.

Access Versus Excel, and Relational Databases

Both Access and Excel contain powerful tools that enable you to extract the information you need and arrange it in a way that makes it easy to analyze. An important part of becoming a proficient Office user is learning which of these applications to use to accomplish a task.

In this section, you will learn how to decide whether to use Access or Excel by examining the distinct advantages of each application. Ideally, the type of data and the type of functionality you require should determine which program will work best.

Knowing When to Use Access or Excel to Manage Data

You are probably familiar with working in an Excel spreadsheet. You type the column headings, enter the data, perhaps add a formula or two, and then add totals to the bottom. Once the data has been entered, you can apply a filter, sort the data, or start all over—similar to what you learned to do in Access with filters. It is true that you can accomplish many of the same tasks using either Excel or Access. Although the two programs have much in common, they each have distinct advantages. How do you choose whether to use Access or Excel? The choice you make may ultimately depend on how well you know Access. Users who know Excel only are more likely to use a spreadsheet even if a database would be better. When database features are used in Excel, they are generally used on data that is in one table. When the data is better suited to be on two or more tables, then using Access is preferable. Learning how to use Access will be beneficial to you because it will enable you to work more efficiently with large groups of data.

Select the Software to Use

A contact list (for example, name, address, phone number) created in Excel may serve your needs just fine in the beginning. Each time you enter a new contact, you can add another row to the bottom of your worksheet. You can sort the list by last name for easier look-up of names. In Excel, you can easily move an entire column, insert a new column, or copy and paste data from one cell to another. This is the "ease of use" characteristic of Excel.

If you need to expand the information in Excel to keep track of each time you contacted someone on your contact list, you may need an additional worksheet. This additional sheet would only list the contacts whom you have contacted and some information about the nature of the contact. Which contact was it? When was the contact made? Was it a phone contact or a face-to-face meeting? As you track these entries, your worksheet will contain a reference to the first worksheet using the contact name.

If a contact is deleted on the first worksheet, that contact's information will still remain on the second worksheet, unless someone remembers to remove it. Similarly, information could be added about a contact on the second worksheet without the contact being officially entered into the first worksheet. As the quantity and complexity of the data increase, the need to organize your data logically also increases.

Access provides built-in tools to help organize data better than Excel. One tool that helps Access organize data is the ability to create relationships between tables. A *relationship* is a connection between two tables using a field that is common to the two tables. The benefit of a relationship is the ability to efficiently combine data from related tables for the purpose of creating queries, forms, and reports. Relationships are the reason Access is referred to as a relational database.

Use Access

STEP 1 > Use Access to manage data when you:

- Require multiple related tables to store your data.
- Have a large amount of data.
- Need to connect to and retrieve data from external databases, such as Microsoft SQL Server.
- Need to group, sort, and total data based on various parameters.
- Have an application that requires multiple users to connect to one data source at the same time.

Use Excel

Use Excel to manage data when you:

- Need only one worksheet to handle all of your data.
- Have mostly numeric data—for example, you need to maintain an expense statement.
- Require subtotals and totals in your worksheet.
- Want to primarily run a series of "what if" scenarios on your data.
- Need to create complex charts and/or graphs.

Understanding Relational Power

In the previous section, we compared Excel worksheets to Access relational databases. Access has the ability to create relationships between two tables, whereas Excel does not. Access is known as a *relational database management system* (RDBMS); using an RDBMS, you can manage groups of data (tables) and set rules (relationships) between tables. When relational databases are designed properly, users can easily combine data from multiple tables to create queries, forms, and reports.

Good database design begins with grouping data into the correct tables. This practice, known as *normalization*, will take time to learn, but over time you will begin to understand the fundamentals. The design of a relational database management system is illustrated in Figure 10.22, which shows the table design of the Northwind Traders database. The tables have been created, the field names have been added, and the data types have been set. The diagram shows the relationships that were created between tables using *join lines*. Join lines enable you to create a relationship between two tables using a common field. Figure 10.22 also shows the join lines between related tables as a series of lines connecting common fields. For example, the Suppliers table is joined to the Products table using the common field SupplierID. If you examine some of the connections, you will see that the EmployeeID is linked to the Orders table by a join line. This means that you can produce a report displaying all orders for a customer and the employee who entered the order. The Orders table is joined to the Order Details table where the OrderID is the common field. The Products table is joined to the Order Details table where the ProductID is the common field. These table connections enable you to query the database for information stored in multiple tables. This feature gives the manager the ability to ask questions like "How many different beverages were shipped last week?" or "What was the total revenue generated from seafood orders last year?"

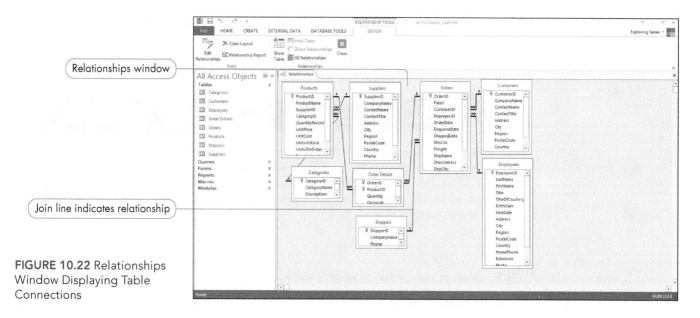

Relationships window

Join line indicates relationship

FIGURE 10.22 Relationships Window Displaying Table Connections

Use the Relationships Window

Relationships are set in the Relationships window by the database developer after the tables have been created but before any sample data is entered. The most common method of connecting two tables is to connect the primary key from one table to the foreign key of another. A *foreign key* is a field in one table that is also the primary key of another table. In the previous figure, Figure 10.22, the SupplierID (primary key) in the Suppliers table is joined to the SupplierID (foreign key) in the Products table. Remember, a primary key is a field that uniquely identifies each record in a table.

To create a relationship between two tables, follow these guidelines:

1. Click Relationships in the Relationships group on the DATABASE TOOLS tab.
2. Add the two tables that you want to join together to the Relationships window.
3. Drag the common field (e.g., SupplierID) from the primary table (e.g., Suppliers) onto the common field (e.g., SupplierID) of the related table (e.g., Products). The data types of the common fields must be the same.
4. Check the Enforce Referential Integrity check box.
5. Close the Relationships window.

 STEP 2»

> ### TIP View Join Lines
>
> Databases with many tables with relationships may make it difficult to see the join lines between tables. Tables may be repositioned to make it easier to see the join lines. To reposition a table, drag the table by its table name to the new position.

Enforce Referential Integrity

STEP 3» Enforce referential integrity is one of three options you can select when setting a table relationship. When *enforce referential integrity* is checked, Access ensures that data cannot be entered into a related table unless it first exists in the primary table. For example, in Figure 10.22 you cannot enter a product into the Products table using a SupplierID that does not exist in the Suppliers table. This rule ensures the integrity of the data in the database and improves overall data accuracy. Referential integrity also prohibits users from deleting a record in one table if it has records in related tables.

In Hands-on Exercise 3, you examine the strengths of Access and Excel in more detail so that you can better determine when to use which application to complete a given task. You will also explore relationships between tables and learn about the power of relational data.

TIP Create Sample Data

When learning database skills, starting with a smaller set of sample data prior to entering all company records can be helpful. A small amount of data gives you the ability to check the tables and quickly see if your results are correct. Even though the data amounts are small, as you test the database tables and relationships, the results will prove useful as you work with larger data sets.

Quick
Concepts

1. How can you determine when to use Access or Excel to manage data? *p. 509*
2. Explain the term RDBMS. *p. 510*
3. What is the purpose of a join line? *p. 510*

Hands-On Exercises

 Watch the Video for this Hands-On Exercise!

 MyITLab® HOE3 Training

3 Access Versus Excel, and Relational Databases

In this exercise, you review the relationships set in the Northwind Traders database. This will help you learn more about the overall design of the database. Examining the relationships will also help you understand why Access rather than Excel is used by Northwind Traders for data management.

Skills covered: Know When to Use Access or Excel to Manage Data • Use the Relationships Window, Use Filter by Form with a Comparison Operator, and Reapply a Saved Filter • Enforce Referential Integrity

STEP 1 ≫ KNOW WHEN TO USE ACCESS OR EXCEL TO MANAGE DATA

In this exercise, you examine the connections between the tables in the Northwind Traders database and review the reasons that Access was selected as the application for this data. Refer to Figure 10.23 as you complete Step 1.

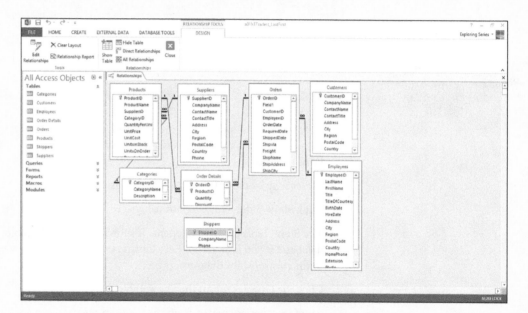

FIGURE 10.23 Relationships Window for the Northwind Database

a. Open the *a01h2Traders_LastFirst* database if you closed it after the last Hands-On Exercise and save it as **a01h3Traders_LastFirst**, changing *h2* to *h3*.

b. Click the **DATABASE TOOLS tab** and click **Relationships** in the Relationships group.

c. Examine the join lines showing the relationships that connect the various tables. For example, the Orders table is connected to the Order Details table.

Examining the number of tables in a database and their relationships is a good way to determine whether you need to use Excel or Access for your data. Because this data needs more than one table, involves a large amount of connected data, needs to group, sort, and total data based on various parameters, and needs to allow multiple users to connect to one data source at the same time, it is better to manipulate this data using Access rather than using Excel.

Use the Relationships window to move tables to make the join lines easier to view. To reinforce your filter skills, use *Filter by Form* to solve more complex questions about the Northwind data. After you retrieve the records, save the *Filter by Form* specifications so that you can reapply the filter later. Refer to Figure 10.24 as you complete Step 2.

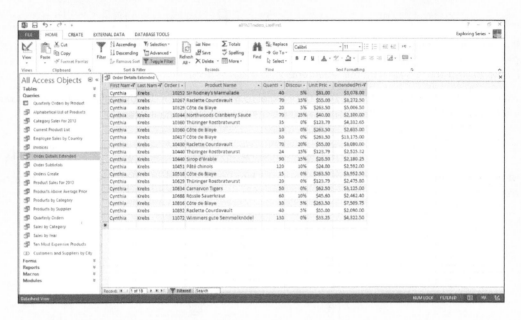

FIGURE 10.24 Query Results with Your Name and Extended Price >$2,000

a. Reposition the Shippers table beneath the Orders table by dragging it to the right by its table name. Reposition the Categories table beneath the Order Details table by dragging it to the right by its table name.

   Tables may be repositioned to make it easier to see the join lines creating the relationships.

b. Click **Show Table** in the Relationships group on the RELATIONSHIPS TOOLS DESIGN tab.

   The Show Table dialog box opens. It shows you the eight tables that are available in the database. If you look in the Relationships window, you will see that all eight tables are open in the relationships diagram.

c. Click the **Queries tab** in the Show Table dialog box.

   All of the queries created from the tables in the database are listed in the Show Table dialog box. You could add all of the queries to the Relationships window. Things might become cluttered, but you could tell at a glance from where the queries get their information.

d. Close the Show Table dialog box.

e. Click the **Shutter Bar Open/Close button** in the Navigation Pane to open the Navigation Pane, if necessary.

f. Click **All Access Objects** on the Navigation Pane and click **Tables and Related Views**.

   You now see each table and all the queries, forms, and reports that are based on each table. If a query is created using more than one table, it appears multiple times in the Navigation Pane.

g. Close the Relationships window. Save the changes to the design. Click **All Tables** on the Navigation Pane and click **Object Type**.

h. Collapse the Tables group in the Navigation Pane, expand the **Queries** group, and then double-click the **Order Details Extended query**.

i. Click **Advanced** in the Sort & Filter group, select **Filter by Form**, click in the first row under the Last Name field, and then select your last name.

j. Scroll right (or press **Tab**) until the Extended Price field is visible. Click in the first row in the Extended Price field and type **>2000**.

The Extended Price field shows the purchased amount for each item ordered. If an item sold for $15 and a customer ordered 10, the Extended Price would display $150.

k. Click **Toggle Filter** in the Sort & Filter group. Examine the filtered results.

Your comparison operator, >2000, identified 18 items ordered where the extended price exceeded $2,000.

l. Close the Order Details Extended query by clicking the **Close (X) button**. Click **Yes** to save changes.

m. Open the Order Details Extended query again.

The filter disengages when you close and reopen the object. However, because you opted to save the changes before closing, the filter has been stored with the query. You may reapply the filter at any time by clicking the Toggle Filter command (until the next filter replaces the current one).

n. Click **Toggle Filter** in the Sort & Filter group. Compare your results to Figure 10.24.

o. Save and close the query.

STEP 3 ≫ ENFORCE REFERENTIAL INTEGRITY

You need an additional relationship created between the Orders table and the Customers table. You create the relationship and enforce referential integrity. Refer to Figure 10.25 as you complete Step 3.

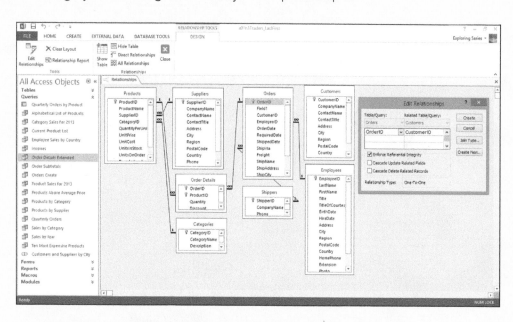

FIGURE 10.25 Relationship Created Between Orders Table and Customers Table

a. Click the **DATABASE TOOLS tab** and click **Relationships** in the Relationships group.

b. Locate the CustomerID field in the Orders table and drag it to the CustomerID field (primary key) in the Customers table.

The Edit Relationships dialog box opens. It shows that the Table/Query is from the Customers table and the related Table/Query comes from the Orders table. The relationship type is displayed at the bottom of the dialog box and indicates that this will be a One-To-Many relationship.

c. Click **Enforce Referential Integrity**.

Access will now ensure that data cannot be entered into the related table (Orders) unless it first exists in the primary table (Customers).

d. Click **Create**.

A join line displays between the Orders and Customers tables.

e. Click the **FILE tab** and click **Compact & Repair Database**. Click **Yes** if asked if you want to save changes to the layout of Relationships.

f. Click the **FILE tab**, click **Save As**, and then click **Save Database As** under *File Types* if necessary. Double-click **Back Up Database** in the Advanced group to open the Save As dialog box.

g. Verify the *Save in* folder displays the location where you want your backup file saved and click **Save**.

A duplicate copy of the database is saved with the default file name that is the original file name followed by the current date.

h. Exit Access.

Access Database Creation

Now that you have examined the fundamentals of an Access database and explored the power of relational databases, it is time to create one! In this section, you explore the benefits of creating a database using each of the methods discussed in the next section.

Creating a Database

When you first start Access, the Backstage view opens and provides you with three methods for creating a new database. These methods are:

- Creating a custom Web app
- Creating a blank desktop database
- Creating a database from a template

Creating a *custom Web app* enables you to create a database that you can build and then use and share with others through the Web. Creating a blank desktop database lets you create a database specific to your needs. Rather than starting from scratch by creating a blank desktop database, you may want to use a template to create a new database. An Access *template* is a predefined database that includes professionally designed tables, forms, reports, and other objects that you can use to jumpstart the creation of your database.

Figure 10.26 shows the options for creating a custom Web app, a blank desktop database, and multiple templates from which you can select the method for which you want to create a database.

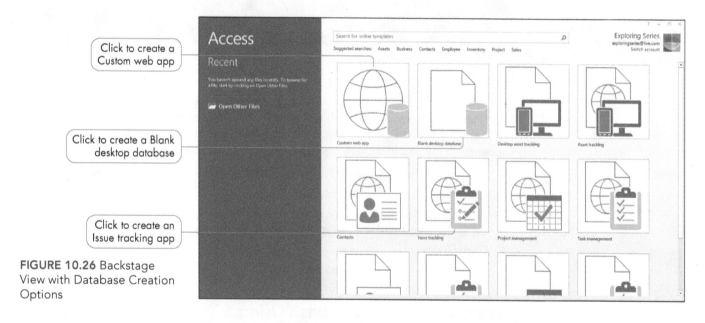

FIGURE 10.26 Backstage View with Database Creation Options

Click to create a Custom web app

Click to create a Blank desktop database

Click to create an Issue tracking app

Create a Web Application Using a Template

Creating a Web app (application) is new in Access 2013. An Access Web app is a new type of database that lets you build a browser-based database application— you can create a database in the cloud that you and others can access and use simultaneously. This requires that you use a host server such as SharePoint (a Web application platform developed by Microsoft) or Office 365 (a cloud service edition of SharePoint).

To create a Web app, click *Custom web app* in the Backstage view, give your app a name, and then choose a location. Once you click Create, a blank database opens. You then create the tables that will serve as the foundation of your database. The easiest way to add a table is to use the Access library of Table Templates. Each of the templates in the library includes tables, fields, and views that you will need to create an app. Some templates also include related tables.

As an alternative to creating a Web app from scratch, you can select a Web app template from the Backstage view. These templates are fully functional Web databases. Click one of the Web app template tiles and an introduction screen appears that previews the datasheet, provides a description of the purpose of the datasheet, lets you know the download size of the database, and even displays how users like you have rated the database. You give the app a name and select the Web location where the app is to be saved. Finally, you create the app. When you have completed the database, click Launch App in the View group on the Home tab. You can then use it and share it on the Web. Figure 10.27 shows the introduction screen for the Asset tracking template. This template requires SharePoint so that you can share content with others.

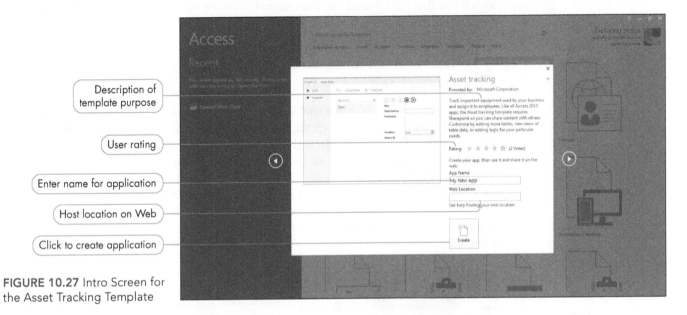

FIGURE 10.27 Intro Screen for the Asset Tracking Template

Create a Blank Desktop Database

To create a blank desktop database specific to your needs, click *Blank desktop database* in the Backstage view. Access opens to a blank table in Datasheet view where you can add data. You can refine the table in Design view. You would then create additional tables and objects as necessary. To create a blank desktop database, do the following:

1. Open Access or click the FILE tab to open the Backstage view and click New.
2. Click the *Blank desktop* database tile.
3. Enter the file name for the file in the text box, click the Browse button to navigate to the folder where you want to store the database file, and then click OK.
4. Click Create.
5. Enter data in the empty table that displays.

Create a Desktop Database Using a Template

Using a template to start a database saves you a great deal of creation time. Working with a template can also help a new Access user become familiar with database design. Templates are available from the Backstage view, where you can select from a variety of templates or search online for more templates.

Access also provides templates for desktop use. To create a desktop database from a template, do the following:

1. Open Access or click the FILE tab to open the Backstage view and click New.
2. Click the database template you want to use.
3. Enter the file name for the file in the text box, click the Browse button to navigate to the folder where you want to store the database file, and then click OK.

4. Click Create to download the template.

5. Open the database and click Enable Content in the Security Warning message bar if you trust the source of the database.

Once the database is open, you may see a Getting Started page that includes links you can use to learn more about the database. A new Access user can gain valuable information by watching any associated videos and clicking provided hyperlinks. When finished reviewing the learning materials, close the Getting Started page to view the database. Figure 10.28 displays the Getting Started page included with the *Desktop task management* template. Two videos are provided to aid you in using and modifying the database. Because this database contains a Contacts table, there is a hyperlink to a wizard that will import contacts from Microsoft Outlook (if you use Microsoft Outlook). Links are available that will connect you with experts, enable you to get free advice from a forum, and get more help from Microsoft .com. The Getting Started page also includes a button you can click to open a survey that provides feedback to Microsoft. Close the Getting Started page to return to the database.

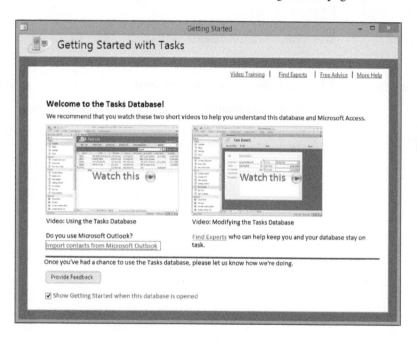

FIGURE 10.28 Getting Started Page for Desktop Task Management Template

STEP 2»

Because you downloaded a template, some objects will have already been created. You can work with these objects just as you did in the first three sections of this chapter. For example, you can enter data directly into any existing table in the database by opening the table, clicking in the first empty field, typing the data, tabbing to the next empty field, and then typing the data for the next field. You can also open any form that is part of the downloaded template and enter the data directly in the forms. Some templates will include queries and reports. Edit any object to meet your requirements.

STEP 3»

Once the database is opened, review the objects listed in the Navigation Pane. Change the Navigation Pane category from Object Type to *Tables and Related Views* to become familiar with the relationships between the tables and other database objects. Note the tables and the objects that are based on them.

After noting the objects in the database, open the Relationships window to see the connections between them. Once you are familiar with the database design, you can enter your data.

Figure 10.29 displays the open Task Management database with the Navigation Pane set to display *Tables and Related Views*. The Tasks table displays with its related queries, forms, and reports. The Relationships window shows the relationship between the Contacts table and the Tasks table.

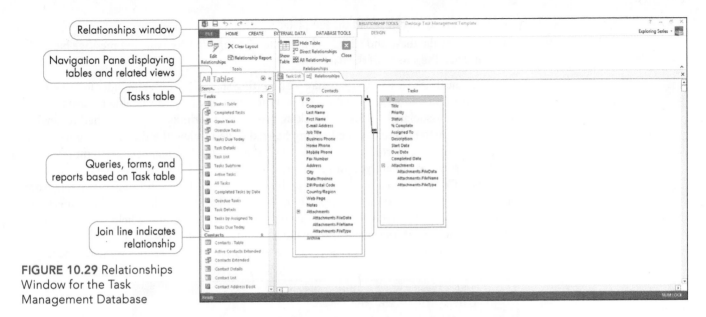

Relationships window

Navigation Pane displaying tables and related views

Tasks table

Queries, forms, and reports based on Task table

Join line indicates relationship

FIGURE 10.29 Relationships Window for the Task Management Database

Quick Concepts

1. Name the three methods for creating a new database. *p. 517*

2. What is a custom Web app, and what is required to build a custom Web app? *p. 517*

3. What are two benefits of using a template to create a database? *p. 518*

Hands-On Exercises

4 Access Database Creation

After working with the Northwind Traders database on the job, you decide to use Access to create a personal contact database. Rather than start from scratch, you use an Access Contact Manager desktop template to jumpstart your database creation. A Web app is not necessary because you do not want to share your contacts with others.

Skills covered: Create a Desktop Database Using a Template • Add Records to a Downloaded Desktop Database Template • Explore the Database Objects in a Downloaded Desktop Database Template

STEP 1 ≫ CREATE A DESKTOP DATABASE USING A TEMPLATE

You locate an Access desktop template that you can use to create your personal contact database. This template not only allows you to store names, addresses, telephone numbers, and other information, but also lets you categorize your contacts, send e-mail messages, and create maps of addresses. You download and save the template. Refer to Figure 10.30 as you complete Step 1.

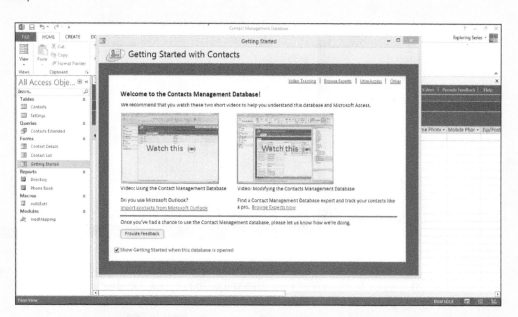

FIGURE 10.30 Desktop Contacts Intro Screen

a. Open Access. Scroll down until you see the *Desktop contacts* template and click the template tile.

   The Create Intro Screen page for the Desktop contacts database opens.

b. Click the **Browse icon** to navigate to the folder where you are saving your files, enter **a01h4Contacts_LastFirst** as the file name, and then click **OK**.

c. Click **Create** to download the template.

d. Click **Enable Content** on the Security Warning message bar.

   The *Getting Started with Contacts* page displays, providing you with videos you can watch to learn how to use and modify the database as well as other helpful links.

> **TROUBLESHOOTING:** If the Getting Started page does not display, click Getting Started in the Forms category on the Navigation Pane.

> **TROUBLESHOOTING:** The Getting Started page opens every time you open the Contacts Management database. To close this page until you want to view it again, clear the *Show Getting Started when this database is opened* check box at the bottom-left corner of the dialog box before closing the Getting Started page.

   e. Close the Getting Started page.

      The database displays with the Contact List table open.

STEP 2 ➤➤ ADD RECORDS TO A DOWNLOADED DESKTOP DATABASE TEMPLATE

Because the database opens in the Contact List form, you decide to begin by entering a contact—your dentist—in the form. Refer to Figure 10.31 as you complete Step 2.

FIGURE 10.31 Contact Details Form

   a. Click in the empty first field of the first row. Enter the following information, pressing **Tab** between each entry. Do not press Tab after entering the ZIP/Postal Code.

Field Name	Value to Type
First Name	Tanya
Last Name	Machuca
Company	Hobblecreek Mountain Dentistry
Job Title	D.D.S.
Category	Business (select from list)
E-mail Address	HMDentistry@email.com
Business Phone	801-555-8102
Home Phone	(leave blank)
Mobile Phone	801-555-8921
ZIP/Postal Code	84664

   b. Click **Save and Close**.

   c. Double-click **Contact List** in the Forms group on the Navigation Pane.

d. Click **Open** in the first field of Dr. Machuca's record.

Open is a hyperlink to a different form in the database. The Contact Details form opens, displaying Dr. Machuca's information. More fields are available for you to use to store information.

e. Enter the following additional information to the record:

Field Name	Value to Type
Street	56 West 200 North
City	Mapleton
State/Province	UT
Country/Region	USA
Notes	Available Tuesday - Friday 7 a.m. to 4 p.m.

f. Click the **Click to Map hyperlink** to view a map to Dr. Machuca's office. Close the map.

Bing displays a map to the address in the record. You can get directions, locate nearby businesses, and use many other options.

g. Click **Save and Close** in the top center of the form to close the Contact Details form.

The record is saved.

h. Click **New Contact** beneath the Contact List title bar.

The Contact Details form opens to a blank record.

i. Enter the following information for a new record, pressing **Tab** to move between fields. Some fields will be blank.

Field Name	Value to Type
First Name	Rowan
Last Name	Westmoreland
Company	Phoenix Aesthetics
Job Title	Aesthetician
Mobile Phone	801-555-2221
Street	425 North Main Street
City	Springville
State/Province	UT
ZIP/Postal Code	84663
Category	Personal
E-mail Address	Rowan55W5@email.com
Notes	Recommended by Michelle

j. Click **Save and Close.**

STEP 3 ▶▶ EXPLORE THE DATABASE OBJECTS IN A DOWNLOADED DESKTOP DATABASE TEMPLATE

You explore the objects created by the template so that you understand the organization of the database. Refer to Figure 10.32 as you complete Step 3.

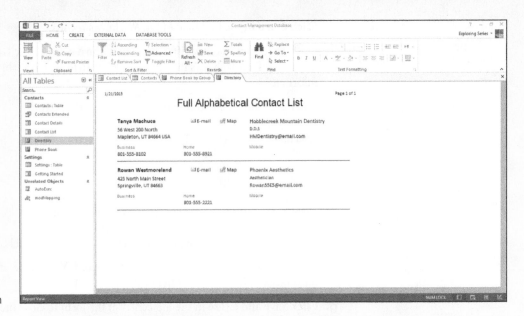

FIGURE 10.32 Directory Form

a. Double-click the **Contacts table** in the Navigation Pane to open it.

The information you entered using the Contact List form and the Contact Details form displays in the Contacts table.

b. Click the **Reports group** in the Navigation Pane to expand the list of reports, if necessary.

The list of reports contained in the database file opens.

c. Double-click **Phone Book** in the Navigation Pane to open it.

The Phone Book report opens displaying the contact name and phone information organized by category.

d. Double-click the **Directory report** in the Navigation Pane to open it.

The Directory report opens, displaying a full alphabetical contact list. The Directory report was designed to display more fields than the Phone Book, but it is not organized by category.

e. Click **All Access Objects** on the Navigation Pane and select **Tables and Related Views**.

You can now see the objects that are based on the Contacts table.

f. Right-click the **Directory report tab** and click **Close All**.

g. Exit Access and submit your work based on your instructor's directions.

After reading this chapter, you have accomplished the following objectives:

1. **Understand database fundamentals.**
   - A database is a collection of data organized as meaningful information that can be accessed, managed, stored, queried, sorted, and reported.
   - Organize information in a database and recognize Access objects: An Access database is a structured collection of six types of objects—tables, forms, queries, reports, macros, and modules.
   - The foundation of a database is its tables, the objects in which data is stored. Each table in the database is composed of records, and each record is in turn comprised of fields.
   - The primary key in a table is the field (or combination of fields) that makes every record in a table unique.
   - Examine the Access interface: Objects are organized and listed in the Navigation Pane. Access also uses a Tabbed Documents interface in which each object that is open has its own tab.
   - Explore Access views: The Datasheet view enables the user to view, add, edit, and delete records, whereas the Design view is used to create and modify a table's design by specifying the fields it will contain, the fields' data types, and their associated properties.
   - Open an Access file and work with Content Security: When a database is opened from a location that has not been designated as a trusted location or that does not have a digital signature from a publisher you can trust, Access displays a message bar with a security warning. Click the Enable Content button if you trust the database's source.

2. **Use an existing database.**
   - Understand the difference between working in storage and memory: Access works primarily from storage. Records can be added, modified, or deleted in the database, and as the information is entered it is automatically saved.
   - Add, edit, and delete records: A pencil icon displays in the row selector box to indicate when you are in editing mode. Moving to another record or clicking Save on the Quick Access Toolbar saves the changes.
   - To add a new record, click *New (blank) record* on the navigation bar. To delete a record, click the row selector and click Delete in the Records group on the Home tab.
   - Save As, Compact and Repair, and Back Up Access files: *Compact and Repair* reduces the size of the database, and Back Up creates a duplicate copy of the database.

3. **Sort table data on one or multiple fields.**
   - Sorting changes the order of information, and information may be sorted by one or more fields.

4. **Create, modify, and remove filters.**
   - A filter is a set of criteria that is applied to a table to display a subset of records in that table.
   - *Filter by Selection* displays only the records that match the selected criteria.
   - *Filter by Form* displays records based on multiple criteria and enables the user to apply logical operators and use comparison operators.

5. **Know when to use Access or Excel to manage data.**
   - Use Access to manage data when you require multiple related tables to store your data; have a large amount of data; need to connect to and retrieve data from external databases; need to group, sort, and total data based on various parameters; and/or have an application that requires multiple users to connect to one data source.
   - Use Excel to manage data when you need one worksheet to handle all of your data; have mostly numeric data; require subtotals and totals in your worksheet; want to primarily run a series of "what if" scenarios on your data; and/or need to create complex charts and/or graphs.

6. **Understand relational power.**
   - Use the Relationships window: A relationship is a connection between two tables using a common field. The benefit of a relationship is to efficiently combine data from related tables for the purpose of creating queries, forms, and reports.
   - Enforce referential integrity: Enforcing referential integrity when setting a table relationship ensures that data cannot be entered into a related table unless it first exists in the primary table.

7. **Create a database.**
   - Create a Web application using a template: Creating a custom Web app enables you to create a database that you can build and use and share with others through the Web.
   - Creating a blank desktop database: Creating a blank desktop database lets you create a database specific to your needs.
   - Create a desktop database using a template: A template is a predefined database that includes professionally designed tables, forms, reports, and other objects that you can use to jumpstart the creation of your database.

Key Terms Matching

Match the key terms with their definitions. Write the key term letter by the appropriate numbered definition.

a. Back Up Database
b. Compact and Repair
c. Custom Web app
d. Datasheet view
e. Design view
f. Field
g. Filter by Form
h. Filter by Selection
i. Form
j. Navigation Pane
k. Object

l. Primary key
m. Query
n. Record
o. Relational database management system (RDBMS)
p. Relationship
q. Report
r. Sort
s. Table
t. Template

1. _____ View that enables you to add, edit, and delete the records of a table. **p. 486**

2. _____ An Access object that enables you to enter, modify, or delete table data. **p. 484**

3. _____ An Access utility that reduces the size of the database and can repair a corrupt database. **p. 491**

4. _____ A main component that is created and used to make a database function. **p. 483**

5. _____ A filtering method that displays records based on multiple criteria **p. 502**

6. _____ A system that uses the relational model to manage groups of data (tables) and rules (relationships) between tables. **p. 510**

7. _____ A database that can be built, used, and shared with others through the use of a host server. **p. 517**

8. _____ An object that contains professional-looking formatted information from underlying tables or queries. **p. 484**

9. _____ An object used to store data, and the foundation of every database. **p. 483**

10. _____ An Access utility that creates a duplicate copy of the database. **p. 491**

11. _____ A predefined database that includes professionally designed tables, forms, reports, and other objects. **p. 517**

12. _____ A filtering method that displays only records that match selected criteria. **p. 501**

13. _____ A connection between two tables using a common field. **p. 509**

14. _____ A method of listing records in a specific sequence. **p. 500**

15. _____ View that enables you to create tables, add and delete fields, and modify field properties. **p. 488**

16. _____ An Access interface element that organizes and lists the database objects in a database. **p. 483**

17. _____ A question you ask that can help you find and retrieve table data meeting conditions you specify. **p. 484**

18. _____ The smallest data element in a table, such as first name, last name, address, or phone number. **p. 483**

19. _____ Complete set of all the fields (data elements) about one person, place, event, or concept. **p. 483**

20. _____ The field (or combination of fields) that uniquely identifies each record in a table. **p. 488**

Multiple Choice

1. Which sequence represents the hierarchy of terms, from smallest to largest?

   (a) Database, table, record, field

   (b) Field, record, table, database

   (c) Record, field, table, database

   (d) Field, record, database, table

2. You edit several records in an Access table. When should you execute the Save command?

   (a) Immediately after you edit a record

   (b) When you close the table

   (c) Once at the end of the session

   (d) Records are saved automatically; the save command is not required.

3. Which of the following is *not* true of an Access database?

   (a) Short Text, Number, AutoNumber, and Currency are valid data types.

   (b) Every record in a table has the same fields as every other record.

   (c) Every table in a database contains the same number of records as every other table.

   (d) Each table should contain a primary key; however, a primary key is not required.

4. Which of the following is *true* regarding the record selector box?

   (a) An orange border surrounds the record selector box and the active record.

   (b) A pencil symbol indicates that the current record already has been saved.

   (c) An asterisk indicates the first record in the table.

   (d) An empty square indicates that the current record is selected.

5. Which of the following will be accepted as valid during data entry?

   (a) Adding a record with a duplicate primary key

   (b) Entering text into a numeric field

   (c) Entering numbers into a text field

   (d) Omitting an entry in a required field

6. You have finished an Access assignment and wish to turn it in to your instructor for evaluation. As you prepare to transfer the file, you discover that it has more than doubled in size. You should:

   (a) Delete extra tables or reports or fields to make the file smaller.

   (b) Zip the database file prior to sending it to your instructor.

   (c) Compact and repair the database before sending it to your instructor.

   (d) Turn it in; the size does not matter.

7. Which of the following conditions is available through *Filter by Selection*?

   (a) Equals condition

   (b) Delete condition

   (c) AND condition

   (d) OR condition

8. An Employees table is open in Datasheet view. You want to sort the names alphabetically by last name and then by first name (e.g., Smith, Andrew). To do this, you must:

   (a) First sort ascending on first name and then on last name.

   (b) First sort descending on first name and then on last name.

   (c) First sort ascending on last name and then on first name.

   (d) First sort descending on last name and then on first name.

9. Which of the following is *not* true when creating relationships between tables?

   (a) Join lines create a relationship between two tables.

   (b) The common fields used to create a relationship must both be primary keys.

   (c) The data types of common fields must be the same.

   (d) Enforcing referential integrity ensures that data cannot be entered into a related table unless it first exists in the primary table.

10. All of the following statements are *true* about creating a database *except*:

    (a) Creating a custom Web app requires that you use a host server.

    (b) When creating a blank desktop database, Access opens to a blank table in Datasheet view.

    (c) Using a template to create a database saves time because it includes predefined objects.

    (d) The objects provided in a template cannot be modified.

Practice Exercises

1 Hotel Rewards

FROM SCRATCH

The Lakes Hotel and Conference Center caters to upscale business travelers and provides stylish hotel suites, sophisticated meeting and reception facilities, and state-of-the-art media equipment. The hotel is launching a rewards club to help the marketing department track the purchasing patterns of its most loyal customers. All of the hotel transactions will be stored in an Access database. Your task is to create a member table and enter sample customers. You will practice filtering on the table data. This exercise follows the same set of skills as used in Hands-On Exercises 1 and 2 in the chapter. Refer to Figure 10.33 as you complete this exercise.

ID	LastName	FirstName	Address	City	State	Zip	Phone	DateOfMembership
1	Guerassio	Janine	1012 TRADERS TRAIL	GRAHAM	NC	27253		1/26/2015
2	Gutierrez	Antonio	102 PENNYPACKER CT	ELIZABETH CITY	NC	27909	555-387-6394	1/29/2016
3	Sigman	Hanni	1922 WRIGHTSVILLE AVE	CARY	NC	27512	555-784-8851	7/30/2016
4	O'Brien	Lovie	3413 KISTLER COURT	WILMINGTON	NC	28409	555-227-8335	2/13/2015
5	Ratanaphruks	Kritika	4444 LLOYD CT	RALEIGH	NC	27609		3/18/2014
6	Koski	Janice	3904 HUNT CHASE CT	RALEIGH	NC	27612		7/3/2016
7	Tulowiecki	Jerry	775 BEAR RIDGE TRAIL	RALEIGH	NC	27607	555-762-9373	5/21/2016
8	Yingling	Bev	PO BOX 7045	SALISBURY	NC	28146		2/17/2014
9	Gray	Bob	100 BIRDIE COURT	RALEIGH	NC	27612	555-787-7688	9/1/2015
10	Hauser	Bob	10008 WHITESTONE RD	RALEIGH	NC	27612	555-783-8286	3/1/2015
*	(New)							

FIGURE 10.33 Enter Data into the Members Table

a. Open Access and click **Blank desktop database**.

b. Type **a01p1Rewards_LastFirst** in the **File Name box**. Click the **Browse icon**. Navigate to the location where you are saving your files in the File New Database dialog box, click **OK** to close the dialog box, and then click **Create** to create the new database.

c. Click **View** in the Views group on the TABLE TOOLS FIELDS tab to switch to Design view. Type **Members** in the **Save As dialog box** and click **OK**.

d. Type **LastName** under the ID field and press **Tab**. Accept **Short Text** as the Data Type. Type **FirstName** in the third row and press **Tab**. Accept **Short Text** as the Data Type.

e. Type the next five fields into the Field Name column: **Address**, **City**, **State**, **Zip**, and **Phone**. Accept **Short Text** as the Data Type for each of these fields.

f. Type **DateOfMembership** as the last Field Name and select **Date/Time** as the Data Type.

g. Click **View** in the Views group to switch to Datasheet view. Click **Yes** to save the table. Type the data as shown in Figure 10.33. Increase the column widths to fit the data as necessary. Press **Tab** to move to the next field.

h. Find a record that displays *Raleigh* as the value in the City field. Click **Raleigh** to select that data value.

i. Click **Selection** in the Sort & Filter group on the HOME tab. Select **Equals "Raleigh"**.

j. Find a record that displays *27612* as the value in the Zip field. Click **27612** to select that data value.

k. Click **Selection** in the Sort & Filter group on the HOME tab. Select **Equals "27612"**.

l. Click any value in the FirstName field. Click **Ascending** in the Sort & Filter group on the HOME tab. Click any value in the LastName field. Click **Ascending** in the Sort & Filter group on the HOME tab.

m. Click the **FILE tab**, click **Print**, and then click **Print Preview** to preview the sorted and filtered table.

n. Click **Close Print Preview** in the Close Preview group.

o. Close the table and save the changes.

p. Click the **FILE tab** and click **Compact and Repair Database** under *Advanced*.

q. Click the **FILE tab**, click **Save As**, and then double-click **Back Up Database**.

r. Click **Save** to accept the default backup file name with today's date.

s. Click the **FILE tab** and click **Exit** (to exit Access). Submit the database based on your instructor's directions.

The Custom Coffee Company provides coffee, tea, and snacks to offices in Miami. Custom Coffee also provides and maintains the equipment for brewing the beverages. The firm has a reputation for providing outstanding customer service. To improve customer service even further, the owner recently purchased an Access database to keep track of customers, orders, and products. This database will replace the Excel spreadsheets currently maintained by the office manager. The Excel spreadsheets are out of date, and they do not allow for data validation while data is being entered. The company hired you to verify and enter all the Excel data into the Access database. This exercise follows the same set of skills as used in Hands-On Exercises 1–3 in the chapter. Refer to Figure 10.34 as you complete this exercise.

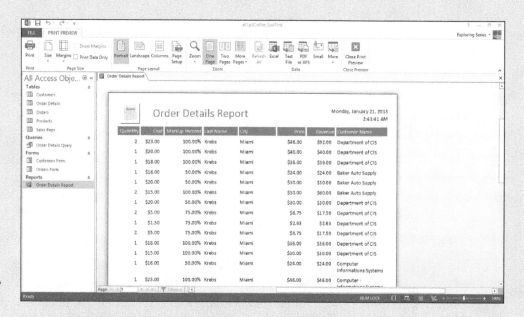

FIGURE 10.34 Order Details Report Filtered for *YourName* and *Miami*

a. Open the *a01p2Coffee* file and save the database as **a01p2Coffee_LastFirst**.

b. Click the **DATABASE TOOLS tab** and click **Relationships** in the Relationships group. Review the table relationships. Take note of the join line between the Customers and Orders tables.

c. Click **Close** in the Relationships group.

d. Double-click the **Sales Reps table** in the Navigation Pane to open it. Replace *YourName* with your name in both the LastName and FirstName fields. For example, as the Access author, I used the name Cynthia Krebs in place of FirstName LastName. Close the table by clicking the **Close (X) button** on the right side of the Sales Reps window.

e. Double-click the **Customers Form** to open it. Click **New (blank) record** in the navigation bar at the bottom of the window. Add a new record by typing the following information; press **Tab** after each field.

Customer Name:	*your name* Company
Contact:	*your name*
Email:	*yourname*@email.com
Address1:	123 Main St
Address2:	(leave blank)
City:	Miami
State:	FL
Zip Code:	33133
Phone:	(305) 555-1234

Fax:	(leave blank)
Service Start Date:	01/17/2016
Credit Rating:	A
Sales Rep ID:	2

Note the pencil in the top-left margin of the form window. This symbol indicates the new record has not been saved. Press **Tab**. The pencil symbol disappears, and the new customer is automatically saved to the table.

f. Close the Customers Form.

g. Double-click the **Orders Form** to open it. Click **New (blank) record** in the navigation bar at the bottom of the window. Add a new record by typing the following information:

Customer ID:	15 (Access will convert it to C0015)
Payment Type:	Cash (select using the arrow)
Comments:	Ship this order in 2 days
Product ID:	4 (Access will convert it to P0004)
Quantity:	2

h. Add a second product using the following information:

Product ID:	6 (Access will convert it to P0006)
Quantity:	1

i. Close the form.

j. Double-click the **Order Details Report** to open it in Report view. Click your name in the Last Name field, click **Selection** in the Sort & Filter group, and then click **Equals "Your Name"**.

k. Right-click **Miami** in the City field and select **Equals "Miami"** from the shortcut menu.

l. Click the **FILE tab**, click **Print**, and then click **Print Preview**.

m. Click **Close Print Preview** in the Close Preview group. Close the report.

n. Click the **FILE tab** and click **Compact & Repair Database**.

o. Click the **FILE tab**, click **Save As**, and then double-click **Back Up Database**. Use the default backup file name.

p. Close Access. Submit based on your instructor's directions.

3 Camping Trip

FROM SCRATCH

You and your friends have decided to spend your annual reunion camping at the Wawona Campground in Yosemite National Park. Wawona Campground is an extremely popular campground. Campground reservations are available in blocks of one month at a time, up to five months in advance, on the 15th of each month at 7 AM Pacific time. Nearly all reservations are filled the first day they become available, usually within seconds or minutes after 7 AM. Realizing that making reservations is a high-priority, critical task, and that there are many other tasks that must be completed before you can have a successful trip, your group decides to use the Access Task Management Database to begin getting organized for their trip on September 15, 2015. Other tasks can be entered at a later time. This exercise follows the same set of skills as used in Hands-On Exercises 3 and 4 in the chapter. Refer to Figures 10.35–10.38 as you complete this exercise.

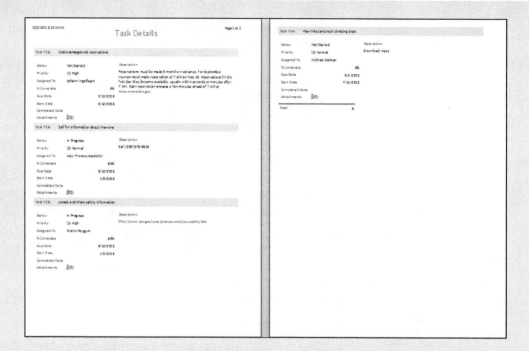

FIGURE 10.35 Task Details Report

a. Open Access and click the **Desktop task management template** in the Access Backstage view.

b. Type **a01p3Camping_LastFirst** in the **File name box**. Click the **Browse icon**. Navigate to the location where you are saving your files in the File New Database dialog box, click **OK** to close the dialog box, and then click **Create** to create the new database.

c. Click the **Watch this arrow** for the *Using the Tasks Database* template video on the left side of the Getting Started page. If the Getting Started page does not open, open the Getting Started form in the Forms group in the Navigation Pane. Click **Watch this>>** and watch the video. Close the video when you have finished watching it. Click **Close** again to return to the *Getting Started with Tasks* page.

d. Remove the check in the *Show Getting Started when this database is opened* check box so that the page does not automatically display in the future. If you want to view Getting Started again, you can click **Getting Started** in the Forms category on the Navigation Pane. Click the **Close (X) button**.

e. Click **Relationships** in the Relationships group on the DATABASE TOOLS tab and note the relationship between the Contacts table and the Tasks table. Close the Relationships window.

f. Double-click **Contact List** in the Forms category on the Navigation Pane. Type the information for each field in the Contact list form using the information displayed in Figure 10.36, pressing **Tab** between each field.

FIGURE 10.36 Contact List

g. Close the Contact List form. The Task List form displays because it was the form open when you downloaded the database.

TROUBLESHOOTING: If the Task List form does not display, double-click the Task List form in the Navigation Pane to open it.

h. Click the **Shutter Bar Open/Close button** to close the Navigation Pane, which enables you to see more table fields.

i. Enter the information for each field in the Task List form using the information displayed in Figure 10.37. In the Priority field, Status field, and Assigned To field, click the arrow and select the list of options. When typing the Start Date and Due Date, type the date and add **7 AM** after the date. Although the date does not show in the table, it is required.

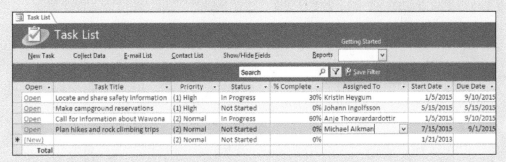

FIGURE 10.37 Task List Form

j. Close the Tasks table and click the **Shutter Bar Open/Close button** to open the Navigation Pane.

k. Double-click **Task Details** in the Forms category in the Navigation Pane.

l. Refer to Figure 10.38 to enter the information in the **Description box** and close the Task Details form.

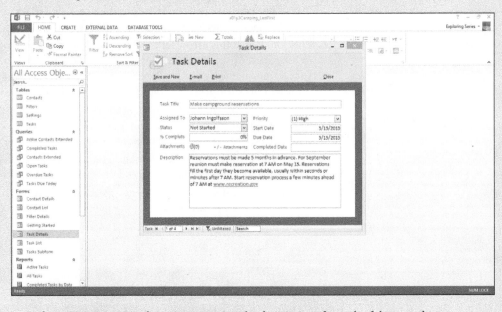

FIGURE 10.38 Description in Task Details Form

m. Refer to Figure 10.35 and continue entering the descriptions for each of the records.

n. Double-click **Task Details** in the Reports category in the Navigation Pane to view the report displaying the details about the tasks you have created. Scroll down to see all tasks.

o. Click the **FILE tab**, click **Print**, and then click **Print Preview**.

p. Click **Two Pages** in the Zoom group on the Print Preview tab. Note the report format groups the information by Task Title.

q. Click **Close Print Preview** in the Close Preview group. Close the report.

r. Click the **FILE tab** and click **Compact & Repair Database**.

s. Click the **FILE tab**, click **Save As**, and then double-click **Back Up Database**. Use the default backup file name.

t. Close Access. Submit based on your instructor's directions.

1 | Home Sales

You are the senior partner in a large, independent real estate firm that specializes in home sales. Most of your time is spent supervising the agents who work for your firm. The firm needs to create a database to hold all of the information on the properties it has listed. You will use the database to help find properties that match the goals of your customers. You will create the database, create two tables, add data to both tables, and create a relationship. Refer to Figure 10.39 as you complete this exercise.

FIGURE 10.39 Properties Table

a. Open Access and click **Blank desktop database**. Type **a01m1Homes_LastFirst** in the **File Name box**. Click **Browse** and navigate to the location where you are saving your files. Click **OK** to close the dialog box and click **Create** to create the new database.

b. Switch to Design view. Type **Properties** in the **Save As dialog box** and click **OK**.

c. Type **DateListed** under the ID field and press **Tab**. Select **Date/Time** as the Data Type.

d. Type the remainder of the fields and Data Types as shown:

Field Name	Data Type
DateSold	Date/Time
ListPrice	Currency
SalesPrice	Currency
SqFeet	Number
Beds	Number
Baths	Number
Address	Short Text
SubDivision	Number
AgentID	Number
Style	Short Text
Construction	Short Text
Garage	Short Text
YearBuilt	Number

e. Switch to Datasheet view. Type the first 10 records as shown in Figure 10.39.

f. Open the *a01m1Properties.xlsx* workbook file in Excel. Click **row 2**, press and hold the **left mouse button**, and then drag through **row 70** so that all the data rows are selected. Click **Copy** in the Clipboard group on the HOME tab. Click **Yes** to save the data to the Clipboard when prompted. Close the Excel file.

g. Return to Access and click on the **asterisk (*)** on the first new row of the Properties table. Click **Paste** in the Clipboard group to paste all 69 rows into the Properties table. Save and close the table.

h. Click **Table** in the Tables group on the CREATE tab. Click **View** in the Views group on the TABLE TOOLS FIELDS tab to switch to Design view. Save the table as **Agents**. Change the primary key from ID to **AgentID**. Add the following fields and switch to Datasheet view. Save changes to the table design when prompted.

Field Name	Data Type
FirstName	Short Text
LastName	Short Text
Title	Short Text

i. Enter the following data in the Agents table and close the table.

AgentID	FirstName	LastName	Title
1	Kia	Hart	Broker
2	Keith	Martin	Agent
3	Kim	Yang	Agent
4	Steven	Dougherty	Agent in Training
5	Angela	Scott	Agent in Training
6	Juan	Resario	President

j. Click the **DATABASE TOOLS tab** and click **Relationships** in the Relationships group. Add both tables to the Relationships window and close the Show Table dialog box.

k. Drag the bottom border of the Properties table downward until all fields display. Drag the **AgentID field** from the Agents table and drop it onto the **AgentID field** in the Properties table. Click the **Enforce Referential Integrity check box** in the Edit Relationships dialog box to activate it. Click **Create** and close the Relationships window. Click **Yes** to save your changes.

l. Open the **Properties** table. Click **Advanced** in the Sort & Filter group and click **Filter By Form**. Set the criteria to identify properties with a list price less than $300,000 and with two bedrooms. (You will use the expression <300000 for the criteria of the list price.) Display the results and sort by ascending list price. Save and close the table.

m. Compact, repair, and back up the database.

n. Exit Access. Submit the database based on your instructor's directions.

2 National Conference

The Association of Higher Education will host its National Conference on your campus next year. To facilitate the conference, the information technology department has replaced last year's Excel spreadsheets with an Access database containing information on the rooms, speakers, and sessions. Your assignment is to create a room itinerary that will list all of the sessions, dates, and times for each room. The list will be posted on the door of each room for the duration of the conference. Refer to Figure 10.40 as you complete this exercise.

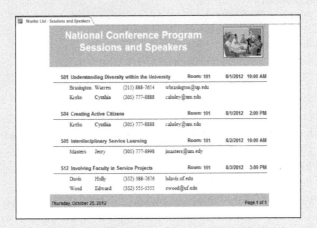

FIGURE 10.40 Sessions and Speakers Report—Room 101

a. Open the *a01m2NatConf* file and save the database as **a01m2NatConf_LastFirst**.

b. Open the Relationships window.

c. Review the objects in the database to see if any of the existing objects will provide the room itinerary information displayed in Figure 10.40.

d. Open the SessionSpeaker table. Scroll to the first blank record at the bottom of the table and enter a new record using SpeakerID **99** and SessionID **09**. (Note: Speaker 99 does not exist.) How does Access respond? Close the dialog box, recognizing that you are not saving this record. Close the SessionSpeaker table. In the Relationships window, right-click the join line between the Speakers table and SessionSpeaker table and click **Delete**. Click **Yes** to permanently delete the selected relationship from the database. Close the Relationships window. Open the SessionSpeaker table and enter the same record again. How does Access respond this time? Close the SessionSpeaker table.

e. Open the Speakers table. Find and replace *YourName* with your name. Close the Speakers table.

f. Open the Speaker–Session Query and apply a filter to identify the sessions where you or Holly Davis are the speakers. Use *Filter by Form* and the Or tab. (Nine records should display.)

g. Sort the filtered results in ascending order by the RoomID field and save and close the query.

h. Open the Master List–Sessions and Speakers report. Right-click the **Master List–Sessions and Speakers tab** and select **Report View**.

i. Apply a filter that limits the report to sessions in Room 101 only.

j. Click the **FILE tab**, click **Print**, and then click **Print Preview**. Compare the report to Figure 10.40 and make any corrections necessary. Close Print Preview and close the report.

k. Compact and repair the database.

l. Back up the database. Use the default backup file name.

m. Exit Access. Submit based on your instructor's directions.

3 Used Cell Phones for Sale

You and a few of your classmates decide to start a new business selling used cell phones, MP3 players, and accessories. You will use an Access database to track your inventory. To begin, one person in your group will locate the Access database for this exercise, complete steps b through f, and then post the database to a OneDrive folder. The next person in your group will retrieve the revised database and also complete steps b through f (and so on until everyone has completed steps b through f). After everyone has completed steps b through f, you will retrieve the database again and complete step g. At the completion of this exercise, each person will submit his or her own Word document containing the answers to the questions below.

a. Open the *a01m3Phones* database and save it as **a01m3PhonesGroupX_LastFirst**. (Replace *X* with the number assigned to your group by your instructor.)

b. Open the Inventory table and review the records in the table. Take note of the data in the TypeOfDevice column. Close the table and open the DeviceOptions table. Review the data and close the table.

c. Open the Relationships window. What is the benefit of the relationship between the Inventory table and the DeviceOptions table? Create a Word document with both the question and your answer. After you complete this exercise, you will submit this Word document to your instructor using the file name **a01m3PhonesAnswers_LastFirst**. Close the Relationships window.

d. Open the Inventory Form and add the information about your cell phone to the table (or search the Internet for any model if you do not have a cell phone) in the first new blank record. Enter your name in the SellerName field. With your information showing in the form, take a screenshot of the form using the Snipping Tool. Paste the image into the Word document you created in step c. Close the form.

e. Open the Inventory Report by Manufacturer in Report view. Filter the records for only items that have not been sold. Take a screenshot using the Snipping Tool and paste the image into the Word document. Close the report, close the database, and then exit Access.

f. Create a folder on your OneDrive account named **Exploring Access** and share the folder with other members in your group and the instructor. Upload the database to this new folder and notify another person in your group. The next person will complete steps b through f, and then the next person, until all group members have added their information.

g. After all the new phone records have been added, each person in the group should download the **a01m3PhonesGroupX** database again and use filters to answer the following questions. Add the questions and your answers to the Word document you created.

1. How many phones are still for sale? _____

2. How many phones are made by Apple or Samsung? _____

3. How many phones were sold in the first half of 2013? _____ List the ID numbers _____

4. Sort the phones from lowest to highest asking price. Which phone is the least expensive? _____ Most expensive? _____.

5. How many items are not phones? _____

h. Use e-mail or text messaging to communicate with the other members in your group if you have any questions.

i. Submit the Word document based on your instructor's directions.

Beyond the Classroom

Northwind Revenue Report

RESEARCH CASE

Open the *a01b2NWind* file and save the database as **a01b2NWind_LastFirst**. Open the Employees table and replace *YourName* with your first and last names. Before you can filter the Revenue report, you need to update the criterion in the underlying query to match the dates in the database. Right-click the **Revenue query** in the Navigation Pane and click **Design view** in the shortcut menu. Scroll to the right until you see *OrderDate*. Right-click in the **Criteria row** under *OrderDate* and click **Zoom**. Change the criterion to **Between#1/1/2015#And#3/31/2015#** and click **OK**. Click **Run** in the Results group on the Query Tools Design tab and save the query. Open the Revenue report. Use the tools that you have learned in this chapter to filter the report for only your sales of Confections. Close the report. Compact, repair, and back up your database and exit Access.

Lugo Computer Sales

DISASTER RECOVERY

You are having trouble with an Access 2013 database. One of the employees accidentally changed the CustomerID of Lugo Computer Sales. This change caused a problem in one of the relationships. Open the *a01b3Recover* file and save the database as **a01b3Recover_LastFirst**. Open the Customers and Orders tables and examine the data. Change the Lugo Computer Sales CustomerID in the Customers table back to the original number of 6. Reset the relationship between the Customers table and the Orders table and enforce referential integrity. Compact, repair, and back up your database and exit Access. Submit the database based on your instructor's directions.

Financial Literacy

SOFT SKILLS CASE

The Cambridge Resources Group stated that surveyed executives ranked the "toll on productivity caused by financial stress" as one of the "most critical unaddressed issues in the workplace today." Dr. E. Thomas Garman*, the president of Personal Finance Employee Education Foundation, stated that "60% of employees live paycheck to paycheck" and that research shows that "those with more financial distress report poor health; financially distressed workers (40–50%) report that their financial problems cause their health woes; and that positive changes in financial behaviors are related to improved health."

Tracking your income and your expenses enables you to see where your money is going. With this information you can create a budget that will help you reach your goals. To aid you with this process, Microsoft created a downloadable Personal Account Ledger template. This database includes a form that enables you to record transactions; reports to display transactions, expenses by category, and income by category; and a tax report. Open *a01b4Ledger*, a database based on the Microsoft Personal Account Ledger, and save it as **a01b4Ledger_LastFirst**. Use the Account Transaction List to enter your income and expenses for the previous month. Then view the Income by Category report and the Expenses by Category report. Compact, repair, and back up your database and exit Access. Submit the database based on your instructor's directions.

* Employee Financial Wellness slideshare presentation, http://www.slideshare.net/irwink/Employee-Financial-Wellness, by Dr. E. Thomas Garman, President, Personal Finance Employee Education Foundation.

Capstone Exercise

Your boss expressed concern about the accuracy of the inventory reports in the bookstore. He needs you to open the inventory database, make modifications to some records, and determine if the changes you make carry through to the other objects in the database. You will make changes to a form and verify those changes in a table, a query, and a report. When you have verified that the changes update automatically, you will compact and repair the database and make a backup of it.

Database File Setup

You will open an original database file and save the database with a new name, replace an existing author's name with your name, create a table, create table relationships, sort, and apply a filter by selection.

a. Open the *a01c1Books* file and save the database as **a01c1Books_LastFirst**.

b. Create a new table in Design view. Save the table as **Publishers**. Change the primary key from ID to **PubID** with a Data Type of **Short Text**. Add the following fields and switch to Datasheet view. Save changes to the table design when prompted.

Field Name	Data Type
PubName	Short Text
PubAddress	Short Text
PubCity	Short Text
PubState	Short Text
PubZIP	Short Text

c. Enter the following data in the Publishers table and close the table.

PubID	PubName	PubAddress	PubCity	PubState	PubZIP
BB	Bantam Books	1540 Broadway	New York	NY	10036
FS	Farrar, Straus and Giroux	12 Union Square West	New York	NY	10003
KN	Knopf	299 Park Avenue	New York	NY	10171
LB	Little, Brown and Company	1271 Avenue of the Americas	New York	NY	10020
PH	Pearson/ Prentice Hall	1 Lake Street	Upper Saddle	NJ	07458
SS	Simon & Schuster	100 Front Street	Riverside	NY	08075

d. Open the Maintain Authors form.

e. Navigate to Record 7 and replace *YourName* with your name.

f. Add a new Title: **Technology in Action**. The ISBN is **0-13-148905-4**, the PubID is **PH**, the PublDate is **2015**, the Price is $89.95 (just type **89.95**, no $), and StockAmt is **95** units. Move to any other record to save the new record. Close the form.

g. Open the Maintain Authors form again and navigate to Record 7. The changes are there because Access works from storage, not memory. Close the form again.

Sort a Query and Apply a Filter by Selection

You need to reorder a detail query so that the results are sorted alphabetically by the publisher name.

a. Open the Publishers, Books, and Authors Query.

b. Click in any record in the PubName column and sort the field in ascending order.

c. Check to make sure that four books list you as the author.

d. Click your name in the Author's Last Name field and filter the records to show only your books.

e. Close the query and save the changes.

View a Report

You need to examine the Publishers, Books, and Authors Report to determine if the changes you made in the Maintain Authors form appear in the report.

a. Open the Publishers, Books, and Authors Report.

b. Check to make sure that the report shows four books listing you as the author.

c. View the layout of the report in Print Preview.

d. Close the report.

Filter a Table

You need to examine the Books table to determine if the changes you made in the Maintain Authors form carried through to the related table. You also will filter the table to display books published after 2010 with fewer than 100 copies in inventory.

a. Open the Books table.

b. Use *Filter by Form* to create a filter that will identify all books published after 2010 with fewer than 100 items in stock.

c. Apply the filter and preview the filtered table.

d. Close the table and save the changes.

Compact and Repair a Database and Back Up a Database

Now that you are satisfied that any changes made to a form or query carry through to the table, you are ready to compact, repair, and back up your file.

a. Compact and repair your database.

b. Create a backup copy of your database, accept the default file name, and save it.

c. Exit Access. Submit based on your instructor's directions.

Tables and Queries in Relational Databases

Yuri Arcurs/Shutterstock

CHAPTER **11**

Designing Databases and Extracting Data

OBJECTIVES AFTER YOU READ THIS CHAPTER, YOU WILL BE ABLE TO:

1. Design a table p. 540
2. Create and modify tables p. 544
3. Share data p. 555
4. Establish table relationships p. 558
5. Create a single-table query p. 569
6. Specify query criteria for different data types p. 571

7. Understand query sort order p. 575
8. Run, copy, and modify a query p. 575
9. Use the Query Wizard p. 576
10. Create a multitable query p. 582
11. Modify a multitable query p. 583

CASE STUDY | Bank Audit

During a year-end review, a bank auditor uncovers mishandled funds at Commonwealth Federal Bank in Wilmington, Delaware. In order to analyze the data in more detail, the auditor asks you to create an Access database so he can enter the compromised accounts, the associated customers, and the involved employees. Once the new database is created and all the data are entered, you will help the auditor answer questions by creating and running queries.

As you begin, you realize that some of the data are contained in Excel spreadsheets. After discussing this with the auditor, you decide importing these data directly into the new database would be best. Importing from Excel into Access is commonplace and should work well. Importing will also help avoid errors that are associated with data entry. Once the Excel data have been imported, you will use queries to determine which data do not belong in the database. Unaffected records will be deleted.

This chapter introduces the Bank database case study to present the basic principles of table and query design. You will use tables and forms to input data, and you will create queries and reports to extract information from the database in a useful and organized way. The value of that information depends entirely on the quality of the underlying data—the tables.

Table Design, Creation, and Modification

Good database design begins with the tables. Tables provide the framework for all of the activities you perform in a database. If the framework is poorly designed, the rest of the database will be poorly designed as well. Whether you are experienced in designing tables or just learning how, the process should not be done haphazardly. You should follow a systematic approach when creating tables for a database. This process will take practice; however, over time, you will begin to see the patterns and eventually see the similarities among all databases.

In this section, you will learn the principles of good table design. You will review essential guidelines used when creating tables. After developing and testing the table design on paper, you will implement that design in Access. The first step is to list all the tables you need for the database and list all the fields in each table. While you learned to create tables in the previous chapter, in this chapter, you will learn to refine them by changing the properties of various fields. You will also be introduced to the concept of data validation. You want to make sure the data entered into the database are valid for the field and valid for the organization. Allowing invalid data into the tables will only cause problems later.

Designing a Table

Recall that a table is a collection of records, with each record made up of a number of fields. During the table design process, think of the specific fields you need in each table; list the fields under the correct table and assign each field a data type (such as short text, number, or date) as well as its size (length) or format. The order of the fields within the table and the specific field names are not significant because they can be changed later. What is important is that the tables contain all necessary fields so that the system can produce the required information.

For example, consider the design process necessary to create a database for a bank. Most likely you have a bank account and know that the bank maintains data about you. Your bank has your name, address, phone number, and Social Security number. It also knows what accounts you have (checking, savings, money market), if you have a credit card with that bank, and what its balance is. Additionally, your bank keeps information about its branches around the city or state. If you think about the data your bank maintains, you could make a list of the categories of data needed to store that information. These categories for the bank—customers, accounts, branches—become the tables in the bank's database. A bank's customer list is an example of a table: It contains a record for each bank customer.

After the tables have been identified, add the necessary fields using these six guidelines. (These guidelines are discussed in detail in the following paragraphs.)

- Include the necessary data.
- Design for now and for the future.
- Store data in their smallest parts.
- Add calculated fields to a table.
- Design to accommodate date arithmetic.
- Link tables using common fields.

Figure 11.1 shows a customer table and two other tables found in a sample bank database. It also lists fields that would be needed in each table record.

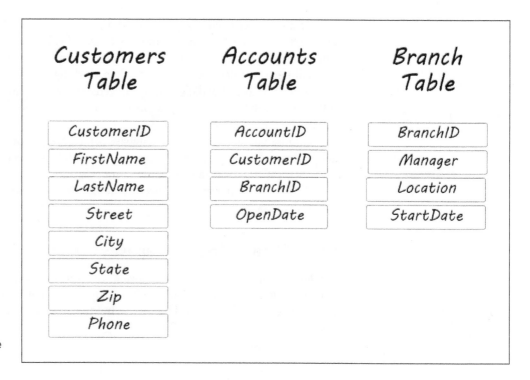

FIGURE 11.1 Rough Draft of Tables and Fields in a Sample Database

Include Necessary Data

A good way to determine what data are necessary in tables is to consider the output you need. It will probably be necessary for you to create professional-looking reports for others, so begin by creating a rough draft of the reports you will need. Then design tables that contain the fields necessary to create those reports. In other words, ask yourself what information will be expected from the system and determine the data required to produce that information. Consider, for example, the tables and fields in Figure 11.1. Is there required information that could not be generated from those tables?

- You can determine which branch a customer uses because the Accounts table includes the CustomerID and the BranchID.
- You can determine who manages a particular branch and which accounts are located there because the Branch table contains the Manager and Location fields.
- You can determine how long a customer has banked with the branch because the date he or she opened the account is stored in the Accounts table.
- You cannot generate the monthly bank statement. In order to generate a customer bank statement (showing all deposits and withdrawals for the month), you would need to add an additional table—an Account Activity table.
- You cannot e-mail a customer because the Customers table does not contain an E-mail field.

If you discover a missing field, such as the E-mail field, you can insert a row anywhere in the appropriate table and add the missing field. The databases found in a real bank are more complex, with more tables and more fields; however, the concepts illustrated here apply both to our sample bank database and to real bank databases.

Design for Now and for the Future

As the data requirements of an organization evolve over time, the information systems that hold the data must change as well. When designing a database, try to anticipate the future needs of the system and build in the flexibility to satisfy those demands. For example, when you add a text field, make sure that the number of characters allocated is sufficient to accommodate future expansion. On the other hand, if you include all the possible fields that anyone might ever need, you could drive up the cost of the database. Each additional field can increase the cost of the database, because it will require additional employee time to enter and maintain the data. The additional fields will also require more storage space, which you will need to calculate, especially when working with larger databases. Good database design must balance the data collection needs of the company with the cost associated with collection and storage. Plans must also include the frequency and cost necessary to modify and update the database.

Suppose you are designing a database for a college. You would need to store each student's name, address, and phone number. You would also need to store multiple phone numbers for most students—a cell phone number, a work number, and an emergency number. As a database designer, you will need to design the tables to accommodate multiple entries for similar data.

Store Data in Their Smallest Parts

The table design in Figure 11.1 divides a customer's name into two fields (FirstName and LastName) to reference each field individually. You might think it easier to use a single field consisting of both the first and last name, but that approach is too limiting. Consider a list of customers stored as a single field:

- Sue Grater
- Rick Grater
- Nancy Gallagher
- Harry Weigner
- Barb Shank
- Pete Shank

The first problem in this approach is the lack of flexibility: You could not easily create a salutation for a letter of the form *Dear Sue* or *Dear Ms. Gallagher* because the first and last names are not accessible individually.

A second difficulty is that the list of customers cannot be easily displayed in alphabetical order by last name because the last name begins in the middle of the field. The names could easily be alphabetized by first name because the first name is at the beginning of the field. However, the most common way to sort names is by the last name, which can be done more efficiently if the last name is stored as a separate field.

Think of how an address might be used. The city, state, and postal code should always be stored as separate fields. Any type of mass mailing requires you to sort on ZIP codes to take advantage of bulk mail. Other applications may require you to select records from a particular state or postal code, which can be done more efficiently if you store the data as separate fields. Often database users enter the postal code, and the database automatically retrieves the city and state information. You may need to direct a mailing only to a neighborhood or to a single street. The guideline is simple: Store data in their smallest parts.

Add Calculated Fields to a Table

A *calculated field* produces a value from an expression or function that references one or more existing fields. Access enables you to store calculated fields in a table using the calculated data type. An example of a calculated field can be found in the bank database. Suppose the bank pays its customers 1.0% interest on the principal each month. A calculated field, such as Monthly Interest, could store the expression Principal × 0.01. The interest amount would then appear on the customer's monthly bank statement.

Storing calculated data in a table enables you to add the data easily to queries, forms, and reports without the trouble of an additional calculation. Storing calculated data in a table may increase the size of the database slightly, but the benefits may outweigh this drawback. In the chapters ahead, you will examine calculations and calculated fields in greater detail. You will learn when to add calculated fields to a table and when to avoid them.

Design to Accommodate Date Arithmetic

Calculated fields are frequently created with numeric data, as the preceding Monthly Interest field example illustrates. You can also create calculated fields using date/time data. If you want to store the length of time a customer has been a customer, you would first create a field to hold the start date for each customer. Next, you would create a calculated field that contains an expression that subtracts the start date from today's date. The resulting calculation would store the number of days each customer has been a customer. Divide the results by 365 to convert days to years. If you want to calculate days to years and account for leap year, you could divide the results by 365.25.

This same concept applies to bank accounts; a bank is likely to store the OpenDate for each account in the Accounts table, as shown in Figure 11.1. Using this date, you can subtract the open date from today's date and calculate the number of days the account has been open. (Again, divide the results by 365 to convert to years.) If you open the Accounts table at least one day later, the results of the calculated field will be different.

A person's age is another example of a calculated field using date arithmetic—the date of birth is subtracted from today's date and the result is divided by 365. It might seem easier to store a person's age rather than the birth date to avoid the calculation. But that would be a mistake because age changes over time and would need to be updated each time age changes. Storing the date of birth is much better because the data remains *constant*. You can use *date arithmetic* to subtract one date from another to find out the number of days, months, or years that have lapsed between them. You can also add or subtract a constant from a date.

Plan for Common Fields Between Tables

As you create the tables and fields for the database, keep in mind that the tables will be joined in relationships using common fields. Draw a line between common fields to indicate the joins, as shown in Figure 11.2. These join lines will be created in Access when you learn to create table relationships later in the chapter. For now, you should name the common fields the same and make sure they have the same data type. For example, CustomerID in the Customers table will join to the CustomerID field in the Accounts table. CustomerID must have the same data type (in this case number/long integer) in both tables; otherwise, the join line will not be allowed.

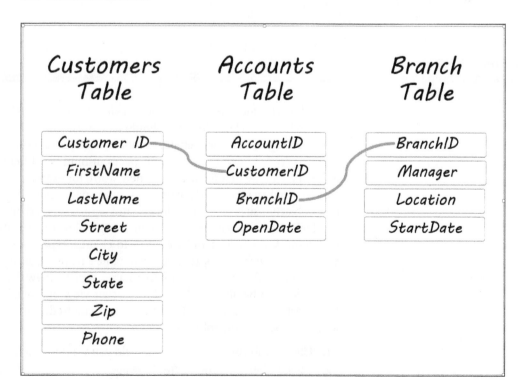

FIGURE 11.2 Create Relationships Using Common Fields

Avoid *data redundancy*, which is the unnecessary storing of duplicate data in two or more tables. You should avoid duplicate information in multiple tables in a database, because errors may result. Suppose the customer address data were stored in both the Customers and Accounts tables. If a customer moved to a new address, it is possible that the address would be updated in only one of the two tables. The result would be inconsistent and unreliable data. Depending on which table served as the source for the output, either the new or the old address might be given to someone requesting the information. Storing the address in only one table is more reliable.

Creating and Modifying Tables

Tables can be created in a new blank database or in an existing database. You can create a table by:

STEP 1

- Typing a field name in a row in Design view.
- Entering table data into a new row in Datasheet view.
- Importing data from another database or application such as Excel.

Regardless of how a table is first created, you can always modify it later to include a new field or change an existing field. Figure 11.3 shows a table created by entering fields in Design view.

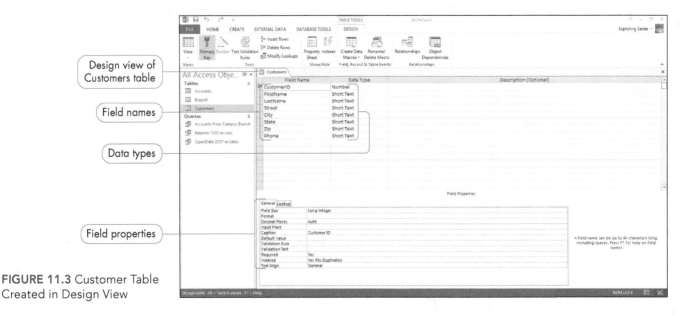

FIGURE 11.3 Customer Table Created in Design View

STEP 4

When you add a new field in Design view, the field must be given a field name to identify the data it holds. The field name should be descriptive of the data and can be up to 64 characters in length, including letters, numbers, and spaces. Database developers use *CamelCase notation* for field names. Instead of spaces in multiword field names, use uppercase letters to distinguish the first letter of each new word, for example, ProductCost or LastName. It is best to avoid spaces in field names, because spaces can cause problems when creating the other objects—such as queries, forms, and reports—based on tables.

Fields may be renamed either in Design view or in Datasheet view. In Design view, double-click the field name you want to change, type the new field name, and then click Save on the Quick Access Toolbar. To rename a field in Datasheet view, double-click the field selector of the field that you want to rename, type the new field name, and then press Enter.

Fields can be also be deleted in Design view or Datasheet view. To delete a field in Datasheet view, select the field or fields you want to delete and press Delete. To delete fields in Design view, do the following:

1. Click the Record Selector of the field you want to delete to select it.
2. Click Delete Rows in the Tools group.

3. Click Yes in the message box that appears if you want to permanently delete the field(s). Click No if you do not want to delete the field(s).

4. Click Yes in the second message box that will appear if the selected field you are deleting is a primary key. Click No if you do not want to delete the primary key.

 TIP Freeze Fields in an Access Database

To keep a field viewable while you are scrolling through a table, select the field or fields you want to freeze, right-click, and then click Freeze Fields. If you want the field(s) to remain frozen when you are finished working, save the changes when you close the table. To unfreeze all fields, right-click the field(s) and select Unfreeze All Fields.

Determine Data Type

Every field also has a *data type* property that determines the type of data that can be entered and the operations that can be performed on that data. Access recognizes 12 data types. Table 11.1 lists these data types, their uses, and examples of the data type.

TABLE 11.1 Data Types and Uses

Data Type	Description	Example
Short Text	Stores alphanumeric data, such as a customer's name or address. It can contain alphabetic characters, numbers, and/or special characters (e.g., an apostrophe in O'Malley). Social Security numbers, telephone numbers, and postal codes should be designated as text fields since they are not used in calculations and often contain special characters such as hyphens and parentheses. A short text field can hold up to 255 characters. Formerly Text data type.	2184 Walnut Street
Long Text	Lengthy text or combinations of text and numbers, such as several sentences or paragraphs; used to hold descriptive data. Formerly Memo data type.	A description of product packaging
Number	Contains a value that can be used in a calculation, such as the number of credits a course is worth. The contents are restricted to numbers, a decimal point, and a plus or minus sign.	12
Date/Time	Holds dates or times and enables the values to be used in date or time arithmetic.	10/31/2016 1:30:00 AM
Currency	Used for fields that contain monetary values.	$1,200
AutoNumber	A special data type used to assign the next consecutive number each time you add a record. The value of an AutoNumber field is unique for each record in the file.	1, 2, 3
Yes/No	Assumes one of two values, such as Yes or No, True or False, or On or Off (also known as a Boolean). For example, is a student on the Dean's list: Yes or No.	Yes
OLE Object	Contains an object created by another application. OLE objects include spreadsheets, pictures, sounds, and graphics.	JPG image
Hyperlink	Stores a Web address (URL) or the path to a folder or file. Hyperlink fields can be clicked to retrieve a Web page or to launch a file stored locally.	http://www.keithmast.com
Attachment	Used to store multiple images, spreadsheet files, Word documents, and other types of supported files.	An Excel workbook
Calculated	The results of an expression that references one or more existing fields.	[IntRate] + 0.25
Lookup Wizard	Creates a field that enables you to choose a value from another table or from a list of values by using a list box or a combo box.	Customers table with an AccountID field that looks up the Account ID from an Accounts table

Establish a Primary Key

STEP 2» As you learned earlier, the primary key is the field (or combination of fields) that uniquely identifies each record in a table. Access does not require that each table have a primary key. However, good database design usually includes a primary key in each table. You should select unique and infrequently changing data for the primary key. For example, a complete address (street, city, state, and postal code) may be unique but would not make a good primary key because it is subject to change when someone moves.

You probably would not use a person's name as the primary key, because several people could have the same name. A customer's account number, on the other hand, is unique and is a frequent choice for the primary key, as in the Customers table in this chapter. The primary key can be easily identified in many tables—for example, a PartNumber in a parts table, the ISBN in the book database of a bookstore, or a StudentID that uniquely identifies a student. When no primary key occurs naturally, you can create a primary key field with the AutoNumber data type. The *AutoNumber* data type is a number that automatically increments each time a record is added.

In Figure 11.4, the book's ISBN is the natural primary key for the book table because no two book titles can have the same ISBN. This field uniquely identifies the records in the table. Figure 11.5 depicts the Speakers table, where no unique field can be identified from the data. Because of this, you can add the SpeakerID field with an AutoNumber data type. Access automatically numbers each speaker record sequentially with a unique ID as each record is added.

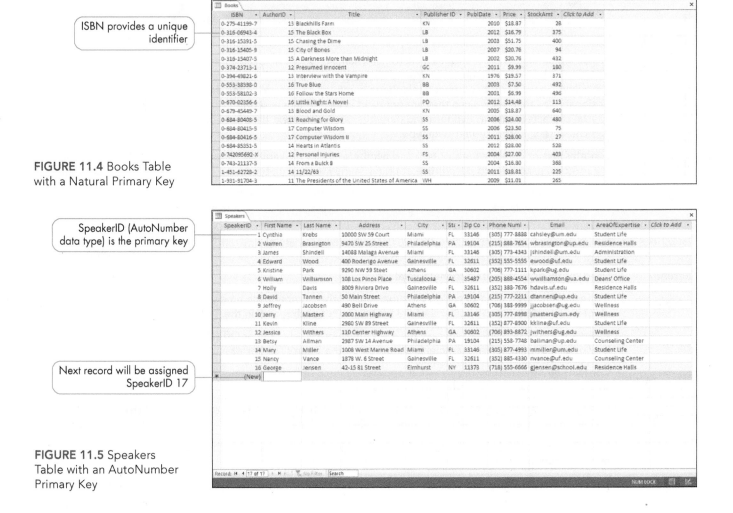

FIGURE 11.4 Books Table with a Natural Primary Key

ISBN provides a unique identifier

SpeakerID (AutoNumber data type) is the primary key

Next record will be assigned SpeakerID 17

FIGURE 11.5 Speakers Table with an AutoNumber Primary Key

Explore a Foreign Key

A *foreign key* is a field in one table that is also the primary key of another table. The CustomerID is the primary key in the Customers table. It serves to uniquely identify each customer. It also appears as a foreign key in a related table. For example, the Accounts table contains the CustomerID field to establish which customer owns the account. A CustomerID can appear only once in the Customers table, but it may appear multiple times in the Accounts table (when viewed in Datasheet view) because one customer may own multiple accounts (checking, money market, home equity). Therefore, the CustomerID is the primary key in the Customers table and a foreign key in the Accounts table.

If you were asked to create an Access database for the speakers at a national conference, you would create a database with the tables Speakers and SessionSpeaker. You would add a primary key field to the Speakers table (SpeakerID) along with a speaker's FirstName and LastName fields; you would also add two fields to the SessionSpeaker table (SpeakerID and SessionID). The SpeakerID field in the Speakers table is a primary key and would not allow duplicates; the SpeakerID field in the SessionSpeaker table is a foreign key and would allow duplicates so that a speaker may speak more than once at the conference. The SpeakerID in the SessionSpeaker table enables you to join the two tables in a relationship. Figure 11.6 shows portions of the Speakers and SessionSpeaker tables.

SpeakerID is the primary key of the Speakers table (no duplicates)

SpeakerID is a foreign key in the Session Speaker table so speakers can be assigned multiple sessions

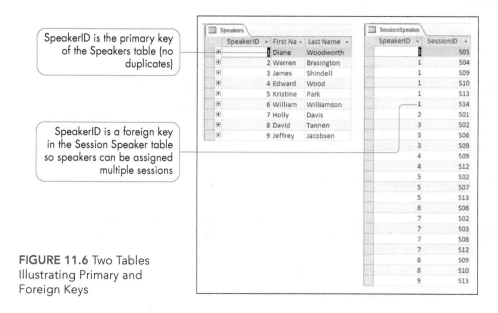

FIGURE 11.6 Two Tables Illustrating Primary and Foreign Keys

Work with Field Properties

STEP 3 》

While a field's data type determines the type of data that can be entered and the operations that can be performed on that data, it is its *field properties* that determine how the field looks and behaves.

Field Size is a commonly changed field property. A field with a *short text data type* can hold up to 255 characters; however, you can limit the characters by reducing the field size property. For example, you would limit the State field to only two characters because all state abbreviations are two letters. A field with a *number data type* can be set to Integer to display the field contents as integers from –32,768 to 32,768 or to Long Integer for larger values.

You can set a *caption property* to create a label more readable than a field. The caption displays at the top of a table or query column in Datasheet view and when the field is used in a report or form. For example, a field named ProductCostPerUnit could have the caption *Per Unit Product Cost*. Even if a caption is used, however, you must use the actual field name, ProductCostPerUnit, in any calculation.

TIP Best Fit Columns

If a field name is cut off in Datasheet view, you can adjust the column width by positioning the pointer on the vertical border on the right side of the column. When the pointer displays as a two-headed arrow, double-click the border. You can also click More in the Records group on the Home tab. Select Field Width and click Best Fit in the Column Width dialog box.

Set the validation rule property to restrict data entry in a field to ensure the correct type of data are entered or that the data do not violate other enforced properties. The *validation rule* checks the data entered when the user exits the field. If the data entered violate the validation rule, an error message displays and prevents the invalid data from being entered into the field. For example, if you have set the data type for a field as Number and then try to enter text in the field, you will receive an error message telling you that the value you entered does not match the Number data type in the column.

The field properties are set to default values according to the data type, but you can modify them if necessary. Common property types are defined in Table 11.2.

TABLE 11.2 Common Access Table Property Types and Descriptions

Property Type	Description
Field Size	Determines the maximum characters of a text field or the format of a number field.
Format	Changes the way a field is displayed or printed but does not affect the stored value.
Input Mask	Simplifies data entry by providing literal characters that are typed for every entry, such as hyphens in a Social Security Number or slashes in a date. It also imposes data validation by ensuring that data entered conform to the mask.
Caption	Enables an alternate name to be displayed other than the field name; alternate name appears in datasheets, forms, and reports.
Default Value	Enters automatically a predetermined value for a field each time a new record is added to the table. For example, if most customers live in Los Angeles, the default value for the City field could be set to Los Angeles to save data entry time and accuracy.
Validation Rule	Requires data entered to conform to a specified rule.
Validation Text	Specifies the error message that is displayed when the validation rule is violated.
Required	Indicates that a value for this field must be entered.
Allow Zero Length	Allows entry of zero length text strings ("") in a Hyperlink, or Short or Long Text fields.
Indexed	Increases the efficiency of a search on the designated field.
Expression	Used for calculated fields only. Enters the expression you want Access to evaluate and store.
Result Type	Used for calculated fields only. Enters the format for the calculated field results.

Enter Table Records in Datasheet View

STEP 5 >> While Design view is used to create and modify the table structure by enabling you to add and edit fields and set field properties, Datasheet view is used to add, edit, and delete records. As you have learned, the Datasheet view of an Access table resembles an Excel spreadsheet and displays data in a grid format—rows represent records and columns represent fields. Datasheet view indicates the current record using a gold border; you can select a record by clicking the record selector on the left side of each record. Use the new blank record (marked with an asterisk) at the end of the table to add a new record.

In Hands-On Exercise 1, you will create a new database and enter fields into a table. Then you will switch to the table's Design view to add additional fields and modify selected field properties of various fields within the table. Finally, you will enter data in the table in Datasheet view.

Quick Concepts

1. What is meant by "Design for now and the future" when designing database fields? *p. 541*

2. What is the difference between a primary key and a foreign key? *p. 547*

3. What is a field property? Which field property creates a more readable label that displays in the top row in Datasheet view and in forms and reports? *p. 547*

Hands-On Exercises

Watch the Video for this Hands-On Exercise!

MyITLab®
HOE1 Training

1 Table Design, Creation, and Modification

Assisting the bank auditor at Commonwealth Federal Bank as he investigates the mishandled funds will be a great opportunity for you to showcase your Access skills. Be sure to check your work each step of the way, because your work will come under substantial scrutiny. Do a good job with this Access project and more opportunities might come your way.

Skills covered: Create a Table in Datasheet View • Delete a Field and Set a Table's Primary Key • Work with Field Properties • Create a New Field in Design View • Modify the Table in Datasheet View

STEP 1 ≫ CREATE A TABLE IN DATASHEET VIEW

You create a new desktop database to store information about the mishandled funds database. You enter the data for the first record (BranchID, Manager, and Location). Refer to Figure 11.7 as you complete Step 1.

Step h: Type the data directly into the datasheet

Step i: Save the table as Branch

FIGURE 11.7 Enter Data into the Branch Table in Datasheet View

a. Start Microsoft Office Access 2013 and click **Blank desktop database**.

b. Type **a02h1Bank_LastFirst** into the **File Name box**.

c. Click **Browse** to find the folder location designated by your instructor and click **OK**. Click **Create** to create the new database.

   Access will create the new database named *a02h1Bank_LastFirst* and a new table will automatically open in Datasheet view.

d. Click **Click to Add** and select **Short Text** as the Data type.

   Click to Add changes to *Field1*. *Field1* is selected to make it easier to change the field name.

e. Type **BranchID** and press **Tab**.

   A list of Data types for the third column opens so that you can select the data type for the third column.

f. Select **Short Text**, type **Manager**, and then press **Tab**.

g. Select **Short Text**, type **Location**, and then click in the first column next to the New Record asterisk.

h. Enter the data for the new table as shown in Figure 11.7, letting Access assign the ID field for each new record. Replace *YourLastName* with your own last name.

   Entering data in Datasheet view provides an easy way to create the table initially. You can now modify the table in Design view as described in the next several steps.

i. Click **Save** on the Quick Access Toolbar. Type **Branch** in the **Save As dialog box** and click **OK**.

STEP 2 ≫ DELETE A FIELD AND SET A TABLE'S PRIMARY KEY

It is possible to modify tables even after data have been entered; however, pay attention to the messages from Access after you make a design change. In this step, you will be modifying the Branch table. You examine the design of the table and realize that the BranchID field is a unique identifier, making the ID field redundant. You delete the ID field and make the BranchID field the primary key field. Refer to Figure 11.8 as you complete Step 2.

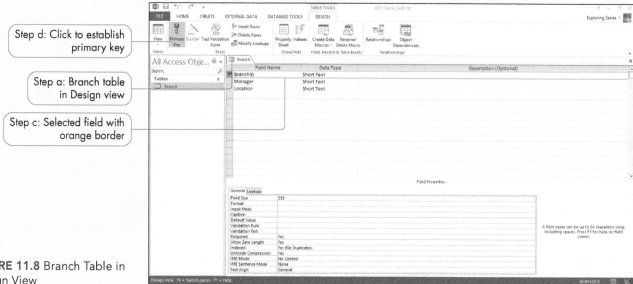

Step d: Click to establish primary key

Step a: Branch table in Design view

Step c: Selected field with orange border

FIGURE 11.8 Branch Table in Design View

a. Click **View** in the Views group to switch to the Design view of the Branch table.

The Field Name for each of the four fields displays along with the Data Type.

b. Click the **ID field** to select it, if necessary. Click **Delete Rows** in the Tools group. Click **Yes** to both warning messages.

Access responds with a warning that you are about to permanently delete a field and a second warning that the field is the primary key. You delete the field because you will set the BranchID field as the primary key.

c. Click the **BranchID field,** if necessary.

The cell field name now has a orange border, as shown in Figure 11.8.

d. Click **Primary Key** in the Tools group on the DESIGN tab.

You set the BranchID as the primary key. The Indexed property in the *Field Properties* section at the bottom of the design window displays *Yes (No Duplicates)*.

e. Click **Save** on the Quick Access Toolbar to save the table.

 **Shortcut Menu**

You can right-click a row selector to display a shortcut menu to copy a field, set the primary key, insert or delete rows, or to access field properties. Use the shortcut menu to make these specific changes to the design of a table.

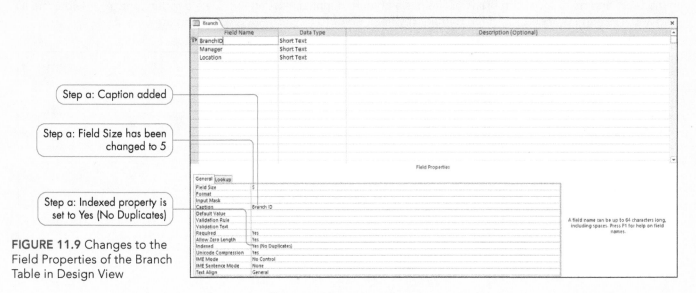

STEP 3 ≫ WORK WITH FIELD PROPERTIES

You need to modify the table design further to comply with the bank auditor's specifications. Be aware of messages from Access that indicate you may lose data. Refer to Figure 11.9 as you complete Step 3.

Step a: Caption added

Step a: Field Size has been changed to 5

Step a: Indexed property is set to Yes (No Duplicates)

FIGURE 11.9 Changes to the Field Properties of the Branch Table in Design View

a. Click the **BranchID field name** in the top section of the design window; modify the BranchID field properties in the bottom of the design window.

- Click in the **Field Size property** and change *255* to **5**.
- Click in the **Caption property** and type **Branch ID**. Make sure *Branch* and *ID* have a space between them.
  A caption provides a more descriptive field name. It will appear as the column heading in Datasheet view.
- Check the Indexed property; confirm it is *Yes (No Duplicates)*.

b. Click the **Manager field name** at the top of the window; modify the following field properties:

- Click in the **Field Size property** and change *255* to **30**.
- Click in the **Caption property** and type **Manager's Name**.

c. Click the **Location field name** and modify the following field properties:

- Click in the **Field Size property** and change *255* to **30**.
- Click in the **Caption property** and type **Branch Location**.

STEP 4 ≫ CREATE A NEW FIELD IN DESIGN VIEW

You notify the auditor that a date field is missing in your new table. Modify the table to add the new field. The data can be entered at a later time. Refer to Figure 11.10 as you complete Step 4.

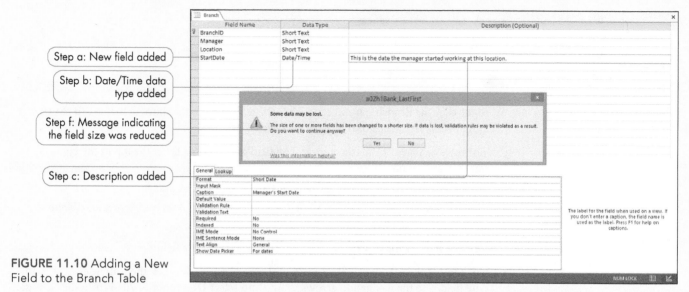

FIGURE 11.10 Adding a New Field to the Branch Table

Step a: New field added

Step b: Date/Time data type added

Step f: Message indicating the field size was reduced

Step c: Description added

a. Click in the first blank row below the Location field name and type **StartDate**.

You added a new field to the table.

b. Press **Tab** to move to the Data Type column. Click the **Data Type arrow** and select **Date/Time**.

TIP **Keyboard Shortcut for Data Types**

You also can type the first letter of the data type, such as d for Date/Time, s for Short Text, or n for Number. To use the keyboard shortcut, click on the field name and press Tab to advance to the Data Type column. Next, type the first letter of the data type.

---

c. Press **Tab** to move to the Description column and type **This is the date the manager started working at this location.**

d. Click the **Format property**, click the arrow, and then select **Short Date** from the list of date formats.

e. Click in the **Caption property** and type **Manager's Start Date**.

f. Click **Save** on the Quick Access Toolbar.

A warning dialog box opens to indicate that "Some data may be lost" because the size of the BranchID, Manager, and Location field properties were shortened. It asks if you want to continue anyway. Always read the Access warning! In this case, you can click Yes to continue because you know that the existing data are no longer than the new field sizes.

g. Click **Yes** in the warning box.

STEP 5 » MODIFY THE TABLE IN DATASHEET VIEW

As you work with the auditor, you will modify tables in the bank database from time to time. To modify the table, you will need to switch between Design view and Datasheet view. Refer to Figure 11.11 as you complete Step 5.

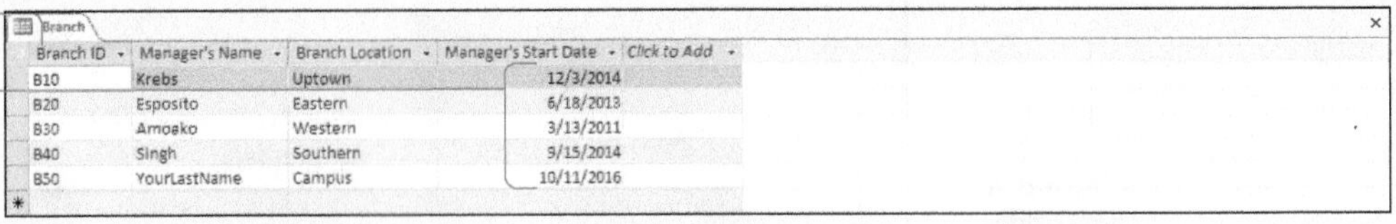

Step b: Expanded fields

Step d: Start dates

FIGURE 11.11 Start Dates
Added to the Branch Table

Branch ID ▾	Manager's Name ▾	Branch Location ▾	Manager's Start Date ▾	Click to Add ▾
B10	Krebs	Uptown	12/3/2014	
B20	Esposito	Eastern	6/18/2013	
B30	Amosko	Western	3/13/2011	
B40	Singh	Southern	9/15/2014	
B50	YourLastName	Campus	10/11/2016	

a. Right-click the **Branch tab** and select **Datasheet View** from the shortcut menu. (To return to Design view, right-click the tab again and select Design view.)

The table displays in Datasheet view. The field captions display at the top of the columns, but they are cut off.

b. Double-click the border between *Branch ID* and *Manager's Name*, the border between *Manager's Name* and *Branch Location*, the border between *Branch Location* and *Manager's Start Date*, and the border after *Manager's Start Date*.

The columns shrink or expand to display the best fit for the field name.

c. Click inside the **Manager's Start Date** in the first record and click the **Calendar** next to the date field. Use the navigation arrows to find and select **December 3, 2014** from the calendar.

You can also enter the dates by typing them directly into the StartDate field.

d. Type the start date directly in each field for the rest of the managers, as shown in Figure 11.11.

e. Click the **Close (X) button** at the top-right corner of the datasheet, below the Ribbon.

TROUBLESHOOTING: If you accidentally click the Close (X) button on top of the Ribbon, you will exit Access completely. To start again, launch Access and click the first file in the Recent list.

---

f. Double-click the **Branch table** in the Navigation Pane to open the table. Check the start dates.

The start dates are still there even though you did not save your work in the previous step. Access saves the data to your storage location as soon as you move off the current record or close an object.

g. Click the **FILE tab**, click **Print**, and then click **Print Preview**.

Occasionally, users will print an Access table. However, database developers usually create reports to print table data.

h. Click **Close Print Preview** and close the Branch table.

i. Keep the database open if you plan to continue with Hands-On Exercise 2. If not, close the database and exit Access.

Multiple-Table Databases

In Figure 11.1, the sample bank database contains three tables—Customers, Accounts, and Branch. You created one table, the Branch table, in the previous section using the Datasheet view and modified the table fields in Design view. You will create the two remaining tables using a different method—importing data from Excel. In this section, you will learn how to import data from Excel, modify tables, create indexes, create relationships between tables, and enforce referential integrity.

Sharing Data

Most companies store some type of data in Excel spreadsheets. Often, the data stored in those spreadsheets can be more efficiently managed in an Access database. Fortunately, Access provides you with a wizard that guides you through the process of importing data from Excel. The wizard can also guide you as you import data from other Access databases. You can import tables, queries, forms, reports, pages, macros, and modules from another database.

Import an Excel Spreadsheet

STEP 1 »
STEP 2 »

Figures 11.12 through 11.17 show the steps of the Get External Data – Excel Spreadsheet feature. Launch the feature by clicking the External Data tab and clicking Excel in the Import & Link group. Figure 11.12 shows the first screen of the Get External Data – Excel Spreadsheet feature. In this step, you specify the source of the data. Locate the Excel file you want to import by clicking Browse. Then choose between three options for the incoming data: *Import the source data into a new table in the current database*; *Append a copy of the records to the table*, which adds the data to an existing table; or *Link to the data source by creating a linked table*, which creates a link to the Excel source. Importing or appending data stores a copy of the data in Access, whereas linking the data keeps the data in the original file and Access retrieves the data each time the database is opened.

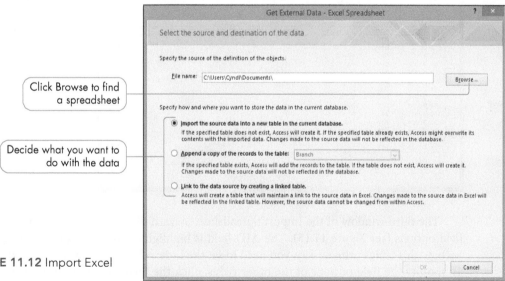

Click Browse to find a spreadsheet

Decide what you want to do with the data

FIGURE 11.12 Import Excel Data

After you locate and select an Excel workbook, accept the default option (*Import the source data into a new table in the current database*) and click OK. The Import Spreadsheet Wizard dialog box launches and displays a list of the worksheets in the specified workbook. Select the worksheet you want to import and click Next. Figure 11.13 shows the Accounts worksheet selected. The bottom of the Import Spreadsheet Wizard dialog box displays a preview of the data stored in the specified worksheet.

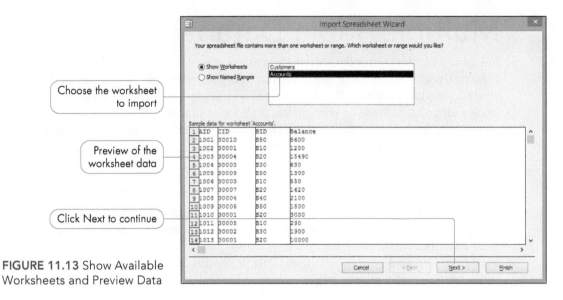

Choose the worksheet to import

Preview of the worksheet data

Click Next to continue

FIGURE 11.13 Show Available Worksheets and Preview Data

Although a well-designed spreadsheet may include descriptive column headings that can be used as field names, not all spreadsheets are ready to import. You may have to revise the spreadsheet before importing it. The second window of the Import Spreadsheet Wizard dialog box contains a check box that enables you to convert the first row of column headings to field names in Access (see Figure 11.14). If a column heading row exists in the spreadsheet, check the box. If no column headings exist, leave the check box unchecked, and the data will import using Field1, Field2, Field3, and so forth as the field names.

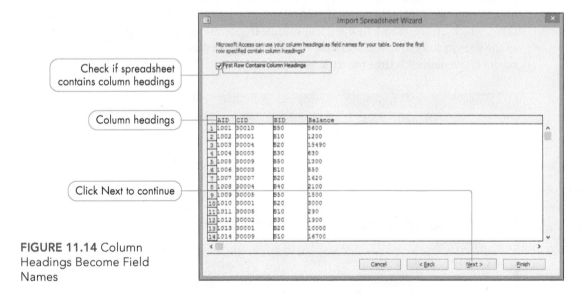

Check if spreadsheet contains column headings

Column headings

Click Next to continue

FIGURE 11.14 Column Headings Become Field Names

The third window of the Import Spreadsheet Wizard dialog box enables you to specify field options (see Figure 11.15). The AID field is highlighted in this figure. Because it will become this table's primary key, you need to set the Indexed Property to *Yes (No Duplicates)*. To modify the field options of the other fields, click the Field Name column heading and make the changes. Not all Access table properties are supported by the wizard. You may need to open the table in Design view after importing it to make any additional field property changes.

When you set the primary key in Access, the *indexed property* is automatically set to *Yes (No Duplicates)*. The indexed property setting enables quick sorting in primary key order and quick retrieval based on the primary key. For non–primary key fields, it may be beneficial to set the Indexed property to *Yes (Duplicates OK)*. Again, Access uses indexing to sort and retrieve data quickly based on the indexed field. As a general rule, indexed fields are usually foreign keys and are numeric.

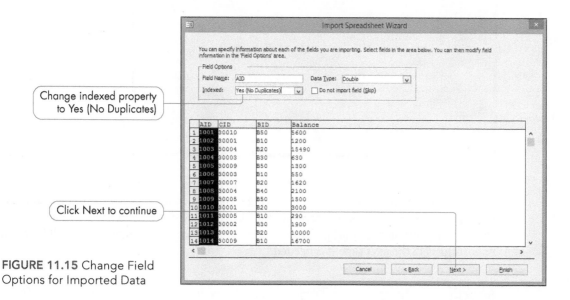

FIGURE 11.15 Change Field Options for Imported Data

The fourth window of the Import Spreadsheet Wizard dialog box enables you to choose a primary key before the import takes place (see Figure 11.16). If the option *Let Access add primary key* is selected, Access will generate an AutoNumber field and designate it as the primary key. Otherwise, you can designate a field to be the primary key or choose to have no primary key. In the import depicted in the Figure 11.16, the Excel data have a unique identifier (AID) that will become the table's primary key.

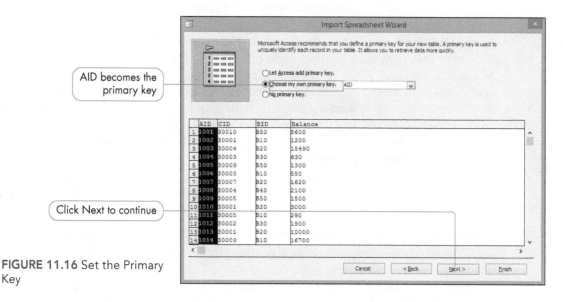

FIGURE 11.16 Set the Primary Key

Use the final window of the Import Spreadsheet Wizard to name the Access table. If the worksheet in the Excel workbook was named, Access uses the worksheet name as the table name (see Figure 11.17).

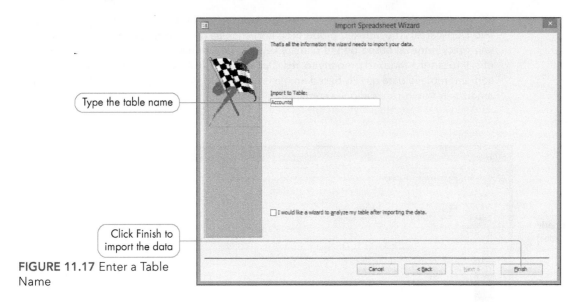

Type the table name

Click Finish to import the data

FIGURE 11.17 Enter a Table Name

Finally, the Wizard will ask if you wish to save the import steps. If the same worksheet is imported from Excel to Access on a recurring basis, you could save the parameters and use them again. To save the import steps, such as the indexing option and any new field names, click Save Import Steps in the Save Import Steps group. Saving the import steps will help you import the data the next time it is needed.

Modify an Imported Table's Design and Add Data

STEP 3 >> Importing data saves typing and prevents errors that may occur while entering data, but modifications will usually be required. After you have imported a table, open the table and examine the design to see if changes need to be made. You may need to modify the table by renaming fields so that they are more meaningful. To rename a field in Datasheet view, right-click the arrow next to the field name and click Rename Field. Type the new field name. To rename a field in Design view, select the field name and type the new name. In the bank example, you would change the name of the AID field to AccountID. Switch to Design view to modify the data type and field size.

STEP 4 >> You may need to add new fields or delete unnecessary fields. To add a new field in Datasheet view, right-click the field name to the right of where you want the new field to be added. Click Insert Field. To delete a field in Datasheet view, right-click the name of the field you want to delete and click Delete Field. To create a new field in Design view, click in the row below where you want the new field to be added and click Insert Rows in the Tools group on the Design tab. To delete a row in Design view, click in the row you want to delete and click Delete Rows in the Tools group on the Design tab. After making the modifications, you can add any data needed to the table.

Establishing Table Relationships

As previously discussed, the benefit of a relationship is to efficiently combine data from related tables for the purpose of creating queries, forms, and reports. Because this is such an important concept in designing and creating relational databases, this chapter reviews creating relationships and enforcing referential integrity. To ensure you are creating redundancy, you should store like data items together in the same table. In the example we are using, the customer data are stored in the Customers table. The Branch table stores data about the bank's branches, management, and locations. The Accounts table stores data about account ownership and balances.

STEP 5»
Once you have created the tables by storing like data items together, you will be able to recognize that some tables have common fields with others. Our Accounts table shares a common field with the Customers table—the CustomerID. It also shares a common field with the Branch table—BranchID. These common fields can be used to establish relationships between two tables.

Once you determine the common fields, you drag the field name from one table to the field name on the table you want to be joined.

Figure 11.18 shows the Bank database with relationships created by joining common fields.

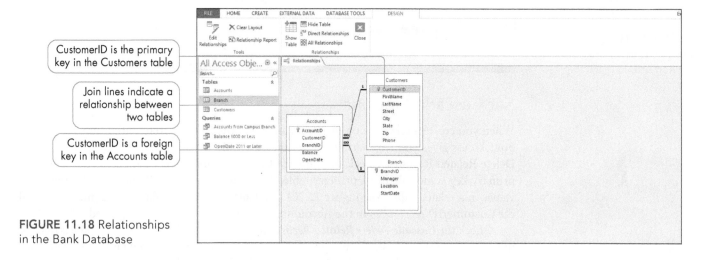

FIGURE 11.18 Relationships in the Bank Database

The primary key of a table plays a significant role when setting relationships. You cannot join two tables unless a primary key has been set in the primary table. In our Bank database, the CustomerID has been set as the primary key in the Customers table. Therefore, a relationship can be set between the Customers table and the Accounts table. Similarly, the Branch table can be joined to the Accounts table because BranchID has been set as the primary key in the Branch table.

The other side of the relationship join line is most often a foreign key of the related table. A foreign key is a field in one table that is also the primary key of another table. In the previous example, CustomerID in the Accounts table is a foreign key; BranchID in the Accounts table is a foreign key. Relationships between tables will almost always be set using primary and foreign keys.

Establish Referential Integrity

When you create a relationship in Access, the Edit Relationships dialog box displays. The first check box, Enforce Referential Integrity, should be checked in most cases. Remember, *referential integrity* enforces rules in a database that are used to preserve relationships between tables when records are changed.

STEP 6»
When referential integrity is enforced, you cannot enter a foreign key value in a related table unless the primary key value exists in the primary table. In the case of the Bank database, a customer's account information (which includes CustomerID) cannot be entered into the Accounts table unless the customer information is first entered into the Customers table. If you attempt to enter an account prior to entering the customer information, an error will appear, as shown in Figure 11.19. When referential integrity is enforced, you cannot delete a record in one table if it has related records.

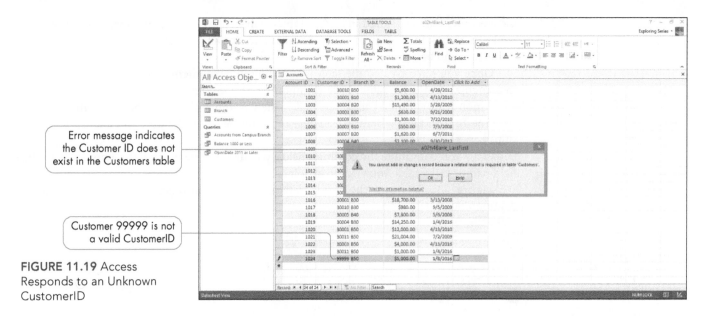

Error message indicates the Customer ID does not exist in the Customers table

Customer 99999 is not a valid CustomerID

FIGURE 11.19 Access Responds to an Unknown CustomerID

Set Cascade Options

When you create a relationship in Access and click the Enforce Referential Integrity checkbox, Access gives you two additional options: Cascade Update Related Fields and Cascade Delete Related Records. Check the *Cascade Update Related Fields* option so that when the primary key is modified in a primary table, Access will automatically update all foreign key values in a related table (see Figure 11.20). If a CustomerID is updated for some reason, all the CustomerID references in the Accounts table will automatically be updated.

Check the *Cascade Delete Related Records* option so that when the primary key is deleted in a primary table, Access will automatically delete all records in related tables that reference the primary key (see Figure 11.20). If one branch of a bank closes and its record is deleted from the Branch table, any account that still remains with this branch would be deleted. Access will give a warning first and enable you to avoid the action. This may be a desired business rule, but it should be set with caution.

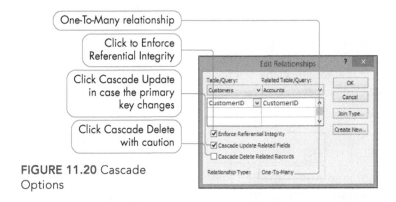

One-To-Many relationship

Click to Enforce Referential Integrity

Click Cascade Update in case the primary key changes

Click Cascade Delete with caution

FIGURE 11.20 Cascade Options

Establish a One-to-Many Relationship

Figure 11.20 also shows that the relationship that will be created will be a one-to-many relationship. Access provides three different relationships for joining your data: one-to-one, one-to-many, and many-to-many. The most common type by far is the one-to-many relationship. A *one-to-many relationship* is established when the primary key value in the primary table can match many of the foreign key values in the related table.

For example, a bank customer will be entered into the Customers table once and only once. The primary key value, which is also the customer's CustomerID number, might be 1585. That same customer could set up a checking, savings, and money market account.

With each account, the CustomerID (1585) is required and therefore will occur three times in the Accounts table. The value appears once in the Customers table and three times in the Accounts table. Therefore, the relationship between Customers and Accounts would be described as one to many.

Table 11.3 lists and describes all three types of relationships you can create between Access tables.

TABLE 11.3	Relationship Types
Relationship Type	**Description**
One-to-Many	The primary key table must have only one occurrence of each value. For example, each customer must have a unique identification number in the Customers table, or each employee must have a unique EmployeeID in the Employee table. The foreign key field in the second table may have repeating values. For example, one customer may have many different account numbers, or one employee can perform many services.
One-to-One	Two different tables use the same primary key. Exactly one record exists in the second table for each record in the first table. Sometimes security reasons require a table be split into two related tables. For example, anyone in the company can look in the Employee table and find the employee's office number, department assignment, or telephone extension. However, only a few people need to have access to the employee's network login password, salary, Social Security number, performance review, or marital status. Tables containing this information would use the same unique identifier to identify each employee.
Many-to-Many	This is an artificially constructed relationship giving many matching records in each direction between tables. It requires construction of a third table called a junction table. For example, a database might have a table for employees and one for projects. Several employees might be assigned to one project, but one employee might also be assigned to many different projects. When Access connects to databases using Oracle or other software, you find this relationship type.

Figure 11.21 shows the Relationships window for the Bank database and all the relationships created using referential integrity. The join line between the CustomerID field in the Customers table and the CustomerID field in the Accounts table indicates that a one-to-many relationship has been set. You can rearrange the tables by dragging the tables by the title bar. You can switch the positions of the Branch and Accounts tables in the Relationships window without changing the relationship itself.

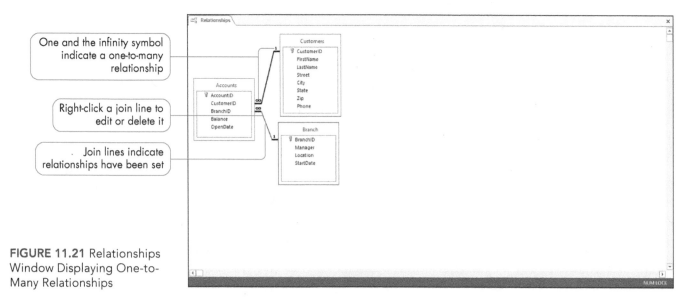

One and the infinity symbol indicate a one-to-many relationship

Right-click a join line to edit or delete it

Join lines indicate relationships have been set

FIGURE 11.21 Relationships Window Displaying One-to-Many Relationships

TIP **Navigating Between the Relationships Window and a Table's Design**

When you right-click on a table's title bar in the Relationships window, the shortcut menu offers you a chance to open the table in Design view. This is a convenient feature because if you want to link one table to another table, the joined fields must have the same data type. This shortcut enables you to check the fields and revise them if necessary if a table contains a field with the wrong data type.

In the following Hands-On Exercise, you will create two additional tables in the Bank database by importing data from an Excel spreadsheet and from an Access database. You will establish and modify field properties. Then you will connect the newly imported data to the Branch table by establishing relationships between the tables.

 Quick Concepts

1. Describe a scenario that may require you to import Excel data into Access. *p. 555*

2. What is the purpose of setting a relationship between two tables? *p. 558*

3. Why would you enforce referential integrity when setting a relationship? *p. 559*

4. Give an example of two database tables that would contain a one-to-many relationship. Describe the relationship. *pp. 560–561*

Hands-On Exercises

2 Multiple-Table Databases

You created a new Bank database, and you created a new Branch table. Now you are ready to import additional tables—one from an Excel spreadsheet and one from an Access database. Assume that the data are formatted correctly and are structured properly so that you can begin the import process.

Skills covered: Import Excel Data • Import Data from an Access Database • Modify an Imported Table's Design and Add Data • Add Data to an Imported Table • Establish Table Relationships • Test Referential Integrity

---

STEP 1 >> IMPORT EXCEL DATA

You and the auditor have discovered several of Commonwealth's files that contain customer data. These files need to be analyzed, so you decide to import the data into Access. In this exercise, you import an Excel spreadsheet into the Bank database. Refer to Figure 11.22 as you complete Step 1.

FIGURE 11.22 Imported Customers Table

a. Open *a02h1Bank_LastFirst* if you closed it at the end of Hands-On Exercise 1. Click the **FILE tab**, click **Save As**, and then click **Save As** in the *Save Database As* section. Type **a02h2Bank_LastFirst**, changing *h1 to h2*. Click **Save**.

b. If necessary, click **Enable Content** below the Ribbon to indicate you trust the contents of the database

> **TROUBLESHOOTING:** If you make any major mistakes in this exercise, you can close the file, open *a02h1Bank_LastFirst* again, and then start this exercise over.

c. Click the **EXTERNAL DATA tab** and click **Excel** in the Import & Link group to launch the Get External Data – Excel Spreadsheet feature. Select the **Import the source data into a new table in the current database option**, if necessary.

d. Click **Browse** and go to the student data folder. Select the *a02h2Customers* workbook. Click **Open** and click **OK** to open the Import Spreadsheet Wizard.

e. Ensure that the *First Row Contains Column Headings* check box is checked to tell Access that column headings exist in the Excel file.

The field names CID, FirstName, LastName, Street, City, State, ZIP, and Phone will import from Excel along with the data stored in the rows in the worksheet. The field names will be modified later in Access.

f. Click **Next**.

g. Ensure that *CID* is displayed in the Field Name box in Field Options. Click the **Indexed arrow** and select **Yes (No Duplicates)**. Click **Next**.

The CID (CustomerID) will become the primary key in this table. It needs to be a unique identifier, so we must change the properties to no duplicates.

h. Click the **Choose my own primary key option**. Make sure that the CID field is selected. Click **Next**.

The final screen of the Import Spreadsheet Wizard asks you to name your table. The name of the Excel worksheet was Customers, and Access defaults to the worksheet name. It is an acceptable name.

i. Click **Finish** to accept the Customers table name.

A dialog box opens asking if you wish to save the steps of this import to use again. If this were sales data that was collected in Excel and updated to the database on a weekly basis, saving the import steps would save time. You do not need to save this example.

j. Click the **Close (X) button**.

The new table displays in the Navigation Pane and resides in the Bank database.

k. Open the imported Customers table in Datasheet view and double-click the border between each of the field names to adjust the columns to Best fit. Compare your table to Figure 11.22.

l. Close the table.

STEP 2 >> IMPORT DATA FROM AN ACCESS DATABASE

The Customers spreadsheet that you imported contains customer information. The auditor asks you to import an Access database table that contains account information related to the mishandled funds. You use the Import Wizard to import the database table. Refer to Figure 11.23 as you complete Step 2.

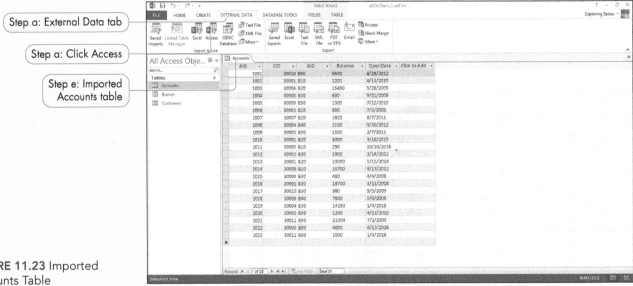

FIGURE 11.23 Imported Accounts Table

a. Click the **EXTERNAL DATA tab** and click **Access** in the Import & Link group to launch the Get External Data – Access Database feature. Select the **Import tables, queries, forms, reports, macros, and modules into the current database option**, if necessary.

b. Click **Browse** and go to the student data folder. Select the *a02h2Accounts* database. Click **Open** and click **OK** to open the Import Objects dialog box.

The Accounts table is active; you will import this table.

c. Ensure that the Accounts table is selected and click **OK**.

d. Click **Close** on the Save Import Steps dialog box.

The Navigation Pane contains three tables: Accounts, Branch, and Customers.

e. Open the imported Accounts table in Datasheet view and compare it to Figure 11.23.

STEP 3 >> MODIFY AN IMPORTED TABLE'S DESIGN AND ADD DATA

When importing tables from either Excel or Access, the fields may have different data types and property settings than required to create table relationships. You need to modify the tables so that each field has the correct data type and field size. Refer to Figure 11.24 as you complete Step 3.

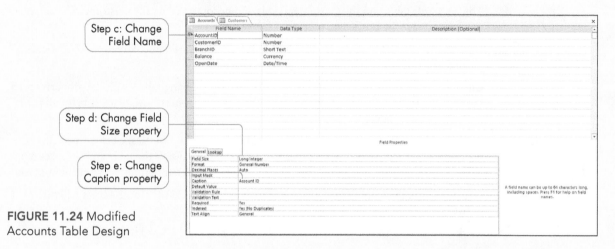

FIGURE 11.24 Modified Accounts Table Design

a. Right-click the **Accounts table** in the Navigation Pane.

b. Click **Design View** to open the table in Design view.

The Accounts table displays with the primary key AID selected.

c. Change the AID field name to **AccountID**.

d. Change the Field Size property to **Long Integer** in the Field Properties at the bottom of the Design window.

Long Integer ensures that there will be enough numbers as the number of customers grows over time and may exceed 32,768 (the upper limit for Integer values).

e. Type **Account ID** in the **Caption property box** for the AccountID field. The caption contains a space between *Account* and *ID*.

f. Change the CID field name to **CustomerID**.

g. Change the Field Size property to **Long Integer** in the Field Properties at the bottom of the Design window.

You can select the Field Size option using the arrow, or you can type the first letter of the option you want. For example, type l for Long Integer or s for Single. Make sure the current option is completely selected before you type the letter.

h. Type **Customer ID** in the **Caption property box** for the CustomerID field. The caption contains a space between *Customer* and *ID*.

i. Click the **BID field**. Change the BID field name to **BranchID**.

j. Type **5** in the **Field Size property box** in the Field Properties.

k. Type **Branch ID** in the **Caption property box** for the Branch ID field.

l. Change the Data Type of the Balance field to **Currency**.

The Currency data type is used for fields that contain monetary values.

m. Change the Data Type of the OpenDate field to **Date/Time** and add **Short Date** in the Format field property. Type **Open Date** in the **Caption property box**.

The OpenDate field stores the date that each account was opened.

n. Click **View** in the Views group to switch to Datasheet view. Read the messages and click **Yes** twice.

In this case, it is OK to click Yes because the shortened fields will not cut off any data. Leave the table open.

o. Right-click the **Customers table** in the Navigation Pane and select **Design View** from the shortcut menu.

p. Change the CID field name to **CustomerID**. Change the Field Size property of the CustomerID field to **Long Integer** and add a caption, **Customer ID**. Take note of the intentional space between *Customer* and *ID*.

The Accounts table and the Customers table will be joined using the CustomerID field. Both fields must have the same data type.

q. Change the Field Size property to **20** for the FirstName, LastName, Street, and City fields. Change the Field Size for State to **2**.

r. Change the data type for ZIP and Phone to **Short Text**. Change the Field size property to **15** for both fields. Remove the @ symbol from the Format property where it exists for all fields in the Customers table.

s. Click the **Phone field name** and click **Input Mask** in Field Properties. Click **ellipsis (...)** on the right side to launch the Input Mask Wizard. Click **Yes** to save the table and click **Yes** to the *Some data may be lost* warning. Click **Finish** to apply the default phone number Input Mask.

The phone number input mask enables users to enter 6105551212, and Access will display it as (610)555-1212.

t. Click **Save** to save the design changes to the Customers table. Read the warning box and click **Yes**.

STEP 4 ≫ ADD DATA TO AN IMPORTED TABLE

Now that you have created the Access tables, you add records. You may also need to update and delete records if you and the auditor decide the information is no longer needed. Refer to Figure 11.25 as you complete Step 4.

Step b: Enter yourself as a new customer

FIGURE 11.25 Customers Table Displaying Your Information

a. Click **View** in the Views group to display the Customers table in Datasheet view.

The asterisk at the bottom of the table data in the row selector area is the indicator of a place to enter a new record.

b. Click the **Customer ID field** in the record after *30010*. Type **30011**. Fill in the rest of the data using your information as the customer. You may use a fictitious address and phone number.

Note the phone number format. The input mask you set formats the phone number.

c. Close the Customers table. The Accounts table tab is open.

> **TROUBLESHOOTING:** If the Accounts table is not open, double-click Accounts in the Navigation Pane.

d. Locate the new record indicator—the * in the row selector—and click in the **Account ID** column. Type **1024**. Type **30011** as the Customer ID and **B50** as the Branch ID. Type **14005** for the Balance field value. Type **8/7/2015** for the OpenDate.

e. Add the following records to the Accounts table:

Account ID	Customer ID	Branch ID	Balance	Open Date
1025	30006	B40	$11,010	3/13/2013
1026	30007	B20	$7,400	5/1/2014

f. Close the Accounts table; keep the database open.

STEP 5 ≫ ESTABLISH TABLE RELATIONSHIPS

The tables for the bank investigation have been designed. Now you will need to establish connections between the tables. Look at the primary and foreign keys as a guide. Refer to Figure 11.26 as you complete Step 5.

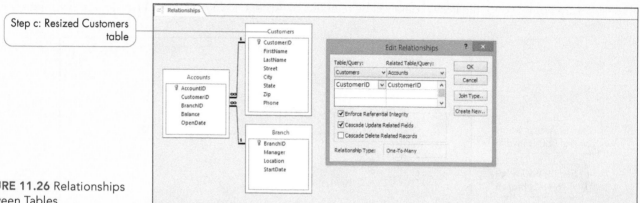

FIGURE 11.26 Relationships Between Tables

a. Click the **DATABASE TOOLS tab** and click **Relationships** in the Relationships group.

The Relationships window opens and the Show Table dialog box appears.

> **TROUBLESHOOTING:** If the Show Table dialog box does not open, click Show Table in the Relationships group on the Relationships Tools Design tab.

b. Double-click each of the three tables displayed in the Show Table dialog box to add them to the Relationships window. (Alternatively, click a table and click **Add**.) Click **Close** in the Show Table dialog box.

> **TROUBLESHOOTING:** If you have a duplicate table, click the title bar of the duplicated table and press Delete.

c. Resize the Customers table box so all of the fields are visible. Arrange the tables as shown in Figure 11.26.

d. Drag the **BranchID field** in the Branch table onto the BranchID field in the Accounts table. The Edit Relationships dialog box opens. Click the **Enforce Referential Integrity** and **Cascade Update Related Fields check boxes**. Click **Create**.

A black line displays, joining the two tables. It has a 1 at the end near the Branch table and an infinity symbol on the end next to the Accounts table. You have established a one-to-many relationship between the Branch and Accounts tables.

e. Drag the **CustomerID field** in the Customers table onto the CustomerID field in the Accounts table. The Edit Relationships dialog box opens. Click the **Enforce Referential Integrity** and **Cascade Update Related Fields check boxes**. Click **Create**.

You have established a one-to-many relationship between the Customers and Accounts tables. A customer will have only a single CustomerID number. The same customer may have many different accounts: Savings, Checking, CDs, and so forth.

> **TROUBLESHOOTING:** If you get an error message when you click Create, verify that the data types of the joined fields are the same. To check the data types from the Relationships window, right-click the title bar of a table and select Table Design from the shortcut menu. Modify the data type and field size of the join fields if necessary.

    f. Click **Save** on the Quick Access Toolbar to save the changes to the relationships. Close the Relationships window.

STEP 6 » TEST REFERENTIAL INTEGRITY

The design of the Bank database must be 100% correct; otherwise, data entry may be compromised. Even though you are confident that the table relationships are correct, you decide to test them by entering some invalid data. If the relationships are not working, the invalid data will be rejected by Access. Refer to Figure 11.27 as you complete Step 6.

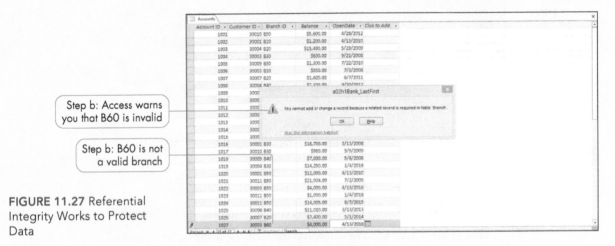

Step b: Access warns you that B60 is invalid

Step b: B60 is not a valid branch

FIGURE 11.27 Referential Integrity Works to Protect Data

    a. Double-click the **Accounts table** to open it in Datasheet view.

    b. Add a new record, pressing **Tab** after each field: Account ID: **1027**, Customer ID: **30003**, Branch: **B60**, Balance: **4000**, OpenDate: **4/13/2016**.

    You attempted to enter a nonexistent BranchID and were not allowed to make that error. A warning message is telling you that a related record in the Branch table is required because the Accounts table and the Branch table are connected by a relationship with Enforce Referential Integrity checked.

    c. Click **OK**. Double-click the **Branch table** in the Navigation Pane and examine the data in the BranchID field. Notice the Branch table has no B60 record. Close the Branch table.

    d. Replace *B60* with **B50** in the new Accounts record and press **Tab** three times. As soon as the focus moves to the next record, the pencil symbol disappears and your data are saved.

    You successfully identified a BranchID that Access recognizes. Because referential integrity between the Accounts and Branch tables has been enforced, Access looks at each data entry item in a foreign key and matches it to a corresponding value in the table where it is the primary key. In step b, you attempted to enter a nonexistent BranchID and were not allowed to make that error. In step d, you entered a valid BranchID. Access examined the index for the BranchID in the Branch table and found a corresponding value for B50.

    e. Close the Accounts table. Reopen the Accounts table; you will find that the record you just entered for 1027 has been saved. Close the table.

    You have established a one-to-many relationship between the Customers and Accounts tables. A customer will have only a single CustomerID number. The same customer may have many different accounts: Savings, Checking, CDs, and so forth.

    f. Close all open tables, if necessary.

    g. Keep the database open if you plan to continue with Hands-On Exercise 3. If not, close the database and exit Access.

Single-Table Queries

If you wanted to see which customers currently have an account with a balance over $5,000, you could find the answer by creating an Access query. A *query* enables you to ask questions about the data stored in a database and then provides the answers to the questions by providing subsets or summaries of data. Because data are stored in tables in a database, you always begin a query by asking, "Which table holds the data I want?" For the question about account balances over $5,000, you would reference the Accounts table. If you want to invite customers in a certain ZIP code to the Grand Opening of a new branch, you could create a query based on the Customers table.

You use the *Query Design view* to create queries. The Query Design view is divided into two parts: The top portion displays the tables, and the bottom portion (known as the query design grid) displays the fields and the criteria. You select only the fields you want arranged in the order that you want the resulting data displayed. The design grid also enables you to sort the records based on one or more fields. You can also create calculated fields to display data based on expressions that use the fields in the underlying table. For example, you could calculate the monthly interest earned on each bank account.

In this section, you will use the Query Design view and the Query Wizard to create queries that display only data that you select. Multitable queries will be covered in the next section.

Creating a Single-Table Query

You can create a single-table query in two ways—by using the Simple Query Wizard or the Query Design tool in the Queries group on the Create tab. The Query Design tool is the most flexible way to create a query. You can add criteria to a query while in the Query Design view. After you design a query, you can display the results of the query by switching to Datasheet view. A query's datasheet looks and acts like a table's datasheet, except that it is usually a subset of the records found in the entire table. The subset shows only the records that match the criteria that were added in the query design. The subset may contain different sorting of the records than the sorting in the underlying table. Datasheet view allows you to enter a new record, modify an existing record, or delete a record. Any changes made in Datasheet view are reflected in the underlying table that the query is based upon.

STEP 3 ⟫   Be aware that query results display the actual records that are stored in the underlying table(s). Being able to correct an error immediately while it is displayed in query results is an advantage. You save time by not having to close the query, open the table, find the error, fix it, and then run the query again. However, you should use caution when editing records in query results since you will be changing the table data.

Create a Single-Table Select Query

The Query Design tool is used to create *select queries*, a type of query that displays only the records that match criteria entered in Query Design view. To create a select query using the Query Design tool, do the following:

STEP 2 ⟫
1. Click the CREATE tab.
2. Click Query Design in the Queries group.
3. Select the table you need in your query from the Show Table dialog box.
4. Click Add to add the table to the top section of the query design and close the Show Table dialog box.
5. Drag the fields needed from the table to the query design grid (or alternatively, double-click the field names); then add criteria and sorting options.
6. Click Run in the Results group to show the results in Datasheet view.

Use Query Design View

The Query Design view consists of two parts. The top portion contains tables with their respective field names. If a query contains more than one table, the join lines between tables will be displayed as they were created in the Relationships window.

The bottom portion (known as the query design grid) contains columns and rows. Each field in the query has its own column and contains multiple rows. The rows permit you to control the query results.

- The **Field row** displays the field name.
- The **Table row** displays the data source.
- The **Sort row** enables you to sort in ascending or descending order.
- The **Show row** controls whether the field will be displayed in the query results.
- The **Criteria row** is used to set the rules that determine which records will be selected, such as customers with account balances greater than $5,000.

Figure 11.28 displays the query design grid with the Show Table dialog box open. The Accounts table has been added from the Show Table dialog box. Figure 11.29 shows the Design view of a sample query with four fields, with a criterion set for one field and sorting set on another. The results of the query are shown in Datasheet view, as shown in Figure 11.30.

TIP **Examine the Records**

An experienced Access user always examines the records returned in the query results. Verify that the records in the query results match the criteria that you specified in Design view. As you add additional criteria, the number of records returned will usually decrease.

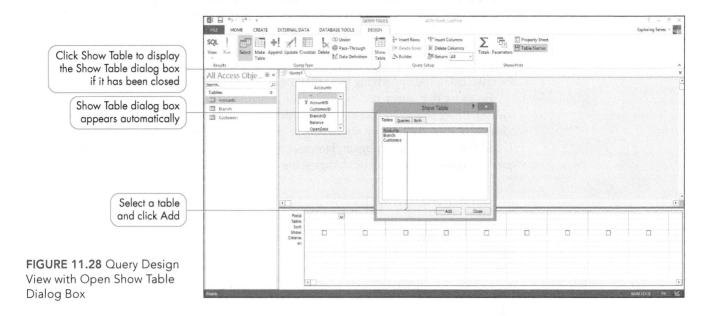

Click Show Table to display the Show Table dialog box if it has been closed

Show Table dialog box appears automatically

Select a table and click Add

FIGURE 11.28 Query Design View with Open Show Table Dialog Box

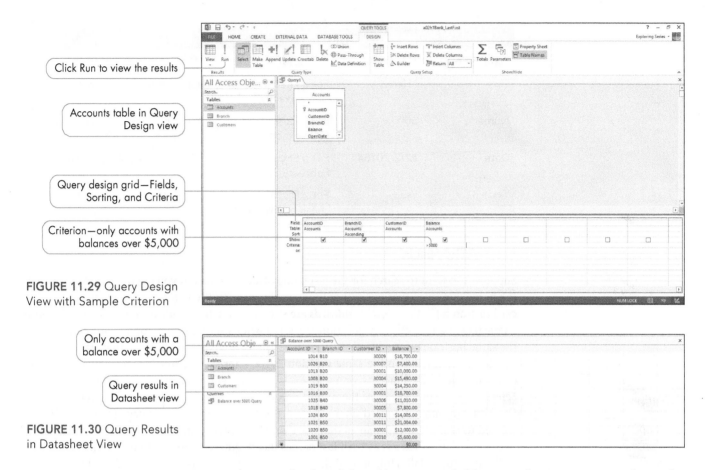

Click Run to view the results

Accounts table in Query Design view

Query design grid—Fields, Sorting, and Criteria

Criterion—only accounts with balances over $5,000

FIGURE 11.29 Query Design View with Sample Criterion

Only accounts with a balance over $5,000

Query results in Datasheet view

FIGURE 11.30 Query Results in Datasheet View

When you developed the tables, you toggled between the Design view and Datasheet view. Similarly, you will toggle between Design view and Datasheet view when you create queries. Use Design view to specify the criteria; you can use the results that display in Datasheet view to answer a question or to make a decision about the organization. Use Datasheet view to see the results of your query. Each time you need to fine-tune the query, switch back to Design view, make a change, and then test the results in Datasheet view. After you are satisfied with the query results, you may want to save the query so it can become a permanent part of the database and can be used later.

Specifying Query Criteria for Different Data Types

When specifying the criteria for a query, you may need to include a *delimiter*—a special character that surrounds a criterion's value. The delimiter needed is determined by the field data type, and Access will automatically enter the delimiter for you for some data types. Text fields require quotation marks before and after the text. Access automatically adds the quotation marks around text, but to ensure that the correct delimiter is used, you may want to include the delimiters yourself.

Use plain digits (no delimiter) for the criteria of a numeric field, currency, or AutoNumber. You can enter numeric criteria with or without a decimal point and with or without a minus sign. Commas and dollar signs are not allowed.

When the criterion is in a date field, you enclose the criterion in pound signs, such as #10/14/2016#. Access accepts a date with or without the pound signs, but if you enter 1/1/2016 without the pound signs, Access will automatically add the pound signs when you move to another column in the design grid. The date value can be entered using any allowed format, such as February 2, 2016, 2/2/2016, or 2-Feb-16. You enter criteria for a Yes/No field as Yes or No. See Table 11.4 for query criteria and examples.

TABLE 11.4 Query Criteria

Data Type	Criteria	Example
Text	"Harry"	For a FirstName field, displays only text that matches Harry exactly.
Numeric	5000	For a Quantity field, displays only numbers that match 5000 exactly.
Date	#2/2/2015#	For a ShippedDate field, shows orders shipped on February 2, 2015.
Yes/No	Yes	For a Discontinued field, returns records where the check box is selected.

Use Wildcards

Suppose you want to search for the last name of a customer, but you are not sure how to spell the name; however, you know that the name starts with the letters Sm. You can use a wildcard to search for the name. *Wildcards* are special characters that can represent one or more characters in a text value. A question mark is a wildcard that stands for a single character in the same position as the question mark, whereas an asterisk is a wildcard that stands for any number of characters in the same position as the asterisk. Use brackets to match any single character within the brackets, or use an exclamation mark inside brackets to match any character not in the brackets. Use the pound sign to match any single numeric character.

You can enter wildcard characters in the Criteria row of a query. Therefore, if you wanted to search for just names that start with the letters Sm, you can specify the criterion in the LastName field as Sm*. All last names that begin with Sm would display. For example, H?ll will return Hall, Hill, and Hull, whereas S*nd will return Sand, Stand, and StoryLand. Table 11.5 shows more query examples that use wildcards.

TABLE 11.5 Query Criteria Using Wildcards

Character	Description	Example	Result
*	Matches for any number of characters in the same position as the asterisk	Sm*	Small, Smiley, Smith, Smithson
?	Matches for a single character in the same position as the question mark	H?ll	Hall, Hill, Hull
[ ]	Matches any single character within the brackets	F[ae]ll	Fall and Fell, but not Fill or Full
[!]	Matches any character not in the brackets	F[!ae]ll	Fill and Full, but not Fall or Fell

Use Comparison Operators in Queries

A comparison operator, such as equal (=), not equal (<>), greater than (>), less than (<), greater than or equal to (>=), and less than or equal to (<=), can be used in the criteria of a query. Comparison operators enable you to limit the query results to only those records that meet the criteria. For example, if you only want to see accounts that have a balance greater than $5,000, you would type >5000 in the Criteria row. Table 11.6 shows more comparison operator examples as well as other sample expressions.

TABLE 11.6 Comparison Operators in Queries

Expression	Example
=10	Equals 10
<>10	Not equal to 10
>10	Greater than 10
>=10	Greater than or equal to 10
<10	Less than 10
<=10	Less than or equal to 10

Work with Null

Sometimes finding what is missing is an important part of making a decision. For example, if you need to know which orders have been completed but not shipped, you would create a query to find the orders with a missing ShipDate. Are there missing phone numbers or addresses for some of your customers? Create a query to find customers with a missing PhoneNumber. The term that Access uses for a blank field is *null*. Table 11.7 gives two illustrations of when to use the null criterion in a query.

TABLE 11.7 Establishing Null Criteria Expressions

Expression	Description	Example
Is Null	Use to find blank fields	For an Employee field in the Customers table when the customer has not been assigned a sales representative.
Is Not Null	Used to find fields with data	For a ShipDate field; a value inserted indicated the order was shipped to the customer.

Establish AND, OR, and NOT Criteria

Remember the earlier question, "Which customers currently have an account with a balance over $5,000?" This question was answered by creating a query with a single criterion, as shown in Figure 11.29. At times, questions are more specific and require queries with multiple criteria. For example, you may need to know "Which customers from the Eastern branch currently have an account with a balance over $5,000?" To answer this question, you need to specify criteria in multiple fields using the *AND logical operator*. When the criteria are in the same row of the query design grid, Access interprets the instructions using the AND operator. This means that the query results will display only records that match *all* criteria.

When you have multiple sets of criteria and you need to satisfy one set only, use the *OR logical operator*. The query results will display records that match any of the specified criteria. To use the OR operator, type your expression into the Criteria row, separating the criteria with the OR operator. Table 11.8 shows an example of an OR operator created using this method. You can also type the first expression into the Criteria row and then type the subsequent expression by using the Or row in the design grid. Figure 11.31b displays an example of an OR operator using this method.

The *NOT logical operator* returns all records except the specified criteria. For example, "Not Eastern" would return all accounts except those opened at the Eastern branch.

TABLE 11.8 AND, OR, and NOT Queries

Logical Operator	Example	Result
AND	"Eastern" AND "Campus"	For a Branch field, returns all records for the Eastern and Campus branches.
AND	>5000 AND <10000	For a Balance field, returns all accounts with a balance greater than $5,000 and less than $10,000.
OR	5000 OR 10000	For a Balance field, returns all accounts with a balance of exactly $5,000 or $10,000.
NOT	Not "Campus"	For a Branch field, returns all records except those in the Campus branch.

The first example in Figure 11.31 shows a query with an AND logical operator (criteria on the same row are implicitly joined by AND). It will return all of the B20 branch accounts with balances over $5,000. (Both conditions must be met for the record to be included.) The second example in Figure 11.31 shows a query with an OR logical operator. It will return all of the B20 branch accounts regardless of balance plus all accounts at any branch with a balance over $5,000. (One condition must be met for a record to be included.) The third example in Figure 11.31 shows a query that uses the NOT logical operator. It will return all of the accounts—excluding the B20 branch—with a balance over $5,000. The last example in Figure 11.31 shows a query that combines AND and OR logical operators. The top row will return B20 branch accounts with a balance over $5,000, and the second row will return B30 branch accounts with a balance over $15,000.

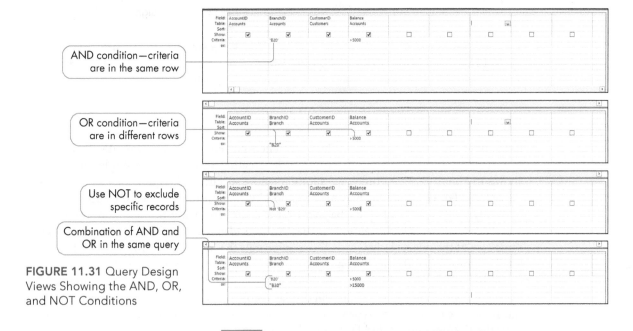

AND condition—criteria are in the same row

OR condition—criteria are in different rows

Use NOT to exclude specific records

Combination of AND and OR in the same query

FIGURE 11.31 Query Design Views Showing the AND, OR, and NOT Conditions

TIP Finding Values in a Date Range

To find the values contained within a data range, use the > (greater than) and < (less than) operators. For example, to find the values of a date after January 1, 2015, and before December 31, 2015, use the criterion >1/1/2015 and <12/31/2015. You can also use the BETWEEN operator. For example BETWEEN 1/1/2015 and 12/31/2015.

Understanding Query Sort Order

The *query sort order* determines the order of records in a query's Datasheet view. You can change the order of records by specifying the sort order in the Design view. When you want to sort using more than one field, the sort order is determined from left to right. The order of columns should be considered when first creating the query. For example, a query sorted by LastName and then by FirstName must have those two fields in the correct order in the design grid. You can change the order of the query fields in the design grid to change the sort order of the query results.

STEP 2»

To change the order of fields, select the column you want to move by clicking the column selector. Release the mouse, then click again and drag the selected field to its new location. To insert additional columns in the design grid, select a column and click Insert Columns in the Query Setup group. The inserted column will insert to the left of the selected column. To delete a column, click the column selector to select the column and click the Delete Columns button on the Design tab or press Delete on the keyboard.

Running, Copying, and Modifying a Query

Several ways exist to run a query. One method is to click Run in the Results group when you are in Design view. Another method is to locate the query in the Navigation Pane and double-click it. A similar method is to select the query and press Enter.

After you create a query, you may want to create a duplicate copy to use as the basis for creating a similar query. Duplicating a query saves time when you need the same tables and fields but with slightly different criteria.

Run a Query

After you create a query and save it, you can run it directly from the Design view. You run a query by clicking the Run command (the red exclamation point) in the Results group on the Query Tools Design tab. You can also run a query from the Navigation Pane. Locate the query you want to run and double-click the query. The results will display as a tab in the main window.

Copy a Query

Sometimes you have a one-of-a-kind question about your data. You would create a query to answer this question and then delete the query. However, sometimes you need a series of queries in which each query is similar to the first. For example, you need a list of accounts in each branch. In a case like this, you create a query for one branch and then save a copy of the query and give it a new name. Finally, you would change the criteria to match the second branch. To accomplish this, do the following:

1. Open the query you want to copy.
2. Click the FILE tab and click Save As.
3. Click Save Object As in the *File Types* section.
4. Ensure Save Object As is selected in the *Database File Types* section and click Save As.
5. Type the name you want to use for the new query in the Save As dialog box and click OK (see Figure 11.32).
6. Switch to Design view and modify the query criteria.

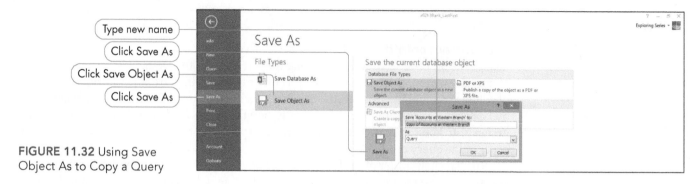

FIGURE 11.32 Using Save Object As to Copy a Query

You can also right-click the original query in the Navigation Pane and click Copy. Click in the Navigation Pane again and click Paste. Type a name for the new query in the Paste As dialog box.

Using the Query Wizard

STEP 1》 You may also create a query using the Query Wizard. Like all of the Microsoft wizards, the *Simple Query Wizard* guides you through the query design process. The wizard is helpful for creating basic queries that do not require criteria. After the query is created using the Wizard, you can switch to Design view and add criteria manually. Even if you initiate the query with a wizard, you will need to learn how to modify it in Design view. Often, copying an existing query and making slight modifications to its design is much faster than starting at the beginning with the wizard. You also will need to know how to add additional tables and fields to an existing query when conditions change. To launch the Query Wizard, click the Create tab and click Query Wizard in the Queries group (see Figure 11.33).

FIGURE 11.33 Launching the Query Wizard

Select the Simple Query Wizard in the Query Wizard dialog box, as shown in Figure 11.34.

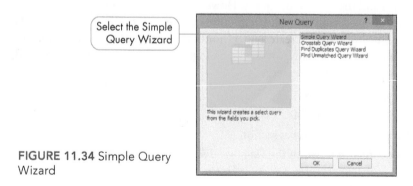

FIGURE 11.34 Simple Query Wizard

In the first step of the Simple Query Wizard dialog box, you specify the tables or queries and fields needed in your query. When you select a table from the Tables/Queries arrow (queries can also be based on other queries), a list of the table's fields displays in the Available Fields list box. See Figures 11.35 and 11.36.

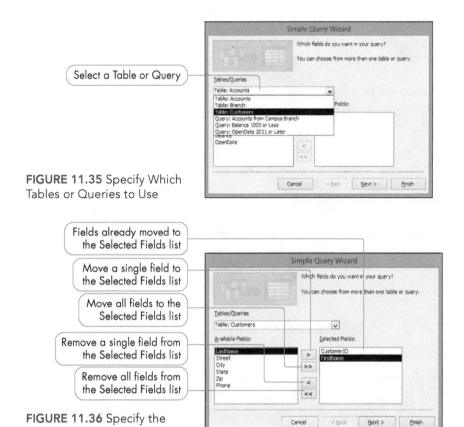

FIGURE 11.35 Specify Which Tables or Queries to Use

Select a Table or Query

Fields already moved to the Selected Fields list

Move a single field to the Selected Fields list

Move all fields to the Selected Fields list

Remove a single field from the Selected Fields list

Remove all fields from the Selected Fields list

FIGURE 11.36 Specify the Fields for the Query

Select the necessary fields and add them to the Selected Fields list box using the directional arrows shown in Figure 11.36.

In the next screen (shown in Figure 11.37), you choose between a detail and a summary query. The detail query shows every field of every record in the result. The summary query enables you to group data and view only summary records. For example, if you were interested in the total funds deposited at each of the bank branches, you would set the query to Summary, click Summary Options, and then click Sum on the Balance field. Access would then sum the balances of all accounts for each branch.

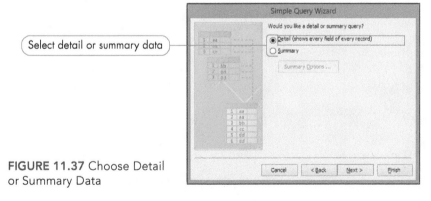

Select detail or summary data

FIGURE 11.37 Choose Detail or Summary Data

The final dialog box of the Simple Query Wizard asks for the name of the query. Assign a descriptive name to your queries so that you know what each does by looking at the query name. See Figure 11.38.

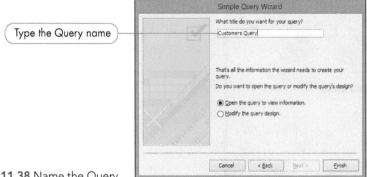

Type the Query name

FIGURE 11.38 Name the Query

The next Hands-On Exercise enables you to create and run queries in order to find answers to questions you have about your data. You will use the Query Wizard to create a basic query and modify the query in Query Design view by adding an additional field and by adding query criteria.

Quick
Concepts ✓

1. Define a query. Give an example. *p. 569*

2. Give an example of how to use the criteria row to find certain records in a table. *p. 570*

3. When would you need to use the "is null" and "is not null" criteria? *p. 573*

4. When would you want to copy a query? *p. 575*

Hands-On Exercises

 Watch the Video for this Hands-On Exercise!

 MyITLab® HOE3 Training

3 Single-Table Queries

The tables and table relationships have been created, and some data have been entered. Now, you need to begin the process of analyzing the bank data for the auditor. You will do so using queries. You decide to begin with the Accounts table.

Skills covered: Create a Query Using a Wizard • Specify Query Criteria and Query Sort Order • Change Query Data

STEP 1 》 CREATE A QUERY USING A WIZARD

You decide to start with the Query Wizard, knowing you can always alter the design of the query later in Query Design view. You will show the results to the auditor using Datasheet view. Refer to Figure 11.39 as you complete Step 1.

Step b: Click Query Wizard

Step 3: Selected fields

FIGURE 11.39 Query Results Before Criteria Are Applied

a. Open *a02h2Bank_LastFirst* if you closed it at the end of Hands-On Exercise 2. Save the database as **a02h3Bank_LastFirst**, changing *h2* to *h3*.

b. Click the **CREATE tab** and click **Query Wizard** in the Queries group to launch the New Query wizard.

The New Query Wizard dialog box opens. Simple Query Wizard is selected by default.

c. Click **OK**.

d. Verify that *Table: Accounts* is selected in the Tables/Query box.

e. Select **AccountID** from the **Available Fields list** and click >. Repeat the process with CustomerID, BranchID, and Balance.

The four fields should now display in the Selected Fields list box.

f. Click **Next**.

g. Confirm *Detail* is selected and click **Next**.

h. Name the query **Accounts from Campus Branch**. Click **Finish**.

This query name describes the data in the query results. Your query should have four fields: AccountID, CustomerID, BranchID, and Balance. The Navigation bar indicates 27 records meet the query criteria.

STEP 2 ≫ SPECIFY QUERY CRITERIA AND QUERY SORT ORDER

The auditor indicated that the problem seems to be confined to the Campus branch. You use this knowledge to revise the query to display only Campus accounts. Refer to Figure 11.40 as you complete Step 2.

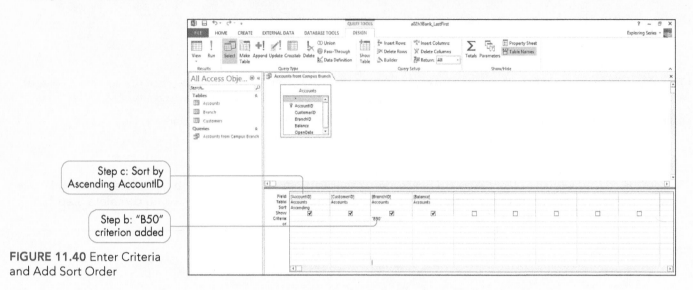

Step c: Sort by Ascending AccountID

Step b: "B50" criterion added

FIGURE 11.40 Enter Criteria and Add Sort Order

a. Click the **HOME tab** and click **View** in the Views group to view the Accounts from Campus Branch query in Design view.

   You have created the Campus Branch Customers query to view only those accounts at the Campus branch. However, other branches' accounts also display. You need to limit the query results to only the records of interest.

b. Click in the **Criteria row** (fifth row) in the BranchID column and type **B50**.

   B50 is the BranchID for the Campus branch. Access queries are not case sensitive; therefore, b50 and B50 will produce the same results. Access adds quotation marks around text criteria.

c. Click in the **Sort row** (third row) in the AccountID column and select **Ascending**.

d. Click **Run** in the Results group.

   You should see nine records, all from Branch B50, in the query results.

STEP 3 ≫ CHANGE QUERY DATA

When the query results are on the screen, the auditor notices that some of the data are incorrect, and one of the accounts is missing. From your experience with Access, you explain to the auditor that the data can be changed directly in a query rather than switching back to the table. Refer to Figure 11.41 as you complete Step 3.

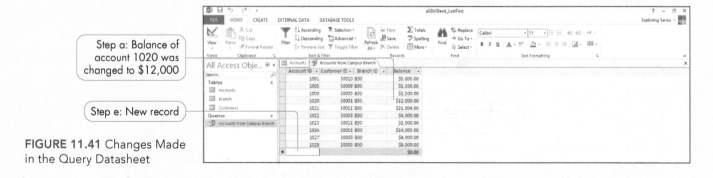

Step a: Balance of account 1020 was changed to $12,000

Step e: New record

FIGURE 11.41 Changes Made in the Query Datasheet

a. Click on the **Balance field** in the record for account 1020. Change *$1,200* to **$12,000**. Press **Enter**. Save and close the query.

You are modifying the record directly in the query results.

b. Double-click the **Accounts table** in the Navigation Pane to open it.

Only one account shows a $12,000 balance. The Account ID is 1020 and the Customer ID is 30001. The change you made in the Accounts table from the Campus Branch query datasheet automatically changed the data stored in the underlying table.

c. Open the Customers table. Find the name of the customer whose CustomerID is 30001. Note that the account belongs to Allison Millward. Close the Customers table.

d. Add a new record to the Accounts table with the following data: **1028** (Account ID), **30005** (Customer ID), **B50** (Branch ID), and **8/4/2016** (Open Date). Press **Tab**.

> **TROUBLESHOOTING:** If the Accounts table is not open, double-click Accounts in the Navigation Pane.

The new record is added to the Accounts table.

e. Double-click the **Accounts from Campus Branch query** in the Navigation Pane.

Customer 30005 now shows two accounts: one with a balance of $1,500 and one with a balance of $8,000.

f. Close the Accounts from Campus Branch query and close the Accounts table.

g. Keep the database open if you plan to continue with Hands-On Exercise 4. If not, close the database and exit Access.

Multitable Queries

Multitable queries contain two or more tables. They enable you to take advantage of the relationships that have been set in your database. When you need to extract information from a database with a query, most times you will need to pull the data from multiple tables to provide the answers you need. One table may contain the core information that you need, while another table may contain the related data that makes the query relevant to the users.

For example, the sample bank database contains three tables: Customers, Accounts, and Branch. You connected the tables through relationships in order to store data efficiently and enforce consistent data entry. The Accounts table lists the balances of each account at the bank—the key financial information. However, the Accounts table does not list the contact information of the owner of the account. Therefore, the Customers table is needed to provide the additional information.

Creating a Multitable Query

Creating a multitable query is similar to creating a single-table query; however, choosing the right tables and managing the table relationships will require some additional skills. First, you should only include related tables in a multitable query. *Related tables* are tables that are joined in a relationship using a common field. As a rule, related tables should already be established when you create a multitable query. Using Figure 11.42 as a guide, creating a query with the Accounts and Branch tables would be acceptable, as would using Accounts and Customers tables, or Accounts, Branch, and Customers tables. All three scenarios include related tables. Creating a query with the Branch and Customers tables would not be acceptable because these tables are *not* directly related. To create a multitable query, do the following:

1. Click the CREATE tab.
2. Click Query Design in the Queries group.
3. Select the table you need in your query from the Show Table dialog box.
4. Click Add to add the table to the top section of the query design.
5. Select the next table you want to add to the query and click Add. Continue selecting and adding tables to the top section of the query design until all the tables you need display.
6. Drag the fields needed from the tables to the query design grid (or alternatively, double-click the field names); then add criteria and sorting options.
7. Click Run in the Results group to show the results in Datasheet view.

> ### TIP | Print the Relationship Report to Help Create a Multitable Query
>
> When creating a multitable query, you should only include related tables. As a guide, you can print the Relationship Report in the Tools group on the Relationship Tools Design tab when the Relationships window is open. This report will help you determine which tables are related in your database.

Refer to Figure 11.31 (the top image) showing the results of the query "Which customers from the Campus branch have an account with a balance over $5,000?" To make this report more understandable to others, we can modify the query by adding the Branch Location (in place of the BranchID) and the Customer LastName (in place of the CustomerID). To make these changes, we would need to add the Branch table (which contains the Location field) and the Customers table (which contains the LastName field) to the query design.

Add Additional Tables to a Query

STEP 1 »
To modify a saved query, open the query in Design view. If you wanted to change the Balance Over $5000 query as discussed earlier, first open the query in Design view. To add additional tables to a query, open the Navigation Pane (if necessary) and drag tables directly into the top portion of the query design grid. For example, the Branch and Customers tables were added to the query, as shown in Figure 11.42. The join lines between tables indicate that relationships were previously set in the Relationships window.

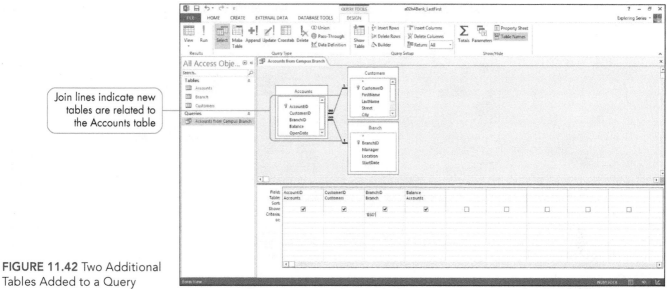

Join lines indicate new tables are related to the Accounts table

FIGURE 11.42 Two Additional Tables Added to a Query

Modifying a Multitable Query

STEP 3 »
After creating a multitable query, you may find that you did not include all of the fields you needed, or you may find that you included fields that are unnecessary and complicate the results. You may find that other fields could be included that would make the results more understandable to others. To modify multitable queries, you use the same techniques you learned for single-table queries. Add tables using the Show Table dialog box; remove tables by clicking the unwanted table and pressing Delete. Add fields by double-clicking the field you want; remove fields by clicking the column selector and pressing Delete. Join lines between related tables should display automatically in a query if the relationships were previously established, as shown in Figure 11.42.

TIP Changes in Multitable Queries Do Not Affect Relationships

When you add two or more tables to a query, join lines appear automatically. You can delete the join lines in a query with no impact on the relationships themselves. Deleting a join line only affects the relationships in the individual query. The next time you create a query with the same tables, the join lines will be restored. And, if you open the Relationships window, you will find the join lines intact.

Add and Delete Fields in a Multitable Query

In Figure 11.43, three tables, as well as the join lines between the tables, display in the top pane of the Query Design view. All the fields from each of the tables are now available to be used in the query design grid. Figure 11.43 shows that Location (from the Branch table) replaced BranchID and LastName (from the Customers table) replaced CustomerID to make the results more useful. The BranchID was deleted from the query; therefore, the "B50" criterion was removed as well. "Campus" was added to the Location field's criteria row in order to extract the same results. Because criteria values are not case sensitive, typing "campus" is the same as typing "Campus," and both will return the same results. The results of the revised query are shown in Figure 11.44.

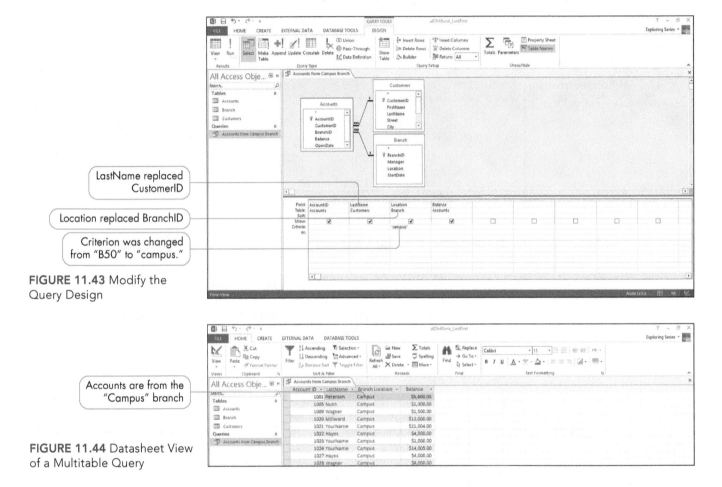

LastName replaced CustomerID

Location replaced BranchID

Criterion was changed from "B50" to "campus."

FIGURE 11.43 Modify the Query Design

Accounts are from the "Campus" branch

FIGURE 11.44 Datasheet View of a Multitable Query

Add Join Lines in a Multitable Query

In Figure 11.45, two tables are added to the query design, but no join line connects them. The results of the query will be unpredictable and will display more records than expected. The Customers table contains 11 records, and the Branch table contains 5 records. Because Access does not know how to interpret the unrelated tables, the results will show 55 records—every possible combination of customer and branch (11 × 5). See Figure 11.46.

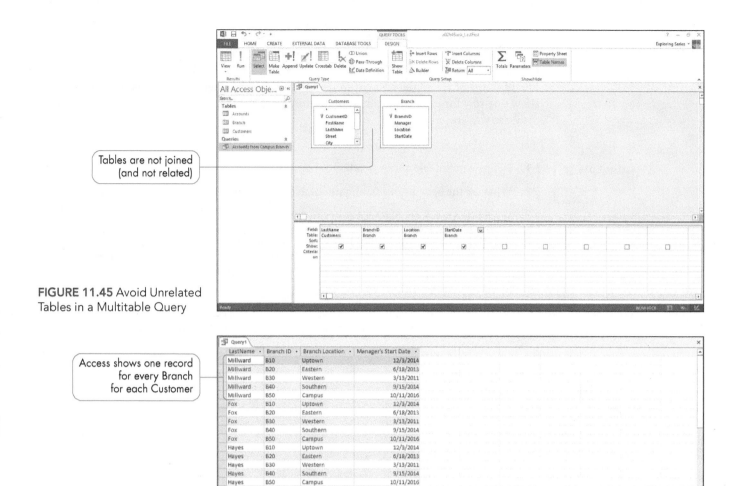

FIGURE 11.45 Avoid Unrelated Tables in a Multitable Query

> Tables are not joined (and not related)

> Access shows one record for every Branch for each Customer

> Result shows 55 records

FIGURE 11.46 Query Result with Unrelated Tables

To fix this problem, you can create join lines using the existing tables if the tables facilitate this by having common fields. In a situation like this, in which there are no common fields, you must add an additional table that will provide a join between all three tables. In the Branch query, you can add the Accounts table, which will facilitate a join between the two existing tables, Customers and Branch. As soon as the third table is added to the query design, the join lines appear automatically, as shown in Figure 11.43.

Over time, your database will grow, and additional tables will be added. Occasionally, new tables are added to the database but not added to the Relationships window. When queries are created with the new tables, join lines will not be established. When this happens, add join lines to the new tables. Or you can create temporary join lines in the query design. These join lines will provide a temporary relationship between two tables and enable Access to interpret the query properly.

Get Answers Using a Multitable Query

STEP 4 ▶

You can get key information from your database using a multitable query. For example, if you want to know how many orders each customer placed since the database was created, you would create a new query and add the Customers and Orders tables to the Query Design view. After you verify that the join lines are correct, you add the CustomerID field from the Customers table and the OrderID field from the Order table to the query design grid.

When you run the query, the results show duplicates in the CustomerID column because customers place multiple orders. Then return to the Query Design view and click Totals in the Show/Hide group. Both columns show the Group By option in the Total row. Change the total row of the OrderID field to Count and run the query again. This time the results show one row for each customer and the number of orders each customer placed since the database was created.

Quick
Concepts

1. Define a multitable query. *p. 582*

2. What are the benefits of creating multitable queries? *p. 582*

3. What is the result of creating a query with two unrelated tables? *p. 584*

4. Describe the purpose adding a join line in a multitable query. *p. 585*

CHAPTER 11 • Tables and Queries in Relational Databases

Hands-On Exercises

4 Multitable Queries

Based on the auditor's request, you will need to evaluate the data further. This requires creating queries that are based on multiple tables rather than on a single table. You decide to open an existing query, add additional tables, and then save the query with a new name.

Skills covered: Add Additional Tables to a Query • Create a Multitable Query • Modify a Multitable Query • Get Answers Using a Multitable Query

---

STEP 1 ❯❯ ADD ADDITIONAL TABLES TO A QUERY

The previous query was based on the Accounts table, but now you need to add information to the query that is in the Branch and Customers tables. You will need to add the Branch and Customers tables to the query. Refer to Figure 11.47 as you complete Step 1.

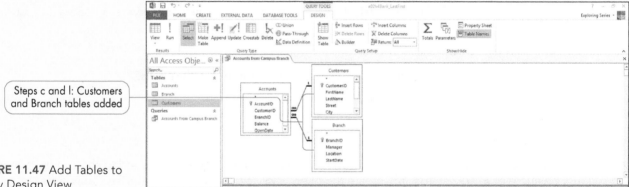

Steps c and l: Customers and Branch tables added

FIGURE 11.47 Add Tables to Query Design View

a. Open *a02h3Bank_LastFirst* if you closed it at the end of Hands-On Exercise 3. Save the database as **a02h4Bank_LastFirst**, changing *h3* to *h4*.

b. Right-click the **Accounts from Campus Branch query** in the Navigation Pane and select **Design View** from the shortcut menu.

c. Drag the **Branch table** from the Navigation Pane to the top pane of the query design grid next to the Accounts table.

   A join line connects the Branch table to the Accounts table. The query inherits the join lines from the relationships created in the Relationships window.

d. Drag the **Location field** from the Branch table to the first empty column in the design grid.

   The Location field should be positioned to the right of the Balance column.

e. Click the **Show check box** under the BranchID field to clear the check box and hide this field in the results.

   The BranchID field is no longer needed because the Location field provides the same information. Because you unchecked the BranchID show check box, the BranchID field will not display the next time the query is opened.

f. Delete the B50 criterion in the BranchID field.

g. Type **Campus** as a criterion in the Location field and press **Enter**.

   Access adds quotation marks around *Campus* for you; quotes are required for text criteria. You are substituting the Location criterion (*Campus*) in place of the BranchID criterion (B50).

h. Remove Ascending from the AccountID sort row. Click in the **Sort row** of the Balance field. Click the arrow and select **Descending**.

i. Click **Run** in the Results group.

The BranchID field does not display in the Datasheet view because you hid the field in step e. Only Campus accounts should display in the datasheet (10 records). Next, you will add the Customer LastName and delete the CustomerID from the query.

j. Save the changes to the query design.

k. Click **View** in the Views group to return to the Design view.

The BranchID field has been removed from the grid.

l. Drag the **Customers table** from the Navigation Pane to the top section of the query design grid and reposition the tables so that the join lines are not blocked (see Figure 11.47).

The one-to-many relationship lines automatically connect the Customers table to the Accounts table (similar to step c on the previous page).

m. Drag the **LastName field** in the Customers table to the second column in the design grid.

The LastName field should be positioned to the right of the AccountID field.

n. Click the column selector in the CustomerID field to select it. Press **Delete**.

The CustomerID field is no longer needed in the results because we added the LastName field.

o. Click **Run** in the Results group.

The last names of the customers now display in the results.

p. Save and close the query.

STEP 2 ❯❯ CREATE A MULTITABLE QUERY

After discussing the query results with the auditor, you realize that another query is needed to show those customers with account balances of $1,000 or less. You create the query and view the results in Datasheet view. Refer to Figure 11.48 as you complete Step 2.

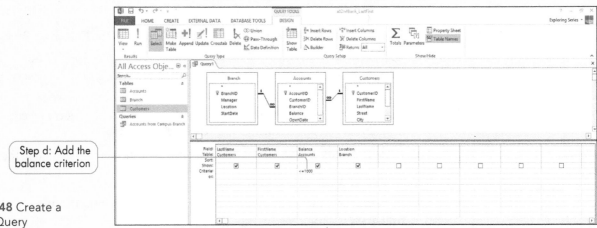

Step d: Add the balance criterion

FIGURE 11.48 Create a Multitable Query

a. Click the **CREATE tab** and click **Query Design** in the Queries group.

b. Double-click the **Branch table name** in the Show Table dialog box and double-click **Accounts** and **Customers** to add all three to the Query Design view. Click **Close** in the Show Table dialog box.

Three tables were added to the query.

   c. Double-click the following fields to add them to the design grid: **LastName**, **FirstName**, **Balance**, and **Location**.

   d. Type **<=1000** in the **Criteria row** of the Balance column.

   e. Click **Run** in the Results group to see the query results.

      Six records that have a balance of $1,000 or less display.

   f. Click **Save** on the Quick Access Toolbar and type **Balance 1000 or Less** as the Query Name in the **Save As dialog box**. Click **OK**.

STEP 3 ≫ MODIFY A MULTITABLE QUERY

The auditor requests additional changes to the Balance 1000 or Less query you just created. You will modify the criteria to display the accounts that were opened after January 1, 2011, with balances of $2,000 or less. Refer to Figure 11.49 as you complete Step 3.

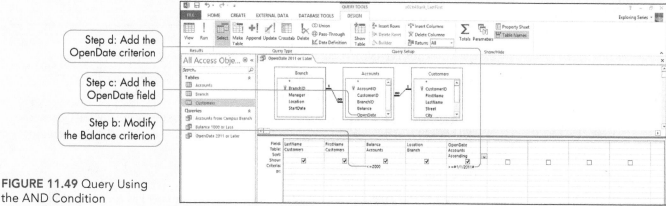

FIGURE 11.49 Query Using the AND Condition

   a. Click **View** in the Views group to switch the *Balance 1000 or Less* query to Design view.

   b. Type **<=2000** in place of *<=1000* in the **Criteria row** of the Balance field.

   c. Double-click the **OpenDate field** in the Accounts table in the top section of the Query Design view to add it to the first blank column in the design grid.

   d. Type **>=1/1/2011** in the **Criteria row** of the OpenDate field to extract only accounts that have been opened since January 2011.

      After you type the expression and then move to a different column, Access will add the # symbols around the date automatically.

   e. Click **Run** in the Results group to display the results of the query.

      Five records display in the query results.

   f. Click the **FILE tab**, click **Save As**, click **Save Object As**, and then click **Save As**. Type **OpenDate 2011 or Later** as the query name. Click **OK**.

   g. Click **View** in the Views group to return to the Design view of the query.

   h. Click in the **Sort row** of the OpenDate field and select **Ascending**.

   i. Click **Run** in the Results group.

      The records are sorted from the earliest open date after January 1, 2011, to the most recent open date.

   j. Save and close the query.

STEP 4 ≫ GET ANSWERS USING A MULTITABLE QUERY

The auditor wants to know the number of accounts each customer has opened. You create a query using a Totals row to obtain these data. Refer to Figure 11.50 as you complete Step 4.

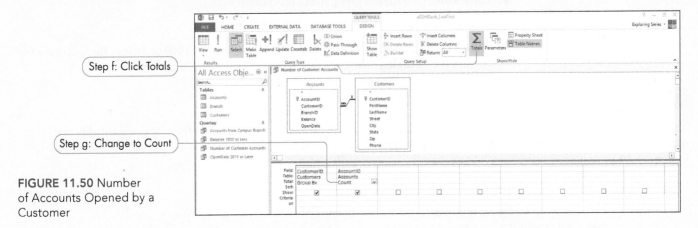

Step f: Click Totals

Step g: Change to Count

FIGURE 11.50 Number of Accounts Opened by a Customer

a. Click the **CREATE tab** and click **Query Design** in the Queries group.

b. Add the Accounts table and the Customers table to the top section of the Query Design view. Click **Close** in the Show Table dialog box.

c. Double-click the **CustomerID** in the Customers table in the top section of the Query Design view to add it to the first blank column in the design grid and double-click the **AccountID** in the Accounts table to add it to the second column.

d. Click **Run** in the Results group.

   The results show there are 28 records. Every account a customer has opened is displayed. The auditor only wants the total number of accounts a customer has, so you need to modify the query.

e. Click **View** in the Views group to return to the Design view of the query.

f. Click **Totals** in the Show/Hide group.

   Both columns show the Group By option in the Total row.

g. Click **Group By** in the Total row of the AccountID field and select **Count**.

h. Click **Run** in the Results group.

   The results show one row for each customer and the number of accounts each customer has opened since the database was created.

i. Click **Save** on the Quick Access Toolbar and type **Number of Customer Accounts** as the query name. Close the query.

j. Submit based on your instructor's directions and close Access.

Chapter Objectives Review

After reading this chapter, you have accomplished the following objectives:

1. **Design a table.**
   - Include necessary data: Consider the output requirements when creating table structure. Determine the data required to produce the expected information.
   - Design for now and for the future: When designing a database, try to anticipate the future needs of the system and build in the flexibility to satisfy those demands.
   - Store data in its smallest parts: Store data in its smallest parts to make it more flexible. Storing a full name in a Name field is more limiting than storing a first name in a separate FirstName field and a last name in a separate LastName field.
   - Add calculated fields to a table: A calculated field produces a value from an expression or function that references one or more existing fields. Storing calculated data in a table enables you to add the data easily to queries, forms, and reports without the trouble of an additional calculation.
   - Design to accommodate date arithmetic: Calculated fields are frequently created with numeric data. You can use date arithmetic to subtract one date from another to find out the number of days, months, or years that have lapsed between them. You can also add or subtract a constant from a date.
   - Plan for common fields between tables: Tables are joined in relationships using common fields. Name the common fields with the same name and make sure they have the same data type.

2. **Create and modify tables.**
   - Create tables: Create tables in Datasheet view or Design view. You can also import data from another database or an application such as Excel.
   - Determine data type: Data type properties determine the type of data that can be entered and the operations that can be performed on that data. Access recognizes 12 data types.
   - Establish a primary key: The primary key is the field that uniquely identifies each record in a table.
   - Explore a foreign key: A foreign key is a field in one table that is also the primary key of another table.
   - Work with field properties: Field properties determine how the field looks and behaves. Examples of field properties are the field size property and the caption property.
   - Enter table records in Datasheet view: Datasheet view is used to add, edit, and delete records. Design view is used to create and modify the table structure by enabling you to add and edit fields and set field properties.

3. **Share data.**
   - Import data: You can import data from other applications such as an Excel spreadsheet or import data from another database by using the Import Wizard.
   - Modify an imported table's design and add data: After importing a table, examine the design and make necessary modifications. Modifications may include changing a field name, adding new fields, or deleting unnecessary fields.

4. **Establish table relationships.**
   - Set relationships in the Relationships window: Use Show Table to add tables to the Relationships window. Drag a field name from one table to the corresponding field name in another table to join the tables.
   - Establish referential integrity: Referential integrity enforces rules in a database that are used to preserve relationships between tables when records are changed.
   - Set cascade options: The Cascade Update Related Fields option ensures that when the primary key is modified in a primary table, Access will automatically update all foreign key values in a related table. The Cascade Delete Related Records option ensures that when the primary key is deleted in a primary table, Access will automatically delete all records in related tables that reference the primary key.
   - Establish a one-to-many relationship: A one-to-many relationship is established when the primary key value in the primary table can match many of the foreign key values in the related table. One-to-one and many-to-many are also relationship possibilities, but one-to-many relationships are the most common.

5. **Create a single-table query.**
   - Create a single-table select query: A single-table select query uses fields from one table to display only those records that match certain criteria.
   - Use Query Design view: Use Query Design view to create and modify a query. The top portion of the view contains tables with their respective field names and displays the join lines between tables. The bottom portion, known as the query design grid, contains columns and rows that you use to control the query results.

6. **Specify query criteria for different data types.**
   - Different data types require different syntax: Date fields are enclosed in pound signs (#) and text fields in quotations (""). Numeric and currency fields require no delimiters.
   - Use wildcards: Wildcards are special characters that can represent one or more characters in a text value. A question mark is a wildcard that stands for a single character in the same position as the question mark, while an asterisk is a wildcard that stands for any number of characters in the same position as the asterisk.
   - Use comparison operators in queries: Comparison operators such as equal (=), not equal (<>), greater than (>), less than (<), greater than or equal to (>=), and less than or equal to (<=) signs can be used in the criteria of a query to limit the query results to only those records that meet the criteria.

- Work with null: Access uses the term *null* for a blank field. Null criteria can be used to find missing information.
- Establish AND, OR, and NOT criteria: The AND, OR, and NOT logical operators are used when queries require multiple criteria. The AND logical operator returns only records that meet all criteria. The OR logical operator returns records meeting any of the specified criteria. The NOT logical operator returns all records except the specified criteria.

7. Understand query sort order.

- Query sort order: The query sort order determines the order of records in a query's Datasheet view. You can change the order of records by specifying the sort order in Design view.
- Determining sort order: The sort order is determined from the order of the fields from left to right. Move the field columns to position them in left to right sort order.

8. Run, copy, and modify a Query.

- Run a query: To obtain the results for a query, you must run the query. To run the query, click Run in the Results group when you are in Design view. Another method is to locate the query in the Navigation Pane and double-click it. A similar method is to select the query and press Enter.
- Copy a query: To save time, after specifying tables, fields, and conditions for one query, copy the query, rename it, and then modify the fields and criteria in the second query.

9. Use the Query Wizard.

- Create a query using the Query Wizard: The Query Wizard is an alternative method for creating queries. It enables you to select tables and fields from lists. The last step of the wizard prompts you to save the query.

10. Create a multitable query.

- Creating a multitable query: Multitable queries contain two or more tables enabling you to take advantage of the relationships that have been set in your database.
- Add additional tables to a query: Open the Navigation Pane and drag the tables from the Navigation Pane directly into the top section of the Query Design view.

11. Modify a multitable query.

- Add and delete fields in a multitable query: Multitable queries may need to be modified. Add fields by double-clicking the field name in the table you want; remove fields by clicking the column selector and pressing Delete.
- Add join lines in a multitable query: If the tables have a common field, create join lines by dragging the field name of one common field onto the field name of the other table. Or you can add an additional table that will provide a join between all three tables.
- Get answers using a multitable query: Use the total row options of a field such as Count to get answers.

Match the key terms with their definitions. Write the key term letter by the appropriate numbered definition.

a. AND logical operator
b. AutoNumber
c. CamelCase notation
d. Caption property
e. Cascade Update Related Fields
f. Criteria row
g. Data redundancy
h. Data type
i. Field property
j. Foreign key

k. Multitable query
l. Number data type
m. Null
n. One-to-many relationship
o. OR logical operator
p. Query
q. Referential Integrity
r. Simple Query Wizard
s. Sort row
t. Wildcard

1. _____ A special character that can represent one or more characters in the criterion of a query. **p. 572**

2. _____ A characteristic of a field that determines how a field looks and behaves. **p. 547**

3. _____ Returns only records that meet all criteria. **p. 573**

4. _____ A row in the Query Design view that determines which records will be selected. **p. 570**

5. _____ Determines the type of data that can be entered and the operations that can be performed on that data. **p. 545**

6. _____ Used to create a more readable label that displays in the top row in Datasheet view and in forms and reports. **p. 547**

7. _____ Enables you to ask questions about the data stored in a database. **p. 569**

8. _____ The term *Access* uses to describe a blank field. **p. 573**

9. _____ A data type that is a number that automatically increments each time a record is added. **p. 546**

10. _____ The unnecessary storing of duplicate data in two or more tables. **p. 544**

11. _____ A data type that can store only numerical data. **p. 547**

12. _____ A relationship established when the primary key value in the primary table can match many of the foreign key values in the related table. **p. 560**

13. _____ A field in one table that is also the primary key of another table. **p. 547**

14. _____ An option that directs Access to automatically update all foreign key values in a related table when the primary key value is modified in a primary table. **p. 560**

15. _____ Rules in a database that are used to preserve relationships between tables when records are changed. **p. 559**

16. _____ Uses no spaces in multiword field names, but uses uppercase letters to distinguish the first letter of each new word. **p. 544**

17. _____ A row in the Query Design view that enables you to reorder data in ascending or descending order. **p. 570**

18. _____ Contains two or more tables, enabling you to take advantage of the relationships that have been set in your database. **p. 582**

19. _____ Returns records meeting any of the specified criteria. **p. 573**

20. _____ Provides dialog boxes to guide you through the query design process. **p. 569**

Multiple Choice

1. All of the following are suggested guidelines for table design *except*:

   (a) Include all necessary data.

   (b) Store data in its smallest parts.

   (c) Avoid date arithmetic.

   (d) Link tables using common fields.

2. Which of the following determines the type of data that can be entered and the operations that can be performed on that data?

   (a) Field properties

   (b) Data type

   (c) Caption property

   (d) Normalization

3. When entering, deleting, or editing table data:

   (a) The table must be in Design view.

   (b) The table must be in Datasheet view.

   (c) The table may be in either Datasheet or Design view.

   (d) Data may only be entered in a form.

4. When importing data into Access, which of the following statements is *true*?

   (a) The Import Wizard only works for Excel files.

   (b) The Import Wizard is found on the Create tab.

   (c) You can assign a primary key while you are importing Excel data.

   (d) The wizard will import the data in one step after you select the file.

5. The main reason to enforce referential integrity in Access is to:

   (a) Limit the number of records in a table.

   (b) Make it possible to delete records.

   (c) Keep your database safe from unauthorized users.

   (d) Keep invalid data from being entered into a table.

6. An illustration of a one-to-many relationship would be a:

   (a) Person changes his/her primary address.

   (b) Customer may have multiple orders.

   (c) Bank branch location has an internal BranchID code.

   (d) Balance field is totaled for all accounts for each person.

7. A query's specifications providing instructions about which records to include must be entered on the:

   (a) Table row of the query design grid.

   (b) Show row of the query design grid.

   (c) Sort row of the query design grid.

   (d) Criteria row of the query design grid.

8. When adding Value criteria to the Query Design view, the value you enter must be delimited by:

   (a) Nothing ().

   (b) Pound signs (#).

   (c) Quotes (" ").

   (d) At signs (@).

9. It is more efficient to make a copy of an existing query rather than create a new query when which of the following is *true*?

   (a) The existing query contains only one table.

   (b) The existing query and the new query use the same tables and fields.

   (c) The existing query and the new query have the exact same criteria.

   (d) The original query is no longer being used.

10. Which of the following is *true* for the Query Wizard?

    (a) You can only select tables as a source.

    (b) No criteria can be added.

    (c) Fields from multiple tables are not allowed.

    (d) You do not need a summary.

Practice Exercises

1 Our Corner Bookstore

FROM SCRATCH

Tom and Erin Mullaney own and operate a bookstore in Philadelphia, Pennsylvania. Erin asked you to help her create an Access database because of your experience in this class. You believe that you can help her by creating a database and importing the Excel spreadsheets they use to store the publishers and the books that they sell. You determine that a third table—for authors—is also required. Your task is to design and populate the three tables, set the table relationships, and enforce referential integrity. If you have problems, reread the detailed directions presented in the chapter. This exercise follows the same set of skills as used in Hands-On Exercises 1 and 2 in the chapter. Refer to Figure 11.51 as you complete this exercise.

FIGURE 11.51 Books Relationships Window

a. Open Access and click **Blank desktop database**. Type **a02p1Books_LastFirst** in the **File Name box**. Click **Browse** to locate your student data files folder in the File New Database dialog box, click **OK** to close the dialog box, and then click **Create** to create the new database.

b. Type **11** in the **Click to Add column** and click **Click to Add**. The field name becomes *Field1*, and *Click to Add* now appears as the third column. Click in the third column, type **Benchloss**, and then press **Tab**. The process repeats for the fourth column; type **Michael R.** and press **Tab** twice.

c. The cursor returns to the first column where *(New)* is selected. Press **Tab**. Type the rest of the data using the following table. These data will become the records of the Author table.

ID	Field1	Field2	Field3
1	11	Brenchloss	Michael R.
(New)	12	Turow	Scott
	13	Rice	Anne
	14	King	Stephen
	15	Connelly	Michael
	16	Rice	Luanne
	17	*your last name*	*your first name*

d. Click **Save** on the Quick Access Toolbar. Type **Author** in the **Save As dialog box** and click **OK**.

e. Click **View** in the Views group to switch to the Design view of the Author table.

f. Select **Field1**—in the second row—in the top portion of the table design and type **AuthorID** to rename the field. In the *Field Properties* section in the lower portion of the table design, type **Author ID** in the **Caption property box** and verify that *Long Integer* displays for the Field Size property.

g. Select **Field2** and type **LastName** to rename the field. In the *Field Properties* section in the bottom portion of the Design view, type **Author's Last Name** in the **Caption property box** and type **20** as the field size.

h. Select **Field3** and type **FirstName** to rename the field. In the *Field Properties* section in the bottom portion of the table design, type **Author's First Name** as the caption and type **15** as the field size.

i. Click the **ID field row selector** (which shows the primary key) to select the row and click **Delete Rows** in the Tools group. Click **Yes** twice to confirm both messages.

j. Click the **AuthorID row selector** and click **Primary Key** in the Tools group to reset the primary key.

k. Click **Save** on the Quick Access Toolbar to save the design changes. Click **Yes** to the *Some data may be lost* message. Close the table.

l. Click the **EXTERNAL DATA tab** and click **Excel** in the Import & Link group to launch the Get External Data – Excel Spreadsheet feature. Verify the *Import the source data into a new table in the current database* option is selected, click **Browse**, and then go to the student data folder. Select the *a02p1Books* workbook, click **Open**, and then click **OK**. This workbook contains two worksheets. Follow these steps:

- Select the **Publishers worksheet** and click **Next**.
- Click the **First Row Contains Column Headings check box** and click **Next**.
- Select the **PubID field**, click the **Indexed arrow**, select **Yes (No Duplicates)**, and then click **Next**.
- Click the **Choose my own primary key arrow**, select **PubID**, if necessary, and then click **Next**.
- Accept the name *Publishers* for the table name, click **Finish**, and then click **Close** without saving the import steps.

m. Repeat the Import Wizard to import the Books worksheet from the *a02p1Books* workbook into the Access database. Follow these steps:

- Select the **Books worksheet** and click **Next**.
- Ensure the *First Row Contains Column Headings* check box is checked and click **Next**.
- Click on the **ISBN column**, set the Indexed property box to **Yes (No Duplicates)**, and then click **Next**.
- Click the **Choose my own primary key arrow**, select **ISBN** as the primary key field, and then click **Next**.
- Accept the name *Books* as the table name. Click **Finish** and click **Close** without saving the import steps.

n. Right-click the **Books table** in the Navigation Pane and select **Design View**. Make the following changes:

- Change the PubID field name to **PublisherID**.
- Change the Caption property to **Publisher ID.**
- Change the PublisherID Field Size property to **2.**
- Click the **ISBN field** and change the Field Size property to **13.**
- Change the AuthorCode field name to **AuthorID.**
- Change the AuthorID Field Size property to **Long Integer.**
- Click the **ISBN field row selector** (which shows the primary key) to select the row. Drag the row up to the first position.
- Click **Save** on the Quick Access Toolbar to save the design changes to the Books table. Click **Yes** to the *Some data may be lost* warning.
- Close the table.

o. Right-click the **Publishers table** in the Navigation Pane and select **Design View**. Make the following changes:

- Change the PubID field name to **PublisherID**.
- Change the PublisherID Field Size property to **2.**
- Change the Caption property to **Publisher's ID**.
- Change the Field Size property to **50** for the PubName and PubAddress fields.
- Change the Pub Address field name to **PubAddress** (remove the space).
- Change the PubCity Field Size property to **30.**
- Change the PubState Field Size property to **2.**
- Change the Pub ZIP field name to **PubZIP** (remove the space).
- Click **Save** on the Quick Access Toolbar to save the design changes to the Publishers table. Click **Yes** to the *Some data may be lost* warning. Close all open tables.

p. Click the **DATABASE TOOLS tab** and click **Relationships** in the Relationships group. Click **Show Table** if necessary. Follow these steps:

- Double-click each table name in the Show Table dialog box to add it to the Relationships window and close the Show Table dialog box.
- Drag the **AuthorID field** from the Author table onto the AuthorID field in the Books table.

- Click the **Enforce Referential Integrity** and **Cascade Update Related Fields check boxes** in the Edit Relationships dialog box. Click **Create** to create a one-to-many relationship between the Author and Books tables.
- Drag the **PublisherID field** from the Publishers table onto the PublisherID field in the Books table.
- Click the **Enforce Referential Integrity** and **Cascade Update Related Fields check boxes** in the Edit Relationships dialog box. Click **Create** to create a one-to-many relationship between the Publishers and Books tables.
- Click **Save** on the Quick Access Toolbar to save the changes to the Relationships window and click **Close**.

q. Click the **FILE tab** and click **Close** to exit Access.

r. Submit based on your instructor's directions.

2 Morgan Insurance Company

The Morgan Insurance Company offers a full range of insurance services in four locations: Miami, Boston, Chicago, and Philadelphia. They store all of the firm's employee data in an Excel spreadsheet. This file contains employee name and address, job performance, salary, and title. The firm is converting from Excel to Access. A database file containing two of the tables already exists; your job is to import the employee data from Excel for the third table. Once imported, you need to modify field properties and set new relationships. The owner of the company, Victor Reed, is concerned that some of the Atlanta and Boston salaries may be below the guidelines published by the national office. He asks that you investigate the salaries of the two offices and create a separate query for each city. If you have problems, reread the detailed directions presented in the chapter. This exercise follows the same set of skills as used in Hands-On Exercises 2–4 in the chapter. Refer to Figure 11.52 as you complete this exercise.

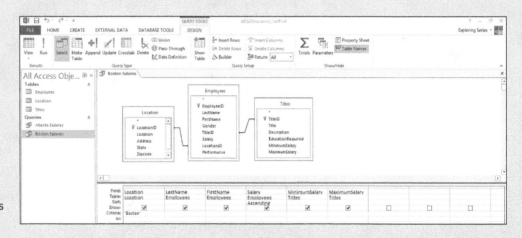

FIGURE 11.52 Boston Salaries Query Design

a. Open *a02p2Insurance*. Click the **FILE tab**, click **Save As**, and then click **Save As** again to save the database as **a02p2Insurance_LastFirst**. Double-click the **Location table** and look at the contents to become familiar with the field names and the type of information stored in the table. Repeat with the Titles table.

b. Click the **EXTERNAL DATA tab**, click **Excel** in the Import & Link group, and then do the following:
- Click **Browse** and locate the *a02p2Employees* workbook in your student data files location. Select the file, click **Open**, and then click **OK**.
- Select the **Employees worksheet**, if necessary, and click **Next**.
- Click the **First Row Contains Column Headings check box** and click **Next**.
- Click the **Indexed arrow** for the EmployeeID field, select **Yes (No Duplicates)**, and then click **Next**.

- Click **Choose my own primary key arrow**, select the **EmployeeID** as the primary key, and then click **Next**.
- Accept the name *Employees* for the table name, click **Finish**, and then click **Close** without saving the import steps.

c. Double-click the **Employees table** in the Navigation Pane, click the **HOME tab**, and then click **View** in the Views group to switch to the Design view of the Employees table. Make the following changes:
- Click the **LastName field** and change the Field Size property to **20**.
- Change the Caption property to **Last Name**.
- Click the **FirstName field** and change the Field Size property to **20**.
- Change the Caption property to **First Name**.
- Click the **LocationID field** and change the Field Size property to **3**.
- Change the Caption property to **Location ID**.
- Click the **TitleID field** and change the Field Size property to **3**.
- Change the Caption property to **Title ID**.
- Change the Salary field data type to **Currency** and change *General Number* in the Format property in field properties to **Currency**.
- Save the design changes. Click **Yes** to the *Some data may be lost* warning.

d. Click **View** in the Views group to view the Employees table in Datasheet view and examine the data. Click any record in the Title ID and click **Ascending** in the Sort & Filter group on the HOME tab. Multiple employees are associated with the T01, T02, T03, and T04 titles.

e. Double-click the **Titles table** in the Navigation Pane to open it in Datasheet view. Notice the T04 title is not in the list.

f. Add a new record in the first blank record at the bottom of the Titles table. Use the following data:
- Type **T04** in the **TitleID field**.
- Type **Senior Account Rep** in the **Title field**.
- Type **A marketing position requiring a technical background and at least three years of experience** in the **Description field**.
- Type **Four-year degree** in the **Education Requirements field**.
- Type **45000** in the **Minimum Salary field**.
- Type **75000** in the **Maximum Salary field**.

g. Close all tables. Click **Yes** if you are asked to save changes to the Employees table.

h. Click the **DATABASE TOOLS tab** and click **Relationships** in the Relationships group. Click **Show Table** if necessary. Follow these steps:
- Double-click each table name in the Show Table dialog box to add them to the Relationships window and close the Show Table dialog box.
- Adjust the height of the tables so that all fields display.
- Drag the **LocationID field** in the Location table onto the LocationID field in the Employees table.
- Click the **Enforce Referential Integrity** and **Cascade Update Related Fields check boxes** in the Edit Relationships dialog box. Click **Create** to create a one-to-many relationship between the Location and Employees tables.
- Drag the **TitleID field** in the Titles table onto the TitleID field in the Employees table.
- Click the **Enforce Referential Integrity** and **Cascade Update Related Fields check boxes** in the Edit Relationships dialog box. Click **Create** to create a one-to-many relationship between the Titles and Employees tables.
- Click **Save** on the Quick Access Toolbar to save the changes to the Relationships window and close the Relationships window.

i. Click the **CREATE tab** and click the **Query Wizard** in the Queries group. Follow these steps:
- Select **Simple Query Wizard** and click **OK**.
- Select **Table: Employees** in the Tables/Queries box, if necessary.
- Double-click **LastName** in the **Available Fields list** to move it to the Selected Fields list.
- Double-click **FirstName** in the **Available Fields list** to move it to the Selected Fields list.

- Double-click **LocationID** in the **Available Fields list** to move it to the Selected Fields list.
- Click **Next**.
- Select the **Detail (shows every field of every record) option**, if necessary, and click **Next**.
- Type **Employees Location** as the query title and click **Finish**.

j. Click the **CREATE tab** and click the **Query Wizard** in the Queries group. Follow these steps:
   - Select **Simple Query Wizard** and click **OK**.
   - Select **Table: Location** in the Tables/Queries box.
   - Double-click **Location** in the **Available Fields list** to move it to the Selected Fields list.
   - Select **Table: Employees** in the Tables/Queries box.
   - Double-click **LastName, FirstName**, and **Salary**.
   - Select **Table: Titles** in the Tables/Queries box.
   - Double-click **MinimumSalary** and **MaximumSalary**. Click **Next**.
   - Select the **Detail (shows every field of every record) option**, if necessary, and click **Next**.
   - Type **Atlanta Salaries** as the query title and click **Finish**.

k. Click the **HOME tab** and click **View** to switch to the Design view of the Atlanta Salaries Query. In the Criteria row of the Location field, type **Atlanta**. Click in the **Sort row** in the Salary field and select **Ascending**. Click **Run** in the Results group on the DESIGN tab. Visually inspect the data to see if any of the Atlanta employees have a salary less than the minimum or greater than the maximum when compared to the published salary range. These salaries will need to be updated later. Save and close the query.

l. Right-click on the **Atlanta Salaries query** in the Navigation Pane and select **Copy**. Right-click a blank area in the Navigation Pane and select **Paste**. In the Paste As dialog box, type **Boston Salaries** for the query name. Click **OK**.

m. Right-click on the **Boston Salaries query** in the Navigation Pane and select **Design View**. In the Criteria row of the Location field, replace *Atlanta* with **Boston**. Click **Run** in the Results group on the DESIGN tab. Visually inspect the data to see if any of the Boston employees have a salary less than the minimum or greater than the maximum when compared to the published salary range. Save and close the query.

n. Click the **FILE tab** and click **Close** to exit Access.

o. Submit based on your instructor's directions.

Mid-Level Exercises

1 My Game Collection

ANALYSIS
CASE

Over the years, you have collected quite a few video games, so you cataloged them in an Access database. After opening the database, you create two tables—one to identify the game system that plays your game and the other to identify the category or genre of the game. Then, you will join each table in a relationship so that you can query the database. Refer to Figure 11.53 as you complete this exercise.

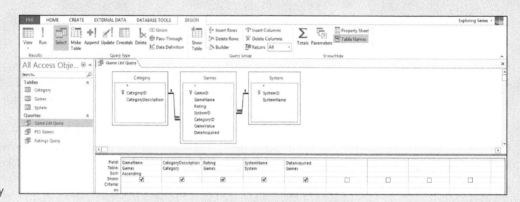

FIGURE 11.53 Game List Query

a. Open *a02m1Games* and save the database as **a02m1Games_LastFirst**. Open the *Games* table and review the fields containing the game information.

b. Click the **CREATE tab** and click **Table Design** in the Tables group.

c. Type **SystemID** for the first Field Name and select **Number** as the Data Type.

d. Type **SystemName** for the second Field Name and accept **Short Text** as the Data Type.

e. Change to Design view. Delete the ID row. Make **SystemID** the primary key and change the Data Type to **AutoNumber**. Add the caption **System ID**.

f. Change the SystemName Field Size property to **15**. Add the caption **System Name**, making sure there is a space between System and Name. Save the table as **System**, saving the changes to the table design. Switch to Datasheet view.

g. Add the system names to the System table as shown below, letting Access use AutoNumber to create the SystemID field. Close the table.

System ID	System Name
1	XBOX 360
2	PS3
3	Wii
4	NES
5	PC Game
6	Nintendo 3DS

h. Click the **CREATE tab** and click **Table Design** in the Tables group. Delete the existing ID row. Type **CategoryID** for the first Field Name and select **AutoNumber** as the Data Type. Set the CategoryID as the **Primary Key**.

i. Type **CategoryDescription** for the second Field Name and accept **Short Text** as the Data Type. Change the Field Size property to **25**. Add the caption **Category Description**, making sure there is a space between Category and Description. Save the table as **Category**, saving the changes to the table design. Switch to Datasheet view.

j. Add the category descriptions to the Category table as shown below, letting Access use AutoNumber to create the CategoryID field. Close the table.

CategoryID	Category Description
1	Action
2	Adventure
3	Arcade
4	Racing
5	Rhythm
6	Role-playing
7	Simulation
8	Sports

k. Click the **DATABASE TOOLS tab** and click **Relationships** in the Relationships group. Add all three tables to the Relationships window and close the Show Table dialog box. Create a one-to-many relationship between CategoryID in the Category table and CategoryID in the Games table. Enforce referential integrity and cascade update related fields.

l. Create a one-to-many relationship between SystemID in the System table and SystemID in the Games table. Enforce referential integrity and cascade update related fields. Close the Relationships window, saving changes.

m. Use the Query Wizard to create a simple query using the Games table. Use the following fields in the query: GameName, Rating. Save the query using the title **Ratings Query**.

n. Switch to Query Design view. Sort the rating field in ascending order and run the query. Close the query, saving the changes to the design of the Ratings Query.

o. Create a multitable query in Design view using all three tables. Use the following fields: GameName, CategoryDescription, Rating, SystemName, and DateAcquired.

p. Sort the query in Ascending order by GameName and run the query. Save the query as **Game List Query** and close the query.

q. Copy the **Game List Query** and paste it in the Navigation Pane using the name **PS3 Games**. Modify the query in Design view by using **PS3** as the criteria for SystemName. Remove the sort by GameName and sort in ascending order by CategoryDescription. The query results should include 7 records.

r. Close the PS3 Games query, saving the changes to the design.

 s. Assume you are going home for Thanksgiving and you want to take your Wii gaming system and games home with you—but you only want to take home games with a rating of Everyone. Create a query named **Thanksgiving Games** that shows the name of the game, its rating, the category description of the games, and the system name. The results of the query will tell you which games to pack.

t. Submit based on your instructor's directions.

2 The Prestige Hotel

The Prestige Hotel chain caters to upscale business travelers and provides state-of-the-art conference, meeting, and reception facilities. It prides itself on its international, four-star cuisine. Last year, it began a member reward club to help the marketing department track the purchasing patterns of its most loyal customers. All of the hotel transactions are stored in the database. Your task is to help the managers of the Prestige Hotel in Denver and Chicago identify their customers who stayed in a room last year and who had three persons in their party. Refer to Figure 11.54 as you complete this exercise.

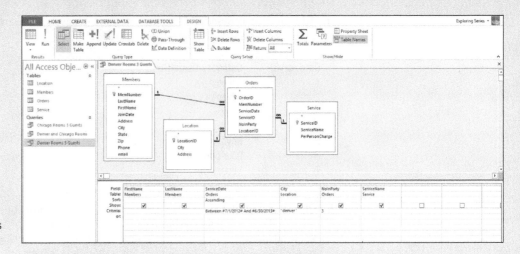

FIGURE 11.54 Denver Rooms 3 Guests Query

a. Open *a02m2Hotel* and save the file as **a02m2Hotel_LastFirst**. Review the data contained in the three tables. Specifically, look for the tables and fields containing the information you need: dates of stays in Denver suites, the members' names, and the numbers in the parties.

b. Import the location data from the Excel file *a02m2Location* into your database as a new table. The first row does contain column headings. Set the LocationID Indexed property to **Yes (No Duplicates)** and set the Data Type to **Long Integer**. Select the **LocationID field** as the primary key. Name the table **Location**. Do not save the import steps.

c. Open the Relationships window and create a relationship between the Location table and the Orders table using the LocationID field. Enforce referential integrity and select **Cascade Update Related Fields**. Create a relationship between the Orders and Members tables using the MemNumber field, ensuring that you enforce referential integrity and cascade update related fields. Create a relationship between the Orders and Service tables using the ServiceID field, ensuring that you enforce referential integrity and cascade update related fields. Save and close the Relationships window.

d. Open the Members table and find Bryan Gray's name. Replace his name with your own first and last names. Use Find to locate Nicole Lee's name and replace it with your name. Close the table.

 **DISCOVER**

e. Create a query using the following fields: ServiceDate (Orders table), City (Location table), NoInParty (Orders table), ServiceName (Service table), FirstName (Members table), and LastName (Members table). Set the criteria to limit the output to **Denver**. Use the Between command to only show services from **7/1/2012** to **6/30/2013**. Set the Number in Party criterion to **3**. Sort the results in ascending order by the Service Date. Compare your query to Figure 11.54.

f. Run the query and examine the number of records in the status bar at the bottom of the query. It should display *154*. If your number of records is different, examine the criteria.

g. Change the order of the query fields so that they display as FirstName, LastName, ServiceDate, City, NoInParty, and ServiceName.

h. Save the query as **Denver Rooms 3 Guests**. Close the query and copy and paste it, renaming the new query **Chicago Rooms 3 Guests**; one of your colleagues in Chicago asked for your help in analyzing the guest data.

i. Open the Chicago Rooms 3 Guests query in Design view and change the criterion for Denver to **Chicago**. Run and save the changes. You should have 179 results.

 **DISCOVER**

j. Combine the two previous queries into a third query named **Denver and Chicago Rooms 3 Guests**. Use the criteria from the two individual queries to create a combination AND–OR condition. The records in the combined query should equal the sum of the records in the two individual queries (333 records).

k. Submit based on your instructor's directions.

3 | Used Cell Phones for Sale

COLLABORATION
CASE

ANALYSIS
CASE

You and a few of your classmates started a new business selling used cell phones, MP3 players, and accessories. You have been using an Access database to track your inventory. You decide to improve the data entry process by adding three additional tables. After the new tables are added and the relationships set, you will create several queries to analyze the data. In order to collaborate with the other members of your group, you will post an Access database and two Excel files to a OneDrive folder. At the completion of this exercise, each person will submit his or her own Word document containing the answers to the questions below.

a. Open the *a02m3Phones* database and save the file as **a02m3Phones_GroupX**. Close the database. (This step will be completed by only one person in your group. Replace *X* with the number assigned to your group by your instructor.) Create a folder on your OneDrive account named **Exploring Access** and share the folder with the other members in your group and the instructor. Upload the database to this new folder and notify the other members in your group.

b. Download the database from the Exploring Access OneDrive folder created in step a and save it locally as **a02m3Phones_GroupX_LastFirst**. (Everyone in the group will complete this step.) Open the database, open the Inventory table, and than review the records in the table. Take note of the data in the TypeOfDevice column; this field is joined to the DeviceOptions table, and the *enforce referential integrity* option has been set. Only the options in the DeviceOptions table are allowed to be entered. What other fields in this table could be joined to a table in the same way? Type your answer into a Word document named **a02m3Phones_Answers_LastFirst**.

c. Import the data in the *a02m3Carriers* Excel spreadsheet into a new table named **Carriers**. Let Access add a primary key field (ID). Open the table and verify that the data imported correctly. Change the ID field to **CarrierID**. Save and close the Carriers table.

d. Open the Inventory table in Design view and add a new field under the Carrier field named **CarrierID**. Set the Data Type to **Number**. Save and close the table. Open the Relationships window and the Carriers table. Create a relationship between the Carriers table and the Inventory table using the CarrierID field. Enforce referential integrity. Take a screen shot of the Relationships window using the Snipping Tool and paste the image into the Word document you created in step b. Close the Relationships window.

e. Open the Inventory table and the Carriers table. Using the CarrierID field in the Carriers table, enter the correct CarrierID into each record in the Inventory table.

f. Repeat steps c, d, and e for the fields Manufacturer and Color. To do this, one member of the group must create an Excel spreadsheet named **a02m3Manufacturers**, which contains all the manufacturers found in the Inventory table. Another member of the group must create an Excel spreadsheet named **a02m3Colors**, which contains all the colors found in the Inventory table. Both of these Excel spreadsheets must be saved to the Exploring Access folder created in step a so all members can access the data.

g. Create relationships between the tables based on common fields. Take a screen shot of the Relationships window using the Snipping Tool and paste the image into the Word document. Close the Relationships window.

h. After all the new tables have been added, each person in the group should create all of the following queries. Make sure the text fields from the supporting tables appear in the queries (not the ID fields). Save each query as noted below. Take a screen shot of the datasheet of each query using the Snipping Tool and paste the image into the Word document.

   1. Display all the phones that are still for sale (SellDate is Null). Save as **qry1 Phones For Sale**.
   2. Display all the phones that are not made by Apple. Save as **qry2 Not Apple Phones**.
   3. List the Manufacturer and Model and asking price of sold phones; also include phones that are less than $50. Sort by asking price; only include tables that are required. Save as **qry3 Phones Sold or less than $50**.
   4. Display the phones that were purchased before 4/1/2012. Exclude the sold phones. Sort by purchase date. Save as **qry4 Obsolete Phones**.

i. Use e-mail or text messaging to communicate with other members in your group if you have any questions.

j. Exit all applications. Submit both the Word document and the database based on your instructor's directions.

Beyond the Classroom

Database Administrator Position

RESEARCH CASE →

FROM SCRATCH

You arrive at Secure Systems, Inc., for a database administrator position interview. After meeting the human resources coordinator, you are given a test to demonstrate your skills in Access. You are asked to create a database from scratch to keep track of all the candidates for the positions currently open at Secure Systems. Use the Internet to search for information about database management. One useful site is published by the federal government's Bureau of Labor Statistics. It compiles an Occupational Outlook Handbook describing various positions, the type of working environment, the education necessary, salary information, and the projected growth. The Web site is http://www.bls.gov/ooh. After researching the database administrator position requirement, create a database using these requirements:

a. Name the database **a02b2Admin_LastFirst**.

b. Create three tables including these fields: Candidates (CandidateID, FirstName, LastName, Phone, Email), JobOpenings (Job OpeningID, JobName, Required Skill, HourlyPayRate, DataPosted, Supervisor), and Interviews (InterviewSequenceID, CandidateID, JobOpeningID, InterviewedBy, DateOfInterview, Rank).

c. Set the table relationships.

d. Add 10 candidates—yourself and 9 other students in your class.

e. Add the Database Administrator job and four other sample jobs.

f. Add eight sample interviews—four for the Database Administrator position and four others. Rank each candidate on a scale of 1 to 5 (5 is highest).

g. Create a query that lists the LastName, FirstName, JobOpeningID, InterviewedBy, DateofInterview, and Rank fields. Display only Database Administrator interviews with a ranking of 4 or 5. Sort by last name and first name. Run the query.

h. Compact and repair the database. Close Access. Submit based on your instructor's directions.

May Beverage Sales

DISASTER RECOVERY +

A coworker called you into his office, explained that he was having difficulty with Microsoft Access 2013, and asked you to look at his work. Open *a02b3Traders* and save it as **a02b3Traders_LastFirst**. It contains two queries, *May 2015 Orders of Beverages and Confections* and *2015 Beverage Sales by Ship Country*. The May 2015 Orders of Beverages and Confections query is supposed to have only information from May 2015. You find other dates included in the results. Change the criteria to exclude the other dates. The 2015 Beverage Sales by Ship Country query returns no results. Check the criteria in all fields and modify so that the correct results are returned. After you find and correct the error(s), compact and repair the database. Close Access. Submit based on your instructor's directions.

Conflict Database

SOFT SKILLS

After watching the Conflict: Sexual Harassment video, search the Web for the Equal Employment Opportunities Commission (EEOC) government site. Open the EEOC site and read the *About EEOC: Overview* information. Open a Word document and save it as **a02b4Harrassment_Answers_LastFirst**. Type a paragraph about the responsibilities of the EEOC.

Locate the *EEOC Laws, Regulations, Guidance & MOUs* page. The *Discrimination by Type* section includes a list of hyperlinks to discrimination type pages—pages that include laws, regulations and policy guidance, and also fact sheets, Q&As, best practices, and other information organized by basis of discrimination. Select a discrimination link and review the material on the page. Type two to three additional paragraphs in the Word document to summarize what you have read. Be sure to use good grammar, punctuation, and spelling in your document. Save the Word document and submit based on your instructor's directions.

Capstone Exercise

The Morris Arboretum in Chestnut Hill, Pennsylvania, tracks donors in Excel. They also use Excel to store a list of plants in stock. As donors contribute funds to the Arboretum, they can elect to receive a plant gift from the Arboretum. These plants are both rare plants and hard-to-find old favorites, and they are part of the annual appeal and membership drive to benefit the Arboretum's programs. The organization has grown, and the files are too large and inefficient to handle in Excel. Your task will be to begin the conversion of the files from Excel to Access.

Create a New Database

You need to examine the data in the Excel worksheets to determine which fields will become the primary keys in each table and which fields will become the foreign keys. Primary and foreign keys are used to form the relationships between tables.

a. Open the *a02c1Donors* Excel workbook.

b. Open the *a02c1Plants* Excel workbook.

c. Examine the data in each worksheet and identify the column that will become the primary key in an Access table. Identify the foreign keys in each table.

d. Create a new, blank database named **a02c1Arbor_LastFirst**.

Create a New Table

Use the new blank table created automatically by Access to hold the donations as they are received from the donors.

a. Switch to Design view and save the table as **Donations**.

b. Add the remaining field names in Design view. Note: The data for this table will be added later in this exercise.

   - Change *ID* to **DonationID** with the **AutoNumber Data Type**.

   - Add **DonorID** (a foreign key) with the **Number Data Type** and a field size of **Long Integer**.

   - Add **PlantID** (a foreign key) as **Number Data** and a field size of **Long Integer**.

   - Enter two additional fields with an appropriate data type and field properties. Hint: You need the date of donation and the amount of donation.

c. Verify the primary key is *DonationID*.

d. Save the table. Close the table.

Import Data from Excel

You need to use the Import Spreadsheet Data Wizard twice to import a worksheet from each Excel workbook into Access. You need to select the worksheets, specify the primary keys, set the indexing option, and name the newly imported tables (see Figures 11.12 through 11.17).

a. Click the **EXTERNAL DATA tab a**nd click **Excel** in the Import & Link group.

b. Locate and select the *a02c1Donors* workbook.

c. Set the DonorID field Indexed option to **Yes (No Duplicates)**.

d. Select **DonorID** as the primary key when prompted.

e. Accept the table name *Donors*.

f. Import the *a02c1Plants* file, set the **ID field** as the primary key, and then change the indexing option to **Yes (No Duplicates)**.

g. Accept the table name *Plants*.

h. Open each table in Datasheet view to examine the data.

i. Change the ID field name in the Plants table to **PlantID**.

Create Relationships

You need to create the relationships between the tables using the Relationships window. Identify the primary key fields in each table and connect them with their foreign key counterparts in related tables. Enforce referential integrity and cascade and update related fields.

a. Open the Donors table in Design view and change the Field Size property for DonorID to **Long Integer** so it matches the Field Size property of DonorID in the Donations table.

b. Open the Plants table in Design view and change the Field Size property for PlantID to **Long Integer** so it matches the Field Size property for PlantID in the Donations table.

c. Close the open tables and open the Relationships window.

d. Add the three tables to the Relationships window using the Show Table dialog box. Close the Show Tables dialog box.

e. Drag the **DonorID field** in the Donors table onto the DonorID field in the Donations table. Enforce referential integrity and cascade and update related fields. Drag the **PlantID field** from the Plants table onto the PlantID field of the Donations table. Enforce referential integrity and check the **Cascade Update Related Fields option**.

f. Close the Relationships window and save your changes.

Add Sample Data to the Donations Table

Add 10 records to the Donations table.

a. Add the following records to the Donations table.

Donation ID	Donor ID	Plant ID	Date Of Donation	Amount Of Donation
10	8228	611	3/1/2015	$150
18	5448	190	3/1/2015	$15
6	4091	457	3/12/2015	$125
7	11976	205	3/14/2015	$100
1	1000	25	3/17/2015	$120
12	1444	38	3/19/2015	$50
2	1444	38	4/3/2015	$50
4	10520	49	4/12/2015	$460
5	3072	102	4/19/2015	$450
21	1204	25	4/22/2012	$120

b. Sort the Donations table by the AmountOfDonation field in descending order.

Use the Query Wizard

Use the Query Wizard to create a query of all donations greater than $100 in the Donations table. Use the following guidelines:

a. Include the DonorID and AmountOfDonation fields.

b. Name the query **Donations Over 100**.

c. Add criteria to include only donations of more than $100.

d. Sort by ascending AmountOfDonation.

e. Save and close the query.

Create a Query in Design View

You need to create a query that identifies the people who made a donation after April 1, 2015. The query should list the date of the donation, donor's full name (LastName, FirstName), phone number, the amount of the donation, and name of the plant they want. Sort the query by date of donation, then by donor last name. This list will be given to the Arboretum staff so they can notify the donors that a plant is ready for pickup.

a. Click the **CREATE tab** and click **Query Design** in the Queries group.

b. Add the tables and fields necessary to produce the query as stated previously. Name the query **Plant Pickup List**.

c. Run and print the query from Datasheet view.

Modify a Query in Design View

a. Copy the Plant Pickup List query on the Navigation Pane and paste it using **ENewsletter** as the query name.

b. Open the ENewsletter query in Design view and delete the DateofDonation column.

c. Add the ENewsletter field to the design and set it to sort in Ascending order. Position the ENewsletter field on the grid so that the query sorts first by ENewsletter and then by LastName.

d. Compact and repair the database. Close Access.

e. Submit based on your instructor's directions.

Customize, Analyze, and Summarize Query Data

Creating and Using Queries to Make Decisions

OBJECTIVES

OBJECTIVES AFTER YOU READ THIS CHAPTER, YOU WILL BE ABLE TO:

1. Create a calculated field in a query p. 610
2. Format and save calculated results p. 613
3. Create expressions with the Expression Builder p. 621

4. Use built-in functions in Access p. 623
5. Add aggregate functions to datasheets p. 631
6. Create queries with aggregate functions p. 632

CASE STUDY | Housing Slump Means Opportunity for College Students

Two students from Passaic County Community College (PCCC) decided they would take advantage of the declining housing market. After taking several business courses at PCCC and a weekend seminar in real estate investing, Donald Carter and Matthew Nevoso were ready to test their skills in the marketplace. Don and Matt had a simple strategy—buy distressed properties at a significant discount, then resell the properties for a profit one year later when the market rebounds.

As they drove through the surrounding neighborhoods, if they noticed a For Sale sign in a yard, they would call the listing agent and ask for the key information such as the asking price, the number of bedrooms, square feet, and days on the market. Because they were just starting out, they decided to target houses that were priced at $150,000 or below and only houses that had been on the market at least six months.

For the first two months, they gathered lots of information and began to get a feel for the houses and prices in the area. Some neighborhoods were definitely more distressed than others! But they still had not made any offers. The two PCCC investors realized they needed a more scientific approach to finding an investment property. Based on a tip from the real estate seminar, they decide to create a database using Access 2013, using data from free lists of homes for sale. They would then like to use Access to help them find houses that meet their criteria. Once the data is in Access, you can help Don and Matt easily identify the qualifying properties. This new database approach should help them become more successful and hopefully help them acquire their first investment property.

Calculations and Expressions

One reason you might choose Excel over a program like Word is for the ability to perform calculations. At first glance, you may not see an obvious location for you to enter a calculation in Access. However, Access includes many of the same built-in calculations and functions that Excel does.

So, why do you need to create calculated fields? Similar to Excel, there are going to be times when you have to process data into information. For example, it could be as simple as needing to calculate a paycheck amount. If you have one field storing the number of hours worked and another field storing the hourly pay rate, you would be able to multiply them together to get the total amount the person is owed. Basic calculations such as these can be done using a query, so you do not have to rely on doing calculations by hand, which can lead to mistakes.

Unfortunately, calculations may not always be that easy. We did not consider some of the common deductions, such as Social Security, Medicare/FICA, federal and state income taxes, unemployment insurance, and possibly union dues. Some of these may be a flat rate, and others may be calculated based on your paycheck amount.

Expressions go beyond simple mathematical functions. Access includes extremely powerful logical functions as well. For example, your employees will claim a certain number of allowances. Based on the number of allowances an employee claims, the amount deducted from the paycheck will be different. This advanced topic will not be covered in this chapter.

When working with Access, there will be times when you need to create arithmetic calculations—using expressions and functions—in your database. In Access 2013, you can add calculations to tables, queries, forms, and reports. Often, rather than storing a calculated value, you would instead store the components of it and calculate the field when necessary. For example, if you have a list price and amount ordered, you would not need to also store the total amount due, because this is the list price multiplied by the amount ordered. Calculating fields rather than storing them will reduce the likelihood of errors and inconsistencies and also save space, as you are storing less information.

In this section, you will learn about the order of operations and how to create a calculated field in a query.

Creating a Calculated Field in a Query

When creating a query, in addition to using fields from tables, you may also need to create a calculation based on the fields from one or more tables. For example, a table might contain the times when employees clock in and out of work. You could create a calculated field (as defined in an earlier chapter) to determine, or calculate, how many hours each employee worked by subtracting the ClockIn field from the ClockOut field. You create calculated fields in the Design view of a query. A formula used to calculate new fields from the values in existing fields is known as an *expression*. An expression can consist of a number of different elements to produce the desired output. The elements used in an expression may include the following:

- Identifiers (the names of fields, controls, or properties)
- Arithmetic operators (for example, *, /, +, or −)
- Functions (built-in functions like Date or Pmt)
- Values that do not change, known as *constants* (numbers such as 30 or 0.5)

You can use calculations to create a new value based on an existing field, verify data entered, set grouping levels in reports, or help set query criteria.

Understand the Order of Operations

The *order of operations* determines the sequence by which operations are calculated in an expression. You may remember PEMDAS from a math class, or the mnemonic device "Please Excuse My Dear Aunt Sally." Evaluate expressions in parentheses first, then exponents, then multiplication and division, and, finally, addition and subtraction. Table 12.1 shows some examples of the order of operations. You must have a solid understanding of these rules in order to create calculated fields in Access. Access, like Excel, uses the following symbols:

- Parentheses   ( )
- Exponentiation   ^
- Multiplication   *
- Division   /
- Addition   +
- Subtraction   –

TABLE 12.1   Examples of Order of Operations

Expression	Order to Perform Calculations	Output
=2+3*3	Multiply first and then add.	11
=(2+3)*3	Add the values inside the parentheses first and then multiply.	15
=2+2^3	Evaluate the exponent first, $2^3=2*2*2$ (or 8). Then add.	10
=10/2+3	Divide first and then add.	8
=10/(2+3)	Add first to simplify the parenthetical expression and then divide.	2
=10*2–3*2	Multiply first and then subtract.	14

Build Expressions with Correct Syntax

Expressions are entered in the first row of the query design grid. You must follow the correct *syntax*, which dictates the structure and components required to perform the necessary calculations in an equation or evaluate expressions. You can create expressions to perform calculations using field names, constants, and functions. If you use a field name, such as Balance, in an expression, you must spell the field name correctly; otherwise, Access displays an error. Access ignores spaces in calculations.

For example, if you worked at a company that was planning on allowing customers to pay off their balance in 12 monthly payments, you would divide the balance by 12. However, let's say you wanted to add a 3.5% surcharge. In this case, you would multiply the balance by 0.035 (3.5%) and then divide that total by 12. An example of an expression with correct syntax is:

STEP 1 »

Balance*0.035/12

If you type the preceding function into a line in a query and save the query, you may be surprised to see Access add a few things to the line (see Figure 12.1):

Expr1: [Balance]*0.035/12

Access made a few changes to your entry. First, it removed extra spaces. Secondly, Access added brackets [ ] around the Balance field, which Access uses to indicate a field name. In addition, you see that Access added *Expr1:* to the start of the line. This is how Access assigns a column heading to this field. If you were to run the query, the column heading would be *Expr1*. As this is not a descriptive name, it would probably be better to include your own title. If you wanted to name this column MonthlySurcharge, you would start the expression with the name, followed by a colon, followed by the expression:

MonthlySurcharge: Balance*0.035/12

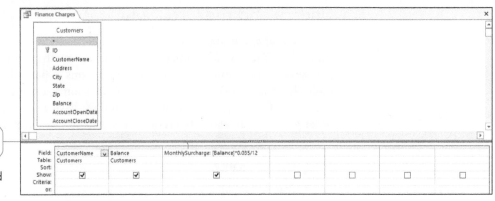

Field calculates
monthly surcharge

FIGURE 12.1 Calculated Field
in a Query Design

TIP | Avoid Spaces in Calculated Field Names

Although you can use spaces in calculated field names, it is a good habit not to use spaces. For example, use NewPrice: [Price]*1.1 rather than New Price: [Price]*1.1. If you avoid spaces in calculated field names, it will be easier to reference these fields in other queries, related forms, and related reports. If you want a column heading to have spaces in it, you should set the Caption property, which will be discussed later in this section.

Again, if you saved the query, Access would add brackets around the Balance field.

In calculated fields, the parts of the formula are usually a constant (for example, 0.035 and 12 in the preceding example), a field name (for example, Balance), or another calculated field. Figure 12.1 shows the MonthlySurcharge field, calculated by multiplying the Balance field by 0.035 (or 3.5%) and dividing by 12. This calculation shows what a customer would pay as a monthly surcharge if you offered him or her the monthly payments and added a 3.5% fee.

The arithmetic operators, the * symbol (multiply) and the / symbol (divide), first multiply [Balance] by 0.035 and then divide the result by 12. There is no real issue in this example with order of operations because the order of operations states that multiplication and division are at the same level of precedence. In other words, if you state 12*3/3, whether you do the multiplication or division first, the result will be exactly the same (12).

The query results, as shown in Figure 12.2, display a decimal number in the MonthlySurcharge column. Notice the results are not formatted well. This will be addressed later in this section.

CustomerName	Balance	MonthlySurcharge
Terri Mccoy	$24,286.00	70.8341666666667
Willie Mann	$47,041.00	137.202916666667
Michael Warren	$26,888.00	78.4233333333333
Tammy Mason	$28,255.00	82.4104166666667
Ashley Smith	$38,108.00	111.148333333333
Paul Johnson	$38,664.00	112.77
Leroy Morrison	$8,070.00	23.5375
Phyllis Daniel	$19,166.00	55.9008333333333
Ryan Weaver	$34,000.00	99.1666666666667
Aaron Jordan	$39,889.00	116.342916666667
Howard Hernandez	$2,296.00	6.69666666666667
Francisco Byrd	$17,146.00	50.0091666666667
Jacob Santos	$49,218.00	143.5525
Willie Anderson	$40,940.00	119.408333333333
Oscar Porter	$12,064.00	35.1866666666667
Evelyn Moore	$42,199.00	123.080416666667
Cheryl Carr	$40,620.00	118.475
Ana Keller	$49,509.00	144.40125
Glenn Brewer	$24,820.00	72.3916666666667
Peter Dean	$48,987.00	142.87875
Sheila Turner	$32,572.00	95.0016666666667
Jason Rodgers	$28,864.00	84.1866666666667
Joel Gonzales	$31,350.00	91.4375
Dolores Hayes	$13,745.00	40.0895833333333
Nancy Daniels	$4,639.00	13.5304166666667
Vivian Cannon	$24,358.00	71.0441666666667

MonthlySurcharge
shows many digits

FIGURE 12.2 Results of a
Calculated Field in a Query

Another example of when to use a calculated field is calculating a price increase for a product or service. Suppose you need to calculate a 10% price increase on certain products you sell. You could name the calculated field NewPrice and use the expression (CurrentPrice) + (CurrentPrice × 0.10). The first segment represents the current price, and the second segment adds an additional 10%. (Recall that to get 10% of a number, you would multiply by 0.10.) The expression would be entered into the query design grid as follows:

NewPrice: [CurrentPrice] + [CurrentPrice]*0.10

Note that if you are adept at math, you may find other ways to calculate this increase.

TIP | Use Zoom (Shift+F2) to View Long Expressions

To see the entire calculated field expression, click the field in Query Design view and press Shift+F2. A new window will appear to enable you to easily see and edit the entire contents of the cell. Access refers to this window as the Zoom dialog box, as shown in Figure 12.3.

Zoom can also be used in a number of other contexts. If you are ever having trouble viewing the entirety of a text box, try using Shift+F2 to expand it. Once you are done modifying a field, click the X in the top-right corner of the Zoom dialog box.

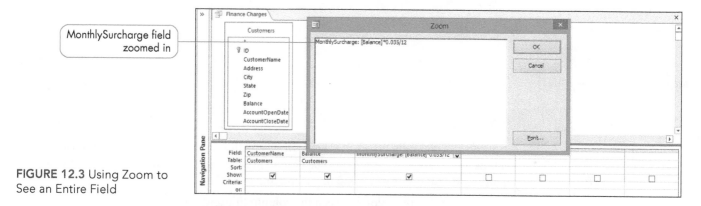

MonthlySurcharge field zoomed in

FIGURE 12.3 Using Zoom to See an Entire Field

Formatting and Saving Calculated Results

In the previous example, we saw inconsistent results in the formatting, with some results showing only two decimal places and others showing many decimal places. In Figure 12.2, the MonthlySurcharge field was extremely difficult to read. Part of the purpose of queries is to perform calculations, but an overlooked portion of that is the formatting. You can create a clever calculation, but if it is not labeled and formatted correctly, it may leave your users confused. Spending a few moments formatting your output will make your query more usable.

There is a way to give Access instructions as to how to format the field. You can use the *Property Sheet* to do so. The Property Sheet enables you to change settings such as number format, number of decimal places, and caption, among many others. You can select a predefined format (for example, currency), change the number of decimal places, and also change the caption, as you did in the earlier chapter on tables. To format the calculated results:

STEP 2 »
1. Open the query in Design view.
2. Click in the calculated field cell (the cell you just created).
3. On the QUERY TOOLS DESIGN tab, click Property Sheet in the Show/Hide group.
4. To change the format, click the *Format property* arrow and select your desired format. For numeric fields, the Decimal Places property will allow you to choose exactly how many decimal places display.

5. To change the caption, click in the text box next to the caption and type your desired column heading. This will override the column name, much like the caption property does for a field name in a table, as shown in a previous chapter.

Formats vary based on the data type. A currency field will have options related to number format, whereas a date/time field will have options related to changing the display of the date and/or time. Figure 12.4 shows the Property Sheet options related to a numeric field.

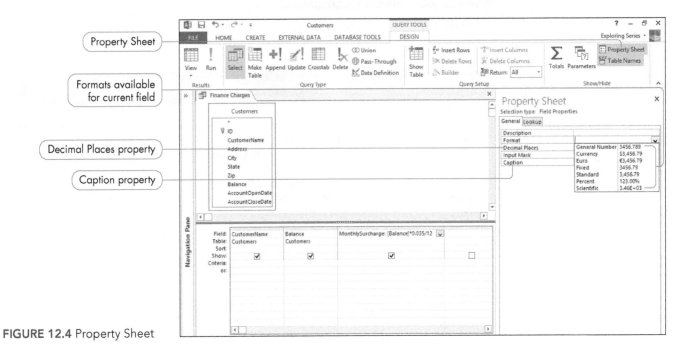

FIGURE 12.4 Property Sheet

Recover from Common Errors

A number of common errors can occur while creating calculated fields. Access may not provide as much assistance as you may be used to in cases like this. The following are three common errors that occur when you begin creating formulas.

STEP 3 »

- Forgetting the colon between the column title and the formula
  - A correct formula would look like this:

    Expr1: [Balance]*0.035/12

    If you forget the colon, the formula looks like this instead:

    Expr1 [Balance]*0.035/12

    and you will get an error about invalid syntax.

- Typing a field name incorrectly
  - If your field name is Balance and you mistype it, you will not get an error until you attempt to run the query. You may end up with a formula that looks like this:

    Expr1: [Baalnce]*0.035/12

  - When you run the query, you will be prompted by Access to give a value for Baalnce.

- Forgetting the order of operations
  - If you do not check your formulas, you may get bad values. For example, the following would not produce the expected output:

    Expr2: [NumberOfDays] + 7/365

  - If you need addition to be done before division, you must remember the parentheses:

    Expr2: ([NumberOfDays] + 7)/365

Verify Calculated Results

STEP 4 » After your query runs, look at the field values in the Datasheet view and look at the calculated values. Ask yourself, "Does the data make sense?" Assume you are calculating a mortgage payment for a $300,000 house, with monthly payments for 20 years. If your formula is incorrect, you may end up calculating a monthly payment such as $30,000. If you look at your data, you should say to yourself, "Does it make sense for me to pay $30,000 a month for a mortgage?" or perhaps "Does it make sense that, on a $300,000 loan, my total repayment is $7,200,000 ($30,000 a month times 12 months a year times 20 years)?" In a real-world scenario, you will not be given step-by-step directions, and you will need to apply critical thinking skills to your work. Access will calculate exactly what you tell it to calculate, even if you make logical errors in the calculation. Although it will catch some errors, it will not catch or note logic errors.

Use a calculator to manually calculate some of the results in the calculated fields and compare the answers to the datasheet results. Another method to verify the results is to copy and paste all or part of the datasheet into Excel. Recreate the calculations in Excel and compare the answers to the query results in Access. The Access calculated field, the calculator, and the Excel calculations should all return identical results.

In the first Hands-On Exercise, you will create a query with a calculated field, format the results, learn how to recover from common errors, and verify your results.

Quick
Concepts

1. Briefly describe the order of operations. Give an example of how order of operations makes a difference in a calculation. ***p. 611***

2. When might you need a calculated field in a query? Give an example. ***p. 611***

3. Define syntax. How does Access respond to incorrect syntax? ***p. 611***

4. Why is it important to verify calculated results? ***p. 615***

Hands-On Exercises

Watch the Video for this Hands-On Exercise!

MyITLab®
HOE1 Training

1 Calculations and Expressions

Using the data from the homes for sale lists that Don and Matt acquired, you are able to help them target properties that meet their criteria. As you examine the data, you discover other ways to analyze the properties. You create several queries and present your results to the two investors for their comments.

Skills covered: Create a Query with a Calculated Field • Format and Save Calculated Results • Recover from Common Errors • Verify the Calculated Results

STEP 1 >> CREATE A QUERY WITH A CALCULATED FIELD

You begin your analysis by creating a query using the Properties and Agents tables. The Properties table contains all the properties the investors will evaluate; the Agents table contains a list of real estate agents who represent the properties' sellers. In this exercise, add the fields you need and only show properties that have not been sold. Refer to Figure 12.5 as you complete Step 1.

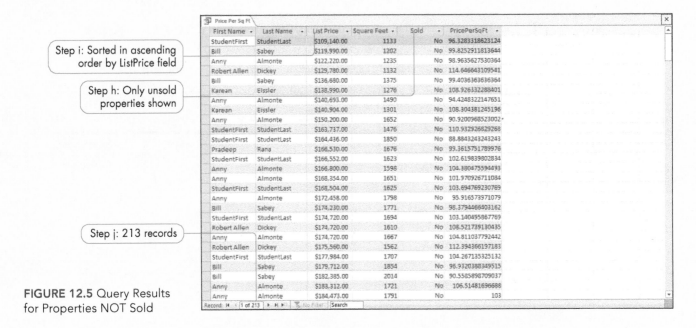

FIGURE 12.5 Query Results for Properties NOT Sold

a. Open *a03h1Property*. Save the database as **a03h1Property_LastFirst**.

> **TROUBLESHOOTING:** Throughout the remainder of this chapter and textbook, click Enable Content whenever you are working with student files.

> **TROUBLESHOOTING:** If you make any major mistakes in this exercise, you can delete the *a03h1Property_LastFirst* file, repeat step a above, and then start this exercise over.

b. Open the Agents table and replace *Angela Scott* with your name. Close the table.

c. Click the **CREATE tab** and click **Query Design** in the Queries group to create a new query.

The Show Table dialog box opens so you can specify the table(s) and/or queries to include in the query design.

d. Select the **Agents table** and click **Add**. Select the **Properties table** and click **Add**. Close the Show Table dialog box.

e. Double-click the **FirstName** and **LastName fields** in the Agents table to add them to the design grid.

f. Double-click the **ListPrice**, **SqFeet**, and **Sold fields** in the Properties table to add them to the query design grid.

g. Click **Run** in the Results group to display the results in Datasheet view.

You should see 303 properties in the results.

h. Switch to Design view. Type **No** in the Criteria row of the Sold field.

i. Select **Ascending** from the Sort row of the ListPrice field.

j. Click **Run** to see the results.

You only want to see properties that were not sold. There should now be 213 properties in the datasheet.

k. Click **Save** on the Quick Access Toolbar and type **Price Per Sq Ft** as the Query Name in the Save As dialog box. Click **OK.**

l. Switch to Design view. Click in the top row of the first blank column of the query design grid and use **Shift+F2** to show the Zoom dialog box. Type **PricePerSqFt: ListPrice/SqFeet** and click **OK.**

Access inserts square brackets around the fields for you. The new field divides the values in the ListPrice field by the values in the SqFeet field. The : after *PricePerSqFt* is required.

m. Click **Run** in the Results group to view the results.

The new calculated field, PricePerSqFt, is displayed. Compare your results to those shown in Figure 12.5.

TROUBLESHOOTING: If you see pound signs (#####) in an Access column, use the vertical lines between column indicators to increase the width.

TROUBLESHOOTING: If, when you run the query, you are prompted for PricePerSqFt, cancel and return to Design view. Ensure you have entered the formula from step l to the field line of the query, not the criteria line.

---

n. Save the changes to the query and close the query.

STEP 2 >> FORMAT AND SAVE CALCULATED RESULTS

Don and Matt would like the field formatted differently. You will change the format to Currency and add a caption to the calculated field. Refer to Figure 12.6 as you complete Step 2.

Steps d–e: PricePerSqFt field formatted as Currency with added caption

Price Per Sq Ft Formatted					
First Name	Last Name	List Price	Square Feet	Sold	Price Per Sq Ft
StudentFirst	StudentLast	$109,140.00	1133	No	$96.33
Bill	Sabey	$119,990.00	1202	No	$99.83
Anny	Almonte	$122,220.00	1235	No	$98.96
Robert Allen	Dickey	$129,780.00	1132	No	$114.65
Bill	Sabey	$136,680.00	1375	No	$99.40
Karean	Eissler	$138,990.00	1276	No	$108.93
Anny	Almonte	$140,693.00	1490	No	$94.42
Karean	Eissler	$140,904.00	1301	No	$108.30
Anny	Almonte	$150,200.00	1652	No	$90.92
StudentFirst	StudentLast	$163,737.00	1476	No	$110.93
StudentFirst	StudentLast	$164,436.00	1850	No	$88.88
Pradeep	Rana	$166,530.00	1676	No	$99.36
StudentFirst	StudentLast	$166,552.00	1623	No	$102.62
Anny	Almonte	$166,800.00	1598	No	$104.38
Anny	Almonte	$168,354.00	1651	No	$101.97
StudentFirst	StudentLast	$168,504.00	1625	No	$103.69
Anny	Almonte	$172,458.00	1798	No	$95.92
Bill	Sabey	$174,230.00	1771	No	$98.38
StudentFirst	StudentLast	$174,720.00	1694	No	$103.14
Robert Allen	Dickey	$174,720.00	1610	No	$108.52
Anny	Almonte	$174,720.00	1667	No	$104.81
Robert Allen	Dickey	$175,560.00	1562	No	$112.39
StudentFirst	StudentLast	$177,984.00	1707	No	$104.27
Bill	Sabey	$179,712.00	1854	No	$96.93
Bill	Sabey	$182,385.00	2014	No	$90.56
Anny	Almonte	$183,312.00	1721	No	$106.51
Anny	Almonte	$184,473.00	1791	No	$103.00

FIGURE 12.6 Results of Calculated Field Creation

a. Make a copy of the Price Per Sq Ft query. Name the copy **Price Per Sq Ft Formatted**.

b. Open the Price Per Sq Ft Formatted query in Design view.

c. Click in the **PricePerSqFt calculated field cell**. Click **Property Sheet** in the Show/Hide group on the DESIGN tab.

   The Property Sheet displays on the right side of your screen.

d. Click the **Format box**. Click the **Format property arrow** and select **Currency**.

e. Click in the **Caption box** and type **Price Per Sq Ft**. Press **Enter**. Close the Property Sheet.

f. Click **Run** to view your changes.

   The calculated field values are formatted as Currency, and the column heading displays *Price Per Sq Ft* instead of *PricePerSqFt*.

g. Save the changes to the query.

STEP 3 >> RECOVER FROM COMMON ERRORS

A few errors arise as you test the new calculated fields. You check the spelling of the field names in the calculated fields because that is a common mistake. Refer to Figure 12.7 as you complete Step 3.

First Name	Last Name	List Price	Square Feet	Sold	Price Per Sq Ft	Wrong Price Per Sq Ft
StudentFirst	StudentLast	$109,140.00	1133	No	$96.33	$100.00
Bill	Sabey	$119,990.00	1202	No	$99.83	$100.00
Anny	Almonte	$122,220.00	1235	No	$98.96	$100.00
Robert Allen	Dickey	$129,780.00	1132	No	$114.65	$100.00
Bill	Sabey	$136,680.00	1375	No	$99.40	$100.00
Karean	Eissler	$138,990.00	1276	No	$108.93	$100.00
Anny	Almonte	$140,693.00	1490	No	$94.42	$100.00
Karean	Eissler	$140,904.00	1301	No	$108.30	$100.00
Anny	Almonte	$150,200.00	1652	No	$90.92	$100.00
StudentFirst	StudentLast	$163,737.00	1476	No	$110.93	$100.00
StudentFirst	StudentLast	$164,436.00	1850	No	$88.88	$100.00
Pradeep	Rana	$166,530.00	1676	No	$99.36	$100.00
StudentFirst	StudentLast	$166,552.00	1623	No	$102.62	$100.00
Anny	Almonte	$166,800.00	1598	No	$104.38	$100.00
Anny	Almonte	$168,354.00	1651	No	$101.97	$100.00
StudentFirst	StudentLast	$168,504.00	1625	No	$103.69	$100.00
Anny	Almonte	$172,458.00	1798	No	$95.92	$100.00
Bill	Sabey	$174,230.00	1771	No	$98.38	$100.00
StudentFirst	StudentLast	$174,720.00	1694	No	$103.14	$100.00
Robert Allen	Dickey	$174,720.00	1610	No	$108.52	$100.00
Anny	Almonte	$174,720.00	1667	No	$104.81	$100.00
Robert Allen	Dickey	$175,560.00	1562	No	$112.39	$100.00
StudentFirst	StudentLast	$177,984.00	1707	No	$104.27	$100.00
Bill	Sabey	$179,712.00	1854	No	$96.93	$100.00
Bill	Sabey	$182,385.00	2014	No	$90.56	$100.00
Anny	Almonte	$183,312.00	1721	No	$106.51	$100.00
Anny	Almonte	$184,473.00	1791	No	$103.00	$100.00

Record: 1 of 213 — No Filter — Search

Step g: Same results ($100.00) for every record

FIGURE 12.7 Results of a Misspelled Field Name

a. Switch to Design view of the Price Per Sq Ft Formatted query. Scroll to the first blank column of the query design grid and click in the top row.

b. Use **Shift+F2** to display the Zoom dialog box. Type **WrongPricePerSqFt: xListPrice/ xSqFeet**. Click the **Close (X) button** in the top-right corner of the Zoom dialog box.

Be sure that you added the extra *x*'s to the field names. You are intentionally misspelling the field names to see how Access will respond. Access inserts square brackets around the field names for you.

c. Click **Property Sheet** in the Show/Hide group of the DESIGN tab. Click the **Format box**. From the menu, select **Currency**. Click in the **Caption box** and type **Wrong Price Per Sq Ft**. Close the Property Sheet.

d. Click **Run** in the Results group.

You should see the Enter Parameter Value dialog box. The dialog box indicates that Access does not recognize xListPrice in the tables defined for this query in the first record. When Access does not recognize a field name, it will ask you to supply a value.

e. Type **100000** in the first parameter box. Press **Enter** or click **OK**.

Another Enter Parameter Value dialog box displays, asking that you supply a value for xSqFeet. Again, this error occurs because the tables defined for this query do not contain an xSqFeet field.

f. Type **1000** in the second parameter box and press **Enter**.

The query has the necessary information to run and returns the results in Datasheet view.

g. Examine the results of the calculation for *Wrong Price Per Sq Ft*. You may have to scroll right to see the results.

All of the records show 100 because you entered the values 100000 and 1000, respectively, into the parameter boxes. The two values are treated as constants and give the same results for all the records.

h. Return to Design view. Press **Shift+F2** to zoom. Correct the errors in the WrongPricePerSqFt field by changing the formula to **WrongPricePerSqFt: [ListPrice]/ [SqFeet]**. Click the **Close (X) button** in the top-right corner of the Zoom dialog box to close it.

i. Run and save the query. Close the query.

The calculated values in the last two columns should be the same.

Because you are in charge of the Access database, you decide to verify your data prior to showing it to the investors. You use two methods to check your calculations: estimation and checking your results using Excel. Refer to Figure 12.8 as you complete Step 4.

Step e: Column G results should match first 10 results in column F

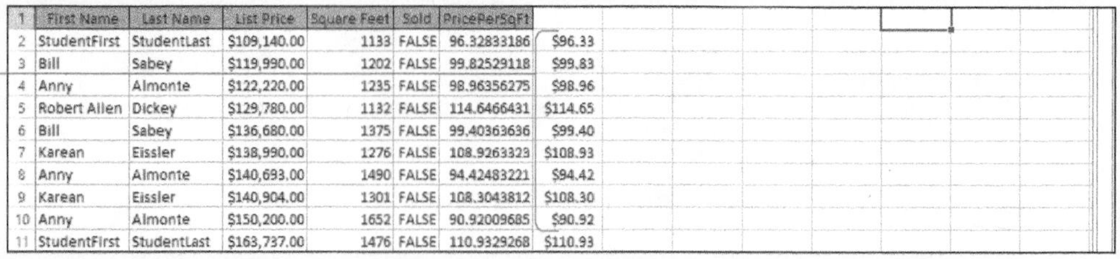

	First Name	Last Name	List Price	Square Feet	Sold	PricePerSqFt	
1							
2	StudentFirst	StudentLast	$109,140.00	1133	FALSE	96.32833186	$96.33
3	Bill	Sabey	$119,990.00	1202	FALSE	99.82529118	$99.83
4	Anny	Almonte	$122,220.00	1235	FALSE	98.96356275	$98.96
5	Robert Allen	Dickey	$129,780.00	1132	FALSE	114.6466431	$114.65
6	Bill	Sabey	$136,680.00	1375	FALSE	99.40363636	$99.40
7	Karean	Eissler	$138,990.00	1276	FALSE	108.9263323	$108.93
8	Anny	Almonte	$140,693.00	1490	FALSE	94.42483221	$94.42
9	Karean	Eissler	$140,904.00	1301	FALSE	108.3043812	$108.30
10	Anny	Almonte	$150,200.00	1652	FALSE	90.92009685	$90.92
11	StudentFirst	StudentLast	$163,737.00	1476	FALSE	110.9329268	$110.93

FIGURE 12.8 Results Validated in Excel

a. Open the Price Per Sq Ft query in Datasheet view. Examine the PricePerSqFt field.

One of the ways to verify the accuracy of the calculated data is to ask yourself if the numbers make sense.

b. Locate the second record with *Bill Sabey* as the listing agent, an asking price of *$119,990*, and square footage of *1202*. Ask yourself if the calculated value of *$99.83* makes sense.

The sale price is $119,990, and the square footage is 1202. You can verify the calculated field easily by rounding the two numbers (to 120,000 and 1,200) and dividing the values in your head (120,000 divided by 1,200 = 100) to verify that the calculated value, $99.83 per square foot, makes sense.

> **TROUBLESHOOTING:** If the second record is not the one listed above, ensure you have sorted the query by the List Price in ascending order, as specified in Step 1i.

c. Open a new, blank workbook in Excel and switch to Access. Drag over the record selector for the first 10 records (the tenth record has a list price of $163,737). Click **Copy** in the Clipboard group on the HOME tab.

You will verify the calculation in the first 10 records by pasting the results in Excel.

d. Switch to Excel and, click **Paste** in the Clipboard group on the HOME tab.

The field names display in the first row, and the 10 records display in the next 10 rows. The fields are located in columns A–F. The calculated field results are pasted in column F as values rather than as a formula.

> **TROUBLESHOOTING:** If you see pound signs (#####) in an Excel column, use the vertical lines between column indicators to increase the width.

e. Type =C2/D2 in **cell G2** and press **Enter**. Copy the formula from **cell G2** and paste it into **cells G3 to G11**.

The formula divides the list price by the square feet. Compare the results in columns F and G. The numbers should be the same, except for a slight difference due to rounding.

> **TROUBLESHOOTING:** If the values differ, look at both the Excel and Access formulas. Determine which is correct, and then find and fix the error in the incorrect formula.

f. Save the Excel workbook as **a03Property_LastFirst**. Exit Excel.

g. Keep the database open if you plan to continue with the next Hands-On Exercise. If not, close the database and exit Access.

The Expression Builder and Functions

In the last Hands-On Exercise, you calculated the price per square foot for real estate properties. That simple calculation helped you to evaluate all the properties on the investment list. You were able to type the expression manually.

When you encounter more complex expressions, you can use the *Expression Builder* tool to help you create more complicated expressions. When you create an expression in the field cell, you must increase the column width to see the entire expression. The Expression Builder's size enables you to easily see complex formulas and functions in their entirety. In addition, it provides easy access to objects, operators, functions, and explanations for functions.

In this section, you will learn how to create expressions using the Expression Builder. You also will learn how to use built-in functions.

Creating Expressions with the Expression Builder

Launch the Expression Builder while in the query design grid to assist with creating a calculated field (or other expression). (See "Launch the Expression Builder" later in this section for directions.) The Expression Builder helps you create expressions by supplying you with the fields, operators, and functions you need to create them. When you use the Expression Builder to help you create expressions, you can eliminate spelling errors in field names. Another advantage is when you are inserting functions; functions require specific arguments in a specific order. When you insert a function using the Expression Builder, the builder gives you placeholders that tell you which values belong where.

You may not always need the Expression Builder. As you become familiar with programs like Access, some of the more common tasks may become second nature to you. Rather than clicking to find what you need, you may be able to do your day-to-day work without the aid of the Expression Builder. However, when working with a less familiar calculation, having this tool gives you extra support.

Though you will learn about the Expression Builder in queries in this chapter, this tool can be used in many other areas. You can also use the Expression Builder when working with forms and reports. For example, if you need to perform a calculation in a form or report, you can launch the Expression Builder to assist you with this task. The same skills you learn here can be applied there as well.

TIP | Missing Field Names

If you have not yet saved your query, you may not see the names of the fields you are working with. This is especially true of any calculated fields you want to use as part of another expression. If you cannot see a field you need to use, exit the Expression Builder, save the query, and close and reopen the query. Once you reenter the Expression Builder, you should see the missing fields.

Create an Expression

The left column of the Expression Builder dialog box contains Expression Elements (see Figure 12.9), which include the built-in functions, the tables and other objects from the current database, and common expressions. Select an item in this column.

The middle column displays the Expression Categories based on the item selected in the Expression Elements box (see Figure 12.9). For example, when the Built-In Functions item is selected in the Expression Elements box, the available built-in function categories, such as the Math category, are displayed in the Expression Categories box.

The right column displays the Expression Values, if any, for the categories that you selected in the Expression Categories box (see Figure 12.9). For example, if you click Built-In Functions in the Expression Elements box and click Date/Time in the Expression Categories box, the Expression Values box lists all of the built-in functions in the Date/Time category.

You can create an expression by manually typing text in the expression box or by double-clicking the elements from the bottom section in the Expression Builder dialog box. For example, to create a calculated field using the fields in the tables, type the calculated field name and type a colon. Next, click the desired table listed in the Expression Elements section and double-click the field you want. Click the Operators item in the Expression Elements section and choose an operator (such as + or *) from the Expression Categories section (or just type the operator). The Expression Builder is flexible and will enable you to find what you need while still enabling you to modify the expression manually.

Calculated fields are relatively simple to create, and most Access developers can create them without the Expression Builder. The main reason to use the builder for a calculated field is to eliminate spelling errors in field names. Using functions in Access almost always requires the Expression Builder because the syntax of functions can be difficult to remember. When you double-click the Functions command in the Expression Elements box and click Built-In Functions, the Expression Categories box lists all the available functions in Access. The Expression Values box lists the functions in each of the categories. When you find the function you need, double-click it and the function displays in the expression box. You can see the «placeholder text» where the arguments belong; replace each placeholder text with the argument values, either numbers or fields from a table.

Launch the Expression Builder

STEP 1>> To launch the Expression Builder:

1. Open a query in Design view (or create a new query).
2. Verify the QUERY TOOLS DESIGN tab is selected on the Ribbon.
3. Click the top cell of a blank column (also known as the Field cell, because it appears in the row labeled Field) where you would like your expression to appear.
4. Click Builder in the Query Setup group, and the Expression Builder launches (see Figure 12.9). (You can also launch the Expression Builder by right-clicking the cell where you want the expression and selecting Build from the shortcut menu.)

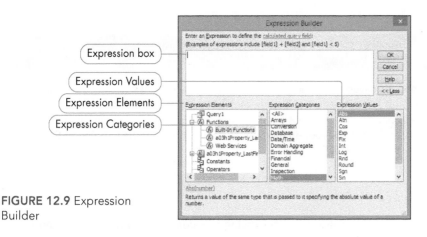

FIGURE 12.9 Expression Builder

5. The top section of the Expression Builder dialog box contains a rectangular area (known as the *expression box*) where you create an expression. You can type your expression in the expression box manually, or you can use the Expression Elements, Expression Categories, and Expression Values in the bottom portion of the Expression Builder. The bottom area allows you to browse for functions, tables, queries, and more. Refer to Figure 12.9.

6. Double-click an item in the *Expression Categories* or *Expression Values* section to add it automatically to the expression box, thus allowing you to use this interface to avoid typographical errors.

7. After you create the expression, click OK to close the Expression Builder window. The expression is then entered into the current cell in the query design grid. From the query design, click Run in the Results group to view the results (in Datasheet view). If the results are incorrect, you can return to Design view and use the Expression Builder again to correct the expression.

Using Built-In Functions in Access

STEP 2>>

Similar to Excel, a number of functions are built into Access. A **function** is a predefined computation that performs a complex calculation. It produces a result based on inputs known as arguments. An **argument** is any data that is needed to produce the output for a function. The term *argument*, outside of computers, can mean a fact. For example, in court, you may have a judge ask a lawyer to present his argument. Similarly, Access will need arguments, or facts, to execute a function. Arguments can be a variable (such as a field name) or a constant (such as a number). Some functions require no arguments, but many require at least one. Some functions have optional arguments, which are not required but may be necessary for your task.

Many of the tasks that are built in are tasks that would otherwise be difficult to perform. If you had to figure out the payment of a loan or determine the year portion of a date without functions, it would not be an easy task.

Once you identify what you need a function to do, you can check the Built-In Functions in the Expression Builder to see if the function exists. If it does, add the function to the expression box and replace the «placeholder text» with the argument values. Functions work the same in Access and Excel and other programming languages (such as Visual Basic). There are nearly 150 built-in functions in Access, and many of them will not apply to the task you are performing. Be aware that if you want to perform complex operations, there may be a function that can do it for you. In cases like this, search engines or Microsoft Help are extremely useful. This chapter will demonstrate one function.

Calculate Payments with the Pmt Function

Figure 12.10 shows the **Pmt function**, which calculates the periodic loan payment given the interest rate per period (for example, monthly), term of the loan (in months), and the original value of the loan (the principal). To use this function, you will need to supply at least three arguments as field names from underlying tables or as constants:

- The first argument is the interest rate per period. Interest rates are usually stated as annual rates, so you will need to convert the annual interest rate to the rate per period. For example, if a loan is paid monthly, you can calculate the rate by dividing the yearly rate by 12.

- The second argument is the number of periods. Because loan terms are usually stated in years, you will need to multiply the number of years by the number of payments per year. For example, a monthly payment would be calculated as the number of years multiplied by 12.

- The third argument is the present value—or principal—of the loan. It is the amount a customer is borrowing.

- The last two arguments—future value and type—are both optional, so they are usually 0 or blank. The future value shows the amount the borrower will owe after the final payment has been made. The type tells Access whether the payment is made at the beginning or the end of the period.

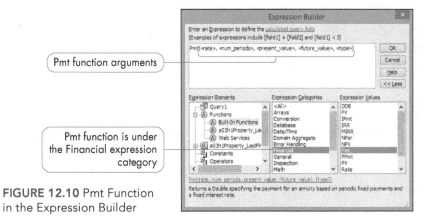

Pmt function arguments

Pmt function is under the Financial expression category

FIGURE 12.10 Pmt Function in the Expression Builder

The following example shows how to use the Pmt function to calculate the monthly payment on a $12,500 loan, at a 5.0% interest rate, with a four-year loan term.

Function: Pmt(*rate, num_periods, present_value, future_value, type*)

Example: Pmt(0.06/12, 5*12, 12500)

The Pmt function will return a negative value (as a loan payment is considered a debit). If you would like to display this as a positive number, you will need to negate it.

Table 12.2 describes the arguments for the Pmt function in more detail.

TABLE 12.2	Arguments of the Pmt Function
Part	**Description**
( )	Items inside the parentheses are arguments for the function. The arguments are separated by commas. Some arguments are optional; some arguments have a default value. In the Pmt function, the first three arguments are required and the last two are optional.
rate	Required. Expression or value specifying interest rate per period, usually monthly. A mortgage with an annual percentage rate of **6.0%** with monthly payments would have a rate entered as **0.06/12**, since the rate of 6% would be entered as .06, and because there are 12 months in a year. A loan with a 4% interest rate paid quarterly would be expressed as .04/4 for the same reason. A common cause of issues with this function is that people forget to divide the annual percentage rate by the number of periods in a year.
num_periods	Required. Expression or integer value specifying total number of payment periods in the loan. For example, monthly payments on a five-year car loan give a total of 5 * 12 (or 60) payment periods. Quarterly payments on a six-year loan would give a total of 6 * 4 (or 24) payment periods.
present_value	Required. Expression or value specifying the present value of the money you borrow. If you borrow $12,500 for a car, the value would be 12500.
future_value	*Optional* (can be left blank). Expression or value specifying the future value after you've made the final payment. Most consumer loans have a future value of $0 after the final payment. However, if you want to save $50,000 over 18 years for your child's education, then 50000 is the future value. Zero is assumed if left blank.
type	*Optional* (can be left blank). Value (0 or 1) identifying when payments are due. Use 0 if payments are due at the end of the payment period (the default), or 1 if payments are due at the beginning of the period. Zero is assumed if left blank.

In the second Hands-On Exercise, you will practice using the Expression Builder to add and modify a field, and use a built-in function.

Quick Concepts ✓

1. List two benefits of creating expressions with the Expression Builder. ***p. 621***

2. Give an example of a built-in function. ***p. 622***

3. What is an argument in a function? Give an example. ***p. 623***

4. Describe a scenario where you might use the Pmt function. ***p. 623***

Hands-On Exercises

Watch the Video
for this Hands-
On Exercise!

MyITLab®
HOE2 Training

2 The Expression Builder and Functions

When Don and Matt ask you to calculate the price per bedroom and the price per room for each property, you use the Expression Builder to make the task easier. You also add two additional fields that calculate the days on market and the estimated commission for each property.

Skills covered: Use the Expression Builder to Add and Modify a Field • Use Built-In Functions

STEP 1 ≫ USE THE EXPRESSION BUILDER TO ADD AND MODIFY A FIELD

You create a copy of the Price Per Sq Ft Formatted query from the previous Hands-On Exercise and paste it using a new name. You will add a few more calculated fields to the new query. You will create one calculation to determine the price per bedroom for each house. You will create a second field to calculate the price per room. For this calculation, you will assume that each property has a kitchen, a living room, a dining room, and the listed bedrooms and bathrooms. The calculations you will create are shown in Figure 12.11. Your expected output is shown in Figure 12.12.

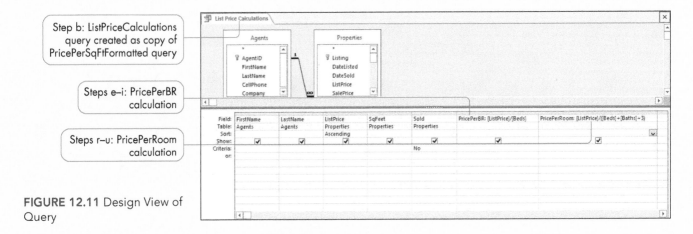

FIGURE 12.11 Design View of Query

a. Open *a03h1Property_LastFirst* if you closed it at the end of Hands-On Exercise 1 and save it as **a03h2Property_LastFirst**, changing *h1* to *h2*.

b. Create a copy of the Price Per Sq Ft Formatted query with the name **List Price Calculations**.

   The new query is displayed in the Navigation Pane. The name of the query suggests it should contain calculations based on each property's list price.

c. Open the List Price Calculations query in Design view. Click the **WrongPricePerSqFt field**. Click **Delete Columns** in the Query Setup group on the QUERY TOOLS DESIGN tab.

> **TROUBLESHOOTING:** If instead of the column being deleted, a new row named *Delete* appears on the bottom half of the screen, close the query without saving, open in Design view once more, and ensure you are clicking Delete Columns in the Query Setup group. If you click Delete under Query Type, you will get very different results.

d. Click in the top cell in the PricePerSqFt column and click **Builder** in the Query Setup group.

   The Expression Builder dialog box opens, displaying the current formula.

e. Change the PricePerSqFt field name to **PricePerBR**.

f. Double-click the **[SqFeet] field** in the expression and press **Delete**.

g. Click the **plus sign** (+) under Expression Elements, next to the *a03h2Property_LastFirst* database in the Expression Elements box, to expand the list. Click + next to *Tables* and click the table named **Properties**.

The fields from the Properties table are now listed in the middle column (Expression Categories).

h. Double-click the **Beds field** to add it to the expression box.

The expression now reads *PricePerBR: [ListPrice]/[Properties]![Beds]*.

i. Highlight the **[Properties]! prefix** in front of *Beds* and press **Delete**.

The expression now reads *PricePerBR: [ListPrice]/[Beds]*. As the Beds field name is unique within our query, the table name is not necessary. Removing this makes the query easier to read. If a field named Beds appeared in more than one table in our query, removing the table name would cause problems.

j. Click **OK** and click **Run** to view the query results.

Notice the column heading still reads Price Per Sq Ft. Also notice the column's contents are formatted as Currency. These settings were copied when we copied the query.

k. Switch to Design view and ensure the **PricePerBR field** is selected. Click **Property Sheet** in the Show/Hide group and change the **Caption** to **Price Per Bedroom**. Close the Property Sheet. Run the query and examine the changes.

The PricePerBR column now has an appropriate caption.

l. Switch to Design view. Select the entire **PricePerBR expression**, right-click the selected expression, and then select **Copy**. Right-click in the top cell of the next blank column and select **Paste**.

You will edit the copy so that it reflects the price per room. As stated already, you assume the kitchen, living room, dining room, and the bedrooms and bathrooms will make up the number of rooms. Your final formula would be the list price divided by the total number of rooms, which is the number of bedrooms (in the Beds field), plus the number of bathrooms (found in the Baths field), plus 3 (a constant representing the kitchen, living room, and dining room).

m. Click **Builder** in the Query Setup group.

n. Change the PricePerBR field name to **PricePerRoom**.

o. Add **parentheses** before the [Beds] portion of the formula. Type a **plus sign** (+) after *[Beds]*.

As you want the addition to be done first, the order of operations states we must enclose the addition in parentheses. The expression box should read *PricePerRoom: [ListPrice]/([Beds]+*

p. Click the **plus sign** (+) next to the *a03h2Property_LastFirst* database in the Expression Elements box to expand the list. Click the **plus sign** (+) next to *Tables* and click the **Properties table**.

The fields from the Properties table are now listed in the Expression Categories box.

q. Double-click the **Baths field** to add it to the expression box.

The expression now reads *PricePerRoom: [ListPrice]/([Beds]+[Properties]![Baths]*.

r. Type another plus sign after *[Baths]* and type **3)**.

The expression now reads *PricePerRoom: [ListPrice]/([Beds]+[Properties]![Baths]+3)*.

s. Delete the [Properties]! portion of the expression and click **OK** to close the Expression Builder.

The expression now reads *PricePerRoom: [ListPrice]/([Beds]+[Baths]+3)*.

t. Click **Property Sheet**. Type **Price Per Room** in the **Caption box**. Close the Property Sheet.

u. Run the query. Widen the PricePerRoom column if necessary in order to see all the values.

Step i: Price Per Bedroom results

Step u: Price Per Room results

FIGURE 12.12 Final Results of Query

First Name	Last Name	List Price	Square Feet	Sold	Price Per Bedroom	Price Per Room
StudentFirst	StudentLast	$109,140.00	1133	No	$54,570.00	$18,190.00
Bill	Sabey	$119,990.00	1202	No	$59,995.00	$17,141.43
Anny	Almonte	$122,220.00	1235	No	$61,110.00	$17,460.00
Robert Allen	Dickey	$129,780.00	1132	No	$64,890.00	$18,540.00
Bill	Sabey	$136,680.00	1375	No	$68,340.00	$22,780.00
Karean	Eissler	$138,990.00	1276	No	$69,495.00	$19,855.71
Anny	Almonte	$140,693.00	1490	No	$70,346.50	$20,099.00
Karean	Eissler	$140,904.00	1301	No	$70,452.00	$23,484.00
Anny	Almonte	$150,200.00	1652	No	$75,100.00	$21,457.14
StudentFirst	StudentLast	$163,737.00	1476	No	$81,868.50	$27,289.50
StudentFirst	StudentLast	$164,436.00	1850	No	$82,218.00	$27,406.00
Pradeep	Rana	$166,530.00	1676	No	$83,265.00	$27,755.00
StudentFirst	StudentLast	$166,552.00	1623	No	$83,276.00	$27,758.67
Anny	Almonte	$166,800.00	1598	No	$83,400.00	$27,800.00
Anny	Almonte	$168,354.00	1651	No	$84,177.00	$24,050.57
StudentFirst	StudentLast	$168,504.00	1625	No	$84,252.00	$28,084.00
Anny	Almonte	$172,458.00	1798	No	$86,229.00	$24,636.86
Bill	Sabey	$174,230.00	1771	No	$87,115.00	$29,038.33
StudentFirst	StudentLast	$174,720.00	1694	No	$87,360.00	$29,120.00
Robert Allen	Dickey	$174,720.00	1610	No	$87,360.00	$29,120.00
Anny	Almonte	$174,720.00	1667	No	$87,360.00	$29,120.00
Robert Allen	Dickey	$175,560.00	1562	No	$87,780.00	$25,080.00
StudentFirst	StudentLast	$177,984.00	1707	No	$88,992.00	$29,664.00
Bill	Sabey	$179,712.00	1854	No	$89,856.00	$25,673.14
Bill	Sabey	$182,385.00	2014	No	$45,596.25	$22,798.13
Anny	Almonte	$183,312.00	1721	No	$91,656.00	$30,552.00
Anny	Almonte	$184,473.00	1791	No	$92,236.50	$26,353.29

Record: ◄ 1 of 213 ► ►► ⊠ No Filter   Search

v. Save and close the query.

TIP | **Switching Between Object Views**

You can switch between object views quickly by clicking View, or you can click the View arrow and select the desired view from the list. Another way to switch between views is to right-click the object tab and select the view from the shortcut menu.

TIP | **Expression Builder and Property Sheet**

You can launch the Expression Builder by either clicking Builder in the Query Setup group on the Design tab or by right-clicking in the top row of the query design grid and selecting Build. Similarly, you can display the Property Sheet by clicking Property Sheet in the Show/Hide group on the Design tab or by right-clicking the top row of the query design grid and selecting Properties from the shortcut menu.

STEP 2 ≫ USE BUILT-IN FUNCTIONS

Don and Matt feel like they are close to making an offer on a house. They would like to restrict the query to houses that cost $150,000 or less. They would also like to calculate the estimated mortgage payment for each house. You create this calculation using the Pmt function. You will use the Pmt function to calculate an estimated house payment for each of the sold properties. You make the following assumptions: 100% of the sale price will be financed, a 30-year term, monthly payments, and a fixed 6.0% annual interest rate. Refer to Figures 12.13 and 12.14 as you complete Step 2.

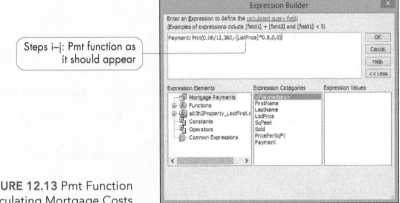

Steps i–j: Pmt function as it should appear

FIGURE 12.13 Pmt Function Calculating Mortgage Costs

a. Create a copy of the Price Per Sq Ft Formatted query named **Mortgage Payments**.

The new query is displayed in the Navigation Pane.

b. Right-click **Mortgage Payments** and select **Design View**.

c. Delete the WrongPricePerSqFt field.

The WrongPricePerSqFt field is not needed for this query.

> **TROUBLESHOOTING:** If you do not see the WrongPricePerSqFt field, ensure you copied the correct query.

d. Type **<=150000** in the Criteria row of the ListPrice column. Press **Enter**.

The query, when it is run, will show only the houses that cost $150,000 or less.

e. Click in the top cell of the first blank column. Click **Builder** in the Query Setup group to open the Expression Builder dialog box.

f. Double-click **Functions** in the Expression Elements box and click **Built-In Functions**.

g. Click **Financial** in the Expression Categories box.

h. Double-click **Pmt** in the Expression Values box.

The expression box displays:

Pmt(«rate», «num_periods», «present_value», «future_value», «type»)

i. Position the insertion point before the Pmt function. Type **Payment:** to the left of the Pmt function.

The expression box now displays:

Payment:Pmt(«rate», «num_periods», «present_value», «future_value», «type»)

> **TROUBLESHOOTING:** If you forget to add the calculated field name to the left of the expression, Access will add *Expr1* to the front of your expression for you. You can edit the Expr1 name later, after the Expression Builder is closed.

j. Click each argument to select it and substitute the appropriate information. Make sure there is a comma between each argument.

Argument	Replacement Value
«rate»	0.06/12
«num_periods»	360
«present_value»	[ListPrice]*0.8
«future_value»	0
«type»	0

Note the loan is a 30-year loan with 12 payments per year, hence the 360 value for the number of payments. Also note, Don and Matt plan on financing 80% of the cost, putting 20% down. Therefore, you need to multiply the list price times 0.8 (80%).

k. Examine Figure 12.13 to make sure that you have entered the correct arguments. Click **OK**.

l. Click **OK**. Open the **Property Sheet** for *Payment* and change the format to **Currency**. Close the Property Sheet. **Run** the query.

Notice the payment amounts are negative numbers (displayed in parentheses). You will edit the formula to change the negative payment values to positive.

m. Right-click the **Mortgage Payments tab** and select **Design View**. Click **Builder**. Add a **minus sign (−)** to the left of *[ListPrice]* and click **OK**.

By adding the negative sign in front of the ListPrice field, you ensure the value is displayed as a positive number. The expression now reads *Payment: Pmt(0.06/12,360, −[ListPrice]*0.8,0,0)*.

The calculated field values should now appear as positive values formatted as currency, as shown in Figure 12.14.

> Steps l–n: Payment field displayed as a positive number, formatted as Currency

First Name	Last Name	List Price	Square Feet	Sold	Price Per Sq Ft	Payment
StudentFirst	StudentLast	$109,140.00	1133	No	$96.33	$523.48
Bill	Sabey	$119,990.00	1202	No	$99.83	$575.52
Anny	Almonte	$122,220.00	1235	No	$98.96	$586.22
Robert Allen	Dickey	$129,780.00	1132	No	$114.65	$622.48
Bill	Sabey	$136,680.00	1375	No	$99.40	$655.57
Karean	Eissler	$138,990.00	1276	No	$108.93	$666.65
Anny	Almonte	$140,693.00	1490	No	$94.42	$674.82
Karean	Eissler	$140,904.00	1301	No	$108.30	$675.83

FIGURE 12.14 Results of Mortgage Payments Query

n. Click **OK**. Run the query and examine the results.

The query displays a column containing the calculated monthly mortgage payment, formatted as currency.

o. Save and close the query. Keep the database open if you plan to continue with the next Hands-On Exercise. If not, close the database and exit Access.

Aggregate Functions

Aggregate functions perform calculations on an entire column of data and return a single value. Aggregate functions—such as Sum, Avg, and Count—are used when you need to evaluate a group of record values rather than the individual records in a table or query.

Access refers to aggregate functions as Totals. Totals can be added to the Datasheet view of a query, or they can be added to a query's Design view. Based on the data type, different aggregate functions will be available. Numeric fields are eligible for all of the functions, whereas Short Text fields are not. A list of common aggregate functions is shown in Table 12.4.

A car dealer's monthly inventory report is a good example of a report that might contain aggregate information. The cars would be grouped by model, then by options package and color. At the end of the report, a summary page would list the count of cars in each model for quick reference by the sales reps. In the property database, aggregate information could be grouped by county or by subdivision. For example, the average home price per county could be presented in a query or a report. This would give prospective buyers a good idea of home prices in their target counties. Almost every company or organization that uses a database will require some type of aggregate data.

TABLE 12.4 Common Aggregate Functions

Function	Description	Use with Data Type(s)
AVG	Calculates the average value for a column. The function ignores null values.	Number, Currency, Date/Time
COUNT	Counts the number of items in a column. The function ignores null values.	All data types except a column of multivalued lists.
MAXIMUM	Returns the item with the highest value. For text data, the highest value is "Z." The function ignores null values.	Number, Currency, Date/Time, Short Text
MINIMUM	Returns the item with the lowest value. For text data, the lowest value is "a." The function ignores null values.	Number, Currency, Date/Time, Short Text
SUM	Adds the items in a column. Works only on numeric and currency data.	Number, Currency

In this section, you will learn how to create and work with aggregate functions. Specifically, you will learn how to use the Total row and create a totals query.

Adding Aggregate Functions to Datasheets

Aggregate functions are most commonly used in tables, queries, and reports. Occasionally, aggregate functions are also added to the *form footer* section of forms. Aggregate data helps users evaluate the values in a single record as compared to the aggregate of all the records. If you are considering buying a property in Bergen County, New Jersey, for $150,000, and the average price of a property in that county is $450,000, you know you are getting a good deal (or buying a bad property).

Access provides two methods of adding aggregate functions to a query—a *Total row*, which displays the results of the aggregate function as the last row in the Datasheet view of a table or query, and a totals query created in Query Design view.

The first method enables you to add a Total row to the Datasheet view. This method is quick and easy and has the advantage of showing the total information while still showing the individual records. Adding a Total row to a query or table can be accomplished by most users, even those who are not familiar with designing a query. Note the Total row values cannot be modified; you can change the aggregate function displayed there, but you cannot overwrite the numbers.

Add a Total Row in a Query or Table

STEP 1 > Figure 12.15 shows the Total row added to the Datasheet view of a query. You can choose any of the aggregate functions that apply to numeric fields. Follow these steps to add a Total row to a query or table:

1. Ensure you are viewing the query in Datasheet view.
2. Click Totals in the Records group on the HOME tab. The Total row is added at the bottom of the datasheet, below the new record row of the query or table.
3. In the new Total row, you can select one of the aggregate functions by clicking in the cell and clicking the arrow. The list of aggregate functions includes Sum, Avg, Count, and others.

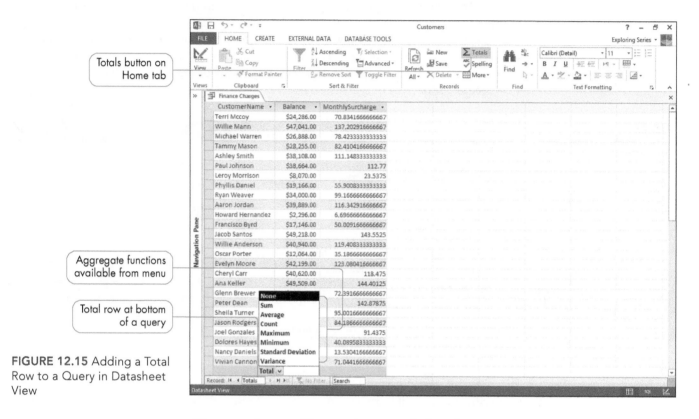

FIGURE 12.15 Adding a Total Row to a Query in Datasheet View

Creating Queries with Aggregate Functions

The second method to display aggregate functions requires you to alter the design of a query and add a Total row in the Query Design view. Once the totals data is assembled, you can use it to make decisions. For example, you can use the Count function to show the number of houses sold. You could also use the Avg function to show the average sale price for houses. This method has the advantage of enabling you to group your data by categories.

Many times, you will need to find some sort of averages for fields, and you may need to do more in-depth statistics than just an overall set as we did in the previous few pages. Instead of wanting to see the average sale price for houses, you may want to see the average sale price by city. Using the total row in the previous example, this is not feasible. Another limitation of the previous example is that I might want to see the average sale price, minimum sale price, and maximum sale price. Using the previous method, we would have to put the sale price field into our query three times, leading to repeated columns.

Instead of showing detail, we can quickly see the overall statistics for the entire table or query. For example, if you want to see the number of listings, average value, and the average size in square feet for all properties in your table, you can run a totals query to get that data and not see details. Instead of doing that, we can create a different type of query to summarize our data.

Create a Basic Totals Query

A *totals query* contains an additional row in the query design grid and is used to display aggregate data when the query is run. Figure 12.16 shows a totals query in Design view, and Figure 12.17 shows the results.

To create a Totals query:

1. Create a query in Design view and add the fields for which you want to get statistics. For example, in the preceding example, we would add the Listing, List Price, and Square Feet fields.
2. Click Totals in the Show/Hide group on the QUERY TOOLS DESIGN tab to display the total row. A new row should display in your query between the Table and Sort options. You will notice it defaults to Group By.
3. For each field, select the menu next to Group By and select the aggregate function you want applied to that field. For example, we want to count the number of listings and average both the list price and square feet values.
4. If you would like to apply specific formats, display the Property Sheet (as we did earlier in this chapter) and adjust the settings for each field.
5. Run the query to see your results.

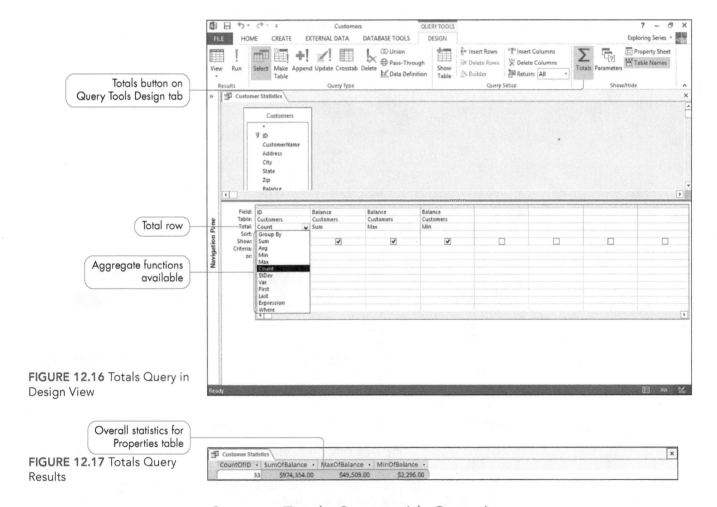

FIGURE 12.16 Totals Query in Design View

FIGURE 12.17 Totals Query Results

Create a Totals Query with Grouping

Grouping a query allows you to summarize your data by the values of a field. For example, you want to see the results not for the entire table, but instead by state. You can add the State field as a grouping level, and Access will show you the statistics you request for each state.

To group an existing query, add the field you wish to group by to the query in Design view. You would then verify the Total row displays Group By (see Figure 12.18). So if you want to see the results by state, add the State field to the query and leave the Total with the default of Group By. You may want to move this column to the beginning, as it will make your query easier to read.

Figure 12.18 shows the Design view of a totals query with five columns, one of which is the grouping field. Figure 12.19 shows the results of this query.

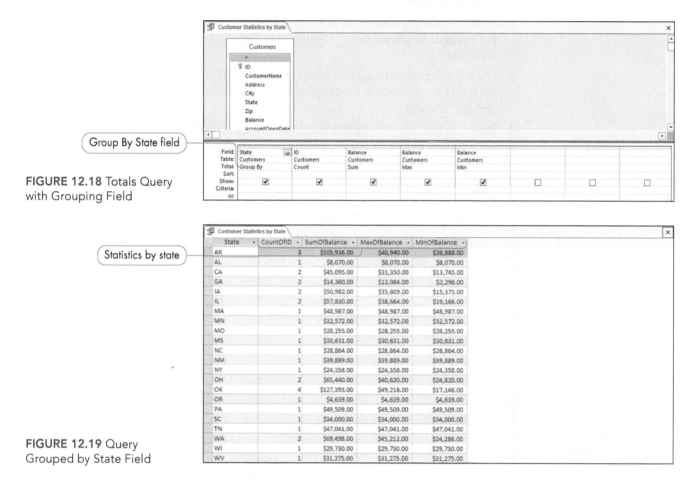

Group By State field

FIGURE 12.18 Totals Query with Grouping Field

Statistics by state

FIGURE 12.19 Query Grouped by State Field

TIP Too Much Grouping

Beware that the more grouping levels you add, the less valuable the data is probably going to be; a typical totals query will group by only a few columns. As the purpose of grouping is to get some sort of aggregate data (such as a sum) for related data, grouping by more fields leads to less data being summarized.

Create a Totals Query with a Condition

Totals queries can provide even better information if you add criteria. For example, if you wanted to see the number of houses, average price, and average square feet for only the unsold properties, grouped by state, you can add the Sold field to the query. You would set the criteria to No to indicate that the Sold field is no. You should select Where from the menu in the Total row for any field you add to which you wish to apply criteria. Figure 12.20 shows a query with a condition added, and Figure 12.21 shows the results. You can compare this to Figure 12.19 to see the change in results.

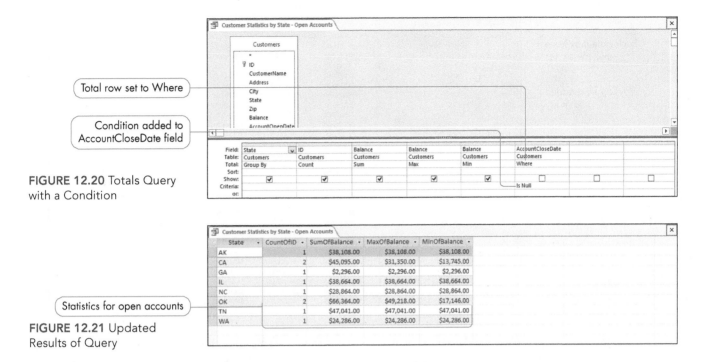

Total row set to Where

Condition added to AccountCloseDate field

FIGURE 12.20 Totals Query with a Condition

Statistics for open accounts

FIGURE 12.21 Updated Results of Query

Create a Totals Query with Multiple Grouping Levels

At times, you may want to add multiple grouping fields. For example, instead of grouping by State, you might want to group by City. However, if you group by city, customers with the same city name in different states would be grouped together. For example, all 50 states have a location named Greenville. If you grouped by city, all customers with a city of Greenville, regardless of state, would appear as a group. This is probably not your intention. Instead, you probably would want to see results by City and State, and thus would want to add multiple grouping levels. Figure 12.22 shows a second grouping level, and Figure 12.23 shows the results of the query if we group by State and then by City. Notice the multiple Greenville results.

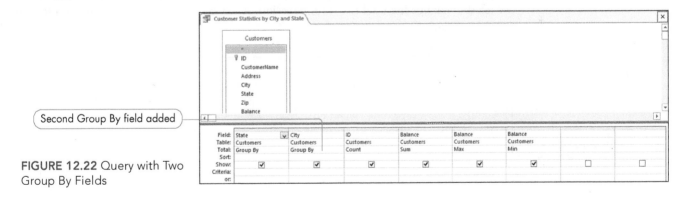

Second Group By field added

FIGURE 12.22 Query with Two Group By Fields

State	City	CountOfID	SumOfBalance	MaxOfBalance	MinOfBalance
AK	Greenville	2	$67,828.00	$40,940.00	$26,888.00
AK	Kaktovik	1	$38,108.00	$38,108.00	$38,108.00
AL	Greenville	1	$8,070.00	$8,070.00	$8,070.00
CA	Los Angeles	1	$13,745.00	$13,745.00	$13,745.00
CA	San Diego	1	$31,350.00	$31,350.00	$31,350.00
GA	Austell	1	$2,296.00	$2,296.00	$2,296.00
GA	Leary	1	$12,064.00	$12,064.00	$12,064.00
IA	Albert City	1	$15,373.00	$15,373.00	$15,373.00
IA	Iowa City	1	$35,609.00	$35,609.00	$35,609.00
IL	Champaign	2	$57,830.00	$38,664.00	$19,166.00
MA	Southampton	1	$48,987.00	$48,987.00	$48,987.00
MN	Beltrami	1	$32,572.00	$32,572.00	$32,572.00
MO	De Kalb	1	$28,255.00	$28,255.00	$28,255.00
MS	Meridian	1	$30,631.00	$30,631.00	$30,631.00
NC	Raleigh	1	$28,864.00	$28,864.00	$28,864.00
NM	Bard	1	$39,889.00	$39,889.00	$39,889.00
NY	Saint Bonavent	1	$24,358.00	$24,358.00	$24,358.00
OH	Canton	1	$40,620.00	$40,620.00	$40,620.00
OH	Cincinnati	1	$24,820.00	$24,820.00	$24,820.00
OK	Albany	1	$17,146.00	$17,146.00	$17,146.00
OK	Canadian	1	$42,199.00	$42,199.00	$42,199.00
OK	Lahoma	1	$18,830.00	$18,830.00	$18,830.00
OK	Rufe	1	$49,218.00	$49,218.00	$49,218.00
OR	Fall Creek	1	$4,639.00	$4,639.00	$4,639.00
PA	Pine Bank	1	$49,509.00	$49,509.00	$49,509.00
SC	Clemson	1	$34,000.00	$34,000.00	$34,000.00
TN	Auburntown	1	$47,041.00	$47,041.00	$47,041.00

Each state may have multiple entries

City field added to query

FIGURE 12.23 Results of Query with Two Group By Fields

Add a Calculated Field to a Totals Query

STEP 3 >> Once you have created a totals query, you can create calculated fields as you did earlier in the chapter. Often, you will want to apply an aggregate function to an existing field, such as summing up the values in a field. However, there may be times when you would prefer to apply an aggregate function to a calculation rather than a field.

We will use a customer purchases database to demonstrate this. When working with a customer order database, you may have a field for each order containing the total order cost and another field for each order containing the shipping cost. If you use the Sum aggregate function and group by the customer ID, you would have the total amount of their orders, and then as a separate column the total cost of the shipping they have paid. Instead of doing that, you may prefer to first create a calculated field that adds the total order cost and shipping cost for each order, and then group by a CustomerName. You will notice in Figure 12.24 we need to change the total row to Expression. After making that change, your results will resemble Figure 12.25.

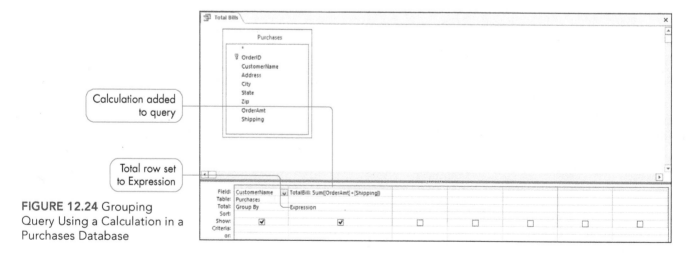

Calculation added to query

Total row set to Expression

FIGURE 12.24 Grouping Query Using a Calculation in a Purchases Database

Results are each customer's total bill

Total Bills	
CustomerName	TotalBill
Alice Ray	$688.99
Alicia Byrd	$810.50
Amber Ingram	$506.50
Annette Gibson	$720.99
Arthur Powell	$477.99
Beth Vaughn	$203.99
Carla Black	$478.50
Crystal Delgado	$166.99
Esther Bennett	$198.50
Eva Turner	$673.99
Florence Douglas	$633.99
Frances Foster	$317.50
Gina West	$629.99
Gloria Medina	$615.99
Harold Wolfe	$432.50
Heather Davidson	$343.50
Jamie Wheeler	$243.99
Jeanette Griffin	$436.50
Keith Strickland	$349.50
Lawrence Payne	$390.50
Leonard Delgado	$161.50
Lynn Brooks	$363.50
Marvin Santiago	$757.98
Megan Wheeler	$720.99
Phillip Medina	$676.50
Steve Mills	$674.50
Thelma Burgess	$529.99

FIGURE 12.25 Results of Grouping Query with a Calculation in a Purchases Database

In the third Hands-On Exercise, you will add aggregate functions to datasheets, create a totals query, and add grouping, conditions, and calculated fields to totals queries.

Quick Concepts

1. What are the benefits of aggregate functions? Give an example. *p. 631*

2. How do you add a Total row to a datasheet? *p. 632*

3. What is a totals query? *p. 633*

4. What is the difference between a query with a Total row and a totals query? *p. 633*

Watch the Video for this Hands-On Exercise!

MyITLab®
HOE3 Training

3 Aggregate Functions

The investors decide it would be helpful to analyze the property lists they purchased. Some of the lists do not have homes that match their target criteria. The investors will either need to purchase new lists or alter their criteria. You create several totals queries to evaluate the property lists.

Skills covered: Add Aggregate Functions to Datasheets • Create a Totals Query with Grouping and Conditions • Add a Calculated Field to a Totals Query

---

STEP 1 ≫ ADD AGGREGATE FUNCTIONS TO DATASHEETS

You begin your property list analysis by creating a total row in the Datasheet view of the Mortgage Payments query. This will give you a variety of aggregate information for each column. Refer to Figure 12.26 as you complete Step 1.

Step g: Average of PricePerSqFt
Step f: Count of Listing
Step e: Average of ListPrice
Step c: Total row

FIGURE 12.26 Total Row Added to Query Datasheet

a. Open *a03h2Property_LastFirst* if you closed it at the end of Hands-On Exercise 2 and save it as **a03h3Property_LastFirst**, changing *h2* to *h3*.

b. Right-click the **Mortgage Payments query** in the Navigation Pane and select **Design View**. Drag the **Listing field** from the Properties table to the fifth column.

   The Listing field is now in the fifth column, between the SqFeet and Sold fields. The other columns shift to the right.

> **TROUBLESHOOTING:** If you drag the Listing field to the wrong position, you can drag it again to the correct location.

c. Switch to Datasheet view. Click **Totals**, in the Records group on the HOME tab to display the Total row.

   The Total row displays as the last row of the query results.

d. Click in the cell that intersects the Total row and the List Price column.

e. Click the arrow and select **Average** to display the average value of all the properties that have not sold. Widen the List Price column if you can't see the entire total value.

   The average list price of all properties is $129,799.63.

f. Click the arrow in the Total row in the Listing column and select **Count** from the list.

   The count of properties in this datasheet is 8.

g. Click in the **Total row** in the Price Per Sq Ft column. Click the arrow and select **Average** to display the average price per square foot.

   The average price per square foot is $102.57.

h. Save and close the query.

STEP 2 >> CREATE A TOTALS QUERY WITH GROUPING AND CONDITIONS

You create a totals query to help Don and Matt evaluate the properties in groups. Refer to Figure 12.27 and Figure 12.28 as you complete Step 2.

FIGURE 12.27 Overall Results Query

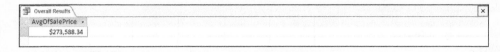

a. Click **Query Design** in the Queries group of the CREATE tab.

You create a new query in Query Design; the Show Table dialog box opens.

b. Add the Properties table from the Show Table dialog box. Close the Show Table dialog box.

c. Add the SalePrice and Sold fields from the Properties table to the query design grid.

d. Click **Totals** in the Show/Hide group of the QUERY TOOLS DESIGN tab to show the Total row.

A new row labeled Totals displays at the bottom of the screen in the design grid, between the Table and Sort rows. Each field will have Group By listed in the new row by default.

e. Click the **Group By arrow** in the SalePrice column Total row and select **Avg.**

f. Click the **Group By arrow** in the Sold column Total row and select **Where**. Type **Yes** in the Criteria row.

This criterion will limit the results to sold houses only.

g. Click in the **SalePrice field** and click **Property Sheet** in the Show/Hide group. Change the SalePrice format to **Currency**. Close the Property Sheet. Run the query and compare your results to Figure 12.27.

The results show an overall average of $273,588.34 for the sold properties in the database.

h. Click **Save** on the Quick Access Toolbar and type **Overall Results** as the Query Name in the Save As dialog box. Click **OK**. Close the query.

i. Click **Query Design** in the Query group of the HOME tab to create a new query.

j. Add the Properties table and the Lists table from the Show Table dialog box. Close the Show Table dialog box.

k. Add the NameOfList field from the Lists table and the SalePrice, Listing, and Sold fields from the Properties table to the query design grid.

l. Click **Totals** on the QUERY TOOLS DESIGN tab in the Show/Hide group to show the Total row.

A new row labeled Total appears at the bottom of the screen in the design grid between the Table and Sort rows.

m. Change the Total row for *SalePrice* to **Avg.**

n. Change the Total row for *Listing* to **Count**.

o. Change the Total row for *Sold* to **Where**. Type **Yes** in the Criteria row.

This criterion will limit the results to sold houses only.

p. Click in the **SalePrice field** and click **Property Sheet** in the Show/Hide group. Change the SalePrice format to **Currency**.

q. Change the caption of the Listing column to **Number Sold**. Run the query and widen the columns as shown in Figure 12.28.

Notice Major Houses has the only average sale price under $200,000. As Don and Matt are hoping to focus on inexpensive properties, they will focus on properties offered by this source. Notice the query results show the number of properties sold in each source, in addition to the average sale price. This will help determine which sources have been more effective.

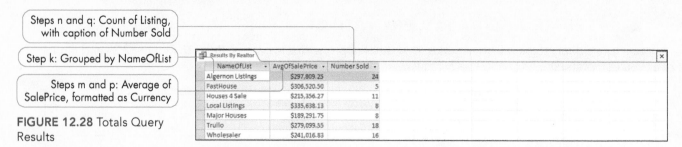

Steps n and q: Count of Listing, with caption of Number Sold

Step k: Grouped by NameOfList

Steps m and p: Average of SalePrice, formatted as Currency

FIGURE 12.28 Totals Query Results

> **r.** Click **Save** on the Quick Access Toolbar and type **Results By Realtor** as the Query Name in the Save As dialog box. Click **OK**. Keep the query open for the next step.

STEP 3 ≫ ADD A CALCULATED FIELD TO A TOTALS QUERY

The previous query shows the average value of the properties by realtor. However, Don and Matt learned at the seminar they attended that the longer a property has been on the market, the better your chances of negotiating a better price. You will revise the query to include the average number of days on the market for each realtor. Refer to Figure 12.29 as you complete Step 3.

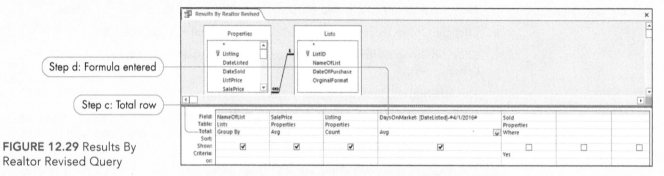

Step d: Formula entered

Step c: Total row

FIGURE 12.29 Results By Realtor Revised Query

> **a.** Click the **FILE tab**, click **Save As**, and then click **Save Object As**. Click **Save As**, and in the *Save 'Results By Realtor' to:* box, type **Results By Realtor Revised**.
>
> **b.** Switch to the Datasheet view for the new Results By Realtor Revised query, if necessary.
>
> **c.** Click **Totals** in the Records group of the HOME tab. Change the Total to **Sum** in the Number Sold column.
>
>   The total number of houses sold (90) now displays at the bottom of the Number Sold column.
>
> **d.** Switch to Design view. In the first blank column, type **DaysOnMarket: [DateListed] – #4/1/2016#** to create a new calculated field. Change the Total row to **Avg**.
>
>   The DaysOnMarket field will show the average number of days on the market for each realtor's listings.
>
> **e.** Display the Property Sheet for the DaysOnMarket field and change the Format property to **Fixed**. Change the Decimal Places property to **0**. Close the Property Sheet.

> **TROUBLESHOOTING:** If you do not see a Decimal Places property immediately beneath the Format property, change the format to Fixed, save and close the query, and then reopen the query. Refer to Figure 12.4 for the location of Decimal Places.

> **f.** Run the query and examine the DaysOnMarket field.
>
>   Major Houses listings have an average of 117 days on the market. The combination of inexpensive prices and properties that do not sell quickly may help Don and Matt negotiate with the realtor.
>
> **g.** Save and close the query.
>
> **h.** Exit Access. Submit based on your instructor's directions.

Chapter Objectives Review

After reading this chapter, you have accomplished the following objectives:

1. **Create a calculated field in a query.**
   - Calculations can be based on fields, constants, and/or functions.
   - Understand the order of operations: Calculated fields follow the same order of operations as mathematical equations—parentheses, then exponentiation, then multiplication and division, and finally addition and subtraction.
   - Build expressions with correct syntax: Expressions must be written using proper syntax—the rules governing the way you give instructions to Access.

2. **Format and save calculated results.**
   - Calculated results may not have the format you want; change the properties of a calculated field using the Property Sheet.
   - Recover from common errors: Common errors include forgetting the colon in the appropriate location, spelling errors, and misuse of the order of operations.
   - Verify calculated results: Always check the results of your equation; Access will check for syntax errors, but not logic errors.

3. **Create expressions with the Expression Builder.**
   - Expression Builder helps create complex expressions.
   - Create an expression: Expression Builder allows you to choose fields and built-in functions easily, and gives you a larger screen to view your expression.
   - Launch the Expression Builder: Clicking the Builder button will open the tool.

4. **Use built-in functions in Access.**
   - Access includes functions, or predefined computations that perform complex calculations.
   - There are almost 150 built-in functions in Access.
   - Some require arguments: inputs (often fields or constants) given to a function.
   - Calculate payments with the Pmt Function: The Pmt function accepts the rate per term, number of payments, and loan amount and calculates a loan payment.

5. **Add aggregate functions to datasheets.**
   - Aggregate functions perform calculations on an entire column of data and return a single value.
   - Include functions such as Sum, Avg, and Count.
   - Add a total row in a query or table: The total row displays at the bottom of a query or table; it can perform any aggregate function on each column.

6. **Create queries with aggregate functions.**
   - This gives you more control over application of your aggregate functions.
   - Create a basic totals query: Create a query as usual and click the Totals button in Design view.
   - Create a totals query with grouping: Grouping allows you to summarize your data by the values of a field; instead of showing overall averages, add state as a grouping field and see averages for each state.
   - Create a totals query with a condition: Conditions can be added to totals queries, such as only showing listings with the Sold field equal to No.
   - Create a totals query with multiple grouping levels: You can add multiple grouping levels; for example, you could group by State and then by City to get more detailed results.
   - Add a calculated field to a totals query: You can apply an aggregate function to the results of a calculation; for example, subtract a date from today's date to get the number of days a listing is active and calculate the overall average of days listings are active.

Key Terms Matching

Match the key terms with their definitions. Write the key term letter by the appropriate numbered definition.

a. Aggregate Function
b. Argument
c. Constant
d. Expression
e. Expression Builder
f. Function
g. Grouping

h. Order of Operations
i. Pmt Function
j. Property Sheet
k. Syntax
l. Total Row
m. Totals Query

1. _____ A value that does not change. **p. 610**

2. _____ A formula used to calculate new fields from the values in existing fields. **p. 610**

3. _____ Determines the sequence by which operations are calculated in an expression. **p. 611**

4. _____ Dictates the structure and components required to perform the necessary calculations in an equation or evaluate expressions. **p. 611**

5. _____ Enables you to change settings such as number format, number of decimal places, and caption. **p. 613**

6. _____ An Access tool that helps you create more complicated expressions. **p. 621**

7. _____ A predefined computation that performs a complex calculation. Almost 150 are built into Access. **p. 623**

8. _____ Any data needed to produce output for a function. **p. 623**

9. _____ Calculates the periodic loan payment given the interest rate per period, term of the loan in months, and the original value of the loan. **p. 623**

10. _____ Performs calculations on an entire column of data and returns a single value. Includes functions such as Sum, Avg, and Count. **p. 631**

11. _____ Displays aggregate function results as the last row in the Datasheet view of a table or query. **p. 631**

12. _____ Makes an additional row available in the query design grid. Used to display aggregate data when the query is run. **p. 633**

13. _____ Allows you to summarize your data by the values of a field. **p. 633**

Multiple Choice

1. Which of the following correctly identifies the rules for the order of operations?

   (a) Parentheses, exponentiation, addition, subtraction, multiplication, division

   (b) Exponentiation, parentheses, addition, subtraction, multiplication, division

   (c) Addition, subtraction, multiplication, division, exponentiation, parentheses

   (d) Parentheses, exponentiation, multiplication, division, addition, subtraction

2. What is the result of the following expression?
   $(3 * 5) + 7 - 2 - 6 / 2$

   (a) 17

   (b) 7

   (c) 14.5

   (d) 13

3. Which of the following *cannot* be adjusted in the Property Sheet?

   (a) Number of decimal places

   (b) Mathematical expression

   (c) Caption

   (d) Number format (for example, Currency)

4. Which of the following is *not* an aggregate function?

   (a) Pmt

   (b) Avg

   (c) Count

   (d) Min

5. Which of the following can be added to a totals query?

   (a) Conditions

   (b) Grouping fields

   (c) Aggregate functions

   (d) All of the above can be added to a totals query

6. Which statement about a totals query is *true*?

   (a) A totals query is created in Datasheet view.

   (b) A totals query may contain several grouping fields but only one aggregate field.

   (c) A totals query is limited to only two fields, one grouping field and one aggregate field.

   (d) A totals query may contain several grouping fields and several aggregate fields.

7. Which of the following statements is *true*?

   (a) A total order cost would be a common field to group by.

   (b) A last name would be a common field to group by.

   (c) For best results, add as many group by fields as possible.

   (d) None of the above statements is true.

8. After creating a calculated field, you run the query and a Parameter dialog box appears on your screen. How do you respond to the Parameter dialog box?

   (a) Click OK to make the parameter box go away.

   (b) Look for a possible typing error in the calculated expression.

   (c) Type numbers in the Parameter box and click OK.

   (d) Close the query without saving changes. Reopen it and try running the query again.

9. A query contains student names. You run the query and while in Datasheet view, you notice a spelling error on one of the student's names. You correct the error in Datasheet view. Which statement is *true*?

   (a) The name is correctly spelled in this query but will be misspelled in the table and all other queries based on the table.

   (b) The name is correctly spelled in this query and any other queries, but will remain misspelled in the table.

   (c) You cannot edit data in a query.

   (d) The name is correctly spelled in the table and in all queries based on the table.

10. Which of the following about the Total row in the query design grid is *false*?

    (a) The Total row enables you to apply aggregate functions to the fields.

    (b) The Total row does not display by default in all new queries.

    (c) The Total row is located between the Table and Sort rows.

    (d) The Total row cannot be applied to numeric fields.

Practice Exercises

1 Comfort Insurance

The Comfort Insurance Agency is a mid-sized company with offices located across the country. Each employee receives a performance review annually. The review determines employee eligibility for salary increases and the annual performance bonus. The employee data is stored in an Access database, which is used by the human resources department to monitor and maintain employee records. Your task is to calculate the salary increase for each employee; you will also calculate the average salary for each position. This exercise follows the same set of skills as used in Hands-On Exercises 1 and 2 in the chapter. Refer to Figure 12.30 as you complete this exercise.

Last Name	First Name	Performance	Salary	2016 Increase	New Salary
Lacher	Tom	Good	$31,200.00	3.00%	$32,136.00
Fantis	Laurie	Good	$28,000.00	3.00%	$28,840.00
Fleming	Karen	Average	$41,100.00	3.00%	$42,333.00
Mc Key	Boo	Good	$39,600.00	3.00%	$40,788.00
Daniels	Phil	Good	$42,600.00	3.00%	$43,878.00
Park	Johnny	Excellent	$48,400.00	3.00%	$49,852.00
Johnson	Debbie	Excellent	$39,700.00	3.00%	$40,891.00
Drubin	Lolly	Good	$37,000.00	3.00%	$38,110.00
Titley	David	Good	$40,200.00	3.00%	$41,406.00
Grippando	Joan	Average	$26,100.00	3.00%	$26,883.00
Block	Leonard	Excellent	$26,200.00	3.00%	$26,986.00
Mills	Jack	Average	$44,600.00	3.00%	$45,938.00
Nagel	Mimi	Average	$46,200.00	3.00%	$47,586.00
Rammos	Mitzi	Excellent	$32,500.00	3.00%	$33,475.00
Vieth	Paula	Good	$40,400.00	3.00%	$41,612.00
Novicheck	Deborah	Good	$46,800.00	3.00%	$48,204.00
Brumbaugh	Paige	Average	$49,300.00	3.00%	$50,779.00
Abrams	Wendy	Good	$47,500.00	3.00%	$48,925.00
Harrison	Jenifer	Excellent	$44,800.00	3.00%	$46,144.00
Gander	John	Average	$38,400.00	3.00%	$39,552.00
Sell	Mike	Excellent	$43,500.00	3.00%	$44,805.00
Smith	Denise	Average	$45,200.00	3.00%	$46,556.00
Pawley	Eleanor	Excellent	$42,700.00	3.00%	$43,981.00
Harris	Jennifer	Average	$34,900.00	3.00%	$35,947.00
North	Randy	Excellent	$31,700.00	3.00%	$32,651.00
Shuffield	Jan	Good	$33,700.00	3.00%	$34,711.00
Barnes	Jeb	Excellent	$46,900.00	3.00%	$48,307.00

Record: 1 of 311 ▶ ▶| No Filter Search

FIGURE 12.30 Raises and Bonuses Query

a. Open *a03p1Insurance*. Save the database as **a03p1Insurance_LastFirst**.

b. Examine the Relationships for the database. Notice the table structure, relationships, and fields. Once you are familiar with the database, close the Relationships window.

c. Create a new query in Design view. Add the Employees and Titles tables.

d. Add the LastName, FirstName, Performance, and Salary fields from the Employees table to the query. Add the 2016Increase field from the Titles table to the query.

e. Click the top row of the first blank column in the query design grid and type **NewSalary:[Salary]+ [Salary]*[2016Increase]** to create a calculated field that adds the existing salary to the increase. You may opt to use the Expression Builder if you prefer.

f. Click **Run** in the Results group to run the query. Look at the output in the Datasheet view. Verify that your answers are correct. Notice that the fourth column heading displays *2016 Increase*.

   This is the caption for the 2016Increase field in the Titles table that was carried over to the query. When a caption exists for a field in the table Design view, the caption also displays in the Query Datasheet view instead of the field name in the query.

g. Switch back to Design view. Click in the **NewSalary calculated field**, display the Property Sheet, and then change the format to **Currency**. Type **New Salary** in the **Caption box**. Close the Property Sheet.

h. Save the query as **Raises and Bonuses**. Close the query.

i. Create a new query in Design view. Add the Employees and Titles tables.

   You will create a query to show the average salary by position.

j. Add the TitleName field from the Titles table. From the Employees table, add the Salary field.

k. Display the Total row. Change the Total row for Salary to **Avg**. Leave the TitleName field set to **Group By**.

l. Click the **Salary field** and display the Property Sheet. Change the format for the field to **Currency**.

m. Run the query. Save the query as **Average Salary By Position** and close the query.

n. Exit Access and submit based on your instructor's directions.

2 | Analyze Orders

You are the marketing manager of your company, and you must use the order information from an Access database to analyze sales trends. You need to determine the order revenue for all orders, grouped by Ship Country. The company would also like to check to see if there are order delays related to a specific employee. You must analyze shipping performance based on the number of days it takes to ship each order. This exercise follows the same set of skills as used in Hands-On Exercises 2 and 3 in the chapter. Refer to Figure 12.31 as you complete this exercise.

FIGURE 12.31 Shipping Issues Query

a. Create a new blank desktop database named **a03p2Orders_LastFirst**.

You will be shown a blank table in Datasheet view.

b. Click **View** in the Views group to switch to Design view. Save the table as **Orders**.

c. Change the first Field Name to **OrderID** and change the Data Type to **Number**. Type **CustomerID** in the second row and press **Tab**. Accept **Short Text** as the Data Type. Type **EmployeeID** in the third row and press **Tab**. Select **Number** for the Data Type.

d. Type and format the remainder of the fields as follows:

OrderDate	Date/Time
ShippedDate	Date/Time
ShipVia	Number
Revenue	Currency
ShipCountry	Short Text

e. Click **View** in the Views group to switch to Datasheet view. Click **Yes** to save the table. Add the three records as shown in the following table. Press **Tab** to move to the next field.

Order ID	Customer ID	Employee ID	Order Date	Shipped Date	Ship Via	Revenue	Ship Country
10248	WILMK	5	1/6/2017	1/19/2017	1	$142.86	Belgium
10249	TRADH	6	1/7/2017	1/10/2017	2	$205.38	Germany
10250	HANAR	4	1/10/2017	1/30/2017	2	$58.60	Venezuela

f. Open the *a03p2Orders* Excel file and click **Enable Editing**, if necessary. Click and hold **row 2** and drag through **row 828** so that all of the data rows are selected. Click **Copy** in the Clipboard group.

g. Return to Access and click on the **asterisk (*)** on the fourth row of the Orders table. Click **Paste** in the Clipboard group and click **Yes** to confirm that you want to paste all 827 rows into the Orders table. Save and close the table, and then close the spreadsheet and Excel. If prompted to save the data in the clipboard, click **No**.

h. Click the **CREATE tab** and click **Query Design** in the Queries group to start a new query. The Show Table dialog box opens. Add the Orders table and close the Show Table dialog box.

i. Add EmployeeID to the query and sort the table by EmployeeID in ascending order.

j. Use the Expression Builder to create a new calculated field. Type the following: **TimeToShip: [ShippedDate]-[OrderDate]**

Run the query and verify that TimeToShip is displaying valid values.

k. Switch back to Design view. Add the criteria **>21** to the TimeToShip field. Run the query and compare your results with Figure 12.31.

The results do not show a pattern of one employee's orders being delayed.

l. Save the query as **Shipping Issues**. Close the query.

m.Click the **CREATE tab** and click **Query Design** in the Queries group to start a new query. The Show Table dialog box opens. Add the Orders table and close the Show Table dialog box. Click **Totals** in the Show/Hide group.

n. Insert the ShipCountry and Revenue fields from the Orders table.

o. Verify the value for ShipCountry is set to **Group By** in the Totals row in Design view and verify that the value for the Revenue field is set to **Sum**.

p. Click in the **Revenue field**. Display the Property Sheet and change the caption to **Total Revenue**.

q. Click **Run** to see the results and save the query as **Revenue by Ship Country**. Close the query.

r. Exit Access and submit based on your instructor's directions.

1 Small Business Loans

ANALYSIS
CASE

FROM
SCRATCH

You are the manager of the small business loan department for the U.S. government. You need to calculate the payments for the loans that are currently on the books. To do this, you will need to create a query and add the Pmt function to calculate the loan payments for each loan. You will also summarize each loan by loan type (M=Mortgage, C=Car, and O=Other). Refer to Figure 12.32 as you complete this exercise.

Company	LoanID	Amount	InterestRate	Term	LoanClass	Payment
Jones and Co	1	29,000.00	5.90%	15	M	$243.15
Elements, Inc.	2	23,000.00	5.25%	5	C	$436.68
Godshall Meats, LLC	3	24,000.00	4.50%	3	C	$713.93
Godshall Meats, LLC	4	12,000.00	3.99%	10	O	$121.44
Godshall Meats, LLC	5	60,000.00	5.50%	30	M	$340.67
Elements, Inc.	6	4,000.00	6.50%	5	O	$78.26
Jones and Co	7	43,000.00	5.50%	5	O	$821.35
Jones and Co	8	37,000.00	5.80%	30	M	$217.10
Jones and Co	9	15,000.00	4.75%	3	O	$447.88
Jones and Co	10	8,000.00	5.50%	15	M	$65.37
Godshall Meats, LLC	11	34,000.00	5.00%	3	C	$1,019.01
Godshall Meats, LLC	12	13,000.00	7.99%	5	O	$263.53
Jones and Co	13	46,000.00	6.50%	5	C	$900.04
Godshall Meats, LLC	14	56,000.00	5.99%	15	M	$472.26
Godshall Meats, LLC	15	54,000.00	6.25%	15	M	$463.01
Jones and Co	16	39,000.00	6.50%	15	M	$339.73
Jones and Co	17	21,000.00	6.00%	30	M	$125.91
Godshall Meats, LLC	18	27,000.00	5.50%	3	O	$815.29
Elements, Inc.	19	44,000.00	5.50%	5	C	$840.45
Godshall Meats, LLC	20	22,000.00	6.25%	4	C	$519.20
Godshall Meats, LLC	21	6,000.00	6.75%	4	C	$142.98
Godshall Meats, LLC	22	46,000.00	6.50%	15	M	$400.71
Jones and Co	23	25,000.00	5.00%	15	M	$197.70
Jones and Co	24	11,000.00	5.55%	30	M	$62.80
Jones and Co	25	52,000.00	4.99%	15	M	$410.94
Total		751,000.00	5.74%	12		

FIGURE 12.32 Loan Payments
Query Results

a. Open Access and create a new blank desktop database named **a03m1Loans_LastFirst**.
   Access will display a table named Table1 with one field, ID.

b. Switch to Design view. Type **Customers** in the **Save As dialog box** and click **OK**.

c. Change the first Field Name to **CustomerID** and accept **AutoNumber** as the Data Type. Type **Company** in the second row and press **Tab**. Accept **Short Text** as the Data Type. Type **FirstName** in the third row and press **Tab**. Accept **Short Text** as the Data Type.

d. Type the remainder of the fields:

LastName	Short Text
City	Short Text
State	Short Text
Zip	Short Text

e. Verify the first field is set as the primary key.

f. Switch to Datasheet view. Click **Yes** to save the table. Add the records as shown in the following table. Note you will allow Access to assign an ID. Once you have entered the records, close the Customers table.

Company	FirstName	LastName	City	State	Zip
Jones and Co	Robert	Paterson	Greensboro	NC	27401
Elements, Inc.	Merve	Kana	Paterson	NJ	07505
Godshall Meats, LLC	Francisco	De La Cruz	Beverly Hills	CA	90210

DISCOVER

g. Click the **External Data tab** and click **Excel** in the Import & Link group. Click **Browse** to locate the *a03m1Loans* spreadsheet. Select the database and click **Open** at the bottom of the dialog box.

h. Ensure the *Import the source data into a new table in the current database option* is selected and click **OK**. Click **Next** three times, until you are asked to add a primary key. From the *Choose my own Primary Key* menu, select **LoanID** (this should be the default option). Click **Next** once more and click **Finish**. Click **Close** in the Save Import Steps dialog box.

i. Open the Loans table in Design view. Select the **InterestRate field** and change the format to **Percent**. Change the field size for the CustomerID field to **Long Integer**. Click **Yes** when prompted that some data may be lost. Save and close the table.

j. Click the **Database Tools tab** and click **Relationships** in the Relationships group. Add both tables to the Relationships window and close the Show Table dialog box.

k. Drag the **CustomerID field** from the Customers table and drop it onto the CustomerID field in the Loans table. Check the **Enforce Referential Integrity check box** in the Edit Relationships dialog box and click **Create**. Save and close the Relationships window.

l. Create a query using the two tables that will calculate the payment amount for each loan. Add the following fields: **Company**, **LoanID**, **Amount**, **InterestRate**, **Term**, and **LoanClass**. Sort the query by LoanID in ascending order. Save the query as **Loan Payments**.

m. Add a calculated field named **Payment** in the first blank column to calculate the loan payment for each loan, using the Expression Builder. Use the Pmt function. Insert the appropriate field names in place of the placeholder arguments. Assume the loans have monthly payments (12 payments per year). Ensure the payment displays as a positive number. Run the query.

The first loan should have a value of approximately $243.15 (the extra decimal places will be removed shortly). Refer to Figure 12.32. If your number does not match up, reexamine your formula.

> **TROUBLESHOOTING:** If you cannot see the fields from your current query, ensure you have saved the query. Try closing and reopening the query.

n. Switch to Design view and change the display to **Currency format**. Run the query again to verify your changes. Compare your results to Figure 12.32.

o. Switch to Datasheet view and add a **Totals row**. Use it to calculate the sum of the amount column, the average interest rate, and the average term. Save and close the query.

p. Create a copy of Loan Payments. Save the new query as **Loan Payments Summary**.

q. Open the Loan Payments Summary query in Design view and rearrange the columns as follows: LoanClass, LoanID, Amount, and InterestRate. Delete columns CompanyName, Term, and Payment. Click **Totals** in the Show/Hide group. Change the Total row from left to right as follows: Group By, Count, Sum, and Avg. Run the query.

As we sorted the previous query by LoanID in Ascending order, this query will have the same sort by default.

r. Switch to Design view and display the Property Sheet. For the LoanID field, change the caption to **Loans**. For the Amount field, change the caption to **Total Amount** and change the format to **Currency**. For the InterestRate field, change the caption to **Avg Interest Rate** and change the format to **Percent**. Run the query. Save and close the query.

s. Exit Access, and submit based on your instructor's directions.

2 Investment Properties

You are in charge of LGS Investment's database, which contains all of the information on the properties your firm has listed and sold. Your task is to determine the length of time each property was on the market before it sold. You also need to calculate the sales commission from each property sold. Two agents will receive commission on each transaction: the listing agent and the selling agent. You also need to summarize the sales data by employee and calculate the average number of days each employee's sales were on the market prior to selling and the total commission earned by the employees. Refer to Figure 12.33 as you complete this exercise.

FIGURE 12.33 Sales Summary Query

Subdivision	Total Sales	Days on Market	Listing Commission	Selling Commission
The Orchards	$1,288,000.00	22.75	$45,080.00	$32,200.00
Fair Brook	$1,053,900.00	24.75	$36,886.50	$26,347.50
Eagle Valley	$4,012,000.00	39.00	$140,420.00	$100,300.00
Wood	$1,428,650.00	47.91	$50,002.75	$35,716.25
Red Canyon	$3,790,000.00	52.00	$132,650.00	$94,750.00
Total	$11,572,550.00		$405,039.25	$289,313.75

a. Open *a03m2Homes*. Save the database as **a03m2Homes_LastFirst**.

b. Create a new query, add the necessary tables, and then add the following fields: from the Agents table, add the LastName field; from the Properties table, the DateListed, DateSold, SalePrice, SellingAgent, and ListingAgent fields; and from the SubDivision table, the Subdivision field.

c. Add criteria to the table to ensure the DateSold field is not empty (in other words, properties that have not been sold). Format the SalePrice field as **Currency**. Save the query as **Sales Report**.

d. Create a calculated field using the Expression Builder named **DaysOnMarket** by subtracting DateListed from DateSold. This will calculate the number of days each sold property was on the market when it sold. Add a caption of **Days on Market**.

e. Calculate the commissions for the selling and listing agents using two calculated fields. The listing commission rate is **3.5%** of the sale price, and the selling commission rate is **2.5%** of the sale price. You can type these in directly or use the Expression Builder. Name the newly created fields **ListComm** and **SellComm**. These fields contain similar expressions. They need to be named differently so that the proper agent—the listing agent or the selling agent—gets paid. Add captions and format the fields as **Currency**.

f. Save the query after you verify that your calculations are correct. In Datasheet view, add the Total row. Calculate the average number of days on the market and the sum for the SalePrice and the two commission fields. Save and close the query.

g. Create a copy of the Sales Report query named **Sales Summary by Last Name**. Remove the DateListed, SellingAgent, ListingAgent, and Subdivision fields.

h. Display the Total row. Group by LastName and change the DateSold field Total row to **Where**, so the condition carries over. Show the sum of SalePrice, the average of DaysOnMarket, and the sum for both ListComm and SellComm. Change the caption for the SalePrice field to **Total Sales** and format the DaysOnMarket field as **Fixed**. Run the query. Adjust column widths as necessary.

i. Adjust the Total row in the Datasheet view so it shows the sum of TotalSales. Save the query.

DISCOVER

j. Create a copy of the Sales Summary by Last Name query named **Sales Summary by Subdivision**. Modify the query so the grouping is based on the Subdivision field, not LastName. Sort the query results so the fewest Days on Market is first and the most Days on Market is last. Limit the results to the top five rows.

k. Exit Access and submit based on your instructor's directions.

---

3 Political Pollsters

COLLABORATION CASE

You are working with a group that would like to analyze survey results. You are specifically looking for trends in the data based on gender, political affiliation, and income level. To demonstrate the power of Access, you and your group will perform a small survey, add the results to a database, and create some queries to demonstrate how grouping can help get results.

a. Individually, open the *a03t1Survey.docx* file. Collect 10 responses each (unless directed to do otherwise by your instructor). You should try to survey a diverse group of people. You can do this survey via e-mail, Facebook, or another appropriate method. Bring the collected data to your group.

b. Open the *a03t1Survey* database and save the database as **a03t1Survey_GroupName**. Use the Enter New Survey Result form to enter all of your information into the existing database. There are four records to start your database.

c. Open the Questions By Gender query. Notice your average for question 1 is a number between 1 and 3. As your survey document listed Agree as a 3, Neutral as 2, and Disagree as 1, the higher the value, the more strongly people agree with the question. Modify the query so that you display the average of Question2, Question3, Question4, and Question5. Change the format for the new fields to **Fixed**.

d. Create a query named **Questions By Party**, using the Questions By Gender query as a guide, grouping by the PoliticalAffiliation field rather than the Gender field.

e. Create a query named **Questions By Income Level**, using the Questions By Gender query as a guide, grouping by the IncomeLevel field rather than the Gender field.

f. Examine your results. Discuss the results with your group and type up your conclusions in a new Word document named **a03t1SurveyResults_GroupName**. You should be able to make around five conclusions. An example of a conclusion might be that people of lower income levels are less interested in being taxed to support free Internet than people of higher income.

g. Exit Access and Word and submit based on your instructor's directions.

Beyond the Classroom

Too Many Digits

RESEARCH CASE

This chapter introduced you to calculated fields. Open the database *a03b2Interest* and save the database as **a03b2Interest_LastFirst**. Open the Monthly Interest query in Datasheet view. Notice the multiple digits to the right of the decimal in the Monthly Interest column; there should only be two digits. Search the Internet to find a function that will resolve this rounding problem. You only want to display two digits to the right of the decimal (even when you click on a Monthly Interest value). Apply your changes to the Monthly Interest field, change the format to **Currency**, and then run the query to test your changes. Save the query as **Monthly Interest Revised**. If you manage to find a solution, add a second column named **MonthlyInterestRounded** that rounds to the nearest dollar. Close the query, close the database, and then exit Access. Submit your work based on your instructor's directions.

Payroll Summary Needed

DISASTER RECOVERY

You were given an Excel spreadsheet that contains paycheck information for your company. Your task is to summarize this data by employee Social Security Number (SSN) and report your results to your supervisor. Open the spreadsheet *a03b3Paychecks* and examine the data. Select all the data and copy the data. You will use Access to summarize the data in this spreadsheet. Open the Access database named *a03b3Payroll* and save it as **a03b3Payroll_LastFirst**. Open the Payroll table, select the first row, and then paste the records. Create a new totals query that summarizes the data by SSN; include the count of pay periods (using the ID field) and the sum of each currency field. Do not include the PayDate field in this query. Create a calculated field named **Total Compensation**, which totals all assets the employees have, including pay, 401(k) retirement, and health benefits. Add appropriate captions to shorten the default captions. Run the query and save it as **Payroll Summary**. Close the query, close the database, and then exit Access. Submit the database based on your instructor's directions.

Customer Service Dialog

SOFT SKILLS CASE S

Passaic County Technology Services (PCTS) provides technical support for a number of local companies. Part of their customer service evaluation involves logging how calls are closed and a quick, one-question survey given to customers at the end of a call, asking them to rate their experience from 1 (poor) to 5 (excellent). To evaluate the effectiveness of their operation, they have asked you to create some queries to help evaluate the performance of the company. Open the database *a03b4PCTS* and save the database as **a03b4PCTS_LastFirst**.

1. Create a query to show each technician and his or her effectiveness.
   - List each technician's first and last names, the number of calls, and the average of the customer's satisfaction for all calls assigned to the rep.
   - Format the average in Standard format and sort by the average so the highest average customer satisfaction appears first.
   - Save the query as **Tech Effectiveness**.

2. Create a query to show how effective the company is by call type.
   - List the call type's description (for example, Hardware Support) and the number of calls and average customer satisfaction for all calls of that type.
   - Format the average in Standard format and sort by the average so the highest average customer satisfaction appears first.
   - Save the query as **Call Type Effectiveness**.

3. Create a query to show how satisfied each customer is.

- List the company name and the number of calls and average customer satisfaction for all calls.
- Format the average in Standard format and sort by the average so the highest average customer satisfaction appears first.
- Save the query as **Customer Happiness**.

Now that you have created these queries, your supervisor should be able to quickly determine which technicians have the happiest customers, which call types the company is most effective on, and which customers are less happy than others. Close the queries, close the database, and then exit Access. Submit the database based on your instructor's directions.

Capstone Exercise

Northwind Traders, an international gourmet food distributor, is concerned about shipping delays over the past six months. Review the orders over the past six months and identify any order that was not shipped within 30 days. Each customer that falls within that time frame will be called to inquire about any problems the delay may have caused. In addition, you will create an order summary and an order summary by country.

Database File Setup

Open the food database, use Save As to make a copy of the database, and then use the new database to complete this capstone exercise. You will add yourself to the employee database.

a. Locate and open *a03c1Food* and save the database as **a03c1Food_LastFirst**.

b. Open the Employees table. Add yourself as an employee. Fill in all information, with the hire date as today. Set your *Title* to **Technical Aide**, extension to **1144**, and the Reports To field to **Buchanan, Steven**. Leave the EmployeePicture field blank.

c. Close the Employees table.

Shipping Efficiency Query

You need to create a query to calculate the number of days between the date an order was placed and the date the order was shipped for each order. As you create the query, run the query at several intervals so you can verify that the data look correct. The result of your work will be a list of orders that took more than three weeks to ship. The salespeople will be calling each customer to see if there was any problem with their order.

a. Create a query using Query Design. From the Customers table, include the fields CompanyName, ContactName, ContactTitle, and Phone. From the Orders table, include the fields OrderID, OrderDate, and ShippedDate.

b. Run the query and examine the records. Save the query as **Shipping Efficiency**.

c. Add a calculated field named **DaysToShip** to calculate the number of days taken to fill each order. (*Hint*: The expression will include the OrderDate and the ShippedDate; the results will not contain negative numbers.)

d. Run the query and examine the results. Does the data in the DaysToShip field look accurate? Save the query.

e. Add criteria to limit the query results to include any order that took more than 30 days to ship.

f. Add the Quantity field from the Order Details table and the ProductName field from the Products table to the query. Sort the query by ascending OrderID. When the sales reps contact these customers, these two fields will provide useful information about the orders.

g. Switch to Datasheet view to view the final results. This list will be distributed to the sales reps so they can contact the customers. In Design view, add the caption **Days to Ship** to the DaysToShip field.

h. Save and close the query.

Order Summary Query

You need to create an Order Summary that will show the total amount of each order in one column and the total discount amount in another column. This query will require four tables: Orders, Order Details, Products, and Customers. Query to determine if employees are following the employee discount policy. You will group the data by employee name, count the orders, show the total dollars, and show the total discount amount. You will then determine which employees are following the company guidelines.

a. Create a query using Query Design and add the four tables above. Add the fields OrderID and OrderDate. Set both fields' Total row to **Group By**.

b. Add a calculated field in the third column. Name the field **ExtendedAmount**. This field should multiply the number of items ordered by the price per item. This will calculate the total amount for each order. Format the calculated field as **Currency** and change the caption to **Total Dollars**. Change the Total row to **Sum**.

c. Add a calculated field in the fourth column. Name the field **DiscountAmount**. The field should multiply the number of items ordered, the price per item, and the discount field. This will calculate the total discount for each order. Format the calculated field as **Currency** and add a caption of **Discount Amt**. Change the Total row to **Sum**.

d. Run the query. Save the query as **Order Summary**. Return to Design view.

e. Add criteria to the OrderDate field so only orders made between 1/1/2016 and 12/31/2016 are displayed. Change the Total row to **Where**. This expression will display only orders that were created in 2016.

f. Run the query and view the results. Save and close the query.

Order Financing Query

Northwind is considering offering financing options to their customers with 5% interest, to be paid over 12 months.

a. Create a copy of the Order Summary query named **Order Financing**.

b. Switch to Design view of the new query and remove the DiscountAmount field.

c. Add a new field using the Expression Builder named **SamplePayment**. Insert the Pmt function with the following parameters:

- Use **.05/12** for the rate argument (5% interest, paid monthly)

- Use the number **12** for the num_periods argument (12 months)

- Use the calculated field **ExtendedAmount** for the present_value

d. Change the Total row to **Expression** for the SamplePayment field.

e. Change the Format for the SamplePayment field to **Currency**.

f. Save and close the query.

Order Summary by Country Query

You need to create one additional query based on the Order Summary query you created in a previous step. This new query will enable you to analyze the orders by country.

a. Create a copy of the Order Summary query named **Order Summary by Country**.

b. Replace the OrderID field with the Country field in Design view of the new query.

c. Run the query and examine the summary records; there should be 21 countries listed.

d. Switch to Design view and change the sort order so that the country with the highest ExtendedAmount is first and the country with the lowest ExtendedAmount is last.

e. Run the query and verify the results.

f. Save and close the query.

g. Exit Access and submit based on your instructor's directions.

Creating and Using Professional Forms and Reports

CHAPTER **13**

Moving Beyond Tables and Queries

Yuri Arcurs/Shutterstock

OBJECTIVES AFTER YOU READ THIS CHAPTER, YOU WILL BE ABLE TO:

1. Create forms using form tools p. 656

2. Use form views p. 663

3. Work with a form layout control p. 666

4. Sort records in a form p. 668

5. Create reports using report tools p. 676

6. Use report views p. 683

7. Modify a report p. 685

8. Sort records in a report p. 688

CASE STUDY | Coffee Shop Starts New Business

The La Vida Mocha coffee shop in Paterson, New Jersey, once was an ordinary coffee shop selling retail coffee, tea, and pastries to its loyal customers in northern New Jersey. Then, in 2012, owner Ryung Park decided to use her knowledge of the coffee industry to sell coffee products to businesses in her area. This new venture grew quickly and soon became 25% of her annual revenue. Realizing that this new business would need more of her time each day, she decided to create an Access database to help track her customer, product, and order information.

With the help of a student from Passaic County Community College, she created a database with tables to hold data for customers, products, sales reps, and orders. She is currently using these tables to enter and retrieve information.

Ryung wants to have one of her employees, Nabil, manage the database. However, she does not want him to work in the tables; she wants him to work with forms. Ryung heard that forms have an advantage over tables because they can be designed to show one record at a time—this will reduce data-entry errors. Ryung would also like to create several reports for her own benefit so she can stay on top of the business by reviewing the reports each week.

You have been hired to help Ryung create the new forms and reports that she needs for the business. She will describe the forms and reports to you in detail and also provide written instructions. You will be expected to work independently to create the forms and reports.

Form Basics

A *form* is a database object that is used to add data into or edit data in a table. Most Access database applications use forms rather than tables for data entry and for looking up information. Three main reasons exist for using forms rather than tables for adding, updating, and deleting data. They are:

- You are less likely to edit the wrong record by mistake.
- You can create a form that shows data from more than one table simultaneously.
- You can create Access forms to match paper forms.

If you are adding data using a table with many columns, you could jump to the wrong record in the middle of a column accidentally. For example, you could enter the data for one record correctly for the first 10 fields but then jump to the row above and overwrite existing data for the remaining field values unintentionally. In this case, two records would have incorrect or incomplete data. A form will not allow this type of error because most forms restrict entry to one record at a time.

Many forms require two tables as their record source. For example, you may want to view a customer's details (name, address, e-mail, phone, etc.) as well as all of the orders he or she has placed. This would require using data from both the Customers and the Orders tables in one form. Similarly, you may want to view the header information for an order while also viewing the detail line items for the order. This would require data from both the Orders and Order Details tables. Both of these examples enable a user to view two record sources at the same time and make changes—additions, edits, or deletions—to one or both sources of data.

Finally, when paper forms are used to collect information, it is a good idea to design the electronic forms to match the paper forms. This will make data entry more efficient and reliable and ease the transition from paper form to computer form. Access forms can be designed to emulate the paper documents already in use in an organization. This facilitates the simultaneous use of both paper forms and electronic data. Databases do not necessarily eliminate paper forms; they supplement and coexist with them.

In this section, you will learn the basics of form design. You will discover multiple methods to create and modify Access forms.

Creating Forms Using Form Tools

Access provides a variety of options for creating forms. There are a number of built-in layouts that you can choose from. Database designers may eventually develop a preference for one or two types of form layouts, but keep in mind you have a lot of options if needed. You will want to find a balance between creating a form that is simple while still powerful enough to be of use.

Access provides 14 different tools for creating forms. You can find these options in the Forms group on the Create tab. The Forms group contains four of the most common form tools (Form, Form Design, Blank Form, and Form Wizard), a list of Navigation forms, and More Forms, as shown in Figure 13.1. Navigation forms provides a list of six templates to create a user interface for a database; the More Forms command lists four additional form tools (Multiple Items, Datasheet, Split Form, and Modal Dialog). Select a table or query, click one of the tools, and Access will create a form using the selected table or query. The most common of these tools, the *Form tool*, is used to create data-entry forms for customers, employees, products, and other primary tables.

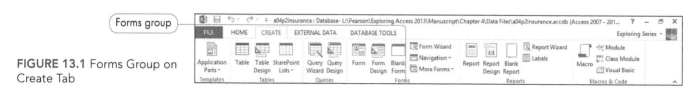

FIGURE 13.1 Forms Group on Create Tab

A complete list of all the Form tools available in Access is found in the Form Tools Reference at the end of this section. Many of the tools will be covered in this chapter. Some tools will not be covered, however, because they are not commonly used or because they are beyond the scope of this chapter (e.g., Form Design, Blank Form, Navigation forms, and Modal Dialog form). Use Microsoft Access Help to find more information about Form tools not covered in this chapter.

> ## TIP | Usability Testing
>
> After a database object (such as a form) is finalized, it should be tested by both the database designer and the end users. The designer should be certain the report meets any criteria the users have given him or her. The designer should also browse through the records to make sure the values in all records (and not just the first record) display correctly. Likewise, the end users should have the opportunity to test the form and provide feedback. After all, they will be the ones using it, so the database designer has a responsibility to ensure the end users are comfortable with the object.

Ideally, a form should simplify data entry. Creating a form is a collaborative process between the form designer and the form users. This process continues throughout the life of the form, because the data needs of an organization may change. Forms designed long ago to collect information for a new customer account may not have an e-mail field; the form would have to be modified to include an e-mail field. The form designer needs to strike a balance between collecting the information users need to do their jobs and cluttering the form with extraneous fields. The users of the data know what they need and usually offer good feedback about which fields should be on a form. If you listen to their suggestions, your forms will function more effectively, the users' work will be easier, and your data will contain fewer data-entry errors.

After discussing the form with the users, it will help you to create the form in Access if you sketch the form first. After sketching the form, you will have a better idea of which form tool to use to create the form. After the form is created, use the sketch to determine which fields are required and in what the order of fields should be.

Identify a Record Source

Before you create a form, you must identify the record source. A *record source* is the table or query that supplies the records for a form or report. You may also see the record source referred to as a data source in certain help files and instructions. Use a table if you want to include all the records from a single table. Use a query if you need to filter the records in a table, if you need to combine records from two or more related tables, or if you do not want to display all fields.

For example, if a sales rep wants to create a form that displays customers from a single state only—where his customers reside—he should base the form on a query. Or, if a parts manager needs to review only parts with a zero on-hand quantity, he could create a form based on a query that includes only records with on-hand equal to zero.

Use the Form Tool

 As noted earlier, the Form tool is the most common tool for creating forms. To use the Form tool:

1. Select a table or query from the Navigation Pane
2. On the CREATE tab, in the Forms group, click Form.

Based on that table or query, Access automatically creates a new form. You may need to modify the form slightly, but you can create a stacked layout form in a just one click. A *stacked layout* displays fields in a vertical column. Because this is a form, it will display one record at a time, as shown in Figure 13.2. The other type of layout you may use is a *tabular layout*, which displays data horizontally across the page.

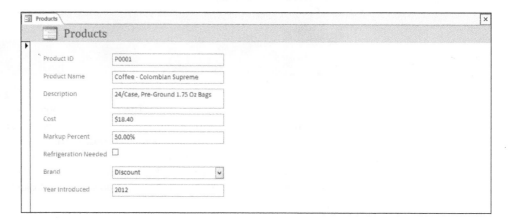

FIGURE 13.2 Form with a Stacked Layout

Understand Controls

Notice in Figure 13.3 that each field has a label on the left and a text box on the right. These are referred to as controls. *Controls* are the text boxes, buttons, boxes, and other tools you use to add, edit, and display the data in a form or report. In Figure 13.3, Product ID, Product Name, Description, and the rest of the field labels are controls. In addition, the boxes containing the values for each field (P0001, Coffee–Colombian Supreme, etc.) are all controls. More specifically, the form locations that hold data are generally text box controls, and the text in front of those, marking what the field means, are label controls.

FIGURE 13.3 Form Controls

A *layout control* provides guides to help keep controls aligned horizontally and vertically and give your form a uniform appearance. The fields are all aligned in Figure 13.3 because a layout control keeps them that way. Picture the layout control as a bookcase, with each field being a shelf on the bookcase.

Work with Form Views

There are three different views of a form available. The first, *Form view*, is a simplified interface primarily used for data entry. This view does not enable you to make changes to the layout. As such, the Form view is an excellent way for users to interact with the form. This ensures they do not accidentally change the form layout. Figure 13.4 shows a form in Form view. Notice forms can include features such as drop-down lists.

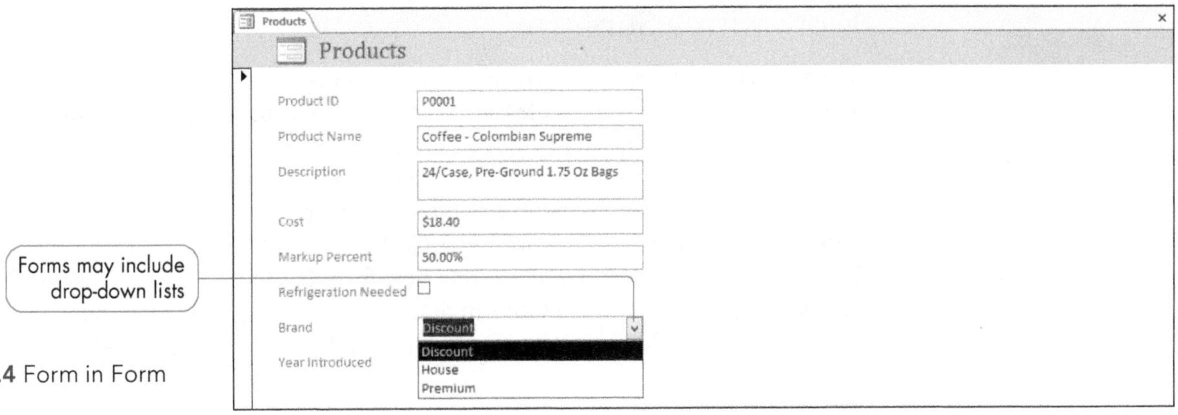

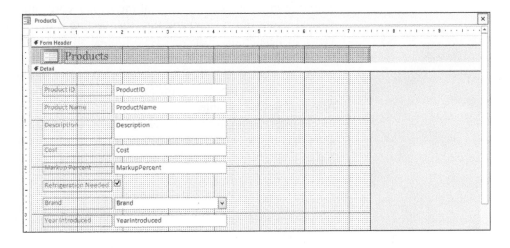

FIGURE 13.4 Form in Form View

> Forms may include drop-down lists

The second view, *Layout view,* enables users to make changes to the layout while viewing the data on the form. Reports have a similar view with the same name. This will be discussed later in the chapter. Layout view is useful for testing the functionality of the form and adjusting sizes of fields as needed. In the previous section, you were shown how to create a form using the Form Tool. When you do this, Access opens the form in Layout view ready for customizing. Figure 13.5 shows a form in Layout view.

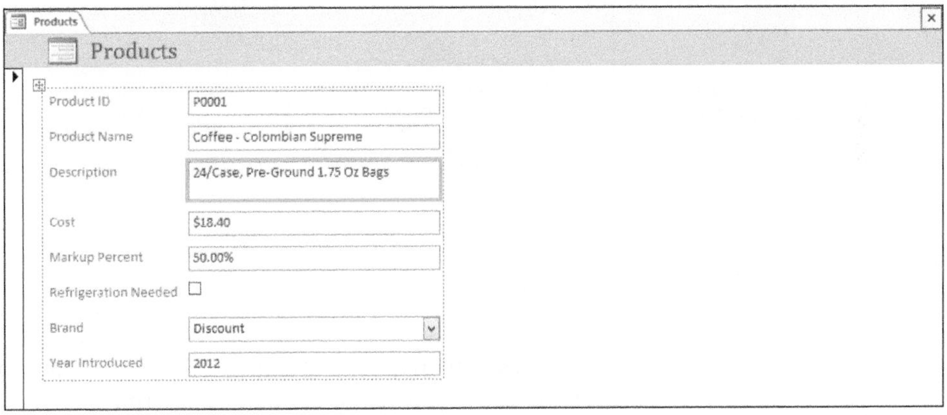

FIGURE 13.5 Form in Layout View

The third view, *Design view,* allows you to change advanced design settings you cannot see in the Layout view, such as a background image. Reports also have a Design view, which will also be discussed later in this chapter. Design view is a much more powerful way of changing the form layout. It is more complex than Layout view, so you would likely use Design view only when you need to perform advanced form layout adjustments. Figure 13.6 shows a form in Design view.

FIGURE 13.6 Form in Design View

These three views will be described in more detail later in this chapter.

Work with a Subform

When you use the Form tool to create a form, Access analyzes the table relationships you created in the database. If the table that the main form is based upon is related to another table through a relationship, then Access automatically adds a subform to the main form. The subform displays records in the related table, generally laid out in a table, similar to an Excel spreadsheet. For example, assume you have sales representatives stored in a SalesReps table and customer information stored in a Customers table. Also assume a relationship exists between the two tables. If you create a new form based on SalesReps using the Form tool, Access will add a Customers subform to the bottom of the main form, showing all customers assigned to each sales representative (see Figure 13.7).

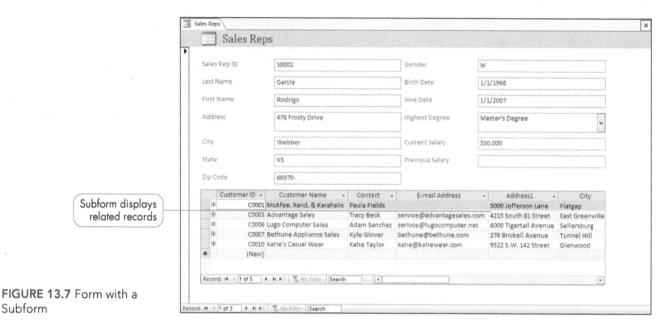

FIGURE 13.7 Form with a Subform

At times, you may want the subform as part of your form; at other times, you may want to remove it. To remove a subform from a form:

1. Switch to Design view.
2. Click anywhere inside the subform.
3. Press Delete.

Create a Split Form

A *split form* combines two views of the same record source—one section is displayed in a stacked layout (form view) and the other section is displayed in a tabular layout (datasheet view). By default, the form view is positioned on the top and the datasheet view is displayed on the bottom; however, the form's page orientation can be changed from horizontal to vertical in Layout view. If you select a record in the top half of the form, the same record will be selected in the bottom half of the form and vice versa. For example, if you create a split form based on an Orders table, you can select an Order in the datasheet section and then see the order's information in the *Form view* section (see Figure 13.8). This gives you the option to enter data in the Form view while being able to navigate between orders more quickly. The top and bottom halves are synchronized at all times.

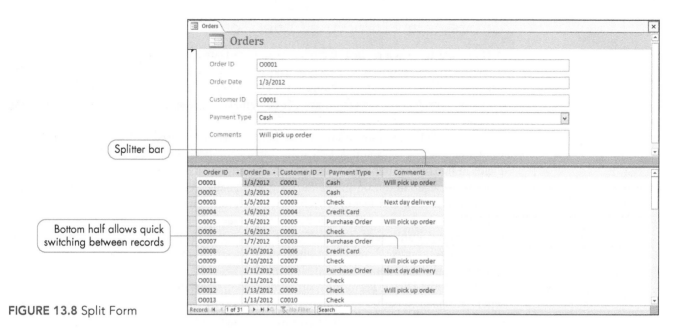

Splitter bar

Bottom half allows quick switching between records

FIGURE 13.8 Split Form

To create a split form, do the following:

1. Select a table or query in the Navigation Pane.
2. Click the CREATE tab.
3. Click More Forms in the Forms group.
4. Select Split Form.

Once you have completed those steps, a new split form displays. You can add, edit, or delete records in either section. The *splitter bar* divides the form into two halves. Users can adjust the splitter bar up or down unless the form designer disables this option.

Create a Multiple Items Form

A *Multiple Items form* displays multiple records in a tabular layout similar to a table's Datasheet view. However, a Multiple Items form gives you more customization options than a datasheet, such as the ability to add graphical elements, buttons, and other controls. Figure 13.9 shows a Multiple Items form created from the Employees table.

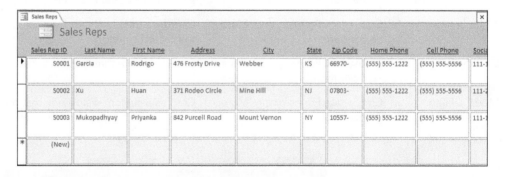

FIGURE 13.9 Multiple Items Form

To create a Multiple Items form, do the following:

1. Select a table or query from the Navigation Pane.
2. Click the CREATE tab.
3. Click More Forms in the Forms group.
4. Select Multiple Items from the list of options.

Create Forms Using the Other Form Tools

A Datasheet form is a replica of a table or query's Datasheet view except that it still retains some of the form properties. Database designers can also use the Datasheet form to display data in a table-like format but change the form properties to not allow a record to be deleted. This would protect the data from accidental damage while still providing the users with the familiar Datasheet view.

The Form Design tool and the Blank Form tools can be used to create a form manually. Click one of these tools and Access will open a completely blank form. Click Add Existing Fields in the Tools group on the Design tab and add the necessary fields.

The Navigation option in the Forms group enables you to create user interface forms that have the look and feel of a Web-based form and enable users to open and close the objects of a database. In other words, you could set up a form that allows users to click on the forms you want them to view. This is an excellent option to simplify the database for data-entry personnel who may not understand the program. These forms are also useful for setting up an Access database on the Internet.

The Modal Dialog Form tool can be used to create a dialog box. This feature is useful when you need to gather information from the user before working with another object. Dialog boxes are common in all Microsoft Office applications.

REFERENCE | Form Tools

Form Tool	Location	Use
Form	Create tab, Forms group	Creates a form with a stacked layout displaying all of the fields in the record source.
Form Design	Create tab, Forms group	Create a new blank form in Design view.
Blank Form	Create tab, Forms group	Create a new blank form in Layout view.
Form Wizard	Create tab, Forms group	Answer a series of questions and Access will create a custom form for you.
Navigation	Create tab, Forms group, Navigation button	Create user-interface forms that can also be used on the Internet. Six different Navigation form layouts are available from the drop-down list.
Split Form	Create tab, Forms group, More Forms button	Creates a two-part form with a stacked layout in one section and a tabular layout in the other.
Multiple Items	Create tab, Forms group, More Forms button	Creates a tabular layout form that includes all of the fields from the record source.
Datasheet	Create tab, Forms group, More Forms button	Creates a form that resembles the datasheet of a table or query.
Modal Dialog	Create tab, Forms group, More Forms button	Creates a custom dialog box that forces the user to respond before working with another object.

 TIP **Print with Caution!**

Users can print a form by clicking the File tab and selecting the Print option. However, printing from a form should be done with caution. Forms are not generally designed for printing, so you may end up with hundreds of pages of printouts. A form with a stacked layout of 1,000 records could print thousands of pages unless you choose the Selected Record(s) option in the Print dialog box. The Selected Record(s) option, as shown in Figure 13.10, will only print the current record (or selected records).

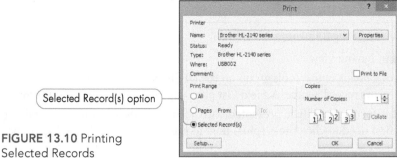

Selected Record(s) option

FIGURE 13.10 Printing Selected Records

Using Form Views

Access provides different views for a form, similar to the different views in tables and queries. Tables and queries have Design view and Datasheet view. Most forms have Layout view, Form view, and Design view.

As you work with the form tools to create and modify forms, you will often need to switch between the three form views in Access: Layout view, Form view, and Design view. Most of your design work will be done in Layout view; occasionally, you will switch to Design view to add a more advanced feature, such as a background, or to use a layout option that is otherwise unavailable. Users of the form will only work in Form view. There should be no reason for a user to switch to Layout or Design view. Modifications to the form should be done by the designated form designer.

After a form is generated by a Form tool, you may need to modify it. Commonly, you may add a field, remove a field, change the order of fields, change the width of a field, modify the theme, or modify label text. These changes can be made in a form's Layout view. Advanced changes, such as changing headers or footers or adding a background image, can be made in a form's Design view.

Edit Data in Form View

STEP 2 Use Form view to add, edit, and delete data in a form; the layout and design of the form cannot be changed in this view. Recall from a previous chapter that you can move from one field to another field by pressing Tab on your keyboard or clicking the desired field with your mouse.

Alter a Form in Layout View

Use Layout view to alter the form design while still viewing the data. You use Layout view to add or delete fields in a form, modify field properties, change the column widths, and enhance a form by adding a color scheme or styling. While you are working in Layout view, you can see the data as it would appear in Form view, but you cannot edit the data in Layout view. Seeing the data in Layout view makes it easier to size controls, for example, to ensure the data is visible. It is good practice to test a form in Form view after making changes in Layout view.

Use the Form Layout Tools Tabs

Forms have a number of options you can use to format. Once you are in Layout or Design view, you will have access to the report layout tools. You have three tabs available:

- Design: Use this tab to make changes to the design of the form, such as adding sorting, changing themes, and inserting additional controls.
- Arrange: Use this tab to change the layout of a form, to move fields, or to insert space.
- Format: Use this tab to change the font; add or remove bolding, italics, or underlining; change font size; change font color or background; adjust text alignment; or add a background image.

Add a Field to a Form

STEP 3 » To add a field to a form, do the following:

1. Open the form in Layout view.
2. Click Add Existing Fields in the Tools group on the DESIGN tab to reveal the available fields from the form's record source. A Field List pane appears at the right of your screen.
3. For a single-table form, you will be presented with a list of fields. For a multiple-table form, you will first need to click the + (plus) next to the appropriate table to locate the desired field.
4. Drag the new field to the precise location on the form, using the shaded line (the color may vary, based on your Office configuration) as a guide for the position of the new field. The other fields will automatically adjust to make room for the new field.

Depending on the layout of the form, the shaded line will appear vertically (tabular layouts) or horizontally (stacked).

Delete a Field from a Form

To delete a field, do the following:

1. Switch to Layout view.
2. Click the text box control of the field to be deleted (note the shaded border around the control).
3. Click the Select Row option on the Layout tab in the Rows & Columns group.
4. Press Delete. The other fields will automatically adjust to close the gap around the deleted field.

Adjust Column Widths in a Form

When column widths are adjusted in a form with a stacked layout, all columns will increase and decrease together. Therefore, it is best to make sure that field columns are wide enough to accommodate the widest value in the table. For example, if a form contains information such as a customer's first name, last name, address, city, state, ZIP, phone, and e-mail address, you will need to make sure the longest address and the longest e-mail address are completely visible (because those fields are likely to contain the longest data values).

To decrease column widths in a form with a stacked layout, do the following:

1. Open the form in Layout view.
2. Click the text box control of the first field to select it.
3. Move the mouse over the right border of the field until the mouse pointer turns into a double arrow.
4. Drag the right edge to the left or right until you arrive at the desired width.

You will notice that all the fields change as you change the width of the first field. All fields that are part of the layout will have a standard width. If you wanted to resize one specific field, you would need to remove that field from the layout control. Note that "removing a field from the layout control" does not mean "removing a field from the form." Recall that the layout control keeps each field in place. If you remove a field from the layout control, it stays on the form but can be moved more freely.

Modify Form Controls using the Format Tab

When you view a form in Layout view, the Form Layout Tools tab displays the Design tab, Arrange tab, and Format tab. The Format tab, shown in Figure 13.11, contains a series of commands that enable you change the font, display, and alignment of the controls on a form. This is useful if you need to quickly change the look of one cell. For example, if you have a form that shows the information about the sale of a vehicle, you might want to emphasize the net profit of each transaction.

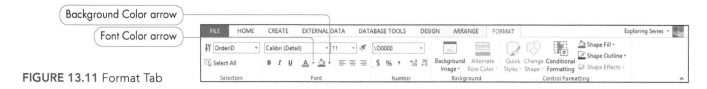

FIGURE 13.11 Format Tab

From this tab, you can change a number of properties. For example, you can perform these tasks, and more:

- Change the font size: Click the Font Size arrow in the Font group.
- Change emphasis: In the Font group, add bold, italics, or underlining.
- Change alignment: In the Font group, choose left, center, or right align.
- Change a control's background color: Click the Background Color arrow (refer to Figure 13.11) and select a color for the background.
- Change a control's font color: Click the Font Color arrow (refer to Figure 13.11) and select a color for the cell's font.
- Change number format: In the Number group, change to currency, percentage, or add commas; increase or decrease decimal places.

Selecting Controls

Controls, as mentioned, include both the labels identifying a field and the text box displaying field values. There may be times you want to select multiple controls. You will notice when you click on one control and click on another that the original control is deselected. If you need to select multiple controls, click on the first control you wish to select, hold down CTRL on your keyboard, and then click on the other controls you wish to select. Once they are selected, you can perform many tasks, such as formatting or deletion.

Add a Theme to a Form

You can apply a theme to a form in order to give the form a more professional finish. A **theme** is a defined set of colors, fonts, and graphics that can be applied to a form (or report). Click Themes in the Themes group on the Design tab, select a theme from the Themes Gallery, and Access will apply the theme to the form. Each theme has a name; you can determine the name of a theme by pointing the mouse to a theme and waiting for the tip to pop up, showing the name.

You can apply a theme to a single form or to all the forms in your database that share a common theme. Applying the same theme to all forms will provide a consistent look to your database; most users prefer a consistent theme when using Access forms. The same themes found in Access are also available in Excel, Word, and PowerPoint. Therefore, you can achieve a uniform look across all Office applications. Themes can be customized and saved so that the theme you create can be used again. Click the Save Current Theme command as shown in Figure 13.12 to do so.

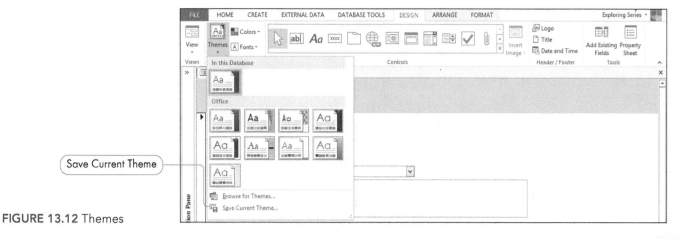

Save Current Theme

FIGURE 13.12 Themes

Add Styling to a Form

Modifying the font size of labels, changing the font color of labels, and adding a background color can enhance a form and also make it more usable. It is best to choose a familiar font family, such as Arial or Calibri, for both the form label controls and the text box controls. Apply bold to the labels in order to help the user distinguish labels from the text boxes. You should also consider right-aligning the labels and left-aligning the text box controls to reduce distance between the label and field, as illustrated in Figure 13.13. You may also want to separate the primary key field from the rest of the form by providing a sufficient visual boundary.

One note of caution: Try to avoid what graphic artists refer to as the "ransom note effect." Using too many font families, font sizes, colors, and other effects can take away from your design.

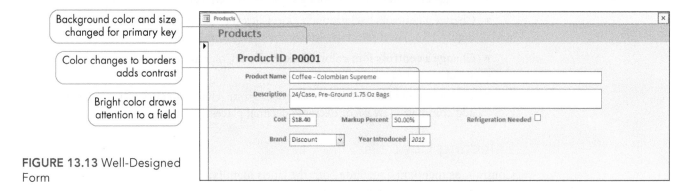

Background color and size changed for primary key

Color changes to borders adds contrast

Bright color draws attention to a field

FIGURE 13.13 Well-Designed Form

Working with a Form Layout Control

Whenever you use one of the form tools to create a new form, Access will add a layout control to help align the fields. Recall that the layout control helps keep controls aligned in order to give your form a uniform appearance. The layout control provides structure for the fields but is restrictive. If you wish to have more control over the location of your fields, you can remove the layout control and position the controls manually on the grid.

Modify a Form Using the Arrange Tab

The Arrange tab appears in both Layout view and Design view. Use this tab to change the layout of a form, to move fields up and down, to insert a space above or below your current position, or to insert a space to the left or the right of the current field. To use these commands, first open a form in Layout view or Design view and click the Arrange tab. Next, select a field or fields and click the appropriate command.

The Table group contains commands that enable you to add gridlines to a form's layout, to change a form's layout from stacked to tabular (and vice versa), or to remove a form's layout. The Remove Layout command is only available in Design view.

To change the arrangement of a form, do the following:

1. Open the form in Layout view.
2. Click any of the field text boxes.
3. Click the ARRANGE tab.
4. Click Select Layout in the Rows & Columns group.
5. Click Tabular or Stacked in the Table group.

To remove a form layout control, do the following:

1. Switch to Design view (if you are not in Design view, you will not see the Remove Layout option).
2. Click on one of the fields that is currently part of the layout.
3. On the ARRANGE tab, click Select Layout in the Rows & Columns group.
4. Click Remove Layout in the Table group.
5. Switch to Layout view to arrange fields.

If you have removed the layout control or have a form that never had one, you can add one if you do the following:

1. Switch to Layout view or Design view (you can switch in either view).
2. Select all the controls you would like added back to the layout control, such as the field labels and text boxes. Hold down CTRL on your keyboard and click on each control, or click the FORMAT tab and in the Selection group, click Select All if you want to add everything to a layout.
3. On the ARRANGE tab, in the Table group, click Tabular or Stacked

The Rows & Columns group contains commands that enable you to insert rows and columns inside a form's layout. For example, in a form with a stacked layout, you may want to separate some fields from the rest of the fields. To do this, you could select a text box and click Insert Below. This will create a space after the selected field. This group also contains the Select Layout, Select Column, and Select Row commands. In Figure 13.14, three rows have been inserted above the Cost field.

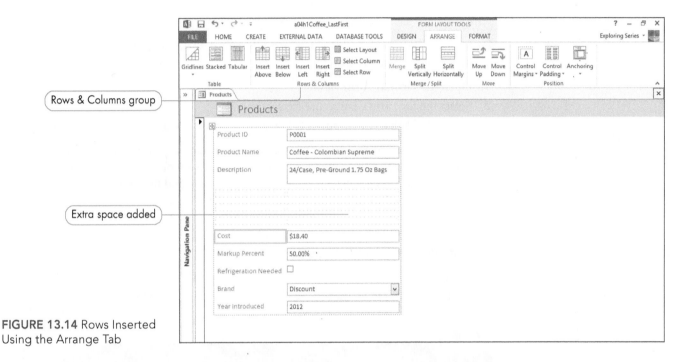

FIGURE 13.14 Rows Inserted Using the Arrange Tab

The Move group contains two commands that enable you to move a field up or down in a stacked layout. For example, if you want to move the second field in a stacked layout to the first position, select the second field's text box and label and click Move Up in the Move group. Moving fields up or down in a form may cause unexpected results; you can always use the Undo command if you need to revert back to a previous layout.

The Position group contains commands that enable you to modify the margins and the padding of controls in a form. This group also contains the Anchoring command, which enables you to change where the form's controls appear on the screen. By default, forms are anchored at the top left; however, you can change this to any of the nine options using the anchoring command.

TIP | Apply a Background Image to a Form

To apply a Background Image to a form, open the form in Design view, click the Format tab, and then click Background Image in the Background group. Next, click Browse to locate the image you want to apply to the form. Once the image has been applied to the form, you can change the properties of the image so that the image is anchored and sized correctly.

Sorting Records in a Form

When a form is created using a Form tool, the sort order of the records in the form is dependent on the sort order of the record source—a table or a query. Tables are usually sorted by the primary key, whereas queries can be sorted in a variety of ways. Adding and removing sorts are shown in Figure 13.15.

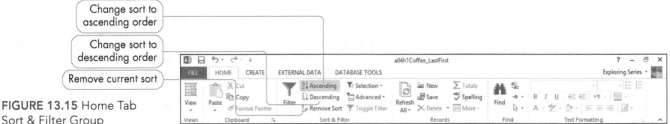

FIGURE 13.15 Home Tab Sort & Filter Group

Sorting by a Single Field

You can easily sort on a single field, in ascending or descending order.

To sort by a single field, do the following:

1. Open the form in Form view.
2. Select the field you want to use for sorting.
3. On the HOME tab, in the Sort & Filter group, click Ascending or Descending.

If the form is based on a query, you can instead modify the underlying query's sort order. This method enables you to create a more advanced sort order based on multiple fields. Open the query in Design view, add the sorting you want, and then save and close the query.

Remove Sorting in a Form

To remove the sort order in a form, do the following:

1. Switch to Form view.
2. On the HOME tab, in the Sort & Filter group, click Remove Sort.

TIP | Inconsistent Sorting Due to Spaces

Including extra spaces when you enter values into fields can cause issues with sorting. To Access, the following values are not the same:

Little Falls, NJ 07424

Little Falls, NJ 07424

Notice the extra space after the word *Little*. If you attempt to sort, these cities will end up in different places in the sort. The first Little Falls (without the extra space) would appear between Little Egg Harbor Township and Little Ferry. However, the second version would end up above Little Egg Harbor Township, because Access treats the space as a different character.

Inconsistent spacing can cause inconsistent sorting. Try to remember that when performing data entry. If you inherit a database with this issue, you might consider performing a Replace, replacing two spaces with one.

Quick
Concepts ✓

1. How does a form simplify data entry (when compared to entering data into a table)? *p. 656*

2. What is the record source of a form? *p. 657*

3. What is the difference between Layout view and Design view? *pp. 658–659*

4. What is the difference between a form with a subform and a split form? *p. 660*

5. What is a layout control? What are the pros and cons of a layout control? *p. 666*

Hands-On Exercises

1 Form Basics

It is your first day on the job at La Vida Mocha. After talking with Ryung about her data-entry needs, you decide to create several sample forms with different formats. You will show each form to Ryung and Nabil to get feedback and see if they have a preference.

Skills covered: Create Forms Using Form Tools • Use Form Views • Work with a Form Layout Control • Sort Records in a Form

You will create some forms to help Ryung and Nabil with their data entry process. After discussing their needs, you created some sketches that you will implement. Refer to Figure 13.16 as you complete Step 1.

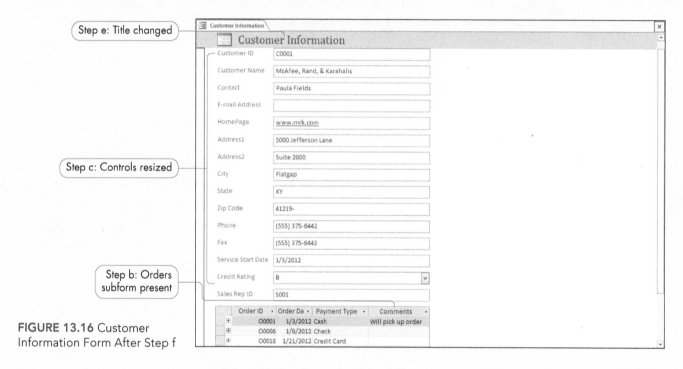

FIGURE 13.16 Customer Information Form After Step f

a. Open *a04h1Coffee*. Click the **FILE tab**, select **Save As**, and click **Save As**. Type **a04h1Coffee_LastFirst** as the file name. Click **Save**.

> **TROUBLESHOOTING:** Throughout the remainder of this chapter and textbook, click Enable Content whenever you are working with student files.

> **TROUBLESHOOTING:** If you make any major mistakes in this exercise, you can close the file, repeat step a above, and then start over.

b. Click the **Customers table** in the Navigation Pane. Click the **CREATE tab** and click **Form** in the Forms group.

> Access creates a new form with two record sources—Customers (with stacked layout, on top) and Orders (with datasheet layout, below). Access found a one-to-many relationship between the Customers and Orders tables. The form opens in Layout view.

c. Click the top text box containing *C0001* if it is not already selected. The text box is outlined with a shaded border. Move the mouse to the right edge of the shaded border until the mouse pointer changes to a double-headed arrow. Drag the right edge to the left until the text box is approximately half of its original size.

All the text boxes and the subform at the bottom adjust in size when you adjust the top text box. This is a characteristic of Layout view—enabling you to easily modify all controls at once.

> **TROUBLESHOOTING:** You may need to maximize the Access window or close the Navigation Pane if the right edge of the text box is not visible.

d. Ensure the labels at the left all appear without being cut off. If they are cut off, adjust the size of the labels like you did in step c.

e. Click **Save** in the Quick Access Toolbar, and then type **Customer Information** as the form name in the **Save As dialog box**. Click **OK**.

f. Click the **Customers title** at the top of the form to select it, click again, and then change the title to **Customer Information**. Press **Enter** to accept the change. Your form should now look like Figure 13.16. Close the form.

> **TROUBLESHOOTING:** If you make a mistake that you cannot easily recover from, consider deleting the form and starting over. The Form tool makes it easy to start over again.

g. Verify the Customers table is selected in the Navigation Pane. Click the **CREATE tab** and click **More Forms** in the Forms group. Select **Split Form**.

Access creates a new form with a split view, one view in stacked layout and one view laid out like a datasheet.

h. Click anywhere on the Coulter Office Supplies customer record in the bottom portion of the form (record 14). Note: You may need to scroll down to see this record.

The top portion shows all the information for this customer.

i. Click the **Customers title** at the top of the form to select it, click **Customers** again, and then change the title to **Customers - Split View**. Press **Enter** to accept the change.

j. Click **Save** on the Quick Access Toolbar and type **Customers - Split View** in the **Form Name box**. Click **OK**. Close the form.

k. Click the **Products table** in the Navigation Pane. Click the **CREATE tab**, click **More Forms** in the Forms group, and then select **Multiple Items**.

Access creates a new multiple-item form based on the Products table. The form resembles a table's Datasheet view.

l. Click the **Products title** at the top of the form to select it, click again on **Products**, and then change the title to **Products - Multiple Items**. Press **Enter** to save the title.

m. Save the form as **Products - Multiple Items** and close the form.

n. Click the **Orders table** in the Navigation Pane. Click **Form** in the Forms group on the CREATE tab.

A form with a subform showing each line of the order is created.

o. Switch to Design view. Click anywhere inside the subform and press **Delete** on your keyboard.

The subform is removed.

p. Save the form as **Order Information**. Close all open objects.

Now that you have created three forms, you will show Nabil how to use the forms to perform data entry.

a. Right-click the **Customer Information** form in the Navigation Pane and click **Open**. Advance to the sixth customer, *Lugo Computer Sales*, using the **Next Record button** on the Navigation Bar at the bottom of the form.

> **TROUBLESHOOTING:** Two Navigation bars exist, one for the main form and one for the subform. Make sure you use the bottom-most one that shows 14 records.

b. Double-click the **Customers table** in the Navigation Pane.

Two tabs now display in the main window. You will compare the table data and the form data while you make changes to both.

c. Verify the sixth record of the Customers table is *Lugo Computer Sales*, which corresponds to the sixth record in the Customer Information form. Click the tabs to switch between the table and the form.

d. Click the **Customer Information tab** and replace *Adam Sanchez*, the contact for Lugo Computer Sales, with your name. Advance to the next record to save the changes. Click the **Customers tab** to see that the contact name changed in the table as well.

The contact field and the other fields on the Customer Information form automatically change the data in the underlying table.

> **TROUBLESHOOTING:** If the change to Adam Sanchez does not display in the Customers table, check the Customer Information form to see if the pencil displays in the left margin. If it does, save the record by advancing to the next customer and recheck to see if the name has changed.

e. Close the Customer Information form and the Customers table.

f. Open the Customers – Split View form. In the bottom portion of the split form, click **Lugo Computer Sales**, the sixth record. Notice the top portion now displays the information for Lugo Computer Sales. Notice there is an error in the e-mail address—*service* is misspelled. In the top portion of the form, change the e-mail address to **service@lugocomputer.net**.

g. Click another record in the bottom pane and click back on **Lugo Computer Sales**.

The pencil disappears from the record selector box and the changes are saved to the table.

STEP 3 >> USE LAYOUT VIEW TO MODIFY A FORM LAYOUT

You will make some changes to the layouts based on recommendations Nabil gave you after seeing the forms in action. You will also add a missing field to the main table and add it to the form. Refer to Figure 13.17 as you complete Step 3.

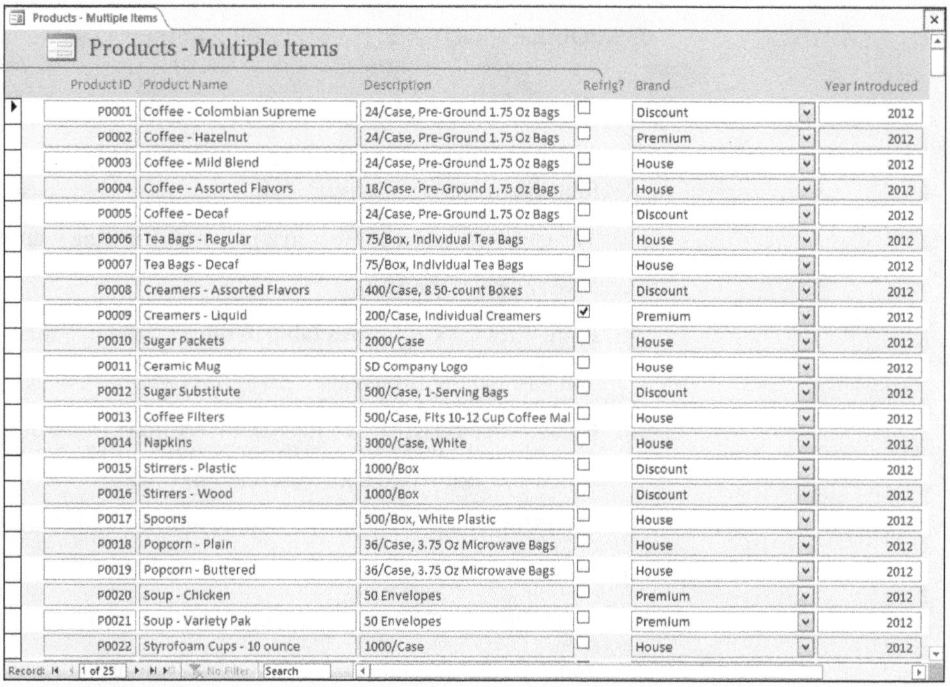

Step d: Refrig? column resized

FIGURE 13.17 Final Version of Products—Multiple Items Report

a. Switch the Customers – Split View form to Layout view. Move your mouse over the splitter bar, the border between the top and bottom portions of the window. When the pointer shape changes to a double-headed arrow, drag the **splitter bar** up until it almost touches the Sales Rep ID field. Save and close the form.

b. Open the Products – Multiple Items form in Layout view. Move the mouse over the bottom edge of cell P0001 until the pointer shape changes to a two-headed arrow. Drag the bottom edge up to reduce the height of the rows so they are as tall as they need to be to accommodate the information.

Changing the height of one row affects the height of all the rows.

c. Click anywhere on the Cost column and click **Select Column** in the Rows & Columns group on the ARRANGE tab. Press **Delete** to remove the column. Repeat the process to delete *MarkupPercent*.

d. Click the **Refrigeration Needed label** to select it. Change the label to the abbreviation **Refrig?**. Shrink the field so it is as wide as necessary. Save and close the form.

You removed fields from the Products – Multiple Items form and the other fields adjust to maintain an even distribution (after you remove the blank space).

e. Open the Customer Information form in Layout view.

f. Click **Themes** in the Themes group on the DESIGN tab. Right-click the **Slice theme** and click **Apply Theme to This Object Only**.

The font and color scheme adjust to match this theme.

> **TROUBLESHOOTING:** Recall that you can determine which theme is named Slice by pointing the mouse to a theme and waiting for a tip to display. Themes are displayed in alphabetical order.

g. Click **Shape Fill** in the Control Formatting group on the FORMAT tab. Click **Light Turquoise, Background 2**.

The background color of the CustomerID field changes to light turquoise.

> **TROUBLESHOOTING:** If you do not see a Light Turquoise, Background 2 in the first row, ensure you have selected the Slice theme.

> **TROUBLESHOOTING:** If the entire background changes to blue, undo and ensure you have selected the control containing *C0001*.

h. Select the **Customer Name field** (which should be *McAfee, Rand, & Karahalis*). Change the font size to **16**.

 The customer name appears in a larger font, setting it apart from the other fields.

i. Save and close the form.

j. Right-click the **Customers table** in the Navigation Pane and click **Design View**.

 You will add the HomePage field to the Customers table.

k. Click the **Address1 field** and click **Insert Rows** in the Tools group.

 A new row is inserted above the Address1 field.

l. Type **HomePage** in the blank **Field Name box** and choose **Hyperlink** as the Data Type.

m. Save and close the Customers table.

n. Right-click the **Customer Information form** in the Navigation Pane and click **Layout View**.

 You will add the HomePage field to the Customer Information form.

o. Click **Add Existing Fields** in the Tools group on the DESIGN tab to display the Field List pane (if necessary).

p. Click the **HomePage field**. Drag the field from the Field List pane to the form, below the E-mail Address field, until a shaded line displays between *E-mail Address* and *Address1*, and release the mouse. Close the Field List pane.

 Access shows a shaded line to help you place the field in the correct location.

> **TROUBLESHOOTING:** If the placement of this field does not look correct, you can use the Undo button and try again.

q. Switch to Form view. Press **Tab** until you reach the HomePage field and type www.mrk.com into the field. Save and close the form.

r. Click the **Revenue query** in the Navigation Pane. Click **Form** in the Forms group on the CREATE tab to create a new form based on this query.

s. Display the form in Design view. Select all text box field controls (from *Last Name* down to *Revenue*) by clicking on the first field (Last Name), holding down **CTRL** on your keyboard, and clicking on each of the other controls. Click **Remove Layout** in the Table group on the ARRANGE tab. Switch to Layout view.

> **TROUBLESHOOTING:** Recall the Remove Layout option only appears in Design view, so if you do not see the option, ensure you are in Design view.

t. Resize the controls individually so they are approximately the same size as shown in Figure 13.18.

u. Click the **Price control**. Hold down **CTRL** and click the **Revenue control**, the **Price label**, and the **Revenue label**. Drag the fields to the locations shown in Figure 13.18. Switch to Form view.

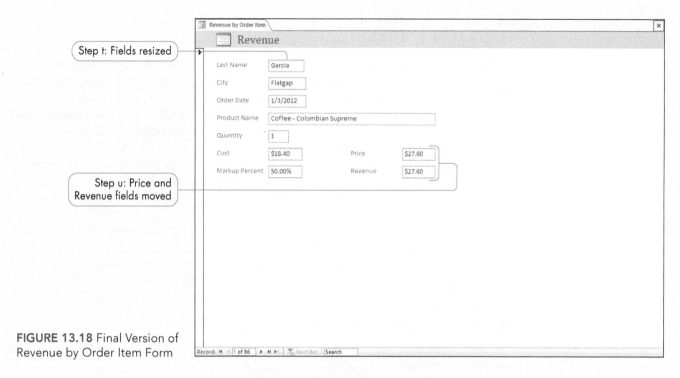

Step t: Fields resized

Step u: Price and Revenue fields moved

FIGURE 13.18 Final Version of Revenue by Order Item Form

v. Save the form as **Revenue by Order Item**. Close the form.

STEP 4 » USE A CONTROL LAYOUT AND SORT RECORDS IN A FORM

Ryung tested the Customer Information form and likes the way it is working. She asks you to change the sorting to make it easier to find customers with a similar customer name. She also has an old form that she hopes you can make easier to read but keep in the vertical format.

a. Open the Sales Reps form in Layout view. Notice the form is not laid out well.

b. Click **Select All** in the Selection group on the FORMAT tab.

All 14 controls are outlined.

c. Click **Tabular** in the Table group on the ARRANGE tab.

The controls are lined up horizontally.

d. Click **Stacked** in the Table group on the ARRANGE tab. Switch to Form view.

Ryung wanted the form laid out vertically. The controls are lined up vertically and are much easier to read.

e. Save and close the form.

f. Open the Customer Information form in Form view. Click **Next record** in the Navigation bar at the bottom several times to advance through the records.

Take note that the customers are in Customer ID order.

g. Click **First record** in the Navigation bar to return to customer *McAfee, Rand, & Karahalis*.

h. Click the **Customer Name field** and click **Ascending** in the Sort & Filter group on the HOME tab.

Advantage Sales displays, as they are the first customer name in alphabetical order.

i. Click **Next record** in the Navigation bar at the bottom to advance through the records.

The records are in Customer Name order.

j. Save and close the Customer Information form.

k. Keep the database open if you plan to continue with the next Hands-On Exercise. If not, close the database and exit Access.

Report Basics

By now, you know how to plan a database, create a table, establish relationships between tables, enter data into tables, and extract data using queries. You generated output by printing table and query datasheets. You also learned how to create several types of data-entry forms. These forms can also be used for inquiries about the data in a database. In this section, you will learn how to create professional reports using the report-writing tools in Access.

A *report* is a document that displays information from a database in a format that outputs meaningful information to its readers. Access reports can be printed, viewed on screen, or even saved as a file. Much like a report you might do for a class, Access does research (gets information from the tables or queries) and organizes and presents it in a meaningful way (the final report, formatted for on-screen viewing or for printing). Reports are unable to change data in your database; a report is designed for output of information only, whether to the screen, to the printer, or to a file.

The following are all examples of reports that might be created in Access:

1. A telephone directory sorted by last name
2. A customer list grouped by sales rep
3. An employee list sorted by most years of service
4. A financial statement
5. A bill or invoice
6. A bar chart showing sales over the past 12 months
7. A shipping label
8. A letter to customers reminding them about a past due payment

Although you can print information from forms, information printed may not be easily understood or economical in terms of paper use. Most of the printed documents generated by Access will come from reports. Reports can be enhanced to help the reader understand and analyze the data. For example, if you print the Datasheet view from the Customers table, you will be able to locate the key information about each customer. However, using report tools, you can group the customers by sales rep and highlight the customers who have not placed an order in six months. This is an example of converting a list of customers into an effective business tool. To increase business, the sales reps could contact their customers who have not ordered in six months and review the findings with the sales manager. A sales report could be run each month to see if the strategy has helped produce any new business.

In this section, you will create reports in Access by first identifying a record source, then sketching the report, and finally choosing a Report tool. You will learn how to modify a report by adding and deleting fields, resizing columns, and adding a color scheme. You will also learn about the report sections, the report views, and controls on reports. After having worked through forms in the earlier section on forms, you will discover that there are many similarities between forms and reports.

Creating Reports Using Report Tools

Access provides five different report tools for creating reports. The report tools are found on the Create tab, in the Reports group, as shown in Figure 13.19. Click one of these tools and Access will base the report using the table or query that is currently selected. The most common of the tools, the *Report tool*, is used to instantly create a tabular report based on the table or query currently selected. The Report Design tool is used to create a new blank report in Design view. This tool is used by advanced users who want to create a blank report with no help from Access. The Blank Report tool is used to create a new blank report so that you can insert fields and controls manually and design the report. The Report Wizard tool will ask a series of questions and help you create a report based on your answers. The Labels tool is used to create a page of labels using one of the preformatted templates provided by Access. Table 13.1 provides a summary of the five report tools and their usage.

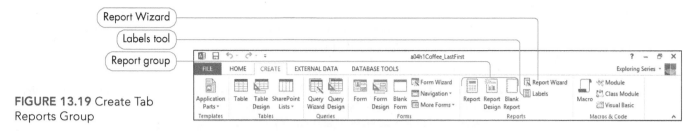

Report Wizard

Labels tool

Report group

FIGURE 13.19 Create Tab Reports Group

After you create a report using one of the report tools, you can perform modifications in Layout view or Design view.

Report Tool	Usage
Report	Create a tabular report showing all of the fields in the record source.
Report Design	Create a new blank report in Design view. Add fields and controls manually.
Blank Report	Create a new blank report in Layout view. Add fields and controls manually.
Report Wizard	Answer a series of questions and Access will design a custom report for you.
Labels	Choose a preformatted label template and create a sheet of labels.

TABLE 13.1 Report Tools and Their Usage

Before you create a report in Access, you should ask these questions:

- What is the purpose of the report?
- Who will use the report?
- Which tables are needed for the report?
- What information needs to be included?
- How will the report be distributed? Will users pull the information directly from Access, or will they receive it through e-mail, fax, or the Internet?
- Will the results be converted to Word, Excel, HTML, or another format?

In the *Forms* section of this chapter, you learned that it is helpful to talk to users and sketch an Access form before you launch Access. The same holds true for creating an Access report. Users can give you solid feedback, and creating a sketch will help you determine which report tool to use to create the report.

The first step in planning your report is to identify the record source. You may use one or more tables, queries, or a combination of tables and queries as the report's record source. Sometimes, a single table contains all of the records you need for the report. Other times, you will need to incorporate several tables. When multiple tables are needed to create a report, you can add all the necessary tables into a single query and then base the report on that query. (As stated earlier, multiple tables in a query must be related, as indicated with join lines. Tables with no join lines usually indicate an incorrect record source.)

Reports can also contain graphics as well as text and numeric data. For example, you can add a company logo. After you identify the record source, you also need to specify which graphic images are needed (and the location of the images).

Use the Report Tool

STEP 1 After you sketch the report, you can decide which report tool is appropriate to produce the desired report. Access provides several tools that you can use to create a report (refer to Figure 13.20). Which one you select depends on the layout of the report, the record source, and the complexity of the report design.

The easiest way to create a report is with the Report tool. The Report tool is used to instantly create a tabular report based on the table or query currently selected. To create a report using the Report tool, do the following:

1. Select a table or query in the Navigation Pane.
2. Click the CREATE tab and click Report in the Reports group. Access creates a tabular layout report instantly. Notice, this type of report displays data horizontally across the page in a landscape view, as shown in Figure 13.20.

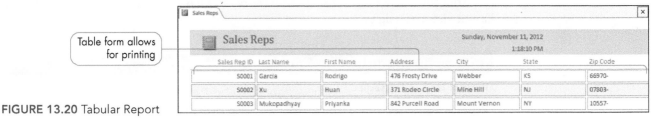

FIGURE 13.20 Tabular Report

If you prefer, you can display a report using a stacked layout, which displays fields in a vertical column. This type of report is less common, as it would result in longer printouts. The number of records on one page depends on the number of records in the record source. You can also force a new page at the start of each record.

Use the Report Wizard to Create a Basic Report

You can also create a professional report with the Report Wizard. The **Report Wizard** asks you questions and then uses your answers to generate a customized report. The wizard uses six dialog boxes to collect information about your report. After thinking through the structure, the layout, and the record source, you are ready to launch the Report Wizard.

1. Select the report's record source in the Navigation Pane and click Report Wizard in the Reports group on the CREATE tab.

   The wizard opens with the table or query (the record source) displayed in the first dialog box. Although you chose the record source before you started, the first dialog box enables you to select fields from additional tables or queries.

2. Choose the fields you want to include in the report. Click the Tables/Queries drop-down list to display a list of available tables or queries. As with the query wizard you used in a previous chapter, you can click > to choose a single field, >> to choose all fields, < to remove a field, and << to remove all fields from the report. See Figure 13.21. Set the desired fields and click Next.

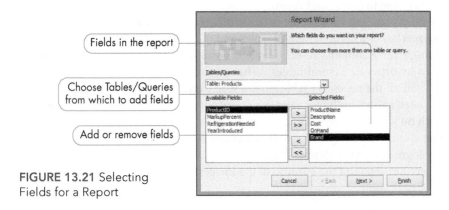

FIGURE 13.21 Selecting Fields for a Report

3. The next dialog box, shown in Figure 13.22, asks, "Do you want to add any grouping levels?" As you learned in a previous chapter, grouping lets you organize and summarize your data, based on values in a field. For a basic report, you will not select any grouping fields and instead just click Next.

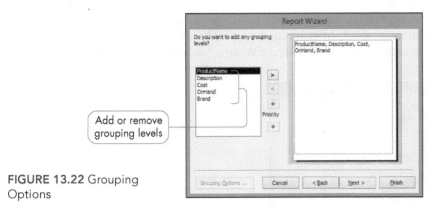

FIGURE 13.22 Grouping
Options

Add or remove
grouping levels

4. The next dialog box, shown in Figure 13.23, asks "What sort order do you want for your records?" For the sort options, specify which field you want to sort by first and optionally add a second, third, and fourth sort. For each field, choose ascending order and/or descending order. Click on the word Ascending and it will toggle to Descending; clicking again will switch back to Ascending. Set the desired sort options and click Next.

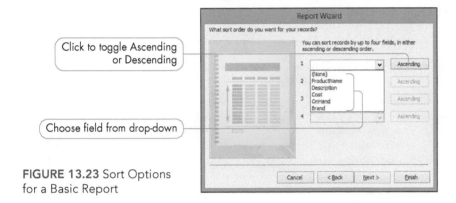

Click to toggle Ascending
or Descending

Choose field from drop-down

FIGURE 13.23 Sort Options
for a Basic Report

5. The next dialog box will determine the report's appearance. You will be given the option to select Columnar, Tabular, or Justified as the layout.

- Columnar will display the information in a column. This leads to reports that are easier to read, but long printouts.
- Tabular will display the data in a table format. This is good for saving space, but it may be difficult to fit all fields on one printed page.
- Justified will display the information in a column as well. If you have Long Text fields, this is a good option to ensure all your data fits.

Tabular is the option you choose to fit the report on as few pages as possible. Clicking an option will give you a general preview in the preview area. You can also select the orientation for the report, either Portrait or Landscape (see Figure 13.24). Select an appropriate format for the report. Set the desired options and click Next.

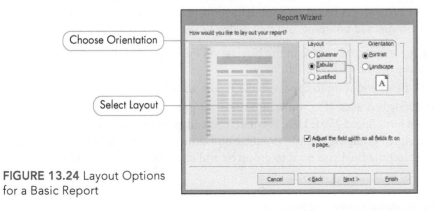

Choose Orientation

Select Layout

FIGURE 13.24 Layout Options
for a Basic Report

6. Decide on an appropriate name for the report. Type a descriptive report name so you can easily determine what information is in the report based on the title. This step, shown in Figure 13.25, is the last step in the Report Wizard. Name the report and click Finish.

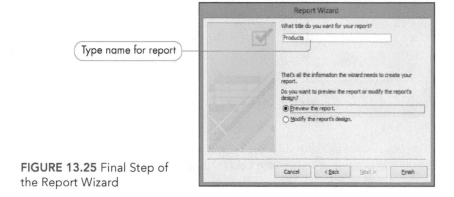

Type name for report

FIGURE 13.25 Final Step of the Report Wizard

Now that you have stepped through the wizard, you will get a report incorporating all the options you chose, as shown in Figure 13.26. You may need to adjust the size of fields, as some may not be fully displayed.

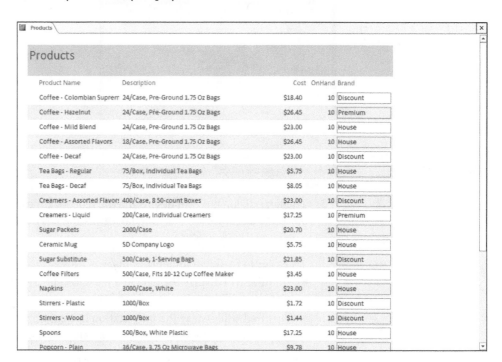

FIGURE 13.26 Results of Report Wizard

Use the Report Wizard with Grouping

In the previous example, we created a basic report using the Report Wizard. However, we can use grouping if we want to summarize our report by a certain field. We can also display overall totals and percentages based on a predefined format. The Report Wizard still has six dialog boxes when you add grouping, but two dialog boxes will change.

1. Select the report's record source in the Navigation Pane and click Report Wizard in the Reports group on the CREATE tab.
2. Choose the fields you want to appear in the report and click Next.
3. The next dialog box asks, "Do you want to add any grouping levels?" In the previous example, we just clicked Next. Here is where you add grouping. As we learned in a previous chapter, grouping lets you organize and summarize your data based on values in a field. Select the field you want to group by and click the > button to add the new

group. If you need a second or third grouping level, add those field names in order. The order in which you select the groups dictates the order of display in the report. Figure 13.27 shows the sort options for a grouped report. In this specific example, records are being grouped by the Brand. Once you have selected the appropriate options, click Next.

4. Because we have specified grouping, the next dialog box asks, "What sort order and summary information do you want for detail records?" Here, you can click Summary Options if you want to add aggregate functions (e.g., sum, average, minimum, and maximum) and to specify whether you want to see detail records on the report or only the aggregate results (see Figure 13.28). You can also choose to calculate percentages, so if you had one group that made up half your sales, you would see 50%. Click OK to return to the Report Wizard. The sort options are the same as before. Set the appropriate options and click Next.

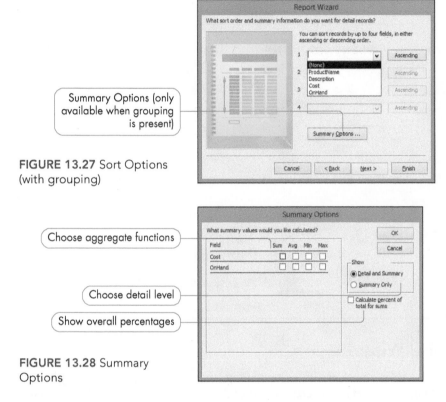

Summary Options (only available when grouping is present)

FIGURE 13.27 Sort Options (with grouping)

Choose aggregate functions

Choose detail level

Show overall percentages

FIGURE 13.28 Summary Options

5. The next dialog box, shown in Figure 13.29, will determine the report's appearance. If you have selected grouping, you will be prompted to select the layout from three options:

- Stepped Layout will display column headings at the top of the page and keep the grouping field(s) in their own row.
- Block Layout will include the grouping field(s) inline with the data, saving some space when printing. It has one set of column headings at the top of each page.
- Outline Layout will display the grouping field(s) on their own separate rows and has column headings inside each group. This leads to a longer report when printing but may help make the report easier to read.

Clicking any of these layouts will give you a general preview in the preview area. The option to choose Portrait or Landscape is still available. Click Next.

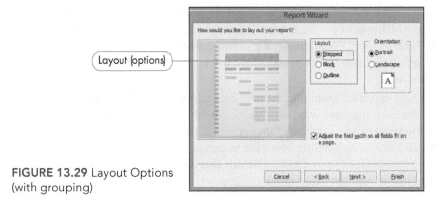

FIGURE 13.29 Layout Options (with grouping)

6. Decide on an appropriate name for the report. Type a descriptive report name. Click Finish. Your grouped report will resemble Figure 13.30.

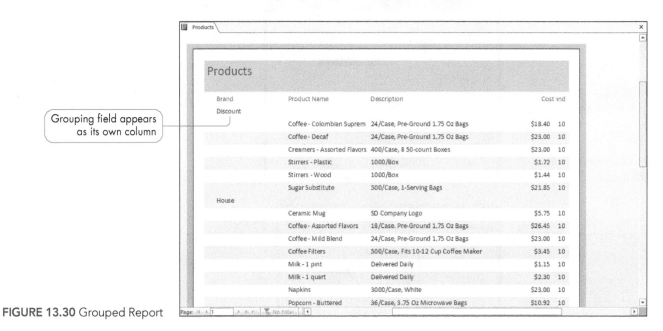

FIGURE 13.30 Grouped Report

Use the Label Wizard

The *Label Wizard* enables you to easily create mailing labels, name tags, and other specialized tags. A *mailing label report* is a specialized report that comes preformatted to coordinate with name-brand labels, such as Avery. Access includes most common labels built into the program. Even if you purchase a store brand from an office supply store, they will generally state the comparable Avery label number.

To use the Label Wizard, do the following:

1. Select the table or query that will serve as the record source for the report.
2. Click Labels in the Reports group on the CREATE tab.
3. Select the manufacturer, the product number, and the label type and click Next.
4. Choose the font type and size and click Next.
5. Add the fields to the label template, as shown in Figure 13.31. You will need to place the fields exactly as you wish them to appear, including adding a comma between City and State and pressing Enter after the CustomerName.
6. Add any sort fields and click Next.
7. Name the report and click Finish to generate your labels. The results are shown in Figure 13.32.

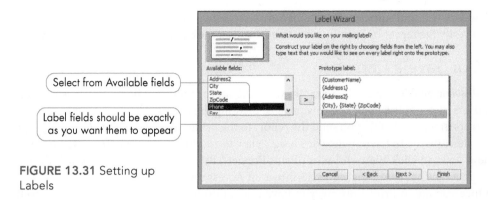

Select from Available fields

Label fields should be exactly as you want them to appear

FIGURE 13.31 Setting up Labels

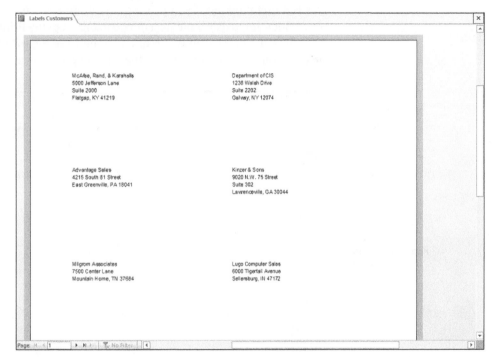

FIGURE 13.32 Output of Label Wizard

Using Report Views

As you work with the report tools to create and modify reports, you will find the need to frequently switch between the four report views in Access—Layout view, Print Preview, Design view, and Report view. Most of your design work will be done in Layout view, but occasionally, you will need to switch to Design view to apply a more advanced feature, such as a calculated field. Users of the report will use Print Preview or Report view. There should be no reason for a user to switch to Layout view or Design view. Modifications to the report should be done by the designated report designer. To switch between the four views, click the View arrow in the Views group and select the desired view.

View a Report in Report View

Report view enables you to view a report onscreen in a continuous page layout. Report view is similar to Form view for forms. However, because the data shown in a report cannot be changed, it is simply a way of viewing the information without having to worry about accidentally moving a control. In addition, using report view allows quick access to filtering options.

Alter a Report in Layout View

Use Layout view to alter the report design while still viewing the data. You should use Layout view to add or delete fields in the report, modify field properties, change the column widths, sort, and filter data by excluding certain records. Although Layout view appears similar to Print

Preview, you will find sufficient variations between the two views, so that you will still always need to verify the report in Print Preview to evaluate all the changes made in Layout view.

Print or Save a Report in Print Preview

STEP 2 » *Print Preview* enables you to see exactly what the report will look like when it is printed. Most users prefer to use Print Preview prior to printing the report. This enables you to intercept errors in reports before you send the report to the printer. You cannot modify the design in this view; switch to Layout view or Design view to modify the design. To switch to Print Preview, you can click View and select Print Preview. By default, Print Preview will display all the pages in the report. Figure 13.33 shows an Access report in Print Preview.

Once you are in Print Preview, you have the option to save the report to a file as well. This is a useful option if you plan on distributing some of your information electronically but do not want to distribute the entire database. On the Print Preview tab in the Data group, you will find a number of different data types. See Figure 13.33. Simply choose the type of file you wish to create, and choose the directory and file name.

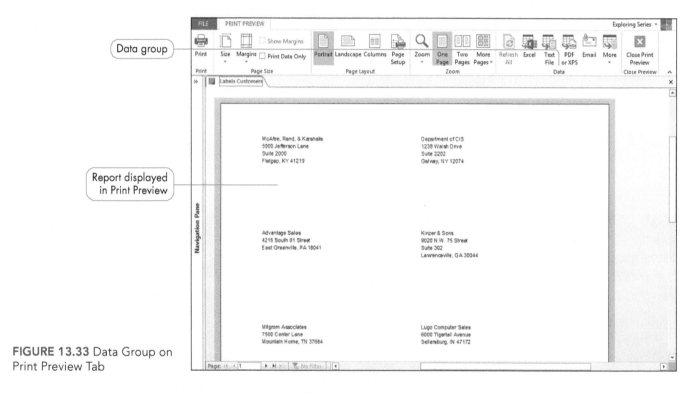

FIGURE 13.33 Data Group on Print Preview Tab

Commonly used formats include Excel, Word, or Portable Document Format (PDF). *Portable Document Format (PDF)* is a file type that was created for exchanging documents independent of software applications and operating system environment. In other words, you can e-mail files in this format to users running Mac operating system or a Linux operating system, and they can open it, even if they do not have Microsoft Office. Acrobat files often open in a program called Adobe Reader, a free tool that displays PDF files.

Because databases contain a great deal of information, Access reports may become very long, requiring many pages to print. Experienced Access users always use Print Preview prior to printing their reports. Some reports may require hundreds of pages to print. Other reports may be formatted incorrectly, and a blank page may print after each page of information. It would be better to correct this problem prior to sending it to the printer.

Modifying a Report

After a report is generated by one of the report tools, you may need to modify it. Similar to forms, the common changes to a report are add a field, remove a field, change the order of fields, change the width of a field, and modify the title. Much like a form, the Report has many options you can use to format a report. Once you are in Layout or Design view, you will have access to the report layout tools. You have four tabs available:

- Design: Use this tab to make changes to the design of the report, such as adding sorting, changing themes, and inserting additional controls.
- Arrange: Use this tab to change the layout of a report, to move fields up and down, to insert a space above or below your current position, or to insert a space to the left or the right of the current field.
- Format: Use this tab to change the font; add or remove bolding, italics, or underlining; change font size; change font color or background; adjust text alignment; or add a background image.
- Page Setup: Use this tab to change paper size, margins, page orientation, or to add columns.

Modify a Report Using the Arrange Tab

The Arrange tab displays in both Layout view and Design view. To use these commands, first open a report in Layout view or Design view and click the Format tab. Next, select a field or fields and click the appropriate command. Some key commands are highlighted in Figure 13.34.

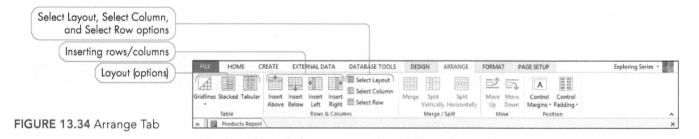

FIGURE 13.34 Arrange Tab

The Table group contains commands that enable you to add gridlines to a report's layout, to change a report's layout from stacked to tabular (and vice versa), or to remove a report's layout. The Remove Layout command is available in Design view only. For example, if a report was created with a tabular layout, you could change it to a stacked layout by doing the following:

STEP 3 ⟩⟩

1. Open the report in Layout view.
2. Click the ARRANGE tab.
3. Click on any text box in the *Detail* section.
4. Click Select Layout in the Rows & Columns group.
5. Click Stacked in the Table group.

The Rows & Columns group contains commands that enable you to insert rows and columns inside a report's layout. For example, in a report with a stacked layout, you may want to separate the first three fields from the rest of the fields. To do this, you could select the third text box and click Insert Below. This will create a space after the third field. This group also contains the Select Layout, Select Column, and Select Row commands.

The Merge/Split group contains commands that enable you to merge and split the cells on a report. There are times when you may want to deviate from the basic row and column formats that the Access Report Wizards create. In this case, you can change the layout of the report using the merge cells and split cell commands. These commands do not change the actual controls, only the layout of the controls.

The Move group contains two commands that enable you to move a field up or down in a stacked layout. For example, if you want to move the second field in a stacked layout to the first position, select the second field's text box and label, and then click Move Up in the Move group. Moving fields up or down in a report may cause unexpected results; you can always use the undo command if you need to revert back to the beginning.

The Position group contains commands that enable you to modify the margins and the padding of controls in a report. This group also contains the Anchoring command, which enables you to change where the report's controls appear on the screen. By default, reports are anchored at the top left; however, you can change this to any of the nine options using the anchoring command.

Modify Report Controls using the Format Tab

The Format tab contains a series of commands that enable you change the font, display, and alignment of the controls on a report, as shown in Figure 13.35. This is useful if you need to quickly change the look of one cell. For example, you may have an important field you want to emphasize. To do so, do the following:

1. Switch to Layout view (or Design view).
2. Select the field you wish to format.
3. Click the FORMAT tab.
4. Change the format as desired. You can format the text as you would in Microsoft Word.

FIGURE 13.35 Format Tab

> ## TIP Apply a Background Image to a Report
>
> To apply a Background Image to a report, open the report in Layout view (or Design view), click the Format tab, and then click Background Image in the Background group. Next, click Browse to locate the image you want to apply to the report. Once the image has been applied to the report, you can change the properties of the image so that the image is anchored and sized correctly.

Add a Field to a Report

Adding a field to a report with a tabular layout is similar to adding a field to a form with a tabular layout. To add a field to a report, do the following:

1. Switch to Layout view.
2. On the DESIGN tab, in the Tools group, click Add Existing Fields to reveal the available fields in the report's record source. The Field List pane will display on the right-hand side of your screen.
3. For a single-table report, you will be presented with a list of fields. For a multiple-table report, you will first need to click the + (plus) next to the appropriate table to locate the desired field.
4. Drag the new field to a precise location on the report, using the vertical shaded line as a guide for the position of the new field, and release the mouse. The other fields will automatically adjust to make room for the new field.

The process of adding a field to a report with a stacked layout is the same as a tabular layout. The only difference is the shaded line will appear horizontally.

Delete a Field from a Report

To delete a field from the *Detail* section of a tabular report, do the following:

1. Switch to the Layout view (or Design view) of the report.
2. Click the text box of the field to be deleted. Click Select Column in the Rows & Columns group on the ARRANGE tab. Note the shaded border appears around the field and the label for the field.
3. With the shaded border visible, press Delete on your keyboard. The field disappears and the other fields fill in the gap.

Adjust Column Widths in a Report

You can adjust the width of each column in a tabular report individually so that each column is wide enough to accommodate the widest value. For example, if a report contains first name, last name, address and city, and email address, you will need to make sure the longest value in each field is completely visible. Scroll through the records to make sure this is the case.

To modify column widths in a tabular report, do the following:

1. Switch to the Layout view (or Design view) of the report.
2. Click the text box of the field you want to adjust. The field will have a shaded border around it, indicating it is selected.
3. Move the mouse to the right border of the selected field; when the mouse pointer turns to a double arrow, drag the edge to the right (to increase) or the left (to decrease) until you arrive at the desired width.

Changing Margins and Orientation

Sometimes, you may wish to print a page in Landscape or adjust the margins rather than adjusting widths. You will notice the Page Setup tab has these options. In the Page Size group, you can change the margins, and in the Page Layout group, you can choose Portrait or Landscape. See Figure 13.36 for locations of commonly used tools on this tab.

Page Layout group

FIGURE 13.36 Report Layout Tools Page Setup Tab

Add a Theme to the Report

You can enhance the report's appearance by applying one of the themes provided by Access. To apply a theme, do the following:

1. Switch to Layout view (or Design view).
2. Click Themes in the Themes group on the DESIGN tab. Scroll through the themes until you find a theme you like; hover over one of the options to see a quick preview of the current report using the current theme. (This is easier to preview in Layout view.)
3. Right-click a theme and select *Apply Theme to This Object Only*. You can also apply the theme to all objects.

Work with a Report Layout Control

Whenever you use one of the report tools to create a new report, Access will add a layout control to help align the fields. Layout controls in reports work the same as layout controls in forms. As discussed earlier in this chapter, the layout control provides guides to help keep controls aligned horizontally and vertically and give your report a uniform appearance.

There are times when you may want to remove the layout control from a report in order to position the fields without aligning them to each other. If you want to remove the layout control from a report, do the following:

1. Switch to Design view (this is not available in Layout view).
2. Click anywhere inside the layout control you want to remove.
3. Click Select Layout in the Rows & Columns group on the ARRANGE tab.
4. In the Table group, click Remove Layout and the layout control is gone. All of the controls are still on the report, but the rectangle binding them together is gone.

You can add a layout control to a report by first selecting all the controls you want to keep together. Then, click Stacked or Tabular in the Table group and the layout control appears.

Sorting Records in a Report

When a report is created using the Report tool, the sort order of the records in the report is initially dependent on the sort order of the record source—similar to the way records are sorted in a form. The primary key of the record source usually dictates the sort order. However, a report has an additional feature for sorting. While in Layout view or Design view, click Group & Sort in the Grouping & Totals group on the Design tab. The Group, Sort, and Total pane displays at the bottom of the report. This section enables you to set the sort order for the report and override the sorting in the report's record source. Note that if you did not use the Report Wizard, this is how you would add grouping and totals to a report.

Sorting is important because sorting by a primary key may not be intuitive. For example, sorting by a field like LastName might be a better choice than a primary key so users see the records are in alphabetical order by LastName.

Change the Sorting in a Report

STEP 4 ►► If you want to change the sorting in the report, do the following:

1. Switch to Layout view.
2. On the DESIGN tab, in the Grouping & Totals group, click Group & Sort to display the *Group, Sort, and Total* section, as shown in Figure 13.37. This will appear at the bottom of the report.

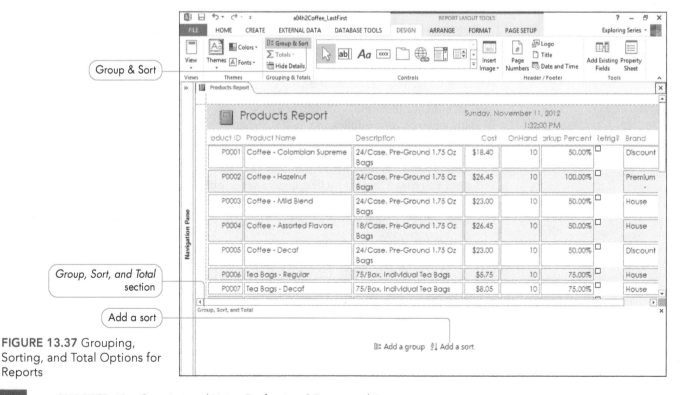

FIGURE 13.37 Grouping, Sorting, and Total Options for Reports

3. Click *Add a sort* and select the field you wish to sort by, which you can change as shown in Figure 13.38. The default sort order is ascending.

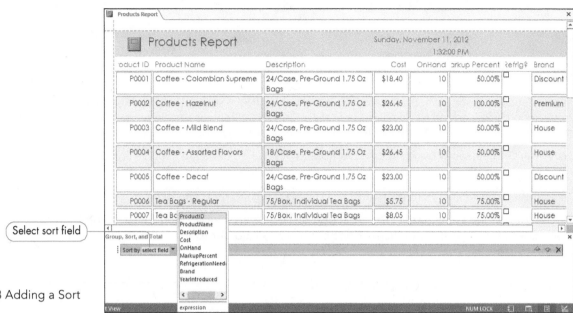

Select sort field

FIGURE 13.38 Adding a Sort to a Report

4. If you wish to add a second sort, click *Add a Sort* again. For example, you could sort first by Brand and then by ProductName, as shown in Figure 13.39.

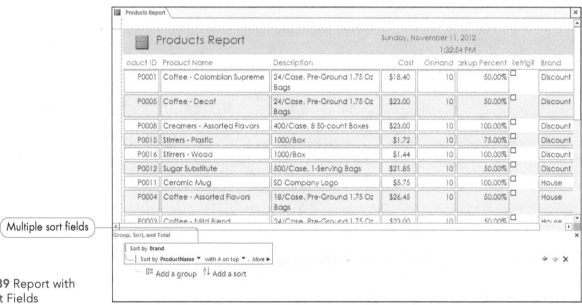

Multiple sort fields

FIGURE 13.39 Report with Multiple Sort Fields

Quick Concepts

1. Compare controls in forms and controls in reports. ***pp. 664, 686***

2. What are the benefits of using the report wizard? ***p. 678***

3. What is the difference between Print Preview and Report view? ***pp. 683–684***

4. What are the benefits of a report layout control when modifying a report? ***pp. 687–688***

5. Why is sorting the records in a report important? ***p. 688***

Watch the Video
for this Hands-
On Exercise!

MyITLab®
HOE2 Training

2 Report Basics

You create a Products report using the Access Report tool to help Ryung stay on top of the key data for her business. After Access creates the report, you modify the column widths so the entire report fits on one page (portrait or landscape, depending on the report). You also use the Report Wizard tool to create other reports for Ryung.

Skills covered: Create Reports Using Report Tools • Use Report Views • Modify a Report • Sort Records in a Report

You use the Report tool to create an Access report to help Ryung manage her product information. This report is especially useful for determining which products she needs to order to fill upcoming orders. Refer to Figure 13.40 as you complete Step 1.

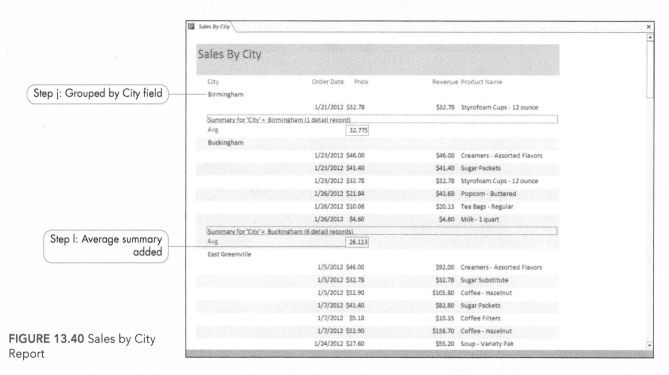

Step j: Grouped by City field

Step l: Average summary added

FIGURE 13.40 Sales by City Report

a. Open *a04h1Coffee_LastFirst* if you closed it at the end of Hands-On Exercise 1. Click the **FILE tab**, select **Save As**, and then click **Save As**. Type **a04h2Coffee_LastFirst** as the file name, changing *h1* to *h2*. Click **Save**.

b. Select the **Products table** in the Navigation Pane. Click the **CREATE tab** and click **Report** in the Reports group.

   Access creates a new tabular layout report based on the Products table. The report opens in Layout view ready to edit.

c. Click the **Products title** at the top of the report to select it, click again on **Products**, and then change the title to **Products Report**. Press **Enter** to accept the change.

d. Right-click the **Products report tab** and select **Print Preview**.

   The report is too wide for the page; you will exit Print Preview and change the orientation to Landscape.

e. Click **Close Print Preview**.

f. Click the **PAGE SETUP tab** and click **Landscape** in the Page Layout group.

The report changes to Landscape orientation. Most of the columns now fit onto one page. You will make further revisions to the report later on so that it fits on one page.

g. Save the report as **Products Report**. Close the report.

h. Select the **Revenue query** in the Navigation Pane. Click the **CREATE tab** and click **Report Wizard** in the Reports group.

The Report Wizard launches.

i. Click the **City field** and click the **> button** to add the City field to the report. Repeat the same process for the **OrderDate, Price, Revenue,** and **ProductName fields**. Click **Next**.

j. Select **City** and click the **> button** to add grouping by city. Click **Next**.

k. Select **OrderDate** for the sort order and leave the order as **Ascending**. Click **Summary Options**.

l. Click the **Avg check box** on the Price row to summarize the Price field. Click **OK**.

m. Click **Next**. Click **Next** again to accept the default layout.

n. Type **Sales by City** for the title of the report. Click **Finish**.

The report is displayed in Print Preview mode. Some of the data values and labels cannot be seen. Next, you will adjust the controls.

o. Click **Close Print Preview**.

p. Switch to Layout view if necessary and adjust the controls so all the field values are visible as shown in Figure 13.40.

q. Display the report in Print Preview to verify your changes.

r. Save and close the report.

STEP 2 ≫ USING REPORT VIEWS

The Products report you created for La Vida Mocha looks very good, according to Ryung. However, she does not have Access at home and would like to have a copy of the report saved so she can bring it home. You will save a copy of the report for her.

a. Open the **Products Report** and switch to **Print Preview**. Click **PDF or XPS** in the Data group on the PRINT PREVIEW tab. Enter the file name **a04h2Products_LastFirst** and click **Publish**.

Windows will open the report in your system's default PDF viewer, which may be Adobe Reader or the Windows 8.1.1 Reader app.

b. Switch back to Access, if necessary. Click **Close** when asked if you want to save the export steps.

c. Click **Close Print Preview** and close the report.

STEP 3 ≫ MODIFYING A REPORT

Ryung realized the Products table is missing a field. She would like you to add this to the table and update the report to reflect the new field. She would also like to make sure the report fits nicely onto one landscape page. She has also asked you to show her some sample color schemes.

a. Right-click the **Products table** and select **Design view**.

You need to add the OnHand field to the Products table.

b. Click the **MarkupPercent field** and click **Insert Rows** in the Tools group on the DESIGN tab.

A new blank row displays above the MarkupPercent field.

c. Type **OnHand** in the **Field Name box** and select **Number** as the Data Type.

d. Save the table. Click **View** to change to Datasheet view.

The new OnHand column appears empty in each row. Next, you will add sample data to the new field.

e. Fill in the number **10** for each item's OnHand field.

f. Close the Products table.

g. Right-click the **Products Report** and select **Layout view**.

h. Click **Add Existing Fields** in the Tools group on the DESIGN tab unless the Field List already appears on the right of your screen.

i. Drag the **OnHand field** from the Field List pane between the Cost and MarkupPercent fields. Close the Field List pane.

Because of the tabular layout control, Access adjusts all the columns to make room for the new OnHand field.

j. Display the report in Print Preview.

The report is still too wide for a single page.

k. Click **Close Print Preview**. Switch to Layout view if necessary.

l. Click anywhere on the **Year Introduced column**. Click the **ARRANGE tab** and click **Select Column** in the Rows & Columns group. Press **Delete** to remove the column.

The Year Introduced column is removed from the report and the other fields fill the empty space.

> **TROUBLESHOOTING:** If you cannot see the Year Introduced column, try scrolling to the right.

m. Click the **ProductID column heading** and drag the right border to the left until the Product ID heading still fits, but any extra white space is removed.

n. Click the **Refrigeration Needed column heading** and rename the column **Refrig?**. Adjust the column width of the Refrig? column so any extra white space is removed.

o. Click **Themes** in the Themes group on the DESIGN tab.

The available predefined themes display.

p. Right-click the **Organic theme** and choose **Apply Theme to This Object Only**. Display the report in Print Preview.

Access reformats the report using the Organic theme.

> **TROUBLESHOOTING:** If you cannot figure out which theme is which, you can hover the mouse over each theme and a ScreenTip will display the theme name.

q. Click **Close Print Preview**. Click the **FILE tab**, select **Save As**, select **Save Object As**, and then click **Save As**. Type **Products Organic** as the report name and click **OK**.

You saved the report with one theme. Now, you will apply a second theme to the report and save it with a different name.

r. Switch to Layout view and click **Themes** in the Themes group to apply a different theme.

s. Right-click the **Retrospect theme** and choose **Apply Theme to This Object Only**. Display the report in Print Preview.

If we do not tell Access to apply the theme to this object only, all objects will change.

t. Click **Close Print Preview**. Click the **FILE tab**, select **Save As**, select **Save Object As**, and then click **Save As**. Type **Products Retrospect** as the report name and click **OK**. Close the report.

You will be able to show Ryung two different themes.

STEP 4 ≫ SORTING RECORDS IN A REPORT

Ryung would like the Products Report report to be sorted by Product Name order (rather than ProductID order). You change the sort order and preview again to see the results.

a. Open **Products Report** in Layout view.

> **TROUBLESHOOTING:** If you cannot see the Products Report, click the Shutter Bar to maximize the Navigation Pane.

b. Click **Group & Sort** in the Grouping & Totals group on the DESIGN tab.

The *Add a group* and *Add a sort* options appear at the bottom of the report.

> **TROUBLESHOOTING:** If the options do not appear, they may have been showing. Try clicking Group & Sort again.

c. Click **Add a sort**.

A new Sort bar displays at the bottom of the report.

d. Select **Brand** from the list.

The report is now sorted by Brand in Ascending order (with Discount on top).

e. Click **Add a group**.

f. Select **Brand** from the list.

The report is now grouped by Brand.

g. Display the report in Print Preview.

h. Close Print Preview and save and close the report.

i. Close the database. Submit the database and the PDF file *a04h2Products_LastFirst* based on your instructor's directions.

Chapter Objectives Review

After reading this chapter, you have accomplished the following objectives:

1. **Create forms using form tools.**
   - A form is used to add data to or edit data in a table.
   - Access provides 14 different tools for creating forms.
   - If you use a form, you are less likely to edit the wrong record.
   - Forms can show data from multiple tables at once.
   - Forms can be customized to match a paper form.
   - Identify a record source: A record source is the table or query that supplies the records.
   - Use the Form tool: The Form tool creates a basic form.
   - Understand controls: Controls are the text boxes, buttons, boxes, and other tools you use to add, edit, and display data in a form or report.
   - Work with form views: Form view is a simplified interface used for data entry, but it allows no changes. Layout view allows users to make changes to the layout while viewing the data on the form. Design view allows you to change advanced design settings you cannot see in the Layout view.
   - Work with a subform: A subform displays data from a related table for each record in the main table.

2. **Create a split form: A split form combines two views of the same record source—one section is displayed in a stacked layout and the other section is displayed in a tabular layout.**
   - Create a multiple-item form: This form displays multiple records in a tabular layout similar to a table's Datasheet view, with more customization options.
   - Create forms using the other form tools: A Datasheet form is a replica of a table or query's Datasheet view except that it still retains some of the form properties. The Form Design tool and the Blank Form tools can be used to create a form manually. The Navigation option in the Forms group enables you to create user interface forms that have the look and feel of a Web-based form and enable users to open and close the objects of a database. The Modal Dialog Form tool can be used to create a dialog box.

3. **Use form views.**
   - Edit data in Form view: Most users will work in Form view. This allows changes to data but not to design elements.
   - Alter a form in Layout view: Layout view allows you to change the design of a form while viewing data.
   - Add a field to a form: Fields can be added to an existing form using the Field List.
   - Delete a field from a form: Fields can be removed, but you may need to select the entire control to avoid leaving empty space in the form.
   - Adjust column widths in a form: Column widths often need to be adjusted. Numeric fields may show up as #### if the value cannot be displayed in the box.
   - Use the Form Layout tools tabs: There are three Form Layout tabs that allow you to manipulate the design of a form.

   - Modify form controls using the Format tab: The Format tab allows changes to the font, including bold, italic, underlining, font size, font color, font background, and alignment.
   - Select controls: Controls can be selected manually or by using the Arrange tab.
   - Add a theme to a form: Themes can be applied to a single form or to all objects in the database.
   - Add styling to a form: Forms can have many types of styles applied. Take care to avoid too many styles on a single form, as it can distract from the form.

4. **Work with a form layout control.**
   - Modify a form using the Arrange tab: The Arrange tab appears in both Layout view and Design view and allows you to change form layout, field order, and spacing options.
   - The Table group lets you add gridlines, change from stacked to tabular layout (and vice versa), or remove a form's layout.
   - The Move group contains lets you move fields.
   - The Position group lets you modify the margins and the padding of controls in a form.

5. **Sort records in form.**
   - Default sort order is the sort order of the data source (table, query, etc.).
   - Sort by a single field: Forms can be sorted by a single field in either ascending or descending order.
   - Remove sorting in a form: Sorts can be removed from a form at any point.

6. **Create reports using report tools.**
   - A report is a document that displays information from a database in a format that outputs meaningful information to its readers.
   - Access reports can be printed, viewed on screen, or saved as files.
   - Reports cannot change data in your database.
   - Use the Report tool: Access has five report tools: The Report tool instantly creates a tabular report based on the table or query currently selected. The Report Design tool creates a new blank report in Design view. The Blank Report tool creates a new blank report so that you can insert fields and controls manually and design the report. The Report Wizard tool helps you create a report. The Labels tool creates a page of mailing labels using a template.
   - Use the Report Wizard to create a report: The Report Wizard will guide you step by step through creating a report, asking questions and generating output.
   - Use the Report Wizard with grouping: The Report Wizard options will change when you add grouping. It will also allow summary options such as creating a sum of a field for each grouping level.
   - Use the Label Wizard: The Label Wizard can produce printable labels. Access includes predefined standard formats for common labels.

7. **Use report views.**
   - View a report in Report view: Report view is ideal for viewing data onscreen. Neither data nor design can be changed.
   - Alter a report in Layout view: Layout view allows you to change the design of a report while viewing data.
   - Print or save a report in Print Preview: Print Preview shows the way the report will display when printed. It also allows you to save the report as a file in a number of formats.

8. **Modify a report.**
   - Modify a report using the Design tab: The Design tab allows you to add or change sorting, change report theme, and insert additional controls.
   - Modify a report using the Arrange tab: The Arrange tab allows you to change the report layout, move fields, and insert spaces.
   - Modify report controls using the Format tab: The Format tab allows changes to the font, including bold, italic, underlining, font size, font color, font background, and alignment.
   - Add a field to a report: Fields can be added to an existing report using the Field List.

   - Delete a field from a report: Fields can be removed, but you may need to select the entire control to avoid leaving empty space in the report.
   - Adjust column widths in a report: Column widths often need to be adjusted. Numeric fields may show up as #### if the value cannot be displayed in the box.
   - Change margins and orientation: You can display the report in portrait or landscape format and increase or decrease margin size.
   - Add a theme to the report: Themes can be applied to a single report or to all objects in the database.
   - Work with a Report Layout control: The Layout control keeps the fields neatly spaced, making it harder to place fields in an exact location but keeping a standard format.

9. **Sort records in a report.**
   - Default sort order for reports is the sort order of the record source.
   - Change the sorting in a report: Sorting can be done by a single or by multiple fields.

Key Terms Matching

Match the key terms with their definitions. Write the key term letter by the appropriate numbered definition.

a. Controls
b. Design view
c. Form
d. Form tool
e. Form view
f. Label Wizard
g. Layout control
h. Layout view
i. Multiple Items form
j. Portable Document Format (PDF)

k. Print Preview
l. Record source
m. Report
n. Report tool
o. Report view
p. Report Wizard
q. Split form
r. Stacked layout
s. Tabular layout
t. Theme

1. _____ A database object that is used to add data into or edit data in a table. **p. 656**

2. _____ Used to create data entry forms for customers, employees, products, and other primary tables. **p. 656**

3. _____ The table or query that supplies the records for a form or report. **p. 657**

4. _____ Displays fields in a vertical column. **p. 658**

5. _____ Displays data horizontally. **p. 658**

6. _____ The text boxes, buttons, boxes, and other tools you use to add, edit, and display the data in a form or report. **p. 658**

7. _____ Provides guides to help keep controls aligned horizontally and vertically and give your form a uniform appearance. **p. 658**

8. _____ A simplified interface primarily used for data entry; does not allow you to make changes to the layout. **p. 658**

9. _____ Enables users to make changes to a layout while viewing the data on the form or report. **p. 659**

10. _____ Enables you to change advanced design settings you cannot see in the Layout view, such as a background image. **p. 659**

11. _____ Combines two views of the same record source—one section is displayed in a stacked layout and the other section is displayed in a tabular layout. **p. 660**

12. _____ Displays multiple records in a tabular layout similar to a table's Datasheet view, with more customization options. **p. 661**

13. _____ A defined set of colors, fonts, and graphics that can be applied to a form or report. **p. 665**

14. _____ A document that displays information from a database in a format that outputs meaningful information to its readers. **p. 676**

15. _____ Used to instantly create a tabular report based on the table or query currently selected. **p. 676**

16. _____ Asks you questions and then uses your answers to generate a customized report. **p. 678**

17. _____ Enables you to easily create mailing labels, name tags, and other specialized tags. **p. 682**

18. _____ Enables you to see what a printed report will look like in a continuous page layout. **p. 683**

19. _____ Enables you to see exactly what the report will look like when it is printed. **p. 684**

20. _____ A file type that was created for exchanging documents independent of software applications and operating system environment. **p. 684**

Multiple Choice

1. The table or query that supplies the records for a form or report is also known as the:
    (a) Control.
    (b) Record Source.
    (c) Theme.
    (d) Tabular Layout.

2. Which of the following statements is *false*?
    (a) Both forms and reports can use tabular and stacked layouts.
    (b) A stacked layout displays data in a vertical column.
    (c) A tabular layout displays data horizontally.
    (d) Stacked layouts are more common for reports because they will use less paper when printed.

3. Which of the following is *not* an example of a control?
    (a) A text box on a form
    (b) Buttons on a report
    (c) A report
    (d) A box on a report

4. The simplest interface you can use to modify control widths in a form is in:
    (a) Layout view.
    (b) Form view.
    (c) Design view.
    (d) Report view.

5. Which of the following views is the most powerful, but also the most complicated?
    (a) Design view.
    (b) Layout view.
    (c) Form view/Report view.
    (d) Print Preview.

6. Which of the following statements about reports are *false*?
    (a) Reports can be saved to a file on your computer.
    (b) Reports are primarily used to modify data.

    (c) Reports can produce output in a number of ways, including mailing labels.
    (d) Reports can be created simply using the Report tool.

7. Use the _____ to see exactly what the printed report will look like before printing.
    (a) Report tool
    (b) Report Wizard
    (c) Report view
    (d) Print Preview

8. If you have a client working on a Mac system, which of the following file formats would be the best choice to use to ensure the client can open it?
    (a) Microsoft Word
    (b) Microsoft Excel
    (c) Microsoft Access
    (d) Portable Document Format (PDF)

9. Which of the following statements is *false*?
    (a) Reports are generally used for printing, emailing, or viewing data on the screen.
    (b) Layout controls for forms and reports are the defined sets of colors, fonts, and graphics.
    (c) Forms are often used for inputting data.
    (d) Forms and reports both include controls, such as text boxes, that can be resized.

10. Which of the following statements is *false*?
    (a) You can use grouping to show a list of properties by state.
    (b) Sorting can be done on both forms and reports.
    (c) Sorting can be done in ascending or descending order.
    (d) You can either group or sort (but not both).

Practice Exercises

1 Financial Management

You are working as a customer service representative for a financial management firm. Your task is to contact a list of prospective customers and introduce yourself and the services of your company. You will create a form to help you view one customer at a time while also helping add and update the data. After creating the form, you will customize it and add sorting. You will also create a report to show you all the data on one screen, for viewing purposes. This exercise follows the same set of skills as used in Hands-On Exercises 1 and 2 in the chapter. Refer to Figure 13.41 as you complete this exercise.

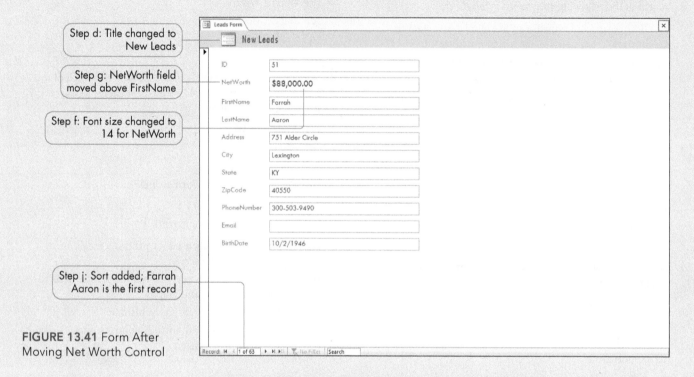

Step d: Title changed to New Leads

Step g: NetWorth field moved above FirstName

Step f: Font size changed to 14 for NetWorth

Step j: Sort added; Farrah Aaron is the first record

FIGURE 13.41 Form After Moving Net Worth Control

a. Start Access and open **a04p1Prospects**. Save the database as **a04p1Prospects_LastFirst**.

b. Click the **Leads table**. Click the **CREATE tab** and click **Form** in the Forms group.

A new form based on the Leads table displays in Layout view.

c. Click the **ID text box** and drag the right border of the first field to the left to shrink the column by approximately half of its original size.

The other columns will shrink as well.

d. Change the title of the form to **New Leads**.

e. Click **Themes** in the Themes group of the DESIGN tab. Select the **Integral theme** (first row, third column).

f. Change the font size to **14** for the NetWorth text box control.

g. Click **Select Row** in the Rows & Columns group on the ARRANGE tab. Click **Move Up** in the Move group on the ARRANGE tab until *NetWorth* appears above *First*.

> **TROUBLESHOOTING:** If both items do not move together, undo, ensure both are selected, and then follow the instructions in step g.

NetWorth should now appear above the FirstName. See Figure 13.41.

h. Save the form as **Leads Form**. Switch to Form view.

i. Navigate to record 63. Enter your first and last names in the appropriate fields. Leave the e-mail address blank.

j. Click in the **Last field** (if necessary) and click **Ascending** in the Sort & Filter group of the HOME tab Farrah Aaron should be the first record displayed unless your last name appears before hers alphabetically.

k. Save and close the form.

l. Click the **Leads table**. Click **Report** in the Reports group on the CREATE tab.

A new report is created based on the Leads table.

m. Make fields as small as possible to remove extra white space. Do not try to fit the entire report all on one page, as you will be using this for on-screen viewing only.

n. Save the report as **Leads Report**. Close the report.

o. Exit Access. Submit the database based on your instructor's directions.

2 Comfort Insurance

The Human Resources department of the Comfort Insurance Agency has initiated its annual employee performance reviews. You will create a form for them to help organize input and a report showing employee salary increases and bonuses. The employee data, along with forms and reports, are stored in an Access database. You need to prepare a report showing employee raises and bonuses by city. This exercise follows the same set of skills as used in Hands-On Exercises 1 and 2 in this chapter. Refer to Figure 13.42 as you complete this exercise.

Step k: Location is a grouping level

Location	LastName	FirstName	HireDate	Salary	2012Increase	2012Raise	YearHired	YearsWorked
L01								
	Abrams		5/24/2012	$47,500.00	3.00%	1425	2012	0
	Anderson	Vicki	9/21/2008	$47,900.00	4.00%	1916	2008	4
	Bichette	Susan	9/10/2012	$61,500.00	4.00%	2460	2012	0
	Block	Leonard	12/13/2010	$26,200.00	3.00%	786	2010	2
	Brown	Patricia	6/12/2011	$20,100.00	5.00%	1005	2011	1
	Brumbaugh	Paige	12/25/2009	$49,300.00	3.00%	1479	2009	3
	Daniels	Phil	2/5/2011	$42,600.00	3.00%	1278	2011	1
	Davis	Martha	6/14/2010	$51,900.00	4.00%	2076	2010	2
	Drubin	Lolly	9/12/2009	$37,000.00	3.00%	1110	2009	3
	Fantis	Laurie	1/11/2011	$28,000.00	3.00%	840	2011	1
	Fleming	Karen	12/15/2009	$41,100.00	3.00%	1233	2009	3
	Gander	John	12/31/2008	$38,400.00	3.00%	1152	2008	4
	Grippando	Joan	8/30/2010	$26,100.00	3.00%	783	2010	2
	Harrison	Jenifer	10/19/2012	$44,800.00	3.00%	1344	2012	0
	Imber	Elise	1/22/2011	$63,700.00	4.00%	2548	2011	1
	Johnshon	Billy	4/28/2012	$21,800.00	5.00%	1090	2012	0
	Johnson	Debbie	6/23/2012	$39,700.00	3.00%	1191	2012	0
	Lacher	Tom	3/7/2011	$31,200.00	3.00%	936	2011	1
	Mc Key	Boo	7/29/2012	$39,600.00	3.00%	1188	2012	0
	McCammon	Johnny	6/22/2012	$43,100.00	4.00%	1724	2012	0
	Mills	Jack	11/6/2008	$44,600.00	3.00%	1338	2008	4
	Nagel	Mimi	12/29/2010	$46,200.00	3.00%	1386	2010	2
	Newman	Adam	10/12/2006	$45,000.00	4.00%	1800	2006	6
	Novicheck	Deborah	11/25/2008	$46,800.00	3.00%	1404	2008	4

FIGURE 13.42 Final Employee Compensation Report

a. Open *a04p2Insurance*. Save the database as **a04p2Insurance_LastFirst**.

b. Select the **Locations table**. Click the **CREATE tab** and click **Form** in the Forms group.

A new form based on the Locations table opens in Layout view.

c. Click the **LocationID text box** containing *L01*. Move the mouse to the right edge of the shaded border until the mouse pointer changes to a double-headed arrow. Drag the right edge to the left to reduce the size of the text box to approximately half of its original size.

The LocationID field and all the other fields should become smaller.

d. Click the subform at the bottom of the form. Press **Delete** to delete the subform.

e. Click **Themes** in the Themes group on the DESIGN tab. Right-click the **Wisp theme** (third row, first column) and select **Apply Theme to This Object Only**.

f. Save the form as **Locations**. Close the form.

g. Select the **Locations table**. Click the **CREATE tab** and click **Report** in the Reports group.

A new tabular layout report based on the Locations table opens in Layout view.

h. Click the **LocationID label** and drag the right border of the label to the left to reduce the size of the control to approximately half of its original size.

i. Repeat the sizing process with the **Zipcode label** and the **OfficePhone label**. Adjust the other columns if necessary until there are no controls on the right side of the vertical dashed line.

j. Display the report in Print Preview. Verify that the report is only one page wide. Save the report as **Locations** and close the report.

k. Select the **Employees Query**. Click the **CREATE tab** and click **Report Wizard** in the Reports group to launch the Report Wizard. Respond to the questions as follows:

- Click (>>) to add all the fields to the Selected Fields box. Click **Next**.
- Accept grouping by Location. Click **Next**.
- Select **LastName** for the first sort order and **FirstName** for the second. Click **Summary Options**.

TROUBLESHOOTING: If you do not see summary options, click Back and click Summary Options at the bottom of the dialog box.

- Click **Sum** for Salary, **Avg** for 2012Increase, and **Avg** for YearsWorked. Accept all other defaults. Click **OK**. Click **Next**.
- Accept the Stepped layout. Change Orientation to **Landscape**. Click **Next**.
- Type **Employee Compensation** for the title of the report. Click **Finish**.

The report is displayed in Print Preview mode. Some of the columns are too narrow. Next, you will adjust the columns.

l. Click **Close Print Preview**. Switch to Layout view.

m. Adjust the column widths so that all the data values are showing and the report appears on one page. Some of the columns will need to be reduced, and some will need to be widened.

n. Click **Themes** in the Themes group on the DESIGN tab. Right-click the **Slice theme** and choose **Apply Theme to This Object Only**.

o. Display the report in Print Preview. Close the Navigation Pane and verify that the report is still one page wide. Compare your report to Figure 13.42. Adjust column widths to display all values.

p. Save and close the Employee Compensation report. Close the database.

q. Exit Access. Submit based on your instructor's directions.

1 Hotel Chain

ANALYSIS CASE

You are the general manager of a large hotel chain. You track revenue by categories, such as conference room rentals and weddings. You need to create a report that shows which locations are earning the most revenue in each category. You will also create a report to show you details of your three newest areas: St. Paul, St. Louis, and Seattle.

a. Open *a04m1Rewards*. Save the database as **a04m1Rewards_LastFirst**.

b. Select the **Members table** and create a Multiple Items form. Save the form as **Maintain Members**.

c. Modify the form in Layout view as follows:
- Change the MemNumber label to **MemID** and reduce the MemNumber column width.
- Adjust the column widths to eliminate extra white space.
- Delete the form icon (the picture next to the title of the form) in the Form Header.

d. Change the sorting on the MemberSince control so that the members who joined most recently are displayed first.

DISCOVER

e. Click on the **LastName field**. Change the Control Padding to **Wide**. Hint: Search **Control Padding Wide** in Access Help.

The controls have some extra space between them.

f. Save and close the form.

g. Select the **Revenue query** and create a report using the Report Wizard. Answer the wizard prompts as follows:
- Include all fields.
- Add grouping by City and by ServiceName.
- Add a Sum to the Revenue field and check the **Summary Only option**.
- Choose **Outline Layout**.
- Name the report **Revenue by City and Service**.

h. Scroll through all the pages to check the layout of the report while in Print Preview mode.

i. Exit Print Preview. Switch to Layout view and delete the NumInParty and PerPersonCharge controls.

j. Change the font size, font color, and/or background color of the Sum control (not the Revenue control) so the control stands out from the other controls.

k. Change the font size, font color, and/or background color of the Grand Total control (found at the end of the report) so the control stands out as well.

l. Change the sort on the report, so that it sorts by city in descending order—that is, so that the last city alphabetically (St. Paul) is displayed first.

m. Examine the data in the report to determine which city of St. Paul, St. Louis, and Seattle has the highest Sum of event revenue. You will use this information to modify a query.

n. Modify the Totals by Service query so the criteria for the City field is the city you determined had the highest sum from St. Paul, St. Louis, or Seattle. Save and close the query.

o. Create a report using the Report tool based on the Totals by Service query. Name the report **Targeted City**.

p. Close the report. Close the database.

q. Exit Access. Submit based on your instructor's directions.

2 Benefit Auction

FROM SCRATCH

You are helping to organize a benefit auction to raise money for families who lost their homes in a natural disaster. The information for the auction is currently stored in an Excel spreadsheet, but you have volunteered to migrate this to Access. You will create a database that will store the data from Excel in an Access database. You will create a form to manage the data-entry process. You also need to create two reports: one that lists the items collected in each category and one for labels so you can send the donors a thank-you letter after the auction.

a. Open Access and create a new database named **a04m2Auction_LastFirst**.

   A new table appears with an ID column.

b. Switch to Design view. Type **Items** in the **Save As dialog box** and click **OK**.

c. Change the ID Field Name to **ItemID**. Type **Description** in the second row and press **Tab**. Accept **Short Text** as the Data Type. Type **50** in the **Field Size property** in Field Properties.

d. Type the remainder of the fields and adjust the data types as shown:

Field Name	Data Type
DateOfDonation	Date/Time
Category	Short Text
Price	Currency
DonorName	Short Text
DonorAddress1	Short Text
DonorAddress2	Short Text

e. Open Excel. Open the **a04m2_Items** file. Examine the length of the Category, DonorName, DonorAddress1, and DonorAddress2 columns. Determine how many characters are needed for each field, and round to the nearest 5. For example, if a field needs 23 characters, you would round up to 25. You will use this to change field sizes in the table.

f. Change the field size for the Category, DonorName, DonorAddress1, and DonorAddress2 to the sizes you chose in step e. Save the table.

g. Copy and paste the rows from the Excel file into the table. Resize the columns so all data is visible. Close the table.

> **TROUBLESHOOTING:** Recall that you must click the Record Selector (pencil icon, to the left of a blank row) to paste data.

> **TROUBLESHOOTING:** Once you have pasted the data, ensure your chosen field sizes did not cause you to lose data. If so, update the field size, delete the records you pasted in, and then repeat step g.

h. Verify that the Items table is selected. Create a new form using the Form tool.

i. Change the layout of the form to a **Tabular Layout**. Resize field widths to reduce extra space. It is acceptable for field values to appear on two lines.

j. Change the title of the form to **Items for Auction**.

DISCOVER

k. Add conditional formatting so that each Price that is greater than 90 has a text color of **Green**. Use the Green color in the first row of the options.

l. Save the form as **Auction Items Form**.

m. Switch to Form view. Create a new record with the following information. Note it will automatically assign an ItemID of 27 for you.

Description	DateOfDonation	Category	Price	DonorName	DonorAddress1	DonorAddress2
iPad	12/31/2016	House	$400	Staples	500 Market St	Brick, NJ 08723

n. Add a sort to the form, so the lowest priced items appear first. Close the form.

o. Select the **Items table** in the Navigation Pane and create a report using the Report Wizard. Include all fields except the donor address fields, group by Category, include the Sum of Price as a Summary Option, accept the default layout, and then save the report **Auction Items by Category**.

p. Switch to Layout view and adjust the controls so all data is visible. Preview the report to verify the column widths are correct.

q. Sort the report so the least expensive items are shown first. Save and close the report.

r. Create mailing labels based on the Avery 5660 template. Place the donor name on the first line, address on the second, and city, state, and ZIP on the third line. Sort the labels by DonorName. Name the report **Donor Labels**. After you create the labels, display them in Print Preview mode verify everything will fit onto the label template. Close the label report.

s. Exit Access. Submit the database based on your instructor's directions.

3 Used Cell Phones for Sale

COLLABORATION CASE

You and a few of your classmates started a new business selling used cell phones, MP3 players, and accessories. You have been using an Access database to track your inventory. You need to create several forms and reports to increase database efficiency and analysis. You have used Access forms and reports as part of your classwork, but you would like to experiment with them as they apply to you in a real-world scenario.

a. Choose one unique type of form and one unique type of report each. Based on your experience in class, you saw there were a number of different types of forms and reports that can be created. Choose one each from the following:

Forms: Form tool, Form Wizard, Multiple Items Form, Split Form

Reports: Report Tool, Report Wizard, Label Wizard

b. Open Access and open the *a04t1Phones* database individually. Save the file as **a04t1Phones_LastFirst**. Each of you will create your forms and reports in an individual database.

c. Create a form and a report based on the Inventory table, using the type of form and report you chose in step a, unless you chose Label Wizard. If you chose Label Wizard, you should create a report based on the Mailing List table, using Avery 8660 as your destination label.

d. Save the form and report as **LastFirst**, replacing Last and First with your last and first names.

e. Make the report as attractive and useful as possible. You may want to change sorting, add grouping (to reports), remove or add a layout control, change formatting options, and/or change the background color. Modify the form and report, save the changes, and exit Access.

f. Meet as a group. Open the *a04t1Phones* database and save the file as **a04t1Phones_GroupName**.

g. Import the form and report from each of your databases.

Your *a04t1Phones_GroupName* file will now have one form and one report for each student.

h. Examine the forms and reports each of you created.

i. Examine your results. Determine which forms and reports you would keep, if this were the real world. Rename the forms and reports you would keep as **Keep_LastFirst** and rename the ones you would discard as **Discard_LastFirst**. Do not delete the forms and reports you will not use.

j. Modify the forms and reports you plan to keep as a group, if necessary. Save the changes and close all forms and reports. Ensure each student has a copy of the final *a04t1Phones_GroupName* database.

k. Exit Access and submit both the *a04t1Phones_GroupName* and *a04t1Phones_LastFirst* databases based on your instructor's directions.

Beyond the Classroom

Create a Split Form

RESEARCH CASE

FROM SCRATCH

This chapter introduced you to Access forms, including the split form. It is possible to turn an existing form into a split form if you modify a few form properties. Perform an Internet search to find the steps to convert a form to a split form. First, create a new database and name the file **a04b2Split_LastFirst**. Next, import *only* the Books table and Books form from the *a04b2BooksImport* database. To import the objects, click the **External Data tab** and click **Access** in the Import & Link group. After the new objects have been imported, use the information from the Internet to convert the Books form into a split form. Make sure the datasheet is on the bottom half. Change the form so it sorts by Title in ascending order. Save the form as **Split Form Books**. Close Access. Submit the database based on your instructor's directions.

Properties by City

DISASTER RECOVERY

Munesh, a co-worker, is having difficulty with an Access report and asked you for your assistance. He was trying to fix the report and seems to have made things worse. Open the *a04b3Sales* database and save the file as **a04b3Sales_LastFirst**. In the new database, open Properties Report in Report View. Notice Munesh moved fields around and the report does not fit on one page. In addition, there is a big gap between two fields and he moved the Bed and Bath fields so they are basically on top of one another. Add all of the fields to a Tabular Layout. Add grouping by City. Sort the report by Year Built in descending order. Change the report to Landscape orientation and adjust the column widths so they all fit onto one page. Save the new report as **Properties by City**. Close Access. Submit the database based on your instructor's directions.

Performance Reviews

SOFT SKILLS CASE S

Passaic County Medical Monitoring provides visiting nurse care for patients in and around Passaic County, New Jersey. They have recently moved their records into an Access database. The director of Human Resources, Farrah Hassan, brings the nurses in yearly for a performance review. Employees are rated by a survey given to patients, asking them to rate the nurses on a scale of 1 (poor) to 5 (superb). You have been asked to create a one-page summary report to show the average of each employee's ratings. You will open her *a04b4Perform* database and save it as **a04b4Perform_LastFirst**. Use the Report Wizard to create a report based on the Performance and Nurses tables, group by the nurse, and add summary options to average the results for Promptness, Attitude, Knowledge, and Gentleness. The final report should display the NurseID, NurseFirst, and NurseLast fields and the averages for each of the four columns. You will also want to format each of the columns in the final report so they show two decimal places. You calculated the results by hand for nurse 1, Lan Wang, and her averages were 3.00 for Promptness, 3.11 for Attitude, 3.67 for Knowledge, and 3.67 for Gentleness, so when you create your report, you can check that it shows the correct data. Save the report as **Overall Ratings**, close Access, and submit the database based on your instructor's directions.

Capstone Exercise

Your boss asked you to prepare a schedule for each speaker for the national conference being hosted next year on your campus. She wants to mail the schedules to the speakers so that they can provide feedback on the schedule prior to its publication. You assure her that you can accomplish this task with Access.

Database File Setup

You need to copy an original database file, rename the copied file, and then open the copied database to complete this capstone exercise. After you open the copied database, you replace an existing employee's name with your name.

a. Open *a04c1_NatConf*.

b. Save the database as **a04c1NatConf_LastFirst**.

c. Open the Speakers table.

d. Find and replace *YourName* with your name. Close the table.

Create and Customize a Form

You need to create a form to add and update Speakers. Use the Form tool to create the form and modify the form as explained. You will also add a layout to an existing form.

a. Select the **Speakers table** as the record source for the form.

b. Use the Form tool to create a new stacked form.

c. Change the title to **Enter/Edit Speakers**.

d. Reduce the width of the text box controls to approximately half of their original size.

e. Delete the Sessions subform.

f. View the form and data in Form view. Sort the records by LastName in ascending order.

g. Save the form as **Edit Speakers**. Close the form.

h. Open the Room Information form in Layout view. The form does not have a Form Layout. Select all controls and apply the **Stacked Layout**.

i. Save and close the form.

Create a Report

You need to create a report based on the Speaker and Room Schedule query. You decide to use the Report Wizard to accomplish this task. You will also need to email the schedule to the presenters, so you will save the report as a PDF.

a. Select the **Speaker and Room Schedule query** as the record source for the report.

b. Activate the **Report Wizard** and use the following options as you go through the Wizard:

- Select all of the available fields for the report.
- View the data by Speakers.
- Accept LastName and FirstName as grouping levels.
- Use **Date** as the primary sort field in ascending order.
- Accept the Stepped and Portrait options.
- Save the report as **Speaker Schedule**.
- Switch to Layout view and apply the **Organic theme** to only this report.

c. Preview the report. Switch to Layout view. Adjust the column widths if necessary.

d. Switch to Print Preview and save the report as a PDF named **a04c1Speaker_LastFirst**.

e. When the PDF displays, close the program that displays it and return to Access. Exit Print Preview. Close the report.

Add an Additional Field

You realize the session times were not included in the query. You add the field to the query and then start over with the Report Wizard.

a. Open the Speaker and Room Schedule query in Design view.

b. Add the **StartingTime field** in the Sessions table to the design grid, after the Date field. Run the query.

c. Save and close the query.

d. Click the **Speaker and Room Schedule query**. Start the Report Wizard again and use the following options:

- Select all of the available fields for the report.
- View the data by Speakers.
- Use the LastName, FirstName fields as the primary grouping level.
- Use Date as the primary sort field in ascending order.
- Use StartingTime as the secondary sort field in Ascending order.
- Select the **Stepped** and **Portrait options**.
- Name the report **Speaker Schedule Revised**.
- Switch to Layout view and apply the **Facet theme** (first row, second column) to only this report.

e. Adjust the column widths in Layout view so that all the data is visible.

f. Add a space to the column heading labels as needed. For example, the column LastName should read Last Name.

g. Save and close the report. Close the database.

h. Exit Access. Submit the database and PDF based on your instructor's directions.

Action and Specialized Queries

CHAPTER 14

Moving Beyond the Select Query

Yuri Arcurs/Shutterstock

OBJECTIVES | AFTER YOU READ THIS CHAPTER, YOU WILL BE ABLE TO:

1. Determine when to use an action query p. 708
2. Update data with an update query p. 710
3. Add records to a table with an append query p. 713
4. Create a table with a make table query p. 716

5. Delete records with a delete query p. 717
6. Summarize data with a crosstab query p. 727
7. Find duplicate records with a query p. 731
8. Find unmatched records with a query p. 733

CASE STUDY | Replacement China, Inc.

Replacement China, Inc., is an international firm that sells china, crystal, and flatware replacement pieces. You are the database administrator for Replacement China, Inc., and need to perform several database management operations. The most urgent is the need to increase retail prices for a key manufacturer, Spode China, by 5 percent. You will use an update query to make this price increase; you will create other action queries to make additional changes to the firm's database.

Before you run the action queries, you decide to make a backup copy of the database. If a problem exists with any of the queries, you will be able to easily recover from the error by reverting to the backup copy. In addition to backing up the database as a precaution, you need to develop a method of verifying that each action query works properly. One method of verifying an action query is to check the values before running the update query and again after running it, ensuring that the values are updated properly.

You will also create another special type of query known as the crosstab query; a crosstab query will summarize data in the Replacement China, Inc., database and help the managers evaluate the sales and other company statistics. Finally, you will create two queries that will reveal tables with missing data and tables with duplicate data.

Action Queries

When you create a query, by default you are creating a select query. You begin your query design by selecting the necessary tables and then selecting the required fields to add to the query design grid. Select queries provide a subset of the data that answers most questions that users ask about the data in their databases. A select query is also flexible; you can update the underlying table data if you see an error or discover a blank field value. Another advantage of a select query is that you can create a query for one condition—for example, banquet sales in Boston hotels—and then copy the query, rename the copy, and change the criteria to extract data for a second city, for example, Miami.

Access provides four additional query types—update, append, make table, and delete—that you can use to add, edit, or delete data. The four queries are collectively referred to as action queries. An *action query* adds, edits, or deletes data in a database. You use these queries to update records that meet certain criteria, to append records to a table, to make a new table, and to delete specific records from a table. Because action queries change data, Access gives a warning when you attempt to run one. Access warns you that you are about to change data in the specified number of records and gives you a chance to cancel the changes.

TIP Database Administrator Career

A database administrator (DBA) helps manage databases, including performing backups, security checks, and upgrades to keep data both safe and accessible. According to the U.S. Department of Labor (www.bls.gov/ooh/computer-and-information-technology/database-administrators.htm), you need a bachelor's degree in Management Information Technology, Information Systems, or Computer Science to work in this field. This Web site also contains salary information.

In this section, you will learn about action queries and how they are used to maintain databases. Specifically, you will create the following types of action queries: update, append, make table, and delete.

Determining When to Use an Action Query

Four main action queries can be used to maintain a database:

- **Update query.** An update query is used to update or change data automatically based on criteria that you specify. Rather than modifying data manually or using the find and replace tool, the update query is fast and accurate.

- **Append query.** An append query is used for adding records to an existing table. Records can be selected from various sources, such as external databases and spreadsheets. Rather than entering data manually or performing multiple copy-and-paste operations to a table, the append query is an automated process.

- **Make Table query.** A make table query automatically creates a new table from data that already exist in a database. You can create the new table in the current or another database. For example, a make table query can use criteria to make a table that archives older records that need to be stored outside of the current table. The process is automated and saves the trouble of tedious copy-and-paste operations. A make table query overwrites existing data in a table of the same name.

- **Delete query.** A delete query removes records from a table based on criteria that you specify. For example, after a make table query is run to create records in another table, you may want to remove those same records from the current table. The delete query saves the chore of having to locate and delete records manually.

The Replacement China, Inc., database, like most Access databases, requires some type of regular maintenance—usually performed by the DBA or another person assigned to these tasks. For example, customer orders that were entered last month but not filled might now be outdated. Over time, those outdated orders must be dealt with so they are not just taking up space in the database. One way to handle this type of outdated data is to move it from the primary order table to an inactive order table. You can accomplish this task using a make table query, an append query, and a delete query. First, design a make table query to create an inactive orders table based on existing data, create an append query to add future outdated orders to the inactive orders table, and then create a delete query to remove the outdated orders from the primary order table.

Another condition that exists in the Replacement China, Inc., database (and many Access databases) is null (i.e., blank) values in numeric data fields. In a list of products, each with a cost and a retail price, it is not uncommon for one of the fields to contain a null value. Access does not always calculate properly when a null is in the list of values. It is usually better to enter the value zero rather than have a null value. When null values exist, you can use an update query to replace null values with a zero. First, find all the records with null values using a select query, and then create an update query that will replace the null values with zeros. This is a good alternative to a manual or some other filter-and-replace operation. Once the update query has been created, it can be used on a regular basis to remedy this condition.

Recognize the Benefits of an Action Query

One situation that requires an action query is when an end user is required to enter the same information into many records. For example, at Replacement China, Inc., if all of the customers who had Julia as their sales representative are now going to be handled by Susan, then Julia will need to be replaced by Susan for each of her customers. An employee could complete this task manually, or you could create an action query and replace "Julia" with "Susan" automatically. To handle this situation, create a select query that lists all the customers who have Julia as their sales representative. Next, change the select query to an update query and enter Susan as the new sales representative. Run the update query, and the task is finished! Once an update query has been created, it can be used repeatedly or modified to handle different situations.

A student database in a college is another situation where an Access designer needs to use action queries. When students enroll in a school or program, they are classified as current students and are entered into the Students table. After graduation, the school likely moves them to a Graduates table. An append query is the easiest way to move records from one table to another. Create a select query to select all the records from the Students table in which the graduation date is not blank (i.e., the student *has* a graduation date). Change the select query to an append query, specify the Graduates table as the *append to* table, and then run the query. The students are now in the Graduates table. Use a delete query to remove the students from the Students table (to avoid storing duplicate data).

Back Up a Database When Testing an Action Query

STEP 1» Action queries locate and alter data that meet specific criteria. You cannot undo updates or deletions performed with an action query. Therefore, you should exercise caution when executing an action query. Before running an action query, it is best to back up the entire database. This provides you with some insurance in case you need to recover from a mistake. After the backup is made, you usually want to create a simple select query first to test your criteria and determine which data will be modified, appended, or deleted before switching to an action query. Once you run an action query, you are committing yourself to an irreversible change.

Updating Data with an Update Query

An *update query* changes the data values in one or more fields for all records that meet specific criteria. For example, the phone company announces that all of your customers in a specific area code will now have a different area code. You construct an update query to identify records of all customers who live in the specific area code and then change their existing area code to the new area code. Another example might be in a database storing information about student athletes and their academic eligibility. At the end of each semester, you would create an update query to identify all academically eligible athletes based on their grade point average (GPA). All athletes with a GPA of 2.5 or higher would be updated to eligible.

Create a Select Query Before Running an Update Query

Prior to updating data in a table, you may first want to locate the records that need to be modified. For example, you discover that one or more orders have a missing order date—key information required to process the order. To find other orders with a missing order date, you would first create a select query.

To create a select query, do the following:

1. Click Query Design in the Queries group on the CREATE tab.
2. Add the order data table to the query design and add all fields to the query design grid.
3. Add Is Null to the criterion of the order date field, as shown in Figure 14.1.
4. Run the query to see how many orders have a missing order date, as shown in Figure 14.2.

You could then ask a customer service employee to research the orders with missing dates, perhaps by talking with user 8580, the employee who entered the orders.

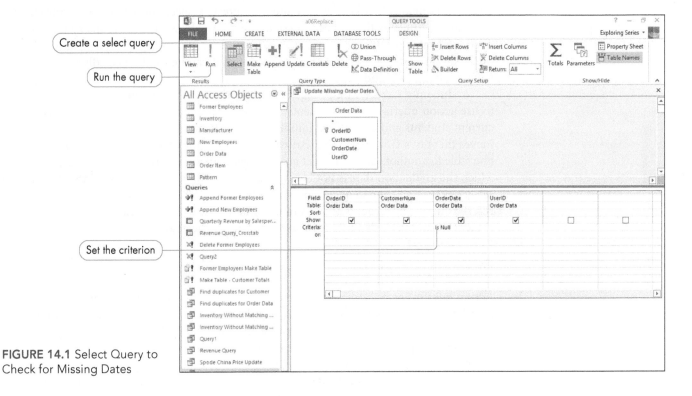

FIGURE 14.1 Select Query to Check for Missing Dates

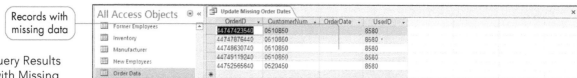

FIGURE 14.2 Query Results Show Records with Missing Dates

Records with missing data

Convert a Select Query to an Update Query

STEP 2»

Your goal is to update records with a missing order date. Once the records with a missing order date are found by a select query, you decide to convert it to an update query and insert the current date into any record with a blank order date so that the orders can be processed.

To create the update query, do the following:

1. View the select query in Design view (as shown in Figure 14.1).
2. Click Update in the Query Type group.
3. Enter the new value into the Update To row. In the missing order date example, type the Date() function into the Update To row of the OrderDate field (as shown in Figure 14.3).
4. Click Run in the Results group. (If you want to verify which records the update query will affect before running the query, test the query as described in the next section.)

The current date is inserted into the OrderDate field for all records with a missing order date.

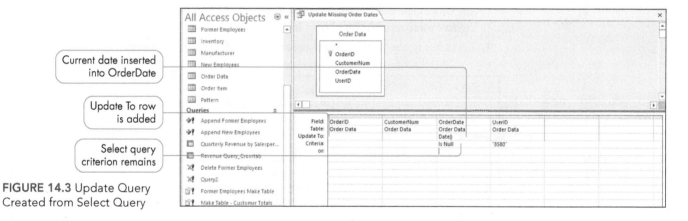

Current date inserted into OrderDate

Update To row is added

Select query criterion remains

FIGURE 14.3 Update Query Created from Select Query

Test an Update Query

STEP 3»

You can test an update query (before clicking Run) and verify that the correct records will be updated by switching to Datasheet view first. Once an update query is run, you cannot undo the action, so it is important to view the eligible records beforehand.

To test an update query before running it, do the following:

From Design view, click View in the Results group and click Datasheet view.

Datasheet view will look different than usual—most of the columns that were showing in the Datasheet view of the select query are no longer showing in the Datasheet view of the update query (see Figure 14.4). Only the column and records that conform to the Update To criteria are showing. You can use this information to evaluate the number of records that will be updated when you run the update query. Look at the number of records shown in the navigation bar at the bottom of the Datasheet view. If the number of records is what you expect, then it is safe to run the update query.

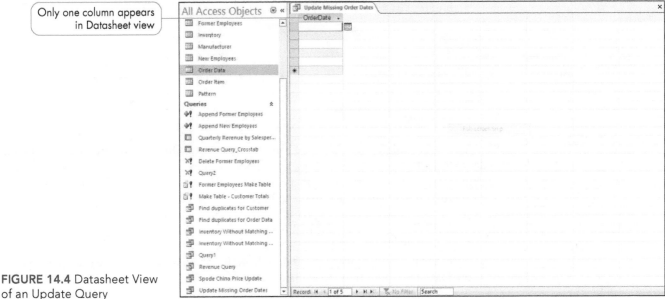

Only one column appears
in Datasheet view

FIGURE 14.4 Datasheet View
of an Update Query

To run the update query, do the following:

1. Return to the query Design view.
2. Verify that Update is selected in the Query Type group.
3. Click Run in the Results group. The five records will have the current date inserted into the order date field, after you click Yes to the Access message *Are you sure you want to update these records?* (as shown in Figure 14.5).
4. Click Yes to the warning message and the update query executes.

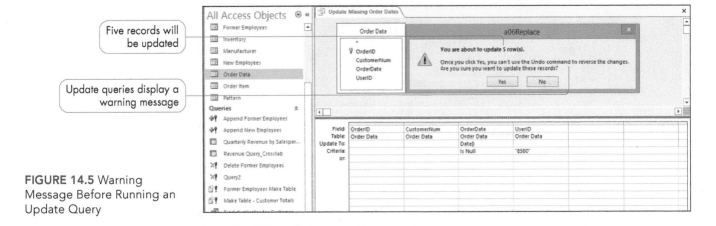

Five records will
be updated

Update queries display a
warning message

FIGURE 14.5 Warning
Message Before Running an
Update Query

 TIP **Add a New Field Before Running an Update Query**

Backing up the database prior to running an update query is the best precaution. Additionally, there may be times when adding a new field to a table may be a practical option. For example, if you are reducing the values of retail prices by 15 percent, you lose the original prices after changing them with an update query. To avoid this, add a new field to the table named Retail Original (for example). Then create an update query that updates the Retail Original field with the current retail price. Next, run the update query to decrease the current retail prices by 15 percent. Now you have both the original retail price (Retail Original) and the new retail price (Retail New).

Verify an Update Query

Running an action query from Design view does not display a view of the results; Access simply returns you to the query design window. No records (with the new data) are displayed. One way to test the results would be to create a query to locate the updated records. Click Select in the Query Type group and modify the query's criteria to select the updated data. In the sample database, we inserted the current date into the missing order date fields. You would change the order date criterion from Is Null to today's date and run the query to view the corrected records.

Another method is to try to locate the original records prior to their being updated and discovering that those records no longer exist in their original state. In the example, you could select orders for User (employee) 8580 where the order dates are null. With Is Null as the criterion in the order date field, enter 8580 in the User ID criteria row and run the query. The query results show that there are no longer records for this user with missing (null) order dates (as shown in Figure 14.6).

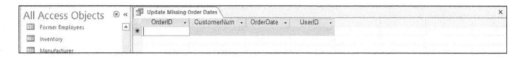

FIGURE 14.6 Verify the Data After an Update Query

TIP Do Not Rerun Action Queries

After you run an action query, it might appear that nothing has happened except that the warning box disappears. You might be tempted to click Run again—but you should not; you may find that data is changed again unnecessarily. For example, if you created an update query to lower the sale price of all products by 15 percent, entering *[Sale Price] * .85* into the Update To row for the sale price field would work correctly. However, running the query a second time would lower the price an additional 15 percent from the current price. In this case, the total reduction would be a 27.75 percent discount (lower than the intended 15 percent).

Adding Records to a Table with an Append Query

STEP 4 »

Another type of action query is the append query. An *append query* copies records from one or more tables (the source) and adds them to an existing table (the destination). The appended records appear in the destination table in primary key order, or they are added to the bottom of the table if no primary key exists. If any appended record violates the primary key rule or another rule created for the destination table, the record is rejected. For example, you might use an append query to copy employee records in the Replacement China, Inc., database. Suppose the company hires new employees each week. The company may place new hires into a Candidates table until the background checks are complete. Once the checks are completed, the candidates can be appended to the Employees table and then deleted from the Candidates table. Moving records from one table to another can be accomplished with the combination of an append query and a delete query. Append queries are frequently used in conjunction with delete queries. If you use an append query to copy a record from one table to another, the original record still exists. The same data is now stored in two different places—a practice that must be avoided in a database. After the criteria for an append query are established, you can reuse the same criteria to create a delete query and delete the records from the source table. This is a common practice when working with append queries.

Often, organizations store the active records (today's or this week's activities) in one table and then append them to a more permanent table after they are completed. The tables involved with an append query—the source and destination—usually contain the same field names. In most cases, the data types of the source fields must match the data types of the destination fields. The rules for appending are as follows:

- Data types of the fields in both tables must match in most cases; however, some exceptions to this rule exist.

- All the normal rules for adding a new record to the destination table apply. For example, the records are not added if a value is missing in the source table when the field is required in the destination table.

- If a field from the source table does not exist in the destination table, Access leaves a blank in the Append To row, and you will need to manually specify the destination field name (or just delete the unneeded source field from the query design grid). If the destination table has non required fields that are not in the source table, the record appends, and the missing field values are blank.

- The destination table should not contain an AutoNumber field. An AutoNumber in the source table should append to a Number field in the destination table.

Create a Select Query Before Running an Append Query

Similar to an update query, the first step in creating an append query is to create a select query. You can use one or multiple tables for the data source. Next, select the fields you want to append from the table(s) to the query design grid. Enter the criteria to filter only the records you want to append. For example, if Replacement China, Inc., wanted to move its former employees from the Employees table to the Former Employees table, it could create a select query, and then add criteria to find employees where the termination date is not null. The results of this query are shown in Datasheet view in Figure 14.7.

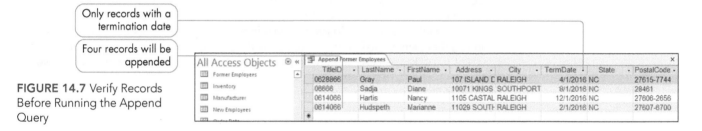

FIGURE 14.7 Verify Records Before Running the Append Query

Set Append To Fields in an Append Query

After you verify that the correct records are selected, switch to Design view, and then change the select query to an append query.

To convert the select query to an append query, do the following:

1. In Design view, click Append in the Query Type group.
2. Select the destination table using the table name arrow and click OK.

Figure 14.8 shows the Append dialog box that displays, in which you specify the destination table.

When you change to an append query, Access removes the Show row in the query design grid and adds the Append To row in its place. If the fields in the source and destination tables are the same, Access automatically inserts the correct field names into the Append To row, as shown in Figure 14.9.

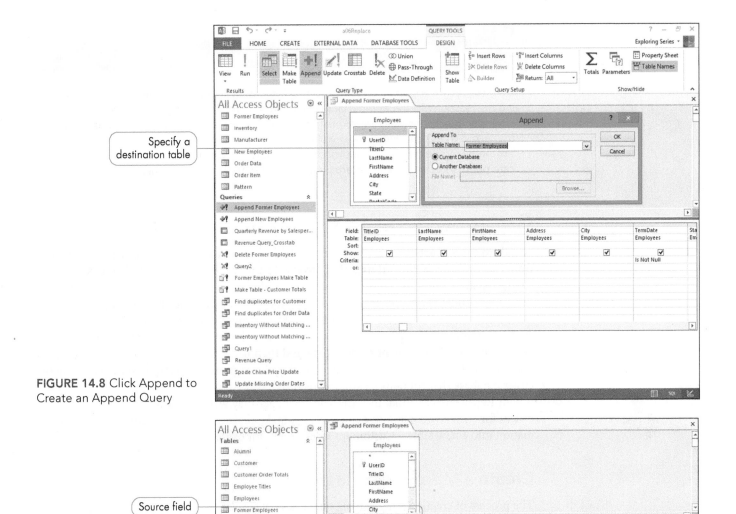

Specify a destination table

FIGURE 14.8 Click Append to Create an Append Query

Source field

Append To row

Destination field

FIGURE 14.9 Source Fields Append to Destination Fields

Run an Append Query

If you need to verify the records to be appended, you can click View in the Results group to double-check in Datasheet view. After verifying the records, switch back to Design view.

To run an append query, do the following:

1. In Design view, click Run in the Results group. You will receive a warning message telling you that you are about to append the number of records selected, as shown in Figure 14.10.
2. Click Yes to continue. As with all the action queries, you cannot undo the action after it is run.
3. Save and close the append query (if required).
4. Open the destination table and verify that the appended records are in the table.

Four rows will be appended

Append query warning message

FIGURE 14.10 Warning Message Appears When You Run an Append Query

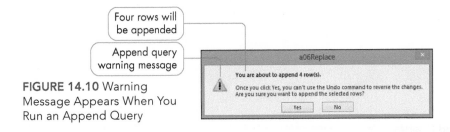

Creating a Table with a Make Table Query

The third type of action query is the make table query. A *make table query* selects records from one or more tables and uses them to create a new table. Suppose that your school has a large database that stores information about students. The database has information about the classes students are registered for each term, their majors, and their emergency contact information. The Business and Technology Department needs to know the names of the students enrolled in its programs. You can use a make table query to extract the Business and Technology Department student data and then use it to create a new table. Subsequent searches can be done on the new table, reducing the response time required by searching the larger database that contains all student records.

At Replacement China, Inc., the sales manager may want to know the total year-to-date orders for each customer. You could create a make table query that would insert this information into a new table—Customer Order Totals, for example.

Create a Make Table Query

STEP 5 » The process of creating a make table query is very similar to creating an append query. The difference is that a make table query creates the structure of the table and then adds the records to the table. An append query requires the destination table to exist first; otherwise, it cannot append additional records. You can use the make table query to copy some or all records from a source table to a destination table even if the destination table does not exist. If the destination table exists and you run the make table query, Access prompts you before it deletes the original table. If you click Yes, Access deletes the source table and replaces it with data specified by the make table query.

To create a make table query, do the following:

1. Create a select query; specify the tables and field names that you want to add to the new table to the query design window.
2. Specify the criteria that will result in selecting the correct records for your new table.
3. In Design view, click Make Table in the Query Type group.
4. Specify the table name that you want to create in the Table Name box.
5. Click OK.

Figure 14.11 displays the setup for a make table query that will copy aggregate order data to a new table.

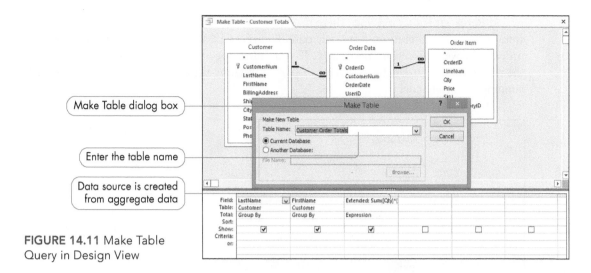

Make Table dialog box

Enter the table name

Data source is created from aggregate data

FIGURE 14.11 Make Table Query in Design View

Test and Run a Make Table Query

As with the other action queries, you should preview the datasheet prior to running the query to verify that the records are those that you intend to insert into a new table.

To test and run a make table query, do the following:

1. Click View in the Results group to view the records in Datasheet view.
2. After you verify that the records are correct, click View again to return to Design view.
3. Click Run in the Results group and Access displays a warning telling you that you are about to append records to a new table.
4. Click Yes and the new table is created.
5. Open the new table and verify the records are correct.
6. Save and close the query (if required).

If you run the same make table query at a later date, the first table is replaced with a new, up-to-date table.

Deleting Records with a Delete Query

STEP 6 ›› The final type of action query is the delete query. A *delete query* selects records from a table, and then removes them from the table. Sometimes it is necessary to identify and delete data in a database. However, it should always be done with caution. For example, if you copy the Replacement China, Inc., database inactive customers from the Customers table to the Inactive Customers table using an append query, you will want to delete those records from the Customers table. Take precautions prior to running a delete query. If you create a backup copy of the database prior to running a delete query, you can always recover from an error.

Create a Delete Query

The delete query begins the same way as all of the other action queries, with a select query.
To create a delete query, do the following:

1. Create a select query; specify the tables and field names that you want to remove from the table in the query design window.
2. Specify the criteria in the fields that will result in deleting the correct records from your table.
3. In Design view, click Delete in the Query Type group.

At Replacement China, Inc., there may be times when they need to remove orders that were incorrectly entered on a specific date. Figure 14.12 shows the criterion to delete the orders that were placed on 6/10/2016. If you fail to specify a criterion, Access deletes all the records in the Orders table. Access displays a warning message and enables you to avoid running the delete query.

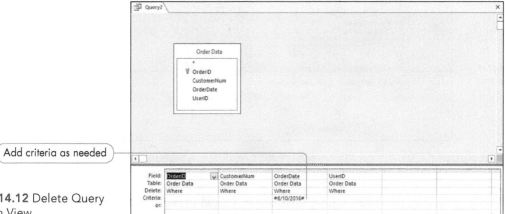

Add criteria as needed

FIGURE 14.12 Delete Query in Design View

Test and Run a Delete Query

As with the other action queries, always view the records to be deleted in Datasheet view prior to running the delete query. After you verify the number of records in the datasheet, run the query.

To run the delete query, do the following:

1. Switch to Design view, if you were testing the query in Datasheet view.
2. Click Run in the Results group to run the query and delete the records.
3. Click Yes when the warning message appears. Verify the results of the delete query by opening the table to confirm that the records were deleted.
4. Save and close the query (if required).

TIP Action Query Icons

Access denotes the action queries differently from select queries by displaying a specific icon for each action query type in the Navigation Pane (see Figure 14.13). This may prevent users from accidentally running an action query and getting unexpected results. For example, if an update query is created to increase prices by 10 percent, running the query a second time would increase those prices again. Exercise caution when running action queries.

Action query icons

FIGURE 14.13 Action Query Icons

You will experiment with creating and running action queries in Hands-On Exercise 1 using the data from Replacement China, Inc. You will run an update query to identify all of the products in inventory from a specified manufacturer and increase their prices by

5 percent. You will use an append query to add new employees to the Employees table. Next, you will make a table containing the employees who are no longer with the firm. You will use a delete query to remove the employees from the Employees table who no longer work for Replacement China, Inc.

Quick
Concepts

1. What is a benefit of creating an append query? *p. 708*

2. What is a potential disadvantage of running an update query? *p. 712*

3. What is a good strategy for handling mistakes that can occur while running action queries? *p. 712*

Hands-On Exercises

1 Action Queries

Several maintenance tasks are required at Replacement China, Inc. Before work begins, you decide to back up the database to make it easy to recover from a mistake. Each task requires an action query. After you create and run each query, you verify the changes by checking the records in the modified table.

Skills covered: Back Up a Database When Testing an Action Query • Create an Update Query • Test an Update Query • Create an Append Query • Create a Make Table Query • Create a Delete Query

---

STEP 1 ❯❯ BACK UP A DATABASE WHEN TESTING AN ACTION QUERY

Create a backup copy of the Replacement China, Inc., database before you create any action queries. If you make a mistake along the way, revert to the original file and start again. Refer to Figure 14.14 as you complete Step 1.

Step b: Click Back Up
Database

FIGURE 14.14 Create a
Backup Copy of the Database

a. Open *a06h1Replace*. Click **Save As** on the FILE tab, click **Save As**, and then type **a06h1Replace_LastFirst**. Click **Save**.

> **TROUBLESHOOTING:** Throughout the remainder of this chapter and textbook, click Enable Content whenever you are working with student files.

> **TROUBLESHOOTING:** If you make any major mistakes in this exercise, you can close the file, repeat step a above, and then start over.

b. Click **Save As** on the FILE tab, and double-click **Back Up Database**.

Before you execute an action query, it is recommended that you make a backup copy of the entire database first. If a problem occurs, you can use the backup copy to recover.

c. Click **Save** to accept the default file name for the backup copy of the *a06h1Replace_LastFirst_date* database.

A backup copy of the database now exists in your default folder.

d. Verify the backup file exists in your default folder.

STEP 2 ≫ CREATE AN UPDATE QUERY

One of your manufacturers, Spode China, has increased its prices for the upcoming year. You decide to increase your retail prices as well. You create an update query to increase the retail price by 5 percent but only for items that are supplied by Spode China. Refer to Figure 14.15 as you complete Step 2.

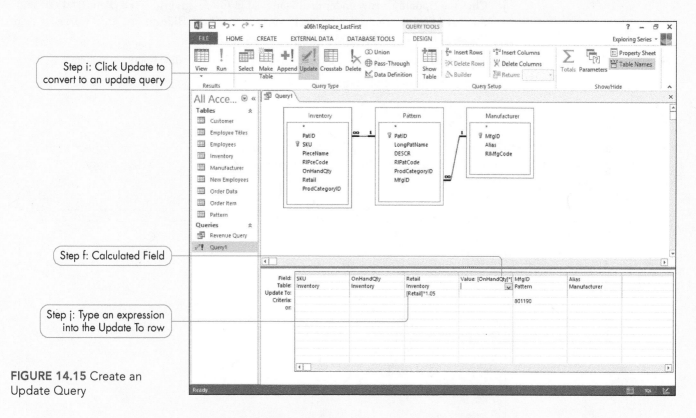

FIGURE 14.15 Create an Update Query

a. Click **Query Design** in the Queries group on the CREATE tab.

The Show Table dialog box opens.

b. Double-click the **Inventory, Pattern**, and **Manufacturer tables** to add these tables to the query design space. Close the Show Table dialog box.

c. Add the SKU, OnHandQty, and Retail fields from the Inventory table, MfgID field from the Pattern table, and Alias field from the Manufacturer table to the design grid. Type **801190** in the **Criteria row** of the MfgID column.

You added the criteria to select only Spode China pieces to update the prices. The MfgID for Spode China is 801190.

d. Switch to Datasheet view and verify the correct records are selected.

The results include 1,129 Spode China records.

e. Switch to Design view. Click the **MfgID column** and click **Insert Columns** in the Query Setup group.

A new blank column appears between Retail and MfgID.

f. Type **Value: [OnHandQty]*[Retail]** in the first row of the new blank column. Click **Property Sheet** in the Show/Hide group. Select **Currency** from the list in the Format box and close the Property Sheet.

You created a calculated field so that you can check the total value of the inventory before and after the update.

g. Switch to Datasheet view. Click **Totals** in the Records group. Advance to the last record.

h. Click in the **Total row** of the Value column, click the arrow, and then select **Sum**.

The total of the Value column is $911,415.88. The value after the update should be $956,986.67 (911,415.88 × 1.05).

i. Click **View** to return to Design view. Click **Update** in the Query Type group.

You changed the query type from a select to an update query. The Sort and Show rows are replaced by the Update To row in the grid.

j. Click the **Update To row** under the Retail field in the design grid. Type **[Retail] * 1.05**. With the Retail field selected, click **Property Sheet** in the Show/Hide group. Select **Currency** from the list in the Format box and close the Property Sheet.

The expression will replace the current retail value with a value 5 percent higher.

k. Compare your screen to Figure 14.15.

STEP 3 ➤ TEST AN UPDATE QUERY

You created an update query to increase the retail price of Spode China products by 5 percent, but you want to verify the values before you run the query. Once you update the prices, you will not be able to undo the changes. Refer to Figure 14.16 as you complete Step 3.

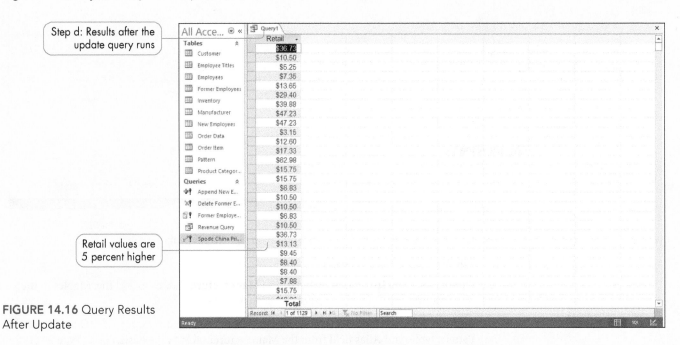

FIGURE 14.16 Query Results After Update

a. Switch to Datasheet view and examine the records before running the query.

You should see a list of retail prices ($34.98, $10.00, $5.00, $7.00, etc.) but no other columns. Access only displays the columns that have a value in the Update To row. These are the current prices that will be updated.

b. Click **View** to return to Design view.

c. Click **Run** in the Results group to execute the query. Click **Yes** in response to the *You are about to update 1129 row(s)* warning.

Although it may seem as though nothing happened, your prices have changed.

d. View the results in Datasheet view.

The first four retail prices are now $36.73, $10.50, $5.25, and $7.35, as shown in Figure 14.16. These prices are 5 percent higher than the original retail prices you saw in step a above.

e. Return to Design view. Click **Select** in the Query Type group.

f. Switch to Datasheet view.

The prices in the Retail column reflect the updated prices, and the bottom of the Retail column is now $956,986.67, which verifies that the update query worked correctly.

g. Return to Design view.

h. Click **Update** in the Query Type group to change back to an update query. Save the query as **Spode China Price Update**. Close the query.

The query icon in the Navigation Pane indicates the query is an update query.

STEP 4 ›› CREATE AN APPEND QUERY

Replacement China, Inc., hired several new employees who were placed into the New Employees table for a 30-day probation period. The probation period is over, and now you need to add them to the Employees table. Refer to Figure 14.17 as you complete Step 4.

Step i: Append query will add four records

FIGURE 14.17 New Employees to Be Appended to the Employees Table

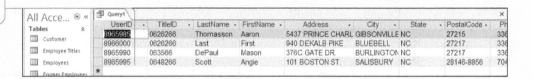

> **TROUBLESHOOTING:** You could make a backup copy of the database to revert back to in the event of an error. You backed up the database at the beginning of this exercise, but you may want another backup in case the append query causes a problem. If you complete this step on the same day as you completed the last step, Access adds_(1) to the end of the backup file name to distinguish it from the earlier file name.

a. Open the New Employees table in Datasheet view. Add yourself as a new record. Type **8966000** in the **UserID field**; **0626266** in the **TitleID field**; your last name, first name, address, city, state, postal code, and phone number in the respective name fields; and **9/11/2016** in the **HireDate field**.

b. Close the New Employees table.

c. Open the Employees table and note the total records in the navigation bar at the bottom of the window.

The navigation bar shows 115 current employees.

d. Close the Employees table.

e. Click **Query Design** in the Queries group on the CREATE tab. Double-click the **New Employees table**. Close the Show Table dialog box.

You have begun to create a select query.

f. Click **Append** in the Query Type group.

You need to change the query design to an append query to add the newly hired employees to the Employees table. The Append dialog box opens, prompting you to supply the destination table name.

g. Click the **Table Name arrow** and select **Employees**. Verify the Current Database option is selected and click **OK**.

The Append To row appears on the design grid, ready for you to add fields. You need all of the fields in the New Employees table added to the Employees table.

h. Double-click the title bar of the New Employees table in the top portion of the Design view window. All of the fields are selected. Drag the selected fields to the first field box in the design grid.

i. Click **View** in the Results group and preview the data you are about to append.

You should see 4 rows and 10 fields, as shown in Figure 14.17.

j. Click **View** in the Views group to return to Design view.

k. Click **Run** in the Results group to run the query. Click **Yes** in response to the *You are about to append 4 row(s)* warning.

l. Open the Employees table. Sort the table in descending order (Newest to Oldest) by the HireDate field and make sure the four newest records were added.

The Employees table should now contain a total of 119 employees. Your own name should be one of the top four records.

m. Click the **Query1 tab** and click **Save** on the Quick Access Toolbar. Save the query as **Append New Employees**. Close the open objects. Save the design of the New Employees table.

The query icon in the Navigation Pane indicates the query is an append query.

STEP 5 ≫ CREATE A MAKE TABLE QUERY

Replacement China, Inc., needs to create a Former Employees table for all employees who are no longer with the company. The records of these former employees are currently stored in the Employees table. You need to move them to a Former Employees table. Refer to Figure 14.18 as you complete Step 5.

Step j: Nine records added to the Former Employees table

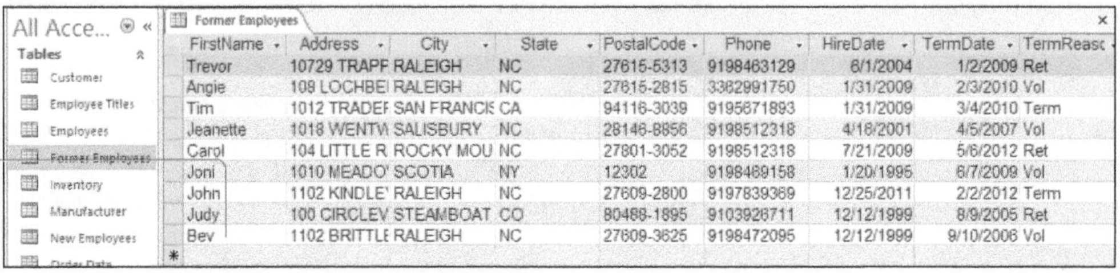

FIGURE 14.18 Use Make Table to Create a New Table

a. Click **Query Design** in the Queries group on the CREATE tab.

b. Double-click the **Employees table** to add it to the query. Close the Show Table dialog box.

Some of the employees listed in the Employees table no longer work for Replacement China, Inc. You need to retain this information but do not want these records included in the Employees table; the records will be stored in the archived Former Employees table.

c. Double-click the title bar of the Employees table in the top portion of the Design view window to select all the fields. Drag the selected fields to the first field box in the design grid.

d. Type **Is Not Null** in the **Criteria row** of the TermDate field.

This criterion will select only those employees with a value in the termination date field.

e. Display the results in Datasheet view.

You should find that nine employees are no longer with the company. These are the employees you want to move to a new table using a make table query.

f. Click **View** to switch back to Design view.

g. Click **Make Table** in the Query Type group.

The Make Table dialog box opens and asks that you name and provide storage location information for the new table. You want to archive this data, but the new table can reside in the same database.

h. Type **Former Employees** in the **Table Name box**. Make sure the Current Database option is selected. Click **OK**.

i. Click **Run** in the Results group to run the query. Click **Yes** in response to the *You are about to paste 9 row(s) into a new table* warning.

j. Examine the Navigation Pane to make sure that the new Former Employees table exists. Open the Former Employees table to verify the nine former employees are present, as shown in Figure 14.18. Close the table.

> **TROUBLESHOOTING:** If your table did not come out properly, delete the query and the newly created table. You can try this query again by beginning from Step 5b. Be sure to check that the correct criterion is entered to locate employees with termination dates.

k. Save the query as **Former Employees Make Table**.

The query icon in the Navigation Pane indicates the query is a make table query.

l. Close the query.

STEP 6 ≫ CREATE A DELETE QUERY

You moved the former employees from the Employees table to the Former Employees table in the Replacement China, Inc., database. Now you need to delete the former employees from the Employees table. It is not a good practice to have the same data stored in two different tables. Refer to Figure 14.19 as you complete Step 6.

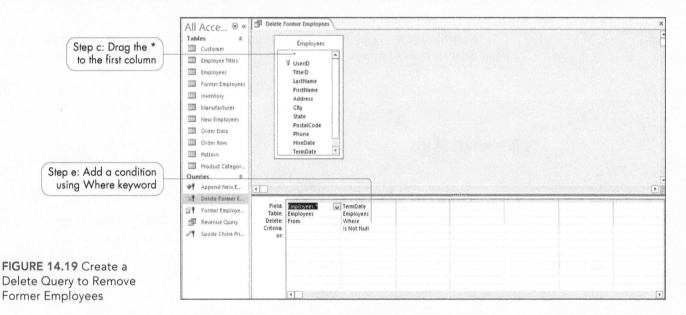

FIGURE 14.19 Create a Delete Query to Remove Former Employees

a. Click **Query Design** in the Queries group on the CREATE tab.

b. Double-click the **Employees table** in the Show Table dialog box to add it to the query. Close the Show Table dialog box.

c. Drag the * from the Employees table to the first column of the query design grid.

The * field only takes up one column in the design grid. The * field represents all the fields in the Employees table. This is a shortcut for adding all of the fields to the design grid in one step rather than one by one.

d. Drag the **TermDate field** from the Employees table to the second column of the query design grid.

You need to add the TermDate a second time to use it to set the criteria for the select query.

e. Type **Is Not Null** in the **Criteria row** for the TermDate field. Click **View** to switch to Datasheet view.

You created a select query to make sure you have correctly identified the nine records for deletion prior to changing it to a delete query. Nine records are shown in Datasheet view.

f. Switch to Design view. Click **Delete** in the Query Type group.

The Delete row now contains From in the Employees.* column and Where in the TermDate column. This delete query will delete all records in the Employees table that have a termination date.

g. Click **Run** in the Results group. Click **Yes** in response to the *You are about to delete 9 row(s) from the specified table* warning.

You deleted the nine former employees from the Employees table.

h. Save the query as **Delete Former Employees**. Close the query.

i. Open the Employees table and verify that the total employees has been reduced from 119 to 110. Close the table.

j. Click **Compact & Repair Database** on the FILE tab.

k. Click **Save As** on the FILE tab, and double-click **Back Up Database**. Name the backup **a06h1Replace_LastFirst_date_(1)**.

You just created a backup of the database you used to complete Hands-On Exercise 1. The *a06h1Replace_LastFirst* database remains open. If you complete this step on the same day as you worked the last step, Access adds_*(1)* to the end of the backup file name to distinguish it from the earlier file name.

l. Keep the database open if you plan to continue with Hands-On Exercise 2. If not, close the database and exit Access.

Queries for Special Conditions

This section will improve your overall effectiveness with a database by introducing you to three types of queries that are used for special conditions.

A crosstab query calculates data using a sum, average, or other function and groups the results by two sets of values. In this section, you will learn how to construct a crosstab query that displays aggregate data in a row-and-column format where each row and column presents values that you select from your database. An unmatched record is a record in one table without a matching record in a related table. A duplicate record is one where the same information is entered extraneously in a table, usually by data entry error. You will also create two special queries: one to find unmatched records and one to find duplicate records.

Summarizing Data with a Crosstab Query

STEP 1 »

You can present aggregate data to the user with a crosstab query. A *crosstab query* summarizes a data source into a grid of rows and columns; the intersection of each row and column displays the aggregate data. A crosstab query is usually created to show trends in values (e.g., sales) over time. For example, to evaluate the sales force at Replacement China, Inc., you might want to construct a crosstab query to examine the revenue generated by each salesperson over a specific period of time. The salespersons' names would be listed along the left side of the grid (the rows). The name of each quarter (or month, for example) would be listed along the top of the grid (the columns). The intersection of the rows and columns displays the total or average revenue for each salesperson for each quarter (or month) of the year. This intersecting cell is the heart of the crosstab query. Crosstab queries can be based on a table or a query.

Group and Summarize Data

The grouping in a crosstab query comes from the definitions of row and column headings. *Row headings* display field names along the left side of a crosstab query. *Column headings* display field names along the top of a crosstab query. The summarizing or aggregating data in a crosstab query is displayed at the intersection of the rows and columns. The type of data that is displayed depends on which aggregate function you choose when you create the crosstab query—count, sum, and average are a few examples. If you want to know the quarterly sales for each salesperson for the current year, use salesperson as the row heading, the order date as the column heading, and the total quarterly sales in dollars as the intersecting values. When you assign a date field to the column heading, Access gives you an option for summarizing by year, quarter, month, or date. You can also add rows to give the crosstab query additional levels of grouping.

TIP | Choosing a Data Source for a Crosstab Query

Crosstab queries work best when you select a data source that has at least two grouping fields. For example, if you want to evaluate a baseball team's performance over the past five years, you could create a crosstab query. The rows could list the category of the game—preseason, conference, nonconference—and the columns could list each of the past five years. The intersection of each category with each year would give you the count of the games won. If you wish to break down the crosstab query even further, you could add the Home/Away field to the rows—the data would be grouped first by game category, and then by home/away games. Then, the query could provide some additional information about the team's effectiveness while playing at home or away.

Use the Crosstab Query Wizard

You will almost always use the Crosstab Query Wizard to build a crosstab query, although it can be built from scratch using the query design grid. As with any query wizard, you first need to identify the source of the data that will be the basis of the crosstab query. Unlike other queries, you can only reference one object (table or query) as the data source in a crosstab query. Therefore, if you want to use fields stored in different tables, you must first combine the required data in a query. Once the data are combined in a single source, you can create the crosstab query.

To create a crosstab query, do the following:

1. Click the Query Wizard in the Queries group on the CREATE tab.
2. When the New Query dialog box appears, select Crosstab Query Wizard.
3. Click OK, as shown in Figure 14.20.

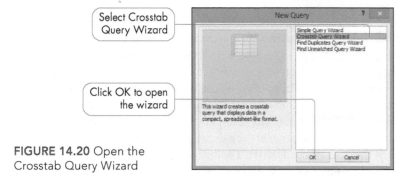

FIGURE 14.20 Open the Crosstab Query Wizard

4. Identify the data source and click Next. You can display tables, queries, or a combination of both by selecting the appropriate view (see Figure 14.21).
5. In the next step, shown in Figure 14.22, identify up to three row heading fields. To make a selection, double-click the field name or click the > button. Click Next. Access limits the number of row heading fields to three and the number of column headings to one. You can have as many aggregate fields as you want, but more than two or three makes the crosstab query difficult to read.
6. Select the field for the column headings, as shown in Figure 14.23. Click Next.
7. If the field contains date data, the next window will ask for the date interval (see Figure 14.24). Click Next. In this example, the sales data for each salesperson will be summarized by quarter.
8. Choose the field to use in a calculation at the intersection of each row and column; then choose what type of aggregate function to apply, such as Avg, Count, or Sum. Click Next. Figure 14.25 shows the result of selecting the Revenue field and the Sum function.
9. Name the query and provide information on how you want to view the new query (see Figure 14.26).
10. Close the query.

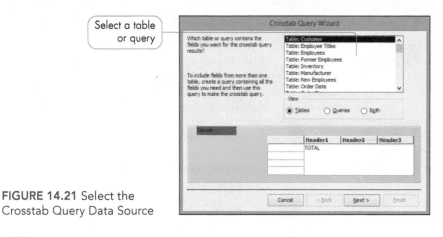

FIGURE 14.21 Select the Crosstab Query Data Source

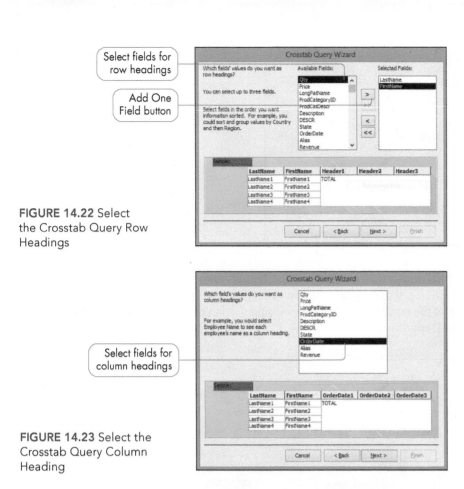

Select fields for row headings

Add One Field button

FIGURE 14.22 Select the Crosstab Query Row Headings

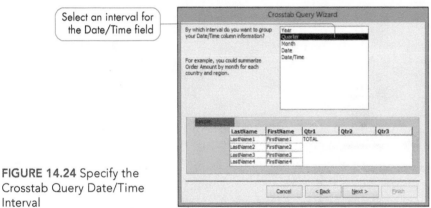

Select fields for column headings

FIGURE 14.23 Select the Crosstab Query Column Heading

Select an interval for the Date/Time field

FIGURE 14.24 Specify the Crosstab Query Date/Time Interval

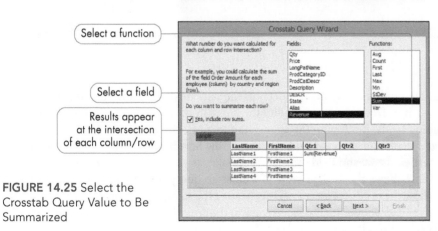

Select a function

Select a field

Results appear at the intersection of each column/row

FIGURE 14.25 Select the Crosstab Query Value to Be Summarized

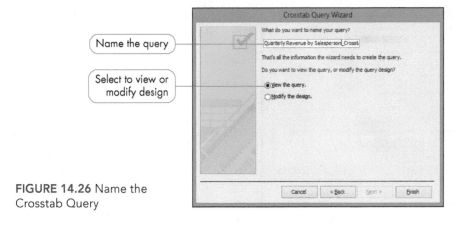

Name the query

Select to view or modify design

FIGURE 14.26 Name the Crosstab Query

Figure 14.27 shows the results of a crosstab query with the total quarterly sales for each salesperson. The Total of Revenue column displays totals for each salesperson for the entire year. To format the results as currency, you would need to modify the format property of the sales fields in Design view.

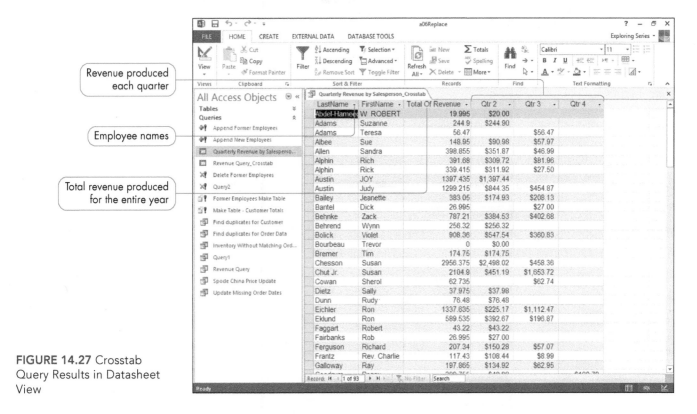

Revenue produced each quarter

Employee names

Total revenue produced for the entire year

FIGURE 14.27 Crosstab Query Results in Datasheet View

Modify a Crosstab Query

STEP 2 ›› You may want to modify the format property of the sales fields or change the organization of the query. Switch to Design view to modify the crosstab query design by changing row and column heading fields, modifying the aggregate function, or altering the field selection for the aggregate calculation. You can add additional row heading fields to the crosstab query. Modify properties, fields, and field order for a crosstab as you would in any query.

Figure 14.28 shows the Design view of a crosstab query. The crosstab query has been modified to show the product category IDs instead of the salesperson's names as the first row heading. Figure 14.29 shows the Datasheet view of the crosstab query once it has been modified, and all calculations have been formatted as currency.

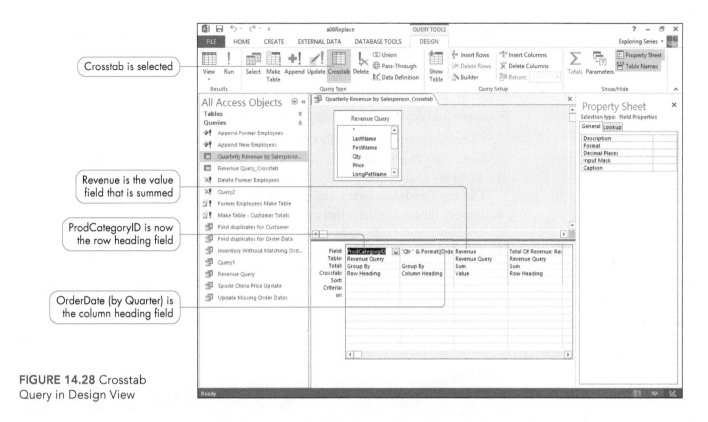

Crosstab is selected

Revenue is the value field that is summed

ProdCategoryID is now the row heading field

OrderDate (by Quarter) is the column heading field

FIGURE 14.28 Crosstab Query in Design View

FIGURE 14.29 Edited Crosstab Query in Datasheet View

ProdCatego	Total Of Revenue	Qtr 1	Qtr 2	Qtr 3
1	$31,114.33	$23.00	$18,198.41	$12,892.93
2	$26,744.52	$88.29	$14,471.53	$12,184.70
3	$15,026.88	$49.49	$7,878.41	$7,098.97

Finding Duplicate Records with a Query

If two records with the same name and address are in a table, that may indicate a duplicate entry. You might expect Access to restrict a user from entering a record into a table with the same name and address; however, because many tables use unique values as the ID number for each record, as long as the ID is different, a user would be able to enter one, two, three, or more records with the same name and address. Access can create a query to display records that are potential duplicate records, for example, a duplicated order.

Sometimes data is entered more than once by mistake. However, not all duplicated data in a database is the result of an error. Some duplication occurs naturally. For example, the CustomerID field is the unique identifier in the Customer table; no two customers can have the same ID number. However, the CustomerID field also appears as a foreign key field in the Orders table. Because of the one-to-many relationship between the Customer table and the Orders table, the CustomerID can repeat in the Orders table. One customer may place many orders. Repeating data values in a foreign key on the many side of a one-to-many relationship is standard database design—duplication is expected.

Additionally, some data values repeat naturally in a table. The city field will contain many records with duplicating values. The LastName field may contain records with the same name, such as Smith, Lee, or Rodriguez. These duplicated data values are not errors. Not all duplicated data values are problematic; however, there may be occasions when you will need to find and manage unwanted duplicates.

Use a Find Duplicate Records Query

STEP 3 You can use a *find duplicates query* to help identify duplicate values in a table. If you inherit a poorly designed database and are unable to enforce referential integrity between tables, you can run find duplicates query to identify the duplicate values in the primary key field candidate. Once you identify the problem records, you can fix or eliminate them and then attempt to enforce referential integrity. Finding duplicate fields and knowing what to do with them remains one of the challenges of good database design.

Create a Find Duplicates Query Using the Wizard

To create a find duplicates query, do the following:

1. Click the Query Wizard in the Queries group on the CREATE tab.
2. In the New Query dialog box, select Find Duplicates Query Wizard, and then click OK.
3. Select the table or query that contains the data source for your query, such as Customer, and click Next (see Figure 14.30).
4. Identify the field or fields that might contain duplicate information, such as LastName and FirstName, as shown in Figure 14.31. Click Next.
5. Select additional fields you want to see in the query results, shown in Figure 14.32. Click Next.
6. Name the query and decide how you want to view it initially (see Figure 14.33). Click Finish. The results are shown in Figure 14.34. The first two records for Susan Agner have the same address; therefore, one of them should probably be removed.
7. Close the query.

TIP **Deleting Duplicate Records**

Use caution when deleting duplicate records. For example, if two customers in a table have the same exact details but unique ID (primary key) fields, records (such as orders) may be stored using both customer IDs. Be sure to ensure that when you delete the duplicated customer record, you do not delete associated orders in a related table. Associate the orders with the customer record that you are keeping.

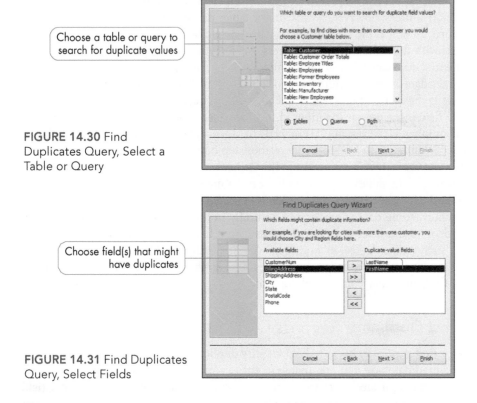

Choose a table or query to search for duplicate values

FIGURE 14.30 Find Duplicates Query, Select a Table or Query

Choose field(s) that might have duplicates

FIGURE 14.31 Find Duplicates Query, Select Fields

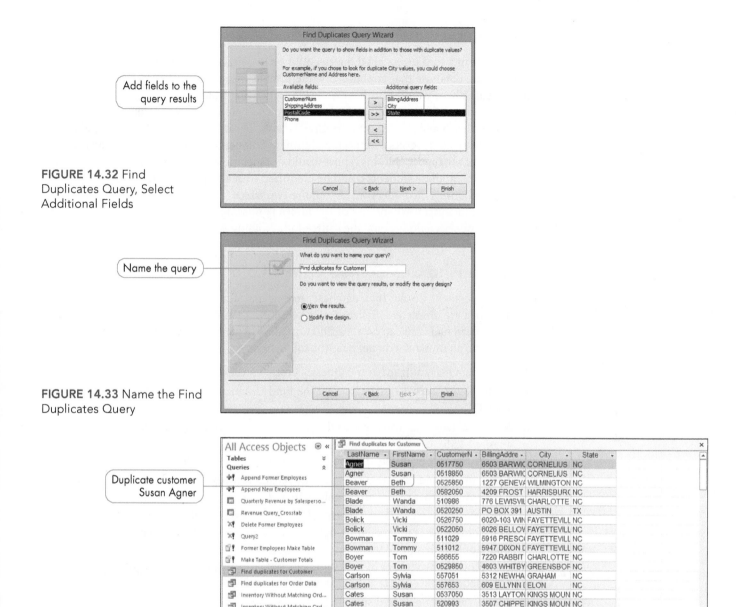

FIGURE 14.32 Find Duplicates Query, Select Additional Fields

FIGURE 14.33 Name the Find Duplicates Query

FIGURE 14.34 Duplicate Customers

Finding Unmatched Records with a Query

It is possible for a company to run reports that show which customers did *not* place an order in the past week, or in the previous month, or in the past 12 months, or ever. No matter how a company decides to handle this group of customers, it could be useful to know how many customers who receive their catalog have never placed an order. Access comes with a special query wizard that helps you find these customers. A *find unmatched query* compares records in two related tables and displays the records found in one table but not the other.

Use a Find Unmatched Query

STEP 4 ≫ Another use of a find unmatched query could be in a grade-book database. Your instructor might have a database that contains a Student table with all the relevant student information. The database would also have a Grades table that holds all the grades for each student. Throughout the semester, as students complete their assignments, the instructor enters the score for each assignment into the Grades table. Periodically, the instructor could run a report showing all the grades for each assignment and perhaps showing the average score at the bottom of the report. But this report would not include students who have not completed each assignment; these students could be identified with a find unmatched query.

The find unmatched query would require two tables (Students and Grades) with a common field (StudentID) where one of the tables is missing information (Grades). The find unmatched query could become the source for a Missing Assignments Report.

Create a Find Unmatched Query Using the Wizard

In the Replacement China, Inc., database, management may want to know which items in the inventory are obsolete. *Obsolete* could be defined as *items that the company stocks that have never been sold.* You can create a find unmatched query to identify these obsolete items.

To create an unmatched query, do the following:

1. Click the Query Wizard in the Queries group on the CREATE tab.
2. In the New Query dialog box, select the Find Unmatched Query Wizard, and then click OK.
3. Select the table that will serve as the primary table source for this query (see Figure 14.35). Click Next. The first table is the one with the records you want to see in the results—for example, the one with inventory items that have never sold.
4. Select the second table that contains the related records—for example, the table that can show whether or not an inventory item was sold (see Figure 14.36). Click Next.
5. Click the appropriate field in each field list, if necessary. Click Matching Fields to determine what is the matching field you want to use. Click Next. The find unmatched query only works if the two tables share a common field. Usually, the two tables are related to each other in a relationship, but a relationship is not required. Access automatically recognizes the common field (see Figure 14.37).
6. Identify which fields to display in the query output. Use the One Field arrow to move the fields you want from the *Available fields* box to the *Selected fields* box, as shown in Figure 14.38. Click Next. In this case, three fields have been selected for the query.
7. Name the query (see Figure 14.39), and then click Finish to view the results.

Figure 14.40 displays the query results.

Choose a table that contains records you want in the query results

FIGURE 14.35 To Find Unmatched Records, Choose a Primary Table First

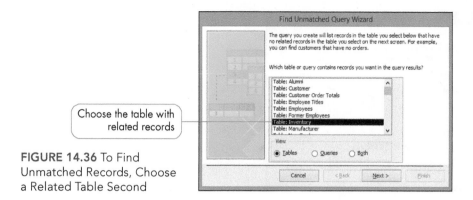

Choose the table with related records

FIGURE 14.36 To Find Unmatched Records, Choose a Related Table Second

The results will show which items in the inventory have no sales. These items can be returned to the manufacturer, discounted in order to sell them, or used as a write-off.

TIP Which Table Do I Choose First?

The first screen of the Find Unmatched Query Wizard asks you *Which table or query contains records you want in the query results?* Choosing this first table is not always an easy task. Select the table that contains records that may be unmatched. The second screen asks, *Which table or query contains the related records?* When you choose the second table, choose a table that shares a common field with the first one. If the two tables have more than one common field candidate, you will need to carefully select which fields you want Access to use. If you make a mistake, delete the query, start over, and then try reversing the order of the two tables.

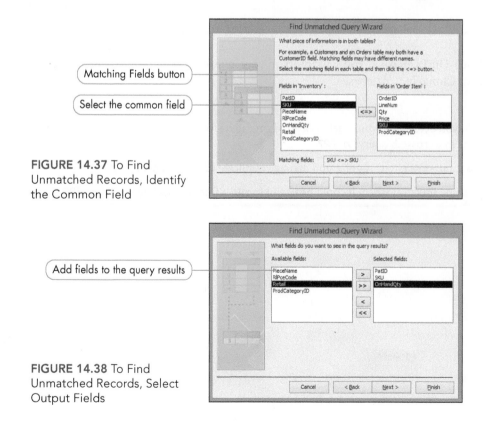

Matching Fields button

Select the common field

FIGURE 14.37 To Find Unmatched Records, Identify the Common Field

Add fields to the query results

FIGURE 14.38 To Find Unmatched Records, Select Output Fields

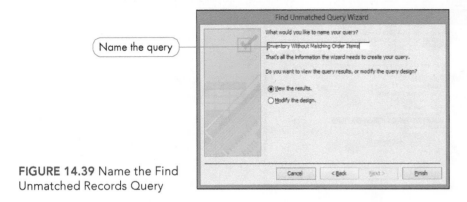

FIGURE 14.39 Name the Find Unmatched Records Query

Name the query

Inventory items that have not sold

FIGURE 14.40 Results of the Obsolete Inventory Query

In Hands-On Exercise 2, you will improve your querying skills as you work with the Replacement China, Inc., database.

Quick Concepts

1. How do you determine which field is a good candidate for the intersecting rows and columns in a crosstab query? *p. 727*

2. Why is it important to recognize and manage duplicate data in a database? *p. 731*

3. What is one situation where it could be useful to run a find unmatched query? *p. 733*

Hands-On Exercises

Watch the Video for this Hands-On Exercise!

MyITLab®
HOE2 Training

2 Queries for Special Conditions

Replacement China, Inc., has asked you to review their database and make a few improvements. You decide to create a crosstab query to help them look up employee information more easily. You also summarize their revenue data by state to help them analyze sales history. Finally, you check for unmatched data and duplicate data using the built-in query tools.

Skills covered: Use the Crosstab Query Wizard • Edit a Crosstab Query • Create a Find Duplicate Records Query Using the Wizard • Create a Find Unmatched Query Using the Wizard

STEP 1 >> USE THE CROSSTAB QUERY WIZARD

You need to analyze the revenue generated by each salesperson at Replacement China, Inc. You decide to break down the results by state. This type of summary can be accomplished using a crosstab query. Refer to Figure 14.41 as you complete Step 1.

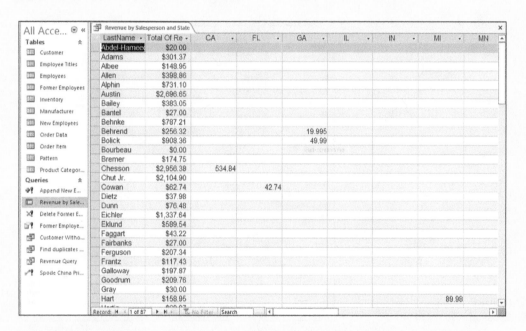

FIGURE 14.41 Crosstab Query Results

a. Open *a06h1Replace_LastFirst* if you closed it at the end of Hands-On Exercise 1. Click **Save As** on the FILE tab, click **Save As**, and then type **a06h2Replace_LastFirst**, changing *h1* to *h2*. Click **Save**.

b. Click **Query Wizard** in the Queries group on the CREATE tab.

c. Select the **Crosstab Query Wizard**. Click **OK**.

The Crosstab Query Wizard opens..

d. Click **Queries** in the *View* section of the Crosstab Query Wizard dialog box. Select **Query: Revenue Query**. Click **Next**.

You selected the Revenue query as the data source that contains revenue by salesperson and state for the crosstab query.

e. Double-click the **LastName field** in the Available Fields box to move it to the Selected Fields box. Click **Next**.

You selected the LastName field as the row heading. The query summarizes the data for each salesperson's last name.

f. Click the **State field** to select it as the column heading. Click **Next**.

You selected the State field as the column heading.

g. Click the **Revenue field** in the Fields box to select it as the summarizing field. Click **Sum** in the Functions box to specify which aggregate function to perform. Click **Next**.

You directed the crosstab query to show you the sum of revenue for each salesperson and for each state.

h. Change the query name to **Revenue by Salesperson and State**. Make sure the *View the query* option is selected. Click **Finish**.

i. Examine the results.

The data shows the sum of revenue for each salesperson in each state. However, the results are cumbersome to view. You will edit the crosstab query in the next step.

STEP 2 ›› EDIT A CROSSTAB QUERY

The sales reps at Replacement China, Inc., would like to change the column heading field from State to ProdCategoryID. This will help the sales reps identify the sales for each product category and also reduce the number of columns in the crosstab query. Refer to Figure 14.42 as you complete Step 2.

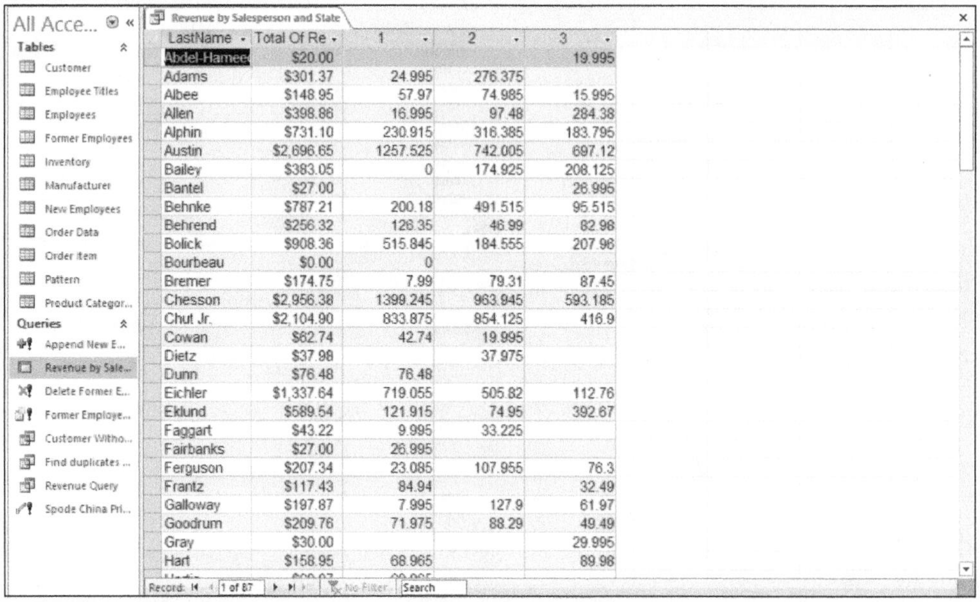

LastName	Total Of Re	1	2	3
Abdel-Hameed	$20.00			19.995
Adams	$301.37	24.995	276.375	
Albee	$148.95	57.97	74.985	15.995
Allen	$398.86	16.995	97.48	284.38
Alphin	$731.10	230.915	316.385	183.795
Austin	$2,696.65	1257.525	742.005	697.12
Bailey	$383.05	0	174.925	208.125
Bantel	$27.00			26.995
Behnke	$787.21	200.18	491.515	95.515
Behrend	$256.32	126.35	46.99	82.98
Bolick	$908.36	515.845	184.555	207.96
Bourbeau	$0.00	0		
Bremer	$174.75	7.99	79.31	87.45
Chesson	$2,956.38	1399.245	963.945	593.185
Chut Jr.	$2,104.90	833.875	854.125	416.9
Cowan	$62.74	42.74	19.995	
Dietz	$37.98		37.975	
Dunn	$76.48	76.48		
Eichler	$1,337.64	719.055	505.82	112.76
Eklund	$589.54	121.915	74.95	392.67
Faggart	$43.22	9.995	33.225	
Fairbanks	$27.00	26.995		
Ferguson	$207.34	23.085	107.955	76.3
Frantz	$117.43	84.94		32.49
Galloway	$197.87	7.995	127.9	61.97
Goodrum	$209.76	71.975	88.29	49.49
Gray	$30.00			29.995
Hart	$158.95	68.965		89.98

FIGURE 14.42 Revised Crosstab Query Results

a. Switch to Design view.

b. Click the arrow in the Field row of the State column in the query design grid and select **ProdCategoryID**.

The columns now show the product category IDs rather than the state names, reducing the number of columns.

c. Click in the **Total of Revenue field**, open the Property Sheet, and then change the Format field property on the General tab to **Currency**. Close the Property Sheet.

d. Click **Run** in the Results group to see the new results. Double-click the right border of the *Total of Revenue* column so all of the data displays.

e. Save the changes and close the query.

STEP 3 ≫ CREATE A FIND DUPLICATE RECORDS QUERY USING THE WIZARD

One of the data entry employees believes duplicate entries are present in the Pattern table. You create a query to look for duplicates in the LongPatName field in the Pattern table. If duplicates do exist, the company will need to move all orders to one Pattern and then delete the other Pattern. Refer to Figure 14.43 as you complete Step 3.

Step e: Two duplicates exist in the LongPatName field

FIGURE 14.43 Results of the Find Duplicate Records Query

a. Click **Query Wizard** on the CREATE tab and select **Find Duplicates Query Wizard** to create a find duplicates query. Click **OK**.

b. Click **Table: Pattern** (scroll down, if necessary). Click **Next**.

c. Double-click the **LongPatName** in the Available fields box to move it to the Duplicate-value fields box. Click **Next**.

d. Click >> to move the rest of the fields in the table from the Available fields box to the Additional query fields box. Click **Next**.

e. Click **Finish** to accept the default name, *Find duplicates for Pattern*, and the option to view the results.

The query runs and opens in Datasheet view. It contains four records showing two duplicate LongPatName fields.

f. Save the query. Close the query.

STEP 4 ≫ CREATE A FIND UNMATCHED QUERY USING THE WIZARD

The Marketing Manager at Replacement China, Inc., asked you to identify the customers who have not placed orders. You create a find unmatched query to find the customers who have no records in the Order Data table. Someone from the Marketing Department will contact these customers and offer them an incentive to place an order. Refer to Figure 14.44 as you complete Step 4.

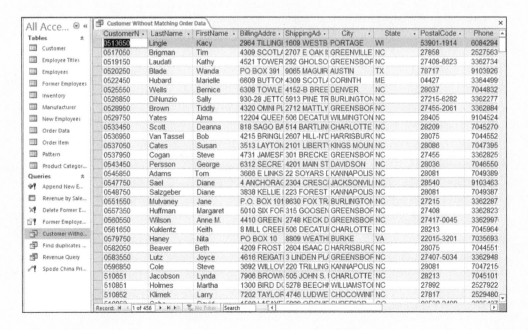

FIGURE 14.44 Customers Who Have Not Ordered

a. Click **Query Wizard** in the Queries group on the CREATE tab. Select the **Find Unmatched Query Wizard** in the New Query dialog box and click **OK**.

You need to create a find unmatched query to find the customers who have not placed an order.

b. Click **Table: Customer** to select the Customer table. Click **Next**.

You selected the Customer table as the first table. You will select the Order Data table next so you can find customers who have not ordered.

c. Click **Table: Order Data** and click **Next**.

You selected the Order Data table as the second table so you can find customers who have not ordered.

d. Click **Next** at the next screen.

Access identifies the common field (CustomerNum) that exists in both tables.

e. Click >> to add all of the fields to the query. Click **Next**.

f. Click **Finish** to accept the default name and the option to view the results.

456 customers have not placed an order.

g. Save the query. Close the query.

h. Click **Compact & Repair Database** on the FILE tab.

i. Close the database. Close Access.

j. Submit based on your instructor's directions.

Chapter Objectives Review

After reading this chapter, you have accomplished the following objectives:

1. **Determine when to use an action query.**
   - Recognize the benefits of an action query: Action queries add, edit, or delete the data in a database. These four queries—update, append, make table, and delete—are used for updating records that meet certain criteria, for appending records to a table, for making a new table, and for deleting specific records from a table.
   - Back up a database when testing an action query: Action queries change data in your database, so it is important to back up your database in case it needs to be restored.

2. **Update data with an update query.**
   - Create a select query before running an update query: Create a select query to define the fields and criteria to be used in your update query.
   - Convert a select query to an update query: An update query changes the data values in one or more fields for all records that meet a specific criterion. The update query defines precisely how field values will be updated.
   - Test an update query: View the update query in Datasheet view to determine which records will be affected before you run it.
   - Verify an update query: Open the table to determine the results of the updates.

3. **Add records to a table with an append query.**
   - Create a select query before running an append query: Create a select query to define the fields and criteria to be used in your append query.
   - Set Append To fields in an append query: An append query selects records from one or more tables and adds them to another table. The append query will define precisely how fields and records will be appended.
   - Run an Append Query: If you need to verify the records to be appended, you can click View in the Results group to double-check in Datasheet view.

4. **Create a table with a make table query.**
   - Create a make table query: A make table query selects records from one or more tables and uses them to create a new table.

   - Test and run a make table query: View the make table query in Datasheet view to determine which records will be added to the new table before you run it.

5. **Delete records with a delete query.**
   - Create a delete query: A delete query selects records from a table and then removes them from the table.
   - Test and run a delete query: View the delete query in Datasheet view to determine which records will be deleted from the table before you run it.

6. **Summarize data with a crosstab query.**
   - Group and summarize data: A crosstab query summarizes a data source into a grid of rows and columns; the intersection of each row and column displays valuable aggregate data.
   - Use the Crosstab Query Wizard: The wizard guides you through the steps of creating the crosstab query, including setting the row and column headings.
   - Modify a crosstab query: In Design view, you can modify the row/column headings of the query, format fields, and summarize the data in different ways.

7. **Find duplicate records with a query.**
   - Use a find duplicate records query: The Find Duplicates Query Wizard is used to help identify duplicated values in a table. However, not all duplicated data in a database are the result of an error.
   - Create a find duplicates query using the wizard: The wizard guides you through the steps of creating the query, including identifying which fields to search for duplicated data.

8. **Find unmatched records with a query.**
   - Use a find unmatched query: The Find Unmatched Query Wizard creates a query that compares records in two related tables and returns the records found in one table but not the other.
   - Create a find unmatched query using the wizard: The wizard guides you through the steps of creating the query, including identifying which fields to search for unmatched data.

Key Terms Matching

Match the key terms with their definitions. Write the key term letter by the appropriate numbered definition.

a. Action query
b. Append query
c. Column headings
d. Crosstab query
e. Delete query

f. Find duplicates query
g. Find unmatched query
h. Make table query
i. Row headings
j. Update query

1. _____ A query that selects records from one or more tables (the source) and adds them to an existing table (the destination). **p. 713**

2. _____ A query that compares records in two related tables, and then displays the records found in one table but not the other. **p. 733**

3. _____ A query that summarizes a data source into a few key rows and columns; the intersection of each row and column displays aggregate data. **p. 727**

4. _____ A query that selects records from one or more tables and uses them to create a new table. **p. 716**

5. _____ The field names displayed along the left side of a crosstab query. **p. 727**

6. _____ A query that selects records from a table and then removes them from the table. **p. 717**

7. _____ The field name displayed at the top of a crosstab query. **p. 727**

8. _____ A query that adds, updates, or deletes data in a database. **p. 735**

9. _____ A query that changes the data values in one or more fields for all records that meet specific criteria. **p. 710**

10. _____ A query that helps you identify repeated values in a table. **p. 731**

Multiple Choice

1. Which one of the following tasks could not be completed with an action query?

   (a) Deleting records from a table
   (b) Updating records in a table
   (c) Displaying data based on a value entered at run time
   (d) Creating a new table based on a group of selected records

2. Which statement is true about action queries?

   (a) Users use action queries more frequently than database administrators.
   (b) You can run an action query as many times as you like.
   (c) A delete query is not an action query.
   (d) Action queries should be executed with caution because you cannot undo their changes.

3. Which query below is used as a basis to create the other three?

   (a) Select query
   (b) Update query
   (c) Delete query
   (d) Append query

4. Your company merged with another company, and now the two customer lists are combined into one table. Because the two companies had many of the same customers, the customer table now contains many duplicate customers with different account numbers. What is the best way to resolve this problem?

   (a) Delete duplicate customers manually.
   (b) Create a select query showing all customers in alphabetical order and then run a delete query to delete every other record.
   (c) It will not affect overall performance of the database to have duplicated records, so leave the table as is.
   (d) Use a find duplicates query to locate duplicate customers. Delete one of the duplicates.

5. Why is it important to monitor how many times an update query is executed?

   (a) Update queries are capable of changing values (such as prices) more than one time.
   (b) Update queries can be used to delete records from your tables.
   (c) It is not important; you can always undo the results of an update query.
   (d) An update query can erase your table and create a new one in its place.

6. Which statement is true about action queries?

   (a) An append query is usually run after an update query.
   (b) A delete query is usually run before an update query.
   (c) A delete query is usually run after an append query.
   (d) Make table queries are usually constructed from an update query.

7. Why would you use an update query?

   (a) Because users need to be able to select records based on varied selection criteria
   (b) To determine which records may need to be deleted from the database
   (c) To summarize the data in a firm's database to help managers evaluate their financial position
   (d) To increase retail prices in a firm's database

8. How do you create a crosstab query?

   (a) Click Crosstab Query on the Create tab.
   (b) Click Query Wizard and select Crosstab Query Wizard for the query type.
   (c) Click Crosstab Query on the Database Tools tab.
   (d) Create a select query and convert it to a crosstab query.

9. What is an unmatched record?

   (a) A record that contains the primary key in the one table
   (b) A record that requires deletion when running a delete query
   (c) A duplicated record that cannot be connected to a parent record
   (d) A record in one table without a matching record in a related table

10. What is the best way to find students who have not attended a certain class?

    (a) Create a select query of attendance and compare the results to the student roster.
    (b) Create a select query of attendance and use the query to create an update query.
    (c) Create a select query of attendance for the students in the class. Then create a find duplicates query using the attendance table.
    (d) Create a find unmatched query using the student and attendance tables.

Practice Exercises

1 National Bank

You are the DBA for a national bank. The bank has decided to decrease mortgage loans by a half percent. You use an update query to modify the mortgage rates. In addition, you decide to move all mortgages from the loans table to a new mortgages table. You delete the mortgages from the loans table after they are moved. This exercise follows the same set of skills as used in Hands-On Exercise 1 in the chapter. Refer to Figures 14.45 and 14.46 as you complete this exercise.

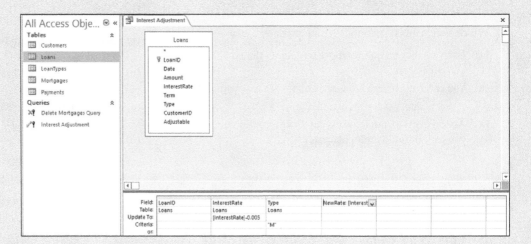

FIGURE 14.45 Update Query to Decrease Rates by 0.50 Percent

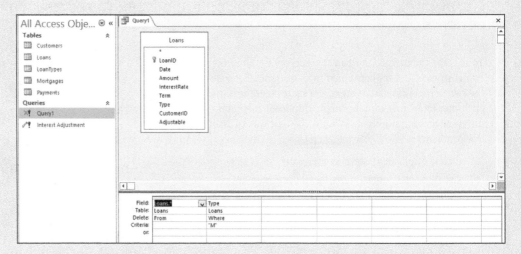

FIGURE 14.46 Query Design to Delete Mortgages from Loans Table

a. Open *a06p1Bank*. Click **Save As** on the FILE tab, click **Save As**, and then type **a06p1Bank_LastFirst**. Click **Save**.

b. Click **Query Design** in the Queries group on the CREATE tab. Double-click the **Loans table** in the Show Table dialog box to add it to the query. Close the Show Table dialog box.

c. Double-click the **LoanID**, **InterestRate**, and **Type fields**. Click **Run** in the Results group. Save the query as **Interest Adjustment**.

d. Switch to Design view. Type **M** in the **Criteria row** of the Type column.

   Entering *M* in the Criteria row of the Type column will isolate only those loans that are mortgages.

e. Click in the **Field row** of the fourth column and type **NewRate: [InterestRate] - 0.0050**. Press **Enter**.

   You have created a new field with the calculation for the new interest rate, which decreases by 0.50 percent.

f. Click **Property Sheet** in the Show/Hide group with the calculated field column selected. Change the Format property to **Percent**. Close the Property Sheet.

g. Click **Run** in the Results group and examine the results of the NewRate calculated field.

h. Switch to Design view. Click **Update** in the Query Type group. Click in the **Update To row** of the InterestRate field and type **[InterestRate] - 0.0050**.

The update query changes the existing interest rates to the lower interest rates calculated in the NewRate field. Compare your query design to Figure 14.45.

i. Click **View** in the Results group to verify that 12 records will be updated. Switch back to Design view.

j. Click **Run** in the Results group. Click **Yes** in response to the Warning box. Save and close the query.

k. Open the Loans table and verify the Mortgage loan interest rates are 0.50 percent lower. Close the table.

l. Click **Query Design** in the Queries group on the CREATE tab. Double-click the **Loans table** in the Show Table dialog box. Close the Show Table dialog box.

m. Double-click the title bar of the Loans table to select all the fields and drag them to the first column in the design grid.

n. Click **Run** in the Results group to run the query.

o. Switch back to Design view. Type **M** in the **Criteria row** of the Type column. Click **Run** in the Results group to run the query.

You only want to see the mortgages in the query results.

p. Switch back to Design view. Click **Make Table** in the Query Type group and type **Mortgages** as the new table name. Accept the default setting of Current Database and click **OK**.

q. Switch to Datasheet view to verify that only the 12 mortgage loans will be affected.

r. Switch to Design view. Click **Run** in the Results group. Click **Yes** in response to the Warning box.

s. Double-click the **Mortgages table** in the Navigation Pane. Verify that the 12 mortgages are in the table. Close the table.

t. Click **Delete** in the Query Type group on the DESIGN tab to change the make table query to a delete query.

u. Delete all the columns in the query design grid except the Type column.

The Type column contains the criterion you need for the delete query.

v. Drag the *** field** from the Loans table to the first column in the query design grid.

Compare your query design to Figure 14.46.

w. Click **Run** in the Results group. Click **Yes** in response to the Warning box.

x. Save the query as **Delete Mortgages Query**. Close the query.

y. Compact and repair the database. Close the database. Close Access.

z. Submit based on your instructor's directions.

---

2 Break Room Suppliers, Inc.

Break Room Suppliers, Inc., is a small service organization that provides coffee, tea, and snacks to local businesses. You have been asked to review the database and create several queries; these queries can be run periodically by the owner. This exercise follows the same set of skills as used in Hands-On Exercises 1 and 2 in the chapter. Refer to Figures 14.47 and 14.48 as you complete this exercise.

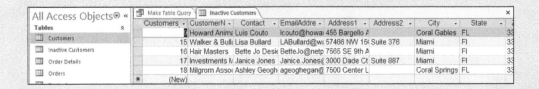

FIGURE 14.47 Inactive Customers Table

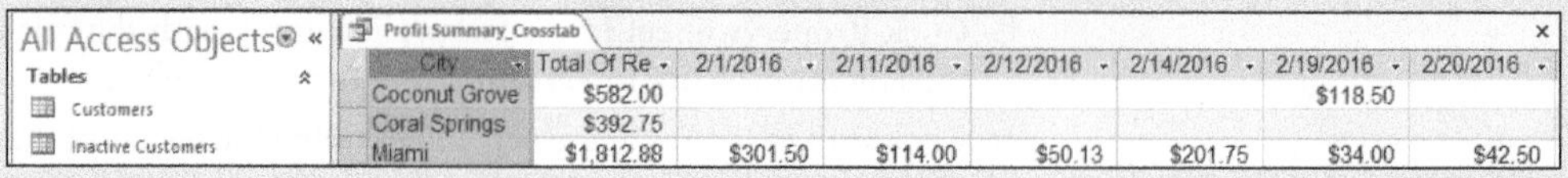

FIGURE 14.48 Crosstab Query
Showing Profit for Each City

City	Total Of Re	2/1/2016	2/11/2016	2/12/2016	2/14/2016	2/19/2016	2/20/2016
Coconut Grove	$582.00					$118.50	
Coral Springs	$392.75						
Miami	$1,812.88	$301.50	$114.00	$50.13	$201.75	$34.00	$42.50

a. Open *a06p2Coffee*. Click **Save As** on the FILE tab, click **Save As**, and then type **a06p2Coffee_ LastFirst**. Click **Save**.

b. Double-click the **Sales Reps table** to open it. Replace *Your_Name* with your name. Close the table.

c. Click **Query Wizard** in the Queries group on the CREATE tab. Click **Find Unmatched Query Wizard**, click **OK**, and then answer the wizard questions as follows:

- Select **Table: Customers** as the first table. Click **Next**.
- Select **Table: Orders** as the second table. Click **Next**.
- Accept the CustomerID field as the common field. Click **Next**.
- Click **>>** to move all of the fields in the Available fields box to the Selected fields box. Click **Next**.
- Accept *Customers Without Matching Orders* as the query name and click **Finish** to display the four inactive customers. Leave the Customers Without Matching Orders query open.

d. Switch to Design view. Click **Make Table** in the Query Type group and follow these steps:

- Type **Inactive Customers** in the **Table Name box**. Click **OK**.
- Click **View** in the Results group to verify that four customers are shown.
- Click **View** to return to Design view.
- Click **Run** in the Results group to run the make table query.
- Click **Yes** in response to the Warning box.
- Click **Save As** on the FILE tab, click **Save Object As**, and then click **Save As**. Save the copy of the query with the name **Make Table Query**. Click **OK**.

e. Open the Inactive Customers table to verify that the four records have been archived. Close the table.

f. Ensure the Customers Without Matching Orders query is open. Click the **DESIGN tab**, click **Delete** in the Query Type group, and then follow these steps:

- Right-click the **Orders table** and select **Remove Table**.
- Type **9 Or 15 Or 16 Or 17** into the **Criteria row** of the CustomerID column.
- Click **View** in the Results group to verify that four customers are shown.
- Click **View** to return to Design view.
- Click **Run** in the Results group to run the delete query.
- Click **Yes** in response to the Warning box.
- Click **Save As** on the FILE tab, click **Save Object As**, and then click **Save As**. Save the copy of the query with the name **Delete Inactive Customers Query**.
- Close the query.

You have deleted the inactive customers (IDs 9, 15, 16, and 17) from the Customers table.

g. Create a copy of the Delete Inactive Customers Query and rename it as **Append Inactive Customers Query**.

- View the query in Design view.
- Click **Append** in the Query Type group. Append to Inactive Customers and click **OK**.
- Delete the existing criterion and type **5** into the **Criteria row** of the CustomerID column.
- Click **View** in the Results group to verify that one customer is shown.
- Click **View** to return to Design view.
- Click **Run** in the Results group to run the append query.
- Click **Yes** in response to the Warning box.
- Save and close the query.

You have appended CustomerID 5 to the Inactive Customers table, as shown in Figure 14.47. Note that because CustomerID is an AutoNumber field in the Inactive Customers table, the record will be renumbered when appended to that table.

h. Click **Query Wizard** in the Queries group on the CREATE tab. Click **Crosstab Query Wizard**, click **OK**, and then follow these steps:

- Click **Queries** in the *View* section.
- Click **Query: Profit Summary**. Click **Next**.
- Click **City** and click > to select it as the Row heading. Click **Next**.
- Click **OrderDate** to select it for the Column heading. Click **Next**.
- In the next screen, click **Date** and click **Next**.
- Click **Revenue** as the calculated field and click **Sum** as the aggregate function. Click **Next**.
- Click **Finish** to accept *Profit Summary_Crosstab* as the query name and view the query results. Compare your results to Figure 14.48.
- Save and close the query.

i. Click **Query Wizard** in the Queries group on the CREATE tab. Click **Find Duplicates Query Wizard**, click **OK**, and then follow these steps:

- Click **Table: Customers**. Click **Next**.
- Click **Contact** and click > to search for duplicates in this field. Click **Next**.
- Click >> to indicate you want to see all the additional fields. Click **Next**.
- Type **Find contact duplicates in Customers** as the query name. Click **Finish**.
- Close the query.

j. Compact and repair the database.

k. Close the database. Close Access.

l. Submit based on your instructor's directions.

1 Northwind Traders

Northwind Traders is a small international specialty foods distribution firm. Management has decided to close their North and South American operations and concentrate on their European markets. They have asked you to update certain customer records and to move all deactivated customers to another table. Once you move the records, you will delete them from the original table. Refer to Figure 14.49 as you complete this exercise.

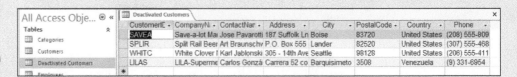

FIGURE 14.49 Deactivated Customers Table Created with Action Queries

a. Open *a06m1Exporters*. Click **Save As** on the FILE tab, click **Save As**, and then type **a06m1Exporters_LastFirst**. Click **Save**.

b. Create a select query based on all of the fields from the Customers table. Add criteria to show only customers in the USA. Run the query.

c. Change the query to an update query that replaces all instances of *USA* with **United States**. Run the query. Save the query as **Update US Customers**. Close the query.

d. Create a make table query that is based on all of the fields in the Customers table. Name the new table **Deactivated Customers**. Add criteria to select only United States customers. Run the query and save it as **Make Table Query**. Close the query.

e. Make a copy of the Make Table Query in the Navigation Pane and name the copy **Append Query**. Right-click the new **Append Query** and select **Design View** from the list.

f. Change the query type to **Append**. Append records to the Deactivated Customers table. Change the criteria of the Country field to **Venezuela**. Run the query. Save and close the query.

g. Make a copy of the Append Query in the Navigation Pane and name the copy **Delete Query**. Right-click the new **Delete Query** and choose **Design View** from the list.

h. Change the query type to **Delete**. Change the Country criteria to **United States Or Venezuela**. Delete all the columns in the query design grid except the Country column. Run the query. Save and close the query. Open the Deactivated Customers table to view the records added by the make table and append queries. Close the table.

i. Close the database. Close Access.

j. Submit based on your instructor's directions.

2 Hotel Chain

ANALYSIS CASE

You are assisting the general manager of a large hotel chain. You need to perform several tasks for the general manager including calculating the total revenue for each service for each city. You also need to find duplicate names in the members table. Refer to Figures 14.50 and 14.51 as you complete this exercise.

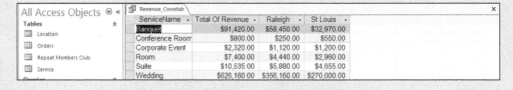

FIGURE 14.50 Crosstab Query Displays Revenue by Service and City

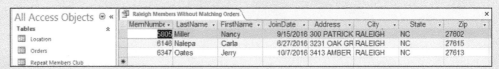

FIGURE 14.51 Raleigh Members Without Matching Orders

a. Open *a06m2Rewards*. Click **Save As** on the FILE tab, click **Save As**, and then type **a06m2Rewards_LastFirst**. Click **Save**.

b. Create a crosstab query based on the Revenue query. Use the ServiceName field for the row heading, the City field for the column heading, and the Revenue field for the column and row intersection. Sum the Revenue field. Save the query as **Revenue_Crosstab**.

c. Format the Revenue and Total of Revenue crosstab values as **Currency**. Run the query. Compare your results to Figure 14.50. Save and close the Revenue_Crosstab query.

DISCOVER

d. Create a copy of the Revenue_Crosstab query and save it as **Revenue_Crosstab2**.

e. Modify the query so that the City field is the row heading and the ServiceName field is the column heading. Run the query, save the query, and close it.

f. Create a find unmatched query that displays repeat members from Raleigh. Records from the Repeat Members Club table should display in the results. Include all fields from the table. Test the query and save it as **Raleigh Members Without Matching Orders**. Compare your results to Figure 14.51. Print the results of the query and submit to your instructor.

g. Create a copy of the Raleigh Members Without Matching Orders query and save it as **Charlotte Members Without Matching Orders**.

h. Modify the query so that Charlotte members who have not used any hotel services are displayed in the results.

i. Create a find duplicates query that displays any locations that have the same city and address. Display the LocationID field as an additional field in the query. Run the query and save it as **Find Duplicate Locations**.

j. Change the Address for LocationID 15 to **Downtown**, in the query results. Close the query.

k. Close the database. Close Access.

l. Submit based on your instructor's directions.

3 Car Dealership

COLLABORATION CASE

You have been asked to modify a car dealership database that tracks employee data, sales records, and vehicle information. You and your team will identify new hires in the database and move them to a separate table. You will summarize data in the database and locate unmatched records. Refer to Figure 14.52 as you complete this exercise.

FIGURE 14.52 Vehicles Without Matching Sales Agreements

VehicleID	VehicleYear	VehicleMake	VehicleModel	VehicleColor	VehicleCost	VehicleSalePrice
1000	2013	Honda	Accord	Gray	$25,000.00	$26,999.00
1002	2013	Honda	Accord	Red	$23,500.00	$27,500.00
1003	2012	Honda	Accord EX	Black	$24,900.00	$28,950.00
1004	2011	Honda	Civic	White	$11,300.00	$14,500.00
1007	2012	BMW	325i	White	$25,000.00	$32,000.00
1008	2013	BMW	528i	Black	$28,000.00	$35,900.00
1009	2010	BMW	M3	Red	$25,900.00	$31,500.00

a. Open *a06m3Collaboration*. Click **Save As** on the FILE tab, click **Save As**, and then type **a06m3Collaboration_GroupName**. As a team, study the existing database and the relationships between the tables. Open each table and study the data that you will be working with.

Assign the following two tasks to a team member:

b. Create a select query based on all of the fields from the Employees table. Add criteria to show only employees whose Active status is No. Run the query.

c. Convert the select query a make table query. Name the new table **Hires Not Activated**. Run the query and save it as **Make Table Query_LastFirst**. Close the query. Open the Hires Not Activated table to verify the results.

Assign the following three tasks to a team member:

d. Set the Active status of Employee ID 3 (Jim Delsor) to **No** in the Employees table. Close the table.

e. Make a copy of the Make Table Query_LastFirst in the Navigation Pane and name the copy **Append Query_LastFirst**. Right-click the new append query and choose **Design View** from the list.

f. Change the query type to **Append**. Append records to the Hires Not Activated table. Modify the criteria to select Employee ID 3 and delete the existing criterion. Run the query. Save and close the query.

Assign the following two tasks to a team member:

g. Make a copy of the Append Query_LastFirst in the Navigation Pane and name the copy **Delete Query_LastFirst**. Right-click the new delete query and choose **Design View** from the list.

h. Change the query type to **Delete**. Modify the criteria to show only employees whose Active status is No and delete the existing criterion. Run the query. Save and close the query. Open the Employees table and note that the inactive employees are deleted.

Assign the following two tasks to a team member:

i. Create a crosstab query based on the Available Inventory query. Use the VehicleMake field for the row heading, the VehicleYear field for the column heading, and the VehicleSalePrice field for the column and row intersection. Average the VehicleSalePrice field. Save the query as **Available Inventory_Crosstab_LastFirst**.

j. Set the caption of the Total Of VehicleSalePrice: [VehicleSalePrice] field to **Average Sale Price**. Save and close the query.

k. Collaborate with your team to determine what would be the best way to portray vehicles that have no sales agreement. Create an unmatched query to view these records, and include all of the fields from the Vehicles table. Accept the default query name. Finish and then close the query.

l. Compact and repair the database. Close the database. Exit Access. Submit the database based on your instructor's directions.

Beyond the Classroom

Find Duplicate Data in a Database

RESEARCH CASE

In this chapter, you learned about the difference between valid and invalid duplicates in a database. Go to www.microsoft.com and search for **duplicate data in Access 2013**. Locate the article *Find duplicate records with a query* that discusses the Find Duplicates Query Wizard. Read through the article and write a brief summary of your findings in a Word document; save the file as **a06b2Duplicate_LastFirst**. Close the document. Submit based on your instructor's directions.

Prohibit Duplicate Append

DISASTER RECOVERY

Northwind Traders is an international specialty foods distributor that relies on an Access 2013 database to process its orders. A make table query moved all the owners from the Customers table to a new Customer Owners table. A colleague converted the make table query to an append query and ran it again (expecting it would not add another set of records). Unfortunately, it did add a second set of owners to the table, and now every owner is duplicated. What is the best way to fix this problem? You need to retain the append query and run it once in a while in case a new owner was added to the database. Running the append query should not add any duplicate records to the Customer Owners table. Open *a06b3Food* and save it as **a06b3Food_LastFirst**. Correct the problem in the table. When you are finished, compact, repair, and close your database. Submit based on your instructor's directions.

Cover Letters and Resume Tips

SOFT SKILLS CASE

You want to determine how many of the new employees in your database have no resumes on file with the Human Resources Department. You decide to create a make table query with their personal information so that they can be contacted by HR. Open *a6b4Resumes*. Save a copy of the database as **a6b4Resumes_FirstLast**. Create the query based on the New Employees table and include the following fields: FirstName, LastName, Email, DateOfHire, and ResumeOnFile (in that order). Hide the ResumeOnFile field in the query results. Set the query to create a table named **Missing Resume**. Save the query as **Missing Resume_Make Table**. Run the query to create the table and close the query. Close the database. Exit Access. Submit the database *a6b4Resumes_FirstLast* based on your instructor's directions.

Capstone Exercise

Northwind Traders is a small international gourmet foods whole-saler. You will update the database by increasing the price of all of the beverage and dairy products. You will make a table of discontinued products. You will also summarize profits by salesperson and category and identify products that have no orders.

Database File Setup

Open the original database file, save a copy with a new file name, and then open the copied database to complete this capstone exercise.

a. Open *a06c1Prices* and save it as **a06c1Prices_LastFirst**.

Identify and Update Selected Category Prices

Create a select query to identify all of the products in the beverage and dairy categories, and then create an update query to increase their prices.

a. Create a select query that includes the CategoryID and CategoryName from the Categories table and the UnitPrice and ProductName fields from the Products table. Run the query and note the CategoryIDs for Beverages and Dairy.

b. Add the appropriate CategoryID criterion to limit the query output to only Beverages.

c. Convert the query to an update query. Update the UnitPrice for beverages only by increasing it by 5 percent. View the query in Datasheet view prior to running it to make sure you are updating the correct records. Return to Design view and run the query.

d. Update the UnitPrice for dairy products only by increasing it by 4 percent. View the query in Datasheet view prior to running it to make sure you are updating the correct records. Return to Design view and run the query.

e. Save the query as **Update Prices**. Close the query.

Create a New Table

Identify the discontinued products and create a new table to store them.

a. Create a select query that identifies all of the discontinued products. Include all fields from the Products table.

b. Convert the select query to a make table query.

c. Name the new table **Discontinued Products**. Run the query.

d. Save the query as **Make Discontinued Products Table**. Close the query.

e. Make a copy of the Make Discontinued Products Table query and save it as **Append Discontinued Products Table**. Open the Append Discontinued Products Table query in Design view. Convert the make table query to an append query. The query will append to the Discontinued Products table.

f. Modify the criteria to append Boston Crab Meat as a product, using the SupplierID from the Products table. Run the query, save it, and then close it.

g. Make a copy of the Append Discontinued Products Table query and save it as **Delete Discontinued Products**. Open the Delete Discontinued Products query in Design view. Convert the append query to a delete query.

h. Modify the criteria to delete the discontinued products, as well as the record for Boston Crab Meat using its SupplierID (*Hint:* There will be two criteria). Run, save, and close the query.

Calculate Summary Statistics

Create a crosstab query that shows profits by salesperson and category.

a. Open the Profit query in Design view and add the **LastName field** from the Employees table to the last column of the design grid. Run, save, and close the query.

b. Use the query wizard to create a crosstab query based on the Profit query that shows total profit by LastName (row heading) and CategoryName (column heading). Name the query **Profit_Crosstab**.

c. Modify the query to display **CategoryName** as a row heading field and **LastName** as a column heading field. Run, save, and close the query.

Create a Find Unmatched Query

a. Create a query to find out if any of the products have no current order details. Add all of the fields from the Products table to the results.

b. Save the query as **Products With No Orders**. Run the query and close it.

c. Close the database. Close Access.

d. Submit based on your instructor's directions.

Advanced Forms and Reports

CHAPTER 15

Moving Beyond the Basics

Yuri Arcurs/Shutterstock

OBJECTIVES AFTER YOU READ THIS CHAPTER, YOU WILL BE ABLE TO:

1. Restrict edits in a form p. 754
2. Create a drop-down menu p. 756
3. Set the tab order p. 759

4. Use subforms p. 760
5. Use advanced controls p. 769
6. Use sections p. 773

CASE STUDY | Technical Services

Yellowstone County Technical Services is a small company that provides technical support for a number of businesses in Yellowstone County, Montana. As one of the company's supervisors, you have been tasked with updating the customer tracking database to expand the input and output capabilities of the system.

In your experience with the company, you have seen some of the common errors users make when performing data entry and have also seen what is effective and what is not effective in forms. In addition, you have seen which reports users utilize and have heard suggestions about changes they would like made.

Creating a database is difficult, but updating a database and making it more user-friendly can be the difference between a tool that is accepted and a tool that is rejected. As any good database administrator realizes, being proactive and helping users prevent errors is critical. In addition, finding ways to extract more information from the same amount of data is important as well. Being able to interpret and present the information in a database so management can use it can be what makes or breaks your career as a database administrator.

In your role as supervisor, you also want to lead your technicians by example, and implementing improvements in your database is a good start. After implementing the changes, you can use the database as a case study to train your technicians in effective database design.

Advanced Forms

For basic database solutions, a simple form created with the Form tool will handle most needs. However, at times you need to go beyond the basics. For example, you can create a form that enables users to look up information but not change it, thereby providing a measure of security. You do not have to worry about users accidentally changing data. You can change a field to a lookup field, finding values in another table or a list of values. However, there may be times where you do not need the lookup in the table but would like it in a form. This can be done through the use of a combo box. Another part of improving data entry is making a form easy to navigate. Sometimes when you tab through a form, you may not end up in the desired field. You can change the tab order in a form to make data entry more efficient. You can also create and manipulate subforms, which show related records from other tables. Part of your goal when administering a database is to make the database simple and powerful, and forms provide that functionality. You will use Design view to make most of the changes in this chapter.

Restricting Edits in a Form

One method of protecting data in a database is to restrict casual users from editing the data. Casual users may need access to the data to look up information such as a person's address or phone number or to review the details of an order. However, the people who need to look up information may be people you do not want adding, editing, and deleting records. When too many users make changes to the data, the data can become unreliable and difficult to maintain. If only a select group of users is allowed to enter and edit data, maintaining the integrity of the data is much easier.

Most databases have data entry forms. For example, a customer form might be created in a bank's database to enable customer information to be entered. If a mistake is made, data entry personnel can find the record with the mistake and fix the error. The form does not require permission or a password to make an edit. Perhaps other employees at the bank also need to look up information—for example, a phone number to contact a customer. The person making these calls will need to look up the phone number of a customer without making any changes to the data. When users need to look up information without making changes, it is best to create a copy of the original form and then restrict editing on the copy. A form that enables users to view but not change data is a ***read-only form***. Incorporating read-only forms in a database helps avoid accidental changes to data. You may ask why you would create a read-only form instead of simply creating a report. Remember that forms are preferred because they show one record at a time, and they enable searches.

In addition to setting the form so data cannot be changed, you as the designer have two other questions to answer. Do you want to allow users to delete records using this form? Do you want to allow users to add new records using this form? Even if a form has restricted editing, it still enables adding and deleting records. These options can be switched off as well.

Create a Read-Only Form

To create a read-only form, do the following:

STEP 1 »
1. Open the form in Layout view.
2. Click the Property Sheet in the Tools group on the DESIGN tab.
3. Select Form in the *Selection type* box at the top of the Property Sheet.
4. Click the Allow Edits property on the Data tab.
5. Change the Allow Edits property to No, as shown in Figure 15.1.
6. Change the Allow Additions and Allow Deletions properties to No (if desired).
7. Switch to Form view to test the form.

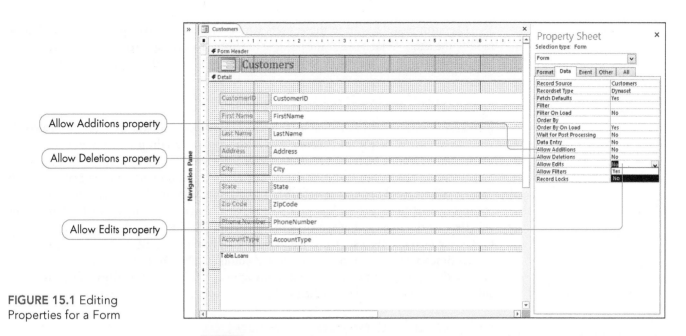

FIGURE 15.1 Editing Properties for a Form

It is suggested that you change the form title and name to indicate it is read-only. Otherwise, you can frustrate users who might open the form and wonder what they are doing wrong!

To test the changes to the form, switch to Form view, and then attempt to change the data in the first record. If you attempt to change the address, for example, nothing happens. In addition, if you changed the Allow Additions and Allow Deletions properties to No, you can see the results of this change when you attempt to click Delete in the Records group on the Home tab—Delete is no longer available. Normally, you add a record in a form by clicking the *New (blank) record* button in the navigation bar at the bottom of the form window. However, because the Allow Additions property is set to No, the option has been disabled. Figure 15.2 shows a read-only form. You will notice it is not obvious it is read-only. Editing the form title to indicate it is read-only will help.

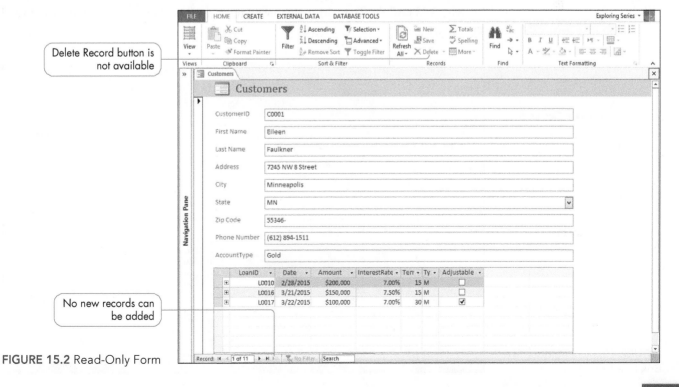

FIGURE 15.2 Read-Only Form

The form is still useful to those users who only need to look up information (but not modify the data). In fact, that is the point of the form. To look up a record, click in the Search box in the navigation bar and type some key words to identify the required record.

Creating a Drop-Down Menu

If you create a form based on a table with a lookup field, the lookup field becomes a combo box control on the new form. A *combo box control* provides a drop-down menu displaying a list of options from which the user can choose a single value. The combo box control forces a user to choose an item from the list if the Limit To List property on the Data tab of the Property Sheet is set to Yes (the default). If you do not want to restrict users to items on the options list, set the Limit To List property to No. To make the combo box field even more effective, set the Required property of the underlying field to Yes—the user will not be able to skip the field and the user will have to choose an item on the list.

At times a combo box control is created automatically. For example, if you base a form on an existing lookup field, the combo box appears without extra effort. If it is not done automatically, you may find situations where it is useful to have a combo box.

Convert a Text Box to a Combo Box

At times, a text box on a form should be converted to a combo box. This can happen when the data you are collecting may not appear to contain repeating data at first. As you enter transactions over time, you may realize that a field does have repeating data and that a combo box may be appropriate. The desire to make input easier for the user should be weighed against creating a drop-down menu that is too long. For example, the state field will sometimes be a combo box. Fifty states and the District of Columbia make up the United States, and you may prefer not to have a drop-down menu containing 51 items. However, if the customers that are entered in your database are located in only a subset of the 50 states, you may be able to include a subset of the states.

Before you convert a text box to a combo box, you should first create a new table and enter the values for the option list, much like you do for lookup fields. Then, do the following:

STEP 2 »

1. Open the form in Design view (or Layout view) and right-click the text box you want to convert.
2. From the shortcut menu, click the Change To option and select Combo Box, as shown in Figure 15.3.

The field now displays with an arrow on the right side of the text box. It does not yet do anything, however.

FIGURE 15.3 Changing a Text Box to a Combo Box

Customize a Converted Combo Box

Once you have converted a text box to a combo box, you still have changes to make to enable the options. For example, you likely want to ensure that users can only enter values appearing on the menu. Though optional, these enable you to help improve data entry. Figure 15.4 shows three properties you can set to customize a combo box, and Figure 15.5 shows how a combo box appears in form view. To set a source for a combo box, do the following:

1. Switch to Design view of the form.
2. Click the Property Sheet in the Tools group on the DESIGN tab.
3. Select a Row Source on the Data tab.
4. Switch to Form view to test the combo box.

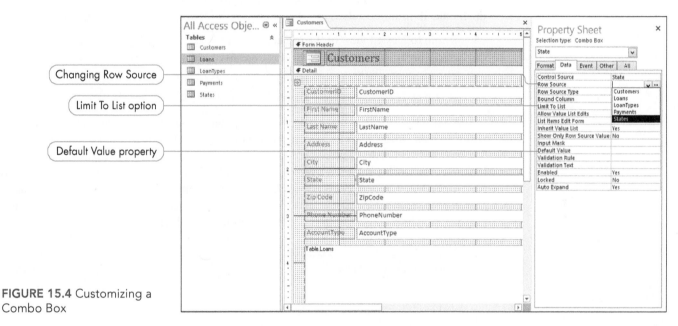

FIGURE 15.4 Customizing a Combo Box

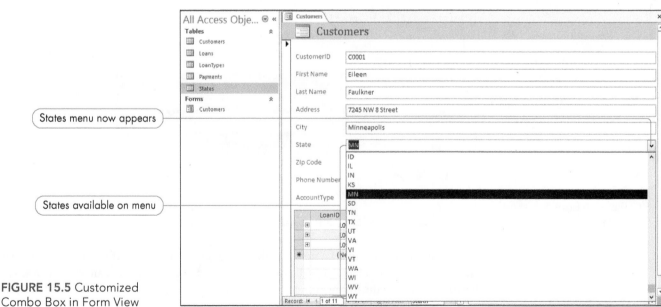

FIGURE 15.5 Customized Combo Box in Form View

TIP Display More Values for Combo Boxes

There are 16 items by default on a combo box menu. If your list contains more than 16 items, users will have to scroll to find the appropriate value. If you prefer to increase this number, switch to Layout or Design view, click the text box for your combo box field, and ensure that the Property Sheet is displayed. If not, on the Form Design Tools Design tab in the Tools group, click Property Sheet. Find the property named List Rows on the Format tab and change the number from 16 to a more appropriate number.

As described earlier, you may want to ensure your users only enter values that exist in the menu. To limit the values to the contents of the source table, do the following:

1. Switch to Design view of the form.
2. Click the Property Sheet in the Tools group on the DESIGN tab.
3. Change the Limit To List property to Yes on the Data tab.
4. Switch to Form view to test the combo box.

What if the available states have been restricted to the states that are represented by the customers, and a customer from a different state—one not on the list—takes out a loan? If you have set the Limit To List option, Access generates an error, as shown in Figure 15.6. Similar to lookup fields, storing values in a separate table makes it very easy to change the values allowed in a combo box if the values ever need changing. For example, you may have initially dealt with customers in Idaho, Montana, and Wyoming. If you ever need to add Oregon and Washington to the combo box, you can simply add new rows to the table storing the state names.

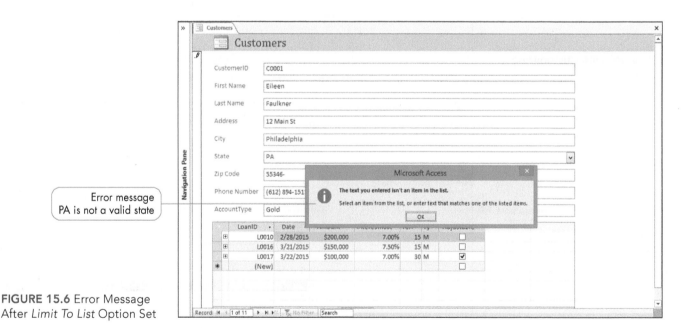

FIGURE 15.6 Error Message After *Limit To List* Option Set

You may also want to set a default value to appear on the form. If you have already set a value for a field on the table, it will appear in the form, but if not, you can set a default value on a form by doing the following:

1. Switch to Design view of the form.
2. Click the Property Sheet in the Tools group on the DESIGN tab.
3. Enter a Default Value on the Data tab.
4. Switch to Form view to test the combo box.

As a database designer, you have some freedom in the design choices you make. If you decide that a combo box with 50+ rows is too much for your form, you may instead just add data validation. You may allow the user to type what they want but require them to enter one of the valid state abbreviations. Your table's data validation will be much longer in this case, but you could set the Validation Rule to IN("AK","AL","AR","AZ" (and continue to "WY")) and give a descriptive Validation Text. Of course, in that case, users might have to go look up the abbreviation for a state (they might not remember, for example, that Maine is ME, not MA). These are simply two tools you have in your toolbox, and it is a matter of style and situation when you need to choose one.

Setting the Tab Order

When entering data into a table, users press Tab to advance from one field to the next. Data cannot be entered out of order unless you click a field with the mouse instead of pressing Tab. The *tab order* is the sequential advancing in a form from one field or control to the next when you press Tab. When working with forms, the designer must remember to check the tab order before delivering the form to the end users; when a form is created, the initial tab order is not necessarily the order that is most useful to the user.

Set the Tab Order

STEP 3» Sometimes, Access sets the tab order in a way that makes little sense. You may enter data in the first field, hit Tab, and end up in the bottom text box. This is something that frustrates users but is easily fixed. The first step you should take if this occurs is to have Access automatically set the tab order. To automatically set the tab order in a form, do the following:

1. Switch to Design view.
2. Click Tab Order in the Tools group on the DESIGN tab. This displays the Tab Order dialog box showing all the controls in each section of the form, as shown in Figure 15.7.
3. Click Detail to display the tab order for the fields.
4. Click Auto Order if the form has a Stacked layout and you want to enter data from top to bottom.
5. Click OK to accept the changes.

Tab order for fields

Auto Order

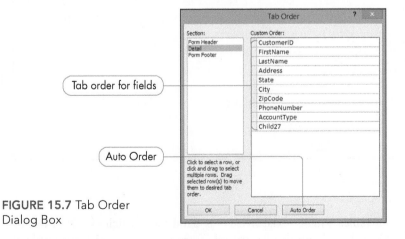

FIGURE 15.7 Tab Order Dialog Box

Access does its best to set the tab order properly, but at times it does not work as you might require. For example, Auto Order does not work well if you have a two-column form. If you need to create a customized tab order, do the following:

1. Switch to Design view.
2. Click Tab Order in the Tools group on the DESIGN tab.
3. Click Detail to display the tab order for the fields.
4. Click the field selector to the left of a field name, release the mouse, and then drag the field to the desired position in the tab order. For example, if two fields are next to each other but in the wrong order, click the second field, release the mouse, and then drag the second field on top of the first one.
5. Click OK to accept the changes.

Remove a Tab Stop

At times, you want the tab order to skip a field completely. For example, if you add a calculated field to the form, you would not want to stop at this field. Calculated fields do not require data entry. Another example occurs when you have an AutoNumber field as the primary key. Your user does not need to add data there, so it should not have a tab stop.

To remove the Tab Stop property of a field, do the following:

1. Switch to Layout view (or Design view).
2. Click the field you want to remove.
3. Click Property Sheet in the Tools group on the DESIGN tab stop.
4. Click the Other tab in the Property Sheet.
5. Locate the Tab Stop property and change the property setting to No, as shown in Figure 15.8.
6. Return to Form view and test the change by pressing Tab to advance through the fields on the form. The field you modified should be skipped when you press Tab.

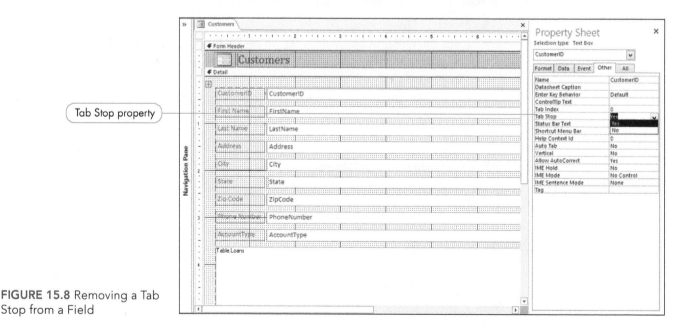

FIGURE 15.8 Removing a Tab Stop from a Field

Using Subforms

Relationships between tables usually exist in Access databases, which can lead to more complicated forms. How should you display records from related tables? Commonly, the main form displays records from a related table using a *subform*. Subforms are generally laid out in a tabular fashion and are used when a relationship exists between two tables, as shown in Figure 15.9.

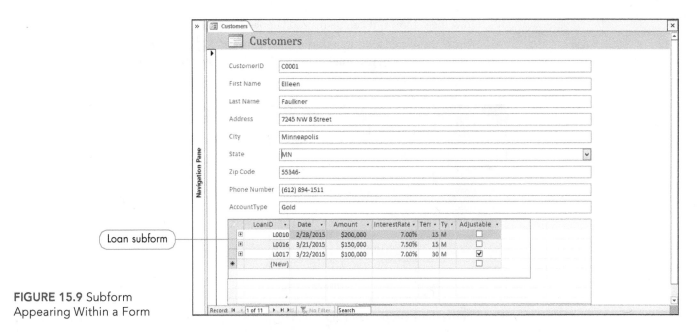

FIGURE 15.9 Subform Appearing Within a Form

Loan subform

Subforms are created by the Form tool automatically. They also can be created by the Form Wizard. If a relationship exists and you choose fields from two different tables using the Form Wizard, it automatically assumes you want a form with a subform. You can also manually add a subform to any form using the Subform/Subreport tool. To manually add a subform using the Subform/Subreport tool, do the following, assuming a relationship exists between the two tables:

STEP 4 ▸▸ 1. Open the form in Design view.
2. Click the Subform/Subreport tool in the Controls group on the DESIGN tab, as shown in Figure 15.10. Depending on your screen resolution, you may need to click More.

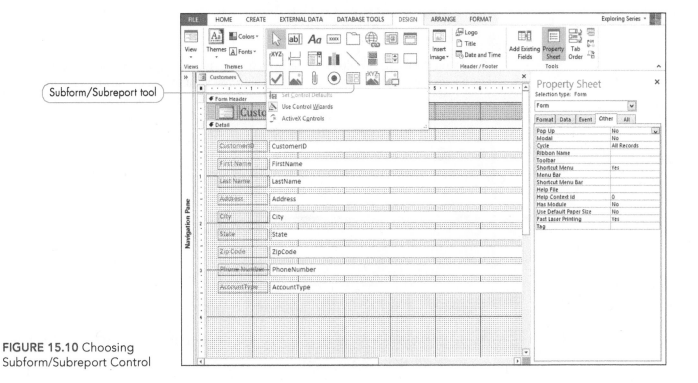

Subform/Subreport tool

FIGURE 15.10 Choosing Subform/Subreport Control

3. Draw the subform. It can be resized later as needed.

4. Choose the source for the subform. You can use an existing form or view data in a table or query. Assuming you want to use a table, click that option and click Next, as shown in Figure 15.11.

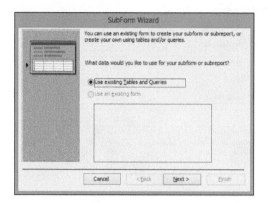

FIGURE 15.11 SubForm Wizard: Choosing Source

5. Choose the appropriate fields from the table (or query) source, as shown in Figure 15.12. Click Next.

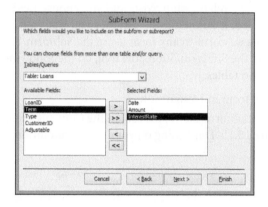

FIGURE 15.12 SubForm Wizard: Choosing Fields

6. Assuming a relationship exists between the two tables, you will be shown a connection between the tables. Choose the relationship you want to use, as shown in Figure 15.13. Click Next.

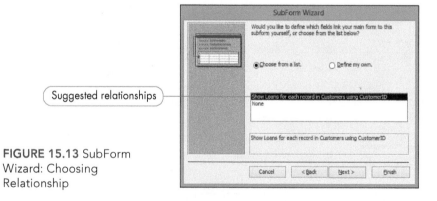

Suggested relationships

FIGURE 15.13 SubForm Wizard: Choosing Relationship

7. Accept the default name or create your own name for the subform. Click Finish. Your results will resemble Figure 15.14.

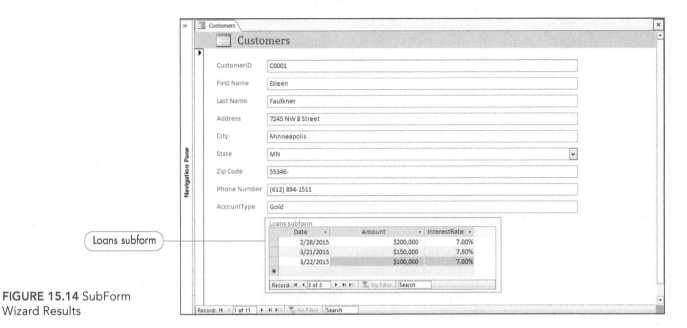

FIGURE 15.14 SubForm
Wizard Results

You can change the size of the subform or the size of the fields in the subform as necessary. It will display in tabular fashion. The changes are easier to make in Layout view, as you can see the data as it appears in the subform.

*Quick
Concepts*

1. Why create a read-only copy of a form? *p. 754*

2. What does a combo box control do? *p. 756*

3. What is one reason the Auto Order option of the tab order may not work? *p. 759*

4. What does a subform do? *p. 760*

Hands-On Exercises

1 Advanced Forms

You have decided to create a lookup form for customer data. You will also create a form with a drop-down menu to enable users to help record customer call satisfaction. You will repair an old form that has problems with tab ordering. You will also create a form with a subform.

Skills covered: Restrict Edits in a Form • Create a Drop-Down Menu • Set the Tab Order • Use Subforms

STEP 1 » RESTRICT EDITS IN A FORM

You have decided to use the Form tool to create a Customers form. This form will enable you to look up customer information. You will make this read-only so you do not accidentally make errors when looking up information. Refer to Figure 15.15 as you complete Step 1.

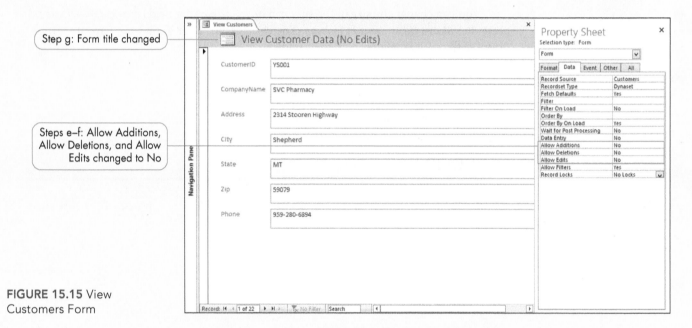

FIGURE 15.15 View Customers Form

a. Open *a07h1Yellowstone* and save it as **a07h1Yellowstone_LastFirst**.

b. Select the **Customers table** in the Navigation Pane. Click the **CREATE tab** and click **Form** in the Forms group.

   Access creates a new form based on the Customers table. The form opens in Layout view, ready to edit.

c. Click anywhere in the subform at the bottom of the window, click the border of the subform, and then press **Delete** to delete the subform.

> **TROUBLESHOOTING**: If you are prompted to confirm deleting of records, press No and ensure you have clicked the border before pressing Delete.

d. Click **Property Sheet** on the DESIGN tab in the Tools group if it is not already displayed.

   The Property Sheet displays on the right side of your screen.

e. Click the **Data tab**, if necessary. Click in the **Allow Edits box**, which currently displays *Yes*, and click the drop-down menu at the right. Change the value to **No**.

f. Repeat step e to change the **Allow Additions** and **Allow Deletions property values** to **No**. Close the Property Sheet.

g. Change the title of the form to **View Customer Data (No Edits)**. Compare your results to Figure 15.15.

h. Switch to Form view.

i. Attempt to type in the **CompanyName box**.

   You should not be able to change the field value.

j. Attempt to add and delete a record.

   You should not be able to add or delete a record.

k. Click **Save** in the Quick Access Toolbar and save the form as **View Customers**. Close the form.

STEP 2 ≫ CREATE A DROP-DOWN MENU

You will use the Form tool to create an Access form to help manage customer call data. This form will enable you to record customer data. You will implement this using a drop-down menu. Refer to Figure 15.16 as you complete Step 2.

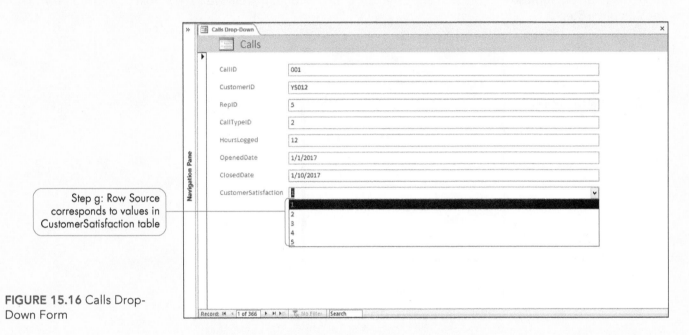

Step g: Row Source corresponds to values in CustomerSatisfaction table

FIGURE 15.16 Calls Drop-Down Form

a. Select the **Calls table** in the Navigation Pane. Click the **CREATE tab** and click **Form** in the Forms group.

   Access creates a new form based on the Calls table.

b. Right-click the **CustomerSatisfaction text box**, click the **Change To option**, and then select **Combo Box**.

   The CustomerSatisfaction text box changes to a combo box with an arrow on the right side of the box.

c. Click **Property Sheet** on the DESIGN tab in the Tools group if it is not already displayed.

d. Click the **Row Source property** on the Data tab of the Property Sheet, click the arrow, and then select **Satisfaction Results**.

e. Click the **Limit To List property** and change the value to **Yes**.

f. Switch to Form view.

g. Click in the **CustomerSatisfaction field**. Notice an arrow now appears on the right of the box. Click the arrow and notice values of 1, 2, 3, 4, and 5 appear, as shown in Figure 15.16.

h. Type the value **6** for the **CustomerSatisfaction field** and press **Tab**.

Access will display an error message that the text you entered is not a value on the list.

> **TROUBLESHOOTING**: If Access does permit the value to be entered, ensure you set the Limit To List property to Yes.

i. Click **OK**. Change the value for the first record's CustomerSatisfaction field to **2** and press **Tab**.

The value will save properly.

j. Save the form as **Calls Drop-Down**, and close the form.

STEP 3 ≫ SET THE TAB ORDER

The users of the current Edit Customers report have reported problems with the tab order. You will fix the tab order. You will also fix an old form so that the tabs appear in the correct order and remove a tab stop. Refer to Figure 15.17 as you complete Step 3.

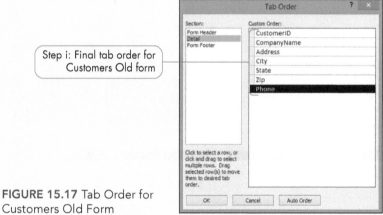

Step i: Final tab order for Customers Old form

FIGURE 15.17 Tab Order for Customers Old Form

a. Open the Edit Customers form in Form view.

b. Click the **CustomerID box**. Press **Tab**.

When you press Tab, Access brings you to the State field.

c. Press **Tab** five more times, noticing where the cursor moves each time.

The fields are not displayed in a logical order.

d. Switch to Design view and click **Tab Order** in the Tools group on the DESIGN tab.

e. Click **Detail** and click **Auto Order**. Click **OK**.

Because this is a Stacked Layout form, Access changes the tab order so it moves down one field at a time.

f. Switch to Form view. Press **Tab** six times and verify that the tab order progresses in a logical order. Save and close the form.

g. Open the Customers Old form in Form view. Press **Tab**.

The form moves to the Phone field. You will switch the tab order so Phone appears last.

h. Switch to Design view. Click **Tab Order** in the Tools group on the DESIGN tab. Click **Detail** and click **Auto Order**.

Notice *Phone* is now at the beginning of the tab order, which is not the logical location for it.

i. Click the **Row Selector** to the left of the Phone field. Drag the **Phone field** beneath the Zip field. Your tab order should match Figure 15.17. Click **OK**.

j. Click the **CustomerID field**. Display the Property Sheet.

k. Click the **Other tab** in the Property Sheet. Locate the Tab Stop property and change the property setting to **No**.

You will no longer be able to access the CustomerID field by pressing Tab.

l. Switch to Form view. Tab through the fields, ensuring the fields display in the correct order and that pressing Tab does not bring you to the CustomerID field.

m. Save and close the form.

STEP 4 ≫ USE SUBFORMS

The Edit Customers form does not display the related call information for each customer. You will modify it so the subform containing the information appears. Refer to Figure 15.18 as you complete Step 4.

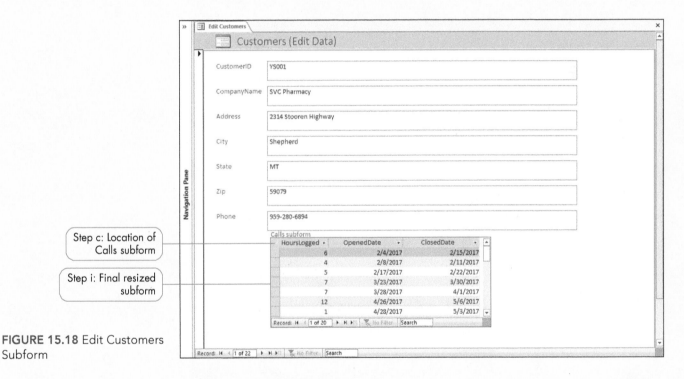

Step c: Location of Calls subform

Step i: Final resized subform

FIGURE 15.18 Edit Customers Subform

a. Open the Edit Customers form in Design view.

b. Click the **Subform/Subreport tool** in the Controls group on the DESIGN tab. If it is not visible, you may need to scroll or click the **More button** at the bottom-right of the Controls box.

c. Draw a box in the location shown in Figure 15.18. The size does not matter, as it will be resized later.

The Subform Wizard dialog box displays.

d. Select **Use existing Tables and Queries** and click **Next**.

e. Click the **Tables/Queries arrow** and select **Table: Calls**. Double-click the **HoursLogged, OpenedDate**, and **ClosedDate fields**. Click **Next**.

f. Click **Next** to accept the default relationship.

g. Accept the default Calls subform name and click **Finish**.

h. Switch to Layout view. Notice the Calls subform appears at the bottom of the screen.

i. Resize the subform and the fields to be approximately the size shown in Figure 15.18.

j. Save and close the form.

k. Keep the database open if you plan to continue with Hands-On Exercise 2. If not, close the database and exit Access.

Controls and Sections

As you work with tools to create and modify forms and reports, you will often need to switch between the three views in Access—Form or Report view, Layout view, and Design view. You use Layout view to perform most changes, but Design view gives you, as a designer, a higher level of control.

To lay out forms and reports, to display fields, and to display field labels, you use basic controls such as text boxes and labels. However, other types of controls exist. You can add formatting controls as well as controls that perform calculations using the same functions found in the Expression Builder.

In this section, you will examine the different form and report sections. As you learn how to create forms and reports, placing fields and labels in the correct section will become a habit. You may have to use trial and error at first, switching between different views until the form or report is working correctly.

The overlap between forms and reports will be easy to see. The same functionality applies to both, so the skills you use in forms can be applied to reports and vice versa.

Using Advanced Controls

Whether you are dealing with a form or report, some features are common to both. A number of common controls are available. When you use the form and report wizards to create basic objects, the resulting forms and reports contain a number of controls that you did not add yourself.

Both forms and reports have a text box control, which displays the data found in record source (often, a table). Although the term *text box* may imply it only displays Short Text values, it can display numeric data, currency, and dates, depending on the field's data type.

The label control is a word or phrase to describe the data associated with a text box. For a field in a form or report, the label control defaults to the caption you set for a field. If you have not set a caption for a field, the label will default to the field name.

Forms and reports also have layout controls. The layout control keeps the fields together in an orderly fashion, enabling you to move fields without having to worry about lining fields up.

Identify Control Types

Both label controls and text box controls are known as **bound controls**. A bound control is a control that is connected to a field in a table or query. Outside of computers, the term *bound* can refer to two objects tied together, so you can see where this term comes from. A bound control changes each time a new record is displayed, as the value is dynamic.

Forms and reports also contain **unbound controls**. An unbound control is a control not tied to a specific field. Generally, this refers to decorative elements, such as the title of the report. An unbound control stays the same as you switch between records. Some other examples of unbound controls are lines, pictures, and other non-data-related elements.

 TIP **Remove the Tab Stop from Unbound Controls**

In most cases, you will want to remove the tab stop from an unbound control. Unbound controls do not require data entry, so there is no reason for the cursor to stop on them.

A *calculated control* contains an expression that generates a calculated result. Calculated controls can also be applied to forms or reports and include aggregate functions such as Sum, Min, Max, and Average. These are basic calculated controls. More advanced calculated controls can contain a combination of functions, constants, and field names from the record source. Figure 15.19 shows each of these types of controls.

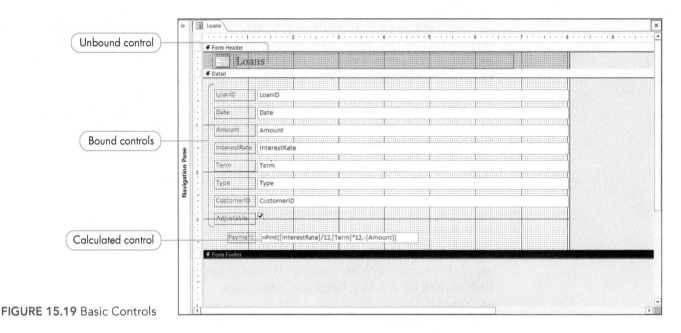

FIGURE 15.19 Basic Controls

Despite having the name *control* in the name, bound, unbound, and calculated controls are not found on the Controls group on the Design tab, which is available in Layout or Design view. Each of these is a category of controls. Recall a text box control is an example of a bound control because it is connected to a field.

Add Emphasis to a Form or Report

When using the Form or Report tools to create an automatic form or report, you have a number of default controls. The title, the form/report icon, and each field are examples. In addition, the form or report has a layout control.

If you want to add emphasis to your form or report, the Line control and Rectangle control are two options. The Line control will allow you to insert a line into your form or report, and the Rectangle will allow you to add a rectangle. After inserting these into an object, you can modify the shape to have a different line color, line thickness, and line type (such as dashed or dotted), and in the case of rectangles you can change the fill color. You will only find these options in Design view; they are not available in Layout view. To add a line or rectangle shape to a form or report, do the following:

STEP 1 1. Switch to Design view.

STEP 2 2. Click the DESIGN tab.

3. In the Controls group, select the Line or Rectangle control, as shown in Figure 15.20. You may need to click More or scroll to see this, depending on your screen configuration.

4. In the form or report, drag the mouse from the desired start point to the desired end point.

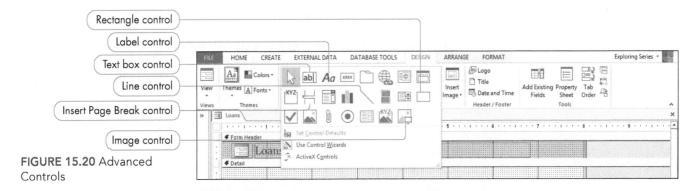

FIGURE 15.20 Advanced Controls

Labels pointing to the controls (top to bottom):
- Rectangle control
- Label control
- Text box control
- Line control
- Insert Page Break control
- Image control

Your line or rectangle will appear. Once you have added a line or rectangle, you can format it by doing the following:

1. Switch to Design view.
2. Click the line or rectangle you wish to format.
3. Click the FORMAT tab.
4. In the Control Formatting group, choose the Shape Outline menu to change the color, thickness, and line type for the rectangle or line. Choose Shape Fill to add a fill color to a rectangle.

Add Text and Images to a Form or Report

Both forms and reports have the option to include text and images.

In addition to the existing label controls, you may wish to add some sort of explanatory text to a form or report. Instead of (or in addition to) a validation rule, you can add text providing guidance for your users. As this text is not tied to a specific field and is unchanging, it is considered a label. To add text to a form or report, do the following:

1. Switch to Design view.
2. Click the DESIGN tab.
3. In the Controls group, click the Label control, as shown in Figure 15.20. You may need to click More or scroll to see this, depending on your screen configuration.
4. Drag the mouse from the desired start point to the desired end point.
5. Type the text you would like to appear in the label.

Images can be useful especially when dealing with corporate forms and reports. Companies commonly use the same logo and colors on official publications. When creating a form or report, you can insert an image file containing the company logo or any other image. Often, the image is inserted in the Form Header or Report Header, so it displays once when printed or viewed on the screen. The Form Header and Report Header will be discussed further in this chapter. To add an image to a form or report, do the following:

1. Switch to Design view.
2. Click the DESIGN tab.
3. In the Controls group, click the Image control, as shown in Figure 15.20. You may need to click More or scroll to see this, depending on your screen configuration.
4. Drag the mouse from the desired start point to the desired end point. The Insert Picture dialog box appears.
5. Browse to the location containing the image and click Open.
6. Resize the image control as necessary.

Add a Calculated Control

Forms and reports based on a query can display calculated fields like any other field. However, some forms and reports are based on a table rather than a query. In this case, you can add a calculated field using a text box. The Expression Builder and its functions can be used similarly to how they are used in queries.

To add a calculated control to a form or report using the Expression Builder, do the following:

1. Switch to Design view.
2. Click the DESIGN tab.
3. In the Controls group, click the Text Box control, as shown in Figure 15.20. You may need to click More or scroll to see this, depending on your screen configuration.
4. Drag the mouse from the desired start point to the desired end point. The word *Unbound* appears in the text box. Access also displays a label by default. You can choose to delete or modify the label as necessary.
5. Display the Property Sheet.
6. Click the Data tab on the Property Sheet and click the Ellipsis (…) found next to the Control Source property to open the Expression Builder.
7. Create the desired expression.

Note that if you are comfortable with functions, you do not have to use the Expression Builder. You could simply type the formula into the text box, preceded by an equal sign. For example, you could type =Date() to show the current date.

If you want to format the results of the function (for example, change the number of decimal places for a numeric field), do the following:

1. Switch to Design view.
2. Click the text box you wish to format.
3. Click Property Sheet on the DESIGN tab in the Tools group.
4. To change the format, click the Format property on the Property Sheet's Format tab. To change decimal places for a numeric field, click the Decimal Places property.

Fix Layout Errors After Adding Controls

When dragging a new text box label to a report, you may find it puts the label in the same row as the data rows. If this happens, you can click Tabular Layout in the Table group of the Arrange tab while both the label and text box controls are selected.

Add a Page Break Control

Pagination can be important for forms and reports. Instead of being unsure where a page will break when printed, you can add a page break at a certain location. To add a page break to a form or report, do the following:

1. Open the report in Design view.
2. On the DESIGN tab, click the Insert Page Break control, as shown in Figure 15.20. You may need to click More or scroll to see this, depending on your screen configuration.
3. Click the mouse in the section of the form or report where you want the page break. When you click the Insert Page Break control, the mouse pointer changes to a cross-hair with a small report (even in forms) icon.
4. After you click the form or report, a series of six dots appears on the left margin.

To remove a page break, click the six dots and press Delete.

TIP | Changing Default Behavior of Controls

Controls have a number of default behaviors. For example, when inserting a text box, a label always appears unless you change the property. You can change default properties for any control by viewing a form or report in Design view, clicking the control, and instead of clicking to place the control, display the Property Sheet. Other common changes may be the size of the control; border appearance, thickness, and color; and text and background color, depending on the type of control. If you find yourself having to change properties to the same thing often, change the default behavior.

Using Sections

A *section* is a part of a form or report that can be manipulated separately from other parts of a form or report. Basic forms have three sections, and basic reports contain five sections. Sections are visible in Design view. Each section can be collapsed or expanded as needed.

Identify the Default Sections

STEP 3 ≫

STEP 4 ≫

One section common to forms and reports is the *Form Header* (for forms) or the *Report Header* (for reports). The *Form Header* section and the *Report Header* section are similar in that they are headers that display one time at the top of each form or report. This section contains the title by default. Column headings (labels) are also located in this section for reports as well as some types of forms. When a form or report is printed, the Form Header or Report Header displays only once immediately before the first record appearing on a printout.

Similarly, the *Form Footer* and *Report Footer* sections are footers that display one time at the bottom of the form or report. This section is left blank by default for forms and may contain some sort of aggregate function (such as Count) for a report. When a form or report is printed the Form Header or Form Footer appears once, in this case after the final record, regardless of the number of pages.

Another default section is the *Page Header* section. The Page Header is a header that appears once at the top of each page in a form or report. This is more commonly used for reports, as they are designed for printing. Page Headers are switched off by default for forms but can be switched on as necessary.

The *Page Footer* is a footer that appears once at the bottom of each page in a form or report. As with the Page Header, the Page Footer is much more common on reports. The Page Footer is also switched off by default for forms.

The distinction between the Form/Report and Page headers and footers can be confusing at first. If you had a 10-page form or report, each page would display a Page Header, while only the first page would display the Form/Report Header. Likewise, the same report would display the Page Footer on each page while displaying the Form/Report Footer once after the final record.

The *Detail section* displays the records in the record source. The *Detail* section displays in between the headers and footers sections in both forms and reports. Figure 15.21 shows the various form sections in Design view, and Figure 15.22 shows them as they appear when printed. Figure 15.23 shows the report sections in Design view, and Figure 15.24 shows them as they appear when printed.

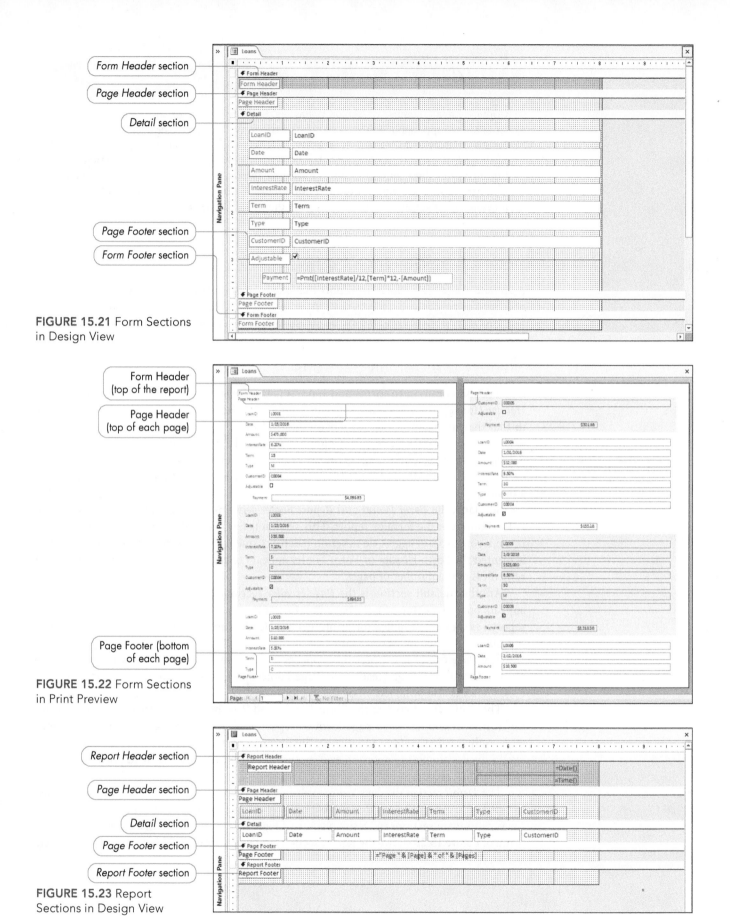

FIGURE 15.21 Form Sections in Design View

FIGURE 15.22 Form Sections in Print Preview

FIGURE 15.23 Report Sections in Design View

Labels in Figure 15.21:
- Form Header section
- Page Header section
- Detail section
- Page Footer section
- Form Footer section

Labels in Figure 15.22:
- Form Header (top of the report)
- Page Header (top of each page)
- Page Footer (bottom of each page)

Labels in Figure 15.23:
- Report Header section
- Page Header section
- Detail section
- Page Footer section
- Report Footer section

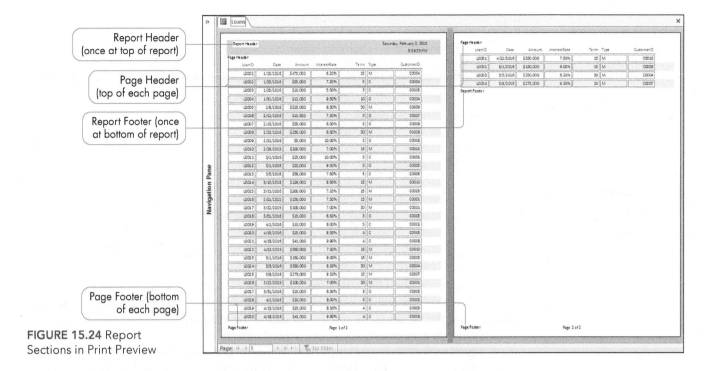

Report Header (once at top of report)

Page Header (top of each page)

Report Footer (once at bottom of report)

Page Footer (bottom of each page)

FIGURE 15.24 Report Sections in Print Preview

Show, Hide, and Resize Sections

Forms and reports display the *Detail* and *Form/Report Header* and *Footer* sections by default. Reports also include the Page Header/Footer by default. Right-clicking a blank area of the form or report enables you to switch on or off sections. Note that when you switch a section off, it deletes all controls in the section. The header and footer sections are tied together; if you remove the Form or Report Header, the Form or Report Footer also disappears. See Figure 15.25 for an illustration in Form Design view and Figure 15.26 for Report Design view.

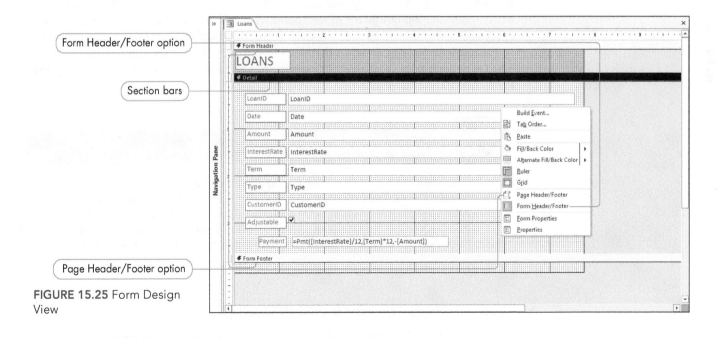

Form Header/Footer option

Section bars

Page Header/Footer option

FIGURE 15.25 Form Design View

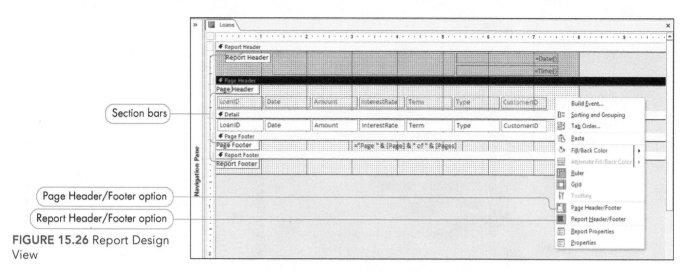

FIGURE 15.26 Report Design View

Section bars

Page Header/Footer option

Report Header/Footer option

In reports, although the *Detail* section cannot be removed, you can hide it from Print Preview, Layout view, and Design view. This is helpful when a report output, for example, contains data with totals at the end. For example, you may display the sum of the values in a field. If you only need to output the totals of each category and not the values of every record, this is a good option. To show Details only, click Hide Details in the Grouping & Totals group on the Design tab. Click Hide Details again to redisplay hidden details. Note that this option is not available for forms.

Within a form or report, you may want to change the height or width of portions of a section. The width is a global property. You cannot change the width of one section without changing it for the entire object. However, you can change the height of each section independently. In Figures 15.25 and 15.26, each gray *section bar* marks the top boundary of a section. Section bars appear gray in these figures, but they can appear in different colors based on your Office setup. You can expand or collapse the space between report sections by moving your mouse over the section bar and dragging to the desired location. The top bar denotes the top boundary of the header. The bottom bar displays the top boundary of the footer. The grid-like area under the bars shows the space allotted to that section. If you decide that the allotted space for a particular section is not needed, you can collapse that section fully so that the section bars are touching. The section remains in the report's design but will not take up any room on the Print Preview or the printed page.

 **Footer Confusion**

In Design view, the *Form Footer* or *Report Footer* section is located below the *Page Footer* section. However, in Print Preview, the Form Footer or Report Footer is positioned above the Page Footer. This may cause some confusion at first; however, the *Form Footer* or *Report Footer* section will be needed to produce grand totals at the end of a report. The Form Footer or Report Footer will only appear one time—at the end of a form or report.

Add a Group Header/Footer to Reports

The Report Wizard and the Group & Sort button are used to add grouping to a report. In addition to the five main sections previously listed, you can also add a custom *Group Header* and *Group Footer* section to a report. Because you cannot add grouping to forms, you will not have the option to add a Group Header or Footer to a form. To add a Group Header, do the following:

1. Switch to Layout view.
2. Click the Group & Sort button on the Grouping & Totals group of the DESIGN tab.
3. Click *Add a group* in the *Group, Sort, and Total* pane at the bottom of the screen.
4. Select the field to group by.
5. Note that even though you have done most work in this chapter in Design view, doing the grouping in Layout view saves you a few steps.

Once you have added grouping, a **Group Header** section appears just above the *Detail* section in Design view, along with the name of the field by which you are grouping. This section appears once each time the grouping field value changes, and the group header prints with the new value. For example, in a Loan report grouped by Type, the group header prints once for each Type, with the loans of that type following. If you select the Type field as a custom group, the section is named Type Header, as shown in Figure 15.27.

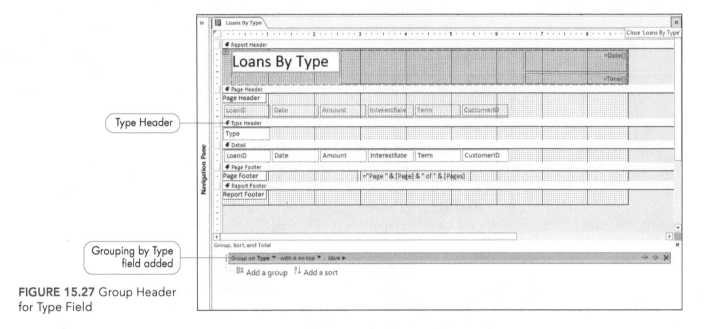

FIGURE 15.27 Group Header for Type Field

A **Group Footer** section does not show by default. It appears just below the *Detail* section in Design view, but only when you select this option in the *Group, Sort, and Total* pane. As with the Group Header, the Group Footer appears once for each distinct value in the grouping field. To display the Group Footer, do the following:

1. Switch to Layout or Design view.
2. Click the More arrow on the *Group, Sort, and Total* pane
3. Switch the option that currently reads *without a footer section* to *with a footer section*, as shown in Figure 15.28.

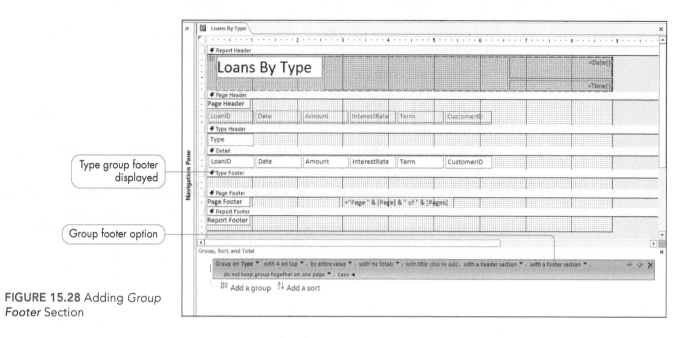

FIGURE 15.28 Adding *Group Footer* Section

Labels pointing to the figure:
- Type group footer displayed
- Group footer option

The group footer is useful for totaling the data at the end of each group. If a group of physicians is part of a major practice, it would be good to know how many physicians are assigned to each specialization. The group footer could display the count of physicians for each specialization.

Add Totals to a Group Footer/Report Footer

Often, reports require totals at the group level and/or at the grand total level. For example, the Physicians Report might contain a count of physicians in each Specialization group and again at the end of the report.

To add totals to a report, do the following:

1. If you have not done so, create the group section required for the totals.
2. Switch to Design view.
3. Click the More arrow on the *Group, Sort, and Total* pane
4. Switch the option that currently reads *without a footer section* to *with a footer section*, as shown in Figure 15.29.

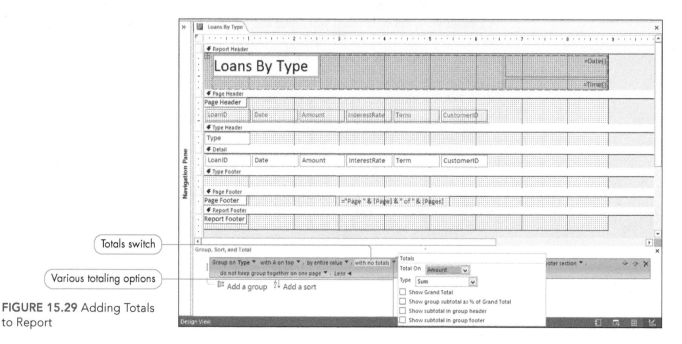

FIGURE 15.29 Adding Totals to Report

Labels pointing to the figure:
- Totals switch
- Various totaling options

5. Select the appropriate total option. Figure 15.30 shows the count (Count Records) for the LoanID field added to the Type Footer and Report Footer.

Count of loans in Type Footer

Overall count displayed in Report Footer

Show Grand Total setting

Show subtotal in group footer setting

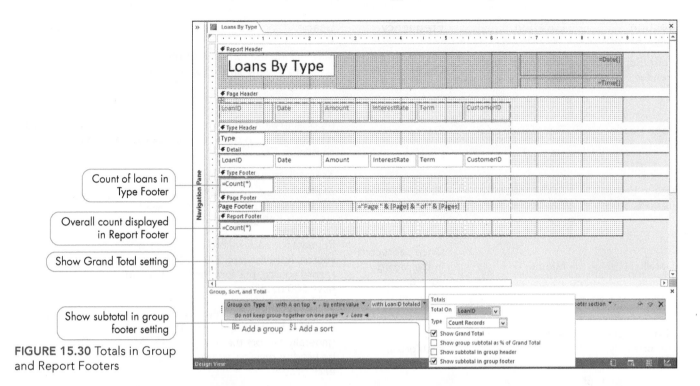

FIGURE 15.30 Totals in Group and Report Footers

TIP | Add a Page Break to a Group Footer

A page break is commonly used in a group footer. Doing so causes each group to print on a separate page. For example, if you had a report grouped by customer, the report would print each customer's data on a separate page (rather than continuing with the next customer on the same page). This type of report is useful when the information is distributed to each customer. In the case that a customer's information takes up more than one page, the page break is inserted after each customer's information.

Section	Location	Frequency	Usage	Default
Form/Report Header	Top of the form/ report	Once	May include the form/report title, the company's name and logo, and the run date and time.	On
Page Header	Top of each page	Once per page	Generally contains the column headings in reports. In a multipage report, the labels repeat at the top of each page to provide continuity.	On (reports) Off (forms)
Group Header (reports only)	At the start of each new group	At the start of each group	Available in reports only. Prints the value of each unique instance for a grouped field. A report grouped by state would print up to 50 unique state names.	Off
Detail	Middle	Once per record in the record source	Repeats for each record in the record source. If there were 500 records in the record source, the form or report would have 500 detail listings.	On
Group Footer (reports only)	At the end of each group	At the end of each group	Available in reports only. Repeats for each record in the record source. This section generally mirrors the group header. May be used to provide aggregate statistics for each group.	Off
Page Footer	Bottom of each page	Once per page	Generally used to print page numbers.	On (reports) Off (forms)
Form/Report Footer	End of the form/ report	Once	Often used to print grand totals or other aggregate information for the records.	On

Quick Concepts ✓

1. What is the difference between controls in forms and controls in reports? *p. 769*
2. What is the difference between a bound control and an unbound control? *p. 769*
3. What is the purpose of a calculated control? *p. 770*
4. List the five default sections of a report. *p. 773*
5. What do the Group Header and Footer do? *pp. 776–777*

Hands-On Exercises

Watch the Video
for this Hands-
On Exercise!

MyITLab®
HOE2 Training

2 Controls and Sections

You have decided to modify reports to add calculations, and to modify the different header and footer sections of forms and reports to improve the print and on-screen readability.

Skills covered: Use Advanced Controls in Forms • Use Advanced Controls in Reports • Use Sections in Forms • Use Sections in Reports

STEP 1 ❯❯ USE ADVANCED CONTROLS IN FORMS

You will be making changes to an existing form and a calculated control to determine if a call is Open or Closed. Refer to Figure 15.31 as you complete Step 1.

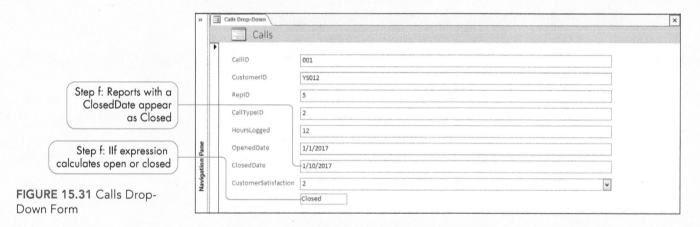

Step f: Reports with a ClosedDate appear as Closed

Step f: IIf expression calculates open or closed

FIGURE 15.31 Calls Drop-Down Form

a. Open *a07h1Yellowstone_LastFirst* if you closed it at the end of Hands-On Exercise 1. Save the database as **a07h2Yellowstone_LastFirst**, changing *h1* to *h2*.

b. Open the Calls Drop-Down form in Design view.

c. Drag the end of the *Detail* section (appearing right above the Form Footer) to about 4" on the vertical toolbar.

d. Click **Text Box** in the Controls group on the DESIGN tab. Click beneath the last control in the form to insert the control. It should be placed approximately where it appears in Figure 15.31.

> **TROUBLESHOOTING:** If you are unable to see the Text Box control, click the More button in the Controls group and select the Text Box control.

e. Display the Property Sheet. Click the **Data tab** on the Property Sheet, click in the **Control Source box**, and then click the **Ellipsis (...)** found next to the Control Source property.

f. Type **IIf(IsNull([ClosedDate]),"Open","Closed")** in the **Expression Builder**. Click **OK**.

This expression displays Open when the ClosedDate is null (in other words, when no value exists in the ClosedDate field) and Closed otherwise.

g. Delete the label for the new control. The control has a default name of *Text* followed by a two-digit number.

h. Switch to Form view. Ensure the first few records display *Closed*. Click the **Last Record Navigation button** and ensure the last record in the table has a value of *Open*.

i. Save and close the form.

STEP 2 ≫ USE ADVANCED CONTROLS IN REPORTS

You will make changes to an existing report to display the number of days each call has been open. Refer to Figure 15.32 as you complete Step 2.

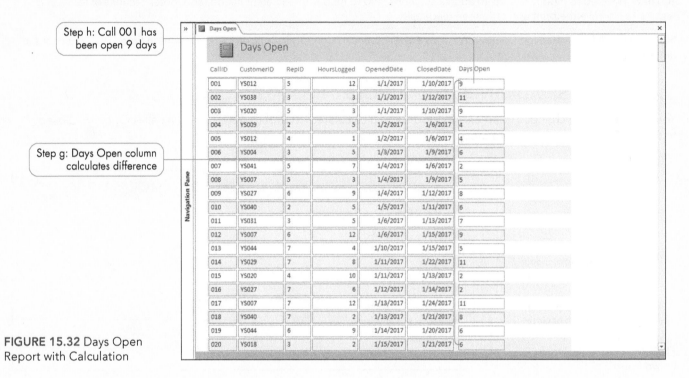

Step h: Call 001 has been open 9 days

Step g: Days Open column calculates difference

FIGURE 15.32 Days Open Report with Calculation

a. Open the Days Open report in Design view.

b. Click the **Text Box control** in the Controls group on the DESIGN tab. Click to the right of the ClosedDate text box in the *Detail* section of the report to add a new field.

TROUBLESHOOTING: If you are unable to see the Text Box control, click the More button in the Controls group and select the Text Box control.

---

c. Click the **Tabular button** in the Table group on the ARRANGE tab.

The new field lines up after the final column in the report.

d. Click the **label control** for the new column. Delete the existing text and type **Days Open**.

e. Click in the **text box control** for the new column. Display the Property Sheet.

f. Click the **Data tab** on the Property Sheet and click **Control Source**. Click the **Ellipses (. . .)** to launch the Expression Builder.

g. Type **=[ClosedDate]-[OpenedDate]** in the **Expression box**. Click **OK**.

h. Switch to Report view. Verify the calculation correctly displays the number of days each call was open, as shown in Figure 15.32.

i. Save and close the report.

You will adjust an existing form by adding a logo to the form header and adding a page header. Refer to Figure 15.33 as you complete Step 3.

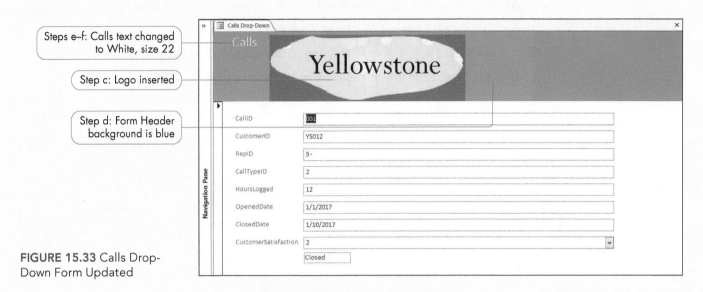

Steps e–f: Calls text changed to White, size 22

Step c: Logo inserted

Step d: Form Header background is blue

FIGURE 15.33 Calls Drop-Down Form Updated

a. Open the Calls Drop-Down form in Design view.

b. Click the **form logo** in the *Form Header* section and press **Delete**.

   The form logo disappears.

c. Click the **Image control** in the Controls group on the DESIGN tab. Click to the right of the word *Calls* in the Form Header. Browse to the location of your data files and select **a07h2Logo**.

   A logo for Yellowstone appears in the report header.

d. Click the grey background of the Form Header. Click the **Shape Fill arrow** in the Control Formatting group on the FORMAT tab. Select **Blue, Accent 1** (first row, fifth column).

e. Click the **Calls label**. Click the **Font Color arrow** in the Font group on the FORMAT tab. Select **White, Background 1**. Recall you can see the names for each color by pointing to a color and waiting for the ScreenTip to appear.

f. Click the **Font Size arrow** in the Font group on the FORMAT tab. Change the size to **22**.

g. Switch to Form view and compare your form to Figure 15.33.

h. Switch to Design view. Right-click a blank area and select **Page Header/Footer**.

   A *Page Header* section appears above the *Detail* section, and a *Page Footer* section appears below the *Detail* section.

i. Click the **Label control** in the Controls group on the DESIGN tab. Click the left side of the Page Footer. Type **Created by First Last**, replacing *First* with your first name and *Last* with your last name.

j. Switch to Form view.

   The page footer is not displayed because it will only appear when printed.

k. Click the **FILE tab** and click **Print**. Click **Print Preview**.

   The footer should appear on each page. You will notice the form is too wide to fit on one page left to right. When printed, this might lead to extra pages.

l. Switch to Design view. Click the **CallID text box** and change the width to **5.5"** on the top ruler.

All other controls resize as well.

m. Point to the right edge of the *Detail* section and drag it to about 7.5" on the top ruler.

n. Click the **FILE tab** and click **Print**. Click **Print Preview**.

As a printed page in Portrait is 8.5" wide, this will now fit on one page wide.

o. Click **Close Print Preview** and save and close the form.

STEP 4 ≫ USE SECTIONS IN REPORTS

You will create a new report based on the Calls table and use the Group Headers and Footers to summarize the data. Refer to Figure 15.34 as you complete Step 4.

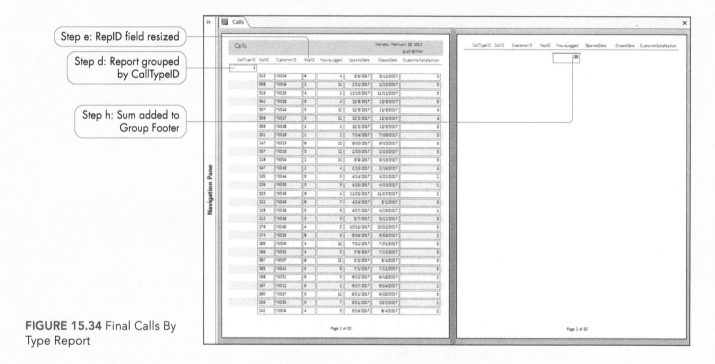

Step e: RepID field resized

Step d: Report grouped by CallTypeID

Step h: Sum added to Group Footer

FIGURE 15.34 Final Calls By Type Report

a. Click the **Calls table**. Click the **Report tool** on the Reports group of the CREATE tab.

b. Delete the report icon from the Report Header.

c. Click **Group & Sort** in the Grouping & Totals group on the DESIGN tab if it is not already displayed.

The *Group, Sort, and Total* pane appears at the bottom of the report.

d. Click **Add a group** in the *Group, Sort and Total* pane and select **CallTypeID**.

The report will be grouped by the type of call.

e. Resize the RepID field width so it takes up only as much room as necessary.

The report should fit on one page, left to right.

f. Switch to Design view.

Notice a CallTypeID Header appears between the *Page Header* and *Detail* sections.

g. Click the **More arrow** in the *Group, Sort, and Total* pane. Click the **without a footer section arrow** and switch to **with a footer section**.

A CallTypeID footer appears between the *Detail* and *Page Footer* sections.

h. Click the **HoursLogged text box**. Click **Totals** in the Grouping & Totals group on the DESIGN tab and select **Sum**.

A Sum function appears in both the CallTypeID Footer and the Report Footer.

i. Resize the CallTypeID Footer and Report Footer to be about 1" tall.

j. Resize the text boxes for the new sum fields to be about double the current height.

k. Click the **Insert Page Break control** in the Controls group on the DESIGN tab. Click the bottom of the CallTypeID Footer.

Six small dots appear on the left of the CallTypeID Footer.

l. Display the report in Print Preview.

TROUBLESHOOTING: If you get an error message stating *The section width is greater than the page width, and there are no items in the additional space, so some pages may be blank.*, try making the rows slightly less tall.

All calls with a CallTypeID appear on page 1, with a total of 188 hours appearing on page 2. Scroll to page 4 and notice a total of 208 hours for all calls with a CallTypeID of 2. Your results should resemble Figure 15.34.

m. Save the report as **Calls By Type** and close the report.

n. Exit Access. Submit based on your instructor's directions.

Chapter Objectives Review

After reading this chapter, you have accomplished the following objectives:

1. **Restricting edits in a form.**
   - Create a read-only form: Read-only forms enable users to view but not change data to help prevent erroneous data entry.

2. **Creating a drop-down menu.**
   - Convert a text box to a combo box: A combo box control provides a drop-down menu that displays a list of options from which the user can choose a single value.
   - Customize a converted combo box: Information can be looked up in a table or, less commonly, added manually. You can restrict to only the provided values using the Limit To List option.

3. **Setting the tab order.**
   - Set the tab order: Tab enables users to advance from one field to the next in a form. The tab order is the sequential advancing in a form from one field or control to the next when you press Tab. Changing the tab order may become useful in some instances.
   - Remove a tab stop: Tab stops can be removed from any field. Oftentimes, they are removed from fields that do not require data entry.

4. **Using subforms.**
   - Form can display records from a related table using a subform.
   - Subforms are generally laid out in a tabular fashion and are used when a relationship exists between two tables.

5. **Using advanced controls.**
   - Identify control types: Label controls and text box controls are known as bound controls. A bound control is a control that is connected to a field in a table or query. An unbound control is a control not tied to a specific field, often decorative elements such as titles, lines, pictures, and other decorative objects.
   - Add emphasis to a form or report: The Line and Rectangle controls are among the options to add emphasis.
   - Add text and images to a form or report: Text can be added using a Label control, and images can be added using the Image control.

- Add a calculated control: A calculated control is placed inside a text box that contains an expression that generates a calculated result and can contain functions, constants, or field names from the record source. Calculated controls can use the Expression Builder to help create complex expressions.
- Fix layout errors after adding controls: When adding controls, you may need to add them to a layout to maintain a consistent layout.
- Add a page break control: You can specify exactly where to add a page break using the Page Break control.

6. **Using sections.**
   - Identify the default sections: A section is a part of a form or report that can be manipulated separately from other parts of the form or report. They are viewable in Design view. The *Form Header* section and the *Report Header* section are headers that display one time at the top of each form or report. The Form Header and Report Header appear only once on printouts immediately before the first record appearing on a printout. *Form Footer* and *Report Footer* sections are footers that display one time at the bottom of the form or report. When a form or report is printed the Form Header and Form Footer appear once regardless of the number of pages. The Page Header is a header that appears once at the top of each page in a form or report. The Page Footer is a footer that appears once at the bottom of each page in a form or report. The *Detail* section displays the records in the record source.
   - Show, hide, and resize sections: You can show any missing section by right-clicking and selecting the missing section. Most sections can be hidden.
   - Add a Group Header/Footer to reports: The *Group Header* section appears just above the *Detail* section in Design view, along with the name of the field by which you are grouping. The *Group Header* section appears once each time the grouping field value changes. The *Group Footer* section appears just below the *Detail* section in Design view. Group Headers and Footers are only available in reports.
   - Add totals to a Group Footer/Report Footer: Group Footers (hidden by default) are commonly used for totals.

Key Terms Matching

Match the key terms with their definitions. Write the key term letter by the appropriate numbered definition.

a. Bound control
b. Calculated control
c. Combo box control
d. *Detail* section
e. Form Footer
f. Form Header
g. Group Footer
h. Group Header
i. Page Footer

j. Page Header
k. Read-only form
l. Report Footer
m. Report Header
n. Section
o. Section bar
p. Subform
q. Tab order
r. Unbound control

1. _____ A form that enables users to view but not change data. **p. 754**

2. _____ Provides a drop-down menu displaying a list of options from which the user can choose a single value. **p. 756**

3. _____ The sequential advancing in a form from one field or control to the next when you press Tab. **p. 759**

4. _____ Records displayed that are related to records in a main form. **p. 760**

5. _____ A control that is connected to a field in a table or query. **p. 769**

6. _____ A control not tied to a specific field. **p. 769**

7. _____ A control containing an expression that generates a calculated result. **p. 770**

8. _____ Part of a form or report that can be manipulated separately from other parts of the form or report. **p. 773**

9. _____ A header that displays once at the top of each form. **p. 773**

10. _____ A header that displays once at the top of each report. **p. 773**

11. _____ A footer that displays one time at the bottom of a form. **p. 773**

12. _____ A footer that displays one time at the bottom of a report. **p. 773**

13. _____ A header that appears once at the top of each page in a form or report. **p. 773**

14. _____ A footer that appears once at the bottom of each page in a form or report. **p. 773**

15. _____ Displays the records in the record source. **p. 773**

16. _____ Marks the top boundary of a section in a form or report. **p. 776**

17. _____ Appears just above the *Detail* section in Design view, along with the name of the field by which you are grouping. Appears once each time the grouping field value changes. **p. 777**

18. _____ Appears just below the *Detail* section in Design view. Appears once each time the grouping field value changes. **p. 777**

Multiple Choice

1. A form that is read-only enables you to:

   (a) Change formatting.
   (b) Change data.
   (c) View records.
   (d) All of the above

2. A combo box enables you to:

   (a) Add a drop-down menu.
   (b) Perform calculations.
   (c) Add headers to a form.
   (d) Create a read-only form.

3. Which of the following statements about tab order is false?

   (a) Tab order can be automatically assigned.
   (b) Fields can have their tab stop removed.
   (c) Tab order can be arranged in any order you want.
   (d) None of the above

4. Which of the following would most likely not be a subform?

   (a) A list of patients for a doctor
   (b) A list of orders for each customer
   (c) A list of employees for a location
   (d) A list of birth mothers for a child

5. A control connected to a field in a table or query is a(n):

   (a) Bound control.
   (b) Calculated control.
   (c) Rectangle control.
   (d) Unbound control.

6. A control containing =*Date()* is most likely to be a(n):

   (a) Bound control.
   (b) Calculated control.
   (c) Rectangle control.
   (d) Unbound control.

7. Which statement is false about controls?

   (a) The *Detail* section displays the values of records.
   (b) A label control is used for text, such as titles.
   (c) A calculated field is created with a text box control.
   (d) Forms cannot display calculated controls.

8. Which of the following prints once per report?

   (a) Form Header
   (b) Group Header
   (c) Page Header
   (d) Report Header

9. Which of the following prints on every page of a form?

   (a) Form Header
   (b) Group Header
   (c) Page Header
   (d) Report Header

10. Which of these is not available in an Access form?

    (a) *Detail* section
    (b) *Group Header* section
    (c) *Form Header* section
    (d) *Page Footer* section

Practice Exercises

1 La Vida Mocha

FROM SCRATCH

You are helping La Vida Mocha, a small coffee supply store, migrate to Access. You will help them add data validation and create two forms, one for data entry and one for viewing data. This exercise follows the same set of skills as used in Hands-On Exercises 1 and 2 in the chapter. Refer to Figure 15.35 as you complete this exercise.

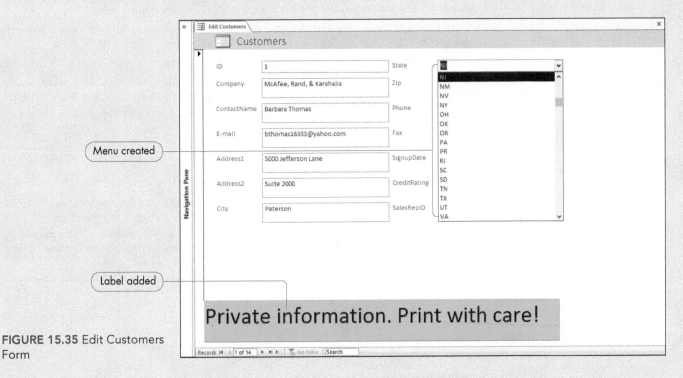

FIGURE 15.35 Edit Customers Form

a. Open Access and create a new database named **a07p1Coffee_LastFirst**.

b. Import the text file *a07p1States* into the database. Name the field **StateName** and choose the StateName field as the primary key. Save the table as **State**. Accept all other default properties.

c. Import the text file *a07p1Customers* into the database. Ensure you check the **First Row Contains Field Names option**, accept default field names, and choose **ID** when asked to select a primary key. Name the table **Customers**.

d. Click the **Customers table** in the Navigation pane. Click **Form** in the Forms group on the CREATE tab. Save the form as **Edit Customers**.

e. Right-click the **State text box**, select **Change To**, and then select **Combo Box**. Click the **Property Sheet button** in the Tools group on the DESIGN tab.

f. Change the **Row Source property** to **State**. Change the **Limit To List property** to **Yes**. Switch to Form view.

g. Change the City for the first customer to **Paterson**, the State to **NJ**, and the Zip to **07505**. You may notice the tab order does not work correctly for this form.

h. Switch to Design view. Click **Tab Order** in the Tools group on the DESIGN tab. Click the **Row Selector** to the left of the State field and drag it below the City field. Click **OK**.

i. Drag the **section bar** below the Form Footer down to approximately 1" on the vertical ruler.

j. Click the **Label control** in the Controls group on the DESIGN tab. Click in the top-left corner of the *Form Footer* section. Type the text **Private information. Print with care!** in the label.

k. Click the border of the label you created in step j to select the entire control. Click the **Font Size menu** in the Font group on the FORMAT tab. Change the font size for the Label control to **36**. Resize the control so all information is displayed on one line.

l. Click the **Font Color menu** in the Font group on the FORMAT tab. Select the **Black, Text 1 color** in the first row.

m. Click the **Background Color menu** in the Font group on the FORMAT tab. Select the **Gold, Accent 4 color** in the first row. Switch to Form view and compare your form to Figure 15.35.

n. Save and close the form. Create a copy of the form named **View Customers**. Open View Customers in Design view.

o. Change the title at the top of the form to **Customers (View Only)**.

p. Display the Property Sheet. Ensure the drop-down at the top of the Property Sheet displays *Form*. Click the **Data tab** and change the options **Allow Additions**, **Allow Deletions**, and **Allow Edits** to **No** to create a read-only form. Switch to Form view and ensure you cannot change data.

q. Save and close the form. Exit Access. Submit the database based on your instructor's directions.

2 Northwind Traders

You are a technical supervisor at Northwind Traders. The technician who handles most Access tasks just went on paternity leave, and he was unable to address user changes before going on leave. You will create a form and report based on user requests. This exercise follows the same set of skills as used in Hands-On Exercises 1 and 2 in the chapter. Refer to Figure 15.36 as you complete this exercise.

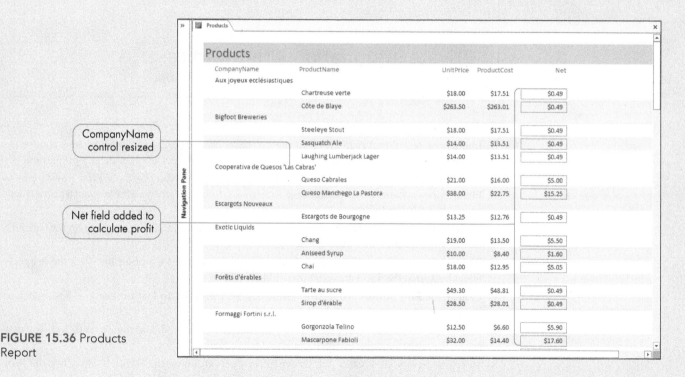

FIGURE 15.36 Products Report

a. Open *a07p2Traders*. Save the database as **a07p2Traders_LastFirst**.

b. Open the Products by Category form in Design view.

c. Use the section bar to increase the size of the *Detail* section to about 5" vertically.

d. Click the **Subform/Subreport tool** in the Controls group on the DESIGN tab. Click below the top-left corner of the Description label.

e. Answer the Subform Wizard as follows:

- Select **Use existing Tables and Queries** and click **Next**.
- Select **Table:Products** from the Tables/Queries list. Double-click the **ProductName**, **QuantityPerUnit, UnitPrice, UnitsInStock,** and **UnitsOnOrder fields**. Click **Next**.
- Select the default relationship (show Products for each record in Categories using CategoryID). Click **Next**.
- Accept the default name of *Products subform*. Click **Finish**.

f. Switch to Layout view. Resize the columns in the subform so all fields are displayed.

g. Save and close the form.

h. Open the Products report in Layout view. Click **Group & Sort** in the Grouping & Totals group on the DESIGN tab. Click **Add a group** in the *Group, Sort and Total* pane. Select **CompanyName**. Notice the CompanyName field is not wide enough to display all values.

i. Switch to Design view. Change the width of the CompanyName field (displayed in the CompanyName Header) to **4"** on the horizontal ruler.

j. Click the **Text Box control** in the Controls group on the DESIGN tab. Click to the right of the ProductCost box.

k. Click **Tabular** in the Table group on the ARRANGE tab.

l. Click in the label for the control created in step j. Change the text in the label from the existing text (which should be *Text* followed by two numbers) to **Net**.

m. Click the text box for the new field and type **=UnitPrice-ProductCost** in the box.

n. Display the Property Sheet by clicking the **Property Sheet button** in the Tools group on the DESIGN tab.

o. Click the **Format button** on the Property Sheet. Change the format to **Currency** and change the **Decimal Places property** to **2**.

p. Switch to Report view. Compare your report to Figure 15.36.

q. Save and close the report.

r. Close the database. Exit Access.

s. Submit based on your instructor's directions.

Mid-Level Exercises

1 Red Cliffs City Hotels

ANALYSIS CASE

You are the general manager of a large hotel chain. You track revenue by categories: hotel rooms, conference rooms, and weddings. You need to create a form that includes a drop-down menu for the state and the company logo in the header, uses the company colors, and has a correct tab order. You also plan on modifying a report so it displays the number of years that each customer has been a member.

a. Open *a07m1Rewards*. Save the database as **a07m1Rewards_LastFirst**.

b. Select the **Members table** and create a form using the Form tool. Save the form as **Maintain Members**.

c. Switch to Design view. Change the State text box to a combo box.

d. Change the Row Source to **States**.

e. Delete the form logo and the label control (containing the word *Members*) from the *Form Header* section.

f. Insert an Image control in the top-left corner of the *Form Header* section. Insert the **a07m1Logo** file.

DISCOVER

g. Change the background color of the *Detail* section to the orange color found in the first row (*Orange, Accent 6*). Note: Select all the labels by drawing a box around them in Design view. Change the font color of the labels to **Black, Text 1**. Change the border width of the labels to **4 pt** and the border color to **Blue, Accent 1**.

h. Switch to Form view. Ensure the form appears correctly. Verify the tab order works as expected by pressing **Tab** to visit each field. Save and close the form.

i. Open the Members By State report in Design view.

j. Add a formula in the **Time as Member box** to determine the number of years they have been a member. Use **#12/31/2017#** as the current date (recall dates must be surrounded by # signs), subtract the MemberSince field, and divide the result by **365**.

k. Change the format of the formula you created in step k to display as **Standard format** with 1 decimal place.

l. Add grouping by the State field. Ensure you remove the State label from the Page Header.

m. Switch to Report view. Ensure the values displayed make sense. For example, member Melissa Remaklus been a member since 11/8/2006, so she has been a member for slightly more than 11 years (assuming it is 12/31/2017).

n. Save and close the report.

o. Open the *a07m1Analysis* document in Word and save as **a07m1Analysis_LastFirst**. Use the database objects you created to answer the questions. Save and close the document.

p. Close the database. Exit Access. Submit based on your instructor's directions.

2 Replacement Parts

You are working as a stockperson in the warehouse for Replacement Parts. You have been given an internship in the information technology department. You have been tasked with making modifications to the company's database. As you are hoping to move from being a stockperson to being a member of the technology staff, you want to impress and go above and beyond what has been asked of you.

a. Open *a07m2Replace*. Save the database as **a07m2Replace_LastFirst**.

b. Create a new form based on the Employees table. Save the form as **Employees Lookup**.

c. Delete the subform. Change the form to be read-only, ensuring users cannot add, delete, or edit records.

d. Change the title in the Form Header to **Employees (Lookup Only)**. Save and close the form.

e. Open the Customer Orders report in Design view.

f. Insert the **a07m2Logo image** in the Report Header to the right of the Customer Orders text.

g. Display the Group Footer. Display the sum of the Qty field in the Group Footer. Add a label that displays **Total Qty Ordered** to the left of the Qty sum.

h. Add a new Text Box control after the Price field. Click **Tabular** in the Table group on the ARRANGE tab.

i. Change the label for the new control to **Line Total**. Add a formula in the text box to multiply the Qty field by the Price field.

j. Change the format of the Line Total to **Currency**.

k. Use the Line control to add a horizontal line at the bottom of the *Group Footer* section.

l. Switch to Report view and ensure the Total Qty Ordered values appear correctly. Switch to Design view.

DISCOVER  **m.** Add a Sparse Dots border to the Total Qty Ordered text boxes. Add a Special Effect of **Shadowed**. Save and close the report.

n. Exit Access. Submit the database based on your instructor's directions.

3 Ramos Hospital

COLLABORATION CASE

You are working for a local hospital in the information technology department. The founder, Waynet Ramos, has asked your team to help her put together some forms and reports. As she is very busy, she is hoping your team can independently develop some reports and work together to implement and revise them. After discussions with her, you realize she is asking for grouped reports.

a. Waynet needs a report based on which doctors are assigned to each patient, a report showing all medications and who they are prescribed to, and a report showing each patient with the medications they are on. Each group member will create one report.

b. Open Access and open *a07m3Ramos* individually. Save the file as **a07m3Ramos_LastFirst**. Each of you will create your report in an individual database.

c. Create a report using the Report Wizard based on the appropriate tables. Add grouping as necessary.

d. Save the report as **LastFirst**, replacing *Last* and *First* with your last and first names.

e. Make the report as attractive and useful as possible. You may want to perform tasks such as adding subtotals to the group or report footer, changing sorting, removing or add a layout control, changing formatting options, and changing the background color. Modify the report, save the changes, and then exit Access.

f. Meet as a group. Open *a07m3Ramos* and save the file as **a07m3Ramos_GroupName**.

g. Import the report from each of your databases.

Your *a07m3Ramos_GroupName* file will now have one report for each student.

h. Examine the reports each of you created.

i. Work with your group to improve the reports as necessary. Ensure that you take a critical eye to what your group members came up with and help them improve their report.

j. Save the changes and close all reports. Ensure each student has a copy of the final *a07m3Ramos_GroupName* database.

k. Exit Access and submit both the *a07m3Ramos_GroupName* and *a07m3Ramos_LastFirst* databases based on your instructor's directions.

Beyond the Classroom

Create a Tabbed Form

RESEARCH CASE

Cindy Livesey has a Web site at LivingRichWithCoupons.com where she posts coupon deals. She also has a coupon database that she maintains in Access, which she uses to keep track of her own stockpile. Cindy has contacted you, as one of the users of her Web site, to assist her in organizing the way she inputs coupons. Open the *a07b2Coupons* database and save it as **a07b2Coupons_LastFirst**.

1. Research tabbed forms in Access help or on the Internet. You will create a form based on the Products table, with a tabbed form below. The tabbed form will have two tabs. One tab should display the contents of the related Coupon table as a subform, and the second tab should display the Stockpile Information table. Save the form as **Coupon Reference**.

2. Cindy would like a field on the Stockpile Information tab to display *Yes* when it is time to restock and *No* when it is not. You can accomplish this by inserting a text box field and using the IIf function, displaying *Yes* when the NumberInStockpile is less than the RestockNumber field.

Close the database and close Access. Submit based on your instructor's directions.

Products Database

DISASTER RECOVERY

A new hire for your company is performing data entry for company products. Her system crashed, and the information technology department was able to restore the database from an old backup. She has asked you for help in fixing the database. She has noticed a few problems with the Products Ordered form:

1. The form's tab order does not work properly.

2. The Total On-Hand Value at the top of the page is used to display a value and no longer does. It used to display with two decimal places and no dollar sign. In addition, a lot of extra space exists at the top of the screen between the title and data.

3. The form no longer displays the current date and time at the top right of each page when printed.

4. The subform field widths are too small.

Open *a07b3Food* and save it as **a07b3Food_LastFirst**. Repair the errors above and save and close the database. Submit based on your instructor's directions.

Health Care Privacy

SOFT SKILLS CASE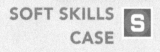

The Woodland Park Hospital is working on a database system to keep track of patients, illnesses, and the doctor assigned to treat the patient. As the technology lead on this project, the group evaluating the database would like your thoughts on how to implement forms and reports. The evaluating committee will be looking at the HIPAA Protected Health Information (PHI) regulation when deciding whether your solution is acceptable. Create forms and reports as specified below and examine the HIPAA PHI regulations. In addition, consider what information you think should be available for each type of user. Open *a07b4Medications* and save it as **a07b4Medications_LastFirst**. Create forms and reports to meet the following specifications. Choose only the fields that you think each group needs based on your research.

1. Doctors need a report showing patient information. Save the report as **Doctor Patient List** and ensure the report title is *Doctor Patient List* as well.

2. Nurses need a report showing medications, doses, and room numbers for each patient. Save the report as **Medications By Room** and change the report title to **Medications by Room**.

3. Front-desk personnel want to enter new patients using a form. Save the form as **Intake**.

4. The hospital needs to provide statistics about how many people are hospitalized with each type of illness to various agencies. Save the report as **Illness Statistics** and change the report title to **Illness Statistics** as well.

Exit Access. Submit the database based on your instructor's directions.

Capstone Exercise

The Human Resources department has asked you to assist them in updating the database they have been using. They need to create a form that can be used to find information but not change information. They have an existing form that they would like to enhance, and they need to be able to present supervisors with a list of employees who report to them. You will assist them in these tasks.

Database File Setup

You will save a copy of the original database and open the database to complete this capstone exercise.

a. Open *a07c1Prices*.

b. Save the database as **a07c1Prices_LastFirst**.

Restrict Edits in a Form

You will create a form to view employees. Use the Form tool to create the form, and then switch the form to be read-only.

a. Select the Employees table and use the Form tool to create a new form.

b. Change the title to **View Employees**.

c. Delete the Orders subform.

d. Change the **Allow Edits**, **Allow Additions**, and **Allow Deletions** settings to **No**.

e. View the form and data in Form view.

f. Save the form as **View Employees** and close the form.

Create a Drop-Down Menu and Set Tab Order

You will modify an existing form to implement a drop-down menu and fix the tab order.

a. Create a new table named **Countries**. Rename the default ID field to **Country** and change the data type to **Short Text**. Enter two records, **UK** and **USA**. Close the table.

b. Open the Update Employees form in Design view.

c. Change the Country field to a combo box.

d. Set the Row Source to **Countries** and the Limit To List property to **Yes**.

e. Fix the tab order so the Postal Code field comes before the Country field. Save and close the form.

Use Controls and Sections

You have been asked to add some privacy information to the bottom of the View Employees form and make some design changes. You have also been asked to create a report for managers that shows the name of all employees who work for them and calculates the number of years the employees have been employed at the company.

a. Open the View Employees form in Design view. Add a new label control in the left-side of the Form Footer that displays the text **Personnel information is considered private and printouts should be shredded after use**.

b. Change the font color to **Black, Text 1** and bold the text.

c. Save and close the form.

d. Create a new report based on the Employees table using the Report Wizard. Select the **FirstName**, **LastName**, **HireDate**, and **HomePhone fields**. Select all other default options.

e. Switch to Layout view. Add grouping by the ReportsTo field.

f. Switch to Design view. Display the Group Footer. Display the count of the First Name field in the Report Footer.

g. Add an Insert Page Break control at the bottom of the ReportsTo footer.

h. Resize the Home Phone field so the right side lines up with the 6" on the horizontal ruler.

i. Add a new Text Box control to the right of the Home Phone box. Use the Tabular button in the Table group on the ARRANGE tab to place it correctly.

j. Change the label for the field to **Years Employed**.

k. Add a formula in the text box to calculate the number of years the employee has been employed, assuming the current date is #12/31/2017#. Format the field as **Standard** with 1 decimal place.

l. Close and save the report. Close the database. Exit Access.

m. Submit based on your instructor's directions.

Get Connected

CHAPTER 16

Exchanging Data Between Access and Other Applications

OBJECTIVES AFTER YOU READ THIS CHAPTER, YOU WILL BE ABLE TO:

1. Create a Hyperlink field p. 798
2. Add an Attachment field p. 800
3. Add attachment controls to forms and reports p. 803
4. Export data to Excel p. 813
5. Export data to Word p. 817
6. Export data to a PDF or XPS document p. 820

7. Export objects to another Access database p. 823
8. Link to an Access table p. 834
9. Link to an Excel spreadsheet p. 837
10. Import an Excel spreadsheet p. 840
11. Import a text file p. 843

CASE STUDY | Property Management Data Exchange

The Blackwood Maintenance Service (BMS) is a property management company located in Pineville, North Carolina. The owners would like to attract new customers by expanding the services they offer. Many of the properties that are maintained by BMS belong to residents' associations.

Your task is to contact the board members of each association and ask them if you can send information about the new services. You will also ask permission to send the homeowners a flyer by regular mail.

After contacting each association, you send the association manager a list of the new services that BMS can offer the homeowners. You also need to create a list of homeowners who BMS will contact by mail. You can prepare the information in a variety of ways, so you need to ask each association its preferred format. Information will also be sent to BMS in a variety of formats, and you will need to incorporate the new data into the database.

Connecting Access to External Files

In many cases, it is necessary or desirable to connect to data that exists apart from an Access database. Access provides several ways that you can access data, Web sites, or files from within your database. Access supports a *hyperlink* data type that enables you to quickly link to any file on your computer or to any Web page on the Internet. The data you enter as a hyperlink can be a path to any file on your computer, the location of a Web page on an intranet, an e-mail address, or a URL. A *uniform resource locator (URL)* is the location of a Web site or Web page on the Internet. When you click a hyperlink field value while in Datasheet view, Access launches the program required to display the file or Web page.

If you have a database that contains a Customers table, you can add a hyperlink field to store the Web site address of each customer. When you need information about the customer—the address, phone number, or contact information—you can quickly access the customer Web site by clicking the hyperlink. If the hyperlink is an e-mail address, Access launches a new e-mail window and automatically adds the customer's e-mail address into the To field. You can also link to an Excel spreadsheet that contains a list of the most recent invoices for the customer.

Access also offers you the option of attaching files to a record in a database through an attachment field. An attachment field enables you to attach multiple files of different types. Rather than links that direct you outside of your database, attachments are stored within the database file itself. No limit exists as to the number of files you can attach. For customers, you could attach a photo of the president or CEO, or a photo of a key contact that you work with. You can also attach other document formats, such as Word documents, including contracts or specifications for a product, or scanned documents that are in PDF format.

Users can easily interact with these documents by double-clicking on the appropriate attachment field. A dialog box appears with options to add, remove, open, or save a file. Choose the appropriate file, and then choose the action you want to take.

In this section, you will create a hyperlink field to store Web site addresses. In addition, you will learn how to attach photos and documents to records. Finally, you will learn how to attach files and use an attachment control in forms and reports.

Creating a Hyperlink Field

STEP 1 ≫ If you were working in a Customers table, you could add a Hyperlink field in Design view of the table to store the customers' Web sites. Figure 16.1 shows the hyperlink data type selection for the field name CustomerWebsite. After you add the hyperlink field, save the changes and switch to Datasheet view, where you can add the URLs, as shown in Figure 16.2.

Add a Hyperlink Field in Design View

To add a Hyperlink field in Access, do the following:

1. Open the table in Design view and add the new field name to the table.
2. Select Hyperlink from the Data Type list.
3. Save the changes and switch to Datasheet view.
4. Add the data values to the new hyperlink field.
5. Click a hyperlink value and Access launches the appropriate program, such as a Web browser or Excel, and enables you to interact with the file.
6. If you make any changes to the file, save the changes within the host application. For example, if you launch an Excel spreadsheet from within Access, you can make changes to the spreadsheet and then save your changes in Excel.

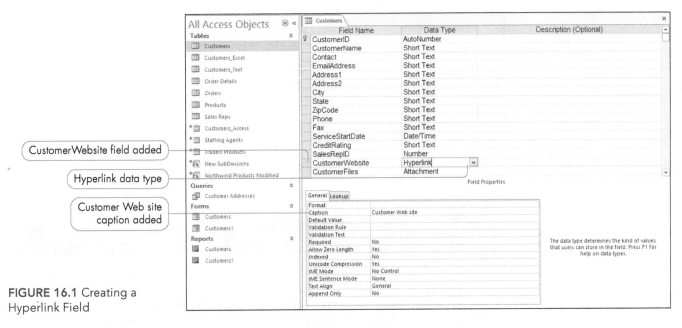

CustomerWebsite field added

Hyperlink data type

Customer Web site caption added

FIGURE 16.1 Creating a Hyperlink Field

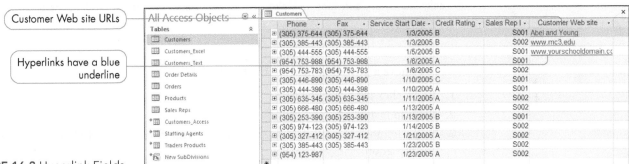

Customer Web site URLs

Hyperlinks have a blue underline

FIGURE 16.2 Hyperlink Fields

Edit a Hyperlink in Datasheet View

STEP 2 ≫

When you attempt to edit a hyperlink by clicking it, you may accidentally launch the software application instead of just editing the hyperlink value.

To edit a hyperlink value, do the following:

1. Right-click the hyperlink field.
2. Point to *Hyperlink*.
3. Select Edit Hyperlink. The Edit Hyperlink dialog box displays as shown in Figure 16.3. Several options exist in the dialog box; however, the two options that are most commonly used are the *Text to display* box and the Address box.
4. In the *Text to display* box, change the *Text to display* value to modify what the user sees when he or she views the data in Datasheet view (for a table), Form view (for a form), or Print Preview (for a report).
5. In the Address box, enter the actual address that Access uses to locate and launch a file and open it with the appropriate software.
6. Click ScreenTip to create a ScreenTip that will display when you point your mouse over the hyperlink text. This is similar to the ScreenTips that appear when you hover your mouse over commands on the Ribbon.
7. Click OK.

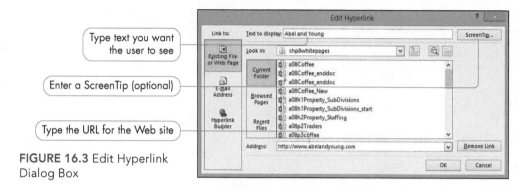

Type text you want the user to see

Enter a ScreenTip (optional)

Type the URL for the Web site

FIGURE 16.3 Edit Hyperlink Dialog Box

TIP   Working with a Hyperlink Field

Working with hyperlink fields can be frustrating for an end user. The user may accidentally click to open a program when he or she only wants to edit the hyperlink. For this reason, some database designers define hyperlink fields as text fields. Users can still store the URLs, e-mail addresses, and file name paths, but the references will not automatically launch any software. Users must copy and paste the references into the appropriate application.

To remove a hyperlink field, do the following:

1. Right-click the hyperlink field.
2. Point to *Hyperlink*.
3. Select Remove Hyperlink. Access will remove the current hyperlink without asking for confirmation.

Other options for manipulating a hyperlink field exist in the shortcut list that displays when you right-click a hyperlink; however, editing and removing a hyperlink field are the most commonly used.

Adding an Attachment Field

STEP 3>> An Access database is primarily used to store and analyze data and to retrieve information. This data is usually typed directly into the tables or entered using an Access form. Sometimes you may want to store a reference to an external file—an image, a scanned document, an Excel spreadsheet, a PDF document—and then be able to open that file from within Access. These situations can be handled by adding an attachment field to a table. An *attachment field* is similar to an attachment in an e-mail; you can use an Access attachment to attach multiple files of any format and then launch those files from within Access. The files are actually copied into the database itself. Keep in mind that Access is not able to analyze the data within these external files; Access can only open the files. To review the documents, you need to use another program.

The size of your database grows when you attach files. Some file types are compressed by Access when you attach them (such as Excel and Word), and other file types increase the database size byte for byte (such as JPEG and other photo formats). You can monitor the increase in size using these steps:

1. Compact the database.
2. Check the size of the database file.
3. Add the file attachment.
4. Check the size of the database file again.

If the database grows too large, you can remove some attachments (such as JPEGs), resize the files, and reattach the files in a smaller format. JPEG attachments are one of the leading causes for "bloating" in an Access database. Remember to compact your database after you add and remove attachments.

Add an Attachment Field in Design View

If you were working with a Customers table and you wanted to store a photo of the owner, the office building, and the master contract in Access, in Design view you could add a new field named CustomerFiles and select the data type *Attachment*, as shown in Figure 16.4. Save the changes, and then switch to Datasheet view so you can add the files to the new attachment field. A paperclip icon with the number of files attached is shown in the New Attachment column. All records, except record 6, show (0) attachments because no files are attached yet (see Figure 16.5).

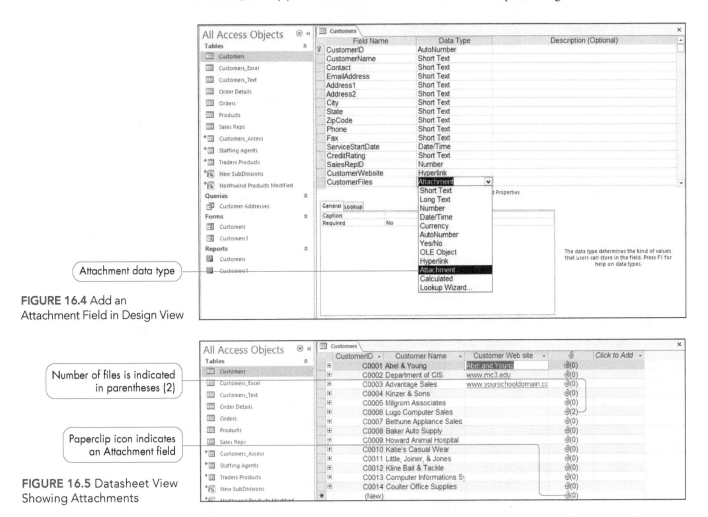

FIGURE 16.4 Add an Attachment Field in Design View

Attachment data type

Number of files is indicated in parentheses (2)

Paperclip icon indicates an Attachment field

FIGURE 16.5 Datasheet View Showing Attachments

Add or Edit Attachments in Datasheet View

 Suppose you have a database that stores all the customer information for your business. You want to store a photo of the owner, a photo of the exterior of the main building, a map with directions to the business, and a Word document containing the price structure for each company. The directions file was created using Google Maps and then saved as a PDF document. You can attach all of the files relating to each customer's record.

To attach a file to a record, do the following:

1. Double-click the attachment field's paperclip icon to open the Attachments dialog box, shown in Figure 16.6.
2. Click Add to add the first attachment.
3. Use the Choose File dialog box to locate and select the file.

4. Click Open to attach the file to the record.
5. Click Add again to add the next file and each additional file. In the previous example, you would need to click Add four times to add the two photos, the map, and the price structure document.
6. Click OK to close the Attachments dialog box. The paperclip icon would now show that (4) files are attached to the current record.
7. Click the record below the current record to save the attached files.

Click Add to attach files

FIGURE 16.6 Attachments Dialog Box

To view or edit attached files, do the following:

1. Double-click the attachment field's paperclip icon to open the Attachments dialog box.
2. Select the file to modify.
3. Click Open. For example, if you click the photo of the owner, and then click Open, you can modify the photo using your computer's default picture manager software.
4. Save and close the file once the change has been made.
5. Click OK in the Attachments dialog box.
6. In the Save Attachment dialog box, click Yes to save your changes (see Figure 16.7).
7. Click the record below the current record to save the changes.

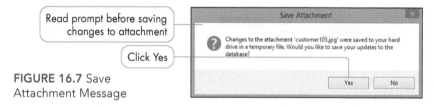

Read prompt before saving changes to attachment

Click Yes

FIGURE 16.7 Save Attachment Message

Remove Attachments in Datasheet View

STEP 5 >> To remove an attached file, do the following:

1. Double-click the attachment field's paperclip icon to open the Attachments dialog box.
2. Select the file to remove and click Remove.
3. Click OK.
4. Click the record below the current record to save the changes.

The number of files shown next to the paperclip is reduced by one.

TABLE 16.1	Using the Attachments Dialog Box
Add	Click to add one or more files to a record.
Remove	Click to remove previously attached files.
Open	Click to launch the appropriate application and open the file. If you try to close the Attachments dialog box with the file open, you will receive a warning that your changes may not be saved. If you are sure you have saved your changes, click OK. You will receive a message that the changes were saved to your hard drive in a temporary file. Access asks if you would like to save your updates to the database (see Figure 16.7).
Save As	Use to save the attached file to a local storage location. You must remember to add it back into the database if you make changes.
Save All	Save all of the attachments in a record to a local, temporary folder.

TIP | **Deleting Temporary Files**

Each time you open an attachment file, Access creates a temporary file on your computer's hard drive. You can remove these temporary files by launching the desktop version of Windows Internet Explorer. Click Tools and select *Internet options*. On the General tab, click Delete in the *Browsing history* section. In the next dialog box, delete the temporary Internet files and Web site files and close the dialog box. Close the remaining dialog boxes to return to Internet Explorer.

Adding Attachment Controls to Forms and Reports

STEP 6 » In a form or report, you can interact with attachments using an attachment control. An **attachment control** is a control that lets you manage attached files in forms and reports. In a form, the attachment control enables you to add, edit, and delete attachments the same way you can in a table. If the attachment is a photo, the control displays the photo as you navigate through the records. If the attachment is a document, you will only see an icon representing the application that was used to create the file. When you click an attachment control in Form view, the Attachment toolbar displays arrows that enable you to advance through the attachments. The Attachment toolbar also has a paperclip icon that you can click to open the Attachments dialog box. This dialog box is the same one that opens when you click an attachment field in a table.

In a report, the attachment field displays the first file only in Print Preview. If the first attachment is a photo, the control displays the photo; if the first file is a document, an icon representing the application is displayed. The Attachment toolbar does not appear in Print Preview. To see the Attachment toolbar and advance through multiple attachments in a report, close Print Preview, and then switch to Report view. Report view enables you to advance through multiple attachments. In a form, switch to Form view to work with the Attachment toolbar.

Add an Attachment Control to a Form

To add an attachment control to a form, do the following:

1. Open the form in Layout view.
2. Click Add Existing Fields in the Tools group on the DESIGN tab.
3. In the Field List, the attachment field appears as a parent field with three child fields. The expand symbol (+) enables you to expand and collapse the child fields.
4. Drag the parent field name to the form, and then drop it in the desired location, as shown in Figure 16.8. Access adds the bound attachment control and the associated label to the form.
5. Resize the bound control, if necessary, to ensure that the images display correctly.
6. Save your changes, and then switch to Form view to view your changes (see Figure 16.9).
7. Return to Layout view for additional modifications if necessary.

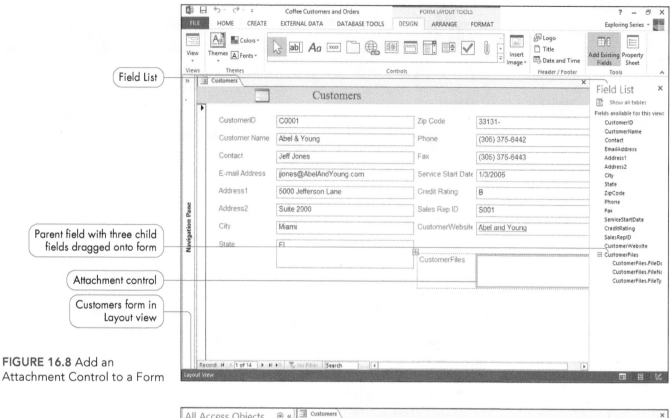

Field List

Parent field with three child fields dragged onto form

Attachment control

Customers form in Layout view

FIGURE 16.8 Add an Attachment Control to a Form

Customers form in Form view

Attachment control displays image

FIGURE 16.9 Attachment Control in Form View

Add an Attachment Field to a Report

STEP 7 »   To add an attachment field to an existing report, do the following:

1. Open the report in Layout view.
2. Click Add Existing Fields in the Tools group on the DESIGN tab.
3. Drag the parent field name to the report, and then drop it in the desired location.
4. When the attachment control is in place, click the control to view the Attachment toolbar, as shown in Figure 16.10. Attachments can also be viewed in Report view of the report.

5. Using the Attachment toolbar, click the *next* and *previous* arrows to advance from one attachment to the next, or click the paperclip icon to open the Attachments dialog box. You should reduce the size of the attachment control in a report because a report usually displays multiple records on one page. If a user needs a larger view of a thumbnail, he or she can always review the photo in Layout view by opening the Attachments dialog box.

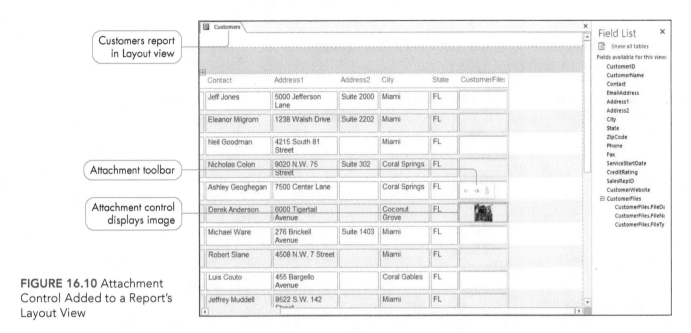

Customers report in Layout view

Attachment toolbar

Attachment control displays image

FIGURE 16.10 Attachment Control Added to a Report's Layout View

In Hands-On Exercise 1, you will work with the database from the Blackwood property management company. You will add and edit a Hyperlink field that will link properties to the appropriate school district's Web page. You will create and use an Attachment field (some with multiple attachments) in an Access table, and you will add attachment controls to a form and a report.

Quick
Concepts

1. What is the major difference between a linked file and an attachment? *p. 798*

2. What is a potential disadvantage of storing attachments in your databases? *p. 800*

3. In which view of a report is the Attachment toolbar available? *p. 803*

Hands-On Exercises

Watch the Video
for this Hands-
On Exercise!

MyITLab®
HOE1 Training

1 Connecting Access to External Files

Blackwood Maintenance Service wants to add a link to a Web site for each subdivision and a link to the school district that each subdivision resides in. You will also add a photo of each property that BMS now serves. Finally, you will add a photo and related documents to the record of each BMS agent.

Skills covered: Add a Hyperlink Field in Design View • Edit a Hyperlink in Datasheet View • Add an Attachment Field in Design View • Add or Edit Attachments in Datasheet View • Remove Attachments in Datasheet View • Add an Attachment Control in Layout View • Add an Attachment Field in a Form or Report

STEP 1 ≫ ADD A HYPERLINK FIELD IN DESIGN VIEW

Create a new field that will link to a Web site for each subdivision served by Blackwood. Also add a link to the school district Web site for each subdivision. Refer to Figure 16.11 as you complete Step 1.

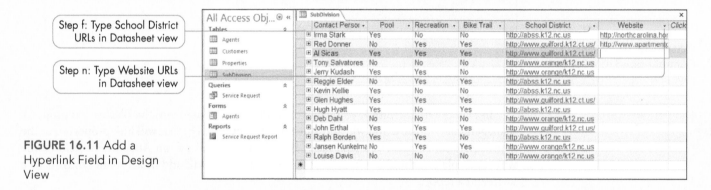

FIGURE 16.11 Add a Hyperlink Field in Design View

a. Open *a08h1Property*. Click the **FILE tab**, click **Save As**, click **Save As**, and then type **a08h1Property_LastFirst**. Click **Save**.

> **TROUBLESHOOTING:** Throughout the remainder of this chapter and textbook, click Enable Content whenever you are working with student files. If you make any major mistakes in this exercise, you can close the file, open *a08h1Property* again, and then start this exercise over.

b. Open the Agents table and replace *Your_Name* with your name in both the FirstName and LastName fields. Close the Agents table.

c. Open the SubDivision table in Design view. In the blank row below the BikeTrail field name, type **SchoolDistrict**. Click the **Data Type arrow** and select **Hyperlink**.

d. Type **School District** in the **Caption property box** in the Field Properties window in the bottom portion of the Table Design view.

e. Save the changes to the table. Switch to Datasheet view.

You are ready to add the school districts' Web site addresses to the new hyperlink field.

f. Type **http://abss.k12.nc.us** into the **School District field** for records 1, 6, 7, 9, and 12.

Fair Brook, North Point, Red Canyon, The Links, and The Pines are all located in the Alamance-Burlington School System.

g. Type **http://www.guilford.k12.ct.us** into the **School District field** for records 2, 3, 8, and 11.

King's Forest, Dale, Seeley Lake, and The Orchards are in the Guilford District.

h. Type **http://www.orange.k12.nc.us** into the **School District field** for the remaining records (records 4, 5, 10, 13, and 14).

The remaining subdivisions are in the Orange County School District.

> **TROUBLESHOOTING:** If you make a mistake, do not click in the School District field to correct it. Instead, click in the BikeTrail column and press Tab to select the field that contains an error. Retype the information.

i. Test the accuracy of the URLs by clicking the **School District hyperlink** in records 1 and 2. If the security window appears, click **Yes** to continue.

The browser opens and the school district's Web site opens. Close the browser window.

j. Widen the School District field so all the data is displayed, and then compare your screen to Figure 16.11.

k. Switch to Design view.

l. Type **Website** in the first blank field under *School District*. Select **Hyperlink** as the data type.

You added a second hyperlink field for each community's Web site.

m. Save the changes to the table. Switch to Datasheet view.

You are ready to add the community Web site addresses to the new hyperlink field.

n. Type **http://northcarolina.hometownlocator.com/nc/catawba/fairbrook.cfm** into the **Website field** of record 1.

This hyperlink points to the nearby community.

o. Type **http://www.apartmentguide.com/neighborhoods/North-carolina-Greensboro-Kings-Forests** into the **Website field** of record 2.

This hyperlink lists information about the surrounding community.

STEP 2 ≫ EDIT A HYPERLINK IN DATASHEET VIEW

You realized that you entered an incorrect URL for the Guilford schools. The current URL links point to schools in Connecticut, not in North Carolina. You will fix the links in this step so that the URL links to schools in North Carolina. Refer to Figure 16.12 as you complete Step 2.

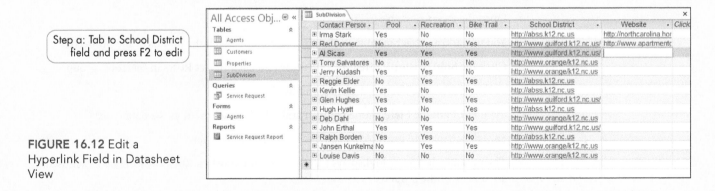

FIGURE 16.12 Edit a Hyperlink Field in Datasheet View

a. Click in the **BikeTrail column** of record 2 and press **Tab** to select the School District field. Press **F2** and edit the link so it reads **http://www.guilford.k12.nc.us**.

The *ct* segment of the hyperlink was changed to *nc*. The hyperlink is enclosed with pound signs (#), which Access uses to activate the link when clicked.

b. Click in the **BikeTrail column** of record 3 to save your changes. Test the new hyperlink by clicking the **School District field** in record 2, *http://www.guilford.k12.nc.us.*

The link now points to the correct school district. Close the browser window. You will use another method to edit the remaining Guilford URLs.

c. Right-click the **http://www.guilford.k12.ct.us** hyperlink in record 3, point to *Hyperlink*, and then select **Edit Hyperlink** from the shortcut menu.

The Edit Hyperlink dialog box opens.

d. Change the *ct* segment of the hyperlink to **nc** in the Address field at the bottom of the dialog box. Click **OK** to accept your changes and press the down arrow to save your changes.

The Text to display changes.

e. Test the modified URL by clicking **http://www.guilford.k12.nc.us hyperlink** in record 3.

The link now points to the correct school district. Close the browser window.

f. Edit the remaining Guilford URLs (change *ct* to *nc*) using the Edit Hyperlink dialog box. Compare your results to Figure 16.12.

g. Close the SubDivision table.

STEP 3 ≫ ADD AN ATTACHMENT FIELD IN DESIGN VIEW

BMS has collected photos of its properties for the past several years. The photos are stored in a folder where employees can access them as needed. The owners have asked you to create an attachment field so you can attach each photo to its corresponding property. Refer to Figure 16.13 as you complete Step 3.

FIGURE 16.13 Add an Attachment Field in Design View

a. Open the Properties table in Design view.

You will add an attachment field that enables you to attach the photos of the properties.

b. Click the **SubDivisionID field row selector** and click **Insert Rows** in the Tools group.

A new row is added between Listing and SubDivisionID.

c. Type **Photo** in the **Field Name column** and select **Attachment** as the data type.

d. Save the changes to the table design. Switch to Datasheet view.

The new attachment field displays a paperclip symbol with a (0), indicating no attachments are on any of the property records.

In this step, you will attach the photos to the corresponding properties. Having these photos attached to the properties enables the agents to access them when working with the property owners. You will add 13 photos now and the other photos later. Refer to Figure 16.14 as you complete Step 4.

Step a: Double-click paperclip icon to open Attachments dialog box

Step d: Double-click file in dialog box to view attached photo

Step b: Click Add to add one or more attachments

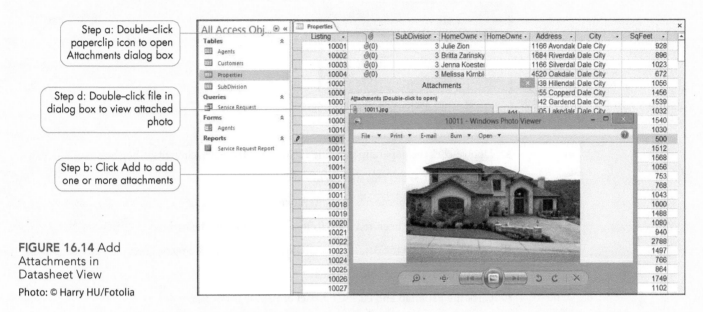

FIGURE 16.14 Add Attachments in Datasheet View

Photo: © Harry HU/Fotolia

a. Double-click the **paperclip icon** in the Photo field in the record for listing 10011 to open the Attachments dialog box.

b. Click **Add**. Locate the *10011.jpg* photo found in the a08h1Photos folder. Double-click the file to add it to the Attachments dialog box.

The file displays in the Attachments dialog box.

c. Click **OK** to close the Attachments dialog box, and then click the record for listing 10012 to save the record.

d. Double-click the **paperclip** in record 11 to open the Attachments dialog box again. Double-click the *10011.jpg* photo to open your computer's default photo software.

Compare your screen to Figure 16.14.

e. Close the photo software and click **OK** in the Attachments dialog box.

f. Double-click the **paperclip** in listing 10043.

g. Click **Add** in the Attachment dialog box, and then locate and attach photo *10043.jpg* to the record. Click **OK**.

h. Double-click the **paperclip** in listing 10067 and attach photo *10067.jpg* to the record.

i. Add the corresponding photos to the following records: 10865, 10888, 10899, 10935, 10968, 11028, 11042, 11118, 11141, and 11171.

j. Select the record for listing 10025. Double-click the **paperclip** to open the Attachments dialog box. Click **Add** and add photo *10025a.jpg* to the Attachments dialog box. Before clicking OK to attach the photo, click **Add** in the Attachments dialog box to add a second attachment to the record. Double-click *10025b.jpg* to add it to the Attachments dialog box. Click **OK** to add both photo attachments to the record. Click the record for listing 10026 to save the record.

STEP 5 ➤➤ REMOVE ATTACHMENTS IN DATASHEET VIEW

One of the properties was sold, and the new owners are not going to use BMS to manage their property. You decide to remove the photos from this property. Refer to Figure 16.15 as you complete Step 5.

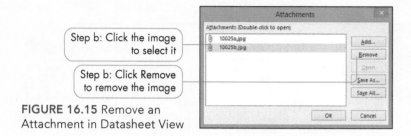

Step b: Click the image to select it

Step b: Click Remove to remove the image

FIGURE 16.15 Remove an Attachment in Datasheet View

a. Double-click the **paperclip** in listing 10025 to open the Attachments dialog box.

b. Click the first photo and click **Remove**.

c. Click the second photo and click **Remove**.

   Both photos have been removed from the Attachments dialog box.

d. Click **OK** to close the Attachments dialog box and click the record below to save the record.

e. Close the Properties table.

f. Click the **FILE tab** and click **Compact & Repair Database**.

   You decide to compact the database because adding and removing attachments can increase the size of the database.

STEP 6 ➤➤ ADD AN ATTACHMENT CONTROL IN LAYOUT VIEW

BMS asks you to create a report showing the properties with an outstanding service request. You decide to include a photo of each property, but only a thumbnail will appear in the report. Refer to Figure 16.16 as you complete Step 6.

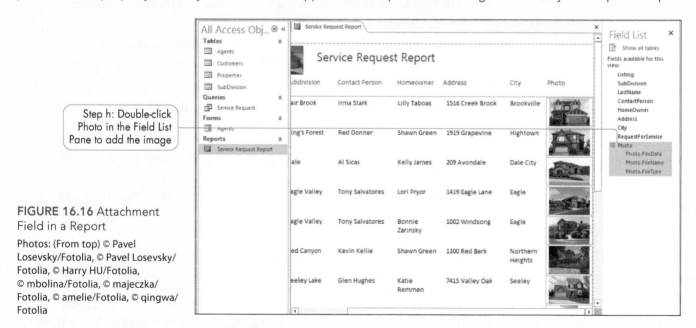

Step h: Double-click Photo in the Field List Pane to add the image

FIGURE 16.16 Attachment Field in a Report

Photos: (From top) © Pavel Losevsky/Fotolia, © Pavel Losevsky/Fotolia, © Harry HU/Fotolia, © mbolina/Fotolia, © majeczka/Fotolia, © amelie/Fotolia, © qingwa/Fotolia

a. Open the Service Request query in Design view. Change the criterion from *Your_name* to your last name.

b. Switch to Datasheet view and examine the query results.

   Thirteen properties display with you as the manager. The Photo field is missing; you must return to Design view to add it to the query design.

c. Switch to Design view.

d. Drag the **Photo field** from the Properties table and drop it into the first blank column in the query design grid.

> **TROUBLESHOOTING:** If you drag one of the three child fields, delete the column and try again. Make sure you add the parent photo field, the field with a (+) or (–) symbol to its left.

e. Switch to Datasheet view and examine the query results again. Save and close the query.

f. Double-click **Service Request Report** and switch to Layout view.

g. Click **Add Existing Fields** in the Tools group.

h. Click **Brookville** to select the City column. Double-click **Photo** in the Field List pane to add the field to the right side of the report.

> **TROUBLESHOOTING:** If you double-click one of the three child fields, click Undo and try again. Make sure you double-click the parent photo field, the field with a (+) or (–) symbol to its left.

The Photo field becomes the last column on the right of the report. Most of the photos are positioned on the right side of the right margin line. You will resize the other columns to reduce the layout width to one page.

i. Click **Add Existing Fields** in the Tools group to close the Field List window. Reduce the width of the Listing column by dragging the right border of the Listing column heading to the left.

j. Reduce the width of the City column until no photos are positioned on the second page.

k. View the report in Print Preview.

All the fields now fit onto one page.

l. Click **Close Print Preview** in the Close Preview group. Save and close the report.

STEP 7 ➤➤ USE AN ATTACHMENT FIELD IN A FORM OR REPORT

Blackwood wants to add a photo of each agent to the database. They also want to attach the latest performance evaluation to each employee's record. Refer to Figure 16.17 as you complete Step 7.

FIGURE 16.17 Attachment Field in a Form

Photo: © Rido/Fotolia

a. Open the Agents table in Design view. Add a field named **RelatedFiles** in the first blank row under *CellPhone*. Select **Attachment Data Type**. In the *Field Properties* section, type **Photo and Related Files** in the **Caption property**.

You added an attachment field to store the photo and performance review for each agent.

b. Save the table changes, and then switch to Datasheet view.

You need to attach a photo and a Word file for each employee.

c. Double-click the **paperclip** in the first record, for Juan Rosario. The Attachments dialog box opens. Click **Add**. Locate and open the *a08h1Agents* folder. Find and double-click *juan.jpg* to attach it. Click **OK** to close the Attachments dialog box and click another record to save the current record.

The paperclip now shows that (1) file is attached to Juan's record. Next, add a photo and a Word file to Kia Hart's record.

d. Double-click the **paperclip** in Kia Hart's record to open the Attachments dialog box. Click **Add**. Locate the *kia.jpg* photo and attach it to the record by double-clicking the file. Click **Add** again and attach the document *Kia Hart Performance Evaluation*. Click **OK** to close the Attachments dialog box and click another record to save the current record.

Kia's record should indicate (2) attachments.

e. Attach the remaining agents' photos to their records. Use the photo named *your_name* for your photo. Attach the *Your_Name Performance Evaluation* document to your record as well. Close the table.

f. Open the Agents form in Design view. Click the **ID field** to activate the Layout Selector (the small square with a cross inside, located to the left of the first field).

You will move all the fields to the right.

g. Click **Layout Selector** and drag the fields as a group to the right.

Use Figure 16.17 (the completed form) as a guide as you reposition the fields.

h. Click **Add Existing Fields** in the Tools group to open the Field List.

i. Drag the **RelatedFiles field** to the left of the fields you just moved.

The field is added to the left side of the form. You need to reposition the label and the control separately.

j. Move the **RelatedFiles control** to the top of the form using the small solid square at the top-left of the control. Resize the control using Figure 16.17 (the completed form) as a guide.

> **TROUBLESHOOTING:** If the label follows the attachment control, release the mouse and try again. Verify you are dragging the attachment using the small solid square.

k. Drag the **Photo and Related Files label** to the bottom of the control, as shown in Figure 16.17. Click the **FORMAT tab** and click **Center** in the Font group to center align the label text.

l. Switch to Form view. Click **Next record** in the Navigation bar to advance to record 2, Kia Hart's record.

This record has two attachments. The Word file displays as an icon, and the photo is not displayed.

m. Double-click the **Word icon** to open the Attachments dialog box. Click **Open**. Kia's overall rating is *Good*. Close the Word file. Click **Kia.jpg** and click **Open**. Close the photo file. Click **OK** in the Attachments dialog box.

n. Click the **Attachment control** to activate the Attachment toolbar. Click the **green arrow** to display the next attachment.

Kia's photo displays.

o. Click **Next record** in the Navigation bar to advance to your record. Double-click the Attachment control to open the Attachments dialog box. Click each attachment and click **Open** to view each file. Close the Attachments dialog box when you are finished.

p. Save and close the form.

q. Click the **FILE tab** and click **Compact & Repair Database**.

r. Keep the database open if you plan to continue with Hand-On Exercise 2. If not, close the database and exit Access.

Exporting Data to Office and Other Applications

Using Access to collect and store data, to extract information, and to analyze information is useful for any organization. The accounting department of a company will always need to track sales, inventory, materials, and labor so it can report the financial statements to management each month. Access can handle this task. In addition, the sales department will need to process orders and track profitability based on each order and on categories of products. Access can handle this task as well. If management wants to know who its best customers are based on sales for the current year, Access can provide this information, too, using a query and a report.

But what happens when this information must be shared with the other departments or with other companies? How can the accountants deliver database information to others who might not be familiar with using Access or even have the software? One way to deliver information is via hard copies. However, this does not work if the recipient wants to manipulate the data him- or herself to analyze it further from a different angle. A common way to distribute data stored in an Access database is to export the data to another application.

In this section, you will learn how to export Access data to Excel and Word. Because these two applications are part of the Microsoft Office Suite, exporting from Access is straightforward. In addition to exporting to Excel and Word, this section will show you how to create a PDF or XPS document and how to export objects from one Access database to another Access database.

Exporting Data to Excel

Exporting data from Access to Excel is generally uncomplicated because the data in Access is usually structured in a manner that Excel understands. However, a few special situations exist when exporting to Excel; these situations will be discussed in the section that follows.

Select a Record Source to Export to Excel

If the record source you want to export to Excel is a table, such as the Customers table shown in Figure 16.18, then the export-to-Excel process is fast and easy. When you export a table to Excel, the field names become the column headings and the table records become the rows in the Excel spreadsheet.

To export a table to Excel, do the following:

1. Select the table in the Navigation Pane (or open the table first).
2. Click Excel in the Export group on the EXTERNAL DATA tab. Access opens the Export – Excel Spreadsheet dialog box to guide you through the export process.
3. Specify the file name and destination and the format for the exported file. Specify whether to export the data with formatting and layout. This option preserves most formatting and layout information applied in Access. Otherwise, the file opens using default Excel formatting.
4. Specify if you want to open the destination file after the export operation is complete. This option opens the resulting file. Otherwise, you would need to open it from within its application.
5. Specify if you want to export only the selected records (if you have selected one or more records in the datasheet).
6. Click OK.

When you export a table from Access, all of the columns and all the records in the table are exported, even if the table is open and not all of the data is visible (as shown in Figure 16.18). The end result is a new Excel worksheet containing all of the columns and all of the records in the Customers table, as shown in Figure 16.19.

FIGURE 16.18 Customers Table in Access Before Exporting to Excel

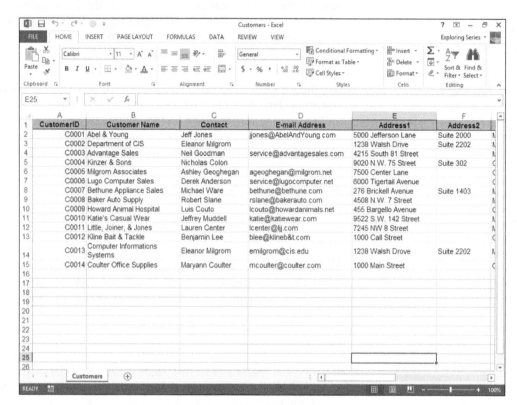

FIGURE 16.19 Customers Table Exported to Excel

STEP 1 »

If you want to export only a subset of the Customers table, you can filter a table or select specific records before exporting. Alternatively, you could create a query to then export to Excel. For example, if you only need the address fields for customers in a certain zip code, you can create a query and then save it. Select the query, and then export the query records to Excel.

Export a Query to Excel

To export a query to Excel, do the following:

1. Select the query in the Navigation Pane (or open the query first).
2. Click Excel in the Export group on the EXTERNAL DATA tab. Access opens the Export – Excel Spreadsheet dialog box (shown in Figure 16.20) to guide you through the export process.
3. Specify the file name and destination and the format for the exported file.
4. Specify whether to export the data with formatting and layout.
5. Specify if you want to open the destination file after the export operation is complete (see Figure 16.21).
6. Specify if you want to export only the selected records (if you have selected one or more records in the datasheet).
7. Click OK.

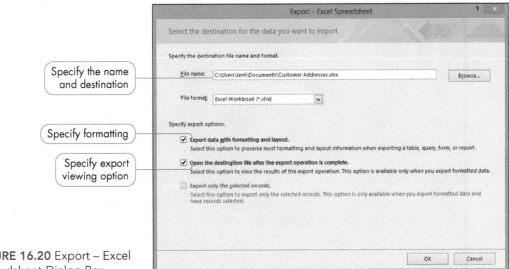

Specify the name and destination

Specify formatting

Specify export viewing option

FIGURE 16.20 Export – Excel Spreadsheet Dialog Box

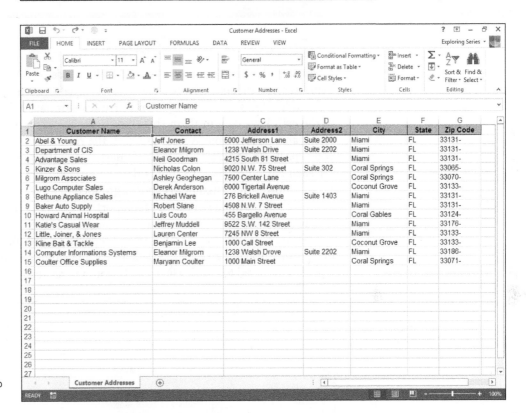

FIGURE 16.21 Customer Addresses Query Exported to Excel

The Excel spreadsheet will display. Once you are finished reviewing the exported Excel spreadsheet, and then return to the Access window, one final screen requires a response. In Figure 16.22, Access asks you, *Do you want to save these export steps?* Click the *Save export steps* check box if you want to repeat the same export process at a later time. Saving export steps is useful if you need to repeatedly export the same query. The saved steps are stored under Saved Exports in the Export group.

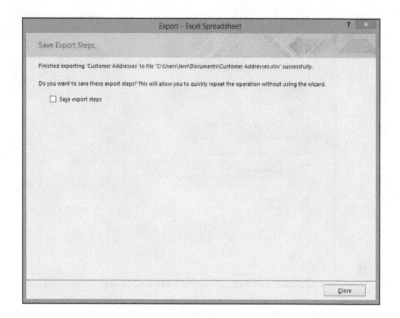

FIGURE 16.22 Save Export Steps Dialog Box

Export Forms and Reports to Excel

STEP 2 Exporting tables and queries to Excel usually yields predictable and consistent results. The main reason is the similarity between an Access datasheet and an Excel worksheet. Both have column headings, and both have multiple rows of data below the column headings. Most of the cells have data in them (blank cells are the exception). However, when you export forms and reports from Access to Excel, the results can be unpredictable. For example, if you export a form that contains Customers information and a subform showing the Orders for each customer, the Customers data exports but the Orders (subform data) does not. Furthermore, if you attempt to export a grouped report in Access, the grouping in Excel may not match the grouping in the Access report. You can either accept the results from the form or report, or redo the export using the underlying record source. The underlying tables and queries are more reliable than forms and reports. Figure 16.23 shows an Access form based on Customers and the related Orders for each customer. Figure 16.24 shows the same form after it is exported to Excel. The records from the related (Orders) table do not display.

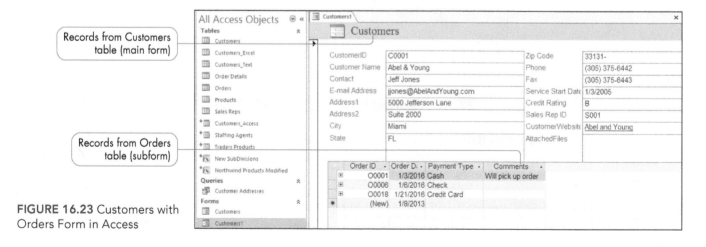

FIGURE 16.23 Customers with Orders Form in Access

Records from Customers table (main form)

Records from Orders table (subform)

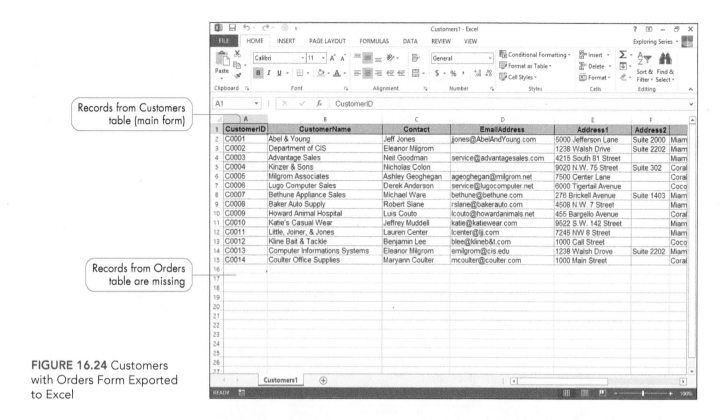

Records from Customers table (main form)

Records from Orders table are missing

FIGURE 16.24 Customers with Orders Form Exported to Excel

Exporting Data to Word

Exporting data from Access to Word is similar to exporting data to Excel, except that you are not able to analyze the data as you can in Excel. Once the data is exported to Word, you will most likely use the data as is for reporting purposes rather than for analysis. Although you can modify the data in the table cells, those changes do not update the totals or other calculated fields (as they do in Excel).

The objects you select to export from Access to Word should have a tabular layout—tables, queries, and tabular reports fit this description. Although other object types do export to Word, the results are unpredictable and poorly formatted. If you are uncertain about which type of objects to export to Word, select any object in Access and export it to Word to see if it is properly formatted. If the data is usable, you can keep the Word document. If the data is not what you wanted, just close the file without saving and try again with a different layout.

When you export an object from Access to Word, Access creates a file in the RTF format. *Rich Text Format (RTF)* is a format that enables documents created in one software application to be opened with a different software application. The RTF format was introduced in 1987 by Microsoft and is now supported by Windows, Macintosh, open source, Unix, and other environments. RTF is a useful format for basic formatted text documents such as instruction manuals, résumés, letters, and other documents. These documents support special text formatting such as bold, italic, and underline. RTF documents also support left-, center-, and right-justified text. Furthermore, font specifications and document margins are supported in RTF documents.

When you export data from Access to Word, the RTF format is used and the file's extension will be .rtf. If you double-click the file, Windows opens Word by default and then displays the contents of the file. Word is the default software application for the RTF extension.

To convert an RTF file to a Word document, do the following:

1. From within Word, click the FILE tab.
2. Click Save As.
3. Change the *Save as type* to Word Document.

From that point forward, the document retains the Word format.

Select a Record Source to Export to Word

STEP 3 ≫ Similar to exporting to Excel, exporting Access tables and queries to Word is much simpler (as compared to exporting forms and reports). For example, if you need to add the Products table from an Access database into a Word document, as shown in Figure 16.25, the export-to-Word process is fast and easy. When you export a table to Word, Access creates an RTF file and inserts a table into the document. For the Products table, the field names become the column headings and the records become the table rows in the RTF file.

You can export tabular reports to Word; Access preserves the report's grouping aggregate functions. Some of the formatting may be lost. Columnar forms and reports do not export to Word properly; however, you can test the export of these objects to see if they produce usable data.

Click the More button, and then select Word from the list

FIGURE 16.25 Product Data in Access

Export Tables and Queries to Word

Exporting tables and queries to Word is similar to exporting tables and queries to Excel.

To export a table or query to Word, do the following:

1. Select the table or query in the Navigation Pane (or open the table or query first) and click the EXTERNAL DATA tab.
2. Click the More button in the Export group.
3. Select Word. Access opens the Export – RTF dialog box (shown in Figure 16.26) to guide you through the export process.

4. Specify the file name, destination, and format for the exported file.

5. Specify if you want to open the destination file after the export operation is complete (see Figure 16.26).

6. Specify if you want to export only the selected records (if you have selected one or more records in the datasheet).

7. Click OK.

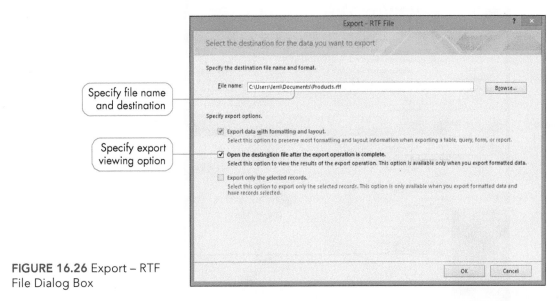

Specify file name and destination

Specify export viewing option

FIGURE 16.26 Export – RTF File Dialog Box

Modify an RTF File in Word

STEP 3 ≫

After you export an Access table to an RTF file, you can edit the file in Word and add additional text to the Products table content. If you need to send the products list to a few vendors to check current prices, you can insert a few blank lines above the Products table and type the To, From, and Subject lines as shown in Figure 16.27. Because the Products table was inserted at the top of the page, to insert lines above the table, click immediately before the first value in the first cell of the table and press Enter three times. The table moves down to make room for the To, From, and Subject lines. Type the rest of the information and save the document.

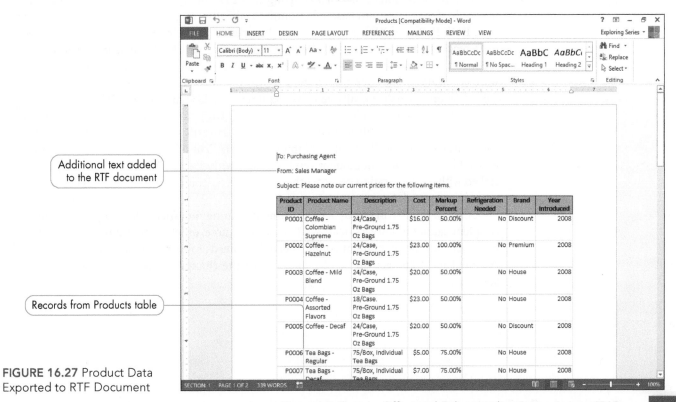

Additional text added to the RTF document

Records from Products table

FIGURE 16.27 Product Data Exported to RTF Document

When you save an RTF file, you might want to change the file type to Word Document so that you can take full advantage of Word's features and formatting tools.

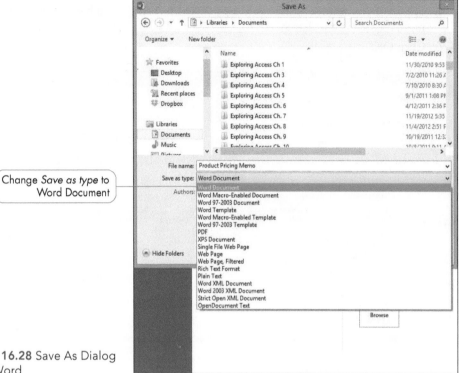

Change *Save as type* to Word Document

FIGURE 16.28 Save As Dialog Box in Word

Exporting Data to a PDF or XPS Document

Exporting data from Access to a PDF or XPS document is similar to exporting data to Word, except that you are not able to edit the exported documents. When you export from Access to Word or Excel, you can modify the exported files. This is not the case with PDF and XPS documents.

STEP 4 Two main reasons exist for exporting to a PDF or XPS document. First, these documents do not require purchase of a commercial software application to view the information. Both PDF and XPS documents can be opened by their respective document readers. Both readers are available as free downloads to users. *Portable Document Format (PDF)* is a file format created by Adobe Systems in 1993 for document exchange independent of software application and operating system environment. PDF documents can be viewed with Adobe Reader, which is available online at http://get.adobe.com/reader/. Windows Reader, an alternative to Adobe Reader, may be preinstalled with your operating system. *XML Paper Specification (XPS)* is a file format developed by Microsoft and designed to display a printed page onscreen identically on any computer platform. The XPS format is considered an alternative to PDF. An XPS document can be viewed with the XPS Viewer, which may be preinstalled with your operating system; otherwise it is available as a free download online at www.microsoft.com/whdc/xps/viewxps.mspx.

Second, neither PDF nor XPS documents can be modified after they are created. The recipient cannot modify a document (a contract, quote, or letter) that should only be revised by the creator. If a document contains errors or needs to be revised for another reason, the recipient must contact the sender and ask for the changes to be made using the original software.

Select an Object to Export

Tables, queries, forms, and reports can all be exported to a PDF or XPS document. However, the number of pages should be checked when the objects are exported. If you attempt to export one record in a form, you will be surprised to find the results contain all the records in the record source. Reports tend to be a good choice for creating PDF and XPS documents, particularly if they do not need modification or data analysis.

Export to a PDF or XPS Document

To export to a PDF or XPS document, do the following:

1. Select the object that you want to export and click the EXTERNAL DATA tab.
2. Click PDF or XPS in the Export group. The Publish as PDF or XPS dialog box opens, as shown in Figure 16.29.
3. Select the folder where the document should be saved, type the name of the exported document, and then select the document type, either PDF or XPS Document.
4. Click the *Open file after publishing* check box.
5. Click Publish to create the document.

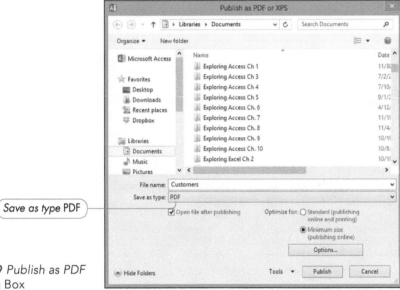

FIGURE 16.29 *Publish as PDF or XPS* Dialog Box

A document opens using the reader associated with the document type (PDF or XPS). The document contains multiple pages if the source has multiple pages. If the document is too wide, then two pages may be required to display one page of data. See Figure 16.30 as an example of a PDF document and Figure 16.31 as an example of an XPS document.

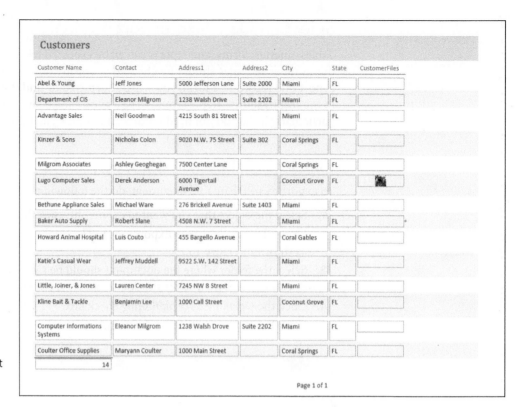

FIGURE 16.30 PDF Document Created from an Access Report

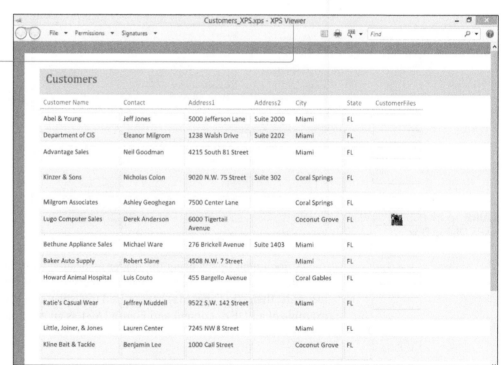

XPS documents are viewed with the XPS Viewer

FIGURE 16.31 XPS Document Created from an Access Report

TIP Viewing XPS Documents

XPS documents can be viewed with your browser (e.g., Internet Explorer) or Windows Reader if the XPS Viewer has not been installed. XPS documents are not as widely used and distributed as PDF documents. For that reason, PDF documents are the preferred format when exporting this type of document from Access.

Exporting Objects to Another Access Database

STEP 5 »

After you create a database for one organization, you may be able to use the structure of some objects in a different database. For example, many business databases require an Employees table, a Customers table, and an Orders table. Companies also need a data-entry form for each of those three tables. There may be common reports that could also be exported from one database to another—for example, an Employee List report and a Customer List report. Exporting objects from one Access database to another saves time because you do not have to create the objects (tables, forms, reports) from scratch. You do not have to set the field names and data types (which Access refers to as the definition). You may have to modify the imported objects slightly to match the requirements of the new database.

When you export tables to another database, the Export dialog box asks if you want to export the data along with the definition. Usually, you will not want the data exported to the new database. After the tables are successfully exported, you can delete unwanted fields and add new fields to create the table structure you need for the new organization. Forms and reports need to be modified as well. Open the forms and reports in Layout view, and then delete any fields that were removed from the underlying tables. Add any new fields to the forms and reports that were added to the tables. You are now ready to populate the new tables either by adding data directly into the tables or by entering data using the forms.

Export Tables to Another Database

Before you can export a table to another database, you must first create the new database (or export the table to an existing database).

To create the new database, do the following:

1. Start Access and click *Blank desktop database* to create a new database.
2. Specify the location and type the name of the new database. You will have to navigate to the location of the new database when you export a table.
3. Click Create.
4. Close the blank target database.

To export a table from one database to another, do the following:

1. Select the table in the Navigation Pane.
2. Click the EXTERNAL DATA tab.
3. Click Access in the Export group.
4. The Export – Access Database dialog box appears (see Figure 16.32).
5. Click Browse to locate the destination file, click the file to select it, and then click Save.
6. Click OK to proceed to the next dialog box, shown in Figure 16.33. The second dialog box asks for the name of the table (you can accept the default name) and whether to export the Definition and Data or Definition Only.
7. Click OK in the second dialog box; the table is then exported to the destination database.
8. Return to the Access window. Close the Save Export Steps window without saving the steps.

To verify that the exported table is now in the destination database, locate and open the destination database. In the Navigation Pane, locate the exported table. Double-click the table to open it. After you verify the table was exported correctly, close the table, and then close the database. Return to the original database and export the next object.

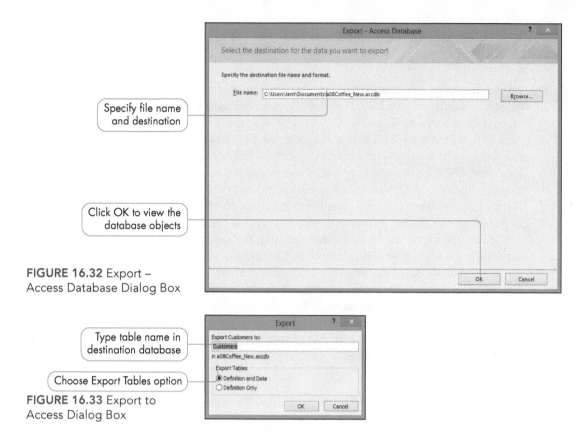

Specify file name and destination

Click OK to view the database objects

FIGURE 16.32 Export – Access Database Dialog Box

Type table name in destination database

Choose Export Tables option

FIGURE 16.33 Export to Access Dialog Box

Export Other Objects to Another Database

STEP 6 ❯❯ To export other objects from one Access database to another, do the following:

1. Select the object (query, form, or report) in the Navigation Pane.
2. Click the EXTERNAL DATA tab.
3. Click Access in the Export group. The Export – Access Database dialog box appears (see Figure 16.32).
4. Click Browse to locate the destination file, click the file to select it, and then click Save.
5. Click OK to proceed to the next dialog box, shown in Figure 16.34. The second dialog box asks for the name of the object (you can accept the default name or type a new name).
6. Click OK in the second dialog box; the table is then exported to the destination database.
7. Return to the Access window. Close the Save Export Steps window without saving the steps.

Verify that the exported object is in the destination database by opening the destination database. In the Navigation Pane, locate the exported object. After you verify the object was exported correctly, return to the original database, and then open the original database to export the next object.

In Hands-On Exercise 2, you will export table data to Excel and export query data into Word using the same real estate database you used for Hands-On Exercise 1. You will also export data to a PDF document and export objects from the real estate database to another database. Verify that the objects were exported successfully by opening the destination database.

Type object name in
destination database

FIGURE 16.34 Export Dialog
Box for Form

Quick
Concepts

1. What is one advantage to exporting Access data to Excel? *p. 813*

2. Why would you want to have an Access report exported to PDF format? *p. 820*

3. Why would you decide to export the definition of a table to a different database, but not the data? *p. 823*

Hands-On Exercises

 Watch the Video for this Hands-On Exercise!

 MyITLab® HOE2 Training

2 Exporting Data to Office Applications

Blackwood Maintenance Service wants to contact the homeowners from the subdivisions they serve to tell them about their new services. You will create several formats, depending on the preference of the subdivision contact person. Some prefer an Excel spreadsheet, some prefer a Word document, one prefers PDF, and one prefers data in an Access table.

Skills covered: Export a Query to Excel • Export a Report to Excel • Export a Query to Word and Modify an RTF File in Word • Export to a PDF or XPS Document • Export a Table to Another Database • Export a Form to Another Database

STEP 1 >> EXPORT A QUERY TO EXCEL

Create a new query that lists all the homeowners in The Woodlands subdivision and export it to an Excel spreadsheet. Refer to Figure 16.35 as you complete Step 1.

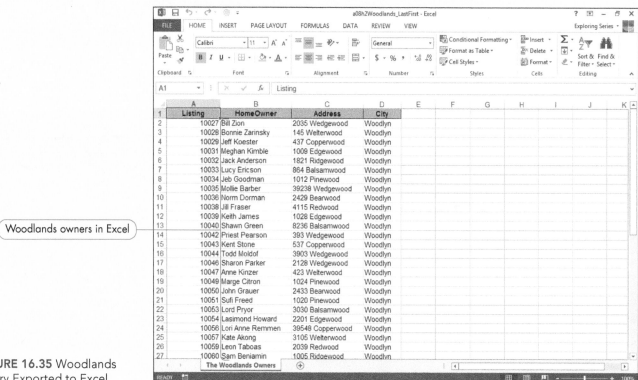

FIGURE 16.35 Woodlands Query Exported to Excel

a. Open *a08h1Property_LastFirst* if you closed it at the end of Hands-On Exercise 1. Click the **FILE tab**, click **Save As**, click **Save As**, and then type **a08h2Property_LastFirst**, changing the *h1* to *h2*.

TROUBLESHOOTING: If you did not complete Hands-On Exercise 1, go back and complete it now. When you are finished, continue with Hands-On Exercise 2. If you make any major mistakes in this exercise, you can close the file, open *a08h1Property_LastFirst* again, and then start this exercise over.

---

b. Click the **CREATE tab** and click **Query Design** in the Queries group. Add the Properties table to the query design and close the Show Table dialog box.

c. Double-click the **SubDivisonID, Listing, HomeOwner, Address**, and **City fields** to add them to the query design grid.

d. Type **14** into the **Criteria row** of the SubDivisionID field. Uncheck the **Show check box**. Save the query as **The Woodlands Owners**.

You entered 14 in the Criteria row, which represents The Woodlands subdivision.

e. Run the query and widen the columns of the query so all the data values are visible.

When you export to Excel, the columns show all the data if the column widths are wide enough in Access.

f. Click the **EXTERNAL DATA tab** and click **Excel** in the Export group. Click **Browse** to choose the export location. Type **a08h2Woodlands_LastFirst** in the **File name box**. Click **Save**.

> **TROUBLESHOOTING:** If you inadvertently click Excel in the Import & Link group, cancel the dialog box and click Excel in the Export group.

g. Click the **Export data with formatting and layout** and **Open the destination file after the export operation is complete check boxes** in the Export – Excel Spreadsheet dialog box. Click **OK**.

A new Excel spreadsheet window opens showing The Woodlands owners' data.

> **TROUBLESHOOTING:** If you attempt to create an Excel file that already exists, Access warns you and asks you, *Do you want to replace the existing one?* If you attempt to create an Excel file that is already open, Access displays a warning, *Microsoft Office Access can't save the output data...* Close the open Excel file and try again.

h. Click **Microsoft Access** on the taskbar to return to Access. Click **Close** to close the Save Export Steps dialog box without saving.

i. Close the query. Save the query if you are asked.

j. Close the workbook and close Excel.

You need to send the Service Request Report to one of the BMS subcontractors. You will export the report to Excel. Refer to Figure 16.36 as you complete Step 2.

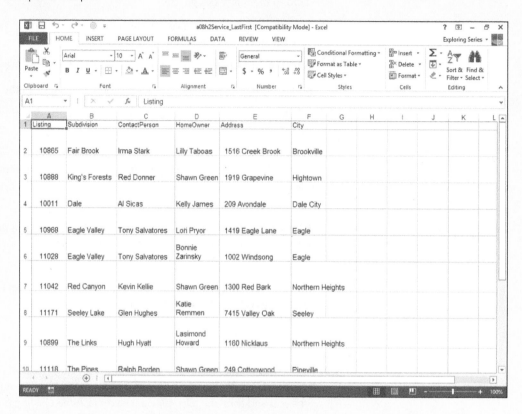

FIGURE 16.36 Report Exported to Excel

a. Double-click the **Service Request Report** in the Navigation Pane to open it.

You will export this report to Excel.

b. Click the **EXTERNAL DATA tab**.

c. Click **Excel** in the Export group.

d. Click **Browse**. Choose a location to save the export file. Change the file name to **a08h2Service_LastFirst**. Click **Save**. Click the **Open the destination file after the export operation is complete check box** in the Export – Excel Spreadsheet dialog box. Click **OK**.

A new Excel spreadsheet window opens, showing the Service Request Report data. The photos are missing, and the report title was deleted.

e. Click **Microsoft Access** on the taskbar to return to Access. Click **Close** to close the Save Export Steps dialog box without saving.

Compare the Excel report with your report in Access.

f. Close the report.

g. Close the workbook and close Excel.

You will need to create a query showing all homes with a tile roof built in or before 1997; these roofs may need to be repaired or replaced. Export the query results to Word. Modify the exported document to include the typical memo elements. Refer to Figure 16.37 as you complete Step 3.

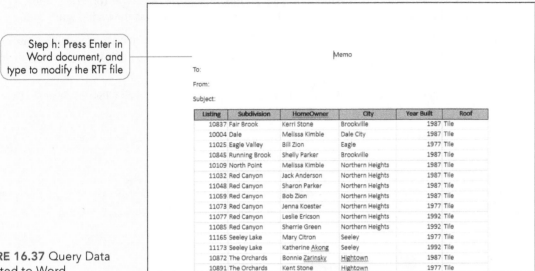

Step h: Press Enter in Word document, and type to modify the RTF file

Memo

To:

From:

Subject:

Listing	Subdivision	HomeOwner	City	Year Built	Roof
10837	Fair Brook	Kerri Stone	Brookville	1987	Tile
10004	Dale	Melissa Kimble	Dale City	1987	Tile
11025	Eagle Valley	Bill Zion	Eagle	1977	Tile
10845	Running Brook	Shelly Parker	Brookville	1987	Tile
10109	North Point	Melissa Kimble	Northern Heights	1987	Tile
11032	Red Canyon	Jack Anderson	Northern Heights	1987	Tile
11048	Red Canyon	Sharon Parker	Northern Heights	1987	Tile
11059	Red Canyon	Bob Zion	Northern Heights	1987	Tile
11073	Red Canyon	Jenna Koester	Northern Heights	1977	Tile
11077	Red Canyon	Leslie Ericson	Northern Heights	1992	Tile
11085	Red Canyon	Sherrie Green	Northern Heights	1992	Tile
11165	Seeley Lake	Mary Citron	Seeley	1977	Tile
11173	Seeley Lake	Katherine Akong	Seeley	1992	Tile
10872	The Orchards	Bonnie Zarinsky	Hightown	1987	Tile
10891	The Orchards	Kent Stone	Hightown	1977	Tile

FIGURE 16.37 Query Data Exported to Word

a. Click the **CREATE tab** and click **Query Design** in the Queries group. Add the Properties table and the SubDivision table to the query design and close the Show Table dialog box.

b. Double-click the fields **Listing**, **HomeOwner**, **City**, **YearBuilt**, and **Roof** in the Properties table and drag **SubDivision** from the SubDivision table to the second column in the query design grid.

The other fields shift to the right to make room for the SubDivision field.

> **TROUBLESHOOTING:** If you inadvertently add the SubDivision field to the last column of the query design grid, point over the thin gray bar above the field name and when the downward-pointing arrow appears, click to select the column. Point in the selected column and click and drag to move the column into the correct position.

c. Type **Tile** in the **Criteria row** of the Roof column and type **<=1997** in the **Criteria row** of the YearBuilt column.

You only want to see properties with a tile roof that were built on or before 1997.

d. Save the query as **Properties Built on or Before 1997**.

e. Run the query. Widen the columns of the query so all the data values are visible.

When you export to Word, the columns show all the data if the column widths are wide enough in Access and the total width of the exported table does not exceed the Word document width.

f. Click the **EXTERNAL DATA tab**, click the **More button** in the Export group, and then select **Word** from the displayed list.

You will use the list of properties to create a memo to send to the roofer so he can inspect the roofs for damage.

g. Click **Browse** to choose a location to save the export file. Type **a08h2Sub_LastFirst** in the **File name box**. Click **Save**. Click the **Open the destination file after the export operation is complete check box** in the Export – RTF File dialog box. Click **OK**.

A new Word window opens, showing the Properties Built on or Before 1997 data.

TROUBLESHOOTING: If you attempt to create a Word file that already exists, Access warns you and asks you, *Do you want to replace the existing one?* If you attempt to create a Word file that is already open, Access displays a warning, *Microsoft Office Access can't save the output data...* Close the open Word file and try again.

h. Press **Enter** one time in Word, type **Memo**. Press **Enter** and type **To:**. Press **Enter**, type **From:**, press **Enter**, type **Subject:**, and then center *Memo*, as shown in Figure 16.37.

i. Click the **FILE tab** and click **Save As** to save the new Word document as **a08h2Sub_LastFirst**. Change the *Save as type* to **Word Document**. Click **OK** in the warning dialog box. Close Word.

j. Click **Access** in the Windows taskbar to return to Access. Click **Close** to close the Save Export Steps dialog box without saving.

k. Close the query. Save the query if you are asked.

STEP 4 ›› EXPORT TO A PDF OR XPS DOCUMENT

You need to send the Service Request Report to one of the BMS contractors. The contractor asks that you send him the report in a PDF format file because he does not own Microsoft Office. Refer to Figure 16.38 as you complete Step 4.

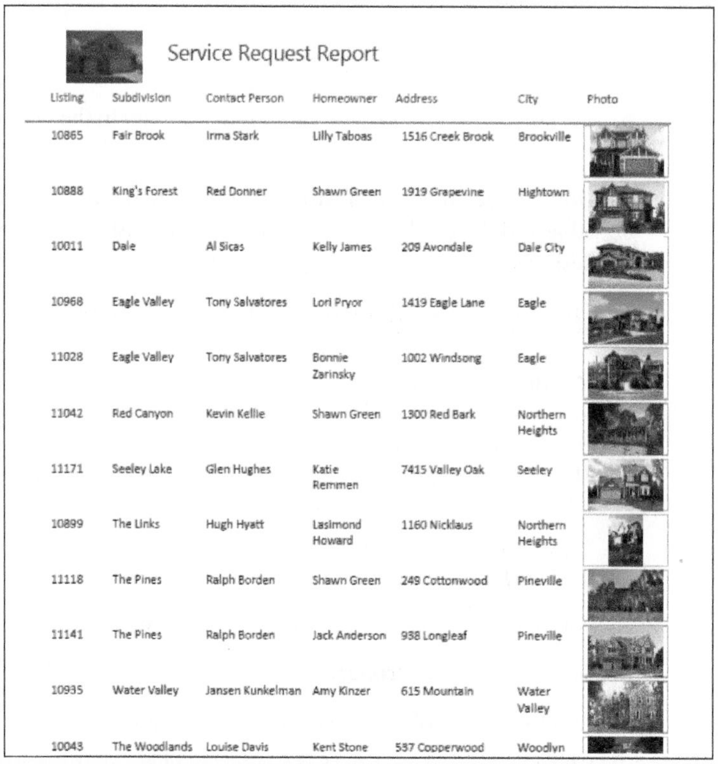

Service Request Report

Listing	Subdivision	Contact Person	Homeowner	Address	City	Photo
10865	Fair Brook	Irma Stark	Lilly Taboas	1516 Creek Brook	Brookville	
10888	King's Forest	Red Donner	Shawn Green	1919 Grapevine	Hightown	
10011	Dale	Al Sicas	Kelly James	209 Avondale	Dale City	
10968	Eagle Valley	Tony Salvatores	Lori Pryor	1419 Eagle Lane	Eagle	
11028	Eagle Valley	Tony Salvatores	Bonnie Zarinsky	1002 Windsong	Eagle	
11042	Red Canyon	Kevin Kellie	Shawn Green	1300 Red Bark	Northern Heights	
11171	Seeley Lake	Glen Hughes	Katie Remmen	7415 Valley Oak	Seeley	
10899	The Links	Hugh Hyatt	Laslmond Howard	1160 Nicklaus	Northern Heights	
11118	The Pines	Ralph Borden	Shawn Green	249 Cottonwood	Pineville	
11141	The Pines	Ralph Borden	Jack Anderson	938 Longleaf	Pineville	
10935	Water Valley	Jansen Kunkelman	Amy Kinzer	615 Mountain	Water Valley	
10043	The Woodlands	Louise Davis	Kent Stone	537 Copperwood	Woodlyn	

FIGURE 16.38 Service Request Report Exported to PDF

Photos: (Left) © Pavel Losevsky/Fotolia; (Right, from bottom) © qingwa/Fotolia, © Maisna/Fotolia, © pics721/Fotolia, © Nomad_Soul/Fotolia, © Pavel Losevsky/Fotolia

a. Select the **Service Request Report** in the Navigation Pane.

   You will use this report to create a PDF document.

b. Click the **EXTERNAL DATA tab** and click **PDF or XPS** in the Export group.

c. Navigate to the folder where you are saving your files.

d. Change the file name to **a08h2Service_LastFirst** and select **PDF** for the *Save as type*. Click **Publish**.

   A new PDF document is created in the folder where you are saving your files.

e. Click **Close** to close the Save Export Steps dialog box without saving.

f. Close the report.

Blackwood's landscaping contractor asked you for a list of all properties for which BMS provides landscaping services. Because his office manager knows Access, he asks you to send him the information in an Access database. Refer to Figure 16.39 as you complete Step 5.

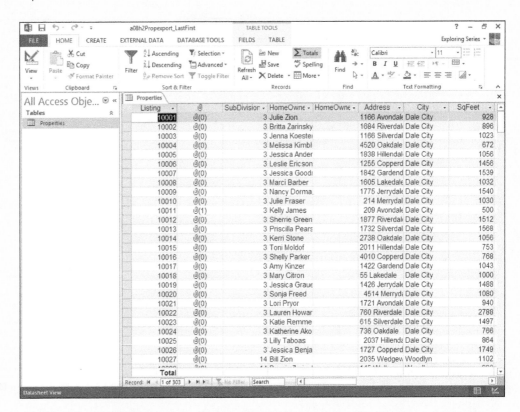

FIGURE 16.39 Destination Database with the Properties Table

a. Close the *a08h2Property_LastFirst* database, if necessary. Open the *a08h2Propexport* database. Save it as **a08h2Propexport_LastFirst** in the folder where you are saving your solution files. Verify that this database does not contain any tables. Close *a08h2Propexport_LastFirst*. Open *a08h2Property_LastFirst*. Select, but do not open, the **Properties table** in the Navigation Pane.

b. Click the **EXTERNAL DATA tab** and click **Access** in the Export group.

The Export – Access Database dialog box appears.

c. Click **Browse** to locate the destination database file. Select the *a08h2Propexport_LastFirst* database and click **Save**. When you return to the Export – Access Database dialog box, click **OK**.

The Export dialog box displays, asking for additional information about the table you are exporting.

d. Confirm that *Properties* is in the *Export Properties to* box. Accept the **Definition and Data option**. Click **OK**.

You are sending the properties data to the landscaping contractor, and he will need all of the properties data.

e. Click **Close** to close the Save Export Steps dialog box without saving.

The table should have been exported, and next you want to verify that it is in the destination database.

f. Close *a08h2Property_LastFirst*. Locate *a08h2Propexport_LastFirst* and open the database. Open the Properties table.

Compare your findings to Figure 16.39.

g. Close the *a08h2Propexport_LastFirst* database.

h. Open the *a08h2Property_LastFirst* database.

The landscaping contractor would like you to send him a form to make it easier to work with the properties data. You will use the Form Tool to quickly make a form with stacked layout. You will export the form to the same destination database as in Step 5. Refer to Figure 16.40 as you complete Step 6.

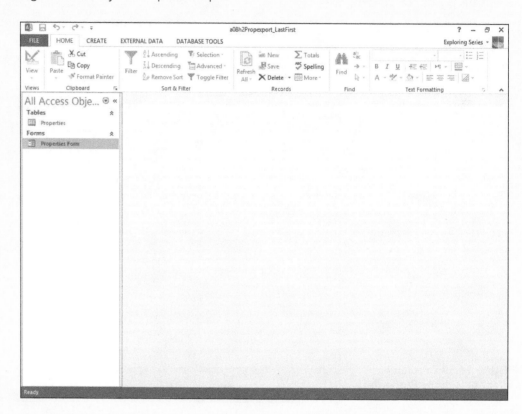

FIGURE 16.40 Destination Database with the Properties Form

a. Click to select the **Properties table** in the Navigation Pane in the *a08h2Property_LastFirst* database.

b. Click the **CREATE tab** and click **Form** in the Forms group.

Access creates a new stacked layout form based on the Properties table.

c. Reduce the width of the Listing control by clicking on the right border and dragging it to the left. Reduce the width by 50%.

d. Select the last four fields (text box and label)—**DateServiceStarted**, **RequestForService**, **SellingAgent**, and **ListingAgent**—one at a time and press **Delete** to delete the fields from the form.

e. Save the form as **Properties Form**. Close the form. Select the **Properties Form** in the Navigation Pane.

f. Click the **EXTERNAL DATA tab** and click **Access** in the Export group.

The Export – Access Database dialog box appears.

g. Click **Browse** to locate the destination database file. Select the *a08h2Propexport_LastFirst* database and click **Save**. When you return to the Export – Access Database dialog box, click **OK**.

The Export dialog box appears, asking you to type the name of the form you are exporting.

h. Confirm that *Properties Form* is in the *Export Properties Form to* box. Click **OK**.

You accept the default name Properties Form.

i. Click **Close** to close the Save Export Steps dialog box without saving.

The form should have been exported, and next you want to verify that it is in the destination database.

j. Close the *a08h2Property_LastFirst* database. Locate *a08h2Propexport_LastFirst* and open the database. Verify the Properties Form is in the database.

Compare your screen to Figure 16.40.

k. Open the form to view the data.

l. Close the form.

m. Click the **FILE tab** and click **Compact & Repair Database**.

n. If you plan to continue with Hands-On Exercise 3, close the database but keep Access open.

Importing Data into Access

In the previous section, you learned about the benefits of exporting information from Access to Excel, from Access to Word, from Access to PDF or XPS, and from one Access database to another Access database. Sometimes you need the opposite process—*importing* data into Access, which enables you to copy external data into your database without linking it to its source file. A variety of data formats can be imported into Access. You will learn how to import the three most common formats: Access, Excel, and text.

When you work with Access, most of the data entry is achieved by typing directly into the tables or forms. However, at times, you may want to import Access database objects from another database into your Access database. If the other objects are tables, you can import the table from the other database into your database and then append that data to your tables. When you append the data to your tables, you may only need a subset of the fields, and you may also use criteria to limit the number of records you append. Create a form or a report based on the imported data if you plan to use the information as stand-alone data (with no connection to the other tables in the database).

You may also receive data in an Excel spreadsheet that can be imported directly into your Access database. Once the data is imported into Access, you can append that data to another table and consequently save a lot of data-entry time. Alternatively, you can use the imported Excel data as a stand-alone table; a stand-alone table can be used to create other objects—queries, forms, or reports.

You may also want to import and use text files in your Access databases rather than typing the data that originates from this type of source file.

In this section, you will learn how to link data from one Access database to another. You will also learn to access data in Excel when using Access by creating a link to and importing an Excel worksheet. Finally, you will learn how to import data into Access using a Text file.

Linking to an Access Table

When a table in another database is relevant to your database, two options are available. One is that you can import the table from the external database into your database; the other is to create a link to a table in another Access database. Importing a table from an external database increases the size of your database; the table could be so large that your database may run less efficiently. *Linking* lets you connect to a table without having to import the table data into your database. You can only link to the tables in another Access database; you cannot link to queries, forms, reports, macros, or modules.

When you link to a table in another Access database, Access creates a new table, called a *linked table*, which maintains a connection to the source table. You cannot change the structure of a linked table in the destination database (e.g., you cannot add or delete a field in a linked table, and you cannot modify the data type of a field). Any changes you make to the data in the source database are reflected in the linked table in the destination database, and vice versa.

A link to an Access table enables edits to the table in the source database from within the destination database. This is in contrast to a link to an Excel spreadsheet. You cannot edit a linked spreadsheet from within Access. The ability to link to Access tables is important because databases are sometimes intentionally split so that nontable objects reside in one database, whereas tables reside in another. To join the two databases, links are created from the database *without* tables to the database *with* tables. Users can add, delete, and edit data (in the linked tables) as if the tables resided in the first database (when they actually reside in the second).

Examine the Tables in the Source Database

STEP 1 » Before you link to tables in another Access database, it is best to examine the tables in the source database first. To examine the Access tables, open the source database—the same way you open any Access database—and examine the data in the table(s). Double-click the table that contains the information you need, as shown in Figure 16.41. Make sure the contents, field names, and other elements are correct prior to linking to the table.

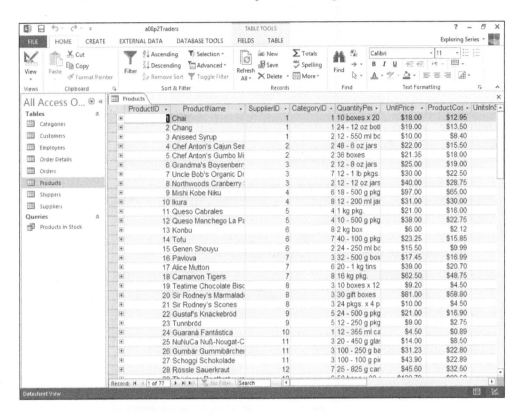

FIGURE 16.41 Products Table in External Database

If the data in the source table looks like it is generally compatible with a table in your database, you can add the linked data to your table. To add the new data into your existing table, you can append all or only a subset of the new table records to your table. You accomplish this by creating an append query based on the linked Access table. An append query is a special query that adds records to an existing table.

Link to an Access Table

STEP 2 » After you examine the data in the source table—the data you want to link to Access—you are ready to create a link from within your Access database.

To link to an Access table in another database, do the following:

1. Click the EXTERNAL DATA tab.
2. Click Access in the Import & Link group. The Get External Data – Access Database dialog box opens, as shown in Figure 16.42.
3. Click *Link to the data source by creating a linked table*.
4. Click Browse to locate the Access database you want to link to.
5. Click the file to select it and click Open to specify this file as the source of the data.
6. Click the *Link to the data source by creating a linked table* option and click OK. The Link Tables dialog box appears, as shown in Figure 16.43.
7. Select the table you want to link to and click OK. Click Select All if the database contains multiple tables and you want to link to all of them.

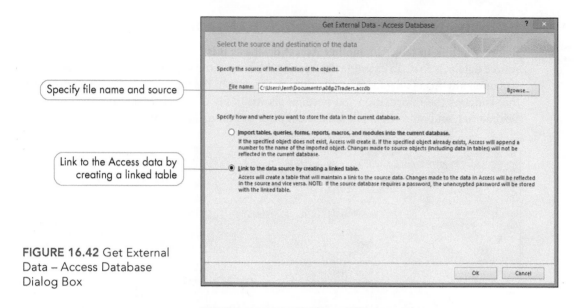

FIGURE 16.42 Get External Data – Access Database Dialog Box

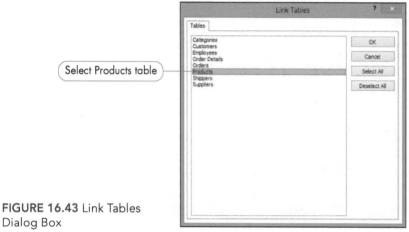

FIGURE 16.43 Link Tables Dialog Box

Once the link is created, you will see a special arrow icon next to the table name in the Navigation Pane that indicates the table is linked to an Access table (see Figure 16.44). Because the name of the linked table, Products, is the same as that of a table that already exists in your Access database, Access adds the number 1 to the end of the table name. Therefore, Access renames the linked table Products1. If you link to another table with the same name, Products, Access renames the third table Products2. To distinguish the linked Products table from the existing Products table, the second table could be renamed (as Traders Products, for example), as shown in Figure 16.45.

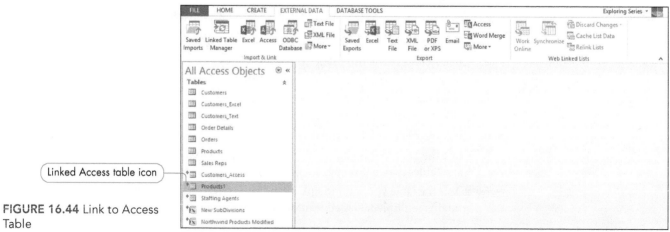

FIGURE 16.44 Link to Access Table

FIGURE 16.45 Link to Access Table—Renamed

Linking to an Excel Spreadsheet

If you have an Access database and you want to import data from an Excel spreadsheet that contains information related to your database, you have three options. You can manually enter the information contained in the spreadsheet into the database tables; you can create a link from Access to Excel that enables you to update tables or create reports based on the data in the Excel spreadsheet; or you can import the data into your Access database to manipulate the data prior to appending it to the tables.

Linking and importing may appear to produce the same results; however, some differences do exist with regard to the resulting size of the database and the ability to modify data. Linking enables you to view the Excel data without increasing the size of the Access database. Importing a large Excel worksheet may increase the Access database substantially (linking to the same spreadsheet does not affect the size of the Access file). Importing an Excel sheet enables you to modify the data prior to appending it to a table. Linking does not enable you to update data from within Access; if errors exist in the worksheet, you must correct the errors in Excel and redisplay the linked table in Access.

Verify the Format of an Excel Spreadsheet

You find that some new property subdivisions are opening in your region, and you may want to target them for new business. You have obtained a spreadsheet that contains initial details, and you want to add the new data to your database. First open the spreadsheet in Excel and examine the data, as shown in Figure 16.46.

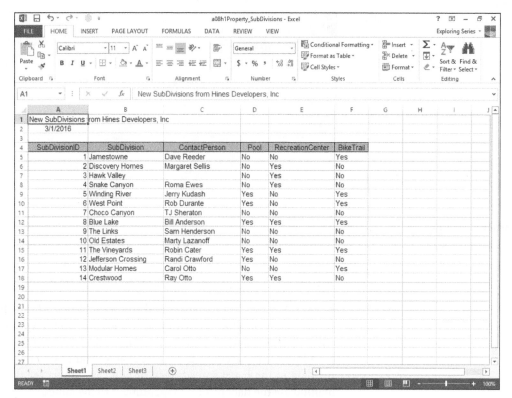

FIGURE 16.46 Property SubDivisions Spreadsheet to Import into Access

STEP 3 >>

Before linking to the spreadsheet, you want to be sure the data is organized so that the import will be successful. The data should be in continuous rows and columns with no blank rows, columns, or extraneous explanatory text. Ideally, the column headings and data formats should be an exact match to those in your database and in the same order, particularly if you are planning to merge the linked spreadsheet into an existing table. The data in the Excel spreadsheet contains titles in cells A1 and A2 and a blank row in row 3. These first three rows will not import properly and should be deleted prior to importing the data. However, it is a good idea to create a backup copy of the original spreadsheet before deleting the rows. This enables you to look up the original data in case this information is needed at another time. In the sheet to be linked, delete the title and blank rows, then save and close the Excel spreadsheet. The results should match those shown in Figure 16.47.

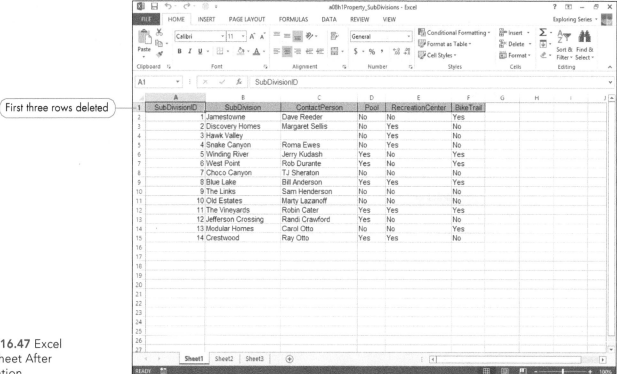

FIGURE 16.47 Excel Spreadsheet After Modification

Link to an Excel Spreadsheet

STEP 4 »

After you modify the Excel spreadsheet so the data will properly link to Access, you are ready to create a link from within Access.

To link the Excel spreadsheet to Access, do the following:

1. Click the EXTERNAL DATA tab and click Excel in the Import & Link group. The Get External Data – Excel Spreadsheet dialog box launches as shown in Figure 16.48.
2. Click Browse to locate the Excel file you want to link to, click the file to select it, and then click Open to specify this file as the source of the data.
3. Click the *Link to the data source…* option and click OK. The Link Spreadsheet Wizard launches as shown in Figure 16.49.
4. Select the worksheet from the list of worksheets shown at the top of the dialog box and click Next.
5. Click First Row Contains Column Headings and click Next. The column headings of the Excel spreadsheet become the field names in the Access table.
6. Enter the new table name in the Linked Table Name box, as shown in Figure 16.50, and click Finish.

Because Access can only link to one sheet at a time, you might have to create multiple links, one for each worksheet. Make sure you label the links with descriptive names.

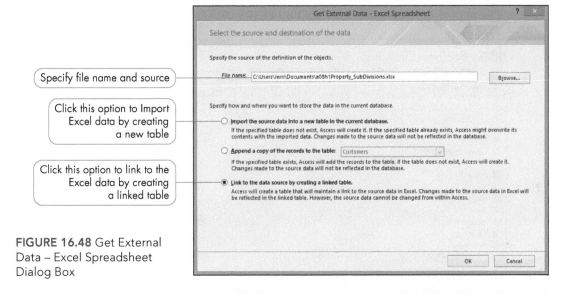

FIGURE 16.48 Get External Data – Excel Spreadsheet Dialog Box

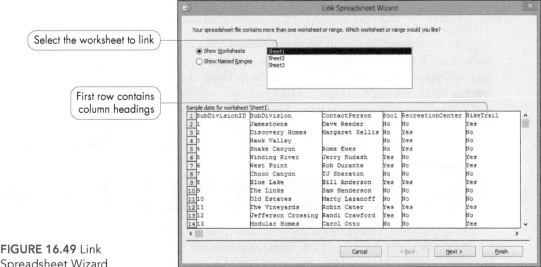

FIGURE 16.49 Link Spreadsheet Wizard

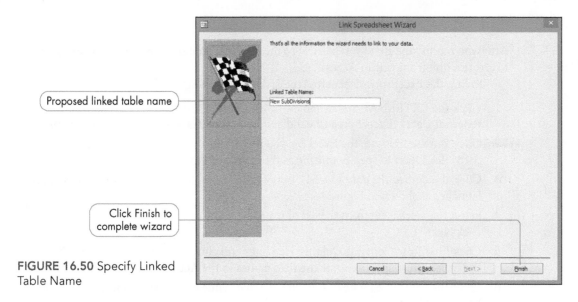

Proposed linked table name

Click Finish to complete wizard

FIGURE 16.50 Specify Linked Table Name

Once the link is created, you will see a special arrow icon next to the table name in the Navigation Pane that indicates the table is linked to the Excel file (see Figure 16.51). Double-click the table name and the table opens. The data looks similar to data in the other tables, even though the data resides in an external Excel file. Although you have the linked table open in Access, you can still open the file in Excel (and vice versa).

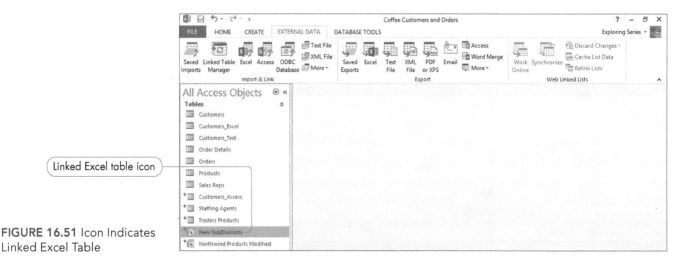

Linked Excel table icon

FIGURE 16.51 Icon Indicates Linked Excel Table

Importing an Excel Spreadsheet

Suppose you receive data in an Excel spreadsheet from another branch of your company and want to work with it in your Access database. In addition to linking to an Excel spreadsheet, you can import a spreadsheet into your Access database. Importing a large Excel worksheet may increase the database file size substantially; however, one reason why you would import an Excel spreadsheet is because you have more control over the imported data. The imported spreadsheet is actually a copy of the original spreadsheet, with no dependency on the external source. For that reason you are able to manipulate the data as necessary once it is available in your database.

TIP | Appending Excel Data to Your Database

When importing a spreadsheet into your database, if a comparable table exists, you can choose to append a copy of the Excel records to the table. In the Get External Data – Excel Spreadsheet dialog box, click the *Append a copy of the records to the table* option and select the table to which you want the records added.

Examine the Spreadsheet Before Importing

STEP 5 ⟩⟩
Always examine the Excel spreadsheet (as shown in Figure 16.52) before attempting to import it into Access. You want to be sure there are no extra rows of data that do not comply with the format of an Access table. You also need to delete any blank rows to ensure that the data to import is continuous and check that the column headings appear in the first row of the spreadsheet.

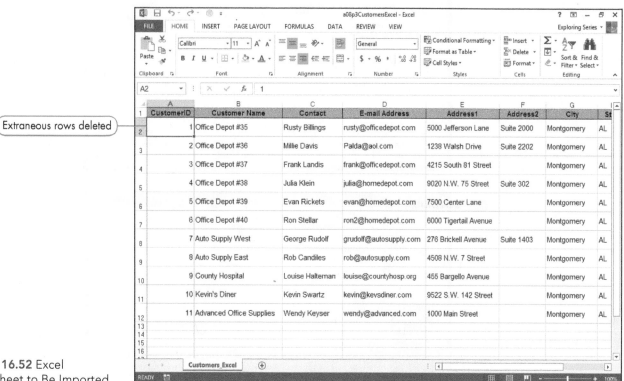

Extraneous rows deleted

FIGURE 16.52 Excel Spreadsheet to Be Imported

Import a Spreadsheet into Access

After you examine the Excel spreadsheet to determine that the data will properly import to Access, you are ready to create the imported table.

To import the Excel spreadsheet to Access, do the following:

1. Click the EXTERNAL DATA tab.
2. Click Excel in the Import & Link group. The Get External Data – Excel Spreadsheet dialog box launches as shown in Figure 16.48.
3. Click Browse to locate the Excel file you want to import, click the file to select it, and then click Open to specify this file as the source of the data.
4. Click the *Import the source data...* option and click OK. The Import Spreadsheet Wizard launches.
5. Select the worksheet from the list of worksheets shown at the top of the dialog box (if necessary) and click Next.
6. Click the First Row Contains Column Headings check box and click Next two times (see Figure 16.53). The column headings of the Excel spreadsheet become the field names in the Access table.
7. Click the *Choose my own primary key* option if the imported data has a field that is acceptable as a primary key (as shown in Figure 16.54) and click Next. Access sets the value in the first column of the spreadsheet (for example, CustomerID) as the primary key field of the table. You can also allow Access to set the primary key if no value that is eligible to be a key field exists, or to set no primary key at all.
8. Enter the new table name in the Import to Table box, as shown in Figure 16.55, and click Finish.
9. Click Close when prompted to Save Import Steps.

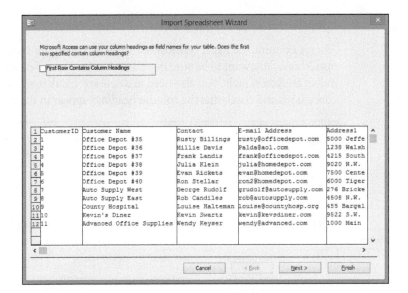

FIGURE 16.53 Import Spreadsheet Wizard

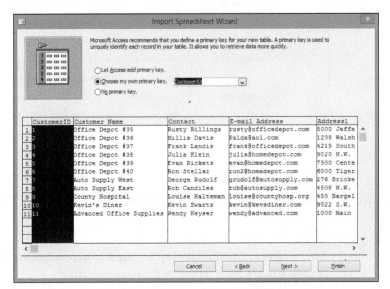

FIGURE 16.54 Choose My Own Primary Key Option

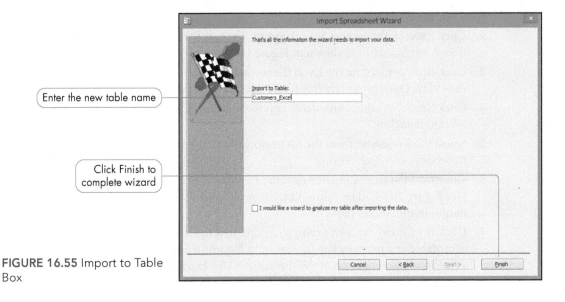

Enter the new table name

Click Finish to complete wizard

FIGURE 16.55 Import to Table Box

Importing a Text File

In the preceding examples, you learned how to link to a table in another Access database and to link to and import an Excel spreadsheet. In this example, you will import a text file directly into your existing Access database. *Text files* are common methods of exchanging information between two computer systems. Text files are usually created by computer software, not manually by humans, and usually contain consistent formatting.

The two most common text file types are comma-separated values (CSV) and fixed-length files. *CSV text files* use a comma to separate one column from the next column, enabling the receiving software to distinguish one set of field values from the next. *Fixed-length text files* allocate a certain number of characters for each field. A fixed-length file containing company data might contain the fields Company Name with 25 characters allocated, Address with 20 characters allocated, City with 20 characters allocated, Region with 2 characters allocated, and Postal Code with 10 characters allocated. Any values with fewer than the allocated characters have spaces added to the end of the value, and any value that is longer than its allocated characters is cut off at the position where the characters exceed the maximum allowed.

Examine the Text File Before Importing

STEP 6 If you receive a text file that needs to be imported into Access, you should examine the file first before performing the import routine. You need to confirm that the contents of the text file are relevant to your database. Also, verify that the format of the file is consistent and that the fields and data values correspond to your Access tables. A text file of the CSV type usually has a .csv extension. If you double-click a CSV file, Excel, the default software application associated with CSV files, opens the file. You can examine the file using Excel. To see the file in its native format, right-click the file, click *Open with*, and then click Notepad from the shortcut menu.

For example, suppose the file NewCustomers.csv contains a list of new prospects for your company. Rather than open the file using the default software, Excel, you could open the file in Notepad to view the comma-separated text.

To open the CSV file in Notepad, do the following:

1. Right-click the file in File Explorer.
2. Point to *Open with*.
3. Click Notepad. The file opens in Notepad, as shown in Figure 16.56.

The data contains field names in the first row—Customer ID, Customer Name, Contact, and so forth—with data values starting in the second row. Each row contains commas separating one column from the next.

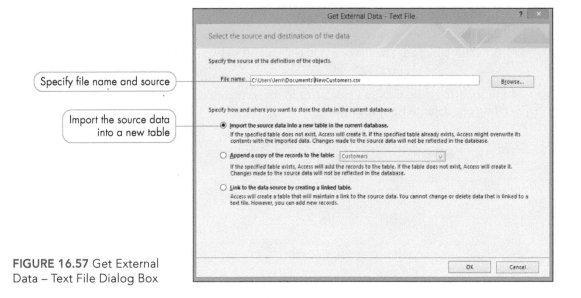

FIGURE 16.56 CSV File
Opened with Notepad

Import a Text File into Access

STEP 7 »
After you examine the data in the CSV file you are ready to import the data into your Access database.

To import a text file into an Access database, do the following:

1. Click the EXTERNAL DATA tab.
2. Click Text File in the Import & Link group. The Get External Data – Text File dialog box launches, as shown in Figure 16.57.
3. Click Browse to locate the CSV file you want to import (e.g., NewCustomers.csv), click the file to select it, and then click Open to specify this file as the source of the data.
4. Click the *Import the source data into a new table…* option and click OK. The Import Text Wizard dialog box appears as shown in Figure 16.58.
5. Click Next to proceed through the questions in the wizard.
6. Click the *First row contains field names* check box and click Next two times.
7. Click the *Choose my own primary key* option and click Next. Access sets the value in the first field name of the text file, if it is acceptable, as the primary key field of the table. You can also allow Access to set the primary key if no value that is eligible to be a key field exists, or to set no primary key at all.
8. Enter the new table name in the *Import to Table* box and click Finish.
9. Click Close when shown the Save Import Steps prompt. The new table appears in the Navigation Pane, as shown in Figure 16.59.

Specify file name and source

Import the source data
into a new table

FIGURE 16.57 Get External
Data – Text File Dialog Box

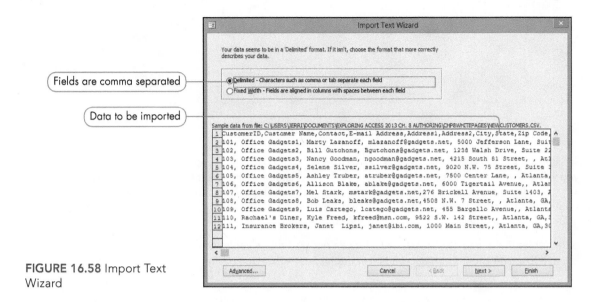

FIGURE 16.58 Import Text
Wizard

Fields are comma separated

Data to be imported

New imported table

FIGURE 16.59 Table Imported
from CSV File

Quick
Concepts

1. What would be a benefit of importing a spreadsheet into your database rather than linking it? *p. 840*

2. Why is it important to examine a spreadsheet before importing it into Access? *p. 841*

3. How is the data organized in a CSV file? *p. 843*

3 Importing Data into Access

Blackwood Maintenance Service is adding additional subdivisions to its portfolio. It will need several new employees to manage the new subdivisions—you will review the list of agents provided in an Access database and link it to the BMS database. BMS has obtained some subdivision information in an Excel spreadsheet, which you will link and import to the database. Another spreadsheet containing potential properties to be inspected also needs to be imported. Finally, BMS purchased a list of properties that might need its services. You need to import the CSV list into the current database.

Skills covered: Examine the Tables in the Source Database • Link to an Access Table • Verify the Format of an Excel Spreadsheet • Link to an Excel Spreadsheet • Examine and Import a Spreadsheet into Access • Examine the Text File Before Importing • Import a Text File into Access

STEP 1 ≫ EXAMINE THE TABLES IN THE SOURCE DATABASE

BMS needs to hire additional agents. It received an Access database from a staffing company with a list of possible agents. You will need to review the data first before you add the data to the Blackwood database. Refer to Figure 16.60 as you complete Step 1.

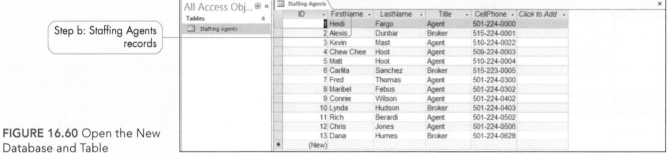

FIGURE 16.60 Open the New Database and Table

a. Open the *a08h3Propstaff* database file.

Access opens the *a08h3Propstaff* database, and the staffing agents table displays in the Navigation Pane.

b. Open the Staffing Agents table in Datasheet view.

Thirteen agents are in the table.

c. Close the Staffing Agents table. Click the **FILE tab**, click **Save As**, click **Save As**, and then type **a08h3Propstaff_LastFirst**. Save the database in the folder where you are saving your solution files. Close the database.

STEP 2 ≫ LINK TO AN ACCESS TABLE

After examining the data from the staffing company, Blackwood wants to link the data to its database. You will create a link to the table in the staffing database; you will then append the data into the Agents table in the Blackwood database. Refer to Figure 16.61 as you complete Step 2.

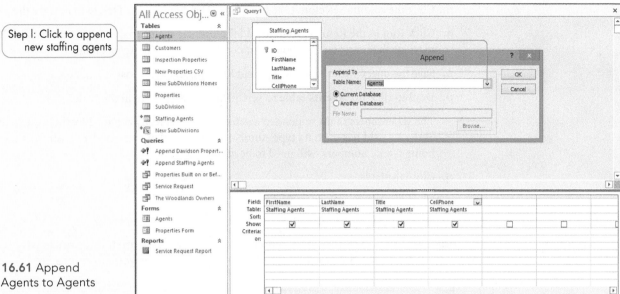

Step I: Click to append new staffing agents

FIGURE 16.61 Append Staffing Agents to Agents Table

a. Open *a08h2Property_LastFirst*. Click the **FILE tab**, click **Save As**, click **Save As**, and then type **a08h3Property_LastFirst**, changing the *h2* to *h3*.

> **TROUBLESHOOTING:** If you did not complete Hands-On Exercises 1 and 2, go back and complete them now. When you are finished, continue with Hands-On Exercise 3.

b. Click the **EXTERNAL DATA tab** in the *a08h3Property_LastFirst* database and click **Access** in the Import & Link group.

c. Click **Browse** to locate the *a08h3Propstaff_LastFirst* database. Click the file to select it and click **Open**.

d. Select the **Link to the data source… option** and click **OK**.

e. Select the **Staffing Agents table** in the Link Tables dialog box and click **OK**.

You created a link to the Staffing Agents table in the staffing database.

f. Double-click the **Staffing Agents table** in the Navigation Pane.

You are now prepared to add the new agents to the Agents table so that all of the agents can be merged into one table.

g. Close the Staffing Agents table.

h. Click the **CREATE tab** and click **Query Design** in the Queries group. Add Staffing Agents to the query design and close the Show Table dialog box.

You created a select query, which you will convert to an append query.

i. Double-click the title bar of the Staffing Agents table to select all the fields. Drag the fields to the query design grid.

j. Switch to Datasheet view.

The new staffing agents are listed as expected.

k. Switch back to Design view.

l. Click **Append** in the Query Type group and select **Agents** using the Table Name arrow. Click **OK**.

The *Append to* row appears in the query design grid with the corresponding field names listed. Some of the new IDs are the same as the existing IDs. You decide to remove the ID field from the append query.

m. Click the column selector at the top of the ID column. Press **Delete** to remove the column.

n. Click **Run** in the Results group to add the staffing agents to the Agents table. Click **Yes** in the message that says you are about to append 13 rows to the Agents table.

o. Save the query with the name **Append Staffing Agents**. Close the query.

p. Double-click the **Agents table** to verify the new agents are in the table.

The ID numbers of the appended agents are automatically assigned by the Agents table, as the ID field has the data type AutoNumber. Note that some of the missing data, such as home phone numbers, will need to be added later.

q. Close the table.

STEP 3 ≫ VERIFY THE FORMAT OF AN EXCEL SPREADSHEET

You will open the list of new subdivisions that BMS received in an Excel spreadsheet format and decide whether you want to add the information to your existing subdivision table. Refer to Figure 16.62 as you complete Step 3.

> Step c: Click Delete in the Cells group on the Home tab

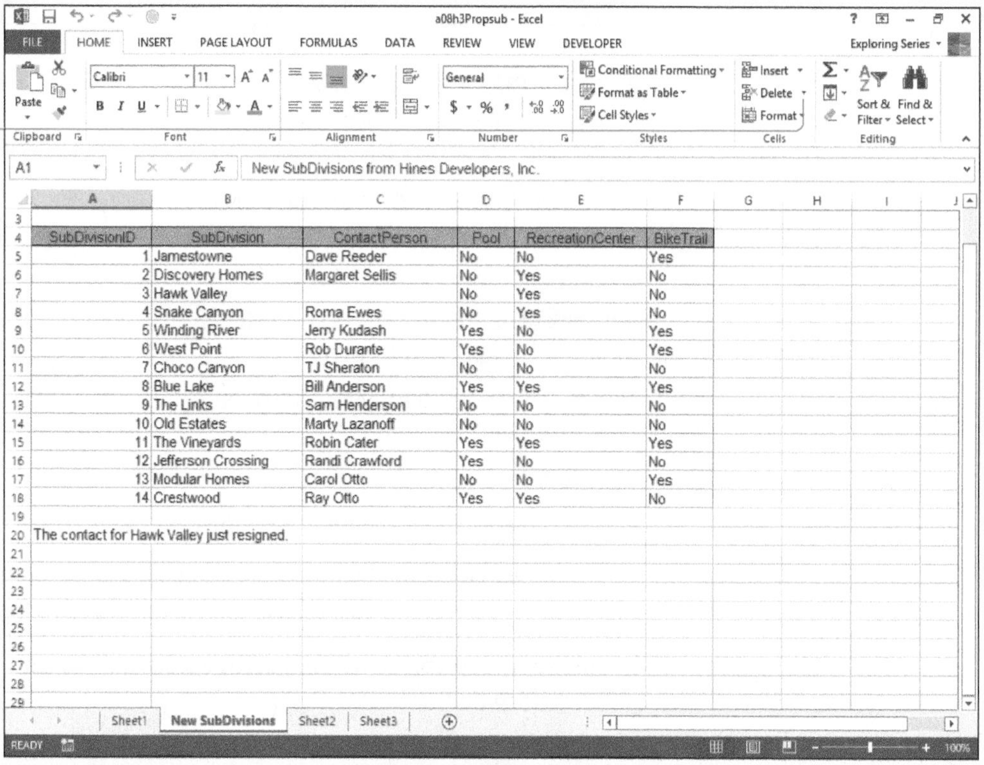

FIGURE 16.62 Copied Excel Worksheet to Be Modified

a. Open the Excel workbook *a08h3Propsub*. Click the **FILE tab**, click **Save As**, click **Save As**, click **Browse** to navigate to correct folder, click enter the file name **a08h3Propsub_LastFirst**, and then click Save.

You need to decide if the data will fit into the existing subdivision table and whether the data is formatted properly and does not contain extraneous rows.

b. Click **Enable Editing** in the Excel window, if necessary. Right-click the **Sheet1 tab**. Select **Move or Copy**. Select **Sheet2** in the *Before sheet:* box and click the **Create a copy check box**. Click **OK**. Double-click the copied sheet tab, rename the worksheet **New SubDivisions**, and then press **Enter**.

The new worksheet is the second worksheet.

c. Click the **New SubDivisions tab**, if necessary. Select the first three rows of the worksheet. Click **Delete** in the Cells group on the HOME tab, as shown in Figure 16.62.

The first row of a spreadsheet must contain column headings that can be recognized as field names by Access.

d. Click **cell A17**, which contains *The contact for Hawk Valley just resigned*. Press **Delete**.

There should not be any data after the last row of formatted data.

e. Save and close the workbook, and exit Excel.

The Excel spreadsheet can now be linked to the Access database.

STEP 4 ≫ LINK TO AN EXCEL SPREADSHEET

You decide to create a link to the new subdivisions worksheet. You will then import the data into your Access database. You will use the linked worksheet to create a new table in the database. If the linked Excel spreadsheet is updated later, you could run the Make Table query to overwrite the table with the new data. Refer to Figure 16.63 as you complete Step 4.

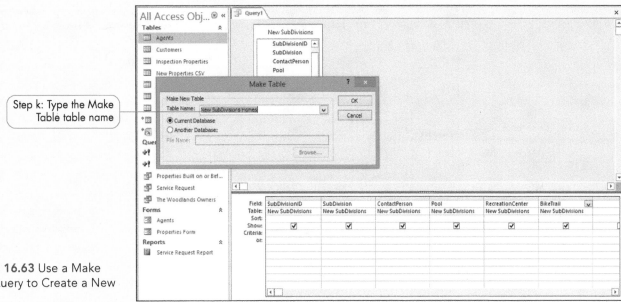

Step k: Type the Make Table table name

FIGURE 16.63 Use a Make Table Query to Create a New Table

a. Click **Access** in the Windows taskbar and click the **EXTERNAL DATA tab**.

b. Click **Excel** in the Import & Link group.

c. Click **Browse** to locate the spreadsheet *a08h3Propsub_LastFirst*. Click **Open**.

d. Select the **Link to the data source… option** and click **OK**.

e. Select **New SubDivisions** in the Show Worksheets box of the Link Spreadsheet Wizard. Click **Next**.

You chose the revised worksheet for the link.

f. Click the **First Row Contains Column Headings check box**. Click **Next**.

g. Accept the name *New SubDivisions* for the Access linked table name. Click **Finish**. Click **OK** in the message box that appears.

The Excel linked icon appears next to the New SubDivisions table.

h. Click the **CREATE tab** and click **Query Design** in the Queries group. Add the New SubDivisions table to the query design and close the Show Table dialog box.

You decide to create a new table from the linked spreadsheet using a Make Table query.

i. Add all the fields from the New SubDivisions table to the query design grid. Switch to Datasheet view to examine the records.

j. Switch back to Design view.

k. Click **Make Table** in the Query Type group. Type **New SubDivisions Homes** in the **Table Name box**, as shown in Figure 16.63. With the Current Database option selected, click **OK**. Click **Run** in the Results group and click **Yes** to the warning message. Close the Make Table query without saving the changes.

The Excel spreadsheet data is now an Access table.

STEP 5 ≫ EXAMINE AND IMPORT A SPREADSHEET INTO ACCESS

Blackwood received an Excel spreadsheet containing a list of potential new properties to be inspected. You need to examine the data prior to adding it to BMS's database; for now, the imported data will be used as a stand-alone table. Refer to Figures 16.64 and 16.65 as you complete Step 5.

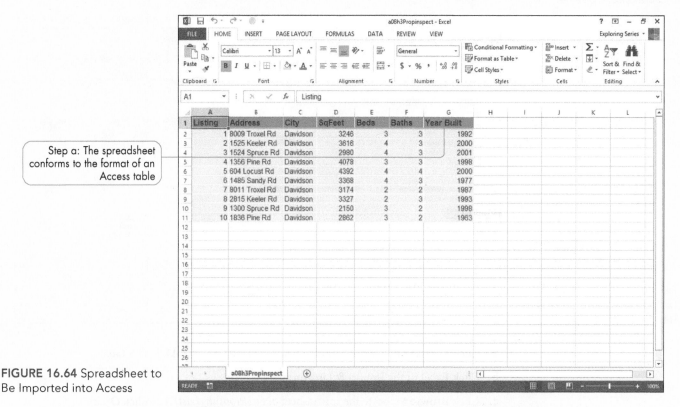

Step a: The spreadsheet conforms to the format of an Access table

FIGURE 16.64 Spreadsheet to Be Imported into Access

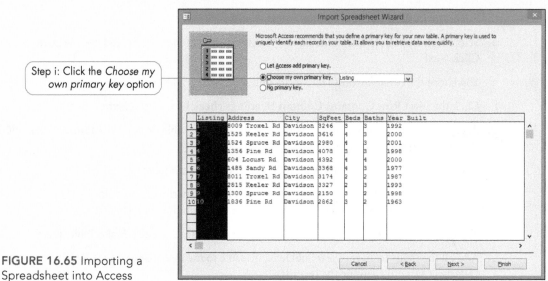

Step i: Click the *Choose my own primary key* option

FIGURE 16.65 Importing a Spreadsheet into Access

a. Open the *a08h3Propinspect* workbook.

The spreadsheet conforms to the format of an Access table, so you do not need to make any changes to it at this time.

b. Close the workbook and exit Excel without making any changes to the file.

c. Click **Access** in the Windows taskbar and click the **EXTERNAL DATA tab**.

d. Click **Excel** in the Import & Link group.

e. Click **Browse** to locate the spreadsheet *a08h3Propinspect*. Click **Open**.

f. Select the **Import the source data into a new table in the current database option** and click **OK**.

g. Ensure *First Row Contains Column Headings* is checked and click **Next** in the Import Spreadsheet Wizard.

The first row of the spreadsheet contains column headings that will be used as the field names for the Access table.

h. Click **Next**.

i. Click the **Choose my own primary key option** and click **Next**.

Access sets the value in the first column of the spreadsheet, Listing, as the primary key field of the table.

j. Enter the new table name, **Inspection Properties**, in the *Import to Table* box and click **Finish**.

k. Click **Close** in the Save Import Steps dialog box.

The imported table appears in the Navigation Pane.

STEP 6 ⟫ EXAMINE THE TEXT FILE BEFORE IMPORTING

Blackwood wants to add additional properties to its database. You want to examine the data prior to adding it to the database. The new data is in a text file. Refer to Figure 16.66 as you complete Step 6.

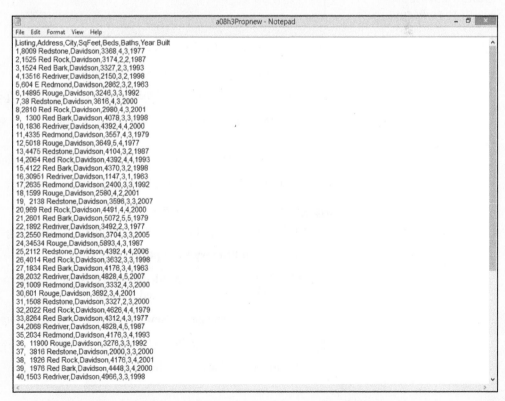

FIGURE 16.66 CSV File Opened in Notepad

a. Open *a08h3Propnew.csv*.

b. Exit Excel without making any changes to the file.

c. Right-click the *a08h3Propnew.csv* file in File Explorer, choose **Open with**, and then click **Notepad** from the shortcut menu.

You decide to examine the file in its native format using Notepad. The file has consistent formatting for importing into Access.

d. Close Notepad.

STEP 7 》 IMPORT A TEXT FILE INTO ACCESS

The BMS owners want to import and then append these properties to the Properties table in the Blackwood database. The Listing values will have to be modified when the data is appended so that they are higher than the existing values in the table. Refer to Figure 16.67 as you complete Step 7.

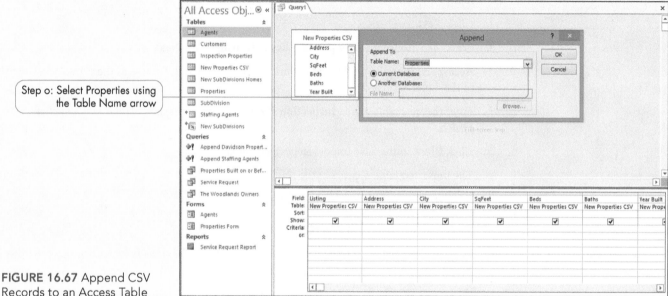

Step o: Select Properties using the Table Name arrow

FIGURE 16.67 Append CSV Records to an Access Table

a. Return to Access. Click the **EXTERNAL DATA tab**.

b. Click **Text File** in the Import & Link group.

c. Click **Browse** to locate the *a08h3Propnew.csv* file. Click **Open**.

d. Select the **Import the source data into a new table in the current database option** and click **OK**.

The Import Text Wizard starts. Delimited should be selected by default.

e. Click **Next** to accept the default options in this dialog box.

f. Click the **First Row Contains Field Names check box**. Click **Next**.

g. Click **Next** to accept the default field options in this dialog box.

h. Click the **No Primary Key option**. Click **Next**.

When the records are appended into an existing table in your database, a unique value is assigned to each of the imported records.

i. Enter the new table name, **New Properties CSV**, in the *Import to Table* box and click **Finish**.

j. Click **Close** in the Save Import Steps dialog box.

The imported table appears in the Navigation Pane.

k. Click the **CREATE tab** and click **Query Design** in the Queries group. Add **New Properties CSV** to the query design and close the Show Table dialog box.

You created a select query, which you will convert to an append query.

l. Double-click the title bar of the New Properties CSV table to select all the fields. Drag the fields to the query design grid.

m. Switch to Datasheet view.

The new properties are listed as expected.

n. Switch to Design view.

o. Click **Append** in the Query Type group and select **Properties** using the Table Name arrow. Click **OK**.

The *Append to* row appears in the design grid with the corresponding field names listed. The new listing values need to be modified so they conform to the format of the existing listings. You decide to add 11300 to each new listing number using a calculated field.

p. Select the **Listing field name** in the first column. Type the calculated field: **Listing2: [Listing] + 11300**.

q. Switch to Datasheet view to see the results of the calculated field.

All of the listing values are now higher than the listing numbers of the existing properties.

r. Switch to Design view.

s. Click **Run** in the Results group to add the new (Davidson) properties to the Properties table.

t. Click **Yes** in response to the *You are about to append 58 row(s)* message.

u. Save the query with the name **Append Davidson Properties**. Close the query.

v. Click the **FILE tab** and click **Compact & Repair Database**.

w. Close the database. Exit Access.

x. Submit *a08h3Property_LastFirst* based on your instructor's directions.

Chapter Objectives Review

After reading this chapter, you have accomplished the following objectives:

1. **Create a hyperlink field.**
   - Add a hyperlink field in Design view: A hyperlink in a table or form launches the appropriate software and enables you to interact with the file.
   - Edit a hyperlink field in Datasheet view: Edit a hyperlink value if it navigates to an incorrect Web page, file, or location.

2. **Add an attachment field.**
   - Add an attachment field in Design view: An attachment field stores a reference to an external file, and you can open that file from within Access.
   - Add or edit attachments in Datasheet view: Manage your attachments from the datasheet using the Attachments dialog box.
   - Remove attachments in Datasheet view: Attachments can be removed using the Attachments dialog box.

3. **Add attachment controls to forms and reports.**
   - Add an attachment control to a form: An attachment control lets you manage attached files in forms.
   - Add an attachment field to a report: You can also manage attached files in reports. In a report, only the first file displays in Print Preview, and you have to navigate to the others.

4. **Export data to Excel.**
   - Select a record source to export to Excel: Tables, queries, forms, and reports can all be exported to Excel if their formats are compatible with spreadsheets.
   - Export a query to Excel: Tables and queries tend to export well to Excel as their datasheet formats are compatible with spreadsheets.
   - Export forms and reports to Excel: Subforms or grouped data may not export or display correctly.

5. **Export data to Word.**
   - Select a record source to export to Word: Data that has been exported to Word cannot always be modified or analyzed.
   - Export tables and queries to Word: Export objects that have a tabular layout (e.g., tables and queries).
   - Modify an RTF file in Word: When an object is exported to Word, Access creates a file in Rich Text Format that opens in Word by default.

6. **Export data to a PDF or XPS document.**
   - Select an object to export: You are not able to edit the data exported to a PDF or XPS document.
   - Export to a PDF or XPS document: PDF and XPS documents can be opened by their respective readers.

7. **Export objects to another Access database.**
   - Export tables to another database: After you create a table for one database, you may be able to use it again (definition or both definition and data) for your next database.
   - Export other objects to another database: There may be common queries, forms, or reports that could also be exported from one database to another.

8. **Link to an Access table.**
   - Examine the tables in the source database: Ensure that the data and format are relevant to your database.
   - Link to an Access table: Linking lets you connect to a table without having to import the table data into your database.

9. **Link to an Excel spreadsheet.**
   - Verify the format of an Excel spreadsheet: Ensure that the data will display properly in Access; delete extraneous or blank rows.
   - Link to an Excel spreadsheet: Create a link from Access to Excel that enables you to view Excel data in Access.

10. **Import an Excel spreadsheet.**
    - Examine the spreadsheet before importing: Ensure that the data will display properly in Access.
    - Import a spreadsheet into Access: Import the data into your Access database to evaluate it before appending it to the tables.

11. **Import a text file.**
    - Examine the text file before importing: Ensure that the data is eligible to be separated into columns and is consistent from row to row.
    - Import a text file into Access: You are able to manipulate the data after it is imported into Access without changing the original text file.

Key Terms Matching

Match the key terms with their definitions. Write the key term letter by the appropriate numbered definition.

a. Attachment control
b. Attachment field
c. CSV text file
d. Fixed-length text file
e. Hyperlink
f. Importing

g. Linking
h. Portable Document Format (PDF)
i. Rich Text Format (RTF)
j. Text file
k. Uniform resource locator (URL)
l. XML Paper Specification (XPS)

1. _____ A file format developed by Microsoft and designed to display a printed page onscreen identically on any computer platform. **p. 820**

2. _____ Uses a comma to separate one column from the next column, enabling the receiving software to distinguish one set of field values from the next. **p. 843**

3. _____ Data type that enables you to quickly link to any file on your computer or to any Web page on the Internet. **p. 798**

4. _____ A common method of exchanging data between two computer systems. **p. 843**

5. _____ The location of a Web site or Web page on the Internet. **p. 798**

6. _____ Process that enables you connect to a table without having to import the table data into your database. **p. 834**

7. _____ A format that enables documents created in one software application to be opened with a different software application. **p. 817**

8. _____ This process may result in increasing the size of the Access database substantially. **p. 798**

9. _____ A file format created by Adobe Systems for document exchange independent of software application and operating system environment. **p. 820**

10. _____ Similar to an attachment in an e-mail; you can use it to attach multiple files of any format and then launch those files from within Access. **p. 800**

11. _____ Allocates a certain number of characters for each field. **p. 843**

12. _____ A control that lets you manage attached files in forms and reports. **p. 803**

Multiple Choice

1. Which statement about hyperlink fields is false?

   (a) Hyperlinks can launch Web pages on the Internet.

   (b) Hyperlinks can launch Excel spreadsheets.

   (c) Editing a hyperlink must be done in Design view.

   (d) Hyperlinks can be modified using the right-click option.

2. Which statement about attachments is true?

   (a) You can attach only one file per record in a table.

   (b) You can use attachment files in forms and reports, but you must first define them in the table.

   (c) Attached photos display as thumbnails in queries.

   (d) Attachment files do not increase the size of an Access database.

3. You need to attach an employee's most recent performance review to her record in the Employees table. What is the correct action?

   (a) Open the Employees table, add an OLE field, and then attach the document to the employee's record in Datasheet view of the table.

   (b) Open the Employees table, add an attachment field, and then attach the document to the employee's record in Design view of the table.

   (c) Open the Employees table, add an attachment field, and then attach the document to the employee's record in Datasheet view of the table.

   (d) Open the Employees table, add a hyperlink field, and then attach the document to the employee's record in Datasheet view of the table.

4. What is the primary difference between an imported table and a linked table?

   (a) Data in an imported table can be modified from Access; data in a linked table cannot be modified.

   (b) Both types increase the size of the database.

   (c) Users cannot create queries with a linked table.

   (d) The data in imported tables resides inside the database; the data in linked tables resides outside the database.

5. You have exported an Access table to Excel because:

   (a) You cannot create reports in Access.

   (b) It can be analyzed by a user who does not know Access or own the software.

   (c) Data cannot be sorted or filtered in Access.

   (d) The Access database has grown too large.

6. What is the default format when you export data to Word?

   (a) PDF

   (b) RTF

   (c) DOC

   (d) DOCX

7. What is the main difference between a PDF document and an XPS document?

   (a) PDF does not require reader software to open the documents.

   (b) PDF documents can be opened with an Internet browser.

   (c) XPS documents show a replica of what the printed document looks like.

   (d) One format was created by Adobe (PDF) and the other by Microsoft (XPS).

8. You have imported an Excel spreadsheet named *Inventory* into your database. It displays in the Navigation Pane as

   (a) The Inventory table.

   (b) The Inventory form.

   (c) The Inventory report.

   (d) A linked table.

9. Which type of objects can be exported from one database to another?

   (a) Tables only

   (b) Tables and queries

   (c) All objects

   (d) Reports only

10. Importing a text file

   (a) Requires the Import Wizard.

   (b) Can only be done with a CSV file.

   (c) Is limited to files with 999 rows or less.

   (d) Is similar to importing a Word file.

Practice Exercises

1 Houston Bank Customer Updates

As database administrator for Houston Bank, your manager wants you to attach photos of the customers to the records in the Customers table. You will create an attachment field in the Customers table and then attach the photos to each record. You will also create an e-mail field for the customers and add your own e-mail address to the table. This exercise follows the same set of skills as used in Hands-On Exercise 1 in the chapter. Refer to Figure 16.68 as you complete this exercise.

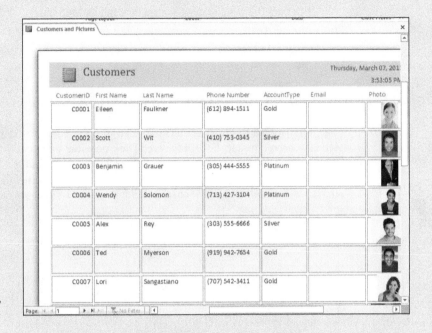

FIGURE 16.68 Hyperlink and Attachment Control in a Report

Photos: (From top) Fotolia, Fotolia, © carlos Restrepo/Fotolia, © Paul Hill/Fotolia, © Rido/Fotolia, Fotolia, © Rido/Fotolia

a. Open *a08p1Bank*. Click the **FILE tab**, click **Save As**, click **Save As**, and then type **a08p1Bank_ LastFirst**. Click **Save**.

b. Open the Customers table in Datasheet view and replace *Your_Name* with your name. Switch to Design view.

c. Type **Email** in the first blank row of the Field Name column. Select **Hyperlink** as the Data Type.

d. Add another field, **Photo**, under *Email*, and then select **Attachment** as the Data Type.

e. Save the table. Switch to Datasheet view.

f. Type your e-mail address into the Email column of the eighth record.

g. Double-click the **paperclip** in the first record. Click **Add** in the Attachments dialog box. Locate and open the *a08p1Customer_photos* folder. Double-click the file named *C0001.jpg* to attach it to the record and click **OK** in the Attachments dialog box.

h. Double-click the **paperclip** in the second record. Click **Add**. Double-click the file named *C0002.jpg* to attach it to the record and click **OK**.

i. Repeat until all of the records have photos attached. Use either the provided picture for record 8 or attach a photo of yourself.

j. Click the **CREATE tab** and click **Report** in the Reports group to create a new report.

k. Modify the report in Layout view. Delete the Address, City, State, and Zip Code columns by clicking each column heading, pressing **Shift**, clicking the first text box below it, and then pressing **Delete**. Delete the empty columns by clicking the column heading of each one and pressing **Delete**.

l. Shrink the remaining columns so all of the fields will fit on one page. Display the report in Print Preview to verify that all columns fit on one page.

> **TROUBLESHOOTING:** If empty columns remain in the report in Layout view, click the empty column heading of each one and press Delete. If the report does not fit onto one page, switch to Design view and drag the page numbers text box to the left. Then reduce the width of the report grid until the report fits on one page.

m. Save the report as **Customers and Pictures**. Close the report. Close the Customers table.

n. Click the **FILE tab** and click **Compact & Repair Database**.

o. Close the database. Exit Access.

p. Submit based on your instructor's directions.

2 International Gourmet Traders

The International Gourmet Traders is a small specialty foods distribution firm. Management wants to send its current product line list to several new potential suppliers. You will need to create several output formats for the product line list so that the new suppliers can receive the information in any one of the following formats: Excel, Word, PDF, or Access. This exercise follows the same set of skills as used in Hands-On Exercise 2 in the chapter. Refer to Figure 16.69 as you complete this exercise.

To: Product Suppliers

From: International Gourmet Traders

Subject: Request for competitive products

Category Name	ProductName	Wholesale Cost	UnitsInStock
Beverages	Chai	$12.95	39
Beverages	Chang	$13.50	17
Beverages	Chartreuse verte	$17.51	69
Beverages	Côte de Blaye	$263.01	17
Beverages	Ipoh Coffee	$45.51	17
Beverages	Lakkalikööri	$17.51	57
Beverages	Laughing Lumberjack Lager	$13.51	52
Beverages	Outback Lager	$14.51	15
Beverages	Rhönbräu Klosterbier	$7.26	125
Beverages	Sasquatch Ale	$13.51	111
Beverages	Steeleye Stout	$17.51	20
Condiments	Aniseed Syrup	$8.40	13
Condiments	Chef Anton's Cajun Seasoning	$15.50	53
Condiments	Genen Shouyu	$9.99	39
Condiments	Grandma's Boysenberry Spread	$19.00	120

FIGURE 16.69 Product Pricing Request in Word Format

a. Open *a08p2Traders*. Click the **FILE tab**, click **Save As**, click **Save As**, and then type **a08p2 Traders_LastFirst**. Click **Save**.

b. Open the Current Product Line query, examine the records in Datasheet view, and then close the query. Verify that the Current Product Line query is selected in the Navigation Pane before you complete each step below.

c. Export the product information to an Excel format as follows:
- Click the **EXTERNAL DATA tab**.
- Click **Excel** in the Export group.
- Click **Browse** to open the File Save dialog box.
- Navigate to the location where you are saving your files.
- Type **a08p2Prodline_LastFirst** as the file name.
- Verify that the *Save as type* is set as Excel Workbook.
- Click **Save** to return to the Export – Excel Spreadsheet dialog box.
- Click the **Export data with formatting…** and **Open the destination file… check boxes**.
- Click **OK**.

- Verify that the data exported correctly to Excel and exit Excel. (The Excel file is automatically saved.)
- Click **Close** in the Save Export Steps dialog box in Access.

d. Export the product information to a Word format as follows:
- Click the **EXTERNAL DATA tab**.
- Click the **More button** in the Export group and select **Word** from the list.
- Click **Browse** to open the File Save dialog box.
  - Navigate to the location where you are saving your files.
  - Type **a08p2Prodline_LastFirst** as the file name.
  - Verify that the *Save as type* is set as Rich Text Format.
  - Click **Save** to return to the Export – RTF File dialog box.
- Click the **Open the destination file… check box**.
- Click **OK**.
- Verify that the data exported correctly to Word, press **Enter**, and then type the To, From, and Subject lines as shown in Figure 16.69.
- Click the **FILE tab** and click **Save As**.
- Navigate to the location where you are saving your files and type **a08p2Prodline_LastFirst** as the file name.
- Change the file type to Word Document.
- Click **Save**. Click **OK** in the compatibility message box.
- Close the Word document.
- Click **Close** in the Save Export Steps dialog box in Access.

e. Export the product information to a PDF format as follows:
- Click the **EXTERNAL DATA tab**.
- Click **PDF or XPS** in the Export group.
- Navigate to the location where you are saving your files.
- Type **a08p2Prodline_LastFirst** as the file name.
- Verify that the *Save as type* is set to PDF.
- Click **Publish**.
- Verify that the data exported correctly. Navigate to where you are saving your files in File Explorer and double-click the file to open it in your reader software.

> **TROUBLESHOOTING:** If all of the columns do not fit onto one page, return to the Current Product Line query and reduce the column widths. Publish to PDF again.

- Close the reader program.
- Click **Close** in the Save Export Steps dialog box in Access.

f. To export the product information to another Access database, follow these steps:
- Open the Current Product Line query in Design view.
- Click **Make Table** in the Query Type group to create a new table.
- Type **Products to Export** in the **Table Name box**, and with the Current Database option selected, click **OK**.
- Click **Run** in the Results group.
- Click **Yes** in response to the *You are about to paste 68 rows* message.
- Click the **FILE tab**, click **Save As**, click **Save Object As**, and then click **Save As**.
- Type **Make Table Products in Stock** as the query name and click **OK**. Close the query.
- Select the **Products to Export table** in the Navigation Pane and click the **EXTERNAL DATA tab**.
- Use File Explorer to locate and open *a08p2Prodstock*. Save it as **a08p2Prodstock_LastFirst**.
- Close *a08p2Prodstock_LastFirst* and return to the *a08p2Traders_LastFirst* database.
- Click **Access** in the Export group.
- Click **Browse** in the Export – Access Database dialog box.
  - Locate and select the *a08p2Prodstock_LastFirst* file.
  - Click **Save** to return to the Export – Access Database dialog box.

- Click **OK**.
- Click **OK** to accept the *Products to Export* table name and the *Definition and Data* option.
- Click **Close** in the Save Export Steps dialog box.

g. Click the **FILE tab** and click **Compact & Repair Database**.

h. Close the database.

i. Open the *a08p2Prodstock_LastFirst* database. Verify that the table exported correctly.

j. Close the database. Exit Access.

k. Submit based on your instructor's directions.

3 Break Room Suppliers, Inc.

Break Room Suppliers, Inc., provides coffee, tea, beverages, and snacks to businesses in its area. In an effort to expand their business, the owners have purchased several customer-prospect lists. You will need to link and import the prospect lists into Access so the owners can determine how best to use them in their database. You will also import an Excel spreadsheet containing newly developed sales rep information. This exercise follows the same set of skills as used in Hands-On Exercise 3 in the chapter. Refer to Figure 16.70 as you complete this exercise.

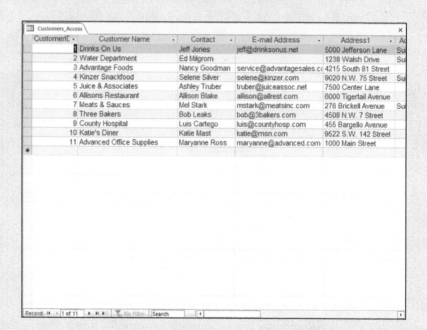

FIGURE 16.70 Customers Imported from Another Access Database

a. Open *a08p3Coffee*. Click the **FILE tab**, click **Save As**, click **Save As**, and then type **a08p3Coffee_LastFirst**. Click **Save**.

b. Click the **EXTERNAL DATA tab** and click **Excel** in the Import & Link group.

c. Click **Browse** in the Get External Data – Excel Spreadsheet dialog box and locate the file *a08p3Custexcel*.

d. Select the file and click **Open** to return to the Get External Data dialog box.

e. Click the **Link to the data source by creating a linked table option**. Click **OK**.

f. Click the **First Row Contains Column Headings check box**. Click **Next**.

g. Confirm **Customers_Excel** is the Linked Table Name. Click **Finish**. Click **OK** in the message box.

h. Double-click the **Customers_Excel table** in the Navigation Pane to view the customer records. Close the table.

i. Click the **EXTERNAL DATA tab** and click **Excel** in the Import & Link group.

j. Click **Browse** in the Get External Data – Excel Spreadsheet dialog box and locate the file *a08p3Repsexcel*.

k. Select the file and click **Open** to return to the Get External Data dialog box.

l. Click the **Import the source data into a new table in the current database option**. Click **OK**.

m. Click the **First Row Contains Column Headings check box**. Click **Next** two times.

n. Click the **Choose my own primary key option**. Click **Next**.

o. Confirm **Sales Reps** is the *Import to Table* name. Click **Finish**. Click **Close** in the Save Import Steps dialog box.

p. Double-click the **Sales Reps table** in the Navigation Pane to view the records. Close the table.

q. Click **Access** in the Import & Link group on the EXTERNAL DATA tab.

r. Click **Browse** in the Get External Data – Access Database dialog box and locate the file *a08p3Custaccess*.

s. Select the file and click **Open** to return to the Get External Data dialog box.

t. Click the **Link to the data source by creating a linked table option**. Click **OK**.

u. Click **Customers_Access** in the Link Tables dialog box. Click **OK**.

v. Double-click the **Customers_Access table** in the Navigation Pane to view the customer records. Close the table.

w. Click **Text File** in the Import & Link group on the External Data tab.

x. Click **Browse** in the Get External Data – Text File dialog box and locate the file *a08p3Custtext.csv*.

y. Select the file and click **Open** to return to the Get External Data dialog box. Verify that the *Import the source data into a new table in the current database* option is selected. Click **OK**.

z. Click **Next** when the Import Text Wizard appears.

aa. Click the **First Row Contains Field Names check box**. Click **Next**.

bb. Click **Next** to confirm the field options.

cc. Click the **No primary key option** in the next dialog box. Click **Next**.

dd. Change the *Import to Table* name to **Customers_Text**. Click **Finish**. Click **Close** in the Save Import Steps dialog box. Close the window.

ee. Double-click the **Customers_Text table** in the Navigation Pane to view the customer records. Close the table.

ff. Click the **FILE tab** and click **Compact & Repair Database**.

gg. Close the database. Exit Access.

hh. Submit based on your instructor's directions.

1 Morrison Arboretum

ANALYSIS CASE

The Morrison Arboretum at NC University wants to add a few new features to its database. They want to add photos of the plants to the Plant Descriptions table and a hyperlink field that points to a Web site that describes each plant. You also need to create a report showing the plant names, the corresponding hyperlinks, and the plant photos. You will export this report to Word, but because you notice that the photos will not export to Word, you will publish the report as a PDF document to distribute via e-mail to members. Finally, you will export a query to Excel to be used as a mailing list. Refer to Figure 16.71 as you complete this exercise.

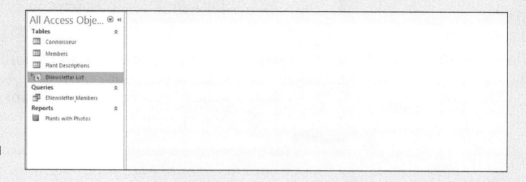

FIGURE 16.71 Navigation Pane with Report and Linked Table

a. Open the file *a08m1Arbor*. Save it as **a08m1Arbor_LastFirst**.

b. Create a new hyperlink field named **PlantLink** in the Plant Descriptions table below the PlantName field.

c. Create a new attachment field named **Picture** in the Plant Descriptions table below the PlantLink field.

DISCOVER

d. Visit Wikipedia.org and perform a search on **viburnum**. Copy the URL and paste it into the correct PlantLink field in Datasheet view.

e. Use the Attachments dialog box to add the appropriate photo for each plant. The photos are in the folder named *a08m1Plant_Photos*.

f. Create a basic report based on the Plant Descriptions table. Set the title of the report as **Plants with Links and Pictures**.

g. Center the report title text in the control and delete the logo to the left of the title control. Save the report as **Plants with Photos**. Close the report. Export the *Plants with Photos* report to Word and save the document as **a08m1Plants_LastFirst**. Note that no pictures were exported and close Word. Close the Save Export Steps dialog box without saving the export steps. Write a short paragraph in Word that discusses why it could be useful to save the export steps. Use Access Help as necessary to research this feature. Save the document as **a08m1Exports_LastFirst**.

h. Publish the report in PDF format and save the document as **a08m1Plants_LastFirst**. View the PDF report in your reader program, note that the pictures were exported, and then close the reader. Close the Save Export Steps dialog box without saving the export steps.

i. Export the query ENewsletter Members to Excel to use as mailing list and save the workbook as **a08m1Email_LastFirst**. Review the exported data and close Excel. Close the Save Export Steps dialog box without saving the export steps. Import the Excel spreadsheet back into the database as a linked table named **ENewsletter List**, using the first row headings as field names.

j. Open the ENewsletter List table and close the table. Compact and repair the database.

k. Close the database. Exit Access.

l. Submit based on your instructor's directions.

ANALYSIS
CASE

As the database manager of a hotel chain, you monitor the services ordered using a summary query. The hotel chain's manager asks you to send him a summary of the Raleigh location orders as an Excel spreadsheet. He also asks you to export the Repeat Members Club table to a different database. Several hotels in Los Angeles are for sale, and you decide to import their order data to determine their activity levels. Refer to Figure 16.72 as you complete this exercise.

FIGURE 16.72 Navigation Pane with Linked and Imported Data

a. Open *a08m2Hotel* and save it as **a08m2Hotel_LastFirst** in the folder where you are saving your files. Open *a08m2Hotelexport*. Save the database as **a08m2Hotelexport_LastFirst**. Close *a08h2Hotelexport_LastFirst* and return to the *a08m2Hotel_LastFirst* database.

b. Export the Repeat Members Club table to another Access database, *a08m2Hotelexport_LastFirst*. Verify that the table was exported correctly and return to the *a08m2Hotel_LastFirst* database. Do not save the export steps.

c. Modify the *Summary by ServiceID* query so that it displays only orders from location 3 (which is Raleigh). Save, run, and then close the query. Export the query to Excel and save the workbook as **a08m2Raleighorders_LastFirst** in the folder where you are saving your solution files.

d. Review the exported data and close Excel. Do not save the export steps. Import the Excel spreadsheet back into the database as a linked table named **Raleigh Property Updates**, with the first row headings as field names. Open the Raleigh Property Updates table and close the table. Do not save the import steps.

e. Open *a08m2Ordersexcel.xslx*. Exit Excel and return to *a08m2Hotel_LastFirst*. Import the Excel spreadsheet as a table named *Orders_Excel* with the first row as column headings and OrderID as the primary key field. Do not save the import steps.

f. Open *a08m2Ordersaccess*. Close *a08m2Ordersaccess* and return to *a08m2Hotel_LastFirst*. Create a link to the *Orders_Access* table in the *a08m2Ordersaccess* database. Do not save the import steps.

g. Open *a08m2Orderstext.csv*. Exit Excel and return to *a08m2Hotel_LastFirst*. Import the data as **Orders_Text** from the *a08m2Orderstext.csv* text file using the first row headings as field names and **OrderID** as the primary key field into the database. Do not save the import steps.

 h. Save a copy of the file *a08m2Orderstext* as **a08m2Orderstext_LastFirst** with the text file format (.txt). Edit the file using the Notepad program to delete the first record, *OrderID 4001*, and reimport the modified text file into your database as **Orders_Text**. Overwrite the original table when prompted. Write a short paragraph in Word that explains why it is important to edit a text file before it is imported into Access. Save the document as **a08m2Orderstext_LastFirst**.

i. Compact and repair the database. Close the database. Exit Access.

j. Submit based on your instructor's directions.

3 Loan-Tracking Database

COLLABORATION CASE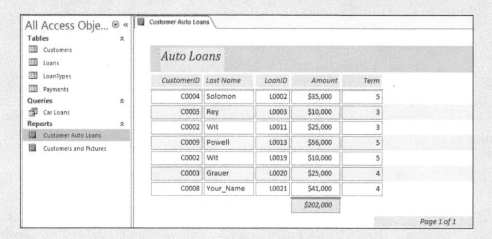

You have been asked to modify a loan-tracking database that tracks customer data, loan records, and payment information. You and your team will modify and import a spreadsheet and a text file into the database. You will add a hyperlink field that will store an e-mail address for each customer. You will then use imported data to create a query in the database, create a report based on the query, and then export the report to a Word document. Refer to Figure 16.73 as you complete this exercise.

FIGURE 16.73 Customer Auto Loans Report Includes Imported Data

a. Open *a08m3Collaboration* and save it as **a08m3Collaboration_GroupName**. As a team, study the existing database and the relationship between the Customers and Loans tables. You will add two new tables to the database by importing external data.

Assign the next two tasks to a team member.

b. Open the text file named *a08m3LoanTypes.txt* and save a copy of the file as *a08m3LoanTypes_LastFirst.txt*. Modify the text file so that instead of the existing separators, commas will specify where the values should be separated. Save your changes.

c. Create a table in the database by importing the modified text file named *a08m3LoanTypes_LastFirst.txt*. Use the first row of the file as field names and **Type** as the primary key and name the table **LoanTypes**. Accept all other default options. Do not save the import steps.

Assign the next two tasks to a team member.

d. Open the workbook named *a08m3Payments* and save a copy of the file as *a08m3Payments_LastFirst*. Modify the workbook so that it will import properly to an Access database. Save your changes.

e. Create a new table in the database by importing the workbook named *a08m3Payments_LastFirst*. Use the first row of the worksheet as column headings, ensure that PaymentID is set as the primary key, and them import the table as **Payments**. Accept all other default options. Do not save the import steps. Change the field size of the LoanID field to Long Integer. If a warning message appears, proceed with the change and then save and close the table.

Assign the next two tasks to a team member.

f. Add a Hyperlink field named **EmailAddress** below the PhoneNumber field in the Customers table.

g. Enter your own first and last names and your personal e-mail address in the appropriate fields for record C0008. Remove the existing attachment from the Photo field and add your own personal photo. Close the table.

Assign the next two tasks to a team member.

h. Add the LoanTypes and Payment tables to the Relationships window. Create a relationship between the Loans and Payments table, enforcing referential integrity. Create a relationship between LoanTypes and Loans, enforcing referential integrity. Save and close the Relationships window.

i. Create a query in Design view. Add the Customers, Loans, and LoanTypes tables to the query window. Add the following fields in this order: CustomerID, LastName, LoanID, Amount, Term, and LoanName. Set the criteria so that customers who have car loans will display in the results. Run the query, save it as **Car Loans**, and then close it.

j. Collaborate with your team to determine what would be the best way to portray the Car Loans query results in a report. Create the report and format it appropriately. Adjust the column widths so that they all fit within the page but the data is still visible. Delete the LoanName column and the Date and Time fields from the report.

k. Switch to Design view and move the page numbering control to the left so that its right edge is just inside the 7-inch mark on the horizontal ruler. Drag the right edge of the report to the left so that it is just inside the 7-inch mark on the ruler. View the report in Print Preview; the report should consist of one page.

l. Modify the report title as **Auto Loans** and delete the logo to the left of the title, if necessary

m. Save the report as **a08m3CustomerAutoLoans_LastFirst** and close the report. Export the report as a Word document using the same name and save it as a Word document. Close the report and exit Word. Do not save the export steps.

n. Compact and repair the database. Close the database. Exit Access. Submit the database and documents based on your instructor's directions.

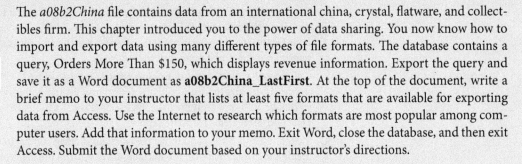

Beyond the Classroom

Exporting from Access

RESEARCH CASE

The *a08b2China* file contains data from an international china, crystal, flatware, and collectibles firm. This chapter introduced you to the power of data sharing. You now know how to import and export data using many different types of file formats. The database contains a query, Orders More Than $150, which displays revenue information. Export the query and save it as a Word document as **a08b2China_LastFirst**. At the top of the document, write a brief memo to your instructor that lists at least five formats that are available for exporting data from Access. Use the Internet to research which formats are most popular among computer users. Add that information to your memo. Exit Word, close the database, and then exit Access. Submit the Word document based on your instructor's directions.

Exporting to Word

DISASTER RECOVERY

Your colleague needs you to export a report from Access to Word to provide him with the most recent sales data. Open *a08b3Real*. Export the Sales Report to Word. Save the Word document as **a08b3Real_LastFirst**. Compact, repair, and then close the database. Exit Access. Submit the Word document based on your instructor's directions.

Workplace Etiquette

SOFT SKILLS CASE

You want to determine how many of the new employees in the *a08b4Etiquette* database require a workplace etiquette in-service. Open *a08b4Etiquette*. Modify the Require Etiquette Inservice query so that only employees who have *not* had etiquette training display in the results. Export the query results to Excel. Save the Excel workbook as **Require Etiquette Inservice_LastFirst**. Close Excel. Compact, repair, and then close the database. Exit Access. Submit the Excel workbook based on your instructor's directions.

You work as an associate database manager at Replacement China, Inc. This firm specializes in finding difficult-to-replace, no-longer-manufactured china, crystal, silver, and collectibles. You need to add a hyperlink field that will store a URL for each manufacturer's Web site. The HR department manager wants to store a photo and the most recent performance review for each employee. You also need to export select inventory items in three different formats. Finally, you will import information from Excel, Access, and text files. Compact and repair the database and make a backup of it when you are finished.

Database File Setup

Make a copy of the original database file, rename the copy, and then open the copy. After you open the copied database, you will replace an existing employee's name with your name.

a. Open *a08c1Replace* and save it as **a08c1Replace_LastFirst**.

b. Open the Employees table.

c. Navigate to record 21 and replace *Your_Name* with your name. Save the record and close the table.

Create Attachment and Hyperlink Fields

Add a hyperlink field to the Manufacturer table to store each company's Web site address. Add an attachment field to the Employees table to store the employee's performance reviews and photos.

a. Create a new field in the Manufacturer table after RlMfgCode named **Website** with the Hyperlink data type. Save the table.

b. Switch to Datasheet view, add the Web site **http://www.lenox.com** to the Lenox China record (7), and then add **http://www.waterford.com** to the Waterford Crystal record (14). Click each link to make sure it launches a browser and locates the appropriate Web site. Close the table.

c. Create a new field in the Employees table after HireDate named **Files** with the Attachment data type. Save the table.

d. Switch to Datasheet view and use the Find command to locate the record for UserID 822680. Add the Word document named *822680.doc* and the picture file named *822680.jpg* to the Files field. The files you need are in the a08c1Reviews folder. Additional attachments will be added in the future.

e. Create a basic form based on the Employees table that will open in Layout view. Delete the subform. Navigate to the record for UserID 822680 (record 21) and use the Attachment toolbar to display the Word document and the picture file.

f. Save the form as **Employees**. Close the form and the table.

Export a Filtered Table to Excel, Word, and PDF

You need to filter the Inventory table and then export the records to three formats: Excel, Word, and PDF. This information will be used to get prices on items that have no on-hand quantity.

a. Use *Filter by Selection* to display records in the Inventory table where the Category equals *Crystal*. Filter the records further to display Crystal where the OH (on-hand) value equals *0* (three records will display). Leave the filtered table open for the next three steps.

b. Export the filtered records to an Excel file. Save the file as **a08c1Crystal_LastFirst**. Do not save the export steps.

c. Export the same filtered records to a Word file. Press **Enter** one time and add the title **Crystal with 0 on hand** to the Word file. Save the file as a Word document with the name **a08c1Crystal_LastFirst**. Do not save the export steps.

d. Export the filtered records to a PDF document. Save the file as **a08c1Crystal_LastFirst**. Do not save the export steps.

e. Close the Inventory table without saving the changes.

Import and Link Data from Excel, Access, and a Text File

You need to import new customer records from Excel and Access. You also will import customer records from a text file.

a. Create a linked table in the database by importing the workbook named *a08c1Customers*. Use the first row of the Customers1 worksheet as row headings and accept all other default options.

b. Create a linked table in the database by importing the Customers2 table from the database named *a08c1Customers*.

c. Create a table in the database by importing the text file named *a08c1Textcust.csv*. Use the first row of the file as field names, **CustomerNum** as the primary key, and name the table **Customers Text**. Accept all other default options.

d. Compact and repair the database.

e. Close the database. Exit Access.

f. Submit based on your instructor's directions.

Fine-Tuning the Database

Analyzing and Improving Database Performance

OBJECTIVES | AFTER YOU READ THIS CHAPTER, YOU WILL BE ABLE TO:

1. Verify first normal form p. 870
2. Verify second normal form p. 873
3. Verify third normal form p. 874
4. Create relationships p. 876
5. Use the Database Documenter tool p. 881
6. Use the Performance Analyzer tool p. 883
7. Use the Table Analyzer tool p. 885
8. Use the Database Splitter tool p. 888
9. Create a menu system p. 895
10. Encrypt and password-protect a database p. 898
11. Digitally sign and publish a database p. 900
12. Save a database as an ACCDE file p. 901

CASE STUDY | The Metropolitan Zoo

Your job as the information manager of the Metropolitan Zoo is to maintain the records for all of the animals at the zoo. The zoo maintains its records in an Access 2013 database, which you have been using for the past two months. The database was created by a former employee who learned about Access by taking a night course at a local community college. The forms and reports have been working well, according to Director of Field Programs, Selene Platt. Selene has worked at the Metropolitan Zoo for 27 years, and she provides you with the information about each animal. She hired you to help with the daily upkeep of the database; she also wants to evaluate the design and performance of the database.

Your tasks include entering new animals, updating changes to existing records, and archiving records for animals that leave the zoo. As you work with the Access database and become familiar with the tables, the table relationships, the data-entry forms, and the reports, you start to look for ways to improve the performance of the database. You also look for ways to protect the data that already exists in the database. These improvements will help you complete the daily tasks of the database; they may also help your boss, Selene, get faster and more reliable results from the database.

Database Normalization

In an earlier chapter, you used common sense to determine which fields to include in each table. The process changes when you deal with a more complex system. Database designers generally start by performing customer interviews, reviewing existing documents, examining existing files, and applying their own knowledge to create a list of potential fields. They then identify potential primary keys and divide the fields into tables. They then go through a process to refine the tables and remove issues. *Normalization* is the formal process of deciding which fields should be grouped together into which tables. Experienced database designers may instinctively create tables that follow the rules of normalization. Less experienced designers generally use the process of normalization to guide them in the process of creating the database. The benefits of normalization are:

- Minimization of data redundancy
- Improvement of referential integrity enforcement
- Ease of maintaining data (add, update, delete)
- Accommodation of future growth of a database

Though this sounds straightforward, it can present challenges. Many colleges and universities have multiple graduate-level database classes to train future database designers in this process.

Following the rules of normalization while creating tables in Access helps you design tables that are free from anomalies. An *anomaly* is an error or inconsistency within a database. Many times, these errors occur when you add, edit, and delete data. Assume a spreadsheet is keeping track of company orders, one order per row. Repeat customers would lead to multiple references to the same customer. Mixed in among thousands of orders, we might have the following information for customer Faten Bader:

9/1/15	Faten Bader	West Paterson, NJ	#456789	3	$12.50
9/10/15	Faten Bader	West Paterson, NJ	#894561	1	$2.95
9/25/15	Faten Bader	West Paterson, NJ	#981156	1	$.95

Faten may call in and change her address, saying her town name changed from West Paterson to Woodland Park, and this introduces an update problem (anomaly). How does the database know which record to update—the first, the second, the third, or all three? A user might try to update the records manually, but this might produce an anomaly as well if only one or two of the three records are changed. If the town's name has changed, should it change for all other customers?

In this section, you will learn the first three rules of normalization. These rules are known as *normal forms* and indicate the current state of a table. The first three normal forms are referred to as first normal form (1NF), second normal form (2NF), and third normal form (3NF). By definition, a table cannot be in 2NF unless it is already in 1NF, and it cannot be in 3NF unless it is in 2NF.

A table that meets 1NF criteria is better than a table that does not. Similarly, a table that meets 2NF criteria is better than a table that is in 1NF, and a table that meets 3NF criteria is better than a table that is in 2NF. There are five normal forms; however, the majority of database designs only require the first three normal forms.

Verifying First Normal Form

STEP 1 ≫ First normal form is the first rule to identify and correct. It can be demonstrated by using an Excel spreadsheet that contains information about authors, books, and publishers (see Figure 17.1). In the spreadsheet, Dan Brown is listed as an AuthorName in column C; the titles of the books that Brown authored are listed on row 5 in column D. The remaining fields contain additional information related to the books. This example would not pass the

1NF test because column D—including the books that Brown authored—has multiple values in a single cell. Brown, the author, is listed once, and the books he wrote are listed in one cell. Even titles on two lines in the same cell are considered multiple values in one cell. If this Excel spreadsheet were imported into Access, the corresponding Access table with repeating groups would be as shown in Figure 17.2. This table shows the same condition with repeating values in the Title field. Repeating groups are not allowed in a normalized table.

Two values in the same cell

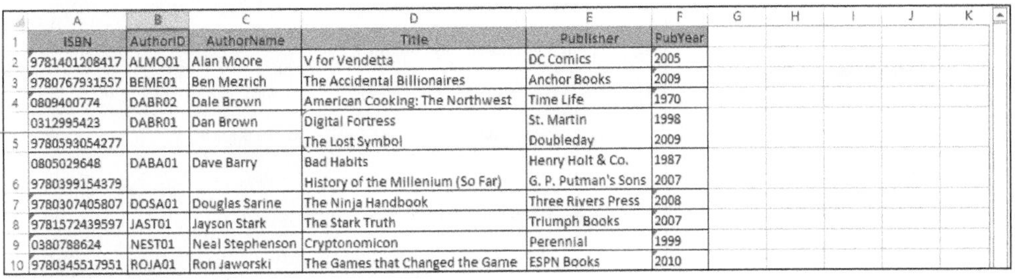

	A	B	C	D	E	F
1	ISBN	AuthorID	AuthorName	Title	Publisher	PubYear
2	9781401208417	ALMO01	Alan Moore	V for Vendetta	DC Comics	2005
3	9780767931557	BEME01	Ben Mezrich	The Accidental Billionaires	Anchor Books	2009
4	0809400774	DABR02	Dale Brown	American Cooking: The Northwest	Time Life	1970
5	0312995423 9780593054277	DABR01	Dan Brown	Digital Fortress The Lost Symbol	St. Martin Doubleday	1998 2009
6	0805029648 9780399154379	DABA01	Dave Barry	Bad Habits History of the Millenium (So Far)	Henry Holt & Co. G. P. Putman's Sons	1987 2007
7	9780307405807	DOSA01	Douglas Sarine	The Ninja Handbook	Three Rivers Press	2008
8	9781572439597	JAST01	Jayson Stark	The Stark Truth	Triumph Books	2007
9	0380788624	NEST01	Neal Stephenson	Cryptonomicon	Perennial	1999
10	9780345517951	ROJA01	Ron Jaworski	The Games that Changed the Game	ESPN Books	2010

FIGURE 17.1 Excel Spreadsheet with Repeating Groups

Two values in the same record

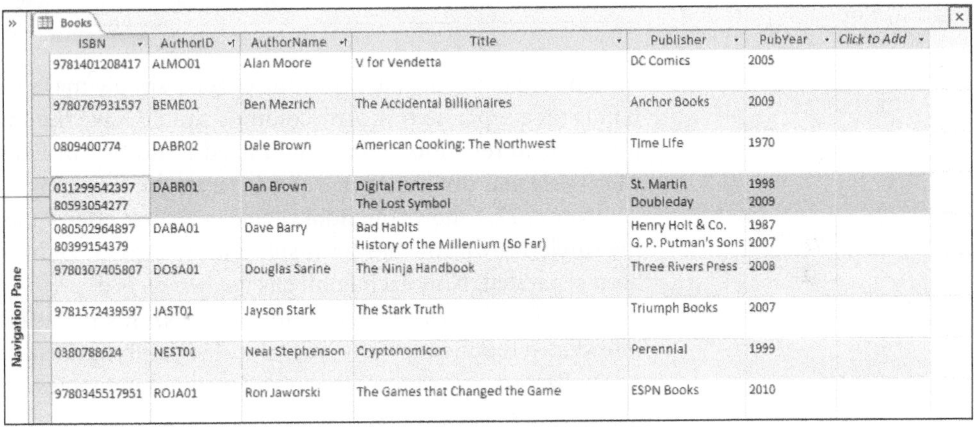

Books

ISBN	AuthorID	AuthorName	Title	Publisher	PubYear	Click to Add
9781401208417	ALMO01	Alan Moore	V for Vendetta	DC Comics	2005	
9780767931557	BEME01	Ben Mezrich	The Accidental Billionaires	Anchor Books	2009	
0809400774	DABR02	Dale Brown	American Cooking: The Northwest	Time Life	1970	
031299542397 80593054277	DABR01	Dan Brown	Digital Fortress The Lost Symbol	St. Martin Doubleday	1998 2009	
080502964897 80399154379	DABA01	Dave Barry	Bad Habits History of the Millenium (So Far)	Henry Holt & Co. G. P. Putman's Sons	1987 2007	
9780307405807	DOSA01	Douglas Sarine	The Ninja Handbook	Three Rivers Press	2008	
9781572439597	JAST01	Jayson Stark	The Stark Truth	Triumph Books	2007	
0380788624	NEST01	Neal Stephenson	Cryptonomicon	Perennial	1999	
9780345517951	ROJA01	Ron Jaworski	The Games that Changed the Game	ESPN Books	2010	

FIGURE 17.2 Access Table with Repeating Groups

We define ***first normal form (1NF)*** as a table that contains no repeating groups or repeating columns. In the book example, the Title column might be replaced with Title1, Title2, and Title3. This might appear to correct the repeating groups problem because each cell contains one piece of information; however, this type of design still violates 1NF and must be corrected. In this example, it is still difficult to find data efficiently.

TIP Multivalued Data Types in Access

Access enables you to create a multivalued field using the Lookup Wizard data type. This data type enables you to enter multiple values into a single field for one record. This data type may appear to break the rules of 1NF, but remember that multivalued fields are handled with special invisible tables Access creates in the background. Although multivalued fields can be useful at times, remember to avoid them if you plan to upgrade to a more powerful database (e.g., SQL Server) in the future.

There are several problems with tables that have repeating groups—it is difficult to add new entries, it is difficult to update existing entries, and it is difficult to properly extract information when running queries. For example, if you want see the information for *Digital Fortress*, you could create a filter or query searching for those results. However, Access considers them to be part of the same record, and you would also see the book *The Lost Symbol*. As a matter of fact, when you attempt to filter your data (as shown in Figure 17.3), you would immediately notice the two book names listed as one piece of data. Similar problems would exist with queries searching for a specific book. In other words, there is no easy way to only show the information for *Digital Fortress*. This occurs because all the books by one author are contained in the same record.

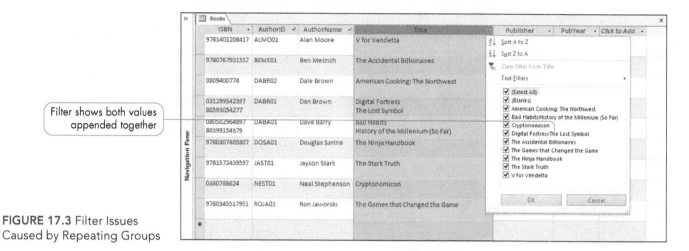

Filter shows both values appended together

FIGURE 17.3 Filter Issues Caused by Repeating Groups

To fix a table that has repeating groups, simply make sure each unique piece of information is on a separate row. Any columns should have the missing information added, even if this leads to repetition. You would need to do this in Excel before importing to Access, or alternately add rows in Access and separate the repeating data into individual rows.

Figure 17.4 shows the Books table in Access after it has been put into first normal form; the single Brown row has been split into two rows, and the books by the same author have been separated. Now each book has its own record.

At this point, although the table is in 1NF, it still has redundancy issues. In fact, we have introduced redundancy into our table. However, because normalization is a process, further normalization will remove the introduced redundancies.

Two records created from original

FIGURE 17.4 Books Table in First Normal Form

The following situations may violate 1NF:

- Multiple values in the same field separated by commas or some other identifier

  - An Authors field listing **Poatsy, Krebs, Cameron, and Williams** is a violation of 1NF.

  - An Address2 field listing **Paterson, NJ 07501** is a violation of 1NF.

  - A Teaching field that contains the following values for the same class, on two lines is a violation of 1NF:
    Cameron
    Siegel

- Multiple columns in the same record containing the same sort of data

  - A table with an Author1 field set to **Poatsy**, Author2 field set to **Krebs**, Author3 field set to **Cameron**, and Author4 field set to **Williams** is a violation of 1NF.

Our focus will be on the more obvious examples, such as multiple values in the field separated by commas or values on separate lines.

Verifying Second Normal Form

STEP 2 » A table is in *second normal form (2NF)* if it meets 1NF criteria and all non-key fields are functionally dependent on the entire primary key. *Functional dependency* occurs when the value of one field is determined by the value of another. A *non-key field* is any field that is not part of the primary key. Therefore, a table with a single-field primary key is usually in 2NF. Because many tables have a single-field primary key, 2NF often requires no changes to a table. However, some tables have a *composite key*, a primary key that is made of two or more fields. Tables with a composite key may require some changes.

Most bookstore databases contain information about location and quantity in stock. Therefore, we have expanded the earlier example to include three extra fields, as shown in Figure 17.5. For the purposes of this example, assume the bookstore has two locations, one in Paterson and one in Wanaque. Because this more realistic version of the table has the location added, a problem now exists. Notice in Figure 17.5 that the ISBN cannot be the primary key for this table because the same book (with the same ISBN) can appear in both locations. In this case, a good option is to use a combination of two fields as the primary key. The composite key for this table would be ISBN plus the location, which uniquely identifies each row.

Because this table has a composite key, you need to ensure all fields are functionally dependent on the entire primary key. To find out the number of books on hand for any specific title, you need to know both the ISBN and the location. Likewise, to find the aisle in which a book is stored, you would need both the ISBN and the location. However, a book's title is independent of the location. Regardless of whether it is in Paterson or Wanaque, the book with an ISBN of 0312995423 is always *Digital Fortress*. The same goes for the rest of the fields. Notice in Figure 17.5 that all the information related to the book *Digital Fortress* is repeated—the AuthorName, Title, Publisher, and PubYear. One data-entry error can lead to inconsistent data.

FIGURE 17.5 Books Table Including Location and Stock Information

If you look up the ISBN 0312995423, whether in this database, on an online bookstore such as Amazon, or in a Barnes & Noble retail store, you should always find the same title, publisher, and author name of the book. Therefore, the title, publisher, and author name are functionally dependent on the ISBN, not the combination of ISBN and location. In other words, these fields are each characteristics of the book.

Amazon may have the same book in its inventory as our bookstore in Paterson, but the book's location, the number on hand, and the aisle will be different or possibly not present. This is because the location, number on hand, and the aisle are not characteristics of the book. Instead, these are characteristics of the book as it exists in a bookstore.

Second normal form tells you that when fields are functionally dependent upon part of a primary key, you need to remove those fields from the table. Most of the time, this results in new tables, though it is possible to move fields into another existing table.

To resolve the problem, you need to create two tables. The first table you will name Books. The Books table should contain the fields ISBN, AuthorID, AuthorName, Title, Publisher, and PubYear. The primary key of this table is ISBN. See Figure 17.6.

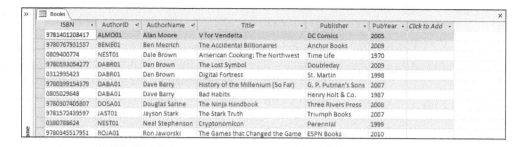

FIGURE 17.6 Books Table in Second Normal Form

The second table you will name Stock. This table contains the fields ISBN, Location, OnHand, and Aisle, as shown in Figure 17.7. The primary key for this table is a composite key, the combination of ISBN and Location.

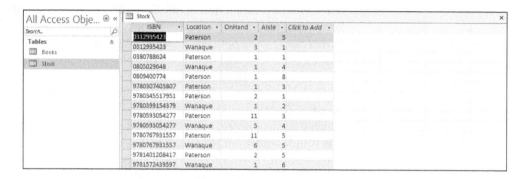

FIGURE 17.7 Newly Created Stock Table

Notice that the data, once divided into two tables, has less repetition of book information.

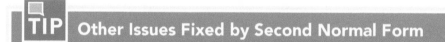

TIP | Other Issues Fixed by Second Normal Form

For simplicity's sake, this example has focused on composite key issues. There are other situations in which 2NF may require changes. In Figure 17.5, just adding an AutoNumber field labelled as the primary key would not solve the issue that the ISBN would still determine some of the information, and the combination of ISBN and location would determine some of the information. Examples will focus on the composite key issues that 2NF fixes.

Verifying Third Normal Form

STEP 3>> A table is in *third normal form (3NF)* if it meets 2NF criteria and no transitive dependencies exist. *Transitive dependencies* occur when the value of one non-key field is functionally dependent on the value of another non-key field. AuthorName in the example is dependent on AuthorID and, therefore, is an example of a transitive dependency. Whenever you know the AuthorID, the AuthorName is automatically known. Therefore, to conform to 3NF, AuthorName must be moved to another table, as shown in Figure 17.8. The new table contains two fields: AuthorID and AuthorName. The Books table can now reference the author using the AuthorID field, as shown in Figure 17.9. The Books table is in 3NF because the transitive dependency was removed. In effect, moving to 3NF requires some work, as a new table often needs to be created and data moved. For a large database, this may require creation of a Make Table query (see the *Action Queries* section of this textbook for more information). In the worst case, this could require large amounts of tedious data entry. However, the trade-off is less repeated data, which leads to fewer anomalies. For example, if you had a typographical error for an author's name (say, Steven King instead of Stephen King), you would only need to change the spelling in one place to correct it.

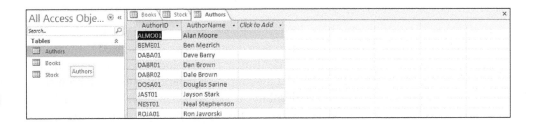

FIGURE 17.8 Newly Created Author Table

FIGURE 17.9 Books Table in Third Normal Form

Another way to handle a conversion to 3NF is to delete fields that may not be necessary. In this specific case, you probably want to keep the AuthorID. In other cases, ask yourself if there is an extra field that can be eliminated. Table 17.1 presents a summary of the three normal forms covered in this chapter.

TABLE 17.1 Normalization Summary

Form	What It Does	Notes
First Normal Form	Removes repeating groups	Introduces redundancy, which is fixed by later normal forms.
Second Normal Form	Removes dependencies on part of a composite primary key	Commonly an issue when a table has a composite key. If the primary key is a single field, a table is usually in 2NF. Changes usually result in added tables.
Third Normal Form	Removes dependencies on any field that is not a primary key	Changes usually result in new tables.

TIP City, State, ZIP, 3NF?

For most locations in the United States, if you have the ZIP code, you can look up the city and state. This might lead you to believe that this is a transitive dependency. However, on some rare occasions this is not true. For example, the ZIP code 42223 covers parts of Christian County, Kentucky, and Montgomery County, Tennessee. In this case, the same ZIP code not only crosses county borders, it also crosses state lines! Note that in this case, this oddity has to do with an army base that crosses state borders. Due to issues such as these, it is safe to consider a database with the city, state, and ZIP in the same table to be in 3NF.

On the other hand, if you have two customers who live in North Brunswick, NJ, one person doing data entry might type it into the database as North Brunswick and the other may abbreviate it as N Brunswick. If you created a filter or query to locate all towns listed as North Brunswick, only one of those two customers would appear. The argument for putting ZIP in a separate table is to avoid issues such as that.

Creating Relationships

STEP 4 » If you have created new tables, you will need to create relationships between the tables. This should be done after completion of the normalization process. The tables should be connected, and the Enforce Referential Integrity option should be checked. Figure 17.10 shows the relationships in the Books database after normalization. This is not done automatically, so you should set this up as you did in an earlier chapter.

Creating relationships can also be a way to test your normalization. Normalization should not result in data loss, so if you cannot create a relationship between the tables, there is likely an issue with the way you have normalized.

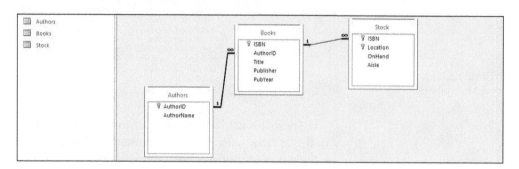

FIGURE 17.10 Relationships in Books Database

In Hands-On Exercise 1, you will work with the Metropolitan Zoo's database to make sure its tables are normalized. The database has been functioning for over two years, so you will have to preserve the existing data when you modify any table. Your boss will work with you to determine which information is important and which data can be discarded.

Quick
Concepts

1. What is the purpose of normalizing a database? *p. 870*

2. What problems does first normal form fix? *p. 871*

3. What problems does second normal form fix? *p. 873*

4. What problems does third normal form fix? *p. 874*

Hands-On Exercise

Watch the Video for this Hands-On Exercise!

MyITLab®
HOE1 Training

1 Database Normalization

Your job at the Metropolitan Zoo has been fun and challenging. You have been making daily updates to the zoo's database with the help of your boss, Selene Platt. Based on your understanding of the rules of normalization, you decide to recommend some design changes to the database.

Skills covered: Verify First Normal Form • Verify Second Normal Form • Verify Third Normal Form • Create Relationships

---

STEP 1 ≫ VERIFY FIRST NORMAL FORM

Your boss has asked you to review the table structure to see if any changes should be made. You decide to apply the rules of normalization to the Animals table, starting with 1NF—eliminate any repeating groups. Refer to Figures 17.11–17.13 as you complete Step 1.

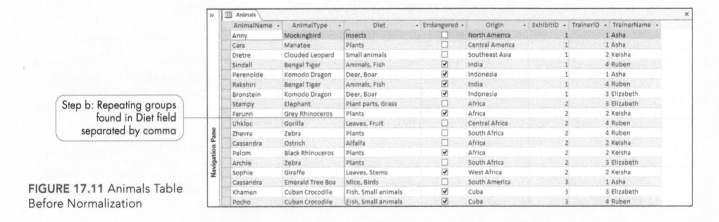

Step b: Repeating groups found in Diet field separated by comma

FIGURE 17.11 Animals Table Before Normalization

Step c: Diet field removed from table—was previously after AnimalType field

FIGURE 17.12 Animals Table in First Normal Form

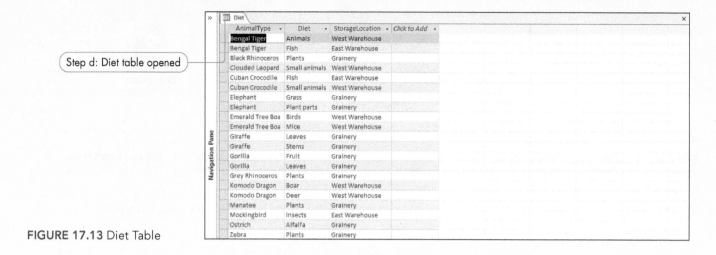

Step d: Diet table opened

FIGURE 17.13 Diet Table

a. Open *a09h1Zoo*. Save the database as **a09h1Zoo_LastFirst**.

> **TROUBLESHOOTING:** If you make any major mistakes in this exercise, you can close the *a09h1Zoo_LastFirst* file and repeat the exercise.

b. Open the Animals table in Datasheet view. Look for repeating groups in the Animals table.

Examining Figure 17.11, you can see the Diet field has multiple values separated by commas. This qualifies as a repeating group. This information needs to be added to a new table and removed from this table. For simplicity's sake, the information for animal diets has been added to a table called Diet, so you will only need to remove the Diet field from the Animal table to conform to 1NF.

c. Delete the Diet field in the Animals table. Click **Yes** when asked for confirmation.

Your Animals table should now match Figure 17.12, and the table now meets 1NF criteria. You deleted the Diet field because it contained repeating values. Repeating values violate 1NF.

d. Open the Diet table in Datasheet view.

For the purposes of this exercise, the data is already in the Diet table as shown in Figure 17.13. This table has been provided to expedite the normalization process.

STEP 2 ≫ VERIFY SECOND NORMAL FORM

After you remove the Diet field, you will examine the Animals table to apply the second normalization rule. Refer to Figures 17.14 and 17.15 as you complete Step 2.

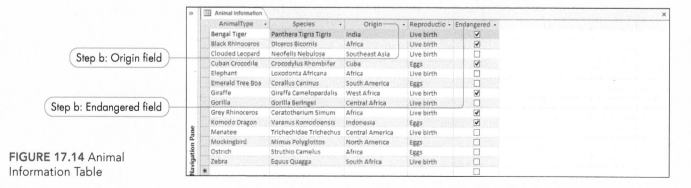

Step b: Origin field

Step b: Endangered field

FIGURE 17.14 Animal Information Table

Step d: Origin and Endangered fields removed

AnimalName	AnimalType	ExhibitID	TrainerID	TrainerName
Anny	Mockingbird	1	1	Asha
Archie	Zebra	2	3	Elizabeth
Bronstein	Komodo Dragon	1	3	Elizabeth
Cara	Manatee	1	1	Asha
Cassandra	Emerald Tree Boa	3	1	Asha
Cassandra	Ostrich	2	2	Kelsha
Dietre	Clouded Leopard	1	2	Kelsha
Farunn	White Rhinoceros	2	2	Kelsha
Khamen	Cuban Crocodile	3	3	Elizabeth
Palom	Black Rhinoceros	2	2	Kelsha
Perenolde	Komodo Dragon	1	1	Asha
Pocho	Cuban Crocodile	3	4	Ruben
Rakshiri	Bengal Tiger	1	4	Ruben
Sindall	Bengal Tiger	1	4	Ruben
Sophie	Giraffe	2	2	Kelsha
Stampy	Elephant	2	3	Elizabeth
Uhkloc	Gorilla	2	4	Ruben
Zhevra	Zebra	2	4	Ruben

FIGURE 17.15 Animals Table in Second Normal Form

a. Switch to Design view, if necessary, for the Animals table. Notice this table has a composite key. Examine the Animals table to look for any non-key fields that are not functionally dependent on the entire primary key.

The primary key for this table is a composite key. Notice in Figure 17.12 that there are two animals named Cassandra, so the combination of AnimalName and AnimalType is the only way to uniquely identify any animal. As there is a composite key in this table, you must check to make sure it is in 2NF.

Origin, Diet, and Endangered are all determined by AnimalType and are attributes of a type of animal, not a specific animal. ExhibitID, TrainerID, and TrainerName are attributes of a specific animal.

b. Open the Animal Information table in Datasheet view. Note this table includes the Origin and Endangered fields as well as other fields regarding animals. See Figure 17.14.

In reality, you may have to create a separate table for this information, but this table is provided to avoid tedious data entry.

c. Close the Animal Information table.

d. Examine the Animals table. This table is not in 2NF because some fields are dependent on part of the primary key. Delete the Origin and Endangered fields, clicking **Yes** in response to the warning.

You delete these two fields because they are not functionally dependent on the entire primary key.

e. Save the Animals table. Switch to Datasheet view.

Your table should match Figure 17.15.

All the remaining fields are functionally dependent on the entire primary key. Therefore, the table now meets 2NF criteria.

STEP 3 ›› VERIFY THIRD NORMAL FORM

The final step to improve the zoo's Animals table is to apply 3NF: the value of a non-key field cannot be functionally dependent on the value of another non-key field.

a. Switch to the Datasheet view for the Animals table. Look for any non-key field values that are functionally dependent on another non-key field value.

TrainerName (non-key) is functionally dependent on TrainerID (non-key). If you know the TrainerID, you automatically know the TrainerName. For example, if you enter value 1 for the TrainerID, then the trainer's name will always be Asha. A Trainers table already exists.

b. Switch to Design view in the Animals table.

c. Delete the TrainerName field, clicking **Yes** in response to the warning.

You delete the TrainerName field because it is functionally dependent on the TrainerID field and therefore is not allowed in the Animals table. Normally, this would then require you to set up a new table, but as you already have a Trainers table, you can simply delete the TrainerName field. Note that this may not always be the case.

d. Save and close the Animals table.

The table now meets 3NF criteria.

STEP 4 ❯❯ CREATE RELATIONSHIPS

You will now create relationships for the tables in the database. Because there are three tables with the AnimalType field, there may be some confusion as to how to establish the proper relationships between tables to ensure proper database function.

a. Click **Relationships** in the Relationships group on the DATABASE TOOLS tab to show the Relationships window.

> **TROUBLESHOOTING:** If all the tables are not closed, you will get a warning about tables being locked. If you receive this warning, exit the Relationships window, close all open tables, and repeat step a.

b. Click **Show Table**. Add each of the four tables to the layout and close the Show Table dialog box.

c. Drag the **AnimalType field** from the Animal Information table to the AnimalType field in the Animals table.

The Animals and Animal Information tables are related by the common AnimalType field.

d. Select the **Enforce Referential Integrity** and **Cascade Update Related Fields options**. Click **Create** to create this relationship.

e. Repeat steps c and d to connect the AnimalType field in the Animal Information table to the AnimalType field in the Diet table.

You may also notice the Animals and Trainers tables are not yet linked. You are leaving these tables unlinked intentionally.

f. Save the relationships and close the Relationships window.

g. Keep the database open if you plan to continue with Hands-On Exercise 2. If not, close the database and exit Access.

Built-In Analysis and Design Tools

A supervisor asks you to create a survey in the database to store suggestions from visitors about their experience while visiting the zoo. Then another department hears about the survey and asks you to add their items to the survey. As new tables, queries, forms, and reports are added to the database, its performance may decline. This slower performance may be due to the fact that Access databases are often created by users—sales managers, accountants, scientists, and production managers—who lack formal training about how to design an Access database. For example, a scientist who creates a database with 10 tables might not understand how to join the tables to produce efficient results.

Even if a database is in 3NF, deficiencies that cause the database to perform poorly may exist. For example, even though the rules of normalization dictate how to design tables, setting relationships may be applied incorrectly. This affects performance. Some IT administrators may try to compensate for a poorly designed database by migrating to an enterprise-level Database Management System (DBMS), such as Microsoft SQL Server or Oracle.

Moving to a DBMS may have a positive net effect on the speed of processing; however, the design problems that existed in Access will still exist. It is best to resolve the design issues first (in Access) and then evaluate whether Access can handle the processing demands of the database. If it can, other reasons to use Access rather than move to an enterprise-level DBMS may exist. These reasons include wizards to help create tables, forms, and reports and a graphical user interface (GUI) that is intuitive to Access users. Also, Access can run on a desktop computer and does not require its own dedicated server as enterprise-level DBMS programs do. Another reason is cost. Microsoft SQL Server and Oracle are much more expensive than Access. If you recommend migrating to one of those solutions, it is best to be sure it is worth the investment.

Sometimes, you can fix problems using the built-in Access tools. For example, you can split an Access database into two database files. If a number of users are accessing the same database, splitting the database may improve performance. One file would contain all the tables and reside on a server, while the other would reside with each user. Users could create their own queries, forms, and reports on their local machines but still access the same data everyone else is using. This could save your company money, which is always a plus.

Access provides three useful tools that database administrators can use to improve the performance of a database—the Database Documenter tool, the Performance Analyzer tool (found as the Analyze Performance icon), and the Table Analyzer tool (found as the Analyze Table icon). In this section, you will learn how to use these three tools, which can be found in the Analyze group on the Database Tools tab, as shown in Figure 17.16. Also in this section, you will learn how to split an Access database into two databases using the Database Splitter tool. The Database Splitter tool is shown in Figure 17.16 on the Database Tools tab, in the Move Data group, with the name Access Database.

FIGURE 17.16 Database Analysis Tools

Using the Database Documenter Tool

STEP 1 ≫ The **Database Documenter** creates a report that contains detailed information for each selected object. When you run the Database Documenter, you can specify which object group you want to see and which specific objects within the selected group you want to document. The Documenter creates a report showing the field names, data types, properties, indexes, and permissions for each of the selected tables. If you run the Documenter for the entire zoo database, the report generated is between 15 and 20 pages long. In other words, the important information can get lost, so it is important to choose only the information you want to see. A common use for the Database Documenter is to verify and update the properties of one object using a printout of the properties of another similar object.

Start the Database Documenter

To use the Database Documenter, click Database Documenter in the Analyze group on the Database Tools tab. The Documenter dialog box opens so that you can select objects to include in the report (see Figure 17.17). Each tab in the Documenter dialog box represents a database object that can be documented. After you select the objects you want to analyze, click OK to generate the report.

Tables tab

Select All picks all tables at once

Use Options to customize report

FIGURE 17.17 Database Documenter Dialog Box

The Documenter creates a report that contains detailed information about the tables and other selected objects in your database; the report opens in Print Preview mode, as shown in Figure 17.18. This shows a large amount of detail about the table and fields, likely more than you need for the type of analysis you are performing. Access enables you to specify which items to include and which to skip. To select the items to be included, click Options, as shown in Figure 17.17. Once you click Options, the Print Table Definition dialog box displays; using the options available, specify which items you want to see on the report. For example, if you want to minimize the information on the report, uncheck all the *Include for Table* items, select the second option in the *Include for Fields* section, and then select nothing in the *Include for Indexes* section (see Figure 17.19). The result is a report that is 4 or 5 pages long, as compared to 20 pages when all the items were checked.

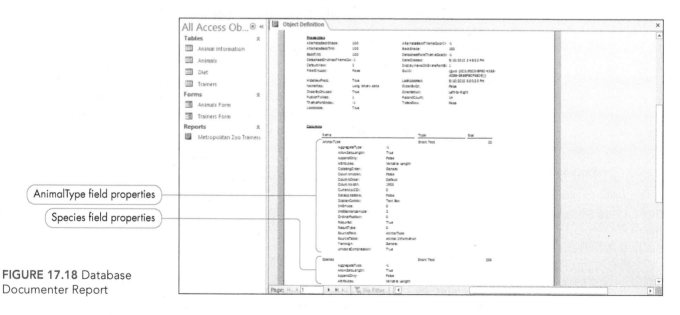

AnimalType field properties

Species field properties

FIGURE 17.18 Database Documenter Report

Although the Documenter starts in Print Preview mode, also notice on the Print Preview tab options to save the report in a number of formats, including as a PDF or XPS file. This is especially useful if you need to share the results of a report with someone else electronically. See Table 17.2 for more details about the Database Documenter options.

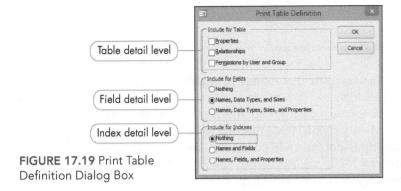

FIGURE 17.19 Print Table Definition Dialog Box

TABLE 17.2 Database Documenter Options

Option	Function
Include for Table: Properties	Options for table properties, including coloring, number of records, and date of last update.
Include for Table: Relationships	Documents table relationships, including which fields are common between tables and type of relationship, such as one to many.
Include for Table: Permissions by Users and Group	Shows permissions for the tables based on users and/ or groups. If your database does not have user-based permissions, this is not worth leaving checked.
Include for Fields: Nothing	Includes no detail about the fields in the selected tables.
Include for Fields: Names, Data Types, and Sizes	Includes field names, data types and field sizes for each field in the selected tables.
Include for Fields: Names, Data Types, Sizes, and Properties	Includes field names, data type, and field size for each field in the selected tables and options such as whether a zero-length value (or null value) is allowed, column width, and text alignment. This makes the report much longer.
Include for Indexes: Nothing	Includes no detail about the indexes in the selected tables.
Include for Indexes: Names and Fields	Includes the names of all indexes and the fields with which they are associated.
Include for Indexes: Names, Fields, and Properties	Includes the names of all indexes, the fields they are associated with, and the index properties, including the number of distinct index values and whether the index is required and must be unique. This makes the report much longer.

Using the Performance Analyzer Tool

STEP 2>> The Database Documenter is useful for listing the properties of each object in a database. However, the Documenter does not identify any flaws in the design of the database. To evaluate the design of the database, you can use the Performance Analyzer. The *Performance Analyzer* evaluates a database and makes recommendations for optimizing the database. Figure 17.20 shows the Performance Analyzer dialog box, where you can select what you would like to analyze.

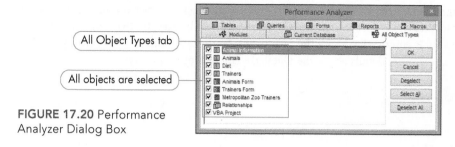

FIGURE 17.20 Performance Analyzer Dialog Box

The Performance Analyzer lists three kinds of analysis results—recommendations, suggestions, and ideas (see Figure 17.21). When you click an item in the Analysis Results list, information about the proposed optimization is displayed in the Analysis Notes box. Suggestion optimizations have potential trade-offs that you should consider before performing them. To view a description of the trade-offs, click a suggestion in the list and read the information in the Analysis Notes box. Access can perform recommendations and suggestions automatically for you; idea optimizations must be performed manually by you.

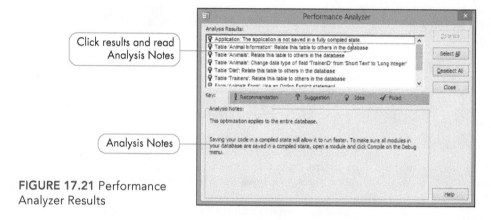

FIGURE 17.21 Performance Analyzer Results

Start the Performance Analyzer

To launch the Performance Analyzer, click Analyze Performance in the Analyze group on the Database Tools tab (refer to Figure 17.16) to display the Performance Analyzer dialog box shown in Figure 17.20. The Tables tab is selected by default. There are tabs for Queries, Forms, Reports, Macros, Modules, Current Database, and All Object Types. Often, the tables are the cause of slowdowns in databases, so the Tables tab is usually the first place to start analyzing performance. Performing searches using queries on poorly designed tables can result in performance issues. The Performance Analyzer attempts to find these issues.

If users inform you that the database generally runs slowly (e.g., reports take a long time to complete), you might choose to analyze the All Object Types tab in an attempt to improve performance. It is possible that forms and reports can have issues as well.

After you select objects for analysis and click OK in the Performance Analyzer dialog box, the dialog box displays an Analysis Notes box, as shown in Figure 17.21. The analysis results in three different types of potential solutions. An Analysis Note provides a brief description of a potential problem and its possible solution. Table 17.3 shows more detail about the three result types you may see if you run the Performance Analyzer.

TABLE 17.3	Performance Analyzer Result Types
Recommendation	Read the Analysis Notes, click the specific recommendation, and then click Optimize. The item's icon changes to Fixed after optimization.
Suggestion	Read the Analysis Notes, click the specific suggestion, and then click Optimize. The item's icon changes to Fixed after optimization.
Idea	Read the Analysis Notes and determine how you will manually implement this idea into your database. Access does not optimize ideas, as these materially change the database design. These require manual changes.

You optimize the database by clicking the result items and then clicking Optimize after you read the Analysis Notes. On occasion, you will find that an optimization results in a trade-off that affects your database in ways you might not consider. For example, changing an existing field named TrainerID with a data type of Short Text to a data type of Long Integer may erase existing data that does not fit the new data type. You may have TrainerIDs that are nonnumeric, and these would be erased from the database. However, changing data types as recommended does improve performance.

Also note that the Performance Analyzer does not catch all problems. Though a useful tool, the Performance Analyzer may miss some issues, so think of this tool as a supplement to your own analysis, not a replacement for it.

TIP Back Up Database Before Optimizing It

Before optimizing your database by using the recommendations, suggestions, and ideas of the Performance Analyzer, it is best to back up your database. That way, you can revert back to the copy if the optimization yields unexpected results. It is also a good practice to read the Analysis Notes before executing any of the analysis recommendations or suggestions.

Add an Index

An item that appears frequently in the Analysis Notes box is *Add an index*. This is a simple change to a field (or fields) in a table that could improve performance when implemented. An **index** reduces the time it takes to run queries and reports. It is similar to the index in the back of this textbook. Generally, you should add an index to any field that will be searched often. For example, in a college database, a student's name would likely be indexed, but not a phone number. However, in a cell phone service provider's database, a phone number would probably be indexed because customer service representatives might use it to find a customer.

On one hand, for reports and queries with a large record source, adding an index can save substantial time. On the other hand, adding more indexes to a table can decrease database performance because each time you add a new record to a database the index must be sorted. In a large database, this may result in a longer wait time before a record is saved. A database of the size of the zoo database may not need an index, but in a larger project this is a common suggestion.

Using the Table Analyzer Tool

The *Table Analyzer* analyzes the tables in a database and normalizes them for you. Normalizing an existing table involves splitting a table into smaller, related tables, with each table focused on a single topic of information, as you did in the first section of this chapter.

As stated earlier, a normalized database has a number of advantages over an unnormalized one. First, updating information is faster and easier because fewer data changes are required.

Second, only the minimum information is stored; therefore, the database is smaller. Finally, a normalized database holds more reliable data because data is stored in only one place.

Although the Table Analyzer helps you create a normalized database, you may want to modify the decisions the Table Analyzer makes if you have database design experience. You can rename tables, split tables, rearrange fields in tables, and create relationships between tables. You can modify Table Analyzer decisions during every step of the normalization process.

Start the Table Analyzer

To start the Table Analyzer, click Analyze Table in the Analyze group on the Database Tools tab. Step one of the Table Analyzer Wizard opens with an explanation of the pitfalls of duplicating information. The output from this process should be tables that pass through normalization, resulting in the creation of additional tables in your database. The Table Analyzer Wizard explains problems for which it will search, describes how it will attempt to fix problems it identifies, and asks you to identify a table for analysis. You can take some control of the process by deciding which fields should be included in new tables created by the Table Analyzer Wizard, or you can choose to let the wizard decide on your behalf.

You could advance through the entire Table Analyzer Wizard accepting the defaults, but this is uncommon. The wizard will offer suggestions, but it is best to think about whether they make sense in your database. It is best to run the Table Analyzer before you attempt any normalization. If you have already created tables and have an incomplete normalization, you may not get a solid recommendation.

Step Through the Table Analyzer Wizard

If you choose to let the Table Analyzer Wizard normalize the tables in your database, the Table Analyzer Wizard runs through the following process:

Step 1. The Table Analyzer Wizard asks you to choose a table (see Figure 17.22). The wizard then breaks the table into a set of smaller tables. Each of these smaller tables contains the minimum set of information that should be grouped together.

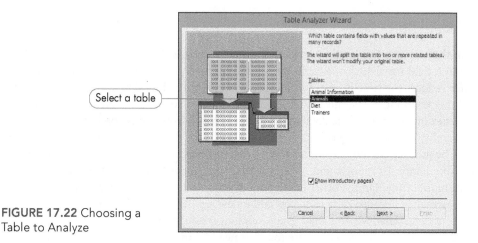

Select a table

FIGURE 17.22 Choosing a Table to Analyze

Step 2. You can direct the wizard to decide what fields go in what tables, as shown in Figure 17.23. The other option is for you to decide how to divide the table into smaller tables. Access makes a recommendation, but if you prefer, you can do the breakdown yourself.

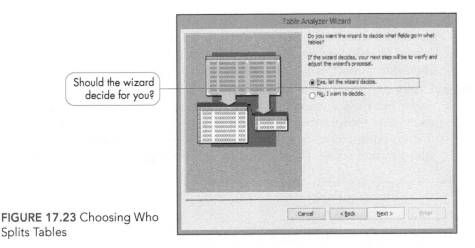

FIGURE 17.23 Choosing Who Splits Tables

Step 3. If you tell the wizard to decide for you, the wizard divides the table and creates relationships that control how the new tables are linked, as shown in Figure 17.24. These relationships enforce referential integrity (data consistency) with cascading updates. The wizard does not automatically add cascading deletes to the relationships because of the risk that you may accidentally delete large portions of data. You can rename the tables in this step. If you prefer to set the cascading deletes option, you must do so yourself.

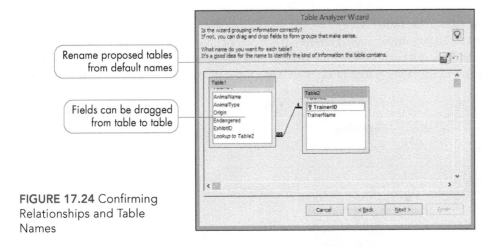

FIGURE 17.24 Confirming Relationships and Table Names

Step 4. The wizard proposes tables and fields, and asks you to confirm the primary keys in each table, as shown in Figure 17.25.

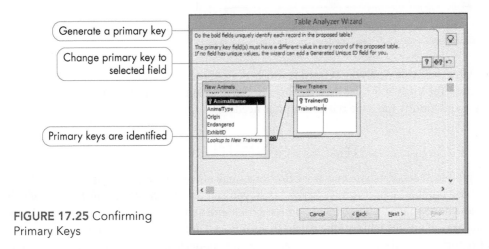

FIGURE 17.25 Confirming Primary Keys

Step 5. In the next step, the wizard searches the new tables for inconsistent data (for example, the same customer with two different phone numbers) and presents a list of records that you can change or accept. If there are no problems with inconsistent data, this step does not appear.

Step 6. Finally, you can choose to create a query that simulates the original table. The wizard first backs up the original table and renames it by appending "_OLD" to its name. Then the wizard creates a query using the original table name. This ensures that any existing forms or reports based on the original table work with the new table structure as well. The results of the wizard might resemble Figure 17.26.

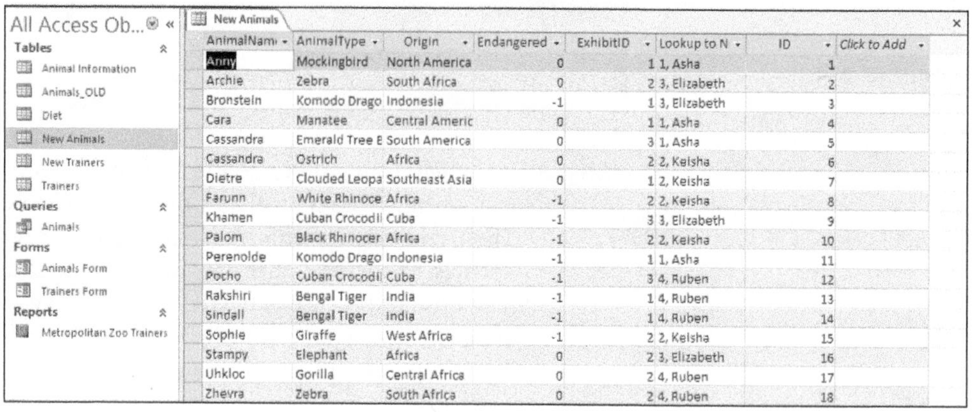

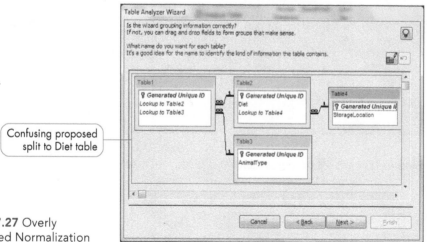

FIGURE 17.26 New Animals Table

As you can see from Figure 17.27, the underlying tables may look messier than the ones you created through normalization. However, if you do not know how to perform normalization, or if the database is straightforward, the analyzer tool would be preferable. Either way, it is important to check the tables Access recommends and not just accept them without viewing.

FIGURE 17.27 Overly Complicated Normalization

After the Table Analyzer Wizard is finished, examine the new table structure. Click the Database Tools tab and click Relationships in the Relationships group. From there, you can review and modify the table relationships as needed.

Using the Database Splitter Tool

STEP 4 ›› A single-file Access database may work fine for a small office with a handful of users. However, when the number of users grows beyond that, you can use the **Database Splitter** tool, which enables you to split a database into two files: a back-end and a front-end database. A **back-end database** contains the tables of the database. A **front-end database** contains the queries, forms, and reports of the database. The two databases are connected, with the forms, queries, and reports stored in the front-end database and the tables stored in the back-end database. You could then have multiple front-end databases using one back-end database.

The main reason to split an Access database is to improve development and maintenance. When a developer works with a single-file Access database, all users must exit the database while the developer makes changes. This can be inefficient for the developer and disruptive for the users. The front end of a split database can be modified while users continue to work. Once the changes to the front end are completed, the new file is distributed to the users (to replace the existing front-end database file).

This approach offers other advantages as well. Splitting the database may improve the speed at which the database processes data and returns results. A report that takes two minutes to display in a single-file database may take only one minute in a split database. There are many other reasons to support splitting a database into two files, as outlined in Table 17.4. The back-end database is typically placed on a server, and a front-end database is placed on each individual user's computer. The front-end database contains links to the tables in the back end.

TABLE 17.4	Reasons to Split an Access Database into Two Files
Improved Performance	The performance of the database usually improves because only the data is sent across the network—not the queries, forms, reports, macros, and modules.
Greater Data Availability	When only the data is sent across the network, database edits are completed more quickly, which makes the data available quicker.
Enhanced Security	If you store the back-end database on a server, you can use the server's security features to help protect your data. Because users access the back-end database by using linked tables, it is less likely that intruders can obtain unauthorized access to the data.
Improved Reliability	If a user encounters a problem and the database closes unexpectedly, any database file corruption is usually limited to the front-end database. Because the user only accesses data in the back-end database by using linked tables, the back-end database file is much less likely to become corrupted. In addition, servers are generally backed up in a business environment; a client machine may not be.
Flexible Development Environment	Because each user works with a separate copy of the front-end database, each user can independently develop queries, forms, reports, and other database objects without affecting other users. Also, developers can distribute an updated version of the front-end database without affecting the data in the back-end database.

Start the Database Splitter

The Database Splitter is not identified by name on the Access Ribbon. To start the Database Splitter, click the Database Tools tab and click Access Database in the Move Data group. The first screen explains what the Database Splitter Wizard does and gives a brief summary of the benefits of a split database. The Database Splitter starts as shown in Figure 17.28.

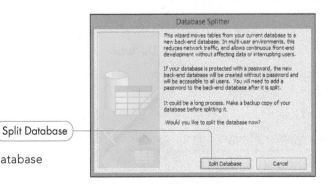

FIGURE 17.28 Database Splitter Wizard

In the next step, the wizard asks you to name the new back-end database. Designate the database name and location for the back-end database or just accept the default file name that Access suggests—the original name plus the suffix "be" for "back-end" (see Figure 17.29).

Work with the Front-End Database

After Access creates the back end, the front-end database remains open. The tables that existed in the original database have been replaced with linked tables with the same table names. Linked tables have an arrow icon to indicate they are linked to another Access database (see Figure 17.30). When you point to a table name, a ScreenTip shows the path to the physical table to which your front-end database is linked. As you add data to the linked tables using the front-end database, the data becomes available to other users of the back-end tables.

Note that if you use the front-end database on a different machine, or if you move the files into a different folder, you may get an error stating the file path is not valid. The back-end database is generally stored on a networked server, so this is not an issue in the real world unless the file is moved on the server.

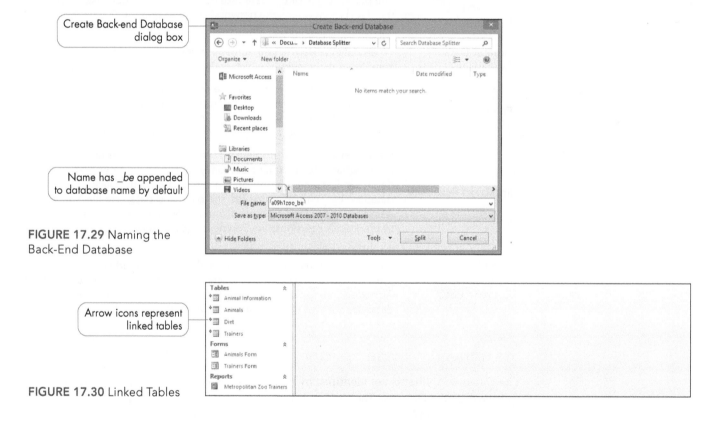

Create Back-end Database dialog box

Name has _be appended to database name by default

FIGURE 17.29 Naming the Back-End Database

Arrow icons represent linked tables

FIGURE 17.30 Linked Tables

In Hands-On Exercise 2, you will use the built-in analysis and design tools to analyze a database. You will also split a database into a front end and a back end.

Quick Concepts

1. Describe three reasons to use the Database Documenter tool. ***p. 881***

2. Define the three possible analyzer result types the Performance Analyzer tool might propose. ***p. 884***

3. How does the Table Analyzer tool make you more productive? ***p. 885***

4. Why would a database administrator choose to split a database? ***p. 888***

Hands-On Exercise

2 Built-In Analysis and Design Tools

The Metropolitan Zoo database has been working well, but you decide to examine the database to see if more improvements can be made. You use the built-in tools to analyze the database; you also decide to split the database into two files. Before you begin, you make a copy of the database so the original format will be safe in case you make a mistake.

Skills covered: Use the Database Documenter Tool • Use the Performance Analyzer Tool • Use the Table Analyzer Tool • Use the Database Splitter Tool

---

STEP 1 ≫ USE THE DATABASE DOCUMENTER TOOL

You will create a report with the Database Documenter to show information on relationships. You will save this report as a PDF file. Refer to Figure 17.31 and Figure 17.32 as you complete Step 1.

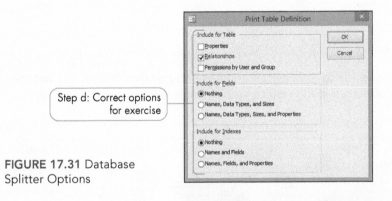

FIGURE 17.31 Database Splitter Options

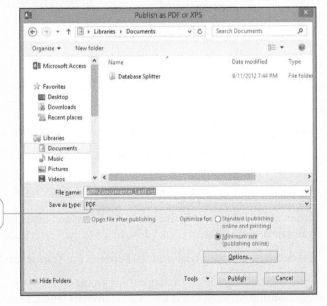

FIGURE 17.32 Saving Report as PDF

a. Open *a09h1Zoo_LastFirst* if you closed it at the end of Hands-On Exercise 1. Save the database as **a09h2Zoo_LastFirst**, changing *h1* to *h2*. Click **Save**.

b. Click **Database Documenter** in the Analyze group on the DATABASE TOOLS tab. Click the **All Objects Types tab**.

c. Click **Select All** on the All Object Types tab and click **Options**.

d. Check the **Relationships box** in the *Include for Table* section. Uncheck checkboxes for *Properties* and *Permission by User and Group*, if necessary. Click **Nothing** in the *Include for Fields* section and click **Nothing** in the *Include for Indexes* section. Your dialog box should resemble Figure 17.31. Click **OK**. Click **OK** to run the report.

You have changed the options so only the required information is present in the report.

e. Select **PDF or XPS** in the Data group on the PRINT PREVIEW tab. Select **PDF** as the option for *Save as type* and type **a09h2ZooDocumenter_LastFirst** for the file name. Click **Publish** to save the file, as shown in Figure 17.32.

This enables you to save the report.

TROUBLESHOOTING: After saving the report, it may open in Adobe Reader or Adobe Acrobat. If this happens, close the program and return to Access.

---

f. Click **Close** on the next screen, which asks you if you want to save the steps.

g. Click **Close Print Preview** in the Close Preview group to close the report.

STEP 2 ≫ USE THE PERFORMANCE ANALYZER TOOL

To evaluate the performance of the zoo database, you decide to run the Performance Analyzer tool. You run the analyzer and then review the recommendations, suggestions, and ideas in the results. You will implement some of the results. Refer to Figure 17.33 as you complete Step 2.

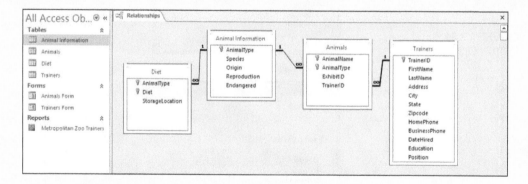

FIGURE 17.33 Final Relationships for Zoo Database

a. Click the **DATABASE TOOLS tab** and click **Analyze Performance** in the Analyze group.

b. Click the **All Object Types tab**, click **Select All**, and then click **OK** to start the Performance Analyzer.

The results window displays ideas to improve the zoo database.

c. Review the results of the Performance Analyzer and take note of the idea regarding relating Trainers to another table. Click **Close** to close the Performance Analyzer dialog box.

You decide to establish relationships between the Trainers and Animals tables.

d. Click **Relationships** in the Relationships group on the DATABASE TOOLS tab and create a relationship between the Trainers and Animals tables, using the common field TrainerID. Ensure the Enforce Referential Integrity and Cascade Update Related Fields options are set.

Your relationships should now match Figure 17.33. The tables may appear in a different order or of a different height in your database.

e. Save and close the Relationships window.

f. Repeat the procedure in steps a and b above to run the Performance Analyzer again and see if the results are different this time.

The idea to relate tables is gone.

g. Close the Performance Analyzer dialog box.

STEP 3 ≫ USE THE TABLE ANALYZER TOOL

You decide to test the design of the tables in the zoo database. To do this, you will open an older version of the database, run the Table Analyzer, and then compare the results to the current database. Refer to Figure 17.34 as you complete Step 3.

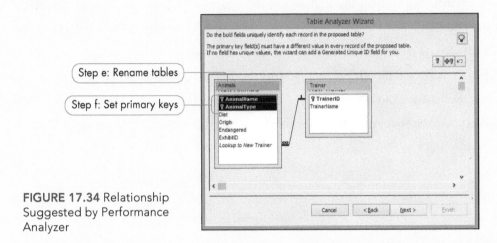

FIGURE 17.34 Relationship Suggested by Performance Analyzer

a. Open *a09h2ZooAnalyzer*. Save the database as **a09h2ZooAnalyzer_LastFirst**.

b. Click the **DATABASE TOOLS tab** and click **Analyze Table** in the Analyze group.

The Table Analyzer Wizard starts.

c. Click **Next** twice.

Access shows a screen asking you to select tables.

d. Select the **ZooAnimals table**. Click **Next** twice.

The ZooAnimals table has been split into three tables.

e. Click the **Rename Table icon**, type **Animals** as the name of Table1, and then click **OK**. Select **Table2** and use the same steps to rename Table2 **Animal Information**. Select **Table3** and rename it **Trainers**. Click **Next**.

f. Click the **AnimalID field** in the Animals table and click the **Set Unique Identifier icon** to set the primary key. Click the **AnimalType field** in the Animal Information table and use the same process to set the primary key. Click **Next**.

Note that Access correctly identified the primary key for the Trainers table, so there is no need to set that manually.

g. Select the **No, don't create the query option** and click **Finish**. Click **OK** in response to the warning message.

This normalization is similar to the one you did in Hands-On Exercise 1, but it did not fix the repeating groups issue in the Diet field. However, if you had no understanding of normalization, using the Table Analyzer helps achieve the goal of reducing data redundancies.

h. Close the database.

i. Submit based on your instructor's directions.

You decide to split the zoo database to see if the performance of the database improves. You use the Database Splitter to divide the database into a front-end and a back-end file.

a. Open *a09h2Zoo_LastFirst*. Save the database as **a09h2ZooSplit_LastFirst**.

The new database is displayed.

b. Click the **DATABASE TOOLS tab** and click **Access Database** in the Move Data group.

The Database Splitter Wizard starts.

c. Click **Split Database**. Accept *a09h2ZooSplit_LastFirst_be* as the file name and click **Split**.

The Database Splitter splits the database into two files.

d. Click **OK**.

The database is split successfully.

e. Open the tables and the other objects to verify the database is working properly.

f. Close the database. Close Access.

g. Submit based on your instructor's directions.

Database Security

Computer security can be defined as the protection of data from unauthorized access, change, or destruction and can be divided into two general categories: physical security and logical security. Physical security involves protecting assets you can touch, such as computers, storage devices, backup tapes, and the office safe. Logical security protects the information that resides on the physical devices, including databases and other computer software. Security measures need to be taken to protect your assets against both physical and logical threats.

Database security is a specialty within computer security that protects a database application from unintended use. Unintended use includes unauthorized viewing of data, unauthorized copying and selling of data, malicious attacks, destruction of data by employees, and inadvertent mistakes made by employees.

In this section, you will learn several techniques available in Access to keep your database application safe. These techniques include:

- Creating a navigation form.
- Encrypting and password protecting a database.
- Digitally signing and publishing the database.
- Saving a database as an ACCDE file.

Creating a Menu System

Most database users prefer a menu system for opening and closing forms and reports, especially forms and reports that are used every day. This can be accomplished using a *navigation form*, which is a tabbed menu system that ties the objects in the database together so that the database is easy to use. The interface displays a menu enabling a nontechnical person to open the various objects within the database and to move easily from one object to another. The form is quite powerful, but it is also easy to create. When you create a navigation form, you simply drag and drop forms and reports onto tabs. An added benefit of a navigation form is that it can be easily converted to a Web form if the Access database is deployed on a company intranet or on the Internet. Navigation forms have the look and feel of a web form.

TIP Switchboards: Another Menu System

Navigation forms were introduced in Access 2010. Before that point, users would use a switchboard to do what the navigation form accomplishes. If you are using a database that is more established, you may find a switchboard as the primary method of interacting with the database rather than a navigation form.

Microsoft removed the Switchboard Manager from the Ribbon when it introduced navigation forms. If you ever need to create or manage a switchboard, follow these steps to display the Switchboard Manager:

1. Click the FILE tab and click Options.
2. Click Customize Ribbon.
3. Select All Commands from the *Choose commands from* option. See Figure 17.35.
4. Scroll down until you see Switchboard Manager.
5. Select Switchboard Manager.
6. On the right, expand the Database Tools group.
7. Click Database Tools.
8. Click New Group.
9. Rename *New Group* as Switchboard.
10. Click Switchboard (Custom).
11. Click Add. The Switchboard Manager is added to the Ribbon as shown in Figure 17.36.

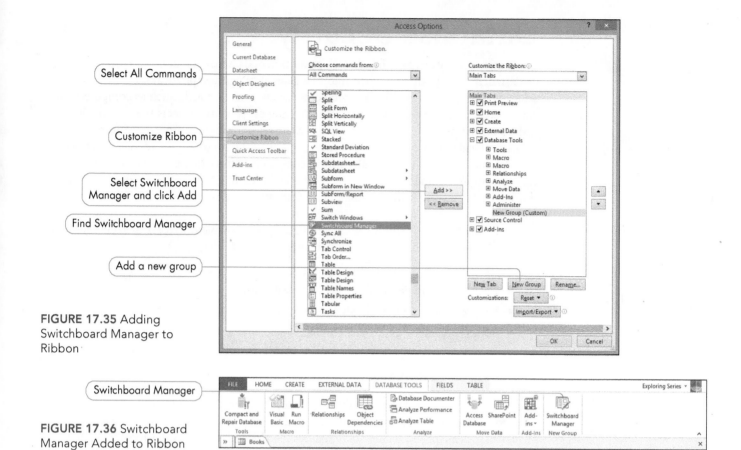

FIGURE 17.35 Adding Switchboard Manager to Ribbon

- Select All Commands
- Customize Ribbon
- Select Switchboard Manager and click Add
- Find Switchboard Manager
- Add a new group

- Switchboard Manager

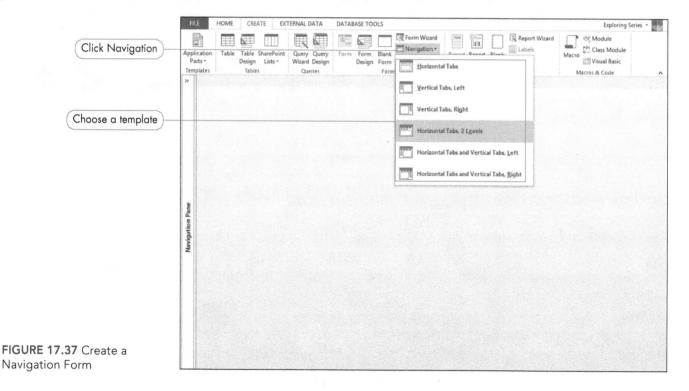

FIGURE 17.36 Switchboard Manager Added to Ribbon

To create a navigation form, click the Create tab and click Navigation in the Forms group. Select one of the six preset templates (as shown in Figure 17.37) and Access creates the basic structure of the navigation form.

- Click Navigation
- Choose a template

FIGURE 17.37 Create a Navigation Form

Create a Navigation Form

For example, choose the first template on the list, Horizontal Tabs, and Access creates a navigation form with [Add New] at the top-left corner of the page. Drag an object from the Navigation Pane onto [Add New], and Access displays the object in the main viewing area, as shown in Figure 17.38. Drag the next object from the Navigation Pane onto [Add New] and Access displays that object. Continue adding the remainder of the objects you want on the navigation form. Switch to Form view and click each tab to view and test each object (see Figure 17.38). Save and close the form.

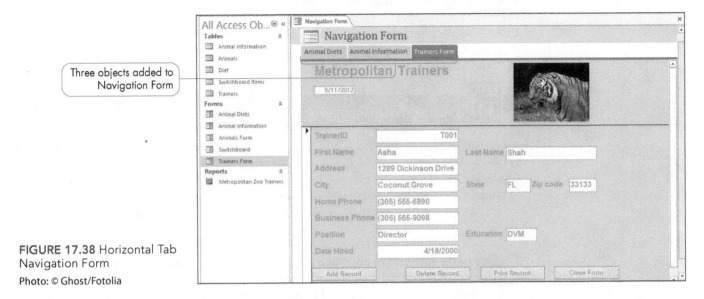

Three objects added to Navigation Form

FIGURE 17.38 Horizontal Tab Navigation Form

Photo: © Ghost/Fotolia

Start a Navigation Form Automatically

To start the navigation form automatically when the database starts, click the File tab and click Options. Click Current Database and select the name of the navigation form using the Display Form option, as shown in Figure 17.39. Click OK to close the Access Options window.

Note that any form, not only a navigation form, can be set to display automatically. Also note that this applies to the current database, so each database can have different forms set to launch on startup.

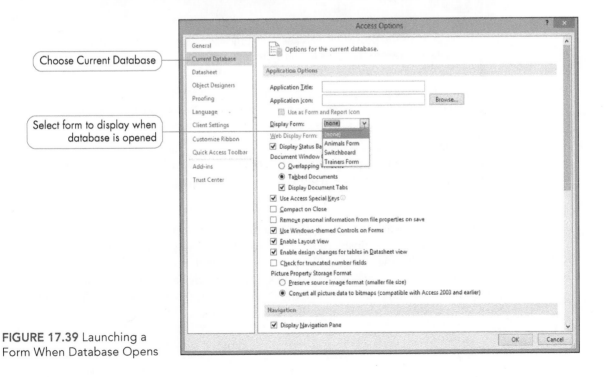

Choose Current Database

Select form to display when database is opened

FIGURE 17.39 Launching a Form When Database Opens

Encrypting and Password Protecting a Database

Access 2013 incorporates encryption methods to help keep your databases secure. *Encryption* is the process of altering digital information using an algorithm to make it unreadable to anyone except those who possess the key (password). As the point of encryption is to protect your data, you need to choose a password when setting up encryption. Encrypting a database makes its contents unreadable to other programs and is especially useful if you intend to distribute your database via e-mail or store your database on removable media such as a USB flash drive. Because millions of secret codes (or passwords) can be generated, an encrypted database is difficult to break.

TIP Lost Your Password?

There are a number of software applications that attempt to find a password for a database. However, the more secure the password, the longer it takes to recover. It may take days or weeks for a password to be recovered, but that is better than losing data permanently. Also keep in mind that the same tool you can use to recover a legitimately lost password can be used by anyone, so a strong password helps prevent unauthorized access.

One of the methods to encrypt a database is to assign a password to the file. Adding a password to an Access database prevents unauthorized access to the file. Passwords typically include a combination of letters and numbers. A good password should be impossible for unauthorized users to guess. For example, use at least eight characters that combine uppercase and lowercase letters, numbers, and symbols to make the password more difficult for others to guess. An example of a weak password is Eric1999 (the author's name and year of graduation). A stronger password is Exp2013@r$. Be sure to record the passwords you assign to your database.

TIP Password Security

The purpose of the password is to keep unauthorized users from using the database. If you create a password that uses letters, numbers, and symbols, make sure your own password does not keep you from accessing your own data!

Writing down the password on a sticky note and leaving it on your monitor is not a good choice for protecting a truly secure password. If you write down your passwords, store them in a secure location such as a locked file cabinet or a safe.

You can download or purchase a client tool to manage your passwords or use a secure online password manager. Of course, tools like that require a password, so make sure you do not forget the password that protects your passwords.

Adding a password and encryption to a database is easily done, but it requires that the database be opened in exclusive mode. *Open Exclusive* mode guarantees that you are the only one currently using the database. To open a database with exclusive access, click the File tab, click Open, click Computer, and then click Browse to display the Open dialog box. Locate the database you want to open, click the Open arrow at the bottom of the dialog box, and then select Open Exclusive from the list (see Figure 17.40).

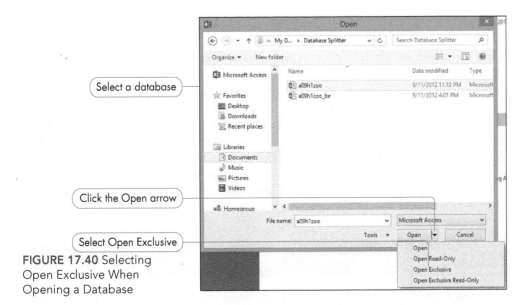

Select a database

Click the Open arrow

Select Open Exclusive

FIGURE 17.40 Selecting Open Exclusive When Opening a Database

After opening a database in exclusive mode, you are ready to assign a password. To accomplish this, click the File tab, click Info, and then click *Encrypt with Password*, as shown in Figure 17.41. The Set Database Password dialog box opens so that you can enter and verify a password. The database is encrypted when you click OK in the Set Database Password dialog box. Once you have set the password, close the database and then open it again without exclusive access. When you open the database, the Password Required dialog box appears. You must type the correct password and click OK to open the database.

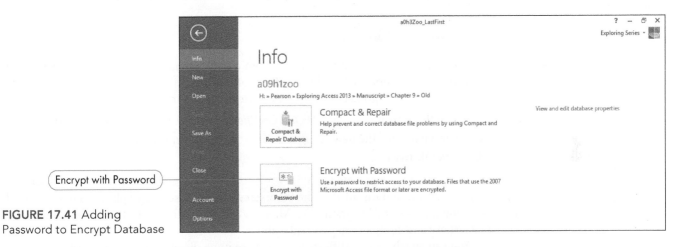

Encrypt with Password

FIGURE 17.41 Adding Password to Encrypt Database

TIP Removing a Password

If you want to remove a password, you must open the database using the Open Exclusive option. Click the File tab, click Info, and then click Decrypt Database. In the Unset Database Password dialog box, type the password and click OK. The database password has been removed. You need the database password to do this, of course.

Digitally Signing and Publishing a Database

STEP 3 ***Digital signatures*** are electronic, encryption-based, secure stamps of authentication that confirm who created the file, that the file is valid, and that no changes have been made to the file after its authentication. You can apply digital signatures to databases, documents, spreadsheets, or macros that you create. By digitally signing and distributing your database, you assure other users that the database has not been tampered with. In other words, if users trust the person who created the digital signature, they can trust your database by enabling any macros or Visual Basic for Applications (VBA) code to run when they use the database.

You can either create a signature yourself or purchase one. A ***certification authority (CA)*** is a commercial company, such as VeriSign, that issues and validates identities using digital signatures for a fee.

TIP | Should I Purchase a Digital Signature?

Choose a CA if you need high-level security. Most countries have stringent laws that regulate CAs so that purchasers can be sure that their digital signatures are valid. Many software manufacturers purchase digital signatures, so when you install their software, you are shown the name of the software publisher. As only the publisher can digitally sign the software, the signature enables users to trust the source of software.

Digital signatures are also used in banking and other fields. If you have a need to assure others that you are the sender of a file and it has not been tampered with, a digital certificate might be a better choice than self-certification. Having an independent group verifying your identity and preventing digital forgeries may be worth the cost.

Use the SelfCert Tool

If you do not have a security certificate from a commercial vendor, you can create one by using the SelfCert tool (included with Microsoft Office).

To create a self-signed certificate, complete the following:

1. From the Start screen, type *Digital Certificate for VBA Projects.* Click the tool to start it.
2. Type a name for the new certificate into the *Your certificate's name* box.
3. Click OK twice.

If the Digital Certificate for VBA Projects tool does not appear on the Start screen, it is possible it was not installed to the Start screen. If not, use File Explorer to navigate to the following location: C:\Program Files\Microsoft Office\Office15. In that folder, double-click SelfCert.exe and complete steps 2 and 3 above.

You can attach your certificate to a database immediately before you distribute it to your users. Keep in mind that a digital signature does not prove that you own the database. By use of a timestamp, it can prove that you were the last person to modify it. You provide the timestamp information to others when you distribute, or publish, your database. By examining the timestamp on your database, you can prove that it has or has not been modified since you applied your signature. A ***timestamp*** is a combination of the date and time that is encrypted as part of the digital signature. For a timestamp to be truly valid to others, it must be passed through a timestamping service provider. Again, this can be a commercial entity or a server located on your network. Further discussion of this process is outside the scope of this textbook.

Apply a Digital Signature

You can digitally sign and publish your database simultaneously from within Access 2013. To digitally sign and publish your database, click the File tab, click Save As, and then double-click *Package and Sign.* If the Select Certificate dialog box opens, select an existing certificate and click OK. The database is packaged and converted to the .accdc file format and digitally signed with your certificate.

Saving a Database as an ACCDE File

STEP 4 »

Access 2013 enables the use of the file extension .accde. Creating an **Access Database Executable (ACCDE)** file will remove all VBA source code, prohibit users from making design and name changes to forms or reports within the database, and prohibit users from creating new forms and reports. Users can execute the VBA code, but they cannot modify it. The ACCDE file type was first introduced in Access 2007.

Double-click Make ACCDE

FIGURE 17.42 Saving Access Database as ACCDE File

Create an ACCDE File

You can create a database with the .accde file extension within Access 2013. This is a simple process that saves your existing database with the new file extension, making a copy of the last saved edition of your database. To create an ACCDE file, click the File tab, click Save As, and then double-click Make ACCDE (see Figure 17.42). The Save As dialog box opens. The *File name* box displays the same main name as the original database with the .accde extension. The *Save as type* box displays *ACCDE File (*.accde)*. Click Save to save the database with the .accde file format. Note you cannot create an ACCDE file unless you have clicked the Enable Content button. As ACCDE files can cause potentially dangerous code to be executed, you first need to assure Access the file is trustworthy.

If you do not have exclusive use of the database before you convert the database to the .accde file format, you receive a message telling you that another user has the database open. The process stops.

Keep the Original Database File Safe

When the database has been converted to .accde, it cannot be converted back to its source format (.accdb). Therefore, keep your original database—the database as it existed when it was converted to the .accde file format—in a safe place. This backup is needed if one or more of its objects (forms, reports, or VBA code) needs to be changed. Without your original database, you would not be able to make these changes. You would be forced to create the database again. Users would not be able to alter the design of forms and reports, nor would they be able to change the VBA code.

In Hands-On Exercise 3, you will practice all of the security measures discussed in this section. Table 17.5 recaps the highlights from this section.

TABLE 17.5	Security Measures and Their Intended Results
Digital Signature	Provides proof to others of when you last modified the database. Not very secure without password protection.
Make ACCDE	Removes Visual Basic code from the database and stops users from making changes to database forms and reports.
Password Protect	Makes the database unreadable by encrypting the database. Users must enter a password to open the database.

Quick Concepts

1. List two advantages of a navigation form. ***p. 895***

2. Describe two reasons you might choose to digitally sign a database. ***p. 900***

3. Describe the problems that can be prevented by creating an ACCDE file. ***p. 901***

Hands-On Exercise

3 Database Security

Management has asked you for a plan to protect the database from accidental deletes, intrusions, and theft. You decide to put several safety and security measures into action, including the addition of a password to protect against unauthorized use of the database.

Skills covered: Create a Menu System • Encrypt and Password-Protect a Database • Digitally Sign and Publish a Database • Save a Database as an ACCDE File

STEP 1 ≫ CREATE A MENU SYSTEM

You decide to create a navigation form to make it easier to open the daily forms and reports. You ask the employees which objects they use the most, and then add them to the navigation form. You decide to use the Horizontal Tabs template. Refer to Figure 17.43 as you complete Step 1.

Step g: Final Navigation Form with five tabs

FIGURE 17.43 Navigation Form in Zoo Database

a. Open *a09h2Zoo_LastFirst*. Save the database as **a09h3Zoo_LastFirst**, changing *h2* to *h3*.

b. Select the **Animals table** and create a basic report using the Report tool. Save the report as **Animals Report**. Close the report.

c. Repeat step b to create a report based on the Diet table. Save the report as **Diet Report**. Close the report.

d. Repeat step b to create a report based on the Animal Information table. Save the report as **Animal Information Report**. Close the report.

e. Click the **CREATE tab** and click **Navigation** in the Forms group. Select the **Horizontal Tabs option** (the first item on the list).

A new Horizontal Tabs navigation form appears in the workspace.

f. Drag the **Trainers Form** from the Navigation Pane to [Add New].

g. Repeat step g to add Animals Report, Diet Report, Animal Information Report, and Zoo Trainers Report, in that order.

> **TROUBLESHOOTING:** If the Field List appears and covers your form, you can close it.

    h. Switch to Form view and test the navigation form by clicking each tab.

       Compare your results to Figure 17.43.

    i. Save and close the navigation form with the default name.

STEP 2 ≫ ENCRYPT AND PASSWORD-PROTECT A DATABASE

Selene asked you to add a password to the database. Several new employees have just been hired, and she wants to restrict their access to the database for the first six weeks. You discuss the password with Selene and decide to use a combination of letters, numbers, and symbols. Refer to Figure 17.44 as you complete Step 2.

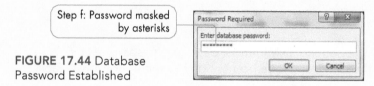

FIGURE 17.44 Database
Password Established

    a. Click **Encrypt with Password** on the FILE tab.

> **TROUBLESHOOTING:** A message appears telling you that you must have the database open for exclusive use. Close the file and open it again using the Open Exclusive option.

    b. Click **OK**. Click **Close Database** on the FILE tab. Click **Computer**. Click **Browse**. Locate the *a09h3Zoo_LastFirst* database, click the **Open arrow** at the bottom of the dialog box, and then select **Open Exclusive** from the list. Refer to Figure 17.40 if you cannot find this option.

    c. Click **Encrypt with Password** on the FILE tab.

       This time the warning message should not appear.

    d. Type the password **exploring** in the **Password box** and type the same password in the **Verify box**. Click **OK** to set the password and encrypt the database. Click **OK** in response to the warning message.

       You need to test the password to be sure that it works.

    e. Close the database and open it again.

       The Password Required dialog box opens, prompting you to enter the password to open the database.

    f. Type **exploring** in the **Enter database password box** and click **OK**.

STEP 3 ≫ DIGITALLY SIGN AND PUBLISH A DATABASE

You suggest to Selene that she add a digital signature to the database. You explain that the database content will be trusted when users from other departments start to use it. Refer to Figure 17.45 as you complete Step 3.

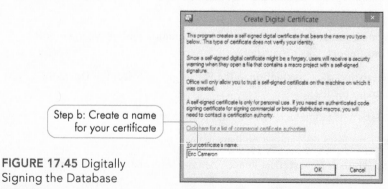

FIGURE 17.45 Digitally
Signing the Database

a. Type **Digital Certificate for VBA Projects** in the **Start screen**. Click the tool to start it.

> **TROUBLESHOOTING:** If Digital Certificate for VBA Projects is not linked on your Start screen, use File Explorer to browse to the C:\Program Files\Microsoft Office\Office15 folder. Double-click SelfCert.exe.

b. Type your full name in the **Your certificate's name box** and click **OK**.

The *Your Name Success* dialog box appears, confirming that you successfully created a new certificate.

c. Click **OK**.

d. Click **Save As** on the FILE tab, and double-click **Package and Sign**.

e. Select the certificate you created in step b, if prompted. Click **OK**.

A new ACCDC file name is suggested using the current database.

f. Click **Create** to accept the new database name with the attached certificate.

A digitally signed database is created in the background; the original database remains open.

STEP 4 >> DIGITALLY SIGN A DATABASE

You decide to make the database more secure digitally signing it and saving it as an ACCDE file. This type of file prohibits the zoo employees from making changes by mistake (or intentionally). Refer to Figure 17.42 as you complete Step 4.

a. Click **Save As** on the FILE tab, and then double-click **Make ACCDE**.

The Save As dialog box opens. The default *Save as type* is ACCDE File (*.accde), and the suggested file name is *a09h3Zoo_LastFirst.accde*.

> **TROUBLESHOOTING:** If your file extensions are hidden, your file name will not show *accde* on the end of the file. Make sure the *Save as type* is ACCDE File.

b. Click **Save** to create the *a09h3Zoo_LastFirst.accde* database file.

c. Click **Close** on the FILE tab.

d. Locate and open the *a09h3Zoo_LastFirst.accde* file you created.

You are prompted for the database password. After you type the password, click Open if a security notice appears.

e. Test the ACCDE file by opening the Animals Form. Right-click the **ANIMALS FORM tab** and observe that *Design View* and *Layout View* are is missing from the shortcut menu.

f. Close the form.

g. Close the file and exit Access.

h. Submit based on your instructor's directions.

Chapter Objectives Review

After reading this chapter, you have accomplished the following objectives:

1. **Verify first normal form**
   - The first step to normalizing a table, which removes repeating groups.

2. **Verify second normal form**
   - Requires 1NF. Criteria is that all non-key fields must be functionally dependent on the entire primary key. If no composite key exists, the table is often in 2NF.

3. **Verify third normal form**
   - Requires 2NF. Removes transitive dependencies, or dependencies on non-key fields.

4. **Create relationships**
   - After normalization, relationships exist between your tables. If a table cannot be connected to others, there is likely a problem with your normalization.

5. **Use the Database Documenter tool**
   - Start the Database Documenter: Database Documenter creates a report containing detailed information for each selected object. Database Documenter can be run on specific objects (for example, only tables, or only forms and reports). Users can select varying levels of detail.

6. **Use the Performance Analyzer tool**
   - Start the Performance Analyzer: Performance Analyzer evaluates a database and makes optimization recommendations.
   - Add an index: Performance Analyzer may recommend adding an index, which will speed up searches such as queries or filters.

7. **Use the Table Analyzer tool**
   - Start the Table Analyzer: The Table Analyzer guides the user through the normalization process. This is a great tool for users with no experience with normalization.
   - Step through the Table Analyzer Wizard: The wizard enables you to split tables, rename newly created tables, rearrange fields in the new tables, and create relationships.

8. **Use the Database Splitter tool**
   - Start the Database Splitter tool: The Database Splitter tool is useful when the number of database users grows beyond a few. The tool splits a database into two files—a front-end database containing queries, forms, and reports, and a back-end database containing tables. Splitting a database may improve the speed of data processing. The back-end database is generally on a server.
   - Work with the front-end database: The front-end database is typically on each user's machine. The front-end database enables users to create their own queries, forms, and reports if necessary. The front end links to back-end tables, which can be shared between users.

9. **Create a menu system**
   - Create a Navigation form: Navigation forms help users open important forms and reports quickly. Choose one of six prebuilt layouts. Drag and drop forms and reports directly on tabs. A navigation form can be easily converted to a Web form.
   - Starting a Navigation form automatically: Navigation forms can start automatically when a database opens to help provide guidance to users.

10. **Encrypt and password-protect a database**
    - Encryption alters digital information using an algorithm, making it unreadable without the key (secret code). Encrypted databases are very difficult to break in to. Encryption is suggested especially if a database is sent via e-mail or put on removable storage such as a USB drive.

11. **Digitally sign and publish a database**
    - Use the SelfCert tool: SelfCert creates a personal signature. The signature can be applied to databases as well as other Office files.
    - Apply a digital signature: Once a certificate is created, it can be applied to a database. Doing so creates an ACCDC file, indicating it has been digitally signed.

12. **Save a database as an ACCDE file**
    - Create an ACCDE file: An ACCDE file is an executable form of the database—objects such as forms, reports, and VBA code cannot be changed. Saving as an ACCDE file adds an extra layer of protection.
    - Keep the original database file safe: Once created, an ACCDE file does not let you modify objects (forms, reports, and VBA code), so the original ACCDB must be kept safe. If the ACCDB file disappears, you will have to recreate your database objects.

Key Terms Matching

Match the key terms with their definitions. Write the key term letter by the appropriate numbered definition.

a. Access Database Executable (ACCDE)
b. Anomaly
c. Back-end database
d. Certification authority (CA)
e. Composite key
f. Database Documenter
g. Database Splitter
h. Digital signatures
i. Encryption
j. First normal form (1NF)

k. Front-end database
l. Functional dependency
m. Navigation form
n. Non-key field
o. Normalization
p. Performance Analyzer
q. Second normal form (2NF)
r. Table Analyzer
s. Third normal form (3NF)
t. Transitive dependencies

1. _____ A commercial company, such as VeriSign, that issues and validates identities using digital signatures for a fee. **p. 900**

2. _____ A file that has had all VBA source code removed, prohibits users from making design and name changes to forms or reports within the database, and prohibits users from creating new forms and reports. **p. 901**

3. _____ A tabbed menu that ties the objects in the database together so that the database is easy to use. **p. 895**

4. _____ A primary key that is made up of two or more fields. **p. 873**

5. _____ A tool that creates a report containing detailed information for each selected object. **p. 881**

6. _____ An error or inconsistency that occurs when you add, edit, and delete data. **p. 870**

7. _____ Analyzes the tables in a database and normalizes them for you. **p. 885**

8. _____ Any field that is not part of the primary key. **p. 873**

9. _____ Contains the queries, forms, and reports of the database. **p. 888**

10. _____ Contains the tables of the database. Often stored on a server or network location. **p. 888**

11. _____ Electronic, encryption-based, secure stamps of authentication that confirm who created the file, that the file is valid, and that no changes have been made to the file after its authentication. **p. 899**

12. _____ Enables you to split a database into two files—a back-end database, which contains the data tables, and a front-end database. **p. 888**

13. _____ Evaluates a database and then makes recommendations for optimizing the database. **p. 883**

14. _____ Occur when the value of one non-key field is functionally dependent on the value of another non-key field. **p. 874**

15. _____ Satisfied when a table contains no repeating groups or repeating columns. **p. 871**

16. _____ Satisfied when a table meets 2NF criteria and no transitive dependencies exist. **p. 874**

17. _____ Satisfied when a table that meets 1NF criteria and all non-key fields are functionally dependent on the entire primary key. **p. 873**

18. _____ The formal process of deciding which fields should be grouped together into which tables. **p. 870**

19. _____ The process of altering digital information using an algorithm to make it unreadable to anyone except those who possess the key (or secret code). **p. 897**

20. _____ When the value of one field is determined by the value of another. **p. 873**

Multiple Choice

1. Which of the following statements about normalization is false?

   (a) A database in 3NF must also be in 1NF.
   (b) There are only three normal forms.
   (c) Normalization reduces redundancy.
   (d) The Table Analyzer can help normalize tables.

2. A table is considered the most normalized when it is in which form?

   (a) 2NF
   (b) 1NF
   (c) 3NF
   (d) Unnormalized

3. Normalization can be defined as:

   (a) Eliminating repetition of data.
   (b) Adding a layer of security to a database.
   (c) Transforming tables into forms.
   (d) A database with multiple tables.

4. The Performance Analyzer:

   (a) Lists the properties of every object in the database.
   (b) Locates places where the database can be optimized.
   (c) Searches for rows of repeating data and suggests design changes to improve performance.
   (d) Is a wizard that provides step-by-step instructions on the creation of tables and forms.

5. The Database Documenter:

   (a) Lists the properties of every object in the database.
   (b) Locates places where the database can be optimized.
   (c) Searches for rows of repeating data and suggests design changes to improve performance.
   (d) Is a wizard that provides step-by-step instructions on the creation of tables and forms.

6. The Table Analyzer:

   (a) Lists the properties of every object in the database.
   (b) Locates places where the database can be optimized.
   (c) Normalizes a database.
   (d) Is a wizard that provides step-by-step instructions on the creation of tables and forms.

7. Which of the following describes a digital signature?

   (a) A scanned copy of the database owner's signature
   (b) Provided by Microsoft when you purchase Office 2013
   (c) Provides a timestamp that can help prove who last modified the database
   (d) An e-mail that details who last made changes to the attached database

8. Which of the following is true about encrypted databases?

   (a) Database encryption alters the contents of the database so that it cannot be opened without a password.
   (b) Encrypted databases can be broken into with ease.
   (c) The contents of encrypted databases cannot be modified.
   (d) Databases can be encrypted but not have a password assigned.

9. Which password is strongest?

   (a) MyAuntSally
   (b) Ginger125
   (c) Mypassword11
   (d) 5*m6notX

10. You open a database with exclusive access. What can other users do?

    (a) Other users can open the database and make changes to it.
    (b) Other users cannot open the database when it is already open with exclusive access.
    (c) No rules apply. Exclusive access is a database setting that can be turned on or off.
    (d) Other users can open but cannot modify the database.

1 Info Labs

Info Labs, a clinical studies company in Mississippi, employs 14 employees; most employees fall in the categories of manager, account rep, or trainee. The employee database holds information about each employee, including their salary and gender, their title, and their location. You have been asked to review the database to see if the employee table was designed properly. This exercise follows the same set of skills as used in Hands-On Exercises 1 and 2 in the chapter. Refer to Figure 17.46 as you complete this exercise.

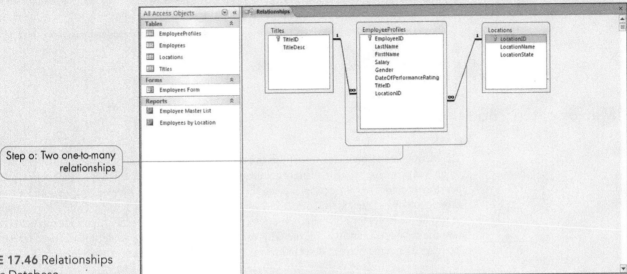

FIGURE 17.46 Relationships in Clinic Database

a. Open *a09p1Clinic*. Save the database as **a09p1Clinic_LastFirst**.

b. Open the Employees table in Datasheet view and examine the data. Determine if the data meets the three normalization rules: 1NF, 2NF, and 3NF.

c. Close the Employees table. You decide to use the Table Analyzer for help with normalizing the Employees table.

d. Click **Analyze Table** in the Analyze group on the DATABASE TOOLS tab. When the first wizard screen appears, click **Next** twice.

e. Select the **Employees table** when the *Which table contains fields with values that are repeated in many records* screen appears. Click **Next** twice.

f. Verify the Employees table has been split into three tables on the next screen.

g. Click **Table1**, click the **Rename Table icon**, and then type **Employee Profiles** as the new name of this table. Click **OK**.

h. Click **Table2**, click the **Rename Table icon**, and then type **Locations** as the new name of this table. Click **OK**.

i. Click **Table3**, click the **Rename Table icon**, and then type **Titles** as the new name of this table. Click **OK**.

j. Click **Next**.

k. Click **LocationID** in the Locations table and click the **Set Unique Identifier icon** to set LocationID as the primary key.

l. Click **EmployeeID** in the EmployeeProfiles table and click the **Set Unique Identifier icon** to set EmployeeID as the primary key.

m. Click **Next**. Select the **No, don't create the query option**. Click **Finish**. Click **OK** when the information message appears.

n. Review the new tables and confirm that the Analyzer moved fields from the Employees table into the two new lookup tables. Close all the tables.

o. Click **Relationships** on the DATABASE TOOLS tab in the Relationships group. Click **All Relationships** to reveal the relationships created by the Table Analyzer. Close the Relationships window and click **No**.

p. Click **Info** on the FILE tab, and click **Encrypt with Password**. Access displays the message *You must have the database open for exclusive use*. Click **OK**. Close the database. Use the Open Exclusive option to open the database.

q. Click **Info** on the FILE tab, and click **Encrypt with Password**. Use **exploring** as the password, in all lowercase letters. Click **OK**. Click **OK** in response to the *Row level locking will be ignored* message.

r. Close the database and reopen it. Type **exploring** in the **Enter database password box**. Close the database and close Access.

s. Submit based on your instructor's directions.

2 Metropolitan Zoo Members

The Metropolitan Zoo invites its patrons to become members of the zoo. For a donation of $50 per year for an individual, or $100 for a family membership, members are entitled to special discounts and member-only promotions. For example, when the pygmy hippos were delivered to the zoo, members were allowed to observe their arrival before the rest of the public. Your task is to review the members database to review the tables for normalization errors, check the performance, to create a lookup field, and then save the database as an ACCDE file. This exercise follows the same set of skills as used in Hands-On Exercises 1–3 in the chapter. Refer to Figures 17.47 and 17.48 as you complete this exercise.

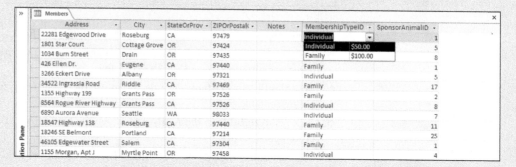

FIGURE 17.47 Lookup Field in Membership Table

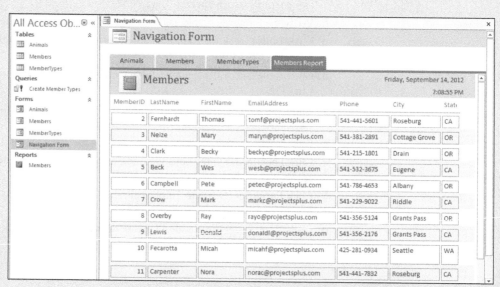

FIGURE 17.48 Navigation Form in Members Database

a. Open *a09p2Members*. Save the database as **a09p2Members_LastFirst**.

b. Open the Members table and examine the data. Determine if the data meets the three normalization rules: 1NF, 2NF, and 3NF.

c. Close the Members table. You decide to normalize the table manually.

d. Click **Query Design** in the Queries group on the CREATE tab. Add the Members table to the query design and close the Show Table dialog box.

e. Add the MembershipTypeID, MembershipTypeName, and MembershipDonation fields to the query design grid. Run the query. Take note of the repeating rows of data.

f. Switch to Design view. Click **Totals** in the Show/Hide group to eliminate the duplicate rows. Run the query. Only the unique rows show in the results.

g. Switch to Design view. Click **Make Table** in the Query Type group and type **MemberTypes** in the **Table Name box**. Click **OK**. Click **Run** in the Results group to create the MemberTypes table. Click **Yes** to the warning message. You created a second table (MemberTypes) to help normalize the Members table.

h. Save the query as **Create Member Types**. Close the query.

i. Open the MemberTypes table in Design view. Set the MembershipTypeID field as the primary key. Save and close the table.

j. Open the Members table in Design view and use the Lookup Wizard to join the Members table to the MemberTypes table in a relationship. Complete the following steps:
   - Change the MembershipTypeID Data Type to *Lookup Wizard*.
   - Click **Next** in the first Lookup Wizard step, select the **MemberTypes table** in the next step, and then click **Next**.
   - Click the >> **button** to include all fields in the Lookup field. Click **Next** three times.
   - Click **Finish** and click **Yes** to save the table. The two tables are now joined using the MembershipTypeID field.

k. Switch to Datasheet view. Click the **MembershipTypeID field** in the first row and verify the Lookup field is working. Next, you will delete the redundant fields in the Members table.

l. Switch to Design view. Select the **MembershipTypeName** and **MembershipDonation fields**. Click **Delete Rows** in the Tools group. Click **Yes** to confirm the deletion. Save and close the table.

m. Create a basic form using the Form button for each of the three tables in the database using the Form tool. Delete any subforms that appear automatically.

n. Create a basic report based on the Members table using the Report tool. Include MemberID, LastName, FirstName, EmailAddress, Phone, City, and StateOrProvince, in that order.

o. Use these four new objects to create a navigation form using the Horizontal Tabs template (see Figure 17.45). Edit the fourth tab and change the caption to **Members Report**. Close the Navigation Pane. Switch to Form view and test the new navigation form. Close the navigation form.

p. Click the **DATABASE TOOLS tab** and click **Analyze Performance**. Click the **All Object Types tab**, click **Select All**, and then click **OK**. The first idea in the Results window suggests you save your application as an MDE file, which is called ACCDE in Access 2013.

q. Close the Results dialog box.

r. Click **Save As** on the FILE tab, and double-click **Make ACCDE**. Click **Save**. The ACCDE file is saved in the same location as the original file with the same name, *a09p2Members_LastFirst*.

s. Close the database and close Access.

t. Submit based on your instructor's directions.

1 The Computer Store

 **ANALYSIS CASE**

The Computer Store, based in Florida, sells computer products to individuals and businesses. You have been hired to assist with the daily computer operations, including management of the order processing database. Your assignment is to analyze the database, create a front end for the users, and transfer the tables to a back-end database. After splitting the database, you recommend a navigation form to open the database objects. Refer to Figure 17.49 as you complete this exercise.

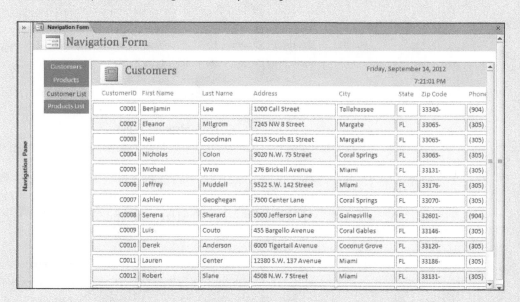

FIGURE 17.49 Navigation Form in Computers Database

a. Open *a09m1Computers*. Click **Save Database As** on the FILE tab, and type **a09m1Computers_LastFirst**. Click **Save**.

b. Open the Database Documenter. Click **Options** and ensure none of the Include for Table items are selected. Select the **Names, Data Types, and Sizes option** in the *Include for Fields* section and select nothing in the *Include for Indexes* section. Click **OK**. Click the **Customers check box** and click **OK**. In the generated report, take note of the Size (the third column) of each field. Notice the values for the ZipCode and PhoneNumber field sizes in the Customers table. Close the generated report after viewing it.

⭐ c. Open the Customers table in Design view and increase the field size to an appropriate size. The field size should be large enough to accommodate all data but small enough so users can not enter extra characters. Save and close the table.

d. Click **Access Database** in the Move Data group and click **Split Database** to split the database into a front-end and a back-end database. Keep the default back-end name, which adds the suffix *be* to the current database name. The front-end Navigation Pane shows linked table icons, similar to those in Figure 17.30.

e. Open the Customers table and type your name as the next customer. Close the table. Open the back-end database and verify your name is in the Customers table. Close the back-end database.

> **TROUBLESHOOTING:** If you use the front-end database on another machine, you may get an error stating the file path is not valid. Use the techniques learned in a previous chapter to link the front-end database to the back-end database.

f. Open the front-end database again and create three objects: a Customers form using the Customers table, a Products form using the Products table, and a Customer List report using the Customers table.

g. Create a navigation form using the Vertical Tabs, Left template. Add the Customers form, followed by the Products form, followed by the Customer List report, followed by the Products List report.

h. Test the navigation form in Form view (compare to Figure 17.49). Save and close the form.

i. Add the navigation form to the Display Form option in the Access Options page so the navigation form opens when the database opens. Test the feature by closing and opening the database. Refer to Figure 17.37 if necessary.

j. Close the database.

k. Submit based on your instructor's directions.

2 | Boats for All Seasons

The owners of Boats for All Seasons would like to improve their database. They would like to add some additional forms and reports and also modify their main table. They are having a problem because customers who bought boats from them years ago are returning to purchase again. The owners are unsure how to record a second transaction for the same customer. After the modifications are completed, they would like you to create a navigation form and also make suggestions for making the database more secure. Refer to Figure 17.50 as you complete this exercise.

FIGURE 17.50 Deleting Redundant Fields in Customers Table

a. Open *a09m2Boats*. Save the database as **a09m2Boats_LastFirst**.

b. Open the Customers table and review the contents of the table. Make a list of any problems that may cause data-entry errors. Does the table need to be normalized? You will split the customers table into two tables: the Customers table and the BoatPurchases table.

c. Open the Customer Purchases query and examine the results. The owners are trying to use this query to enter purchases. They are confused because the boat purchase data is comingled with the Customers table. Also, some of the customers are still prospects and have not even purchased a boat yet. You will fix the problem in the steps below.

d. Modify the Customer Purchases query so it only shows fields with values. Run the query. Your query should list only customers who purchased a boat (56 records).

e. Switch to Design view. Click **Make Table** and type **BoatPurchases** in the **Table name box**. Click **OK**. Run the query and click **Yes** at the warning. Save and close the query.

f. Open the BoatPurchases table in Design view and change the CustomerID Data Type to **Number**. Save the table and switch to Datasheet view. Sort the records by CustomerID, locate the three customers who purchased more than one boat (Billingslea, Mcdowell, and Windon), and then update their CustomerIDs so that both purchases show the smaller ID. For example, change the second Billingslea CustomerID from *62* to **2**.

DISCOVER

g. Change the CustomerID field in the BoatPurchases table to a Lookup Wizard displaying CustomerID, LastName, and FirstName, sorted by LastName and then by FirstName. Hide the key column. Save the table and click **Yes** at the prompt. Your field should show the customer LastName and FirstName when you click in the CustomerID field.

h. Switch to Datasheet view. Verify that the name in column 1 matches the names in columns 2 and 3. If it does, switch to Design view and delete the **LastName** and **FirstName fields**. These two fields were for reference only until you verified the data matched the column 1 data. Save and close the BoatPurchases table.

i. Open the Customers table in Design view and delete the **BoatType**, **BoatPurchaseDate**, and **BoatPurchaseAmount fields**. This information is not needed in the Customers table because it now exists in the BoatPurchases table.

j. Save the table and switch to Datasheet view. Sort the table by Ascending LastName. Locate the three customers who purchased more than one boat (Billingslea, Mcdowell, and Windon) and delete the three duplicate records with the larger CustomerID. For example, delete the second Billingslea record with a CustomerID of *62*.

k. Close the database and reopen it using the Open Exclusive option. Encrypt the database with a password of **exploring**.

l. Create a new form and a new report using the BoatPurchases table.

m. Use the information in the *Add the Switchboard Manager* section to create a switchboard using the Switchboard Manager. Add the Boat Purchases form, the Boat Purchases report, the Customer Data Entry form, and the Customers and Prospects report to the switchboard. Modify the Access options so the switchboard automatically opens when the database opens. Close and reopen the database to test the switchboard.

n. Click **Save As** on the FILE tab, and make an ACCDE file. The ACCDE file is saved in the same location as the original file.

o. Close the database and close Access.

p. Submit based on your instructor's directions.

3 | Normalizing a Database

COLLABORATION CASE

The Specialty Foods, Ltd., company has a large database that has not been normalized. The company's recent hires have been given the task of trying to normalize the database.

a. Open the *a09m3Orders* database and save it as **a09m3Orders_GroupName**. (This step should be completed by only one person in your group. Replace *GroupName* with the name or number assigned to your group by your instructor.)

b. Examine the contents of the CustomerOrders table. Create a list of fields in the database. This database, with over 2,100 rows of information, contains a large amount of redundancy. Some companies, Specialty Foods included, create a database and do not normalize until the amount of data becomes unmanageable.

c. Each member of the group should take the list of fields, examine them separately, and create an initial guess as to what the final tables will look like. Be sure to identify potential primary keys for each table.

d. Come together as a group and discuss your proposals. Reach a consensus on the final design. Put this aside for the moment.

e. Each student should separately attempt to convert the database from the unnormalized state to 1NF.

f. Come together as a group and discuss your proposals. Reach a consensus on the design after 1NF. Be sure to identify primary keys. Open Microsoft Word and open *a09m3Normalization*. Record your proposal in the section labeled *First Normal Form* and save it as **a09m3Normalization_ GroupName**. For example, the table titles shown in Figure 17.46 would be described like this:

Table Name: Titles

Fields: TitleID, TitleDesc

Primary Key: TitleID

g. Attempt to convert the database from the 1NF group settled on in step f to 2NF. Do this separately.

h. Come together as a group and discuss your proposals. Reach a consensus on the design after 2NF. Be sure to identify primary keys. Record the proposal in the *a09m3Normalization_GroupName* document in the section labeled *Second Normal Form*.

i. Each student should separately attempt to convert the database from the 2NF the group settled on in step h to 3NF.

j. Come together as a group and discuss your proposals. Reach a consensus on the design after 3NF. Be sure to identify primary keys. Record the proposal in the *a09m3Normalization_GroupName* document in the section labeled *Third Normal Form*.

k. Run the Analyze Table tool in Access on the CustomerOrders table. Name the tables appropriately. Accept the default primary keys proposed. Do not create a query when prompted. Examine the tables created and the relationships between the tables. Discuss as a group what (if anything) differs between your proposal and that proposed by Access. In the *a09m3Normalization_GroupName* document in the *Comparison* section, summarize the differences and attempt to explain why Access has different results than your proposal. Given the choice, would you use your proposal or the one provided by Access? Why?

l. Exit Word. Exit Access. Submit the Word document and the Access database based on your instructor's directions.

Beyond the Classroom

Switchboard Versus Navigation Form

RESEARCH CASE

Your company uses an Access 2013 database to store its customer and sales information. The Accounting Department uses and maintains this database. Three other departments—Marketing, Sales, and Production—also need access to the database. Some users have asked for a switchboard, and others have asked for a navigation form. The accounting department does not have experience with creating either of these forms. Your assignment is to do online research to determine which menu system is better for your company: a switchboard or a navigation form. Create a Word document named **a09b2Switchboard_LastFirst**, giving a brief summary of the two menu systems and recommending which one is better for the company.

Troubleshoot: ACCDE File Errors

DISASTER RECOVERY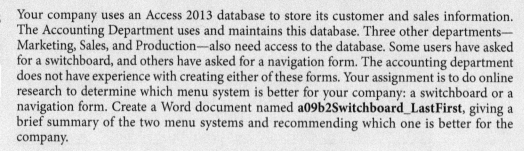

Keith Hernandez, the manager of a local collectibles store, has contacted you about a database issue he has. His former technology support person set up a database for him on his USB flash drive. When he brought the file home, he was shown the following error:

> The database was created with the 32-bit version of Access. Please open it with the 32-bit version of Microsoft Access.

He tried then recreating the ACCDE from his home machine, but when he brought it to work, he was given the following error:

> The database was created with the 64-bit version of Access. Please open it with the 64-bit version of Microsoft Access.

Keith is frustrated and is hoping you can find out if there is a way for him to create an Access Database Executable that works on both the 32-bit and 64-bit versions of the program. If there is no way to do this, he is hoping you might have recommendations on how he should work with these ACCDE files. Write up your findings in a Word document and save it as **a09b3Collect_LastFirst**. Note he does not want you to fix the issue; he is just interested in finding out if this can be done or not. Keith has provided you with *a09b3Collect* (the original database), *a09b3Collect64* (which works on 64-bit editions of Access but not 32-bit editions), and *a09b3Collect32* (which works on 32-bit editions of Access but not 64-bit editions). However, you should only submit the final Word document to your instructor.

Interview Questions

SOFT SKILLS CASE

You are a database administrator at a large company. The company is hiring a new entry-level database administrator, and your supervisor, Keith Mast, has asked you to draft questions to be asked during the interview. Specifically, he would like questions that an entry-level person should be expected to answer. You have decided you will ask them a question about normalization, another about database performance, a third about splitting databases, and a fourth about encryption. Your boss has asked to see the questions (and ideal answers) before the interview. Create a new Word document named **a09b4Interview_LastFirst**. Create the four questions you would ask an interviewee to explain during an interview, and provide optimal answers for the four questions. Submit based on your instructor's directions.

Capstone Exercise

Your company handles room registration, speaker coordination, and other functions for national conferences that are held at your campus throughout the year. The sales department mails schedules to speakers and building coordinators. The speaker database was modified by unauthorized personnel, and some of the changes need to be reversed. For example, all of the relationships were deleted; they need to be recreated. You have been asked to analyze the database, fix the relationships, and make the database more secure to avoid this situation in the future. The database tables may already be normalized; however, you need to examine the tables to verify this.

Restore Database Relationships

You open the original database and use Save As to create a copy of the original.

a. Open *a09c1NatConf* and save the database as **a09c1NatConf_LastFirst**.

b. Open each table in the database and look for normalization errors.

c. Open the Relationships window. Notice there are currently no relationships.

d. Add the Speakers, SessionSpeaker, Sessions, and Rooms tables to the Relationships window. Restore relationships by dragging the primary key from the primary table onto the foreign key of a related table.

e. Enforce *Referential Integrity* and *Cascade Update Related Fields* for each relationship you create.

f. Save the changes and close the Relationships window.

Analyze Database Performance

You want to verify that the database performs properly when it is used in a production environment. Run Performance Analyzer and take note of the recommendations, suggestions, and ideas in the analysis results.

a. Open the Performance Analyzer dialog box, click the **All Object Types tab**, click **Select All**, and then click **OK**.

b. Verify that the first item on the list (an idea) suggests creating an MDE file, which is called ACCDE in Access 2013. You will create an ACCDE file later.

c. Verify the third item on the list (an idea) suggests you change the data type of RoomID in the Sessions table from *Short Text* to **Long Integer**. You decide not to make this change.

> **TROUBLESHOOTING:** If changing the data type of RoomID is not the third idea, ensure you set the options properly in step a.

d. Close the Performance Analyzer.

Split the Database

Splitting the database by creating a back end and a front end enables users to customize their individual front-end databases; the back end (the tables) remains safe and secure.

a. Split the database, accepting the default back-end name *a09c1NatConf_LastFirst_be*. The front-end copy of the database remains open.

b. Look for the linked tables in the front-end copy of the database.

Create the Navigation Form

You need to create a navigation form that displays a new form and the three reports in the database. Add the navigation form to the Display Form option to make the navigation form appear whenever the database opens.

a. Create a new form based on the Speakers table.

b. Save the form as **Add or Edit Speakers**.

c. Create a navigation form based on the Horizontal Tabs template.

d. Drag the new **Add or Edit Speakers form** to the first tab position.

e. Drag the reports to fill the next three tab positions.

f. Switch to Form view and test the navigation form. Save the navigation form with the default name and close it.

g. Set the database to open the navigation form when the database opens. This setting can be found in Options on the FILE tab. Click the **Current Database tab** and update the Display Form option.

h. Test the navigation form by closing and then reopening the database.

Encrypt the Database with a Password and Create the ACCDE File

Make sure you have the database open with exclusive access before completing these steps. You need to encrypt the front-end database with a password. In addition, you want to convert the front-end database to the ACCDE file format.

a. Display the Set Database Password dialog box.

b. Set the database password to **exploring**. Type the same password in both text boxes. Click **OK** at the next prompt.

c. Close and reopen the database to test the password.

d. Convert the front-end database to an ACCDE file format. A new database file with extension .accde is created in the background.

e. Close the database. Close Access.

f. Submit based on your instructor's directions.

Index